The Complete
Mental Health
Directory

2010/2011

Seventh Edition

The Complete Mental Health Directory

A Comprehensive
Source Book for
Professionals and Individuals

A Sedgwick Press Book

Grey House Publishing

PUBLISHER:	Leslie Mackenzie
EDITOR:	Richard Gottlieb
EDITORIAL DIRECTOR:	Laura Mars
PRODUCTION MANAGER:	Jefferson Martin
MEDICAL EDITOR:	Dr. Nada Stotland
PRODUCTION ASSISTANTS:	Jennifer Consolato, Kristen Thatcher, Erica Schneider
MARKETING DIRECTOR:	Jessica Moody

Grey House Publishing, Inc.
4919 Route 22
Amenia, NY 12501
518.789.8700
FAX 845.373.6390
www.greyhouse.com
e-mail: books@greyhouse.com

First edition printed 1999
Seventh edition printed 2010

Biennial
Spine title: The complete mental health directory
    v.27.5
"A comprehensive source book for individuals and professionals"
Includes indexes
ISSN: 1538-0556

1. Mental health services—United States—Directories.

RA790.6.C625
362—dc21   2001-233121
ISBN: 978-1-59237-544-8   softcover

Table of Contents

SECTION ONE: Disorders

Each disorder chapter includes a detailed description and some or all of the following categories: *Association & Agencies; Books; Periodicals & Pamphlets; Research Centers; Support Groups & Hot Lines; Video & Audio; Web Sites.* See *Diagnostic Categories* in the front matter for a complete list of disorders covered.

Introduction

This is the seventh edition of *The Complete Mental Health Directory*. This unique reference directory provides comprehensive coverage of 19 broad mental health disorder categories, from Adjustment Disorders to Tic Disorders. Within these categories are more than 70 specific disorders, including Obsessive Compulsive Disorder, Asperger's Syndrome, Bipolar Disorder, Postpartum Depression, Schizophrenia, Somatization Disorder, and Paraphilias.

A winner of the **2009 Annual National Health Information Awards**, this new edition includes a chapter on *Pediatric and Adolescent Issues*, with an introduction on disorders diagnosed in children and teenagers, and signs and symptoms to look for. This directory also includes a chapter on *Suicide* which, although not a mental disorder, is the consequence of some mental disorders, and involves a complex interaction of factors.

Praise for previous edition:

> *"...This directory would be useful to libraries providing consumer health information and [to] medical libraries. It would also be valuable to professionals and patients..."*
>
> Cheryl A. Capitani, Chief Librarian
> Harrisburg Hospital

> *"[Despite] online resources...certain times and situations call for a print resource, especially in the field of mental health services. Having one in hand is helpful. ...The introductory essay's...thoughtful questions and comments can open many topics to discussion and searches for further information. [The] section ... on professional services includes a wealth of resources. Summing up: Recommended. All levels."*
>
> Choice Magazine

Coverage of 70-plus disorders include clear, concise descriptions, all updated with the most current diagnoses and treatment methods. Users will find a variety of disorder-specific resources, including Associations, Books, Periodicals, Research Centers, and Support Groups. In addition to disorder-specific resources, *The Complete Mental Health Directory* includes Professional Services, Publishers, Facilities, Clinical Management and Pharmaceutical Companies.

Medical Editor Dr. Nada Stotland has more than 30 years experience in the mental health field, as Professor of Psychiatry at Chicago's Rush Medical Center, past President of the American Psychiatric Association, and author of many books and articles. We are deeply grateful for her input, which has made this edition easier to use, current and comprehensive. Her knowledge of treatments and medications adds unsurpassed value to this important work.

In addition to more than 4,500 listings, *The Complete Mental Health Directory* includes an article written by Dr. Stotland, **Developments and Controversies in Mental Health, 2010** that discusses perception and reality of mental disease, who's to blame for crimes committed by mental patients, psychiatric medications, and whether substance abuse is a disease or moral weakness. Following this article is a **Bill of Rights for Children's Mental Health Disorders and their Families**, created by a coalition for children's mental health. Plus, **Mental Disorders by Diagnostic Category** educates patient and professional about categorical diagnoses, symptoms and treatments.

SECTION ONE: Disorders

This section consists of 21 chapters dealing with broad categories of mental health issues from Adjustment Disorders to Tic Disorders. Each chapter begins with a description, written in clear, accessible language and includes symptoms, prevalence and treatment options. These descriptions include information on specific syndromes within a general category, such as Post Traumatic Stress Disorder and Social Anxiety Disorder within the Anxiety Disorders chapter. Following the descriptions are specific resources relevant to the disorder, including Associations, Books, Government Agencies, Periodicals, Pamphlets, Support Groups, Hot Lines, Resource Centers, Audio & Video Tapes, and Web Sites.

SECTIONS TWO & THREE: Associations, Organizations, Government Agencies
More than 1,000 National Associations, and Federal and State Agencies are profiled in these sections that offer general mental health services and support for patients and their families.

SECTION FOUR: Professional Support & Services
This section provides resources that support the many different professionals in the mental heath field. Included are specific chapters on Accreditation and Quality Assurance, Associations, Books, Conferences and Meetings, Periodicals, Training and Recruitment, Audio & VideoTapes, Web Sties, and Workbooks and Manuals.

SECTION FIVE: Publishers
This section lists major publishers of books and magazines that focus on health care or mental health issues. This material is suitable for both professionals in the mental health industry as well as patients and their network community.

SECTION SIX: Facilities
This section lists major facilities and hospitals, arranged by state, which provide treatment for persons with mental health disorders.

SECTION SEVEN: Clinical Management
Here you will find products and services that support the Clinical Management aspect of the mental health industry, including Directories and Databases, Management Companies, and Information Services, which provide patient and medical data, as well as marketing information.

SECTION EIGHT: Pharmaceuticals Companies
This section offers information on the pharmaceutical companies that manufacture drugs to treat mental health disorders. This data is presented in two ways: First, alphabetically by company name, including address, phone, fax, web site, and a list of specific drugs manufactured. Second, alphabetically by name of drug, including the disorder it is typically prescribed for, and reference to the company or companies that manufacture it.

INDEXES: Disorder Index lists entries by disorders and disorder categories. **Entry** Index is an alphabetical list of all entries. **Geographic Index** lists entries by state.

This information in this revised edition is crucial for those suffering from a mental condition and their support network, including professionals who diagnose and treat mental disorders. It combines, in a single volume, disorder descriptions written in clear, layman's terms, and a wide variety of resources. Here's where you'll find where to go and who to ask – for the most diagnosed mental health disorders in the country.

For even easier access to date, *The Complete Mental Health Directory* is available in our new online database platform, http://gold.greyhouse.com. Subscribers have access to all of this health information, and can search by geographic area, disorder, contacts, keyword and so much more. With this new, online database, locating mental health resources has never been faster or easier.

Developments and Controversies in Mental Health, 2010

By Nada L. Stotland, MD, MPH

Developments in mental health have created more controversy than those in any other area of medicine. Although there has been a good deal of progress in recent years, psychiatric medications and other treatments are misunderstood. Psychiatric disorders and therapies are often stigmatized. There are concerns about whether too many children and adults are being diagnosed with psychiatric conditions, as well as concerns about particular effects of psychiatric medications on children and pregnant women.

New rules, resulting from the passage of a national bill requiring equal treatment of mental illness and other medical illnesses by insurance carriers, take effect July 1, 2010. Inarguably, this is a very important statement by the federal government, but implementation will depend on the interpretation of 'equality' by those carriers and the availability of psychiatric and other mental health services.

Reality of Mental Illness

Mental disorders can be diagnosed as accurately as most other medical disorders. We have increasing evidence from brain imaging and other tests that mental illnesses are associated with changes in the brain. As in other branches of medicine, there is an ongoing attempt to improve the classification and diagnosis of psychiatric disorders. *The American Psychiatric Association Diagnostic and Statistical Manual of Mental Disorders* is currently in its fourth edition (*DSM IV*). An early draft of the fifth edition, expected to be published in 2013, has recently been released electronically for professional and public comment. This manual is used throughout the country and in many other parts of the world, providing a common system for health care professionals and researchers. The criteria for diagnoses are derived from complete reviews of the medical evidence followed by field trials in which draft criteria are tested in real clinical situations. Diagnoses are based on the symptoms experienced by patients and observed by others, recognizing that manifestations of illness vary between the genders and among cultures.

The *DSM* includes a category, 'Mental Disorders Secondary to a Medical Condition.' The brain, which governs thinking, feeling, and behavior, is an organ that interacts with all the other organs in the body. For example, an excess of thyroid hormones makes an individual jumpy and overactive, while a deficiency of the same hormones decreases an individual's energy and activity in ways that mimic clinical depression. People with liver or kidney failure become confused and disoriented. All individuals should have a primary care physician with whom they check in when mental symptoms appear, to identify any underlying physical medical conditions and thus treat the correct cause of the symptoms. We are learning more every day about the genetic factors in mental illnesses and responses to treatments. There are early indications that we may be able to match the individual to the most effective treatment on the basis of genetic studies.

We all need to be aware of active (and, unfortunately, sometimes effective) efforts on the part of small groups to convince the public that mental illnesses are not real and that mental health treatments are dangerous. Accurate information is freely available from primary care physicians, textbooks, the National Institutes of Health, and the web sites of professional organizations. Any or all of these resources should be consulted before making any decisions regarding mental illness.

All medical illnesses can be more or less serious. Some people 'tough it out' when treatment could prevent great suffering and disability. Others seek medical care for every minor symptom. Either extreme response can be problematic. No diagnosis should be given until the individual with symptoms has had a thorough examination, including laboratory tests where indicated, and all factors, such as social conflicts and traumas, contributing to the symptoms, have been identified and addressed. In the area of mental health, people are generally reluctant to seek care until they are in physical pain or having trouble with day-to-day activities. Like most other medications, such as antibiotics, psychiatric medications can be both underused, when people who are ill do not seek treatment, and overused, when prescribed without a full evaluation. Many people with psychiatric disorders do not seek care until they have suffered for months or years; many more are never diagnosed and, therefore, never treated.

A prominent controversy in treating the mental health of children concerns attention deficit/hyperactivity disorder(ADHD), specifically if and how much to medicate. Prescribing medication should never be the first response when a child is restless or inattentive. This behavior may result from family conflict, a poor fit between the school and the child, or a problem such as poor eyesight or hearing. ADHD should only be diagnosed when the child's behavior is not normal for his or her level of development. Children with ADHD cannot learn, and they disrupt the learning of others in the classroom. Other children do not want to play with them. The diagnosis and treatment of ADHD, when present, can restore family harmony and enable the child to continue on a normal developmental path.

We often see media accounts describing a so-called 'epidemic' of one or another psychiatric disorder, such as depression or autism. Since definitions and counting methods change over time, and increasing awareness brings increasing numbers of cases to medical attention, it is very difficult to judge whether the incidence of disorders has actually changed, and, if so, why. Studies in these areas are under way that can help answer the question "Are psychiatric diagnoses a substitute for normal responses to the ups and downs of life and are too many medications being prescribed?"

Alcoholism & Substance Abuse

Alcohol and substance abuse are diagnoses in the DSM. These defined mental illnesses are associated with observable changes in brain function. Motivated patients can be successfully treated, both by professionals and with the help of programs such as Alcoholics Anonymous.

Screening for Mental Disorders

Screening is a technique used in many areas of medicine. A simple, quick, inexpensive test or observation is used to identify individuals who are at risk for a particular condition such as diabetes , hypertension, or depression. Screening does not provide a diagnosis. A positive screening means that an individual should be fully evaluated by a professional. Screening saves lives. Parents, teachers, and pediatricians do informal screening of children all the time, determining if a child able to see the blackboard, hear instructions, pay attention, interact with other children. It is ultimately up to the individual or parents to decide how to proceed after a positive screening.

Treating Mental Disorders

Treatments for mental illnesses are highly effective. They can relieve suffering and restore function. Many mental illnesses are chronic or recurrent, like many other medical disorders for which people seek treatment, such as asthma, hypertension, and diabetes. Like treatments for those disorders, mental health treatment not only reduces or eliminates symptoms, but also prevents serious complications such as job loss, family loss, homelessness, and suicide.

Effects of Psychiatric Medications

The function of psychiatric medications is to restore people to their own normal levels of emotion, thinking, and behavior. An antidepressant will not make a person who is not depressed any happier. Antipsychotic medications diminish or eliminate the hallucinations, delusions, and confusion that make life miserable for people with schizophrenia and other psychoses. Lithium evens out the feelings and behaviors of people with bipolar, or manic-depressive, disorders, who otherwise ricochet between severe highs and lows that can ruin their lives and the lives of their loved ones. Medication for ADHD enables a child to concentrate and to sit long enough to learn and work with others, and not simply a sedative used to control children.

Addictiveness of Psychiatric Medication

When a person is addicted to a substance, the effects of the substance diminish over time. The person wakes in the morning craving the substance, craves larger and larger amounts, and can be driven to lie or steal in order to get it. There is only one class of psychiatric medication -- benzodiazepines or so-called 'minor tranquilizers' -- which can be addicting. Even with these medications, however, addiction is highly unusual. The effects of psychiatric medications are reversible. Medications should be taken as long as the disorder is expected to last. If discontinued earlier, the signs and symptoms often return. Medications should be tapered under medical supervision rather than stopped abruptly, so that the brain and other organs can readjust. People with persistent or recurrent illnesses may choose to take medication indefinitely to avoid the return of symptoms.

Safety of Psychiatric Treatments

All medications can have side or adverse effects. These differ from person to person, and medication may have to be adjusted until the right balance is found. Patients on any kind of medication, especially for depression, should be followed carefully. Overdoses of lithium and some older antidepressants such as amitryptiline can be fatal. The newer, selective serotonin reuptake inhibitors (SSRIs) antidepressants are considered quite safe.

It is important to note that, several years ago, the United States Food and Drug Administration (FDA) issued warnings about the use of SSRIs in young people. These warnings, however, are controversial and studies that led to concerns about a relationship between SSRIs and suicidality have serious scientific flaws. The FDA warnings confuse thoughts of suicide, which are very common in young people, and actual suicide. More recent warnings by the FDA include the dangers, including suicide, of untreated depression. Studies of the effects of psychiatric medications on pregnancy, with the exception of lithium and anticonvulsants used to treat bipolar disorders, have generally been reassuring. The small risks associated with these medications must be weighed against the known risks of untreated depression for mother and infant. Most women who discontinue antidepressants during pregnancy suffer relapse. The scientific literature in this area is changing rapidly and treatment decisions must be made on an individual basis.

Electroconvulsive treatment, or ECT, sometimes referred to as 'shock treatment,' is safe and effective. It can save the lives of people with depressions so severe that they do not eat or move, and that do not respond to medication. Current protocols require anesthesia as small doses of electric current are delivered to one side of the brain.

Psychotherapy

The most traditional psychotherapy, *psychodynamic psychotherapy*, is derived from the psychoanalytic theories and techniques of Sigmund Freud and his followers, and informed by more recent scientific findings. Psychodynamic psychotherapy focuses on the individual's unconscious psychological conflicts based on interaction between inborn personality traits and childhood experiences. These conflicts can be observed and analyzed within the therapist-patient relationship. Supportive psychotherapy uses an individual's own coping styles to help with a life crisis.

More contemporary psychotherapies are 'manual-based,' employing standardized systems and time frames. *Cognitive-behavioral psychotherapy* focuses on countering the negative thoughts associated with an individual's symptoms, such as 'There is no hope for me,' "Nobody likes me,' 'Bad things always happen to me.' Often these thoughts become self-fulfilling prophecies and the individual's behavior causes, for example, bad things to happen. In this situation, the therapist first helps the individual to identify these negative thoughts, and then helps the patient question whether they are realistic. Homework entails replacing unrealistic negative thoughts with realistic, optimistic ones, and developing behaviors that reflect that optimism. *Interpersonal psychotherapy* focuses on the relationships in a person's current life.

There is increasing evidence that all these forms of psychotherapy are effective, often as effective as medication for milder episodes of psychiatric illness. Psychotherapy and medication can each lead to the same positive changes in brain function. Unfortunately, health insurance plans can make it difficult to access psychotherapy, and sometimes refuse to reimburse physicians for providing it.

Mental Health Care Professionals

Each category of mental health professional has its own training and licensing requirements. Requirements also vary from state to state. Counselors (marital, family, school, occupational) generally have a bachelor's or master's degree in counseling. Licensed professional social workers have completed a two-year master's degree program. Most psychologist licenses require a Ph.D or Psy.D (Doctor of Psychology) degree. Both social workers and psychologists must have some clinical experience under supervision to attain licenses to practice. Psychiatrists are medical doctors who complete four-year residencies in psychiatry, including work in general medicine, after graduating from medical school. Those who wish to be certified by the American Board of Psychiatry and Neurology must pass written and oral examinations. Among mental health professionals, only psychiatrists can prescribe medication, except in Louisiana and New Mexico, where small numbers of psychologists have been licensed and trained to prescribe.

Spirituality and Mental Health

Spirituality, whether inside or outside organized religion, is a positive factor in mental health. There is no conflict between religion and mental health care. For those who feel more comfortable in a designated 'Christian' environment, for example, there are mental health care providers who identify themselves as 'Christian.'

In summary, mental illnesses are real conditions. They are being diagnosed and treated much better now than at any time in the past. New research continues to improve our understanding and effectiveness.

Bill of Rights for Children's Mental Health Disorders and their Families

The children's mental health coalition has created a Bill of Rights for Children with Mental Health Disorders and their Families. The coalition includes:

American Academy of Child and Adolescent Psychiatry (AACAP)
Autism Society of America (ASA)
Child and Adolescent Bipolar Foundation (CABF)
Children and Adults with Attention-Deficit Hyperactivity Disorder (CHADD)
Federation of Families for Children's Mental Health (FFCMH)
Mental Health America (MHA)
National Alliance on Mental Illness (NAMI).

The Bill of Rights was created because of the inconsistency of accessible mental healthcare services throughout the country. It states:

1. Treatment must be family-driven and child-focused. Families and youth (when appropriate), must have a primary decision-making role in their treatment.
2. Children should receive care in home and community-based settings as close to home as possible.

3. Mental health services are an integral part of a child's overall healthcare. Insurance companies must not discriminate against children with mental illnesses by imposing financial burdens and barriers to treatment, such as differential deductibles, co-pays, annual or lifetime caps, or arbitrary limits on access to medically necessary inpatient and/or outpatient services.
4. Children should receive care from highly-qualified professionals who are acting in the best interest of the child and family, with appropriate informed consent.
5. Parents and children are entitled to as much information as possible about the risks and benefits of all treatment options, including anticipated outcomes.
6. Children receiving medications for mental disorders should be monitored appropriately to optimize the benefit and reduce any risks or potential side effects that may be associated with such treatments.
7. Children and their families should have access to a comprehensive continuum of care, based on their needs, including a full range of psychosocial, behavioral, pharmacological, and educational services, regardless of the cost.
8. Children should receive treatment within a coordinated system of care where all agencies (e.g., health, mental health, child welfare, juvenile justice, and schools, etc.) delivering services work together to support recovery and optimize treatment outcome.
9. Children and families are entitled to an increased investment in high-quality research on the origin, diagnosis, and treatment of childhood disorders.
10. Children and families need and deserve access to mental health professionals with appropriate training and experience. Primary care professionals providing mental health services must have access to consultation and referral resources from qualified mental health professionals.

http://www.aacap.org/cs/root/resources_for_families/patient_bill_of_rights

Disorders by Diagnostic Category

Adjustment Disorders

Alcohol and Substance Abuse & Dependence

Anxiety Disorders
Agoraphobia
General Anxiety Disorder
Obsessive Compulsive Disorder
Panic Disorder
Phobias
Post Traumatic Stress Disorder
Social Anxiety Disorder

Cognitive Disorders
Delirium
Dementia, i.e. Alzheimer's Disease
Amnestic Disorder

Dissociative Disorders
Depersonalization Disorder
Dissociative Amnesia
Dissociative Fugue
Dissociative Identity Disorder

Eating Disorders
Anorexia Nervosa
Bulima Nervosa

Impulse Control Disorders
Kleptomania
Pathological Gambling
Pyromania
Trichotillomania

Mental Disorders Usually Diagnosed in Childhood or Adolescence
Attention Deficit/Hyperactivity Disorder (ADHD)
Austism Spectrum Disorders
Asperger's Syndrome
Autistic Disorder
Conduct Disorder
Tic Disorders
Chronic Motor or Vocal Tic Disorder
Transient Tic Disorder
Tourette's Syndrome

Mood Disorders
Bipolar Depression
Depression
Dythymic Disorder
Major Depression
Postpartum Depression
Premenstrual Dysphoric Disorder

Personality Disorders
Antisocial Personality Disorder
Avoidant Personality Disorder
Borderline Personality Disorder
Dependent Personality Disorder
Histrionic Personality Disorder
Narcissistic Personality Disorder
Obsessive-Compulsive Personality Disorder
Paranoid Personality Disorder
Schizoid Personality Disorder
Schizotypal Personality Disorder

Psychotic Disorders
Brief Psychotic Disorder
Delusional Disorders
Schizoaffective Disorder
Schizophrenia

Psychosomatic Disorders
Hypochondria
Factitious Disorder
Malingering Disorder
Somatization Disorder

Sexual / Gender Identification Disorders
Sexual Desire Disorder
Sexual Arousal Disorder
Orgasmic Disorder Symptom
Sexual Pain Disorder
Paraphilias (Perversions)
Exhibitionism
Fetishism
Frotteurism
Pedophilia
Sexual Masochism
Sexual Sadism
Transvestic Fetishism
Voyeurism

Sleep Disorders
Primary Insomnia
Primary Hypersomnia
Narcolepsy
Breathing-related Sleep Disorder
Circadian Rhythm Sleep Disorder
Substance Abuse Induced Sleep Disorder
Night mare Disorder
Sleep Terror Disorder

Below is a sample listing illustrating the kind of information that is or might be included in an Association entry, with additional fields that apply to publication and trade show listings. Each numbered items of information is described in the paragraphs on the following page.

---

1.   **12345**

2.   **Association for People with Mental Illness**
3.   29 Simmons Street
     Philadelphia, PA 15201

4.   234-555-1111
5.   234-555-1112
6.   800-555-1113
7.   TDD: 234-555-1114
8.   Info@association-mh.com
9.   www.association-mh.com

10.   William Lancaster, Executive Director
      Monty Spitz, Marketing Manager
      Kathleen Morrison, Medical Consultant

11.   Association for Mental Health is funded by the Mental Health Community Support Program. The purpose of the association is to share information about services, providers and ways to cope with mental illnesses. Available services include referrals, professional seminars, support groups, and a variety of publications.

12.   1 M *Members*

13.   *Founded*: 1984

14.   Bi Monthly

15. $59.00

16.   110,000

User's Key

1. **Record Number:** Entries are listed alphabetically within each category and numbered sequentially. The entry number, rather than the page number, are used in the indexes to refer to listings.

2. **Title:** Formal name of association or publication. Where names are completely capitalized, the listing will appear at the beginning of the section. If listing is a publication or trade show, the publisher or sponsoring organization will appear below the title.

3. **Address:** Location or permanent address of the association.

4. **Phone Number:** The listed phone number is usually for the main office of the association, but may also be for the sales, marketing, or public relations office as provided.

5. **Fax Number:** This is listed when provided by the association.

6. **Toll-Free Number:** This is listed when provided by the association.

7. **TDD:** This is listed when provided by the association. It refers to Telephone Device for the Deaf.

8. **E-mail:** This is listed when provided by the association.

9. **Web Site:** This is listed when provided by the association and is also referred to as an URL address. These web sites are accessed through the Internet by typing http://before the URL address.

10. **Key Executives**: Lists key contacts of the association, publication or sponsoring organization.

11. **Description:** This paragraph contains a brief description of the association, their purpose and services.

12. **Members:** Total number of association members.

13. **Founded:** Year association was founded.

14. **Frequency:** If listing is a publication.

15. **Subscription Price:** If listing is a publication.

16. **Circulation**: If listing is a publication.

Adjustment Disorders

Introduction

The experience of stress in life is inevitable and begins in utero. When we are faced with a painful event or situation, we do our best to cope, get through it, and move on. How we cope and how long it takes vary according to the stressful situation and the resources the individual brings to it. In most situations, we respond appropriately to the stressful event or situation and show an adaptive response.

Adjustment Disorders are maladaptive reactions to a stressful event or situation. The adjustment is to a real event or situation (e.g.,the breaking up of a relationship, being laid off), and the disorder signifies that the reaction is more extreme than would be warranted considering the stressor, or it keeps the individual from functioning as usual.

SYMPTOMS

•The development of emotional or behavioral symptoms is in response to an identifiable stressor except bereavement within three months of the appearance of the stressor;
•The emotions or behaviors are significant either because the distress is more extreme than would normally be caused by the stressor, or because the emotions or behaviors are clearly impairing the person's social, school, or work functioning;
•If the symptoms persist for less than six months after the stressor ends, the disorder is considered acute; if symptoms persist for longer than six months, the disorder is considered to be chronic.
•Adjustment Disorders are divided into several subtypes:

•**Depressed Mood** - predominant mood is depression, with symptoms such as tearfulness, hopelessness, sadness, sleep disturbances;
•**Anxiety** - predominant symptoms are edginess, nervousness, worry, or in children, fears of separation from important attachment figures;
•**Anxiety and Depressed Mood** - chief manifestations are a combination of depression and anxiety;
•**Disturbance of Conduct** - predominant symptoms are conduct which involves either a violation of other people's rights (e.g., reckless driving, fighting), or the violation of social norms and rules.

ASSOCIATED FEATURES

Many commonplace events can be stressful (e.g., first day of school, changing jobs). If the stressor is an acute event (like an impending surgical procedure), the onset of the disturbance is usually immediate but may not last more than six months after the stressor ends. If the stressor or its consequences continue (such as a long-term illness), the Adjustment Disorder may also continue. Whatever the nature of the event, it caused the person to feel overwhelmed. A person may be reacting to one or many stressors; the stressor may affect one person or the whole family. The more severe the stressor, the more likely that an Adjustment Disorder will develop. If a person is already vulnerable, e.g., is suffering from a disability or a mental disorder, an Adjustment Disorder is more likely.

The diagnosis of an Adjustment Disorder is called a residual category, meaning that other possible diagnoses must be ruled out first. For example, symptoms that are part of a personality disorder and become worse under stress are not usually considered to be Adjustment Disorders unless they are new types of symptoms for the individual.

There are three questions to consider in diagnosing Adjustment Disorder: How out-of-proportion is the response to the stressor? How long does it go on? To what extent does it impair the person's ability to function in social, workplace, and school settings?

The emotional response may show itself in excessive worry and edginess, excessive sadness and hopelessness or a combination of these. There may also be changes in behavior in response to the stressful event or situation, with the person violating other people's rights or breaking agreed-upon rules and regulations. The emotional response and the changes in behavior persist, even after the stressful event or circumstances have ended. Finally, the response significantly affects the person's normal functioning in social, school or work settings.

Adjustment Disorders increase the risk of suicidal behavior and completed suicide, and they also complicate the course of other medical conditions (for example, patients may not take their medication, eat properly, etc).

PREVALENCE

Men and women of all ages, as well as children, can suffer from this disorder. In outpatient mental health centers the diagnosis of Adjustment Disorder is made in five to twenty percent of patients.

TREATMENT OPTIONS

Anyone who is experiencing one or more stressful events or circumstances, and feels overwhelmed or markedly distressed and cannot function normally, should seek help. A psychiatrist or other mental health professional should make an evaluation including a referral for physical examination if necessary. Treatment prescribed is often psychotherapy and, depending on the circumstances, can include individual, couple, or family therapy. Medication is sometimes prescribed for a few weeks or months. In most instances long-term therapy will not be necessary and the person can expect marked improvement within 8 to 12 sessions.

Associations & Agencies

2 **Alive Alone**
1112 Champaign Drive
Van Wert, OH 45891-2569
419-238-7879
E-mail: alivealone@bright.net
www.alivealone.org

Kay Bevington, Founder

Self-help network of parents who have lost child/children. Provides education and publications to promote communication and healing, assists in resolving grief, and develops the means to reinvest lives for a positive future.

Year Founded: 1988

3   At Health
14241 NE Woodinville-Duvall Road
Suite 104
Woodinville, WA 98072-8564
360-668-3808
888-284-3258
Fax: 360-668-2216
E-mail: support@athealth.com
www.athealth.com

Providing trustworthy online information, tools, and training that enhance the ability of practitioners to furnish high quality, personalized care to those they serve. For the meantl health consumer, find practitioners, treatment center, learn about disorders and conditions, and about medications being used, news and resources.

4   Center For Mental Health Services
SAMSHA's National Mental Health Information Center
PO Box 42557
Washington, DC 20015-557
866-889-2647
800-789-2647
Fax: 240-221-4295
E-mail: info@mentalhealth.org
www.mentalhealth.samhsa.gov

A Kathryn Power, MEd, Director
Edward B Searle, Deputy Director

Information about resources, technical assistance, research, training, networks, and other federal clearing houses, and fact sheets and materials.

5   Center for Family Support (CFS)
333 7th Avenue
9th floor
New York, NY 10001-5004
212-629-7939
Fax: 212-239-2211
E-mail: jortiz@cfsny.org
www.cfsny.org

Steven Vernikoff, Executive Director

An agency that continues to develop new programs to serve families and individuals with their care needs. They currently offer services throughout the New York City region including: New Jersey, Long Island and the Lower Hudson Valley.

6   Center for Loss in Multiple Birth (CLIMB)
PO Box 91377
Anchorage, AK 99509-1377
907-222-5321
E-mail: climb@pobox.alaska.net
www.climb-support.org

Jean Kollantai, Founder

Support by and for parents who have experienced the death of one or more of their twins or higher multiples during pregnance, birth, in infancy, or childhood. Newsletter, information on specialized topics, pen pals, phone support.

7   Center for Mental Health Services (CMHS)
PO Box 2345
Rockville, MD 20847
240-221-4021
800-789-2647
Fax: 240-221-4295
TDD: 866-889-2647
www.mentalhealth.samhsa.gov

A Kathryn Power, MEd, Director
Anna Marsh PhD, Deputy Director
Fran Randolph PhD, Dir, Service & Systems Improveme
Anne Mathews-Younes EdD, Dir, Prevention/Traumatic Stress

CMHS leads Federal efforts to treat mental illnesses by promoting mental health and by preventing the development or worsening of mental illness when possible. Congress created CMHS to bring new hope to adults who have serious mental illnesses and to children with serious emotional disorders. CMHS provides information about mental health via a toll-free the web site, and more than 600 publications. Developed for users of mental health services and their families, the general public, policy makers, providers, and the media.

Year Founded: 1992

8   First Candle/SIDS Alliance
1314 Bedford Avenue
Suite 210
Baltimore, MD 21208-6605
410-415-6628
800-221-7437
E-mail: info@firstcandle.org

Deborah M Boyd, Executive Director
Laura L Reno, Director Marketing/Public Affair

National nonprofit health organization uniting parents, care givers and researchers nationwide with government, business and community service groups to advance infant health and survival. With help from a national network of member and partner organizations, we are working to increase public participation and support in the fight against infant mortality.

9   Grief Recovery After Substance Passing (GRASP)
C/O Patricia Wittberger
1088 Torrey Pines Road
Chula Vista, CA 91915-1404
843-705-2217
Fax: 619-397-3493
E-mail: mom@jennysjourney.org
www.grasphelp.org

Patricia Wittberger, Contact

Support and advocacy group for parents who have suffered the death of a child due to substance abuse. Provides opportunity for parents to share theri greif and experiences without shame or recrimination.

Year Founded: 2002

10   M.I.S.S. Foundation/Center for Loss & Trauma
2525 W Carefree Hwy 7-148
Phoeniz, AZ 85085

623-979-1000
888-455-6577
Fax: 623-979-1001
E-mail: info@missfoundation.org
www.missfoundation.org

Dr Joanne Cacciatore PhD FT LMSW, Founder
Jenny McSpadden

Offers emergency and on-going support for families suffering from the loss of a child. Provides information, referrals, phone support, newsletter, pen pals, literature, advocacy and online chat room support. Information on local group development.

Year Founded: 1995

11   National Association for the Dually Diagnosed (NADD)
132 Fair Street
Kingston, NY 12401-4802
845-331-4336
800-331-5362
Fax: 845-331-4569
E-mail: info@thenadd.org
www.thenadd.org

Robert Fletcher, Executive Director
Donna Nagy, President

Not-for-profit membership association established for professionals, care providers and families to promote understanding of and services for individuals who have developmental disabilities and mental health needs.

12   National Mental Health Consumers' Self-Help Clearinghouse
1211 Chestnut Street
Suite 1207
Philadelphia, PA 19107-4103
215-751-1810
800-553-4539
Fax: 215-636-6312
E-mail: info@mhselfhelp.org
www.mhselfhelp.org

Joseph Rogers, Executive Director

A national consumer technical assistance center that has played a major role in the development of the mental health consumer movement.

Year Founded: 1986

13   National Organization of Parents of Murdered Children
100 E 8th Street
Suite 202
Cincinnati, OH 45202-2129
513-721-5683
888-818-7662
Fax: 513-345-4489
E-mail: natlpomc@aol.com
www.pomc.org

Nancy Ruhe, Executive Director
Ann Reed, VP

Provides self help groups to support persons who survived the violent death of someone close, as they seek to recover.

Newsletter, and court accompaniment also provided in many areas. Offers guidelines for starting local chapters. Parole Block Program and Second Option Service also available.

Year Founded: 1978

14   Save Our Sons And Daughters (SOSAD)
2441 W Grand Blvd
Detroit, MI 48208-1259
313-361-5200
Fax: 313-361-0055
E-mail: sosadb@aol.com

Clementine Barfield, Contact

Crisis intervention and violence prevention program that provides support and advocacy for survivors of homicide or other traumatic loss.

1987 pages

15   Survivors of Loved Ones' Suicides (SOLOS)
PO Box 592
Dumfries, VA 22026-592
703-580-8958
E-mail: solos@1000deaths.com
www.1000deaths.com

Christine Smith, President
Betsy Beasley, VP

Organization to help provide support for the families and friends who have suffered the suicide loss of a loved one.

16   Tender Hearts
Triplet Connection
PO Box 429
Spring City, UT 84662-429
435-851-1105
Fax: 435-462-7466
E-mail: tc@tripletconnection.org
www.tripletconnection.org

Janet L Bleyl, President
Cheryl L Newcomb, Chairman

Network of parents who have lost one or more children in multiple births. Information on selection reduction. Newletter, information and referrals, phone support and pen pals.

17   Triplet Connection
PO Box 429
Spring City, UT 84662-429
435-851-1105
Fax: 435-462-7466
www.tripletconnection.org

Janet L Bleyl, President
Cheryl L Newcomb, Chairman

Network of parents who have lost one or more children in multiple births. Information on selection reduction. Newletter, information and referrals, phone support and pen pals.

Year Founded: 1983

18 UNITE Inc Grief Support
PO Box 65
7600 Central Avenue
Drexel Hill, PA 19026-65

888-488-6483
E-mail: administrator@unitegriefsupport.org
www.unitegriefsupport.org

Barbara Bond-Moury, Chairperson
Joanne Porreca, Administrator

Support for parents grieving miscarriage, stillbirth and infant death. Also provides support for parents through subsequent pregnancies. Group meetings, phone help, newsletter, annual conference. Offers group facilitator and grief counselor training programs. Professional in advisory roles.

Year Founded: 1975

Books

19 After School and More
Resources for Children with Special Needs
116 E 16th Street
5th Floor
New York, NY 10003-2164
212-677-4650
Fax: 212-254-4070
E-mail: info@resourcenyc.org
www.resourcesnyc.org

Rachel Howard, Executive Director

The most complete directory of after school programs for children with disabilities and special needs in the metropolitan New York area focusing on weekend and holiday programs. *$25.00*

ISBN 0-967836-57-3

20 Consumer's Guide to Psychiatric Drugs
New Harbinger Publications
5674 Shattuck Avenue
Oakland, CA 94609-1662
510-652-0215
800-748-6273
Fax: 510-652-5472
E-mail: customerservice@newharbinger.com
www.newharbinger.com

Matthew McKay, Owner

Helps consumers understand what treatment options are available and what side effects to expect. Covers possible interactions with other drugs, medical conditions and other concerns. Explains how each drug works, and offers detailed information about treatments for depression, bipolar disorder, anxiety and sleep disorders, as well as other conditions. *$16.95*

340 pages ISBN 1-572241-11-X

21 Don't Despair on Thursdays: the Children's Grief-Management Book
ADD WareHouse
300 NW 70th Avenue
Suite 102
Plantation, FL 33317-2360
954-792-8944
800-233-9273
Fax: 954-792-8545
E-mail: sales@addwarehouse.com
www.addwarehouse.com

Harvey C Parker, Owner

Children are sure to be comforted by the friendly manner and sensitivity that this book imparts as it explains the grief process to children and helps them understand that grieving is a normal response. For children ages 4-10. *$18.95*

61 pages Year Founded: 1996 ISBN 0-933849-60-5

22 Don't Feed the Monster on Tuesdays: The Children's Self-Esteem Book
ADD WareHouse
300 NW 70th Avenue
Suite 102
Plantation, FL 33317-2360
954-792-8944
800-233-9273
Fax: 954-792-8545
E-mail: sales@addwarehouse.com
www.addwarehouse.com

Harvey C Parker, Owner

Strikes right at the heart of the basic elements of self-esteem. It presents valuable information to children that will help them understand the importance of their self worth. A friendly book that children ages 4 to 10 will love. *$18.95*

55 pages Year Founded: 1991 ISBN 0-933849-38-9

23 Drug Therapy and Adjustment Disorders
Mason Crest Publishers
370 Reed Road
Suite 302
Broomall, PA 19008-4017
610-543-6200
866-627-2665
Fax: 610-543-3878
E-mail: dtaylor@masoncrest.com
www.masoncrest.com

Adolescents are among those who suffer from adjustment disorders, many without knowing what it is or how it affects their lives. This book offers information on the advances in the development of antidepressants with fewer side effects and how their more selective effect on the neurotransmitters of the brain has led to their use in treatment for adjustment disorders.

ISBN 1-590845-80-9

24 Preventing Maladjustment from Infancy Through Adolescence
Sage Publications
2455 Teller Road
Thousand Oaks, CA 91320-2234

805-499-0721
800-818-7243
Fax: 805-499-0871
E-mail: info@sagepub.com
www.sagepub.com

Blaise R Simqu, CEO

Examines the theoretical and historical issues of prevention with children and youth, and delineates those factors which place the individual at risk. Hardcover $109.00 & Paperback $51.95

156 pages Year Founded: 1987 ISBN 0-803928-68-8

25   Stress Response Syndromes: Personality Styles and Interventions
Jason Aronson-Rowman & Littlefield Publishers
200 Park Avenue South
Suite 1109
New York, NY 10003-1512
212-529-3888
E-mail: custerv@rowman.com
www.rowmanlittlefield.com

Neils Aaboe, Manager

Incorporation of the most recent advances in the understanding and treatment of stress response syndromes to date. Describes the general characteristics, including signs and symptoms, and elaborates on treatment techniques that integrate cognitive and dynamic approaches. *$43.00*

451 pages ISBN 0-765703-13-0

26   Transition from School to Post-School Life for Individuals with Disabilities
Charles C Thomas Publisher
PO Box 19265
Springfield, IL 62794-9265
217-789-8980
800-258-8980
Fax: 217-789-9130
www.ccthomas.com

Designed to assist professionals in developing and implementing transition services for students with disabilities. Specifically, this book focuses on the importance of assessment in transition planning and targets the various domains that should be included in any achool-to-work transition assessment. advocates a transdisciplinary school-based approach to transition assessment that involves not only school-based professionals in the assessment process but community agency representatives as well. Available in paperback for $41.95. *$61.95*

300 pages Year Founded: 2004 ISBN 0-398074-80-1

27   Treatment of Stress Response Syndromes
American Psychiatric Publishing, Inc.
1000 Wilson Boulevard
Suite 1825
Arlington, VA 22209-3901
703-907-7322
800-368-5777
Fax: 703-907-1091
E-mail: appi@psych.org
www.appi.org

Robert E Hales MD, Editor-in-Chief
Ron McMillen, Chief Executive Officer
John McDuffie, Editorial Director

A comprehensive clinical guide to treating patients with disorders related to loss, trauma and terror. Author Mardi J Horowitz, MD, is the clinical researcher who is largely responsible for modern concepts of posttraumatic stress disorder (PTSD). In this book he reveals the latest strategies for treating PTSD and expands the coverage to include several related diagnoses. *$27.50*

134 pages Year Founded: 2003 ISBN 1-585621-07-2

28   When A Friend Dies
Free Spirit Publishing
217 Fifth Avenue North
Suite 200
Minneapolis, MN 55401-1299
612-338-2068
Fax: 612-337-5050
E-mail: help4kids@freespirit.com
www.freespirit.com

Judy Galbraith, Owner

The death of a friend is a wrenching event for anyone at any age. Teenagers especially need help coping. This compassionate book answers questions grieving teens often have, like 'How should I be acting?''Is it wrong to go to parties and have fun?' and 'What if I can't handle my grief on my own?' The author has seen her children suffer from the death of a friend, and she knows what teens go through. Also recommended for parents and teachers of teens who have experienced a painful loss. *$9.95*

128 pages

Periodicals & Pamphlets

29   A Journey Together
Bereaved Parents of the USA
C/O Betty R Ewart
326 Longview Avenue
Lewisburg, WV 24901
304-645-3048
E-mail: jbgoodrich@sbcglobal.net
www.bereavedparentsusa.org

Dave Alexander, President 2009-2010
John Goodrich, National Contact
Betty R Ewart, Author

The newsletter contains articles of interest to the bereaved about grief. It also has book reviews and information about upcoming Grief Gatherings and other support groups.

4 per year

30   Journal of Mental Health Research
NADD Press
132 Fair Street
Kingston, NY 12401-4802
845-331-4336
800-331-5362
Fax: 845-334-4569

E-mail: info@thenadd.org
www.thenadd.org

Robert Fletcher, Executive Director

Bi-monthly publication designed to promote interest of professional and parent development with resources for individuals who have the coexistence of mental illness and mental retardation.

4 per year

31   The NADD Bulletin
NADD Press
132 Fair Street
Kingston, NY 12401-4802
845-331-4336
800-331-5362
Fax: 845-334-4569
E-mail: info@thenadd.org
www.thenadd.org

Robert Fletcher, Executive Director

Bi-monthly publication designed to promote interest of professional and parent development with resources for individuals who have the coexistence of mental illness and mental retardation.

6 per year

Support Groups & Hot Lines

32   Bereaved Parents of the USA
PO Box 95
Park Forest, IL 60466-0095
708-748-7866
E-mail: jbgoodrich@sbcglobal.net
www.bereavedparentsusa.org

Dave Alexander, President 2009-2010
John Goodrich, National Contact

BP/USA is a national non-profit self-help group that offers support, understanding, compassion and hope especially to the newly bereaved, whether they are granparents, parents or siblings.

33   Compassionte Friends, Inc
PO Box 3696
Oak Brook, IL 60522-3696
630-990-0010
877-969-0010
Fax: 630-990-0246
E-mail: nationaloffice@compassionatefriends.org
www.compassionatefriends.org

Bereavement support for families grieving the death of a child of any age regardless of cause.

34   Friends for Survival
PO Box 214463
Sacramento, CA 95821-463
916-392-0664
www.friendsforsurvival.org

Marilyn Koenig, Contact

Assists family, friends, and professionals following a suicide death.

35   National SHARE Office
St. Joseph Health Center
300 1st Capitol Drive
Saint Charles, MO 63301-2844
636-947-6164
800-821-6819
Fax: 636-947-7486
E-mail: share@nationalshareoffice.com
www.NationalSHAREOffice.com

Mandy Murphey Brown, President
Susan Pundmann, Executive Director

Pregnancy and infant loss support.

36   Parents of Murdered Children
100 East Eighth Street
Suite 202
Cincinnati, OH 45202-2129
513-721-5683
888-818-7662
Fax: 513-345-4489
E-mail: natlpomc@aol.com
www.pomc.org

Nancy Ruhe, Executive Director

Parents supporting parents who have suffered the loss of a murdered child.

37   Rainbows
2100 Golf Road
Suite 370
Rolling Meadows, IL 60008-4231
847-952-1770
Fax: 847-952-1774
E-mail: info@rainbows.org
www.rainbows.org

Suzy Marta, President

An international, not-for-profit organization that fosters emotional healing among children grieving a loss from a life-altering crisis. Rainbows provides training and curricula for ages 4 through adults: Sunbeams: Preschool edition; Rainbows: Elementary Edition; Spectrum: High School Edition; Kaleidoscope: College age/Adult Edition; Prism: Single/Stepparent Edition and Silver Linings: Community Crisis response Editions.

38   Survivors of Loved Ones' Suicides (SOLOS)
PO Box 592
Dumfries, VA 22026-592
703-580-8958
E-mail: solos@1000deaths.com
www.1000deaths.com

For the families and friends who have suffered the suicide loss of a loved one.

Video & Audio

39 Effective Learning Systems
3451 Bonita Bay Boulevard
Suite 205
Bonita Springs, FL 34134-4354
239-948-1660
800-966-5683
Fax: 239-948-1664
E-mail: info@efflearn.com
www.efflearn.com

Robert E Griswold, President
Deirdre M Griswold, VP

Audio tapes for stress management, deep relaxation, anger control, peace of mind, insomnia, weight and smoking, self-image and self-esteem, positive thinking, health and healing. Since 1972, Effective Learning Systems has helped millions of people take charge of their lives and make positive changes. Over 75 titles available, each with a money-back guarantee. Price range $12-$14.

Web Sites

40 AtHealth.Com
At Health

Providing trustworthy online information, tools, and training that enhance the ability of practitioners to furnish high quality, personalized care to those they serve. For mental health consumers, find practitioners, treatment centers, learn about disorders and medications, news and resources.

41 www.1000deaths.com
Survivors of Loved Ones' Suicides

Group for those who have suffered a suicide loss.

42 www.alivealone.org
Alive Alone

Self-help network of parents who have lost an only child or all of their children. Provides education and publications to promote communication and healing, assists in resolving grief, and develops the means to reinvest lives for a positive future.

43 www.athealth.com
At Health

Provides information and tools to enhance practitioners quality for those whom they serve.

44 www.bereavedparentsusa.org
Bereaved Parents' Network

Designed to aid and suport bereaved parents and their families who are struggling to survive their grief after the death of a child. Information and referrals, newsletter, phone support, conferences, support group meetings. Assistance and guidelines in starting groups.

45 www.cfsny.org
Center for Family Support

Provides services and programs for individuals living with developmental and related disabilities, and for the families that care for them at home.

46 www.climb-support.org
Center for Loss in Multiple Birth

Support by and for parents who have experienced the death of one or more of their twins or higher multiples during pregnance, birth, in infancy, or childhood. Newsletter, information on specialized topics, pen pals, phone support.

47 www.compassionatefriends.org
Compassionate Friends

Organization for those having lost a child.

48 www.counselingforloss.com
Counseling for Loss and Life Changes

Look under articles for reprints of writings and links.

49 www.cyberpsych.org
CyberPsych

CyberPsych presents information about psychoanalysis, psychotherapy and topics like anxiety disorders, substance abuse, homophobia, and traumas. It hosts mental health organizations and individuals with content of interest to the public and professional communities. There is also a free therapist finder service.

50 www.death-dying.com
Death and Dying Grief Support

Information on grief and loss.

51 **www.divorceasfriends.com**
Bill Ferguson's How to Divorce as Friends

Useful information on how to eliminate the anger usually associated with divorce.

52 **www.divorcecentral.com**
Surviving the Emotional Trauma of Divorce

Offers helpful advice and suggestions on what to expect emotionally, and how to deal with the emotional effects of divorce.

53 **www.divorceinfo.com**
Divorce Information

Simply written and covers all the issues.

54 **www.divorcemag.com**
Divorce Magazine

The printed magazine's commercial site.

55 **www.divorcesupport.com**
Divorce Support

Covers all aspects of divorce.

56 **www.friendsforsurvival.org**
Friends for Survival

Assisting anyone who has suffered the loss of a loved one through suicide death.

57 **www.grasphelp.org**
Grief Recovery After A Substance Passing

Support and advocacy group for parents who have suffered the death of a child due to substance abuse. Provides opportunity for parents to share theri grief and experiences without shame or recrimination. They will provide information and suggestions for those wanting to start a similar group elsewhere.

58 **www.griefnet.org**
GriefNet

Useful information on coping with loss.

59 **www.mhselfhelp.org**
National Self-Help Clearinghouse

Encouraging the development and growth of consumer self-help groups.

60 **www.misschildren.org**
Mothers in Sympathy and Support

Help for mothers suffering the loss of a child.

61 **www.missfoundation.org**
MISS Foundation

Offers emergency and on-going support for families suffering from the loss of a child. Provides information, referrals, phone support, newsletter, pen pals, literature, advocacy and online chat room support. Information on local group development. Local support group listings online.

62 **www.nationalshareoffice.com**
National SHARE Office

Pregnancy and infant loss support.

63 **www.planetpsych.com**
PlanetPsych.com

Learn about disorders, their treatments and other topics in psychology. Articles are listed under the related topic areas. Ask a therapist a question for free, or view the directory of professionals in your area. If you are a therapist sign up for the directory. Current features, self-help, interactive, and newsletter archives.

64 **www.pomc.com**
Parents of Murdered Children

Help for anyone who has suffered the loss of a murdered child.

65 **www.psychcentral.com**
Psych Central

Personalized one-stop index for psychology, support, and mental health issues, resources, and people on the Internet.

66 **www.psycom.net/depression.central.grief.html**
Grief and Bereavement

Helpful information for those grieving from the loss of a loved one.

67 **www.rainbows.org**
Rainbows

Group for grieving parents and children.

68 **www.realtionshipjourney.com**
Relationship and Learning Center

Articles on divorce, among other articles.

69 **www.safecrossingsfoundation.org**
Safe Crossings Foundation

For children facing a loved one's death.

70 **www.sidsalliance.org**
First Candle/SIDS Alliance

For those who have suffered the loss of an infant through SIDS.

71 **www.spig.clara.net/guidline.htm**
Guidelines for Separating Parents

Useful information that helps to decrease the stress associated with separation.

72 **www.thenadd.org**
National Association for The Dually Diagnosed: NADD

An association for persons with developmental disabilities and mental health needs.

73 **www.tripletconnection.org**
Tender Hearts

Network of parents who have lost one or more children in multiple births. Information on selection reduction. Newletter, information and referrals, phone support and pen pals.

74 **www.unitegriefsupport.org**
UNITE

Support for parents grieving miscarriage, stillbirth and infant death. Also provides support for parents through subsequent pregnancies. Group meetings, phone help, newsletter, annual conference. Offers group facilitator and grief counselor training programs. Professional in advisory roles.

75 **www.widownet.org**
WidowNet

Help for someone suffering the loss of a spouse.

Alcohol/Substance Abuse & Dependence

Introduction

Substance abuse and addictive disorders are among the most destructive mental disorders in America today, contributing to a host of medical and social problems and to widespread individual suffering. Alcohol, a drug that is widely available and socially approved, is the most abused of all substances, and alcohol addiction is a pervasive mental disorder. Like all addictive disorders, alcohol addiction is characterized by repeated use despite repeated adverse consequences, and by physical and psychological craving.

Alcohol addiction can be treated, but successful recovery is dependent on acceptance by the patient that he or she has an illness; lack of this acceptance is often the greatest stumbling block to treatment.

Relapse is common for several reasons: lack of acceptance of the diagnosis; genetic vulnerability; and social factors. Successful treatment very often requires involvement by the patient in some form of self-help group, such as Alcoholics Anonymous or another 12-step program. The great majority of motivated individuals with these disorders can recover, but it often requires three or more separate episodes of treatment to more or less permanently prevent relapse and lead to recovery.

Scientific understanding of how alcohol works on the body and the brain, and the underlying physiology of addiction, has advanced remarkably in recent years. With the help of brain imaging and other techniques, we can now see that these disorders are associated with structural changes in the brain.

The substances referred to in this section include: amphetamines; marijuana; cocaine (and its purer derivative, crack); hallucinogens, such as LSD; inhalants, such as butane gas or cleaning fluid; opioids, such as morphine, heroin, or codeine; and benzodiazepines like Valium and Zanax. Caffeine and nicotine, both of which have the potential for abuse and dependence, are not included. The United States Food and Drug Administration has proposed adding nicotine to the list of addictive substances they monitor.

SYMPTOMS

Alcohol and Substance Abuse Symptoms:
•Repeated use resulting in inability to fulfill fundamental obligations at work, school, or home, e.g., repeated absences, poor work performance, family neglect;
•Repeated use, resulting in dangerous situation, e.g., driving or operating a machine while impaired;
•Repeated alcohol and substance-related legal problems, e.g., arrests for disorderly conduct;
•Continued use despite persistent social or interpersonal problems worsened by the effects of substance abuse.

Alcohol and Substance Dependence Problems:
•Alcohol or substance is often taken in greater amounts or for a longer period than intended;
•Repeated wish or unsuccessful attempts to control use;
•A great deal of time is taken to get and use alcohol or substance or to recover from its effects;
•Important social, work, or recreational activities are missed because of use;
•Use continues in spite of the person knowing about the persistent psychological or physical problems it causes, e.g., depression induced by cocaine or continued drinking.

Tolerance:
•Need for increased amounts of alcohol or the substance to achieve desired effect;
•Diminished effects with continued use of the same amount of alcohol or substance;
•Alcohol abuse can occur without tolerance, as in binge drinking, a particular problem for young people on college campuses and elsewhere.

Withdrawal:
•Characteristic withdrawal syndrome, prolonged taking and then stopping/reducing alcohol or substance causing physical and mental symptoms;
•Same or a related substance is taken to avoid/alleviate the withdrawal symptoms.

ASSOCIATED FEATURES

Frequently, alcohol abuse and dependence occur together with dependence on other substances, and alcohol may be used to counteract the ill effects of these substances. Depression, anxiety, and sleep disorders are common in alcohol dependence.

Typically, accidents, injuries and suicide accompany alcohol dependence, and it is estimated that half of all traffic accidents involve alcoholic intoxication. Absenteeism, low work productivity and injuries on the job are often caused by alcohol dependence. Alcohol is also the most common cause of preventable birth defects, including fetal alcohol syndrome, according to the American Psychiatric Association.

Women and men tend to have different drinking patterns. Society is more tolerant of male drunkeness than of female; women tend to drink alone and in secret and are more susceptible to medical complications of alcoholism. Alcohol abuse severely damages organ systems including the brain, the liver, the heart, and the digestive tract.

Genetics has a considerable influence on a person's propensity for substance abuse disorders, and such disorders are associated with significant changes in the brain.

Many individuals with substance or alcohol-use disorders take more than one substance and suffer from other mental symptoms and disorders as well. Individuals with a wide variety of mental disorders sometimes abuse drugs as an attempt to medicate themselves. Forty-seven percent of people with Schizophrenia have drug abuse/disorders. People with Antisocial Personality Disorder often abuse substances, including amphetamines such as cocaine. Substance-related disorders can also lead to other mental disorders. Use of the synthetic hallucinogen Ecstasy is associated with acute and paranoid psychoses, and the prolonged use of cocaine (a stimulant) can lead to paranoid psychosis with violent behavior. Substance use and the effects on an individual's employment and relationships, as well as legal difficulties, can precipitate anxiety and mood disorders. Intravenous substance abuse is associated with a high risk of HIV infections and other medical complications.

Chronic drug and alcohol abuse can lead to difficulty in memory and problem solving, and impaired sexual functioning.

Childhood sexual abuse is strongly associated with substance dependence and with a number of other mental symptoms and disorders.

PREVALENCE

Alcohol dependence and abuse are among the most prevalent mental disorders in the general population. One community study in the US found that about eight percent of the adult population had alcohol dependence and about five percent had alcohol abuse at some time in their lives. Approximately six percent had alcohol dependence or abuse during the preceding year.

There are large cultural differences in attitudes toward substances. In some cultures, mood altering drugs, including alcohol, are well accepted; in others they are strictly forbidden.

Those between the ages of 18 and 24 have a high prevalence for abuse of all substances. Early adolescent drug and alcohol use is associated with a slight but significant decline in intellectual abilities. Substance related disorders are more common among males than females. The lifetime prevalence of use of any drugs (aside from alcohol) in the US is 11.9 percent; in males it is twice as high as in females. About thirteen percent of the general population is estimated to use cannabis (marijuana); about seven to nine percent of 18 to 25 year-olds have used amphetamines at least once; eight to 15.5 percent of 26 to 34 year-olds have used hallucinogens like LSD at least once. Inhalants have been used at least once by five percent of the population. Inhalants are used mainly by boys between eight and 19 years old, and especially by 13 to 15 year-olds.

TREATMENT OPTIONS

Diagnosis and treatment of alcohol dependence has improved as understanding of the physiology of addiction has advanced. But successful treatment still relies on acceptance by the patient that he or she has an illness, as well as support from other people who have gone through the same process. For this reason, medical treatment is most often successful when it is accompanied by involvement in a support group, for both the patient and family members; these may include Alcoholics Anonymous (AA) and Al-Anon, 12-step spiritual programs that have gained popularity over the years. Local groups can be found in almost every community and are listed in the phone book and on the Internet. Recently, similar groups have formed that do not emphasize spirituality, as these do, but rely on group support for sobriety.

There is a growing controversy over the need for people who have had an alcohol problem to abstain completely from alcohol for the rest of their lives, one of the central beliefs of AA. Some researchers and clinicians are arguing that it is possible for some former alcoholics to resume controlled social drinking. AA, in the past, has discouraged

members from using psychotropic medications; this is often counterproductive. Many alcohol treatment programs have been developed with men's needs and personalities in mind. Successful programs for women are less confrontational than men's programs and include arrangements for child care.

Treatment for alcoholism has been hospital-based in the past, but has increasingly moved to the outpatient setting. Hospital treatment is necessary for withdrawal when alcohol use has been heavy and steady. Delirium tremens, a consequence of very heavy drinking, can be fatal.

Medical treatment of alcohol dependence may include Anabuse, a drug that makes an individual violently ill if alcohol is used. Group or hospital-based treatment may also be useful, and psychotherapy can help the patient more effectively deal with underlying conflicts and interpersonal problems.

Denial of illness and ambivalence about abstinence can make treatment difficult. A patient's cravings can be overwhelmingly intense, and the individual's social circle is often composed of other substance abusers, making it hard for the individual to maintain relationships while becoming or remaining abstinent — the goal in treatment. A wide range of intervention may be needed, including a general assessment of the drug abuse, and evaluation of medical, social, and psychological problems. It is best to involve partner/family/friends to help the person gain new understanding of the problem and to make the general assessment complete. An explicit treatment plan should be worked out with the person (and partner/family/friends if appropriate) with concrete goals for which the person takes responsibility, which should include not only stopping substance use, but dealing with associated problems concerning health, personal relationships and work.

Associations & Agencies

77 Alcoholics Anonymous (AA): Worldwide
475 Riverside Drive
11th Floor
New York, NY 10115-58
212-870-3400
Fax: 212-870-3003
E-mail: cpc@aa.org
www.aa.org
Don Meurer, VP

A fellowship of men and women who share their experience, strength and hope with each other that they may solve their common problem and help others to recover from alcoholism.

78 American Academy of Addiction Psychiatry (AAAP)
345 Blackstone Boulevard
1st Floor - Weld
Providence, RI 02906-4800
401-524-3076
Fax: 401-272-0922
E-mail: info@aaap.org
www.aaap.org

Kevin A.. Sevarino MD, Head, Treatment Section
Karen P.G. Drexler MD, Head, Education Section
Richard N. Rosenthal MD, Head, Public Policy Section
Laura F. McNicholas MD, PhD, Head, Research Section

Professional membership organization with approximately 1,000 members in the United States and around the world. The membership consists of psychiatrists who work with addiction in their practices, faculty at various academic institutions.

79   American Council on Alcoholism

1000 E. Indian School Road
Phoenix, AZ 85014-4810

800-527-5344
E-mail: info@aca-usa.org
www.aca-usa.org

Lloyd Vacovsky, Executive Director
Percy Menzies, Acting Chairman

ACA is dedicated to educating the public about the effects of alcohol, alcoholism, alcohol abuse & the need for prompt, effective, readily-available & affordable alcoholism treatment.

80   American Public Human Services Association

Ste 4
1133 19th St Nw
Washington, DC 20036-3623
202-682-0100
Fax: 202-289-6555
E-mail: jfriedman@aphsa.org
www.aphsa.org

Karl Kurtz, President
Jerry Friedman, Executive Director

Nonprofit, bipartisan organization of individuals and agencies concerned with human services. Members include all state and many territorial human service agencies, more than 1,200 local agencies and thousands of individuals.

81   Career Assessment & Planning Services
Goodwill Industries-Suncoast

10596 Gandy Boulevard
PO Box 14456
St. Petersburg, FL 33733-4456
727-523-1512
888-279-1988
Fax: 727-577-2749
E-mail: gw.marketing@goodwill-suncoast.com
www.goodwill-suncoast.org

R. Lee Waits, President/CEO
Deborah A Passerini, VP Operations

Provides a comprehensive assessment, which can predict current and future employment and potential adjustment factors for physically, emotionally, or developmentally disabled persons who may be unemployed or underemployed.

82   Center for Family Support (CFS)

333 7th Avenue
New York, NY 10001-5115

212-629-7939
Fax: 212-239-2211
www.cfsny.org

Steven Vernikoff, Executive Director
Melanie Singleton, Human Resources Director

Service agency devoted to the physical well-being and development of the retarded child and the sound mental health of the parents. Helps families with retarded children with all aspects of home care including counseling, referrals, home aide service and consultation. Offers intervention for parents at the birth of a retarded child with in home support, guidance and infant stimulation. Pioneered training of nonprofessional women as home aides to provide supportive services in homes.

83   Center for Mental Health Services (CMHS)

PO Box 2345
Rockville, MD 20847
240-221-4021
800-789-2647
Fax: 240-221-4295
TDD: 866-889-2647
www.mentalhealth.samhsa.gov

A Kathryn Power, MEd, Director
Anna Marsh PhD, Deputy Director
Fran Randolph PhD, Dir, Service & Systems Improveme
Anne Mathews-Younes EdD, Dir, Prevention/Traumatic Stress

CMHS leads Federal efforts to treat mental illnesses by promoting mental health and by preventing the development or worsening of mental illness when possible. Congress created CMHS to bring new hope to adults who have serious mental illnesses and to children with serious emotional disorders. CMHS provides information about mental health via a toll-free the web site, and more than 600 publications. Developed for users of mental health services and their families, the general public, policy makers, providers, and the media.

Year Founded: 1992

84   Grief Recovery After Substance Passing (GRASP)

C/O Patricia Wittberger
1088 Torrey Pines Road
Chula Vista, CA 91915-1404
619-656-8414
Fax: 619-397-3493
E-mail: mom@jennysjourney.org
www.grasphelp.org

Support and advocacy group for parents who have suffered the death of a child due to substance abuse. Provides opportunity for parents to share theri greif and experiences without shame or recrimination. They will provide information and suggestions for those wanting to start a similar group elsewhere.

Year Founded: 2002

85   Mental Health America

2000 N. Beauregard Street
6th Floor
Alexandria, VA 22311

703-684-7722
800-969-6642
Fax: 703-684-5968
E-mail: infoctr@mentalhealthamerica.net
www.mentalhealthamerica.net

David Shern PhD, President/CEO

Formerly known as the National Mental Health Association, dedicated to promoting mental health, preventing mental and substance use conditions and achievving victory over mental illnesses and addictions through advocacy, education, research and service.

86   National Alliance on Mental Illness
3803 N Fairfax Drive
Suite 100
Arlington, VA 22203
703-524-7600
Fax: 703-524-9094
E-mail: info@nami.org
www.nami.org

Mike Fitzpatrick, Executive Director
Lynn Borton, COO

Dedicated to improving the lives of individuals and families affected by mental illness

Year Founded: 1979

87   National Association of Alcohol and Drug Abuse Counselors (NAADAC)
1001 N. Fairfax St.
Suite 201
Alexandria, VA 22314-1587
703-741-7686
800-548-0497
Fax: 703-741-7698
E-mail: naadac@naadac.org
www.naadac.org

Cythina Touhoy, Executive Director
Cynthia Moreno Tuohy, Executive Director

The only professional membership organization that serves counselors who specialize in addiction treatment. With 14,000 members and 47 state affiliates representing more than 80,000 addiction counselors, it is the nation's largest network of alcoholism and drug abuse treatment professionals. Among the organization's national certification programs are the National Certified Addiction Counselor and the Masters Addiction Counselor designations.

88   National Association of State Alcohol and Drug Abuse Directors
1025 Connecticut Avenue NW
Suite 605
Washington, DC 20036-5430
202-293-0090
Fax: 202-293-1250
E-mail: dcoffice@nasadad.org
www.nasadad.org

Robert Morrison, Executive Director
Alan Moghul, Prevention Director
Hollis McMullen, Director Finance

A private, nonprofit educational, scientific and informational organization that serves all state alcoholism and drug agency directors. NASADADs basic purpose is to foster and support the development of effective alcohol and other drug abuse prevention.

Year Founded: 1971

89   National Clearinghouse for Alcohol and Drug Information
PO Box 2345
Rockville, MD 20847-2345

800-729-6686
Fax: 301-468-7394
www.ncadi.samhsa.gov/govpubs/ph317/

Godfrey Jacobs, Deputy Director
John Noble, Project Director

One-stop resource for information about substance abuse prevention and addiction treatment.

90   National Council for Community Behavioral Healthcare
1701 K Street NW
Suite 400
Washington, DC 20006
202-684-7457
Fax: 202-684-7472
E-mail: communications@thenationalcouncil.org
www.thenationalcouncil.org

Linda Rosenberg, President/CEO
Jeannie Campbell, Executive VP

The unifying voice of America's behavioral health organizations. Serves the nation's most vulnerable citizens-more than 6 million adults and children with mental illnesses and addiction disorders

91   National Council on Alcoholism and Drug Dependence
244 East 58th Street
4th Floor
New York, NY 10022-2001
212-269-7797
Fax: 212-269-7510
E-mail: officemanager@ncadd.org
www.ncadd.org

Robert J Lindsey, President/CEO
Leah Brook, Affiliate Services Director
Devora Wooden, Office Manager

Fights the stigma and the disease of alcoholism and other drug addictions. Founded by Marty Mann, the first woman to find long-term sobriety in Alcoholics Anonymous, NCADD provides education, information, intervetion and treatment through offices in New York and Washington, and a nationwide network of Affiliates.

Year Founded: 1944

92   National Institute on Alcohol Abuse and Alcoholism
5635 Fishers Lane
MSC 9304
Bethesda, MD 20892-1

301-443-3860
Fax: 301-443-8774
E-mail: niaaweb-r@exchange.nih.gov
www.niaaa.nih.gov

Ting-Kai Li, Director
Faye Calhoun, Deputy Director

Federal agency that supports research nationwide on alcohol abuse and alcoholism. Includes investigator-initiated research on homeless persons.

93   National Mental Health Consumers' Self-Help Clearinghouse
1211 Chestnut Street
Suite 1207
Philadelphia, PA 19107-4103
215-751-1810
800-553-4539
Fax: 215-636-6312
E-mail: info@mhselfhelp.org
www.mhselfhelp.org

Joseph Rogers, Executive Director

A national consumer technical assistance center that has played a major role in the development of the mental health consumer movement.

Year Founded: 1986

94   National Organization on Fetal Alcohol Syndrome
1200 Eton Ct Nw
Washington, DC 20007-3239
202-785-4585
800-666-6327
Fax: 202-466-6456
E-mail: information@nofas.org
www.nofas.org

Tom Donaldson, President
Kathleen Tavenner Mitchell, Program Director/Spokesperson

Develops and implements innovative prevention and education strategies assessing fetal alcohol syndrome - the leading known preventable cause of mental retardation - including information, resource and referral clearinghouse.

95   SAMHSA's Fetal Alcohol Spectrum Disorders Center for Excellence (FASD)
2101 Gaither Road
Suite 600
Rockville, MD 20850

866-786-7327
E-mail: fasdcenter@samsa.hhs.gov
www.fascenter.samhsa.gov

Patricia Getty, Contact

Focus on exploring innovative service delivery strategies, developing comprehensive systems of care for FASD prevention and treatment, training staff, families and individuals with an FASD, and preventing alcohol use among women of childbearing age. The mission of the FASD Center for Excellence is to facilitate the development and improvement of prevention and treatment, and care systems in

the United States by providing national leadership and facilitating collaboration in the field.
Year Founded: 2001

96   SAMHSA's National Clearinghouse For Alcohol And Drug Information
PO Box 2345
Rockville, MD 20847-2345
240-221-4019
800-729-6686
Fax: 240-221-4292
TDD: 800-487-4889
www.ncadi.samhsa.gov

One-stop resource for information about abuse prevention and addiction treatment.

97   SAMHSA's National Mental Health Information Center
US Department of Health and Human Services
PO Box 42557
Washington, DC 20015-557
240-221-4021
800-789-2647
Fax: 240-221-4295
TDD: 866-889-2647
www.mentalhealth.org

A Kathryn Power MEd, Director
Edward B Searle, Deputy Director

Provides information about mental health via a toll-free telephone number, this web site, and more than 600 publications. Developed for users of mental health services and their families, the general public, policy makers, providers, and the media.

98   Section for Psychiatric and Substance Abuse Services (SPSPAS)
1 N Franklin Street
Chicago, IL 60606-4425
312-422-3000
Fax: 312-422-4796
www.http://www.aha.org/aha/member-center/constituency-

Dick Davidson, President
Pamela Thompson, Executive Director

Institutional members of the American Hospital Association who provide psychiatric substance abuse, clinical psychology and other behavorial health services and assists the AHA in development and implementation of policies and programs.

99   Substance Abuse & Mental Health Services Administration of the US Dept of Health and Human Services (SAMHSA)
1 Choke Cherry Road
Rockville, MD 20857
240-276-2000
www.samhsa.gov

Pamela Hyde JD, Administrator
Eric Broderick DDS, MPH, Deputy Adminstrator

Kana Enomoto MA, Advisor to the Administrator
Elaine Parry MS, Director of Program Services

SAMHSA's mission is to reduce the impact of substance abuse and mental illness on America's communities. The Agency was established by Congress to target effectively substance abuse and mental health services to the people most in need and to translate research in these areas more effectively and more rapidly into the general health care system. SAMHSA has demonstrated that prevention works, treatment is effective, and people recover from mental and substance use disorders. Behavioral health services improve health statuse and reduce health care costs to society. The Agency's programs are carried out through: the Center for Mental Health Services (CMHS); The Centers for Substance Abuse Prevention and Treatment (CSAP/T); and the Office of Applied Studies.

Year Founded: 1992

Books

100 Addiction Workbook: A Step by Step Guide to Quitting Alcohol and Drugs
New Harbinger Publications
5674 Shattuck Avenue
Oakland, CA 94609-1662
510-652-0215
800-748-6273
Fax: 510-652-5472
E-mail: customerservice@newharbinger.com
www.newharbinger.com

Matthew McKay, Owner

This comprehensive workbook explains the facts about addiction and provides simple, step by step directions for working through the stages of the quitting process. *$18.95*
160 pages ISBN 1-572240-43-1

101 Addiction: Why Can't They Just Stop?
Rodale Books
733 Third Avenue
New York, NY 10017-3293
212-697-2040
Fax: 212-682-2237
www.rodale.com

Jim Berra, Senior VP

Addiction offers a comprehensive and provocative look at the impact of chemical dependency on addicts, their loved ones, society, and the economy.
256 pages ISBN 1-594867-15-1

102 Alcohol & Other Drugs: Health Facts
ETR Associates
4 Carbonero Way
Scotts Way, CA 95066-4200
831-438-4060
800-321-4407
Fax: 831-438-3618
E-mail: customerservice@etr.org
www.etr.org

Mary Nelson, President

Offers clear, concise background information on alcohol and other drugs, and provides assessment of the impact on youth. Also, discusses risk and protective factors, current trends, and prevention strategies. *$17.00*

103 Alcohol and the Community
Cambridge University Press
40 W 20th Street
New York, NY 10011-4211
212-924-3900
800-872-7423
Fax: 212-691-3239
E-mail: marketing@cup.org
www.cup.org

The authors challenge the current implicit models used in alcohol problem prevention and demonstrate an ecological perspective of the community as a complex adaptive system composed of interacting subsystems. This volume represents a new and sensible approach to the prevention of alcohol dependence and alcohol-related problems. *$110.00*
197 pages ISBN 0-521591-87-2

104 Alcoholism Sourcebook
Omnigraphics
PO Box 625
Holmes, PA 19043-625

800-234-1340
Fax: 800-875-1340
E-mail: info@omnigraphics.com
www.omnigraphics.com

Omnigraphics is the publisher of the Health Reference Series, a growing consumer health information resource with more than 100 volumes in print. Each title in the series features an easy to understand format, nontechnical language, comprehensive indexing, and resources for further information. Material in each book has been collected from a wide range of government agencies, professional associations, periodicals, and other sources. *$78.00*
613 pages ISBN 0-780803-25-6

105 American Psychiatric Association Practice Guideline for the Treatment of Patients With Substance Use Disorders
American Psychiatric Publishing, Inc.
1000 Wilson Boulevard
Suite 1825
Arlington, VA 22209-3901
703-907-7322
800-368-5777
Fax: 703-907-1091
E-mail: appi@psych.org
www.appi.org

Robert E Hales MD, Editor-in-Chief
Ron McMillen, Chief Executive Officer
John McDuffie, Editorial Director

Offers guidance to psychiatrists caring for patients with substance use disorders. Includes treatment for alcohol, cocaine and opioids addiction. *$29.50*
126 pages ISBN 0-890423-03-2

106 Broken
Penguin
375 Hudson Street
New York, NY 10014-3672
212-366-2000
Fax: 212-366-2933

David Shanks, CEO

Broken tells the story of what happened between then and now-from growing up the privileged son of Bill Moyers to his descent into alcholism and drug addiction, his numerous stabs at getting clean, his many relapses, and how he managed to survive.

ISBN 0-143112-45-7

107 Clinical Supervision in Alcohol and Drug Abuse Counseling
Jossey-Bass / Wiley & Sons
111 River Street
Hoboken, NJ 07030-5790
201-748-6000
Fax: 201-748-6088
E-mail: custserv@wiley.com
www.josseybass.com

This is the throughly revised edition of the groundbreaking, definitive text for supervisors in substance abuse counseling. *$25.95*

400 pages ISBN 0-787973-77-7

108 Concerned Intervention: When Your Loved One Won't Quit Alcohol or Drugs
New Harbinger Publications
5674 Shattuck Avenue
Oakland, CA 94609-1662
510-652-0215
800-748-6273
Fax: 510-652-5472
E-mail: customerservice@newharbinger.com
www.newharbinger.com

Matthew McKay, Owner

Practical guide to group intervention techniques with lessons from experiences of families seeking counseling and treatment. *$13.95*

208 pages ISBN 1-879237-36-9

109 Concise Guide to Treatment of Alcoholism and Addictions
American Psychiatric Publishing, Inc.
1000 Wilson Boulevard
Suite 1825
Arlington, VA 22209-3901
703-907-7322
800-368-5777
Fax: 703-907-1091
E-mail: appi@psych.org
www.appi.org

Robert E Hales MD, Editor-in-Chief
Ron McMillen, Chief Executive Officer
John McDuffie, Editorial Director

Presents information on available treatment options for alcoholism and addictions, substance abuse in the workplace and laboratory testing. *$29.95*

172 pages ISBN 0-880483-26-1

110 Drug Abuse Sourcebook
Omnigraphics
615 Griswold
Detroit, MI 48226-3900

800-234-1340
Fax: 800-875-1340
E-mail: info@omnigraphics.com
www.omnigraphics.com

Health information about illicit substance abuse and the misuse of prescription and over-the-counter medications, including depressants, hallucinogens, inhalants, marijuana, stimulants and anabolic steroids. *$78.00*

608 pages ISBN 0-780807-40-5

111 Dynamics of Addiction
Hazelden
15251 Pleasant Valley Road
PO Box 176
Center City, MN 55012-176
651-213-2400
800-257-7810
Fax: 651-213-4411
E-mail: info@hazelden.org
www.hazelden.org

Pamphlet about addictions.

12 pages ISBN 0-935908-38-2

112 Eye Opener
Hazelden
15251 Pleasant Valley Road
PO Box 176
Center City, MN 55012-176
651-213-4000
800-328-9000
Fax: 651-213-4590
www.hazelden.org

These daily meditations support core concepts of the AA program and help clients review key recovery ideas. *$12.00*

381 pages ISBN 0-894860-23-2

113 Fetal Alcohol Syndrome & Fetal Alcohol Effect
Hazelden
15251 Pleasant Valley Road
PO Box 176
Center City, MN 55012-176
651-213-4000
800-328-9000
Fax: 651-213-4590
E-mail: customersupport@hazelden.org
www.hazelden.org

If you're a chemical dependency counselor or work with women in pregnancy planning or self-care, this resource is filled with facts to help you better meet your clients needs. *$5.25*

48 pages ISBN 0-894869-51-5

114 Getting Beyond Sobriety
Jossey-Bass / Wiley & Sons
111 River Street
Hoboken, NJ 07030-5790
201-748-5774
Fax: 201-748-6088
E-mail: custserv@wiley.com
www.wiley.com

This method will lead to a change in behavior within the individual, while developing and expanding connection with others. *$ 42.50*

198 pages Year Founded: 1997 ISBN 0-787908-40-1

115 Getting Hooked: Rationality and Addiction
Cambridge University Press
40 W 20th Street
New York, NY 10011-4211
212-924-3900
Fax: 212-691-3239
www.cambridge.org

The essays in this volume offer thorough and up-to-date discussion on the relationship between addiction and rationality. Includes contributions from philosophers, psychiatrists, neurobiologists, sociologists and economists. Offers the neurophysiology of addiction, examination of the Becker theory of rational addiction, an argument for a visceral theory of addiction, a discussion of compulsive gambling as a form of addiction, discussions of George Ainslie's theory of hyperbolic discounting, analyses of social causes and policy implications and an investigation into relapse. *$75.00*

296 pages Year Founded: 1999 ISBN 0-521640-08-3

116 Handbook of the Medical Consequences of Alcohol and Drug Abuse
Taylor & Francis
2 Park Square
Milton Park
Oxford, UK

Carlton Erickson, Author

Alcohol is one of the oldest and most widely used psychoactive drugs on earth.

117 Helping Women Recover: Special Edition for Use in the Criminal Justice System
Jossey-Bass / Wiley & Sons
111 River Street
Hoboken, NJ 07030-5790
201-748-6000
Fax: 201-748-6088
E-mail: custserv@wiley.com
www.wiley.com

Designed to meet the unique needs of substance-abusing women. Created for use with women's groups in a variety of correctional settings. Offers mental health professionals, corrections personnel, and program administrators the tools they need to implement this highly effective program.

384 pages ISBN 0-787946-10-5

118 Inside Recovery How the Twelve Step Program Can Work for You
The Rosen Publishing Group
29 E 21st Street
New York, NY 10010-6209
212-777-3017
800-237-9932
Fax: 212-777-0277
E-mail: info@rosenpublishing.com
www.rosenpublishing.com

Roger Rosen, President

A twelve step program to help with the recovery process. *$25.25*

ISBN 0-823926-34-6

119 Inside a Support Group
Rosen Publishing Group
29 E 21st Street
New York, NY 10010-6209
212-777-3017
800-237-9932
Fax: 212-777-0277
E-mail: info@rosenpub.com
www.rosenpublishing.com

Roger Rosen, President

Lists support organizations for children of alcoholics. Explains what to expect at Alateen meetings and support groups for teenagers. *$25.25*

64 pages ISBN 0-823925-08-0

120 Kicking Addictive Habits Once & For All
Jossey-Bass / Wiley & Sons
111 River Street
Hoboken, NJ 07030-5790

800-956-7739
Fax: 800-605-2665
E-mail: custserv@wiley.com
www.wiley.com

All aspects of changing bad habits and developing a balanced lifestyle are addressed in the book. *$22.50*

224 pages ISBN 0-787940-68-2

121 LSD: Still With Us After All These Years
Jossey-Bass / Wiley & Sons
111 River Street
Hoboken, NJ 07030-5790
201-748-6000
Fax: 201-748-6088
E-mail: custserv@wiley.com
www.wiley.com

Facts about LSD. *$21.50*

176 pages ISBN 0-787943-79-7

122 Let's Talk Facts About Substance Abuse & Addiction
American Psychiatric Publishing, Inc.
1000 Wilson Boulevard
Suite 1825
Arlington, VA 22209-3901
703-907-7322
800-368-5777
Fax: 703-907-1091
E-mail: appi@psych.org
www.appi.org

Robert E Hales MD, Editor-in-Chief
Ron McMillen, Chief Executive Officer
John McDuffie, Editorial Director

Straight talk about a difficult subject. *$26.95*

123 Living Skills Recovery Workbook
Elsevier Science
Po Box 28430
Saint Louis, MO 63146-930
314-453-7010
800-545-2522
Fax: 314-453-7095
E-mail: custserv@elsevier.com
www.elsevier.com

Katie Hennessy, Medical Promotions Coordinator

Provides clinicians with the tools necessary to help patients with dual diagnoses acquire basic living skills. Focusing on stress management, time management, activities of daily living, and social skills training, each living skill is taught in relation to how it aids in recovery and relapse prevention for each patient's individual lifestyle and pattern of addiction. Book is now printed as ordered. *$39.95*

224 pages ISBN 0-750671-18-1

124 Living Sober I
Jossey-Bass / Wiley & Sons
111 River Street
Hoboken, NJ 07030-5790
201-748-8677
Fax: 201-748-2665
www.wiley.com

Emphasizes the specific coping skills essential to a client's recovery. *$495.00*

87 pages Year Founded: 1999

125 Living Sober II
Jossey-Bass / Wiley & Sons
111 River Street
Hoboken, NJ 07030-5790
201-748-6000
Fax: 201-748-6088
www.wiley.com

Emphasizes the specific coping skills essential to a client's recovery. *$395.00*

126 Meaning of Addiction
Jossey-Bass / Wiley & Sons
111 River Street
Hoboken, NJ 07030-5790
201-748-6000
Fax: 201-748-6088
www.wiley.com

A controversial and persuasive analysis of addiction.
$30.50

224 pages Year Founded: 1998 ISBN 0-787943-82-7

127 Medical Aspects of Chemical Dependency
Active Parenting Publishers
Hazelden
15251 Pleasant Valley Road
PO Box 176
Center City, MN 55012-176
651-213-4000
800-328-9000
Fax: 651-213-4590
E-mail: info@hazelden.org
www.hazelden.org

This curriculum helps professionals educate clients in treatment and other settings about medical effects of chemical use and abuse. The program includes a video that explains body and brain changes that can occur when using alcohol or other drugs, a workbook that helps clients apply the information from the video to their own situations, a handbook that provides in-depth information on addiction, brain chemistry and the physiological effects of chemical dependency and a pamphlet that answers critical questions clients have about the medical effects of chemical dependency. Available to purchase separately. Program value packages available. *$244.70*

128 Mother's Survival Guide to Recovery: All About Alcohol, Drugs & Babies
New Harbinger Publications
5674 Shattuck Avenue
Oakland, CA 94609-1662
510-652-0215
800-748-6273
Fax: 510-652-5472
E-mail: customerservice@newharbinger.com
www.newharbinger.com

Matthew McKay, Owner

Offers a strong message of hope to help women cope with the challenges of recovering, deal with prenatal care and parenting issues, and take steps toward creating the healthy, happy families they want to have. A must read textbook for healthcare professionals and children's service workers.
$12.95

138 pages ISBN 1-572240-49-0

129 Motivating Behavior Changes Among Illicit-Drug Abusers
American Psychological Association
750 First Street NE
Washington, DC 20002-4242
202-336-5500
800-374-2721

Fax: 202-336-5518
www.apa.org

Norman B Anderson, CEO

Scientifically based method focused on the use of incentives to change behavior. Research in multiple applications of contingency management techniques. Test case of effective utilization of the method in treating illicit-drug abusers. *$39.95*

547 pages Year Founded: 1999 ISBN 1-557985-70-7

130   National Directory of Drug and Alcohol Abuse Treatment Programs
Substance Abuse & Mental Health Services Adminsitration
5600 Fishers Lane
Room 16-105, Office of Applied Stud
Rockville, MD 20857-1
301-443-4795
Fax: 301-443-0284
E-mail: findtreatment@samhsa.gov

Nelba Chavez, Administrator

Directory of substance abuse treatment programs for use by persons seeking treatment and by professionals. Lists facility name, address, telephone number and services offered. Updated annually. Available in paperback. Searchable on-line version on web site.

596 pages 1 per year

131   New Treaments for Chemical Addictions
American Psychiatric Publishing, Inc.
1000 Wilson Boulevard
Suite 1825
Arlington, VA 22209-3901
703-907-7322
800-368-5777
Fax: 703-907-1091
E-mail: appi@psych.org
www.appi.org

Robert E Hales MD, Editor-in-Chief
Ron McMillen, Chief Executive Officer
John McDuffie, Editorial Director

Examines new approaches for an old problem. *$37.50*

248 pages ISBN 0-880488-38-7

132   Points for Parents Perplexed about Drugs
Hazelden
15251 Pleasant Valley Road
PO Box 176
Center City, MN 55012-176
651-213-4000
800-257-7810
Fax: 651-213-4411
E-mail: info@hazelden.org
www.hazelden.org

Clear guidelines help teachers, parents, family members and others recognize, evaluate, and deal with adolescent drug abuse. Excellent support for family counseling programs. *$3.25*

16 pages Year Founded: 1996 ISBN 0-894861-40-9

133   Relapse Prevention for Addictive Behaviors: a Manual for Therapists
Blackwell Publishing
350 Main Street
Malden, MA 02148-5020
781-870-1200
Fax: 781-388-8255

Lisa Bybee, VP

Applies cognitive-behavioral strategies and lifestyle procedures to treat people with addiction problems. *$43.95*

224 pages ISBN 0-632024-84-4

134   Rethinking Substance Abuse: What the Science Shows, and What We Should Do about It
The Guilford Press
72 Spring Street
New York, NY 10012-4019
212-431-9800
800-365-7006
Fax: 212-966-6708
E-mail: info@guilford.com

Bob Matloff, President

Civilizations have long wrestled with problems linked to the use of alcohol and other psychoactive substances, and have made all manner of efforts to control.

ISBN 1-572302-31-3

135   Science of Prevention: Methodological Advances from Alcohol and Substance Research
American Psychological Association
750 First Street NE
Washington, DC 20002-4242
202-336-5500
800-374-2721
Fax: 202-336-5518
E-mail: executiveoffice@apa.org
www.apa.org

Norman B Anderson, CEO

This book explores ways for bringing greater methodological rigor to prevention research, gathering together the analyses and insights of prominent researchers who present examples of the problems and the solutions they have encountered in their own work. *$39.95*

458 pages Year Founded: 1997 ISBN 1-557984-39-5

136   Selfish Brain: Learning from Addiction
Hazelden
15251 Pleasant Valley Road
PO Box 176
Center City, MN 55012-176
651-213-4000
800-328-9000
Fax: 651-213-4590
E-mail: customersupport@hazelden.org
www.hazelden.org

Helps clients or loved ones face addiction and recovery by exploring the biological, historical and cultural aspects of addiction and its destructiveness. *$18.95*

544 pages ISBN 1-568383-63-0

137 Seven Points of Alcoholics Anonymous
Hazelden
15251 Pleasant Valley Road
PO Box 176
Center City, MN 55012-176
651-213-4000
800-328-9000
Fax: 651-213-4590
E-mail: customersupport.org
www.hazelden.org

The 7 points of Alcoholics Anonymous is the final work of Richmond Walker, author of the best-selling beloved book Twenty-Four Hours a Day. This book is the summation of Walker's knowledge on the practice and fundamentals of 12 Step recovery. Topics include an overview and history of A.A., the nature of alcoholism and recovery, the 12 Step way and fellowship, surrender, character defects, amends, living One Day at a Time, and sharing. *$9.95*

103 pages ISBN 0-934125-16-3

138 Sex, Drugs, Gambling and Chocolate: Workbook for Overcoming Addictions
Impact Publishers
PO Box 6016
Atascadero, CA 93423-6016
805-466-5917
800-246-7228
Fax: 805-466-5919
E-mail: info@impactpublishers.com
www.impactpublishers.com

There is an alternative to 12-step. You can reduce almost any type of addictive behavior from drinking to sex, eating, and the Internet. With this practical and effective workbook. Teaches general principles of addictive behavior change, so readers can apply them as often as they need. *$15.95*

240 pages ISBN 1-886230-55-2

139 Sober Siblings: How to Help Your Alcoholic Brother or Sister-and Not Lose Yourself
Da Capo Press
Eleven Cambridge Center
Cambridge, MA 02142
617-252-5200
www.perseusbooksgroup.com

Patricia Olsen, Author
Petros Levounis, Author

An empowering, practical guide to help the brothers and sisters of alcoholics-by a journalist and sibling of two alcoholics, and an addiction specialist

240 pages ISBN 1-600940-55-2

140 Substance Abuse Treatment and the Stages of Change: Selecting and Planning Interventions (Guilford Substance Abuse Series)
The Guilford Press
72 Spring Street
New York, NY 10012-4019
212-431-9800
800-365-7006
Fax: 212-966-6708
E-mail: info@guilford.com

Bob Matloff, President

Alcohol and drug use is a common occurrence in today's society, with such use often associated with a variety of medical, psychological, and social problems.

ISBN 1-593850-97-2

141 Substance Abuse: Information for School Counselors, Social Workers, Therapists, and Counselors
Allyn & Bacon
230 Pearson Parkway
Lebanon, IN 46052-2795

E-mail: pearsonstorecs@pearsoned.com
www.pearsonhighered.com

Gary L Fisher, Author

To provide counselors, social workers, and students with a detailed overview of the alcohol-and-other-drug field. The new edition provides updated coverage and clinical examples to reflect the rapid changes in this area.

ISBN 0-205591-76-0

142 Teach & Reach: Tobacco, Alcohol & Other Drug Prevention
ETR Associates
4 Carbonero Way
Scotts Valley, CA 95066-4200
831-438-4060
800-321-4407
Fax: 831-438-3618
E-mail: customerservice@etr.org
www.etr.org

Mary Nelson, President

Helps to build commitment to stay tobacco, alcohol drug free. Also, looks to peer norms to support healthy, responsible choices, and enhances protective factors that prevent tobacco, alcohol and other drug use *$22.00*

143 Teen Guide to Staying Sober
Rosen Publishing
29 E 21st Street
New York, NY 10010-6209
212-777-3017
800-237-9932
Fax: 212-777-0277
E-mail: info@rosenpub.com
www.rosenpublishing.com

Roger Rosen, President

Helpful tips on how to keep teens from drinking. *$25.25*

64 pages ISBN 0-823927-65-2

144 The Science of Addiction: From Neurobiology to Treatment
W.W. Norton
500 Fifth Avenue
New York, NY 10110-54
212-354-2907
Fax: 212-869-0856

Drake McFeely, CEO

Indivdual chapters look at the general consequences of alcohol abuse, its neuropsychological consequences, effects on the brain, and effects of heavy prenatal alcohol exposure.

ISBN 0-393704-63-7

145 Treating Alcoholism
Jossey-Bass Publishers
10475 Crosspoint Blvd
Indianapolis, IN 46256-3386

877-762-2974
Fax: 800-597-3299
www.josseybass.com

Presents a model of alcoholism treatment to help you guide alcoholics and their families on a path to long term recovery. *$40.00*

448 pages ISBN 0-787938-76-9

146 Twelve-Step Facilitation Handbook
Hazelden Publishing
15251 Pleasant Valley Road
PO Box 176
Center City, MN 55012-176
651-213-4000
800-328-9000
Fax: 651-213-4590
E-mail: customersupport@hazelden.org
www.hazelden.com

This book provides clinicians with the tools they need to encourage chemically dependent clients to take advantage of the healing power of twelve-step programs. Learn how to integrate these time-tested principles into your practice. *$24.95*

214 pages Year Founded: 2003 ISBN 1-592850-96-0

147 Twenty-Four Hours a Day
Hazelden
15251 Pleasant Valley Road
PO Box 176
Center City, MN 55012-176
651-213-4000
800-328-9000
Fax: 651-213-4590
E-mail: customersupport@hazelden.org
www.hazelden.org

Daily meditation in this classic book helps clients develop a solid foundation in a spiritual program, learn to relate the Twelve Steps to their everyday lives and accomplish their treatment and aftercare goals. Includes 366 daily meditations with special consideration and extra encouragement given during holidays. Helps clients find the power to stay sober each day and not to take that first drink. Hardcover - $12.95, Softcover - $10.95.

400 pages ISBN 0-894868-34-9

148 When Parents Have Problems: A Book for Teens and Older Children with an Abusive, Alcoholic, or Mentally Ill Parent
Charles C Thomas Publishers
PO Box 19265
Springfield, IL 62794-9265
217-789-8980
800-258-8980
Fax: 217-789-9130
www.ccthomas.com

This book is written with the idea that intelligent children can use sound ideas to improve thier lives, either on their own or with the help of adults. The author helps the reader be realistic about the sources of a problem, particularly if they are the result of a parents' difficulties. The text covers the kinds of problems that a parent's troubles can causes and offers ideas on how to deal constructively with the challenges. Available in paperback for $23.95. *$39.95*

94 pages Year Founded: 1995 ISBN 0-398059-89-6

149 Woman's Journal, Special Edition for Use in the Criminal Justice System
Jossey-Bass / Wiley & Sons
111 River Street
Hoboken, NJ 07030-5790
201-748-6000
Fax: 201-748-6088
E-mail: customer@wiley.com
www.wiley.com

Designed to meet the unique needs of substance-abusing women. Created for use with women's groups in a variety of correctional settings. Offers mental health professionals, corrections personnel, and program administrators the tools they need to implement this highly effective program. *$23.50*

144 pages Year Founded: 1999 ISBN 0-787946-10-9

150 You Can Free Yourself From Alcohol & Drugs: Work a Program That Keeps You in Charge
New Harbinger Publications
5674 Shattuck Avenue
Oakland, CA 94609-1662
510-652-0215
800-748-6273
Fax: 510-652-5472
E-mail: customerservice@newharbinger.com
www.newharbinger.com

Matthew McKay, Owner

Reworking of the Twelve Steps approach into a program that helps addicts and alcoholics make needed changes in their lifestyle. *$13.95*

214 pages ISBN 1-572241-18-7

151 Your Brain on Drugs
Hazelden
15251 Pleasant Valley Road
PO Box 176
Center City, MN 55012-176
651-213-4000
800-328-9000
Fax: 651-213-4590
E-mail: info@hazelden.org
www.hazelden.org

This pamphlet explains the effects of alcohol and other drugs on the brain through illustrations, activities and exercise that help to reinforce the easy-to-read text. *$4.00*

36 pages

Periodicals & Pamphlets

152 About Alcohol
ETR Associates
4 Carbonero Way
Scotts Valley, CA 95066-4200
831-438-4060
800-321-4407
Fax: 831-438-3618
E-mail: customerservice@etr.org
www.etr.org

Mary Nelson, President

What it is, why it's dangerous, and its negative effects on the body and in prenatal development. Title #079.

153 About Crack Cocaine
ETR Associates
4 Carbonero Way
Scotts Valley, CA 95066-4200
831-438-4060
800-321-4407
Fax: 831-438-3618
E-mail: customerservice@etr.org
www.etr.org

Mary Nelson, President

Describes what crack cocaine is and why it's dangerous and lists the effects on the body. *$16.00*

154 About Drug Addiction
ETR Associates
4 Carbonero Way
Scotts Valley, CA 95066-4200
831-438-4060
800-321-4407
Fax: 831-438-3618
E-mail: customerservice@etr.org
www.etr.org

Mary Nelson, President

Includes answers to commonly asked questions about drug addiction, a 13'x 17' wall chart presents the stages of addiction and recovery, covers denial, withdrawal and relapse. *$18.00*

155 Alateen Talk
Al-Anon Family Group Headquarters
1600 Corporate Landing Parkway
Virginia Beach, VA 23454-5617
757-563-1600
888-425-2666
Fax: 757-563-1655
E-mail: wso@al-anon.org
www.al-anon.alateen.org

Newsletter with articles and drawings created by teenage and preteen Alateen members. Material relates to members' application of twelve step, and principles of Alateen program. Also includes articles by Alateen sponsors. *$7.50*

4 pages 4 per year   ISSN 1054-1411

156 Alcohol ABC's
ETR Associates
4 Carbonero Way
Scotts Valley, CA 95066-4200
831-438-4060
800-321-4407
Fax: 831-438-3618
E-mail: customerservice@etr.org
www.etr.org

Mary Nelson, President

Presents the consequenes of drinking and explains the difference between use and abuse in a straightforward, matter-of-fact way. Title #R712.

157 Alcohol Issues Insights
Beer Marketer's Insights
49 E Maple Ave
Suffern, NY 10901-5507
845-624-2337
Fax: 845-624-2340
E-mail: eric@beerinsights.com
www.beerinsights.com

Benjamin Steinman, Publisher

Newsletter that provides information on the use and misuses of alcohol. Covers such topics as misrepresentation in the media, minimum age requirements, advertising bans, deterrence of drunk driving, and the effects of tax increases on alcoholic beverage consumption. *$375.00*

4 pages 12 per year   ISSN 1067-3105

158 Alcohol Self-Test
ETR Associates
4 Carbonero Way
Scotts Valley, CA 95066-4200
831-438-4060
800-321-4407
Fax: 831-438-3618
E-mail: customerservice@etr.org
www.etr.org

Mary Nelson, President

Thought provoking questions include: What do I know about alcohol? How safely do I drink? When and why do I drink? Title #H259.

159 Alcohol: Incredible Facts
ETR Associates
4 Carbonero Way
Scotts Valley, CA 95066-4200
831-438-4060
800-321-4407
Fax: 831-438-3618
E-mail: customerservice@etr.org
www.etr.org

Mary Nelson, President

Strange but true facts to trigger discussion about alcohol use, social consequences, and risks involved. Title #R719.

160 Alcoholism: A Merry-Go-Round Named Denial
Hazelden
15251 Pleasant Valley Road
PO Box 176
Center City, MN 55012-176
651-213-4000
800-328-9000
Fax: 651-213-4590
E-mail: customersupport.org
www.hazelden.org

This pamphlet provides a clear description of alcoholism and defines the roles of the alcoholic and those affected by chemical dependency. *$2.95*

20 pages ISBN 0-894860-22-4

161 Alcoholism: A Treatable Disease
Hazelden
15251 Pleasant Valley Road
PO Box 176
Center City, MN 55012-176
651-213-4000
800-328-9000
Fax: 651-213-4590
www.hazelden.org

A hard look at the disease of chemical dependence, the confusion and delusion that go with it, intervention and a hopeful conclusion - alcoholism is treatable. *$2.95*

18 pages ISBN 0-935908-37-4

162 American Journal on Addictions
American Academy of Addiction Psychiatry
345 Blackstone Blvd
1st Floor-Weld
Providence, RI 02906
401-524-3076
Fax: 401-272-0922
E-mail: info@aaap.org
www.aaap.org

Martha Bostick, Associate Managing Editor

Covers a wide variety of topics ranging from codependence to genetics, epidemiology to dual diagnostics, etiology to neuroscience, and much more. Features of the journal, all written by experts in the field, include special overview articles, clinical or basic research papers, clinical updates, and book reviews within the area of addictions.

ISSN 1055-0496

163 Binge Drinking: Am I At Risk?
ETR Associates
4 Carbonero Way
Scotts Valley, CA 95066-4200
831-438-4060
800-321-4407
Fax: 831-438-3618
E-mail: customerservice@etr.org
www.etr.org

Mary Nelson, President

Easy-to-follow checklists help students decide if they have a problem with binge drinking, make a plan, and get help. Title #R018.

164 Chalice
Calix Society
2555 Hazelwood Avenue
Saint Paul, MN 55109-2030
651-773-3117
800-398-0524
Fax: 651-777-3069
www.calixsociety.org

Directed toward Catholic and non-Catholic alcoholics who are maintaining their sobriety through affiliation with and participation in Alcoholics Anonymous. Emphasizes the virtue of total abstinence, through contributed stories regarding spiritual and physical recovery. Recurring features include statistics, book announcements, and research. *$15.00*

4-6 pages 24 per year

165 Crossing the Thin Line: Between Social Drinking and Alcoholism
Hazelden
15251 Pleasant Valley Road
PO Box 176
Center City, MN 55012-176
651-213-4000
800-328-9000
Fax: 651-213-4590
www.hazelden.org

This pamphlet explores the physical predisposition to alcoholism, as well as behavioral and emotional changes. *$2.50*

20 pages ISBN 0-894860-77-1

166 Designer Drugs
ETR Associates
4 Carbonero Way
Scotts Valley, CA 95066-4200
831-438-4060
800-321-4407
Fax: 831-438-3618
E-mail: customerservice@etr.org
www.etr.org

Mary Nelson, President

Traces the evolution of designer drugs like China White and MDMA, explains how addiction works and suggests why designer drugs are so addictive. *$16.00*

167 Drinking Facts
ETR Associates
4 Carbonero Way
Scotts Valley, CA 95066-4200
831-438-4060
800-321-4407
Fax: 831-438-3618
E-mail: customerservice@etr.org
www.etr.org

Mary Nelson, President

Addresses changing attitudes about drinking, and examines the basic facts of alcohol. Shows how to avoid risky situations, explains about the blood alcohol levels, and offers tips for curbing consumption. Title #R843

168 Drug ABC's
ETR Associates
4 Carbonero Way
Scotts Valley, CA 95066-4200
831-438-4060
800-321-4407
Fax: 831-438-3618
E-mail: customerservice@etr.org
www.etr.org

Mary Nelson, President

26 good reasons to stay away from drugs, facts of different drugs, and motivation for being drug-free. *$16.00*

169 Drug Dependence, Alcohol Abuse and Alcoholism
Elsevier Publishing
11830 Westline Industrial Drive
St Louis, MO 63146-3313
314-872-8370
800-542-2522
Fax: 314-432-1380
E-mail: usbkinfo@elsevier.com
www.elsevier.com

Erik Engstrom, CEO

This journal aims to provide its readers with a swift, yet complete, current awareness service. This is achieved both by the scope and structure of the journal.

ISSN 0925-5958

170 Drug Facts Pamphlet
ETR Associates
4 Carbonero Way
Scotts Valley, CA 95066-4200
831-438-4060
800-321-4407
Fax: 831-438-3618
E-mail: customerservice@etr.org
www.etr.org

Mary Nelson, President

Overview of 11 of the most commonly abused drugs includes: Description of drug, short-term effects and long-term effects. *$18.00*

171 Drug and Alcohol Dependence
Customer Support Services
PO Box 945
New York, NY 10159-945
212-633-3730
800-654-2452
Fax: 212-633-3680
www.elsevier.com

International journal devoted to publishing original research, scholarly reviews, commentaries and policy analysis in the area of drug, alcohol and tobacco use and dependence. *$239.00*

15 per year   ISSN 0376-8716

172 DrugLink
Facts and Comparisons
111 Westport Plaza
Suite 300
Saint Louis, MO 63146-3024
314-216-2100
800-223-0554
Fax: 314-878-5563
www.drugsfacts.com

DrugLink is an eight-page newsletter that provides abstracts of drug-related articles from various journals. DrugLink allows health care professionals to stay up-to-date on hot topics without having to subscribe to multiple publications. *$52.95*

8 pages   ISBN 1-089559-0 -

173 Drugs: Talking With Your Teen
ETR Associates
4 Carbonero Way
Scotts Valley, CA 95066-4200
831-438-4060
800-321-4407
Fax: 831-438-3618
E-mail: customerservice@etr.org
www.etr.org

Mary Nelson, President

Suggestions for effective communication include: avoid scare tatics, clarify family rules, other alternative for drug use. *$ 16.00*

174 Fetal Alcohol Syndrome & Fetal Alcohol Effect
Hazelden
15251 Pleasant Valley Road
PO Box 176
Center City, MN 55012-176
651-213-4000
800-328-9000
Fax: 651-213-4590
www.hazelden.org

If you're a chemical dependency counselor or work with women in pregnancy planning or self-care, this resource is filled with facts to help you better meet your clients needs. *$5.95*

48 pages   ISBN 0-894869-51-5

175 Five Smart Steps to Safer Drinking
ETR Associates
4 Carbonero Way
Scotts Valley, CA 95066-4200
831-438-4060
800-321-4407
Fax: 831-438-3618
E-mail: customerservice@etr.org
www.etr.org

Mary Nelson, President

Steps to making healthy decisions about alcohol include:
make choices, learn about alcohol, know your limits, have
a plan, and watch for problems. Title # H252.

176 Getting Involved in AA
Hazelden
15251 Pleasant Valley Road
PO Box 176
Center City, MN 55012-176
651-213-4000
800-328-9000
Fax: 651-213-4590
E-mail: customersupport@hazelden.org
www.hazelden.org

Twelve specific suggestions help clients through their early
days in the AA fellowship. Topics include different types of
meetings, expectations, common pitfalls, as well as do's
and don'ts. *$2.95*

24 pages ISBN 0-894861-36-0

177 Getting Started in AA
Hazelden
15251 Pleasant Valley Road
PO Box 176
Center City, MN 55012-176
651-213-4000
800-328-9000
Fax: 651-213-4590
www.hazelden.org

The principles and working of Alcoholics Anonymous provide an excellent resource for clients in early treatment and
as a aftercare tool to provide ongoing support. *$10.95*

160 pages ISBN 1-568380-91-7

178 Getting What You Want From Drinking
ETR Associates
4 Carbonero Way
Scotts Valley, CA 95066-4200
831-438-4060
800-321-4407
Fax: 831-438-3618
E-mail: customerservice@etr.org
www.etr.org

Mary Nelson, President

Practical ideas for drinking more safely, preventing hang-
overs, weight gain, and injuries; blood alcohol chart shows
the effect of alcohol on the mind and body. Title #H220.

179 Hazelden Voice
Hazelden Foundation
PO Box 11
Center City, MN 55012-11
612-213-4000
800-257-7810
Fax: 651-213-4411
E-mail: info@hazelden.org
www.hazelden.org

Reports on Hazelden activities and programs, and discusses
developments and issues in chemical dependency treatment
and prevention. Carries notices of professional education
opportunities, reviews of resources in the field, and a
calendar of events.

180 I Can't Be an Alcoholic Because...
Hazelden
15251 Pleasant Valley Road
PO Box 176
Center City, MN 55012-176
651-213-4000
800-328-9000
Fax: 651-213-4590
www.hazelden.org

This pamphlet describes fallacies and misconceptions
about alcoholism and includes facts and figures about alcohol, its use, and its abuse. Available in Spanish. *$1.95*

9 pages ISBN 0-894861-58-1

181 ICPA Reporter
ICPADD
12501 Old Columbia Pike
Silver Spring, MD 20904-6601
301-680-6719
Fax: 301-680-6707
E-mail: The ICPA@hotmail.com
www.icpa-dd.org

Reports on activities of the Commission worldwide, which
seeks to prevent alcoholism and drug dependency. Recurring features include a calendar of events and notices of
publications available.

4 pages 4 per year

182 Journal of Substance Abuse Treatment
Elsevier Publishing
11830 Westline Industrial Drive
St Louis, MO 63146-3313
314-872-8370
800-545-2522
Fax: 314-432-1380
E-mail: custserv@elsevier.com
www.elsevier.com

Erik Engstrom, CEO

The Journal of Substance Abuse Treatment features original reviews, training and educational articles, special commentary, and especially research articles that are
meaningful to the treatment of nicotine, alcohol, and other
drugs of dependence.

ISSN 0740-5472

183   Marijuana ABC's
ETR Associates
4 Carbonero Way
Scotts Valley, CA 95066-4200
831-438-4060
800-321-4407
Fax: 831-438-3618
E-mail: customerservice@etr.org
www.etr.org

Mary Nelson, President

Discusses the effects of marijuana, legal consequences, and strategies for saying no. *$16.00*

184   Motivational Interviewing: Preparing People to Change Addictive Behavior
Guilford Publications
72 Spring Street
New York, NY 10012-4068
212-431-9800
800-365-7006
Fax: 212-966-6708
E-mail: info@guilford.com

Bob Matloff, President

A nonauthoritarian approach to helping people free up their own motivations and resources, overcome ambivalence and help 'unstuck.' Presents a practical, research-tested approach to effecting change in persons with addictive behaviors. Paperback also available. *$42.00*

419 pages ISBN 1-572305-63-0

185   National Institute of Drug Abuse (NIDA)
6001 Executive Boulevard
Room 5213
Bethesda, MD 20892-1
301-443-6245
Fax: 301-443-7397
E-mail: information@lists.nida.nih.gov
www.drugabuse.gov

Beverly Jackson, Manager
Beverly Jackson, Public Information Director

Covers the areas of drug abuse treatment and prevention research, epidemiology, neuroscience and behavioral research, health services research and AIDS. Seeks to report on advances in the field, identify resources, promote an exchange of information, and improve communications among clinicians, researchers, administrators, and policymakers. Recurring features include synopses of research advances and projects, NIDA news, news of legislative and regulatory developments, and announcements.

186   Real World Drinking
ETR Associates
4 Carbonero Way
Scotts Valley, CA 95066-4200
831-438-4060
800-321-4407
Fax: 831-438-3618
E-mail: customerservice@etr.org
www.etr.org

Mary Nelson, President

Credible young people talk about benefits of not drinking and risks of drinking. Title #R746.

187   Teens and Drinking
ETR Associates
4 Carbonero Way
Scotts Valley, CA 95066-4200
831-438-4060
800-321-4407
Fax: 831-438-3618
E-mail: customerservice@etr.org
www.etr.org

Mary Nelson, President

Includes common sense messages about drinking, binge drinking, and important things to know about drinking. Title #R717.

188   The Prevention Researcher
Integrated Research Services
66 Club Road
Suite 370
Eugene, OR 97401-2464
541-683-9278
800-929-2955
Fax: 541-683-2621
E-mail: info@tpronline.org

Steven Ungerleider

Provides information on behavioral research to health and human services professionals, with a primary emphasis on adolescent substance abuse issues. *$20.00*

12-16 pages 4 per year ISSN 1086-4385

189   Understanding Dissociative Disorders and Addiction
Hazelden Publishing
15251 Pleasant Valley Road
Center City, MN 55012-9640
651-213-4000
800-328-9000
E-mail: customersupport@hazelden.org

A Scott Winter, MD

This booklet discusses the origins and symptoms of dissociation, explains the links between dissociative disorder and chemical dependency. Addresses treatment options available to help in your recovery. The work book includes exercises and activities that help you acknowledge, accept and manage both your chemical dependency and your dissociative disorder. *$2.95*

ISBN 1-572850-14-6

190   When Someone You Care About Abuses Drugs and Alcohol: When to Act, What to Say
Hazelden
15251 Pleasant Valley Road
PO Box 176
Center City, MN 55012-176
651-213-4000
800-328-9000

Fax: 651-213-4590
www.hazelden.org

This pamphlet shows family, friends, and co-workers how to confront someone who may be abusing alcohol or other drugs. *$2.50*

16 pages

191   Why Haven't I Been Able to Help?
Hazelden
15251 Pleasant Valley Road
PO Box 176
Center City, MN 55012-176
651-213-4000
800-328-9000
Fax: 651-213-4590
E-mail: customersupport@hazelden.org
www.hazelden.org

Discusses how spouses of alcoholics are also trapped by deteriorating self-image, unconscious defense, destructive behavior, and offers change, especially through intervention. *$2.95*

12 pages ISBN 0-935908-40-4

Research Centers

192   UAMS Psychiatric Research Institute
5800 W 10th Street
Suite 605
Little Rock, AR 72204-1773
501-660-7559
Fax: 501-660-7542
E-mail: kramerteresal@uams.edu
www.uams.edu

Combining research, education and clinical services into one facility, PRI offers inpatiend and outpatient services, with 40 psychiatric beds, therapy options, and specialized treatment for specific disorders, including: addictive eating, anxiety, deppressive and post-traumatic stress disorders. Research focuses on evidence-based care takes into consideration the education of future medical personnel while relying on research scientists to provide innovative forms of treatment. PRI includes the Center for Addiction Research as well as a methadone clinic.

Support Groups & Hot Lines

193   Adult Children of Alcoholics World Services Organization
PO Box 3216
Torrance, CA 90510-3216
310-534-1815
E-mail: info@adultchildren.org
www.adultchildren.org

A 12-Step and 12-Tradition program for adults raised in an environment including alcohol or other dysfunctions.

194   Al-Anon Family Group National Referral Hotline
1600 Corporate Landing Parkway
Virginia Beach, VA 23454-5617
757-563-1600
Fax: 757-563-1655
E-mail: wso@al-anon.org
www.al-anon.alateen.org

Al - Anon's purpose is to help families and friends of alcoholics recover from the effects of living with the problem drinking of a relative or friend.

195   Alateen and Al-Anon Family Groups
1600 Corporate Landing Parkway
Virginia Beach, VA 23454-5617
757-563-1600
888-425-2666
Fax: 757-563-1655
E-mail: wso@al-anon.org
www.al-anon.alateen.org/sitemap.html

Mary Ann Keller, Director Members Services

A fellowship of men, women, children and adult children affected by another persons drinking.

196   Alcoholics Anonymous (AA): World Services
PO Box 459
New York, NY 10163-459
212-870-3400
www.aa.org

For men and women who share the common problems of alcoholism.

197   Chemically Dependent Anonymous
PO Box 423
Severna Park, MD 21146-423

888-232-4673
E-mail: publicinfo@cdaweb.org
www.cdaweb.org

Twelve-step program for friends and relatives of chemically dependent people.

198   Cocaine Anonymous
3740 Overland Avenue
Suite C
Los Angeles, CA 90034-6377
310-559-5833
Fax: 310-559-2554
E-mail: cawso@ca.org
www.ca.org

Fellowship of men and women who share their experience, stength and hope with each other in hope that they may solve their common problem and help others recover from their addiction.

199 Infoline
United Way of Connecticut
1344 Silas Deane Highway
Rocky Hill, CT 06067-1350
860-571-7500
800-203-1234
Fax: 860-571-7525
www.ctunitedway.org

Richard Porth, CEO

Infoline is a free, confidential, help-by-telephone service for information, referral, and crisis intervention. Trained professionals help callers find information, discover options or deal with a crisis by locating hundreds of services in their area on many different issues, from substance abuse to elder needs to suicide to volunteering in your community. Infoline is certified by the American Association of Suicidology. Operates 24 hours a day, everyday. Multilingual caseworkers are available. For Child Care Infoline, call 1-800-505-1000.

200 Join Together Online
715 Albany Street
580-3rd Floor
Boston, MA 02118
617-437-1500
Fax: 617-437-9394
E-mail: info@jointogether.org
www.jointogether.org

A project of the Boston University School of Public Health, this association's mission is to help reduce substance abuse and gun violence.

201 MADD-Mothers Against Drunk Drivers
511 E John Carpenter Freeway
Suite 700
Irving, TX 75062-8187
214-744-6233
800-438-6233
Fax: 214-869-2206

Charles Hurley, CEO

A crusade against alcohol consumption. Mission is to stop drunk driving, support the victims of the violent crime and prevent underage drinking.

202 Marijuana Anonymous
PO Box 2912
Van Nuys, CA 91404-2912

800-766-6779
E-mail: office@marijuana-anonymous.org
www.marijuana-anonymous.org

Twelve-step program for marijuana addiction.

203 Nar-Anon Family Groups
22527 Crenshaw Blvd
Suite 200B
Torrance, CA 90505
310-534-8188
800-477-6291
Fax: 310-534-8688

E-mail: naranonwso@gmail.com
www.nar-anon.org

Cathy Khaledi, Executive Director

Twelve-step program for families and friends of addicts.

204 Narcotics Anonymous
PO Box 9999
Van Nuys, CA 91409-9099
818-773-9999
Fax: 818-700-0700
www.na.org

For narcotic addicts: Peer support for recovered addicts.

205 Pathways to Promise
5400 Arsenal Street
Saint Louis, MO 63139-1403

Fax: 314-877-6405
E-mail: pathways@mimh.edu
www.pathways2promise.org

Pathways to Promise is an interfaith technical assistance and resource center which offers liturgical and educational materials, program models, and networking information to promote a caring ministry with people with mental illness and their families.

206 Rational Recovery
PO Box 800
Lotus, CA 95651-800
530-621-2667
www.rational.org

Exclusive, worldwide source of counseling, guidance and direct instruction on self-recovery from addiction to alcohol and other drugs through planned, permanent abstinence.

207 SADD: Students Against Destructive Decisions
255 Main Street
Marlborough, MA 01752-5505
508-481-3568
877-723-3462
Fax: 508-481-5759
E-mail: webmaster@sadd.org
www.sadd.org

Penny Wells, Executive Director

Peer leadership organization dedicated to preventing destructive decisions, particularly underage drinking, other drug use, impaired driving, teen violence and teen depression and suicide.

208 SMART-Self Management and Recovery Training
7537 Mentor Avenue
Suite 306
Mentor, OH 44060-5463
440-951-5357
866-951-5357

E-mail: info@smartrecovery.org
www.smartrecovery.org

Shari Allwood, Executive Director

Free face-to-face and online mutual help groups. Helps people recover from all types of addictive behaviors. Also it is an alternative to AA-Alcoholics Anonymous and NA-Narcotics Anonymous.

Video & Audio

209 Alcohol and Sex: Prescription for Poor Decision Making
ETR Associates
4 Carbonero Way
Scotts Valley, CA 95066-4200
831-438-4060
800-321-4407
Fax: 831-438-3618
E-mail: customerservice@etr.org
www.etr.org

Mary Nelson, President

Explains how alcohol use can interfere with healthy decisions about sex and intimacy, as well as describing the effects of alcohol on the brain. Also, includes information about the date rape drug, how alcohol affects relationships, and includes a Teacher Resource Book. *$139.95*

210 Alcohol: the Substance, the Addiction, the Solution
Hazelden
15251 Pleasant Valley Road
PO Box 176
Center City, MN 55012-176
651-213-4000
800-328-9000
Fax: 651-213-4590
www.hazelden.org

Weaves dramatic personal stories of recovery from alcoholism with essential facts about alcohol itself. Emphasizes the impact of using and abusing alcohol in conjunction with other drugs. Educates about the dangers of this legally sanctioned drug, including the myth of safer versions such as wine and beer. *$225.00*

211 Binge Drinking
ETR Associates
4 Carbonero Way
Scotts Valley, CA 95066-4200
831-438-4060
800-321-4407
Fax: 831-438-3618
E-mail: customerservice@etr.org
www.etr.org

Mary Nelson, President

Explains the physiological and psychological effects of alcohol, covers the warning signs for alcohol poisoning and procedures to take to save someone, and delivers a no-nonsense message about why binge drinking is dangerous. Describes the catastrophic realities that can result from party

behavior, such as car crashes, falls, bad decisions and acquaintance rape. *$139.95*

212 Cocaine & Crack: Back from the Abyss
Hazelden
15251 Pleasant Valley Road
PO Box 176
Center City, MN 55012-176
651-213-4000
800-257-7810
Fax: 651-213-4411
E-mail: info@hazelden.org
www.hazelden.org

Provides clients in correctional, educational, and treatment settings an understanding of the history, pharamacology, and medical impact of cocaine/crack use through personal stories of addiction and recovery. Reveals proven methods for overcoming addiction and discusses the best ways to maintain recovery. 46 minutes. *$225.00*

213 Cross Addiction: Back Door to Relapse
Hazelden
15251 Pleasant Valley Road
PO Box 176
Center City, MN 55012-176
651-213-2121
800-328-9000
Fax: 651-213-4590
www.hazelden.org

Presents a overview of the nature of cross-addiction. What it looks like, how it happens and why the addict is so susceptible to it. Explains to clients understanding the impact of different drugs and multiple drugs on the mind and body. *$225.00*

214 Disease of Alcoholism Video
Hazelden
15251 Pleasant Valley Road
PO Box 176
Center City, MN 55012-176
651-213-4000
800-328-9000
Fax: 651-213-4590
www.hazelden.org

This video is used daily in treatment, corporations, and schools. Dr. Ohlms discusses startling and convincing information on the genetic and physiological aspects of alcohol addiction. *$395.00*

215 Effective Learning Systems
3451 Bonita Bay Boulevard
Suite 205
Bonita Springs, FL 34134-4354
239-948-1660
800-966-5683
Fax: 239-948-1664
E-mail: info@efflearn.com
www.efflearn.com

Robert E Griswold, President
Deirdre M Griswold, VP

Audio tapes for stress management, deep relaxation, anger control, peace of mind, insomnia, weight and smoking, self-image and self-esteem, positive thinking, health and healing. Since 1972, Effective Learning Systems has helped millions of people take charge of their lives and make positive changes. Over 75 titles available, each with a money-back guarantee. Price range $12-$14.

216 Fetal Alcohol Syndrome & Fetal Alcohol Effect
Hazelden
15251 Pleasant Valley Road
PO Box 176
Center City, MN 55012-176
651-213-4000
800-328-9000
Fax: 651-213-4590
www.hazelden.org

If you're a chemical dependency counselor or work with women in pregnancy planning or self-care, this resource is filled with facts to help you better meet your clients needs. *$225.00*

217 Fetal Alcohol Syndrome and Effect, Stories of Help and Hope
Hazelden
15251 Pleasant Valley Road
PO Box 176
Center City, MN 55012-176
651-213-4000
800-328-9000
Fax: 651-213-4590
www.hazelden.org

Provides clients with a factual defintion of the medical diagonosis of fetal alcohol syndrome and its effects, including how children are diagnosed and the positive prognosis possible for these children. *$225.00*

218 Heroin: What Am I Going To Do?
Hazelden
15251 Pleasant Valley Road
PO Box 176
Center City, MN 55012-176
651-213-4000
800-328-9000
Fax: 651-213-4590
E-mail: info@hazelden.org
www.hazelden.org

Shares powerful stories and keen insights from recovering heroin addicts and the rewards of clean living. Teaches clients how to use honesty, surrender and responsibility as the power tools for a successful recovery. Deglamorizes heroin use, with a portrait of drug's inevitable degration of the mind, body and spirit. 30 minutes. *$225.00*

219 I'll Quit Tomorrow
Hazelden
15251 Pleasant Valley Road
PO Box 176
Center City, MN 55012-176
651-213-4000
800-328-9000

Fax: 651-213-4590
www.hazelden.org

Show clients the progressive nature of alcoholism through one of the most powerful films ever made about this disease. This three-part video series and facilitator's guide use a dramatic personal story to provide a clear and thorough introduction to the disease concept of alcoholism, enabling the intervention process, treatment and the hope of healing and recovery. *$300.00*

220 Marijuana: Escape to Nowhere
Hazelden
15251 Pleasant Valley Road
PO Box 176
Center City, MN 55012-176
651-213-4000
800-328-9000
Fax: 651-213-4590
E-mail: info@hazelden.org
www.hazelden.org

Challenges myths about marijuana by clearly stating that marijuana is addictive and use results in physical, emotional and spiritual consequences. Explains to clients in simple language the pharmacology of today's more potent marijuana and shares the hope and healing of recovery. 30 minutes. *$225.00*

Year Founded: 1999

221 Medical Aspects of Chemical Dependency Active Parenting Publishers
Hazelden
15251 Pleasant Valley Road
PO Box 176
Center City, MN 55012-176
651-213-2121
800-328-9000
Fax: 651-213-4590
E-mail: info@hazelden.org
www.hazelden.org

This curriculum helps professionals educate clients in treatment and other settings about medical effects of chemical use and abuse. The program includes a video that explains body and brain changes that can occur when using alcohol or other drugs, a workbook that helps clients apply the information from the video to their own situations, a handbook that provides in-depth information on addiction, brain chemistry and the physiological effects of chemical dependency and a pamphlet that answers critical questions clients have about the medical effects of chemical dependency. Available to purchase separately. Program value packages available. *$225.00*

222 Methamphetamine: Decide to Live Prevention Video
Hazelden
15251 Pleasant Valley Road
PO Box 176
Center City, MN 55012-176
651-213-4000
800-328-9000
Fax: 651-213-4590

E-mail: info@hazelden.org
www.hazelden.org

Methamphetamine: Decide to Live presents the latest information on the devastating consequences of meth addiction and the struggles and rewards of recovery. Facts, medical aspects, personal stories, and insights on the recovery process illuminate the path to healing. The video is divided into two parts and is 38 minutes long. *$225.00*

223 Prescription Drugs: Recovery from the Hidden Addiction
Hazelden
15251 Pleasant Valley Road
PO Box 176
Center City, MN 55012-176
651-213-4000
800-328-9000
Fax: 651-213-4590
E-mail: info@hazelden.org
www.hazelden.org

Combines essential facts about prescription drugs with vivid personal stories of addiction and recovery. Classifies prescription medications and gives the corresponding street forms. Offers solutions to problems unique to presciption drugs, addresses the particular needs of older adults and elaborates on the dangers of cross-addiction. 31 minutes. *$225.00*

224 Reality Check: Marijuana Prevention Video
Hazelden
15251 Pleasant Valley Road
PO Box 176
Center City, MN 55012-176
651-213-4000
800-328-9000
Fax: 651-213-4590
E-mail: info@hazelden.org
www.hazelden.org

This video creates a strong message for kids about the dangers of marijuana use. A combination of humor, animated graphics, testimonials and music deliver the facts on the pharmacology of marijuana and both it's short and long use consequences. Suitable for kids grades 7-12. 15 minute video. *$225.00*

225 SmokeFree TV: A Nicotine Prevention Video
Hazelden
15251 Pleasant Valley Road
PO Box 176
Center City, MN 55012-176
651-213-4000
800-328-9000
Fax: 651-213-4590
E-mail: info@hazelden.org
www.hazelden.org

Key facts, consequences of use and refusal skills guide children in understanding why they should avoid nicotine. Animated graphics, stories, humor, and music appeal to young people. Pharmacology of nicotine, its consequences and ways to refuse it are also explored. 15 minute video. *$225.00*

226 Straight Talk About Substance Use and Violence
ADD WareHouse
300 NW 70th Avenue
Suite 102
Plantation, FL 33317-2360
954-792-8944
800-233-9273
Fax: 954-792-8545
E-mail: sales@addwarehouse.com
www.addwarehouse.com

Harvey C Parker, Owner

Substance abuse and violence prevention begins with this three video program featuring the frank testimonials of 19 teens with significant chemical dependency issues who range in age from 13 to 22. In the starkest terms they discuss their most personal issues: substance abuse, sexual abuse, physical abuse, suicide attempts, violent acting out, depression, and abusive relationships. Includes 95 page discussion guide and three 30 minute videos. *$259.00*

227 What Should I Tell My Child About Drinking?
NADD-National Council on Alcoholism and Drug Dependence
22 Cortlandt Street
Suite 801
New York, NY 10007-3128
212-269-7797
800-622-2255
Fax: 212-269-7510
E-mail: national@ncadd.org
www.ncadd.org

A two-part video to help parents and other caregivers improvve their communications skills about alcohol. Includes brochures and a facilitators guide. Approximately 46 minutes. *$59.99*

Web Sites

228 www.Ncadi.Samhsa.Gov
National Clearinghouse for Alcohol & Drug Information

One-stop resource for information about abuse prevention and addiction treatment.

229 www.aa.org
AA-Alcoholics Anonymous

Group sharing their experience, strength and hope with each other to recover from alcoholism.

230 www.aca-usa.org
American Council on Alcoholism

Referrals to DWI classes and treatment centers.

231 www.addictionresourceguide.com
Addiction Resource Guide

Descriptions of inpatient, outpatient programs.

232 www.adultchildren.org
Adult Children of Alcoholics World Services
Organization

12 step and 12 tradition program for adults raised in an environment including alcohol or other dysfunctions.

233 www.al-anon.alateen.org
Al-Anon/Alateen

Program for relatives and friends of persons with alcohol problems.

234 www.alcoholism.about.com/library
Alcohol and the Elderly

Links to other pages relevant to overuse of alcohol and drugs in the elderly.

235 www.cfsny.org
Center for Family Support

Providing care givers with all aspects of service needed.

236 www.doitnow.org/pages/pubhub.hmtl
The Do It Now Foundation

Copies of brochures on drugs, alcohol, smoking, drugs and kids, and street drugs.

237 www.jacsweb.org
Jewish Alcoholics Chemically Dependent Persons

Ten articles dealing with denial and ignorance.

238 www.jointogether.org
Join Together

Alcohol and substance abuse information, legislative alerts, new and updates.

239 www.madd.org
MADD-Mothers Against Drunk Driving

A crusade to stop alcohol consumption, and underage drinking.

240 www.mentalhealth.com
Internet Mental Health

On-line information and a virtual encyclopedia related to mental disorders, possible causes and treatments. News, articles, on-line diagnostic programs and related links. Designed to improve understanding, diagnosis and treatment of mental illness throughout the world. Awarded the Top Site Award and the NetPsych Cutting Edge Site Award.

241 www.mentalhealth.samhsa.gov
SAMHSA's National Mental Health Info Center

Information about resources, technical assistance, research, training, networks, and other federal clearing houses, and fact sheets and materials.

242 www.mhselfhelp.org
National Mental Health Consumers Self-Help
Clearinghouse

Encourages the development and growth of consumer self-help groups.

243 www.naadac.org
National Association of Alcohol and Drug Abuse
Counselors

Its mission is to lead, unify and empower global addiction focused professionals to achieve excellence through education, advocacy, knowledge, standards of practice, ethics, professional development and research. Advocates on behalf of addiction professionals and the people they serve. Establishes and promotes the highest possible standards of practice and qualifications for addiction professionals.

244 **www.nccbh.org**
National Council for Commuity Behavioral Healthcare

A network for sharing information and provding assistance among those working in the healthcare management field.

245 **www.niaaa.nih.gov**
National Institute on Alcohol Abuse & Alcoholism

Supports research nationwide on alcohol abuse and alcoholism.

246 **www.nida.nih.gov**
National Institute on Drug Abuse

Many publications useful for patients. Research Reports, summaries about chemicals and treatments.

247 **www.nida.nih.gov/drugpages**
Commonly Abused Drugs: Street Names for Drugs of Abuse

Current names, periods of detection, medical uses.

248 **www.nofas.org**
National Organization on Fetal Alcohol Syndrome

Develops and implements innovative prevention and education strategies assessing fetal alcohol syndrome.

249 **www.psychcentral.com**
Psych Central

Personalized one-stop index for psychology, support, and mental health issues, resources, and people on the Internet.

250 **www.sadd.org**
SADD-Students Against Destructive Decisions

Peer leadership organization dedicated to preventing destructive decisions.

251 **www.samhsa.gov**
Substance Abuse and Mental Health Services Administration

Provides links to government resources related to substance abuse and mental health.

252 **www.smartrecovery.org**
SMART: Self-Management and Recovery Training

Four-Point program includes maintaining motivation, coping with urges, managing feelings and behavior, balancing momentary/enduring satisfactions.

253 **www.soulselfhelp.on.ca/coda.html**
Souls Self Help Central

Discusses self-help, mental health, issues of co-dependency.

254 **www.unhooked.com**
LifeRing

Offers nonreligious approach with links to groups.

255 **www.well.com**
Web of Addictions

Links to fact sheets from trustworthy sources.

Anxiety Disorders

Introduction

It is perfectly normal to feel worried or nervous sometimes, especially if there is an obvious reason: a loved one is late coming home; a pending yearly evaluation meeting at work; an important social event is looming. Even when you are nervous or anxious with good cause, you continue performing life's functions adequately. Indeed, some anxiety is not only normal, it is necessary, helping us to avoid trouble and danger - like preparing for a test in school, or making sure your child is safely buckled into a car. But if you can't rid yourself of your worry, you worry all the time, and about everything. If people close to you comment that you seem bothered and unlike yourself, or if your nervousness is affecting your relationships and your work, it is time to seek help. Sometimes a person who suffers from persistent anxiety turns to alcohol or other drugs in an effort to seek relief.

Different kinds of Anxiety Disorders have been identified. Several of the most prevalent are discussed in detail below. Treatment is tailored to the particular disorder and has become more effective as a result.

SYMPTOMS

Agoraphobia
•Usually involves fears connected with being outside the home and alone;
•Anxiety about being in places or situations from which it is difficult or embarrassing to escape (e.g., in the middle seat of a row in a theatre) or in which help may not be immediately available (as in an airplane);
•Such situations are avoided or endured with distress and fear of having a panic attack;
•The anxiety significantly interferes with the individual's ability to participate normally in work, domestic, and/or recreational activities.

Social Anxiety Disorder
•Fear of being humiliated or embarrassed in a social situation with strangers or where other people are watching;
•Being in the situation causes intense anxiety, sometimes with panic attacks;
•Realizing that the fear is irrational;
•Unlike simple shyness, the fear leads to avoidance of important or uncomplicated social situations and interferes with the ability to function at work or with friends.

General Anxiety Disorder
•Excessive worry and anxiety on most days for at least six months about several events or activities such as work or school performance;
•Difficulty in controlling the worry;
•The anxiety is connected with at least three of the following: restlessness/feeling on edge; being easily tired; difficulty concentrating; irritability; muscle tension; difficulty falling/staying asleep or restless sleep;
•The anxiety or physical symptoms seriously affect the person's social life, work life, or other important areas.

Phobias
•Persistent, unreasonable, and exaggerated fear of the presence or anticipated presence of a particular object or situation (e.g., snake, flying in an airplane; blood);
•The presence of such an object or situation triggers immediate anxiety which may be a panic attack;
•Knowledge that the fear is exaggerated and unreasonable;
•The phobic situation is either avoided or experienced with extreme distress;
•The avoidance, fearful anticipation, and distress seriously affects the person's normal routine, work and social activities, and relationships.

Panic Disorder
A panic attack is a period of intense fear in which four or more of the following symptoms escalate suddenly, reaching a peak within ten minutes, after which they diminish:
•Palpitations and pounding;
•Rapid heart beat;
•Sweating;
•Trembling or shaking;
•Shortness of breath;
•Feeling of choking;
•Chest pain;
•Nausea;
•Feeling dizzy or faint;
•Feelings of unreality or detachment;
•Fear of losing control or going crazy;
•Fear of dying;
•Numbness or tingling;
•Chills or hot flashes.

Obsessive Compulsive Disorder (OCD)
Individuals with OCD have overwhelming obsessions and/or compulsions. Obsessions are repeated, intrusive, unwanted thoughts that cause distressing emotions such as anxiety or anguish; a compulsion is a ceaseless urge to do something to lessen the anxiety caused by the obsession.
•Recurrent and persistent thoughts, impulses or images that are experienced as intrusive and inapproriate and that cause marked anxiety or distress;
•Thoughts and worries are not simply excessive worries about eal-life problems, but can be inflated misinterpretations of actions and words of others;
•Repetitive behaviors that the person feels driven to perform in response to an obsession, or according to rules that must be applied rigidly;
•The person recognizes that the obsessions or compulsions are unreasonable;
•The obsessions or compulsions cause marked distress, are time consuming, or significantly interfere with the person's normal routine, occupational or academic functioning, or usual social activities.

Post Traumatic Stress Disorder (PTSD)
Traumatic events can stay with us for a long time, and range from common events to the horrific. PTSD consists of of the psychological and phsyiological symptoms that arise from experiencing, witnessing or participating in a traumatic event.
Three basic types of symptoms occur: Re-experiencing, numbing, and/or increased emotional arousal.
Re-experiencing includes:
•Recurrent and intrusive distressing recollections of the event, including images, thoughts or perceptions;
•Recurrent distressing flashbacks, nightmares and/or dreams of the event;
•Acting or feeling as if the traumatic event were recurring Increased arousal includes:
•Intense psychological distress at exposure to internal or external cues that symbolize or resemble an aspect of the

traumatic event;
•Increased physiological reactivity (fast heartbeat or breathing, gastrointestinal distress) on exposure to internal or external cues that symoblize or resemble an aspect of the event;
•Persistent avoidance of stimuli associated with the trauma
Numbing includes:
•Diminished general responsiveness;
•Desensitization of emotional reactiveness;
Increased emotional arousal includes:
•Jumpiness: reacting to ordinary experiences such as loud noises as though they represent danger;
•Bouts of temper: anger with no or insufficient cause
•May experience a dissociative state when in threatening situations, allowing them to have no recollection afterwards;
•Somatic physical complaints linked to no discernable anatomic or physiological explanations;
•May undergo a profound change of personality;
•Duration of the disturbance is more than one month, and it causes clinically significant distress or impairment is social, occupational, or other important settings;
•May also suffer from other distinctive mental illnesses brought on by the PTSD: depression, OCD; social phobia, or substance-abuse.

ASSOCIATED FEATURES

Anxiety can be acute and intense such as the fear of imminent death in a panic attack or it can be experienced as the state of chronic nagging worry in Generalized Anxiety Disorder. Whatever its intensity or frequency, it persists over time. One of the hallmarks of Anxiety Disorders is that the person is unable to control the anxiety, even when he or she knows it is exaggerated and unreasonable, as in Obsessive Compulsive Disorder. To other people, the person may seem edgy, irritable, to have unexpected outbursts of anger, or to be consumed by an unreasonable fear. For the anxious person, the problem takes up time and effort and becomes a major preoccupation. The OCD affected persona can further that time and expenditure of energy in creating a ritual to manage the obsession, such as performing an action a specific number of times in a particular manner. People with PTSD can go to lengths to avoid trigger situations, seriously disrupting normal life.

In addition to the psychological effects (and entangled with them) are the physical effects, that is, a frequent or constant state of physical arousal and tension. This can lead to gastrointestinal upset, headaches, and cardiovascular disease. Using alcohol or drugs to resolve the problem is common but ineffective and dangerous. Anxiety Disorders negatively affect all aspects of life-family, work, and friends.

PREVALENCE

Anxiety Disorders are the most common psychiatric disorders in the U.S. Anxiety Disorders are approximately twice as common in women as in men.

Obsessive Compulsive Disorder usually begins in adolescence or early adulthood, but may begin in childhood. In males the onset is earlier (between 6 and 15 years old) than for women (between 20 and 29), though it is equally common in both.

PTSD can occur at any point in any person's life, and more often occur in women and children than in men. One might imagine that a person would become resistant to the effects of repeated traumas, but in fact each traumatic event furthers the individual's vulnerability over future events.

TREATMENT OPTIONS

It is very important to have a full evaluation so that a proper diagnosis can be made. In general, people should have a primary care evaluation as part of the diagnostic process for all disorders, so as to rule out a general medical condition that could be causing the signs and symptoms. For example, hyperthyroidism can cause anxiety problems; hypothyroidism can look like depression. Self medication with alcohol, tranquilizers, or other drugs is dangerous and can lead to serious drug abuse. Many people who abuse drugs are suffering from an underlying Anxiety Disorder. Treatment will vary depending on which of the Anxiety Disorders is diagnosed. Medications, psychotherapy or both will be prescribed. Some psychotherapies which have proven helpful in certain cases are cognitive-behavioral therapies, including exposure therapy, and eye movement desensitisation reprogramming (EMDR). Benzodiazepines, or minor tranquillizers, can be useful for the acute treatment of anxiety symptoms; care must be taken, because these medications have addictive potential. Selective Serotonin Reuptake Inhibitors, or SSRIs, which were originally developed as Antidepressants, have proved to be effective in several Anxiety Disorders and are now the mainstays of treatment. Since new drugs are frequently introduced, and already approved medications given new therapeutic indications by the USDA, it is wise to consult an expert or recent expert reference before making a treatment decision.

Patients with OCD may benefit from behavioral therapy and/or a variety of medications. Particularly effective is exposure and response prevention therapy, in which a therapist carefully exposes the patient to situations that cause anxiety and provoke the obsessive compulsive behavior. Slowly the patient learns to decrease and eventually end the ritualistic behaviors.

With the PTSD patient, SSRI's are useful in conjunction with behavioral therapies and EMDR. These therapies allow the patient to recognize the thought process that results in the traumatic stress conditions, and over time, learn to experience certain stimuli without distress. Sufferers of PTSD will also benefit from support groups and confidence and esteem building exercises.

It is important to note that suddenly stopping an SSRI can cause rebound symptoms including sleeplessness, headaches, and irritability. Medications should be tapered under the care of a physician.

Associations & Agencies

257 Agoraphobics in Motion
1719 Crooks Road
Royal Oak, MI 48067-1306
248-547-0400
E-mail: anny@ameritech.net
www.aim-hq.org

AIM is a nationwide, nonprofit, support group organization, committed to the support and recovery of those suffering with anxiety disorders, and their families.

258 Anxiety Disorders Association of America
8730 Georgia Avenue
Suite 600
Silver Spring, MD 20910-3643
240-485-1001
www.adaa.org

Alies Muskin, Manager
J. Teichroew, Director, Media Relations and Co

A national non profit organization dedicated exclusively to promoting the prevention, treatment, and cure of anxiety disorders and improving the lives of all people touched by these disorders.

259 Anxiety and Phobia Treatment Center
White Plains Hospital Center
Davis Avenue at E Post Road
White Plains, NY 10601
914-681-1038
E-mail: jchessa@wphospital.org

John Schandler, CEO
Judy Lake Chessa, Coordinator

Treatment groups for individuals suffering from phobias. Deals with fears through contextual therapy, a treatment and study of the phobia in the actual setting in which the phobic reactions occur.

260 Association of Traumatic Stress Specialists
88 Pompton Avenue
Verona, NJ 07044
973-559-9200
E-mail: admin@atss.info
www.atss.info

Lauren De Poto, Administration Director

Helps the traumatized through international service, education and professional development

261 Career Assessment & Planning Services
Goodwill Industries-Suncoast
10596 Gandy Boulevard
PO Box 14456
St. Petersburg, FL 33733-4456
727-523-1512
888-279-1988
Fax: 727-563-9300
E-mail: gw.marketing@goodwill-suncoast.com
www.goodwill-suncoast.org

R Lee Waits, President/CEO
Deborah A Passerini, VP Operations

Provides a comprehensive assessment, which can predict current and future employment and potential adjustment factors for physically, emotionally, or developmentally disabled persons who may be unemployed or underemployed. Assessments evaluate interests, aptitudes, academic achievements, and physical abilities (including dexterity and coordination) through coordinated testing, interviewing and behavioral observations.

262 Center for Family Support (CFS)
333 7th Avenue
New York, NY 10001-5115
212-629-7939
Fax: 212-239-2211
www.cfsny.org

Steven Vernikoff, Executive Director

An agency that continues to develop new programs to serve families and individuals with their care needs. Offering services throughout the New York City Region including: New Jersey, Long Island and the Lower Hudson Valley.

263 Center for Mental Health Services (CMHS)
PO Box 2345
Rockville, MD 20847
240-221-4021
800-789-2647
Fax: 240-221-4295
TDD: 866-889-2647
www.mentalhealth.samhsa.gov

A Kathryn Power, MEd, Director
Anna Marsh PhD, Deputy Director
Fran Randolph PhD, Dir, Service & Systems Improveme
Anne Mathews-Younes EdD, Dir, Prevention/Traumatic Stress

CMHS leads Federal efforts to treat mental illnesses by promoting mental health and by preventing the development or worsening of mental illness when possible. Congress created CMHS to bring new hope to adults who have serious mental illnesses and to children with serious emotional disorders. CMHS provides information about mental health via a toll-free the web site, and more than 600 publications. Developed for users of mental health services and their families, the general public, policy makers, providers, and the media.

Year Founded: 1992

264 E-Productivity-Services.Net
13 NW Barry Road
Kansas City, MO 64155-2728
816-468-4945
E-mail: nld@epsn.net

Nancy L Day, Certified Trauma Specialist

Services include professional skills training in trauma resolutions and personal growth; and individual sessions.

265 Freedom From Fear
308 Seaview Avenue
Staten Island, NY 10305-2246
718-351-1717
Fax: 718-667-8893
E-mail: help@freedomfromfear.org
www.freedomfromfear.org

Jack D Maser PhD, Professor of Psychiatry

The mission of Freedom From Fear is to aid and counsel individuals and their families who suffer from anxiety and depressive illness.

266 International Critical Incident Stress Foundation
3290 Pine Orchard Lane
Suite 106
Ellicott City, MD 21042-2254
410-750-9600
Fax: 410-750-9601
E-mail: info@icisf.org
www.icisf.org

Donald Howell, Executive Director
Stephanie Beam, General Information

A nonprofit, open membership foundation dedicated to the prevention and mitigation of disabling stress by education, training and support services for all emergency service professionals.

267 International Obsessive Compulsive Disorder Foundation
112 Water St
Suite 501
Boston, MA 02109-4206
617-973-5801
Fax: 617-973-5803
E-mail: info@ocfoundation.org
www.ocfoundation.org

Jeff Szymanski, Executive Director
Diane Davey, President

For sufferers of obsessive-compulsive disorder and their families and friends. To educate the public and professional communities about OCD and related disorders; to provide assistance to individuals with OCD and related disorders, their family and friends, and to support research into the causes and effective treatments.

268 International Society for Traumatic Stress Studies
60 Revere Drive
Suite 500
Northbrook, IL 60062-1591
847-480-9028
Fax: 847-480-9282
E-mail: istss@istss.org
www.istss.org

Stuart Turner, President

Provides a forum for sharing research, clinical strategies, public policy concerns and theoretical formulation on trauma in the US and worldwide. Dedicated to discovery and dissemination of knowledge and to the stimulation of policy, program and services.

Year Founded: 1985

269 National Alliance on Mental Illness
2107 Wilson Boulevard
Suite 300
Arlington, VA 22201-3080
703-524-7600
800-950-6264
Fax: 703-524-9094
E-mail: helpline@nami.org
www.nami.org

Michael Fitzpatrick, Executive Director

Nation's leading self-help organization for all those affected by severe brain disorders. Mission is to bring consumers and families with similar experiences together to share information about services, care providers, and ways to cope with the challenges of schizophrenia, manic depression, and other serious mental illnesses.

270 National Anxiety Foundation
3135 Custer Drive
Lexington, KY 40517-4001
859-272-7166

Stephanie Cox MD, President/Medical Director
Linda Vernon Blair, VP

To alleviate suffering and to save lives by educating the public about anxiety disorders.

271 National Association for the Dually Diagnosed (NADD)
132 Fair Street
Kingston, NY 12401-4802
845-331-4336
800-331-5362
Fax: 845-331-4569
E-mail: info@thenadd.org
www.thenadd.org

Robert Fletcher, Executive Director

Nonprofit organization designed to promote interest of professional and parent development with resources for individuals who have the coexistence of mental illness and mental retardation. Provides conference, educational services and training materials to professionals, parents, concerned citizens and service organizations. Formerly known as the National Association for the Dually Diagnosed.

Year Founded: 1983

272 National Mental Health Consumers' Self-Help Clearinghouse
1211 Chestnut Street
Suite 1207
Philadelphia, PA 19107-4103
215-751-1810
800-553-4539
Fax: 215-636-6312
E-mail: info@mhselfhelp.org
www.mhselfhelp.org

Joseph Rogers, Executive Director

A national consumer technical assistance center that has played a major role in the development of the mental health consumer movement.

Year Founded: 1986

273 Obsessive Compulsive Anonymous
PO Box 215
New Hyde Park, NY 11040-215
516-739-0662
E-mail: west24th@aol.com
www.hometown.aol.com/west24th

Jim Broatch, Executive Director

National, nonprofit, self help organization consisting of a fellowship of individuals dedicated to sharing their experience, strength and hope with one another to enable them to solve their common problems and help others recover from OCD.

274 Obsessive Compulsive Information Center
Madison Institute of Medicine
7617 Mineral Point Road
Suite 300
Madison, WI 53717-1623
608-827-2470
E-mail: mim@miminc.org
www.factsforhealth.org

Margarett Baudhuin, Manager

Provides information packets, booklets, patient guides, and telephone information services.

Year Founded: 1990

275 SAMHSA's National Mental Health Information Center
US Department of Health and Human Services
PO Box 42557
Washington, DC 20015-557
240-221-4021
800-789-2647
Fax: 240-221-4295
TDD: 866-889-2647
www.mentalhealth.samhsa.gov

Provides information about mental health via a toll-free telephone number, this web site, and more than 600 publications. Developed for users of mental health services and their families, the general public, policy makers, providers, and the media.

276 Selective Mutism Foundation
PO Box 13133
Sissonville, WV 25360-133

E-mail: sue@selectivemutismfoundation.org
www.selectivemutismfoundation.org

Sue Newman, Co-Founder/Director
Carolyn Miller, Co-Founder/Director

Promote further research, advocacy, social acceptance, and the understanding of Selective Mutism as a debilitating disorder

277 Territorial Apprehensiveness (TERRAP) Programs
14 Wood Lake Square
Houston, TX 77063-3207
713-266-5111
800-274-6242
Fax: 337-474-2782
E-mail: terrap@suddenlink.net
www.terraphouston.com

Shirley G Riff, Director

Developed by Dr. Arthur Hardy in the 1950's, Territorial Apprehensiveness Programs are designed to assist in the treatment of territorial, social and generalized anxieties.

Year Founded: 1981

Books

278 100 Q&A About Panic Disorder
Jones and Bartlett Publishers
40 Tall Pine Drive
Sudbury, MA 01776-2270
978-443-5000
800-832-0034
Fax: 978-443-8000
E-mail: info@jbpub.com
www.jbpub.com

Clayton Jones, CEO

ISBN 0-763727-15-6

279 Acceptance and Commitment Therapy for Anxiety Disorders
New Harbinger Publications
5674 Shattuck Avenue
Oakland, CA 94609-1662
510-652-0215
800-748-6273
Fax: 510-652-5472
E-mail: customerservice@newharbinger.com
www.newharbinger.com

Matthew McKay, Owner

The first step-by-step professional book that teaches how to apply and integrate acceptance and mindfulness for treatment with anxiety disorders. *$58.95*

304 pages ISBN 1-572244-27-5

280 After the Crash: Assessment and Treatment of Motor Vehicle Accident Survivors
American Psychological Publishing
750 1st Street NE
Washington, DC 20002-4242
202-336-5500
800-374-2721
Fax: 202-336-5518
TDD: 202-336-6123
TTY: 202-336-6123
www.apa.org

Norman B Anderson, CEO
Edward J Hickling, PsyD, Author

In this timely second edition, written in a clear and lucid style and illustrated by a wealth of charts, guides, case studies, and clinical advice, the authors report on new, international research and provide updates on their own long-standing research protocols within the groundbreaking Alabny MVA Project. *$59.95*

475 pages Year Founded: 2003 ISBN 1-591470-70-6

281 Aging and Post Traumatic Stress Disorder
American Psychiatric Publishing, Inc.
1000 Wilson Boulevard
Suite 1825
Arlington, VA 22209-3901
703-907-7322
800-368-5777
Fax: 703-907-1091
E-mail: appi@psych.org
www.appi.org

Robert E Hales MD, Editor-in-Chief
Ron McMillen, Chief Executive Officer
John McDuffie, Editorial Director

Provides both literature reviews and data about animal and clinical studies and training for important current concepts of aging, the stress response and the interaction between them. *$37.50*

268 pages ISBN 0-880485-13-2

282 An End to Panic: Breakthrough Techniques for Overcoming Panic Disorder
New Harbinger Publications
5674 Shattuck Avenue
Oakland, CA 94609-1662
510-652-0215
800-748-6273
Fax: 510-652-5472
E-mail: customerservice@newharbinger.com
www.newharbinger.com

Matthew McKay, Owner

A state of the art treatment program covers breathing re-training, taking charge of fear fueling thoughts, overcoming the fear of physical symptoms, coping with phobic situations, avoiding relapse, and living in the here and now. *$18.95*

230 pages ISBN 1-572241-13-6

283 Anxiety & Phobia Workbook
New Harbinger Publications
5674 Shattuck Avenue
Oakland, CA 94609-1662
510-652-0215
800-748-6273
Fax: 510-652-5472
E-mail: customerservice@newharbinger.com
www.newharbinger.com

Matthew McKay, Owner

This comprehensive guide is recommended to those struggling with anxiety disorders. Includes step by step instructions for the crucial cognitive - behavioral techniques that have given real help to hundreds of thousands of readers struggling with anxiety disorders. *$19.95*

448 pages ISBN 1-572240-03-2

284 Anxiety Cure: Eight Step-Program for Getting Well
John Wiley & Sons
605 3rd Avenue
New York, NY 10158-180

212-850-6301
E-mail: info@wiley.com

Anxiety disorders are the most common type of emotional trouble and among the most treatable. Dupont provides a practical guide featuring a step-by-step program for curing the six kinds of anxiety. *$14.95*

256 pages ISBN 0-471247-01-4

285 Anxiety Disorders
Cambridge University Press
40 W 20th Street
New York, NY 10011-4211
212-924-3900
800-872-7423
Fax: 212-691-3239
E-mail: marketing@cup.org
www.cup.org

Stephen Bourne, Chief Press Executive / Director

This comprehensive text covers all the anxiety disorders found in the latest DSM and ICD classifications. Provides detailed information about seven principal disorders, including anxiety in the medically ill. For each disorder, the book covers diagnosis criteria, epidemiology, etiology and pathogenesis, clinical features, natural history and different diagnosis. Describes treatment approaches, both psychological and pharmacological. *$74.95*

354 pages

286 Anxiety and Its Disorders
Guilford Publications
72 Spring Street
New York, NY 10012-4068
212-431-9800
800-365-7006
Fax: 212-966-6708
E-mail: info@guilford.com

Bob Matloff, President

Incorporating recent advances from cognitive science and neurobiology on the mechanisms of anxiety and using emotion theory as basic theoretical framework. Ties theory and research of emerging clinical knowledge to create a new model of anxiety with profound implications for treatment. *$75.00*

700 pages ISBN 1-572304-30-8

287 Anxiety, Phobias, and Panic
Grand Central Publishing
322 South Enterprise Blvd
Lebanon, IN 46052

800-759-0190
www.hachettebookgroupusa.com

Reneau Z Peurifoy, Author

Congratulations! You are about to start a journey along the path to freedom.

ISBN 0-446692-77-8

288 Anxiety, Phobias, and Panic: a Step-By-Step Program for Regaining Control of Your Life
Time Warner Books
3 Center Plaza
Boston, MA 02108-2084

800-759-0190
Fax: 800-331-1664
E-mail: sales@aoltwbg.com
www.twbookmark.com

Helps you identify stress and reduce stress anxiety, recognize and change distorted mental habits, stop thinking and acting like a victim, eliminate the excessive need for approval, make anger your friend and ally, stand up for yourself and feel good about yourself, and conquer your fears and take charge of your life. *$11.00*

363 pages ISBN 0-446670-53-7

289 Beyond Anxiety and Phobia
New Harbinger Publications
5674 Shattuck Avenue
Oakland, CA 94609-1662
510-652-0215
800-748-6273
Fax: 510-652-5472
E-mail: customerservice@newharbinger.com
www.newharbinger.com

Matthew McKay, Owner

Helping people try to get beyond anxiety and their phobia. *$19.95*

264 pages ISBN 1-572242-29-9

290 Biology of Anxiety Disorders
American Psychiatric Publishing, Inc.
1000 Wilson Boulevard
Suite 1825
Arlington, VA 22209-3901
703-907-7322
800-368-5777
Fax: 703-907-1091
E-mail: appi@psych.org
www.appi.org

Robert E Hales MD, Editor-in-Chief
Ron McMillen, Chief Executive Officer
John McDuffie, Editorial Director

Provides the most recent data on the neurobiology and pathophysiology af anxiety from a variety of perspectives. *$30.50*

280 pages Year Founded: 1993 ISBN 0-880484-76-4

291 Boy Who Couldn't Stop Washing
Penguin Group
375 Hudson Street
New York, NY 10014-3672
212-366-2000
800-631-8571
Fax: 212-366-2933
E-mail: online@penguinputnam.com

David Shanks, CEO

The Boy Who Wouldn't Stop Washing: Experience and Treatment of Obsessive-Compulsive Disorder. A comprehensive treatment of obsessive-compulsive disorder that summarizes evidence that the disorder is neurobiological. It also describes the effect of medication combined with behavioral therapy. *$6.99*

304 pages Year Founded: 1991 ISBN 0-451172-02-7

292 Brain Lock: Free Yourself from Obsessive Compulsive Behavior
Harper Collins
10 E 53rd Street
New York, NY 10022-5299
212-207-7000

Brian Murray, Group President
Jeffrey M Schwartz, Author

A simple four-step method for overcoming OCD that is so effective, it's now used in academic treatment centers throughout the world. Proved by brain-imaging tests to actually alter the brain's chemistry, this method dosen't rely on psychopharmaceuticals but cognitive self-therapy and behavior modification to develop new patterns of response. Offers real-life stories of actual patients. Paperback. *$13.00*

256 pages Year Founded: 1997 ISBN 0-060987-11-1

293 Childhood Obsessive Compulsive Disorder
Sage Publications
2455 Teller Road
Thousand Oaks, CA 91320-2234
805-499-0721
800-818-7243
Fax: 805-499-0871
E-mail: info@sagepub.com
www.sagepub.com

Blaise R Simqu, CEO

Childhood Obsessive Compulsive Disorder: Developmental Clinical Psychology and Psychiatry. *$21.95*

ISBN 0-803959-22-2

294 Children and Trauma: Guide for Parents and Professionals
John Wiley & Sons
1 Wiley Drive
Somerset, NJ 08873-1272
732-537-9410
800-225-5945
Fax: 732-302-2300
E-mail: compbks@wiley.com
www.wiley.com

Clifford Kline, Senior VP

Comprehensive guide to the emotional aftermath of children's crises. Discusses warning signs that a child may need professional help, and explores how parents and professionals can help children heal, reviving a sense of well being and safety. *$21.95*

240 pages Year Founded: 1997 ISBN 0-787910-71-6

295 Cognitive Therapy for Depression and Anxiety
American Psychiatric Publishing, Inc.
1000 Wilson Boulevard
Suite 1825
Arlington, VA 22209-3901
703-907-7322
800-368-5777
Fax: 703-907-1091
E-mail: appi@psych.org
www.appi.org

Robert E Hales MD, Editor-in-Chief
Ron McMillen, Chief Executive Officer
John McDuffie, Editorial Director

Detailed guide to using cognitive therapy in the treatment of patients suffering from depression and anxiety - two of the most prevalent disorders encountered in the community. *$44.95*

240 pages ISBN 0-632039-86-8

296 Comorbidity of Mood and Anxiety Disorders
American Psychiatric Publishing, Inc.
1000 Wilson Boulevard
Suite 1825
Arlington, VA 22209-3901
703-907-7322
800-368-5777
Fax: 703-907-1091
E-mail: appi@psych.org
www.appi.org

Robert E Hales MD, Editor-in-Chief
Ron McMillen, Chief Executive Officer
John McDuffie, Editorial Director

Presents a systematic examination of the concurrence of different symptoms and syndromes in patients with anxiety or mood disorders. *$75.00*

868 pages ISBN 0-880483-24-5

297 Compulsive Acts: A Psychiatrist's Tales of Rituals and Obsessions
University of California Press
2120 Berkeley Way
Berkeley, CA 94704-1012
510-642-4247
Fax: 510-643-7127
www.ucpress.edu

Lynne Withey, Director
Elias Aboujaoude MD, Author

The author tells stories inspired by memorable patients he has treated, taking readers from his initial contact through the stages of the doctor-patient relationship. Stories include a man who can't let anyone get within a certain distance of his nose, two kleptomaniacs, an Internet addict who chooses virtual life over real life, a professor with a dangerous gambling habit, and others with equally debilitating compulsive conditions. *$24.95*

191 pages Year Founded: 2008 ISSN 978-0520255678ISBN 0-520255-67-4

298 Concise Guide to Anxiety Disorders
American Psychiatric Publishing, Inc.
1000 Wilson Boulevard
Suite 1825
Arlington, VA 22209-3901
703-907-7322
800-368-5777
Fax: 703-907-1091
E-mail: appi@psych.org
www.appi.org

Robert E Hales MD, Editor-in-Chief
Ron McMillen, Chief Executive Officer
John McDuffie, Editorial Director

Concise Guide to Anxiety Disorders summarizes the latest research and translates it into practical treatment strategies for the best clinical outcomes. Designed for daily use in the clinical setting, it serves as an instant library of current information, quick to access and easy to understand. Every clinician who diagnoses and treats patients with anxiety disorders-including psychiatrists, residents and medical students, psychologists, and mental health professionals-will find this book invaluable for making informed treatment decisions. *$29.95*

272 pages Year Founded: 2003 ISBN 1-585620-80-7

299 Consumer's Guide to Psychiatric Drugs
New Harbinger Publications
5674 Shattuck Avenue
Oakland, CA 94609-1662
510-652-0215
800-748-6273
Fax: 510-652-5472
E-mail: customerservice@newharbinger.com
www.newharbinger.com

Matthew McKay, Owner

Helps consumers understand what treatment options are available and what side effects to expect. Covers possible interactions with other drugs, medical conditions and other concerns. Explains how each drug works, and offers detailed information about treatments for depression, bipolar disorder, anxiety and sleep disorders, as well as other conditions. *$16.95*

340 pages ISBN 1-572241-11-X

300 Coping with Anxiety
New Harbinger Publications
5674 Shattuck Avenue
Oakland, CA 94609-1662
510-652-0215
800-748-6273
Fax: 510-652-5472
E-mail: customerservice@newharbinger.com
www.newharbinger.com

Matthew McKay, Owner

Ten simple steps, proven to help relieve anxiety. *$ 10.95*

176 pages ISBN 1-572243-20-1

301 Coping with Post-Traumatic Stress Disorder
Rosen Publishing Group
29 E 21st Street
New York, NY 10010-6209

212-777-3017
800-237-9932
Fax: 212-777-0277
E-mail: info@rosenpub.com
www.rosenpublishing.com

Roger Rosen, President

$26.50

Year Founded: 2002 ISBN 0-823934-56-X

302 Coping with Social Anxiety: The Definitive Guide to Effective Treatment Options
Holt Paperbacks
175 Fifth Avenue
New York, NY 10010-7703
646-307-5095
Fax: 212-633-0748
E-mail: publicity@hholt.com
www.henryholt.com

Eric Hollander, Author

An essential guide for the 5.3 million American sufferers of social anxiety from a leading psychiatrist and researcher.

ISBN 0-805075-82-8

303 Coping with Trauma: A Guide to Self Understanding
Anxiety Disorders Association of America
8730 Georgia Avenue
Suite 600
Silver Spring, MD 20910-3643
240-485-1001
E-mail: AnxDis@adaa.org
www.adaa.org

Alies Muskin, Manager
Michelle Alonso, Communications/Membership

Book will appeal to survivors of traumatic stress, as well as mental health professionals.

304 Coping with Trauma: A Guide to Self Understanding
American Psychiatric Publishing, Inc.
1000 Wilson Boulevard
Suite 1825
Arlington, VA 22209-3901
703-907-7322
800-368-5777
Fax: 703-907-1091
E-mail: appi@psych.org
www.appi.org

Robert E Hales MD, Editor-in-Chief
Ron McMillen, Chief Executive Officer
John McDuffie, Editorial Director
Jon G Allen, Author

Coping With Trauma is based on more than a decade of Dr. Allen's experience conducting educational groups for persons struggling with psychiatric disorders stemming from trauma. Readers will gain essential knowledge to embark on the process of healing from the complex wounds of trauma, along with a guide to current treatment approaches.
Copyright 2005 *$16.00*

385 pages ISBN 0-880489-96-0

305 Don't Panic: Taking Control of Anxiety Attacks
Anxiety Disorders Association of America
8730 Georgia Avenue
Suite 600
Silver Spring, MD 20910-3643
240-485-1001
E-mail: AnxDis@adaa.org
www.adaa.org

Alies Muskin, Manager
Michelle Alonso, Communications/Marketing

Book on overcoming panic and anxiety.

306 Drug Therapy and Anxiety Disorders
Mason Crest Publishers
370 Reed Road
Suite 302
Broomall, PA 19008-4017
610-543-6200
866-627-2665
Fax: 610-543-3878
E-mail: dtaylor@masoncrest.com
www.masoncrest.com

This volume provides readers with a clear introduction to anxiety disorders. Numerous case studies give insight into the world of mental disorders and helps readers understand the symptoms and treatments of this disorder, which includes: generalized anxiety disorder, social phobia, specific phobia, obsessive-compulsive disorder (covered more extensively in a separate column), post-traumatic stress disorder, and panic disorder.

ISBN 1-590845-61-7

307 Drug Therapy and Obsessive-Compulsive Disorder
Mason Crest Publishers
370 Reed Road
Suite 302
Broomall, PA 19008-4017
610-543-6200
866-627-2665
Fax: 610-543-3878
E-mail: dtaylor@masoncrest.com
www.masoncrest.com

This volume provides readers with a clear and understandable introduction to obsessive-compulsive disorder (OCD). Numerous case studies are included, which give insight into the world of those who experience this disorder; these anecdotes also help readers understand the symptoms and treatments of this disease. Famous historical figures who suffered from OCD, such as Samuel Johnson (1709-1784) and Howard Hughes (1905-1975) are mentioned as well.

ISBN 1-590845-69-2

308 Dying of Embarrassment: Help for Social Anxiety and Social Phobia
New Harbinger Publications
5674 Shattuck Avenue
Oakland, CA 94609-1662

510-652-0215
800-748-6273
Fax: 510-652-5472
E-mail: customerservice@newharbinger.com
www.newharbinger.com

Matthew McKay, Owner

Clear, supportive instructions for assessing your fears, improving or developing new social skills, and changing self defeating thinking patterns. *$13.95*

204 pages ISBN 1-879237-23-7

309 Effecive Treatments for PTSD: Practice Guide lines from the International Society for Traumatic Stress Studies
The Guilford Press
72 Spring Street
New York, NY 10012-4019
212-431-9800
800-365-7006
Fax: 212-966-6708
E-mail: info@guilford.com

Bob Matloff, President

The treatment guidelines presented in this book were developed under the auspices of the PTSD Treatment Guidelines Task Force established by the Board of Directors.

ISBN 1-593850-14-X

310 Effective Treatments for PTSD
Guilford Publications
72 Spring Street
New York, NY 10012-4068
212-431-9800
800-365-7006
Fax: 212-966-6708
E-mail: info@guilford.com

Bob Matloff, President

Represents the collaborative work of experts across a range of theoretical orientations and professional backgrounds. Addresses general treatment considerations and methodological issues, reviews and evaluates the salient literature on treatment approaches for children, adolescents and adults. *$44.00*

379 pages ISBN 1-572305-84-3

311 Emotions Anonymous Book
Emotions Anonymous International Service Center
PO Box 4245
Saint Paul, MN 55104-0245
651-647-9712
Fax: 651-647-1593
E-mail: info@EmotionsAnonymous.org
www.EmotionsAnonymous.org

Karen Mead, Executive Director

The Big Book of EA: A fellowship of men and women who share their experience, strength and hope with each other, that they may solve their common problem and help others recover from emotional illness. *$15.00*

260 pages ISBN 0-960735-65-5

312 Encyclopedia of Phobias, Fears, and Anxieties
Facts on File
132 West 31st Street
17th Floor
New York, NY 10001-3406
212-613-2800
800-322-8755
E-mail: custserv@factsonfile.com

Providing the basic information on common phobias and anxieties, some 2000 entries explain the nature of anxiety disorders, panic attacks, specific phobias, and obsessive-compulsive disorders. *$71.50*

576 pages Year Founded: 2000 ISBN 0-816039-89-5

313 Five Weeks to Healing Stress: the Wellness Option
New Harbinger Publications
5674 Shattuck Avenue
Oakland, CA 94609-1662
510-652-0215
800-748-6273
Fax: 510-652-5472
E-mail: customerservice@newharbinger.com
www.newharbinger.com

Matthew McKay, Owner

This workbook presents a quick and effective, body oriented program for regaining inner strength and calming stress. *$17.95*

216 pages ISBN 1-572240-55-5

314 Flying Without Fear
New Harbinger Publications
5674 Shattuck Avenue
Oakland, CA 94609-1662
510-652-0215
800-748-6273
Fax: 510-652-5472
E-mail: customerservice@newharbinger.com
www.newharbinger.com

Matthew McKay, Owner

Program to confront fears of flying and guides you through first takeoff and later flights. *$13.95*

176 pages ISBN 1-572240-42-3

315 Free from Fears: New Help for Anxiety, Panic and Agoraphobia
Anxiety Disorders Association of America
8730 Georgia Avenue
Suite 600
Silver Spring, MD 20910-3643
240-485-1001
E-mail: AnxDis@adaa.org
www.adaa.org

Alies Muskin, Manager
Michelle Alonso, Communications/Membership

Book shows you how to recognize the avoidance trap, combat fears, and modify your behavior for a lasting cure.

316 **Freeing Your Child from Anxiety: Powerful, Practical Solutions to Overcome Your Child's Fears, Worries, and Phobias**
Broadway Books
1745 Broadway
New York, NY 10019-4368
212-662-0231
E-mail: bwaypub@randomhouse.com

Sherif Isak, Owner
Phillip Stern, Author

317 **Freeing Your Child from Obsessive-Compulsive Disorder: A Powerful, Practical Program for Parents of Children and Adolescents**
Three Rivers Publishing
1745 Broadway
New York, NY 10019
212-782-9000
Fax: 212-940-7408
E-mail: crownpublicity@randomhouse.com
www.crownpublishing.com

Tamar E Chansky, Author

Creates a clear road map to understanding and overcoming OCD based on her successful practice treating hundreds of children and teenages with this disorder. *$15.95*

368 pages ISBN 0-812931-17-3

318 **Funny, You Don't Look Crazy: Life With Obsessive Compulsive Disorder**
Dilligaf Publishing
64 Court Street
Ellsworth, ME 04605
207-667-5031

An honest look at people who live with Obsessive Compulsive Disorder and those who love them.

128 pages Year Founded: 1994 ISBN 0-963907-00-X

319 **Getting Control: Overcoming Your Obsessions and Compulsions**
Penguin Putnam
375 Hudson Street
New York, NY 10014-3672
212-366-2000
800-227-9604
Fax: 212-366-2933

David Shanks, CEO

Updated guide to treating OCD based on clinically proven techniques of behavior therapy. Offers a step-by-step program including assessing symptoms, setting realistic goals and creating specific therapeutic exercises. *$13.95*

272 pages Year Founded: 2000 ISBN 0-452281-77-6

320 **Handbook of Intellectual and Developmental Disabilities (Issued in Clinical Child Psychology)**
Springer Publishing
11 West 42nd Street
15th Floor
New York, NY 10036

877-687-7476
www.springerpub.com

John W Jacobson, Editor
James A Mulick, Editor
Johannes Rojahn, Editor

makes clear the far-reaching impact these disorders have on individuals, their families and society in general. For clinicians, researchers, and advanced-level graduate students, this volume is a must-have resources and reference.

321 **Handbook of PTSD: Science and Practice**
The Guilford Press
72 Spring Street
New York, NY 10012-4019
212-431-9800
800-365-7006
Fax: 212-966-6708
E-mail: info@guilford.com

Bob Matloff, President

Unparalleled in its breadth and depth, this state-of-the-art handbook reviews the latest scientific advances in understanding trauma and PTSD.

ISBN 1-593854-73-0

322 **Haunted by Combat: Understanding PTSD in War Veterans**
Praeger Security International General Interest-Cloth
88 Post Road West
Westport, CT 06880-4208
203-226-3571
www.greenwood.com

Daryl S Paulson, Author

Across history, the condition has been called soldier's heart, shell shock, or combat fatigue.

ISBN 0-275991-87-3

323 **Healing Fear: New Approaches to Overcoming Anxiety**
New Harbinger Publications
5674 Shattuck Avenue
Oakland, CA 94609-1662
510-652-0215
800-748-6273
Fax: 510-652-5472
E-mail: customerservice@newharbinger.com
www.newharbinger.com

Matthew McKay, Owner

Covers a wide range of healing strategies that help you learn how to relinquish control, discover a unique purpose that is bigger than your particular fears, and find ways to restructure your work and home environments to make them more congruent with the real you. *$ 16.95*

416 pages ISBN 1-572241-16-0

324 How to Help Your Loved One Recover from Agoraphobia
Anxiety Disorders Association of America
8730 Georgia Avenue
Suite 600
Silver Spring, MD 20910-3643
240-485-1001
E-mail: AnxDis@adaa.org
www.adaa.org

Alies Muskin, Manager
Michelle Alonso, Communications/Membership

Book is helpful for sufferer and family members to understand what a sufferer is going through.

325 I Can't Get Over It: Handbook for Trauma Survivors
New Harbinger Publications
2674 Shattuck Avenue
Oakland, CA 94609
510-652-0215
800-748-6273
Fax: 510-652-5472
E-mail: customerservice@newharbinger.com
www.newharbinger.com

Matthew McKay, Owner

Guides readers through the healing process of recovering from Post Traumatic Stress Disorder. From the emotional experience to the process of healing, this book is written for survivors of all types of trauma including war, sexual abuse, crime, family violence, rape and natural catastrophes. *$16.95*

416 pages Year Founded: 1996 ISBN 1-572240-58-X

326 Imp of the Mind: Exploring the Silent Epidemic of Obsessive Bad Thoughts
Penguin Putnam
375 Hudson Street
New York, NY 10014-3672
212-366-2000
800-227-9604
Fax: 212-366-2933

David Shanks, CEO

Draws on new advances to explore the causes of obsessive thoughts, and the difference between harmless and dangerous bad thoughts. *$14.00*

176 pages Year Founded: 2002 ISBN 0-525945-62-8

327 Integrative Treatment of Anxiety Disorders
American Psychiatric Publishing, Inc.
1000 Wilson Boulevard
Suite 1825
Arlington, VA 22209-3901
703-907-7322
800-368-5777
Fax: 703-907-1091

E-mail: appi@psych.org
www.appi.org

Robert E Hales MD, Editor-in-Chief
Ron McMillen, Chief Executive Officer
John McDuffie, Editorial Director

An overview of the spectrum of anxiety disorders, and reviews the treatment alternatives. *$67.00*

349 pages Year Founded: 1996 ISBN 0-880487-15-1

328 It's Not All In Your Head: Now Women Can Discover the Real Causes of their Most Misdiagnosed Health Problems
Anxiety Disorders Association of America
8730 Georgia Avenue
Suite 600
Silver Spring, MD 20910-3643
240-485-1001
E-mail: AnxDis@adaa.org
www.adaa.org

Alies Muskin, Manager
Michelle Alonso, Communications/Membership

This book will present you with information about when, how and from whom to seek treatment.

329 Let's Talk Facts About Obsessive Compulsive Disorder
American Psychiatric Publishing, Inc.
1000 Wilson Boulevard
Suite 1825
Arlington, VA 22209-3901
703-907-7322
800-368-5777
Fax: 703-907-1091
E-mail: appi@psych.org
www.appi.org

Robert E Hales MD, Editor-in-Chief
Ron McMillen, Chief Executive Officer
John McDuffie, Editorial Director

$12.50

8 pages ISBN 0-890423-58-X

330 Managing Social Anxiety: A Cognitive Behavioral Therapy Approach Client Workbook (Treatments That Work)
Oxford University Press
2001 Evans Road
Carry, NC 27513-2010
919-677-0977
800-445-9714
Fax: 919-677-2673
E-mail: custserv.us@oup.com

Debra A Hope, Author
Richard G Heimberg, Author

This is a client workbook for those in treatment or considering treatment for social anxiety.

ISBN 0-195183-82-7

331 Managing Traumatic Stress Risk: A Proactive Approach
Charles C Thomas Publishers
PO Box 19265
Springfield, IL 62794-9265
217-789-8980
800-258-8980
Fax: 217-789-9130
www.ccthomas.com

This volume represents the first systematic review of critical incident and disaster hazards, the contextual factors that influence risk, and their implications for traumatic stress risk management. It provides the hazard assessment and risk analysis information which, combined with information on resilience, facilitates the systematic analysis of traumatic stress risk and proactive and methodical development of mitigation and risk reduction strategies. This book is also available in paperback for $41.95. *$61.95*

258 pages Year Founded: 2004 ISBN 0-398075-17-4

332 Master Your Panic and Take Back Your Life: Twelve Treatment Sessions to Overcome High Anxiety
Impact Publishers
PO Box 6016
Atascadero, CA 93423-6016
805-466-5917
800-246-7228
Fax: 805-466-5919
E-mail: info@impactpublishers.com
www.impactpublishers.com

Practical, self empowering book on overcoming agoraphobia and debilitating panic attacks is now completely revised and expanded to include the latest information and research findings on relaxation, breathing, medication and other treatments. *$15.95*

304 pages Year Founded: 1998 ISBN 1-886230-08-0

333 Mastery of Your Anxiety and Panic: Workbook
Oxford University Press
2001 Evans Road
Cary, NC 27513-2010
919-677-0977
800-445-9714
Fax: 919-677-2673
E-mail: custserv.us@oup.com

David H Barlow, Author

If you are prone to panic attacks and constantly worry about when the next attack may come, you may suffer from panic disorder and/or agoraphobia. Though panic disorder seems irrational and uncontrollable, it has been proven that a treatment like the one outlined in this book can help you take control of your life.

ISBN 0-195311-35-3

334 My Quarter-Life Crisis: How an Anxiety Disorder Knocked Me Down, and How I Got Back Up
Tucket Publishing
01776

Lee Wellman, Author

A candid memoir of an All-American athlete who fell victim to a debilitating anxiety disorder and depression. Lee Wellman shares his battle in order to help others, while bashing old stigmas that anxiety is for the weak and timid. Lee outlines 15 strategies, proven and professionaly endorsed, to help overcome anxiety and depression. Available on Amazon.com

224 pages Year Founded: 2007 ISBN 0-978751-57-4

335 No More Butterflies: Overcoming Shyness, Stagefright, Interview Anxiety, and Fear of Public Speaking
New Harbinger Publications
5674 Shattuck Avenue
Oakland, CA 94609-1662
510-652-0215
800-748-6273
Fax: 510-652-5472
E-mail: customerservice@newharbinger.com
www.newharbinger.com

Matthew McKay, Owner

Demonstrates how to pinpoint fears, refute fear - provoking thoughts, and exhibit confidence at interviews and auditions. *$13.95*

176 pages ISBN 1-572240-41-5

336 OCD Workbook: Your Guide to Breaking Free From Obsessive-Compulsive Disorder
New Harbinger Publications
5674 Shattuck Avenue
Oakland, CA 94609-1662
510-652-0215
800-748-6273
Fax: 510-652-5472
E-mail: customerservice@newharbinger.com
www.newharbinger.com

Matthew McKay, Owner
Cherry Pedrick, RN, Author

Offers the latest information about the neurobiological causes of obsessive-compulsive disorder(OCD), new developments in medication and other treatment options for the disorder, and a new chapter outlining cutting-edge daily coping strategies for sufferers. *$19.95*

198 pages ISBN 1-572244-22-4

337 OCD in Children and Adolescents: A Cognitive-Behavioral Treatment Manual
Guilford Publications
72 Spring Street
New York, NY 10012-4068
212-431-9800
800-365-7006
Fax: 212-966-6708
E-mail: info@guilford.com

Bob Matloff, President

Written for clinicians, the book includes tips for parents, and treatment guidelines. The cognitive - behavioral approach to OCD has been problematic for many to understand because patients with symptoms of increased anxiety are told that their treatment initially involves further in-creases in their anxiety levels. The authors provide this in a modified and developmentally appropriate approach. *$32.00*

298 pages

338 Obsessive Compulsive Anonymous
Obsessive Compulsive Anonymous
PO Box 215
New Hyde Park, NY 11040-0910
516-739-0662
E-mail: west24th@aol.com
www.obsessivecompulsiveanonymous.com

Literature for the OCA program. *$19.00*

ISBN 0-962806-62-5

339 Obsessive-Compulsive Disorder Casebook
American Psychiatric Publishing, Inc.
1000 Wilson Boulevard
Suite 1825
Arlington, VA 22209-3901
703-907-7322
800-368-5777
Fax: 703-907-1091
E-mail: appi@psych.org
www.appi.org

Robert E Hales MD, Editor-in-Chief
Ron McMillen, Chief Executive Officer
John McDuffie, Editorial Director

Presents 60 case histories of OCD with a discussion by the author and editors regarding their opinion on each diagnosis. *$39.95*

336 pages ISBN 0-880487-29-1

340 Obsessive-Compulsive Disorder Spectrum
American Psychiatric Publishing, Inc.
1000 Wilson Boulevard
Suite 1825
Arlington, VA 22209-3901
703-907-7322
800-368-5777
Fax: 703-907-1091
E-mail: appi@psych.org
www.appi.org

Robert E Hales MD, Editor-in-Chief
Ron McMillen, Chief Executive Officer
John McDuffie, Editorial Director

Comprehensive examination of OCD, related disorders and treatment regimens. *$68.50*

338 pages ISBN 0-880487-07-0

341 Obsessive-Compulsive Disorder in Children and Adolescents: A Guide
Madison Institute of Medicine
7617 Mineral Point Road
Suite 300
Madison, WI 53717-1623

608-827-2470
E-mail: mim@miminc.org
www.factsforhealth.org

Margarett Baudhuin, Manager

The guide is a comprehensive introduction to obsessive-compulsive disorder for parents who are learning about the illness. Discusses treating symptoms by a combination of behavioral therapy and medication and describes various drugs that can be used with children and adolescents in terms of their effects on brain functioning, symptom control, and side-effects. The book is attuned to the difficulties families of OCD children face. *$5.95*

66 pages ISBN 1-890802-28-X

342 Obsessive-Compulsive Disorder in Children and Adolescents
American Psychiatric Publishing, Inc.
1000 Wilson Boulevard
Suite 1825
Arlington, VA 22209-3901
703-907-7322
800-368-5777
Fax: 703-907-1091
E-mail: appi@psych.org
www.appi.org

Robert E Hales MD, Editor-in-Chief
Ron McMillen, Chief Executive Officer
John McDuffie, Editorial Director

Examines the early development of obsessive - compulsive disorder and describes effective treatments. *$47.50*

360 pages ISBN 0-880482-82-6

343 Obsessive-Compulsive Disorder: Theory, Research and Treatment
Guilford Publications
72 Spring Street
New York, NY 10012-4068
212-431-9800
800-365-7006
Fax: 212-966-6708
E-mail: info@guilford.com

Bob Matloff, President

Part I: Psychopathology and Theoretical Perspectives; Part II: Assessment and Treatment; Part III: Obsessive Compulsive Spectrum Disorders; Appendix: List of Resources. *$50.00*

478 pages ISBN 1-572303-35-2

344 Obsessive-Compulsive Disorders: A Complete Guide to Getting Well and Staying Well
Oxford University Press
2001 Evans Road
Cary, NC 27513-2010
919-677-0977
800-445-9714
Fax: 919-677-2673
E-mail: custserv.us@oup.com

Fred Penzel, Author

In defining obsessive-compulsive disorders (OCDs), our language creates problems, because it treats the terms "obsessive" and "compulsion" very loosely.

345 Obsessive-Compulsive Disorders: Practical Management
Elsevier
Po Box 28430
Saint Louis, MO 63146-930
314-453-7010
800-460-3110
Fax: 314-453-7095
www.elsevier.com

Michael A Jenike, MD, Author
Lee Baer, PhD, Author
Wiliam F Minichiello, EdD, Author

Topics include the clinical picture, illnesses relation to obsessive-compulsive disorder, spectrum disorders, patient and clinical management and pathophysiology and assessment. *$73.00*

886 pages Year Founded: 1998 ISBN 0-815138-40-7

346 Obsessive-Compulsive Disorders: The Latest Assessment and Treatment Strategies
Compact Clinicals
7205 N.W. Waukomis Drive
Kansas City, MI 64151-1463
816-587-0044
800-408-8830
Fax: 816-587-7198
E-mail: customerservice@compactclinicals.com
www.compactclinicals.com

Gail Steketee, Author

Previously considered a rare mental condition, obsessive compulsive disorder (OCD) now appears to be a hidden epidemic with over 6.5 million sufferers.

347 Obsessive-Compulsive Related Disorders
American Psychiatric Publishing, Inc.
1000 Wilson Boulevard
Suite 1825
Arlington, VA 22209-3901
703-907-7322
800-368-5777
Fax: 703-907-1091
E-mail: appi@psych.org
www.appi.org

Robert E Hales MD, Editor-in-Chief
Ron McMillen, Chief Executive Officer
John McDuffie, Editorial Director

Discusses the way compulsivity and impulsivity are understood, diagnosed and treated. *$22.50*

286 pages ISBN 0-880484-02-0

348 Over and Over Again: Understanding Obsessive-Compulsive Disorder
Jossey-Bass/Wiley
111 River Street
Hoboken, NJ 07030-5773

201-748-6000
Fax: 201-748-6088
E-mail: custserv@wiley.com
www.wiley.com

This sensitive and insightful book, the result of the author's years of research and experimentation, is a much needed survival manual for OCD sufferers and the families and friends who share their pain. *$25.00*

240 pages Year Founded: 1997 ISBN 0-787908-76-2

349 Overcoming Anxiety, Depression, and Other Mental Health Disorders in Children and Adults: A New Roadmap for Families and Professionals
Interdesciplinary Council on Development and Learning Disorders
4938 Hampden Lane
Bethesda, MD 20814
301-656-2667
E-mail: info@icdl.com
www.icdl.com

Dr Stanley Greenspan, Author

Reveals strategies for family members as well as professionals from different disciplines to help both children and adults. The most common mental health disorders, including anxiety, depression, obsessive-compulsive patterns, ADD/ADHD, borderline states, and others, are discussed literally with a new set of eyeglasses

168 pages ISBN 0-976775-88-3

350 Overcoming Obsessive-Compulsive Disorder: Client Manual: A Behavioral and Cognitive Protocol for the Treatment of OCD (Best Practices Series)
New Harbinger Publications
5674 Shattuck Avenue
Oakland, CA 94609

800-748-6273
Fax: 800-652-1613
E-mail: customerservice@newharbinger.com
www.newharbinger.com

Matthew McKay PhD, Founder/Author
Gail Steketee PhD, Author

This protocol outlines a fourteen-session treatment for individual adults diagnosed with obsessive-compulsive disorder. This protocol is based on imagined exposure, in vivo exposure, response prevention and avoidance reduction. Copyright 1998 *$15.95*

104 pages ISSN 978-1572241299

351 Panic Disorder and Agoraphobia: A Guide
Madison Institute of Medicine
7617 Mineral Point Road
Suite 300
Madison, WI 53717-1623
608-827-2470
E-mail: mim@miminc.org
www.factsforhealth.org

Margarett Baudhuin, Manager

Learn about the causes of panic disorder and agoraphobia and how patients can overcome these disabling disorders with medications and behavior therapy in this booklet written by leading experts on the subject. *$5.95*

69 pages

352 Panic Disorder: Critical Analysis
Guilford Publications
72 Spring Street
New York, NY 10012-4068
212-431-9800
800-365-7006
Fax: 212-966-6708
E-mail: info@guilford.com

Bob Matloff, President

Provides a comprehensive, integrative exploration of panic disorder. Discusses the phenomenology of the disorder, with extensive reviews of the epidemiology, biological aspects and psychopharmacalogic treatments, followed by detailed explorations of psychological aspects, including predictability and controllability and psychological treatments including cognitive behavioral techniques. *$38.00*

276 pages ISBN 0-898622-63-8

353 Pharmacotherapy for Mood, Anxiety and Cognitive Disorders
American Psychiatric Publishing, Inc.
1000 Wilson Boulevard
Suite 1825
Arlington, VA 22209-3901
703-907-7322
800-368-5777
Fax: 703-907-1091
E-mail: appi@psych.org
www.appi.org

Robert E Hales MD, Editor-in-Chief
Ron McMillen, Chief Executive Officer
John McDuffie, Editorial Director

Takes a critical look at the different medications available for treating mood, anxiety and cognitive disorders. Also, it takes a look at their relevance to pathobiology and the underlying mechanisms, and the limitations. *$99.00*

832 pages Year Founded: 2000 ISBN 0-880488-85-9

354 Phobias and How to Overcome Them: Understanding and Beating Your Fears
New Page Books
3 Tice Road
Po Box 687
Franklin Lakes, NJ 07417
201-848-0310
800-227-3371
www.newpagebooks.com

James Gardner, Author

Do you or does someone you care about suffer from phobias?

ISBN 1-564147-66-5

355 Phobic and Obsessive-Compulsive Disorders: Theory, Research, and Practice
Kluwer Academic/Plenum Publishers
233 Spring Street
New York, NY 10013-1522
212-242-1490

$80.00

Year Founded: 1990 ISBN 0-306410-44-3

356 Post-Traumatic Stress Disorder: Assessment, Differential Diagnosis, and Forensic Evaluation
Professional Resource Press
PO Box 15560
Sarasota, FL 34277-1560
941-343-9601
800-443-3364
Fax: 941-343-9201
E-mail: orders@prpress.com
www.prpress.com

Carroll L Meek, Editor
Debra Fink, Managing Editor

A concise yet thorough examination of PTSD. An excellent resource for psychologists, psychiatrists, and lawyers involved in litigation concerning PTSD. *$26.95*

264 pages Year Founded: 1990 ISBN 0-943158-35-4

357 Posttraumatic Stress Disorder in Litigation: Guidelines for Forensic Assessment
American Psychiatric Publishing, Inc.
1000 Wilson Boulevard
Suite 1825
Arlington, VA 22209-3901
703-907-7322
800-368-5777
Fax: 703-907-1091
E-mail: appi@psych.org
www.appi.org

Robert E Hales MD, Editor-in-Chief
Ron McMillen, Chief Executive Officer
John McDuffie, Editorial Director

This essential collection by 13 leading US experts sheds important new light on forensic guidelines for effective assessment and diagnosis and determination of disability, serving both plaintiffs and defendants in litigation involving PTSD claims. Mental health and legal professionals, third-party payers, and interested laypersons will welcome this balanced approach to a complex and difficult field. *$44.95*

272 pages Year Founded: 2003 ISBN 1-585620-66-1

358 Posttraumatic Stress Disorder: A Guide
Madison Institute of Medicine
7617 Mineral Point Road
Suite 300
Madison, WI 53717-1623
608-827-2470
E-mail: mim@miminc.org
www.factsforhealth.org

Margarett Baudhuin, Manager

This informative guide provides a comprehensive overview of the causes and effective treatments of posttraumatic stress disorder (PTSD). *$5.95*

69 pages

359 Psychiatric Treatment of Victims and Survivors of Sexual Trauma: A Neuro-Bio-Psychological Approach
Charles C Thomas Publishers
PO Box 19265
Springfield, IL 62794-9265
217-789-8980
800-258-8980
Fax: 217-789-9130
www.ccthomas.com

This book originated on the basis of clinical observations and the authors believe that trauma is the region in which psych and soma meet each other and integrate, becoming a single entity. The authors attempt to integrate the psychosocial and bio-neuro-endcrine aspects of human experience, including trauma. Available in paperback for $33.95. *$53.95*

234 pages Year Founded: 2004 ISBN 0-398074-60-7

360 Psychological Trauma
American Psychiatric Publishing, Inc.
1000 Wilson Boulevard
Suite 1825
Arlington, VA 22209-3901
703-907-7322
800-368-5777
Fax: 703-907-1091
E-mail: appi@psych.org
www.appi.org

Robert E Hales MD, Editor-in-Chief
Ron McMillen, Chief Executive Officer
John McDuffie, Editorial Director

Epidemiology of trauma and post-traumatic stress disorder. Evaluation, neuroimaging, neuroendocrinology and pharmacology. *$29.00*

206 pages ISBN 0-880488-37-9

361 Real Illness: Obsessive-Compulsive Disorder
National Institute of Mental Health
6001 Executive Boulevard
Room 8184
Bethesda, MD 20892-1
301-443-4513
866-615-6464
TTY: 301-443-8431
E-mail: nimhinfo@nih.gov

Do you have disturbing thoughts and behaviors you know don't make sense but that you can't seem to control? This easy brochure explains how to get help.

9 pages

362 Rebuilding Shattered Lives: Responsible Treatment of Complex Post-Traumatic and Dissociative Disorders
John Wiley & Sons
1 Wiley Drive
Somerset, NJ 08873-1272
732-537-9410
800-225-5945
Fax: 732-302-2300
E-mail: compbks@wiley.com
www.wiley.com

Clifford Kline, Senior VP

Essential for anyone working in the field of trauma therapy. Part I discusses recent findings about child abuse, the changes in attitudes toward child abuse over the last two decades and the nature of traumatic memory. Part II is an overview of principles of trauma treatment, including symptom control, establishment of boundaries and therapist self - care. Part III covers special topics, such as dissociative identity disorder, controversies, hospitalization and acute care. *$73.95*

288 pages Year Founded: 1998 ISBN 0-471247-32-4

363 Relaxation & Stress Reduction Workbook
New Harbinger Publications
5674 Shattuck Avenue
Oakland, CA 94609-1662
510-652-0215
800-748-6273
Fax: 510-652-5472
E-mail: customerservice@newharbinger.com
www.newharbinger.com

Matthew McKay, Owner

Step by step instructions cover progressive muscle relaxation, meditation, autogenics, visualization, thought stopping, refuting irrational ideas, coping skills training, job stress management, and much more. *$17.95*

256 pages ISBN 1-879237-82-2

364 Rewind, Replay, Repeat: A Memoir of Obsessive-Compulsive Disorder
Hazelden Publishing & Educational Services
PO Box 176
Center City, MN 55012-176
651-213-4200
800-257-7810
Fax: 651-213-4411
E-mail: info@hazelden.org
www.hazelden.org

Jeff Bell, Author

The revealing story of one man's struggle with obsessive-compulsive disorder (OCD) and his hard-won recovery.

365 Risk Factors for Posttraumatic Stress Disorder
American Psychiatric Publishing, Inc.
1000 Wilson Boulevard
Suite 1825
Arlington, VA 22209-3901
703-907-7322
800-368-5777

Fax: 703-907-1091
E-mail: appi@psych.org
www.appi.org

Robert E Hales MD, Editor-in-Chief
Ron McMillen, Chief Executive Officer
John McDuffie, Editorial Director

Strategies to study risk for the development of PTSD including epidemiological risk factors for trauma and PTSD, genetic risk factors for a twin study, family studies, parental PTSD as a risk factor, neurocognitive risk factors and risk factors for the acute biological and psychological response to trauma. *$42.50*

320 pages ISBN 0-880488-16-6

366 School Personnel
Obsessive-Compulsive Foundation
676 State Street
New Haven, CT 06511-6508
203-401-2070
Fax: 203-401-2076
E-mail: info@ocfoundation.org
www.ocfoundation.org

Gail B Adams, Author

School Personnel: A Critical Link in the Identification, Treatment and Management of OCD in Children and Adolescents. Recognizing OCD in the school setting, current treatments, the role of school personnel in identification, assessment, and educational interventions, are thoroughly covered in this brief, but informative booklet especially targeted to educators and guidance counselors. *$4.00*

19 pages Year Founded: 1995 ISBN B-0006QK-6V-6

367 Shy Children, Phobic Adults: Nature and Treatment of Social Phobia
American Psychological Association
750 First Street, NE
Washington, DC 20002-4242
202-336-5500
800-374-2721
Fax: 202-336-5518
TTY: 202-336-6123
www.apa.org

Norman B Anderson, CEO

Medical University of South Charleston. Recent advances in the understanding of social phobia.

ISBN 1-557984-61-1

368 Social Anxiety Disorder: A Guide
Madison Institute of Medicine
7617 Mineral Point Road
Suite 300
Madison, WI 53717-1623
608-827-2470
E-mail: mim@miminc.org
www.factsforhealth.org

Margarett Baudhuin, Manager

Do you fear public speaking or do you avoid social situations because you worry you may do something embarassing or humiliating? Learn how social anxiety disorder, also known as social phobia, is diagnosed and treated

in this thorough publication written by leading experts on the subject. *$5.95*

61 pages

369 Social Phobia: From Shyness to Stage Fright
Anxiety Disorders Association of America
8730 Georgia Avenue
Suite 600
Silver Spring, MD 20910-3643
240-485-1001
E-mail: AnxDis@adaa.org
www.adaa.org

Alies Muskin, Manager
Michelle Alonso, Communications/Membership

Book on social phobia.

370 Stop Obsessing: How to Overcome Your Obsessions and Compulsions
Anxiety Disorders Association of America
8730 Georgia Avenue
Suite 600
Silver Spring, MD 20910-3643
240-485-1001
E-mail: AnxDis@adaa.org
www.adaa.org

Alies Muskin, Manager
Michelle Alonso, Communications/Membership

Book provides knowledgeable descriptions of the steps, the challenges, and the value of self - treatment.

371 Stress Response Syndromes: Personality Styles and Interventions
Jason Aronson-Rowman & Littlefield Publishers
200 Park Avenue South
Suite 1109
New York, NY 10003-1512
212-529-3888
E-mail: custerv@rowman.com
www.rowmanlittlefield.com

Neils Aaboe, Manager

Incorporation of the most recent advances in the understanding and treatment of stress response syndromes to date. Describes the general characteristics, including signs and symptoms, and elaborates on treatment techniques that integrate cognitive and dynamic approaches. *$43.00*

451 pages ISBN 0-765703-13-0

372 Stress-Related Disorders Sourcebook
Omnigraphics
PO Box 625
Holmes, PA 19043-625

800-234-1340
Fax: 800-875-1340
E-mail: info@omnigraphics.com
www.omnigraphics.com

Omnigraphics is the publisher of the Health Reference Series, a growing consumer health information resource with more than 100 volumes in print. Each title in the series features an easy to understand format, nontechnical language, comprehensive indexing and resources for further information. Material in each book has been collected from a wide range of government agencies, professional associations, periodicals, and other sources. *$78.00*

600 pages ISBN 0-780805-60-7

373 Take Charge: Handling a Crisis and Moving Forward
American Institute for Preventive Medicine
30445 Northwestern Highway
Suite 350
Farmington Hills, MI 48334-3107
248-539-1800
Fax: 248-539-1808
E-mail: aipm@healthy.net
www.HealthyLife.com

Don R Powell, PhD, President/CEO
Sue Jackson, VP Marketing

Take Charge helps people effectively live their lives after September 11th. This full color booklet provides just the right amount of information to effectively address the many concerns people have today. It will help people to be prepared for any kind of disaster, be it a terrorist attack, fire or flood. *$4.25*

32 pages

374 Ten Simple Solutions To Panic
New Harbinger Publications
5674 Shattuck Avenue
Oakland, CA 94609-1662
510-652-0215
800-748-6273
Fax: 510-652-5472
E-mail: customerservice@newharbinger.com
www.newharbinger.com

Matthew McKay, Owner

Provides readers who have at one time or another experienced unexplainable, intense mental and physical attacks over time. *$11.95*

152 pages ISBN 1-572243-25-2

375 Textbook of Anxiety Disorders
American Psychiatric Publishing, Inc.
1000 Wilson Boulevard
Suite 1825
Arlington, VA 22209-3901
703-907-7322
800-368-5777
Fax: 703-907-1091
E-mail: appi@psych.org
www.appi.org

Robert E Hales MD, Editor-in-Chief
Ron McMillen, Chief Executive Officer
John McDuffie, Editorial Director

US and international experts cover every major anxiety disorder, compare it with animal behavior and the similarities in the brain that exist, how disorders can relate to age specific groups, and covers the latest developments in understanding and treating these disorders. *$77.00*

544 pages ISBN 0-880488-29-8

376 The 10 Best-Ever Anxiety Management Techniques: Understanding How Your Brain Makes You Anxious and What You Can Do to Change It
W.W. Norton & Company, Inc.
500 Fifth Avenue
New York, NY 10110
212-354-5500
Fax: 212-869-0856
www.books.wwnorton.com

Margaret Wehrenberg, Author

A strategy-filled handbook to understand, manage, and conquer your own your own stress. *$18.95*

Year Founded: 2008 ISSN 9780393705560

377 The Agoraphobia Workbook
New Harbinger Publications
5674 Shattuck Avenue
Oakland, CA 94609-1662
510-652-0215
800-748-6273
Fax: 510-652-5472
E-mail: customerservice@newharbinger.com
www.newharbinger.com

Matthew McKay, Owner

Self-help resource to help readers overcome the disorder in all its forms *$19.95*

200 pages ISBN 1-572243-23-6

378 The American Psychiatric Publishing Textbook of Anxiety Disorders
American Psychiatric Publishing, Inc.
1000 Wilson Boulevard
Suite 1825
Arlington, VA 22209-3901
703-907-7322
800-368-5777
Fax: 703-907-1091
E-mail: appi@psych.org
www.appi.org

Robert E Hales MD, Editor-in-Chief
Ron McMillen, Chief Executive Officer
John McDuffie, Editorial Director

Gives a detailed look at the history, classification, preclinical models, concepts and combined treatment of anxiety disorders. *$92.00*

536 pages Year Founded: 2002 ISBN 0-880488-29-8

379 The Anxiety & Phobia Workbook, 4th Edition
New Harbinger Publications
5674 Shattuck Avenue
Oakland, CA 94609-1662
510-652-0215
800-748-6273
Fax: 510-652-5472
E-mail: customerservice@newharbinger.com
www.newharbinger.com

Matthew McKay, Owner

Research conducted by the National Institute of Mental Health has shown that anxiety disorders are the number one mental health problem among American women and.

ISBN 1-572244-13-5

380   The Imp of the Mind: Exploring the Silent Epidemic of Obsessive Bad Thoughts
Plume
375 Hudson Street
New York, NY 10014
212-366-2372
Fax: 212-366-2933
www.us.penguingroup.com

Clare Ferraro, President
Lee Baer PhD, Author

Dr. Lee Baer combines the latest research with his own extensive experience in treating this widespread syndrome. Drawing on information ranging from new advances in brain technology to pervasive social taboos, Dr. Baer explores the root causes of bad thoughts, why they can spiral out of control, and how to recognize the crucial difference between harmless and dangerous bad thoughts.

176 pages Year Founded: 2002 ISSN 978-0452283077ISBN 0-452283-07-8

381   Tormenting Thoughts and Secret Rituals: The Hidden Epidemic of Obsessive-Compulsive Disorder
Random House
1745 Broadway
3rd Floor
New York, NY 10019-4343
212-782-9000
Fax: 212-302-7985
www.randomhouse.com

Markus Dohle, CEO

Discusses the various forms Obsessive-Compulsive Disorder (OCD) takes and, using the most common focuses of obsession, presents detailed cases whose objects are filth, harm, lust, and blasphemy. He explains how the disorder is currently diagnosed and how it differs from addiction, worrying, and preoccupation. He summarizes the recent findings in the areas of brain biology, neuroimaging and genetics that show OCD to be a distinct chemical disorder of the brain. *$14.95*

336 pages Year Founded: 1999 ISBN 0-440508-47-9

382   Traumatic Stress: Effects of Overwhelming Experience on Mind, Body and Society
Guilford Publications
72 Spring Street
New York, NY 10012-4068
212-431-9800
800-365-7006
Fax: 212-966-6708
E-mail: info@guilford.com

Bob Matloff, President

The current state of research and clinical knowledge on traumatic stress and its treatment. Contributions from lead-

ing authorities summarize knowledge emerging. Addresses the uncertainties and controversies that confront the field of traumatic stress, including the complexity of posttraumatic adaptations and the unproven effectiveness of some approaches to prevention and treatment. *$62.00*

596 pages ISBN 1-572300-88-4

383   Triumph Over Fear: A Book of Help and Hope for People with Anxiety, Panic Attacks, and Phobias
Bantam Dell Publishing Group
1745 Broadway
New York, NY 10019
212-782-9000
E-mail: bdpublicity@randomhouse.com
www.randomhouse.com

Jerilynn Ross, Author

Resource and guide for both lay and professional readers.

296 pages Year Founded: 1994 ISSN 9780553081329ISBN 0-553081-32-2

384   Trust After Trauma: A Guide to Relationships for Survivors and Those Who Love Them
New Harbinger Publications
5674 Shattuck Avenue
Oakland, CA 94609-1662
510-652-0215
800-748-6273
Fax: 510-652-5472
E-mail: customerservice@newharbinger.com
www.newharbinger.com

Matthew McKay, Owner

Survivors guided through process of strengthening existing bonds, building new ones, and ending cycles of withdrawal and isolation. *$17.95*

352 pages Year Founded: 1998 ISBN 1-572241-01-2

385   Understanding Post Traumatic Stress Disorder and Addiction
Sidran Institute
200 E Joppa Road
Suite 207
Baltimore, MD 21286-3107
410-825-8888
888-825-8249
Fax: 410-337-0747
E-mail: sidran@sidran.org
www.sidran.org

Esther Giller, President

This booklet discusses PTSD, how to recognize it and how to begin a dual recovery program from chemical dependency and PTSD. The workbook includes information to enhance your understanding of PTSD, activities to help identify the symptoms of dual disorders, a self evaulation of your recovery process and ways to handle situations that may trigger PTSD. *$7.20*

38 pages

386 What to Do When You Worry Too Much: A Kid's Guide to Overcoming Anxiety
American Psychological Association
750 First Street, NE
Washington, DC 20002-4242
202-336-5500
800-374-2721
Fax: 202-336-5518
TTY: 202-336-6123
www.apa.org

Norman B Anderson, CEO

Interactive self-help book designed to guide 6-12 year olds and thier parents through the techniques most often used in the treatments of generalized anxiety.

387 What to Do When You're Scared and Worried: A Guide for Kids
Free Spirit Publishing
217 Fifth Avenue North, Suite 200
Minneapolis, MN 55401-1299
612-338-2068
800-735-7323
Fax: 612-337-5050
www.freespirit.com

Judy Galbraith, Owner

This book is all about fears and worries: things taht everyone deals with at some point in thier lives.

388 When Once Is Not Enough: Help for Obsessive Compulsives
New Harbinger Publications
5674 Shattuck Avenue
Oakland, CA 94609-1662
510-652-0215
800-748-6273
Fax: 510-652-5472
E-mail: customerservice@newharbinger.com
www.newharbinger.com

Matthew McKay, Owner
Kerrin White, MD, Author

How to recognize and confront fears, using simple rituals, positive coping strategies and handling complications. *$14.95*

229 pages Year Founded: 1990 ISBN 0-934986-87-8

389 When Perfect Isn't Good Enough: Strategies for Coping with Perfectionism
New Harbinger Publications
5674 Shattuck Avenue
Oakland, CA 94609-1662
510-652-0215
800-748-6273
Fax: 510-652-5472
E-mail: customerservice@newharbinger.com
www.newharbinger.com

Matthew McKay, Owner
Richard P Swinson, Author

This step by step guide explores the nature of perfectionism and offers a series of exercises to help you challenge unre-

alistic expectations and work on the specific situations in your life where perfectionism is a problem. *$14.95*

272 pages ISBN 1-572241-24-1

390 Who Gets PTSD? Issues of Posttraumatic Stress Vulnerability
Charles C Thomas Publishers
PO Box 19265
Springfield, IL 62794-9265
217-789-8980
800-258-8980
Fax: 217-789-9130
www.ccthomas.com

This book draws from research and life experiences on trauma vulnerability to better understand how mental health professionals and those concerned with the psychological well-being of others may disentangle the perplexing questions of who gets PTSD, why they do, and how we may prevent or minimize this from happening. This is also available in paperback for $29.95. *$46.95*

216 pages Year Founded: 2006 ISBN 3-980761-89-

391 Worry Control Workbook
New Harbinger Publications
5674 Shattuck Avenue
Oakland, CA 94609-1662
510-652-0215
800-748-6273
Fax: 510-652-5472
E-mail: customerservice@newharbinger.com
www.newharbinger.com

Matthew McKay, Owner

Self help program that shares experiences of people who have developed ways to overcome chronic worry. Step by step format helps identify areas likely to reoccur and develop new skills. *$15.95*

266 pages ISBN 1-572241-20-9

Periodicals & Pamphlets

392 Anxiety Disorders
National Institute of Mental Health
6001 Executive Boulevard
Room 8184
Bethesda, MD 20892-1
301-443-4513
866-615-6464
TTY: 301-443-8431
E-mail: nimhinfo@nih.gov

This brochure helps to identify the symptoms of anxiety disorders, explains the role of research in understanding the causes of these conditions, describes effective treatments, helps you learn how to obtain treatment and work with a doctor or therapist, and suggests ways to make treatment more effective.

393   Anxiety Disorders Fact Sheet
Center for Mental Health Services: Knowledge
Exchange Network
PO Box 42490
Washington, DC 20015

800-789-2647
Fax: 301-984-8796
TDD: 866-889-2647
E-mail: ken@mentalhealth.org
www.mentalhealth.org

This fact sheet presents basic information on the symptoms, formal diagnosis, and treatment for generalized anxiety disorder, panic disorders, phobias, and post-traumatic stress disorder.

3 pages

394   Anxiety Disorders in Children and Adolescents
Center for Mental Health Services: Knowledge
Exchange Network
PO Box 42557
Washington, DC 20015-557

800-789-2647
Fax: 240-747-5470
TDD: 866-889-2647
E-mail: ken@mentalhealth.org
www.mentalhealth.samhsa.gov/

This fact sheet defines anxiety disorders, identifies warning signs, discusses risk factors, describes types of help available, and suggests what parents or other caregivers can do.

3 pages

395   Facts About Anxiety Disorders
National Institute of Mental Health
6001 Executive Boulevard
Room 8184
Bethesda, MD 20892-1
301-443-4513
866-615-6464
TTY: 301-443-8431
E-mail: nimhinfo@nih.gov

Series of fact sheets that provide overviews and descriptions of generalized anxiety disorder, obsessive-compulsive disorder, panic disorder, post-traumatic stress disorder, social phobia, and the Anxiety Disorders Education Program.

396   Families Can Help Children Cope with Fear,
Anxiety
Center for Mental Health Services: Knowledge
Exchange Network
PO Box 42490
Washington, DC 20015

800-789-2647
Fax: 301-984-8796
TDD: 866-889-2647
E-mail: ken@mentalhealth.org
www.mentalhealth.org

This fact sheet defines conduct disorder, identifies risk factors, discusses types of help available, and suggests what

parents or other caregivers to common signs of fear and anxiety.

397   Five Smart Steps to Less Stress
ETR Associates
4 Carbonero Way
Scotts Valley, CA 95066-4200
831-438-4060
800-321-4407
Fax: 831-438-3618
E-mail: customerservice@etr.org
www.etr.org

Mary Nelson, President

Steps to managing stress include: know what stresses you, manage your stress, take care of your body, take care of your feelings, ask for help. *$16.00*

398   Five Ways to Stop Stress
ETR Associates
4 Carbonero Way
Scotts Valley, CA 95066-4200
831-438-4060
800-321-4407
Fax: 831-438-3618
E-mail: customerservice@etr.org
www.etr.org

Mary Nelson, President

An easy to read pamphlet that discusses how to recognize the signs of stress, explains the big and little changes that can produce stress and the different causes of stress.
$16.00

399   Getting What You Want From Stress
ETR Associates
4 Carbonero Way
Scotts Valley, CA 95066-4200
831-438-4060
800-321-4407
Fax: 831-438-3618
E-mail: customerservice@etr.org
www.etr.org

Mary Nelson, President

Includes signs of stress, some stress can be healthy, and when to change, when to adapt. *$16.00*

400   Helping Children and Adolescents Cope with
Violence and Disasters
National Institute of Mental Health
6001 Executive Boulevard
Room 8184
Bethesda, MD 20892-1
301-443-4513
866-615-6464
TTY: 301-443-8431
E-mail: nimhinfo@nih.gov

Fact sheets that discuss children and adolescents' reactions to violence and disasters, emphasizing the wide range of responses and the role that parents, teachers and therapists can play in the healing process.

8-12 pages Year Founded: 1986

401 Journal of Anxiety Disorders
Elsevier Publishing
360 Park Avenue South
New York, NY 10010-1736
212-989-5800
800-325-4177
Fax: 212-633-3820
E-mail: custserv.ehs@elsevier.com

Interdisciplinary journal that publishes research papers dealing with all aspects of anxiety disorders for all age groups (child, adolescent, adult and geriatrics).

8 per year Year Founded: 1987 ISSN 0887-6185

402 Let's Talk Facts About Panic Disorder
American Psychiatric Publishing, Inc.
1000 Wilson Boulevard
Suite 1825
Arlington, VA 22209-3901
703-907-7322
800-368-5777
Fax: 703-907-1091
E-mail: appi@psych.org
www.appi.org

Robert E Hales MD, Editor-in-Chief
Ron McMillen, Chief Executive Officer
John McDuffie, Editorial Director

Contains an overview of the illness, its symptoms, and the illness's effect on family and friends. A biliography and list of resources make them ideal for libraries or patient education. *$29.95*

8 pages ISBN 0-890423-57-1

403 Let's Talk Facts About Post-Traumatic Stress Disorder
American Psychiatric Publishing, Inc.
1000 Wilson Boulevard
Suite 1825
Arlington, VA 22209-3901
703-907-7322
800-368-5777
Fax: 703-907-1091
E-mail: appi@psych.org
www.appi.org

Robert E Hales MD, Editor-in-Chief
Ron McMillen, Chief Executive Officer
John McDuffie, Editorial Director

$12.50

8 pages ISBN 0-890423-63-6

404 OCD Newsletter
676 State Street
New Haven, CT 06511-6508
203-401-2070
Fax: 203-401-2076
E-mail: info@ocfoundation.org
www.ocfoundation.org

For sufferers of obsessive-compulsive disorder and their families and friends.

405 One Hundred One Stress Busters
ETR Associates
4 Carbonero Way
Scotts Valley, CA 95066-4200
831-438-4060
800-321-4407
Fax: 831-438-3618
E-mail: customerservice@etr.org
www.etr.org

Mary Nelson, President

These 101 stress busters were written by students to help fellow students relieve stress: tell a joke, laugh out loud, beat a pillow to smitherines. *$16.00*

406 Panic Attacks
ETR Associates
4 Carbonero Way
Scotts Valley, CA 95066-4200
831-438-4060
800-321-4407
Fax: 831-438-3618
E-mail: customerservice@etr.org
www.etr.org

Mary Nelson, President

Describes causes of panic attacks, including genetics, stress, and drug use; prevention and treatment, and how to stop a panic attack in its tracks. *$16.00*

407 Real Illness: Generalized Anxiety Disorder
National Institute of Mental Health
6001 Executive Boulevard
Room 8184
Bethesda, MD 20892-1
301-443-4513
866-615-6464
TTY: 301-443-8431
E-mail: nimhinfo@nih.gov

If you worry and feel tense a lot, even though others may assure you there are no real problems, you have a treatable disorder. Read this easy pamphlet to learn more.

9 pages

408 Real Illness: Panic Disorder
National Institute of Mental Health
6001 Executive Boulevard
Room 8184
Bethesda, MD 20892-1
301-443-4513
866-615-6464
TTY: 301-443-8431
E-mail: nimhinfo@nih.gov

Do you often have feelings of sudden fear that don't make sense? If so, you may have panic disorder. Read this pamplet of simple information about getting help.

9 pages

409 Real Illness: Post-Traumatic Stress Disorder
National Institute of Mental Health
6001 Executive Boulevard
Room 8184
Bethesda, MD 20892-1
301-443-4513
866-615-6464
TTY: 301-443-8431
E-mail: nimhinfo@nih.gov

Do you avoid reminders of a bad accident, war or another traumatic event? Do you have nightmares, fear, emotional numbness? Read this pamphlet of simple information about how to get help.

9 pages

410 Real Illness: Social Phobia Disorder
National Institute of Mental Health
6001 Executive Boulevard
Room 8184
Bethesda, MD 20892-1
301-443-4513
866-615-6464
TTY: 301-443-8431
E-mail: nimhinfo@nih.gov

Are you terrified of talking in groups or even going to parties because you're afraid people will think badly of you? This simple pamphlet describes how to get help.

9 pages

411 Stress
ETR Associates
4 Carbonero Way
Scotts Valley, CA 95066-4200
831-438-4060
800-321-4407
Fax: 831-438-3618
E-mail: customerservice@etr.org
www.etr.org
Mary Nelson, President

Includes common changes that cause stress, symptoms of stress, and effects on feelings, actions and physical health.

412 Stress Incredible Facts
ETR Associates
4 Carbonero Way
Scotts Valley, CA 95066-4200
831-438-4060
800-321-4407
Fax: 831-438-3618
E-mail: customerservice@etr.org
www.etr.org
Mary Nelson, President

Strange-but-true facts to trigger discussion about how stress affects the body, how to use it and long-term risks. *$18.00*

413 Stress in Hard Times
ETR Associates
4 Carbonero Way
Scotts Valley, CA 95066-4200
831-438-4060
800-321-4407
Fax: 831-438-3618
E-mail: customerservice@etr.org
www.etr.org
Mary Nelson, President

Discusses stress caused by troubling world events, describes short and long term symptoms, and suggests ways to cope. *$ 16.00*

414 Teen Stress!
ETR Associates
4 Carbonero Way
Scotts Valley, CA 95066-4200
831-438-4060
800-321-4407
Fax: 831-438-3618
E-mail: customerservice@etr.org
www.etr.org
Mary Nelson, President

Explains what stress is, outlines the causes and effects and offers ideas for handling stress. *$16.00*

Research Centers

415 UAMS Psychiatric Research Institute
5800 W 10th Street
Suite 605
Little Rock, AR 72204-1773
501-660-7559
Fax: 501-660-7542
E-mail: kramerteresal@uams.edu
www.uams.edu

Combining research, education and clinical services into one facility, PRI offers inpatiend and outpatient services, with 40 psychiatric beds, therapy options, and specialized treatment for specific disorders, including: addictive eating, anxiety, deppressive and post-traumatic stress disorders. Research focuses on evidence-based care takes into consideration the education of future medical personnel while relying on research scientists to provide innovative forms of treatment. PRI includes the Center for Addiction Research as well as a methadone clinic.

Support Groups & Hot Lines

416 Agoraphobics Building Independent Lives
3212 Cutshaw Ave
Richmond, VA 23230-5024
804-257-5591
E-mail: mhav@mhav.org
www.mhav.org

Provides hope, support and advocacy for people suffering from debilitating phobias, panic attacks and/or agoraphobics by establishing self-help groups providing public education.

417 Emotions Anonymous International Service Center
PO Box 4245
Saint Paul, MN 55104-0245
651-647-9712
Fax: 651-647-1593
E-mail: info@EmotionsAnonymous.org
www.EmotionsAnonymous.org

Karen Mead, Executive Director

Fellowship of men and women who share their experience, strength and hope with each other, that they may solve their common problem and help others recover from emotional illness.

418 International OCD Foundation
112 Water Street
Suite 501
Boston, MA 02109
617-973-5801
Fax: 617-973-5803
E-mail: info@ocfoundation.org
www.ocfoundation.org

Diane Davey RN, President

An international not-for-profit organization made up of people with Obsessive Compulsive Disorder and related disorders, as well as their families, friends, professionals and others.

Year Founded: 1986

419 Obsessive-Compulsive Anonymous
PO Box 215
New Hyde Park, NY 11040
516-739-0662
Fax: 212-768-4679
E-mail: west24th@aol.com
www.obsessivecompulsiveanonymous.com

Is a fellowship of people who share their Experience, Strength, and Hope with each other that they may solve their common problem and help others to recover from OCD.

420 Pass-Group
6 Mahogany Drive
Williamsville, NY 14221-2419
716-689-4399

Offers three-month telephone counseling program for panic attack suffers (agoraphobia). 'The Panic Attack Recovery Book' explains the cause and cure for panic attacks.

421 Phobics Anonymous
PO Box 1180
Palm Springs, CA 92263-1180
760-322-2673

Twelve-step program for panic disorders and anxiety. Publications available.

422 Recovery
802 N Dearborn Street
Chicago, IL 60610-3364
312-337-5661
E-mail: inquiries@recovery-inc.com
www.recovery-inc.org

Kathleen Garcia, Executive Director

Techniques for controlling behavior, changing attitudes for recovering mental patients. Systematic method of self-help offered.

Video & Audio

423 Anxiety Disorders
American Counseling Association
5999 Stevenson Avenue
Alexandria, VA 22304-3304
703-823-9800
800-347-6647
Fax: 703-823-0252
TDD: 703-823-6862
E-mail: webmaster@counseling.org
www.counseling.org

Richard Yep, Executive Director

Increase your awareness of anxiety disorders, their symptoms, and effective treatments. Learn the effect these disorders can have on life and how treatment can change the quality of life for people presently suffering from these disorders. Includes 6 audiotapes and a study guide. *$140.00*

424 DSM-IV-TR
American Psychiatric Publishing, Inc.
1000 Wilson Boulevard
Suite 1825
Arlington, VA 22209-3901
703-907-7322
800-368-5777
Fax: 703-907-1091
E-mail: appi@psych.org
www.appi.org

Robert E Hales MD, Editor-in-Chief
Ron McMillen, Chief Executive Officer
John McDuffie, Editorial Director

Series of three clinical programs that reveals additions and changes for mood, psychotic and anxiety disorders. Each video focuses on a different level of disorder as well as giving three 10 minute interviews. Approximately 60 minutes. *$57.00*

Year Founded: 1995 ISBN 0-880488-98-0

425 Driving Far from Home
New Harbinger Publications
5674 Shattuck Avenue
Oakland, CA 94609-1662
510-652-0215
800-748-6273
Fax: 510-652-5472
E-mail: customerservice@newharbinger.com
www.newharbinger.com

Matthew McKay, Owner

120 minute videotape that reduces fear associated with leaving the safety of your home base. *$11.95*

Year Founded: 1995 ISBN 1-572240-14-8

426 Effective Learning Systems
3451 Bonita Bay Boulevard
Suite 205
Bonita Springs, FL 34134-4354
239-948-1660
800-966-5683
Fax: 239-948-1664
E-mail: info@efflearn.com
www.efflearn.com

Robert E Griswold, President
Deirdre M Griswold, VP

Audio tapes for stress management, deep relaxation, anger control, peace of mind, insomnia, weight and smoking, self-image and self-esteem, positive thinking, health and healing. Since 1972, Effective Learning Systems has helped millions of people take charge of their lives and make positive changes. Over 75 titles available, each with a money-back guarantee. Price range $12-$14.

427 Hope & Solutions for Obsessive Compulsive Disorder: Part III
Awareness Foundation for OCD
3N374 Limberi Lane
Afocd c/o Gail Adams
Saint Charles, IL 60175-7655
630-513-9234
www.ocawareness.com

An educational psychologist offers educators effective classroom strategies that school personnel may implement with students who have obsessive compulsive disorder and addresses federal law as it pertains to students with disabilities. *$19.95*

428 Hope and Solutions for OCD
ADD WareHouse
300 NW 70th Avenue
Suite 102
Plantation, FL 33317-2360
954-792-8944
800-233-9273
Fax: 954-792-8545
E-mail: sales@addwarehouse.com
www.addwarehouse.com

Harvey C Parker, Owner

Finally, a video series about obsessive compulsive disorder with some straight forward solutions and advice for individuals with OCD, their families, doctors, and school personnel. Viewers will learn what OCD is and how to treat it. Discusses how OCD can affect students in school and the impact on the family life. 85 minutes. *$89.95*

429 Legacy of Childhood Trauma: Not Always Who They Seem
Research Press
Dept 24 W
PO Box 9177
Champaign, IL 61826-9177
217-352-3273
800-519-2707
Fax: 217-352-1221
E-mail: rp@researchpress.com
www.researchpress.com

Russell Pense, VP Marketing

This powerful video focuses on the connection between so-called "delinquent youth" and the experience of childhood trauma such as emotional, sexual, or physical abuse. It inspires viewers to comprehend the emotional betrayal felt by abused children and encourages caregivers to identify strategies for healing and transformation. *$195.00*

430 Touching Tree
Obsessive-Compulsive Foundation
676 State Street
New Haven, CT 06511-6508
203-401-2070
Fax: 203-401-2076
E-mail: info@ocfoundation.org
www.ocfoundation.org

This video will foster awareness of early onset obsessive-compulsive disorder (OCD) and demonstrate the symptoms and current therapies that are most successful. Typical ritualistic compulsions of children and adolescents such as touching, hand washing, counting, etc. are explained. *$49.95*

Year Founded: 1993

431 Treating Trauma Disorders Effectively
Colin A Ross Institute for Psychological Trauma
1701 Gateway
Suite 349
Richardson, TX 75080-3546
972-918-9588
E-mail: rossinst@rossinst.com
www.rossinst.com

Melissa Caldwell, Manager
Trie Kole

This video illustrates two fundamental treatment principles: attachment to the perpetrator and loss of control shift. For clinicians, the program provides immediately usable techniques for their practices; for the layperson it provides a clear explanation for two consequences of childhood trauma. *$85.00*

432 Understanding and Treating the Hereditary Psychiatric Spectrum Disorders
Hope Press
PO Box 188
Duarte, CA 91009-188
818-303-0644
800-321-4039
Fax: 818-358-3520
www.hopepress.com

David E Comings MD, Presenter

Learn with ten hours of audio tapes from a two day seminar given in May 1997 by David E Comings MD. Tapes cover: ADHD, Tourette Syndrome, Obsessive-Compulsive Disorder, Conduct Disorder, Oppositional Defiant Disorder, Autism and other Hereditary Psychiatric Spectrum Disorders. Eight audio tapes. *$75.00*

Year Founded: 1997

Web Sites

433 **www.apa.org/practice/traumaticstress.html**
American Psychological Association

Provides tips for recovering from disasters and other traumatic events.

434 **www.bcm.tmc.edu/civitas/caregivers.htm**
Caregivers Series

Sophisticated articles describing the effects of childhood trauma on brain development and relationships.

435 **www.cyberpsych.org**
CyberPsych

Presents information about psychoanalysis, psychotherapy and special topics such as anxiety disorders, the problematic use of alcohol, homophobia, and the traumatic effects of racism.

436 **www.factsforhealth.org**
Madison Institute of Medicine

Resource to help identify, understand and treat a number of medical conditions, including social anxiety disorder, posttraumatic stress disorder, alzheimer's disease, and premenstrual dysphoric disorder.

437 **www.goodwill-suncoast.org**
Career Assessment & Planning Services

A comprehensive assessment for the developmentally disabled persons who may be unemployed or underemployed.

438 **www.guidetopsychology.com**
A Guide To Psychlogy & Its Practice

Free information on various types of psychology.

439 **www.healthanxiety.org**
Anxiety and Phobia Treatment Center

Treatment groups for individuals suffering from phobias.

440 **www.healthyminds.org**
Anxiety Disorders

American Psychiatric Association publication diagnostic criteria and treatment.

441 **www.icisf.org**
International Critical Incident Stress Foundation

A nonprofit, open membership foundation dedicated to the prevention and mitigation of disabling stress by education, training and support services for all emergency service professionals. Continuing education and training in emergency mental health services for psychologists, psychiatrists, social workers and licensed professional counselors.

442 **www.intelihealth.com**
Mastering Your Stress Demons

443 **www.jobstresshelp.com**
Job Stress Help

444 **www.lexington-on-line.com**
Panic Disorder

Explains development and treatment of panic disorder.

445 **www.mayoclinic.com**
Mayo Clinic

Provides information on obsessive-compulsive disorder.

446 **www.mentalhealth.Samhsa.Gov**
Center for Mental Health Services Knowledge Exchange Network

Information about resources, technical assistance, research, training, networks and other federal clearinghouses.

447 www.mentalhealth.com
Internet Mental Health

On-line information and a virtual encyclopedia related to mental disorders, possible causes and treatments. News, articles, on-line diagnostic programs and related links. Designed to improve understanding, diagnosis and treatment of mental illness throughout the world. Awarded the Top Site Award and the NetPsych Cutting Edge Site Award.

448 www.nami.org
National Alliance on Mental Illness

From its inception in 1979, NAMI has been dedicated to improving the lives of individuals and families affected by mental illness.

449 www.ncptsd.org
National Center for PTSD

Aims to advance the clinical care and social welfare of U.S. Veterans through research, education and training on PTSD and stress-related disorders

450 www.nimh.nih.gov/anxiety/anxiety/ocd
National Institute of Health

Information on anxiety disorders and OCD.

451 www.nimh.nih.gov/publicat/ocdmenu.cfm
Obsessive-Compulsive Disorder

Introductory handout with treatment recommendations.

452 www.npadnews.com
National Panic/Anxiety Disorder Newsletter

This resource was founded by Phil Darren who collects and collates information of recovered anxiety disorder sufferers who want to distribute some of the lessons that they learned with a view to helping others.

453 www.ocdhope.com/gdlines.htm
Guidelines for Families Coping with OCD

454 www.ocfoundation.org
Obsessive-Compulsive Foundation

An international not-for-profit organization composed of people with obsessive compulsive disorder and related disorders, their families, friends, professionals and other concerned individuals.

455 www.panicattacks.com.au
Anxiety Panic Hub

Information, resources and support.

456 www.panicdisorder.about.com
Agoraphobia: For Friends/Family

457 www.planetpsych.com
Planetpsych.com

Learn about disorders, their treatments and other topics in psychology. Articles are listed under the related topic areas. Ask a therapist a question for free, or view the directory of professionals in your area. If you are a therapist sign up for the directory. Current features, self-help, interactive, and newsletter archives.

458 www.psychcentral.com
Psych Central

Personalized one-stop index for psychology, support, and mental health issues, resources, and people on the Internet.

459 www.ptsdalliance.org
Post Traumatic Stress Disorder Alliance

Website of the Post Traumatic Stress Disorder Alliance.

460 www.selectivemutismfoundation.org
Selective Mutism Foundation

Promotes awareness and understanding for individuals and families affected by mutism.

461   **www.selfhelpmagazine.com/articles/stress**
Meditation, Guided Fantasies, and Other Stress
Reducers

462   **www.sidran.org**
Sidran Institute

Helps people understand, recover from, and treat traumatic
stress (including PTSD), dissociative disorders, and
co-occuring issues, such as addictions, self injury, and
suicidality.

463   **www.sidran.org/trauma.html**
Trauma Resource Area

Resources and Articles on Dissociative Experiences Scale
and Dissociative Identity Disorder, PsychTrauma Glossary
and Traumatic Memories.

464   **www.terraphouston.com**
Territorial Apprehensiveness Programs (TERRAP)

Formed to disseminate information concerning the recognition, causes and treatment of anxieties, fears and phobias.

465   **www.thenadd.org**
NADD: National Association for the Dually
Diagnosed

Promotes interest of professional and parent development
with resources for individuals who have coexistence of
mental illness and mental retardation.

466   **www.trauma-pages.com**
David Baldwin's Trauma Information Pages

Focus primarily on emotional trauma and traumatic stress,
including PTSD (Post-traumatic Stress Disorder) and dissociation, whether following individual traumatic experi-
ence(s) or a large-scale disaster.

ADHD

Introduction

Attention-Deficit/Hyperactivity Disorder (AD/HD) includes (1) a pervasive pattern of inattention, and (2) difficulty in controlling impulses including the impulse to be constantly on the move. Since many chilren are inattentive, impulsive, and rambunctious at times, it is important to note that the disgnosis in not made unless these behaviors are more severe than is typical for a person at a comparable developmental level. The symptoms must appear before age seven.

The problems of hyperactivity show themselves in constant movement, especially among younger children. Preschool children with hyperactivity cannot sit still, even for quiet activities that usually absorb children of the same age, are always on the move and run rather than walk. In older children the intensity of the hyperactivity is reduced but fidgeting, getting up during meals or homework, and excessive talking continue.

People with Attention-Deficit/Hyperactivity Disorder have great difficulty controlling all their impulses, not just the craving for movement and stimulation. They have little sense of time (five minutes seems like hours), and waiting for something is intolerable. Thus, they are impatient, interrupt, make comments out of turn, grab objects from others, clown around, and cause trouble at home, in school, work, and in social settings.

The consequences of ADHD can be severe. From a young age, people with Attention-Deficit/Hyperactivity Disorder tend to experience failure repeatedly, including rejection by peers, resulting in low self-esteem and sometimes more serious problems.

SYMPTOMS

1. Inattention, as compared with others at the same developmental level
•Often fails to attend to details, or makes careless mistakes in schoolwork, work or other activities;
•Often finds it difficult to maintain attention in tasks or play activities;
•Often does not seem to listen when spoken to;
•Often doesn't follow through on instructions and doesn't finish schoolwork, chores, or tasks;
•Often has difficulty organizing tasks or activities;
•Often avoids tasks that demand sustained mental effort, such as schoolwork or homework;
•Often loses things needed for tasks or activities, such as toys and school assignments;
•Often is easily distracted;
•Often is forgetful in daily activities.

2. Hyperactivity, as compared with others at the same developmental level
•Often fidgets with hands or feet, or squirms in chair;
•Often leaves seat in classroom or other situations where remaining seated is expected;
•Often runs or climbs about in situations in which it is inappropriate (among adolescents or adults, this may be a feeling of restlessness);
•Often has difficulty playing or handling leisure activities quietly;
•Often is on the go, moving excessively;
•Often talks excessively.
•Often blurts out answers impulsively before questions are finished;
•Often has difficulty waiting in turn;
•Often intrudes impulsively on others' games, activities or conversations.

Parts of this description may apply to all or most children at times, but behaving in this way nearly all the time wreaks havoc on the child and family. Three distinctions are made in the diagnosis:

Attention-Deficit/Hyperactivity Disorder, Combined Type if six or more items from List (1) and six or more from List (2) are applicable;

Attention-Deficit/Hyperactivity Disorder, Predominantly Inattentive Type if six or more items from List (1) only are applicable;

Attention-Deficit/Hyperactivity Disorder, Predominantly Hyperactive-Impulsive Type if six or more items from List (2) only are applicable.

ASSOCIATED FEATURES

Certain behaviors often go along with Attention-Deficity/Hyperactivity Disorder. The person is often frustrated and angry, exhibiting outbursts of temper and bossiness. To others, the lack of application and inability to finish tasks may look like laziness or irresponsibility. Other conditions may also be associated with the disorder, including Hyperthyroidism (an overactive thyroid). There may be a higher prevalence of anxiety, depression, and learning disorders among people with AD/HD.

A careful assessment and diagnosis by a professional familiar with AD/HD are essential, especially since some of the typical AD/HD behaviors may resemble those of other disorders. Family, school, and other possible problems must be taken into account and addressed. This is a lifelong disorder, though sometimes attenuated in adulthood.

The diagnosis is especially difficult to establish in young children, e.g., at the toddler and preschool level, because behavior that is typical at that age is similar to the symptoms of AD/HD. Children at that age may be extremely active but not develop the disorder.

PREVALENCE

AD/HD occurs in various cultures. It is much more frequent in males than females, with male to female ratios at 4:1 in the general population, and 9:1 in clinic populations. The prevalence among school-age children is from three percent to five percent.

There is emerging literature concerning adult AD/HD, and evidence that some adults can benefit from the same treatments used for children.

TREATMENT OPTIONS

Treatment should be based on an understanding that Attention-Deficit/Hyperactivity Disorder is not intentional, and punishment is not a cure.

The person with AD/HD has great need for external

motivation, consistency, and structure. This should be provided by a professional who is familiar with the disorder. For a school-aged child, it is important to enlist the help of the school in designing a treatment plan which should include concrete steps aimed at developing specific compentencies (e.g., handling time, sequencing, problem-solving, and social interaction).

Medication is often prescribed but should not be the only treatment. Newer preparations of medications, such as Concerta, offer once or twice a day dosing, so that children do not need to take medication during the school day. Since this condition affects all members of the family, the family needs help in providing consistency and structure, and in changing the role of the person with AD/HD as the family member who always gets into trouble.

Current treatments can have a positive impact and, in some cases, transform behaviors so that a formerly chaotic life becomes one over which the person has much greater control and more frequent experience of success.

Associations & Agencies

468 Attention Deficit Disorder Association
15000 Commerce Parkway
Suite C
Mount Laurel, NJ 08054-2212
856-439-9099
Fax: 856-439-0525
E-mail: adda@ahint.com
www.add.org

Linda S Anderson M.A. & MCC, President
Evelyn Polk Green MS.Ed, VP

Provides children, adolescents and adults with ADD information, support groups, publications, videos, and referrals. Also, generates hope, awareness, empowerment and connections worldwide.

469 Center For Mental Health Services
PO Box 42557
Washington, DC 20015-557
240-221-4022
800-789-2647
Fax: 240-221-4295
TDD: 866-889-2647
www.mentalhealth.samhsa.gov

470 Center for Family Support (CFS)
333 7th Avenue
New York, NY 10001-5115
212-629-7939
Fax: 212-239-2211
www.cfsny.org

Steven Vernikoff, Executive Director

An agency that continues to develop new programs to serve families and individuals with their care needs. They offer services throughout the New York City region including: New Jersey, Long Island and the Lower Hudson Valley.

471 Center for Mental Health Services (CMHS)
PO Box 2345
Rockville, MD 20847
240-221-4021
800-789-2647
Fax: 240-221-4295
TDD: 866-889-2647
www.mentalhealth.samhsa.gov

A Kathryn Power, MEd, Director
Anna Marsh PhD, Deputy Director
Fran Randolph PhD, Dir, Service & Systems Improveme
Anne Mathews-Younes EdD, Dir, Prevention/Traumatic Stress

CMHS leads Federal efforts to treat mental illnesses by promoting mental health and by preventing the development or worsening of mental illness when possible. Congress created CMHS to bring new hope to adults who have serious mental illnesses and to children with serious emotional disorders. CMHS provides information about mental health via a toll-free the web site, and more than 600 publications. Developed for users of mental health services and their families, the general public, policy makers, providers, and the media.

Year Founded: 1992

472 Children and Adults with AD/HD (CHADD)
8181 Professional Place
Suite 150
Landover, MD 20785
301-306-7070
800-233-4050
Fax: 301-306-7090
www.chadd.org

E Clarke Ross DPA, CEO
Ruth Hughes PhD, Chief Community Svcs Programs
Marsha Bokman CMP, Director, Meetings & Events
Bryan Goodman MA, Director, Communications & Media

National nonprofit organization representing children and adults with attention deficit/hyperactivity disorder (AD/HD). Available on Facebook and Twitter.

Year Founded: 1987

473 Learning Disabilities Association of America
4156 Library Road
Pittsburgh, PA 15234-1349
412-341-1515
E-mail: info@LDAamerica.org
www.ldaamerica.org

Sheila Buckley, Executive Director
Connie Parr, VP

Educating individuals with learning disabilities and their parents about the nature of the disability and inform them of their rights, encourages research in neuro-physiological and psycological aspects of learning disabilities.

474 National Alliance on Mental Illness
2107 Wilson Boulevard
Suite 300
Arlington, VA 22201-3080
703-524-7600
800-950-6264

Fax: 703-524-9094
E-mail: helpline@nami.org
www.nami.org

Suzanne Vogel-Scibilia, President
Fredrick Sandoval, Vice President

Nation's leading self-help organization for all those affected by severe brain disorders. Mission is to bring consumers and families with similar experiences together to share information about services, care providers, and ways to cope with the challenges of schizophrenia, manic depression, and other serious mental illnesses.

Year Founded: 1979

475 National Association for the Dually Diagnosed (NADD)
132 Fair Street
Kingston, NY 12401-4802
845-331-4336
800-331-5362
Fax: 845-331-4569
E-mail: info@thenadd.org
www.thenadd.org

Robert Fletcher, Executive Director
Donna Nagy PhD, President

Nonprofit organization designed to promote interest of professional and parent development with resources for individuals who have the coexistence of mental illness and mental retardation. Provides conference, educational services and training materials to professionals, parents, concerned citizens and service organizations. Formerly known as the National Association for the Dually Diagnosed.

Year Founded: 1983

476 National Dissemination Center for Children with Disabilities (NICHCY)
PO Box 1492
Washington, DC 20013-1492
202-884-8200
800-695-0285
Fax: 202-884-8441
TTY: 800-695-0285
E-mail: nichcy@aed.org
www.nichcy.org

Suzanne Ripley, Project Director
Lisa Kupper, Author/Editor

Provides support and services for children and youth with physical and mental disabilities, as well as education and training services for their families.

477 National Mental Health Consumers' Self-Help Clearinghouse
1211 Chestnut Street
Suite 1207
Philadelphia, PA 19107-4103
215-751-1810
800-553-4539
Fax: 215-636-6312
E-mail: info@mhselfhelp.org
www.mhselfhelp.org

Joseph Rogers, Executive Director

A national consumer technical assistance center that has played a major role in the development of the mental health consumer movement.

Year Founded: 1986

478 SAMHSA's National Mental Health Information Center
US Department of Health and Human Services
PO Box 42557
Washington, DC 20015-557
240-221-4021
800-789-2647
Fax: 240-221-4295
TDD: 866-889-2647
www.mentalhealth.org

A Kathryn Power MEd, Director
Edward B Searle, Deputy Director

Provides information about mental health via a toll-free telephone number, this web site, and more than 600 publications. Developed for users of mental health services and their families, the general public, policy makers, providers, and the media.

Books

479 AD/HD Forms Book: Identification, Measurement, and Intervention
Research Press
Dept 24 W
PO Box 9177
Champaign, IL 61826-9177
217-352-3273
800-519-2707
Fax: 217-352-1221
E-mail: rp@researchpress.com
www.researchpress.com

Russell Pense, VP Marketing

A collection of intervention procedures and over 30 reproducible forms and checklists for use with any AD/HD program for children or adolescents. Each item is prefaced by a brief description of its purpose and use. The AD/HD Forms Book helps educators, mental health professionals and parents translate their knowledge into action. *$ 25.95*

128 pages ISBN 0-878223-78-9

480 ADD & Learning Disabilities: Reality, Myths, & Controversial Treatments
Bantam Doubleday Dell Publishing
1745 Broadway
New York, NY 10019-4343
212-782-9000

Jeff Rechtzigel, Publisher

For parents of children with learning disabilities and attention deficit disorder - and for educational and medical professionals who encounter these children - two experts in the field have devised a handbook to help identify the very best treatments. *$10.36*

256 pages ISBN 0-385469-31-4

481 ADD & Romance
ADD WareHouse
300 NW 70th Avenue
Suite 102
Plantation, FL 33317-2360
954-792-8944
800-233-9273
Fax: 954-792-8545
E-mail: sales@addwarehouse.com
www.addwarehouse.com

Harvey C Parker, Owner

Romantic relationships are hard enough, but sustaining a stimulating and satisfying romantic relationship can be even more challenging if one partner has ADD. This book discusses how ADD can influence vital aspects of one's romantic life, such as intimacy and communication and provides effective techniques for communication, conflict resolution and ways to cope with ADD in a relationship. *$ 12.95*

230 pages

482 ADD Hyperactivity Handbook for Schools
ADD WareHouse
300 NW 70th Avenue
Suite 102
Plantation, FL 33317-2360
954-792-8944
800-233-9273
Fax: 954-792-8545
E-mail: sales@addwarehouse.com
www.addwarehouse.com

Harvey C Parker, Owner

A must read for anyone interested in learning evaluation methods for ADD and ways to effectively assist children with ADD in regular and special education. Contains an overview of the important facts about ADD and provides practical and proven techniques teachers can use in the classroom to help students and their families. *$29.00*

330 pages

483 ADD Kaleidoscope: The Many Facets of Adult Attention Deficit Disorder
Hope Press
PO Box 188
Duarte, CA 91009-188
818-303-0644
800-321-4039
Fax: 818-358-3520
www.hopepress.com

A comprehensive presentation of all aspects of attention deficit disorder in adults. While often thought of as a childhood disorder, ADD symptoms usually continue into adulthood where they can cause a wide range of problems with personal interactions, work performance, attitude towards one's employer, and interactions with spouses and children. *$24.95*

ISBN 1-878267-03-5

484 ADD Success Stories: Guide to Fulfillment for Families with Attention Deficit Disorder
ADD WareHouse
300 NW 70th Avenue
Suite 102
Plantation, FL 33317-2360
954-792-8944
800-233-9273
Fax: 954-792-8545
E-mail: sales@addwarehouse.com
www.addwarehouse.com

Harvey C Parker, Owner

Real-life stories of people with ADD who achieved success in school, at work, in marriages and relationships. Thousands of interviews and histories as well as new research show children and adults from all walks of life how to reach the next-step, a fulfilling, successful life with ADD. Discover which occupations are best for people with ADD. *$12.00*

250 pages

485 ADD in the Workplace: Choices, Changes and Challenges
ADD WareHouse
300 NW 70th Avenue
Suite 102
Plantation, FL 33317-2360
954-792-8944
800-233-9273
Fax: 954-792-8545
E-mail: sales@addwarehouse.com
www.addwarehouse.com

Harvey C Parker, Owner

It's one thing to deal with ADD in the doctor's office or at home, but quite another 'out there' in the workplace. This unique guide focuses on adults living with ADD, and illustrates various ways to initiate and maintain the best possible work situation. *$24.00*

248 pages

486 ADD/ADHD Checklist: an Easy Reference for Parents & Teachers
ADD WareHouse
300 NW 70th Avenue
Suite 102
Plantation, FL 33317-2360
954-792-8944
800-233-9273
Fax: 954-792-8545
E-mail: sales@addwarehouse.com
www.addwarehouse.com

Harvey C Parker, Owner

This resource for parents and teachers is packed with up-to-date facts, findings and proven strategies and techniques for understanding and helping children and adolescents with attention deficit problems and hyperactivity. *$12.00*

150 pages

487 ADHD Monitoring System
ADD WareHouse
300 NW 70th Avenue
Suite 102
Plantation, FL 33317-2360
954-792-8944
800-233-9273
Fax: 954-792-8545
E-mail: sales@addwarehouse.com
www.addwarehouse.com

Harvey C Parker, Owner

Provides a simple, cost effective way to carefully monitor how well a student with ADHD is doing at school. Parents and teachers will be able to easily track behavior, academic performance, quality of student classwork and homework. Contains monitoring forms along with instructions for use. *$8.95*

488 ADHD Parenting Handbook: Practical Advise for Parents
Taylor Trade Publishing
5360 Manhattan Circle #101
Boulder, CO 80303-4249
303-543-7835
Fax: 303-543-0043
E-mail: rrinehart@rowman.com

Colleen Alexander-Roberts, Author

Practical advice for parents from parents, and proven techniques for raising hyperactive children without losing your temper.

489 ADHD Survival Guide for Parents and Teachers
Hope Press
PO Box 188
Duarte, CA 91009-188
818-303-0644
800-321-4039
Fax: 818-358-3520
www.hopepress.com

Fills an important need expressed by parents, teachers, and other caretakers of ADHD children who have asked for clear, practical, and easily understood strategies to deal with ADHD children.

ISBN 1-878267-43-4

490 ADHD and Teens: Parent's Guide to Making it Through the Tough Years
ADD WareHouse
300 NW 70th Avenue
Suite 102
Plantation, FL 33317-2360
954-792-8944
800-233-9273
Fax: 954-792-8545
E-mail: sales@addwarehouse.com
www.addwarehouse.com

Harvey C Parker, Owner

Unlike the parents of elementary school children with ADHD, parents of ADHD teens must focus on gaining and keeping control of the situation because the risks are increased in severity and consequence. A manual of practical advice to help parents cope with the problems that can arise during these years. *$13.00*

208 pages

491 ADHD and the Nature of Self-Control
Guilford Publications
72 Spring Street
New York, NY 10012-4068
212-431-9800
800-365-7006
Fax: 212-966-6708
E-mail: info@guilford.com

Bob Matloff, President

Provides a radical shift of perspective on ADHD, arguing that the disorder is a developmental problem of self control and that an attention deficit is a secondary characteristic. Combines neuropsychological research and the theory on the executive functions, illustrating how normally functioning individuals are able to bring behavior under the control of time and orient their actions toward the future. *$46.00*

410 pages ISBN 1-572302-50-X

492 ADHD in the Young Child: Driven to Redirection
ADD WareHouse
300 NW 70th Avenue
Suite 102
Plantation, FL 33317-2360
954-792-8944
800-233-9273
Fax: 954-792-8545
E-mail: sales@addwarehouse.com
www.addwarehouse.com

Harvey C Parker, Owner

The authors sensitively and effectively describe what life is like living with a young child with ADHD. With the help of over 75 cartoon illustrations they provide practical solutions to common problems found at home, in school and elsewhere. *$18.95*

202 pages

493 ADHD: A Complete and Authoritative Guide
American Academy Of Pediatrics
141 Northwest Point Boulevard
Elk Grove Village, IL 60007-1098
847-228-0604
www.aap.org

Sherill Tippins, Author

Based on the American Academy of Pediatrics' own clinical practice guidelines for ADHD and written in clear, accessible language, ths book answers the common question: How is ADHD diagnosed? What are today's best treatment options? and Will my child outgrow ADHD?

494 Adventures in Fast Forward: Life, Love and Work for the ADD Adult
ADD WareHouse
300 NW 70th Avenue
Suite 102
Plantation, FL 33317-2360
954-792-8944
800-233-9273
Fax: 954-792-8545
E-mail: sales@addwarehouse.com
www.addwarehouse.com

Harvey C Parker, Owner

For all adults with ADD, this book is designed to be a practical guide for day-to-day life. No matter where you are in the scenario - curious about ADD, just diagnosed or experiencing particular problems, this book will give you effective strategies to help anticipate and negotiate the challenges that come with the condition. Filled with important tools and tactics for self-care and success. *$23.00*

210 pages

495 All About Attention Deficit Disorder: Revised Edition
ADD WareHouse
300 NW 70th Avenue
Suite 102
Plantation, FL 33317-2360
954-792-8944
800-233-9273
Fax: 954-792-8545
E-mail: sales@addwarehouse.com
www.addwarehouse.com

Harvey C Parker, Owner

A practical and comprehensive manual for parents and teachers interested in understanding the facts about ADD. Chapters on home management, the 1-2-3 Magic discipline method, facts about medication management and practical ideas for teachers to use in managing learning and classroom behavior. *$13.00*

165 pages

496 All Kinds of Minds
ADD WareHouse
300 NW 70th Avenue
Suite 102
Plantation, FL 33317-2360
954-792-8944
800-233-9273
Fax: 954-792-8545
E-mail: sales@addwarehouse.com
www.addwarehouse.com

Harvey C Parker, Owner

Primary and elementary students with learning disorders can now gain insight into the difficulties they face in school. This book helps all children understand and respect all kinds of minds and can encourage children with learning disorders to maintain their motivation and keep from developing behavior problems stemming from their learning disorders. *$31.00*

283 pages

497 Answers to Distraction
ADD WareHouse
300 NW 70th Avenue
Suite 102
Plantation, FL 33317-2360
954-792-8944
800-233-9273
Fax: 954-792-8545
E-mail: sales@addwarehouse.com
www.addwarehouse.com

Harvey C Parker, Owner

A user's guide to ADD presented in a question and answer format ideal for parents of children and adolescents with ADD, adults with ADD and teachers who work with students who have ADD. *$13.00*

334 pages

498 Attention Deficit Disorder and Learning Disabilities
Bantam Doubleday Dell Publishing
1745 Broadway
New York, NY 10019-4343
212-782-9000

Jeff Rechtzigel, Publisher

Discusses ADHD and learning disabilities as well as their effective treatments. Warns against nutritional and other alternative treatments. *$12.95*

256 pages ISBN 0-385469-31-4

499 Attention Deficit Hyperactivity Disorder in Children: A Medication Guide
Madison Institute of Medicine
7617 Mineral Point Road
Suite 300
Madison, WI 53717-1623
608-827-2470
E-mail: mim@miminc.org
www.factsforhealth.org

Margarett Baudhuin, Manager

Written for parents, this explains the various medications used commonly to treat ADHD/ADD. It includes a review of the symptoms of ADHD, medication therapy, commonly asked questions, and side effects of medications. *$5.95*

41 pages

500 Attention Deficits and Hyperactivity in Children: Developmental Clinical Psychology and Psychiatry
Sage Publications
2455 Teller Road
Thousand Oaks, CA 91320-2234
805-499-0721
800-818-7243
Fax: 805-499-0871
E-mail: info@sagepub.com
www.sagepub.com

Blaise R Simqu, CEO

Provides background information and evaluates key debates and questions that remain unanswered about ADHD. Includes what tools can be used to gain optimal information about this disorder and which factors predict subsequent functioning in adolescence and adulthood. Advances, challenges and unresolved problems in diverse but relevant areas are analyzed and placed in context. Paperback also available. *$43.95*

161 pages Year Founded: 1993 ISBN 0-803951-96-5

501 Attention-Deficit Hyperactivity Disorder in Adults: A Guide
Madison Institute of Medicine
7617 Mineral Point Road
Suite 300
Madison, WI 53717-1623
608-827-2470
E-mail: mim@miminc.org
www.factsforhealth.org

Margarett Baudhuin, Manager

This guide provides an overview of adult ADHD and how it is treated with medications and other treatment approaches. *$5.95*

58 pages

502 Beyond Ritalin
ADD WareHouse
300 NW 70th Avenue
Suite 102
Plantation, FL 33317-2360
954-792-8944
800-233-9273
Fax: 954-792-8545
E-mail: sales@addwarehouse.com
www.addwarehouse.com

Harvey C Parker, Owner

Beyond Ritalin: Facts About Medication and Other Strategies for Helping Children, Adolescents and Adults with Attention Deficit Disorders. The authors respond to concerns all parents and individuals have about using medication to treat disorders such as ADHD, explain the importance of a treatment program for those with this condition and discuss fads and fallacies in current treatments. *$13.50*

254 pages

503 Birds-Eye View of Life with ADD and ADHD: Advice from Young Survivors, Second Edition
Cherish the Children
PO Box 189
Cedar Bluff, AL 35959-189

Fax: 256-779-5203
E-mail: chirs@chrisdendy.com
www.chrisdendv.com

Chris A Zeigler Dendy, Author

504 Conduct Disorders in Children and Adolescents
American Psychiatric Publishing, Inc.
1000 Wilson Boulevard
Suite 1825
Arlington, VA 22209-3901

703-907-7322
800-368-5777
Fax: 703-907-1091
E-mail: appi@psych.org
www.appi.org

Robert E Hales MD, Editor-in-Chief
Ron McMillen, Chief Executive Officer
John McDuffie, Editorial Director

Examines the phenomenology, etiology, and diagnosis of conduct disorders, and describes therapeutic and preventive interventions. Includes the range of treatments now availaable, including individual, family, group, and behavior therapy; hospitalization; and residential treatment. *$52.00*

448 pages ISBN 0-880485-17-5

505 Consumer's Guide to Psychiatric Drugs
New Harbinger Publications
5674 Shattuck Avenue
Oakland, CA 94609-1662
510-652-0215
800-748-6273
Fax: 510-652-5472
E-mail: customerservice@newharbinger.com
www.newharbinger.com

Matthew McKay, Owner

Helps consumers understand what treatment options are available and what side effects to expect. Covers possible interactions with other drugs, medical conditions and other concerns. Explains how each drug works, and offers detailed information about treatments for depression, bipolar disorder, anxiety and sleep disorders, as well as other conditions. *$16.95*

340 pages ISBN 1-572241-11-X

506 Daredevils and Daydreamers: New Perspectives on Attention Deficit/Hyperactivity Disorder
ADD WareHouse
300 NW 70th Avenue
Suite 102
Plantation, FL 33317-2360
954-792-8944
800-233-9273
Fax: 954-792-8545
E-mail: sales@addwarehouse.com
www.addwarehouse.com

Harvey C Parker, Owner

Summarizes what has been learned about ADHD in the past ten years and explains how parents can use this knowledge to help their child. Explains how to obtain a good evaluation, how to spot coexisting problems like depression and learning disabilities, how to find the right professional to treat your child and answers many other questions about caring for a child with ADHD. *$11.00*

260 pages

507 Distant Drums, Different Drummers: A Guide for Young People with ADHD
ADD WareHouse
300 NW 70th Avenue
Suite 102
Plantation, FL 33317-2360
954-792-8944
800-233-9273
Fax: 954-792-8545
E-mail: sales@addwarehouse.com
www.addwarehouse.com

Harvey C Parker, Owner

This book presents a positive perspective of ADHD - one that stresses the value of individual differences. Written for children and adolescents struggling with ADHD, it offers young readers the opportunity to see themselves in a positive light and motivates them to face challenging problems. Ages 8-14. *$16.00*

48 pages

508 Don't Give Up Kid
ADD WareHouse
300 NW 70th Avenue
Suite 102
Plantation, FL 33317-2360
954-792-8944
800-233-9273
Fax: 954-792-8545
E-mail: sales@addwarehouse.com
www.addwarehouse.com

Harvey C Parker, Owner

Alex, the hero of this book, is one of two million children in the US who have learning disabilities. This book gives children with reading problems and learning disabilities a clear understanding of their difficulties and the necessary courage to learn to live with them. Ages 5-12. *$13.00*

509 Down and Dirty Guide to Adult Attention Deficit Disorder
ADD WareHouse
300 NW 70th Avenue
Suite 102
Plantation, FL 33317-2360
954-792-8944
800-233-9273
Fax: 954-792-8545
E-mail: sales@addwarehouse.com
www.addwarehouse.com

Harvey C Parker, Owner

A book about ADD that is immensely entertaining, informative and uncomplicated. Describes concepts essential to understanding how this disorder is best identified and treated. You'll find a refreshing absence of jargon and an abundance of common sense, practical advice and healthy skepticism. *$17.00*

194 pages

510 Driven to Distraction: Recognizing and Coping with Attention Deficit Disorder from Childhood through Adulthood
ADD WareHouse
300 NW 70th Avenue
Suite 102
Plantation, FL 33317-2360
954-792-8944
800-233-9273
Fax: 954-792-8545
E-mail: sales@addwarehouse.com
www.addwarehouse.com

Harvey C Parker, Owner
John J Ratey MD

Through vivid stories of the experiences of their patients (both adults and children), this books shows the varied forms ADD takes - from the hyperactive search for high stimulation to the floating inattention of daydreaming - and the transforming impact of precise diagnosis and treatment. The authors explain when and how medication can be helpful, and since both authors have ADD, their advice on effective behavior-modification techniques is enriched by their own experience. Also available on audiotape for $16.00. *$13.00*

319 pages

511 Drug Therapy and Childhood & Adolescent Disorders
Mason Crest Publishers
370 Reed Road
Suite 302
Broomall, PA 19008-4017
610-543-6200
866-627-2665
Fax: 610-543-3878
E-mail: dtaylor@masoncrest.com
www.masoncrest.com

This book provides readers with an easy-to-understand introduction to this topic. Numerous case sstudies and examples give insight in the four disorders first diagnosed in childhood and adolescence that can be treated with psychiatric drugs, and helps readers understand the symptoms and treatments of these disorders. The disorders included in this volume are: mental retardation, pervasive developmental disorders, attention-deficit and disruptive behavior disorders and tic disorders.

ISBN 1-590845-63-3

512 Eagle Eyes: A Child's View of Attention Deficit Disorder
ADD WareHouse
300 NW 70th Avenue
Suite 102
Plantation, FL 33317-2360
954-792-8944
800-233-9273
Fax: 954-792-8545
E-mail: sales@addwarehouse.com
www.addwarehouse.com

Harvey C Parker, Owner

This book helps readers of all ages understand ADD and gives practical suggestions for organization, social cues and self calming. Expressive illustrations enhance the book and encourage reluctant readers. Ages 5-12. *$13.00*

513 Eukee the Jumpy, Jumpy Elephant
ADD WareHouse
300 NW 70th Avenue
Suite 102
Plantation, FL 33317-2360
954-792-8944
800-233-9273
Fax: 954-792-8545
E-mail: sales@addwarehouse.com
www.addwarehouse.com

Harvey C Parker, Owner
Esther Trevino

A story about a bright young elephant who is not like all the other elephants. Eukee moves through the jungle like a tornado, unable to pay attention to the other elephants. He begins to feel sad, but gets help after a visit to the doctor who explains why Eukee is so jumpy and hyperactive. With love, support and help, Eukee learns ways to help himself and gain renewed self-esteem. Ideal for ages 3-8. *$15.00*

22 pages

514 Facing AD/HD: A Survival Guide for Parents
Research Press
Dept 24 W
PO Box 9177
Champaign, IL 61826-9177
217-352-3273
800-519-2707
Fax: 217-352-1221
E-mail: rp@researchpress.com
www.researchpress.com

Russell Pense, VP Marketing

Provides parents with the skills they need to help minimize the everyday struggles and frustrations associated with AD/HD. The book addresses structure, routines, setting goals, using charts, persistency with consistency, teamwork, treatment options, medication and more. *$ 14.95*

232 pages ISBN 0-878223-81-9

515 First Star I See
ADD WareHouse
300 NW 70th Avenue
Suite 102
Plantation, FL 33317-2360
954-792-8944
800-233-9273
Fax: 954-792-8545
E-mail: sales@addwarehouse.com
www.addwarehouse.com

Harvey C Parker, Owner

This entertaining and funny look at ADD without hyperactivity is a must-read for middle grade girls with ADD, their teachers and parents. *$11.00*

150 pages

516 Gene Bomb
Hope Press
PO Box 188
Duarte, CA 91009-188
818-303-0644
800-321-4039
Fax: 818-358-3520
www.hopepress.com

Gene Bomb: Does Higher Education and Advanced Technology Accelerate the Selection of Genes for Learning Disorders, Addictive and Disruptive Behaviors? Explores the hypothesis that autism, learning disorders, alcoholism, drug abuse, depression, attention deficit disorder, and other disruptive behavioral disorders are increaseing in frequency because of an increasing selection, in the 20th century, for the genes associated with these conditions. *$29.95*

304 pages ISBN 1-878267-38-8

517 Give Your ADD Teen a Chance: A Guide for Parents of Teenagers with Attention Deficit Disorder
ADD WareHouse
300 NW 70th Avenue
Suite 102
Plantation, FL 33317-2360
954-792-8944
800-233-9273
Fax: 954-792-8545
E-mail: sales@addwarehouse.com
www.addwarehouse.com

Harvey C Parker, Owner

Parenting teenagers is never easy, especially if your teen suffers from ADD. This book provides parents with expert help by showing them how to determine which issues are caused by 'normal' teenager development and which are caused by ADD. *$15.00*

299 pages

518 Grandma's Pet Wildebeest Ate My Homework
ADD WareHouse
300 NW 70th Avenue
Suite 102
Plantation, FL 33317-2360
954-792-8944
800-233-9273
Fax: 954-792-8545
E-mail: sales@addwarehouse.com
www.addwarehouse.com

Harvey C Parker, Owner

Parents and teachers dealing with hyperactive or daydreaming kids will find this book outstanding. As an ADHD adult himself, Quinn draws upon his own experience, making use of straightforward, creative behavioral management techniques, along with a keen sense of humor. A highly informative and enlightened book. *$16.95*

272 pages

519 Healing ADD: Simple Exercises That Will Change Your Daily Life
ADD WareHouse
300 NW 70th Avenue
Suite 102
Plantation, FL 33317-2360
954-792-8944
800-233-9273
Fax: 954-792-8545
E-mail: sales@addwarehouse.com
www.addwarehouse.com

Harvey C Parker, Owner

Presents simple methods involving visualization and positive thinking that can be readily picked up by adults and taught to children with ADD. *$10.00*

178 pages

520 Help 4 ADD@High School
ADD WareHouse
300 NW 70th Avenue
Suite 102
Plantation, FL 33317-2360
954-792-8944
800-233-9273
Fax: 954-792-8545
E-mail: sales@addwarehouse.com
www.addwarehouse.com

Harvey C Parker, Owner

This new book was written for teenagers with ADHD. Designed like a web site, it has short, easy-to-read information packed sections which tell you what you need to know about how to get your life together - for yourself, not for your parents or your teachers. Includes tips on studying, ways your high school can help you succeed, tips on getting along better at home, on dating, exercise and much more. *$19.95*

119 pages

521 HomeTOVA: Attention Screening Test
ADD WareHouse
300 NW 70th Avenue
Suite 102
Plantation, FL 33317-2360
954-792-8944
800-233-9273
Fax: 954-792-8545
E-mail: sales@addwarehouse.com
www.addwarehouse.com

Harvey C Parker, Owner

Screen yourself or your child (ages 4 to 80 plus) for attention problems. After a simple installation on your home computer (Windows 95/98 OS only), the Home TOVA program runs with use of a mouse. Takes 21.6 minutes and measures how fast, accurate and consistent a person is in responding to squares flashing on a screen. Each program is limited to two administrators. *$29.95*

522 How to Do Homework without Throwing Up
ADD WareHouse
300 NW 70th Avenue
Suite 102
Plantation, FL 33317-2360
954-792-8944
800-233-9273
Fax: 954-792-8545
E-mail: sales@addwarehouse.com
www.addwarehouse.com

Harvey C Parker, Owner

Cartoons and witty insights teach important truths about homework and strategies for getting it done. Learn how to make a homework schedule, when to do the hardest homework, where to do homework, the benefits of homework and more. Useful in motivating students with ADD. For ages 8-13. *$9.00*

67 pages

523 Hyperactive Child, Adolescent, and Adult
Oxford University Press
198 Madison Avenue
New York, NY 10016-4341
212-726-6400
800-451-7556

Michael Cunningham, Manager

Discusses symptoms and treatment of ADD/ADHD in children and adults with practical suggestions for the management of children. *$27.00*

172 pages ISBN 0-195042-91-3

524 Hyperactive Children Grown Up: ADHD in Children, Adolescents, and Adults
Guilford Publications
72 Spring Street
New York, NY 10012-4068
212-431-9800
800-365-7006
Fax: 212-966-6708
E-mail: info@guilford.com

Bob Matloff, President

Explores what happens to hyperactive children when they grow to adulthood. Based on the McGill prospective studies, which spans more than 30 years, the volume reports findings on the etiology, treatment and outcome of attention deficits and hyperactivity at all stages of development. Paperback also available. *$44.95*

473 pages ISBN 0-898620-39-2

525 I'm Somebody, Too!
ADD WareHouse
300 NW 70th Avenue
Suite 102
Plantation, FL 33317-2360
954-792-8944
800-233-9273
Fax: 954-792-8545
E-mail: sales@addwarehouse.com
www.addwarehouse.com

Harvey C Parker, Owner

Because it is written for an older, non-ADD audience, this book explains ADD in depth and explains methods to handle the feelings that often result from having a family member with ADD. For children ages 9 and older. *$13.00*

159 pages

526 Is Your Child Hyperactive? Inattentive? Impulsive? Distractible?
ADD WareHouse
300 NW 70th Avenue
Suite 102
Plantation, FL 33317-2360
954-792-8944
800-233-9273
Fax: 954-792-8545
E-mail: sales@addwarehouse.com
www.addwarehouse.com

Harvey C Parker, Owner

Written with compassion and hope, this parent guide prepares you for the process of determining if your child has ADD and guides you in your dealings with educators, doctors and other professionals. *$13.00*

235 pages

527 Learning to Slow Down and Pay Attention
ADD WareHouse
300 NW 70th Avenue
Suite 102
Plantation, FL 33317-2360
954-792-8944
800-233-9273
Fax: 954-792-8545
E-mail: sales@addwarehouse.com
www.addwarehouse.com

Harvey C Parker, Owner

Written for children to read, and illustrated with charming cartoons and activity pages, the book helps children identify problems and explains how their parents, teachers and doctors can help. For children 6-14. *$10.00*

70 pages

528 Living with Attention Deficit Disorder: a Workbook for Adults with ADD
New Harbinger Publications
5674 Shattuck Avenue
Oakland, CA 94609-1662
510-652-0215
800-748-6273
Fax: 510-652-5472
E-mail: customerservice@newharbinger.com
www.newharbinger.com

Matthew McKay, Owner

Includes strategies for handling common problems at work and school, dealing with intimate relationships, and finding support. *$17.95*

176 pages ISBN 1-572240-63-6

529 Medications for Attention Disorders and Related Medical Problems: Comprehensive Handbook
ADD WareHouse
300 NW 70th Avenue
Suite 102
Plantation, FL 33317-2360
954-792-8944
800-233-9273
Fax: 954-792-8545
E-mail: sales@addwarehouse.com
www.addwarehouse.com

Harvey C Parker, Owner

ADHD and ADD are medical conditions and often medical intervention is regarded by most experts as an essential component of the multimodal program for the treatment of these disorders. This text presents a comprehensive look at medications and their use in attention disorders. *$37.00*

420 pages

530 Meeting the ADD Challenge: A Practical Guide for Teachers
Research Press
Dept 24 W
PO Box 9177
Champaign, IL 61826-9177
217-352-3273
800-519-2707
Fax: 217-352-1221
E-mail: rp@researchpress.com
www.researchpress.com

Dr Michael J Asher, Co-Author
Dr Steven B Gordon, Author
Dennis Wiziecki, Marketing

Information on the needs and treatment of children and adolescents with ADD. The book addresses the defining characteristics of ADD, common treatment approaches, myths about ADD, matching intervention to student, use of behavior rating scales and checklists, evaluating interventions, regular versus special class placement, helping students regulate their own behavior and more. Includes case examples. *$21.95*

196 pages ISBN 0-878223-45-2

531 Misunderstood Child: Understanding and Coping with Your Child's Learning Disabilities
ADD WareHouse
300 NW 70th Avenue
Suite 102
Plantation, FL 33317-2360
954-792-8944
800-233-9273
Fax: 954-792-8545
E-mail: sales@addwarehouse.com
www.addwarehouse.com

Harvey C Parker, Owner

In this revised and updated edition you will find promising treatment options for children, adolescents and adults with learning disabilities, discussion of ADHD, pros and cons of using medication, revision to federal and state laws covering discrimination and educational rights, new approaches for those of college age and older. *$15.00*

403 pages

532 My Brother's a World Class Pain: a Sibling's Guide to ADHD
ADD WareHouse
300 NW 70th Avenue
Suite 102
Plantation, FL 33317-2360
954-792-8944
800-233-9273
Fax: 954-792-8545
E-mail: sales@addwarehouse.com
www.addwarehouse.com

Harvey C Parker, Owner

While they frequently bear the brunt of the ADHD child's impulsiveness and distractibility, siblings usually are not afforded opportunities to understand the nature of the problem and to have their own feelings and thoughts addressed. This story shows brothers and sisters how they can play an important role in the family's quest for change. *$12.00*

34 pages

533 Put Yourself in Their Shoes: Understanding Teenagers with Attention Deficit Hyperactivity Disorder
ADD WareHouse
300 NW 70th Avenue
Suite 102
Plantation, FL 33317-2360
954-792-8944
800-233-9273
Fax: 954-792-8545
E-mail: sales@addwarehouse.com
www.addwarehouse.com

Harvey C Parker, Owner

Contains up-to-date information on how ADHD affects the lives of adolescents at home, in school, in the workplace and in social relationships. Chapters discuss how to get a good assessment, controversial treatments and medications for ADHD, building positive communication at home, problem-solving strategies to resolve family conflict, ADHD and the military, study strategies to improve learning, ADHD and delinquency, two hundred educational accommodations for ADHD teens and more. *$19.00*

249 pages

534 RYAN: A Mother's Story of Her Hyperactive/ Tourette Syndrome Child
Hope Press
PO Box 188
Duarte, CA 91009-188
818-303-0644
800-321-4039
Fax: 818-358-3520
www.hopepress.com

A moving and informative story of how a mother struggled with the many behavioral problems presented by her son with Tourette syndrome, ADHD and oppositional defiant disorder. *$9.95*

302 pages ISBN 1-878267-25-6

535 Shelley, The Hyperative Turtle
ADD WareHouse
300 NW 70th Avenue
Suite 102
Plantation, FL 33317-2360
954-792-8944
800-233-9273
Fax: 954-792-8545
E-mail: sales@addwarehouse.com
www.addwarehouse.com

Harvey C Parker, Owner

The story of a bright young turtle who's not like all the other turtles. Shelley moves like a rocket and is unable to sit still for even the shortest periods of time. Because he and the other turtles are unable to understand why he is so wiggly and squirmy, Shelley begins to feel naughty and out of place. But after a visit to the doctor, Shelley learns what 'hyperactive' means and that it is necessary to take special medicine to control that wiggly feeling. Ideal for ages 3-7. *$14.00*

24 pages

536 Sometimes I Drive My Mom Crazy, But I Know She's Crazy About Me
ADD WareHouse
300 NW 70th Avenue
Suite 102
Plantation, FL 33317-2360
954-792-8944
800-233-9273
Fax: 954-792-8545
E-mail: sales@addwarehouse.com
www.addwarehouse.com

Harvey C Parker, Owner

This warm and humorous story of a young boy with ADHD addresses the many difficult and frustrating issues kids like him confront every day - from sitting still in the classroom, to remaining calm, to feeling 'different' from other children. This book is an amusing look at how a youngster with ADHD can develop a sense of self-worth through better understanding of this disorder. Ages 6-12. *$16.00*

129 pages

537 Stuck on Fast Forward: Youth with Attention Deficit/Hyperactivity Disorder
Mason Crest Publishers
370 Reed Road
Suite 302
Broomall, PA 19008-4017
610-543-6200
866-627-2665
Fax: 610-543-3878
E-mail: dtaylor@masoncrest.com
www.masoncrest.com

Provides a comprehensive, yet easy to understand, overview of attention deficit/hyperactivity disorder. ADHD is an increasingly common diagnosis for school-aged and preschool children today, as parents, educators, and medical professionals struggle to deal with children who often don't sit still, don't pay attention, or act impulsively and even inappropriately. The debate over diagnosis and treatment of such symptoms is intense, and Stuck on Fast Forward explores all sides of the issue.

ISBN 1-590847-28-8

538 Succeeding in College with Attention Deficit Disorders: Issues and Strategies for Students, Counselors and Educators
ADD WareHouse
300 NW 70th Avenue
Suite 102
Plantation, FL 33317-2360
954-792-8944
800-233-9273
Fax: 954-792-8545
E-mail: sales@addwarehouse.com
www.addwarehouse.com

Harvey C Parker, Owner

Written for college students, their couselors and educators. Based on the real life experiances of adults who were interviewed as part of a research study, this book offers a vivid picture of how college students with ADD can cope and find success in school. *$18.00*

189 pages

539 Survival Guide for College Students with ADD or LD
ADD WareHouse
300 NW 70th Avenue
Suite 102
Plantation, FL 33317-2360
954-792-8944
800-233-9273
Fax: 954-792-8545
E-mail: sales@addwarehouse.com
www.addwarehouse.com

Harvey C Parker, Owner

A useful guide for high school or college students diagnosed with attention deficit disorder or learning disabilities. Provides the information needed to survive and thrive in a college setting. Full of practical suggestions and tips from an experienced specialist in the field and from college students who also suffer from these difficulties. *$10.00*

56 pages

540 Survival Strategies for Parenting Your ADD Child
Underwood Books
PO Box 1609
Grass Valley, CA 95945-1609

Fax: 530-274-7179
E-mail: timunderwd@cs.com
www.underwoodbooks.com

Survival Strategies for Parenting Your ADD Child: Dealing with Obsessions, Compulsions, Depression, Explosive Behavior and Rage. Provides parents with methods which can heal the fractures and pain that occur in families with troubled children. *$12.95*

268 pages ISBN 1-887424-19-9

541 Taking Charge of ADHD: Complete, Authoritative Guide for Parents
ADD WareHouse
300 NW 70th Avenue
Suite 102
Plantation, FL 33317-2360
954-792-8944
800-233-9273
Fax: 954-792-8545
E-mail: sales@addwarehouse.com
www.addwarehouse.com

Harvey C Parker, Owner

Written for parents who are ready to take charge of their child's life. Strong on advocacy and parental empowerment, this book provides step-by-step methods for managing a child with ADHD in a variety of everyday situations, gives information on medications and discusses numerous techniques for enhancing a child's school performance. *$18.00*

350 pages

542 Teenagers with ADD and ADHD: A Guide for Parents and Professionals
Woodbine House
6510 Bells Mill Road
Bethesda, MD 20817-1636
301-897-3570
800-843-7323
Fax: 301-897-5838
www.woodbinehouse.com

Irv Shapell, Owner

The newly updated and expanded guide to raising a teenager with an attention deficit disorder is more comprehensive than ever. Thousands more parents can rely on Dendy's compassionately presented expertise based on the latest research and decades of her experience as a parent, teacher, school psychologist, and mental health counselor.

543 Teenagers with ADD: A Parent's Guide
Woodbine House
6510 Bells Mill Road
Bethesda, MD 20817-1636
301-897-3570
800-843-7323
Fax: 301-897-5838
E-mail: info@woodbinehouse.com
www.woodbinehouse.com

Irv Shapell, Owner

Double-column book full of information, suggestions and case studies. Lively, upbeat, comprehensive and well targeted to the problems parents face with ADD teenagers. *$18.95*

370 pages ISBN 0-933149-69-7

544 Understanding Girls with Attention Deficit Hyperactivity Disorder
ADD WareHouse
300 NW 70th Avenue
Suite 102
Plantation, FL 33317-2360
954-792-8944
800-233-9273
Fax: 954-792-8545
E-mail: sales@addwarehouse.com
www.addwarehouse.com

Harvey C Parker, Owner

Symptoms of ADHD are often overlooked or misunderstood in girls who are often diagnosed much later, and their ADHD symptoms may go untreated. This groundbreaking book reveals how ADHD affects girls from preschool through high school years. Gender differences are discussed along with issues related to school success, medication treatment, family relationships and susceptibility to other disorders such as anxiety, depression and learning problems. *$19.95*

291 pages

545 Voices From Fatherhood: Fathers, Sons and ADHD
ADD WareHouse
300 NW 70th Avenue
Suite 102
Plantation, FL 33317-2360
954-792-8944
800-233-9273
Fax: 954-792-8545
E-mail: sales@addwarehouse.com
www.addwarehouse.com

Harvey C Parker, Owner
Patricia O Quinn MD

Written to specifically help fathers navigate the complex world of parenting and ADHD, this book helps fathers enhance and deepen their relationships with their sons while providing them with strategies for guiding their sons. *$20.00*

184 pages

546 What Makes Ryan Tick?
Hope Press
PO Box 188
Duarte, CA 91009-188
818-303-0644
800-321-4039
Fax: 818-358-3520
www.hopepress.com

What Makes Ryan Tick? A Family's Triumph over Tourette's Syndrome and Attention Deficit Hyperactivity Disorder. A moving and informative story how a mother struggled with the many behavioral problems presented by her son with Tourettes syndrome, ADHD and oppositional defiant disorder. *$15.95*

303 pages ISBN 1-878267-35-3

547 Women with Attention Deficit Disorder
ADD WareHouse
300 NW 70th Avenue
Suite 102
Plantation, FL 33317-2360
954-792-8944
800-233-9273
Fax: 954-792-8545
E-mail: sales@addwarehouse.com
www.addwarehouse.com

Harvey C Parker, Owner

Combines real-life histories, treatment experiences and recent clinical research to highlight the special challenges facing women with Attention Deficit Disorder. After describing what to look for and what to look out for in treatment and counseling, this book outlines empowering steps that women living with ADD may use to change their lives. Also available on audiotape. 3 hours on 2 cassettes for $20.00. *$12.00*

288 pages

548 You Mean I'm Not Lazy, Stupid or Crazy?
ADD WareHouse
300 NW 70th Avenue
Suite 102
Plantation, FL 33317-2360
954-792-8944
800-233-9273
Fax: 954-792-8545
E-mail: sales@addwarehouse.com
www.addwarehouse.com

Harvey C Parker, Owner
Peggy Ramundo

This book is the first written by ADD adults for ADD adults. A comprehensive guide, it provides accurate information, practical how-to's and moral support. Readers will also get information on unique differences in ADD adults, the impact on their lives, treatment options available for adults, up-to-date research findings and much more. Also available on audiotape. *$14.00*

426 pages

Periodicals & Pamphlets

549 ADDitude Magazine
ADD Warehouse
300 NW 70th Avenue
Suite 102
Plantation, FL 33317-2360
954-792-8944
800-233-9273
Fax: 954-792-8545
E-mail: sales@addwarehouse.com
www.addwarehouse.com

Harvey C Parker, Owner

Provides valuable resource information for professionals-teachers, healthcare providers, employers and others-who interact with AD/HD people everyday. *$19.97*

550 ADHD Report
Guilford Publications
72 Spring Street
New York, NY 10012-4068
212-431-9800
800-365-7006
Fax: 212-966-6708
E-mail: info@guilford.com

Bob Matloff, President

This accessible newsletter provides a single reliable guide to the latest developments, newest topics, and current trends in ADHD. An indispensibe resource, the ADHD Report examines the nature, definition, diagnosis, developmental course, outcomes and etiologies associated with ADHD, as well as changes occuring in the fields of education and clinical management. It includes handouts for clinicians and parents, as well as annotated research findings. *$79.00*

6 per year ISSN 1065-8025

551 Attention-Deficit/Hyperactivity Disorder in Children and Adolescents
Center for Mental Health Services: Knowledge Exchange Network
PO Box 42557
Washington, DC 20015-557

800-789-2647
Fax: 301-984-8796
TDD: 866-889-2647
E-mail: ken@mentalhealth.org
www.mentalhealth.samhsa.gov/publications/

This fact sheet defines attention-deficit/hyperactivity disorder, describes the warning signs, discusses types of help available, and suggests what parents or other caregivers can do.

3 pages Year Founded: 1997

552 Learning Disabilities: A Multidisciplinary Journal
Learning Disabilities Association of America
4156 Library Road
Pittsburgh, PA 15234-1349
412-341-1515
www.ldaamerica.org

Sheila Buckley, Executive Director

The most current research designed for professionals in the field of LD. *$60.00*

553 Treatment of Children with Mental Disorders
National Institute of Mental Health
6001 Executive Boulevard
Room 8184
Bethesda, MD 20892-1
301-443-4513
866-615-6464
TTY: 301-443-8431
E-mail: nimhinfo@nih.gov

A short booklet that contains questions and answers about therapy for children with mental disorders. Includes a chart of mental disorders and medications used.

Support Groups & Hot Lines

554 Children and Adults with AD/HD (CHADD)
8181 Professional Place
Suite 150
Landover, MD 20785-2264
301-306-7070
800-233-4050
Fax: 301-306-7090
www.chadd.org

Non-profit organization serving individuals with AD/HD and their families. Over 16,000 members in 200 local chapters throughout the United States. Chapters offer support for individuals, parents, teachers, professionals, and others. Available on Facebook and Twitter.

Video & Audio

555 ADHD & LD: Powerful Teaching Strategies & Accomodations
ADD Warehouse
300 NW 70the Avenue
Suite 102
Plantation, FL 33317-2360
954-792-8944
800-233-9273
Fax: 954-792-8545
E-mail: sales@addwarehouse.com
www.addwarehouse.com

Harvey C Parker, Owner

Provides instructional strategies for engaging attention and active participation, classroom management and behavioral interventions, gives academic strategies and accomodations, and collaborates teaming for success. 45 minutes. *$129.00*

Year Founded: 2003

556 ADHD-Inclusive Instruction & Collaborative Practices
ADD Warehouse
300 NW 70th Avenue
Suite 102
Plantation, FL 33317-2360
954-792-8944
800-233-9273
Fax: 954-792-8545
E-mail: sales@addwarehouse.com
www.addwarehouse.com

Harvey C Parker, Owner

Describes classroom modifications, teaching strategies, and interventions that can be used to maximize learning and ensure that all students achieve success. 38 minutes. *$99.00*

Year Founded: 1995 ISBN 1-887943-04-8

557 ADHD: What Can We Do?
ADD WareHouse
300 NW 70th Avenue
Suite 102
Plantation, FL 33317-2360
954-792-8944
800-233-9273
Fax: 954-792-8545
E-mail: sales@addwarehouse.com
www.addwarehouse.com

Harvey C Parker, Owner

Can serve as a companion to ADHD: What Do We Know?, this video focuses on the most effective ways to manage ADHD, both in the home and in the classroom. Scenes depict the use of behavior management at home and accommodations and interventions in the classroom which have proven to be effective in the treatment of ADHD. Thirty five minutes. *$95.00*

ISBN 0-898629-72-1

558 ADHD: What Do We Know?
ADD WareHouse
300 NW 70th Avenue
Suite 102
Plantation, FL 33317-2360
954-792-8944
800-233-9273
Fax: 954-792-8545
E-mail: sales@addwarehouse.com
www.addwarehouse.com

Harvey C Parker, Owner

This video provides an overview of the disorder and introduces the viewer to three young people who have ADHD. Discusses how ADHD affects the lives of the children and adults, causes of the disorder, associated problems, outcome in adulthood and provides vivid illustrations of how individuals with ADHD function at home, at school and on the job. Thirty five minutes. *$95.00*

ISBN 0-898629-71-3

559 Adults with Attention Deficit Disorder: ADD Isn't Just Kids Stuff
ADD WareHouse
300 NW 70th Avenue
Suite 102
Plantation, FL 33317-2360
954-792-8944
800-233-9273
Fax: 954-792-8545
E-mail: sales@addwarehouse.com
www.addwarehouse.com

Harvey C Parker, Owner

Explains this often misunderstood condition and the effects it has on one's work, home and social life. With the help of a panel of six adults, four ADD adults and two of their spouses, the book addresses the most common concerns of adults with ADD and provides information that will help families who are experiencing difficulties. 86 minutes. *$ 47.00*

560 Educating Inattentive Children
ADD WareHouse
300 NW 70th Avenue
Suite 102
Plantation, FL 33317-2360
954-792-8944
800-233-9273
Fax: 954-792-8545
E-mail: sales@addwarehouse.com
www.addwarehouse.com

Harvey C Parker, Owner

This two-hour video is ideal for in-service to regular and special educators concerning problems experienced by inattentive elementary and secondary students. Provides educators with information necessary to indentify and evaluate classroom problems caused by inattention and a well-defined set of practical guidelines to help educate children with ADD. *$49.00*

561 Medication for ADHD
ADD WareHouse
300 NW 70th Avenue
Suite 102
Plantation, FL 33317-2360
954-792-8944
800-233-9273
Fax: 954-792-8545
E-mail: sales@addwarehouse.com
www.addwarehouse.com

Harvey C Parker, Owner

This comprehensive DVD addresses the critical questions regarding the use of medication in the treatment of ADD or ADHD. Allows those involved with ADHD to make well-informed and constructive decisions that may deeply change someone's life. *$39.95*

ISBN 1-889140-18-X

562 New Look at ADHD: Inhibition, Time and Self Control
Guilford Publications
72 Spring Street
New York, NY 10012-4068
212-431-9800
800-365-7006
Fax: 212-966-6708
E-mail: info@guilford.com

Bob Matloff, President

This video provides an accessible introduction to Russell A Barkley's influential theory of the nature and origins of ADHD. The program brings to life the conceptual framework delineated in Barkley's other books. Discusses concrete ways that our new understanding of the disorder might facilitate more effective clinical interventions. This lucid, state of the art program is ideal viewing for clinicians, students and inservice trainees, parents of children with ADHD and adults with the disorder. 30 minutes. *$95.00*

Year Founded: 2000 ISBN 1-572304-97-9

563 Outside In: A Look at Adults with Attention Deficit Disorder
ADD Warehouse
300 NW 70th Avenue
Suite 102
Plantation, FL 33317-2360
954-792-8944
800-233-9273
Fax: 954-792-8545
E-mail: sales@addwarehouse.com
www.addwarehouse.com

Harvey C Parker, Owner

Documentary film about adults with ADD and their journeys and the strategies they used to succeed. 29 minutes *$27.95*

564 Understanding and Treating the Hereditary Psychiatric Spectrum Disorders
Hope Press
PO Box 188
Duarte, CA 91009-188
626-303-0644
800-321-4039
Fax: 626-358-3520
E-mail: dcomings@mail.earthlink.net
www.hopepress.com

Learn with 10 hours of audio tapes from a two day seminar given in May 1997 by David E Comings, MD. Tapes cover: ADHD, Tourette Syndrome, Obsessive-Compulsive Disorder, Conduct Disorder, Oppositional Defiant Disorder, Autism and other Hereditary Psychiatric Spectrum Disorders. Eight audio tapes. *$75.00*

Year Founded: 1997

565 Understanding the Defiant Child
Guilford Publications
72 Spring Street
New York, NY 10012-4068
212-431-9800
800-365-7006
Fax: 212-966-6708
E-mail: info@guilford.com

Bob Matloff, President

Presents information on Oppositional Defiant Disorder and Conduct Disorder with scenes of family interactions, showing the nature and causes of these disorders and what can and should be done about it. Thirty five minutes with a manual that contains more information. 30 minutes. *$95.00*

Year Founded: 1997 ISBN 1-572301-66-X

566 Why Won't My Child Pay Attention?
ADD WareHouse
300 NW 70th Avenue
Suite 102
Plantation, FL 33317-2360
954-792-8944
800-233-9273
Fax: 954-792-8545
E-mail: sales@addwarehouse.com
www.addwarehouse.com

Harvey C Parker, Owner

Provides an easy-to-follow explanation concerning the effect ADD has on children at school, home and in the community. Provides guidelines to help parents and professionals successfully and happily manage the problems these behaviors can cause. 76 minutes. *$38.00*

Web Sites

567 www.CHADD.org
Children/Adults with Attention Deficit/Hyperactivity Disorder

568 www.LD-ADD.com
Attention Deficit Disorder and Parenting Site

569 www.aap.org
American Academy of Pediatrics Practice Guidelines on ADHD

Site serves the purpose of giving the public guidelines for diagnosing and evaluating children with possible ADHD.

570 www.add.about.com
Attention Deficit Disorder

Hundreds of sites.

571 www.add.org
Attention Deficit Disorder Association

Provides information, resources and networking to adults with ADHD and to the professionals who work with them.

572 www.additudemag.com
Happy Healthy Lifestyle Magazine for People with ADD

573 www.addvance.com
Answers to Your Questions About ADD

provides answers to questions about ADD, ADHD for families and individuals at every stage of life from preschool through retirement years.

574 www.adhdnews.com/Advocate.htm
Advocating for Your Child

575 www.adhdnews.com/sped.htm
Special Education Rights and Responsibilities

Writing IEP's and TIEPS. Pursuing special education services.

576 www.babycenter.com/rcindex.html
BabyCenter

577 www.cfsny.org
Center for Family Support

Devoted to the physical well-being and development of the retarded child and the sound mental health of parents.

578 www.cyberpsych.org
CyberPsych

Hosts the American Psychoanalyists Foundation, American Association of Suicideology, Society for the Exploration of Psychotherapy Intergration, and Anxiety Disorders Association of America. Also subcategories of the anxiety disorders, as well as general information, including panic disorder, phobias, obsessive compulsive disorder (OCD), social phobia, generalized anxiety disorder, post traumatic stress disorder, and phobias of childhood. Book reviews and links to web pages sharing the topics.

579 www.nami.org
National Alliance on Mental Illness

From its inception in 1979, NAMI has been dedicated to improving the lives of individuals and families affected by mental illness.

580 www.nichcy.org
National Information Center for Children and Youth with Disabilities

Excellent information in English and Spanish.

581 www.nimh.nih.gov/publicat/adhd.cfm
Attention Deficit Hyperactivity Disorder

Thirty page booklet.

582 www.oneaddplace.com
One ADD Place

583 www.planetpsych.com
Planetpsych.com

Learn about disorders, their treatments and other topics in psychology. Articles are listed under the related topic areas. Ask a therapist a question for free, or view the directory of professionals in your area. If you are a therapist sign up for the directory. Current features, self-help, interactive, and newsletter archives.

584 www.psychcentral.com
Psych Central

Personalized one-stop index for psychology, support, and mental health issues, resources, and people on the Internet.

585 www.thenadd.org
National Association for the Dually Diagnosed

Nonprofit organization to promote interests of professional and parent development with resources for individuals who have coexistence of mental illness and mental retardation.

Autism Spectrum Disorders

Introduction

Autism Spectrum Disorders are a distinct group of neurological conditions characterized by impairment in language and communication skills; two of the most common are Autistic Disorder and Asperger's Syndrome.

Autistic Disorder is a pervasive developmental disorder whose main symptoms are a marked lack of interest in connecting, interacting, or communicating with others. People with this disorder cannot share something of interest with other people, rarely make eye contact with others, avoid physical contact, show little facial expression, and do not make friends. Autistic Disorder is a profound, lifelong condition associated with wide ranging and severe disabilities, including behavior problems, such as hyperactivity, obsessive compulsive behavior, self injury, and tics. Although present before age three, the disorder may not be apparent until later, although parents often sense that there is something wrong because of their child's marked lack of interest in social interaction. Very young children with autism not only show no desire for affection and cuddling, but show actual aversion to it. There is no socially directed smiling or facial responsiveness, and no responsiveness to the voices of parents and siblings. As a result, parents may sometimes worry that their child is deaf. Later, the child may be more willing to interact socially, but the quality of interaction is unusual, usually inappropriately intrusive with little understanding of social rules and boundaries. The autistic child seems not to have the abilities and desires that would make it possible for him or her to become a social being. Instead, the child seems locked up in an alien interior world, which is both incomprehensible and inaccessible to parents, siblings and others.

Asperger's Syndrome (AS) is named for Austrian pediatrician Hans Asperger, who in 1944, observed four children who had normal intelligence, but lacked nonverbal communication skills; additionally they did not demonstrate empathy with their peers, and were physically clumsy. Dr. Asperger called the condition 'Autistic psychopathy' and described it as a personality disorder marked by social isolation.

Twin and family studies have shown a genetic predisposition to AS and other ADs, but a specific gene has not yet been identified. Some researchers have proposed that the disorder may stem from abnormalities during critical stages of fetal development, including defects in the genes that control and regulate normal brain growth and growth patterns.

There is no standardized screening tool available to diagnose Asperger's Syndrome. Most doctors rely on the presence of a core group of behaviors to diagnose the syndrome.

SYMPTOMS

Autism: Impairment in the Quality of Social Interaction
•Gross lack of nonverbal behavior (e.g., eye contact, facial expression, body postures, and gestures), which gives meaning to social interaction and social behavior;
•Failure to make friends in age-appropriate ways;
•Lack of spontaneously seeking to share interests or achievements with others (e.g., not showing things to others, not pointing to, or bringing interesting objects to others);
•Lack of social or emotional give and take (e.g., not joining in social play or simple games with others);
•Notable lack of awareness of others. Oblivious of other children (including siblings), of their excitement, distress, or needs.

Autism: Marked Impairment in the Quality of Communication
•Delay in, or lack of, spoken language development. Those who speak cannot initiate or sustain comunication with others;
•Lack of spontaneous make-believe or imitative play common among young children;
•When speech does develop, it may be abnormal and monotonous;
•Repetitive use of language.

Autism: Restricted Repetitive Patterns or Behavior
•Restricted range of interests often fixed on one subject and its facts (e.g., baseball);
•A great deal of exact repetition in play, (e.g., lining up play objects in the same way again and again);
•Resistance and distress if anything in the environment is changed, (e.g., a chair moved to a different place);
•Insistence on following certain rules and routines (e.g., walking to school by the same route each day);
•Repeated body movements (e.g., body rocking, hand clapping);
•Persistent preoccupation with details or parts of objects (e.g., buttons).

Asperger's Syndrome in Contrast to Autism:
Asperger's Syndrome causes two types of symptoms: problems with social interactions and stereotyped, repetitive patterns of behavior. Individuals with AS have limited interests and are preoccupied with a particular subject to the exclusion of other activities. Some other characteristics are:
•Repetitive routines or rituals;
•Peculiarities in speech and language, such as speaking in an overly formal manner or in a monotone, or taking figures of speech literally;
•Socially and emotionally inappropriate behavior and the inability to interact successfully with peers;
•Problems with non-verbal communication, including the restricted use of gestures, limited or inappropriate facial expressions, or a peculiar, stiff gaze;
•Clumsy and uncoordinated motor movements.

ASSOCIATED FEATURES

Autism seems to bring with it an increased risk of other disorders. Seventy-five percent of autistic children have cognitive deficits, and twenty-five percent have cognitive abilities at or above average. Twenty-five percent of individuals with autism also have seizure disorders. The development of intellectual skills is usually uneven. An autistic child may be able to read extremely early, but not be able to comprehend what he or she reads. Other symptoms include hyperactivity, short attention span, impulsivity, aggressiveness, and self injury, such as head banging, hair pulling, and arm biting (particularly in young children). There may be unusual responses to stimuli: less than normal sensitivity to pain but extreme sensitivity to sounds or to being touched. There may be abnormalities in emotional expression, giggling or weeping for no apparent reason, and little or no emotional reaction when one would be expected. Similar abnormal responses may be shown in relation to fear; an absence of fear in response to real danger, but great fearfulness in the presence of harmless objects.

In adolescence or adulthood, people with Autistic Disorder who have the capacity for insight may become depressed when they realize how seriously impaired they are. Autistic Disorder sometimes follows medical and obstetrical problems, such as encephalitis, anoxia (absence of oxygen) during birth, and maternal rubella during pregnancy.There is some evidence of genetic transmission. The disorder is not caused by inappropriate parenting or by routine immunizations.

The person with Asperger's may not develop age-appropriate relationships or attempt to share interests or pleasures with others. He or she may be unable to reciprocate others' feelings, have difficulty using gestures or facial expressions, be extremely preoccupied with a very narrow area of interest, insist upon very rigid routines, make repetitive movements, and focus on parts of objects rather than the objects as a whole.

Asperger's Syndrome does not interfere with the development of language or thinking. However, its symptoms interfere with the individual's social or occupational functioning.

PREVALENCE

By definition, Autistic Disorder is present before age three. There are two to five cases of the disorder per 10,000 births. Rates of autism are four to five times greater among males than females. Females with Autistic Disorder are more likely to be severely retarded than are males with Autistic Disorder. Follow-up studies suggest that only a small percentage of people with Autistic Disorder live independent adult lives. Even the highest functioning adults continue to have problems in social interaction and communication, together with greatly restricted interests and activities. The siblings of people with the disorder are at increased risk.

There is a controversy about the observation that autism is much more frequently diagnosed currently than it was in the past. It is not clear whether this is because the condition has actually become more prevalent, or because cases that were missed in the past are now being identified, or because is it being over-diagnosed.

The incidence of Asperger's Syndrome is estimated to be two out of every 10,000 children. Boys are three to four times more likely than girls to have the disorder. Although diagnosed mainly in children, it is being increasingly diagnosed in adults with other mental health conditions such as depression, obsessive-compulsive disorder, and attention-deficit/hyperactivity disorder.

TREATMENT OPTIONS

It is difficult or unusual to be able to eradicate all the symptoms of Autistic Disorder, but there are many intervention and education programs which help to improve functioning. It is extremely important, however, that a proper assessment and diagnosis be made. Since the disturbance in behavior is so wide ranging, this can require an array of professional skills - psychological, languaage development, neuropsychological, and medical. Such a multiple assessment establishes the presence or absence of other disorders, the level of intellectual functioning, together with individual strengths and weaknesses, and the child's capacity for social and personal self-sufficiency. Since the symptoms of Autistic Disorder vary widely, a proper assessment is the foundation for designing and planning an individually tailored intervention program.

The autistic person may benefit from a combination of educational and behavioral interventions, which may reduce many of the behavioral disturbances, and improve the quality of life for the person and his or her family. In some cases, medication may also be prescribed. The diagnosis of Autistic Disorder can be a shattering experience for any family. The outcome of the diagnosis is open-ended and uncertain and includes a lifetime of care. Every member of the family is affected and it is vital to work with and support them.

Some new, inensive, multi-dimensional treatments are promising, but few people have access to them at this time.

Treatment for Asperger's Syndrome address the core symptoms of the disorder: poor communication skills; obsessive or repetitive routines; and physical clumsiness. No single treatment works best, but the program would include social skills training, cognitive behavioral therapy, medication, occupational/physical therapy, and parent training and support.

Associations & Agencies

587 Asperger's Association of New England (AANE)
85 Main Street
Suite 101
Watertown, MA 02472-4411
617-393-3824
866-597-2263
Fax: 617-393-3827
E-mail: info@aane.org
www.aane.org

Dania Jekel, Executive Director

Fosters awareness, respect, acceptance and support for individuals with AS and related conditions and their families. AANE offers a full array of educational events for people with an interest in Asperger's Syndrome.

588 Asperger's Syndrome Education Network of America (ASPEN)
9 Aspen Circle
Edison, NJ 08820-2832
732-321-0880
E-mail: info@aspennj.org
www.aspennj.org

Lori Shery, President

A non-profit organization which provides families and individuals whose lives are affected by Autism Spectrum Disorders with education about the issues surrounding the disorders; support in knowing that they are not alone, and in helping individuals achieve their maximum potential; advocacy in areas of appropriate educational programs, medical research funding, adult issues and increased public awareness and understanding.

589 Autism Network International
PO Box 35448
Syracuse, NY 13235-448

E-mail: jisincla@syr.edu
www.ani.ac
Jim Sinclair

ANI is an organization run by autistic people, for autistic people. We offer education, peer advocacy, and peer support.

590 Autism Research Foundation
c/o Moss-Rosene Lab, W701
715 Albany Street
Boston, MA 02118-2526
617-414-7012
Fax: 617-414-7207
E-mail: tarf@ladders.org
www.ladders.org

Claudia Persico, Project Manager/Coordinator

A nonprofit, tax-exempt organization dedicated to researching the neurological underpinnings of autism and other related developmental brain disorders. Seeking to rapidly expand and accelerate research into the pervasive developmental disorders.

591 Autism Research Institute
4182 Adams Avenue
San Diego, CA 92116-2599
619-281-7165
866-366-3361
Fax: 619-563-6840
www.autism.com

Steve Edelson, Executive Director

Provides information on Autism and Asperger's Syndrome.

592 Autism Society
4340 East-West Highway
Suite 350
Bethesda, MD 20814
301-657-0881
800-328-8476
Fax: 301-657-0869
E-mail: info#autism-society.org
www.autism-society.org

Lee Grossman, President & CEO
Jennifer Repella, Director of Programs
Hannah Cary, Assoc Dir, Public Policy
Cahterine McKeon, Autism Source Specialist

Promotes lifelong access and opportunities for persons within the autism spectrum and their families, to be fully included, participating members of their communities through advocacy, public awareness, education and research related to autism. Hosts a national conference, publishes a magazine, engages in public policy activities at local, state and federal levels, and provides information and

referral services via phone and email. The Autism Society consists of a nationwide network of local chapters.
Year Founded: 1965

593 Autism Society of America (ASA)
4340 East-West Highway
Suite 350
Bethesda, MD 20814
301-657-0881
800-328-8476
www.autism-society.org

Lee Grossman, President/CEO

The nation's leading grassroots autism organization, exists to improve the lives of all affected by autism.
Year Founded: 1965

594 Autistic Services
4444 Bryant Stratton Way
Williamsville, NY 14221-6013
716-631-5777
888-288-4764
Fax: 716-631-9234
E-mail: veronica@autisticservices.org
www.autisticservices.org

Thomas Mazur, President
Veronica Federiconi, Executive Director

Agency exclusively dedicated to serving the unique lifelong needs of individuals with autism. Also a regional resource for parents, school districts, physicians and other professionals.

595 Center for Family Support (CFS)
333 7th Avenue
New York, NY 10001-5115
212-629-7939
Fax: 212-239-2211
www.cfsny.org

Steven Vernikoff, Executive Director

An agency that continues to develop new programs to serve families and individuals with their care needs. They offer services throughout the New York City region including: New Jersey, Long Island and the Lower Hudson Valley.

596 Center for Mental Health Services (CMHS)
PO Box 2345
Rockville, MD 20847
240-221-4021
800-789-2647
Fax: 240-221-4295
TDD: 866-889-2647
www.mentalhealth.samhsa.gov

A Kathryn Power, MEd, Director
Anna Marsh PhD, Deputy Director
Fran Randolph PhD, Dir, Service & Systems Improveme
Anne Mathews-Younes EdD, Dir, Prevention/Traumatic Stress

CMHS leads Federal efforts to treat mental illnesses by promoting mental health and by preventing the development or worsening of mental illness when possible. Congress created CMHS to bring new hope to adults who have serious mental illnesses and to children with serious emotional disorders. CMHS provides information about mental health via a toll-free the web site, and more than 600 publications. Developed for users of mental health services and their families, the general public, policy makers, providers, and the media.

Year Founded: 1992

597 Community Services for Autistic Adults and Children
8615 East Village Avenue
Montgomery Village, MD 20886-4316
240-912-2220
TTY: 800-735-2258
E-mail: csaac@csaac.org

Ian Paregol, Executive Director
Marcee Smith, Ph.D., Assistant Executive Director of

Enables individuals to achieve to their highest potential and contribute as confident members in their community, instead of living in institutions.

Year Founded: 1979

598 Families for Early Autism Treatment
PO Box 255722
Sacramento, CA 95865-5722
916-491-1033
Fax: 916-581-5029
E-mail: feat@feat.org
www.feat.org

A nonprofit organization of parents and professionals, designed to help families with children who are diagnosed with autism or pervasive developmental disorder.

599 Indiana Resource Center for Autism (IRCA)
Indiana University
2853 E Tenth Street
Bloomington, IN 47408-2601
812-855-6508
800-280-7010
Fax: 812-855-9630
TTY: 812-855-9396
E-mail: prattc@indiana.edu
www.iidc.indiana.edu/irca

Cathy Pratt PhD, Director
Scott Bellini PhD, Assistant Director

Conducts outreach training and consultations, engage in research, develop and disseminate information on behalf of individuals across the autism spectrum, Aspergers syndrome, and other pervasive developmental disorders. Provides communities, organizations, agencies and families with the knowledge and skills to support children and adults in typical early intervention, school, community work and home.

600 More Advanced Autistic People Services (MAAPS)
PO Box 524
Crown Point, IN 46308-524

219-662-1311
Fax: 219-662-0638
E-mail: chart@netnitco.net
www.maapservices.org

Susan J Moreno, President
Mary Anne Neiner, Assistant

Provides information and advice to people with Asperger syndrome, Autism and other pervasive developmental disorders. Provides parents and professionals a way to network with others to learn more within the autism spectrum.

601 National Alliance on Mental Illness
2107 Wilson Boulevard
Suite 300
Arlington, VA 22201-3080
703-524-7600
800-950-6264
Fax: 703-524-9094
E-mail: helpline@nami.org
www.nami.org

Michael Fitzpatrick, Executive Director

Nation's leading self-help organization for all those affected by severe brain disorders. Mission is to bring consumers and families with similar experiences together to share information about services, care providers, and ways to cope with the challenges of schizophrenia, manic depression, and other serious mental illnesses.

Year Founded: 1979

602 National Association for the Dually Diagnosed (NADD)
132 Fair Street
Kingston, NY 12401-4802
845-331-4336
800-331-5362
Fax: 845-331-4569
E-mail: info@thenadd.org
www.thenadd.org

Robert Fletcher, Executive Director
Donna Nagy PhD, President

Nonprofit organization designed to promote interest of professional and parent development with resources for individuals who have the coexistence of mental illness and mental retardation. Provides conference, educational services and training materials to professionals, parents, concerned citizens and service organizations. Formerly known as the National Association for the Dually Diagnosed.

Year Founded: 1983

603 National Institute of Mental Health
National Institutes of Health DHHS
6001 Executive Boulevard Room 8184
MSC 9663
Bethesda, MD 20892-1
301-443-4513
TTY: 301-443-8431
E-mail: nimhinfo@nih.gov

Provides information and support on Autism and Asperger's Syndrome.

604 National Institute of Neurological Disorders and Stroke Brain Information Network (BRAIN)
PO Box 5801
Bethesda, MD 20824-5801
301-496-5751
800-352-9424
TTY: 301-468-5981
www.ninds.nih.gov

605 National Institute on Deafness and Other Communication Disorders Information Clearinghouse
31 Center Drive
MSC 2320
Bethesda, MD 20892-1

800-241-1044
TTY: 800-241-1055
E-mail: nidcinfo@nidcd.nih.gov
www.nidcd.nih.gov

Barry ACHE, Director
Kaylin ADIPIETRO, Director

Support and services for individuals with Autism and Asperger's Syndrome.

606 National Mental Health Consumers' Self-Help Clearinghouse
1211 Chestnut Street
Suite 1207
Philadelphia, PA 19107-4103
215-751-1810
800-553-4539
Fax: 215-636-6312
E-mail: info@mhselfhelp.org
www.mhselfhelp.org

Joseph Rogers, Executive Director

A national consumer technical assistance center that has played a major role in the development of the mental health consumer movement.

Year Founded: 1986

607 New England Center for Children
33 Turnpike Road
Southborough, MA 01772-2108
508-481-1015
Fax: 508-485-3421
E-mail: info@necc.org
www.necc.org

Vincent Strully, Executive Director
Katherine E Foster MEd, Associate Executive Director

Serving students between the ages of 3 and 22 diagnosed with autism, learning disabilities, language delays, mental retardation, behavior disorders and related disabilities; educational curriculum encompasses both the teaching of functional life skills.

608 SAMHSA's National Mental Health Information Center
US Department of Health and Human Services
PO Box 42557
Washington, DC 20015-557
240-221-4021
800-789-2647
Fax: 240-221-4295
TDD: 866-889-2647
www.mentalhealth.org

A Kathryn Power MEd, Director
Edward B Searle, Deputy Director

Provides information about mental health via a toll-free telephone number, this web site, and more than 600 publications. Developed for users of mental health services and their families, the general public, policy makers, providers, and the media.

Books

609 A Book: A Collection of Writings from the Advocate
Autism Society of North Carolina Bookstore
505 Oberlin Road
Suite 230
Raleigh, NC 27605-1345
919-743-0204
800-442-2762
Fax: 919-743-0208

David Lax, Manager

A collection of articles and writings from the Advocate, the national newsletter of the Autism Society of America.
$12.00

610 A Parent's Guide to Asperger Syndrome and High-Functioning Autism
Guilford Press
72 Spring Street
New York, NY 10012-4019
212-431-9800
800-365-7006
Fax: 212-966-6708
E-mail: info@guilford.com

Bob Matloff, President
Geraldine Dawson
James McPartland

How to Meet the Challenges and Help Your Child Thrive. Covers definitions, diagnsosis, causes and treatments as well as living with AS-HFA, channeling a child's strengths, and dealing with home and social world and life as an adult. *$18.95*

278 pages Year Founded: 2002 ISBN 1-572305-31-2

611 Activities for Developing Pre-Skill Concepts in Children with Autism
Autism Society of North Carolina Bookstore
505 Oberlin Road
Suite 230
Raleigh, NC 27605-1345
919-743-0204
800-442-2762
Fax: 919-743-0208

David Lax, Manager

Chapters include auditory development, concept development, social development and visual-motor integration. *$34.00*

612 Adults with Autism
Cambridge University Press
40 W 20th Street
New York, NY 10011-4211
212-924-3900
Fax: 212-691-3239
E-mail: marketing@cup.org
www.cambridge.org

Provides pratical help and guidance specifically for those caring for the growing recognized population of adults with autism. *$ 50.00*

312 pages Year Founded: 1996 ISBN 0-521456-83-5

613 Are You Alone on Purpose?
Autism Society of North Carolina Bookstore
505 Oberlin Road
Suite 230
Raleigh, NC 27605-1345
919-743-0204
800-442-2762
Fax: 919-743-0208

David Lax, Manager

This is the story of Alison, the twin sister of an autistic boy, who develops a friendship with a boy who has become paralyzed. Alison's feelings of isolation from her family and brother are discussed as she develops a true friendship. *$14.95*

614 Aspects of Autism: Biological Research
Autism Society of North Carolina Bookstore
505 Oberlin Road
Suite 230
Raleigh, NC 27605-1345
919-743-0204
800-442-2762
Fax: 919-743-0208

David Lax, Manager

Reviews the evidence for a physical cause of autism and the roles of genetics, magnesium and vitamin B6. *$15.00*

615 Asperger Syndrome
Guilford Publications
72 Spring Street
New York, NY 10012-4068

212-431-9800
800-365-7006
Fax: 212-966-6708
E-mail: info@guilford.com

Bob Matloff, President

Brings together preeminent scholars and practitioners to offer a definitive statement of what is currently known about Asperger syndrome and to highlight promising leads in research and clinical practice. Sifts through the latest developments in theory and research, discussing key diagnostic and conceptual issues and reviewing what is known about behavioral features and neurobiology. The effects of Asperger syndrome on social development, learning and communication are examined. *$48.00*

484 pages ISBN 1-572305-34-7

616 Asperger Syndrome: A Practical Guide for Teachers
ADD WareHouse
300 NW 70th Avenue
Suite 102
Plantation, FL 33317-2360
954-792-8944
800-233-9273
Fax: 954-792-8545
E-mail: sales@addwarehouse.com
www.addwarehouse.com

Harvey C Parker, Owner

A clear and concise guide to effective classroom practice for teachers and support assistants working with children with Asperger Syndrome in school. The authors explain characteristics of children with Asperger Syndrome, discusses methods of assessment and offers practical strategies for effective classroom interventions. *$24.95*

90 pages

617 Asperger's Syndrome: A Guide for Parents and Professionals
ADD WareHouse
300 NW 70th Avenue
Suite 102
Plantation, FL 33317-2360
954-792-8944
800-233-9273
Fax: 954-792-8545
E-mail: sales@addwarehouse.com
www.addwarehouse.com

Harvey C Parker, Owner

Providing a description and analysis of the unusual characteristics of Asperger's syndrome, with strategies to reduce those that are most conspicuous or debilitating. This guide brings together the most relevant and useful information on all aspects of the syndrome, from language and social behavior to motor clumsiness. *$18.95*

223 pages

618 Aspergers Syndrome: A Guide for Educators and Parents, Second Edition
Pro-Ed Publications
8700 Shoal Creek Boulevard
Austin, TX 78757-6897
512-451-3246
800-897-3202
Fax: 512-451-8542
E-mail: info@proedinc.com

Donald D Hammill, Owner

Packed with the current knowledge of a syndrome only recently applied in this country to individuals with significant social and language peculiarities. Will assist special education professionals and parents in understanding the special needs of children with AS, as well as how to address them in the classroom. For families, it offers helpful planning strategies for post secondary schooling. *$28.00*

130 pages

619 Autism
Autism Society of North Carolina Bookstore
505 Oberlin Road
Suite 230
Raleigh, NC 27605-1345
919-743-0204
800-442-2762
Fax: 919-743-0208

David Lax, Manager

In a question-and-answer format, the authors respond to questions about autism asked by countless parents and family members of children and youths with autism. *$26.00*

620 Autism & Asperger Syndrome
Cambridge University Press
40 W 20th Street
New York, NY 10011-4211
212-924-3900
800-872-7423
Fax: 212-691-3239
www.cup.org

Six clinician-researchers present aspects of Asperger Syndrome, one form of autism. Research summaries are enlivened by case studies. *$24.00*

247 pages

621 Autism & Sensing: The Unlost Instinct
Jessica Kingsley Publishers
325 Chestnut Street
Philadelphia, PA 19106-2614
215-625-8900
Fax: 215-625-2940
www.jkp.com

Available in paperback. *$26.95*

200 pages Year Founded: 1998 ISBN 1-853026-12-3

622 Autism Bibliography
TASH
29 W Susquehanna Avenue
Suite 210
Baltimore, MD 21204-5218
410-828-8274
Fax: 410-828-6706
E-mail: info@tash.org
www.tash.org

Three hundred recent references to publications on autism along with brief abstracts. *$9.00*

623 Autism Spectrum
Autism Society of North Carolina Bookstore
505 Oberlin Road
Suite 230
Raleigh, NC 27605-1345
919-743-0204
800-442-2762
Fax: 919-743-0208

David Lax, Manager

An excellent publication for new parents and professionals. *$28.95*

624 Autism Spectrum Disorders: The Complete Guid to Understanding Autism, Asperger's Syndrome, Pervasive Developmental Disorder, and Other ASDs
Penguin Group (USA)
375 Hudson Street
New York, NY 10014-3672
212-366-2000
Fax: 212-366-2933

David Shanks, CEO
Temple Grandin, Author

Twelve years ago, we were in the local doctor's office in a small village in England, where we had just moved.

625 Autism Treatment Guide
Autism Society of North Carolina Bookstore
505 Oberlin Road
Suite 230
Raleigh, NC 27605-1345
919-743-0204
800-442-2762
Fax: 919-743-0208

David Lax, Manager

A comprehensive book covering treatments and methods used to help individuals with autism. *$12.75*

626 Autism and Pervasive Developmental Disorders
Cambridge University Press
40 W 20th Street
New York, NY 10011-4211
212-924-3900
Fax: 212-691-3239
E-mail: marketing@cup.org
www.cup.org

Featuring contributions from leading authorities in the clinical and social sciences, this volume reflects recent progress in the understanding of autism and related conditions, and offers an international perspective on the present state of the discipline. Chapters cover current approaches to definition and diagnosis; prevalence and planning for service delivery; cognitive, genetic and neurobiological features and pathophysiological mechanisms. *$75.00*

294 pages Year Founded: 1998 ISBN 0-521553-86-5

627 Autism: An Inside-Out Approach An Innovative Look at the Mechanics of Autism and its Developmental Cousins
Jessica Kingsley Publishers
325 Chestnut Street
Philadelphia, PA 19106-2614
215-625-8900
Fax: 215-625-2940
www.jkp.com

Marisa Kitsock, Marketing Representative

Written by an autistic person for people with autism and related disorders, carers, and the professionals who work with them, is a practical handbook to understanding, living with and working with autism. *$23.95*

336 pages ISBN 1-853023-87-6

628 Autism: An Introduction to Psychological Theory
Harvard University Press
79 Garden Street
Cambridge, MA 02138-1400
617-495-1000
Fax: 617-495-5898
E-mail: CONTACT_HUP@harvard.edu
www.hup.harvard.edu

William Sisler, President

Provides a concise overview of current psychological theory and research that synthesizes the established work on the biological foundations, cognitive characteristics, and behavioral manifestations of this disorder. *$32.00*

160 pages Year Founded: 1998 ISBN 0-674053-12-5

629 Autism: Explaining the Enigma
Autism Society of North Carolina Bookstore
505 Oberlin Road
Suite 230
Raleigh, NC 27605-1345
919-743-0204
800-442-2762
Fax: 919-743-0208

David Lax, Manager

Explains the nature of autism. *$27.95*

630 Autism: From Tragedy to Triumph
Branden Publishing Company
PO Box 812094
Wellesley, MA 02482-13

Fax: 781-790-1056

E-mail: branden@branden.com
www.branden.com

A new book that deals with the Lovaas method and includes a foreward by Dr. Ivar Lovaas. The book is broken down into two parts, the long road to diagnosis and then treatment. *$12.95*

Year Founded: 1998 ISBN 0-828319-65-0

631 Autism: Identification, Education and Treatment
Autism Society of North Carolina Bookstore
505 Oberlin Road
Suite 230
Raleigh, NC 27605-1345
919-743-0204
800-442-2762
Fax: 919-743-0208

David Lax, Manager

Chapters include medical treatments, early intervention and communication and development in autism. *$36.00*

632 Autism: Nature, Diagnosis and Treatment
Guilford Publications
72 Spring Street
Department 4E
New York, NY 10012-4019
212-431-9800
800-365-7006
Fax: 212-966-6708
E-mail: exam@guilford.com

Bob Matloff, President

Foremost experts explore new perspectives on the nature and treatment of autism. Covering theory, research and the development of hypotheses and models, this book provides a balance between depth and breadth by focusing on questions most central to the field. For each question, an expert examines theoretical issues as well as empirical findings to offer new directions and testable hypotheses for future research. *$52.00*

417 pages ISBN 0-898627-24-9

633 Autism: Strategies for Change
Groden Center
86 Mount Hope Avenue
Providence, RI 02906-1648
401-274-6310
Fax: 401-421-3280
E-mail: grodencenter@grodencenter.org
www.grodencenter.org

June Groden, President

A comprehensive approach to the education and treatment of children with autism and related disorders. Clinicians, parents, and students of autism who are, or want to be advocates for change will find in this book a blueprint, and much detail, on how to bring change about. This applies at the level of program planning and management as well as of clinical or education practice. *$21.95*

634 Autistic Adults at Bittersweet Farms
Haworth Press
10 Alice Street
Binghamton, NY 13904-1503
607-722-5857
800-429-6784
Fax: 607-722-1424
E-mail: getinfo@haworthpressinc.com
www.haworthpress.com

A touching view of an inspirational residential care program for autistic adolescents and adults. *$17.95*

212 pages ISBN 1-560240-57-1

635 Avoiding Unfortunate Situations
Autism Society of North Carolina Bookstore
505 Oberlin Road
Suite 230
Raleigh, NC 27605-1345
919-743-0204
800-442-2762
Fax: 919-743-0208

David Lax, Manager

A collection of tips and information from and about people with autism and other developmental disabilities. *$5.00*

636 Beyond Gentle Teaching
Autism Society of North Carolina Bookstore
505 Oberlin Road
Suite 230
Raleigh, NC 27605-1345
919-743-0204
800-442-2762
Fax: 919-743-0208

David Lax, Manager

A nonaversive approach to helping those in need. *$35.00*

637 Biology of the Autistic Syndromes
Autism Society of North Carolina Bookstore
505 Oberlin Road
Suite 230
Raleigh, NC 27605-1345
919-743-0204
800-442-2762
Fax: 919-743-0208

David Lax, Manager

A revision of the original, classic text in the light of new developments and current knowledge. This book covers the epidemiological, genetic, biochemical, immunological and neuropsychological literature on autism. *$74.95*

638 Camps 2009-2010
Resources for Children with Special Needs
116 E 16th Street
5th Floor
New York, NY 10003-2164
212-677-4650
Fax: 212-254-4070
E-mail: info@resourcenyc.org
www.resourcesnyc.org

Rachel Howard, Executive Director

The guide includes a dozen new camps and updates on more than 300 camps and programs that provide a wide range of summer activities for children with emotional, developmental, learning and physical disabilities, health issues and other special needs. Day camps in the New York metro area are included as well as sleepaway camps in the Northeast. *$25.00*

133 pages Year Founded: 2009 ISBN 0-967836-57-3

639 Children with Autism: A Developmental Perspective
Harvard University Press
79 Garden Street
Cambridge, MA 02138-1400
617-495-1000
Fax: 617-495-5898
E-mail: CONTACT_HUP@harvard.edu
www.hup.harvard.edu

William Sisler, President

Views autism through the lens of developmental psychpathology, a discipline grounded in the belief that studies of normal and abnormal development can inform and enhance one another.

640 Children with Autism: Parents' Guide
Woodbine House
6510 Bells Mill Road
Bethesda, MD 20817-1636
301-897-3570
800-843-7323
Fax: 301-897-5838
E-mail: info@woodbinehouse.com
www.woodbinehouse.com

Irv Shapell, Owner

Recommended as the first book parents should read, this completely revised volume offers information and a complete introduction to autism, while easing the family's fears and concerns as they adjust and cope with their child's disorder. *$14.95*

456 pages ISBN 1-890627-04-6

641 Communication Unbound: How Facilitated Communication Is Challenging Views
Baker & Taylor International
2709 Water Ridge Parkway
Charlotte, NC 28217-4596
704-357-3500
800-775-1800
www.btol.com

Addresses the ways in which we receive persons with autism in our society, our community and our lives. *$18.95*

240 pages

642 Diagnosis and Treatment of Autism
Autism Society of North Carolina Bookstore
505 Oberlin Road
Suite 230
Raleigh, NC 27605-1345

919-743-0204
800-442-2762
Fax: 919-743-0208

David Lax, Manager

Various chapters written by professionals working with autistic children and adults. *$110.00*

643   Facilitated Communication and Technology Guide
Autism Society of North Carolina Bookstore
505 Oberlin Road
Suite 230
Raleigh, NC 27605-1345
919-743-0204
800-442-2762
Fax: 919-743-0208

David Lax, Manager

Chapters include technology and facilitated communication, augmentative and alternative communication, spelling boards, speech synthesizers and software. *$20.00*

644   Fighting for Darla: Challenges for Family Care & Professional Responsibility
Baker & Taylor International
2709 Water Ridge Parkway
Charlotte, NC 28217-4596
704-357-3500
800-775-1800
www.btol.com

Follows the story of Darla, a pregnant adolescent with autism. *$18.95*

176 pages ISBN 0-807733-56-3

645   Fragile Success - Ten Autistic Children, Childhood to Adulthood
Autism Society of North Carolina Bookstore
505 Oberlin Road
Suite 230
Raleigh, NC 27605-1345
919-743-0204
800-442-2762
Fax: 919-743-0208

David Lax, Manager

A book about the lives of autistic children, whom the author has followed from their early years at the Elizabeth Ives School in New Haven, CT, through to adulthood. *$24.95*

646   Getting Started with Facilitated Communication
Syracuse University, Facilitated Communication Institute
370 Huntington Hall
Syracuse, NY 13244-1
315-443-9657
Fax: 315-443-2274
E-mail: fcstaff@sued.syr.edu
www.soeweb.syr.edu/thefci

Describes in detail how to help individuals with autism and/or severe communication difficulties get started with facilitated communication.

647   Handbook of Autism and Pervasive Developmental Disorders
ADD WareHouse
300 NW 70th Avenue
Suite 102
Plantation, FL 33317-2360
954-792-8944
800-233-9273
Fax: 954-792-8545
E-mail: sales@addwarehouse.com
www.addwarehouse.com

Harvey C Parker, Owner

A comprehensive view of all information presently available about autism and other pervasive developmental disorders, drawing on findings and clinical experience from a number of related disciplines psychiatry, psychology, neurobiology and pediatrics. *$95.00*

1092 pages

648   Helping People with Autism Manage Their Behavior
Autism Society of North Carolina Bookstore
505 Oberlin Road
Suite 230
Raleigh, NC 27605-1345
919-743-0204
800-442-2762
Fax: 919-743-0208

David Lax, Manager

Covers the broad topic of helping people with autism manage their behavior. *$7.00*

649   Hidden Child: The Linwood Method for Reaching the Autistic Child
Woodbine House
6510 Bells Mill Road
Bethesda, MD 20817-1636
301-897-3570
800-843-7323
Fax: 301-897-5838
E-mail: info@woodbinehouse.com
www.woodbinehouse.com

Irv Shapell, Owner

Chronicle of the Linwood Children's Center's successful treatment program for autistic children. *$14.95*

286 pages ISBN 0-933149-06-9

650   How to Teach Autistic & Severely Handicapped Children
Autism Society of North Carolina Bookstore
505 Oberlin Road
Suite 230
Raleigh, NC 27605-1345

919-743-0204
800-442-2762
Fax: 919-743-0208

David Lax, Manager

Book provides procedures for effectively assessing and teaching autistic and other severely handicapped children. *$9.00*

651 I'm Not Autistic on the Typewriter
TASH
29 W Susquehanna Avenue
Suite 210
Baltimore, MD 21204-5218
410-828-8274
Fax: 410-828-6706
E-mail: info@tash.org
www.tash.org

Donna Gilles, President
Nancy Weiss, Executive Director
Jorge Pineda, Treasurer
Barbara Ransom, Secretary

An introduction to the facilitated communication training method. *$25.00*

652 Inner Life of Children with Special Needs
Taylor & Francis
325 Chestnut Street
Philadelphia, PA 19106-2614
215-625-8900
Fax: 215-625-2940
www.taylorandfrancis.com

Kevin Bradley, CEO

653 Joey and Sam
Autism Society of North Carolina Bookstore
505 Oberlin Road
Suite 230
Raleigh, NC 27605-1345
919-743-0204
800-442-2762
Fax: 919-743-0208

David Lax, Manager

A beautifully illustrated storybook for children, focusing on a family with two sons, one of whom suffers from autism. *$16.95*

654 Keys to Parenting the Child with Autism
Autism Society of North Carolina Bookstore
505 Oberlin Road
Suite 230
Raleigh, NC 27605-1345
919-743-0204
800-442-2762
Fax: 919-743-0208

David Lax, Manager

This book explains what autism is and how it is diagnosed. *$7.95*

655 Kristy and the Secret of Susan
Autism Society of North Carolina Bookstore
505 Oberlin Road
Suite 230
Raleigh, NC 27605-1345
919-743-0204
800-442-2762
Fax: 919-743-0208

David Lax, Manager

This book discusses Kristy and her new baby-sitting charge, Susan. Susan can't speak but sings beautifully. Susan is autistic. *$ 3.50*

656 Learning and Cognition in Autism
Kluwer Academic/Plenum Publishers
233 Spring Street
New York, NY 10013-1522
212-242-1490

Collection of papers written by experts in the field of autism. Describes the cognitive and educational characteristics of people with autism and explains intervention techniques and strategies. Topics include motivating communication in children with autism and a chapter by a high-functioning woman with autism who discusses special learning problems and unique learning strengths that characterize their development and offers specific suggestions for working with people like herself. *$59.00*

368 pages ISBN 0-306448-71-8

657 Let Community Employment Be the Goal For Individuals with Autism
Autism Society of North Carolina Bookstore
505 Oberlin Road
Suite 230
Raleigh, NC 27605-1345
919-743-0204
800-442-2762
Fax: 919-743-0208

David Lax, Manager

A guide designed for people who are responsible for preparing individuals with autism to enter the work force. *$7.00*

658 Let Me Hear Your Voice
Autism Society of North Carolina Bookstore
505 Oberlin Road
Suite 230
Raleigh, NC 27605-1345
919-743-0204
800-442-2762
Fax: 919-743-0208

David Lax, Manager

The Maruice family's second and third children were diagnosed with autism. This book recounts their experience with a home program using behavior therapy. *$13.95*

659 Letting Go
Autism Society of North Carolina Bookstore
505 Oberlin Road
Suite 230
Raleigh, NC 27605-1345
919-743-0204
800-442-2762
Fax: 919-743-0208

David Lax, Manager

A book of poems about a journey, an emotional road of placing a child in a residential group home for children with autism. *$7.50*

660 Management of Autistic Behavior
Pro-Ed Publications
8700 Shoal Creek Boulevard
Austin, TX 78757-6897
512-451-3246
800-897-3202
Fax: 512-451-8542
E-mail: info@proedinc.com

Donald D Hammill, Owner

Comprehensive and practical book that tells what works best with specific problems. *$41.00*

450 pages ISBN 0-890791-96-1

661 Mindblindness: An Essay on Autism and Theory of Mind
Autism Society of North Carolina Bookstore
505 Oberlin Road
Suite 230
Raleigh, NC 27605-1345
919-743-0204
800-442-2762
Fax: 919-743-0208

David Lax, Manager

Interpretations and research into the theory of mindblindness in children with autism. *$19.95*

300 pages ISBN 0-262023-84-9

662 Mixed Blessings
Autism Society of North Carolina Bookstore
505 Oberlin Road
Suite 230
Raleigh, NC 27605-1345
919-743-0204
800-442-2762
Fax: 919-743-0208

David Lax, Manager

A real-life family discusses the raising of their autistic son. *$19.95*

663 More Laughing and Loving with Autism
Autism Society of North Carolina Bookstore
505 Oberlin Road
Suite 230
Raleigh, NC 27605-1345

919-743-0204
800-442-2762
Fax: 919-743-0208

David Lax, Manager

A collection of warm and humorous parent stories about raising a child with autism. *$9.95*

664 Neurobiology of Autism
Johns Hopkins University Press
2715 N Charles Street
Baltimore, MD 21218-4319
410-516-6900
800-537-5487
Fax: 410-516-6998

William Brody, President

This 2nd edition discusses recent advances in scientific research that point to a neurobiological basis for autism and examines the clinical implications of this research. *$44.95*

272 pages Year Founded: 2005 ISBN 0-801856-80-9

665 News from the Border: a Mother's Memoir of Her Autistic Son
Houghton Mifflin Company
222 Berkeley Street
Boston, MA 02116-3760
617-351-5000
Fax: 617-351-1105

Barry O'Callaghan, CEO

A searingly honest account of the author's family experiences with autism. Raising an autistic child is the central, ongoing drama of her married life in this riveting account of acceptance and coping. *$22.95*

384 pages

666 Nobody Nowhere
Autism Society of North Carolina Bookstore
505 Oberlin Road
Suite 230
Raleigh, NC 27605-1345
919-743-0204
800-442-2762
Fax: 919-743-0208

David Lax, Manager

An autobiography giving readers a tour of the author's life with autism. *$14.00*

667 Parent Survival Manual
Autism Society of North Carolina Bookstore
505 Oberlin Road
Suite 230
Raleigh, NC 27605-1345
919-743-0204
800-442-2762
Fax: 919-743-0208

David Lax, Manager

Compiled from three hundred fifty anecdotes told by parents of autistic and developmentally disabled children. *$38.50*

668 Parent's Guide to Autism
Autism Society of North Carolina Bookstore
505 Oberlin Road
Suite 230
Raleigh, NC 27605-1345
919-743-0204
800-442-2762
Fax: 919-743-0208

David Lax, Manager

An essential handbook for anyone facing autism. *$14.00*

669 Please Don't Say Hello
Human Sciences Press
233 Spring Street
New York, NY 10013-1522
212-620-8000
Fax: 212-807-1047

Paul and his family moved into a new neighborhood. Paul's brother was autistic. The children thought that Eddie was retarded until they learned that there were skills that he could do better than they could. *$10.95*

47 pages ISBN 0-898851-99-8

670 Preschool Issues in Autism
Kluwer Academic/Plenum Publishers
233 Spring Street
New York, NY 10013-1522
212-242-1490

Combines some of the most important theory and data related to the early identifiction and intervention in autism and related disorders. Addresses clinical aspects, parental concerns and legal issues. Helps professionals understand and implement state-of-the-art services for young children and their families. *$54.00*

294 pages ISBN 0-306444-40-2

671 Psychoeducational Profile
Autism Society of North Carolina Bookstore
505 Oberlin Road
Suite 230
Raleigh, NC 27605-1345
919-743-0204
800-442-2762
Fax: 919-743-0208

David Lax, Manager

The PEP-R is a revision of the popular instrument that has been used for over twenty years to assess skills and behavior of autistic and communication-handicapped children who function between the ages of 6 months and 7 years. *$74.00*

672 Reaching the Autistic Child: a Parent Training Program
Brookline Books/Lumen Editions
PO Box 97
Newton Upper Falls, MA 02464-1

800-666-2665
Fax: 617-558-8011
www.brooklinebooks.com

Detailed case studies of social and behavioral change in autistic children and their families show parents how to implement the principles for improved socialization and behavior. Revised and updated 1998. *$15.95*

ISBN 1-571290-56-7

673 Record Books for Individuals with Autism
Indiana Institute on Disability and Community
Indiana University
2853 E Tenth Street
Bloomington, IN 47408-2601
812-855-9396
800-280-7010
Fax: 812-855-9630
TTY: 812-855-9396
E-mail: uap@indiana.edu

David Mank, Executive Director

This book was developed with parent information about an autistic child so that it is organized, easily accessible and can be copied as needed. *$5.00*

37 pages

674 Russell Is Extra Special
Autism Society of North Carolina Bookstore
505 Oberlin Road
Suite 230
Raleigh, NC 27605-1345
919-743-0204
800-442-2762
Fax: 919-743-0208

David Lax, Manager

A sensitive portrayal of an autistic boy written by his father. *$8.95*

675 Schools for Students with Special Needs
Resources for Children with Special Needs
116 E 16th Street
Fifth Floor
New York City, NY 10003-2112
212-677-4650
Fax: 212-254-4070
E-mail: info@resourcesnyc.org
www.resourcesnyc.org

Rachel Howard, Executive Director

The first complete book listing private day and residential schools for parents, caregivers and professionals seeking schools for students 5 and up with developmental, emotional, physical and learning disabilities in the NYC metro area. More than 400 schools and residential programs that serve children in the elementary through high school grades are listed with contact information, ages and populations served, class sizes and student-teacher ratios, special services and diplomas offered. Includes a 46-page section of Schools for Children with Autism Spectrum Disorders, as well as a guide with a list of websites on autism spectrum disorders. *$25.00*

342 pages

676 Sex Education: Issues for the Person with Autism
Indiana Institute on Disability and Community
Indiana University
2853 E Tenth Street
Bloomington, IN 47408-2601
812-855-9396
800-280-7010
Fax: 812-855-9630
TTY: 812-855-9396
E-mail: uap@indiana.edu

David Mank, Executive Director

Discusses issues of sexuality and provides some methods of instruction for persons with autism. *$3.00*

18 pages

677 Siblings of Children with Autism: A Guide for Families
Autism Society of North Carolina Bookstore
505 Oberlin Road
Suite 230
Raleigh, NC 27605-1345
919-743-0204
800-442-2762
Fax: 919-743-0208

David Lax, Manager

Offers information on the needs of a child with autism. *$16.95*

678 Somebody Somewhere
Autism Society of North Carolina Bookstore
505 Oberlin Road
Suite 230
Raleigh, NC 27605-1345
919-743-0204
800-442-2762
Fax: 919-743-0208

David Lax, Manager

Offers a revealing account of the author's battle with autism. *$15.00*

679 Soon Will Come the Light
Autism Society of North Carolina Bookstore
505 Oberlin Road
Suite 230
Raleigh, NC 27605-1345
919-743-0204
800-442-2762
Fax: 919-743-0208

David Lax, Manager

Offers new perspectives on the perplexing disability of autism. *$19.95*

680 Teaching Children with Autism: Strategies to Enhance Communication
Autism Society of North Carolina Bookstore
505 Oberlin Road
Suite 230
Raleigh, NC 27605-1345
919-743-0204
800-442-2762
Fax: 919-743-0208

David Lax, Manager

This valuable new book describes teaching strategies and instructional adaptations which promote communication and socialization in children with autism. *$34.95*

681 Teaching and Mainstreaming Autistic Children
Love Publishing Company
9101 E Kenyon Avenue
Suite 2200
Denver, CO 80237-1854
303-221-7333
Fax: 303-221-7444
E-mail: lpc@lovepublishing.com
www.lovepublishing.com

Stan Love, Owner

Dr Knoblock advocates a highly organized, structured environment for autistic children, with teachers and parents working together. His premise is that the learning and social needs of autistic children must be analyzed and a daily program be designed with interventions that respond to this functional analysis of their behavior. *$39.95*

Year Founded: 1982 ISBN 0-891081-11-9

682 Ten Things Every Child with Autism Wishes You Knew
Future Horizons
721 West Abram Street
Arlington, TX 76013-6995
817-277-0727
800-489-0727
Fax: 817-277-2270
www.fhautism.com

Wayne Gilpin, President

Framed in both humor and compassion, the book defines the top ten characteristics that illuminate the minds and hearts of cildren with autism. Ellen's personal experiences.

683 The Comprehensive Directory
Resources For Children with Special Needs
116 E 16th Street
5th Floor
New York, NY 10003-2164
212-677-4650
Fax: 212-254-4070
E-mail: info@resourcesnyc.org
www.resourcesnyc.org

Rachel Howard, Executive Director

The directory for everyone who needs to find services for children with disabilities and special needs. Designed for parents, caregivers and professionals, it includes more than

2,500 agencies providing more than 4,000 services and programs. *$30.00*

1200 pages ISBN 0-967836-51-4

684 The Hidden Child: Youth with Autism
Mason Crest Publishers
370 Reed Road
Suite 302
Broomall, PA 19008-4017
610-543-6200
866-627-2665
Fax: 610-543-3878
E-mail: dtaylor@masoncrest.com
www.masoncrest.com

Hope is the keyword for the autistic child's future. Through education, early intervention, and continued research, children with autism can live normal lives. Factual information about autism, the Autism Society of America, sibshops, and different educational treatments will expand the reader's knowledge of this condition. A fictional story told from a sibling's point of view helps the reader understand the effects autism has on individuals and family members.

ISBN 1-590847-38-9

685 Thinking In Pictures, Expanded Edition: My Life with Autism
Vintage
1745 Broadway 20th Floor
New York, NY 10019-4368
212-572-2882
800-733-3000
Fax: 212-572-6043
www.randomhouse.com/vintage/index.html

Temple Grandin, Author

ISBN 0-307275-65-5

686 Transition Matters From School to Independence: a Guide & Directory of Services for Children & Youth with Disabilities & Special Needs in the Metro New York Area
Resources for Children with Special Needs
116 E 16th Street
5th Floor
New York, NY 10003-2164
212-677-4650
Fax: 212-254-4070
E-mail: info@resourcesnyc.org
www.resourcesnyc.org

Rachel Howard, Executive Director

Youth with disabilities need special guidance when moving from school to adult life. Transition Matters covers every aspect of moving from high school to the world of postsecondary education, job training, employment and idependent living. This guide for parents, caregivers and educators presents a wealth of information about the transition process, and lists 1,000 agencies and organizations that provide services for youth 14 and up. It explains entitlements and options and helps families navigate systems and procedures. *$15.00*

500 pages ISBN 0-967836-56-5

687 Ultimate Stranger: The Autistic Child
Autism Society of North Carolina Bookstore
505 Oberlin Road
Suite 230
Raleigh, NC 27605-1345
919-743-0204
800-442-2762
Fax: 919-743-0208

David Lax, Manager

Delacato's thesis is that autism is neuro-genic and not psycho-genic in origin. *$10.00*

688 Understanding Autism
Fanlight Productions
4196 Washington Street
Boston, MA 02131-1731
617-469-4999
800-937-4113
Fax: 617-469-3379
E-mail: fanlight@fanlight.com
www.fanlight.com

Parents of children with autism discuss the nature and symptoms of this lifelong disability, and outline a treatment program based on behavior modification principles. *$195.00*

ISBN 1-572951-00-1

689 Until Tomorrow: A Family Lives with Autism
Autism Society of North Carolina Bookstore
505 Oberlin Road
Suite 230
Raleigh, NC 27605-1345
919-743-0204
800-442-2762
Fax: 919-743-0208

David Lax, Manager

The central theme of this book is an effort to show what it is like to live with a child who cannot communicate. *$10.00*

690 When Snow Turns to Rain
Woodbine House
6510 Bells Mill Road
Bethesda, MD 20817-1636
301-897-3570
800-843-7323
Fax: 301-897-5838
E-mail: info@woodbinehouse.com
www.woodbinehouse.com

Irv Shapell, Owner

A gripping personal account of one family's experiences with autism. Chronicles a family's journey from parental bliss to devastation, as they learn that their son has autism. This book delves into diagnosis, treatments, and attitudes toward persons with autism. *$14.95*

250 pages ISBN 0-933149-63-8

691 Winter's Flower
Autism Society of North Carolina Bookstore
505 Oberlin Road
Suite 230
Raleigh, NC 27605-1345
919-743-0204
800-442-2762
Fax: 919-743-0208

David Lax, Manager

The story of Ranae Johnson's quest to rescue her son from a world of silence. A story of love, patience and dedication. *$12.95*

692 Without Reason
Autism Society of North Carolina Bookstore
505 Oberlin Road
Suite 230
Raleigh, NC 27605-1345
919-743-0204
800-442-2762
Fax: 919-743-0208

David Lax, Manager

A story of a family coping with two generations of autism. *$19.95*

Periodicals & Pamphlets

693 Autism Newslink
Autism Society Ontario
1179A King Street W
Suite 004
Toronto, ON
416-246-9592
Fax: 416-246-9417
E-mail: mail@autismsociety.on.ca
www.autismsociety.on.ca

Covers society activities and contains information on autism. Recurring features include news of research, a calendar of events, reports of meetings, and book reviews. *$25.00*

10 pages 4 per year

694 Autism Research Review International
Autism Research Institute
4182 Adams Avenue
San Diego, CA 92116-2599
619-281-7165
Fax: 619-563-6840
www.autism.com

Steve Edelson, Executive Director

Discusses current research and provides information about the causes, diagnosis, and treatment of autism and related disorders. *$18.00*

8 pages 4 per year ISSN 0893-8474

695 Autism Society News
Utah Parent Center
2290 E 4500 S
Suite 110
Salt Lake City, UT 84117-4428
801-272-1051
800-468-1160
Fax: 801-272-8907
www.utahparentcenter.org

Helen Post, Executive Director

Presents news, research information, and legislative updates regarding autism. Recurring features include a calendar of events and columns titled Parent Meetings, What's On in the News, Research News, Parent Corner, Legislative Summary, and A Big Thank You!

8 pages

696 Autism Spectrum Disorders in Children and Adolescents
Center for Mental Health Services: Knowledge Exchange Network
PO Box 42490
Washington, DC 20015

800-789-2647
Fax: 301-984-8796
TDD: 866-889-2647
E-mail: ken@mentalhealth.org
www.mentalhealth.org

This fact sheet defines autism, describes the signs and causes, discusses types of help available, and suggests what parents or other caregivers can do.

2 pages

697 Autism in Children and Adolescents
Center for Mental Health Services: Knowledge Exchange Network
PO Box 42557
Washington, DC 20015-557

800-789-2647
Fax: 301-984-8796
TDD: 866-889-2647
E-mail: ken@mentalhealth.org
www.mentalhealth.org.samhsa.gov

This fact sheet defines autism, describes the signs and causes, discusses types of help available, and suggests what parents or other caregivers can do.

2 pages Year Founded: 1997

698 Facts About Autism
Indiana Institute on Disability and Community
Indiana University
2853 E Tenth Street
Bloomington, IN 47408-2601
812-855-9396
800-280-7010
Fax: 812-855-9630
TTY: 812-855-9396
E-mail: uap@indiana.edu

David Mank, Executive Director

Provides concise information describing autism, diagnosis, needs of the person with autism from diagnosis through adulthood. Information on the Autism Society of America chapters in Indiana are listed in the back, along with a description of the Indiana Resource Center for Autism and suggested books to look for in the local library. Also available in Spanish. *$1.00*

699   Journal of Autism and Developmental Disorders
Springer Science & Business Media
Heidelberger Plate 3
14197 Berlin
Germany,

www.springer.com

Features research and case studies involving the entire spectrum of interventions and advances in the diagnosis and classification of disorders. *$98.00*

6 per year   ISSN 0162-3257

700   MAAP
MAAP Services
PO Box 524
Crown Point, IN 46308-524
219-662-1311
Fax: 219-662-0638
E-mail: chart@netnitco.net
www.maapservices.org

This quarterly newsletter provides the opportunity for parents and professionals to network with families of more advanced individuals with Autism, Asperger's syndrome, and Pervasive developmental disorder. Helps you to learn about more advanced individuals within the autism spectrum. *$22.00*

4 per year

701   Sex Education: Issues for the Person with Autism
Autism Society of North Carolina Bookstore
505 Oberlin Road
Suite 230
Raleigh, NC 27605-1345
919-743-0204
800-442-2762
Fax: 919-743-0208

David Lax, Manager

Discusses issues of sexuality and provides methods of instruction for people with autism. *$4.00*

702   The Source Newsletter
MAAP
PO Box 524
Crown Point, IN 46308-524
219-662-1311
Fax: 219-662-0638
E-mail: chart@netnitco.net

Susan J Moreno, Editor

Newsletter from the Global Information and Support Network for More Advanced Persons with Austism and Asperger's Syndrome.

4 per year

703   Treatment of Children with Mental Disorders
National Institute of Mental Health
6001 Executive Boulevard
Room 8184
Bethesda, MD 20892-1
301-443-4513
866-615-6464
TTY: 301-443-8431
E-mail: nimhinfo@nih.gov

A short booklet that contains questions and answers about therapy for children with mental disorders. Includes a chart of mental disorders and medications used.

Research Centers

704   Facilitated Learning at Syracuse University
Syracuse University, Facilitated Communication Institute
370 Huntington Hall
Syracuse, NY 13244-1
315-443-9657
Fax: 315-443-9218
E-mail: fcstaff@syr.edu
www.thefci.syr.edu

College offering facilitated learning research into communication with persons who have autism or severe disabilities. Offers books, videos and public awareness on research projects.

705   Indiana Resource Center for Autism (IRCA)
Indiana University
2853 E Tenth Street
Bloomington, IN 47408-2601
812-855-6508
800-280-7010
Fax: 812-855-9630
TTY: 812-855-9396
E-mail: prattc@indiana.edu
www.iidc.indiana.edu/irca

Cathy Pratt PhD, Director
Scott Bellini PhD, Assistant Director

Conducts outreach training and consultations, engage in research, develop and disseminate information on behalf of individuals across the autism spectrum, Aspergers syndrome, and other pervasive developmental disorders. Provides communities, organizations, agencies and families with the knowledge and skills to support children and adults in typical early intervention, school, community work and home.

706 TEACCH
CB# 6305
University of NC at Chapel Hill
Chapel Hill, NC 27599-1
919-966-2174
Fax: 919-966-4127
E-mail: teacch@unc.edu
www.teacch.com

Lee Marcus, Clinical Director
Jean Justice, Office Manager

This organization is the division for the treatment and education of autistic and related communication handicapped children.

Video & Audio

707 Asperger's Unplugged, an Interview with Jerry Newport
Program Development Associates
PO Box 2038
Syracuse, NY 13220-2038
315-452-0643
Fax: 315-452-0710
E-mail: info@disabilitytraining.com
www.disabilitytraining.com

Meet the man who answered a question in the film 'Rain Man' - How much is 4,343 x 1,234? - before the autistic savant character played by Dustin Hoffman answered it. Jerry Newport discovered Asperger's Syndrome while watching 'Rain Man' and has since become an engaging speaker and self-help organizer. This inspiring interview, available on VHS or DVD, supports teachers, staff developers and people with high functioning autism. 40 minutes. *$79.95*

708 Autism Spectrum Disorders and the SCERTS
Program Development Associates
PO Box 2038
Syracuse, NY 13220-2038
315-452-0643
800-543-2119
Fax: 315-452-0710
E-mail: info@disabilitytraining.com
www.disabilitytraining.com/autism

Early intervention for children with Autism Spectrum Disorders. Shows a model in action with higher-functioning children who require less support. 105 minutes between three tapes. *$279.00*
Year Founded: 2004

709 Autism in the Classroom
Program Development Associates
PO Box 2038
Syracuse, NY 13220-2038
315-452-0643
800-543-2119
Fax: 315-452-0710
E-mail: info@disabilitytraining.com
www.disabilitytraining.com/autism

Overviews symptoms, behaviors and treatments, and interviews children with autism, along with their parents and their teachers. 16 minutes. *$69.95*
Year Founded: 2004

710 Autism is a World
Program Development Associates
PO Box 2038
Syracuse, NY 13220-2038
315-452-0643
800-543-2119
Fax: 315-452-0710
E-mail: info@disabilitytraining.com
www.disabilitytraining.com/autism

Takes a look inside the life of a woman who lives with the disorder. She explains how she feels, how she relates to others, her obsession and why her behavior can be so very different. Gives teachers and professionals striving to understand Autism Spectrum Disorder a glimpse from the inside out of this developmental disability. 40 minutes & can also be ordered as a DVD with special features. *$99.95*
Year Founded: 2004

711 Autism: A Strange, Silent World
Filmakers Library
124 E 40th Street
New York, NY 10016-1798
212-808-4980
E-mail: info@filmakers.com
www.filmakers.com

Sue Oscar, Manager

British educators and medical personnel offer insight into autism's characteristics and treatment approaches through the cameos of three children. 52 minutes. *$295.00*

712 Autism: A World Apart
Fanlight Productions
2
47 Halifax St
Jamaica Plain, MA 02130-4327
617-469-4999
800-937-4113
Fax: 617-469-3379
E-mail: fanlight@fanlight.com
www.fanlight.com

Kelli English, Publicity Coordinator

In this documentary, three families show us what the textbooks and studies cannot; what it's like to live with autism day after day, raise and love children who may be withdrawn and violent and unable to make personal connections with their families. Video cassette. 29 minutes. *$199.00*
ISBN 1-572950-39-0

713 Autism: Being Friends
Indiana Institute on Disability and Community
Indiana University
2853 E Tenth Street
Bloomington, IN 47408-2601

812-855-9396
800-280-7010
Fax: 812-855-9630
TTY: 812-855-9396
E-mail: uap@indiana.edu

David Mank, Executive Director

This autism awareness videotape was produced specifically for use with young children. The program portrays the abilities of the child with autism and describes ways in which peers can help the child to be a part of the everyday world. *$10.00*

Year Founded: 1991

714   Avoiding The Turbulance: Guiding Families of Children Diagnosed with Autism
Program Development Associates
PO Box 2038
Syracuse, NY 13220-2038
315-452-0643
800-543-2119
Fax: 315-452-0710
E-mail: info@disabilitytraining.com
www.disabilitytraining.com/autism

Focuses primarily on the best strategies of early intervention. Good resources for primary care medical providers and agency professionals involved in early intervention autism programs. 12 minutes. *$79.95*

Year Founded: 2005

715   Breakthroughs: How to Reach Students with Autism
ADD WareHouse
300 NW 70th Avenue
Suite 102
Plantation, FL 33317-2360
954-792-8944
800-233-9273
Fax: 954-792-8545
E-mail: sales@addwarehouse.com
www.addwarehouse.com

Harvey C Parker, Owner

This video is designed for instructors of children with autism, K-12. The program provides a fully-loaded teacher's manual with reproducible lesson plans that will take you through an entire school year as well as an award-winning video that demonstrates the instructional and behavioral techniques recommended in the manual. Covers math, reading, fine motor, self-help, vocational, social and life skills. Features a veteran instructor who was named 'Teacher of the Year' by the Autism Society of America. *$89.00*

716   Children and Autism: Time is Brain
Program Development Associates
PO Box 2038
Syracuse, NY 13220-2038
315-452-0643
800-543-2119
Fax: 315-452-0710
E-mail: info@disabilitytraining.com
www.disabilitytraining.com/autism

Video features Applied Behavior Analysis (ABA) as an autism treatment technique by focusing on two families raising a child with autism. Gives documentation on their interaction with therapists and behavior analysts. 28 minutes. *$99.95*

Year Founded: 2004

717   Dr. Tony Attwood: Asperger's Syndrome Volume 2 DVD
Program Development Associates
PO Box 2038
Syracuse, NY 13220-2038
315-452-0643
Fax: 315-452-0710
E-mail: info@disabilitytraining.com
www.disabilitytraining.com

Following rave national reviews that autism expert Dr. Tony Attwood received for his Volume 1 introduction to Asperger's Syndrome, here's the new DVD of his latest conference presentations. Volume 2 leaps off the DVD screen with Dr. Attwood's interactive, in-depth, theory-of-mind approach to Asperger's. 180 minutes. *$109.95*

718   Going to School with Facilitated Communication
Syracuse University, Facilitated Communication Institute
370 Huntington Hall
Syracuse, NY 13244-1
315-443-9657
Fax: 315-443-2274
E-mail: fcstaff@sued.syr.edu
www.soeweb.syr.edu/thefci

A video in which students with autism and/or severe disabilities illustrate the use of facilitated communication focusing on basic principles fostering facilitated communication.

719   Health Care Desensitization
Indiana Institute on Disability and Community
Indiana University
2853 E Tenth Street
Bloomington, IN 47408-2601
812-855-9396
800-280-7010
Fax: 812-855-9630
TTY: 812-855-9396
E-mail: uap@indiana.edu

David Mank, Executive Director

Training videotape for teachers, parents, health professionals and group home staff showing how the desensitization procedure to medical, dental and optometric exams was applied to preschool and adolescent students with autism and thier successful cooperation with the subsequent health care. *$25.00*

Year Founded: 1989

720 I'm Not Autistic on the Typewriter
Syracuse University, Facilitated Communication Institute
370 Huntington Hall
Syracuse, NY 13244-1
315-443-9657
Fax: 315-443-2274
E-mail: fcstaff@sued.syr.edu
www.soeweb.syr.edu/thefci

A video introducing facilitated communication, a method by which persons with autism express themselves.

721 Interview with Dr. Pauline Filipek
Program Development Associates
PO Box 2038
Syracuse, NY 13220-2038
315-452-0643
800-543-2119
Fax: 315-452-0710
E-mail: info@disabilitytraining.com
www.disabilitytraining.com/autism

An interview that presents early stage developmental autism, with diagnosis and age-level comparisons, research, interventions and myths and false and future treatments. 14 minutes. *$79.95*

Year Founded: 2005

722 Matthew: Guidance for Parents with Autistic Children
Program Development Associates
PO Box 2038
Syracuse, NY 13220-2038
315-452-0643
800-543-2119
Fax: 315-452-0710
E-mail: info@disabilitytraining.com
www.disabilitytraining.com/autism

A resource video guide for parents of autistic children. Shows parents where they should go, who to consult and what did or did not work for Matthew and his parents. 28 minutes. *$79.95*

Year Founded: 2004

723 Rising Above a Diagnosis of Autism
Program Development Associates
PO Box 2038
Syracuse, NY 13220-2038
315-452-0643
800-543-2119
Fax: 315-452-0710
E-mail: info@disabilitytraining.com
www.disabilitytraining.com/autism

Focuses primarily on the period when a child receives a diagnosis of Autism. Meet with others who are involved somehow with autistic children, and hear recommendations from professionals and meet children that have Autism, PDD, Asperger's Syndrome or any other forms of Austism Spectrum Disorder. 30 minutes. *$99.95*

Year Founded: 2005

724 Rylee's Gift - Asperger Syndrome
Program Development Associates
PO Box 2038
Syracuse, NY 13220-2038
315-452-0643
Fax: 315-452-0710
E-mail: info@disabilitytraining.com
www.disabilitytraining.com

This video or DVD spotlights Rylee - through his mother, grandparents, doctor, teacher - and adults with Asperger's Syndrome. Balances views of difficult transitions and meltdown behaviors, with sensory therapy, socialization and the amazing capabilities of people with this syndrome/gift. 56 minutes. *$89.95*

725 Sense of Belonging: Including Students with Autism in Their School Community
Indiana Institute on Disability and Community
Indiana University
2853 E Tenth Street
Bloomington, IN 47408-2601
812-855-9396
800-280-7010
Fax: 812-855-9630
TTY: 812-855-9396
E-mail: uap@indiana.edu

David Mank, Executive Director

Highlights the efforts of two elementary and one middle school student with autism in general education settings. Illustrates the value of inclusion and importance it plays for the future of all students. Practical strategies for teaching students with autism are described. *$40.00*

Year Founded: 1997

726 Straight Talk About Autism with Parents and Kids
ADD WareHouse
300 NW 70th Avenue
Suite 102
Plantation, FL 33317-2360
954-792-8944
800-233-9273
Fax: 954-792-8545
E-mail: sales@addwarehouse.com
www.addwarehouse.com

Harvey C Parker, Owner

These revealing videos contain intimate interviews with parents of kids with autism and the young people themselves. Topics discussed include friends and social isolation, communication difficulties, hypersensitivities, teasing, splinter skills, parent support groups and more. One video focuses on childhood issues, while the second covers adolescent issues. Two 40 minute videos. *$99.00*

727 Struggling with Life: Asperger's Syndrome
Program Development Associates
PO Box 2038
Syracuse, NY 13220-2038
315-452-0643
Fax: 315-452-0710

E-mail: info@disabilitytraining.com
www.disabilitytraining.com
ABC News correspondent Jay Schadler's report on the neurological disorder called Asperger's focuses on the telling line between intense interests and obsessions. The latter may be an early symptom of the syndrome. This closed caption video is grounded on studies by Fred Voklmar at Yale that explore compulsive fixations and unreadable facial expressions, both of which are typical of Asperger's and inhibit normal peer interactions among children. VHS or DVD. 14 minutes. *$ 69.95*

Web Sites

**728   Social Skills Training for Children and
Adolescents with Asperger Syndrome and
Social-Communications Problems**
Autism Asperger Publishing

www.amazon.com
User-friendly book that provides a wealth of ready-to-use activities.

**729   The Asperger Parent: How to Raise a Child
with Asperger Syndrome and Maintain Your
Sense of Humor**
Autism Asperger Publishing Company

www.amazon.com
Great advice for the parent of a child with Asperger's Syndrome.

730   www.aane.org
Asperger's Association of New England

Working advocacy group of Massachusetts parents of adults and teens with AS who have come together with the goal of getting state funding for residential supports for adults with AS. At the present time no state agency will provide these needed supports. Interested parents and AS adults are welcome to join this working group.

731   www.ani.ac
Autism Network International

This organization is run by and for the autistic people. The best advocates for autistic people are autistic people themselves. Provides a forum for autistic people to share information, peer support, tips for coping and problem solving, as well as providing a social outlet for autistic people to explore and participate in autistic social experiences. In addition to promoting self advocacy for high-functioning autistic adults, ANI also works to improve the lives of au-

tistic people who, whether they are too young or because they do not have the communication skills, are not able to advocate for themselves. Helps autistic people by providing information and referrals for parenting and teachers. Also strives to educate the public about autism.

732   www.aspennj.org
Asperger Syndrome Education Network (ASPEN)

Regionally-based non-profit organization headquarted in New Jersey, with 11 local chapters, providing families and those individuals affected with Asperger Syndrome, PDD-NOS, High Function Autism, and related disorders. Provides education about the issues surrounding Asperger Syndrome and other related disorders. Support in knowing that they are not alone and in helping individuals with AS achieve their maximum potential. Advocacy in areas of appropriate educational programs and placement, medical research funding, and increased public awareness and understanding.

733   www.aspergerinfo.com
Aspergers Resource Links

AspergerInfo.com offers a safe place to ask questions, share experiences, and discuss treatments relating to Asperger Syndrome.

734   www.aspergers.com
Aspergers Resource Links

Asperger's Disorder Homepage

735   www.aspergersyndrome.org
Aspergers Resource Links

Barbara Kirby, Founder
A collection of web resources on Asperger's Syndrome and related topics. Hosted by the University of Delaware.

736   www.aspiesforfreedom.com
Aspies for Freedom

Aspies for Freedom (AFF) is a web site with chat rooms, forums and information relating to Austism and Asperger's Syndrome.

737   www.autism-society.org
Autism Society of America

Promotes lifelong access and opportunities for persons within the autism spectrum and their families, to be fully included, participating members of their communities through advocacy, public awareness, education and research related to autism.

738 **www.autism.org**
Center for the Study of Autism (CSA)

Located in the Salem/Portland, Oregon area. Provides information about autism to parents and professionals, and conducts research on the efficacy of various therapeutic interventions. Much of our research is in collaboration with the Autism Research Institute in San Diego, California.

739 **www.autismresearchinstitute.org**
Autism Research Institute

Devoted to conducting research on the causes of autism and on the methods of preventing, diagnosing and treating autism and other severe behavioral disorders of childhood.

740 **www.autismservicescenter.org**
Autism Services Center

Makes available technical assistance in designing programs. Provides supervised apartments, group homes, respite services, independent living programs and job-coached employment.

741 **www.autismspeaks.org**
National Alliance for Autism Research (NAAR)

National nonprofit, tax-exempt organization dedicated to finding the causes, preventions, effective treatments and, ultimately, a cure for the autism spectrum disorders. NAAR's mission is to fund, promote and support biomedical research into autism. Aims to have an aggressive and far-reaching research program. Seeks to encourage scientists outside the field of autism to apply their insights and experience to autism. Publishes a newsletter that focuses on developments in autism research. Supports brain banks and tissue consortium development.

742 **www.autisticservices.com**
Autistic Services

Dedicated to serving the unique lifelong needs of autistic individuals.

743 **www.cfsny.org**
Center for Family Support (CFS)

Devoted to the physical well-being and development of the retarded child and the sound mental health of the parents.

744 **www.csaac.org**
Community Services for Autistic Adults & Children

Enables individuals to achieve their highest potential and contribute as confident members in their community, instead of living in institutions.

745 **www.cyberpsych.org**
CyberPsych

Hosts the American Psychoanalyists Foundation, American Association of Suicideology, Society for the Exploration of Psychotherapy Intergration, and Anxiety Disorders Association of America. Also subcategories of the anxiety disorders, as well as general information, including panic disorder, phobias, obsessive compulsive disorder (OCD), social phobia, generalized anxiety disorder, post traumatic stress disorder, and phobias of childhood. Book reviews and links to web pages sharing the topics.

746 **www.feat.org**
Families for Early Autism Treatment

A nonprofit organization of parents and professionals, designed to help families with children who are diagnosised with autism or pervasive developmental disorder. It offers a network of support for families. FEAT has a Lending Library, with information on autism and also offers Support Meetings on the third Wednesday of each month.

747 **www.iidc.indiana.edu**
Indiana Resource Center for Autism (IRCA)

Conducts outreach training and consultations, engage in research and develop and disseminate info on behalf of individuals across the autism spectrum.

748 **www.ladders.org**
The Autism Research Foundation

A nonprofit, tax-exempt organization dedicated to researching the neurological underpinnings of autism and other related developmental brain disorders. Seeking to rapidly expand and accelerate research into the pervasive developmental disorders. To do this, time and efforts goes into investigating the neuropathology of autism in their laboratories, collecting and redistributing brain tissue to promising research groups for use by projects approved by the Tissue Resource Committee, studies frozen autistic brain tissue collected by TARF. They believe that only aggressive scientific and medical research will reveal the cure for this lifelong disorder.

749   www.maapservices.org
MAAP Services

Provides information and advice to people with Asperger Syndrome, Autism and Pervasive Developmental Disorders. Provides parents and professionals a chance to network with others to learn more within the autism spectrum.

750   www.mentalhealth.Samhsa.Gov
Center for Mental Health Services Knowledge Exchange Network

Information about resources, technical assistance, research, training, networks and other federal clearinghouses and fact sheets and materials.

751   www.mhselfhelp.org
National Mental Health Consumer's Self-Help Clearinghouse

Encourages the development and growth of consumer self-help groups.

752   www.nami.org
National Alliance on Mental Illness

From its inception in 1979, NAMI has been dedicated to improving the lives of individuals and families affected by mental illness.

753   www.necc.org
New England Center for Children

Serves students diagnosed with autism, learning disabilities, language delays, mental retardation, behavior disorders and related disabilities.

754   www.planetpsych.com
Planetpsych.com

Learn about disorders, their treatments and other topics in psychology. Articles are listed under the related topic areas. Ask a therapist a question for free, or view the directory of professionals in your area. If you are a therapist sign up for the directory. Current features, self-help, interactive, and newsletter archives.

755   www.resourcesnyc.org
Resources for Children with Special Needs

Gives a general introduction on autism, educational approaches, available resources, supplementary services, definitions and other related services are included.

756   www.son-rise.org
Son-Rise Autism Treatment Center of America

Training center for autism professionals and parents of autistic children. Programs focus on the design and implementation of home-based/child-centered alternatives.

757   www.thenadd.org
NADD-National Association for the Dually Diagnosed

Promotes the interest of professional and parent development with resources for individuals who have the coexistence of mental illness and mental retardation.

758   www.wrongplanet.net
Wrong Planet

WrongPlanet.net is a web community designed for individuals with Asperger's Syndrome and other PDDs. They provide a forum where members can communicate with each other, may read or submit essays or how-to guides about various subjects, and a chatroom for communication with other Aspies.

Conferences & Meetings

759   Asperger Syndrome Education Network (ASPEN) Conference
9 Aspen Circle
Edison, NJ 08820-2832
732-321-0880

Lori Shery, President
Annual conference.

760   MAAP Services
PO Box 524
Crown Point, IN 46308-524

219-662-1311
Fax: 219-662-0638
E-mail: chart@netnitco.net

MAAP Services Conference on Autism, Asperger Syndrome and Pervasive Development Disorders.

Directories & Databases

761 After School and More
Resources for Children with Special Needs
116 E 16th Street
5th Floor
New York, NY 10003-2164
212-677-4650
Fax: 212-254-4070
E-mail: info@resourcenyc.org
www.resourcesnyc.org

Rachel Howard, Executive Director

The most complete directory of after school programs for children with disabilities and special needs in the metropolitan New York area focusing on weekend and holiday programs. *$15.00*

252 pages ISBN 0-967836-57-3

Cognitive Disorders

Introduction

Cognitive disorders are a group of conditions characterized by impairments in the ability to think, reason, plan and organize. There are three types of cognitive disorders; delirium, dementia (of which Alzheimer's Disease is the most common) and amnestic disorder.

Delirium is a relatively short-term condition in which the level of conciousness waxes and wanes. It is common in patients after surgery or during illness, as with high fever. It resolves when the underlying problem resolves. There are three categories of causes of delirium: a general medical condition; substance-induced; and multiple causes. An amnestic disorder, in contrast to delirium or dementia, is a condition in which only memory is impaired; for instance the person is unable to recall important facts or events, making it difficult to function normally. Dementia is a chronic impairment of multiple cognitive functions. Persons with dementia may have severe memory loss and also be unable to plan or prepare for events or to care for themselves.

Dementia, Alzheimer's type, is a progressive disorder that slowly kills nerve cells in the brain. While definitive treatments are lacking, there is a prodigious amount of research on the condition, some of which suggests that a vaccine may be developed to prevent the condition. Though such hopeful breakthroughs remain distant, there is much that families and patients can do when the condition is recognized and care and support are sought early in the disorder's progression. Since other, serious, treatable disorders can resemble Alzeimer's Disease, it is very important for individuals who are losing cognitive functions to be evaluated by a physician. Early detection of Alzheimer's Disease, with early treatment, may improve the chances for slowing the rate of decline.

Here we will describe only Alzheimer's dementia, the most prevalent Cognitive Disorder.

SYMPTOMS

•Langugage disorders;
•Impaired ability to carry out motor activities despite intact motor function;
•Failure to recognize or identify objects despite intact sensory perception;
•Disturbance in executive functioning (planning, organizing, sequencing, abstracting);
•The deficits cause impairment in social or occupational functioning and represent a decline from previous level of functioning;
•The course is gradual and continuous;
•The deficits are not due to central nervous system conditions such as Parkinson's Disease, other conditions known to cause dementia, and are not substance-induced;
•The deficits do not occur during the course of delirium and are not better accounted for by severe depression or schizophrenia.

ASSOCIATED FEATURES

Dementia, Alzheimer's type, generally begins gradually, not with deficits in cognition but with a marked change in personality. For instance, a person may suddenly become given to fits of anger for no apparent reason.

Soon, however, family and acquaintances may notice that the individual begins to mix up facts, or gets lost driving to a familiar place. In the early stages the afflicted individual may become aware of slipping cognitive functions, adding to confusion, fright and depression. After a period, lapses in memory grow more obvious; patients with Alzheimer's are apt to repeat themselves, and may forget the names of grandchildren or longtime friends. They may also be increasingly agitated and combative when family members or other caretakers try to correct them or help with accustomed tasks. The memory lapses in patients with Alzheimer's differ markedly from those in normal aging: a patient with Alzheimer's may often forget entire experiences and rarely remembers them later; the patient only grudgingly acknowledges lapses. In contrast, the individual with normal aging or depression is extremely concerned about, and may even exaggerate, the extent of memory loss. In Alzheimer's, skills deteriorate and a patient is increasingly unable to follow directions, or care for him/herself. Eventually the disease leads to death.

PREVALENCE

An estimated two percent to four percent of the population over age 65 has dementia, Alzheimer's type. Other types of dementia are believed to be much less common. Prevalance of the condition increases with age, particularly after age 75; in persons over 85, an estimated twenty percent have dementia, Alzheimer's type.

TREATMENT OPTIONS

There is no known cure or definitive treatment for dementia, Alzheimer's type. However, research has suggested avenues that involve drugs, such as THA, Donepezil, and Rivastigmine, for regulating acetylcholine, seratonin or norepinephrine in the brain. According to the American Psychiatric Association, some progress has been seen in slowing the death rate among nerve cells using a chemical known as Alcar (acetyl-l-carnitine). Psychiatrists treating patients with dementia, Alzheimer's type, may also be able to prescribe medications that can treat the depression and anxiety that accompanies the condition. And families are strongly encouraged to take advantage of adjunctive services including support groups, counseling and psychotherapy. There is a high incidence of depression among family members caring at home for persons with Alzheimer's Disease.

Associations & Agencies

763 Alzheimer's Association National Office
225 N Michigan Avenue
Suite 1000
Chicago, IL 60601-7617
312-335-8700
888-572-8566
Fax: 312-335-5886
TDD: 866-403-3073
E-mail: info@alz.org

Harry Johns, CEO

Headquarters for the nation's leading organization for all those suffering with alzheimer's disease and their families and support network. Offers referrals, support groups, workshops, training seminars, publications.

764 Alzheimer's Disease Education and Referral Center
PO Box 8250
Silver Spring, MD 20907-8250
301-495-3311
800-438-4380
Fax: 301-495-3334
TTY: 800-222-4225
E-mail: adear@alzheimers.org
www.alzheimers.org

Alison Serey, Executive Director

The ADEAR Center provides information about Alzheimer's Disease and related disorders to health professionals, patients and their families, and the public.

765 American Health Assistance Foundation
22512 Gateway Center Drive
Clarksburg, MD 20871-2005
301-948-3244
800-437-2423
Fax: 301-258-9454
E-mail: janthony@ahaf.org
www.ahaf.org

Kathy Honaker, Executive Director
Jonathan Rise, Esq, VP
Gayle Handiboe, Manager Of Development

Provides information on treatment, symptoms risk factors and healthy exercises.

766 Center for Family Support (CFS)
333 7th Avenue
New York, NY 10001-5115
212-629-7939
Fax: 212-239-2211
www.cfsny.org

Steven Vernikoff, Executive Director
Melaine Singleton, Director Human Resources

Service agency devoted to the physical well-being and development of the retarded child and the sound mental health of the parents. Helps families with retarded children with all aspects of home care including counseling, referrals, home aide service and consultation. Offers intervention for parents at the birth of a retarded child with in-home support, guidance and infant stimulation. Pioneered training of nonprofessional women as home aides to provide supportive services in homes.

767 Center for Mental Health Services (CMHS)
PO Box 2345
Rockville, MD 20847
240-221-4021
800-789-2647
Fax: 240-221-4295

TDD: 866-889-2647
www.mentalhealth.samhsa.gov

A Kathryn Power, MEd, Director
Anna Marsh PhD, Deputy Director
Fran Randolph PhD, Dir, Service & Systems Improveme
Anne Mathews-Younes EdD, Dir, Prevention/Traumatic Stress

CMHS leads Federal efforts to treat mental illnesses by promoting mental health and by preventing the development or worsening of mental illness when possible. Congress created CMHS to bring new hope to adults who have serious mental illnesses and to children with serious emotional disorders. CMHS provides information about mental health via a toll-free the web site, and more than 600 publications. Developed for users of mental health services and their families, the general public, policy makers, providers, and the media.

Year Founded: 1992

768 National Association Councils on Developmental Disabilities
1660 L Street NW
Suite 700
Washington, DC 20036
202-506-5813
Fax: 202-506-5846
E-mail: info@nacdd.org
www.nacdd.org

Michael Brogioli, CEO

A national membership organization representing the 55 State and Territorial Councils on Developmental Disabilities. An organization with the purpose of promoting and enhancing the outcomes of our member councils in developing and sustaining inclusive communities and self direceted services and supports for individuals with developmental disabilities.

769 National Association for the Dually Diagnosed (NADD)
132 Fair Street
Kingston, NY 12401-4802
845-331-4336
800-331-5362
Fax: 845-331-4569
E-mail: info@thenadd.org
www.thenadd.org

Robert Fletcher, Executive Director

Nonprofit organization designed to promote interest of professional and parent development with resources for individuals who have the coexistence of mental illness and mental retardation. Provides conference, educational services and training materials to professionals, parents, concerned citizens and service organizations. Formerly known as the National Association for the Dually Diagnosed.

Year Founded: 1983

770 National Family Caregivers Association
10400 Connecticut Avenue
Suite 500
Kensington, MD 20895-3944

301-942-6430
800-896-3650
E-mail: info@thefamilycaregiver.org
www.thefamilycaregiver.org

Suzanne Mintz, President
Cindy Fowler, Co-Founder/Secretary

Acts as a support and an advocate for family caregivers.

771 National Institute of Neurological Disorders and Stroke
NIH Neurological Institute
PO Box 5801
Bethesda, MD 20824-5801
301-496-5751
800-352-9424
Fax: 301-402-2186
TTY: 301-468-5981
E-mail: braininfo@ninds.nih.gov
www.ninds.nih.gov

Story C Landis, PhD, Director
Audrey S Penn, MD, Deputy Director

Federal agency that supports research nationwide on disorders of the brain and nervous system. Website has updated neuroscience news and articles.

772 National Mental Health Consumers' Self-Help Clearinghouse
1211 Chestnut Street
Suite 1207
Philadelphia, PA 19107-4103
215-751-1810
800-553-4539
Fax: 215-636-6312
E-mail: info@mhselfhelp.org
www.mhselfhelp.org

Joseph Rogers, Executive Director

A national consumer technical assistance center that has played a major role in the development of the mental health consumer movement.

Year Founded: 1986

773 National Niemann-Pick Disease Foundation
401 Madison Avenue, Suite B
PO Box 49
Ft Atkinson, WI 53538-49
920-563-0930
877-287-3672
Fax: 920-563-0931
E-mail: nnpdf@idcnet.com
www.nnpdf.org

Nadine Hill, Director of Family Services

Offers support and funding for individuals with cognitive disorders and their support network.

774 SAMHSA's National Mental Health Information Center
US Department of Health and Human Services
PO Box 42490
Washington, DC 20015

240-221-4021
800-789-2647
Fax: 240-221-4295
TDD: 866-889-2647
www.mentalhealth.smahsa.gov

Provides information about mental health via a toll-free telephone number, this web site, and more than 600 publications. Developed for users of mental health services and their families, the general public, policy makers, providers, and the media.

Books

775 Agitation in Patients with Dementia: a Practical Guide to Diagnosis and Management
American Psychiatric Publishing, Inc.
1000 Wilson Boulevard
Suite 1825
Arlington, VA 22209-3901
703-907-7322
800-368-5777
Fax: 703-907-1091
E-mail: appi@psych.org
www.appi.org

Robert E Hales MD, Editor-in-Chief
Ron McMillen, Chief Executive Officer
John McDuffie, Editorial Director

Appealing to a wide audience of geriatric psychiatrists, primary care physicians and internists, general practitioners, nurses, social workers, psychologists, pharmacists and mental health care workers and practitioners in hospitals, nursing homes and clinics, this remarkable monograph offers practical direction on assessing and managing agitation in patients with dementia. *$57.00*

250 pages Year Founded: 2003 ISBN 0-880488-43-3

776 Alzheimer's Disease Sourcebook
Omnigraphics
PO Box 625
Holmes, PA 19043-625

800-234-1340
Fax: 800-875-1340
E-mail: info@omnigraphics.com
www.omnigraphics.com

Omnigraphics is the publisher of the Health Reference Series, a growing consumer health information resource with more than 100 volumes in print. Each title in the series features an easy to understand format, nontechnical language, comprehensive indexing and resources for further information. Material in each book has been collected from a wide range of government agencies, professional associations, periodicals, and other sources. *$78.00*

524 pages ISBN 0-780802-23-3

777 Alzheimer's Disease: Activity-Focused Care, Second Edition
Therapeutic Resources
PO Box 16814
Cleveland, OH 44116-814
440-331-7114
888-331-7114
Fax: 440-331-7118
E-mail: contactus@therapeuticresources.com
www.therapeuticresources.com

Katie Hennessy, LCSW, Medical Promotions Coordinator

Provides practical and innovative strategies for care of people with Alzheimer's disease, emphasizing the activities that make up daily living - dressing, toileting, eating, exercising, and communication. The text is written from the viewpoint that activity-focused care promotes the resident's cognitive, physical, psychosocial, and spiritual well-being.

436 pages ISBN 0-750699-08-6

778 American Psychiatric Association Practice Guideline for the Treatment of Patients with Delirium
American Psychiatric Publishing, Inc.
1000 Wilson Boulevard
Suite 1825
Arlington, VA 22209-3901
703-907-7322
800-368-5777
Fax: 703-907-1091
E-mail: appi@psych.org
www.appi.org

Robert E Hales MD, Editor-in-Chief
Ron McMillen, Chief Executive Officer
John McDuffie, Editorial Director

Best practices examined from the group whose vision is a society that has available, accessible quality psychiatric diagnosis and treatment. *$30.95*

75 pages Year Founded: 1999 ISBN 0-890423-13-X

779 Behavioral Complications in Alzheimer's Disease
American Psychiatric Publishing, Inc.
1000 Wilson Boulevard
Suite 1825
Arlington, VA 22209-3901
703-907-7322
800-368-5777
Fax: 703-907-1091
E-mail: appi@psych.org
www.appi.org

Robert E Hales MD, Editor-in-Chief
Ron McMillen, Chief Executive Officer
John McDuffie, Editorial Director

Practical management strategies for the identification, measurement and treatment of behavioral symptoms in patient with Alzheimer's disease. *$36.50*

272 pages Year Founded: 1995 ISBN 0-880484-77-2

780 Care That Works: A Relationship Approach to Persons With Dementia
Johns Hopkins University Press
2715 N Charles Street
Baltimore, MD 21218-4319
410-516-6900
800-537-5487
Fax: 410-516-6998

William Brody, President
Jitka M Zagola, Author

Provides caregivers the information with which they can develop their own approaches, evaluate their effectiveness, and continue to grow in skill and insight. Real life strategies for a challenging task. *$58.00*

272 pages Year Founded: 1999 ISBN 0-801860-25-3

781 Cognitive Therapy in Practice
WW Norton & Company
500 5th Avenue
New York, NY 10110-54
212-354-2907
800-233-4830
Fax: 212-869-0856
E-mail: npd@wwnorton.com

Drake McFeely, CEO

Basic text for graduate studies in psychotherapy, psycholgy nursing social work and counseling. *$29.00*

224 pages Year Founded: 1989 ISBN 0-393700-77-1

782 Dementia: A Clinical Approach
Elsevier Health Sciences
11830 Westline Industrial Drive
St. Louis, MO 63146-3313
314-872-8370
800-568-5136
Fax: 314-432-1380
E-mail: orders@bhusa.com or custserv@bhusa.com
www.elsevier.com

Erik Engstrom, CEO
Jeffrey L Cummings, Author

Third Edition, this is both a scholarly review of the dementias and a practical guide to their diagnosis and treatment. *$99.00*

654 pages Year Founded: 2003 ISBN 0-750674-70-9

783 Disorders of Brain and Mind: Volume 1
Cambridge University Press
40 W 20th Street
New York, NY 10011-4211
212-924-3900
Fax: 212-691-3239
E-mail: marketing@cup.org
www.cup.org

Maria A Ron, Editor
Anthony S David, Editor

Discusses various neuropsychiatry topics where the brain and mind come together. *$65.00*

388 pages Year Founded: 1999 ISBN 0-521778-51-4

784 Drug Therapy and Cognitive Disorders
Mason Crest Publishers
370 Reed Road
Suite 302
Broomall, PA 19008-4017
610-543-6200
866-627-2665
Fax: 610-543-3878
E-mail: dtaylor@masoncrest.com
www.masoncrest.com

Alzheimer's disease is one of the most common cognitive disorder, one that affects millions of people. Patients, caregivers and loved ones all suffer as they experience the devastation of this often misunderstood disease. Researchers are working hard to find a cure for the symptoms of Alzheimer's and other cognitive disorders, and this book describes the most recent research. Coauthored by someone who has experienced the early stages of Alzheimer's firsthand, this volume will give readers a new understanding and appreciation of the treatment options for those who experience a cognitive disorder.

ISBN 1-590845-62-5

785 Progress in Alzheimer's Disease and Similar Conditions
American Psychiatric Publishing, Inc.
1000 Wilson Boulevard
Suite 1825
Arlington, VA 22209-3901
703-907-7322
800-368-5777
Fax: 703-907-1091
E-mail: appi@psych.org
www.appi.org

Robert E Hales MD, Editor-in-Chief
Ron McMillen, Chief Executive Officer
John McDuffie, Editorial Director

Details advances in research on human genetics that is broadening our knowledge of Alzheimer's disease and other related afflictions. Describes disease mechanisms, including prisons, that provide insight into the role environment plays in the development of disease. Includes stories about the pain inflicted by this disease on the patients and their family and friends as well as current efforts in management and treatment. *$77.00*

318 pages Year Founded: 1997 ISBN 0-880487-60-7

786 Treating Complex Cases: The Cognitive Behavioral Therapy Approach
John Wiley & Sons
605 3rd Avenue
New York, NY 10158-180
212-850-6301
E-mail: info@wiley.com
www.wiley.com

Nicholas Tarrierk, Editor
Adrian Wells, Editor
Gillian Haddock, Editor

This book brings together some of the most experiences and expert cognitive behavioral therapists to share their specialist experience of formulation and treatment of complex problems such as co-morbidity, psychotic conditions, and chronic conditions. The experienced clinician will find: evidence-based approaches to assessment and formulation of complex cases; a wide range of problems not restricted to disorder categories, including anger, low self-esteem, abuse and shame; a concern with the realities of clinical practice which involves complex cases that do not fit into simple case conceptualisations or diagnostic categories. Copyright 2000. *$80.00*

456 pages ISBN 0-471978-39-8

787 Victims of Dementia: Service, Support, and Care
Haworth Press
10 Alice Street
Binghamton, NY 13904-1503
607-722-5857
800-429-6784
Fax: 607-721-0012
E-mail: getinfo@haworthpressinc.com
www.haworthpress.com

Jackie Blakeslee, Advertising/Journal Liaison
William M Clemmer, PhD, Editor

Provides an in depth look at the concept, construction and operation of Wesley Hall, a special living area at the Chelsea United Methodist retirement home in Michigan. *$27.95*

155 pages Year Founded: 1993 ISSN 978156024-265-9

Periodicals & Pamphlets

788 Alzheimer's Disease Research and the American Health Assistance Foundation
American Health Assistance Foundation
22512 Gateway Center Drive
Clarksburg, MD 20871-2005
301-948-3244
800-437-2423
Fax: 301-258-9454
E-mail: jwilson@ahaf.org
www.ahaf.org

Kathy Honaker, Executive Director

Provides information on treatment, medication, medical referrals.

Video & Audio

789 A Change of Character
Fanlight Productions
2
47 Halifax St
Jamaica Plain, MA 02130-4327
617-469-4999
Fax: 617-439-3379
E-mail: fanlight@fanlight.com
www.fanlight.com

Truett Allen's personality changed drastically after a series of strokes resulted in damage to the frontal lobes of his brain. this captivating video features neuroscientist Dr. Elkhonon Goldberg, author of The Executive Brain, as well as neurologist and best-selling author Dr. Oliver Sacks.

790 Effective Learning Systems

3451 Bonita Bay Boulevard
Suite 205
Bonita Springs, FL 34134-4354
239-948-1660
800-966-5683
Fax: 239-948-1664
E-mail: info@efflearn.com
www.efflearn.com

Robert E Griswold, President
Deirdre M Griswold, VP

Audio tapes for stress management, deep relaxation, anger control, peace of mind, insomnia, weight and smoking, self-image and self-esteem, positive thinking, health and healing. Since 1972, Effective Learning Systems has helped millions of people take charge of their lives and make positive changes. Over 75 titles available, each with a money-back guarantee. Price range $12-$14.

Web Sites

791 www.Nia.Nih.Gov/Alzheimers
Alzheimer's Disease Education and Referral

Fax: 301-495-3334

A division of the National Institute on Aging of the National Institute of Health. Solid information and a list of federally funded centers for evaluation, referral, treatment.

792 www.aan.com
American Academy of Neurology

Provides information for both professionals and the public on neurology subjects, covering Alzheimer's and Parkinson's diseases to stroke and migraine, includes comprehensive fact sheets.

793 www.agelessdesign.com
Ageless Design

Information on age related diseases such as Alzheimer's disease.

794 www.ahaf.org/alzdis/about/adabout.htm
American Health Assistance Foundation

Alzheimer's resource for patients and caregivers.

795 www.alz.co.uk
Alzheimer's Disease International

Umbrella organization of associations that support people with dementia.

796 www.alzforum.org
Alzheimer Research Forum

Information in layman's terms, plus many references and resources listed.

797 www.alzheimersbooks.com/
Alzheimer's Disease Bookstore

798 www.alzheimersupport.Com
AlzheimerSupport.com

Information and products for people dealing with Alzheimer's Disease.

799 www.biostat.wustl.edu
Washington University - Saint Louis

Page on Alzheimer's information, from basic care to friends and family networking experiences for support.

800 www.cyberpsych.org
CyberPsych

Hosts the American Psychoanalyists Foundation, American Association of Suicideology, Society for the Exploration of Psychotherapy Intergration, and Anxiety Disorders Association of America. Also subcategories of the anxiety disorders, as well as general information, including panic disorder, phobias, obsessive compulsive disorder (OCD), social phobia, generalized anxiety disorder, post traumatic stress disorder, and phobias of childhood. Book reviews and links to web pages sharing the topics.

801 www.elderlyplace.com
Elderly Place

Includes Caregiver's Guide to Alzheimer's.

802 **www.habitsmart.com/cogtitle.html**
Cognitive Therapy Pages

Offers accessible explanations.

803 **www.mayohealth.org/mayo/common/htm/**
MayoClinic.com

Information for dealing with Alzheimer's Disease.

804 **www.mentalhealth.com**
Internet Mental Health

On-line information and a virtual encyclopedia related to mental disorders, possible causes and treatments. News, articles, on-line diagnostic programs and related links. Designed to improve understanding, diagnosis and treatment of mental illness throughout the world. Awarded the Top Site Award and the NetPsych Cutting Edge Site Award.

805 **www.mentalhealth.smahsa.gov**
SMAHSA'S National Mental Health Information Center

US Department of Health and Human Services website with current Alzheimer's information.

806 **www.mindstreet.com/training.html**
Cognitive Therapy: A Multimedia Learning Program

The basics of cognitive therapy are presented.

807 **www.ninds.nih.gov**
National Institute of Neurological Disorders & Stroke

Neuroscience updates and articles.

808 **www.noah-health.org/en/bns/disorders/**
alzheimer.html
Ask NOAH About: Aging and Alzheimer's Disease

Links to brochures on medical problems of the elderly.

809 **www.ohioalzcenter.org/facts.html**
University Memory and Aging Center

Alzheimer's disease fact page.

810 **www.planetpsych.com**
Planetpsych.com

Learn about disorders, their treatments and other topics in psychology. Articles are listed under the related topic areas. Ask a therapist a question for free, or view the directory of professionals in your area. If you are a therapist sign up for the directory. Current features, self-help, interactive, and newsletter archives.

811 **www.psych.org/clin_res/pg_dementia.cfm**
American Psychiatric Association

Practice guidelines for the treatment of patients with Alzheimer's.

812 **www.psychcentral.com**
Psych Central

Personalized one-stop index for psychology, support, and mental health issues, resources, and people on the Internet.

813 **www.rcpsych.ac.uk/info/help/memory**
Royal College of Psychiatrists

Memory and Dementia

814 **www.zarcrom.com/users/alzheimers**
Alzheimer's Outreach

Detailed and practical information.

815 **www.zarcrom.com/users/yeartorem**
Year to Remember

A memorial site covering many aspects of Alzheimer's disease.

Conduct Disorder

Introduction

Conduct disorder is characterized by a repetitive and persistent pattern of behavior in which societal norms and the basic rights of others are violated. These behaviors can include physical harm to people or animals, damage to property, deceitfulness or theft, and extreme violations of rules. It is important to note that troublesome behavior can also result from adverse circumstances; the circumstances need to be fully investigated, and attempts to rectify adversity made, before Conduct Disorder is diagnosed. The diagnosis can be divided into two types, depending on the age of diagnosis: childhood-onset type and adolescent-onset type.

SYMPTOMS

•Aggression to people and animals, including bullying, picking fights, using weapons, physical cruelty to people and animals, stealing or forcing someone into sexual activity;
•Destruction of property;
•Deceitfulness or theft, including breaking into someone's house, lying to obtain goods or favors, or shoplifting;
•Violations of rules, including staying out past curfews, running away from home, and truancy from school.

ASSOCIATED FEATURES

Conduct disorder is often associated with early onset of sexual activity, drinking and smoking. The disorder leads to school disruption, problems with the police, sexually transmitted diseases, unplanned pregnancy, and injury from accidents and fights. Suicide and suicidal attempts are more common among adolescents with Conduct Disorder, probably both because they have a history of abuse and neglect and because their behavior results in adverse consequences. Individuals with Conduct Disorder appear to have little remorse for their acts, though they may learn that expressing guilt can diminish punishment; and they often show little or no empathy for the feelings, wishes, and well-being of others.

PREVALENCE

Prevalence of Conduct Disorder appears to have increased in recent years. For males under 18 years of age, rates range from six percent to sixteen percent; for females, rates range from two percent to nine percent.

TREATMENT OPTIONS

Both psychotherapy and medication can be useful in treating Conduct Disorder. This condition is stressful for family members of the affected child or adolescent; it is crucial that they are supported and involved in the treatment.

Associations & Agencies

817 Association for Behavioral and Cognitive Therapies
305 Seventh Avenue
16th Floor
New York, NY 10001-6008
212-647-1890
Fax: 212-647-1865
E-mail: mebrown@aabt.org
www.aabt.org

Mary Jane Eimer, Executive Director
Mary Ellen Brown, Administration/Convention
Lisa Yarde, Membership

Membership listing of mental health professionals focusing in behavior therapy.

818 Career Assessment & Planning Services
Goodwill Industries-Suncoast
10596 Gandy Boulevard
St. Petersburg, FL 33702-1427
727-523-1512
Fax: 727-563-9300
www.goodwill.org

Lee Waits, President
Jay McCloe, Resource Development

Provides a comprehensive assessment, which can predict current and future employment and potential adjustment factors for physically, emotionally, or developmentally disabled persons who may be unemployed or underemployed. Assessments evaluate interests, aptitudes, academic achievements, and physical abilities (including dexterity and coordination) through coordinated testing, interviewing and behavioral observations.

819 Center for Family Support (CFS)
333 7th Avenue
New York, NY 10001-5115
212-629-7939
Fax: 212-239-2211
www.cfsny.org

Steven Vernikoff, Executive Director
Melanie Singleton, Director Human Resource

Service agency devoted to the physical well-being and development of the retarded child and the sound mental health of the parents. Helps families with retarded children with all aspects of home care including counseling, referrals, home aide service and consultation. Offers intervention for parents at the birth of a retarded child with in-home support, guidance and infant stimulation. Pioneered training of nonprofessional women as home aides to provide supportive services in homes.

820 National Association for the Dually Diagnosed (NADD)
132 Fair Street
Kingston, NY 12401-4802
845-331-4336
800-331-5362
Fax: 845-331-4569
E-mail: info@thenadd.org
www.thenadd.org

Robert Fletcher, Executive Director

Nonprofit organization designed to promote interest of professional and parent development with resources for individuals who have the coexistence of mental illness and mental retardation. Provides conference, educational services and training materials to professionals, parents, concerned citizens and service organizations. Formerly known as the National Association for the Dually Diagnosed.

Year Founded: 1983

821 National Mental Health Consumers' Self-Help Clearinghouse

1211 Chestnut Street
Suite 1207
Philadelphia, PA 19107-4103
215-751-1810
800-553-4539
Fax: 215-636-6312
E-mail: info@mhselfhelp.org
www.mhselfhelp.org

Joseph Rogers, Executive Director

A national consumer technical assistance center that has played a major role in the development of the mental health consumer movement.

Year Founded: 1986

Books

822 Antisocial Behavior by Young People
Cambridge University Press

40 W 20th Street
New York, NY 10011-4211
212-924-3900
Fax: 212-691-3239
E-mail: marketing@cup.org
www.cup.org

Michael Rutter, MRC Child Psychiarty Unit
Ann Hagell
Henri Giller

Written by a child psychiatrist, a criminologist and a social psychologist, this book is a major international review of research evidence on anti-social behavior. Covers all aspects of the field, including descriptions of different types of delinquency and time trends, the state of knowledge on the individuals, social-psychological and cultural factors involved and recent advances in prevention and intervention. *$22.99*

490 pages Year Founded: 1998

823 Bad Men Do What Good Men Dream: a Forensic Psychiatrist Illuminates the Darker Side of Human Behavior
American Psychiatric Publishing, Inc.

1000 Wilson Boulevard
Suite 1825
Arlington, VA 22209-3901
703-907-7322
800-368-5777
Fax: 703-907-1091

E-mail: appi@psych.org
www.appi.org

Robert E Hales MD, Editor-in-Chief
Ron McMillen, Chief Executive Officer
John McDuffie, Editorial Director

Provides insights into the minds of rapists, stalkers, serial killers, psychopaths, professional exploiters, and other individuals whose behavior both frightens and fascinates us. *$32.50*

376 pages Year Founded: 1996 ISBN 0-880489-95-2

824 Conduct Disorders in Childhood and Adolescence, Developmental Clinical Psychology and Psychiatry
Sage Publications

2455 Teller Road
Thousand Oaks, CA 91320-2234
805-499-0721
800-818-7243
Fax: 805-499-0871
E-mail: info@sagepub.com
www.sagepub.com

Blaise R Simqu, CEO
Alan E Kazdin, Author

Conduct disorder is a clinical problem among children and adolescents that includes aggressive acts, theft, vandalism, firesetting, running away, truancy, defying authority and other antisocial behaviors. This book describes the nature of conduct disorder and what is currently known from research and clinical work. Topics include psychiatric diagnosis, parent psychopathology and child-rearing processes. Paperback also available. *$51.95*

191 pages Year Founded: 1995 ISBN 0-803971-81-8

825 Creative Therapy 2: Working with Parents
Impact Publishers

PO Box 6016
Atascadero, CA 93423-6016
805-466-5917
800-246-7228
Fax: 805-466-5919
E-mail: info@impactpublishers.com
www.impactpublishers.com

Kate M Ollier, Psych, Author
Angela M Hobday, Sc, Author

Sequel and companion volume to the authors' highly successful Creative Therapy with Children and Adolesents. Creative Therapy 2 offers practicing therapists a wealth of resources for working with parents whose children are experiencing emotional and/or behavioral problems. The procedures and exercises are carefully crafted to provide help even when the parents have been less than understanding - or perhaps even abusive toward their children. Therapists will find dozens of creative ways to form good working relationships with parents, and to prepare them to help their children. *$21.95*

192 pages Year Founded: 2001 ISBN 1-886230-42-0

826 Difficult Child
Bantam Doubleday Dell Publishing
1745 Broadway
New York, NY 10019-4343
212-782-9000
E-mail: books@randomhouse.com

Jeff Rechtzigel, Publisher
Stanley Turecki, Author

Help for parents dealing with behavioral problems. *$ 17.00*

320 pages Year Founded: 2000 ISBN 0-553380-36-2

827 Dysinhibition Syndrome How to Handle Anger and Rage in Your Child or Spouse
Hope Press
PO Box 188
Duarte, CA 91009-188
818-303-0644
800-321-4039
Fax: 818-358-3520
www.hopepress.com

Rose Wood, Author

How to understand and handle rage and anger in your children or spouse. The book presents behavioral approaches that can be very effective and an understanding that can be family saving. *$24.95*

271 pages Year Founded: 1999 ISBN 1-878267-08-6

828 Helping Parents, Youth, and Teachers Understand Medications for Behavioral and Emotional Problems
American Psychiatric Publishing, Inc.
1000 Wilson Boulevard
Suite 1825
Arlington, VA 22209-3901
703-907-7322
800-368-5777
Fax: 703-907-1091
E-mail: appi@psych.org
www.appi.org

Robert E Hales MD, Editor-in-Chief
Ron McMillen, Chief Executive Officer
John McDuffie, Editorial Director

Resource Book of Medication Information Handouts, Second Edition. Valuable resource for anyone involved in evaluating psychiatric disturbances in children and adolescents. Provides a compilation of information sheets to help promote the dialogue between the patient's family, caregivers and the treating physician. *$62.00*

205 pages Year Founded: 2003 ISBN 1-585620-41-6

829 Preventing Antisocial Behavior Interventions from Birth through Adolescence
Guilford Publications
72 Spring Street
New York, NY 10012-4068
212-431-9800
800-365-7006
Fax: 212-966-6708
E-mail: info@guilford.com

Bob Matloff, President
Joan McCord, Editor
Richard E Tremblay, Editor

Establishes the crucial link between theory, measurement, and intervention. Brings together a collection of studies that utilize experimental approaches for evaluating intervention programs for preventing deviant behavior. Demonstrates both the feasibility and necessity of independent evaluation. Also shows how the information obtained in such studies can be used to test and refine prevailing theories about human behavior in general and behavior changes in particular. *$55.00*

391 pages Year Founded: 1992 ISBN 0-898628-82-2

830 Skills Training for Children with Behavior Disorders
Courage to Change
PO Box 486
Wilkes-Barre, PA 18703-486

800-440-4003
Fax: 800-772-6499
www.couragetochange.com

Michael L Bloomquist, Author

Written for both parents and therapists, this book provides backround, instructions, and many reproducible worksheets. Academic success, anger management, emotional well being and compliance/following rules are covered. *$36.00*

272 pages Year Founded: 1996 ISBN 1-572300-80-9

Periodicals & Pamphlets

831 Conduct Disorder in Children and Adolescents
SAMHSA'S National Mental Health Information Center
PO Box 42557
Washington, DC 20015-557

800-789-2647
Fax: 240-747-5470
TDD: 866-889-2647
E-mail: ken@mentalhealth.org
www.mentalhealth.samhsa.gov

A Kathryn Power, MEd, Director
Edward B Searle, Deputy Director

This fact sheet defines conduct disorder, identifies risk factors, discusses types of help available, and suggests what parents or other caregivers can do.

2 pages

832 Mental, Emotional, and Behavior Disorders in Children and Adolescents
SAMHSA'S National Mental Health Information Center
PO Box 42557
Washington, DC 20015-557

800-789-2647
Fax: 240-747-5470
TDD: 866-889-2647
E-mail: ken@mentalhealth.org
www.mentalhealth.samhsa.gov

A Kathryn Power, MEd, Director
Edward B Searle, Deputy Director

This fact sheet describes mental, emotional, and behavioral problems that can occur during childhood and adolescence and discusses related treatment, support services, and research.

4 pages

833 Treatment of Children with Mental Disorders
National Institute of Mental Health
6001 Executive Boulevard
Room 8184
Bethesda, MD 20892-1
301-443-4513
866-615-6464
TTY: 301-443-8431
E-mail: nimhinfo@nih.gov

Dr Thomas R Insel, Director
Ruth Dubois, Assistant Chief

A short booklet that contains questions and answers about therapy for children with mental disorders. Includes a chart of mental disorders and medications used.

Year Founded: 2004

Research Centers

834 Child & Family Center
Menninger Clinic
2801 Gessner Drive
Houston, TX 77080-2503
713-275-5000
800-351-9058
Fax: 713-275-5117
E-mail: webmaster@menninger.edu

Ian Aitken, CEO

The Center's goals: to further develop emerging understanding of the impact of childhood maltreatment and abuse; to chart primary prevention strategies that will foster healthy patterns of caregiving and attachment and reduce the prevalence of maltreatment and abuse; to develop secondary prevention strategies that will promote early detection of attachment-related problems and effective interventions to avert the development of chronic and severe disorders; and to develop more effective treatment approaches for those individuals whose early attachment problems have eventuated in severe psychopathology.

Video & Audio

835 Active Parenting Now
Active Parenting Publishers
1955 Vaughn Road NW
Suite 108
Kennesaw, GA 30144-7808
770-429-0565
800-825-0060
Fax: 770-429-0334
E-mail: cservice@activeparenting.com

Michael H Popkin, MD, Author

A complete video-based parenting education program curriculum. Helps parents of children ages two to twelve raise responsible, courageous children. Emphasizes nonviolent discipline, conflict resolution and improved communication. With Leader's Guide, videotapes, Parent's Guide and more. Also available in Spanish. *$ 349.00*

Year Founded: 2002 ISBN 1-880283-89-1

836 Aggression Replacement Training Video: A Comprehensive Intervention for Aggressive Youth
Research Press
Dept 24 W
PO Box 9177
Champaign, IL 61826-9177
217-352-3273
800-519-2707
Fax: 217-352-1221
E-mail: rp@researchpress.com
www.researchpress.com

Dennis Wiziecki, Marketing

This staff training video illustrates the training procedures in the Aggression Replacement Training (ART) book. It features scenes of adolescents participating in group sessions for each of ART's three interventions: Prosocial Skills, Anger Control, and Moral Reasoning. A free copy of the book accompanies the video program. *$125.00*

837 Understanding & Managing the Defiant Child
Courage to Change
PO Box 486
Wilkes-Barre, PA 18703-486

800-440-4003
Fax: 800-772-6499
www.couragetochange.com

Russell A Barkley, PhD, Presenter

Understanding and Managing the Defiant Child provides a proven approach to behavior management. *$205.95*

838 Understanding and Treating the Hereditary Psychiatric Spectrum Disorders
Hope Press
PO Box 188
Duarte, CA 91009-188
818-303-0644
800-321-4039
Fax: 818-358-3520
www.hopepress.com

David E Comings MD, Presenter

Learn with ten hours of audio tapes from a two day seminar given in May 1997 by David E Comings, MD. Tapes cover: ADHD, Tourette Syndrome, Obsessive-Compulsive Disorder, Conduct Disorder, Oppositional Defiant Disorder, Autism and other Hereditary Psychiatric Spectrum Disorders. Eight audio tapes. *$75.00*

Year Founded: 1997

Web Sites

839 www.cyberpsych.org
CyberPsych

Hosts the American Psychoanalyists Foundation, American Association of Suicideology, Society for the Exploration of Psychotherapy Intergration, and Anxiety Disorders Association of America. Also subcategories of the anxiety disorders, as well as general information, including panic disorder, phobias, obsessive compulsive disorder (OCD), social phobia, generalized anxiety disorder, post traumatic stress disorder, and phobias of childhood. Book reviews and links to web pages sharing the topics.

840 www.planetpsych.com
PlanetPsych.com

Learn about disorders, their treatments and other topics in psychology. Articles are listed under the related topic areas. Ask a therapist a question for free, or view the directory of professionals in your area. If you are a therapist sign up for the directory. Current features, self-help, interactive, and newsletter archives.

841 www.psychcentral.com
Psych Central

Personalized one-stop index for psychology, support, and mental health issues, resources, and people on the Internet.

Dissociative Disorders

Introduction

Dissociative Disorders are a cluster of mental disorders, characterized by a profound change in consciousness or a disruption in continuity of consciousness. People with a Dissociative Disorder may abruptly take on different personalities, or undergo long periods in which they do not remember anything that happened; in some cases, individuals may embark on lengthy international travels, returning home with no recollection of where they have been or why they had gone.

Dissociative Disorders are uncommon, mysterious and somewhat controversial; reports of Dissociative Disorders have grown more frequent in recent years and a degree of debate surrounds the validity of these reports. Some professionals say the disorders are far more rare than is reported, and that these individuals are highly vulnerable to the suggestions of others.

Dissociative Disorders are believed to be related in many cases to severe trauma, although the historical validity of these cases is difficult to determine. There are five types of Dissociative Disorders: Dissociative Amnesia; Dissociative Fugue; Dissociative Identity Disorder; Depersonalization Disorder; and Dissociative Disorder Not Otherwise Specified.

SYMPTOMS

Dissociative Amnesia
•One or more episodes of inability to recall important personal information, usually of a traumatic or stressful nature, that is too extensive to be explained by ordinary forgetfulness;
•The disturbance does not occur exclusively during the course of any other Dissociative Disorder and is not due to the direct physiological effects of a substance abuse or general medical condition;
•The symptoms cause clinically significant distress or impairment in social, occupational or other important areas of functioning.

Associative Fugue
•A sudden, unexpected travel away from home or work, with inability to recall one's past;
•Confusion about personal identity or assumption of a new identity;
•The disturbance does not occur exclusively during the course of any other Dissociative Disorder and is not due to the direct physiological effects of a substance or a general medical condition;
•The symptoms cause clinically significant distress or impairment in social, occupational, or other important areas of functioning.

Dissociative Identity Disorder
•The presence of two or more distinct identities or personality states that take control of the person's behavior;
•Inability to recall important personal information;
•The disturbance is not due to the direct physiological effects of a substance or a general medical condition.

Depersonalization Disorder

•Persistent or rec urrent experiences of feeling detached from one's body and mental processes;
•During the depersonalization experience, reality testing remains intact;
•The depersonalization causes clinically significant distress or impairment in social, occupational, or other important areas of functioning;
•The depersonalization does not occur during the course of another Dissociative Disorder or as a direct physiological effect of a substance or general medical condition;
•Akin to depersonalization (feeling one is not real) is derealization, which is feeling that one's environment and/or perceptions are not real.

ASSOCIATED FEATURES

Patients with any of the Dissociative Disorders may be depressed, and may experience depersonalization, or a feeling of not being in their own bodies. They often experience impairment in work or interpersonal relationships, and they may practice self-mutilation or have aggressive and suicidal impulses. They may also have symptoms typical of a Mood or Personality Disorder. Individuals with Dissociative Amnesia and Dissociative Identity Disorder (sometimes known as multiple personality disorder) often report severe physical and/or sexual abuse in childhood. Controversy surrounds the accuracy of these reports, in part because of the unreliability of some childhood memories. Individuals with Dissociative Identity Disorder may have symptoms typical of Post-Traumatic Stress Disorder, as well as Mood, Substance Abuse Related, Sexual, Eating or Sleep Disorders.

PREVALENCE

The prevalence of Dissociative Disorders is difficult to ascertain, and subject to controversy. The recent rise in the US in reports of Dissociative Amnesia and Dissociative Identity Disorder related to traumatic childhood abuse has been very controversial. Some say these disorders are overreported, the result of suggestibility in individuals and the unreliability of childhood memories. Others say the disorders are underreported, given the propensity for children and adults to dismiss or forget abusive memories and the tendency of perpetrators to deny or obscure their abusive actions. For Dissociative Fugue, a prevalence rate of 0.2 percent of the population has been reported. Dissociative Identity Disorder is diagnosed three to nine times more frequently in females than in males.

Associations & Agencies

843 Center for Family Support (CFS)
333 7th Avenue
New York, NY 10001-5115
212-629-7939
Fax: 212-239-2211
www.cfsny.org

Steven Vernikoff, Executive Director

An agency that continues to develop new programs to serve families and individuals with their care needs. Currently offering services throughout the New York City region including: New Jersey, Long Island and the Lower Hudson Valley.

844 Center for Mental Health Services (CMHS)
PO Box 2345
Rockville, MD 20847
240-221-4021
800-789-2647
Fax: 240-221-4295
TDD: 866-889-2647
www.mentalhealth.samhsa.gov

A Kathryn Power, MEd, Director
Anna Marsh PhD, Deputy Director
Fran Randolph PhD, Dir, Service & Systems Improveme
Anne Mathews-Younes EdD, Dir, Prevention/Traumatic
Stress

CMHS leads Federal efforts to treat mental illnesses by promoting mental health and by preventing the development or worsening of mental illness when possible. Congress created CMHS to bring new hope to adults who have serious mental illnesses and to children with serious emotional disorders. CMHS provides information about mental health via a toll-free the web site, and more than 600 publications. Developed for users of mental health services and their families, the general public, policy makers, providers, and the media.

Year Founded: 1992

845 International Society for the Study of Dissociation
60 Revere Drive
Suite 500
Northbrook, IL 60062-1591
847-480-0899
Fax: 847-480-9282
E-mail: issd@issd.org
www.issd.org

Steven N. Gold PhD, President
Ruth Blizard PhD, Director

The society is a nonprofit professional association organized for the porposes of: information sharing and international networking of clinicians and researchers; providing professional and public education; promoting research and theory about dissociation.

846 National Association for the Dually Diagnosed (NADD)
132 Fair Street
Kingston, NY 12401-4802
845-331-4336
800-331-5362
Fax: 845-331-4569
E-mail: info@thenadd.org
www.thenadd.org

Robert Fletcher, Executive Director

Nonprofit organization designed to promote interest of professional and parent development with resources for individuals who have the coexistence of mental illness and mental retardation. Provides conference, educational services and training materials to professionals, parents, concerned citizens and service organizations. Formerly known as the National Association for the Dually Diagnosed.

Year Founded: 1983

847 National Mental Health Consumers' Self-Help Clearinghouse
1211 Chestnut Street
Suite 1207
Philadelphia, PA 19107-4103
215-751-1810
800-553-4539
Fax: 215-636-6312
E-mail: info@mhselfhelp.org
www.mhselfhelp.org

Joseph Rogers, Executive Director

A national consumer technical assistance center that has played a major role in the development of the mental health consumer movement.

Year Founded: 1986

848 SAMHSA's National Mental Health Information Center
US Department of Health and Human Services
PO Box 42557
Washington, DC 20015-557
240-221-4021
800-789-2647
Fax: 240-221-4295
TDD: 866-889-2647
www.mentalhealth.samhsa.gov

A Kathryn Power, MEd, Director
Edward B Searle, Deputy Director

Provides information about mental health via a toll-free telephone number, this web site, and more than 600 publications. Developed for users of mental health services and their families, the general public, policy makers, providers, and the media.

Books

849 Amongst Ourselves: A Self-Help Guide to Living with Dissociative Identity Disorder
New Harbinger Publications
5674 Shattuck Avenue
Oakland, CA 94609-1662
510-652-0215
800-748-6273
Fax: 510-652-5472
E-mail: customerservice@newharbinger.com
www.newharbinger.com

Matthew McKay, Owner
Karen Marshall, LCSW, Author

First person perspective of Dissociative Identity Disorder and practical suggestions to come to terms with and improve their lives. *$19.95*

256 pages Year Founded: 1998 ISBN 1-562241-22-5

850 Dissociation
American Psychiatric Publishing, Inc.
1000 Wilson Boulevard
Suite 1825
Arlington, VA 22209-3901
703-907-7322
800-368-5777
Fax: 703-907-1091
E-mail: appi@psych.org
www.appi.org

Robert E Hales MD, Editor-in-Chief
Ron McMillen, Chief Executive Officer
John McDuffie, Editorial Director

Combines cultural anthropology, congitive psychology, neurophysiology, and the study of psychosomatic illness to present the latest information on the dissociative process. Designed for professionals in cross cultural psychiatry and the influence of the mind on the body. *$33.50*

227 pages ISBN 0-880485-57-4

851 Dissociation and the Dissociative Disorders: DSM-V and Beyond
Routledge
270 Madison Avenue
New York, NY 10016-601
212-695-6599

Maura May, Publisher

This book draws together and integrates the most recent scientific and conceptual foundations of dissociation and the dissociative disorders field.

852 Dissociative Child: Diagnosis, Treatment and Management
Sidran Institute
200 E Joppa Road
Suite 207
Baltimore, MD 21286-3107
410-825-8888
888-825-8249
Fax: 410-337-0747
E-mail: sidran@sidran.org
www.sidran.org

Esther Giller, President
J G Goellner, Director Emertius
Stanley Platman, MD, Medical Advisor
Joyanna Silberg, Author

This second groundbreaking edition addresses all aspects of caring for the dissociative child and adolescents. Contributors include experienced and eminent practitioners in the field of childhood DID. The section on diagnosis offers comprehensive coverage of various aspects of diagnosis, including diagnosis taxonomy, differential diagnosis, interviewing, testing and the special problems of male children and adolescents with DID. The section on treatment covers factors associated with positive theraputic outcome, therapeutic phases, the five-domain crisis model, promoting intergration in dissociative children, art therapy and group therapy. Includes ways school personnel can act to help the dissociative child, multiculturalism and other important information. *$35.00*

400 pages

853 Drug Therapy and Dissociative Disorders
Mason Crest Publishers
370 Reed Road
Suite 302
Broomall, PA 19008-4017
610-543-6200
866-627-2665
Fax: 610-543-3878
E-mail: dtaylor@masoncrest.com
www.masoncrest.com

Dissociative disorders are some of the most controversial disorders in psychiatry today. Despite newfound recognition and numerous diagnosis the very existence of these disorders is still hotly debated in some academic circles. these disorders make us question our assumptions about memory, self, and personality, and shed unique light on the mysterious complexities of the human mind. From amnesia to multiple personalities, dissociative disorders present treatment challenges to psychotherapy and psychopharmacology alike. Through stories of individuals' struggles with dissociative disorders, this book provides both historical overview of treatment and reviews the most up-to-date treatments available today.

ISBN 1-590845-64-1

854 Got Parts? An Insider's Guide to Managing Life Successfully with Dissociative Identity Disorder
Loving Healing Press
5145 Pontiac Trail
Ann Arbor, MI 48105-9279
734-929-0881
Fax: 734-663-6861
E-mail: info@lovinghealing.com
www.lovinghealing.com

This book is directed towards people treating Dissociative Identity Disorder.

855 Handbook for the Assessment of Dissociation: a Clinical Guide
American Psychiatric Publishing, Inc.
1000 Wilson Boulevard
Suite 1825
Arlington, VA 22209-3901
703-907-7322
800-368-5777
Fax: 703-907-1091
E-mail: appi@psych.org
www.appi.org

Robert E Hales MD, Editor-in-Chief
Ron McMillen, Chief Executive Officer
John McDuffie, Editorial Director

Offers guidelines for the systematic assessment of dissociation and posttraumatic syndromes for clinicians and researchers. Provides a comprehensive overview of dissociative symptoms and disorders and an introduction to the use of the SCID-D, a diagnostic interview for the dissociative disorders. *$54.00*

433 pages ISBN 0-880486-82-1

856 Lost in the Mirror: An Inside Look at Borderline Personality Disorder
Sidran Institute
200 E Joppa Road
Suite 207
Baltimore, MD 21286-3107
410-825-8888
888-825-8249
Fax: 410-337-0747
E-mail: sidran@sidran.org
www.sidran.org

Esther Giller, President
J G Goellner, Director Emertius
Stanley Platman, MD, Medical Advisor
Richard Moskovitz, MD, Author

Dr. Moskovitz considers BPD to be part of the dissociative continuum, as it has many causes, symptoms and behaviors in common with Dissociative Disorder. This book is intended for people diagnosed with BPD, their families and therapists. Outlines the features of BPD, including abuse histories, dissociation, mood swings, self harm, impulse control problems and many more. Includes an extensive resource section. *$13.95*

190 pages

857 Rebuilding Shattered Lives: Responsible Treatment of Complex Post-Traumatic and Dissociative Disorders
John Wiley & Sons
1 Wiley Drive
Somerset, NJ 08873-1272
732-537-9410
800-225-5945
Fax: 732-302-2300
E-mail: compbks@wiley.com
www.wiley.com

Clifford Kline, Senior VP

Essential for anyone working in the field of trauma therapy. Part I discusses recent findings about child abuse, the changes in attitudes toward child abuse over the last two decades and the nature of traumatic memory. Part II is an overview of principles of trauma treatment, including symptom control, establishment of boundaries and therapist self-care. Part III covers special topics, such as dissociative identity disorder, controversies, hospitalization and acute care. *$ 73.95*

288 pages Year Founded: 1998 ISBN 0-471247-32-4

858 Treatment of Multiple Personality Disorder
American Psychiatric Publishing, Inc.
1000 Wilson Boulevard
Suite 1825
Arlington, VA 22209-3901
703-907-7322
800-368-5777
Fax: 703-907-1091
E-mail: appi@psych.org
www.appi.org

Robert E Hales MD, Editor-in-Chief
Ron McMillen, Chief Executive Officer
John McDuffie, Editorial Director

Authorities in the Multiple Personality Disorder field merge clinical understanding and research into therapeutic approaches that can be employed in clinical practice. *$22.50*

258 pages ISBN 0-880480-96-3

859 Understanding Dissociative Disorders and Addiction
Sidran Institute
200 E Joppa Road
Suite 207
Townson, MD 21286-3107
410-825-8888
888-825-8249
Fax: 410-337-0747
E-mail: sidran@sidran.org
www.sidran.org

Esther Giller, President
J Gila Goellner, Director Emertius
Stanley Plantman, MD, Medical Advisor
A Scott Winter, MD, Author

This booklet discusses the origins and symptoms of dissociation, explains the links between dissociative disorder and chemical dependency. Addresses treatment options available to help in your recovery. The work book includes exercises and activities that help you acknowledge, accept and manage both your chemical dependency and your disociative disorder. *$7.20*

860 Understanding Dissociative Disorders: A Guide for Family Physicians and Healthcare Workers
Crown House Publishing
6 Trowbridge Drive
Suite 5
Bethel, CT 06801-2882
203-778-1300

Mark Tracten, President

This volume outlines common presentations in the family physicians' practice, and offers realistic, practical answers to a multitude of questions.

Video & Audio

861 Different From You
Fanlight Publications
2
47 Halifax St
Jamaica Plain, MA 02130-4327
617-469-4999
Fax: 617-439-3379
E-mail: fanlight@fanlight.com
www.fanlight.com

As a result of the 'deinstituionalization' of mental patients, people with mental illnesses now make up a majority of the homeless in many areas. This video explores the problem through the work of a compassionate physician who cares for mentally ill people living on the streets and in inadequate 'board and care' facilities in Los Angeles.

Resources and Articles on Dissociative Experiences Scale and Dissociative Identity Disorder, PsychTrauma Glossary and Traumatic Memories.

Web Sites

862 **www.cyberpsych.org**
CyberPsych

Hosts the American Psychoanalyists Foundation, American Association of Suicideology, Society for the Exploration of Psychotherapy Intergration, and Anxiety Disorders Association of America. Also subcategories of the anxiety disorders, as well as general information, including panic disorder, phobias, obsessive compulsive disorder (OCD), social phobia, generalized anxiety disorder, post traumatic stress disorder, and phobias of childhood. Book reviews and links to web pages sharing the topics.

863 **www.fmsf.com**
False Memory Syndrome Facts

Access to literature.

864 **www.isst-D.Org**
International Society for the Study of Dissociation

A nonprofit, professional society that promotes research and training in the identification and treatment of dissociative disorders, provides professional and public education about dissociative states, and serves as a catalyst for international communication and cooperation among clinicians and researchers working in this field.

865 **www.planetpsych.com**
Planetpsych.com

Learn about disorders, their treatments and other topics in psychology. Articles are listed under the related topic areas. Ask a therapist a question for free, or view the directory of professionals in your area. If you are a therapist sign up for the directory. Current features, self-help, interactive, and newsletter archives.

866 **www.psychcentral.com**
Psych Central

Personalized one-stop index for psychology, support, and mental health issues, resources, and people on the Internet.

867 **www.sidran.org**
Trauma Resource Area

Eating Disorders

Introduction

Eating is integral to human health, and for many people food is a pleasure that can be enjoyed without too much thought. But an increasing number of people (mostly, but not exclusively, women) have eating disorders, which cause them to use food and dieting in ways that are extremely unhealthy, even life-threatening. The two principal eating disorders are Anorexia Nervosa and Bulimia Nervosa; though different in the symptoms they manifest, the two disorders are quite similar in their underlying pathology: an obsessive concern with food, body image, and body weight.

Many people believe that eating disorders are, in part, culturally determined: in the Western world, and particularly the US, a pervasive cultural preference for slimness causes many people to spend extraordinary amounts of time, money and energy dieting and exercise to stay slim. At the same time, people are flooded with media; celebrations of anorexia, and suggested strategies for remaining thin, can be easily found on the Internet, on television, and in magazines. Cultural preference is likely to exert pressure on people, especially young women, who may be genetically or psychologically predisposed to the illness. It is important to be wary of media, including the Internet, which can expose young people to counterproductive influences. Overeating is another type of Eating Disorder, as it reflects the paradox that, as society values thinness more and more, more and more people are obese. Eating Disorders may do lasting physical damage; because of this, treatment must first restore a patient to a safe and healthy body weight. Treatment of the disorder is a long-term process, involving psychotherapy, family interventions and, for depressed or obsessional patients, antidepressant medication. Fortunately, most people who are appropriately treated can and do recover.

SYMPTOMS

Anorexia Nervosa:
•Refusal to maintain body weight at or above eighty-five percent of a minimally normal weight for age and height;
•Intense fear of gaining weight or becoming fat, even though underweight;
•Disturbance in the way one's body weight or shape is experienced, undue influence of body weight or shape on self-evaluation, or denial of the seriousness of the current low body weight;
•In menstruating females, the absence of at least three consecutive menstrual cycles;
•Physical damage often occurs, such as imbalances in body chemicals, which if severe can cause cardiac arrest; purging often erodes tooth enamel, in which case a dentist might make the diagnosis. Anorexia Nervosa is associated with amenorrhea and infertility, which may lead patients to seek help from a gynecologist, who must then make the diagnosis.

Bulimia Nervosa:
•Recurrent episodes of binge eating characterized by eating more food than most people would eat during a similar period of time and under similar circumstances;
•A sense of loss of control over eating;
•Recurrent inappropriate behavior in order to prevent weight gain, such as self-induced vomiting or misuse of

laxatives, and excessive fasting or exercise;
•The binge-eating and inappropriate behaviors both occur, on average, at least twice a week for three months;
•Self-evaluation is unduly influenced by body shape and weight;
•The disturbance does not occur exclusively during episodes of Anorexia Nervosa.

ASSOCIATED FEATURES

Patients with Anorexia Nervosa may be severely depressed, and may experience insomnia, irritability, and diminished interest in sex. These features may be exacerbated if the patient is severely underweight. People with Eating Disorders also share many of the features of Obsessive Compulsive Disorder. For instance, someone with an Eating Disorder may have an excessive interest in food; they may hoard food, or spend unusual amounts of time reading and researching about foods, recipes and nutrition. People with Anorexia Nervosa may also exhibit a strong need to control their environment, and may be socially and emotionally withdrawn.

Individuals with Bulimia Nervosa are often within the normal weight range, but prior to the development of the disorder they may be overweight. Depression and other Mood Disorders are common among people with bulimia, and patients often ascribe their bulimia to the Mood Disorders. In other cases, however, it appears that the Mood Disorders precede the Eating Disorders. Substance abuse occurs in about one-third of individuals with bulimia.

Anxiety Disorders are common, and fear of social situations can be a precipitating factor in binging episodes.

PREVALENCE

Prevalence studies in females have found rates of 0.5 to one percent for Anorexia Nervosa. There is only limited data for the prevalence of Anorexia Nervosa in males. The prevalence of Bulimia Nervosa among adolescent females is approximately one to three percent. The rate of the disorder among males is approximately one-tenth of that in females.

TREATMENT OPTIONS

Medications, especially the newest SSRIs (Selective Serotonin Reuptake Inhibitors, which were originally developed as antidepressants), have been found to be very effective in the treatment of Eating Disorders. They can help restore and build self-esteem, and thereby help the patient maintain a positive attitude as well as a safe and healthy body image and body weight.

Because of the physical damage that an Eating Disorder can do to a patient, nutritional counseling and monitoring is often vital to restore and maintain proper body weight.

It is critical to recognize that Eating Disorders are, in addition to being life-threatening, extremely complex: simply restoring the patient to an acceptable body weight is not enough. Many patients have complex and conflicting psychological issues that trigger the compulsion to binge, or the morbid fear of gaining weight. These issues need to be addressed by psychotherapy. Forms of psychotherapy that may be useful in treating Eating Disorders include psychodynamic psychotherapy (in which longstanding and sometimes unconscious emotional issues related to the eating disorders are explored) and cognitive behavior therapy, which aims to identify the thought patterns that trigger the Eating Disorder and to establish healthy eating habits. Recent literature suggests that psychotherapeutic approaches are often more effective than medications in the treatment of Anorexia. Family involvement in treatment is critical, and peer pressure can be utilized to compel patients to maintain adequate nutrition. Eating Disorders are serious — untreated Anorexia can kill a patient — and treatment may be required over a course of many years.

Associations & Agencies

869 American Anorexia/Bulimia Association
435 East 61st Street
6th Floor
New York, NY 10065
212-501-8351
800-522-2230
Fax: 212-501-0342

Judith Robinson, RN, PhD, Executive Director

Organization dedicated to increasing the awareness of eating disorders and offering information on prevention and treatment.

870 Anorexia Nervosa and Related Eating Disorders
PO Box 5102
Eugene, OR 97405-102
541-344-1144
E-mail: jarinor@rio.com
www.anred.com

We are a nonprofit organization that provides information about anorexia nervosa, bulimia nervosa, binge eating diorder, and other less-well-known food and weight disorders.

871 Center for Family Support (CFS)
333 7th Avenue
New York, NY 10001-5115
212-629-7939
Fax: 212-239-2211
www.cfsny.org

Steven Vernikoff, Executive Director

An agency that continues to develop new programs to serve families and individuals with their care needs. Currently offering services throughout the New York City region including: New Jersey, Long Island and the Lower Hudson Valley.

872 Center for Mental Health Services (CMHS)
PO Box 2345
Rockville, MD 20847
240-221-4021
800-789-2647
Fax: 240-221-4295
TDD: 866-889-2647
www.mentalhealth.samhsa.gov

A Kathryn Power, MEd, Director
Anna Marsh PhD, Deputy Director

Fran Randolph PhD, Dir, Service & Systems Improveme
Anne Mathews-Younes EdD, Dir, Prevention/Traumatic Stress

CMHS leads Federal efforts to treat mental illnesses by promoting mental health and by preventing the development or worsening of mental illness when possible. Congress created CMHS to bring new hope to adults who have serious mental illnesses and to children with serious emotional disorders. CMHS provides information about mental health via a toll-free the web site, and more than 600 publications. Developed for users of mental health services and their families, the general public, policy makers, providers, and the media.

Year Founded: 1992

873 Change for Good Coaching and Counseling
3801 Connecticut Avenue NW
Washington, DC 20008-4530
202-362-3009
Fax: 202-204-6100
E-mail: brockhansenlcsw@aol.com
www.change-for-good.org

Brock Hansen, LCSW, President

Coaching on learnable emotional skills to see goals clearly, harness resources and get moving toward a successful outcome.

874 Council on Size and Weight Discrimination (CSWD)
PO Box 305
Mount Marion, NY 12456-305
845-679-1209
Fax: 845-679-1206
E-mail: info@cswd.org
www.cswd.org

Miriam Berg, President
Lynn McAfee, Director of Medical Advocacy
William J. Fabrey, Media Project
Nancy Summer, Fund Raising

The Council on Size and Weight Discrimination is a not-for-profit group which works to change people's attitudes about weight. They act as consumer advocates for larger people, especially in the areas of medical treatment, job discrimination, and media images.

875 International Association of Eating Disorders Professionals
PO Box 1295
Pekin, IL 61555-1295
309-346-3341
800-800-8126
Fax: 309-346-2874
E-mail: iaedpmembers@earthlink.net
www.iaedp.com

Bonnie Harken, Managing Director
Emmett R Bishop MD CEDS, President

Offers professional counseling and assistance to the medical community, courts, law enforcement officials, and social welfare agencies.

876 Largesse, The Network for Size Esteem
PO Box 9404
New Haven, CT 06534-404
203-787-1624
E-mail: size_esteem@yahoo.com
www.eskimo.com/~largesse

Karen W Stimson, Director

An international clearinghouse for information on size diversity empowerment. Their mission is to create personal awareness and social change which promotes a positive image, health and equal rights for people of size.

877 National Alliance on Mental Illness
2107 Wilson Boulevard
Suite 300
Arlington, VA 22201-3080
703-524-7600
800-950-6264
Fax: 703-524-9094
E-mail: helpline@nami.org
www.nami.org

Suzanne Vogel-Scibilia, MD, President
Frederick R Sandoval, First VP

Nation's leading self-help organization for all those affected by severe brain disorders. Mission is to bring consumers and families with similar experiences together to share information about services, care providers, and ways to cope with the challenges of schizophrenia, manic depression, and other serious mental illnesses.

Year Founded: 1979

878 National Association for the Dually Diagnosed (NADD)
132 Fair Street
Kingston, NY 12401-4802
845-331-4336
800-331-5362
Fax: 845-331-4569
E-mail: info@thenadd.org
www.thenadd.org

Robert Fletcher, Executive Director
Donna Nagy PhD, President

Nonprofit organization designed to promote interest of professional and parent development with resources for individuals who have the coexistence of mental illness and mental retardation. Provides conference, educational services and training materials to professionals, parents, concerned citizens and service organizations. Formerly known as the National Association for the Dually Diagnosed.

Year Founded: 1983

879 National Association of Anorexia Nervosa and Associated Disorders (ANAD)
PO Box 7
Highland Park, IL 60035-7
847-831-3438
Fax: 847-433-4632
E-mail: anad20@aol.com
www.anad.org

Vivian Hanson Meehan, DSc, President

Sponsors national and local programs to prevent eating disorders and assist people with eating disorders and their families. Provides a national clearinghouse of information and is a grassroots association for laypeople and professionals.

880 National Association to Advance Fat Acceptance (NAAFA)
PO Box 22510
Oakland, CA 94609-5110
916-558-6880
Fax: 415-373-0483
E-mail: naafa@naafa.org
www.naafa.org

Carole Cullum, Co-Chairman
Kara Brewer Allen, Co-Chairman

Nonprofit organization dedicated to improving the quality of life for fat people. Opposes discrimination against fat people including discrimination in advertising, employment, fashion, medicine, insurance, social acceptance, the media, schooling and public accomodations. Monitors legislative activity and litigation affecting fat people. Publications: NAAFA Newsletter, bimonthly. Annual conference and symposium, always mid-August.

881 National Eating Disorders Association
603 Stewart Street
Seattle, WA 98101-1264
206-382-3587
800-931-2237
Fax: 206-829-8501
E-mail: info@NationalEatingDisroders.org
www.nationaleatingdisorders.org

Lynn S Grefe MA, CEO

Offers a national information phone line, an international treatment referral directory, and a support group directory. The organization sponsors an annual conference and offers a speakers' bureau with a wide range of eating disorder.

882 National Institute of Mental Health Eating Disorders Program
Building 10 Room 35231
Bethesda, MD 20892-1
301-496-6081
866-615-6464

Martiz Peterson, Manager

Mission is to reduce the burden of mental illness and behavior disorders through research on mind, brain and behavior. NIMH is committed to educating the public about mental disorders and has developed many booklets and fact sheets that provide the latest research-based information on these illnesses.

883 National Mental Health Consumers' Self-Help Clearinghouse
1211 Chestnut Street
Suite 1207
Philadelphia, PA 19107-4103
215-751-1810
800-553-4539

Fax: 215-636-6312
E-mail: info@mhselfhelp.org
www.mhselfhelp.org

Joseph Rogers, Executive Director

A national consumer technical assistance center that has played a major role in the development of the mental health consumer movement.

Year Founded: 1986

884   SAMHSA's National Mental Health Information Center
US Department of Health and Human Services
PO Box 42557
Washington, DC 20015-557

800-789-2647
Fax: 240-747-5470
TDD: 866-889-2647
E-mail: ken@mentalhealth.org
www.mentalhealth.samhsa.gov

A Kathryn Power, MEd, Director
Edward B Searle, Deputy Director

Information about resources, technical assistance, research, training, networks, and other federal clearing houses, and fact sheets and materials. Information specialists refer callers to mental health resources in their communities as well as state, federal and nonprofit contacts. Staff available Monday through Friday, 8:30 AM - 5:00 PM, EST, excluding federal holidays. After hours, callers may leave messages and an information specialist will return their call.

885   TOPS Club
4575 S 5th Street
PO Box 07360
Milwaukee, WI 53207-360
414-482-4620
800-932-8677
Fax: 414-482-3955
E-mail: topsinteractive@tops.org
www.tops.org

Maggie Lehnert, Wellness Coordinator

TOPS is an international family of all ages, sizes, and shapes from all walk of life. Dedicated to helping each other Take Off and Keep Off Pounds Sensibly. We offer fellowship while you change to a healthier, new lifestyle andlearn to maintain it.

886   We Insist on Natural Shapes
PO Box 19938
Sacramento, CA 95819-938

800-600-9467
E-mail: winsnews@aol.com
www.winsnews.org

Kara Garner, Executive Director

A nonprofit organization educates about normal, healthy shapes.

Books

887   Anorexia Nervosa & Recovery: a Hunger for Meaning
Haworth Press
10 Alice Street
Binghamton, NY 13904-1503
607-722-5857
800-429-6784
Fax: 607-721-0012
E-mail: getinfo@haworthpress.com
www.haworthpress.com

Jackie Blakeslee, Advertising/Journal Liason
Karen Way, MA, Author

Presents the most objective, complete, and compassionate picture of what anorexia nervosa is about. *$19.95*

142 pages   Year Founded: 1993 ISBN 0-918393-95-7

888   Assessment of Eating Disorders
The Guilford Press
72 Spring Street
New York, NY 10012-4019
212-431-9800
800-365-7006
Fax: 212-966-6708
E-mail: info@guilford.com

Bob Matloff, President
James E Mitchell, Author
Carol B Peterson, Author

Provides a clear framework and a range of up-to-date tools for assessing patients with eating disorders.

889   Beyond Anorexia
Cambridge University Press
40 W 20th Street
New York, NY 10011-4211
212-924-3900
800-872-7423
Fax: 212-691-3239
E-mail: marketing@cup.org
www.cup.org

Beyond Anorexia is a sociological exploration of how people recover from what medicince lables 'eating disorders'. *$59.95*

248 pages

890   Binge Eating: Nature, Assessment and Treatment
Guilford Publications
72 Spring Street
New York, NY 10012-4068
212-431-9800
800-365-7006
Fax: 212-966-6708
E-mail: info@guilford.com

Bob Matloff, President

Informative and practical text brings together original and significant contributions from leading experts from a wide variety of fields. Detailed manual covers all those who binge eat, including those who are overweight. *$21.95*

419 pages ISBN 0-898628-58-X

891 Body Image Workbook: An 8 Step Program for Learning to Like Your Looks
New Harbinger Publications
5674 Shattuck Avenue
Oakland, CA 94609-1662
510-652-0215
800-748-6273
Fax: 510-652-5472
E-mail: customerservice@newharbinger.com
www.newharbinger.com

Matthew McKay, Owner

Workbook offering a program to help transform your relationship with your body. *$19.95*

240 pages Year Founded: 1997 ISBN 1-572240-62-8

892 Body Image, Eating Disorders, and Obesity in Youth
APA Books
750 First Street NE
Washington, DC 20002-4241
202-336-5500
800-374-2721
Fax: 202-336-5500
TDD: 202-336-6123
E-mail: order@apa.org
www.apa.org/books

Provides for clinicians including research, assessment and treatment suggestions on body image disturbances and eating disorders in children and adolescents. *$49.95*

517 pages ISBN 1-557987-58-0

893 Brief Therapy and Eating Disorders
Jossey-Bass Publishers
989 Market Street
San Francisco, CA 94103-1708
415-433-1740
Fax: 415-433-0499
www.leadertoleader.org

Debra Hunter, President

Demonstrates how solution-focused brief therapy is one of the more efficient approaches in treating eating disorders. *$36.95*

284 pages ISBN 0-787900-53-2

894 Bulimia
Jossey-Bass Publishers
989 Martket Street
San Francisco, CA 94103-1708
415-433-1740
Fax: 415-433-0499
www.leadertoleader.org

Debra Hunter, President

A step-by-step guide to this complex disease. Filled with practical information and advice, this essential resource of-fers hope to millions of bulimics and their loved ones. *$17.95*

167 pages ISBN 0-787903-61-2

895 Bulimia Nervosa
University of Minnesota Press
111 3rd Avenue S
Suite 290
Minneapolis, MN 55401-2520
612-627-1970
Fax: 612-627-1980
E-mail: ump@tc.umn.edu
www.upress.umn.edu

Doug Armato, Manager

A practical guide for health-care professionals to the diagnosis, treatment and management of bulimia by a leading expert in the field of eating disorders. Hardcover. *$27.95*

188 pages ISBN 0-816616-26-4

896 Bulimia Nervosa & Binge Eating: A Guide To Recovery
New York University Press
838 Broadway
3rd Floor
New York, NY 10003-4812
212-998-2575
Fax: 212-995-3833
www.nyupress.nyu.edu

A self-help book designed to guide bilimics and binge-eaters to recovery. *$35.00*

160 pages ISBN 0-814715-22-2

897 Bulimia: a Guide to Recovery
Gurze Books
PO Box 2238
Carlsbad, CA 92018-2238
760-434-7533
800-756-7533
Fax: 760-434-5476
E-mail: gzcatl@aol.com
www.gurze.net

Lindsey Cohn, Co-Owner Gurze Books

Guidebook offers a complete understanding of bulimia and a plan for recovery. Includes a two-week program to stop binging, things-to-do instead of binging, a two-week guide for support groups, specific advice for loved ones, and Eating Without Fear - Hall's story of self-cure which has inspired thousands of other bulimics. *$14.95*

285 pages ISBN 0-936077-31-X

898 Clinical Handbook of Eating Disorders: An Integrated Approach (Medical Psychiatry, 26)
Informa Healthcare
52 Vanderbilt Avenue
New York, NY 10017-3808
646-443-3976
Fax: 646-661-5054
E-mail: healthcare.enquiries@informa.com
www.informaworld.com

Victoria Sollecito, Manager

Reviews the most current research on the assessment, epidemiology, etiology, risk factors, neurodevelopment, course of illness, and various empirically-based evaluation and treatment approaches relating to eating disorders-studying disordered eating in atypical patient populations, such as men, infants, and the elderly and highlighting gender, cultural, and age-related differences that have appeared in the study of these conditions.

899   Controlling Eating Disorders with Facts, Advice and Resources
Oryx Press
88 Post Road W
Westport, CT 06880-4208
203-226-3571
Fax: 603-431-2214
E-mail: info@oryxpress.com
www.oryxpress.com

900   Conversations with Anorexics: A Compassionate & Hopeful Journey
Jason Aronson
230 Livingston Street
Northvale, NJ 07647-1726

800-782-0015
Fax: 201-767-1576
www.aronson.com

A compassionate and hopeful journey through the theraputic process.In this book Bruch presents some of her most challenging cases, offering deeply moving accounts of the course and cure. *$30.00*

238 pages ISBN 1-568212-61-5

901   Coping with Eating Disorders
Rosen Publishing Group
29 E 21st Street
New York, NY 10010-6209
212-777-3017
Fax: 212-777-0277
E-mail: info@rosenpub.com
www.rosenpublishing.com

Roger Rosen, President

Offers practical suggestions on coping with eating disorders. *$16.95*

ISBN 0-823921-33-6

902   Cult of Thinness
Oxford University Press
198 Madison Avenue
New York, NY 10016-4341
212-726-6400
800-445-9714
TTY: 800-445-9714
E-mail: custserv.us@oup.com

Michael Cunningham, Manager

Discusses eating patterns and disorders and their relationship to emotional states and self-esteem. *$15.95*

208 pages Year Founded: 1997 ISBN 0-195082-41-9

903   Developmental Psychopathology of Eating Disorders: Implications for Research, Prevention and Treatment
Lawrence Erlbaum Associates
10 Industrial Avenue
Mahwah, NJ 07430-2253
201-825-3200
800-926-6577
Fax: 201-236-0072
E-mail: orders@erlbaum.com
www.erlbaum.com

This text provides backround material from developmental psychology and psychopathology - following the theory that eating problems and disorders are typically rooted in childhood. Applications are then outlined, including research, treatment, protective factors and primary prevention. *$79.95*

456 pages ISBN 0-805817-46-8

904   Eating Disorders & Obesity: a Comprehensive Handbook
Guilford Publications
72 Spring Street
New York, NY 10012-4068
212-431-9800
800-365-7006
Fax: 212-966-6708
E-mail: info@guilford.com

Bob Matloff, President

Presents and integrates virtually all that is currently known about eating disorders and obesity in one authorative, accessible and eminently practical volume. *$57.95*

583 pages ISBN 0-898628-50-4

905   Eating Disorders Sourcebook
Omnigraphics
PO Box 625
Holmes, PA 19043-625

800-234-1340
Fax: 800-875-1340
E-mail: info@omnigraphics.com
www.omnigraphics.com

Dawn D Matthews, Editor

Omnigraphics is the publisher of the Health Reference Series, a growing consumer health information resource with more than 100 volumes in print. Each title in the series features an easy to understand format, nontechnical language, comprehensive indexing and resources for further information. Material in each book has been collected from a wide range of government agencies, professional associations, periodicals and other sources. *$78.00*

322 pages Year Founded: 2001 ISBN 0-780803-35-3

**906 Eating Disorders and Obesity, Second Edition :
A Comprehensive Handbook**
The Guilford Press
72 Spring Street
New York, NY 10012-4019
212-431-9800
800-365-7006
Fax: 212-966-6708
E-mail: info@guilford.com

Bob Matloff, President
Christopher Fairburn, Author

This unique handbook presents and integrates virtually all
that is currently known about eating disorders and obesity
in one authoritative, accessible, and eminently practical
volume.

907 Eating Disorders: Reference Sourcebook
Oryx Press
88 Post Road W
Westport, CT 06880-4208
203-226-3571
Fax: 603-431-2214
E-mail: info@oryxpress.com
www.oryxpress.com

Listings of 200 centers and groups for care and treatment of
eating disorders, such as anorexia nervosa, bulimia nervosa,
and compulsive overeating. *$49.95*

**908 Eating Disorders: When Food Turns Against
You**
Franklin Watts
90 Old Sherman Turnpike
Danbury, CT 06816-1

800-621-1115
Fax: 203-797-3657
www.grolier.com
$14.50
96 pages ISBN 0-531111-75-X

**909 Emotional Eating: A Practical Guide to Taking
Control**
Lexington Books
4501 Forbes Boulevard
Suite 200
Lanham, MD 20706-4346
717-794-3800
800-426-6420
Fax: 717-794-3803
www.lexingtonbook.com

Using case histories he explores some of the causes of emotional eating (childhood programming, family life, sexual
abuse) and the manifestos of emotional eating ("sneaky
snaking",grazing, and binging). Of particular interest is the
last chaper, which helps the reader determine whether or
not it is a good or bad time to diet. While not a diet book or
a 12-step primer, this is a tool for developing healthier
ways of handling emotions and food. *$19.95*

200 pages ISBN 0-029002-15-X

910 Encyclopedia of Obesity and Eating Disorders
Facts on File
11 Penn Plaza
New York, NY 10001-2006
212-290-8090
800-322-8755
Fax: 212-678-3633

From abdominoplasty to Zung Rating Scale, this volume
defines and explains these disorders, along with medical
and other problems associated with them. *$50.00*

272 pages

911 Etiology and Treatment of Bulimia Nervosa
Jason Aronson
506 Clement Street
Dunmore, PA 18512
415-387-2272
Fax: 415-387-2377
E-mail: info@greepapplebooks.com
www.aronson.com

$35.00
352 pages ISBN 1-568213-39-5

912 Feminist Perspectives on Eating Disorders
Guilford Publications
72 Spring Street
New York, NY 10012-4068
212-431-9800
800-365-7006
Fax: 212-966-6708
E-mail: info@guilford.com

Bob Matloff, President

Explores the relationship between the anguish of eating
disorder sufferers and the problems of ordinary women.
Examines the sociocultural pressure on women to conform
to culturally ideal body types and how this affects individual self concept. Controversial topics include the relationship between sexual abuse and eating disorders, the use of
medications and the role of hospitalization and 12-step programs. *$ 25.95*

465 pages ISBN 1-572301-82-1

913 Food for Recovery: The Next Step
Crown Publishing Group
201 E 50th Street
New York, NY 10022-7703
212-751-2600

A very practicle guide on every aspect needed by the patient and counselor to utilize nutrition as a therapeutic tool.
$ 14.00
ISBN 0-517586-94-0

914 Golden Cage, The Enigma of Anorexia Nervosa
Random House
1745 Broadway 15-3
New York, NY 10019-4368
212-572-4985
Fax: 212-782-9052
www.randomhouse.com

Markus Bohle, CEO

One of the world's leading authorities offers a vivid and moving account of the causes, effects and treatment of this devastating disease. *$9.00*

ISBN 0-394726-88-X

915 Group Psychotherapy for Eating Disorders
American Psychiatric Publishing, Inc.
1000 Wilson Boulevard
Suite 1825
Arlington, VA 22209-3901
703-907-7322
800-368-5777
Fax: 703-907-1091
E-mail: appi@psych.org
www.appi.org

Robert E Hales MD, Editor-in-Chief
Ron McMillen, Chief Executive Officer
John McDuffie, Editorial Director

The first book to fully explore the use of group therapy in the treatment of eating disorders. *$46.00*

353 pages ISBN 0-880484-19-5

916 Helping Athletes with Eating Disorders
Human Kinetics Publishers
PO Box 5076
Champaign, IL 61825-5076

800-747-4457
Fax: 217-351-1549
E-mail: orders@hkusa.com

Gives readers the information they need to identify and address major eating disorders such as: anorexia, bulimia nervosa, and eating disorders not otherwise specified. *$25.00*

208 pages ISBN 0-873223-83-7

917 Hunger So Wide and Deep
University of Minnesota Press
111 3rd Avenue S
Suite 290
Minneapolis, MN 55401-2520
612-627-1970
Fax: 612-627-1980
E-mail: um@tc.umn.edu
www.upress.umn.edu

Doug Armato, Manager

ISBN 0-816624-35-6

918 Hungry Self; Women, Eating and Identity
Harper Collins
10 E 53rd Street
New York, NY 10022-5299
212-207-7000

Answers the need for help among the five million American women who suffer from eating disorders. Paperback. *$13.00*

256 pages ISBN 0-060925-04-3

919 Insights in the Dynamic Psychotherapy of Anorexia and Bulimia
Jason Aronson
506 Clemant Street
San Francisco, CA 94118-2324
415-387-2272
Fax: 415-387-2377
www.greenapplebooks.com

The clinical insights that guide the dynamic psychotheray of anorexic and bulimic patients. *$45.00*

288 pages ISBN 0-876685-68-8

920 Lifetime Weight Control
New Harbinger Publications
5674 Shattuck Avenue
Oakland, CA 94609-1662
510-652-0215
800-748-6273
Fax: 510-652-5472
E-mail: customerservice@newharbinger.com
www.newharbinger.com

Matthew McKay, Owner

Program of lifetime weight management in seven steps: 1. Eat spontaneously to settle into your 'setpoint' weight. 2. Accept yourself as okay, regardless of your weight. 3. Determine how and why you eat, learning all the reasons besides hunger. 4. Satisfy emotional needs directly, saving food for satisfying real hunger. 5. Improve nutrition. 6. Increase activity. 7. Stick to it. *$13.95*

208 pages Year Founded: 1990 ISBN 0-934986-83-5

921 Making Peace with Food
Harper Collins
10 E 53rd Street
New York, NY 10022-5299
212-207-7000
800-242-7737

For millions of diet-conscious Americans, the scientifically proven, step-by-step guide to overcoming repeated weight loss and gain, binge eating, guilt and anxieties about food and body image. *$15.00*

224 pages ISBN 0-060963-28-X

922 Obesity: Theory and Therapy
Raven Press
I 185 Avenue of the Americas
New York, NY 10013-1209
212-930-9500
800-638-3030
Fax: 212-869-3495
www.lww.com

A classic reference for clinicians dealing with obesity, this volume provides the most up-to-date research, preclinical and clinical information.

500 pages ISBN 0-881678-84-8

923 Overeaters Anonymous
Overeaters Anonymous
350 Third Avenue
PO Box 759
New York, NY 10010-2310
212-946-4599
E-mail: NYOAMentroOffice@yahoo.com

Personal stories demonstrating the struggles overcome and accomplishments made. *$7.50*

204 pages

924 Psychobiology and Treatment of Anorexia Nervosa and Bulimia Nervosa
American Psychiatric Publishing, Inc.
1000 Wilson Boulevard
Suite 1825
Arlington, VA 22209-3901
703-907-7322
800-368-5777
Fax: 703-907-1091
E-mail: appi@psych.org
www.appi.org

Robert E Hales MD, Editor-in-Chief
Ron McMillen, Chief Executive Officer
John McDuffie, Editorial Director

Combines clinical research concerning these distinct disorders and provides an overview of the psychobiology and treatment. *$48.50*

356 pages ISBN 0-880485-06-X

925 Psychodynamic Technique in the Treatment of the Eating Disorders
Jason Aronson
400 Keystone Industrial Park
Dunmore, PA 18512-1507
570-342-1320
800-782-0015
Fax: 201-767-1576
www.aronson.com

Provides a blueprint for the treatment of the eating disorders. *$50.00*

440 pages ISBN 0-876686-22-6

926 Psychosomatic Families: Anorexia Nervosa in Context
Harvard University Press
79 Garden Street
Cambridge, MA 02138-1400
617-495-1000
Fax: 617-495-5898
E-mail: contact_hup@harvard.edu
www.hup.harvard.edu

William Sisler, President

Hardcover. *$38.50*

351 pages ISBN 0-674722-20-5

927 Self-Starvation
Jason Aronson
400 Keystone Industrial Park
Dunmore, PA 18512-1507
570-342-1320
800-782-0015
Fax: 201-767-1576
www.aronson.com

Argues that anorexia nervosa is a social disease reflecting unbearable conflicts within the family. *$30.00*

312 pages ISBN 1-568218-22-2

928 Shame and Anger: The Criticism Connection
Change for Good Coaching and Counseling
3801 Connecticut Avenue NW
Washington, DC 20008-4530
202-362-3009
Fax: 202-204-6100
E-mail: brockhansenlcsw@aol.com
www.change-for-good.org

Brock Hansen LCSW, Author

Coaching on learnable emotional skills to see goals clearly, harness resources and get moving toward a successful outcome. *$16.98*

216 pages ISBN 0-615135-81-6

929 Starving to Death in a Sea of Objects
Jason Aronson
400 Keystone Industrial Park
Dunmore, PA 18512-1507
570-342-1320
800-782-0015
Fax: 201-840-7242
www.aronson.com

Makes the central dilemma clear: how emancipation can come to mean security and pleasure for the anorexic. *$30.00*

464 pages ISBN 0-876684-35-5

930 Surviving an Eating Disorder: Perspectives and Strategies
Harper Collins
10 E 53rd Street
New York, NY 10022-5299
212-207-7000

Addresses the cutting-edge advances made in the field of eating disorders, discusses how the changes in health care have affected treatment and provides additional strategies for dealing with anorexia, bulimia and binge eating disorder. It also includes updated readings and a list of support organizations. A terrrific resource for those suffering from eating disorders, their families and professionals. Paperback. *$13.00*

256 pages ISBN 0-060952-33-4

931 Treating Eating Disorders
Jossey-Bass Publishers
10475 Crosspoint Boulevard
Indianapolis, IN 46256-3386

877-762-2974
Fax: 800-597-3299
E-mail: consumers@wiley.com
www.josseybass.com

Details how some of the most eminent clinicians in the field combine and intergrate a wide variety of contemporary therapies — ranging from psychodynamic to systematic to cognitive behavioral—to successfully treat clients with anorexia nervosa, bulimia nervosa, and binge eating diorders. Filled with up to date information and important approaches to assessment and treatment, the book offers a hands-on approach that cogently illustrates both theory and technique. *$29.95*

416 pages ISBN 0-787903-30-2

932 When Food Is Love
Geneen Roth and Associates
PO Box 2852
Santa Cruz, CA 95063-2852

877-243-6336
Fax: 831-685-8602
E-mail: GeneenRoth@GeneenRoth.com
www.geneenroth.com

Lindsey Cohn, Bookseller

Shows how dieting and compulsive eating often become a subsititue for intimacy. Drawing on painful personal experiece as well as the candid stories of those she has helped in her seminars, Roth claims the crucial issues that surrounds compulsive eating: need for control, dependency on melodrama, desire for what is forbidden, and the belief that the wrong move can mean catastrophe. She shows why many people overeat in an attempt to satisfy their emotional hunger, and why weight loss frequently just uncovers a new set of problems. This book will help readers break destructive, self-perpetuating patterns and learn to satisfy all the hungers - physical and emotional - that makes us human. *$10.00*

205 pages

Periodicals & Pamphlets

933 American Anorexia/Bulimia Association News
425 East 61st Streett
6th Floor
New York, NY 10065-8795
212-501-8351
Fax: 212-501-0342

Offers information on the latest treatments, medications, books, conferences, support groups, and workshops for persons with eating disorders.

934 Anorexia: Am I at Risk?
ETR Associates
4 Carbonero Way
Scotts Valley, CA 95066-4200
831-438-4060
800-321-4407
Fax: 831-438-3618

E-mail: customerservice@etr.org
www.etr.org

Mary Nelson, President

Offers a clear overview of anorexia; Lists symptoms; Explains helath problems.

935 Body Image
ETR Associates
4 Carbonero Way
Scotts Valley, CA 95066-4200
831-438-4060
800-321-4407
Fax: 831-438-3618
E-mail: customerservice@etr.org
www.etr.org

Mary Nelson, President

Discusses the difference between healthy and distorted body image; the link between poor body image and low self esteem; five point list to help people check out their own body image.

936 Bulimia
ETR Associates
4 Carbonero Way
Scotts Valley, CA 95066-4200
831-438-4060
800-321-4407
Fax: 831-438-3618
E-mail: customerservice@etr.org
www.etr.org

Mary Nelson, President

Includes warning signs that someone's bulimic, health consequesnces of bulimia, and how to help a friend.

937 Eating Disorder Sourcebook
Gurze Books
PO Box 2238
Carlsbad, CA 92018-2238
760-434-7533
800-756-7533
Fax: 760-434-5476
E-mail: gzcatl@aol.com
www.bulimia.com

Leigh Cohn, Co-Owner

Includes 125 books and tapes on eating disorders and related subjects for both lay and professional audiences, basic facts about eating disorders, a list of national organizations and treatment facilities. Also publishes a bi-monthly newsletter for clinicians and are executive editors of Eating Disorders the Journal of Treatment and Prevention.

28 pages 1 per year

938 Eating Disorders
ETR Associates
4 Carbonero Way
Scotts Valley, CA 95066-4200
831-438-4060
800-321-4407

Fax: 831-438-3618
E-mail: customerservice@etr.org
www.etr.org

Mary Nelson, President

Includes anorexia and bulimia, eating patterns versus eating disorders, treatment and getting help.

939 Eating Disorders Factsheet
SAMHSA'S National Mental Health Information Center
PO Box 42557
Washington, DC 20015-557

800-789-2647
Fax: 240-747-5470
TDD: 866-889-2647
E-mail: ken@mentalhealth.org
www.mentalhealth.samhsa.gov

A Kathryn Power, MEd, Director
Edward B Searle, Deputy Director

This fact sheet provides basic information on the symptoms, medical complications, formal diagnosis, and treatment for anorexia nervousa and bulimia nervosa.

2 pages

940 Eating Disorders: Facts About Eating Disorders and the Search for Solutions
National Institute of Mental Health
6001 Executive Boulevard
Room 8184
Bethesda, MD 20892-1
301-443-4513
866-615-6464
TTY: 301-443-8431
E-mail: nimhinfo@nih.gov

Eating is controlled by many factors, including appetite, food availability, family, peer, and cultural practices, and attempts at voluntary control. Dieting to a body weight leaner than needed for health is highly promoted by current fashion trends, sales campaigns for special foods, and in some activities and professions. Eating disorders involve serious disturbances in eating behavior, such as extreme and unhealthy reduction of food intake or severe overeating, as well as feelings of distress or extreme concern about body shape or weight. There is help, and there is every hope for recovery.

8 pages

941 Fats of Life
ETR Associates
4 Carbonero Way
Scotts Valley, CA 95066-4200
831-438-4060
800-321-4407
Fax: 831-438-3618
E-mail: customerservice@etr.org
www.etr.org

Mary Nelson, President

Stresses that health, not body weight, is what's important; dispels myths about dieting; includes chart to help people determine their body mass index.

942 Food and Feelings
ETR Associates
4 Carbonero Way
Scotts Valley, CA 95066-4200
831-438-4060
800-321-4407
Fax: 831-438-3618
E-mail: customerservice@etr.org
www.etr.org

Mary Nelson, President

Helps students recognize eating disorders; emphasizes the seriousness of eating disorders; encourages the sufferers to seek treatment.

943 Getting What You Want from Your Body Image
ETR Associates
4 Carbonero Way
Scotts Valley, CA 95066-4200
831-438-4060
800-321-4407
Fax: 831-438-3618
E-mail: customerservice@etr.org
www.etr.org

Mary Nelson, President

Discusses topics such as the influence of the media, the truth about dieting, and body image survival tips.

944 Restrictive Eating
ETR Associates
4 Carbonero Way
Scotts Valley, CA 95066-4200
831-438-4060
800-321-4407
Fax: 831-438-3618
E-mail: customerservice@etr.org
www.etr.org

Mary Nelson, President

Discusses the spectrum of eating patterns, signs of restrictive eating and why it is a problem, how to help a friend, and where to go for help.

945 Teen Image
ETR Associates
4 Carbonero Way
Scotts Valley, CA 95066-4200
831-438-4060
800-321-4407
Fax: 831-438-3618
E-mail: customerservice@etr.org
www.etr.org

Mary Nelson, President

Dispels unrealistic media images; offers ways to boost body image and self esteem; includes tips to maintain a good body image.

946 Working Together
National Association of Anorexia Nervosa and
Associated Disorders
PO Box 7
Highland Park, IL 60035-7
847-831-3438
Fax: 847-433-4632
E-mail: anad20@aol.com
www.anad.org

Dawn Ries, Administrator

Designed for individuals, families, group leaders and professionals concerned with eating disorders. Provides updates on treatments, resources, conferences, programs, articles by therapists, recovered victims, group members and leaders.

2 pages 4 per year

Research Centers

947 Center for the Study of Adolescence
Michael Reese Hospital and Medical Center
Po Box 116059
Atlanta, GA 30368-6059
312-791-2000
E-mail: info@michaelreesehospital.com
www.michaelreesehospital.com

Enrique Beckmann, Chair/Ceo

948 Center for the Study of Anorexia and Bulimia
1841 Broadway 4th Floor
New York, NY 10023-7603
212-333-4466
E-mail: csab@icpnyc.orgg

Established as a division of the Institute for Contemporary Psychotherapy in 1979 and is the oldest non-profit eating disorders clinic in New York City. Using an eclectic approach, the professional staff and affiliates are on the cutting edge of treatment in their field. The treatment staff includes social workers, psychologists, registered nurses and nutritionists, all with special training in the treatment of eating disorders.

949 Eating Disorders Research and Treatment
Program
Michael Reese Hospital and Medical Center
Po Box 116059
Atlanta, GA 30368-6059
312-791-2000
E-mail: info@michaelreesehospital.com
www.michaelreesehospital.com

Enrique Beckmann, Chair/Ceo

950 Obesity Research Center
St. Luke's-Roosevelt Hospital
1090 Amsterdam Avenue 14th Floor
New York, NY 10025-1737
212-523-5366
E-mail: dg108@columbia.edu

Janine Pangburn, Research Project Manager
Tony Sikora, Administrative Assistant

Helps reduce the the incidence of obesity and related diseases through leadership in basic research, clinical research, epidemiology and public health, patient care, and public education.

951 UAMS Psychiatric Research Institute
5800 W 10th Street
Suite 605
Little Rock, AR 72204-1773
501-660-7559
Fax: 501-660-7542
E-mail: kramerteresal@uams.edu
www.uams.edu

Combining research, education and clinical services into one facility, PRI offers inpatiend and outpatient services, with 40 psychiatric beds, therapy options, and specialized treatment for specific disorders, including: addictive eating, anxiety, deppressive and post-traumatic stress disorders. Research focuses on evidence-based care takes into consideration the education of future medical personnel while relying on research scientists to provide innovative forms of treatment. PRI includes the Center for Addiction Research as well as a methadone clinic.

952 University of Pennsylvania Weight and Eating
Disorders Program
3535 Market Street
Suite 3108
Philadelphia, PA 19104-3313
215-898-8094
E-mail: cwilson@mail.med.upenn.edu

Conducts a wide variety of studies on the causes and treatment of weight-related disorders.

Support Groups & Hot Lines

953 Food Addicts Anonymous
4623 Forest Hill Boulevard
Suite 109-4
W Palm Beach, FL 33415-9120
561-967-3871
E-mail: info@foodaddictsanonymous.org
www.foodaddictsanonymous.org

Linda Closy, Manager

The FAA program is based on the belief that food addiction is a bio-chemical disease. We share our experience, strength, and hope with others allows us to recover from this disease.

954 MEDA
92 Pearl Street
Newton, MA 02458-1529
617-558-1881
866-343-6332
E-mail: info@medainc.org
www.medainc.org

MEDA ia a nonprofit organization dedicated to the prevention and treatment of eating disorders and disordered eating. MEDA'S mission is to prevent the continuing spread of eating disorders through educational awareness and early detection. MEDA serves as a support network and resource for clients, loved ones, clinicians, educators and the general public.

955 National Center for Overcoming Overeating
PO Box 1257
Old Chelsea Station
New York, NY 10113-1257
212-875-0442
E-mail: webmaster@overcomingovereating.com
www.overcomingovereating.com

Is an educational and training organization working to end body hatred and dieting.

956 Overeaters Anonymous General Service Office
PO Box 44020
Rio Rancho, NM 87174-4020
505-891-2664
Fax: 505-891-4320
E-mail: info@oa.org
www.oa.org

OA offers a program of recovery from compulsive eating using the Twelve Steps and Twelve Traditions of OA. It addresses physical, emotional and spiritual well-being.

Year Founded: 1960

Video & Audio

957 Eating Disorder Video
Active Parenting Publishers
1955 Vaughn Road NW
Suite 108
Kennesaw, GA 30144-7808
770-429-0565
800-825-0060
Fax: 770-429-0334
E-mail: cservice@activeparenting.com

Features compelling interviews with several young people who have suffered from anorexia nervosa, bulimia and compulsive eating. Discusses the treatments, causes and techniques for prevention with field experts. *$39.95*

ISSN Q6456

958 Eating Disorders: When Food Hurts
Fanlight Productions
2
47 Halifax St
Jamaica Plain, MA 02130-4327
617-469-4999
800-937-4113
Fax: 617-469-3379
E-mail: info@fanlight.com
www.fanlight.com

Ben Achtenberg, President
Nicole Johnson, Publicity Coordinator

People recovering from anorexia and bulimia, together with a therapist specializing in eating disorders, discuss their experiences of confronting these dangerous conditions. Encourages people with eating disorders to get help, as well as educating teachers, counselors, and others who work with young women. *$195.00*

Year Founded: 1996

Web Sites

959 www.anred.com
Anorexia Nervosa and Related Eating Disorders

The factual materials are detailed and organized.

960 www.bulimia.us.com
Bulimia: News & Discussion Forum

Eating disorders forum with news and information about bulimia, anorexia, male and teen eating disorders; treatment, help and resources information, events and inspirational stories.

961 www.closetoyou.org/eatingdisorders
Close to You

Information about eating disorders, anorexia, bulimia, binge eating disorder, and compulsive overeating.

962 www.cyberpsych.org
CyberPsych

Hosts the American Psychoanalysts Foundation, American Association of Suicideology, Society for the Exploration of Psychotherapy Intergration, and Anxiety Disorders Association of America. Also subcategories of the anxiety disorders, as well as general information, including panic disorder, phobias, obsessive compulsive disorder (OCD), social phobia, generalized anxiety disorder, post traumatic stress disorder, and phobias of childhood. Book reviews and links to web pages sharing the topics.

963 **www.edap.org**
Eating Disorders Awareness and Prevention

A source of educational brochures and curriculum materials.

964 **www.gurze.com**
Gurze Bookstore

Hundreds of books on eating disorders.

965 **www.healthyplace.com/Communities/**
Peace, Love, and Hope

Click on Body Views for information on body dysmorphic disorder.

966 **www.kidsource.com/nedo/**
National Eating Disorders Organization

Educational materials on dynamics, causative factors and evaluating treatment options.

967 **www.mentalhelp.net**
Anorexia Nervosa General Information

Introductory text on Anorexia Nervosa.

968 **www.mirror-mirror.org/eatdis.htm**
Mirror, Mirror

Relapse prevention for eating disorders.

969 **www.planetpsych.com**
Planetpsych.com

Learn about disorders, their treatments and other topics in psychology. Articles are listed under the related topic areas. Ask a therapist a question for free, or view the directory of professionals in your area. If you are a therapist sign up for the directory. Current features, self-help, interactive, and newsletter archives.

970 **www.psychcentral.com**
Psych Central

Personalized one-stop index for psychology, support, and mental health issues, resources, and people on the Internet.

971 **www.something-fishy.com**
Something Fishy Music and Publishing

Continuously educating the world on eating disorders to encourage every sufferer towards recovery.

Gender Identity Disorder

Introduction

With a wide scope of questions and confusion surrounding human sexuality and gender-explicit roles in the modern era, many children, adolescents and adults have been perplexed by the concepts of homosexuality and cross-gender identification. Homosexuality is a matter of sexual orientation: whether one is sexually attracted to men or women. The American Psychiatric Association ceased to classify homosexuality as an illness in 1973. Gender identity, in contrast, is a matter of what gender one feels oneself to be; people with Gender Identity Disorder feel that their psychological experience conflicts with the physical body with which they were born. Gender Identity Disorders can have serious social and occupational repercussions.

Diagnosis of Gender Identity Disorder requires two sets of criteria: (1) a heavy and persistent insistence that the individual is, or has a strong desire to be, of the opposite sex, and (2) a constant discomfort about his/her designated sex, a feeling of inappropriateness towards his/her biological designation. Typically, boys meeting critera for the disorder are predisposed to dressing as girls, drawing explicit pictures of females, playing with pre-designated feminine toys, fantasizing and role playing as females and interacting primarily with girls. Girls with the condition tend to participate in contact sports, have an aversion to wearing dresses, are often mistaken for boys due to attire and hair style, and may assert that they will develop in to men. For adolescents and adults, ostracism in school and the workplace is likely to occur, as is a profound inability to associate with others and poor relationships with family members and members of either sex.

There is a sharp divide among persons whose biological gender feels wrong; some insist that this is not a psychiatric disorder but rather a biological variant; others feel strongly that they have a psychiatric disorder. Some of this conviction is driven by the need to demonstrate 'medical necessity' in order for health insurance to cover hormonal or surgical interventions to make the individual look like the gender he or she feels they are.

SYMPTOMS

In boys
•A marked preoccupation with traditionally feminine activites;
•A preference for dressing as a girl;
•Attraction to stereotypical female games and toys;
•Portraying female characters in role playing;
•Assertion he is a girl;
•Insistence on sitting to urinate;
•Displaying disgust for his genitals, wishing to remove them.

In girls
•Aversion to traditional female attire;
•Shared interest in contact games;
•A preference for associating with boys;
•Refusing to urinate sitting down;
•Show little interest in playing with stereotypical female toys such as dolls;
•Assertion that she will grow a penis, not breasts;
•Identification with strong male figures.

In adolescents
•Ostracism in school and social situations;
•Social isolation, peer rejection and peer teasing;
•Significant cross-gender identification and mannerisms;
•Similar symptoms as children.

In adults
•Adoption of social roles, physical appearance, and mannerisms of opposite sex;
•Surgical and/or hormonal manipulation of biological state;
•Discomfort in being regarded by others, or functioning, as his/her designated sex;
•Cross-dressing;
•Transvestic Fetishism.

ASSOCIATED FEATURES

Those who have Gender Identity Disorder are at risk of mental and physical harm resulting, not from the condition itself, but from the reactions of other people to the condition. In children, a manifestation of Separation Anxiety Disorder, Generalized Anxiety Disorder and symptoms of Depression may result. For adolescents, depression and suicidal thoughts or ideas, as well as actual suicide attempts can result from prolonged feelings of ostracism by peers. Relationships with either one or both parents may weaken from resentment, lack of communication and misunderstanding; many with this disorder may drop out of or avoid school due to peer teasing. For many, lives are built around attempts to decrease gender distress. They are often preoccupied with appearance. In extreme cases, males with the disorder perform their own castration. Prostitution has been linked with the disorder because young people who are rejected by their families and ostracized by others may resort to prostitution as the only way to support themselves, a practice which increases the risk of acquiring sexually transmitted diseases. Some people with the disorder resort to substance abuse and other forms of abuse in an attempt to deal with the associated stress.

TREATMENT OPTIONS

Therapists who attempt to pathologize and 'cure' sexual orientation have been generally unsuccessful. So-called conversion therapy can cause more harm than good. In contrast, some people with Gender Identity Disorder decide to live as members of the opposite sex; some choose to undergo sex-change surgery. There is some controversy about the diagnosis; 'transsexual' groups protest that their condition, like homosexuality, should not be classified as a mental disease. Psychological assistance can help individuals to gain acceptance of themselves, and can teach methods of dealing with discrimination, prejudice and violence.

Associations & Agencies

973 Center for Family Support (CFS)
333 7th Avenue
New York, NY 10001-5115
212-629-7939
Fax: 212-239-2211
www.cfsny.org
Steven Vernikoff, Executive Director

An agency that continues to develop new programs to serve families and individuals with their care needs. They currently offer services throughout the New York City region including: New Jersey, Long Island and the Lower Hudson Valley.

974 Center for Mental Health Services (CMHS)

PO Box 2345
Rockville, MD 20847
240-221-4021
800-789-2647
Fax: 240-221-4295
TDD: 866-889-2647
www.mentalhealth.samhsa.gov

A Kathryn Power, MEd, Director
Anna Marsh PhD, Deputy Director
Fran Randolph PhD, Dir, Service & Systems Improveme
Anne Mathews-Younes EdD, Dir, Prevention/Traumatic Stress

CMHS leads Federal efforts to treat mental illnesses by promoting mental health and by preventing the development or worsening of mental illness when possible. Congress created CMHS to bring new hope to adults who have serious mental illnesses and to children with serious emotional disorders. CMHS provides information about mental health via a toll-free the web site, and more than 600 publications. Developed for users of mental health services and their families, the general public, policy makers, providers, and the media.

Year Founded: 1992

975 National Association for the Dually Diagnosed (NADD)

132 Fair Street
Kingston, NY 12401-4802
845-331-4336
800-331-5362
Fax: 845-331-4569
E-mail: info@thenadd.org
www.thenadd.org

Robert Fletcher, Executive Director

Nonprofit organization designed to promote interest of professional and parent development with resources for individuals who have the coexistence of mental illness and mental retardation. Provides conference, educational services and training materials to professionals, parents, concerned citizens and service organizations. Formerly known as the National Association for the Dually Diagnosed.

Year Founded: 1983

976 National Gay and Lesbian Task Force

1325 Massachusetts Avenue NW
Suite 600
Washington, DC 20005-4171
202-393-2241
Fax: 202-393-2241
E-mail: info@TheTaskForce.org
www.thetaskforce.org

Rea Carey, Executive Director
Sandi Greene, Director of Administration

Offers community support for gay and lesbian individuals.

Year Founded: 1973

977 National Institute of Mental Health

6001 Executive Blvd
Room 8184, MSC 9663
Bethesda, MD 20892-1
301-443-4513
TTY: 301-443-8431
E-mail: nimhinfo@nih.gov

Thomas R Insel MD, Director

The mission of the National Institute of Mental Health is to reduce the burden of mental illness and behavioral disorders through research on mind, brain, and behavior.

978 National Mental Health Consumers' Self-Help Clearinghouse

1211 Chestnut Street
Suite 1207
Philadelphia, PA 19107-4103
215-751-1810
800-553-4539
Fax: 215-636-6312
E-mail: info@mhselfhelp.org
www.mhselfhelp.org

A consumer-run national technical assistance center serving the mental health consumer movement. They connect individuals to self-help and advocacy resources, and offer expertise to self-help groups and other peer-run services for mental health consumers.

Year Founded: 1986

979 Parents and Friends of Lesbians and Gays

1726 M Street NW
Suite 400
Washington, DC 20036-4521
202-467-8180
Fax: 202-467-8194
E-mail: info@pflag.org

John R Cepek, President
Nina Sevilla, Executive Office Administrator

Organization of families and friends of lesbian and gay individuals, dedicated to offer support and understanding.

980 Parents, Families and Friends of Lesbians and Gays

1726 M Street NW
Suite 400
Washington, DC 20036-4521
202-467-8180
Fax: 202-467-8194
E-mail: info@pflag.org

John R Cepek, President

A national non-profit organization with over 200,000 members and supporters and over 500 affiliates in the United States.

981 SAMHSA's National Mental Health Information Center
US Department of Health and Human Services
PO Box 42557
Washington, DC 20015-557
240-221-4021
800-789-2647
Fax: 240-221-4295
TDD: 866-889-2647
www.mentalhealth.samhsa.gov

A Kathryn Power MEd, Director
Edward B Searle, Deputy Director

Provides information about mental health via a toll-free telephone number, this web site, and more than 600 publications. Developed for users of mental health services and their families, the general public, policy makers, providers, and the media.

Books

982 Gender Identity Disorder: A Medical Dictionary, Bibliography, and Annotated Research Guide to Internet References
ICON Health Publications
7404 Trade Street
San Diego, CA 92121-3414
858-635-9414

This book was created for medical professionals, students, and members of the general public who want to conduct medical research using the most advanced tools available and spending the least amount of time doing so.

983 Handbook of Sexual and Gender Identity Disorder
John Wiley & Sons
111 River Street
Hoboken, NJ 07030-5790
201-748-6000
Fax: 201-748-6088
E-mail: info@wiley.com
www.wiley.com

William J Pesce, CEO
David L Rowland, Author

The Handbook of Sexual and Gender Identity Disorders provides mental health professionals a comprehensive yet practical guide to the understanding, diagnosis, and treatment of a variety of sexual problems. *$95.00*

984 Identity Without Selfhood
Cambridge University Press
32 Avenue of the Americas
New York, NY 10013-2473
212-924-3900
Fax: 212-691-3239
www.cambridge.org

Richard Ziemacki, President

Situated at the crossroads of feminism, queer theory, and poststructuralist debates around identity, this is a book that shows how key Western concepts such as individuality constrain attempts to deconstruct the self and prevent bisexuality being understood as an identity. *$99.00*
ISBN 0-521623-57-x

Support Groups & Hot Lines

985 TransYouth Family Allies
PO Box 1471
Holland, MI 49422-1471

888-462-8932
E-mail: info@imatyfa.org
www.imatyfa.org

Kim Pearson, Executive Director
Shannon Garcia, President

TYFA empowers children and families by partnering with educators, service providers and communities to develop supportive environments in which gender may be expressed and respected.

Web Sites

986 www.cyberpsych.org
CyberPsych

Presents information about psychoanalysis, psychotherapy and special topics such as anxiety disorders, the problematic use of alcohol, homophobia, and the traumatic effects of racism.

987 www.health.nih.gov
National Institutes of Health

Part of the U.S. Department of Health and Human Services that is the nation's medical research agency-making important medical discoveries that improve health and save lives.

988 www.healthfinder.gov
Healthfinder

Developed by the U.S. Department of Health and Human Services, a key resource for finding the best government and nonprofit health and human services information on the internet.

989 www.intelihealth.com
Aetna InteliHealth

Aetna InteliHealth's mission is to empower people with trusted solutions for healthier lives.

990 www.kidspeace.org
KidsPeace

KidsPeace is a private charity dedicated to serving the be-havioral and mental health needs of children, preadolescents and teens.

991 www.mayohealth.com
Mayo Clinic Health Oasis

Their mission is to empower people to manage their health. They accomplish this by providing useful and up-to-date information and tools that reflect the expertise and standard of excellence of Mayo Clinic.

992 www.nlm.nih.gov
National Library of Medicine

The National Library of Medicine (NLM), on the campus of the National Institutes of Health in Bethesda, Maryland, is the world's largest medical library. The Library collects materials and provides information and research services in all areas of biomedicine and health care

993 www.planetpsych.com
Planet Psych

The online resource for mental health information

994 www.psychcentral.com
Psych Central

The Internet's largest and oldest independent mental health social network created and run by mental health profession-als to guarantee reliable, trusted information and support communities.

Impulse Control Disorders

Introduction

Everyone has experienced a situation in which they are tempted to do something that is harmful to themselves or others. This kind of behavior only becomes a disorder when a person is repeatedly and persistently unable to resist a temptation which is always harmful to them or to others. Usually the person feels a rising tension before acting on the need, feels pleasure and relief when giving in to the impulse and, sometimes, feels remorse and guilt afterwards. Four different disorders are included in this category.

KLEPTOMANIA

Symptoms
•Recurrent failure to resist the impulse to steal objects; often they are objects the individual could have paid for or doesn't particularly want;
•Increased sense of tension immediately before the theft;
•Pleasure and relief during the stealing;
•The theft is not due to anger, delusions or hallucinations.
•Awareness that stealing is senseless and wrong;
•Feelings of depression and guilt after stealing.

Associated Features
Kleptomania should not be confused with thefts which are deliberate and for personal gain, or those that are sometimes done by adolescents on a dare or as a rite of passage. Kleptomania is strongly associated with Depression, Anxiety Disorders, and Eating Disorders.

Prevalence
Kleptomania appears to be very rare; fewer than five percent of shoplifters have the disorder. However, Kleptomania is usually kept secret by the person, so this estimate may be low. It is much more common among females than males and may continue in spite of convictions for shoplifting.

Treatment Options
Behavior therapy, which is psychotherapy focusing on changing the behavior, has had some success, as has anti-depressant medication. A combination of these is most likely to help the person curb the impulse to steal while treating some of the underlying problems.

PYROMANIA

Symptoms
•Purposefully setting fires more than once;
•Increased tension before the deed;
•Fascination with and curiosity about fire and its paraphernalia;
•Pleasure or relief when setting or watching fires;
•The fire is not set for financial gain, revenge, or political reasons.

Associated Features
Many with this disorder make complicated preparations for setting a fire, and seem not to care about the serious consequences. They may get pleasure from the destruction. Most juveniles who set fires also have symptoms of Attention-Deficit/Hyperactivity Disorder or Adjustment Disorder.

Prevalence
Over forty percent of people arrested for arson in the US are under 18, but among children, the disorder is rare. Fire setting occurs mostly among males, and is more common for males with alcohol problems, learning problems and poor social skills.

Treatment Options
There is no agreed-upon best treatment. Pyromania is difficult to treat because the person usually does not take responsibility for the fire setting, and is in denial. Psychotherapy focused on the individual and with the family have been helpful. There is some indication that antidepressants may be effective.

PATHOLOGICAL GAMBLING

Symptoms
•Recurrent gambling;
•Gambling distrupts family, personal and work activities;
•Preoccupation with gambling, thinking about past plays, planning future gambling and how to get money for more gambling;
•Seeks excitement more than money. Bets become bigger and risks greater to produce the needed excitement;
•Gambling continues despite repeated efforts to stop with accompanying restlessness and irritability;
•Person may gamble to escape depression, anxiety, guilt;
•Chasing losses may become a pattern;
•May lie to family, therapists, and others to conceal gambling;
•May turn to criminal behavior (forgery, fraud, theft) to get money for gambling;
•May lose job, relationships, career opportunities;
Bailout behavior, that is turning to family and others, when in desperate financial straits.

Associated Features
Compulsive gamblers are distorted in their thinking. They are superstitious, deny they have a problem, and may be overconfident. They believe that money is the cause of, and solution to, all their problems. They are often competitive and easily bored. They may be extravagantly generous and very concerned with other people's approval. Compulsive gamblers are prone to medical problems connected with stress, such as hypertension and migraine. They also have a higher rate of Attention-Deficit/Hyperactivity Disorder; up to seventy-five percent suffer from Major Depressive Disorder, one third from Bipolar Disorder, and more than fifty percent abuse alcohol. Twenty percent are reported to have attempted suicide.

Prevalence
Gambling takes different forms in different cultures, e.g. cock-fights, horse racing, the stock market. Both males and females can be compulsive gamblers. Men usually begin gambling in adolescence, women somewhat later.
Women are more likely to use gambling as an escape from Depression. The prevalence of pathological gambling is high and rising, now including between one percent and three percent of the adult US population.
It is estimated that half of pathological gamblers are women, though women only make up from two percent to four percent of Gamblers Anonymous. Women may not go to treatment programs because of greater stigma attached to women gamblers.

Treatment Options

It is a difficult disorder to treat, but psychotherapy that concretely targets the behavior had limited success. Gamblers Anonymous, a 12-step program, may enable some to stop gambling. Treatment of the underlying disorders and involving family members may be helpful. It is important to note that, as specified in the American Psychiatric Association's Diagnostic and Statistical Manual of Mental Disorders, a psychiatric diagnosis, includng this one, does not, and is not meant to, exonerate an individual from responsibility for criminal behavior.

TRICHOTILLOMANIA

Symptoms

•Repeated hair pulling so that hair loss is noticeable;
•Increasing tension just before the behavior or when trying to resist it;
•Pleasure or relief when pulling;
•Causes clear distress and problems in personal work, or social functioning.

Associated Features

Examining the hair root, pulling the hair between the teeth, or eating hairs (Trichophagia) may accompany Trichotillomania. Hair pulling is usually done in private or in the presence of close family members. Pain is not usually reported. The hair pulling is mostly denied and concealed by wigs, hairstyling and cosmetics. People with this disorder may also have Major Depressive Disorder, General Anxiety Disorder, Eating Disorder or Mental Retardation.

Prevalence

Among children, both males and females can have the disorder, but among adults, it is far more frequent in females. There are no recent prevalence figures for the general population, but in studies of college students, one percent to two percent have experienced Trichotillomania.

Treatment Options

There is no agreement about the cause of this disorder, making treatment more difficult. Professionals are often not consulted. Variable treatments that have been proposed include behavior therapy, hypnosis, and stress reduction. Medication has sometimes been helpful.

Associations & Agencies

996 Career Assessment & Planning Services
Goodwill Industries-Suncoast
10596 Gandy Boulevard
Po Box 14456
St. Petersburg, FL 33733-4456
727-523-1512
888-279-1988
Fax: 727-563-9300
E-mail: gw.marketing@goodwill-suncoast.com
www.goodwill-suncoast.org

R Lee Waits, President/CEO
Deborah Passerini, VP Operations

Provides a comprehensive assessment, which can predict current and future employment and potential adjustment factors for physically, emotionally or developmentally disabled persons who may be unemployed or underemployed. Assessments evaluate interests, aptitudes, academic achievements, and physical abilities (including dexterity and coordination) through coordinated testing, interviewing and behavioral observations.

997 Center for Family Support (CFS)
333 7th Avenue
New York, NY 10001-5115
212-629-7939
Fax: 212-239-2211
www.cfsny.org

Steven Vernikoff, Executive Director

An agency that continues to develop new programs to serve families and individuals with their care needs. Offering services throughout the New York City region including: New Jersey, Long Island and the Lower Hudson Valley.

998 Center for Mental Health Services (CMHS)
PO Box 2345
Rockville, MD 20847
240-221-4021
800-789-2647
Fax: 240-221-4295
TDD: 866-889-2647
www.mentalhealth.samhsa.gov

A Kathryn Power, MEd, Director
Anna Marsh PhD, Deputy Director
Fran Randolph PhD, Dir, Service & Systems Improveme
Anne Mathews-Younes EdD, Dir, Prevention/Traumatic Stress

CMHS leads Federal efforts to treat mental illnesses by promoting mental health and by preventing the development or worsening of mental illness when possible. Congress created CMHS to bring new hope to adults who have serious mental illnesses and to children with serious emotional disorders. CMHS provides information about mental health via a toll-free the web site, and more than 600 publications. Developed for users of mental health services and their families, the general public, policy makers, providers, and the media.

Year Founded: 1992

999 Mental Health Matters
PO Box 82149
Kenmore, WA 98028-149
425-402-6934
E-mail: info@mental-health-matters.com
www.mental-health-matters.com

Founded to supply information and resources to mental health consumers, professionals, students and supporters.

1000 National Association for the Dually Diagnosed (NADD)
132 Fair Street
Kingston, NY 12401-4802
845-331-4336
800-331-5362
Fax: 845-331-4569
E-mail: info@thenadd.org
www.thenadd.org

Robert Fletcher, Executive Director
Donna Nagy PhD, President

Nonprofit organization designed to promote interest of professional and parent development with resources for individuals who have the coexistence of mental illness and mental retardation. Provides conference, educational services and training materials to professionals, parents, concerned citizens and service organizations. Formerly known as the National Association for the Dually Diagnosed.

Year Founded: 1983

1001 National Mental Health Consumers' Self-Help Clearinghouse

1211 Chestnut Street
Suite 1207
Philadelphia, PA 19107-4103
215-751-1810
800-553-4539
Fax: 215-636-6312
E-mail: info@mhselfhelp.org
www.mhselfhelp.org

Joseph Rogers, Executive Director

A national consumer technical assistance center that has played a major role in the development of the mental health consumer movement.

Year Founded: 1986

1002 SAMHSA's National Mental Health Information Center
US Department of Health and Human Services

PO Box 42557
Washington, DC 20015-557
240-221-4021
800-789-2647
Fax: 240-221-4295
TDD: 866-889-2647
www.mentalhealth.samhsa.gov

A Kathryn Power, MEd, Director
Edward B Searle, Deputy Director

Provides information about mental health via a toll-free telephone number, this web site, and more than 600 publications. Developed for users of mental health services and their families, the general public, policy makers, providers, and the media.

1003 Trichotillomania Learning Center

207 McPherson Street
Suite H
Santa Cruz, CA 95060-5863
831-457-1004
www.trich.org

Christina Pearson, Executive Director
Christina Pearson, Executive Director

Works to improve the quality of life of children, adolescents and adults with trichotillomania and related body-focused repetitive disorders such as skin picking through information dissemination, education, outreach, alliance building, and support of research into the causes and treatment of these disorders.

Year Founded: 1991

1004 Angry All the Time
New Harbinger Publications

5674 Shattuck Avenue
Oakland, CA 94609-1662
510-652-0215
800-748-6273
Fax: 510-652-5472
E-mail: customerservices@newharbinger.com
www.newharbinger.com

Matthew McKay, Owner

An emergency guide for people who have anger control problems. *$12.95*

136 pages

1005 Clinical Manual of Impulse-Control Disorders
American Psychiatric Publishing, Inc.

1000 Wilson Boulevard
Suite 1825
Arlington, VA 22209-3901
703-907-7322
800-368-5777
Fax: 703-907-1091
E-mail: appi@psych.org
www.appi.org

Robert E Hales MD, Editor-in-Chief
Ron McMillen, Chief Executive Officer
John McDuffie, Editorial Director

Focuses on all of the different impulse-control disorders as a group.

1006 Drug Therapy and Impulse Control Disorders
Mason Crest Publishers

370 Reed Road
Suite 302
Broomall, PA 19008-4017

866-627-2665
Fax: 610-543-3878
www.masoncrest.com

Autumn Libal, Author

The stories and information in this book will tell you more about impulse-control disorders, how they affect people's lives, and how they can be treated. *$24.95*

128 pages ISBN 1-590845-66-0

1007 Impulse Control Disorders: A Clinician's Guide to Understanding and Treating Behavioral Addictions
W.W. Norton & Company

500 Fifth Avenue
New York, NY 10110-54
212-354-2907
Fax: 212-869-0856

Drake McFeely, CEO

A comprehensive book on impulse control disorders topic for clinicians provides a screening instrument and a detailed method for assessing and treating them.

1008 Impulsivity and Compulsivity
American Psychiatric Publishing, Inc.
1000 Wilson Boulevard
Suite 1825
Arlington, VA 22209-3901
703-907-7322
800-368-5777
Fax: 703-907-1091
E-mail: appi@psych.org
www.appi.org

Robert E Hales MD, Editor-in-Chief
Ron McMillen, Chief Executive Officer
John McDuffie, Editorial Director

Leading researchers and clinicians share their expertise on the phenomenological, biological, psychodynamic, and treatment aspects of these disorders. *$40.00*

294 pages ISBN 0-880486-76-7

1009 One Hundred Four Activities That Build
Sunburst Media
2 Skyline Drive
Suite 101
Hawthorne, NY 10532-2142

888-367-6368
Fax: 914-347-1805
E-mail: info@Childswork.com
www.Childswork.com

Full of interactive and fun games that can be used to encourage, modification of behavior, increase interaction with others, start discussions and build other life and social skills. *$23.95*

71 pages

1010 Out of Control: Gambling and Other Impulse Control Disorders
Chelsea House Publications
132 West 31st Street
17th Floor
New York, NY 10001-3406

800-322-8755
Fax: 800-678-3633
E-mail: custserv@factsonfile.com
www.chelseahouse.infobasepublishing.com

This Encyclopedia of Psychological Disorders provides information on the history, causes and effects of, and treatment and therapies for problems affecting the human mind. *$35.00*

95 pages Year Founded: 2000 ISBN 0-791053-13-X

1011 Pyromania, Kleptomania, and Other Impulse Control Disorder
Enslow Publishers
40 Industrial Road
Box 398
Berkeley Heights, NJ 07922-1502
908-771-9400
800-398-2504
Fax: 908-771-0925
E-mail: customerservice@enslow.com

Mark Enslow, Owner

Describes the characterisitics of impulsive control disorders, from their early diagnoses and methods of treatment to today's available medications. *$26.60*

128 pages Year Founded: 2002 ISBN 0-766018-99-7

1012 Stop Me Because I Can't Stop Myself: Taking Control of Impulsive Behavior
McGraw-Hill Companies
1221 Avenue of the Americas
New York, NY 10020-1095
212-512-2000
www.mcgraw-hill.com

Harold W McGraw Iii, CEO
Jon E Grant, Author

Offers the latest research and practical help for those who engage in all types of impulse-related behaviors.

1013 When Anger Hurts: Quieting The Storm Within
New Harbinger Publications
5674 Shattuck Avenue
Oakland, CA 94609-1662
510-652-0215
800-748-6273
Fax: 510-652-5472
www.newharbinger.com

Matthew McKay, Owner

Step by step guide to changing habitual anger-controlled thoughts while developing healthier, more effective ways of meeting your needs. *$16.95*

325 pages Year Founded: 2003 ISBN 1-572243-44-9

1014 Youth with Impulse-Control Disorders: On the Spur of the Moment (Helping Youth with Mental, Physical, & Social Disabilities)
Mason Crest Publishers
370 Reed Road
Suite 302
Broomall, PA 19008-4017

866-621-2665
Fax: 610-543-3878
www.masoncrest.com

Kenneth McIntosh, Author
Phyllis Livingston, Author

Support Groups & Hot Lines

1015 Gam-Anon Family Groups International Service Office
PO Box 157
Whitestone, NY 11357-0157
718-352-1671
Fax: 718-746-2571
E-mail: info3@gam-anon.org
www.gam-anon.org

The self-help organization of Gam-Anon is a life saving instrument for the spouse, family or close friends of compulsive gamblers.

1016 Gamblers Anonymous
PO Box 17173
Los Angeles, CA 90017-173
213-386-8789
Fax: 213-386-0030
E-mail: isomain@gamblersanonymous.org
www.gamblersanonymous.org

Fellowship of men and women who share their experience, strength and hope with each other so that they may solve their common problem and help others recover from a gambling problem.

1017 Trichotillomania Learning Center
207 McPherson Street
Suite H
Santa Cruz, CA 95060-5863
831-457-1004
E-mail: info@trich.org
www.trich.org

Christina Pearson, Executive Director

Groups of individuals who get together and help one another understand about their disease. Also, they show each other different ways to prevent a attack from happening.

Video & Audio

1018 A Desperate Act
Trichotillomania Learning Center
303 Potrero Street
Suite 51
Santa Cruz, CA 95060-2760
831-457-1004
Fax: 831-426-4383
E-mail: info@trich.org
www.trich.org

A performance artist with TTM discusses her experiences in front of a live audience. 60 minutes.

1019 Our Personal Stories
Trichotillomania Learning Center
303 Potrero Street
Suite 51
Santa Cruz, CA 95060-2760
831-457-1004
Fax: 831-426-4383
E-mail: info@trich.org
www.trich.org

Documentary detailing 8 women's personal experiences with TTM. 90 minutes. *$28.00*

1020 Trichotillomania: Overview and Introduction to HRT
Trichotillomania Learning Center
303 Potrero Street
Suite 51
Santa Cruz, CA 95060-2760
831-457-1004
Fax: 831-426-4383
E-mail: info@trich.org
www.trich.org

A lecture on behavior therapy and Habit reversal Training for TTM. 120 minutes. *$30.00*

Web Sites

1021 www.apa.org/pubinfo/anger.html
Controlling Anger-Before It Controls You

From the American Psychological Association.

1022 www.cfsny.org
Center for Family Support

A not-for-profit human service agency that provides individualized support services and programs for individuals living with developmental and related disabilities, and for the families that care for them at home.

1023 www.cyberpsych.org
CyberPsych

Presents information about psychoanalysis, psychotherapy and special topics such as anxiety disorders, the problematic use of alcohol, homophobia, and the traumatic effects of racism.

1024 www.goodwill-suncoast.org
Suncoast Residential Training Center

Serves individuals diagnosed as mentally retarded with a secondary diagnosis of pychiatric difficulties as evidenced by problem behavior.

1025 www.members.aol.com/AngriesOut
Get Your Angries Out

Guidelines for kids, teachers, and parents.

1026 www.mentalhealth.org
Center for Mental Health Services Knowledge Exchange Network

Information about resources, technical assistance, research, training, networks and other federal clearinghouses, fact sheets and materials.

1027 www.mentalhelp.net/psyhelp/chap7
Anger and Aggression

Therapeutic approaches.

1028 www.mhselfhelp.org
National Mental Health Consumer's Self-Help Clearinghouse

A national consumer technical assistance center, has played a major role in the development of the mental health consumer movement

1029 www.psychcentral.com
Psych Central

Internet's largest and oldest independent mental health social network created and run by mental health professionals to guarantee reliable, trusted information and support communities to you.

1030 www.stopbitingnails.com
Stop Biting Nails

Online organization created for those who bite their nails. Created a product which is used to prevent nailbiting.

1031 www.thenadd.org
National Association for the Dually Diagnosed

A not-for-profit membership association established for professionals, care providers and families to promote understanding of and services for individuals who have developmental disabilities and mental health needs.

Mood Disorders

Introduction

Mood disorders are psychiatric conditions in which the most prominent symptom is a consistent change in mood - either up, down, or both in alteration. They are common; they cause a large proportion of the disability world-wide, and they can be fatal. These are really whole-body diseases; many other symptoms go along with the mood change. There are changes in sleep, appetite, energy, and concentration, and many people have physical pain during episodes of depression. Some depressed people have irritability rather than sadness. Fortunately, there are effective treatments, both pharmacological and psychotherapeutic.

DEPRESSION

Feelings of sadness are common to everyone, and quite natural in reaction to unfortunate circumstances. The death of a loved one, the end of a relationship, or other traumatic life experiences are bound to bring on the blues. But when feelings of sadness and despair persist beyond a reasonable period, arise for no particular reason, or begin to affect a person's ability to function, help is needed. Depression is a diagnosis made by a psychiatrist or other mental health professional to describe serious and prolonged symptoms of sadness or despair. While it is quite common, it is also a disease that no one should take lightly; depression can be deadly. Many people who are deeply depressed think about or actually try to commit suicide; some commit suicide. Even a relatively mild depresseion, if untreated, can disrupt marriages and relationships or impede careers. Such depressions cost the U.S. economy billions of dollars a year in lost productivity.

Symptoms

Depression is diagnosed when an individual experiences 1) persistent feelings of sadness or 2) loss of interest or pleasure in usual activities, in addition to five of the following symptoms for at least two weeks:
•Significant weight gain or loss unrelated to dieting;
•Inability to sleep or, conversely, sleeping too much;
•Restlessness and agitation;
•Fatigue or loss of energy;
•Feelings of worthlessness or guilt;
•Diminished ability to think or concentrate;
•Recurrentthoughts of death or suicide;
•Distress not caused by a medication or the symptoms of a medical illness.

Associated Features

Because depression can range from mild to severe, people who are depressed may exhibit a variety of behaviors. Often, people who are depressed are tearful, irritable, or brooding. Problems sleeping (either insomnia or sleeping too much) are common. People with Depression may worry unnecessarily about being sick or having a disease, or they may report physical symptoms such as headaches or other pains. Depression can seriously affect people's friendships and intimate relationships.

Depression can make people worry aout having a disease, but this is not a central symptom. Depression very frequently coexists with anxiety disorder. There is a genetic predisposition in some people.

Abuse of alcohol, presription drugs, or illegal drugs is also common among people who are depressed. The most serious risk associated with Depression is the risk of suicide: people who have tried to commit suicide are especially at risk. Individuals who have another mental disorder, such as Schizophrenia, in addition to Depression are also more likely to commit suicide.

Prevalence

Every year, more than 17 million Americans suffer some type of depressive illness. Depression does not discriminate; anyone can have it. Children, adults and the elderly are susceptible. Nevertheless, studies do indicate that women are twice as likely to have Depression as men. Depression has significant adverse effects on children's functioning and development; among adolescents, suicide id believed to be the fifth leading cause of death. Depression is also common among the elderly, and can be treated as an illness distinct from loneliness or sadness that may accompany old age.

Treatment Options

Depression is a medical disease and does not respond to the usual ways we have of cheering up ourselves or others. In fact, attempts to cheer depressed individuals may have the opposite and unfortunate consequence of making them feel worse, often because they are frustrated and feel guilty that others' well-meaning efforts do not help. If a person experiences the symptoms of Depression, he or she should seek treatment from a qualified professional. The vast majority of people with Depression get better when they are treated properly, and virtually everyone gets some relief from their symptoms.

A psychiatrist or other mental health professional should conduct a thorough evaluation, including and interview; a physical examination should be done by a primary care provider. On the basis of a complete evaluation, the appropriate treatment will be prescribed. Most likely, the treatment will be medication or psychotherapy, or both. Antidepressants usually take effect within three to six weeks after treatment has begun; it is important to give medications long enough to work, and to increase dosages or change or add medications ifdepression does not resolve completely.

The natural (untreated) course of a depressive episode is about nine months. Therefore treatment should be continued for at least that length of time even though the individual feels better. If treatment is discontinued prematurely, the depression is very likely to return. Depression is also a recurring disease; the risk of an episode after a first episode is 50%; after two episodes, 67%; and after three, over 90%. Therefore, some patients prefer to continue taking antidepressant medication indefinitely.

Dysthymic disorder is more low-level than chronic, with depressed mood consistently for at least two tears, than major depressive episodes, which last about nine months. Dysthymia can be treated with medication and psychotherapy as well.

Psychotherapy, or talk therapy, may be used to help the patient improve the way he or she thinks about things and deals with specific life problems. Individual, family, or couples therapy may be recommended, depending on the patient's life experiences. If the Depression is not severe, treatment can take a few weeks; if the Depression has been a longstanding problem, it may take much longer, but in many cases, a patient will experience improvement in 10-15 sessions.

POSTPARTUM DEPRESSION

Within days to a year after giving birth, women may experience a spectrum of psychological symptoms related to both the abrupt hormonal changes and the psychological and social demands of motherhood. The mildest of these symptoms, 'baby blues,' is not a psychiatric condition. It consists of a few days of heightened emotionality starting within days after birth and resolving spontaneously. They may become concerned when the emotionality leads to tears, but women with 'baby blues,' and their families, need only reassurance.

Postpartum depression is often a continuation of depression starting during or even before pregnancy. The symptoms, which are listed below, are much the same as those of depression occurring at any other time of life. The fact that the postpartum period is almost always associated with problems with sleep, appetite, libido, energy, and concentration makes those symptoms less useful for diagnosis at this time. Two cardinal questions are: 'Are you feeling sad most of the time?' and 'Are you unable to enjoy things that you usually enjoy?' Women with postpartum depression are preoccupied with concerns about their ability to be good mothers. Unlike an average, tired new mother, the depressed woman cannot enjoy her baby. She is often guilty and reluctant to tell her family about it because she knows she is supposed to appreciate her good fortune and be happy. Severe Postpartum Depression, or Postpartum Psychosis, that causes confusion, disorientation, delusions, and hallucinations, and can cause suicide or infanticide, is a serious medical condition demanding immediate professional attention. Fortunately, there is increasing awareness and understanding of postpartum depression among the general population.

Symptoms
In addition to the symptoms of Depression:
•Preoccupation with concerns of being a good mother;
•Inability to rest while the baby is sleeping;
•Inability to enjoy her baby accompanied with feelings of guilt.

Prevalence
Very mild depression after delivery, or 'baby blues,' affects over half, perhaps up to 90% of postpartum women. Baby blues is actually not depression at all; rather it is a common condition characterized by sensitivity and emotionality, both happy and sad. Postpartum Depression affects approximately 10% of new mothers. Much postpartum depression is a continuation of depression that was already present during pregnancy.

Treatment Options
Treatment for Postpartum Depression is similar to treatment for depression in general. Possible risks of medications taken during pregnancy and breastfeeding have to be weighed against the risks of leaving the depression untreated. Women who discontinue antidepressant medication because they wish to become or have become pregnant are at a very high risk of relapse.

BIPOLAR DISORDER

Bipolar Disorder (Manic Depression) is the name for a group of severe mental illnesses characterized by alterations between depression and manic euphoria or irritability.

The two states are not independent of each other, but part of the same illness. Individuals in the manic phase of Bipolar Disorder may feel exuberant, invincible, or even immortal. They may be awake for days at a time, and be able to work tirelessly; they may rush from one idea to the next carried by a nearly uncontrollable burst of energy that leaves others bewildered and unable to keep up. (Some extraordinarily creative people, Vincent Van Gogh, for example, have had Bipolar Disorder. Whether or not the disorder makes a positive contribution to creativity is a controversial question.)

In the depressed phase which follows a manic high, the patient may be suicidal. The depressed phase of the illness mirrors a major depressive episode. There are three forms of Bipolar Disorders: Bipolar I Disorder, Bipolar II Disorder, and Cyclothymic Disorder. Bipolar II Disorder consists of repeated depressive episodes interspersed with hypomaniac (not full blown mania) episodes. The individual with Cyclothymic Disorder has a history of at least two years of repeated episodes of elevated and depressed mood which don't meet all the criteria for mania or depression but which cause distress and/or decreased ability to function.

A number of researchers are closing in on genetic links to the illness. Like all mental disorders, however, the relationship between genetic physiologic, psychological, and environmental causes is complex. Lithium was the first medication found to be effective; several other medications are now available and effective. Many patients with Bipolar Disorders need a combination of medications to address both the manic and depressive aspects. While medication is quite effective, patients need psychotherapy as well, in order to address issues like compliance with medication, noting early signs of relapse, dealing with friends and family and environmental life stressors.

Symptoms
A **manic episode** consists of the following:

•A distinct period of abnormally and persistently elevated, expansive, or irritable mood, lasting at least one week;
•Inflated self-esteem or grandiosity;
•Decreased need for sleep;
•More talkative than usual;
•Flight of ideas (a succession of topics with little relationship to one another) or a subjective experience that thoughts are racing;
•Distractibility;
•Increase in goal-directed activity;
•Excessive involvement in activities that have a high potential for painful consequences;
•The mood disturbances are severe enough to cause impairment in social or occupational functioning;
•The symptoms are not due to the direct physiological effects of a substance.

The **depressive phase** of Bipolar Disorder consists of the following:

•Depressed mood most othe day, nearly every day, as indicated by either subjective report or observation;
•Markedly diminished interest or pleasure in almost all activities most of the day;
•Significant weight loss when not dieting, or weight gain, or decrease or increase in appetite nearly every day;
•Insomnia or hypersomnia nearly every night;
•Psychomotor agitation or retardation nearly every day;
•Fatigue or loss of evergy nearly every day;
•Feelings of worthlessness or excessive or inappropriate guilt nearly every day.

Associated Features

Bipolar Disorder is a severe mental illness that can cause extreme disruption to individual lives and careers, and to whole families. While manic, patients may spend all of a family's money, borrow great sums, engage in indiscriminate sexual activity, and behave in other ways that leave lasting negative effects. Suicide is a risk factor in the illness, and an estimated 10% to 15% of individuals with Bipolar I Disorder commit suicide. Abuse of children, spouses or other family members, or other types of violence, may occur during the manic phase of the illness. Untreated mania, during which the individual gets no sleep, little or no nutrition, and expends great quantities of energy, can result in death as well.

It is important for patients with depression to be carefully screened for any manic or hypomanic symptoms so that Bipolar Disorder can be diagnosed and the appropriate treatment prescribed. Most people with Bipolar Disorder present, or are referred, for care while in the depressive state; it is essential that any individual diagnosed with depression be carefully evaluated to rule out bipolar disorder before antidepressany medication is prescribed. Antidepressany medication alone can precipitate a manic episode in an individual with Bipolar Disorder. The cycles of mood changes tend to become more frequent, shorter, and more intense as the patient gets older.

Disturbances in work, school or social functioning are common, resulting in frequent school truancy or failure, occupational failure, divorce, or episodic antisocial behavior. A variety of other mental disorders may accompany Bipolar Disorder; these include Anorexia Nervosa, Bulimia Nervosa, Attention Deficit/Hyperactivity Disorder, Panic Disorder, Social Phobia, and Substance-Abuse Related Disorder.

Prevalence

The prevalence of Bipolar I Disorder varies from 0.4% to 0.6% in the community. Community prevalence of Bipolar II Disorder is approximately 0.5%. The prevalence of Cyclothymic Disorder is estimated at 0.4% to 1%, and from 3% to 5% in clinics specializing in mood disorders.

Treatment Options

Lithium is the most commonly prescribed drug for Bipolar Disorder and is effective for stabilizing patients in the manic phase of the illness and preventing mood swings. However, compliance is a problem among patients both because of the nature of the condition (some patients may actually miss the high of their mood swings and other people often envy their enthusiasm, energy, and confidence) and because of the side effects associated with the drug. These include weight gain, excessive thirst, tremors and muscle weakness. Lithium is also very toxic in overdose. Blood levels of lithium must be measured daily

or weekly to begin with, and in at least six-month intervals thereafter. The disruptive nature of the condition also necessitates the use of psychotherapy and family therapy to help patients rebuild relationships, to maintain compliance with treatment and a positive attitude toward living with a chronic illness, and to restore confidence and self-esteem.

Anticonvulsants/mood stabilizers, such as Valproate, Carbamazepine, Lamotrigine, Gabapentin, and Topiramate have also become first-line treatments, as have several antipsychotic medications.

Education of the family is crucial for successful treatment, as is education of patients about the disorder and treatment.

Associations & Agencies

1033 Bipolar Disorders Treatment Information Center
Madison Institute of Medicine
7617 Mineral Point Road
Suite 300
Madison, WI 53717-1623
608-827-2470
E-mail: mim@miminc.org
www.factsforhealth.org

Margarett Baudhuin, Manager
David Katzelnick, Founder

Provides information on mood stabilizers other than lithium for bipolar disorder. With more than 4,000 references on file, the Center collects and disseminates information about all medications and other forms of treatment of bipolar disorder, including divalproex sodium (valproate), carbamazepine, lamotrigine, gabapentin and topiramate.

1034 Career Assessment & Planning Services
Goodwill Industries-Suncoast
10596 Gandy Boulevard
PO Box 14456
St. Petersburg, FL 33733-4456
727-523-1512
888-279-1988
Fax: 727-563-9300
E-mail: gw.marketing@goodwill-suncoast.com
www.goodwill-suncoast.org

R Lee Waits, President/CEO
Deborah Passerini, VP Operations

Provides a comprehensive assessment, which can predict current and future employment and potential adjustment factors for physically, emotionally, or developmentally disabled persons who may be unemployed or underemployed. Assessments evaluate interests, aptitudes, academic achievements, and physical abilities (including dexterity and coordination) through coordinated testing, interviewing and behavioral observations.

1035 Center for Family Support (CFS)
333 7th Avenue
New York, NY 10001-5115

212-629-7939
Fax: 212-239-2211
www.cfsny.org

Steven Vernikoff, Executive Director

An agency that continues to develop new programs to serve families and individuals with their care needs. Currently offering services throughout the New York City region including: New Jersey, Long Island and the Lower Hudson Valley.

1036 Center for Mental Health Services (CMHS)
PO Box 2345
Rockville, MD 20847
240-221-4021
800-789-2647
Fax: 240-221-4295
TDD: 866-889-2647
www.mentalhealth.samhsa.gov

A Kathryn Power, MEd, Director
Anna Marsh PhD, Deputy Director
Fran Randolph PhD, Dir, Service & Systems Improveme
Anne Mathews-Younes EdD, Dir, Prevention/Traumatic
Stress

CMHS leads Federal efforts to treat mental illnesses by promoting mental health and by preventing the development or worsening of mental illness when possible. Congress created CMHS to bring new hope to adults who have serious mental illnesses and to children with serious emotional disorders. CMHS provides information about mental health via a toll-free the web site, and more than 600 publications. Developed for users of mental health services and their families, the general public, policy makers, providers, and the media.

Year Founded: 1992

1037 Child and Adolescent Bipolar Foundation
820 Davis Street
Suite 520
Evanston, IL 60201
847-492-8519
E-mail: cabf@bpkids.org
www.bpkids.org

Susan Resko MM, Executive Director

A not-for-profit organizatoin of families raising children and teens affected by depression, bipolar disorder, and other mood disorders

1038 Depression & Bi-Polar Support Alliance
730 N Franklin Street
Suite 501
Chicago, IL 60654-7225
312-642-0049
800-826-3632
Fax: 312-642-7243
www.dbsalliance.org

Sue Bergeson, President
Ingrid Deetz, Program Manager

Educates patients, families, professionals, and the public concerning the nature of depressive and manic-depressive illnesses as treatable medical diseases, fosters self-help for patients and families, works to eliminate discrimination and

stigma, improves access to care, advocates for research toward the elimination of these illnesses.

1039 Depression & BiPolar Support Alliance
730 N Franklin Street
Suite 501
Chicago, IL 60654-7225
312-642-0049
800-826-3632
Fax: 312-642-7243
E-mail: questions@dbsalliance.org
www.dbsalliance.org

Sue Bergeson, President
Susan Bergeson, VP

Educates patients, families, professionals, and the public concerning the nature of depressive and manic-depressive illnesses as treatable medical diseases, fosters self-help for patients and families, eliminates discrimination and stigma.

1040 Depression & Related Affective Disorders Association (DRADA)
2330 West Joppa Road
Suite 100
Lutherville, MD 21093
410-583-2919
Fax: 410-614-3241
E-mail: drada@jhmi.edu

Catherine Pollock, Executive Director
Elizabeth Boyce, Director Development

Non profit association whose mission is to alleviate the suffering arising from depression and manic depression by assisting self - help groups, providing education and information and lending support to research programs.

1041 Depression After Delivery
91 E Somerset Street
Raritan, NJ 08869-2129
908-575-9121
800-944-4773
Fax: 908-541-9713
E-mail: dadorg@earthlink.net
www.depressionafterdelivery.com

Joyce A Venis, RNC, President
Donna Cangialosi, Office Manager

Twenty four information request line. Free information packet of referrals and volunteer contacts nationwide for women with postpartum disorders.

1042 Depression and Bi-Polar Alliance
730 N Franklin Street
Suite 501
Chicago, IL 60654-7225
312-642-0049
800-826-3632
Fax: 312-642-7243
www.dbsalliance.org

Sue Bergeson, President
Julie Bremer, External Relations Director

Previously called the National Depressive and Manic Depressive Association, the Depression and Bi-Polar Alliance publishes a variety of educational materials for adults and teens on mood disorders, all available free of charge or for a nominial fee. Because the Alliance focuses on the consumer living with a mood disorder, their publications are written in language free from medical and scientific jargon and everything they produce conveys a strong message of hope and optimism.

1043 Freedom From Fear

308 Seaview Avenue
Staten Island, NY 10305-2246
718-351-1717
Fax: 718-667-8893
E-mail: help@freedomfromfear.org
www.freedomfromfear.org

Mary Guardino, Founder/President

The mission of Freedom From Fear is to aid and counsel individuals and their families who suffer from anxiety and depressive illness.

1044 Lithium Information Center
Madison Institute of Medicine

7617 Mineral Point Road
Suite 300
Madison, WI 53717-1623
608-827-2470
E-mail: mim@miminc.org
www.factsforhealth.org

Margarett Baudhuin, Manager
David Katzelnick, Founder

A resource for information on lithium treatment of bipolar disorders and on the other medical and biological applications of lithium. The Center currently has more than 32,000 references on file.

1045 Mental Health Research Association (NARSAD)

60 Cutter Mill Road
Suite 404
Great Neck, NY 11021-3104
516-829-0091
800-829-8289
Fax: 516-487-6930
E-mail: info@narsad.org
www.narsad.org

Constance Lieber, President
Steven G Doochin, Executive Director

The Mental Health Research Association is a nonprofit organization that raises funds for scientific research on severe mental illnesses. It is the largest donor-supported organization in the world dedicated to finding the causes, improved treatments and cures for psychiatric brain and behavior disorders.

1046 NARSAD: The Mental Health Research Association

60 Cutter Mill Road
Suite 404
Great Neck, NY 11021-3104
516-829-0091
800-829-8289
Fax: 516-487-6930
E-mail: info@narsad.org
www.narsad.org

Steve Doochin, Executive Director
Louis Innamorato, CFO

Previously known as the National Alliance for Research on Schizophrenia and Depression, NARSAD is a private, not-for-profit public charity organized for the purpose of raising funds for scientific research into the causes, cures, treatments and prevention of severe psychiatric brain and behavior disorders, such as schizophrenia and depression.

1047 National Alliance on Mental Illness

2107 Wilson Boulevard
Suite 300
Arlington, VA 22201-3080
703-524-7600
800-950-6264
Fax: 703-524-9094
E-mail: helpline@nami.org
www.nami.org

Michael Fitzpatrick, Executive Director

Nation's leading self-help organization for all those affected by severe brain disorders. Mission is to bring consumers and families with similar experiences together to share information about services, care providers, and ways to cope with the challenges of schizophrenia, manic depression, and other serious mental illnesses.

1048 National Assocaition for the Dually Diagnosed

132 Fair Street
Kingston, NY 12401-4802
845-331-4336
800-331-5362
E-mail: nadd@mhv.net
www.thenadd.org

Robert Fletcher, Executive Director
Donna Nagy PhD, President

Nonprofit organization designed to promote interest of professional and parent development with resources for individuals who have the coexistence of mental illness and mental retardation. Provides conference, educational services and training materials to professionals, parents, concerned citizens and service organizations. Formerly known as the National Association for the Dually Diagnosed.

1049 National Association for the Dually Diagnosed (NADD)

132 Fair Street
Kingston, NY 12401-4802
845-331-4336
800-331-5362
Fax: 845-331-4569

E-mail: info@thenadd.org
www.thenadd.org

Robert Fletcher, Executive Director

A not-for-profit membership association established for professionals, care providers and families to promote understanding of and services for individuals who have developmental disabilities and mental health needs.

Year Founded: 1983

1050 National Institute of Mental Health
6001 Executive Boulevard
Room 8184
Bethesda, MD 20892-1
301-443-4513
866-615-6464
TTY: 301-443-8431
E-mail: nimhinfo@nih.gov

Information and resources concerning depression, manic depression, bi-polar disorder and other mental health issues.

1051 National Mental Health Consumers' Self-Help Clearinghouse
1211 Chestnut Street
Suite 1207
Philadelphia, PA 19107-4103
215-751-1810
800-553-4539
Fax: 215-636-6312
E-mail: info@mhselfhelp.org
www.mhselfhelp.org

Joseph Rogers, Executive Director

A national consumer technical assistance center that has played a major role in the development of the mental health consumer movement.

Year Founded: 1986

1052 Postpartum Support International
PO Box 60931
Santa Barbara, CA 93160
805-967-7636
800-944-4773
Fax: 323-204-0635
E-mail: psioffice@postpartum.net
www.postpartum.net

Wendy N Davis, Program Director
Devani Priest, Office Administrator

A non-profit organization whose mission is to promote awareness, prevention and treatment of mental health issues related to childbearing in every country worldwide.

Year Founded: 1987

1053 SAMHSA's National Mental Health Information Center
PO Box 42557
Washington, DC 20015-557
240-221-4025
800-789-2647
Fax: 240-221-4295

TDD: 866-889-2647
TTY: 301-443-9006
www.mentalhealth.org

A Kathryn Power MEd, Director
Edward B Searle, Deputy Director

Provides information about mental health via a toll-free telephone number, this web site, and more than 600 publications. Developed for users of mental health services and their families, the general public, policy makers, providers, and the media.

Books

1054 A Story of Bipolar Disorder (Manic- Depressive Illness) Does this Sound Like You?
National Institute of Mental Health
6001 Executive Boulevard
Room 8184
Bethesda, MD 20892-1
301-443-4513
866-615-6464
TTY: 301-443-8431
E-mail: nimhinfo@nih.gov

Feeling really down sometimes and really up other times? Are these mood changes causing problems at work, school, or home? If yes, you may have bipolar disorder, also called manic-depressive illness.

20 pages

1055 Against Depression
Viking Adult
375 Hudson Street
New York, NY 10014-3658
212-366-2372
Fax: 212-366-2933
www.us.penguingroup.com

Peter D Kramer, Author

1056 An Unquiet Mind: A Memoir of Moods and Madness
Random House
1745 Broadway
New York, NY 10019
212-782-9000
E-mail: ecustomerservice@randomhouse.com
www.randomhouse.com

Kay Redfield Jamison, Author

$15.00

240 pages ISBN 0-679763-30-9

1057 Anxiety and Depression in Adults and Children, Banff International Behavioral Science Series
Sage Publications
2455 Teller Road
Thousand Oaks, CA 91320-2234

805-499-0721
800-818-7243
Fax: 805-499-0871
E-mail: info@sagepub.com
www.sagepub.com

Blaise R Simqu, CEO

Collection of papers by well respected researchers in the field of anxiety and depression. Brings together desparate areas of research and integrates them in an informative and interesting way. Focuses on recent advances in treating anxiety and depression in adults and children. Topics include self-management therapy, assessing and treating sexually abused children and unipolar depression. Integrates empirical research with clinical applications. Paperback also available. *$46.95*

296 pages ISBN 0-803970-20-X

1058 Bipolar Disorder Survival Guide: What You and Your Family Need to Know
The Guilford Press
72 Spring Street
New York, NY 10012-4019
212-431-9800
800-365-7006
Fax: 212-966-6708
E-mail: info@guilford.com

Bob Matloff, President

Gives ideas to the person diagnosed with the disorder how to come to terms with the diagnosis. Also shows who you should confide in and how to recognize mood swings. *$19.95*

322 pages Year Founded: 2002 ISBN 1-572305-25-8

1059 Bipolar Disorder for Dummies
John Wiley and Sons
10475 Crosspoint Blvd
Indianapolis, IN 46256-3386
317-572-3000
Fax: 317-572-4000
www.wiley.com

Lou Peragallo, Manager

Guide explains the brain chemistry behind the disease, and covers the latest medications and therapies. Sound advice and self-help techniques that everyone can use including children to ease and eliminate syptoms, function in a crisis, and plan ahead for manic or depressive episodes. *$19.99*

340 pages Year Founded: 2005 ISBN 0-764584-51-0

1060 Bipolar Disorders: A Guide to Helping Children and Adolescents
ADD WareHouse
300 NW 70th Avenue
Suite 102
Plantation, FL 33317-2360
954-792-8944
800-233-9273
Fax: 954-792-8545
E-mail: sales@addwarehouse.com
www.addwarehouse.com

Harvey C Parker, Owner

A million children and adolescents in the US may have childhood-onset bipolar disorder-including a significant number with ADHD. This new book helps parents and professionals recognize, treat and cope with bipolar disorders. It covers diagnosis, family life, medications, talk therapies, school issues, and other interventions. *$24.95*

340 pages

1061 Bipolar Disorders: Clinical Course and Outcome
American Psychiatric Publishing, Inc.
1000 Wilson Boulevard
Suite 1825
Arlington, VA 22209-3901
703-907-7322
800-368-5777
Fax: 703-907-1091
E-mail: appi@psych.org
www.appi.org

Robert E Hales MD, Editor-in-Chief
Ron McMillen, Chief Executive Officer
John McDuffie, Editorial Director

Provides a concise, up to date summary of affective relapse, comorbid psychopathology, functional disability, and psychosocial outcome in contemporary bipolar disorders. *$49.95*

312 pages ISBN 0-880487-68-2

1062 Bipolar Puzzle Solution
National Alliance on Mental Illness
2107 Wilson Boulevard
Suite 300
Arlington, VA 22201-3080
703-524-7600
800-950-6264
Fax: 703-524-9094
TDD: 703-516-7227
www.nami.org

An informative book on bipolar illness in a 187 question-and-answer format. *$17.00*

1063 Breaking the Patterns of Depression
Random House
1745 Broadway
New York, NY 10019-4343
212-572-4985
800-733-3000
Fax: 212-782-9052
www.randomhouse.com

Markus Bohle, CEO

Presents skills that enable readers to understand and ultimately avert depression's recurring cycles. Focusing on future prevention as well as initial treatment, the book includes over one hundred structured activities to help sufferers learn the skills necessary to become and remain depression-free. Translates the clinical literature on psychotherapy and antidepressant medication into understandable language. Defines what causes depression and clarifies what can be done about it. With this knowledge in hand, readers can control their depression, rather than having depression control them. *$13.95*

362 pages ISBN 0-385483-70-8

1064 Brilliant Madness: Living with Manic-Depressive Illness
Bantam Books
1745 Broadway
3rd Floor
New York, NY 10019-4368
212-782-9000
E-mail: bdpublicity@randomhouse.com

Jeff Rechtzigel, Publisher

1065 Broken Connection: On Death and the Continuity of Life
American Psychiatric Publishing, Inc.
1000 Wilson Boulevard
Suite 1825
Arlington, VA 22209-3901
703-907-7322
800-368-5777
Fax: 703-907-1091
E-mail: appi@psych.org
www.appi.org

Robert E Hales MD, Editor-in-Chief
Ron McMillen, Chief Executive Officer
John McDuffie, Editorial Director

Exploration of the inescapable connections between death and life, the psychiatric disorders that arise from these connections, and the advent of the nuclear age which has jeopardized any attempts to ensure the perpetuation of the self beyond death. *$38.00*

474 pages ISBN 0-880488-74-3

1066 Carbamazepine and Manic Depression: A Guide
Madison Institute of Medicine
7617 Mineral Point Road
Suite 300
Madison, WI 53717-1623
608-827-2470
E-mail: mim@miminc.org
www.factsforhealth.org

Margarett Baudhuin, Manager

A concise guide to the use of carbamazepine for the treatment of manic depression with information about dosing, monitoring and side effects. *$5.95*

32 pages

1067 Clinical Guide to Depression in Children and Adolescents
American Psychiatric Publishing, Inc.
1000 Wilson Boulevard
Suite 1825
Arlington, VA 22209-3901
703-907-7322
800-368-5777
Fax: 703-907-1091
E-mail: appi@psych.org
www.appi.org

Robert E Hales MD, Editor-in-Chief
Ron McMillen, Chief Executive Officer
John McDuffie, Editorial Director

Integrates advances in the recognition, diagnosis, management, and treatment of depressive disorders and bipolar disorders in infancy, childhood, and adolescence. *$39.50*

304 pages ISBN 0-880483-56-3

1068 Consumer's Guide to Psychiatric Drugs
New Harbinger Publications
5674 Shattuck Avenue
Oakland, CA 94609-1662
510-652-0215
800-748-6273
Fax: 510-652-5472
E-mail: customerservice@newharbinger.com
www.newharbinger.com

Matthew McKay, Owner

Helps consumers understand what treatment options are available and what side effects to expect. Covers possible interactions with other drugs, medical conditions and other concerns. Explains how each drug works, and offers detailed information about treatments for depression, bipolar disorder, anxiety and sleep disorders, as well as other conditions. *$16.95*

340 pages ISBN 1-572241-11-X

1069 Depression & Anxiety Management
New Harbinger Publications
5674 Shattuck Avenue
Oakland, CA 94609-1662
510-652-0215
800-748-6273
Fax: 510-652-5472
E-mail: customerservice@newharbinger.com
www.newharbinger.com

Matthew McKay, Owner

Offers step-by-step help for identifying the thoughts that make one anxious and depressed, confronting unrealistic and distorted thinking, and replacing negative mental patterns with healthy, realistic thinking. *$11.95*

ISBN 1-879237-46-6

1070 Depression Workbook: a Guide for Living with Depression
New Harbinger Publications
5674 Shattuck Avenue
Oakland, CA 94609-1662
510-652-0215
800-748-6273
Fax: 510-652-5472
E-mail: customerservice@newharbinger.com
www.newharbinger.com

Matthew McKay, Owner

Based on responses of participants sharing their insights, experiences, and strategies for living with extreme mood swings. *$ 19.95*

352 pages Year Founded: 1992 ISBN 1-572242-68-X

1071 Depression and Its Treatment
Time Warner Books
3 Center Plaza
Boston, MA 02108-2084

800-759-0190
Fax: 800-331-1664
E-mail: sales@aoltwbg.com
www.twbookmark.com

A layman's guide to help one understand and cope with
America's number one mental health problem. *$19.95*

157 pages

1072 Depression, the Mood Disease
Johns Hopkins University Press
2715 N Charles Street
Baltimore, MD 21218-4319
410-516-6900
800-537-5487
Fax: 410-516-6998

William Brody, President

Explores the many faces of an illness that will affect as
many as 36 million Americans at some point in their lives.
Updated to reflect state-of-the-art treatment. *$12.76*

240 pages   ISBN 0-801851-84-X

**1073 Diagnosis and Treatment of Depression in Late
Life: Results of the NIH Consensus
Development Conference**
American Psychiatric Publishing, Inc.
1000 Wilson Boulevard
Suite 1825
Arlington, VA 22209-3901
703-907-7322
800-368-5777
Fax: 703-907-1091
E-mail: appi@psych.org
www.appi.org

Robert E Hales MD, Editor-in-Chief
Ron McMillen, Chief Executive Officer
John McDuffie, Editorial Director

Provides comprehensive studies in early life depression
versus late life depression, the prevalence of depression in
elderly people and the risk factors involved. *$21.95*

536 pages   ISBN 0-880485-56-6

1074 Divalproex and Bipolar Disorder: A Guide
Madison Institute of Medicine
7617 Mineral Point Road
Suite 300
Madison, WI 53717-1623
608-827-2470
E-mail: mim@miminc.org
www.factsforhealth.org

Margarett Baudhuin, Manager

Written by leading experts on bipolar disorder (manic depression) and its treatment, this concise, up-to-date guide
includes the most important information every patient taking divalproex (valproate) for bipolar disorder needs to
know about this medication. *$5.95*

32 pages

1075 Drug Therapy and Postpartum Disorders
Mason Crest Publishers
370 Reed Road
Suite 302
Broomall, PA 19008-4017
610-543-3878
866-627-2665
Fax: 610-543-3878
E-mail: dtaylor@masoncrest.com
www.masoncrest.com

Pregnancy, childbirth and early motherhood are supposed
to be times filled with the joy and wonder of bringing a
new life into the world. Unfortunately, many women find
that the struggles of early motherhood are accompanied by
multiple sorrows that clash with the sentimental ideal. New
mothers may feel alone in their struggles, but depression
after childbirth is far more common than most people realize. This book provides information about the psychiatric
conditions that can accompany new motherhood and the
treatments that can help.

ISBN 1-590846-70-6

1076 Encyclopedia of Depression
Facts on File
132 W 31st Street
17th Floor
New York, NY 10001-3406
212-613-2800
800-322-8755
E-mail: custserv@factsonfile.com

This volume defines and explains all terms and topics relating to depression. *$58.50*

170 pages

**1077 Growing Up Sad: Childhood Depression and Its
Treatment**
WW Norton & Company
500 5th Avenue
New York, NY 10110-54
212-354-2907
800-233-4830
Fax: 212-869-0856
E-mail: npb@wwnorton.com

Drake McFeely, CEO

The authors have updated their classic study, Why Isn't
Johnny Crying? that looks at the symptoms and treatment
of childhood - onset depression. The authors give an authoritative summary of research, counsel prompt diagnosis,
and assert that the disorder is treatable. *$25.00*

216 pages   ISBN 0-393317-88-9

**1078 Guildeline for Treatment of Patients with
Bipolar Disorder**
American Psychiatric Publishing, Inc.
1000 Wilson Boulevard
Suite 1825
Arlington, VA 22209-3901

703-907-7322
800-368-5777
Fax: 703-907-1091
E-mail: appi@psych.org
www.appi.org

Robert E Hales MD, Editor-in-Chief
Ron McMillen, Chief Executive Officer
John McDuffie, Editorial Director

Provides guidance to psychiatrists who treat patients with bipolar I disorder. Summarizes the pharmacologic, somatic, and psychotherapeutic treatments used for patients. *$22.50*

96 pages ISBN 0-890423-02-4

1079 Help Me, I'M Sad: Recognizing, Treating, and Preventing Childhood and Adolescent Depression
Penguin Publishers
375 Hudson Street
New York, NY 10014

800-847-5515
www.us.penguingroup.com

David G Fassler, Author
Lynne Dumas, Co-Author

Discusses how to tell if your child is at risk; how to spot symptoms; depressions link with other problems and its impact on the family; teen suicide; finiding the right diagnosis, therapist, anad treatment; nad what you can do to help

224 pages ISBN 0-140267-63-1

1080 Helping Someone with Mental Illness: A Compassionate Guide for Family, Friends, and Caregivers
Three Rivers Press
1745 Broadway
New York, NY 10019
212-782-9000
E-mail: ecustomerservice@randomhouse.com
www.randomhouse.com

Rosalynn Carter, Author
Susan Golant MA, Co-Author

The authors address the latest breakthroughs in understanding, research, and treatment of schizophrenia, depression, manic depression, panic attacks, obsessive-compulsive disorder, and other mental disorders. *$19.00*

368 pages Year Founded: 1999 ISSN 9780812928983ISBN 0-812928-98-9

1081 Helping Your Depressed Teenager: a Guide for Parents and Caregivers
John Wiley & Sons
1 Wiley Drive
Somerset, NJ 08873-1272
732-537-9410
800-225-5945
Fax: 732-302-2300
E-mail: compbks@wiley.com
www.wiley.com

Clifford Kline, Senior VP
Sarah S Montgomery, Author

The authors, a psychologist and a social worker, contrast clinical depression with normal adolescent mood changes. They deal realistically with teenage suicide and urge prompt intervention. *$ 19.95*

208 pages Year Founded: 1994 ISBN 0-471621-84-6

1082 Lithium and Manic Depression: A Guide
Madison Institute of Medicine
7617 Mineral Point Road
Suite 300
Madison, WI 53717-1623
608-827-2470
E-mail: mim@miminc.org
www.factsforhealth.org

Margarett Baudhuin, Manager

A concise, up-to-date guide written by a leading expert on manic depression (bipolar disorder) and its treatment. This publication includes the most important information every patient taking lithium needs to know about lithium dosing, monitoring and side effects. *$5.95*

31 pages

1083 Living Without Depression & Manic Depression: a Workbook for Maintaining Mood Stability
New Harbinger Publications
5674 Shattuck Avenue
Oakland, CA 94609-1662
510-652-0215
800-748-6273
Fax: 510-652-5472
E-mail: customerservice@newharbinger.com
www.newharbinger.com

Matthew McKay, Owner

Outlines a program that helps people achieve breakthroughs in coping and healing. Contents include: self advocacy, building a network of support, wellness lifestyle, symptom prevention strategies, self-esteem, mood stability, a career that works, trauma resolution, dealing with sleep problems, diet, vitamin and herbal therapies, dealing with stigma, medication side effects, psychotherapy, and counseling alternatives. *$18.95*

263 pages ISBN 1-879237-74-1

1084 Lonely, Sad, and Angry: a Parent's Guide to Depression in Children and Adolescents
ADD Warehouse
300 NW 70th Avenue
Suite 102
Plantation, FL 33317-2360
954-792-8944
800-233-9273
Fax: 954-792-8545
www.addwarehouse.com

Harvey C Parker, Owner

Covers the symptoms of depression, its diagnosis, causes, treatment (including medication), suicide, and management strategies at home and at school. For parents and teenagers. *$14.95*

225 pages

1085 Management of Bipolar Disorder: Pocketbook
American Psychiatric Publishing, Inc.
1000 Wilson Boulevard
Suite 1825
Arlington, VA 22209-3901
703-907-7322
800-368-5777
Fax: 703-907-1091
E-mail: appi@psych.org
www.appi.org

Robert E Hales MD, Editor-in-Chief
Ron McMillen, Chief Executive Officer
John McDuffie, Editorial Director

Contains the need for treatment, what defines bipolar disorders, spectrum of the disorder, getting the best out of treatment, treatment of mania and bipolar depression, preventing new episodes, special problems in treatment, mood stabilizers and case studies. *$ 14.95*

96 pages ISBN 1-853172-74-X

1086 Management of Depression
American Psychiatric Publishing, Inc.
1000 Wilson Boulevard
Suite 1825
Arlington, VA 22209-3901
703-907-7322
800-368-5777
Fax: 703-907-1091
E-mail: appi@psych.org
www.appi.org

Robert E Hales MD, Editor-in-Chief
Ron McMillen, Chief Executive Officer
John McDuffie, Editorial Director

Comprehensive text covers all the important issues in the management of depression. *$39.95*

136 pages ISBN 1-853175-47-1

1087 Mania: Clinical and Research Perspectives
American Psychiatric Publishing, Inc.
1000 Wilson Boulevard
Suite 1825
Arlington, VA 22209-3901
703-907-7322
800-368-5777
Fax: 703-907-1091
E-mail: appi@psych.org
www.appi.org

Robert E Hales MD, Editor-in-Chief
Ron McMillen, Chief Executive Officer
John McDuffie, Editorial Director

Diagnostic considerations, biological aspects, and treatment of mania. *$59.95*

478 pages ISBN 0-880487-28-3

1088 Manic-Depressive Illness: Bipolar Disorders and Recurrent Depression
Oxford University Press
2001 Evans Road
Cary, NC 27513-2010
919-677-0977
800-445-9714
Fax: 919-677-2673
E-mail: custserv.us@oup.com

Frederick K Goodwin, Author

The revolution in psychiatry that began in earnest in the 1960s led to dramatic advances in the understanding and treamtent of manic-depressive illness. Hailed as the most outstanding book in the biomedical sciences when it was originally published in 1990

1089 Mayo Clinic on Depression
Mason Crest Publishers
370 Reed Road
Suite 302
Broomall, PA 19008-4017
866-627-2665
Fax: 610-543-3878
www.masoncrest.com/index.php

Keith G Kramlinger, Author

1090 Mood Apart
Basic Books
387 Park Avenue S
New York, NY 10016-8810
212-340-8100
Fax: 212-340-8115

Elizabeth Maguire, Publisher

An overview of depression and manic depression and the available treatments for them. *$24.00*

363 pages

1091 Mood Apart: Thinker's Guide to Emotion & Its Disorders
Harper Collins
10 E 53rd Street
New York, NY 10022-5299
212-207-7000
E-mail: sales@harpercollins.com

Discussion of depression and mania includes symptoms, human costs, biological underpinnings, and therapies. Authoritatively written, it uses case histories, appendices, and historical references. *$15.00*

ISBN 0-060977-40-X

1092 Natural History of Mania, Depression and Schizophrenia
American Psychiatric Publishing, Inc.
1000 Wilson Boulevard
Suite 1825
Arlington, VA 22209-3901
703-907-7322
800-368-5777
Fax: 703-907-1091

E-mail: appi@psych.org
www.appi.org

Robert E Hales MD, Editor-in-Chief
Ron McMillen, Chief Executive Officer
John McDuffie, Editorial Director

An unusual look at the course of mental illness, based on data from the Iowa 500 Research Project. *$42.50*

336 pages ISBN 0-880487-26-7

1093 Overcoming Anxiety, Depression, and Other Mental Health Disorders in Children and Adults: A New Roadmap for Families and Professionals
Interdesciplinary Council on Development and Learning Disorders
4938 Hampden Lane
Bethesda, MD 20814
301-656-2667
E-mail: info@icdl.com
www.icdl.com

Dr Stanley Greenspan, Author

Reveals strategies for family members as well as professionals from different disciplines to help both children and adults. The most common mental health disorders, including anxiety, depression, obsessive-compulsive patterns, ADD/ADHD, borderline states, and others, are discussed literally with a new set of eyeglasses

168 pages ISBN 0-976775-88-3

1094 Overcoming Depression
Harper Collins
10 E 53rd Street
New York, NY 10022-5299
212-207-7000

Described as one of the most comprehensive books available for the layperson on depression. Covers the full range of mood disorders. *$15.00*

ISBN 0-060927-82-8

1095 Oxcarbazepine and Bipolar Disorder: A Guide
Madison Institute of Medicine
7617 Mineral Point Road
Suite 300
Madison, WI 53717-1623
608-827-2470
E-mail: mim@miminc.org
www.factsforhealth.org

Margarett Baudhuin, Manager

This 31 page booklet provides patients with the information they need to know about the use of oxcarbazepine in the treatment of bipolar disorder, including information about proper dosing, medication management, and possible side effects. *$5.95*

31 pages

1096 Pain Behind the Mask: Overcoming Masculine Depression
Haworth Press
10 Alice Street
Binghamton, NY 13904-1503
607-722-5857
800-429-6784
Fax: 607-721-0012
E-mail: getinfo@haworthpress.com
www.haworthpress.com

Jackie Blakeslee, Advertising/Journal Liason
John Lynch, PhD, Author
Christopher Kilmartin, PhD, Author

Presents a model of masculinity based on the premise that men express depression through behaviors that distort the feelings and human conflicts they experience. *$22.95*

210 pages Year Founded: 1999 ISBN 0-789005-58-1

1097 Pastoral Care of Depression
Haworth Press
10 Alice Street
Binghamton, NY 13904-1503
607-722-5857
800-429-6784
Fax: 800-895-0582
E-mail: getinfo@haworthpressinc.com
www.haworthpress.com

Binford W Gilbert, PhD, Author

Helps caregivers by overcoming the simplistic myths about depressive disorders and probing the real issues. *$17.95*

127 pages Year Founded: 1997 ISBN 0-789002-65-5

1098 Physician's Guide to Depression and Bipolar Disorders
McGraw-Hill Companies
PO Box 182604
Columbus, OH 43218-2604
877-833-5524
Fax: 614-759-3749
E-mail: customer.service@mcgraw-hill.com
www.mcgraw-hill.com

Offers a clear definitive instruction on drug treatments for bipolar disorders with the exact dosages needed. Crucial to a diagnosis and treatment is the ability to identify a patients symptoms. *$59.00*

400 pages Year Founded: 2005 ISBN 0-071441-75-1

1099 Post-Natal Depression: Psychology, Science and the Transition to Motherhood
Routledge
2727 Palisade Avenue
Suite 4H
Bronx, NY 10463-1020
888-765-1209
Fax: 718-796-0971
E-mail: vd6@columbia.edu

$23.95

ISBN 0-415163-62-5

1100 Postpartum Mood Disorders
American Psychiatric Publishing, Inc.
1000 Wilson Boulevard
Suite 1825
Arlington, VA 22209-3901
703-907-7322
800-368-5777
Fax: 703-907-1091
E-mail: appi@psych.orgg
www.appi.org

Robert E Hales MD, Editor-in-Chief
Ron McMillen, Chief Executive Officer
John McDuffie, Editorial Director

Provides thorough coverage of a highly prevalent, but often misunderstood subject. *$38.50*

280 pages ISBN 0-880489-29-4

1101 Practice Guideline for Major Depressive Disorders in Adults
American Psychiatric Publishing, Inc.
1000 Wilson Boulevard
Suite 1825
Arlington, VA 22209-3901
703-907-7322
800-368-5777
Fax: 703-907-1091
E-mail: appi@psych.org
www.appi.org

Robert E Hales MD, Editor-in-Chief
Ron McMillen, Chief Executive Officer
John McDuffie, Editorial Director

Summarizes the specific forms of somatic, psychotherapeutic, psychosocial, and educational treatments developed to deal with major depressive order and its various subtypes. *$22.50*

51 pages ISBN 0-890423-01-6

1102 Predictors of Treatment Response in Mood Disorders
American Psychiatric Publishing, Inc.
1000 Wilson Boulevard
Suite 1825
Arlington, VA 22209-3901
703-907-7322
800-368-5777
Fax: 703-907-1091
E-mail: appi@psych.org
www.appi.org

Robert E Hales MD, Editor-in-Chief
Ron McMillen, Chief Executive Officer
John McDuffie, Editorial Director

Helps clinicians and managed care administrators assign the correct somatic therapy. *$29.00*

224 pages ISBN 0-880484-94-2

1103 Prozac Nation: Young & Depressed in America, a Memoir
Houghton Mifflin Company
222 Berkeley Street
Boston, MA 02116-3760

617-351-5000
Fax: 617-351-1105

Barry O'Callaghan, CEO

Struck with depression at 11, Wurtzel, now 27, chronicles her struggle with the illness. Witty, terrifying and sometimes funny, it tells the story of a young life almost destroyed by depression. *$19.95*

317 pages

1104 Questions & Answers About Depression & Its Treatment
Charles Press Publishers
117 S 17th Street
Suite 310
Philadelphia, PA 19103-5025
215-496-9616
Fax: 215-496-9637
E-mail: mailbox@charlespresspub.com
www.charlespresspub.com

All the questions you'd like to ask, with answers.

136 pages

1105 Seasonal Affective Disorder and Beyond: Light Treatment for SAD and Non-SAD Conditions
American Psychiatric Publishing, Inc.
1000 Wilson Boulevard
Suite 1825
Arlington, VA 22209-3901
703-907-7322
800-368-5777
Fax: 703-907-1091
E-mail: appi@psych.org
www.appi.org

Robert E Hales MD, Editor-in-Chief
Ron McMillen, Chief Executive Officer
John McDuffie, Editorial Director

Summarizes issues around the therapeutic uses of light treatment. *$45.00*

320 pages ISBN 0-880488-67-0

1106 Stories of Depression: Does this Sound Like You?
National Institute of Mental Health
6001 Executive Boulevard
Room 8184
Bethesda, MD 20892-1
301-443-4513
866-615-6464
TTY: 301-443-8431
E-mail: nimhinfo@nih.gov

Are you feeling really sad, tired, and worried most of the time? Are these feelings lasting more than a few days? If yes, you may have depression.

20 pages

1107 Talking to Depression: Simple Ways to Connect When Someone In Your Life Is Depressed
Penguin Group
375 Hudson Street
New York, NY 10014-3657

800-847-5515
www.us.penguingroup.com
Claudia J Strauss, Author

What to say and what not to say when a friend or family member is struggling with depression *$14.00*

224 pages ISBN 0-451209-86-3

1108 Taming Bipolar Disorders
Alpha
1101 Enterprise Drive
Po Box 255
Royersford, PA 19468-255

800-992-9124
www.alphapub.com

Contains cutting-edge research and straightforward advice from the most respectable names on bipolar disorder, along with the most up-to-date information on mental health organizations, support and advocacy groups. *$17.95*

400 pages Year Founded: 2004 ISBN 1-592572-85-5

1109 The Cognitive Behavorial Workbook for Depression: A Step-by-Step Program
New Harbinger Publications
5674 Shattuck Avenue
Oakland, CA 94609-1662
510-652-0215
Fax: 510-652-5472
E-mail: ii.info@ingrambook.com
www.newharbinger.com

Matthew McKay, Owner
Albert Ellis, Author

This type of cognitive behavioral therapy, called rational emotive behavior therapy (REBT) by Ellis, proved especially effective at relieving problems like anger, anxiety, and depression.

1110 Touched with Fire: Manic-Depressive Illness and The Artistic Temperament
Free Press
40 Main Street
Suite 301
Florence, MA 01062-3100
877-888-1533
Fax: 413-585-8904
www.freepress.net

Kay Redfield Jamison, Author

"We of the craft are all crazy." -remarked Lord Byron about himself and his fellow poets.

1111 Treatment Plans and Interventions for Depression and Anxiety Disorders
Guilford Publications
72 Spring Street
New York, NY 10012-4068
212-431-9800
800-365-7006
Fax: 212-966-6708
E-mail: info@guilford.com

Bob Matloff, President

Provides information on treatments for seven frequently encountered disorders: major depression, generalized anxiety, panic, agoraphobia, PTSD, social phobia, specific phobia and OCD. Serving as ready to use treatment packages, chapters describe basic cognitive behavioral therapy techniques and how to tailor them to each disorder. Also featured are diagnostic decision trees, therapist forms for assessment and record keeping, client handouts and homework sheets. *$ 49.50*

332 pages ISBN 1-572305-14-2

1112 Treatment for Chronic Depression: Cognitive Behavioral Analysis System of Psychotherapy (CBASP)
Guilford Publications
72 Spring Street
New York, NY 10012-4068
212-431-9800
800-365-7006
Fax: 212-966-6708
E-mail: info@guilford.com

Bob Matloff, President

This book describes CBASP, a research based psychotherapeutic approach designed to motivate chronically depressed patients to change and help them develop needed problem solving and relationship skills. Filled with illustrative case material that brings challenging clinical situations to life, this book now puts the power of CBASP in the hands of the clinician. Readers are provided with two essential assets: an innovative framework for understanding the patient's psychopathology and a disciplined plan for helping the individual overthrow depression. *$35.00*

326 pages ISBN 1-572305-27-4

1113 When Nothing Matters Anymore: A Survival Guide for Depressed Teens
Free Spirit Publishing
217 5th Avenue N
Suite 200
Minneapolis, MN 55401-1299
612-338-2068
866-735-7323
Fax: 612-337-5050
E-mail: help4kids@freespirit.com
www.freespirit.com

Judy Galbraith, Owner

Written for teens with depression and those who feel despondent, dejected or alone. This powerful book offers help, hope, and potentially lifesaving facts and advice. *$13.95*

176 pages Year Founded: 1998 ISBN 1-575420-36-8

1114 Winter Blues
Guilford Publications
72 Spring Street
New York, NY 10012-4068
212-431-9800
800-365-7006
Fax: 212-966-6708
E-mail: info@guilford.com

Bob Matloff, President

Complete information about Seasonal Affective Disorder
and its treatment. *$14.95*

1115 Yesterday's Tomorrow
Hazelden
15251 Pleasant Valley Road
Center City, MN 55012-9640
651-213-4000
800-822-0080

Meditation book that shows why and how recovery works,
from the author's own experiences. *$12.00*

432 pages ISBN 1-568381-60-3

**1116 You Can Beat Depression: Guide to Prevention
and Recovery**
Impact Publishers
PO Box 6016
Atascadero, CA 93423-6016
805-466-5917
800-246-7228
Fax: 805-466-5919
E-mail: info@impactpublishers.com
www.impactpublishers.com

Includes material on prevention of depression, prevention
of relapse after treatment, brief therapy interventions, exercise, other non medical approaches and the Prozac controversy. Helps readers recognize when and how to help
themsevles, and when to turn to professional treatment.
$14.95

176 pages ISBN 1-886230-40-4

Periodicals & Pamphlets

1117 Bipolar Disorder
National Institute of Mental Health
6001 Executive Boulevard
Room 8184
Bethesda, MD 20892-1
301-443-4513
866-615-6464
TTY: 301-443-8431
E-mail: nimhinfo@nih.gov
www.nimh.nih.gov

A detailed booklet that describes Bipolar Disorder
symptons, causes, and treatments, with information on getting help and coping.

24 pages

**1118 Child and Adolescent Bipolar Disorder: An
Update from the National Institute of Mental
Health**
National Institute of Mental Health
6001 Executive Boulevard
Room 8184
Bethesda, MD 20892-1
301-443-4513
866-615-6464
TTY: 301-443-8431
E-mail: nimhinfo@nih.gov

Research findings, clinical experience, and family accounts
provide substantial evidence that bipolar disorder, also
called manic-depressive illness, can occur in children and
adolescents. Bipolar disorder is difficult to recognize and
diagnose in youth. Better understanding of the diagnosis
and treatment is urgently needed. In pursuit of this goal, the
NIMH is conducting and supporting research on child and
adolescent bioplar disorder.

3 pages Year Founded: 2000

**1119 Coping With Unexpected Events: Depression
& Trauma**
Depression & BiPolar Support Alliance
730 N Franklin Street
Suite 501
Chicago, IL 60654-7225
312-642-0049
800-826-3632
Fax: 312-642-7243
E-mail: programs@dbsalliance.org
www.dbsalliance.org

Sue Bergeson, President

How to cope with depression after trauma, helping others
and preventing suicide.

1120 Coping with Mood Changes Later in Life
Depression and Bipolar Support Alliance
730 N Franklin Street
Suite 501
Chicago, IL 60654-7225
312-642-0049
800-826-3632
Fax: 312-642-7243
www.dbsalliance.org

Sue Bergeson, President

A large print guide that discusses symptoms, causes and
treatment options. Also contains resources that may be
helpful to older adults.

14 pages Year Founded: 2003

**1121 DBSA Support Groups: An Important Step on
the Road to Wellness**
Depression and Bipolar Support Alliance
730 N Franklin Street
Suite 501
Chicago, IL 60654-7225
312-642-0049
800-826-3632

Fax: 312-642-7243
www.dbsalliance.org

Sue Bergeson, President

Support groups for people with depression or bipolar disorder to discuss the experiences, and helpful treatments.

10 pages Year Founded: 2003

1122 Depression
National Institute of Mental Health
6001 Executive Boulevard
Room 8184
Bethesda, MD 20892-1
301-443-4513
866-615-6464
TTY: 301-443-8431
E-mail: nimhinfo@nih.gov

This brochure gives descriptions of major depression, dysthymia and bipolar disorder (manic depression). It lists symptoms, gives possible causes, tells how depression is diagnosed and discusses available treatments. This brochure provides help and hope for the depressed person, family and friends.

23 pages

1123 Depression in Children and Adolescents: A Fact Sheet for Physicians
National Institute of Mental Health
6001 Executive Boulevard
Room 8184
Bethesda, MD 20892-1
301-443-4513
866-615-6464
TTY: 301-443-8431
E-mail: nimhinfo@nih.gov

Discusses the scope of the problem and the screening tools used in evaluating children with depression.

8 pages

1124 Depression: Help On the Way
ETR Associates
4 Carbonero Way
Scotts Valley, CA 95066-4200
831-438-4060
800-321-4407
Fax: 831-438-3618
E-mail: customerservice@etr.org
www.etr.org

Mary Nelson, President

Includes symptoms of minor depression, major depression, and seasonal affective depression; treatment options and medication, and the importance of exercise and laughter. Sold in lots of 50.

1125 Depression: What Every Woman Should Know
National Institute of Mental Health
6001 Executive Boulevard
Room 8184
Bethesda, MD 20892-1

301-443-4513
866-615-6464
TTY: 301-443-8431
E-mail: nimhinfo@nih.gov

This booklet discusses the symptoms of depression and some of the reasons that make women so vulnerable. It also discusses the types of therapy and where to go for help.

24 pages

1126 Finding Peace of Mind: Treatment Strategies for Depression and Bipolar Disorder
Depression and Bipolar Support Alliance
730 N Franklin Street
Suite 501
Chicago, IL 60654-7225
312-642-0049
800-826-3632
Fax: 312-642-7243
www.dbsalliance.org

Sue Bergeson, President

Helps to build a good, cooperative relationship with your doctor by explaining some of the treatments for mood disorders and how they work. Also includes a guide for medication that has been frequently prescribed and new treatments that are being investigated.

20 pages Year Founded: 2003

1127 Getting Better Sleep: What You Need to Know
Depression and Bipolar Support Alliance
730 N Franklin Street
Suite 501
Chicago, IL 60654-7225
312-642-0049
800-826-3632
Fax: 312-642-7243
www.dbsalliance.org

Sue Bergeson, President

Describes some causes of sleep loss, and how sleep loss relates to bipolar disorder and depression. Also provides information on how to get better sleep.

1128 Introduction to Depression and Bipolar Disorder
Depression and Bipolar Support Alliance
730 N Franklin Street
Suite 501
Chicago, IL 60654-7225
312-642-0049
800-826-3632
Fax: 312-642-7243
www.dbsalliance.org

Sue Bergeson, President

Quick and easy-to-read brochure describing syptoms and treatments for mood disorders.

1129 Let's Talk About Depression
National Institute of Mental Health
6001 Executive Boulevard
Room 8184
Bethesda, MD 20892-1
301-443-4513
866-615-6464
TTY: 301-443-8431
E-mail: nimhinfo@nih.gov

Facts about depression, and ways to get help. Target audience is teenaged youth.

1130 Major Depression in Children and Adolescents
SAMHSA's National Mental Health Information Center
PO Box 42557
Washington, DC 20015-557

800-789-2647
Fax: 240-747-5470
TDD: 866-889-2647
E-mail: ken@mentalhealth.org
www.mentalhealth.samhsa.gov

A Kathryn Power, MEd, Director
Edward B Searle, Deputy Director

This fact sheet defines depression and its signs, identifies types of help available, and suggests what parents or other caregivers can do.

2 pages

1131 McMan's Depression and Bipolar Weekly
McMan's Depression and Bipolar Web
PO Box 5093
Kendall Park, NJ 08824-5093

E-mail: mcman@mcmanweb.com
www.mcmanweb.com

John McManamy, Editor/Publisher

Online newsletter devoted to the issues of bipolar and depression disorders. There is no charge, just for you to understand different things about the disorders.

1132 Men and Depression
National Institute of Mental Health
6001 Executive Boulevard
Room 8184
Bethesda, MD 20892-1
301-443-4513
866-615-6464
TTY: 301-443-8431
E-mail: nimhinfo@nih.gov

Have you known a man who is grumpy, irritable, and has no sense of humor? Maybe he drinks too much or abuses drugs. Maybe he physically or verbally abuses his wife and his kids. Maybe he works all the time, or compulsively seeks thrills in high-risk behavior. Or maybe he seems isolated, withdrawn, and no longer interested in the people or activities he used to enjoy. Perhaps this man is you. Talk to a healthcare provider about how you are feeling, and ask for help.

36 pages

1133 Mood Disorders
Center for Mental Health Services: Knowledge Exchange Network
PO Box 42490
Washington, DC 20015

800-789-2647
Fax: 301-984-8796
TDD: 866-889-2647
E-mail: ken@mentalhealth.org
www.mentalhealth.org

This fact sheet provides basic information on the symptoms, formal diagnosis, and treatment for bipolar disorder.

3 pages

1134 Myths and Facts about Depression and Bipolar Disorders
Depression and Bipolar Support Alliance
730 N Franklin Street
Suite 501
Chicago, IL 60654-7225
312-642-0049
800-826-3632
Fax: 312-642-7243
www.dbsalliance.org

Sue Bergeson, President

Gives some myths about depression and bipolar disorder and the truths that combat them.

1135 New Message
Emotions Anonymous
PO Box 4245
Saint Paul, MN 55104-245
651-647-9712
Fax: 651-647-1593
E-mail: info@EmotionsAnonymous.org
www.EmotionsAnonymous.org

Karen Mead, Executive Director

Features stories and articles of recovery, plus the latest news from EA International. *$8.00*

4 per year

1136 Recovering Your Mental Health: a Self-Help Guide
SAMHSA'S National Mental Health Informantion Center
PO Box 42557
Washington, DC 20015-557

800-789-2647
Fax: 240-747-5470
TDD: 866-889-2647
E-mail: ken@mentalhealth.org
www.mentalhealth.samhsa.gov

A Kathryn Power, MEd, Director
Edward B Searle, Deputy Director

This booklet offers tips for understanding symptoms of depression and other conditions and getting help. Also details the advantages of counseling, medications available, options for professional help, relaxation techniques and paths to positive thinking.

32 pages

1137 Storm In My Brain
Depression & Bi-Polar Support Alliance
730 N Franklin Street
Suite 501
Chicago, IL 60654-7225
312-642-0049
800-826-3632
Fax: 312-642-7243
www.dbsalliance.org

Sue Bergeson, President
Ingrid Deetz, Program Director

Pamphlet free on the Internet or by mail. Discusses child or adolesent Bi-Polar symptoms.

1138 What Do These Students Have in Common?
National Institute of Mental Health
6001 Executive Boulevard
Room 8184
Bethesda, MD 20892-1
301-443-4513
866-615-6464
TTY: 301-443-8431
E-mail: nimhinfo@nih.gov

Provides college sutdents with clear descriptions of the most prevalent forms of depression. Discusses symptoms, causes and treatment options. Includes information about suicide and resources for help that are available to most college students.

4 pages

1139 What to do When a Friend is Depressed: Guide for Students
National Institute of Mental Health
6001 Executive Boulevard
Room 8184
Bethesda, MD 20892-1
301-443-4513
866-615-6464
TTY: 301-443-8431
E-mail: nimhinfo@nih.gov

This brochure offers information on depression and its symptoms and suggests things a young person can do to guide a depressed friend in finding help. Especially good for health fairs, health clinics and school health units.

3 pages

1140 You've Just Been Diagnosed...What Now?
Depression and Bipolar Support Alliance
730 N Franklin Street
Suite 501
Chicago, IL 60654-7225
312-642-0049
800-826-3632
Fax: 312-642-7243
www.dbsalliance.org

Sue Bergeson, President

Pamphlet to help you understand about the disorder you have just been diagnosed with. Tells you basic facts about mood disorders and will help you work towards a diagnosis.

19 pages Year Founded: 2002

Research Centers

1141 Bipolar Clinic and Research Program
The Massachusetts General Hospital Bipolar Clinic & Research Program
50 Staniford Street
Suite 580
Boston, MA 02114-2540
617-724-6544

Gary S Sachs, Founder/Director

Dedicated to providing quality clinical care, conducting clinically informative research, and educating our colleagues, patients, as well as the community.

1142 Bipolar Disorders Clinic
Standford School of Medicine
401 Quarry Road
Stanford, CA 94304-1419
650-723-5001

Caroline Paterno, Clinic Chief
Jenifer Culver PhD, Clinical Assistant Professor

Offers an on-going clinical treatment, manage clinical trials and neuroimaging studies, lecture and teach seminar courses at Stanford University and train residents in the School of Medicine.

1143 Bipolar Research at University of Pennsylvania
University of Pennsylvania
Clinical Research Building Room 11
125 S 31st Street Suite 2200
Philadelphia, PA 19104-3413
215-573-3258
E-mail: balthrop@mail.med.upenn.edu

Steven Arnold

A study that invites individuals age 16 or older to participate in a neurobiology and behavior study. The individuals have to have bipolar disorder or schizoaffective disorder.

1144 Epidemiology-Genetics Program in Psychiatry
John Hopkins University School of Medicine
733 N Broadway
Suite G49
Baltimore, MD 21205-1832
410-955-4260

Sandy Muscelli, Manager

The research program is to help characterize the genetic (biochemical) developmental, and environmental components of bipolar disorder. The hope is that once scientists understand the biological causes of this disorder new medications and treatments can be developed.

1145 National Alliance for Research on Schizophrenia and Depression

60 Cutter Mill Road
Suite 404
Great Neck, NY 11021-3104
516-487-3822
800-829-8289
Fax: 516-487-2530
E-mail: info@narsad.org
www.pocli.com

David Schimel, President

NARSAD raises funds for research on schizophrenia, depression, and other serious brain disorders.

1146 Sid W Richardson Institute for Preventive Medicine of the Methodist Hospital

6565 Fannin Street
Houston, TX 77030-2703
713-790-3311

Alan Herd MD, Director

1147 UAMS Psychiatric Research Institute

5800 W 10th Street
Suite 605
Little Rock, AR 72204-1773
501-660-7559
Fax: 501-660-7542
E-mail: kramerteresal@uams.edu
www.uams.edu

Combining research, education and clinical services into one facility, PRI offers inpatiend and outpatient services, with 40 psychiatric beds, therapy options, and specialized treatment for specific disorders, including: addictive eating, anxiety, deppressive and post-traumatic stress disorders. Research focuses on evidence-based care takes into consideration the education of future medical personnel while relying on research scientists to provide innovative forms of treatment. PRI includes the Center for Addiction Research as well as a methadone clinic.

1148 UT Southwestern Medical Center

5323 Harry Hines Blvd
Dallas, TX 75390-7200
817-921-2996

Researching corticosteroid effects on the brain, dual-diagnosed patients, and depression in asthma patients.

1149 University of Texas: Mental Health Clinical Research Center

5323 Harry Hines Boulevard
Dallas, TX 75235
214-648-3111
www.utsouthwestern.edu

Research activity of major and atypical depression.

1150 Yale Mood Disorders Research Program
Department of Psychiatry

300 George Street
New Haven, CT 06511-6624
203-785-2117
www.med.yale.edu

Brings together a multi-disciplinary group of scientists who use a wide variety of research methods in a highly collaborative research effort to study the genetic and environmental factors that contribute to mood disorders.

1151 Yale University: Depression Research Program
Yale University Department of Psychiatry

333 Cedar Street
New Haven, CT 06510-3206
203-785-6069

Arthur Bradus

Successfuly treating people with depression for over three decades. Operated jointly by the Connecticut Mental Health Center and the Yale University School of Medicine, Department of Psychiatry.

Support Groups & Hot Lines

1152 Depressed Anonymous

PO Box 17414
Louisville, KY 40217-414
502-569-1989
E-mail: info@depressedanon.com
www.depressedanon.com

Individuals suffering from depression or anxiety. A self-help organization with meetings and sharing of experiences. Similar to the 12 step program, uses mutual aid as a theraputic healing force. Website offers information on how to form groups in your area.

1153 Emotions Anonymous International Service Center

PO Box 4245
Saint Paul, MN 55104-0245
651-647-9712
Fax: 651-647-1593
E-mail: info@EmotionsAnonymous.org
www.EmotionsAnonymous.org

Karen Mead, Executive Director

Fellowship of men and women who share their experience, strength and hope with each other, that they may solve their common problem and help others recover from emotional illness.

1154 Recovery

802 N Dearborn Street
Chicago, IL 60610-3364
312-337-5661
E-mail: inquiries@recovery-inc.com
www.recovery-inc.org

Kathleen Garcia, Executive Director

Techniques for controlling behavior, changing attitudes for recovering mental patients. Systematic method of self-help offered.

Video & Audio

1155 Bundle of Blues
Fanlight Productions
2
47 Halifax St
Jamaica Plain, MA 02130-4327
617-469-4999
Fax: 617-439-3379
E-mail: fanlight@fanlight.com
www.fanlight.com

The stories in this thoughtful documentary represent a range of experiences from minor postpartum depression through postpartum psychosis. It stresses that PDD can happen to any new mother, but that it can be managed.

1156 Coping with Depression
New Harbinger Publications
5674 Shattuck Avenue
Oakland, CA 94609-1662
510-652-0215
800-748-6273
Fax: 510-652-5472
E-mail: customerservice@newharbinger.com
www.newharbinger.com

Matthew McKay, Owner

60 minute videotape that offers a powerful message of hope for anyone struggling with depression. *$39.95*
Year Founded: 1994 ISBN 1-879237-62-8

1157 Covert Modeling & Covert Reinforcement
New Harbinger Publications
5674 Shattuck Avenue
Oakland, CA 94609-1662
510-652-0215
800-748-6273
Fax: 510-652-5472
E-mail: customerservice@newharbinger.com
www.newharbinger.com

Matthew McKay, Owner

Based on the essential book of cognitive behavioral techniques for effecting change in your life, Thoughts & Feelings. Learn step-by-step protocols for controlling destructive behaviors such as anxiety, obsessional thinking, uncontrolled anger, and depression. *$ 11.95*
ISBN 0-934986-29-0

1158 Dark Glasses and Kaleidoscopes: Living with Manic Depression
Depression and Bipolar Support Alliance
730 N Franklin Street
Suite 501
Chicago, IL 60654-7225

312-642-0049
800-826-3632
Fax: 312-642-7243
www.dbsalliance.org

Sue Bergeson, President

Video featuring people who have bipolar disorder (manic depression) and doctors outlining syptoms and coping strategies. 33 minutes. Copyright 1997. *$5.00*

1159 Day for Night: Recognizing Teenage Depression
DRADA-Depression and Related Affective Disorders Association
2330 W Joppa Road
Suite 100
Lutherville, MD 21093-4614
410-583-2919
Fax: 410-583-2964
E-mail: drada@jhmi.edu
www.drada.org

Catherine Pollock, Executive Director
Sallie Mink, Director Education

Award winning video that provides an in depth look at teenage depression and offers educational support and hope for those who suffer this treatable condition. *$22.50*

1160 Depression and Manic Depression
Fanlight Productions
47 Halifax Street
Boston, MA 02130-4327
617-524-0980
800-937-4113
Fax: 617-524-8838
E-mail: info@fanlight.com
www.fanlight.com

Explores the realities of depression and manic depression, as well as provides an overview of available treatments, and a listing of other resources. *$149.00*

1161 Families Coping with Mental Illness
Mental Illness Education Project
PO Box 470813
Brookline Village, MA 02447-813
617-562-1111
800-343-5540
Fax: 617-779-0061
E-mail: info@miepvideos.org
www.miepvideos.org

Ten family members share their experiences of having a family member with schizophrenia or bipolar disorder. Designed to provide insights and support to other families, the tape also profoundly conveys to professionals the needs of families when mental illness strikes. In two versions: a 22-minute version ideal for short classes and workshops, and a richer 43-minute version with more examples and details. Discounted price for families/consumers. *$99.95*

1162 Living with Depression and Manic Depression
New Harbinger Publications
5674 Shattuck Avenue
Oakland, CA 94609-1662

510-652-0215
800-748-6273
Fax: 510-652-5472
E-mail: customerservice@newharbinger.com
www.newharbinger.com

Matthew McKay, Owner

Describes a program based on years of research and hundreds of interviews with depressed persons. Warm, helpful, and engaging, this tape validates the feelings of people with depression while it encourages positive change. *$11.95*

Year Founded: 1994 ISBN 1-879237-63-6

1163 The Bonnie Tapes Mental Illness in the Family; Recovering from Mental Illness; My Sister is Mentally Ill
The Mental Illness Education Project
PO Box 470813
Brookline Village, MA 02447-813
617-562-1111
E-mail: info@miepvideos.org
www.miepvideos.org

Talks with a young woman with schizophrenia, how it has affected her and her family. Also talks with mental health professionals to see how she is handling everything. Talks about what happens when mental illness enters a family, and how the person with the illness feels, and what are steps to get better. Each video is $99.95

1164 Why Isn't My Child Happy? Video Guide About Childhood Depression
ADD WareHouse
300 NW 70th Avenue
Suite 102
Plantation, FL 33317-2360
954-792-8944
800-233-9273
Fax: 954-792-8545
E-mail: sales@addwarehouse.com
www.addwarehouse.com

Harvey C Parker, Owner

The first of its kind, this new video deals with childhood depression. Informative and frank about this common problem, this book offers helpful guidance for parents and professionals trying to better understand childhood depression. 110 minutes. *$55.00*

1165 Women and Depression
Fanlight Productions
47 Halifax Street
Boston, MA 02130-4327
617-524-0980
800-937-4113
Fax: 617-524-8838
E-mail: info@fanlight.com
www.fanlight.com

Clinical depression affects 19 million Americans, about 10 million of these are women. 28 minute video features women who talk about their own depression, and how it is viewed and handled in the African American community, and a therapist who deals with her own depression. Treat-

ments are explored and practical strategies are offered. *$129.00*
Year Founded: 2000

Web Sites

1166 www.Depressedteens.Com
Depression and Related Affective Disorders Association: DRADA

Educational site dedicated to helping teens, parents and teachers understand symptoms of teenage depression. Provides resources for those ready to seek help.

1167 www.Ifred.Org
National Foundation for Depressive Illness

Support, helplines, and advice.

1168 www.befrienders.org
Samaritans International

Support, helplines, and advice.

1169 www.blarg.net/~charlatn/voices
Voices of Depression

Compilation of writings by people suffering from depression.

1170 www.bpso.org
BPSO-Bipolar Significant Others

Informational site intended to provide information and support to the spouses, families, friends and other loved ones of those who suffer from bi-polar.

1171 www.bpso.org/nomania.htm
How to Avoid a Manic Episode

Provides different ways to avoid an episode, and factors what causes episodes.

1172 www.cfsny.org
Center for Family Services

Devoted to the physical well-being and development of the reatrded child and the sound mental health of the parents.

1173 www.cyberpsych.org
CyberPsych

Hosts the American Psychoanalyists Foundation, American Association of Suicideology, Society for the Exploration of Psychotherapy Intergration, and Anxiety Disorders Association of America. Also subcategories of the anxiety disorders, as well as general information, including panic disorder, phobias, obsessive compulsive disorder (OCD), social phobia, generalized anxiety disorder, post traumatic stress disorder, and phobias of childhood. Book reviews and links to web pages sharing the topics.

1174 www.dbsalliance.org
Depression & Bi-Polar Support Alliance

Mental health news updates and local support group information.

1175 www.emdr.com
EMDR Institute

Discusses EMDR-Eye Movement Desensitization and Reprocessing-as an innovative clinical treatment for trauma, including sexual abuse, domestic violence, combat, crime, and those suffering from a number of other disorders including depressions, addictions, phobias and a variety of self-esteem issues.

1176 www.geocities.com/enchantedforest/1068
Bipolar Kids Homepage

Set of links.

1177 www.goodwill-suncoast.org
Suncoast Residential Training Center

Group home that serves individuals diagnosed as mentally retarded with a secondary diagnosis of psychiatric difficulties as evidenced by problem behavior.

1178 www.klis.com/chandler/pamphlet/dep/
Jim Chandler MD

White paper on depression in children and adolesents.

1179 www.manicdepressive.org
The Massachusetts General Hospital Bipolar Clinic/Research Program

Dedicated to providing quality clinical care, conducting clinically informative research, and educating colleagues, patients and the community.

1180 www.med.yale.edu
Yale University School of Medicine

Research center dedicated to understanding the science of mood disorders.

1181 www.mentalhealth.Samhsa.Gov
Center for Mental Health Services Knowledge Exchange Network

Information about resources, technical assistance, research, training, networks, and other federal clearinghouses, fact sheets and materials.

1182 www.mhselfhelp.org
National Mental Health Consumer's Self-Help Clearinghouse

Encourages the development and growth of consumer self-help groups.

1183 www.miminc.org
Bipolar Disorders Treatment Information Center

Provides information on mood stabilizers other than lithium for bipolar disorders.

1184 www.moodswing.org/bdfaq.html
Bipolar Disorder Frequently Asked Questions

Excellent for those newly diagnosed. Gives information on symptoms, stories, causes and helpful treatments.

1185 www.nami.org
National Alliance on Mental Illness

From its inception in 1979, NAMI has been dedicated to improving the lives of individuals and families affected by mental illness.

1186 www.nimh.nih.gov/publicat/depressionmenu.cfm
National Institute of Mental Health

National Institute of Mental Health offers brochures organized by topic. Depression discusses symptoms, diagnosis, and treatment options.

1187 www.nimh.nih.gov/publist/964033.htm
National Institute of Mental Health

Discusses depression in older years, symptoms, treatment, going for help.

1188 www.planetpsych.com
Planetpsych.com

Learn about disorders, their treatments and other topics in psychology. Articles are listed under the related topic areas. Ask a therapist a question for free, or view the directory of professionals in your area. If you are a therapist sign up for the directory. Current features, self-help, interactive, and newsletter archives.

1189 www.psychcentral.com
Psych Central

Personalized one-stop index for psychology, support, and mental health issues, resources, and people on the Internet.

1190 www.psychologyinfo.com/depression
Psychology Information On-line: Depression

Information on diagnosis, therapy, and medication.

1191 www.psycom.net/depression.central.html
Dr. Ivan's Depression Central

Medication-oriented site. Clearinghouse on all types of depressive disorders.

1192 www.queendom.com/selfhelp/depression/depression.html
Queendom

Articles, information on medication and support groups.

1193 www.shpm.com
Self Help Magazine

Articles and discussion forums, resource links.

1194 www.thenadd.org
NADD: National Association for the Dually Diagnosed

Promotes interest of professional and parent development with resources for individuals who have the coexistence of mental illness and mental retardation.

1195 www.utsouthwestern.edu
UT Southwestern Medical Center

Research to find the corticosteroid effects on the human brain, dual-diagnosed patients, and depression in asthma patients.

1196 www.wingofmadness.com
Wing of Madness: A Depression Guide

Accurate information, advice, support, and personal experiences.

Books

1197 Emotions Anonymous Book
Emotions Anonymous International Service Center
PO Box 4245
Saint Paul, MN 55104-0245
651-647-9712
Fax: 651-647-1593
E-mail: info@EmotionsAnonymous.org
www.EmotionsAnonymous.org

Karen Mead, Executive Director

The Big Book of EA: A fellowship of men and women who share their experience, strength and hope with each other, that they may solve their common problem and help others recover from emotional illness. *$15.00*

260 pages ISBN 0-960735-65-5

Paraphilias (Perversions)

Introduction

Paraphilias are sexual disorders or perversions in which sexual intercourse is not the desired goal. Instead, the desire is to use non-human objects or non-sexual body parts for sexual activities sometimes involving the suffering of, or inflicting pain onto, non-consenting partners.

SYMPTOMS

•Recurrent, intense, sexually arousing fantasies, urges, or behavior involving the particular perversion for at least six months;
•The fantasies, urges, or behavior cause distress and/or disruption in the person's functioning in social, work, and interpersonal areas.

There are eight Paraphilias, described below, categorized as either victimless, or as victimizing someone who has not consented to the sexual activity, with relevant associated features.

Exhibitionism
The exposure of the genitals to a stranger or group of strangers. Sometimes the paraphiliac masturbates during exposure. The onset of this disorder usually occurs before age 18 and becomes less severe after age 40.

Fetishism
Using non-living objects, known as fetishes, for sexual gratification. Objects commonly used by men with the disorder include women's underwear, shoes, or other articles of women's clothing. The person often masturbates while holding, rubbing, or smelling the fetish object. This disorder usually begins in adolescence; it is chronic.

Frotteurism
Sexual arousal, and sometimes masturbation to orgasm, while rubbing against a non-consenting person. The behavior is usually planned to occur in a crowded place, such as on a bus, subway, or in a swimming pool, where detection is less likely. Frotteurism usually begins in adolescence, is most frequent between the ages of 15 and 25, then gradually declines.

Pedophilia
Sexual activity with a prepubertal child, generally 13 years or younger. The pedophiliac, him or herself, must be at least 16 and at least five years older than his victim when the behavior occurs. Pedophiliacs are usually attracted to children in one particular age range.
The frequency of the behavior may be associated with the degree of stress in the person's life. It usually begins in adolescence and is chronic. Pedophiles may be married, but have a higher than average incidence of marital discord.

Sexual Masochism
Acts of being bound, beaten, humiliated, or made to suffer in some other way in order to become sexually aroused. The behaviors can be self-inflicted or performed with a partner, and include physical bondage, blindfolding and humiliation. Masochistic sexual fantasies are likely to have been present since childhood. The activities themselves begin at different times but are common by early adulthood;

they are usually chronic. The severity of the behaviors may increase over time.

Sexual Sadism
Acts in which the person becomes sexually excited through the physical or psychological suffering of someone else. Some Sexual Sadists may conjure up the sadistic fantasies during sexual activity without acting on them. Others act on their sadistic urges with a consenting partner (who may be a Sexual Masochist), or act on their urges with a non-consenting partner. The behavior may involve forcing the other person to crawl, be caged or tortured. Sadistic sexual fantasies are likely to have been present in childhood. The onset of the behavior varies but most commonly occurs by early adulthood. The disorder is usually chronic, and severity tends to increase over time. When the disorder is severe or coupled with Antisocial Personality Disorder, the person is likely to seriously injure or kill his victim.

Transvestic Fetishism
Consists of heterosexual males dressing in women's clothes and makeup then masturbating. When not cross dressed, the man looks like an ordinary masculine man. It is important to note that there is considerable controversy over this diagnosis; some people who cross dress seem to have little distress and function normally. This condition typically begins in childhood or adolescence. Often the cross dressing is not done publicly until adulthood.

Voyeurism
Peeping Tom disorder, involving the act of observing one or more unsuspecting persons (usually strangers) who are naked, in the process of undressing, or engaged in sexual activity, in order for the voyeur to become sexually excited. Sexual activity with the people being observed is not usually sought. The voyeur may masturbate during the observation or later. The onset of this disorder is usually before age 15. It tends to be chronic.

PREVALENCE

Paraphiliacs are almost exclusively male. Very few volunteer to disclose their activities or to seek treatment. It is estimated that most have deficits in interpersonal or sexual relationships. In one study, two thirds were diagnosed with Mood Disorders and fifty percent had alcohol or drug abuse problems.

Recent studies provide evidence that the great majority of Paraphiliacs are active in more than one form of sexually perverse behavior; less than ten percent have only one form; and thirty-eight percent engage in five or more different sexually deviant behaviors. In a survey of college students, it was found that young males often fantasize about forced sex, and almost half have engaged in some form of sexual misconduct or sexual behavior with someone younger than age 14.

At the same time, the incidence and prevalence of some sexual perversions are hard to estimate, or unknown, because they are rarely reported or the people involved do not come into contact with authorities.

TREATMENT OPTIONS

All the Paraphilias are difficult to treat. It is important for the professional making the diagnosis to take a very careful history, and to be sensitive to the presence of other, e.g., personality, disorders. Relapse is common.

Diagnostic techniques can be useful. Penile plethysmography measures the degree of penile erection while the individual is exposed to visual sexual stimuli. Some people are treated in a formal Sex Offenders Program, developed for individuals arrested for and convicted of paraphilias that are crimes. Sometimes treatment occurs within the context of individual therapy where trust can be established. Others have been treated by means of conditioning techniques, e.g., where a fetish object is paired with an aversive stimulus such as mild electric shock. Medication is also used. Pedophilia is sometimes treated through so-called chemocastration which, through the use of female hormones or other medications, diminishes sexual appetite.

Treatment can be difficult because it is associated with the risk of reporting and punishment; many individuals do not have any real interest in being treated. They may deliberately deceive the professional, or deny the problem. Sex offenders are also more likely to exaggerate treatment gains, resist treatment, or end treatment prematurely. The fact that these conditions are classified as mental disorders does not relieve individuals who violate laws of criminal responsibility.

Associations & Agencies

1199 Center for Family Support (CFS)
333 7th Avenue
New York, NY 10001-5115
212-629-7939
Fax: 212-239-2211
www.cfsny.org

Steven Vernikoff, Executive Director

An agency that continues to develop new programs to serve families and individuals with their care needs. They currently offer services throughout the New York City region including: New Jersey, Long Island and the Lower Hudson Valley.

1200 Center for Mental Health Services (CMHS)
PO Box 2345
Rockville, MD 20847
240-221-4021
800-789-2647
Fax: 240-221-4295
TDD: 866-889-2647
www.mentalhealth.samhsa.gov

A Kathryn Power, MEd, Director
Anna Marsh PhD, Deputy Director
Fran Randolph PhD, Dir, Service & Systems Improveme
Anne Mathews-Younes EdD, Dir, Prevention/Traumatic Stress

CMHS leads Federal efforts to treat mental illnesses by promoting mental health and by preventing the development or worsening of mental illness when possible. Congress created CMHS to bring new hope to adults who have serious mental illnesses and to children with serious emotional disorders. CMHS provides information about mental health via a toll-free the web site, and more than 600 publications. Developed for users of mental / health services and their families, the general public, policy makers, providers, and the media.

Year Founded: 1992

1201 National Association for the Dually Diagnosed (NADD)
132 Fair Street
Kingston, NY 12401-4802
845-331-4336
800-331-5362
Fax: 845-331-4569
E-mail: info@thenadd.org
www.thenadd.org

Robert Fletcher, Executive Director

Nonprofit organization designed to promote interest of professional and parent development with resources for individuals who have the coexistence of mental illness and mental retardation. Provides conference, educational services and training materials to professionals, parents, concerned citizens and service organizations. Formerly known as the National Association for the Dually Diagnosed.

Year Founded: 1983

1202 National Mental Health Consumers' Self-Help Clearinghouse
1211 Chestnut Street
Suite 1207
Philadelphia, PA 19107-4103
215-751-1810
800-553-4539
Fax: 215-636-6312
E-mail: info@mhselfhelp.org
www.mhselfhelp.org

Joseph A Rogers, Executive Director

A national consumer technical assistance center that has played a major role in the development of the mental health consumer movement.

Year Founded: 1986

1203 SAMHSA's National Mental Health Information Center
US Department of Health and Human Services
PO Box 42557
Washington, DC 20015-557
240-221-4021
800-789-2647
Fax: 240-221-4295
TDD: 866-889-2647
www.mentalhealth.samhsa.gov

A Kathryn Power, MEd, Director
Edward B Searle, Deputy Director

Provides information about mental health via a toll-free telephone number, this web site, and more than 600 publications. Developed for users of mental health services and their families, the general public, policy makers, providers, and the media.

Books

1204 Perversion (Ideas in Psychoanalysis)
National Book Network
4501 Forbes Boulevard
Suite 200
Lanham, MD 20706-4346
301-459-3366
800-462-6420
Fax: 301-429-5746

Jed Lyons, President
Claire Pajaczkowska, Author

Perversion's relationship to feelings of contempt, triumph, sexual excitement and to shame, revulsion and fear, necessarily make it a troubling concept.

1205 The World of Perversion: Psychoanalysis and the Impossible Absolute of Desire
State University of New York Press
194 Washington Avenue
Suite 305
Albany, NY 12210-2314
518-472-5000
E-mail: info@sunypress.edu

Gary Dunham, Executive Director
James Penney, Author

An original critique of queer theory, from a psychoanalysis perspective.

Web Sites

1206 www.mentalhealth.com
Internet Mental Health

Website offers psychiatric diagnosis in the hope of reaching the two-thirds of individuals with mental illness who do not seek treatment.

1207 www.planetpsych.com
Planetpsych.com

The online resource for mental health information.

1208 www.psychcentral.com
Psych Central

The Internet's largest and oldest independent mental health social network created and run by mental health professionals to guarantee reliable, trusted information and support communities to you.

Personality Disorders

Introduction

Personality is deeply rooted in our sense of ourselves and how others see us; it is formed from a complex intermingling of genetic factors and life experience. Everyone has personality characteristics that are likable and unlikable, attractive and unattractive, to others. By adulthood, most of us have personality traits that are difficult to change. Sometimes, these deeply rooted personality traits can get in the way of our happiness, hinder relationships, and even cause harm to ourselves or others.

For example, a person may have a tendency to be deeply suspicious of other people with no good reason. Another person may assume a haughty, arrogant manner that is difficult to be around. Personality Disorders, by definition, do not cause symptoms, which are experiences that are troublesome to the individual. They consist of whole sets of distorted experiences of the outside world that pervade every or nearly every aspect of a person's life, causing traits and behaviors leading to interpersonal problems which only secondarily cause distress to the individual. The problem is blamed on other people. For example, people with dependent personality disorder feel that they need more care and protection than others, not that they are inordinately demanding of care and protection. People with narcissistic personality disorder feel that others do not respect them, not that they demand more attention and admiration than others; people with paranoid personality disorder feel that others are out to trick and cheat them, not that they are inordinately suspicious; people with obsessive personality disorder feel that others are sloppy, not that they are overly preoccupied with order and tidiness.

A diagnosis of a Personality Disorder should be distinguished from labeling someone as a bad or disagreeable person and not be used to stigmitize people who are simply unpopular, rebellious or otherwise unorthodox. A personality disorder is not simply a personality style, but a condition that interferes with successful living. A Personality Disorder refers to an enduring pattern or experience and behavior that is inflexible, long lasting (often beginning in adolescence or early childhood) and which leads to distress and impairment. Personality disorders frequently co-exist with depression and other mental disorders.

Ten distinct personality disorders have been identified:
•Paranoid Personality Disorder;
•Schiziod Personality Disorder;
•Schizotypal Personality Disorder;
•Antisocial Personality Disorder;
•Borderline Personality Disorder;
•Histrionic Personality Disorder;
•Narcissistic Personality Disorder;
•Avoidant Personality Disorder;
•Dependent Personality Disorder;
•Obsessive-Compulsive Personality Disorder.

SYMPTOMS

An enduring pattern of inner experience and behavior that deviates markedly from the expectations of the individual's culture:
•This pattern is manifested in two or more of the following areas: cognition, affectivity, interpersonal functioning, and impulse control;
•The enduring pattern is inflexible and pervasive across a broad range of personal and social situations;
•The enduring pattern leads to clinically significant distress or impairment in social, occupational, or other important areas of functioning;
•The pattern is stable and of long duration and its onset can be traced back at least to adolescence or early adulthood;
•The enduring pattern is not better accounted for as a manifestation or consequence of another mental disorder;
•The enduring pattern is not due to the direct physiological effects of a substance or a general medical condition.

TREATMENT OPTIONS

Most people who suffer from a Personality Disorder do not see themselves as having psychological problems, and therefore do not seek treatment. For those who do, the most effective treatment is long-term (at least one year) psychotherapy. People with Personality Disorders generally seek treatment only because they are distressed about the behavior of those around them. It is important for a patient to find a mental health professional with expert knowledge and experience in treating personality disorders. Some therapists specialize in treating Borderline Personality Disorder. Antisocial Personality disorder is notably difficult to treat, especially in extreme cases, when the affected individual lacks all concern for others.

Psychotherapy encourages patients to talk about their suspicions, doubts and other personality traits that have a negative impact on their lives, and therefore helps to improve social interactions.

Psychotherapeutic treatment should include attention to family members, stressing the importance of emotional support, reassurance, explanation of the disorder, and advice on how to manage and respond to the patient. Group therapy is helpful in many situations.

Antipsychotic medication can be useful in patients with certain Personality Disorders, specifically Schizotypal and Borderline Disorders.

Associations & Agencies

1210 Career Assessment & Planning Services
Goodwill Industries-Suncoast
10596 Gandy Boulevard
St. Petersburg, FL 33702-1427
727-523-1512
888-279-1988
Fax: 727-563-9300
E-mail: gw.marketing@goodwill-suncoast.org
www.goodwill.org

Lee Waits, President
R Lee Waits, President/CEO

Provides a comprehensive assessment, which can predict current and future employment and potential adjustment factors for physically, emotionally, or developmentally disabled persons who may be unemployed or underemployed. Assessments evaluate interests, aptitudes, academic achievements, and physical abilities (including dexterity and coordination) through coordinated testing, interviewing and behavioral observations.

1211 Center for Family Support (CFS)
333 7th Avenue
New York, NY 10001-5115
212-629-7939
Fax: 212-239-2211
www.cfsny.org

Steven Vernikoff, Executive Director

An agency that continues to develop new programs to serve families and individuals with their care needs. They currently offer services throughout the New York City region including: New Jersey, Long Island and the Lower Hudson Valley.

1212 Center for Mental Health Services (CMHS)
PO Box 2345
Rockville, MD 20847
240-221-4021
800-789-2647
Fax: 240-221-4295
TDD: 866-889-2647
www.mentalhealth.samhsa.gov

A Kathryn Power, MEd, Director
Anna Marsh PhD, Deputy Director
Fran Randolph PhD, Dir, Service & Systems Improveme
Anne Mathews-Younes EdD, Dir, Prevention/Traumatic Stress

CMHS leads Federal efforts to treat mental illnesses by promoting mental health and by preventing the development or worsening of mental illness when possible. Congress created CMHS to bring new hope to adults who have serious mental illnesses and to children with serious emotional disorders. CMHS provides information about mental health via a toll-free the web site, and more than 600 publications. Developed for users of mental health services and their families, the general public, policy makers, providers, and the media.

Year Founded: 1992

1213 National Alliance on Mental Illness
2107 Wilson Boulevard
Suite 300
Arlington, VA 22201-3080
703-524-7600
800-950-6264
Fax: 703-524-9094
E-mail: info@nami.org
www.nami.org

Suzanne Vogel-Scibilia, MD, President
Frederick Sandoval, First VP

Nation's leading self-help organization for all those affected by severe brain disorders. Mission is to bring consumers and families with similar experiences together to share information about services, care providers, and ways to cope with the challenges of schizophrenia, manic depression, and other serious mental illnesses.

Year Founded: 1979

1214 National Association for the Dually Diagnosed (NADD)
132 Fair Street
Kingston, NY 12401-4802
845-331-4336
800-331-5362
Fax: 845-331-4569
E-mail: info@thenadd.org
www.thenadd.org

Robert Fletcher, Executive Director

Nonprofit organization designed to promote interest of professional and parent development with resources for individuals who have the coexistence of mental illness and mental retardation. Provides conference, educational services and training materials to professionals, parents, concerned citizens and service organizations. Formerly known as the National Association for the Dually Diagnosed.

Year Founded: 1983

1215 National Mental Health Consumers' Self-Help Clearinghouse
1211 Chestnut Street
Suite 1207
Philadelphia, PA 19107-4103
215-751-1810
800-553-4539
Fax: 215-636-6312
E-mail: info@mhselfhelp.org
www.mhselfhelp.org

Joseph A Rogers, Executive Director

A national consumer technical assistance center that has played a major role in the development of the mental health consumer movement.

Year Founded: 1986

1216 SAMHSA's National Mental Health Information Center
US Department of Health and Human Services
PO Box 42557
Washington, DC 20015-557
240-221-4021
800-789-2647
Fax: 240-221-4295
TDD: 866-889-2647
www.mentalhealth.samhsa.gov

A Kathryn Power, MEd, Director
Edward B Searle, Deputy Director

Provides information about mental health via a toll-free telephone number, this web site, and more than 600 publications. Developed for users of mental health services and their families, the general public, policy makers, providers, and the media.

Books

1217 Angry Heart: Overcoming Borderline and Addictive Disorders
New Harbinger Publications
5674 Shattuck Avenue
Oakland, CA 94609-1662
510-652-0215
800-748-6273
Fax: 510-652-5472
E-mail: customerservice@newharbinger.com
www.newharbinger.com

Matthew McKay, Owner
Ronald Cohen, PhD, Author

This self help guide uses a variety of exercises and step by step techniques to help individuals with borderline and addictive disorders come to terms with their destructive lifestyle and take steps to break out of its dysfunctional cycle of self defeating thoughts and behavior. *$15.95*

272 pages Year Founded: 1997 ISBN 1-572240-80-6

1218 Assess Dialogue Personality Disorders
Cambridge University Press
40 W 20th Street
New York, NY 10011-4211
212-924-3900
Fax: 212-691-3239
E-mail: information@cup.org
www.cup.org

Cambridge University Press is the printing and publishing house of the University of Cambridge. It is an integral part of the University and is devoted constitutionally to printing and publishing for 'the acquisition, advancement, conservation, and dissemination of knowledge in all subjects'. As such, it is a charitable, not-for-profit organization, free from tax worldwide.

1219 Biology of Personality Disorders, Review of Psychiatry
American Psychiatric Publishing, Inc.
1000 Wilson Boulevard
Suite 1825
Arlington, VA 22209-3901
703-907-7322
800-368-5777
Fax: 703-907-1091
E-mail: appi@psych.org
www.appi.org

Robert E Hales MD, Editor-in-Chief
Ron McMillen, Chief Executive Officer
John McDuffie, Editorial Director

Contents include neurotransmitter function in personality disorders, new biological research strategies for personality disorders, genetics and psychobiology of seven - factor model of personality, psychopharmacological management, and significance of biological research for a biopsychosocial model of personality disorders. *$25.00*

166 pages ISBN 0-880488-35-2

1220 Borderline Personality Disorder
American Psychiatric Publishing, Inc.
1000 Wilson Boulevard
Suite 1825
Arlington, VA 22209-3901
703-907-7322
800-368-5777
Fax: 703-907-1091
E-mail: appi@psych.org
www.appi.org

Robert E Hales MD, Editor-in-Chief
Ron McMillen, Chief Executive Officer
John McDuffie, Editorial Director

Guide to the diagnosis and treatment of borderline personality disorder. *$34.00*

256 pages ISBN 0-880486-89-9

1221 Borderline Personality Disorder: Multidimensional Approach
American Psychiatric Publishing, Inc.
1000 Wilson Boulevard
Suite 1825
Arlington, VA 22209-3901
703-907-7322
800-368-5777
Fax: 703-907-1091
E-mail: appi@psych.org
www.appi.org

Robert E Hales MD, Editor-in-Chief
Ron McMillen, Chief Executive Officer
John McDuffie, Editorial Director

Practical approach to the management of patients with BPD. *$33.00*

288 pages ISBN 0-880486-55-4

1222 Borderline Personality Disorder: A Patient's Guide to Taking Control
WW Norton & Company
500 5th Avenue
New York, NY 10110-54
212-354-2907
800-233-4830
Fax: 212-869-0856
E-mail: npb@wwnorton.com

Drake McFeely, CEO

The Patient's Guide is your clients' means to begin to take command of their lives by following the therapeutic course described in these books. Provides a step-by-step cognitive program wich in worksheets and exercises to facilitate your clients' personal process of self-examination and problem solving.

ISBN 0-393703-53-3

1223 Borderline Personality Disorder: Etilogy and Treatment
American Psychiatric Publishing, Inc.
1000 Wilson Boulevard
Suite 1825
Arlington, VA 22209-3901

703-907-7322
800-368-5777
Fax: 703-907-1091
E-mail: appi@psych.org
www.appi.org

Robert E Hales MD, Editor-in-Chief
Ron McMillen, Chief Executive Officer
John McDuffie, Editorial Director

Provides empirical data as the basis for progress in understanding and treating the borderline patient. *$50.00*

420 pages ISBN 0-880484-08-X

1224 Borderline Personality Disorder: Tailoring the Psychotherapy to the Patient
American Psychiatric Publishing, Inc.
1000 Wilson Boulevard
Suite 1825
Arlington, VA 22209-3901
703-907-7322
800-368-5777
Fax: 703-907-1091
E-mail: appi@psych.org
www.appi.org

Robert E Hales MD, Editor-in-Chief
Ron McMillen, Chief Executive Officer
John McDuffie, Editorial Director

Emphasizes how the clinician should decide between the use of supportive as opposed to expressive techniques, depending upon the characteristics of the patient. *$34.00*

256 pages ISBN 0-880486-89-9

1225 Challenging Behavior
Cambridge University Press
40 W 20th Street
New York, NY 10011-4211
212-924-3900
Fax: 212-691-3239
E-mail: marketing@cup.org
www.cup.org

1226 Clinical Assessment and Management of Severe Personality Disorders
American Psychiatric Publishing, Inc.
1000 Wilson Boulevard
Suite 1825
Arlington, VA 22209-3901
703-907-7322
800-368-5777
Fax: 703-907-1091
E-mail: appi@psych.org
www.appi.org

Robert E Hales MD, Editor-in-Chief
Ron McMillen, Chief Executive Officer
John McDuffie, Editorial Director

Focuses on issues relevant to the clinician in private practice, including the diagnosis of a wide range of personality disorders and alternative management approaches. *$33.00*

260 pages ISBN 0-880484-88-8

1227 Cognitive Analytic Therapy & Borderline Personality Disorder: Model and the Method
John Wiley & Sons
1 Wiley Drive
Somerset, NJ 08873-1272
732-537-9410
800-225-5945
Fax: 732-302-2300
E-mail: compbks@wiley.com
www.wiley.com

Clifford Kline, Senior VP

This book documents CAT's recent theoretical and practical developments is a must for anyone interested in CAT itself and in integrative approaches, for those interested in brief, psychodynamically informed therapy, or indeed for those interested in developments in psychology generally. *$70.00*

206 pages Year Founded: 1997 ISBN 0-471976-18-0

1228 Cognitive Therapy of Personality Disorders, Second Edition
The Guilford Press
72 Spring Street
New York, NY 10012-4019
212-431-9800
800-365-7006
Fax: 212-966-6708
E-mail: info@guilford.com

Bob Matloff, President
Aaron T Beck, Author

Presents a cognitive framework for understanding and treating personality disorders.

1229 Developmental Model of Borderline Personality Disorder: Understanding Variations in Course and Outcome
American Psychiatric Publishing, Inc.
1000 Wilson Boulevard
Suite 1825
Arlington, VA 22209-3901
703-907-7322
800-368-5777
Fax: 703-907-1091
E-mail: appi@psych.org
www.appi.org

Robert E Hales MD, Editor-in-Chief
Ron McMillen, Chief Executive Officer
John McDuffie, Editorial Director

Landmark work on this difficult condition. Emphasizes a developmental approach to BPD based on treatment of inpatients at Chestnut Lodge in Rockville, Maryland, during the years through 1975. Using information gleaned from the original clinical notes and follow-up studies, the authors present four intriguing case studies to chart the etiology, long-term course, and clinical manifestations of BPD. *$34.95*

256 pages Year Founded: 2002 ISBN 0-880485-15-9

1230 Disordered Personalities
Rapid Psychler Press
3560 Pine Grove Avenue
Suite 374
Port Huron, MI 48060-1994
519-667-2335
888-779-2453
Fax: 888-779-2457
E-mail: rapid@psychler.com
www.psychler.com

David Robinson, MD, Publisher

Provides a comprehensive, practical and entertaining overview of the DSM-IV personality disorders. The diagnostic, theoretical and therapeutic principles relevant to understanding character pathology are detailed in the introductory chapters. *$39.95*

428 pages Year Founded: 2005 ISBN 1-894328-09-4

1231 Disorders of Narcissism: Diagnostic, Clinical, and Empirical Implications
American Psychiatric Publishing, Inc.
1000 Wilson Boulevard
Suite 1825
Arlington, VA 22209-3901
703-907-7322
800-368-5777
Fax: 703-907-1091
E-mail: appi@psych.org
www.appi.org

Robert E Hales MD, Editor-in-Chief
Ron McMillen, Chief Executive Officer
John McDuffie, Editorial Director

Addresses important subjects at the forefront of the study of narcissism, including cognitive treatment, normal narcissism, pathological narcissism and suicide, and the connection between pathological narcissism, trauma, and alexithymia. *$42.50*

304 pages ISBN 0-880487-01-1

1232 Drug Therapy and Personality Disorders
Mason Crest Publishers
370 Reed Road
Suite 302
Broomall, PA 19008-4017
610-543-6200
866-627-2665
Fax: 610-543-3878
E-mail: dtaylor@masoncrest.com
www.masoncrest.com

This volume in the series explains the origins, symptoms and treatments of those personality disorders that can benefit from the use of psychiatric medications, including avoidant, paranoid, schizoid, schizotypal, obsessive-compulsive and borderline personality disorders. Case studies and examples of individuals with personality disorders are included to help readers gain a more complete understanding of how these disorders affect actual people.

ISBN 1-590845-71-4

1233 Fatal Flaws: Navigating Destructive Relationships with People with Disorders
American Psychiatric Publishing, Inc.
1000 Wilson Boulevard
Suite 1825
Arlington, VA 22209-3901
703-907-7322
800-368-5777
Fax: 703-907-1091
E-mail: appi@psych.org
www.appi.org

Robert E Hales MD, Editor-in-Chief
Ron McMillen, Chief Executive Officer
John McDuffie, Editorial Director

Featuring case vignettes from nearly 30 years of Dr. Yudofsky's clinical practice and incorporating the knowledge of gifted clinicians, educators, and research scientists with whom he has collaborated throughout that time.

1234 Field Guide to Personality Disorders
Rapid Psychler Press
3560 Pine Grove Avenue
Suite 374
Port Huron, MI 48060-1994
519-667-2335
888-779-2453
Fax: 888-779-2457
E-mail: rapid@psychler.com
www.psychler.com

David Robinson, MD, Publisher

Provides a practical, comprehensive and enjoyable introduction to the DSM-IV-TR personality disorders. Diagnostic, theoretical and therapeutic principles are covered in detail, providing a basis for understanding character pathology. *$19.95*

212 pages Year Founded: 2005 ISBN 1-894328-10-8

1235 Lost in the Mirror: An Inside Look at Borderline Personality Disorder
Sidran Institute
200 E Joppa Road
Suite 207
Baltimore, MD 21286-3107
410-825-8888
888-825-8249
Fax: 410-337-0747
E-mail: sidran@sidran.org
www.sidran.org

Esther Giller, President
J G Goellner, Director Emertius
Stanley Platman, MD, Medical Advisor
Richard Moskovitz, MD, Author

Dr. Moskovitz considers BPD to be part of the dissociative continuum, as it has many causes, symptoms and behaviors in common with Dissociative Disorder. This book is intended for people diagnosed with BPD, their families and therapists. Outlines the features of BPD, including abuse histories, dissociation, mood swings, self harm, impulse control problems and many more. Includes an extensive resource section. *$13.95*

190 pages

1236 Management of Countertransference with Borderline Patients
American Psychiatric Publishing, Inc.
1000 Wilson Boulevard
Suite 1825
Arlington, VA 22209-3901
703-907-7322
800-368-5777
Fax: 703-907-1091
E-mail: appi@psych.org
www.appi.org

Robert E Hales MD, Editor-in-Chief
Ron McMillen, Chief Executive Officer
John McDuffie, Editorial Director

Open and detailed discussion of the emotional reactions that clinicians experience when treating borderline patients. *$34.50*

254 pages ISBN 0-880785-63-9

1237 Personality Disorders in Modern Life
John Wiley & Sons
111 River Street
Hoboken, NJ 07030-5790
201-748-6000
Fax: 201-748-6088
E-mail: info@wiley.com
www.wiley.com

William J Pesce, CEO

Exploring the continuum from normal personality tests to the diagnosis amd treatment of severe cases of personality disorders.

1238 Personality and Psychopathology
American Psychiatric Publishing, Inc.
1000 Wilson Boulevard
Suite 1825
Arlington, VA 22209-3901
703-907-7322
800-368-5777
Fax: 703-907-1091
E-mail: appi@psych.org
www.appi.org

Robert E Hales MD, Editor-in-Chief
Ron McMillen, Chief Executive Officer
John McDuffie, Editorial Director

Compiles the most recent findings from more than 30 internationally recognized experts. Analyzes the association between personality and psychopathology from several interlocking perspective, descriptive, developmental, etiological, and therapeutic. *$58.50*

496 pages ISBN 0-880489-23-5

1239 Role of Sexual Abuse in the Etiology of Borderline Personality Disorder
American Psychiatric Publishing, Inc.
1000 Wilson Boulevard
Suite 1825
Arlington, VA 22209-3901
703-907-7322
800-368-5777
Fax: 703-907-1091

E-mail: appi@psych.org
www.appi.org

Robert E Hales MD, Editor-in-Chief
Ron McMillen, Chief Executive Officer
John McDuffie, Editorial Director

Presenting the latest generation of research findings about the impact of traumatic abuse on the development of BPD. This book focuses on the theoretical basis of BPD, including topics such as childhood factors associated with the development, the relationship of child sexual abuse to dissociation and self-mutilation, severity of childhood abuse, borderline symptoms and family environment. Twenty six contributors cover every aspect of BPD as it relates to childhood sexual abuse. *$65.00*

264 pages Year Founded: 1996 ISBN 0-880484-96-9

1240 Stop Walking on Eggshells
New Harbinger Publications
5674 Shattuck Avenue
Oakland, CA 94609-1662
510-652-0215
800-748-6273
Fax: 510-652-5472
E-mail: customerservice@newharbinger.com
www.newharbinger.com

Matthew McKay, Owner
Paul Mason, MS, Author

Stop Walking on Eggshells: Taking Back Your Life When Someone You Care About Has Borderline Personality Disorder. This guide for the family and friends of those who have BPD is designed to help them understand how the disorder affects their loved ones and recognize what they can do to establish personal limits and enforce boundaries, communicate more effectively, cope with self destructive behavior, and take care of themselves. *$15.95*

272 pages Year Founded: 1998 ISBN 1-572241-08-X

1241 Structured Interview for DSM-IV Personality (SIDP-IV)
American Psychiatric Publishing, Inc.
1000 Wilson Boulevard
Suite 1825
Arlington, VA 22209-3901
703-907-7322
800-368-5777
Fax: 703-907-1091
E-mail: appi@psych.org
www.appi.org

Robert E Hales MD, Editor-in-Chief
Ron McMillen, Chief Executive Officer
John McDuffie, Editorial Director

Semistructured interview uses nonperorative questions to examine behavior and personality traits from the patient's perspective. *$21.95*

48 pages ISBN 0-880489-37-5

1242 The Borderline Personality Disorder Survival Guide
New Harbinger Publications
5674 Shattuck Avenue
Oakland, CA 94609-1662
510-652-0215
800-748-6273
Fax: 510-652-5472
www.newharbinger.com

Matthew McKay, Owner
Alex Chapman, Author
Kim Gratz, Author

The book is organized as a series of answers to questions common to borderline personality disorder sufferers. Later chapters cover several common treatment approaches to borderline personality disorder.

Support Groups & Hot Lines

1243 SAFE Alternatives
7115 W North Avenue
PMB 319
Oak Park, IL 60302-1002
708-366-9066
800-366-8288
Fax: 708-366-9065
E-mail: info@selfinjury.com
www.selfinjury.com

Karen Conterio, CEO
Wendy Lader, PhD, President/Clinical Director
Michelle Seliner, MSW/LCSW, COO

A national organized treatment appraoch, professional network and educational resource base, which is committed to helping you and others achieve an end to self-injurious behavior.

Web Sites

1244 www.cyberpsych.org
CyberPsych

Presents information about psychoanalysis, psychotherapy and special topics such as anxiety disorders, the problematic use of alcohol, homophobia, and the traumatic effects of racism

1245 www.mentalhealth.com
Internet Mental Health

Offers online psychiatric diagnosis in the hope of reaching the two-thirds of individuals with mental illness who do not seek treatment.

1246 www.mhsanctuary.com/borderline
Borderline Personality Disorder Sanctuary

Borderline personality disorder education, communities, support, books, and resources.

1247 www.nimh.nih.gov/publicat/ocdmenu.cfm
Obsessive-Compulsive Disorder

Introductory handout with treatment recommendations.

1248 www.ocdhope.com/gdlines.htm
Guidelines for Families Coping with OCD

1249 www.planetpsych.com
Planetpsych.com

The online resource for mental health information.

1250 www.psychcentral.com
Psych Central

The Internet's largest and oldest independent mental health social network created and run by mental health professionals to guarantee reliable, trusted information and support communities to you.

Psychosomatic (Somatizing) Disorders

Introduction

Officially known as Somatizing Disorders, the disorders in this category are characterized by multiple physical symptoms or the conviction that one is ill despite negative medical examinations and laboratory tests. Those who have a Somatizing Disorder persist in believing they are ill, or experience physical symptoms over long periods, and their beliefs negatively affect all areas of their functioning. Two main types of Somatizing Disorders are Hypochondriasis, which consists of being convinced that one is ill despite evidence to the contrary, and Somatization Disorder, consisting of experiencing physical symptoms without a discernible basis.

Facititious disorder and malingering are also conditions in which physical symptoms are not caused by an identifiable general medical condition, but in these conditions, the symptoms are deliberately and consiously produced. A malingerer deliberately complains or mimics symptoms to achieve a specific goal, such as winning a medical mapractice suit or obtaining disability insurance.

SYMPTOMS

HYPOCHONDRIASIS

- Preocc upation with fears of having a serious illness based on a misinterpretation of bodily symptoms or sensations;
- The preoccupation persists in spite of medical reassurance;
- The preoccupation is a source of distress and difficulty in social, work, and other areas;
- The duration of the preoccupation is at least six months.

SOMATIZATION DISORDER

- A historints beginning before age 30 and continuing over years, resulting in a search for treatment or clear difficulties in social, work or interpersonal areas;
- Four pain symptoms related to at least four anatomical areas or functions;
- Two gastrointestinal problems other than pain, e.g. nausea, diarrhea;
- One sexual sympton other than pain, e.g. irregular menstruation, sexual disinterest, erectile dysfunction;
- One pseudoneurological symptom other than pain, e.g., weakness, double vision;
- Symptoms cannot be explained by a medical condition;
- When a medical condition exists, physical complaints and social difficulties are greater than normal.

ASSOCIATED FEATURES

The person with either of these Somatizing Disorders visits many doctors, but physical examinations and negative lab results neither reassure them nor resolve their symptoms. They often believe they are not getting proper respect or attention, and, indeed, they may be viewed in medical settings as troublesome, because their problems are 'all in their heads.' Persons with these disorders often suffer from anxiety and depression as well. Physical symptoms appearing after the somatization diagnosis is made, however, should not be dismissed completely out of hand. Sufferers can have general medical disorders at the same time as Somatizing Disorders.

The person may be treated by several doctors at once, which can lead to unwitting and possibly dangerous combinations of treatments. There may be suicide threats and attempts, and deteriorating personal relationships. Individuals with these disorders often have associated Personality Disorders, such as Histrionic, Borderline, or Antisocial Personality Disorder.

PREVALENCE

Hypochondriasis is equally common in both sexes. Its prevalence in the general population is not known. In general medical practice, four percent to nine percent of patients have the disorder. It is usually chronic.

Somatization Disorder was once thought to be mainly a disease of women, but occurs in both sexes. It is slightly less common among men in the general population of the US than in other countries, but not uncommon in general medical practice. It is more common among Puerto Rican and Greek men, which suggests that cultural factors influence the sex ratios.

TREATMENT OPTIONS

These disorders are chronic by definition, and are difficult to manage. Repeated reassurance is not successful. The aim is to limit the extent to which the physical concerns and symptoms preoccupy an individual's thoughts and activities, and drain family emotional and financial resources. Individuals suffering from these disorders often resist mental health referral because they interpret it, sometimes correctly, as an indication that their symptoms are not being taken seriously. Treatment, whether by the primary care or mental health professional or both, should focus on maintaining function despite the symptoms. It is important that the psychological management and treatment is coordinated with medical treatment if possible by one physician only; one person should oversee all the medical treatment, including the psychological, so that care does not become fragmented and/or repetitive as the patient sees many different clinicians. Some individuals with Hypochondriasis respond to treatment which combines medication with intensive behavioral and cognitive techniques to manage anxiety and modify beliefs about the origin and course of physical symptoms.

People with hypochondriasis and somatization disorders do not deliberatley produce or falsely complain of physical symptoms; their beliefs and behaviors are engendered by psychological conflict, and often by modeling on someone who was important to them when they were growing up.

Associations & Agencies

1252 Career Assessment & Planning Services
Goodwill Industries-Suncoast
10596 Gandy Boulevard
St. Petersburg, FL 33702-1427
727-523-1512
Fax: 727-563-9300
E-mail: gw.marketing@goodwill-suncoast.com
www.goodwill.org

Lee Waits, President
Loreen M Spencer, Chair Person

Provides a comprehensive assessment, which can predict current and future employment and potential adjustment factors for physically, emotionally, or developmentally disabled persons who may be unemployed or underemployed. Assessments evaluate interests, aptitudes, academic achievements, and physical abilities (including dexterity and coordination) through coordinated testing, interviewing and behavioral observations.

1253 Center for Family Support (CFS)

333 7th Avenue
New York, NY 10001-5115
212-629-7939
Fax: 212-239-2211
www.cfsny.org

Steven Vernikoff, Executive Director

An agency that continues to develop new programs to serve families and individuals with their care needs. They currently offer services throughout the New York City region including: New Jersey, Long Island and the Lower Hudson Valley.

1254 Center for Mental Health Services (CMHS)

PO Box 2345
Rockville, MD 20847
240-221-4021
800-789-2647
Fax: 240-221-4295
TDD: 866-889-2647
www.mentalhealth.samhsa.gov

A Kathryn Power, MEd, Director
Anna Marsh PhD, Deputy Director
Fran Randolph PhD, Dir, Service & Systems Improveme
Anne Mathews-Younes EdD, Dir, Prevention/Traumatic Stress

CMHS leads Federal efforts to treat mental illnesses by promoting mental health and by preventing the development or worsening of mental illness when possible. Congress created CMHS to bring new hope to adults who have serious mental illnesses and to children with serious emotional disorders. CMHS provides information about mental health via a toll-free the web site, and more than 600 publications. Developed for users of mental health services and their families, the general public, policy makers, providers, and the media.

Year Founded: 1992

1255 Deborah MacWilliams

777 Northwest Wall Street
Suite 308
Bend, OR 97701-2760
541-617-0351

Deborah MacWilliams PhD PMHNP

Providing individual psychiatric evaluation, psychotherapy, and medical management for adults and teens. Specializing in thorough assessments and personalized treatment planning.

1256 Institute for Contemporary Psychotherapy

1841 Broadway
4th Floor
New York, NY 10023-7608
212-333-3444
www.icpnyc.org

Ron Taffel PhD, Chairman
Fred Lipschitz, Treasurer/Founder
Mildred Schwartz, Founder

One of the oldest and largest not-for-profit mental health training and treatment facilities in New York City, dedicated to providing high quality therapy at low to moderate cost, offering post-graduate training for therapists, and educating the public about mental health issues.

Year Founded: 1971

1257 Institute for Contemproary Psychotherapy

1841 Broadway 60th Street Fourth Floor
New York, NY 10023
212-333-3444
www.icpnyc.org

Ron Taffel, PhD, Chairman
Fred Lipschitz, Treasurer

ICP is dedicated to providing high quality therapy at low to moderate cost, offering post-graduate training for therapists and educatiing the public about mental health issues.

1258 National Association for the Dually Diagnosed (NADD)

132 Fair Street
Kingston, NY 12401-4802
845-331-4336
800-331-5362
Fax: 845-331-4569
E-mail: info@thenadd.org
www.thenadd.org

Robert Fletcher, Executive Director

Nonprofit organization designed to promote interest of professional and parent development with resources for individuals who have the coexistence of mental illness and mental retardation. Provides conference, educational services and training materials to professionals, parents, concerned citizens and service organizations. Formerly known as the National Association for the Dually Diagnosed.

1259 National Mental Health Consumers' Self-Help Clearinghouse

1211 Chestnut Street
Suite 1207
Philadelphia, PA 19107-4103
215-751-1810
800-553-4539
Fax: 215-636-6312
E-mail: info@mhselfhelp.org
www.mhselfhelp.org

Joseph Rogers, Executive Director

A national consumer technical assistance center that has played a major role in the development of the mental health consumer movement.

Year Founded: 1986

1260 SAMHSA'S National Mental Health Information Center
US Department of Health and Human Services
PO Box 42557
Washington, DC 20015-557

800-789-2647
Fax: 240-747-5470
TDD: 866-889-2647
E-mail: ken@mentalhealth.org
www.mentalhealth.smahsa.org

A Kathryn Power, MEd, Director
Edward B Searle, Deputy Director

Information about resources, technical assistance, research, training, networks, and other federal clearing houses, and fact sheets and materials. Information specialists refer callers to mental health resources in their communities as well as state, federal and nonprofit contacts. Staff available Monday through Friday, 8:30 AM - 5:00 PM, EST, excluding federal holidays. After hours, callers may leave messages and an information specialist will return their call.

Books

1261 Concise Guide to Psychopharmacology
American Psychiatric Publishing, Inc.
1000 Wilson Boulevard
Suite 1825
Arlington, VA 22209-3901
703-907-7322
800-368-5777
Fax: 703-907-1091
E-mail: appi@psych.org
www.appi.org

Robert E Hales MD, Editor-in-Chief
Ron McMillen, Chief Executive Officer
John McDuffie, Editorial Director
Lauren B Marangell MD, Author

The definitive pocket reference for convenient everyday use. This invaluable clinical companion begins with an overview of the general principles relevant to the safe and effective use of psychotropic medications. Subsequent chapters focus on the major classes of psychotropic medications and the disorders for which they are prescribed. *$47.95*

260 pages Year Founded: 2006 ISSN 9781585622559ISBN 1-585622-55-9

1262 Disorders of Simulation: Malingering, Factitious Disorders, and Compensation Neurosis
Psychosocial Press
59 Boston Post Road
Madison, CT 06443-2130
203-245-4000
Fax: 203-245-0775

Grant L Hutchinson, Author

1263 Do No Harm?
Independent Publishing Group
814 N Franklin Street
Chicago, IL 60610-3813
312-337-0747
Fax: 312-337-5985
E-mail: frontdesk@ipgbook.com
www.ipgbook.com

Curt Matthews, President

Munchausen Syndrome by Proxy is the syndrome that causes parents and care workers to harm their children to get attention. Many families are separated after its diagnosis. But has the fertile imagination of social workers and the public turned MSBP into the trendy disorder of our time? *$16.95*

240 pages ISBN 1-901250-48-2

1264 Drug Therapy and Psychosomatic Disorders
Masn Crest Publishers
370 Reed Road
Suite 302
Broomall, PA 19008-4017
610-543-6200
866-627-2665
Fax: 610-543-3878
E-mail: dtaylor@masoncrest.com
www.masoncrest.com

Psychosomatic disorders are complex psychiatric conditions involving the mysterious connection between the body and the brain. From unexplained pain to nonepileptic seizures, the physical symptoms that result from psychopharmacology alike. Through stories of individuals' struggles with psychosomatic disorders combined with easily explained scientific information, this book provides both a historical overview of treatment and reviews the most up-to-date treatments available today.

ISBN 1-590845-73-0

1265 Essentials of Psychosomatic Medicine
American Psychiatric Publishing, Inc.
1000 Wilson Boulevard
Suite 1825
Arlington, VA 22209-3901
703-907-7322
800-368-5777
Fax: 703-907-1091
E-mail: appi@psych.org
www.appi.org

Robert E Hales MD, Editor-in-Chief
Ron McMillen, Chief Executive Officer
John McDuffie, Editorial Director

This book focuses on psychiatric care for medically ill patients.

1266 Hypochondria: Woeful Imaginings
University of California Press
2120 Berkeley Way
Berkeley, CA 94704-5804
510-642-4247
Fax: 510-643-7127

E-mail: askucp@ucpress.edu
www.ucpress.edu

Pamela Wimberly, Plant Manager

Susan Baur illuminates the process by which hypochondriacs come to adopt and maintain illness as a way of life. *$25.00*

260 pages Year Founded: 1989 ISBN 0-520067-51-7

1267 Mind-Body Problems: Psychotherapy with Psychosomatic Disorders
Jason Aronson
230 Livingston Street
Northvale, NJ 07647-1726
570-342-1320
800-782-0015
Fax: 201-767-1576
www.aronson.com

Shows us the causes and treatments of the major pychosomatic symptons. *$70.00*

376 pages ISBN 1-568216-54-8

1268 Munchausen by Proxy: Identification, Intervention, and Case Management
Routledge
270 Madison Avenue
New York, NY 10016-601
212-695-6599

Maura May, Publisher
Louisa Lasher, Author

This step-by-step guide will help you identify and manage cases of this unique form of child maltreatment.

1269 Munchausen's Syndrome by Proxy
World Scientific Publishing Company
27 Warren Street
Suite 401-402
Hackensack, NJ 07601-5477
201-487-9655
800-227-7562
Fax: 201-487-9656
E-mail: wspc@wspc.com
www.wspc.com

Calandri Braswell, Manager

This book reviews the current state of knowledge of Munchausen's Syndrome by Proxy, a type of child abuse which causes wide concern. Two main areas are covered: new directions in research, and treatment of the perpetrator in and outside the family. *$53.00*

ISBN 1-860941-34-6

1270 Phantom Illness: Recognizing, Understanding, and Overcoming Hypochondria
Houghton Mifflin Company
222 Berkeley Street
Boston, MA 02116-3760
617-351-5000
Fax: 617-351-1105
E-mail: inquiries@hmco.com

Barry O'Callaghan, CEO

Offers hope to those who suffer from the debilitating disorder of hypochondria. Carla Cantor's long, dark road to hypochondria began when she crashed a car, killing a friend of hers. She couldn't forgive herself, and a few years later began imagining that she was suffering from Lupus. Many years and two hospitalizations later, she wrote this book not only about her experiences, but about hypochondria in general, now more politely referred to as a 'somatoform disorder'. Paperback. *$15.00*

351 pages ISBN 0-395859-92-1

1271 Playing Sick
Routledge Publishing
270 Madison Avenue
New York, NY 10016-601
212-695-6599

Maura May, Publisher

Taken from bizarre cases of real patients, the first book to chronicle the devastating impact of phony illnesses-factitious disorders and Munchausen syndrome-on patients and caregivers alike. *$ 27.50*

328 pages ISBN 0-415949-34-7

1272 Playing Sick?: Untangling the Web of Munchausen Syndrome, Munchausen by Proxy, Malingering, and Factitious Disorder
Routledge
270 Madison Avenue
New York, NY 10016-601
212-695-6599

Maura May, Publisher

Based on years of research and clinical practice, this book provides the clues that can help practitioners and family members recognize these disorders, avoid invasive procedures, and sort out the motives that drive people to hurt themselves and deceive others.

1273 Somatoform and Factitious Disorders (Review of Psychiatry)
American Psychiatric Publishing, Inc.
1000 Wilson Boulevard
Suite 1825
Arlington, VA 22209-3901
703-907-7322
800-368-5777
Fax: 703-907-1091
E-mail: appi@psych.org
www.appi.org

Robert E Hales MD, Editor-in-Chief
Ron McMillen, Chief Executive Officer
John McDuffie, Editorial Director

Offers clinicians a broad synthesis of the current knowledge about somatoform and factitious disorders.

1274 The Divided Mind: The Epidemic of Mindbody Disorders
HarperCollins Publishers
10 East 53rd Street
New York, NY 10022-5299
212-207-7000
Fax: 212-207-6964
www.harpercollins.com

Brian Murray, CEO

Explores the chasm between the conscious and unconscious minds where psychosomatic ailments originate.

1275 What Your Patients Need to Know about Psychiatric Medications
American Psychiatric Publishing, Inc.
1000 Wilson Boulevard
Suite 1825
Arlington, VA 22209-3901
703-907-7322
800-368-5777
Fax: 703-907-1091
E-mail: appi@psych.org
www.appi.org

Robert E Hales MD, Editor-in-Chief
Ron McMillen, Chief Executive Officer
John McDuffie, Editorial Director

This book includes all major classes of medications, along with detailed information on specific agents - information that's more in-depth and easier to understand than what can be obtained from pharmacies or found on the Internet.
$87.00

441 pages Year Founded: 2009 ISSN 9781585623563

Periodicals & Pamphlets

1276 Asher Meadow Newsletter
18209 Smoke House Court
Germantown, MD 20874-2425

www.ashermeadow.com

Asher Meadow is a wholly-owned non-profit subsidiary of American Marvels, an Internet development company that provides a newsletter for survivors of MSBP.

Support Groups & Hot Lines

1277 Asher Meadow
18209 Smoke House Court
Germantown, MD 20874-2425

www.ashermeadow.com

A wholly-owned non profit subsidiary of American Marvels, and Internet development company that provides resources and links related to Munchausen's Syndrome by Proxy.

Web Sites

1278 www.mbpexpert.com
MBP Expert Services

Expert services from Louisa J Lasher, MA, provides Munchausen by Proxy maltreatment training, case consultation, technical assistance, and expert witness services in an objective manner and in the best interest of the child or children involved.

1279 www.mentalhealth.com
Internet Mental Health

Offers online psychiatric diagnosis in the hope of reaching the two-thirds of individuals with mental illness who do not seek treatment.

1280 www.msbp.com
Mothers Against Munchausen Syndrome by Proxy Allegations

Begun in response to the fast growing number of false allegations of Munchausen Syndrome by Proxy.

1281 www.munchausen.com
Munchause Syndrome

Dr. Marc Feldman's Munchausen Syndrome, Malingering, Factitious Disorder, & Munchausen by Proxy page. Includes articles, related book list, personal stories and links.

1282 www.planetpsych.com
Planetpsych.com

Online resource for mental health information

1283 www.psychcentral.com
Psych Central

The Internet's largest and oldest independent mental health social network created and run by mental health professionals to guarantee reliable, trusted information and support communities to you.

Schizophrenia

Introduction

Schizophrenia is an old term meaning, approximately, 'split personality.' While the name of the diagnosis survives, the concept of split personality is outdated. This is a misuse of the term.

Schizophrenia is a devastating disease of the brain that severely impairs an individual's ability to think, feel and function normally. Though not a common disorder, it is one of the most destructive, disrupting the lives of sufferers, as well as of family members and loved ones. Long misunderstood, people with Schizophrenia and their families have also borne a burden of stigma in addition to the burden of their illness.

Although family and other environmental stressors can play a role in precipitating or exacerbating episodes of illness, theories that the disease is caused by poor parenting have been discredited. Much has been learned about the disease in recent years and treatments have improved markedly.

Schizophrenia is a largely genetically determined disorder of the brain. One theory is that it is a disorder of information processing resulting from a defect in the prefrontal cortex of the brain. Because this system is defective, an individual with Schizophrenia is easily overwhelmed by the amount of information and stimuli coming from the environment. Schizophrenia causes hallucinations, which are sensory experiences in the absence of actual stimuli (hearing voices when no one is speaking), and delusions, which are bizarre beliefs (tThat the individual is God, that the television is conveying messages specifically aimed at the individual, that some power is removing the individual's thoughts from his or her mind). Speech may be tangential or confused. These are called 'positive symptoms.' The individual also loses some normal behaviors and experiences, engaging in little behavior or social interaction. These are called 'negative symptoms.' Schizophrenia is a chronic disease and, once diagnosed, a person often needs treatment the rest of his or her life. However, great strides have been made in treating the disease and many individuals with schizophrenia can hold jobs, marry, parent children, and have gratifying and productive lives.

SYMPTOMS

So-called 'Positive' symptoms (experiences not shared by people in society):
•Delusions or false and bizarre beliefs;
•Hallucinations;

Negative symptoms (the loss of normal behaviors):
•Withdrawing from social contact;
• Speaking less;
•Losing interest in things and the ability to enjoy them;
•Disorganized speech;
•Grossly disorganized or catatonic behavior (extremely agitated or zombie-like);
•The symptoms cause social and occupational dysfunction;
•Signs of the disturbance persist for at least six months;
•The symptoms must not be related to mood or depressive disorders, substance abuse or general medical conditions.

ASSOCIATED FEATURES

People with Schizophrenia, because their disease causes difficulty in perceiving their environment and responding to it normally, often act strange, and have odd beliefs. They sometimes react to stimuli (voices or images originating inside their brains) as though they were originating in their environment; hallucinations and delusions can make a person's behavior appear bizarre to others. Anhedonia, the inability to enjoy pleasurable activities, is common in Schizophrenia, as are sleep disturbances and abnormalities of psychomotor activity. The latter may take the form of pacing, rocking, or immobility. Negative symptoms can be more disabling than positive ones. Family members often become annoyed because they think the individual is just lazy. Schizophrenia takes many forms, and there are a number of subtypes of the illness, including paranoid schizophrenia.

Individuals with untreated Schizophrenia, under the influence of hallucinations and delusions, have a slightly greater propensity for violence than the general population, but only when there is co-existing alcohol or substance abuse, which is quite common. Schizophrenia is known as a heterogenous disease, meaning that the illness takes many forms, depending on a variety of individual characteristics and circumstances. Patients who receive appropriate treatment are not more violent than the general population.

The life expectancy of people with Schizophrenia is shorter than the general population for a varietyof reasons: suicide is common among people with the disease and people with Schizophrenia often have both poor medical care and poor health.

PREVALENCE

The first episode of Schizophrenia usually occurs in teenage years, although some cases may occur in the late thirties or forties. Onset prior to puberty is rare, though cases as early as five year olds have been reported. Women have a later average of onset and a better prognosis. Estimates of the prevalence of Schizophrenia vary widely around the world, but probably about one percent of the world population has the disease.

TREATMENT OPTIONS

Medications can diminish or eliminate many of the positive symptoms of Schizophrenia. Older medications, such as Haldol, are effective and inexpensive, but cause more side effects than newer medications, such as Zyprexa and Geodon. Clozapine was the first and is still one of the most effective treatments, but it causes a low incidence of a life-threatening blood disorder; therefore people who take it must have blood tests at regular intervals. The newer medications are more effective in treating the negative, as well as the positive, symptoms.

Often, patients report that antipsychotic medications make them feel foggy, or lethargic. Antipsychotic medications can have serious side effects, including Tardive Dyskinesia, which consists of involuntary muscular movements. The newer antipsychotic medications are less sedating and have a decreased risk of causing Tardive Dyskinesia, but are associated with significant weight gain and increased risk of diabetes. There is considerable public controversy as to whether the weight gain, and risk of diabetes associated with the newer medications, along with their cost, outweigh their advantages.

Having Schizophrenia interferes with taking care of oneself and getting proper medical care in several ways; Schizophrenia often depletes financial resources so that patients cannot afford medication, nutrition, and medical care. Untreated Schizophrenia can also interfere with an individual's ability to understand signs and symptoms of medical disorders. Compliance with medication is often a problem, and failure to continue taking medication is a major cause of relapse. For this reason, treatment should include supportive therapy, in which a psychiatrist or other mental health professional provides counseling aimed at helping the patient maintain a positive and optimistic attitude focused on staying healthy. Other forms of therapy, such as social skills training, have also found some success and may be useful in helping a person with schizophrenia learn appropriate social and interpersonal behavior. It is important to note that psychotic illness does not necessarily affect all aspects of an individual's thinking. People with schizophrenia may have bizarre beliefs or behaviour in one sphere of life but be perfectly able to make decisions and function in other areas. In addition, it is crucial not to destroy an individual or family's hopes of a normal life by communicating the message that schizophrenia is hopeless.

Paranoid schizophrenia is especially difficult to treat. Paranoia, the irrational conviction that other people, institutions (the FBI), or alien beings are attempting to harm the individual, prevents the individual from forming trusting relationships with care providers and adhering to effective treatment regimens. The individual with paranoid schizophrenia can appear convincingly lucid in order to obtain release from care, while continuing to hold psychotic beliefs.

Associations & Agencies

1285 Career Assessment & Planning Services
Goodwill Industries-Suncoast
10596 Gandy Boulevard
St. Petersburg, FL 33702-1427
727-523-1512
Fax: 727-563-9300
E-mail: gw.marketing@goodwill-suncoast.org
www.goodwill.org

Lee Waits, President
Loreen M Spencer, Chair Person

Provides a comprehensive assessment, which can predict current and future employment and potential adjustment factors for physically, emotionally, or developmentally disabled persons who may be unemployed or underemployed. Assessments evaluate interests, aptitudes, academic achievements, and physical abilities (including dexterity and coordination) through coordinated testing, interviewing and behavioral observations.

1286 Center for Family Support (CFS)
333 7th Avenue
New York, NY 10001-5115
212-629-7939
Fax: 212-239-2211
www.cfsny.org

Steven Vernikoff, Executive Director

An agency that continues to develop new programs to serve families and individuals with their care needs. They currently offer services throughout the New York City region including: New Jersey, Long Island and the Lower Hudson Valley.

1287 Center for Mental Health Services (CMHS)
PO Box 2345
Rockville, MD 20847
240-221-4021
800-789-2647
Fax: 240-221-4295
TDD: 866-889-2647
www.mentalhealth.samhsa.gov

A Kathryn Power, MEd, Director
Anna Marsh PhD, Deputy Director
Fran Randolph PhD, Dir, Service & Systems Improveme
Anne Mathews-Younes EdD, Dir, Prevention/Traumatic Stress

CMHS leads Federal efforts to treat mental illnesses by promoting mental health and by preventing the development or worsening of mental illness when possible. Congress created CMHS to bring new hope to adults who have serious mental illnesses and to children with serious emotional disorders. CMHS provides information about mental health via a toll-free the web site, and more than 600 publications. Developed for users of mental health services and their families, the general public, policy makers, providers, and the media.

Year Founded: 1992

1288 NARSAD: The Mental Health Research Association
60 Cutter Mill Road
Suite 404
Great Neck, NY 11021-3104
516-829-0091
800-829-8289
Fax: 516-487-6930
E-mail: info@narsad.org
www.narsad.org

Steve Doochin, Executive Director
Stephen Doochin, Executive Director

A nonprofit organization that raises funds for scientific research on severe mental illness. It is the largest donor-supported organization in the world dedicated to finding the causes, improved treatments and cures for psychiatric brain and behavior disorders.

1289 National Alliance on Mental Illness
2107 Wilson Boulevard
Suite 300
Arlington, VA 22201-3080
703-524-7600
800-950-6264
Fax: 703-524-9094
E-mail: info@nami.org
www.nami.org

Suzanne Vogel-Scibila, MD, President
Frederick R Sandoval, First VP

Nation's leading self-help organization for all those affected by severe brain disorders. Mission is to bring consumers and families with similar experiences together to share information about services, care providers, and ways to cope with the challenges of schizophrenia, manic depression, and other serious mental illnesses.

Year Founded: 1979

1290 National Association for The Dually Diagnosed (NADD)
132 Fair Street
Kingston, NY 12401-4802
845-331-4336
800-331-5362
Fax: 845-331-4569
E-mail: info@thenadd.org
www.thenadd.org

Robert Fletcher, Executive Director

Nonprofit organization designed to promote interest of professional and parent development with resources for individuals who have the coexistence of mental illness and mental retardation. Provides conference, educational services and training materials to professionals, parents, concerned citizens and service organizations. Formerly known as the National Association for the Dually Diagnosed.

1291 National Mental Health Association
2001 N Beauregard Street
12th Floor
Alexandria, VA 22311-1739
703-684-7722
800-969-6642
Fax: 703-684-5968
TTY: 800-433-5959
E-mail: infoctr@nmha.org
www.mentalhealthamerica.net

David Shern, CEO
Chris Condayn, Communications

Dedicated to improving treatments, understanding and services for adults and children with mental health needs. Working to win political support for funding for school mental health programs. Provides information about a wide range of disorders.

1292 National Mental Health Consumers' Self-Help Clearinghouse
1211 Chestnut Street
Suite 1207
Philadelphia, PA 19107-4103
215-751-1810
800-553-4539
Fax: 215-636-6312
E-mail: info@mhselfhelp.org
www.mhselfhelp.org

Joseph Rogers, Executive Director

A national consumer technical assistance center that has played a major role in the development of the mental health consumer movement.

Year Founded: 1986

1293 SAMHSA'S National Mental Health Information Center
US Department of Health and Human Services
PO Box 42557
Washington, DC 20015-557

800-789-2647
Fax: 240-747-5470
TDD: 866-889-2647
E-mail: ken@mentalhealth.org
www.mentalhealth.samhsa.gov

A Kathryn Power, MEd, Director
Edward B Searle, Deputy Director

Information about resources, technical assistance, research, training, networks, and other federal clearing houses, and fact sheets and materials. Information specialists refer callers to mental health resources in their communities as well as state, federal and nonprofit contacts. Staff available Monday through Friday, 8:30 AM - 5:00 PM, EST, excluding federal holidays. After hours, callers may leave messages and an information specialist will return their call.

Books

1294 Biology of Schizophrenia and Affective Disease
American Psychiatric Publishing, Inc.
1000 Wilson Boulevard
Suite 1825
Arlington, VA 22209-3901
703-907-7322
800-368-5777
Fax: 703-907-1091
E-mail: appi@psych.org
www.appi.org

Robert E Hales MD, Editor-in-Chief
Ron McMillen, Chief Executive Officer
John McDuffie, Editorial Director

Provides a state-of-the-art look at the biological basis of several mental illness from the perspective of the researchers making these discoveries. *$58.50*

464 pages ISBN 0-880487-46-1

1295 Breakthroughs in Antipsychotic Medications: A Guide for Consumers, Families, and Clinicians
National Alliance on Mental Illness
2107 Wilson Boulevard
Suite 300
Arlington, VA 22201-3080
703-524-7600
800-950-6264
Fax: 703-524-9094
TDD: 703-516-7227
E-mail: campaign@nami.org
www.nami.org

Helps consumers and their families weigh the pros and cons of switching from older antipsychotics to newer ones. Answers frequently asked questions about antipsychotics and guides readers through the process of switching. Includes fact sheets on the new medications and their side effects. *$22.95*

207 pages Year Founded: 1999 ISBN 0-393703-03-7

1296 Concept of Schizophrenia: Historical Perspectives
American Psychiatric Publishing, Inc.
1000 Wilson Boulevard
Suite 1825
Arlington, VA 22209-3901
703-907-7322
800-368-5777
Fax: 703-907-1091
E-mail: appi@psych.org
www.appi.org

Robert E Hales MD, Editor-in-Chief
Ron McMillen, Chief Executive Officer
John McDuffie, Editorial Director

$65.00

211 pages

1297 Contemporary Issues in the Treatment of Schizophrenia
American Psychiatric Publishing, Inc.
1000 Wilson Boulevard
Suite 1825
Arlington, VA 22209-3901
703-907-7322
800-368-5777
Fax: 703-907-1091
E-mail: appi@psych.org
www.appi.org

Robert E Hales MD, Editor-in-Chief
Ron McMillen, Chief Executive Officer
John McDuffie, Editorial Director

Covers approaches to the patient by investigating biological, pharmacological and psychosocial treatments. *$99.95*

960 pages ISBN 0-880486-81-3

1298 Drug Therapy and Schizophrenia
Mason Crest Publishers
370 Reed Road
Suite 302
Broomall, PA 19008-4017
610-543-6200
866-627-2665
Fax: 610-543-3878
E-mail: dtaylor@masoncrest.com
www.masoncrest.com

This volume provides a concise description of this disease, which is considered the most severe of the mental disorders. The book also includes a brief account of the disease in history, as well as explanations of how the brain operates and how psychiatric drugs work within the brain. Many case studies are presented to help readers better understand the nature of this difficult and potentially devastating mental disorder.

ISBN 1-590845-74-9

1299 Encyclopedia of Schizophrenia and the Psychotic Disorders
Facts on File
132 W 31st Street
17th Floor
New York, NY 10001-3406
212-613-2800
800-322-8755
E-mail: custserv@factsonfile.com

Details recent theories and research findings on schizophrenia and psychotic disorders, together with a complete overview of the field's history. *$65.00*

368 pages Year Founded: 2000 ISBN 0-816040-70-2

1300 Family Care of Schizophrenia: a Problem-Solving Approach...
Guilford Publications
72 Spring Street
New York, NY 10012-4068
212-431-9800
800-365-7006
Fax: 212-966-6708
E-mail: info@guilford.com

Bob Matloff, President

Falloon and his colleagues have developed a model for the broad-based community treatment of schizophrenia and other severe forms of mental illness that taps this underutilized potential. The goal of their program is not merely the reduction of stress that can trigger florid episodes, but also the restoration of the patient to a level of social functioning that permits employment and socialization with people outside the family. As the author demonstrates, families can, with proper guidance, be taught to modulate intrafamilial stress, whether it derives from family tensions or external life events. *$27.95*

451 pages ISBN 0-898629-23-3

1301 Family Work for Schizophrenia: a Practical Guide
American Psychiatric Publishing, Inc.
1000 Wilson Boulevard
Suite 1825
Arlington, VA 22209-3901
703-907-7322
800-368-5777
Fax: 703-907-1091
E-mail: appi@psych.org
www.appi.org

Robert E Hales MD, Editor-in-Chief
Ron McMillen, Chief Executive Officer
John McDuffie, Editorial Director

1302 First Episode Psychosis
American Psychiatric Publishing, Inc.
1000 Wilson Boulevard
Suite 1825
Arlington, VA 22209-3901
703-907-7322
800-368-5777
Fax: 703-907-1091

E-mail: appi@psych.org
www.appi.org

Robert E Hales MD, Editor-in-Chief
Ron McMillen, Chief Executive Officer
John McDuffie, Editorial Director

Professional discussion of early Psychosis presentation.
$39.95

160 pages ISBN 1-853174-35-1

1303 Group Therapy for Schizophrenic Patients
American Psychiatric Publishing, Inc.
1000 Wilson Boulevard
Suite 1825
Arlington, VA 22209-3901
703-907-7322
800-368-5777
Fax: 703-907-1091
E-mail: appi@psych.org
www.appi.org

Robert E Hales MD, Editor-in-Chief
Ron McMillen, Chief Executive Officer
John McDuffie, Editorial Director

Acquaints mental health practitioners with this cost-effective method of treatment. *$29.00*

192 pages ISBN 0-880481-72-2

1304 Guidelines for the Treatment of Patients with Schizophrenia
American Psychiatric Publishing, Inc.
1000 Wilson Boulevard
Suite 1825
Arlington, VA 22209-3901
703-907-7322
800-368-5777
Fax: 703-907-1091
E-mail: appi@psych.org
www.appi.org

Robert E Hales MD, Editor-in-Chief
Ron McMillen, Chief Executive Officer
John McDuffie, Editorial Director

Provides therapists with a set of patient care strategies that will aid their clinical decison making. Describes the best and most appropriate treatments available to patients.
$22.50

160 pages ISBN 0-890423-09-1

1305 How to Cope with Mental Illness In Your Family: A Guide for Siblings and Offspring
Health Source
1404 K Street, NW
Washington, DC 20005-2401
202-789-7303
800-713-7122
Fax: 202-789-7899
E-mail: healthsourcebooks@psych.org
www.healthsourcebooks.org

This book explores the nature of illnesses such as schizophrenia, major depression, while providing the tools to overcome the devasting effects of growing up or living in a family where they exist. Readers are led through the essen-

tial stages of recovery, from revisiting their childhood to revising their family legacy, and ultimately, to reclaiming their life. *$14.00*

240 pages ISBN 0-874779-23-5

1306 Innovative Approaches for Difficult to Treat Populations
American Psychiatric Publishing, Inc.
1000 Wilson Boulevard
Suite 1825
Arlington, VA 22209-3901
703-907-7322
800-368-5777
Fax: 703-907-1091
E-mail: appi@psych.org
www.appi.org

Robert E Hales MD, Editor-in-Chief
Ron McMillen, Chief Executive Officer
John McDuffie, Editorial Director

Firsthand look at the future direction of clinical services. Focuses on services for individuals who use the highest proportion of mental health resources and for whom traditional services have not been effective. *$65.00*

512 pages ISBN 0-880486-80-5

1307 Me, Myself, and Them: A Firsthand Account of One Young Person's Experience with Schizophrenia (Adolescent Mental Health Initiative)
Oxford University Press
198 Madison Avenue
New York, NY 10016-4341

800-445-9714
Fax: 919-677-1303
E-mail: custserv.us@oup.com
www.oup.com/us

Kurt Snyder, Author
Raquel E Gur, Author
Linda Wasmer Andrews, Author

Offers hope to young people who are struggling with schizophrenia, helping them to understand and manage the challenges of this illness and go on to lead healthy lives.

192 pages ISBN 0-195311-22-1

1308 Natural History of Mania, Depression and Schizophrenia
American Psychiatric Publishing, Inc.
1000 Wilson Boulevard
Suite 1825
Arlington, VA 22209-3901
703-907-7322
800-368-5777
Fax: 703-907-1091
E-mail: appi@psych.org
www.appi.org

Robert E Hales MD, Editor-in-Chief
Ron McMillen, Chief Executive Officer
John McDuffie, Editorial Director

An unusual look at the course of mental illness, based on data from the Iowa 500 Research Project. *$42.50*

336 pages ISBN 0-880487-26-7

1309 New Pharmacotherapy of Schizophrenia
American Psychiatric Publishing, Inc.
1000 Wilson Boulevard
Suite 1825
Arlington, VA 22209-3901
703-907-7322
800-368-5777
Fax: 703-907-1091
E-mail: appi@psych.org
www.appi.org

Robert E Hales MD, Editor-in-Chief
Ron McMillen, Chief Executive Officer
John McDuffie, Editorial Director

Discusses the new class of antipsychotic agents that promise superior efficacy and more favorable side-effects; offers an improved understanding of how to employ existing pharmachotherapeutic agents. *$32.50*

272 pages ISBN 0-880484-91-8

1310 Office Treatment of Schizophrenia
American Psychiatric Publishing, Inc.
1000 Wilson Boulevard
Suite 1825
Arlington, VA 22209-3901
703-907-7322
800-368-5777
Fax: 703-907-1091
E-mail: appi@psych.org
www.appi.org

Robert E Hales MD, Editor-in-Chief
Ron McMillen, Chief Executive Officer
John McDuffie, Editorial Director

Examines options in outpatient treatment of schizophrenic patients. *$31.00*

208 pages

1311 Practicing Psychiatry in the Community: a Manual
American Psychiatric Publishing, Inc.
1000 Wilson Boulevard
Suite 1825
Arlington, VA 22209-3901
703-907-7322
800-368-5777
Fax: 703-907-1091
E-mail: appi@psych.org
www.appi.org

Robert E Hales MD, Editor-in-Chief
Ron McMillen, Chief Executive Officer
John McDuffie, Editorial Director

Addressess the major issues currently facing community psychiatrists. *$67.50*

560 pages ISBN 0-880486-63-5

1312 Prenatal Exposures in Schizophrenia
American Psychiatric Publishing, Inc.
1000 Wilson Boulevard
Suite 1825
Arlington, VA 22209-3901
703-907-7322
800-368-5777
Fax: 703-907-1091
E-mail: appi@psych.org
www.appi.org

Robert E Hales MD, Editor-in-Chief
Ron McMillen, Chief Executive Officer
John McDuffie, Editorial Director

Considers a range of epigenetic elements thought to interact with abnormal genes to produce the onset of illness. Attention to the evidence implicating obstetric complications, prenatal infection, autoimmunity and prenatal malnutrition in brain disorders. *$36.50*

352 pages ISBN 0-880484-99-3

1313 Psychiatric Rehabilitation of Chronic Mental Patients
American Psychiatric Publishing, Inc.
1000 Wilson Boulevard
Suite 1825
Arlington, VA 22209-3901
703-907-7322
800-368-5777
Fax: 703-907-1091
E-mail: appi@psych.org
www.appi.org

Robert E Hales MD, Editor-in-Chief
Ron McMillen, Chief Executive Officer
John McDuffie, Editorial Director

Provides highly detailed prescriptions for assessment and treatment techniques with case examples and learning exercises. *$28.00*

320 pages ISBN 0-880482-01-X

1314 Psychoses and Pervasive Development Disorders in Childhood and Adolescence
American Psychiatric Publishing, Inc.
1000 Wilson Boulevard
Suite 1825
Arlington, VA 22209-3901
703-907-7322
800-368-5777
Fax: 703-907-1091
E-mail: appi@psych.org
www.appi.org

Robert E Hales MD, Editor-in-Chief
Ron McMillen, Chief Executive Officer
John McDuffie, Editorial Director

Provides a concise summary of currently knowledge of psychoses and pervasive developmental disorders of childhood and adolescence. Discusses recent changes in aspects of diagnosis and definition of these disorders, advances in knowledge, and aspects of treatment. *$46.50*

368 pages ISBN 1-882103-01-7

1315 Return From Madness
Jason Aronson
200 Livingston Street
Northvale, NJ 07647
201-767-4093
800-782-1005
Fax: 201-767-1576
www.aronson.com

This book offers a new approach to helping people who have emerged from madness. *$50.00*

256 pages ISBN 1-568216-25-4

1316 Schizophrenia
American Psychiatric Publishing, Inc.
1000 Wilson Boulevard
Suite 1825
Arlington, VA 22209-3901
703-907-7322
800-368-5777
Fax: 703-907-1091
E-mail: appi@psych.org
www.appi.org

Robert E Hales MD, Editor-in-Chief
Ron McMillen, Chief Executive Officer
John McDuffie, Editorial Director

Ideas in treating the disease, and how many patients can lead productive lives without relapse. *$165.00*

760 pages ISBN 0-632032-76-6

1317 Schizophrenia Revealed: From Neurons to Social Interactions
W.W. Norton & Company
500 Fifth Avenue
New York, NY 10110-54
212-354-2907
Fax: 212-869-0856

Drake McFeely, CEO

1318 Schizophrenia and Genetic Risks
National Alliance on Mental Illness
2107 Wilson Boulevard
Suite 300
Arlington, VA 22201-3080
703-524-7600
800-950-6264
Fax: 703-524-9094
TDD: 703-516-7227
E-mail: info@nami.org
www.nami.org

Provides basic facts about schizophrenia and its familial distribution so consumers and mental health workers can become informed enough to initiate appropriate actions. Includes suggested resources.

1319 Schizophrenia and Manic Depressive Disorder
National Alliance for the Mentally Ill
2107 Wilson Boulevard
Suite 300
Arlington, VA 22201-3080

703-525-0686
800-950-6264
TDD: 703-516-7227
E-mail: info@nami.org

Explores the biological roots of mental illness with a primary focus on schizophrenia. *$27.00*

274 pages ISBN 0-465072-85-2

1320 Schizophrenia and Primitive Mental States
Jason Aronson Publishing
276 Livingston Street
Northvale, NJ 07647
570-342-1320
800-782-0015
Fax: 201-767-1576
www.aronson.com

In this volume, renowned therapist Peter Giovacchini shows readers how to do more for psychotic patients than rely on medication to reduce their florid symptoms. Instead, he demonstrates how schizophrenic patients can be offered true cure and the possibility of living a full and related life through intensive psychotherapeutic treatment. *$50.00*

288 pages ISBN 0-765700-27-1

1321 Schizophrenia in a Molecular Age
American Psychiatric Publishing, Inc.
1000 Wilson Boulevard
Suite 1825
Arlington, VA 22209-3901
703-907-7322
800-368-5777
Fax: 703-907-1091
E-mail: appi@psych.org
www.appi.org

Robert E Hales MD, Editor-in-Chief
Ron McMillen, Chief Executive Officer
John McDuffie, Editorial Director

Explores the multidimensional phenotype of schizophrenia, and use of molecular biology and anti-psychotic medications. Reviews the implications of early sensory procesing and subcortical involvement of cognitive dysfuntion in schizophrenia. Functional neuroimaging applied to the syndrome of schizophrenia. *$26.50*

224 pages ISBN 0-880489-61-8

1322 Schizophrenia: From Mind to Molecule
American Psychiatric Publishing, Inc.
1000 Wilson Boulevard
Suite 1825
Arlington, VA 22209-3901
703-907-7322
800-368-5777
Fax: 703-907-1091
E-mail: appi@psych.org
www.appi.org

Robert E Hales MD, Editor-in-Chief
Ron McMillen, Chief Executive Officer
John McDuffie, Editorial Director

Provides a thorough look at schizophrenia that includes neurobehavioral studies, traditional and emerging technologies, psychosocial and medical treatments, and future research opportunities. *$34.00*

278 pages ISBN 0-800489-50-2

1323 Schizophrenia: Straight Talk for Family and Friends
William Morrow & Company
10 East 53rd Street
New York, NY 10022-5244
212-872-1133
Fax: 212-872-1199
www.signal-capital.com

Lists more than 150 local chapters of the National Alliance for the Mentally Ill. *$17.95*

Year Founded: 1985

1324 Stigma and Mental Illness
American Psychiatric Publishing, Inc.
1000 Wilson Boulevard
Suite 1825
Arlington, VA 22209-3901
703-907-7322
800-368-5777
Fax: 703-907-1091
E-mail: appi@psych.org
www.appi.org

Robert E Hales MD, Editor-in-Chief
Ron McMillen, Chief Executive Officer
John McDuffie, Editorial Director

Collection of firsthand accounts on how society has stigmatized mentally ill individuals, their families and their caregivers. *$36.00*

236 pages ISBN 0-880484-05-5

1325 Surviving Schizophrenia: A Manual for Families, Consumers and Providers
Harper Collins
10 E 53rd Street
New York, NY 10022-5299
212-207-7000
800-242-7737

Since its first publication nearly twenty years ago, this has become the standard reference book on this disease, helping thousands of patients, families and mental health professionals to better deal with the condition. Dr. Fuller Torrey explains the nature causes, symptoms, and treatment of this often misunderstood illness. This fully revised 4th edition of Surviving Schizophrenia is a must-have for the multitude of people affected both directly and indirectly by this serious, yet treatable, disorder. *$15.00*

544 pages ISBN 0-060959-19-3

1326 The Complete Family Guide to Schizophrenia: Helping Your Loved One Get the Most Out of Life
The Guilford Press
72 Spring Street
New York, NY 10012-4019

212-431-9800
800-365-7006
Fax: 212-966-6708
E-mail: info@guilford.com

Bob Matloff, President
Kim T Mueser, Author
Susan Gingerich, Author

This book walks readers through a range of treatment and support options that can lead to a better life for the entire family. Individual chapters hightlight special issues for parents, siblings, and partners, while other sections provide tips for dealing with problems including cognitive difficulties, substance abuse, and psychosis.

1327 Treating Schizophrenia
Jossey-Bass / John Wiley & Sons
111 River Street
Hokoken, NJ 07030-5790
201-748-6000
Fax: 201-748-6088
E-mail: custserv@wiley.com
www.wiley.com

Using case studies from their own practices, the contributors describe how to conduct a successful assessment of schizophrenia. They then explore in detail the major treatment methods, including inpatient treatment, individual therapy, family therapy, group therapy, and the crucial role of medication. Th authors also address the timely issue of treating schizophrenia in the era of managed care. *$121.60*

372 pages Year Founded: 1995

1328 Understanding Schizophrenia: Guide to the New Research on Causes & Treatment
Free Press
1120 Avenue of the Americas
New York, NY 10036-6700
800-456-6798
Fax: 800-943-9831
E-mail: consumer.customerservice@simonandschuster.com
www.simonsays.com

Two noted researchers provide an accessible, timely guide to schizophrenia, discussing the nature of the disease, recent advances in understanding brain structure and function, and the latest psychological and drug treatments. *$25.95*

283 pages Year Founded: 1994 ISBN 0-029172-47-0

1329 Water Balance in Schizophrenia
American Psychiatric Publishing, Inc.
1000 Wilson Boulevard
Suite 1825
Arlington, VA 22209-3901
703-907-7322
800-368-5777
Fax: 703-907-1091
E-mail: appi@psych.org
www.appi.org

Robert E Hales MD, Editor-in-Chief
Ron McMillen, Chief Executive Officer
John McDuffie, Editorial Director

Provides clinicians with a consolidated guide to polydipsia - hyponatramia, associated with schizophrenia. *$54.95*

304 pages ISBN 0-880484-85-3

Periodicals & Pamphlets

1330 Schizophrenia
National Institute of Mental Health
6001 Executive Boulevard
Room 8184
Bethesda, MD 20892-1
301-443-4513
866-615-6464
TTY: 301-443-8431
E-mail: nimhinfo@nih.gov

This booklet answers many common questions about schizophrenia, one of the most chronic, severe and disabling mental disorders. Current research-based information is provided for people with schizophrenia, their family members, friends and the general public about the symptoms and diagnosis of schizophrenia, possible causes, treatments and treatment resources.

28 pages Year Founded: 1999

1331 Schizophrenia Bulletin: Superintendent of Documents
Government Printing Office
732 N Capital Street NW
Washington, DC 20401-3
202-512-1417

Bill Lewis, CEO

ISBN 0-160105-89-7

1332 Schizophrenia Fact Sheet
SAMHSA'S National Mental Health Information Center
PO Box 42557
Washington, DC 20015-557

800-789-2647
Fax: 240-747-5470
TDD: 866-889-2647
E-mail: ken@mentalhealth.org
www.mentalhealth.samhsa.gov

A Kathryn Power, MEd, Director
Edward B Searle, Deputy Director

This fact sheet provides information on the symptoms, diagnosis, and treatment for schizophrenia.

2 pages

1333 Schizophrenia Research
11830 Westline Industrial Drive
St Louis, MO 63146-3313
212-633-3730
800-545-2522
Fax: 800-535-9935

E-mail: usbkinfo@elsevier.com
www.elsevier.nl/locate/schres

A publication of new international research that contributes to the understanding of schizophrenia disorders. It is hoped that this journal will aid in bringing together previously separated biological, clinic and psychological research on this disorder, and stimulate the synthesis of these data into cohesive hypotheses.

ISSN 0920-9964

Research Centers

1334 NARSA: The Mental Health Research Association
60 Cutter Mill Road
Suite 404
Great Neck, NY 11021-3104
516-829-0091
800-829-8289
Fax: 516-487-6930
E-mail: info@narsad.org
www.narsad.org

Stephen G Doochin, Executive Vice President
Louis Innamorato, CFO

Previously known as the National Alliance for Research on Schizophrenia and Depression, NARSAD is a private, not-for-profit public charity organized for the purpose of raising funds for scientific research into the causes, cures, treatments and prevention of severe psychiatric brain and behavior disorders, such as schizophrenia and depression

1335 Schizophrenia Research Branch: Division of Clinical and Treatment Research
6001 Executive Boulevard
Room 18 MSC 9663
Bethesda, MD 20892-1
301-443-4513
866-615-6464
Fax: 301-443-5158
TTY: 301-443-8431
E-mail: nimhinfo@nih.gov
www.nimh.nih.gov

Plans, supports, and conducts programs of research, research training, and resource development of schizophrenia and related disorders. Reviews and evaluates research developments in the field and recommends new program directors. Collaborates with organizations in and outside of the National Institute of Mental Health (NIMH) to stimulate work in the field through conferences and workshops.

1336 Schizophrenic Biologic Research Center
James J Peters VA Medical Center
130 W Kingsbridge Road
Bronx, NY 10468-3904
718-584-9000

Maryann Musumeci, Manager

Focuses on mental illness and schizophrenia.

Support Groups & Hot Lines

1337 Family-to-Family: National Alliance on Mental Illness
2107 Wilson Boulevard
Suite 300
Arlington, VA 22201-3080
703-524-7600
Fax: 703-524-9094
E-mail: info@nami.org
www.nami.org

Michael Fitzpatrick, Executive Director
Lynn Borton, COO

A free 12-week course for family caregivers of individuals with severe mental illnesses that discusses the clinical treatment of these illnesses and teaches the knowledge and skills that family members need to cope more effectively.

1338 Schizophrenics Anonymous Forum
Mental Health Association in Michigan
30233 Southfield Road
Suite 220
Southfield, MI 48076-1363
248-647-1711
E-mail: inquiries@nsfoundation.org
www.mha-mi.org

Mark Reinstein, CEO

Self-help organization sponsored by American Schizophrenia Association. Groups are comprised of dignosed schizophrenics who meet to share experiences, strengths and hopes in an effort to help each other cope with common problems and recover from the disease, rehabilitation program follows the 12 principles of Alcoholics Anonymous. Publications: Newsletter, semi-annual. Monthly support group meeting.

Video & Audio

1339 Bonnie Tapes
Mental Illness Education Project
PO Box 470813
Brookline Village, MA 02447-813
617-562-1111
800-343-5540
Fax: 617-779-0061
E-mail: info@miepvideos.org
www.miepvideos.org

Christine Ledoux, Executive Director
Jack Churchill, President
Lucia Miller, Marketing Director

Bonnie's account of coping with schizophrenia will be a revelation to people whose view of mental illness has been shaped by the popular media. She and her family provide an intimate view of a frequently feared, often misrepresented, and much stigmatized illness-and the human side of learning to live with a psychiatric disability. Set of three tapes $143.88 or $59.95 per tape.

Year Founded: 1997

1340 Families Coping with Mental Illness
Mental Illness Education Project
PO Box 470813
Brookline Village, MA 02447-813
617-562-1111
800-343-5540
Fax: 617-779-0061
E-mail: info@miepvideos.org
www.miepvideos.org

Christine Ledoux, Executive Director

10 family members share their experiences of having a family member with schizophrenia or bipolar disorder. Designed to provide insights and support to other families, the tape also profoundly conveys to professionals the needs of families when mental illness strikes. In two versions: a twenty two minute version ideal for short classes and workshops, and a richer forty three minute version with more examples and details. Discounted price for families/consumers. *$68.95*

Year Founded: 1997

Web Sites

1341 www.cyberpsych.org
CyberPsych

Presents information about psychoanalysis, psychotherapy and special topics such as anxiety disorders, the problematic use of alcohol, homophobia, and the traumatic effects of racism.

1342 www.hopkinsmedicine.org/epigen
Epidemology-Genetics Program in Psychiatry

Learn more about research and how you can sign up for various studies.

1343 www.members.aol.com/leonardjk/USA.htm
Schizophrenia Support Organizations

1344 www.mentalhealth.com
Internet Mental Health

Offers online psychiatric diagnosis in the hope of reaching the two-thirds of individuals with mental illness who do not seek treatment.

1345 **www.naminys.org**
National Alliance on Mental Illness

From its inception in 1979, NAMI has been dedicated to
improving the lives of individuals and families affected by
mental illness.

1346 **www.planetpsych.com**
Planetpsych.com

The online resource for mental health information.

1347 **www.psychcentral.com**
Psych Central

The Internet's largest and oldest independent mental health
social network created and run by mental health professionals to guarantee reliable, trusted information and support
communities to you.

1348 **www.schizophrenia.com**
Schizophrenia

A non-profit community providing in-depth information,
support and education related to schizophrenia, a disorder
of the brain and mind.

1349 **www.schizophrenia.com/discuss/**
Schizophrenia

On-line support for patients and families.

1350 **www.schizophrenia.com/newsletter/buckets/**
success.html
Schizophrenia

Success stories including biographical accounts, links to
stories of famous people who have schizophrenia, and personal web pages.

Sexual Disorders

Introduction

It is not possible to know what degree of sexual interest, desire, or activity is 'normal'; at best, we have averages, not indications of the optimal state. A Sexual Disorder is diagnosed when lack of desire or activity is repeated, persists over time and causes distress or interferes with the person's functioning in other important areas of life. Sexual Disorders are divided into four groups: Disorders of Sexual Desire; Disorders of Sexual Arousal; Orgasmic Disorders; and Disorders involving Sexual Pain. It is essential to know whether the problem is lifelong or was precipitated by a recent event, and whether it occurs only with a particular partner or in a particular situation. It is also essential not to make assumptions about sexual activity based on age, socioeconomic status, or sexual orientation. The only way to know about an individual's sexual life is to ask.

SEXUAL DESIRE DISORDERS SYMPTOMS

Hypoactive Sexual Desire Disorder (HSDD)
• Persistent or repeated lack of sexual fantasies and desire for sexual activities;
• The lack of sexual fantasies and desire cause marked distress or interpersonal problems.

Sexual Aversion Disorder (SAD)
• Persistent or repeated extreme aversion to, and avoidance of, all or almost all genital sexual contact with a sexual partner;
• The aversion causes marked distress or interpersonal problems.

Associated Features
The person with a Sexual Desire Disorder commonly has a poor body image and avoids nudity. In HSDD, a person does not initiate sexual activity, or respond to the partner's initiation attempts. The disorder is often associated with the inability to achieve orgasm in women, and the inability to achieve an erection in men. It can also be associated with other psychiatric and medical problems, including a history of sexual trauma and abuse.

Prevalence
HADD is common in both men and women but twice as many women as men report it. It is estimated at twenty percent overall, and as high as sixty-five-percent among those seeking treatment for sexual disorders. The prevalence of SAD is unknown.

SEXUAL AROUSAL DISORDER SYMPTOMS

Female Sexual Arousal Disorder (FSAD)
• Persistent or repeated inability to attain or maintain adequate lubrication-swelling (sexual excitement) response throughout sexual activity;
• The disorder causes clear distress or interpersonal problems.

Male Erectile Disorder (MED)
• Persistent or repeated inability to maintain an adequate erection throughout sexual activity;
• The disorder causes clear distress or interpersonal problems.

Associated Features
While both these disorders are common, men tend to be more upset by it than women. Contributing issues include performance anxiety (especially in men), fear of failure, inadequate stimulation, and relationship conflicts. Other problems are also associated with FSAD and MED, such as childhood sexual trauma, sexual identity concerns, religious orthodoxy, depression, lack of intimacy or trust, and power conflicts. MED is frequently associated with diabetes, peripheral nerve disorders, and hypertension, and is a side effect of a variety of medications; men with MED must be evaluated for these conditions. In addition, the medications used to treat MED are contraindicated in some medical conditions, such as heart conditions.

Prevalence
Prevalence information varies for FSAD. In one study, 13.6 percent of women overall reported a lack of lubrication during most or all sexual activity; twenty-three percent had such problems occasionally; and 4, 4.2 percent of post-menopausal women reported having lubrication problems. In a study of happily married couples, about one third of women complained of difficulty in achieving or maintaining sexual excitement.

Erectile difficulties in men are estimated to be very common, affecting 20-30 million men in the US. The frequency of erectile problems increases steeply with age. In one survey, fifty-two percent of men aged 40-70 reported erectile problems, with three times as many older men reporting difficulties. The disorder is common among married, single, heterosexual and homosexual men.

Treatment Options
In FSAD, a cognitive-behavioral psychotherapy is often recommended, including practical help such as the use of water-soluble lubricating products. Hormone treatment, such as testosterone-estrogen compounds, is sometimes helpful.

An array of treatments is available for Male Erectile Dysfunction, including prosthetic devices for physiological penile problems. In cases of hormonal problems, testosterone treatments have had some results. (However, the use of testosterone to treat sexual disorders in menopausal women is controversial and can have serious side effects.) Viagra is producing success for male erectile dysfunction, as are two newer medications for MED, vardenafil (Levitra) and tadalafil (Cialis).

When sexual problems are limited to a particular partner or situation, psychotherapy (individual or couple) is necessary to resolve the difficulty.

ORGASMIC DISORDER SYMPTOMS

Female and Male Orgasmic Disorders
• Persistent or repeated delay in, or absence of, orgasm despite a normal sexual excitement phase;
• The disorder causes clear distress or interpersonal problems.

Premature Ejaculation
• Persistent or recurring ejaculation with minimal sexual stimulation before, upon, or shortly after penetration and earlier than desired;
• The disorder causes clear distress or interpersonal

problems.

Associated Features

When FOD or MOD occur only in certain situations, difficulty with desire and arousal are often also present.

All of these disorders are associated with poor body image, self-esteem or relationship problems. In FOD or MOD, medical or surgical conditions can also play a role, such as multiple sclerosis, spinal cord injury, surgical prostatectomy (males), and some medications. PE is likely to be very distruptive. Some males may have had the disorder all their lives, for others it may be situational. Few illnesses or drugs are associated with PE.

Prevalence

FOD is probably the most frequent sexual disorder among females. Among those who have sought sex therapy twenty-four percent to thirty-seven percent report the problem. In general population samples, 15.4 percent of premenopausal women report the disorder, and 34.7 percent of postmenopausal women do so. More single than married women report that they have never had an orgasm. There is no association between FOD and race, socioeconomic status, education, or religion. MOD is relatively rare; only three percent to eight percent of men seeking treatment report having the disorder, though there is a higher prevalence among homosexual males (ten percent to fifteen percent).

PE is very common: twenty-five percent to forty percent of adult males report having, or having had, this problem.

Treatment Options

Psychotherapeutic treatments are similar to those for Sexual Desire and Sexual Arousal Disorders. In both males and females with Orgasmic Disorders there may be a lack of desire, performance anxiety, and fear of impregnation or disease. Therapy should take into account contextual and historical information concerning the onset and course of the problem. Cognitive-behavioral methods to help change the assumptions and thinking of the person have sometimes been helpful.

SEXUAL PAIN DISORDER SYMPTOMS

Dyspareunia
•Recurring or persistent pain with sexual intercourse in a male or female;
•The disorder causes clear distress or interpersonal problems.

Vaginismus
•Persistent or recurrent involunatry spasm of the vagina that interferes with sexual intercourse;
•The disorder causes clear distress or interpersonal problems.

Associated Features

Both Dyspareunia and Vaginismus may be associated with lack of desire or arousal. Women with Vaginismus tend to avoid gynecological exams, and the disorder is most often associated with psychological and interpersonal issues. Various physical factors are associated with Dyspareunia, such as pelvic inflammatory disease, hymenal or childbirth-related scarring, and vulvar vestibulitis. Dyspareunia is not a clear symptom of any physical condition. In women it is often combined with Depression and interpersonal conflicts. Other associated psychosocial

factors include religious orthodoxy, low self-esteem, poor body image, poor couple communication, and history of sexual trauma.

Prevalence

Dyspareunia is frequent in females but occurs infrequently in males. Vaginismus is seen quite often in sex therapy clinics - in fifteen percent to seventeen percent of women coming for treatment.

Treatment Options

Probably the most successful treatment for women with these disorders is the reinsertion of a graduated sequence of dilators in the vagina. The woman's sexual partner should be present, and a participant in this treatment. This treatment should be done in conjunction with relaxation training, sensate focusing exercises, (which help people focus on the pleasures of sex rather than the performance) and sex therapy.

General Treatment Options

The professional making the diagnosis of a Sexual Disorder should be trained and experienced in Sexual Disorders and sex therapy. It is important to know whether or not a medical or medication issue is present. However, many with these disorders do not seek treatment. Their lack of desire for sex is often combined with a lack of desire for sex therapy. Even with therapy, relapse is commonly reported. Treatments that have had some success are ones that challenge the cognitive assumptions and distortions of client(s), e.g., that sex should be perfect, that without intercourse and without both partners having an orgasm it isn't real sex. Therapy often also includes sensate focusing in which the person is encouraged and trained to give up the role of agitated spectator to love-making in favor of participating in it. A sexual history should be part of every mental health evaluation, and patients receiving psychotropic medications should be asked about sexual side effects. Having information about sexual function before medication is prescribed will prevent pre-existing sexual problems from being confused with any that may result from medication.

Associations & Agencies

1352 Center for Family Support (CFS)
333 7th Avenue
New York, NY 10001-5115
212-629-7939
Fax: 212-239-2211
www.cfsny.org

Steven Vernikoff, Executive Director

An agency that continutes to develop new programs to serve families and individuals with their care needs. They currently offer services throughout the New York City region including: New Jersey, Long Island and the Lower Hudson Valley.

1353 National Assocaition for the Dually Diagnosed (NADD)
132 Fair Street
Kingston, NY 12401-4802

845-331-4336
800-331-5362
E-mail: info@thenadd.org
www.thenadd.org

Robert Fletcher, Executive Director

Nonprofit organization designed to promote interest of professional and parent development with resources for individuals who have the coexistence of mental illness and mental retardation. Provides conference, educational services and training materials to professionals, parents, concerned citizens and service organizations. Formerly known as the National Association for the Dually Diagnosed.

Year Founded: 1983

1354 National Mental Health Consumers' Self-Help Clearinghouse

1211 Chestnut Street
Suite 1207
Philadelphia, PA 19107-4103
215-751-1810
800-553-4539
Fax: 215-636-6312
E-mail: info@mhselfhelp.org
www.mhselfhelp.org

Joseph A Rogers, Executive Director

A national consumer technical assistance center that has played a major role in the development of the mental health consumer movement.

Year Founded: 1986

1355 SAMHSA'S National Mental Health Information Center
US Department of Health and Human Services

PO Box 42557
Washington, DC 20015-557

800-789-2647
Fax: 240-747-5470
TDD: 866-889-2647
E-mail: ken@mentalhealth.org
www.mentalhealth.samhsa.gov

A Kathryn Power, Director
Edward B Searle, Deputy Director

Information about resources, technical assistance, research, training, networks, and other federal clearing houses, and fact sheets and materials. Information specialists refer callers to mental health resources in their communities as well as state, federal and nonprofit contacts. Staff available Monday through Friday, 8:30 AM - 5:00 PM, EST, excluding federal holidays. After hours, callers may leave messages and an information specialist will return their call.

Books

1356 Back on Track: Boys Dealing with Sexual Abuse

200 E Joppa Road
Suite 207
Baltimore, MD 21286-3107
410-825-8888
888-825-8249
Fax: 410-337-0747
E-mail: sidran@sidran.org
www.sidran.org

Leslie Bailey Wright
Mindy B Loiselle

Written for boys age ten and up, this wookbook addresses adolescent boys directly, answering commonly asked questions, offering concrete suggestions for getting help and dealing with unspoken concerns such as homosexuality. Contains descriptions of what therapy may be like and brief explanations of social services and courts, as well as sections on family and friends. Exercises and interesting graphics break up the text. The book's important message is TELL: Just keep telling until someone listens who STOPS the abuse. *$14.00*

144 pages

1357 Dangerous Sex Offenders: a Task Force Report of the American Psychiatric Association
American Psychiatric Publishing, Inc.

1000 Wilson Boulevard
Suite 1825
Arlington, VA 22209-3901
703-907-7322
800-368-5777
Fax: 703-907-1091
E-mail: appi@psych.org
www.appi.org

Robert E Hales MD, Editor-in-Chief
Ron McMillen, Chief Executive Officer
John McDuffie, Editorial Director

$40.95

224 pages ISBN 0-890422-80-X

1358 Handbook of Sexual and Gender Identity Disorder
John Wiley & Sons

111 River Street
Hoboken, NJ 07030-5790
201-748-6000
Fax: 201-748-6088
E-mail: info@wiley.com
www.wiley.com

William J Pesce, CEO
David L Rowland, Author

The Handbook of Sexual and Gender Identity Disorders provides mental health professionals a comprehensive yet practical guide to the understanding, diagnosis, and treatment of a variety of sexual problems. *$95.00*

1359 Interviewing the Sexually Abused Child
American Psychiatric Publishing, Inc.
1000 Wilson Boulevard
Suite 1825
Arlington, VA 22209-3901
703-907-7322
800-368-5777
Fax: 703-907-1091
E-mail: appi@psych.org
www.appi.org

Robert E Hales MD, Editor-in-Chief
Ron McMillen, Chief Executive Officer
John McDuffie, Editorial Director

Guide for mental health professionals who need to know if a child has been sexually abused. Presents guidelines on the structure of the interview and covers the use of free play, toys, and play materials by focusing on the investigate interview of the suspected victim. *$27.95*

80 pages ISBN 0-880486-12-0

1360 Masculinity and Sexuality: Selected Topics in the Psychology of Men
American Psychiatric Publishing, Inc.
1000 Wilson Boulevard
Suite 1825
Arlington, VA 22209-3901
703-907-7322
800-368-5777
Fax: 703-907-1091
E-mail: appi@psych.org
www.appi.org

Robert E Hales MD, Editor-in-Chief
Ron McMillen, Chief Executive Officer
John McDuffie, Editorial Director

$37.50

200 pages ISBN 0-880489-62-6

1361 Principles and Practice of Sex Therapy
The Guilford Press
72 Spring Street
New York, NY 10012-4019
212-431-9800
800-365-7006
Fax: 212-966-6708
E-mail: info@guilford.com

Bob Matloff, President
Sandra R Leiblum, Author

Provides a comprehensive guide to assessment and treatment of all of the major female and male sexual dysfunctions. *$95.00*

1362 Quickies: The Handbook of Brief Sex Therapy
W.W. Norton & Company
500 Fifth Avenue
New York, NY 10110-54
212-354-2907
Fax: 212-869-0856

Drake McFeely, CEO
Douglas G Flemons, Author

All of the chapters present time-efficient, client-focused approaches supported by case examples, to working with clients with sexual problems.
ISBN 0-393705-27-7

1363 Sexual Aggression
American Psychiatric Publishing, Inc.
1000 Wilson Boulevard
Suite 1825
Arlington, VA 22209-3901
703-907-7322
800-368-5777
Fax: 703-907-1091
E-mail: appi@psych.org
www.appi.org

Robert E Hales MD, Editor-in-Chief
Ron McMillen, Chief Executive Officer
John McDuffie, Editorial Director

Appropriate diagnosis and treatment options are presented. *$64.00*

364 pages ISBN 0-880487-57-7

1364 Sexuality and People with Disabilities
Indiana Institute on Disability and Community
Indiana University
2853 E Tenth Street
Bloomington, IN 47408-2601
812-855-9396
800-280-7010
Fax: 812-855-9630
TTY: 812-855-9396
E-mail: uap@indiana.edu

David Mank, Executive Director

Sexuality information for people with disabilities is available but difficult to find. This publication discusses the importance of having sexuality information available and provides numerous sexuality-related resources. *$5.00*

16 pages

1365 Therapy for Adults Molested as Children: Beyond Survival
Springer Publishing Company
11 West 42nd Street
15th Floor
New York, NY 10036-8002
212-941-7842
877-687-7476
Fax: 212-941-7842
E-mail: contactus@springerpub.com
www.springerpub.com

Sheri W Sussman, SVP Editorial
John Briere, PhD, Author

Substantially expanded and revised, this new edition includes detailed information on how to treat sexual abuse survivors more effectively. Chapters cover topics such as client dissociation during therapy, the false/recovered memory controversy, gender differences in abuse treatment. The appendix analyzes the Trauma Symptom Inventory, a 100 item test of post traumatic stress and other psychological sequelae of traumatic events. *$39.95*

270 pages Year Founded: 1996 ISBN 0-826156-41-X

**1366 Treating Intellectually Disabled Sex Offenders:
A Model Residential Program**
Safer Society Foundation
PO Box 340
Brandon, VT 05733-340
802-247-3132
Fax: 802-247-4233
E-mail: gina@safersociety.org
www.safersociety.org

Gina Brown, Sales/Marketing Manager

Describes how the intensive residential specialized Social
Skills Program at Oregon State Hospital combines the principles of respect, self-help, and experiential learning with
traditional sex-offender treatment methods. *$24.00*

152 pages ISBN 1-884444-30-X

Periodicals & Pamphlets

1367 Family Violence & Sexual Assault Bulletin
Family Violence & Sexual Assault Institute
10065 Old Grove Road
San Diego, CA 92131
858-527-1860
Fax: 858-527-1743
www.fvsai.org

David Westgate, Director

Book club, research and quarterly newsletter. *$35.00*

60-70 pages

Web Sites

1368 www.emdr.com
EMDR Institute

Eye Movement Desensitization and Reprocessing (EMDR)
integrates elements of many effective psychotherapies in
structured protocols that are designed to maximize treatment effects. These include psychodynamic, cognitive behavioral, interpersonal, experiential, and body-centered
therapies.

1369 www.mentalhealth.com
Internet Mental Health

Offers online psychiatric diagnosis in the hope of reaching
the two-thirds of individuals with mental illness who do not
seek treatment.

1370 www.planetpsych.com
Planetpsych.com

Online resource for mental health information.

1371 www.priory.com/sex.htm
Sexual Disorders

Diagnoses and treatments.

1372 www.psychcentral.com
Psych Central

The Internet's largest and oldest independent mental health
social network created and run by mental health professionals to guarantee reliable, trusted information and support communities to you.

1373 www.shrinktank.com
Shrinktank

Psychology-related programs, shareware and freeware.

1374 www.xs4all.nl/~rosalind/cha-assr.html
Support and Information on Sex Reassignement

The purpose of this newsgroup is to provide a supportive
and informative environment for people who are undergoing or who have undergone sex reassignment surgery
(SRS) and for their relatives and significant others.

Sleep Disorders

Introduction

Sleep Disorders are a group of disorders characterized by extreme distruptions in normal sleeping patterns. These include Primary Insomnia, Primary Hypersomnia, Narcolepsy, Breathing-related Sleep Disorder, Circadian Rhythm Sleep Disorder, Substance Abuse Induced Sleep Disorder, Nightmare Disorder and Sleep Terror Disorder. Primary Insomnia consists of the inability to sleep, with excessive daytime sleepiness, for at least one month, as evidenced by either prolonged sleep episodes or daytime sleep episodes that occur almost daily. Narcolepsy is characterized by chronic, involuntary and irresistible sleep attacks; a person with the disorder can suddenly fall asleep at any time of the day and during nearly any activity, including driving a car.

Breathing-related Sleep Disorder is diagnosed when sleep is distrupted by an obstruction of the breathing apparatus. Circadian Rhythm Sleep Disorder is a disruption of normal sleep patterns leading to a mismatch between the schedule required by a person's environment and his or her sleeping patterns; i.e., the individual is irresistibly sleepy when he or she is required to be awake, and awake at those times that he or she should be sleeping. Nightmare Disorder is diagnosed when there is a repeated occurrence of frightening dreams that lead to waking. Sleep Terror Disorder is the repeated occurrence of sleep terrors, or abrupt awakenings from sleeping with a shriek or a cry.

SYMPTOMS

This discussion addresses the disorder with the greatest prevalence: Primary Insomnia. A diagnosis of Primary Insomnia is made if the following criteria are met:

•Difficulty initiating or maintaining sleep or nonrestorative sleep for at least one month;
•The impairment causes clinically significant distress or impairment in social, occupational or other important areas of functioning;
•The disturbance does not occur exclusively during the course of other sleep-related disorders;
•The disturbance is not due to another general medical or psychiatric disorder, or the direct physiological effects of a substance.

ASSOCIATED FEATURES

Individuals with primary insomnia have a history of light sleeping. Interpersonal or work-related problems typically arise because of lack of sleep. Accidents and injuries may result from lack of attentiveness during waking hours, and sleep inducing, tranquillizer, or other medications are liable to be misused or abused. Once general medical problems are ruled out, a careful sleep history will often reveal that the individual has poor sleep habits or is reacting to an adverse life situation. These problems can then be addressed with advice or psychotherapy.

PREVALENCE

Surveys indicate a one-year prevalence of insomnia complaints in thirty percent to forty percent of adults, though the percentage of those who would have a diagnosis of Primary Insomnia is unknown. In clinics specializing in Sleep Disorders, about fifteen percent to twenty-five percent of individuals with chronic insomnia are diagnosed with Primary Insomnia.

TREATMENT OPTIONS

Treatment for Sleep Disorders includes an examination by a primary care physician to determine physical condition and sleeping habits, and a discussion with a somnologist, a professional trained in Sleep Disorders, or other mental health professional, to determine the individual's emotional state.

Referrals may be made to sleep clinics, which can be situated in hospitals, or sleep disorder centers in hospitals, universities or psychiatric institutions. To determine the cause of sleep disturbances, an individual in a sleep clinic or sleep disorder center may undergo interviews, psychological tests and laboratory observation — sleeping in the sleep laboratory while various functions are monitored. Medications that may be part of treatment for Sleep Disorders include drugs known as Hypnotics, or sleeping pills, including temazepam, Ambien, Sonata, and Lunesta. Some medications are more helpful with falling, and others with staying, asleep; a new formulation of Ambien has been developed in an attempt to address both. Sleep medications can lose effectiveness if taken over extended periods; use should always be supervised by a physician. Many cases will resolve with improved sleep hygiene, and treatment of pain and other remediable causes. There is also a new drug, Provigil, which helps people with Narcoleopsy to stay awake.

Associations & Agencies

1376 **American Academy of Sleep Medicine**
One Westbrook Corporate Center
Suite 920
Westchester, IL 60154-5767
708-492-0930
Fax: 708-492-0943
E-mail: inquiries@aasmnet.org
www.aasmnet.org

Jerry Barrett, Executive Director
Jennifer Markkanen, Assistant Executive Director

National not-for-profit professional membership organization dedicated to the advancement of sleep medicine. The Academy's mission is to assure quality care for patients with sleep disorders, promote the advancement of sleep research and provide public and professional education. The AASM delivers programs, information and services to and through its members and advocates sleep medicine supportive policies in the medical community and the public sector.

Year Founded: 1975

1377 **Center for Family Support (CFS)**
333 7th Avenue
New York, NY 10001-5115
212-629-7939
Fax: 212-239-2211
www.cfsny.org

Steven Vernikoff, Executive Director

An agency that continues to develop new programs to serve families and individuals with their care needs. They currently offer services throughout the New York City region including: New Jersey, Long Island and the Lower Hudson Valley.

1378 National Alliance on Mental Illness
2107 Wilson Boulevard
Suite 300
Arlington, VA 22201-3080
703-524-7600
800-950-6264
Fax: 703-524-9094
E-mail: info@nami.org
www.nami.org

Suzanne Vogel-Scibilia, MD, President
Frederick R Sandoval, First VP

Nation's leading self-help organization for all those affected by severe brain disorders. Mission is to bring consumers and families with similar experiences together to share information about services, care providers, and ways to cope with the challenges of schizophrenia, manic depression, and other serious mental illnesses.

Year Founded: 1979

1379 National Association for the Dually Diagnosed (NADD)
132 Fair Street
Kingston, NY 12401-4802
845-331-4336
800-331-5362
Fax: 845-331-4569
E-mail: info@thenadd.org
www.thenadd.org

Robert Fletcher, Executive Director

Nonprofit organization designed to promote interest of professional and parent development with resources for individuals who have the coexistence of mental illness and mental retardation. Provides conference, educational services and training materials to professionals, parents, concerned citizens and service organizations. Formerly known as the National Association for the Dually Diagnosed.

1380 National Mental Health Consumers' Self-Help Clearinghouse
1211 Chestnut Street
Suite 1207
Philadelphia, PA 19107-4103
215-751-1810
800-553-4539
Fax: 215-636-6312
E-mail: info@mhselfhelp.org
www.mhselfhelp.org

Joseph A Rogers, Executive Director

A national consumer technical assistance center that has played a major role in the development of the mental health consumer movement.

Year Founded: 1986

1381 SAMHSA'S National Mental Health Information Center
US Department of Health and Human Services
PO Box 42557
Washington, DC 20015-557

800-789-2647
Fax: 240-747-5470
TDD: 866-889-2647
E-mail: ken@mentalhealth.org
www.mentalhealth.samhsa.gov

A Kathryn Power, MEd, Director
Edward B Searle, Deputy Director

Information about resources, technical assistance, research, training, networks, and other federal clearing houses, and fact sheets and materials. Information specialists refer callers to mental health resources in their communities as well as state, federal and nonprofit contacts. Staff available Monday through Friday, 8:30 AM - 5:00 PM, EST, excluding federal holidays. After hours, callers may leave messages and an information specialist will return their call.

Books

1382 Concise Guide to Evaluation and Management of Sleep Disorders
American Psychiatric Publishing, Inc.
1000 Wilson Boulevard
Suite 1825
Arlington, VA 22209-3901
703-907-7322
800-368-5777
Fax: 703-907-1091
E-mail: appi@psych.org
www.appi.org

Robert E Hales MD, Editor-in-Chief
Ron McMillen, Chief Executive Officer
John McDuffie, Editorial Director

Overview of sleep disorders medicine, sleep physiology and pathology, insomnia complaints, excessive sleepiness disorders, parasomnias, medical and psychiatric disorders and sleep, medications with sedative-hypnotic properties, special problems and populations. *$29.95*

304 pages ISBN 0-880489-06-5

1383 Drug Therapy and Sleep Disorders
Mason Crest Publishers
370 Reed Road
Suite 302
Broomall, PA 19008-4017
610-543-6200
866-627-2665
Fax: 610-543-3878
E-mail: dtaylor@masoncrest.com
www.masoncrest.com

What are sleep disorders? Which drugs do doctors prescribe to treat them? What risks and benefits are involved? This book answers these and other questions by examining various sleep disorders, their symptoms and causes, common treatments, the drugs used to treat them, and how sleep drugs affect the brain.

ISBN 1-590845-76-5

1384 Principles and Practice of Sleep Medicine
Elsevier/WB Saunders Company
Curtis Center, Suite 300E
170 S Independence Mall W
Philadelphia, PA 19106-3323
215-238-7800
800-523-1649
Fax: 800-238-7883
www.us.elsevierhealth.com

Covers the recent advances in basic sciences as well as sleep pathology in adults. Encompasses developments in this rapidly advancing field and also includes topics related to psychiatry, circadian rhythms, cardiovascualr diseases and sleep apnea diagnosis and treatment. Hardcover. *$159.00*

1336 pages Year Founded: 2000 ISBN 0-721676-70-7

1385 Sleep Disorders Sourcebook, Second Edition
Omnigraphics
PO Box 625
Holmes, PA 19043-625

800-234-1340
Fax: 800-875-1340
E-mail: info@omnigraphics.com
www.omnigraphics.com

Amy L Sutton, Editor

Omnigrahphics is the publisher of the Health Reference Series, a growing consumer health information resource with more than 100 volumes in print. Each title in the series features an easy to understand format, nontechnical language, comprehensive indexing and resources for further information. Material in each book has been collected from a wide range of government agencies, professional associations, periodicals and other sources. *$78.00*

567 pages Year Founded: 2005 ISBN 1-780807-43-X

Video & Audio

1386 Effective Learning Systems
3451 Bonita Bay Boulevard
Suite 205
Bonita Springs, FL 34134-4354
239-948-1660
800-966-5683
Fax: 239-948-1664
E-mail: info@efflearn.com
www.efflearn.com

Robert E Griswold, President
Deirdre M Griswold, VP

Audio tapes for stress management, deep relaxation, anger control, peace of mind, insomnia, weight and smoking, self-image and self-esteem, positive thinking, health and healing. Since 1972, Effective Learning Systems has helped millions of people take charge of their lives and make positive changes. Over 75 titles available, each with a money-back guarantee. Price range $12-$14.

Web Sites

1387 www.aasmnet.org
American Academy of Sleep Medicine

A professional society that is dedicated exclusively to the medical subspecialty of sleep medicine.

1388 www.cyberpsych.org
CyberPsych

Presents information about psychoanalysis, psychotherapy and special topics such as anxiety disorders, the problematic use of alcohol, homophobia, and the traumatic effects of racism.

1389 www.mentalhealth.com
Internet Mental Health

Offers on-line psychiatric diagnosis in the hope of reaching the two-thirds of individuals with mental illness who do not seek treatment.

1390 www.nhlbi.nih.gov/about/ncsdr
National Institute of Health National Center on Sleep Disorders

The Center seeks to fulfill its goal of improving the health of Americans by serving four key functions: research, training, technology transfer, and coordination.

1391 www.nlm.nih.gov/medlineplus/sleepdisorders. html
MEDLINEplus on Sleep Disorders

Compilation of links directs you to information on sleep disorders.

1392 www.planetpsych.com
Planetpsych.com

Online resource for mental health information.

1393 **www.psychcentral.com**
Psych Central

The Internet's largest and oldest independent mental health
social network created and run by mental health professionals to guarantee reliable, trusted information and support
communities to you.

Tic Disorders

Introduction

A tic is described as an involuntary, sudden, rapid, recurrent, non-rhythmic motor movement or vocalization. Four disorders are associated with tics: Chronic Motor or Vocal Tic Disorder, Transient Tic Disorder, Tic Disorder Not Otherwise Specified, and Tourette's Syndrome. Tourette's Syndrome is the most extreme case, consisting of multiple motor tics and one or more vocal tics, and will be the focus of this chapter. The vocalizations of Tourette's Syndrome can consist of grunts, obscenities, or other words the individual otherwise would not make. They are disruptive and profoundly embarrassing.

SYMPTOMS

•Multiple motor, as well as one or more vocal tics have been present during the illness, not necessarily at the same time;
•The tics occur many times during a day (often in bouts) nearly every day or intermittently throughout for more than one year, and during this period there was never a tic-free period of more three consecutive months;
•The disturbance causes clear distress or difficulties in social, work, or other areas;
•The onset is before age 18;
•The involuntary movements or vocalizations are not due to the direct effects of a substance (e.g., stimulants) or a general medication condition.

ASSOCIATED FEATURES

Between ten percent and forty percent of people with Tourette's Syndrome also have echolalia (automatically repeating words spoken by others) or echopraxia (imitating someone else's movements). Fewer than ten percent have coprolalia (the involuntary uterance of obscenities).

There seems to be a clear association between tic disorders, such as Tourette's Syndrome, and Obsessive Compulsive Disorder (OCD). As many as twenty percent to thirty percent of people with OCD report having or having had tics, and between five percent and seven percent of those with OCD also have Tourette's Syndrome. In studies of patients with Tourette's Syndrome it was found that thirty-six percent to fifty-two percent also meet the criteria for OCD. This is evidence that Tourette's Syndrome and Obsessive Compulsive Disorder share a genetic basis or some underlying pathological/physiological disturbance. The genetic evidence is further strengthened by the concordance rate in twins (i.e., the likelihood that if one member of the pair has the disorder, the other will also develop it): in identical twins, who have the same genes, the concordance is fifty-three percent, whereas in fraternal twins, who are no more closely related than other siblings, it is eight percent.

Other conditions commonly associated with Tourette's Syndrome are hyperactivity, distractibility, impulsivity, difficulty in learning, emotional disturbances, and social problems. The disorder causes social uneasiness, shame, self-consciousness, and depression. The person may be rejected by others and may develop anxiety about the tics, negatively affecting social, school, and work functioning.

In severe cases, the disorder may interfere with everyday activities like reading and writing.

PREVALENCE

Tourette's Syndrome is reported in a variety of ethnic and cultural groups. It is one and one-half to three times more common in males than females and about 10 times more prevalent in children and adolescents than in adults. Overall prevalence is estimated at between four and five people in 10,000.

While the age of onset can be as early as two years, it commonly begins during childhood or early adolescence. The median age for the development of tics is seven years. The disorder usually lasts for the life of the person, but there may be periods of remission of weeks, months, or years. The severity, frequency, and variability of the tics often diminish during adolescence and adulthood. In some cases, tics can disappear entirely by early adulthood.

TREATMENT OPTIONS

Many treatments have been tried. Haloperidol, an antipsychotic drug, is the most effective; it acts directly on the brain source of the tic, counteracting the overactivity, and can have a calming effect, but also can have unfortunate side effects. In very severe, disabling cases of OCD, brain surgery is an option. SSRIs (Selective Serotonin Reuptake Inhibitors) have also been effective in some cases of Tic Disorders. Symptoms of the disorder usually diminish with increasing age, and many people learn to live with them.

Associations & Agencies

1395 Center for Family Support (CFS)
333 7th Avenue
New York, NY 10001-5115
212-629-7939
Fax: 212-239-2211
www.cfsny.org

Steven Vernikoff, Executive Director

An agency that continues to develop new programs to serve families and individuals with their care needs. They currently offer services throughout the New York City region including: New Jersey, Long Island and the Lower Hudson Valley.

1396 National Alliance on Mental Illness
2107 Wilson Boulevard
Suite 300
Arlington, VA 22201-3080
703-524-7600
800-950-6264
Fax: 703-524-9094
E-mail: info@nami.org
www.nami.org

Joseph Rodgers, Founder/Executive Director
Christine Simirglia, Director

Nation's leading self-help organization for all those affected by severe brain disorders. Mission is to bring consumers and families with similar experiences together to share information about services, care providers, and ways to cope with the challenges of schizophrenia, manic depression, and other serious mental illnesses.

Year Founded: 1979

1397 National Association for the Dually Diagnosed (NADD)

132 Fair Street
Kingston, NY 12401-4802
845-331-4336
800-331-5362
Fax: 845-331-4569
E-mail: info@thenadd.org
www.thenadd.org

Robert Fletcher, Executive Director

Nonprofit organization designed to promote interest of professional and parent development with resources for individuals who have the coexistence of mental illness and mental retardation. Provides conference, educational services and training materials to professionals, parents, concerned citizens and service organizations. Formerly known as the National Association for the Dually Diagnosed.

1398 National Mental Health Consumers' Self-Help Clearinghouse

1211 Chestnut Street
Suite 1207
Philadelphia, PA 19107-4103
215-751-1810
800-553-4539
Fax: 215-636-6312
E-mail: info@mhselfhelp.org
www.mhselfhelp.org

Joseph A Rogers, Executive Director

A national consumer technical assistance center that has played a major role in the development of the mental health consumer movement.

Year Founded: 1986

1399 SAMHSA'S National Mental Health Information Center

US Department of Health and Human Services
PO Box 42557
Washington, DC 20015-557

800-789-2647
Fax: 240-747-5470
TDD: 866-889-2647
E-mail: ken@mentalhealth.org
www.mentalhealth.samhsa.gov

A Kathryn Power, MEd, Director
Edward B Searle, Deputy Director

Information about resources, technical assistance, research, training, networks, and other federal clearing houses, and fact sheets and materials. Information specialists refer callers to mental health resources in their communities as well as state, federal and nonprofit contacts. Staff available Monday through Friday, 8:30 AM - 5:00 PM, EST, excluding federal holidays. After hours, callers may leave messages and an information specialist will return their call.

1400 Tourette Syndrome Association

42-40 Bell Boulevard
Suite 205
Bayside, NY 11361-2874
718-224-2999
888-486-8738
Fax: 718-279-9596
E-mail: ts@tsa-usa.org
www.tsa-usa.org

Judit Ungar, President

National, nonprofit voluntary health organization with 50 chapters in the US and over 45 contacts in other countries. Members include people with TS, their relatives and other interested, concerned supporters.

Year Founded: 1972

Books

1401 Adam and the Magic Marble

Hope Press
PO Box 188
Duarte, CA 91009-188

800-321-4039
Fax: 818-358-3520
E-mail: dcomings@mail.earthlink.net
www.hopepress.com

Exciting reading for all ages, and a must for those who have been diagnosed with Tourette syndrome or other disabilities. An up-beat story of three heros, two with Tourette syndrome, one with cerebral palsy. Constantly taunted by bullies, the boys find a marble full of magic power, they aim a spell at the bullies and the adventure begins. *$6.95*

1402 Children with Tourette Syndrome: A Parent's Guide

ADD WareHouse
300 NW 70th Avenue
Suite 102
Plantation, FL 33317-2360
954-792-8944
800-233-9273
Fax: 954-792-8545
E-mail: sales@addwarehouse.com
www.addwarehouse.com

Harvey C Parker, Owner

The first guide written specifically for parents and other family members is a collaboration by a team of medical specialists, therapists, people with TS, and parents. It provides a complete introduction to TS and how it's diagnosed and treated. Also, chapters on family life, emotions, education and legal rights. *$17.00*

340 pages

1403 Children with Tourette Syndrome: A Parents' Guide

Woodbine House
6510 Bells Mill Road
Bethesda, MD 20817-1636

301-897-3570
800-843-7323
Fax: 301-897-5838
E-mail: info@woodbinehouse.com
www.woodbinehouse.com

Irv Shapell, Owner

Essays discuss the nature of Tourette Syndrome, how it is diagnosed and treated, daily life, family adjustments, and the educational needs of children with Tourette Syndrome.

ISBN 1-890627-36-4

1404 Don't Think About Monkeys: Extraordinary Stories Written by People with Tourette Syndrome
Hope Press
PO Box 188
Duarte, CA 91009-188

800-321-4039
Fax: 626-358-3520
www.hopepress.com

Collection of fourteen stories written by teenager and adults with Tourette syndrome, describing how they have managed to cope and live with disorder. Especially inspiring to others with this and similar disorders. *$12.95*

200 pages ISBN 1-878267-33-7

1405 Echolalia: an Adult's Story of Tourette Syndrome
Hope Press
PO Box 188
Duarte, CA 91009-188
818-303-0644
800-321-4039
Fax: 818-358-3520
www.hopepress.com

Adam Seligman, Author

Story of best selling writer Jackson Evans, who was diagnosed at age 35 as having Tourette syndrome and obsessive-compulsive disorder. At first he is grateful for the answers it brings him, but Jackson soon realizes that the real problems are just beginning. Story is told in a poetic style that captures the rhythms that smooth the Tourette. It ends with the ultimate truth, the answer isn't in being diagnosed, the answer is in living. *$11.95*

165 pages Year Founded: 1991 ISBN 1-878267-31-0

1406 Hi, I'm Adam: a Child's Story of Tourette Syndrome
Hope Press
PO Box 188
Duarte, CA 91009-188
818-303-0644
800-321-4039
Fax: 818-358-3520
www.hopepress.com

Adam Buehrens, Author

Adam Buehrens is ten years old and has Tourette syndrome. Adam wrote and illustrated this book because he wants everyone to know he and other children with

Tourette syndrome are not crazy. They just have a common neurological disorder. If you know a child that has tics, temper tantrums, unreasonable fears, or problems dealing with school, you will find this a reassuring story. *$4.95*

35 pages Year Founded: 1990 ISBN 1-878267-29-9

1407 I Can't Stop!: A Story About Tourette Syndrome
Albert Whitman & Company
6340 Oakton Street
Morton Grove, IL 60068-4272
847-581-0033
800-255-7675
Fax: 847-581-0039
E-mail: mail@awhitmanco.com
www.albertwhitman.com

John Quattrocchi, President

A picture book about tics (and TS, obviously) for kids. The kids portrayed in the book are in elementary school, and I'd say the text is good for grades 2-5, and easily read to kids somewhat younger.

ISBN 0-807536-20-2

1408 Mind of its Own, Tourette's Syndrome: Story and a Guide
Oxford University Press
198 Madison Avenue
New York, NY 10016-4341
212-726-6400
800-451-7556

Michael Cunningham, Manager

Composed of two parts which interdigitate with each other. One part is an on-going story about Michael, a boy with TS, and his family and friends. Michael is a fictional composite character drawn from experience with many patients. Portrays a relatively mild case because the majority of the cases are mild. The second part consists of factual information which we have tried to present in a clear and readable manner. Includes illustration, some tables and other materials that may be of interest.

174 pages ISBN 0-195065-87-5

1409 RYAN: A Mother's Story of Her Hyperactive/ Tourette Syndrome Child
Hope Press
PO Box 188
Duarte, CA 91009-188
818-303-0644
800-321-4039
Fax: 818-358-3520
www.hopepress.com

A moving and informative story of how a mother struggled with the many behavioral problems presented by her son with Tourette syndrome, ADHD and oppositional defiant disorder. *$9.95*

302 pages ISBN 1-878267-25-6

1410 RYAN: a Mother's Story of Her Hyperactive/Tourette Syndrome Child
Hope Press
PO Box 188
Duarte, CA 91009-188
818-303-0644
800-321-4039
Fax: 818-358-3520
E-mail: dcomings@mail.earthlink.net
www.hopepress.com

A moving and informative story of how a mother struggled with the many behavioral problems presented by her son with Tourette syndrome, ADHD and oppositional defiant disorder. *$9.95*

302 pages ISBN 1-878267-25-6

1411 Raising Joshua
Hope Press
PO Box 188
Duarte, CA 91009-188
818-303-0644
800-321-4039
Fax: 818-358-3520
E-mail: dcomings@mail.earthlink.net
www.hopepress.com

A mothers story of Josh, a boy with Tourette Syndrome and Attention Deficit Hyperactivity Disorder. *$14.95*

ISBN 0-965750-17-

1412 Tics and Tourette Syndrome: A Handbook for Parents and Professionals
Jessica Kingsley Publishers
116 Pentonville Road
London,

E-mail: post@jkp.com
www.jkp.com

Uttom Chowdhury, Author

This essential guide to tic disorders and Tourette Syndrome tackles problems faced both at home and at school, such as adjusting to the diagnosis, the effect on siblings and classroom difficulties.

ISBN 1-843102-03-X

1413 Tourette Syndrome
Dilligaf Publishing for Awareness Project
64 Court Street
Ellsworth, ME 04605
207-667-5031
E-mail: awareness@acadia.net

Includes an overview of the syndrome and tips of how to recognize traditional tics in the classroom; evaulation and referral are the basic components of this easy-to-read, basic book for the classroom teacher.

20 pages

1414 Tourette Syndrome and Human Behavior
Hope Press
PO Box 188
Duarte, CA 91009-188
818-303-0644
800-321-4039
Fax: 818-358-3520
E-mail: dcomings@mail.earthlink.net
www.hopepress.com

How Tourette syndrome, a common hereditary disorder, provides insights into the cause and treatment of a wide range of human behavioral problems. It covers diagnosis, associated behaviors including ADHD, learning disorders, dyslexia, conduct disorder, obsessive-compulsive behaviors, alcoholism, drug abuse, obesity, depression, panic attacks, phobias, night terrors, bed wetting, sleep disturbances, lying, stealing, inappropiate sexual behavior, and others, brain structure and chemistry and implications for society. *$39.95*

850 pages ISBN 1-878267-28-0

1415 Tourette's Syndrome, Tics, Obsession, Compulsions: Developmental Psychopathology & Clinical Care
John Wiley & Sons
605 3rd Avenue
New York, NY 10158-180
212-850-6301
E-mail: info@wiley.com

Once thought to be rare, Tourette's Syndeome is now seen as a relatively common childhood disorder either in its complete or partial incarnations. Drawing on the work of contributors hailing from the Yale Unversity Child Psychiatry Department, this edited volume explores the disorder from many perspectives, mapping out the diagnosis, genetics, phenomenology, natural history, and treatment of Tourette's Syndrome. *$189.00*

584 pages ISBN 0-471160-37-7

1416 Tourette's Syndrome: The Facts, Second Edition
Oxford University Press
198 Madison Avenue
New York, NY 10016-4341
212-726-6400
800-451-7556

Michael Cunningham, Manager

Explains the causes of the syndrome, how it is diagnosed, and the ways in which it can be treated. *$19.95*

110 pages Year Founded: 2005 ISBN 0-198523-98-X

1417 Tourette's Syndrome: Tics, Obsessions, Compulsions
ADD WareHouse
300 NW 70th Avenue
Suite 102
Plantation, FL 33317-2360
954-792-8944
800-233-9273
Fax: 954-792-8545

E-mail: sales@addwarehouse.com
www.addwarehouse.com

Harvey C Parker, Owner

Drawing on the work of contributors hailing from the prestigious Yale University Child Psychiatry Department, this edited volume explores the disorder from many perspectives, mapping out the diagnosis, genetics, phenomenology, natural history and treatment of Tourette's Syndrome. *$89.95*

584 pages

1418 Treating Tourette Syndrome and Tic Disorders : A Guide for Practitioners
The Guilford Press
72 Spring Street
New York, NY 10012-4019
212-431-9800
800-365-7006
Fax: 212-966-6708
E-mail: info@guilford.com

Bob Matloff, President

Grounded in a comprehensive model of Tourette syndrome (TS) and related disorders, this state-of-the-art volume provides a multidisciplinary framework for assessment and treatment.

ISBN 1-593854-80-3

1419 What Makes Ryan Tic?
Hope Press
PO Box 188
Duarte, CA 91009-188
818-303-0644
800-321-4039
Fax: 818-358-3520
E-mail: dcomings@mail.earthlink.net
www.hopepress.com

What Makes Ryan Tic?: A Family's Triumph Over Tourette's Syndrome and Attention Deficit Hyperactivity Disorder. A moving and informative story of how a mother struggled with the many behavioral problems presented by her son with Tourette syndrome, ADHD and oppostional defiant disorder. *$15.95*

303 pages ISBN 1-878267-35-3

Support Groups & Hot Lines

1420 Tourette Syndrome Association
42-40 Bell Boulevard
Bayside, NY 11361-2874
718-224-2999
Fax: 718-279-9596
E-mail: ts@tsa-usa.org
www.tsa-usa.org

Judit Ungar, President

A national voluntary non-profit membership organization whose mission is to identify the cause of, find the cure for and control the effects of Tourette Syndrome.

Year Founded: 1972

Video & Audio

1421 After the Diagnosis...The Next Steps
Tourette Syndrome Association
42-40 Bell Boulevard
Suite 205
Bayside, NY 11361-2874
718-224-2999
888-486-8738
Fax: 718-279-9596
E-mail: ts@tsa-usa.org
www.tsa-usa.org

Judit Ungar, President
Gary Frank, EVP
Mark Levine, VP Development
Richard Dreyfuss, Narrator

When the diagnosis is Tourette Syndrome, what do you do first? How do you sort out the complexities of the disorder? Whose advice do you follow? What steps do you take to lead a normal life? Six people with TS—as different as any six people can be—relate the sometimes difficult, but finally triumphant path each took to lead the rich, fulfilling life they now enjoy. Narrated by Academy Award-winning actor, Richard Dreyfuss, the stories are refreshing blends of poignancy, fact, and inspiration illustrating that a diagnosis of TS can be approached with confidence and hope. Includes comments by family and friends, teachers, counselors and leading medical authorities on Tourette Syndrome. A must-see for the newly diagnosed child, teen or adult. *$35.00*

1422 Clinical Counseling: Toward a Better Understanding of TS
Tourette Syndrome Association
42-40 Bell Boulevard
Suite 205
Bayside, NY 11361-2874
718-224-2999
888-486-8738
Fax: 718-279-9596
E-mail: ts@tsa-usa.org
www.tsa-usa.org

Judit Ungar, President
Gary Frank, EVP
Mark Levine, VP Development
Dylan McDermott, Narrator

Certain key issues often surface during the counseling sessions of people wwith TS and their families. These important areas of concern are explored for counselors, social workers, educators, psychologists and other allied professionals. Expert clinical practitioners offer invaluable insights for those working with people affected by Tourette Syndrome. *$30.00*

1423 Complexities of TS Treatment: Physician's Roundtable
Tourette Syndrome Association
42-40 Bell Boulevard
Suite 205
Bayside, NY 11361-2874
718-224-2999
888-486-8738
Fax: 718-279-9596
E-mail: ts@tsa-usa.org
www.tsa-usa.org

Judit Ungar, President
Gary Frank, EVP
Mark Levine, VP Development

Three of the most highly regarded experts in the diagnosis and treatment of Tourette Syndrome offer insight, advice and treatment strategies to fellow physicians and other healthcare professionals. *$ 30.00*

1424 Family Life with Tourette Syndrome... Personal Stories
Tourette Syndrome Association
42-40 Bell Boulevard
Suite 205
Bayside, NY 11361-2874
718-224-2999
888-486-8738
Fax: 718-279-9596
E-mail: ts@tsa-usa.org
www.tsa-usa.org

Judit Ungar, President
Gary Frank, EVP
Mark Levine, VP Development

In extended, in-depth interviews, all the people engagingly profiled in After the Diagnosis. The Next Steps, reveal the individual ways they developed to deal with TS. Each shows us that the key to leading a successful life in spite of having TS, is having a loving, supportive network of family and friends. Available in its entirety or as separate vignettes. *$50.00*

1425 Understanding and Treating the Hereditary Psychiatric Spectrum Disorders
Hope Press
PO Box 188
Duarte, CA 91009-188
818-303-0644
800-321-4039
Fax: 818-358-3520
www.hopepress.com

David E Comings MD, Presenter

Learn with ten hours of audio tapes from a two day seminar given in May 1997 by David E Comings, MD. Tapes cover: ADHD, Tourette Syndrome, Obsessive-Compulsive Disorder, Conduct Disorder, Oppositional Defiant Disorder, Autism and other Hereditary Psychiatric Spectrum Disorders. Eight Audio tapes. *$75.00*

Year Founded: 1997

Web Sites

1426 www.mentalhealth.com
Internet Mental Health

Offers online psychiatric diagnosis in the hope of reaching the two-thirds of individuals with mental illness who do not seek treatment.

1427 www.planetpsych.com
Planetpsych.com

Online resource for mental health information.

1428 www.psychcentral.com
Psych Central

The Internet's largest and oldest independent mental health social network created and run by mental health professionals to guarantee reliable, trusted information and support communities to you.

1429 www.tourette-syndrome.com
Tourette Syndrome

Online community devoted to children and adults with Tourette Syndrome disorder and their families, friends, teachers, and medical professionals. Provides an interactive meeting place for those interested in Tourette Syndrome or people wanting to help others who have TS.

1430 www.tourettesyndrome.net
Tourette Syndrome Plus

Parent and teacher friendly site on Tourette Syndrome, Attention Deficit Disorder, Executive Dysfunction, Obsessive Compulsive Disorder, and related conditions.

1431 www.tsa-usa.org
Tourette Syndrome Association

Web site of the association dedicated to identifying the cause, finding the cure and controlling the effects of TS.

Pediatric & Adolescent Issues

Introduction

The media is full of reports about supposed epidemics of psychiatric medications in children, and, tragically, from time to time, stories of children who commit suicide or murder. Parents, other relatives, guardians, and teachers are understandably concerned about not missing the signs of a treatable disorder while, at the same time, not subjecting the child to unnecessary and potentially stigmatizing diagnosis and treatment. No one can say for sure whether there are more cases of autism or bipolar disorder in children now than ten or twenty years ago. Whenever there is publicity about any medical disorder, the number of diagnoses goes up. Some of those accurately diagnosed would have been overlooked in the past. Others are diagnosed and treated without a full evaluation. The American Academy of Child and Adolescent Psychiatry (http://www.aacap.org/) provides accurate and useful information to help those responsible for children decide: whether a child's behavior is normal for his or her age; if a child is being adversely influenced by circumstances; what is a warning sign for mental disorder; and what constitutes a mental disorder.

In general, a child or adolescent is evaluated not only on the basis of particular behaviors that cause concern, but also with respect to meeting the milestones expected at his or her age. A child should be increasingly able to relate to other people, both children and adults, and to learn. An untreated mental disorder can deprive a child of essential years of social and educational growth. Anyone concerned about a child should start with the child's pediatrician. A child should not be given a diagnosis or prescribed medication without a complete physical health evaluation, specialized observation, and interviews with parents, teachers, and others familiar with the him or her. There is a shortage of fully qualified experts in child and adolescent mental health; it may require considerable persistence to assure that a child receives the attention necessary, but it will be worthwhile. There should be no hesitation to obtain a second opinion. Heatlh professionals should be able to explain why a child was or wasn't given a specific diagnosis, and the pros and cons of the treatment choices.

Note: Vaccinations do not cause autism, and going un-vaccinated exposes both a child to diseases that can be serious, even fatal; and all those the child comes incontact with, before the signs of the disease are evident.

Associations & Agencies

1433 American Academy of Child and Adolescent Psychiatry
3615 Wisconsin Avenue NW
Washington, DC 20016-3007
202-362-1797
800-333-7636

Virginia Anthony, Executive Director
Earl Magee, Administrator
William Bernet, Treasurer

Professional medical organization comprised of child and adolescent psychiatrist trained to promote healthy development and to evaluate, diagnose, and treat children and adolescents and their families who are affected by disorders of feeling, thinking, learning and behavior. Child and adolescent psychiatrists are physicians who are uniquely qualified to integrate knowledge about human behavior, social, and cultural perspectives with scientific, humanistic, and collaborative approaches to diagnosis, treatment and the promotion of mental health.

1434 American Academy of Pediatrics
141 NW Point Boulevard
Elk Grove Village, IL 60007-1098
847-228-0604
E-mail: cme@aap.org
www.aap.org

Ren?e R. Jenkins, MD, President
Errol R. Alden, MD, Executive Director

Provides information on diagnosis and treatment of physical and mental pediatric conditions by offering programs, training, and resources.

1435 American Pediatrics Society
3400 Research Forest Drive
Suite B-7
The Woodlands, TX 77381-4259
281-419-0052
Fax: 281-419-0082
E-mail: info@aps-spr.org
www.aps-spr.org

Debbie Anagnostelis, Executive Director
William W. Hay, Jr., M.D., President

Society of professionals working with pediatric health care issues; offers seminars and a variety of publications.

1436 Association for the Help of Retarded Children
83 Maiden Lane
New York, NY 10038-4812
212-780-2500
Fax: 212-777-5893
E-mail: ahrcnyc@dti.net
www.ahrcnyc.org

Shirley Berenstein, Director
Jennifer Rossiter, Contact

Developmentally disabled children and adults, their families, and interested individuals. Provides support services, training programs, clinics, schools and residential facilities to the developmentally disabled.

1437 Center for Family Support (CFS)
333 7th Avenue
New York, NY 10001-5115
212-629-7939
Fax: 212-239-2211
www.cfsny.org

Steven Vernikoff, Executive Director

An agency that continues to develop new programs to serve families and individuals with their care needs. They currently offer services throughout the New York City Region including: New Jersey, Long Island and the Lower Hudson Valley.

1438 Federation for Children with Special Needs (FCSN)
1135 Tremont Street
Suite 420
Boston, MA 02120-2199
617-236-7210
800-331-0688
Fax: 617-572-2094
E-mail: fcsninfo@fcsn.org
www.fcsn.org

Rich Robison, President

The federation provides information, support, and assistance to parents of children with disabilities, their professional partners and their communities.

1439 Federation of Families for Children's Mental Health
9605 Medical Center Drive
Suite 280
Rockville, MD 20850-6390
240-403-1901
Fax: 240-403-1909
E-mail: ffcmh@ffcmh.org
www.ffcmh.org

Sandra Spencer, Executive Director
Arthur Penn, President

National family-run organization dedicated exclusively to children and adolesents with mental health needs and their families. Our voice speaks through our work in policy, training and technical assistance programs.

1440 Lifespire
350 Fifth Avenue
Suite 301
New York, NY 10118-301
212-741-0100
Fax: 212-242-0696
E-mail: info@lifespire.org
www.lifespire.org

Robert J. Krakow, Chairman

Professionals, parents, siblings, and others interested in mentally retarded and developmentally disabled adults.

1441 Mentally Ill Kids in Distress (MIKID)
2642 E. Thomas Road
Phoenix, AZ 85016
602-253-1240
800-356-4543
Fax: 602-253-1250
E-mail: familyresource@MIKID.org
www.mikid.org

Steve Carter, President, Board of Directors
Vicki L Johnson, Executive Director
Sue Gilbertson, Founder

Mission is to provide support and assistance to families in Arizona with behaviorally challenged children, youth, and young adults.

1442 Michigan Association for Children's Mental Health
6017 W St Joseph Highway
Suite 200
Lansing, MI 48917
517-371-4016
Fax: 517-372-4032
www.acmh-mi.org

Malisa Pearson, Executive Director

Provides information, support, resources, referral and advocacy for children and youth with mental, emotional, or behavioral disorders and their families

Year Founded: 1989

1443 National Child Support Network
PO Box 1018
Fayetteville, AR 72702-1018

800-729-5437
Fax: 479-582-2401
www.childsupport.org

A private bonded, licensed and insured child support collection agency.

1444 National Dissemination Center for Children with Disabilities
PO Box 1492
Washington, DC 20013-1492

800-695-0285
Fax: 202-884-8441
E-mail: nichcy@aed.org
www.nichcy.org/

Suzanne Ripley, Project Director
Lisa Kupper, Author/Editor

Provides support and services for children and youth with physical and mental disabilities, as well as education and training services for their families.

1445 National Technical Assistance Center for Children's Mental Health
Georgetown University Child Development Center
Georgetown University Center for Child a
Box 571485
Washington, DC 20057-1485
202-687-5000
Fax: 202-687-1954
TTY: 202-687-5503
E-mail: gucdc@georgetown.edu
www.http://gucchd.georgetown.edu/programs/ta_center

Integral part of the Georgetown University Center for Child and Human Development at the Georgetown University Medical Center. Nationally recognized for its work in assisting states and communities build systems of care for mental health concerns.

Year Founded: 1984

1446 Parents Helping Parents
Sobrato Center for Nonprofits
1400 Parkmoor Avenue
Suite 1000
San Jose, CA 95126
408-727-5775
Fax: 408-286-1116
www.php.com

Mary Ellen Peterson, Executive Director/CEO

A non-profit, community-based, parent-directed family resource center. Provides lifetime guidance, supports and services to children with any special need, their families and the professionals who serve them.

1447 Pilot Parents: PP
Ollie Webb Center
1941 S 42nd Street
Suite 122
Omaha, NE 68105-2942
402-346-5220
Fax: 402-346-5253
E-mail: jvarner@olliewebb.org
www.olliewebbinc.org

Laurie Ackermann, Executive Director

Parents, professionals and others concerned with providing emotional and peer support to new parents of children with special needs. Sponsors a parent-matching program which allows parents who have had sufficient experience and training.

1448 Research and Training Center for Children's Mental Health
University of South Florida
13303 Bruce B Downs Boulevard
Department of Child and Family
Tampa, FL 33612
813-974-3133
www.usf.edu

Linda Carr, Manager
Albert Duchnowski, Deputy Director

State initiative for clinical studies of pediatric mental health issues.

1449 Research and Training Center on Family Support and Children's Mental Health
Portland State University/Regional Research Institute
PO Box 751
Portland State University
Portland, OR 97207-751
503-725-4040
Fax: 503-725-4180
E-mail: rtcpubs@pdx.edu
www.rtc.pdx.edu

Nicole Ave, Public Information/Outreach
Janet Walker, Director of Research

Dedicated to promoting effective community based, culturally competent, family centered services for families and their children who are or may be affected by mental, emotional or behavioral disorders. This goal is accomplished through collaborative research partnerships with family members, service providers, policy makers, and other concerned persons. Major efforts in dissemination and training include: An annual conference, an award winning web site to share information about child and family mental services and policy issues which includes Focal Point, a national bulletin regarding family support and children's mental health.

1450 Resources for Children with Special Needs
116 E 16th Street
5th Floor
New York, NY 10003-2164
212-677-4650
Fax: 212-254-4070
E-mail: info@resourcesnyc.org
www.resourcesnyc.org

Rachel Howard, Executive Director
Vicky Burton, Executive assitent

Information, referral, advocacy, training, publications for New York City parents of youth with disabilities or special needs and the professionals who work with them. Available online on Facebook, Twitter, Flickr, and Delicious.

1451 United Families for Children's Mental Health
32 Norwich Avenue
Suite 103
Tampa, FL 33612
860-537-6125
86- 43- 078
Fax: 860-537-6130
E-mail: email@familiesunited.org
www.ctfamiliesunited.homestead.com

Jackie Hoope Hage, President
Cheryl Cole, VP

Run by and for caregivers of children with mental health issues. Children with emotional, behavioral, and mental health challenges can thrive at home, school, and in the community with appropriate, timely, and effective resources.

1452 Young Adult Institute and Workshop (YAI)
460 W 34th Street
New York, NY 10001-2382
212-273-6193
866- 49- 456
Fax: 212-947-7524
www.yai.org

Philip Levy, CEO
Philip H. Levy, President/COO

Serves more than 15,000 people of all ages and levels of mental retardation, developmental and learning disabilities. Provides a full range of early intervention, preschool, family supports, employment training and placement, clinical and residential service.

1453 Youth Services International
6000 Cattleridge Drive
Suite 200
Sarasota, FL 34232-6064
941-953-9199
Fax: 941-953-9198
E-mail: YSIWEB@youthservices.com
www.ysii.com

James F Saltey, CEO

Premier provider in the Youth Care Industry of educational and developmental services that change, dramatically, the thinking and behavior of troubled youth.

1454 ZERO TO THREE: National Center for Infants, Toddlers, and Families
2000 M Street NW
Suite 200
Washington, DC 20036
202-638-1144
800-899-4301
Fax: 202-638-0851
E-mail: oto3@presswarehouse.com
www.zerotothree.org

Matthew E Melmed JD, Executive Director
Tammy Mann PhD, Deputy Executive Director

Publishes book, pamphlets, and curricula with a focus on the social and emotional development of infants, toddlers, and their families. Trains professionalsin the infant-family field and issues policy briefs on a myraid of child development topics, both on the national and state levels. Also, provides technical assistance for Early Head Start programs nationwide.

Books

1455 After School and More
Resources for Children with Special Needs
116 E 16th Street
5th Floor
New York, NY 10003-2164
212-677-4650
Fax: 212-254-4070
E-mail: info@resourcenyc.org
www.resourcesnyc.org

Rachel Howard, Executive Director

The most complete directory of after school programs for children with disabilities and special needs in the metropolitan New York area focusing on weekend and holiday programs. *$25.00*

ISBN 0-967836-57-3

1456 Aggression Replacement Training: A Comprehensive Intervention for Aggressive Youth
Research Press
Dept 24 W
PO Box 9177
Champaign, IL 61826-9177

217-352-3273
800-519-2707
Fax: 217-352-1221
E-mail: rp@researchpress.com
www.researchpress.com

Russell Pense, VP Marketing

Aggression Replacement Training (ART) offers a comprehensive intervention program designed to teach adolescents to understand and replace aggression and antisocial behavior with positive alternatives. The book is designed to be user-friendly and teacher-oriented. It contains summaries of ART's outcome evaluations and it discusses recent applications in schools and other settings. *$24.95*

366 pages   ISBN 0-878223-79-7

1457 Bibliotherapy Starter Set
Childs Work/Childs Play
303 Crossways Park Dr
Woodbury, NY 11797-2099

800-962-1141
Fax: 800-262-1886
E-mail: info@Childswork.com
www.Childswork.com

Eight popular books for helping children ages four - twelve. Titles include Self Esteem, Divorce, ADHD, Feelings, and Anger. *$105.00*

1458 Book of Psychotherapeutic Homework
Childs Work/Childs Play
303 Crossways Park Dr
Woodbury, NY 11797-2099

800-962-1141
Fax: 800-262-1886
E-mail: info@Childswork.com
www.Childswork.com

Lawrence E Shapiro, Author

More than 80 home activities to guarantee your therapy won't lose momentum. Appropriate for ages five - ten. *$20.95*

Year Founded: 2001 ISBN 1-882732-55-3

1459 Breaking the Silence: Teaching the Next Generation About Mental Illness
NAMI Queens/Nassau
1983 Marcus Avenue
Lake Success, NY 11042-1016
516-326-0797
E-mail: btslessonplans@aol.com

Janet Susin, President
Janet Susin, Project Director
Lorraine Kaplan, Director Educational Training

Breaking the Silence (BTS) is an innovative teaching package which includes lesson plans, games and posters on serious mental illness for three grade levels: upper elementary, middle and high school. It is designed to fight stigma by putting a human face on mental illness, replacing fear and ridicule with compassion. BTS meets national health standards.

1460 CARE Child and Adolescent Risk Evaluation: A Measure of the Risk for Violent Behavior
Research Press
Dept 24 W
PO Box 9177
Champaign, IL 61826-9177
217-352-3273
800-519-2707
Fax: 217-352-1221
E-mail: rp@researchpress.com
www.researchpress.com

Dennis Wiziecki, Marketing
Dr Kathryn Siefert, Author

The CARE was developed as a prevention tool to identify youth, as early as possible, who are at risk for committing acts of violence. Unlike other evaluation programs, CARE includes a case management planning form that provides the information needed to develop a risk management intervention plan. The CARE Kit includes 25 assessment forms, 25 case management planning forms and manual. *$75.00*

1461 Camps 2009-2010
Resources for Children with Special Needs
116 E 16th Street
5th Floor
New York, NY 10003-2164
212-677-4650
Fax: 212-254-4070
E-mail: info@resourcenyc.org
www.resourcesnyc.org

Rachel Howard, Executive Director

The guide includes a dozen new camps and updates on more than 300 camps and programs that provide a wide range of summer activities for children with emotional, developmental, learning and physical disabilities, health issues and other special needs. Day camps in the New York metro area are included as well as sleepaway camps in the Northeast. *$25.00*

133 pages Year Founded: 2009 ISBN 0-967836-57-3

1462 Children and Trauma: Guide for Parents and Professionals
Courage to Change
375 Stewart Street
PO Box 486
Wilkes-Barres, PA 18703-486

800-440-4003
Fax: 800-772-6499
www.couragetochange.com

Cynthia Monahon, Author

Comprehensive guide to the emotional aftermath of children's crises. Discusses warning signs that a child may need professional help, and explores how parents and professionals can help children heal, reviving a sense of well being and safety. *$19.95*

240 pages Year Founded: 1997 ISBN 0-787910-71-6

1463 Children in Therapy: Using the Family as a Resource
WW Norton & Company
500 5th Avenue
New York, NY 10110-54
212-354-2907
800-233-4830
Fax: 212-869-0856
E-mail: npb@wwnorton.com
www.wwnorton.com

Drake McFeely, CEO

This anthology presents theoretical perspectives of five different competency-based approaches: solution-oriented brief therapy, narrative therapy, collaborative language systems therapy, internal family systems therapy, and emotionally focused family therapy.

ISBN 0-393704-85-8

1464 Childs Work/Childs Play
303 Crossways Park Dr
Woodbury, NY 11797-2099

800-962-1141
Fax: 800-262-1886
E-mail: info@Childswork.com
www.Childswork.com

Catalog of books, games, toys and workbooks relating to child development issues such as recognizing emotions, handling uncertainty, bullies, ADD, shyness, conflicts and other things that children may need some help navigating.

1465 Creative Therapy with Children and Adolescents
Impact Publishers
PO Box 6016
Atascadero, CA 93423-6016
805-466-5917
800-246-7228
Fax: 805-466-5919
E-mail: info@impactpublishers.com
www.impactpublishers.com

Over 100 activities to be used in working with children, adolescents and families. Encourages creativity in therapy and helps therapists facilitate change by gaining rapport with children and other clients who find it difficult to talk about feelings and experiences. *$21.95*

192 pages ISBN 1-886230-19-6

1466 Don't Feed the Monster on Tuesdays: The Children's Self-Esteem Book
ADD WareHouse
300 NW 70th Avenue
Suite 102
Plantation, FL 33317-2360
954-792-8944
800-233-9273
Fax: 954-792-8545
E-mail: sales@addwarehouse.com
www.addwarehouse.com

Harvey C Parker, Owner

Strikes right at the heart of the basic elements of self-esteem. It presents valuable information to children that will help them understand the importance of their self worth. A friendly book that children ages 4 to 10 will love. *$18.95*

55 pages Year Founded: 1991 ISBN 0-933849-38-9

1467 Don't Pop Your Cork on Mondays: The Children's Anti-Stress Book
ADD WareHouse
300 NW 70th Avenue
Suite 102
Plantation, FL 33317-2360
954-792-8944
800-233-9273
Fax: 954-792-8545
E-mail: sales@addwarehouse.com
www.addwarehouse.com

Harvey C Parker, Owner

This book explores the causes and effects of stress and offers children techniques for dealing with everyday stress factors. Bold and colorful cartoons project a blend of sensitivity and broad humor. Ages 4-10. *$18.95*

48 pages Year Founded: 1988 ISBN 0-933849-18-4

1468 Don't Rant and Rave on Wednesdays: The Children's Anger-Control Book
ADD WareHouse
300 NW 70th Avenue
Suite 102
Plantation, FL 33317-2360
954-792-8944
800-233-9273
Fax: 954-792-8545
E-mail: sales@addwarehouse.com
www.addwarehouse.com

Harvey C Parker, Owner

A book that will delight both children and adults. Explains the causes of anger and offers methods that can help children reduce the amount of anger they feel. Gives effective techniques to help young people control their behavior even when they are angry. Ages 5-12. *$18.95*

61 pages Year Founded: 1994 ISBN 0-933849-54-0

1469 Forms for Behavior Analysis with Children
Research Press
Dept 24 W
PO Box 9177
Champaign, IL 61826-9177
217-352-3273
800-519-2707
Fax: 217-352-1221
E-mail: rp@researchpress.com
www.researchpress.com

Dr Joseph Cautela, Author
Dennis Wiziecki, Marketing

A unique collection of 42 reproducible assessment forms designed to aid counselors and therapists in making proper diagnoses and in developing treatment plans for children and adolescents. Different assessment formats are included, ranging from direct observations and interviews to infor-

mant ratings and self-reports. Certain forms are to be filled out by children and adolescents, while others are to be completed by parents, school personnel, significant others or the therapist. *$ 39.95*

208 pages ISBN 0-878222-67-7

1470 Forms-5 Book Set
Childs Work/Childs Play
303 Crossways Park Dr
Woodbury, NY 11797-2099

800-962-1141
Fax: 800-262-1886
E-mail: info@Childswork.com
www.Childswork.com

Five-book pack with reproducible forms titled: Oppositional Child, Children with OCD, Counseling Children, ADHD Child and Socially Fearful Child. *$125.00*

1471 Gangs in Schools: Signs, Symbols and Solutions
Research Press
Dept 24 W
PO Box 9177
Champaign, IL 61826-9177
217-352-3273
800-519-2707
Fax: 217-352-1221
E-mail: rp@researchpress.com
www.researchpress.com

Russell Pense, VP Marketing

Written by noted authority Arnold Goldstein and gang expert Donald Kodluboy, this book is an essential resource for educators and administrators who are concerned about gang presence or the possibility of gang presence in their schools. The book describes effective gang prevention and intervention strategies. It includes a helpful checklist on how to recognize early gang presence in schools. And it presents a comprehensive plan for maximizing school safety. *$19.95*

256 pages ISBN 0-878223-82-7

1472 Gender Respect Workbook
Childs Work/Childs Play
303 Crossways Park Dr
Woodbury, NY 11797-2099

800-962-1141
Fax: 800-262-1886
E-mail: info@Childswork.com
www.Childswork.com

Over 100 activities appropriate for ages 8 and up, to help teachers and counselors raise consciousness of sexisim and sexist practices. *$20.95*

1473 I Wish Daddy Didn't Drink So Much
Childs Work/Childs Play
303 Crossways Park Dr
Woodbury, NY 11797-2099

800-962-1141
Fax: 800-262-1886
E-mail: info@Childswork.com
www.Childswork.com

Judith Vigna, Author

Realistic and sensitive book about how a girl handles disappointment in her father's problems. Ages 6 - 12. *$6.95*

ISBN 0-807535-26-5

1474 I'm Somebody, Too!
ADD WareHouse
300 NW 70th Avenue
Suite 102
Plantation, FL 33317-2360
954-792-8944
800-233-9273
Fax: 954-792-8545
E-mail: sales@addwarehouse.com
www.addwarehouse.com

Harvey C Parker, Owner

Because it is written for an older, non-ADD audience, this book explains ADD in depth and explains methods to handle the feelings that often result from having a family member with ADD. For children ages 9 and older. *$13.00*

159 pages

1475 Kid Power Tactics for Dealing with Depression & Parent's Survival Guide to Childhood Depression
Childs Work/Childs Play
303 Crossways Park Dr
Woodbury, NY 11797-2099

800-962-1141
Fax: 800-262-1886
E-mail: info@Childswork.com
www.Childswork.com

Nicholas Dubuque, Author
Susan Dubuque, Author

Two-volume set was wriiten by a child who suffered from depression and his mother. Plain language and a wealth of information for children ages 8 and over, plus their parents and teachers. *$12.95*

47 pages Year Founded: 1996 ISBN 1-882732-48-0

1476 My Body is Mine, My Feelings are Mine
Childs Work/Childs Play
303 Crossways Park Dr
Woodbury, NY 11797-2099

800-962-1141
Fax: 800-262-1886
E-mail: info@Childswork.com
www.Childswork.com

Susan Hoke, Author
Bruce Van Patter, Illustrator
Charles Brenna, Designer

For ages 3 - 8. First part to be read to children, the second part teaches adults how to educate children about body

safety. Sexual victimization can be prevented through explanation of how to identify inappropriate touching and what to do about it. *$20.95*

78 pages Year Founded: 1995 ISBN 1-882732-24-3

1477 My Listening Friend: A Story About the Benefits of Counseling
Childs Work/Childs Play
303 Crossways Park Dr
Woodbury, NY 11797-2099

800-962-1141
Fax: 800-262-1886
E-mail: info@Childswork.com
www.Childswork.com

P J Michaels, Author
Anna Dewdney, Illustrator

For ages five - twelve, explores the feelings a child has the first time they see a counselor. Written from the point of view of the child. *$14.50*

57 pages Year Founded: 2001 ISBN 1-588150-43-7

1478 Preventing Maladjustment from Infancy Through Adolescence
Sage Publications
2455 Teller Road
Thousand Oaks, CA 91320-2234
805-499-0721
800-818-7243
Fax: 805-499-0871
E-mail: info@sagepub.com
www.sagepub.com

Blaise R Simqu, CEO

Examines the theoretical and historical issues of prevention with children and youth, and delineates those factors which place the individual at risk. Hardcover $109.00 & Paperback $51.95

156 pages Year Founded: 1987 ISBN 0-803928-68-8

1479 Saddest Time
Childs Work/Childs Play
303 Crossways Park Dr
Woodbury, NY 11797-2099

800-962-1141
Fax: 800-262-1886
E-mail: info@Childswork.com
www.Childswork.com

Norma Simon, Author

Helps children ages 6 - 12 understand that death is sad and sometimes tragic, but it is also part of life. *$13.95*

Year Founded: 1999 ISBN 0-613141-80-6

1480 Schools for Students with Special Needs
Resources for Children with Special Needs
116 E 16th Street
Fifth Floor
New York City, NY 10003-2112

212-677-4650
Fax: 212-254-4070
E-mail: info@resourcesnyc.org
www.resourcesnyc.org
Rachel Howard, Executive Director

The first complete book listing private day and residential schools for parents, caregivers and professionals seeking schools for students 5 and up with developmental, emotional, physical and learning disabilities in the NYC metro area. More than 400 schools and residential programs that serve children in the elementary through high school grades are listed with contact information, ages and populations served, class sizes and student-teacher ratios, special services and diplomas offered. Includes a 46-page section of Schools for Children with Autism Spectrum Disorders, as well as a guide with a list of websites on autism spectrum disorders. *$25.00*

342 pages

1481 Teen Relationship Workbook
Childs Work/Childs Play
303 Crossways Park Dr
Woodbury, NY 11797-2099
516-349-5520
800-962-1141
Fax: 800-262-1886
E-mail: info@childswork.com
www.childswork.com

A reproducible workbook, this hands-on tool helps teens develop healthy relationships and prevent dating abuse and domestic violence. *$44.95*

135 pages

1482 Thirteen Steps to Help Families Stop Fightin Solve Problems Peacefully
Childs Work/Childs Play
303 Crossways Park Dr
Woodbury, NY 11797-2099

800-962-1141
Fax: 800-262-1886
E-mail: info@Childswork.com
www.Childswork.com

Sharon Hernes Silverman, Author

Candid views on why families fight, and solutions to conflict. *$15.95*

Year Founded: 2001 ISBN 1-882732-77-4

1483 What Works When with Children and Adolescents: A Handbook of Individual Counseling Techniques
Research Press
Dept 24 W
PO Box 9177
Champaign, IL 61826-9177
217-352-3273
800-519-2707
Fax: 217-352-1221
E-mail: rp@researchpress.com
www.researchpress.com

Dennis Wiziecki, Marketing
Dr Ann Vernon, Author

This practical handbook is designed for counselors, social workers and psychologists in schools and mental health settings. It offers over 100 creative activities and effective interventions for individual counseling with children and adolescents (ages 6-18). Dr. Vernon provides strategies for establishing a therapeutic relationship with students who are sometimes apprehensive or opposed to counseling. Several case studies are included to help illustrate the counseling techniques and interventions. The book also includes a chapter on working with parents and teachers. *$39.95*

344 pages ISBN 0-878224-38-6

Periodicals & Pamphlets

1484 Conduct Disorder in Children and Adolescents
Center for Mental Health Services: Knowledge Exchange Network
PO Box 42490
Washington, DC 20015

800-789-2647
Fax: 301-984-8796
TDD: 866-889-2647
E-mail: ken@mentalhealth.org
www.mentalhealth.org

This fact sheet defines conduct disorder, identifies risk factors, discusses types of help available, and suggests what parents or other caregivers can do.

2 pages

1485 Families Can Help Children Cope with Fear, Anxiety
Center for Mental Health Services: Knowledge Exchange Network
PO Box 42557
Washington, DC 20015-557

800-789-2647
Fax: 301-984-8796
TDD: 866-889-2647
E-mail: ken@mentalhealth.org
www.mentalhealth.org

This fact sheet defines conduct disorder, identifies risk factors, discusses types of help available, and suggests what parents or other caregivers to common signs of fear and anxiety.

1 pages Year Founded: 2002

1486 Helping Hand
Performance Resource Press
1270 Rankin Drive
Suite F
Troy, MI 48083-2843
248-588-7733
800-453-7733
Fax: 248-588-6633
www.prponline.net

Educates teachers and parents about child and adolescents behavioral health.

4 pages 9 per year

1487 Major Depression in Children and Adolescents
Center for Mental Health Services: Knowledge Exchange Network
PO Box 42557
Washington, DC 20015-557

800-789-2647
Fax: 301-984-8796
TDD: 866-889-2647
E-mail: ken@mentalhealth.org
www.mentalhealth.org

This fact sheet defines depression and its signs, identifies types of help available, and suggests what parents or other caregivers can do.

2 pages Year Founded: 1997

1488 Mental, Emotional, and Behavior Disorders in Children and Adolescents
Center for Mental Health Services: Knowledge Exchange Network
PO Box 42557
Washington, DC 20015-557

800-789-2647
Fax: 301-984-8796
TDD: 866-889-2647
E-mail: ken@mentalhealth.org
www.mentalhealth.org

This fact sheet describes mental, emotional, and behavioral problems that can occur during childhood and adolescence and discusses related treatment, support services, and research.

4 pages Year Founded: 1996

1489 Treatment of Children with Mental Disorders
National Institute of Mental Health
6001 Executive Boulevard
Room 8184
Bethesda, MD 20892-1
301-443-4513
866-615-6464
TTY: 301-443-8431
E-mail: nimhinfo@nih.gov

Ruth Dubois, Assistant Chief

A short booklet that contains questions and answers about therapy for children with mental disorders. Includes a chart of mental disorders and medications used.

Support Groups & Hot Lines

1490 Alateen and Al-Anon Family Groups
1600 Corporate Landing Parkway
Virginia Beach, VA 23454-5617

757-563-1600
888-425-2666
Fax: 757-563-1655
E-mail: wso@al-anon.org
www.al-anon.alateen.org/sitemap.html

Mary Ann Keller, Director Members Services

A fellowship of men, women, children and adult children affected by another persons drinking.

1491 Girls and Boys Town of New York
444 Park Avenue South
Suite 801
New York, NY 10016-7491
212-725-4260
800-448-3000
Fax: 212-725-4385
E-mail: Hotline@girlsandboystown.org

Cynthia Armijo, Executive Director

Crisis intervention and referrals.

1492 Just Say No International
1777 North California Blvd.
Suite 210
Walnut Creek, CA 94596-4150
510-939-6666
800-258-2766
E-mail: kci.org/meth_info/sites/drug_hotline.htm
www.justsayno.org/ and also

Provides numerous links to National Hotlines and Helplines in addition to Websites containing information on drug addiction/abuse, drug treatment/rehabilitation programs and centers, and also information on alcohol addiction/treatment and detox programs.

1493 Kidspeace National Centers
5300 Kidspeace Drive
Orefield, PA 18069-2098

800-854-3123
Fax: 610-391-8280
E-mail: kpinfo@kidspeace.org.
www.kidspeace.org

C T O'Donnell II, President
Michael J Vogel, Chairman

KidsPeace is a private, not-for-profit charity dedicated to serving the critical behavioral and mental health needs of children, preadolescents and teens. Since 1882, KidsPeace has been helping kids develop the confidence and skills they need to overcome crisis. KidsPeace provides specialized residential treatment services and a comprehensive range of treatment programs and educational services to help families help kids anticipate and avoid crisis whenever possible.

1494 National Youth Crisis Hotline
5331 Mount Alifan Drive
San Diego, CA 92111-2622

800-448-4663
www.1800hithome.com/

Information and referral for runaways, and for youth and parents with problems.

1495 Rainbows

1111 Tower Road
Schaumburg, IL 60173-4305
708-310-1880
Fax: 847-952-1774
E-mail: info@rainbows.org
www.rainbows.org/rainbows.html

Suzy Yehl Marta, Founder/President
Jessica Grata, Director of Administration

Peer support groups for adults and children who are grieving.

1496 SADD: Students Against Destructive Decisions

255 Main Street
Marlboro, MA 01752-5505
508-481-3568
Fax: 508-481-5759
E-mail: info@sadd.org
www.sadd.org

Penny Wells, Executive Director
Tiffany Corey, Student Leadership Council
Tinnelle Bombard, Marketing
Marlene Connelly, Family Focus Program

SADD's mission is to provide students with the best prevention and intervention tools possible to deal with the issues of underage drinking, other drug use, impaired driving and other destructive decisions, depression and suicide.

Video & Audio

1497 Aggression Replacement Training Video: A Comprehensive Intervention for Aggressive Youth

Research Press
Dept 24 W
PO Box 9177
Champaign, IL 61826-9177
217-352-3273
800-519-2707
Fax: 217-352-1221
E-mail: rp@researchpress.com
www.researchpress.com

Dennis Wiziecki, Marketing

This staff training video illustrates the training procedures in the Aggression Replacement Training (ART) book.It features scenes of adolescents participating in group sessions for each of ART's three interventions: Prosocial Skills, Anger Control, and Moral Reasoning. A free copy of the book accompanies the video program. *$125.00*

1498 Are the Kids Alright?

Fanlight Productions
2
47 Halifax St
Jamaica Plain, MA 02130-4327
617-469-4999
Fax: 617-439-3379
E-mail: fanlight@fanlight.com
www.fanlight.com

Filmed in courtrooms, correctional institutions, treatment centers, and family homes, this searing documentary documents the results of the tragic decline in mental health services for children and adolescents at risk.

1499 Children: Experts on Divorce

Courage to Change
375 Stewart Street
PO Box 486
Wilkes Barres, PA 18703-486

800-440-4003
Fax: 800-772-6499
www.couragetochange.com/

Dede L Pitts, CEO

Children of divorced parents are interviewed about their feelings and views of how adults can relate to their children during and after a separation and divorce. The information on this video can help to prevent some of the long-term harm that they may feel. Ages of these children are four to fifteen. 38 minutes. *$34.95*

1500 Chill: Straight Talk About Stress

Childs Work/Childs Play
303 Crossways Park Dr
Woodbury, NY 11797-2099

800-962-1141
Fax: 800-262-1886
E-mail: info@Childswork.com
www.Childswork.com

Encourages youth to recognize, analyze and handle the stresses in their lives. 22 minutes. *$96.95*

1501 Fetal Alcohol Syndrome & Fetal Alcohol Effect

Hazelden
15251 Pleasant Valley Road
PO Box 176
Center City, MN 55012-176
651-213-4000
800-328-9000
Fax: 651-213-4590
www.hazelden.org

If you're a chemical dependency counselor or work with women in pregnancy planning or self-care, this resource is filled with facts to help you better meet your clients needs. *$225.00*

1502 Legacy of Childhood Trauma: Not Always Who They Seem
Research Press
Dept 24 W
PO Box 9177
Champaign, IL 61826-9177
217-352-3273
800-519-2707
Fax: 217-352-1221
E-mail: rp@researchpress.com
www.researchpress.com

Russell Pense, VP Marketing

This powerful video focuses on the connection between so-called "delinquent youth" and the experience of childhood trauma such as emotional, sexual, or physical abuse. It inspires viewers to comprehend the emotional betrayal felt by abused children and encourages caregivers to identify strategies for healing and transformation. *$195.00*

1503 Why Isn't My Child Happy? Video Guide About Childhood Depression
ADD WareHouse
300 NW 70th Avenue
Suite 102
Plantation, FL 33317-2360
954-792-8944
800-233-9273
Fax: 954-792-8545
E-mail: sales@addwarehouse.com
www.addwarehouse.com

Harvey C Parker, Owner

The first of its kind, this new video deals with childhood depression. Informative and frank about this common problem, this book offers helpful guidance for parents and professionals trying to better understand childhood depression. 110 minutes. *$55.00*

Web Sites

1504 www.Al-Anon-Alateen.org
Al-Anon and Alateen

AA literature may serve as an introduction.

1505 www.CHADD.org
CHADD: Children/Adults with Attention Deficit/Hyperactivity Disorder

1506 www.aacap.org
American Academy of Child and Adolescent Psychiatry

Represents over 6,000 child and adolescent psychiatrists, brochures availible online which provide concise and up-to-date material on issues ranging from children who suffer from depression and teen suicide to stepfamily problems and child sexual abuse.

1507 www.abcparenting.com
ABCs of Parenting

1508 www.aboutteensnow.com/dramas
Teen Dramas

Realistic conflicts played out and discussed by a therapist.

1509 www.adhdnews.com.ssi.htm
Social Security

Applying for disability benefits for children with ADHD.

1510 www.adhdnews.com/Advocate.htm
Advocating for Your Child

1511 www.adhdnews.com/sped.htm
Special Education Rights and Responsibilities

Writing IEP's and TIEPS. Pursuing special education services.

1512 www.cfc-efc.ca/docs/00000095.htm
Helping Your Child Cope with Separation and Divorce

1513 www.couns.uiuc.edu
Self-Help Brochures

Address issues teens deal with.

1514 www.divorcedfather.com
Still a Dad

For divorced fathers.

1515 www.duanev/family/dads.html
So What are Dads Good For

1516 www.education.indiana.edu/cas/adol/adol.html
Adolescence Directory On-Line

A collection of documents on the growth and development of adolescents.

1517 www.ericps.crc.uiuc.edu/npin/index.html
NPIN: National Parent Information Network

Information on education.

1518 www.ericps.crc.uiuc.edu/npin/library/texts.html
NPIN Resources for Parents: Full Texts of Parenting-Related Material

1519 www.fathermag.com
Fathering Magazine

Hundreds of articles online.

1520 www.fathers.com
Fatherhood Project

1521 www.flyingsolo.com
Flying Solo

Site on single parenting.

1522 www.freedomvillageusa.com
Freedom Village USA

Faith-based home for troubled teens.

1523 www.fsbassociates.com/fsg/whydivorce.html
Breaking the News

Clear rules on how not to tell kids about divorce.

1524 www.geocities.com/enchantedforest/1068
Bipolar Kids Homepage

Set of links.

1525 www.home.clara.net/spig/guidline.htm
Guidelines for Separating Parents

1526 www.hometown.aol.com/DrgnKprl/BPCAT.html
Bipolar Children and Teens Homepage

1527 www.ianrpubs.unl.edu/family/nf223.htm
Supporting Stepfamilies: What Do the Children Feel

Deals with emotions of children in blended families.

1528 www.kidshealth.org/kid/feeling/index.html
Dealing with Feelings

Ten readings. Examples are: Why Am I So Sad; Are You Shy; Am I Too Fat or Too Thin; and A Kid's Guide to Divorce.

1529 www.kidsource.com/kidsource/pages/parenting
Parenting: General Parenting Articles

1530 www.klis.com/chandler/pamphlet/bipolar/bipolarpamphlet.html
Bipolar Affective Disorder in Children and Adolescents

An introduction for families.

1531 www.klis.com/chandler/pamphlet/bipolar/bipolarpamphlet.htm
Depression in Children and Adolescents

1532 **www.klis.com/chandler/pamphlet/panic/**
Panic Disorder, Separation, Anxiety Disorder, and
Agoraphobia

Parents News publication.

1533 **www.magicnet.net/~hedyyumi/child.html**
Learning to Get Along for the Best Interest of the
Child

1541 **www.oznet.ksu.edu/library/famlf2/**
Family Life Library

1542 **www.parentcity.com/read/library**
Parent City Library

1534 **www.mentalhealth.org/publications/allpubs/**
Attention-Deficit/Hyperactiviy Disorder in
Children and Adolescents

Many articles on parenting.

Lists symptoms very fully.

1543 **www.parenthoodweb.com**
ParenthoodWeb

1535 **www.muextension.missouri.edu/xpor/hesguide/**
Focus on Kids: The Effects of Divorce on Children

Focusing on early childhood.

Discusses stresses on kids.

1544 **www.parenthoodweb.com/**
Blended Families

1536 **www.naturalchild.com/home**
Natural Child Project

Resolving conflicts.

Articles by experts.

1545 **www.people1.org**
People First of Oregon

1537 **www.nichcy.org**
National Information Center for Children and
Youth with Disabilities

A self-advocacy organization of developmentally disabled
people who have joined together to learn how to speak for
themselves.

Excellent information in English and Spanish.

1546 **www.personal.psu.edu/faculty**
Family Relations

1538 **www.nnfr.org/curriculum/topics/sep_div.html**
Coping with Separation and Divorce: A Parenting
Seminar

Information parenting and family problems.

1547 **www.positive-way.com/step.htm**
Stepfamily Information

1539 **www.nospank.org/toc.htm**
Project NoSpank

Introduction and tips for stepfathers, stepmothers and re-
married parents.

Site for those against paddling in schools.

1548 **www.pta.org/commonsense**
Common Sense: Strategies for Raising
Alcoholic/Drug-/Free Children

1540 **www.npin.org/pnews/pnews997/**
Temper Tantrums: What Causes Them and How
Can You Respond?

Drug facts, warning signs, and guidance.

1549 **www.stepfamily.org/tensteps.htm**
Ten Steps for Steps

Guidelines for stepfamilies.

1550 **www.stepfamilyinfo.org/sitemap.htm**
Stepfamily Information

1551 **www.teenwire.com/index.asp**
Teenwire

Information on relationships and sexuality.

1552 **www.todaysparent.com**
Today's Parent Online

1553 **www.users.aol.com:80/jimams/**
Questions from Adolescents about ADD

Responses to children's questions.

1554 **www.users.aol.com:80/jimams/answers1**
Questions from Younger Children about ADD

Responses to children's questions.

1555 **www.wholefamily.com/kidteencenter/**
About Teens Now

Addresses important issues in teens lives.

1556 **www.worldcollegehealth.org**
World Health College

Dedicated to adolescent health issues including learning disabilities and grief. Written by experts.

1557 **www2.mc.duke.edu/pcaad**
Duke University's Program in Child and
Adolescent Anxiety Disorder

1558 **After School and More**
Resources for Children with Special Needs
116 E 16th Street
5th Floor
New York, NY 10003-2164
212-677-4650
Fax: 212-254-4070
E-mail: info@resourcenyc.org
www.resourcesnyc.org
Rachel Howard, Executive Director

The most complete directory of after school programs for children with disabilities and special needs in the metropolitan New York area focusing on weekend and holiday programs. *$15.00*

252 pages ISBN 0-967836-57-3

Suicide

Introduction

Suicide is an event, not a mental disorder, but it is the lethal consequence of some mental disorders. Suicide involves a complex interaction of psychological, neurological, medical, social, and family factors.

Most professionals distinguish at least two suicide groups: those who actually kill themselves, i.e. completed suicides; and those who attempt it, usually harming themselves, but survive. Those who succeed in killing themselves are nearly always suffering from one or more psychiatric disorders, most commonly depression, often along with alcohol or substance abuse. Some individuals plan suicide very carefully, taking steps to insure that they will not be discovered and rescued, and they use lethal means (shooting themselves, or jumping from high places). Some act impulsively, reacting to a life disappointment by jumping off a nearby bridge. Some suicide attempts or gestures use means that make discovery and rescue probable, and are not likely to be lethal (e.g. taking insufficient pills). Some people make repeated suicide attempts. Unfortunately, recurrent suicidal gestures cannot be dismissed; each unsuccesful attempt increases the likelihood of a completed suicide.

ASSOCIATED FEATURES

Nine of ten suicides are associated with some form of mental disorder, especially Depression, Schizophrenia, Alcohol/Substance Abuse, Bipolar Disorder, and Anxiety Disorders. In addition, Personality Disorders have been diagnosed in one-third to one-half of people who kill themselves. These suicides often occur in younger people who live in an environment where drug and alcohol abuse, as well as violence, are common. The most common personality disorders associated with suicide are Borderline Personality Disorder, Antisocial Personality Disorder, and Narcissistic Personality Disorder. Among people with schizophrenia, especially those suffering from Paranoid Schizophrenia, suicide is the main reason for premature death.

Drug and alcohol abuse is risk factor for suicide. In a recent study among 113 young people who killed themselves in California, fifty-five percent had some kind of substance abuse problems, usually long-standing and including several different drugs.

Some suicides result from insufficiently treated, severe, debilitating, or terminal physical illness. The pain, restricted function, and dread of dependence can all contribute to suicidal behavior, especially in illnesses such as Huntington's Disease, cancer, MS, spinal cord injuries and AIDS. Some or many of these risk factors are present in most completed suicides. Depression and suicide are not inevitable for people with severe general medical diagnoses. The recognition and treatment of depression, when it does occur, can prevent many suicides.

PREVALENCE

Suicide is the ninth leading cause of death in the United States and the third leading cause among 15-24 year-olds. It is estimated that over five million people have suicidal thoughts, though there are only 30,000 deaths from it each year. This may be a serious underestimate, however, since suicide is still stigmatized and often goes unreported. In the general population there are 11.2 suicides reported for every 100,000 people. The incidence among 5-14 year-olds is 0.7 percent per 100,000; even very young children can commit suicide. The rate among 15-19 year-olds, 13.2 percent per 100,000, has recently increased sharply. Boys are more likely to complete suicide than girls, largely because they use more lethal means, such as firearms. Compared to other countries, guns are particularly common in the U.S. as a means of suicide. Children who kill themselves often have a history of antisocial behavior, and depression and suicide is more common in their families than in families in general.

More males than females commit suicide, both among adults and adolescents. Among adults, the most likely suicides are among men who are widowed, divorced, or single, who lack social support, who are unemployed, who have a diagnosed mental disorder (especially Depression), who have a physical illness, a family history of suicide, who are in psychological turmoil, who have made previous attempts, who use or abuse alcohol, and/or who have easy access to firearms. Among adolescents, the most likely suicides are married males (or unwed and pregnant females), who have suffered from parental abuse or absence, who have academic problems, affect disorders (especially Bipolar Disorder), who are substance abusers, suffer from AD/HD or epilepsy, who have Conduct Disorder, problems with impulse control, a family history of suicide, and/or access to firearms. Keeping guns in the home is a suicide risk for both males and females.

Elderly people (those over age 65) are more likely than any other age group to commit suicide. While only twelve percent of the population is elderly, twenty percent of all those who kill themselve are elderly. As in other population groups, elderly men are more likely to kill themselves than elderly woman but the difference between the sexes is much bigger in this age group than in other age groups. Among all ages, the rate of suicide for men is about 20 per 100,000 and for women five per 100,000. Among the elderly, the rate for men is about 42 per 100,000 and for women about six and one-half per 100,000. Thus the great overall gender differences become even bigger among the elderly and more so as the elderly get older. The highest rate of suicide is among elderly white men, probably because their economic and social status drops severely with age, and because they may lack good social support systems and be reluctant to ask for help.

Although all the factors discussed here are risk factors, it should be kept in mind that 99.9 percent of those at risk do not commit suicide.

TREATMENT OPTIONS

Considering the risk factors, a professional must first make a careful assessment, taking all the risk factors into account, including the availabilty of weapons, pill and other lethal means, as well as whether or not the person has conveyed the intention to commit suicide, and whether the method the patient plans to use is available (one can only jump off a bridge if there is a bridge, or drive into a wall if one has access to a vehicle). Every individual who feels that life is not worth living, or who is contemplating suicide, should be asked about guns in the home and should be encouraged to remove them. The same is true for medications that are dangerous in overdose.

Someone who has no thought of death or has thoughts of death that are not connected with suicide is at a lower risk than someone who is thinking about suicide. Among those who are thinking of it, those who have not worked out the means of committing suicide are at a lower risk than those who have thought of a specific method of carrying it out. Treatment is partly based on the level of intervention that is believed to be required. If the person is seriously depressed and is also anxious, tense and angry, and in overwhelming psychological anguish, the risk is more acute. The first priority is to ensure the safety of the client. To that end, hospitalization may be necessary.

After safety is assured, treatment is aimed at the underlying disorder. It may include psychological support, medication, and other therapies: group, art, dance/movement, music. Professional treatment should involve working with the family when possible, and other medical staff, e.g. a physician, and should include regular reassessments.

In cases of Personality Disorders, there may be anger and aggression, and the suicidal thoughts and ideas may be chronic or repetitive. This is a particular strain on professionals, patients, and family. They all must work together to understand the chronocity of the condition, and the fact that suicide cannot always be prevented. It is essential to develop a working alliance between the therapist and client, based on trust, mutual respect, and on the client's belief that the therapist genuinely cares about him/her. At the same time, the therapist must set limits on patient demands to prevent 'burn out'.

Reassessments include getting information from other professionals involved in treating the patient, including medication with the prescribing physician, and from family members or others significant in the life of the client who should participate in planning and following up. Assessment must also include assessment of the client's ability to understand and participate in the treatment, information about his/her psychological state (hopeless, despairing, depressed) and cognitive competence.

Associations & Agencies

1560 National Alliance on Mental Illness
2107 Wilson Boulevard
Suite 300
Arlington, VA 22201-3080
703-524-7600
800-950-6264
Fax: 703-524-9094
E-mail: info@nami.org
www.nami.org

Suzanne Vogel-Scibilia, MD, President
Frederick R Sandoval, First VP

Nation's leading self-help organization for all those affected by severe brain disorders. Mission is to bring consumers and families with similar experiences together to share information about services, care providers, and ways to cope with the challenges of schizophrenia, manic depression, and other serious mental illnesses.

Year Founded: 1979

1561 National Mental Health Consumers' Self-Help Clearinghouse
1211 Chestnut Street
Suite 1207
Philadelphia, PA 19107-4103
215-751-1810
800-553-4539
Fax: 215-636-6312
E-mail: info@mhselfhelp.org
www.mhselfhelp.org

Joseph Rogers, Executive Director

A national consumer technical assistance center that has played a major role in the development of the mental health consumer movement.

Year Founded: 1986

1562 SAMHSA'S National Mental Health Information Center
US Department of Health and Human Services
PO Box 42557
Washington, DC 20015-557

800-789-2647
Fax: 240-747-5470
TDD: 866-889-2647
E-mail: ken@mentalhealth.org
www.mentalhealth.samhsa.gov

A Kathryn Power, MEd, Director
Edward B Searle, Deputy Director

Information about resources, technical assistance, research, training, networks, and other federal clearing houses, and fact sheets and materials. Information specialists refer callers to mental health resources in their communities as well as state, federal and nonprofit contacts. Staff available Monday through Friday, 8:30 AM - 5:00 PM, EST, excluding federal holidays. After hours, callers may leave messages and an information specialist will return their call.

1563 Survivors of Loved Ones' Suicides (SOLOS)
PO Box 592
Dumfries, VA 22026-592
703-580-8958
E-mail: solos@1000deaths.com
www.1000deaths.com

Christine Smith, President
Betsy Beasley, VP

Organization to help provide support for the families and friends who have suffered the suicide loss of a loved one.

Books

1564 Adolescent Suicide
American Psychiatric Publishing, Inc.
1000 Wilson Boulevard
Suite 1825
Arlington, VA 22209-3901

703-907-7322
800-368-5777
Fax: 703-907-1091
E-mail: appi@psych.org
www.appi.org

Robert E Hales MD, Editor-in-Chief
Ron McMillen, Chief Executive Officer
John McDuffie, Editorial Director

Presents techniques that allow psychiatrists and other professionals to respond to signs of distress with timely therapeutic intervention. *$38.95*

212 pages ISBN 0-873182-08-1

1565 Adolescent Suicide: A School-Based Approach to Assessment and Intervention
Research Press
Dept 24 W
PO Box 9177
Champaign, IL 61826-9177
217-352-3273
800-519-2707
Fax: 217-352-1221
E-mail: rp@researchpress.com
www.researchpress.com

Dennis Wiziecki, Marketing
Dr William G Kirk, Author

Presents the information required to accurately identify potentially suicidal adolescents and provides the skills necessary for effective intervention. The book includes many case examples derived from information provided by parents, mental health professionals and educators, as well as adolescents who have considered suicide or survived suicide attempts. An essential resource for school counseling staff, psychologists, teachers and administrators. *$16.95*

190 pages ISBN 0-878223-36-3

1566 Anatomy of Suicide: Silence of the Heart
Charles C Thomas Publisher
2600 S First Street
Springfield, IL 62704-4730
217-789-8980
800-258-8980
Fax: 217-789-9130
E-mail: books@ccthomas.com
www.ccthomas.com

Michael P Thomas, President

The author explores the scope of this problem which involves clinical and ethical issues; the myth of depression; the path to suicide; unfinished business; staying alive; early warnings; first interventions; the self-contract; cases in point; and the future of suicide. Written for psychologists, counselors, and mental health professionals, this book is an excellent resource that will further our understanding of suicide and seek new ways for prevention. *$42.95*

170 pages Year Founded: 1998 ISSN 0-398-06803-8ISBN 0-398068-02-X

1567 Exubernace: The Passion for Life
Knopf Publishing Group
1745 Broadway
New York, NY 10019-4343
212-782-9000
Fax: 212-940-7390
E-mail: knopfpublicity@randomhouse.com

Sonny Mehta, Executive Director

It is a curious request to make of God. Shield your joyous ones, asks the Anglican prayer: Shield your joyous ones. God more usually is asked to watch over those who are ill or in despair, as indeed the rest of the prayer makes clear.

1568 Harvard Medical School Guide to Suicide Assessment and Intervention
Jossey-Bass / Wiley & Sons
111 River Street
Hoboken, NJ 07030-5790
201-748-6000
Fax: 201-748-6088
E-mail: consumers@wiley.com
www.wiley.com

Presents a multidimensional model of suicide assessment by offering clear techniques for intervention in both inpatient and outpatient settings. Also describes the use of psychopharmacology and prevention in the context of managed care. *$59.95*

736 pages Year Founded: 1998 ISBN 0-787943-03-7

1569 In the Wake of Suicide
Jossey-Bass / Wiley & Sons
111 River Street
Hoboken, NJ 07030-5790
201-748-6000
Fax: 201-748-6088
E-mail: consumers@wiley.com
www.wiley.com

Breathtaking stories of incredible power for anyone struggling to find the meaning in the suicide death of a loved one and for all readers seeking writing that moves and inspires. *$27.00*

256 pages Year Founded: 1998 ISBN 0-787940-52-6

1570 Left Alive: After a Suicide Death in the Family
Charles C Thomas Publisher
2600 S 1st Street
Springfield, IL 62704-4730
217-789-8980
800-258-8980
Fax: 217-789-9130
E-mail: books@ccthomas.com
www.ccthomas.com

Michael P Thomas, President

$21.95

120 pages ISBN 0-398066-50-7

1571 My Son...My Son: A Guide to Healing After Death, Loss, or Suicide
Bolton Press Atlanta
1090 Crest Brook Lane
Roswell, GA 30075-3403
770-645-1886
E-mail: contactus@boltonpress.com
www.boltonpress.com

John Bolton, Owner

A moving story of love, loss and recovery that will grab your heart, nourish your soul and open your eyes. A must read for anyone who has experienced a great loss and is trying to find some path out of the darkness of their despair or to understand those that are.

ISBN 0-961632-60-7

1572 Night Falls Fast: Understanding Suicide
Vintage Books A Division Of Random House
1745 Broadway
20th Floor
New York, NY 10019-4368
212-782-9000
800-733-3000
Fax: 212-302-7985
www.randomhouse.com

Markus Dohle, CEO

No one knows who the first was to slash the throat with a piece of flint, take a handful of poison berries, or intentionally drop.

ISBN 0-375701-47-8

1573 No Time to Say Goodbye: Surviving the Suicide of a Loved One
Broadway Books a Division of Random House
1745 Broadway
New York, NY 10019-4368
212-572-4985
Fax: 212-782-9052
E-mail: bwaypub@randomhouse.com
www.randomhouse.com

Markus Bohle, CEO

In the days following my husband's suicide, I remembered a documentary about cancer patients that I had seen several years before.

1574 Suicidal Patient: Principles of Assesment, Treatment, and Case Management
American Psychiatric Publishing, Inc.
1000 Wilson Boulevard
Suite 1825
Arlington, VA 22209-3901
703-907-7322
800-368-5777
Fax: 703-907-1091
E-mail: appi@psych.org
www.appi.org

Robert E Hales MD, Editor-in-Chief
Ron McMillen, Chief Executive Officer
John McDuffie, Editorial Director

Presents a clinical approach and valuable assessment strategies and techniques. Demonstrates an easy to use innovative clinical model with specific stages of treatment and associated interventions outlined for inpatient and outpatient settings. *$45.50*

282 pages ISBN 0-800485-54-X

1575 Suicide Over the Life Cycle
American Psychiatric Publishing, Inc.
1000 Wilson Boulevard
Suite 1825
Arlington, VA 22209-3901
703-907-7322
800-368-5777
Fax: 703-907-1091
E-mail: appi@psych.org
www.appi.org

Robert E Hales MD, Editor-in-Chief
Ron McMillen, Chief Executive Officer
John McDuffie, Editorial Director

Helps readers understand risk factors and treatment of suicidal patients. *$82.50*

836 pages ISBN 0-880483-07-5

1576 Understanding and Preventing Suicide: New Perspectives
Charles C Thomas Publisher
2600 S 1st Street
Springfield, IL 62704-4730
217-789-8980
800-258-8980
Fax: 217-789-9130
E-mail: books@ccthomas.com
www.ccthomas.com

Michael P Thomas, President

Seven perspectives for understanding and preventing suicidal behavior, illustrating their implications for prevention. This book discusses suicide from a crimnological perspective, and whether the theories in it have any applicability to suicidal behavior, both in futhering our understanding of suicide and in seeing new ways to prevent suicide. Armed with this information, we may move far toward understanding and preventing suicide in the twenty-first century. *$35.95*

137 pages Year Founded: 1990 ISSN 0-398-06235-8ISBN 0-398057-09-5

1577 Why Suicide? Answers to 200 of the Most Frequently Asked Questions about Suicide
HarperCollins
10 East 53rd Street
New York, NY 10022
212-207-7000
www.harpercolllins.com

Eric Marcus, Author

$14.95

ISBN 0-062511-66-9

Periodicals & Pamphlets

1578 Suicide Talk: What To Do If You Hear It
ETR Associates
4 Carbonero Way
Scotts Valley, CA 95066-4200
831-438-4060
800-321-4407
Fax: 831-438-3618
E-mail: customerservice@etr.org
www.etr.org

Mary Nelson, President

Includes suicide warning signs, how to help a friend, and ways to relieve stress. *$16.00*

1579 Suicide: Fast Fact 3
SAMHSA'S National Mental Health Information Center
PO Box 42557
Washington, DC 20015-557

800-789-2647
Fax: 240-747-5470
TDD: 866-889-2647
E-mail: ken@mentalhealth.org
www.mentalhealth.samhsa.org

A Kathryn Power MEd, Director
Edward B Searle, Deputy Director

This fact card provides statistics and a list of resources on suicide.

Year Founded: 2000

1580 Suicide: Who Is at Risk?
ETR Associates
4 Carbonero Way
Scotts Valley, CA 95066-4200
831-438-4060
800-321-4407
Fax: 831-438-3618
E-mail: customerservice@etr.org
www.etr.org

Mary Nelson, President

Includes warning signs, symptoms, and what to do. *$ 16.00*

Research Centers

1581 American Foundation for Suicide Prevention (SPAN USA)
1010 Vermont Avenue NW
Suite 408
Washington, DC 20005
202-449-3600
Fax: 202-449-3601
E-mail: info@spanusa.org
www.afsp.org

Robert Getsbia, Executive Director
John Madigan, Senior Dir, Public Policy
Trevor Summerfield, Manager, Public Policy

SPAN USA is dedicated to preventing suicide through public education and awareness, community engagement, and federal, state and local grassroots advocacy. By empowering those who have been touched by suicide, SPAN USA seeks to advance the implementation of the National Strategy for Suicide Prevention.

Year Founded: 1996

Support Groups & Hot Lines

1582 Covenant House Nineline
460 West 41st Street
New York, NY 10036-6898
212-613-0300
800-999-9999
Fax: 212-629-3756
E-mail: info@covenanthouseny.org
www.covenanthouse.com

Samone Thompson, Manager

Nationwide crisis/suicide hotline.

1583 Friends for Survival
PO Box 214463
Sacramento, CA 95821-463
916-392-0664
www.friendsforsurvival.org

Marilyn Koenig, Director

An organization of people who have been affected by a death caused by suicide. Dedicated to providing a variety of peer support services that comfort those in grief, encourage healing and growth, foster the development of skills to cope with a loss and educate the entire community regarding the impact of suicide.

1584 NineLine
460 W 41st Street
New York, NY 10036-6801
212-613-0300
800-999-9999
www.nineline.org

Bruce J Henry, Executive Director

Nationwide crisis/suicide hotline.

1585 Survivors of Loved Ones' Suicides (SOLOS)
PO Box 592
Dumfries, VA 22026-592

E-mail: solos@1000deaths.com
www.1000deaths.com

Christine Smith, PhD, President

Provide help and support to Survivors of Loved Ones Suicides(SOLOS) through outreach, education and research.

Web Sites

1586 www.1000deaths.com
Survivors of Loved Ones' Suicides

Group for those who have suffered a suicide loss.

1587 www.friendsforsurvival.org
Friends for Survival

Assisting anyone who has suffered the loss of a loved one
through suicide death.

Associations & Organizations

National

1588 Bellefaire Jewish Children's Bureau
22001 Fairmount Boulevard
Shaker Heights, OH 44118-4819
216-932-6152

Adam G Jacobs PhD, Executive Vp
Larry Pollock, President

A nonprofit mental health agency committed to serving the needs of children, youth and their families through an array of child welfare and behavioral health services. Provides its services without regard to race, religion, sex or national origin.

1589 AAMR: American Association on Mental Retardation
444 N Capitol Street NW
Suite 846
Washington, DC 20001-1569
202-637-0475
800-424-3688
Fax: 202-637-0585
E-mail: dcroser@aaidd.org

Paul Aitken, Director Finance/Administration
Doreen Croser, Executive Director
Bruce Appelgren, Director Publications

Promotes progressive policies, sound research, effective practices, and universal human rights for people with intellectual disabilities.

1590 Action Autonomie
#208 1260, rue Sainte-Catherine
Montreal, QC, ZZ
514-525-5060
Fax: 514-525-5580

Offers services for the protection and promotion of mental health rights.

1591 Advocates for Human Potential
323 Boston Post Road
Sudbury, MA 01776-3022
978-443-0055
Fax: 978-443-4722
E-mail: nshifman@ahpnet.com
www.ahpnet.com

Neal Shifman, Owner

Under contract with the Center for Mental Health Services (CMHS), Advocates for Human Potential (AHP) provides technical assistance to states and local providers regarding the Projects for Assistance in Transition from Homelessness (PATH) Program.

1592 Aleppos Foundation
39 Fairway E
Colts Neck, NJ 07722-1418
732-946-4489
Fax: 732-946-3344
E-mail: ilynch@monmouth.com
www.aleppos.org

Focuses on self-education: to learn about our inner and outer selves; to face up to our past; and to learn to communicate our true selves to others.

1593 Alliance of Genetic Support Groups
4301 Connecticut Avenue NW
Suite 404
Washington, DC 20008-2369
202-966-5557
800-336-4363
Fax: 202-966-8553
E-mail: info@geneticalliance.org
www.geneticalliance.org

A non-profit coalition of voluntary genetic support groups, consumers and professionals addressing the needs of individuals and families affected by genetic disorders from a national perspective. Specializes in linking people intrested in generic conditions with organization which can provide support and information.

1594 American Academy of Child and Adolescent Psychiatry
3615 Wisconsin Avenue NW
Washington, DC 20016-3007
202-362-1797
E-mail: communications@aacap.org

Robert Hendren, President
David Herzog, Secretary
William Bernet, Treasurer

Information is provided as a public service to aid in the understanding and treatment of the developmental, behavioral, and mental disorders which affect an estimated 7 to 12 million children and adolescents at any given time in the United States.

1595 American Academy of Pediatrics
141 NW Point Boulevard
Elk Grove Village, IL 60007-1098
847-228-0604
E-mail: cme@aap.org
www.aap.org

Provides information on diagnosis and treatment of physical and mental pediatric conditions by offering programs, training, and resources.

1596 American Association for Geriatric Psychiatry
7910 Woodmont Avenue
Suite 1050
Bethesda, MD 20814-3069
301-654-7850
Fax: 301-654-4137

E-mail: main@aagponline.org
www.aagponline.org

Christine De Vries, Manager
Annie Williams, Administrative Assistant

American Association for Geriatric Psychiatry (AAGP) is a national association representing and serving its members and the field of geriatric psychiatry. It is dedicated to promoting the mental health and well-being of older people and improving the care of those with late life mental disorders. AAGP enhances the knowledge base and standards of practice in geriatric psychiatry through education and research and by advocating for meeting the mental health needs of older Americans.

1597 American Association of Psychiatric Services for Children (AAPSC)
2345 Crystal Drive
Suite 250
Arlington, VA 22202-4815
703-412-2400
Fax: 703-412-2401

Christine James-Brown, President/CEO

Fosters prevention and treatment of mental and emotional disorders of the child, adolescent and family and furthers the development and application of clinical knowledge. Researches and supports projects dealing with child and adolescent mental health. Sponsors educational programs and compiles statistics. Publications: AAPSC Membership Directory, annual. AAPSC Newsletter, bimonthly. Child Psychiatry and Human Development, quarterly. Annual conference and exhibit usually in February or March.

1598 American Association on Intellectual and Developmental Disabilities (AAIDD)
501 3rd Street NW
Suite 200
Washington, DC 20001

800-424-3688
Fax: 202-387-2193
E-mail: anam@aaidd.org
www.aamr.org

M Doreen Croser, Executive Director

AAIDD promotes progressive policies, sound research, effective practices and universal human rights for people with intellectual and developmental disabilities.

1599 American Holistic Health Association
PO Box 17400
Anaheim, CA 92817-7400
714-779-6152
E-mail: mail@ahha.org
www.ahha.org

Michael Morton, PhD., President
Suzan Walter, Secretary/Treasurer

Promotes holistic principles honoring the whole person and encouraging people to actively participate in their own health and healthcare.

1600 American Managed Behavioral Healthcare Association
1101 Pennsylvania Avenue NW
6th Floor
Washington, DC 20004-2544
202-756-7726
Fax: 202-756-7308
E-mail: info@abhw.org

Pamela Greenberg, President/CEO

Represents and promotes the interests of specialty managed behavioral health care organizations.

1601 American Network of Community Options and Resources (ANCOR)
1101 King Street
Suite 380
Alexandria, VA 22314-2962
703-532-7850
Fax: 703-535-7860
E-mail: ancor@ancor.org
www.ancor.org

Represents providers of care to persons with disabilities (including MR/NH). Promotes high standard of ethics. Conducts educational programs.

1602 American Pediatrics Society
3400 Research Forest Drive
Suite B-7
The Woodlands, TX 77381-4259
281-419-0052
Fax: 281-419-0082
E-mail: info@aps-spr.org
www.aps-spr.org

Larry Shapiro, M.D., President
Elizabeth McAnarney, M.D., Vice President

Society of professionals working with pediatric health care issues; offers seminars and a variety of publications.

1603 American Psychiatric Association
1000 Wilston Boulevard
Suite 1825
Arlington, VA 22209-3924
703-248-0760
Fax: 703-907-1085
E-mail: apa@psych.org
www.psych.org

Tara L Burkholder, Marketing

Medical specialty society recognized world-wide. Both U.S. and international member physicians work together to ensure humane care and effective treatment for all persons with mental disorder, including mental retardation and substance-related disorders.

1604 American Psychological Association
750 1st Street NE
Washington, DC 20002-4242
202-336-5500
800-374-2721
Fax: 202-336-5518
TDD: 202-336-6123

TTY: 202-336-6123
www.apa.org

Norman B Anderson, CEO

Largest scienctific and professional organziation representing psychology in the United States and is the world's largest association of psychologists. Works to advance psychology as a science, as a profession, and as a means of promoting human welfare.

1605 American Speech-Language-Hearing Association

2200 Research Blvd
Rockville, MD 20850-3289
301-269-5700
800-638-8255
Fax: 301-296-8580
TTY: 301-296-5650
E-mail: actioncenter@asha.org
www.asha.org

Arlene A Pietranton, Executive Director

ASHA is the professional, scientific and credentialing association for 140,000 members and affiliates who are audiologists, spech-language pathoologists and speech, language and hearing scientists.

Year Founded: 1925

1606 Association for the Help of Retarded Children

200 Park Avenue S
Suite 1201
New York, NY 10003-1524
212-477-9696
E-mail: ahrcnyc@dti.net

Shirley Berenstein, Director

Offer disabled individuals day to day living that is as rich, absorbing and worthwhile as possible, with an emphasis on helping clients live up to their maximum potential in the community.

1607 Association of Mental Health Librarians (AMHL)

13301 Bruce B Downs Blvd
Tampa, FL 33612-3807
813-974-4471
Fax: 813-974-7242
E-mail: hanson@fmhi.usf.edu
www.fmhi.usf.edu/amhl

Ardis Hanson, President

An organization that is working in the field of mental health information delivery. Its members come from a variety of settings. AMHL provides opportunities for its members to enhance their professional skills; encourage research activities in mental health librarianship; and strengthens the role of the librarian within the mental health community.

1608 Bazelon Center for Mental Health Law

1101 15th Street NW
Suite 1212
Washington, DC 20005-5002

202-467-5730
Fax: 202-223-0409
E-mail: webmaster@bazelon.org
www.bazelon.org

Robert Berstein, Executive Director
Albert Archie, Operations Manager

National legal advocate for people with mental disabilities. Through precedent-setting litigation and in the public policy arena, the Bazelon Center works to advance and preserve the rights of people with mental illnesses and development disabilities.

1609 Best Buddies International (BBI)

100 SE 2nd Street
#1990
Miami, FL 33131-2100
305-374-2233
800-892-8339
Fax: 305-374-5305
E-mail: LaverneLewis@BestBuddies.org
www.bestbuddies.org

Anthony Shriver, President
J.R. Fry, Director

A nonprofit organization dedicated to enhancing the lives of people with intellectual disabilities by providing opportunities for one-to-one friendships and integrated employment.

1610 Bethesda Lutheran Homes and Services

700 Hoffman Drive
Watertown, WI 53094-6204
920-261-3050
800-369-4636

John E Bauer, CEO

Provides religious education, habilitation services, therapeutic services, vocational training and residential care for persons with mental retardation. Paid summer co-op positions in nursing, social work, psychology, special education, recreation, Christian education. Provides free information and referral services nationwide for parents, pastors, teachers, and mental retardation professionals.

1611 Black Mental Health Alliance (BMHA)

733 W 40th Street
Suite 10
Baltimore, MD 21211-2107
410-338-2642

Tracee Bryant, Executive Director

Seeks to increase clinicians, clergy, educators and social service professionals awareness of African-Americans mental health needs and concerns on issues including stress, violence, racism, substance abuse and parenting. Provides consultation, public information and resource referrals. Publications: Visions, quarterly. Annual meeting and dinner-dance. Annual Optimal Mental Health for African American Families Conference.

1612 Canadian Art Therapy Association

26 Earl Grey Road
Toronto ON, ZZ

416-461-9420

www.catainfo.ca

Nick Zwaagstra, President

To encourage and sponsor activities which enhance the progressive development of professional standards of art therapy, practice, training, research, publications & conferences.

1613 Canadian Federation of Mental Health Nurses

#104 1185 Eglinton Avenue E
Toronto ON, ZZ
416-426-7029
Fax: 416-426-7280
E-mail: info@cfmhn.ca
www.cfmhn.org

Sharyn Chapman, Treasurer/Membership

National voice for psychiatric and mental health nursing.

1614 Canadian Mental Health Association

#810 8 King Street E
Toronto ON, ZZ
416-484-7750
Fax: 416-484-4617
E-mail: info@cmha.ca
www.cmha.ca

Penelope Marrett, CEO

Promote mental health as well as support the resilience and recovery of people experiencing mental illness, through advocacy, education, research and service.

1615 Center for Attitudinal Healing (CAH)

33 Buchanan Drive
Sausalito, CA 94965-1650
415-331-6161
Fax: 415-331-4545
E-mail: home123@aol.com
www.attitudinalhealing.org

Don Gowewy, Executive Director

Nonsectarian organization established to supplement traditional health care by offering free attitudinal healing services for children and adults with life-threatening illnesses or other crisis. Offers support groups and arranges home and hospital visits for children, youth and adults. Publications: Advice to Doctors and Other Big People, book. Another Look at the Rainbow, book. Rainbow Connection, newsletter, three times a year. There is a Rainbow Behind Every Dark Cloud, book. Workshops, five times a year.

1616 Center for Family Support (CFS)

333 Seventh Avenue
9th Floor
New York, NY 10001-5004
212-629-7939
Fax: 212-239-2211
www.cfsny.org

Steven Vernikoff, Executive Director

A not-for-profit human service agency that provides individualized support services and programs for individuals living with developmental and related disabilities, and for the families that care for them at home.

1617 Center for Mental Health Services (CMHS)

PO Box 2345
Rockville, MD 20847
240-221-4021
800-789-2647
Fax: 240-221-4295
TDD: 866-889-2647
www.mentalhealth.samhsa.gov

A Kathryn Power, MEd, Director
Anna Marsh PhD, Deputy Director
Fran Randolph PhD, Dir, Service & Systems Improveme
Anne Mathews-Younes EdD, Dir, Prevention/Traumatic Stress

CMHS leads Federal efforts to treat mental illnesses by promoting mental health and by preventing the development or worsening of mental illness when possible. Congress created CMHS to bring new hope to adults who have serious mental illnesses and to children with serious emotional disorders. CMHS provides information about mental health via a toll-free the web site, and more than 600 publications. Developed for users of mental health services and their families, the general public, policy makers, providers, and the media.

Year Founded: 1992

1618 Center for the Study of Issues in Public Mental Health
Nathan S Kline Institute for Psychiatric Research

140 Old Orangeburg Road
Orangeburg, NY 10962-1157
845-398-5478
E-mail: siegel@nki.rfmh.org

Carole Siegel, PhD, Director
Kim Hopper, PhD, Co-Director
Dixianne Penney, Administrator Director

The Center is committed to developing and conducting research within the contents of a rigorous research program that is strongly influenced by the requirements of a public mental health system and, in turn, influences the development of policy and practice in this arena.

1619 Centre for Addiction & Mental Health

33 Russell Street
Toronto ON, ZZ
416-535-8501
800-463-6273
E-mail: public_affairs@camh.net
www.camh.net

Paul Beeston, Chair

Provide treatment for and research into substance abuse and mental health issues.

1620 Child & Parent Resource Institute

600 Sanatorium Road
London ON, ZZ
519-858-2774
Fax: 519-858-3913

Anne Stark, Administrator

Enhance the quality of life of children and youth with complex mental health or developmental challenges.

1621 Child Welfare League of America

2345 Crystal Drive
Suite 250
Arlington, VA 22202-4815
703-412-2400

Christine James-Brown, CEO

Oldest and largest membership-based child welfare organization. Committed to engaging people everywhere in promoting the well-being of children, youth, and their families, and protecting every child from harm.

1622 Christian Horizons

Po Box 150367
Grand Rapids, MI 49515-367
616-956-7063
Fax: 616-956-7063
E-mail: info@christianhorizonsinc.org
www.christianhorizonsinc.org

A Christian organization dedicated to enriching the lives of people with mental impairments. Provides day programs, camping ministries, and Bible studies. Assists churches in identifying persons with special needs and supports parents of those with special needs.

1623 Coalition of Voluntary Mental Health Agencies

90 Broad Street
8th Floor
New York, NY 10004-2205
212-742-1600
Fax: 212-742-2080
E-mail: mailbox@cvmha.org
www.cvmha.org/

An umbrella advocacy organization of New York City's mental health community, representing over 100 non-profit community based mental health agencies that serve more than 500,000 clients in the five boroughs of New York City. Founded in 1972, the Coalition is entirely membership supported with limited foundation and government funding for special purpose advocacy and assistance projects.

1624 Community Access

666 Broadway
3rd Floor
New York, NY 10004-3412
212-228-1351
Fax: 212-780-1412
www.communityaccess.org

Steve Coe, Executive Director

A nonprofit agency providing housing and advocacy for people with psychiatric disabilities. Provides 430 affordable housing units for people with psychiatric disabilities, families with disabilities, and low income people from local neighborhoods.

1625 Community Service Options

6845 S Western Ave
Chicago, IL 60636-3117
773-471-4700
Fax: 773-471-4770
TDD: 773-471-4722
www.cso1.org

Contracts with the Illinois Department if Human Services (IDHS) to provide preadmission screening, eligibility determination and service coordination for people with developmental disabilities, in Chicago.

Year Founded: 1989

1626 Council for Learning Disabilities

11184 Antioch Road
Box 405
Overland Park, KS 66210
913-491-1011
Fax: 913-491-1012
E-mail: cldinfo@ie-events.com
www.cldinternational.org

Christina Curran, President
Linda Nease, Executive Director

An international organization concerned about issues related to students with learning disabilities.

1627 Council on Quality and Leadership

100 W Road
Suite 335
Towson, MD 21204
410-583-0060
Fax: 410-832-7226
E-mail: info@thecouncil.org
www.thecouncil.org

James F Gardner PhD, President/CEO

An international not-for-profit organization that brings together providers, professionals, advocates and other leaders in the disability field whose vision is community inclusion, dignity and quality of life for people with intellectual and developmental disabilities and people with mental illness.

1628 Emotions Anonymous International Service Center

PO Box 4245
Saint Paul, MN 55104-0245
651-647-9712
Fax: 651-647-1593
E-mail: info@EmotionsAnonymous.org
www.EmotionsAnonymous.org

Karen Mead, Executive Director

Fellowship of men and women who share their experience, strength and hope with each other, that they may solve their common problem and help others recover from emotional illness.

1629 Eye Movement Desensitization and Reprocessing International Association (EMDRIA)
PO Box 141925
Austin, TX 78714-1925
512-451-5200
Fax: 512-451-5256
E-mail: info@emdria.org
www.emdria.org

Carol York, Executive Director
Rosalie Thomas, President

The primary objective of EMDRIA is to establish, maintain and promote the highest standards of excellence and integrity in Eye Movement Desensitization and Reprocessing practice, research and education.

1630 Families Anonymous
PO Box 3475
Culver City, CA 90231-3475

Fax: 310-815-9682
E-mail: famanon@familiesanonymous.org
www.familiesanonymous.org

For concerned relatives and friends of youth with drug abuse or related behavior problems.

1631 Family Advocacy & Support Association
PO Box 74884
Washington, DC 20056-4884
202-576-6065

Phyllis Morgan, President

Self-help, nonprofit, support, education and advocacy organization comprised of parents/family members and service providers dedicated to improving the quality of life for children and youth with emotional, behavioral and learning disabilities.

1632 Family Violence & Sexual Assault Institute
6160 Cornerstone Court E
San Diego, CA 92121-3720
858-623-2777
Fax: 858-646-0761
www.fvsai.org

David Westgate, Director

Book club, research, and quarterly newsletter.

1633 Federation for Children with Special Needs (FCSN)
1135 Tremont Street
Suite 420
Boston, MA 02120-2199
617-236-7210
800-331-0688
Fax: 617-572-2094
E-mail: fcsninfo@fcsn.org
www.fcsn.org

Rich Robison, President

The federation provides information, support, and assistance to parents of children with disabilities, their professional partners and their communities.

1634 Federation of Families for Children's Mental Health
9605 Medical Center Drive
Rockville, MD 20850-6390
240-403-1901
Fax: 240-403-1909
E-mail: ffcmh@ffcmh.org
www.ffcmh.org

Sandra Spencer, Executive Director
Kameisha Bennett, Associate Dir of Development

National family-run organization dedicated exclusively to children and adolescents with mental health needs and their families. Our voice speaks through our work in policy, training and technical assistance programs. Publishes a quarterly newsletter and sponsors an annual conference and exhibits.

1635 Gam-Anon Family Groups International Service Office
PO Box 157
Whitestone, NY 11357-0157
718-352-1671
Fax: 718-746-2571
E-mail: info3@gam-anon.org
www.gam-anon.org

The self-help organization of Gam-Anon is a life saving instrument for the spouse, family or close friends of compulsive gamblers.

1636 Healing for Survivors
Po Box 8405
Fresno, CA 93747-8405
559-442-3600
Fax: 559-442-3600
E-mail: hfshope@email.com
www.hfshope.org

Jan Kister, Director
Tammie Wineland, Administrative Assistant

Support center for adults who were physically, emotionally, or sexually abused as children. Provides weekly support groups, weekend workshops, individual counseling, partners groups and couples groups.

1637 Hincks-Dellcrest Centre
440 Jarvis Street
Toronto ON, ZZ
416-924-1164
Fax: 416-924-8208
E-mail: info@hincksdellcrest.org
www.hincksdellcrest.org

John F Spekkens, Executive Director

Provides mental health prevention and early intervention programs for infants, children and youth.

1638 Hong Fook Mental Health Association
1065 McNicoll Avenue
Scarborough ON, ZZ
416-493-4242
Fax: 416-493-2214
E-mail: info@hongfook.ca
www.hongfook.ca

Raymond CY Chung MSW RSW, Executive Director

To achieve optimal mental health status through activities of direct services, promotion and prevention.

1639 Human Services Research Institute
2336 Massachusetts Avenue
Cambridge, MA 02140-1886
617-876-0426
Fax: 617-491-7902
E-mail: sjohniken@hsri.org
www.hsri.org

Val Bradley, President

Assists state and federal government to enhance services and support people with mental illness and people with mental retardation.

1640 Information Centers for Lithium, Bipolar Disorders Treatment & Obsessive Compulsive Disorder
Madison Institute of Medicine
7617 Mineral Point Road
Suite 300
Madison, WI 53717-1623
608-827-2470
E-mail: mim@miminc.org
www.factsforhealth.org

Margarett Baudhuin, Manager

The Information Centers publish information / booklets. Authored by experts on each disorder, these patient guides offer information about various psychiatric disorders and their treatments, and address the questions most frequently asked by patients and their families.

1641 Inner Peace Movement of Canada
#1106 100 Bronson Avenue
Ottawa ON, ZZ
613-238-7844
Fax: 613-238-7445

Rita Bunbury, Office Manager

Promote self-help techniques; to organize self-help programs for the public.

1642 Institute of Living Anxiety Disorders Center
Hartford Hospital
200 Retreat Avenue
Hartford, CT 06106-3309
860-545-2629
800-673-2411

David A Pepper, Director

Provides evaluation and treatment for individuals suffering from anxiety disorders as well as training and education for clinicians.

1643 International Photo Therapy Association
Photo Therapy Centre
#205 1300 Richards Street
Vancouver BC, ZZ
604-689-9709
Fax: 604-633-1505
E-mail: jweiser@phototherapy-centre.com
www.phototherapy-centre.com

Judy Weiser, Chair

Educate about therapeutic uses of still & video photography.

1644 International Society of Psychiatric-Mental Health Nurses
1211 Locust Street
Philadelphia, PA 19107-5409
215-545-2843
800-826-2950
Fax: 215-545-8107
E-mail: info@ispn-psych.org
www.ispn-psych.org

Lynette Jack PhD, RN, CARN, President
Geraldine S Pearson PhD, RN, CS, Secratary
Mary Jo Regan-Kubinski PhD, RN, Treasurer

To unite and enhance the presence and the voice of specialty psychiatric mental health nurses while influencing healthcare policy to promote equitable, evidence-based and effective treatment and care for individuals, families and communities.

1645 Judge Baker Children's Center
3 Blackfan Circle
Boston, MA 02115
617-232-8390
Fax: 617-232-8399
E-mail: info@jbcc.harvard.edu
www.jbcc.harvard.edu

Stewart Hauser, MD, PhD, President
Kevin Lee Hepner, VP

A nonprofit organization dedicated to improving the lives of children whose emotional and behavioral problems threaten to limit their potential.

1646 Learning Disabilities Association of America
4156 Library Road
Pittsburgh, PA 15234-1349
412-341-1515
E-mail: info@ldaamerica.org
www.LDAAmerica.org

Sheila Buckley, Executive Director

Offers information and referral services to the learning disabled. Free pamphlets, fact sheets and bibliography regarding learning disabilities.

1647 Life Development Institute
18001 N 79th Avenue, Suite E71
Phoenix, AZ 85308-8396

623-773-2774
Fax: 623-773-2788
E-mail: LDIinARIZ@aol.com

Robert Crawford, CEO

Serves older adolescents and adults with learning disabilities and related disorders. Conducts programs to assist individuals to achieve careers/employment commensurate with capabilities and independent status.

1648 Lifespire

345 Hudson Street
3rd Floor
New York, NY 10014-7476
212-741-0100
Fax: 212-463-9814
E-mail: info@lifespire.org
www.lifespire.com

Professionals, parents, siblings, and others interested in mentally retarded and developmentally disabled adults. Offers professionally supervised programs for mentally retarded and developmentally disabled adults including vocational rehabilitation, dual diagnosis programs, job placement, rehabilitation workshops, activities for daily living, day treatment, day training, supported work, and family support programs.

1649 Menninger Clinic

2801 Gessner
PO Box 809045
Houston, TX 77280-9045
713-275-5000
800-351-9058
Fax: 713-275-5107
www.menninger.edu

Dr. Herbert Spohn, Director

A national specialty psychiatric care facility offering diagnostic and treatment programs for adoloscents and adults.

1650 Mental Health and Aging Network (MHAN) of the American Society on Aging (ASA)
Ameican Society on Aging
833 Market Street
Suite 511
San Francisco, CA 94105-2938
415-974-9600
800-537-9728
Fax: 415-974-0300
E-mail: info@asaging.org
www.asaging.org

Bob Stein, Executive Director
Robert Lowe, Director Of Operations

Dedicated to improving the supportive interventions for older adults with mental health problems and their caregivers by: Creating a cadre of professionals with expertise in geriatric mental health, Assuring that service professionals are multi capable, Improving the systems of care, Providing a voice for the underserved and Advocating for the services that advance quality of life for our clients.

1651 Mental Illness Education Project

PO Box 470813
Brookline Village, MA 02447-813
617-562-1111
800-343-5540
Fax: 617-779-0061
E-mail: info@miepvideos.org
www.miepvideos.org

Christine Ledoux, Executive Director

Engaged in the production of video-based educational and support materials for the following specific populations: people with psychiatric disabilities; families, mental health professionals, special audiences, and the general public. The Project's videos are designed to be used in hospital, clinical and educational settings, and at home by individuals and families.

1652 Nathan S Kline Institute for Psychiatric Research

140 Old Orangeburg Road
Orangeburg, NY 10962-1157
845-398-5500
Fax: 845-398-5510
E-mail: webmaster@nki.rfmh.org
www.rfmh.org/nki

Bennett L Leventhal, MD, Deputy Director

Research programs in Alzheimers disease, analytical psychopharmacology, basic and clinical neuroimaging, cellular and molecular neurobiology, clinical trial data management, co-occuring disorders and many other mental health studies.

1653 National Alliance on Mental Illness

2107 Wilson Boulevard
Suite 300
Arlington, VA 22201-3080
703-524-7600
Fax: 703-524-9094
www.nami.org

Michael Fitzpatrick, Executive Director
Lynn Borton, COO

Dedicated to the eradication of mental illnesses and to the improvement of the quality of life of all whose lives are affected by these diseases.

Year Founded: 1979

1654 National Association for Rural Mental Health

300 33rd Avenue South
Suite 101
Waite Park, MN 56387
320-202-1820
Fax: 320-202-1833
E-mail: info@narmh.org
www.narmh.org

Rick Peterson, President
LuAnn Rice, Manager

Provides a forum for rural mental health professionals and advocates to: identify and solve challenges; work cooperatively toward improving the delivery of rural mental health services; promote the unique needs and concerns of rural mental health policy and practice issues. Sponsors an annual conference where rural mental health professionals benefit from the sharing of knowledge and resources.

Year Founded: 1977

1655 National Association for the Dually Diagnosed (NADD)

132 Fair Street
Kingston, NY 12401-4802
845-331-4336
800-331-5362
Fax: 845-331-4569
E-mail: info@thenadd.org
www.thenadd.org

Robert Fletcher, Executive Director

A not-for-profit membership association established for professionals, care providers and families to promote understanding of and services for individuals who have developmental disabilities and mental health needs.

Year Founded: 1983

1656 National Association of Protection and Advocacy Systems

900 2nd Street NE
Suite 211
Washington, DC 20002-3560
202-408-9514
Fax: 202-408-9520
TDD: 202-408-9521
E-mail: info@napas.org
www.ndrn.org

Curtis Decker, Executive Director

NAPAS was established under the Protection and Advocacy for Individuals with Mental Illness (PAIMI) Act. PAIMI programs protect and advocate for the legal rights of persons with mental illness. The programs investigate reports of abuse or neglect and provide technical assistance, information, and legal counseling. Publishes a free, quarterly newsletter, P&A News.

1657 National Association of State Mental Health Program Directors

66 Canal Center Plaza
Suite 302
Alexandria, VA 22314-1568
703-739-2120
Fax: 703-548-9517
E-mail: roy.praschil@nasmhpd.org
www.nasmhpd.org

Robert W Glover, Executive Director
Roy Praschil, Director Operations

Nonprofit membership organization that adovacates at the national level for the collective interests of state mental health agency commissioners and staff. Operates under a cooperative agreement with the National Governor's Association. NASMHPD is committed to working with other stakeholders to improve public mental health systems and the lives of persons with serious mental illnesses who access these and other systems. Its core services focus on legislative advocacy, technical assistance and information dissemination.

Year Founded: 1959

1658 National Association of Therapeutic Wilderness Camps

698 Dinner Bell-Ohiopyle Road
Ohiopyle, PA 15470-1006

E-mail: info@natwc.org
www.natwc.org

Represents nearly fifty therapeutic wilderness camps located all over the US. We believe therapeutic wilderness camps represent the most effective method to help troubled young people change the way they deal with their parents, school, and other authorities.

1659 National Center for Learning Disabilities

381 Park Avenue S
Room 1401
New York, NY 10016-8829
212-545-7504
888-575-7373
Fax: 212-545-9665
www.ncld.org

James Wendorf, Executive Director

National, non profit organization dedicated to improving the lives of those affected by learning didabilities (LD). Services include national information and referral, public outreach and communications, legislative advocacy and public policy. Its mission is to promote public awareness and understanding of learning disabilities and to provide national leadership on behalf of children and adults with LD so they may achieve thier potential and enjoy full participation in society. Our website offers a free monthly e mail newsletter, and much more information for contacts and referrals.

1660 National Center on Addiction and Substance Abuse at Columbia University

633 3rd Avenue
19th Floor
New York, NY 10017-8155
212-841-5200
Fax: 212-956-8020
E-mail: info@casacolumbia.org
www.casacolumbia.org

William H Foster, CEO
Richard Mulieri, Communications

Unique think/action tank that engages all disiplines to study every form of substance abuse as it affects our society.

1661 National Child Support Network

PO Box 1018
Fayetteville, AR 72702-1018

800-729-5437
Fax: 479-582-2401
www.childsupport.org

A private bonded, insured and licensed child support collection agency.

1662 National Council for Community Behavioral Healthcare
12300 Twinbrook Parkway
Suite 320
Rockville, MD 20852-1606
301-984-6200
Fax: 301-881-7159
E-mail: lindare@nccbh.org
www.nccbh.org

Linda Rosenberg, CEO
David Schuerholz, Marketing/Communications

Behavioral healthcare administrators. Publishes the Journal of Behavioral Health Sciences and Research, ABHM Leader. Annual training conferences. See web for additional information.

1663 National Empowerment Center
599 Canal Street
Lawrence, MA 01840-1244
978-685-1494
800-769-3728
Fax: 978-681-6426

Dan Fisher, Executive Director
Debbie Whittle, Director

Consumer/survivor/ex-patient run organization that carries a message of recovery, empowerment, hope and healing to people who have been diagnosed with mental illness; and provide information and technical assistance to individuals and groups involved in consumer empowerment activities

1664 National GAINS Center for People with Co-Occurring Disorders in the Justice System
345 Delaware Avenue
Delmar, NY 12054-1905
518-439-7415
800-311-4246
Fax: 518-439-7612
E-mail: sdavidson@prainc.com
www.gainsctr.com

Joseph J Cocozza PhD, Co-Director
Henry Steadman PhD, Co-Director
Susan Davidson, Division Manager

Center is a national focus for the collection and dissemination of information about effective, integrated mental health and substance abuse services for people with co-ocurring disorders who come in contact with the criminal justice system, including law enforcement, jails, prisons, and community corrections. The center is operated by Policy Research, Inc. of Delmar, NY and is supported by the National Institute of Corrections, the Center for Substance Abuse Treatment and the Center for Mental Health Services.

1665 National Institute of Drug Abuse (NIDA)
6001 Executive Boulevard
Room 5213
Bethesda, MD 20892-1
301-443-6245
Fax: 301-443-7397

E-mail: information@lists.nida.nih.gov
www.drugabuse.gov
Beverly Jackson, Manager

Covers the areas of drug abuse treatment and prevention research, epidemiology, neuroscience and behavioral research, health services research and AIDS. Seeks to report on advances in the field, identify resources, promote an exchange of information, and improve communications among clinicians, researchers, administrators, and policymakers. Recurring features include synopses of research advances and projects, NIDA news, news of legislative and regulatory developments, and announcements.

1666 National Institute of Mental Health Information Resources and Inquiries Branch
6001 Executive Boulevard
Room 8184
Bethesda, MD 20892-1
301-443-4513
866-615-6464
TTY: 301-443-8431
E-mail: nimhinfo@nih.gov

One of 27 components of the National Institutes of Health, the Federal government's principal biomedical and behavioral research agency.

1667 National Mental Health Association
2000 N Beauregard Street
6th Floor
Alexandria, VA 22311-1748
703-684-7722
800-969-6642
Fax: 703-684-5968
TTY: 800-433-5959
www.mentalhealthamerica.net

David Shern, CEO
Kate Gaston, VP Afiliate Services

Dedicated to improving treatments, understanding and services for adults and children with mental health needs. Working to win political support for funding for school mental health programs. Provides information about a wide range of disorders, such as panic disorder, obsessive-compulsive disorder, post traumatic stress, generalized anxiety disorder and phobias. Also advocates for programs to diagnose and treat children in juvenile justice systems.

1668 National Mental Health Consumers' Self-Help Clearinghouse
1211 Chestnut Street
Suite 1207
Philadelphia, PA 19107-4103
215-751-1810
800-553-4539
Fax: 215-636-6312
E-mail: info@mhselfhelp.org
www.mhselfhelp.org

Joseph Rogers, Executive Director

A national consumer technical assistance center that has played a major role in the development of the mental health consumer movement.

Year Founded: 1986

1669 National Network for Mental Health
#604 55 King Street
St. Catharine ON, ZZ
905-682-2423
888-406-4663
Fax: 905-682-7469
E-mail: info@nnmh.ca
www.nnmh.ca

Constance McKnight, Executive Director

Advocate, educate and provide expertise and resources for increased health and well-being of the Canadian mental health consumer.

1670 National Organization on Disability
888 Sixteenth Street NW
Suite 800
Washington, DC 20006
202-293-5960
Fax: 202-293-7999
TTY: 202-293-5968
E-mail: ability@nod.org
www.nod.org

Tom Ridge, Chairman
Carol Glazer, President

The mission of the National Organization on Disability (NOD) is to expand the participation and contribution of America's 54 million men, women and children with disabilities in all aspects of life. By raising disability awareness through programs and information, together we can work toward closing the participation gaps.

Year Founded: 1982

1671 National Rehabilitation Association
633 S Washington Street
Alexandria, VA 22314-4109
703-836-0850
Fax: 703-836-0848
TDD: 703-836-0849
E-mail: info@nationalrehab.org

Patrica Leahy, Executive Director
John D'Angelo, Director Operations

Concerned with the rights of people with disabilities, our mission is to provide advocacy, awareness and career advancement for professionals in the fields of rehabilitation. Our members include rehab counselors, physical, speech and occupational therapists, job trainers, consultants, independent living instructors and other professionals involved in the advocacy of programs and services for people with disabilities.

1672 National Resource Center on Homelessness & Mental Illness
345 Delaware Avenue
Delmar, NY 12054-1905
518-439-7415
800-444-7415
Fax: 518-439-7612
E-mail: nrc@prainc.com
www.nrchmi.samhsa.gov

Francine Williams, Director
Deborah Dennis, VP/Project Director

Provides technical assistance and comprehensive information concerning the treatment, services and housing needs of persons who are homeless and who have serious mental illnesses. The Resource Center provides technical assistance to CHS grantees, provides or arranges technical assistance on the development of housing and services for special needs populations; maintains an extensive bibliographic database of published and unpublished materials, develops workshops and training institutes on the coordination of services and housing for homeless persons with mental illnesses, and responds to requests for information.

1673 National Self-Help Clearinghouse Graduate School and University Center
365 5th Avenue
Suite 3300
New York, NY 10016-4309
212-817-1822
E-mail: info@selfhelpweb.org
www.selfhelpweb.org

Audrey Gardner, Co Director
Frank Riessman, Co Director

Facilitates access to self-help groups and increases the awareness of the importance of mutual support. The clearinghouse provides services by: assisting human service agencies on self-help principles, conducting training for self-help group leaders and group facilitators, researches the effectiveness of self-help and relationships with formal caregiving systems and provides media outreach.

Year Founded: 1976

1674 National Technical Assistance Center for Children's Mental Health
Georgetown University Child Development Center
3307 M Street NW
Washington, DC 20007-3539
202-724-8783
TTY: 202-687-5503
E-mail: gucdc@georgetown.edu

Integral part of the Georgetown University Center for Child and Human Development at the Georgetown University Medical Center. Nationally recognized for its work in assisting states and communities build systems of care for mental health concerns.

Year Founded: 1984

1675 New Hope Foundation
PO Box 201
Kensington, MD 20895-201
301-946-6395
Fax: 301-946-1402
E-mail: newhope@nhfi.org
www.newhopfoundationinc.org

Daphne Stegmaier, Volunteer

Nonprofit organization integrates the many techniques proven effective in dealing with serious mental problems. Presents an innovative, replicable program designed to maximize the ability of chronically ill mental patients to achieve stable, self supporting lives in the community.

1676 PRO Behavioral Health
7600 E Eastman Avenue
Denver, CO 80231-4376
303-695-6007
888-687-6755
Fax: 303-695-0100
www.probh.com

Mari Teitelman LCSW, Business Development

PRO Behavioral Health is one of the nation's leading mental health and substance abuse managed care firms. Founded and directed by behavioral health clinicians and managers, PRO brings a clinically driven behavioral health service model to the market. Client organizations enjoy the benefits of PRO's client-specific customized programs, highly responsible customer service, behavioral health care coordinated with medical care, continuous quality improvement and reduced costs.

1677 Parents Helping Parents
Sobrato Center for Nonprofits
1400 Parkmoor Avenue
Suite 100
San Jose, CA 95126
408-727-5775
Fax: 408-286-1116
www.php.com

Mary Ellen Peterson MA, Executive Director/CEO

A non-profit, community-based, parent-directed family resource center. Provides lifetime guidance, supports and services to children with any special need, their families and the professionals who serve them.

1678 Parents for Children's Mental Health
#309 40 St. Clair Avenue E
Toronto ON, ZZ
416-921-2109
Fax: 416-921-7600
E-mail: parents@parentsforchildrensmentalhealth.org
www.parentsforchildrensmentalhealth.org

Provide voice for children & their families who face the challenges of mental health problems in Ontario.

1679 Partnership for Workplace Mental Health
1000 Wilson Blvd
Suite 1825
Arlington, VA 22209-3901
703-907-8561
Fax: 703-907-1089
E-mail: mleftwich@psych.org
www.workplacementalhealth.org

Clare Miller, Director
Mary Claire Kraft, Promgram Manager

A program of the American Psychiatric Foundation, the Partnership advances effective employer approaches to mental health, delivering educational materials and providing a forum to explore mental health issues and share solutions. It promotes the business case for quality mental health care, including early recognition, access to care and effective treatment.

1680 Phoenix Care Systems, Inc: Willowglen Academy
1744 N Farwell Avenue
Milwaukee, WI 53202-1806
414-225-4460
866-225-4459
Fax: 414-225-4475
E-mail: john.yopps@phoenixcaresystems.com
www.phoenixcaresystems.com

Leonard Dziubla, CEO
Lin Daley, Exec Director-Wisconsin
Kathleen Tresemer, Exec Director-Illinois
Dwayne Mueller, Exec Director-Indiana

As a wholly owned subsidiary of Phoenix Care Systems, Inc, Willowglen Academy provides therapeutic residential treatment and educational services to children, adolescents and young adults with mental health, emotional, cognitive and developmental disabilities. Our accrediting bodies include COA, CARF and JCAHO.

1681 Professional Assistance Center for Education (PACE)
National-Louis University
2840 Sheridan Road
Evanston, IL 60201
847-256-5150
E-mail: cburns@nl.edu

Carol Burns, Director

Non-credit, non degree, two-year postsecondary program for students with learning disabilities. The program prepares young adults for careers as aides in preschools or human service agencies. In addition to professional preparation coursework, the curriculum also focuses on social skills and independent living skills. Students receive a certificate of completion at the conclusion of the program. College residential life is an integral part of the program. Transitional program where appropriate.

1682 Psychiatric Clinical Research Center
University of Illinois at Chicago
1740 W Taylor Street
Medical Center
Chicago, IL 60612-7232
312-996-3801
800-842-1002

Russell D Brown, Director

The Center offers those whose quality of life is affected by severe mental disorders the opportunity to receive an accurate diagnosis and treatment for their condition using the latest methods of care. Those who participate in the clinical research give our staff the opportunity to learn more about these serious mental disorders.

1683 Reclamation
2502 Waterford Drive
San Antonio, TX 78217-5037
210-822-3569
www.community-2.webtv/stigmanet/

Don H Culwell, Director

Former mental patients and interested others. Seeks to eliminate the stigma of mental illness and reclaim members' dignity. Serves as a voice for mental health patients in consumer, social and political affairs. Helps members to live outside a hospital setting by providing assistance in the areas of resocialization, employment and housing. Monitors the media and encourages positive media coverage. Publications: Positive Visibility, quarterly newsletter. Annual Reclamation conference.

1684 Recovery
802 N Dearborn Street
Chicago, IL 60610-3364
312-337-5661
E-mail: inquiries@recovery-inc.com
www.recovery-inc.org

Kathleen Garcia, Executive Director
Maurine Pyle

Recovery method is to help prevent relapses in former mental patients and to forestall chronicity in nervous patients. Recovery provides training in a systematic method of self-help aftercare for these patients, based on the system of self-help principles described in Low's book, Mental Health Through Will Training.

1685 Refuah
PO Box 1212
Randolph, MA 02368-1212
781-961-2815
Fax: 781-986-5070
E-mail: nblrefuah@aol.com
www.refuahboston.org

Nancy Blake Lewis, Executive Director

Expanding network of concerned Jewish family members and friends with loved ones of any race or creed suffering from chronic mental illness.

1686 Research Center for Severe Mental Illnesses
11301 Wilshire Boulevard #116
W LA VA Medical Center, Building 208 R
Los Angeles, CA 90073-1003
310-477-7927
E-mail: rpl@ucla.edu
www.npi.ucla.edu/crc/products/products

Robert Paul Liberman MD, Director
Jim Mintz PhD, Associate Director

For more than 20 years the center has given priority to the design, validation and dissemination of the practical, user-friendly assesment, treatment and rehabilitation techniques for practitioners.

1687 Research and Training Center on Family Support and Children's Mental Health
Portland State University/Regional Research Institute
PO Box 751
Portland State University
Portland, OR 97207-751
503-725-4040
Fax: 503-725-4180

E-mail: gordon@pdx.edu
www.rtc.pdx.edu

Lynwood Gordon, Public Information/Outreach
Janet Walker, Editor

Dedicated to promoting effective community based, culturally competent, family centered services for families and their children who are or may be affected by mental, emotional or behavioral disorders. This goal is accomplished through collaborative research partnerships with family members, service providers, policy makers, and other concerned persons. Major efforts in dissemination and training include: An annual conference, an award winning web site to share information about child and family mental services and policy issues which includes Focal Point, a national bulletin regarding family support and children's mental health.

1688 Resources for Children with Special Needs
116 E 16th Street
5th Floor
New York, NY 10003-2164
212-677-4650
Fax: 212-254-4070
E-mail: info@resourcesnyc.org
www.resourcesnyc.org

Rachel Howard, Executive Director
Dianne Littwin, Director Publications

Information, referral, advocacy, training, publications for New York City parents of youth with disabilities or special needs and the professionals who work with them.

1689 Sidran Traumatic Stress Institute
200 E Joppa Road
Suite 207
Towson, MD 21286-3107
410-825-8888
888-825-8249
Fax: 410-337-0747
E-mail: sidran@sidran.org
www.sidran.org

Esther Giller, President

A nonprofit charitable organization devoted to education, advocacy and research to benefit people who are suffering from injuries of traumatic stress. Whether caused by family violence, crime, disaster, war or any other overwhelming experience, the disabling effects of trauma can be overcome with understanding, support and appropriate treatment. To support people with traumatic stress conditions and to educate mental health professionals and the public. Sidran has developed many service, training and bookshelf information sources.

1690 Systems Advocacy
National Mental Health Consumers' Self-Help Clearinghouse
1211 Chestnut Street
Suite 1000
Philadelphia, PA 19107-4103
215-751-1810
800-553-4539
Fax: 212-636-6312

E-mail: THEKEY@delphi.com
www.mhselfhelp.org

A consumer-run national technical assistance center serving the mental health consumer movement. Help connect individuals to self-help and advocacy resources, and we offer expertise to self-help groups and other peer-run services for mental health consumers.

1691 Thresholds
4101 N Ravenswood Avenue
Chicago, IL 60613
773-572-5500
E-mail: thresholds@thresholds.org
www.thresholds.org

Anthony M Zipple, CEO

Serves people with severe and persistent mental illness with a range of programs designed with the individual's recovery as a goal.

1692 United Families for Children's Mental Health
13301 Bruce B Downs Boulevard
FMHI Box 2, Room 2514
Tampa, FL 33612-3807
813-974-2428
E-mail: ffcmh@earthlink.net

Carol Baier

Nonprofit family organization run by and for caregivers of children with mental health issues.

1693 Voice of the Retarded
5005 Newport Drive
Suite 108
Rolling Meadows, IL 60008-3837
847-253-6020
Fax: 847-253-6054
E-mail: vor@compuserve.com
www.vor.net

Tamie Hopp, Executive Director
Nancy Ward, President

VOR is a national advocacy organization. Its mission is to ensure quality care and choice in services and supports received by people with mental retardation. Through a weekly e-mail update, a quarterly newsletter and frequent action alerts, we empower our members and coordinate grass roots advocacy. Membership is $25 per year.

1694 Warren Grant Magnuson Clinical Center
9000 Rockville Pike
Building 10, Room 1C255
Bethesda, MD 20892-1
301-496-2563
Fax: 301-402-2984
E-mail: occc@cc.nih.gov
www.cc.nih.gov

Established as the research hospital of the National Institutes of Health. Designed with patient care facilities close to research laboratories so new findings of basic and clinical scientists can be quickly applied to the treatment of patients. Upon referral by physicians, patients are admitted to NIH clinical studies.

Year Founded: 1953

1695 Women's Counselling, Referral and Education Centre
489 College Street
Suite 303B
Toronto ON M6G 1A5, ZZ
416-534-7501
Fax: 416-534-7501
E-mail: generalmail@wcrec.org
www.wcrec.org

Strives to empower women by addressing the systemic barriers that affect their quality of life. Offers free in-house counselling, information, and educational services.

Year Founded: 1976

1696 World Federation for Mental Health Secretariat
12940 Harbor Drive
Suite 101
Woodbridge, VA 22192
703-494-6515
Fax: 703-494-6518
E-mail: info@wfmh.com
www.wfmh.org

Anthony Fowke, President

An international membership organization founded to advance, among all peoples and nations, the prevention of mental and emotional disorders, the proper treatment and care of those with such disorders, and the promotion of mental health.

1697 Young Adult Institute and Workshop (YAI)
460 W 34th Street
New York, NY 10001-2382
212-273-6193
Fax: 212-947-7524
www.yai.org

Philip Levy, CEO
Phil Levy, President/COO

Serves more than 15,000 people of all ages and levels of mental retardation, developmental and learning disabilities. Provides a full range of early intervention, preschool, family supports, employment training and placement, clinical and residential services, as well as recreation and camping services. YAI/National Intitute for People with Disabilities is also a professional organization, nationally renowned for its publications, conferences, training seminars, video training tapes and innovative television programs.

1698 Youth Services International
1819 Main Street
Suite 1000
Sarasota, FL 34236-5999
941-953-9199
Fax: 941-953-9198
E-mail: YSIWEB@youthservices.com
www.youthservices.com

Premier provider in the youth care industry of educational and developmental services that change, dramatically, the thinking and behavior of troubled youth.

1699 ZERO TO THREE: National Center for Infants, Toddlers, and Families

2000 M Street NW
Suite 200
Washington, DC 20036-3380
202-638-1144
800-899-4301
Fax: 202-638-0851
E-mail: oto3@presswarehouse.com
www.zerotothree.org

Matthew E Melmed JD, Executive Director
Tammy Mann PhD, Deputy Executive Director

Publishes book, pamphlets, and curricula with a focus on the social and emotional development of infants, toddlers, and their families. Publications include the Diagnostic Classification of Mental Health and Developmental Disorders of Infancy and Early Childhood, Revised, Early Development and the Brain, Caring for Infants and Toddlers in Groups, Learning Happens (DVD), adn the Magic of Everyday Moments. Publishes the Zero to Three journal (six yearly issues), a theme-based professional publication, sponsors the National Training Institute, an annual professional training conference in December, provides resources for parents and offers a fellows program.

By State

Alabama

1700 Horizons School

2111 University Boulevard
Birmingham, AL 35233-3107
205-322-6606
800-822-6242
Fax: 205-322-6605
www.horizonsschool.org

Marie McElheny, Admissions Coordinator
Jade Carter, Director

College based, non degree program for students with specific learning disabilities and other mild learning problems. This specially-designed, two-year program prepares individuals for successful transitions to the community. Classes teach life skills, social skills and career training.

1701 Mental Health Board of North Central Alabama

4110 Highway 31 South
PO Box 2479
Decatur, AL 35602-2479
256-355-5904
800-365-6008
Fax: 256-355-6092
E-mail: mentalhealth@mhcna.org
www.mhcnca.org

1702 Mental Health Center of North Central Alabama

4110 Highway 31 S
Decatur, AL 35603
256-355-6091
800-337-3162
E-mail: mentalhealth@mhcna.org
www.mhcnca.org

Provides treatment, education and assitance to people affected by mental health problems.

Year Founded: 1967

1703 National Alliance on Mental Illness: Alabama

4122 Wall Street
Montgomery, AL 36106-2861
334-396-4797
800-626-4199
Fax: 334-396-4794
E-mail: terri@namialabama.org
www.namialabama.org

Greg Carlson, President
Terri Beasley, Executive Director

An organization comprised of local support and advocacy groups throughout the state dedicated to improving the quality of life for persons with a mental illness in Alabama.

Alaska

1704 Alaska Alliance for the Mentally Ill

144 W 15th Avenue
Suite B
Anchorage, AK 99501-5106
907-277-1300
Fax: 907-277-1400
E-mail: info@nami-alaska.org
www.nami-alaska.org

Beth LaCross, Board President
Yvonne Evans, Support Group Facilitator

Mission is to bring consumers and families with similar experiences together to share information about services, care providers, and ways to cope with the challenges of schizophrenia, manic depression, and other serious mental illnesses.

1705 Mental Health Association in Alaska

4045 Lake Otis Parkway
Suite 209
Anchorage, AK 99508-5227
907-563-0880
Fax: 907-563-0881
www.alaska.net/~mhaa/

1706 National Alliance on Mental Illness: Alaska

144 W 15th Avenue
Anchorage, AK 99501-5106
907-277-1300
800-478-4462
Fax: 907-277-1400
E-mail: info@nami-alaska.org
www.nami.org/sites/alaska

Jeanette Grasto, President

A nonprofit, support, education and advocacy organization of consumers, families and friends of people with severe brain disorders such as schizophrenia, schizoaffective disorder, bipolar disorder, major depressive disorder, obsessive-compulsive disorder, panic and anxiety disorders and attention deficit/hyperactivity disorder.

Arizona

1707 Arizona Alliance for the Mentally Ill

2210 N 7th Street
Phoenix, AZ 85006-1604
602-244-8166
800-626-5022
Fax: 602-244-9264
E-mail: azami@azami.org
www.az.nami.org

Sue Davis, Executive Director
Joan Abbot, Membership

Advocacy, education and support groups for families in Arizona who have loved ones dealing with mental health concerns.

1708 Community Partnership of Southern Arizona

4575 E Broadway
Tucson, AZ 85711-3509
520-318-6900
Fax: 520-325-1441
E-mail: nogra@cpsa-rhba.org
www.cpsa-rhba.org

Neal Cash, CEO
Judy Johnson PhD, Deputy Director

Administrative organization responsible for the coordination of behavioral health treatment and preventitive services in southern and southeastern Arizona. We are a local community based nonprofit organization that is dedicated to ensuring the provision of accessible high quality and cost effective behavioral health services for adults and children.

1709 Devereux Arizona Treatment Network

11000 N Scottsdale Road
Suite 260
Scottsdale, AZ 85254-6200
480-998-2920
800-345-1292
Fax: 480-443-5587
www.devereux.org

Jim Cole, Executive Director

National non-profit treatment centers for emotional disorders.

1710 K'E Project: Chinle

PO Box 1757
Chinle, AZ 86503
520-781-6377
Fax: 520-781-4259

Shirley Etsitty

Chinle children and families advocacy corporation.

1711 K'E Project: Fort Defiance

PO Box 309
Fort Defiance, AZ 86504
520-729-2138
Fax: 520-729-5606

Janet Hillis

Children and families advocacy corporation.

1712 K'E Project: Tuba City

PO Box 3937
Tuba City, AZ 86045
520-283-5415
Fax: 520-283-5413

Rueben McCabe

Childrens and families advocacy corporation.

1713 K'E Project: Window Rock

HC 63, Box E
Window Rock, AZ 86047
520-657-3234
Fax: 520-657-3207

Jayne Clark

Children and families advocacy corporation.

1714 Mental Health Association of Arizona

6411 E Thomas Road
Scottsdale, AZ 85251-6005
480-994-4407
800-642-4407
Fax: 480-994-4744
www.mhaarizona.org

Charles Japson, Executive Director
Julie Clark, Community Education

Allfiliate of the National Mental Health Association, we support all people with mental disorders to achieve respect and dignity, to reach their full potential and to be free from stigma and prejudice.

Year Founded: 1954

1715 Mentally Ill Kids in Distress (MIKID)

2642 E. Thomas Road
Phoenix, AZ 85016
602-253-1240
800-356-4543
Fax: 602-253-1250
E-mail: familyresource@MIKID.org
www.mikid.org

Steve Carter, President, Board of Directors
Vicki L Johnson, Executive Director
Sue Gilbertson, Founder

Mission is to provide support and assistance to families in Arizona with behaviorally challenged children, youth, and young adults.

1716 National Alliance on Mental Illness: Arizona
2210 N 7th Street
Phoenix, AZ 85006-1604
602-244-8166
800-626-5022
Fax: 602-244-9264
E-mail: namiaz@namiaz.org
www.namiaz.org

Cheryl Fanning, President

The mission of NAMI Arizona shall be to serve as an alliance of local Arizona Affiliates of NAMI and their members and associate members who are dedicated to the eradication of mental illnesses and to the improvement of the quality of life of persons whose lives are affected by these diseases.

Arkansas

1717 Arkansas Alliance for the Mentally Ill
1012 Autumn Road
Suite 1
Little Rock, AR 72211-3704
501-661-1548
800-844-0381
Fax: 501-664-0264
E-mail: karnold@nami.org
www.ar.nami.org

Rick Owen, President
Kim Arnold, Executive Director

Dedicated to improving the lives of individuals and families affected by mental illness.

1718 National Alliance on Mental Illness: Arkansas
1012 Autumn Road
Suite 1
Little Rock, AR 72211-3704
501-661-1548
800-844-0381
Fax: 501-664-0264
E-mail: karnold@nami.org
www.ar.nami.org

Rick Owen, President
Kim Arnold, Executive Director

A non-profit, grassroots organization dedicated to improving the lives of persons with severe mental illness, their families, and their communities. Formerly known as Arkansas Alliance for the Mentally Ill (AAMI), NAMI Arkansas operates a statewide organization and coordinates a network of affiliates, support groups and field services throughout the state.

California

1719 Assistance League of Southern California
1360 North Street
Andrews Plaza
Hollywood, CA 90028-8529
323-469-1970
Fax: 323-469-5896
E-mail: email@assistanceleague.net
www.assistanceleague.net

Sandy Doerschlag, Executive Director
Janet Harrison, Public Relations

Provides mental health services to childeren over 5 years of age, individuals and families. Parent education and domestic violence classes are available. Services in English, Spanish and Armenian.

Year Founded: 1919

1720 California Alliance for the Mentally Ill
National Alliance for the Mentally Ill
1111 Howe Avenue
Suite 475
Sacramento, CA 95825-8544
916-567-0163
Fax: 916-567-1757
E-mail: grace. mcandrews@namicalifornia.org
www.namicalifornia.org

Laurie Flynn, Executive Director

Nation's leading self-help organization for all those affected by severe brain disorders. Mission is to bring consumers and families with similar experiences together to share information about services, care providers, and ways to cope with the challenges of schizophrenia, manic depression, and other serious mental illnesses. The California office answers questions from hundreds of individuals and groups outside NAMI who turn to us for accurate information about mental illness, NAMI affiliates near them, and where to turn for help.

Year Founded: 1977

1721 California Association of Marriage and Family Therapists
7901 Raytheon Road
San Diego, CA 92111-1606
858-292-2638
Fax: 858-292-2666
www.camft.org

Mary Riemersma, Executive Director

Independent professional organization representing the interests of licensed marriage and family therapists. Dedicated to advancing the profession as an art and a science, to maintaining high standards of professional ethics, to upholding the qualifications for the profession and to expanding the recognition and awareness of the profession.

1722 California Association of Social Rehabilitation Agencies
815 Marina Vista, Suite D
PO Box 388
Martinez, CA 94553-38
925-229-2300
Fax: 925-229-9088
E-mail: casra@casra.org
www.casra.org

Betty Dahlquist, Executive Director
Peggy Harris, Executive Assistant
Dave Hosseini, Public Policy
Sheryle Stafford, Public Policy

Dedicated to improving services and social conditions for people with psychiatric disabilities by promoting their recovery, rehabilitation and rights. A diagnosis is not a destiny.

1723 California Health Information Association

1915 N Fine Avenue
Suite 104
Fresno, CA 93727-1565
559-251-5038
E-mail: info@californiahia.org
www.californiahia.org

Lavonne La Moureaux, Executive Director
Marilyn R Taylor, Operations Manager

Nonprofit association that provides leadership, education, resources and advocacy for California's health information management professionals. Contributes to the delivery of quality patient care through excellence in health information management practice.

1724 California Institute for Mental Health

2030 J Street
Sacramento, CA 95811-3120
916-556-3480
Fax: 916-446-4519
E-mail: sgoodwin@cimh.org
www.cimh.org

Sandra Naylor-Goodwin, Executive Director
Bill Carter, Deputy Director
Ed Diksa, Director Training

Promoting excellence in mental health services through training, technical assistances, research and policy development.

1725 California Psychiatric Association (CPA)

1400 K Street
Suite 302
Sacramento, CA 95814-3916
916-442-5196
E-mail: calpsych@worldnet.att.net
www.calpsych.org

Barbara Gard, Executive Director
Randall Hagar, Director Government Relations

Represents psychiatrists and the interests of their patients as those interests are affected by state government. CPA is area six of the American Psychiatric Association, and is composed of members of APA's five district branches in California.

1726 California Psychological Association

1231 I Street
Suite 204
Sacramento, CA 95814-2933
916-286-7979
Fax: 916-286-7971
E-mail: membership@cpapsych.org
www.cpapsych.org

Jo Linder-Crow PhD, Executive Director
Patricia VanWoerkom, Administration Director

A non-profit professional association for licensed psychologists and others affiliated with the delivery of psychological services.

Year Founded: 1948

1727 California Women's Commission on Addictions

14622 Victory Boulevard
Van Nuys, CA 91411-1621
818-376-0470

1728 Calnet

3625 East Thousand Oaks Blvd
Suite 178
Westlake Village, CA 91362
805-778-0055
Fax: 805-778-0054
www.calnetcare.com

Brent Lamb, President

A not-for-profit network founded to connect accredited mental health and chemical dependency treatment providers with insurers and managed care organizations

Year Founded: 1983

1729 Community Resource Council

1945 Palo Verde Avenue
Suite 202
Long Beach, CA 90815-3445
562-431-8080

Barry Leedy, Executive Director

Agency provides groups and classes to all ages. Sliding fee scale.

1730 Filipino American Service Group

135 N Park View Street
Los Angeles, CA 90026-5215
213-487-9804
Fax: 213-487-9806
E-mail: fasgi@fasgi.org
www.fasgi.org

Susan Dilges, Executive Director
Bryan Jones, Directo, Transitional Programs

FASGI focuses on promoting the physical health and mental well-being of underserved, low-income seniors. It aims to improve the quality of life of all members of the community in Historic Filipinotown and the Greater Los Angeles Area.

Year Founded: 1981

1731 Five Acres: Boys and Girls Aid Society of Los Angeles County

760 W Mountain View Street
Altadena, CA 91001-4925
323-681-4827
TTY: 626-204-1375
E-mail: for5acres@earthlink.com
www.5acres.org

Robert Ketch, Executive Director
Sandi Zaslow, Assistant Executive Director
Cathy Clement, Director Development

Works to: prevent child abuse and neglect, care for, treat and educate emotionally disturbed, abused and neglected children and their families in residential and outreach programs, advance the welfare of children and families by research, advocacy and collaboration, strive for the highest standards of excellence by professionals and volunteers, and provide research and educational resources to families, the community and professionals for the prevention and treatment of child abuse and neglect.

Year Founded: 1888

1732 Gold Coast Alliance for the Mentally Ill

520 N Main Street, Room 203
PO Box 1088
Angels Camp, CA 95222-1088
209-736-4264
Fax: 209-736-4264
E-mail: gcami@goldrush.com
www.nami.org

Laurie Flynn, Executive Director

Local chapter of the national self-help organization (NAMI) for all those affected by severe brain disorders. Mission is to bring consumers and families with similar experiences together to share information about services, care providers, and ways to cope with the challenges of schizophrenia, manic depression, and other serious mental illnesses.

1733 Health Services Agency: Mental Health

1080 Emeline Avenue
Santa Cruz, CA 95060-1966
831-454-4000
Fax: 831-454-4770
TDD: 831-454-2123
E-mail: info@santacruzhealth.org
www.santacruzhealth.org

Rama Khalsa PhD, Health Services Administrator
David McNutt MD, County Health Officer

Exists to protect and improve the health of the people in Santa Cruz County. Provides programs in environmental health, public health, medical care, substance abuse prevention and treatment, and mental health. Clients are entitled to information on the costs of care and their options for getting health insurance coverage through a variety of programs.

1734 Langley Porter Psychiatric Institute at UCSF Parnassus Campus

University of California
401 Parnassus Avenue
San Francisco, CA 94143-2211
415-476-7520

Leonard S Zegans, Director

Conducts clinical studies of psychiatric disorders.

1735 Nation Alliance on Mental Illness: California

101 Hurley Way
Suite 195
Sacramento, CA 95825

916-567-0163
Fax: 916-567-1757
E-mail: membership@namicalifornia.org
www.namicalifornia.org

Ralph Nelson, President
Grace McAndrews, Executive Director

An organization of families and individuals whose lives have been affected by serious mental illness. We advocate for lives of quality and respect, without discrimination and stigma, for all our constituents. We provide leadership in advocacy, legislation, policy development, education and support throughout California.

1736 National Association of Mental Illness: California

1111 Howe Avenue
Suite 475
Sacramento, CA 95825-8544
916-567-0163
Fax: 916-567-1757
E-mail: grace.mcandrews@namicalifornia.org
www.namicalifornia.org

Grace McAndrews, Executive Director

Provides support, information and education for families of seriously mentally ill individuals. NAMI California's efforts focus on support, referral, advocacy, research and education. Available are the Journal Magazine, videos, educational classes, and support groups.

1737 National Health Foundation

Hospital Association of Southern California
6633 Telephone Road
Suite 210
Ventura, CA 93003-5569
805-650-1243
Fax: 805-650-6456
E-mail: mclark@hasc.org
www.hasc.org

Monty Clark, Regional Vice President

Charitable affiliate whose mission is to improve and enhance the health of the underserved by developing and supporting inovative programs that can become independently viable, systemic solutions to gaps in healthcare access and delivery and have potential to be replicated nationally.

1738 Northern California Psychiatric Society

1631 Ocean Avenue
San Francisco, CA 94112-1796
415-334-2418
E-mail: info@ncps.org
www.ncps.org

Marvin Firestone, President
Byron Whittlin, VP
Janice Tagart, Executive Director

A district branch of the American Psychiatric Association. A nonprofit organization that tries to improve the treatment, rehabilitation, and care of the mentally ill, the developmentally disabled, and the emotionally disturbed.

1739 Orange County Psychiatric Society
300 S Flower Street
Orange, CA 92868-3417
714-978-3016
www.ocps.org

Holly Appelbaum, Manager

Works to improve public awareness of mental illness and increase financial support.

1740 UCLA Department of Psychiatry & Biobehavioral Sciences
C8-871 Neuropsychiatry Institute
Box 951759
Los Angeles, CA 90095-1759
310-825-0511
www.psychiatry.ucla.edu

Programs for clinical research treatment for adults and children suffering from psychiatric illness.

1741 United Advocates for Children of California
1401 El Camino Avenue
Suite 340
Sacramento, CA 95815-2746
916-643-1530
Fax: 916-643-1592
TTY: 916-643-1532
E-mail: information@uacc4families.org
www.uacc4families.org

A nonprofit organization that works on behalf of children and youth with serious emotional disturbances and their families.

Colorado

1742 Adolescent and Family Institute of Colorado
10001 W 32nd Avenue
Wheat Ridge, CO 80033-5601
303-238-1231
Fax: 303-238-0500
www.aficonline.com

Mary Panio, Administrator

A licensed and accredited adolescent psychiatric and substance abuse 24 hour facility.

1743 CAFCA
1120 Lincoln Street
Suite 701
Denver, CO 80203-2137
720-570-8402
Fax: 720-570-8408
E-mail: info@cafca.net
www.cafca.net

Skip Barber, Executive Director
Arnie Goldstein, President
Jerry Yager, Vice President

The services provided by member agencies include: adoption, alcohol and drug treatment, day treatment, education, family support and preservation, foster care, group homes, independent living, kinship care, mental health treatment and counseling, pregnancy counseling, residential care at all levels, services for homeless and runaway youth, services for sexually reactive youth, sexual abuse services and transitional living.

1744 CHINS UP Youth and Family Services
10 North Farragut Avenue
Colorado Springs, CO 80909
719-636-2122
Fax: 719-634-0482
E-mail: info@griffithcenters.org
www.chinsup.org

Beth Millern, CEO
Lee Patke, COO of Residential Services
Ken Lingle, Community Programs Director
Laura Patke, Chief Clinical Director

A division of The Griffith Centers for Children, Chins Up is a nonprofit multi-service agency serving children and families in the child welfare and juvenile justice systems. Chins Up strives to heal the broken lives of children and families.

Year Founded: 1974

1745 Colorado Health Networks-Value Options
7150 Campus Drive
Suite 300
Colorado Springs, CO 80920-6553

800-804-5040
Fax: 719-538-1433
www.valueoptions.com

CHN is comprised of partnerships between ValueOptions and seven community mental health centers.

1746 Craig Counseling & Biofeedback Services
611 Breeze Street
Craig, CO 81625-2503
970-824-7475
Fax: 970-824-7475
E-mail: drhadlee@hotmail.com

Frank Hadley MA, DAPA, Director
Bert Dech MD, Medical Director

Full-service mental health and biofeedback center with two male and one female therapist and a board certified adult, adolescent and child psychiatrist.

1747 Federation of Families for Children's Mental Health: Colorado Chapter
2950 Tennyson Street
Denver, CO 80212
303-572-0302
888-569-7500
Fax: 303-433-1605
E-mail: tdillingham@coloradofederation.org
www.coloradofederation.org

Tom Dillingham, Executive Director

To promote mental health for all children, youth and families.

1748 Mental Health Association of Colorado
6795 E Tennessee Avenue
Suite 425
Denver, CO 80224-1614
303-377-3040
800-456-3249
Fax: 303-377-4920
www.mhacolorado.org

Jeanne Mueller Rohner, Executive Director
Michelle Hoffer, Director Development
Kristen Gravatt, Director Community Relations

A nonprofit association providing leadership to address the full range of mental health issues in Colorado. The association is a catalyst for improving diagnosis, care and treatment for people of all ages with mental health problems.

1749 National Alliance on Mental Illness: Colorado
1100 Fillmore Street
Suite 201
Denver, CO 80206-3334
303-321-3104
888-566-6261
Fax: 303-321-0912
E-mail: lberumen@nami.org
www.namicolorado.org

Dennis Hofts, President
Lacey Berumen, Executive Director

A statewide nonprofit organization whose mission is to give strength and hope to individuals with mental illness and their families.

Connecticut

1750 Connecticut Families United for Children's Mental Health
131 Main Street Extension
Middletown, CT 06457
860-343-7330
Fax: 860-343-7805
E-mail: dgarfield@familiesunited.org
www.ctfamiliesunited.homestead.com

Deirdre Cotter Garfield, Executive Director

Helps families achieve better outcomes for their children and youth who are experiencing social, emotional and behavioral challenges through support, training, empowerment, enrichment, and referral programs.

1751 Connecticut National Alliance on Mental Illness
241 Main Street
5th Floor
Hartford, CT 06106
860-882-0236
800-215-3021
E-mail: namicted@namict.org
www.nami.org

Kate Mattias MPH JD, Executive Director

Supports families and consumers whose lives are impacted by serious mental illness; educate families, people with mental illnesses and the general public about brain disorders such as schizophrenia, bipolar disorder, obsessive compulsive disorder, and severe depression among other

and advocate for improved treatment and services for all individuals with mental illnesses, including increased research that will lead to more effective treatment.

1752 Family & Community Alliance Project
110 Washington Street
Hartford, CT 06106-4405
860-566-6810

Support group for families who have children with a mental illness.

1753 Mental Health Association: Connecticut
1480 Bedford Street
Stamford, CT 06905-4714
203-323-0124
Fax: 203-323-0383

To advocate and work for everyone's mental health.

1754 National Alliance on Mental Illness: Connecticut
241 Main Street
5th Floor
Hartford, CT 06106-1897
860-882-0236
800-215-3021
Fax: 860-882-0240
E-mail: namicted@namict.org
www.namict.org

Ralph Oriola, President
Kate Mattias, Executive Director

NAMI-CT is the only Connecticut organization affiliated with NAMI, the nation's leading grassroots family and consumer organization dedicated to improving the lives of people with serious mental illnesses and their families.

1755 Thames Valley Programs
1 Ohio Avenue
Norwich, CT 06360-1567
860-886-4850
866-445-2616
www.natchaug.org

Corey Gartner, Manager

The Thames Valley Programs offer a continuum of care services with the goal of stabilization for children and adolescents who suffer from a broad range of behavioral and emotional problems. Programs utilize a positive, goal oriented approach to treatment that emphasizes patients' strength and success in the effort to maintain recovery and desired outcomes. Individualized, highly structured treatment programs offered at Thames Valley include: Partial Hospital Program, Intensive Outpatient Program, and Extended Day Program.

1756 Women's Support Services
158 Gay Street
PO Box 341
Sharon, CT 06069-341

860-364-1080
Fax: 860-364-5767
E-mail: wssdv@snet.net

Judy Sheridan, Director

Support and advocacy for those affected by domestic violence and abuse as well as women in transition in the towns of Cannan, Cornwall, Kent, North Cannan, Salisbury, and Sharon, CT and nearby NY and MA.

Delaware

1757 Delaware Alliance for the Mentally Ill

2400 W 4th Street
Wilmington, DE 19805-3306
302-427-0787
888-427-2643
Fax: 302-427-2075
E-mail: namide@namide.org
www.namide.org

John P Smoots, President
Richard Taylor, Vice President
Rita A Marocco, Executive Director

A statewide organization of families, mental health consumers, friends and professionals dedicated to improving the quality of life for those affected by life changing brain diseases such as schizophrenia, bipolar disorder and major depression.

1758 Delaware Guidance Services for Children and Youth

1156 Walker Road
Dover, DE 19904-6540
302-678-9316
Fax: 302-678-9317
www.delawareguidance.com

To provide quality mental health services for children, youth and their families.

1759 Mental Health Association of Delaware

100 W 10th Street
Wilmington, DE 19801-6603
302-654-6833

Jim Lafferty, Executive Director

To deliver mental health education, advocacy and support, and to collaborate to provide mental health leadership in Delaware

1760 National Alliance on Mental Illness: Delaware

2400 W 4th Street
Wilmington, DE 19805-3306
302-427-0787
888-427-2643
Fax: 302-427-2075
E-mail: namide@namide.org
www.namide.org

Edward McNally, President
Rita Marocco, Executive Director

A statewide organization of families, mental health consumers, friends, and professionals dedicated to improving the quality of life for those affected by life-changing brain diseases such as schizophrenia, bipolar disorder, and major depression.

1761 National Association of Social Workers: Delaware Chapter

3301 Green Street
Claymont, DE 19703-2052
302-792-0646
E-mail: naswae@aol.com
www.naswde.org

Ed Huffman, Executive Director

Works to enhance the professional growth and development of its members, to create and maintain professional standards, and to advance sound social policies.

District of Columbia

1762 DC Alliance for the Mentally Ill

422 8th Street SE
2nd Floor
Washington, DC 20003-2832
202-546-0646
Fax: 202-546-6817
E-mail: namidc@junc.com
www.nami.org/about/namidc

Adria A Green, President
Nancy Head, Executive Director

Nation's leading self-help organization for all those affected by severe brain disorders. Mission is to bring consumers and families with similar experiences together to share information about services, care providers, and ways to cope with the challenges of schizophrenia, manic depression, and other serious mental illnesses.

1763 Department of Health and Human Services/OAS

200 Independence Avenue SW
Washington, DC 20201-4
202-619-0257
877-696-6775
www.dhhs.gov

The DHHS is the United States government's principal agency for protecting the health of all Americans and providing essential human services, especially for those who are least able to help themselves.

1764 Family Advocacy & Support Association

1289 Brentwood Road NE
Washington, DC 20018-1031
202-526-5436
Fax: 202-265-7877
www.mentalhealth.org

Comprehensive community mental health services program for children and their families.

1765 National Alliance on Mental Illness: District of Columbia
422 8th Street SE
2nd Floor
Washington, DC 20003-2832
202-546-0646
Fax: 202-546-6817
E-mail: namidc@juno.com
www.nami.org/about.namidc

Adrian Green, President
Steven Newman, Executive Director

Established in 1978 as D.C. Threshold, NAMI-DC has been serving the families of persons with mental illness in the nation's capital for over a quarter century.

Florida

1766 Department of Human Services For Youth & Families
2929 NW 17th Avenue
Miami, FL 33142
305-633-6481
Fax: 305-633-5632

1767 Family Network on Disabilities
2196 Main St
Suite K
Dunedin, FL 34698-5694
727-523-1130
800-825-5736
Fax: 727-523-8687
E-mail: fnd@fndusa.org
www.fndusa.org

Rich LaBelle, Executive Director
Tammy Blackburn, Executive Assistant
Tara Bremer, Director of Programs
Joe Hecker, Director of Finance

Family Network on Disabilities is a national network of individuals of all ages who may be at-risk, have disabilities, or have special needs, and their families, professionals and concerned citizens. The mission of Family Network on Disabilities is to ensure through collaboration that individuals have full access to family-driven support, education, information, resources and advocacy, and to serve families of children with disabilities ages birth through 26, who have a full range of disabilities as described in section 602.3 of IDEA.

1768 Florida Alcohol and Drug Abuse Association
2868-1 Mahan Drive
Suite 100
Tallahassee, FL 32308
850-878-2196
Fax: 850-878-6584
E-mail: fadaa@fadaa.org
www.fadaa.org

Mark Fontaine, Executive Director

Statewide membership organization that represents more than 100 community-based substance abuse treatment and prevention agencies throughout Florida. FADAA has provided advocacy for substance abuse programs and the cli-

ents they serve for the past 30 years, as well as quality training programs for substance abuse professionals and up-to-date information on substance abuse to the general public.

1769 Florida Federation of Families for Children's Mental Health
734 Shadeville Highway
Crawfordville, FL 32327-2405
850-926-3514
877-926-3514
Fax: 413-480-2947
E-mail: ejwells@sprynet.com
www.fifionline.org

Conni Wells

A nationally affiliated parent-run organization focused on the needs of children and youth with emotional, behavioral or mental disorders and their families.

1770 Florida Health Care Association
307 W Park Avenue
Tallahassee, FL 32301-1457
850-224-3907
Fax: 850-681-2075
www.fhca.org

Bill Phelan, Executive Director

FHCA is dedicated to providing the highest quality care for elderly, chronically ill, and disabled individuals.

1771 Florida Health Information Management Association
7510 Ehrlich Road
Tampa, FL 33625-1462
813-792-9550
Fax: 813-792-9442
E-mail: fhima@infionline.net
www.fhima.org

Holly Woemmel, MA RHIA, President
Anita Doupnik, RHIA, Director
Carolyn Glavan, MS RHIA, Executive Director

Fosters professional development for its members, promotes privacy and quality of health information through education, communication and advocacy.

1772 Florida National Alliance for the Mentally Ill
316 E Park Avenue
Tallahassee, FL 32301
850-671-4445
877-626-4352
Fax: 850-671-5272
www.namifl.org

Judi Evans, Executive Director
Nichole Theis
Carol Weber

Nation's leading self-help organization for all those affected by severe brain disorders. Mission is to bring consumers and families with similar experiences together to share information about services, care providers, and ways to cope with the challenges of schizophrenia, manic depression, and other serious mental illnesses.

1773 Mental Health Association of West Florida

840 W Lakeview Avenue
Pensacola, FL 32501-1967
850-438-9879
Fax: 850-438-5901

Offers special information and referrals for families of mental health.

1774 National Alliance on Mental Illness: Florida

1615 Village Square Boulevard
Suite 6
Tallahassee, FL 32309-2770
850-671-4445
877-626-4352
Fax: 850-671-5272
E-mail: namifl@namifl.org
www.namifl.org

Linda McKinnon, President

Contains thirty-four affiliates in communities throughout Florida that provide education, advocacy, and support groups for people with mental illness and their loved ones.

1775 National Association of Social Workers Florida Chapter

1931 Dellwood Drive
Tallahassee, FL 32303-4815
850-224-2400
800-352-6279
Fax: 850-561-6279
E-mail: naswfl@naswfl.org
www.naswfl.org

Jim Akin, Executive Director

NASW is a membership organization for professional social workers in Florida. NASWFL provides: continuing education, information center, advocacy for employment and legislation.

Georgia

1776 Georgia Association of Homes and Services for Children

34 Peachtree Street NW
Suite 710
Atlanta, GA 30303-2331
404-572-6170
Fax: 404-572-6171
E-mail: norman@gahsc.org
www.gahsc.org

Normer Adams, Executive Director

GAHSC is an association that is dedicated to supporting those who care for children who are at risk of abuse and neglect. Member agencies of GAHSC include family foster care, community group homes, education programs and others.

1777 Georgia National Alliance for the Mentally Ill

3050 Presidential Drive
Suite 202
Atlanta, GA 30340-3916
770-234-0855
800-728-1052
Fax: 770-234-0237
E-mail: andymont@nami.org
www.nami.org or www.namigeorgia.org

Nora Haynes, President
Jean Dervan, Office Manager

NAMI is nonprofit, grassroots, self-help, support and advocacy organization of consumers, families and friends of people with severe mental illnesses such as schizophrenia, bipolar disorder, major despressive disorder, and other severe and persistent mental illnesses that affect the brain.

1778 Georgia Parent Support Network

1381 Metropolitan Parkway
Atlanta, GA 30310-4455
404-758-4500
800-832-8645
Fax: 404-758-6833
E-mail: slsmith2@ix.netcom.com
www.gpsn.org

Sue Smith, CEO
Kathy Dennis, Vice President
Linda Seay, Secretary/Treasurer

The Georgia Parent Support Network is dedicated to providing support, education and advocacy for children and youth with mental illness, emotional disturbances and behavioral difference and their families.

1779 Grady Health Systems: Central Fulton CMHC

80 Jesse Hill Jr Drive S.E.
Atlanta, GA 30303-3031
404-616-4307
www.gradyhealthsystem.org

Michael Young, CEO
Clayton Sheptherd, Treasurer

Grady Health System improves the health of the community by providing quality, comprehensive health care in a compassionate, culturally competent, ethical and fiscally responsible manner. Grady maintains its commitment to the underserved of Fulton and DeKalb counties, while also providing care for residents of metro Atlanta and Georgia. Grady leads through its clinical exellence, innovative research and progressive medical education and training.

1780 National Alliance on Mental Illness: Georgia

3050 Presidential Drive
Suite 202
Atlanta, GA 30340-3916
770-234-0855
800-728-1052
Fax: 770-234-0237
E-mail: nami-ga@nami.org
www.namiga.org

Nora Hayes, President

The purpose of NAMI Georgia, Inc. is to relieve the suffering and improve the quality of life for mentally ill Georgians and their families.

Hawaii

1781 Hawaii Families As Allies
PO Box 700310
Kapolei, HI 96709-310
808-487-8785
866-361-8825
Fax: 808-487-0514
www.mentalhealth.org

Sharon Nobriga, Co Executive Director

Parent Advocacy group for those with children who have mental disorders.

1782 National Alliance on Mental Illness: Hawaii
770 Kapiolani Boulevard
Suite 613
Honolulu, HI 96813-5212
808-591-1297
Fax: 808-591-2058
E-mail: namihawaii@hawaiiantel.net
www.namihawaii.org

Marjorie Au, President
Eileen Uchima, Executive Director

Nation's leading self-help organization for people living with mental illness and their families. Provides education, support and advocacy for consumers, families and care givers on the challanges of living with schizophrenia, bipolar, and other serious mental illnesses.

Idaho

1783 Idaho Alliance for the Mentally Ill
PO Box 68
Albion, ID 83311-68
208-673-6672
800-572-9940
Fax: 208-673-6685
www.nami.org

Laurie Flynn, Executive Director

NAMI Idaho is a non-profit, tax exempt family organization for people with brain disorders.

1784 National Alliance on Mental Illness: Idaho
260 Skyline Drive
Pocatello, ID 83204-4808
208-232-5791
E-mail: zrmagee@cableone.net
www.nami.org/sites/namiidaho

Doug Call, President

A nationwide organization dedicated to support, education and advocacy on behalf of people with a mental illness and their families.

Illinois

1785 Allendale Association
PO Box 1088
Lake Villa, IL 60046-1088
847-356-2351
888-255-3631
Fax: 847-356-0289
www.allendale4kids.org

Mary Shahbazian, President
Ronald Howard, VP Residential Programs
Dr. Pat Taglione, VP Clinical/Community Services

The Allendale Association is a private, non-profit organization dedicated to the excellence and innovation in the care, education, treatment and advocacy for troubled children, youth and their families.

1786 Baby Fold
108 E Wilow Street
PO Box 327
Normal, IL 61761-327
309-452-1170
Fax: 309-452-0115
E-mail: info@thebabyfold.org

The Baby Fold is a multi-service agency that provides Residential, Special Education, Child Welfare, and Family Support Services to children and families in central Illinois.

1787 Chaddock
205 S 24th Street
Quincy, IL 62301-4492
217-222-0034
888-242-3625
Fax: 217-222-3865
E-mail: dreed@chaddock.org
www.chaddock.org

Gene Simon, President/CEO

A faith-based, not-for-profit organization dedicated to providing hope and healing to children and families. Chaddock specializes in developmental trauma and attachment and provides a wide-range of services including child and adolescent residential treatment, independent living program, group home, special education school serving children 6 to 21, three levles of foster care and adoption

1788 Chicago Child Care Society
5467 S University Avenue
Chicago, IL 60615-5193
773-643-0452
Fax: 773-643-0620
www.cccsociety.org

Nancy Johnstone, Executive Director
Robert L Rinder, Vice President
Mary O'Brian Pearlman, Vice President
Judith Lavender, Secretary

Chicago Child Care Society exists to protect vulnerable children and strengthen their families. We strive to be among the premier providers of high quality and effective child welfare services. We believe the quality of life for future generations depends upon the quality of care provided for children today. We believe children should be provided with services and opportunities that will enable them to reach their optimism physical, mental and social development. We believe all the children are entitled to the protection and nurturing care of adults, preferably within their birth families. However, if family can't fulfill these basic functions, we believe society, by either public or private means should provide the best alternative care.

1789 Children's Home Association of Illinois

2130 N Knoxville Avenue
Peoria, IL 61603-2497
309-685-1047
Fax: 309-687-7299
www.chail.org

Clete Winkelmann, President

Nonprofit, non-sectarian multiple program and social service organization. Giving children a childhood and future by protecting them, teaching them, healing them and by building strong communities and loving families.

1790 Coalition of Illinois Counselors Organization

PO Box 1086
Northbrook, IL 60065-1086
815-787-0515
E-mail: imhca@imhca.org
www.cico-il.org

Daniel Stasi, Executive Director

The Coalition has as its purpose representation of and advocacy for all Illinois counselros and master's level psychologists, their organization and their clients, in relations to government in all its branches and agencies; relevant segments of the private sector, such as insurance, managed care, business and industry, and other mental health providers, health and human services organization and professions

1791 Family Service Association of Greater Elgin Area

22 S Spring Street
Elgin, IL 60120-6412
847-695-3680
E-mail: JZahm@fsaelgin.org
www.fsaelgin.org

Lisa La Forge, Executive Director
Dr. Sandra Angelo, Dir. Consumer Credit Counseling
Jon A Zahm, Developmental/Community Rel.

A non-profit agancy, Family Service Association has served the Greater Elgin Area since 1931. Supported both publicly and privately, most of the funding is received from such local sources as United Ways, corporate and individual contributions and client fees.

1792 Human Resources Development Institute

222 S Jefferson Street
Chicago, IL 60661-5603
312-441-9009
Fax: 312-441-9019
www.hrdi.org

Ollie M Knight, CEO
Kimberly Sutton PhD, Sr VP Clinical/Program Support

Community based behavioral health and human services organization. This nonprofit agency on the south side of Chi-

cago, is concerned with mental health and substance abuse solutuions. Offering more than 40 programs at 20 sites.

Year Founded: 1974

1793 Illinois Alcoholism and Drug Dependency Association

937 S 2nd Street
Springfield, IL 62704-2701
217-528-7335
Fax: 217-528-7340
www.iadda.org

Sara Howe, CEO
Sara Moscato, Associate Director
Pel Thomas, Business Manage
May Jo Pevey, Prevention Coordinator

IADDA is a statewide organization established in 1967 respresenting more than 100 prevention and treatment agencies, as well as individuals who are interested in the substance abuse field. The Association advocates for sound public policy that will create healthier families and safer communites. IADDA members educate government officials in Springfield and Washington, and work to increase the public understanding of substance abuse and addiction.

1794 Illinois Alliance for the Mentally Ill

730 E Vine Street
Suite 209
Springfield, IL 62703-2492
217-522-1403
800-346-4572
Fax: 217-522-3598
E-mail: namiill@sbcglobal.net
www.il.namil.org

Tom Lambert, President

We are committed to a future where recovery is the expected outcome and when mental illness can be prevented or cured. We envision a nation where everyone with a mental illness will have access to early detection and the effective treatment and support essential to live, work, learn and participate fully in their community.

1795 Illinois Federation of Families for Children's Mental Health

PO Box 413
McHenry, IL 60051
815-344-3200
Fax: 847-497-4690
E-mail: cshep@sbcglobal.net
www.iffcmh.nt

Cynthia Sheppard, Executive Director
Stephanie Frank, Associate Director

Dedicated exclusively to helping children with mental health needs and their families achieve a better quality of life.

1796 Larkin Center

1212 Larkin Avenue
Elgin, IL 60123-6098

847-695-5656
Fax: 847-695-0897
www.larkincenter.org

Dennis L Graf MS, Executive Director
Richard Peterson MSW, Executive Director
Martine Lyle, Admissions And QA Director
Michelle Potter MS LCPC, Clinical Director

Our mission is achieved through the efforts of Larkins Center's team of skilled professionals in creative cooperation with the community.

1797 Little City Foundation (LCF)
1760 W Algonquin Road
Palatine, IL 60067-4799
847-358-5510
Fax: 847-358-3291
E-mail: people@littlecity.org
www.littlecity.org

Shawn Jeffers, Administrator
Alex Gianaras, Vice President
Fred G Lebed, Secretary
Quentin Johnson, Treasurer

The mission of Little City Foundation is to provide state of the art services to help children and adults with mental retardation or other developmental emotional and behavioral challenges to lead meaningful, productive, and dignified lives.

1798 Metropolitan Family Services
14 E Jackson Boulevard
Chicago, IL 60604-2259
312-986-4340
Fax: 312-986-4187
E-mail: contactus@metrofamily.org
www.metrofamily.org

Richard L Jones PhD, President and CEO
Nancy Kim Philips, Chief Operating Officer
Denis Hurley, Chife Financial Offcer
Evelyn Engler, Vice President, Human ResourcesS

Our mission is to help Chicago - area families become strong, stable and self-sufficient.

1799 National Alliance on Mental Illness: Illinois
218 W Lawrence Avenue
Springfield, IL 62704-2612
217-522-1403
800-346-4572
Fax: 217-522-3598
E-mail: namiil@sbcglobal.net
www.il.nami.org

Carolyn Jakopin, President
Lora Thomas, Executive Director

A state-wide organization comprised of local Illinois Affiliates dedicated to the task of eradicating mental illness and improving the lives of persons with mental illness and their families.

Indiana

1800 Indiana Resource Center for Autism (IRCA)
Indiana University
2853 E Tenth Street
Bloomington, IN 47408-2601
812-855-6508
800-280-7010
Fax: 812-855-9630
TTY: 812-855-9396
E-mail: prattc@indiana.edu
www.iidc.indiana.edu/irca

Cathy Pratt PhD, Director
Scott Bellini PhD, Assistant Director

Conducts outreach training and consultations, engage in research, develop and disseminate information on behalf of individuals across the autism spectrum, Aspergers syndrome, and other pervasive developmental disorders. Provides communities, organizations, agencies and families with the knowledge and skills to support children and adults in typical early intervention, school, community work and home.

1801 Indiana University Psychiatric Management
PO Box 2087
Indianapolis, IN 46206-2087
317-278-9100
800-230-4876
Fax: 317-278-9142
E-mail: iupm@iupui.edu
www.iupui.edu/

IUPM is a managed mental health program development within Indiana University which links quality mental health and substance abuse providers in the community with a superior academic psychiatric program.

1802 Mental Health Association in Marion County Consumer Services
2506 Willowbrook Parkway
Suite 100
Indianapolis, IN 46205-1542
317-251-0005
Fax: 317-254-2800
www.mcmha.org

Shary Johnson, President
Dan Collins, Vice President
Mike Simmons, Secretary
David Vonnegut-Gabovitch, Treasurer

The mission of the Association is to provide education, advocacy and service through programs designed to promote health; positively affect public attiudes and perceptions of mental illness through support and knowledge; and improve care and treatment of persons with mental ilness.

1803 National Alliance on Mental Illness: Indiana
PO Box 22697
Indianapolis, IN 46222-697
317-925-9399
800-677-6442
Fax: 317-925-9398
E-mail: nami-in@nami.org
www.namiindiana.org

Harriet Rosen, President
Pamela McConey, Executive Director

Dedicated to improving the quality of life for those persons who are affected by mental illness.

including schizophrenia, schizoaffective disorder, schizophreniform disorder and schizotypal personality.

Iowa

1804 Iowa Alliance for the Mentally Ill
5911 Meredith Drive
Suite E
Des Moines, IA 50322-1903
515-254-0417
800-417-0417
E-mail: namiiowa@mchsi.com

Margaret Stout, Executive Director
Margaret Stout, Executive Director

NAMI is dedicated to the education of mental illnesses and to the improvement of the quality of life of all whose lives are affected by these diseases.

1805 Iowa Federation of Families for Children's Mental Health
106 South Booth
PO Box 362
Anamosa, IA 52205
319-462-2187
888-400-6302
Fax: 319-462-6789
E-mail: help@iffcmh.org
www.iffcmh.orgl

Our mission is to link families to community, county and state partners for needed support and services; and to promote system change that will enable families to live in a safe, stable and respectful environment.

1806 National Alliance on Mental Illness: Iowa
5911 Meredith Drive
Suite E
Des Moines, IA 50322-1903
515-254-0417
800-417-0417
Fax: 515-254-1103
E-mail: namiiowa@mchsi.com
www.namiiowa.com

Bruce Sieleni, President
Margaret Stout, Executive Director

Mission is to raise public awareness and concern about mental illness, to foster research, to improve treatment and to upgrade the system of care for the people of Iowa.

1807 University of Iowa, Mental Health: Clinical Research Center
University of Iowa Hospitals & Clinics
200 Hawkins Drive
Iowa City, IA 52242-1007
319-356-3574
877-575-2864

Dr. Nancy C Andreassen, Director

We seek to improve the precision with which specific disease categories are defined and to increase our understanding of their underlying mechanisms and causes. Our primary emphasis is on schizophrenia spectrum disorders,

Kansas

1808 Keys for Networking: Kansas Parent Information & Resource Center
2311 West 33rd Street
Topeka, KS 66611
785-233-8732
800-499-8732
Fax: 785-235-6659
E-mail: jadams@keys.org
www.keys.org

Jane Adams, Manager

A non-profit organization providing information, support, and training to families in Kansas whose children who have educational, emotional, and/or behavioral problems.

1809 National Alliance on Mental Illness: Kansas
PO Box 675
Topeka, KS 66601-675
785-233-0755
800-539-2660
Fax: 785-233-4804
E-mail: namikansas@nami.org
www.namikansas.org

Rick e Cagan, Executive Director

Nation's leading self-help membership organization for all those affected by severe brain disorders. Mission is to provide peer support, education, advocacy and research on behalf of persons affected by serious mental illness and their family members.

Kentucky

1810 Children's Alliance
420 Capitol Avenue
Frankfort, KY 40601-2837
502-875-3399
E-mail: melissa.lawson@childrensallianceky.org

Bart Baldwin, President
Melissa Lawson, Member Services
Nannette Lenington, Business Manager
David Graves, Chairman

Our mission is to shape public policy, inform constituencies and provide leadership in advocacy for Kentucky's children and families.

1811 KY-SPIN
10301-B Deering Road
Louisville, KY 40272-4000
502-937-6894
800-525-7746
Fax: 502-937-6464
E-mail: spininc@aol.com
www.kyspin.com

Non-profit organization dedicated to promoting programs which will enable persons with disabilities and their families to enhance their quality of life.

1812 Kentucky Alliance for the Mentally Ill
10510 LeGrange Road
Building 103
Louisville, KY 40223-1277
502-245-5284
800-257-5081
Fax: 502-245-6390
E-mail: namiky@mindspring.com
www.nami.org

Carol Carrithers, Executive Director
Lois Anderson, President

Nation's leading self-help organization for all those affected by severe brain disorders. Mission is to bring consumers and families with similar experiences together to share information about services, care providers, and ways to cope with the challenges of schizophrenia, manic depression, and other serious mental illnesses.

1813 Kentucky IMPACT
275 E Main Street
Frankfort, KY 40621-1
502-564-7610
Fax: 502-564-9010
E-mail: elizabeth.cloyd@uky.edu
www.ihdi.uky.edu/kydrm/contact_us.htm

Elizabeth Cloyd, Director

Kentucky IMPACT is a statewide program which coordinates services for children with severe emotional disabilities and their families.

1814 Kentucky Partnership for Families and Children
207 Homes Street
1st Floor
Frankfort, KY 40621
502-875-1320
800-369-0855
Fax: 502-875-1399
E-mail: kpfc@kypartneship.org
www.kypartnership.org

Carol W Cecil, Executive Director
Kate Tilton, Program Coordinator

Non-profit organization focused on the need of children and youth with emotional, behavioral or mental disorders and their families. Kentucky state chapter of the Federation of Families for Children's Mental Health.

1815 Kentucky Psychiatric Association
PO Box 198
Frankfort, KY 40602-198
502-695-4843
877-597-7924
Fax: 502-695-4441
E-mail: waltonkpa@aol.com
www.kyppsych.org

Tom Brown, President
Theresa Walton, Executive Director

A non-profit association of medical doctors who have completed a psychiatry residency.

1816 National Alliance on Mental Illness: Kentucky
10510 Lagrange Road
Building 103
Louisville, KY 40223-1277
502-245-5284
800-257-5081
Fax: 502-245-6390
E-mail: ccarrithers@bellsouth.net
www.ky.nami.org

Phillip Gunning, President
Carol Carrithers, Executive Director

NAMI Kentucky is a self-help organization that is part of a nation-wide network devoted to improving the lives of the seriously mentally ill and decreasing the prevailing stigma associated with mental illness.

1817 National Association of Social Workers: Kentucky Chapter
304 West Liberty Street
Suite 201
Louisville, KY 40202-3035

800-526-8098
Fax: 502-589-3602
E-mail: naswky@aol.com
www.naswky.org

Professional membership organization, for state social workers.

1818 ValueOptions
240 Corporate Boulevard
Norfolk, VA 23502-4847
757-459-5100
www.valueoptions.com

Barbara B Hill, CEO
Michael D Alfano, COO

Supports the unique needs of client organizations with traditional managed care products, integrated behavioral health care services, as well as wellness and prevention initiatives and work/life programs.

Louisiana

1819 Louisiana Alliance for the Mentally Ill
PO Box 64585
Baton Rouge, LA 70896-4585
504-343-6928
www.la.nami.org

Diane Pitts, President

Nation's leading self-help organization for all those affected by severe brain disorders. Mission is to bring consumers and families with similar experiences together to share information about services, care providers, and ways to cope with the challenges of schizophrenia, manic depression, and other serious mental illnesses.

1820 Louisiana Federation of Families for Children's Mental Health
5627 Superior Drive
Suite A-2
Baton Rouge, LA 70816-6085
225-293-3508
800-224-4010
Fax: 225-293-3510
www.laffcmh.org

A parent-run organization focused on the needs of children and youth with emmotional, behavioral or mental disorders and their families.

Year Founded: 1991

1821 National Alliance on Mental Illness: Louisiana
PO Box 40517
Baton Rouge, LA 70835-0517
225-291-6262
866-851-6264
Fax: 225-291-6244
E-mail: namilouisiana@bellsouth.net
www.namilouisiana.org

Catherine Tridico, President
Jennifer Jantz, Executive Director

Dedicated to the eradication of mental illnesses and to the improvement of the quality of life for persons of all ages who are affected by mental illnesses

Maine

1822 Maine Psychiatric Association
PO Box 190
Manchester, ME 04351-190
207-622-7743
Fax: 207-622-3332
E-mail: weldridge@mainemed.com

Warene Chase Eldridge, Executive Secretary

To provide treatment for all persons with mental disorder, including mental retardation and substance-related disorders.

1823 National Alliance on Mental Illness: Maine
1 Bangor Street
Augusta, ME 04330-4701
207-622-5767
800-464-5767
Fax: 207-621-8430
E-mail: info@namimaine.org
www.namimaine.org

Julie O'Brien, President
Carol Carothers, Executive Director

Dedicated to improving the lives of all people affected by mental illness NAMI Maine provides services across the entire state of Maine. Available on Twitter and FaceBook.

1824 United Families for Children's Mental Health
PO Box 2107
Augusta, ME 04338-2107

207-622-3309
Fax: 207-622-1661
www.ffcmh.org/local.htm

Pat Hunt

Non-profit organization providing statewide individual emotional suuport, information and referrals, help in locating services, news regarding children's mental health issues and current events, support groups, newsletter, family and professional collaborations, family and systems advocacy, family member participation in policy and system development.

Maryland

1825 Community Behavioral Health Association of Maryland: CBH
18 Egges Lane
Cantonsville, MD 21228-4511
410-788-1865
E-mail: mdcbh@aol.com

Herbert Cromwell, Executive Director

Professional association for Maryland's network of community behavioral health programs operating in the public and private sectors.

1826 Families Involved Together
2219 Maryland Avenue
Baltimore, MD 21218-5627
410-235-5222
Fax: 410-235-4222
E-mail: diane@familiesinvolved.org

Diane Sakwa

Parents of children with special needs.

1827 Health Resources and Services Administration
Parklawn Building
5600 Fishers Lane
Rockville, MD 20857-1
301-594-4110

Donald L Weaver, Administrator
Stephen Smith, Senior Advisor

The Health Resources and Services Administration's mission is to improve and expand access to quality health care for all.

1828 Maryland Psychiatric Research Center
PO Box 21247
Baltimore, MD 21228-747
410-402-7666
Fax: 410-402-7198
www.mprc.umaryland.edu

Dr. William Carpenter Jr, Director

To study the manifestations, causes, and innovative treatment of zchizophrenia.

1829 Mental Health Association of Maryland
711 W 40th Street
Suite 460
Baltimore, MD 21211-2199
410-235-1178
800-572-6426
Fax: 410-235-1180
E-mail: info@mhamd.org
www.mhamd.org

Linda Raines, Executive Director
Diane Cabot, Regional Director
Linda Raines, Executive Director

The Mental Health Association of Maryland is dedicated to promoting mental health, preventing mental disorders and achieving victory over mental illness through advocacy, education, research and service.

1830 National Alliance on Mental Illness: Maryland
10630 Little Patuxent Pkwy
Suite 475
Columbia, MD 21044-3264
410-884-8691
877-878-2371
Fax: 410-884-8695
E-mail: info@namimd.org
www.namimd.org

Janet Edelman, President
Lynn Albizo, Executive Director

A grassroots organization dedicated to education, support and advocacy for persons with mental illnesses, their families and the wider community.

1831 National Association of Social Workers: Maryland Chapter
5740 Executive Drive
Suite 208
Baltimore, MD 21228-1767
410-788-1066
800-867-6776
E-mail: nasw.md@verizon.net
www.nasw-md.org

Daphne Mc Clellan, Executive Director

The mission of the NASW-MD chapter is to support, promote and advocate for the social work profession and its clients, promote just and equitable social policies and for the health and welfare of the people of Maryland.

1832 National Federation of Families for Children's Mental Health
Attn: Marion Mealing, Admin Asst
9605 Medical Center Drive
Rockville, MD 20850
240-403-1901
Fax: 240-403-1909
E-mail: ffcmh@ffcmh.org
www.ffcmh.org/

Sandra Spencer, Executive Director
Kameisha Bennett, Assoc Dir Development & Outreach

A national family-run organization serves to: provide advocacy at the national level for the rights of children and youth with emotional, behavioral and mental health chal-

lenges and their families; provide leadership and technical assistance to a nation-wide network of family run organizations; and collaborate with family run and other child serving organization to transform mental health care in America. The vision of the Federation is, through a family driven approach, to obtain the needed support and services for children and youth with these challenges in order for these children to grow up healthy and be able to maximize their potential.

1833 Sheppard Pratt Health System
6501 N Charles Street
Baltimore, MD 21204-6893
410-938-3800
888-938-4207
E-mail: info@sheppardpratt.org
www.sheppardpratt.org

Steven S Sharfstein, CEO
Dr Robert Roca, VP & Medical Director

Private, nonprofit behavioral health system with inpatients, partial outpatient, residential, crisis, contract management.

1834 Survey & Analysis Branch
5600 Fishers Lane
Rockwall II Suite 15C
Rockville, MD 20857-1
301-443-3343
Fax: 301-443-7926
www.samhsa.gov

Dr. Ronald Manderscheid, Branch Chief

Federally funded agency studying mental health issues.

Massachusetts

1835 Bridgewell
471 Broadway
Lynn, MA 01904-2649
781-599-4240
Fax: 781-593-5731
E-mail: info@bridgewell.org
www.bridgewell.org

Robert Stearns, CEO

Private, non-profit corporation that provides residential, clinical, recreation, day and employment, work training, affordable housing, and multi-cultural and community education services for people with disabilities, their families, and advocates in Northeastern Massachusetts.

1836 CASCAP
678 Massachusetts Avenue
Floor 10
Cambridge, MA 02139-3338
617-492-5559
Fax: 617-492-6928
TTY: 617-234-2992
E-mail: info@cascap.org
www.cascap.org

Michael Haran, Executive Director

Committed to improving the quality of life for members of the community who may be disadvantaged by poverty, disability, or age. Our purpose is to help thos we serve achieve optimal levels of personal autonomy and community integration.

Year Founded: 1973

1837 Concord Family and Youth Services A Division of Justice Resource Institute
380 Massachusetts Avenue
Acton, MA 01720-3743
978-263-3006
Fax: 978-263-3088
www.jri.org

Greg Canfield, Manager

Concord Family and Youth Services, a division of the non-profit Justice Resource Institute, Inc., has been providing help to adolescents, young adults and families since 1814. Programs include a group home for boys, a therapeutic high school in Acton, two residential schools for girls, as well as, parenting and adoption support services through First Connections.

1838 Depression and Bipolar Support Alliance of Boston
115 Mill Street
PO Box 102
Belmont, MA 02478
617-855-2795
Fax: 617-855-3666
E-mail: info@dbsaboston.org
www.dbsaboston.org

Terry Landers, President
Steve Lappen, Vice President
Dennis Hagler, Treasurer

DBSA-BOSTON is a resource for people with affective disorders and their families and friends.

1839 Jewish Family and Children's Services
1430 Main Street
Waltham, MA 02451
781-647-5327
www.jfcsboston.org

Cares for individuals and families by providing exceptional human service and health care programs, guided by Jewish traditions of social responsibility, compassion, and respect for all members of the community. Available on FaceBook.

1840 Massachusetts Alliance for the Mentally Ill
400 W Cummings Park
Suite 6650
Woburn, MA 01801-6528
781-938-4048
800-370-9085
Fax: 781-938-4069
E-mail: namimass@aol.com
www.namimass.org

Laurie Martinelli, Executive Director
Philip Hadley, President

Nation's leading self-help organization for all those affected by severe brain disorders. Mission is to bring con-sumers and families with similar experiences together to share information about services, care providers, and ways to cope with the challenges of schizophrenia, manic depression, and other serious mental illnesses.

1841 Massachusetts Behavioral Health Partnership
120 Front Street
Suite 315
Worcester, MA 01608-1424
508-890-6400
Fax: 508-890-6410
www.masspartnership.com

Elizabeth O'Brien, Manager

The Massachusetts Behavioral Health Partnership manages the mental health and substance abuse services for MassHealth Members who select the Division's Primary Care Clinician Plan.

1842 Mental Health and Substance Abuse Corporations of Massachusetts
251 W Central Street
Natick, MA 01760-3758
508-647-8385

Vicker Di Gravio Iii, CEO

To promote community-based mental health and substance abuse services as the most appropriate, clinically effective, and cost-sensitive method for providing care to individuals in need.

1843 National Alliance on Mental Illness: Massachusetts
400 West Cummings Park
Suite 6650
Woburn, MA 01801-6528
781-938-4048
800-370-9085
Fax: 781-938-4069
E-mail: namimass@aol.com
www.namimass.org

Phil Hadley, President
Toby Fisher, Executive Director

A nonprofit grassroots education and advocacy group dedicated to improving the quality of life for people affected by mental illness.

1844 Parent Professional Advocacy League
59 Temple Place
Suite 664
Boston, MA 02111-1344
617-542-7860
800-537-0446
Fax: 617-542-7832
E-mail: info@ppal.net
www.http://ppal.net

Provides support, education, and advocacy around issues related to children's mental health

Michigan

1845 Borgess Behavioral Medicine Services
1521 Gull Road
Kalamazoo, MI 49048-1640
269-226-8135
Fax: 269-226-7396
www.borgess.com

Paul Spaude, CEO
Denise Crawford MSW, Referal Development Division

Offers patients and families a wide array of services to address their mental health concerns.

1846 Boysville of Michigan
8759 Clinton Macon Road
Clinton, MI 49236-9569
517-423-7451
Fax: 517-423-5442
E-mail: djablons@boysville.org
www.boysville.org

David Jablonski, Director of Communications
Francis Boylan, President/CEO

Boysville of Michigan works with one thousand plus boys and girls and their families on a daily basis in both residential and community based programs throughout Michigan and northwestern Ohio.

1847 Justice in Mental Health Organizations
421 Seymour Avenue
Lansing, MI 48933-1116
517-371-2794
800-831-8035
Fax: 517-371-5770
E-mail: jimhojim@aol.com

Lisa Howell, Executive Director

The JMHO is a non-profit 501 (c) (3) organization in Lansing, Michigan. It is an advocacy group, as well as a mutual self-help organization that offers a network of support to thousands of individuals living in the community.

1848 Lapeer County Community Mental Health Center
1570 Suncrest Drive
Lapeer, MI 48446-1154
810-667-0500
Fax: 810-664-8728
E-mail: iccmhc@tir.com

Michael Vizena, Executive Director
Lauren J Emmons, Associate Director

Comprehensive community mental health services to children and adults of all ages. Services are limited to Lapeer County residents. Most insurance plans are honored. A sliding fee schedule is applied for those without insurance benefits. The center is licensed by the state of Michigan and is fully accredited by JCAHO.

1849 Macomb County Community Mental Health
10 N Main
5th Floor
Mt Clemens, MI 48043-5673

586-469-5258
Fax: 586-307-3898
www.macombcountymi.gov

Ricco Bono, Manager

Provides a wide variety of mental health treatment and support services to adults and children with mental illness, developmental disabilities, and substance abuse treatment needs.

1850 Manic Depressive and Depressive Association of Metropolitan Detroit
PO Box 32531
Detroit, MI 48232-531
734-284-5563
www.mdda-metro-detroit.org

Educates patients, families, and professionals, and the public concerning the nature of depressive and manic-depressive illness as treatable medical diseases; to foster self-help for patients and families; to eliminate discrimination and stigma; to improve access to care; and to advocate for research toward the elimination of these illnesses.

1851 Metropolitan Area Chapter of Federation of Families for Children's Mental Health
5504 Kreger
Sterling Heights, MI 48310-5733
810-978-1221
www.ffcmh.org/local.htm

Pat Boyer

Dedicated to children and adolescents with mental health needs and their families.

1852 Michigan Alliance for the Mentally Ill
921 N Washington Avenue
Lansing, MI 48906-5137
517-485-4049
800-331-4264
Fax: 517-485-2333
E-mail: namimichigan@acd.net
www.mi.nami.org

Hubert Huebl, President

Nation's leading self-help organization for all those affected by severe brain disorders. Mission is to bring consumers and families with similar experiences together to share information about services, care providers, and ways to cope with the challenges of schizophrenia, manic depression, and other serious mental illnesses.

1853 Michigan Association for Children with Emotional Disorders: MACED
230233 Southfield Road
Suite 219
Southfield, MI 48076
248-433-2200
Fax: 248-433-2299
E-mail: info@michkids.org
www.michkids.org

Samuel L Davis, Clinical Director

Ensures that children with serious emotional disorders receive appropriate mental health and educational services so that they reach their full potential. To provide support to families and to encourage community understanding of the need for specialized programs for their children.

1854 Michigan Association for Children's Mental Health

6017 W St Joseph Highway
Suite 200
Lansing, MI 48823-3104
517-336-7222
800-782-0883
Fax: 517-336-8884
www.acmh-mi.org

Robin Laurain, Family Advocacy Consultant

Provides information, support, resources, referral and advocacy for children and youth with mental, emotional, or behavioral disorders and their families

1855 National Alliance on Mental Illness: Michigan

921 N Washington Avenue
Lansing, MI 48906-5137
517-485-4049
800-331-4264
Fax: 517-485-2333
E-mail: namimichigan@acd.net
www.mi.nami.org

Hubert Huebl, President

To assist affiliates, provide support, promote education, pursue advocacy and encourage research on mental illness.

1856 Northpointe Behavioral Healthcare Systems

715 Pyle Drive
Kingsford, MI 49802-4456
906-774-0522
Fax: 906-779-1306
E-mail: info@nbhs.org
www.nbhs.org

Karen Thekan, CEO

Michigan Community Mental Health agency serving Dickinson, Menominee and Iron counties. Provides a full spectrum of managed behavioral healthcare services to the chronically mentally ill and developmentally disabled. A corporate services division provides employee assistance programs both in Michigan and outside the state.

1857 Southwest Counseling & Development Services

1700 Waterman Street
Detroit, MI 48209-2022
313-841-8900
Fax: 313-841-3756
www.swsol.org

John Vancamp, CEO
Graciela Villalobos, Program Director of Outpatient

A mental health agency working to promote community well being. The mission is to enhance the well being of individuals, families and the community by providing effec-

tive leadership and innovative, quality mental health services.

1858 Woodlands Behavioral Healthcare Network

960 M-60 East
Cassopolis, MI 49031-9339
269-445-3043
www.woodlandsbhn.org

Kathy Boes, CEO

Provides community mental health services.

Minnesota

1859 NASW Minnesota Chapter

Iris Park Place, Suite 340
1885 University Avenue W
Saint Paul, MN 55104-3489
651-293-1935
E-mail: email@naswmn.org
www.naswpress.org

Alan Ingram, Executive Director

To promote the profession of Social Work by establishing and maintaining professional standards and by advancing the authority and credibility of Social Work; to provide services to its members by supplying opportunities for professional development and leadership and by enhancing communication among its members; to advocate for clients by promoting political action and community education.

1860 National Alliance on Mental Illness: Minnesota

800 Transfer Road
Suite 7A
Saint Paul, MN 55114-1414
651-645-2948
888-473-0237
Fax: 651-645-7379
E-mail: nami-mn@nami.org
www.namimn.org

David Hartford, President
Sue Abderholden, Executive Director

A non-profit organization dedicated to improving the lives of adults and children with mental illness and their families. NAMI-MN offers programs of education, support and advocacy, and supports research efforts.

1861 North American Training Institute: Division of the Minnesota Council on Compulsive Gambling

314 W Superior Street
Suite 702
Duluth, MN 55802-1868
218-722-1503
888-989-9234
Fax: 218-722-0346
E-mail: info@nati.org
www.nati.org

Elizabeth George, Executive Director

The NATI conducts web based clinical courses to provide specific knowledge and advanced training leading to national certification for professionals in the prevention, treatment, and rehabilitation of patholgical gamblers.

1862 Pacer Center
8161 Normandale Boulevard
Minneapolis, MN 55437-1044
952-838-9000
800-537-2237
Fax: 952-838-0199
TTY: 952-838-0190
E-mail: pacer@pacer.org
www.pacer.org

Paula Goldberg, Executive Director

To expand opportunities and anhance the quality of life of children and young adults with disabilities and their families, based on the concept of parents helping parents.

Mississippi

1863 Mississippi Alliance for the Mentally Ill
411 Briarwood Drive
Suite 401
Jackson, MI 39206-3058
601-899-9058
800-357-0388
Fax: 601-956-6380
E-mail: namimiss1@aol.com
www.nami.org

Teri Brister, Executive Director
Annette Giessner, President

Nation's leading self-help organization for all those affected by severe brain disorders. Mission is to bring consumers and families with similar experiences together to share information about services, care providers, and ways to cope with the challenges of schizophrenia, manic depression, and other serious mental illnesses.

1864 Mississippi Families as Allies
5166 Keele Street
Suite B100
Jackson, MS 39206-4319
601-981-1618
800-833-9671
Fax: 601-981-1696
E-mail: msfam@netdoor.com
www.msfaacmh.org

Tessie Schweitzer, Executive Director

To provide information and emotional support to families, provide education and training for families and professionals and advocate for improvements in the System of Care for Mississippi's children.

1865 National Alliance on Mental Illness: Mississippi
411 Briarwood Drive
Suite 401
Jackson, MS 39206-3058
601-899-9058
803-570-3884
Fax: 601-956-6380

E-mail: namimiss1@aol.com
www.nami.org/sites/namimississippi

Anette Giessner, President
Shirley Montgomery, Executive Director

Missouri

1866 Depressive and Bipolar Support Alliance (DBSA)
730 N Franklin Street
Suite 501
Chicago, IL 60654-7225

800-826-3632
Fax: 312-642-7243
E-mail: info@dbsalliance.org
www.dbsalliance.org

Peter Ashenden, President & CEO
Allen Daniels, EdD, Executive Vice President
Ingrid Deetz, Director, Chapter Relations
Allen Doederlein, Vice President, Development

The Depression and Bipolar Support Alliance is the leading patient-directed national organization focusing on the most prevalent mental illnesses. The organization fosters an environment of understanding about the impact and management of these life threatening illnesses by providing up-to-date, scientifically based tools and information written in language the general public can understand.

Year Founded: 1985

1867 Mental Health Association of Greater St. Louis
1905 S Grand Boulevard
Saint Louis, MO 63104-1542
314-773-1399
Fax: 314-773-5930
E-mail: mhagstleaol.com
www.mhagstl.org

James E House Ii, Executive Director

The Mental Health Association (MHA) of Greater St. Louis serves St. Louis City and the counties of St. Louis, St. Charles, Lincoln, Warren, Franklin and Jefferson. Services include educational literature/reference library, referrals to mental health professionals and self-help groups, representative payee services, educational course (BRIDGES), speakers bureau and more.

1868 Missouri Alliance for the Mentally Ill
1001 SW Boulevard
Suite E
Jefferson City, MO 65109-2501
314-634-7727
800-374-2138
Fax: 573-761-5636
E-mail: mocami@aol.com

Steven R Wilhelm, President
Cindi Keele, Executive Director

The Missouri Coalition of Alliance for the Mentally Ill is a family organization for persons with brain disorders. It has 15 active chapters throughout Missouri.

1869 Missouri Institute of Mental Health
5400 Arsenal Street
Saint Louis, MO 63139
314-877-6401
Fax: 314-877-6405
www.mimh.edu

Dedicated to providing research, evaluation, policy and training expertise to the Missouri Department of Mental Health, other state agencies, service provider agencies, and other organizations and individuals seeking information related to mental health and other related policy areas.

1870 Missouri Statewide Parent Advisory Network: MO-SPAN
440 A Rue Street Francois
Florissant, MO 63031-5018
314-972-0600
Fax: 314-972-0606
www.mo.span.org

Donna Dittrich, Executive Director
Tina Var Vera, Administrative Assistant

The mission of MO-SPAN is to improve the lives of children and youth with serious emotional disorders and their families by supporting and mobilizing families through training, education, advocacy and systems change. MO-SPAN is a statewide, nonprofit organization which is directed by a Board of Directors, the majority of who are parents of children with severe emotional disabilities.

1871 National Alliance on Mental Illness: Missouri
1001 Southwest Boulevard
Suite E
Jefferson City, MO 65109-2501
573-634-7727
800-374-2138
Fax: 573-761-5636
E-mail: sonyabaumgartner@yahoo.com

Tim Harlan, President
Cindi Keele, Executive Director

Montana

1872 Family Support Network
3302 4th Avenue
Suite 103
Billings, MT 59101-1214
406-256-7783
Fax: 406-256-9879
www.ffcmh.org/local.htm

Barbara Sample, Executive Director

Dedicated to children and adolescents with mental health needs and their families.

1873 Mental Health Association of Montana
205 Haggerty Lane Suite 170
PO Box 88
Bozeman, MT 59771
406-587-7774
E-mail: info@montanamentalhealth.org
www.montanamentalhealth.org

Jana Lehman, Interim Executive Director

A statewide education and advocacy organization. Mission is to work for good mental health for all; and for social justice as well as quality services for persons with mental illnesses.

1874 Montana Alliance for the Mentally Ill
554 Toole Court
Helena, MT 59602-6946
406-443-7871
888-280-6264
Fax: 406-862-6357
E-mail: namimt@ixi.net
www.mt.nami.org

Gary Mihelish, President

1875 National Alliance on Mental Illness: Montana
616 Helena Avenue
Suite 218
Helena, MT 59601-3654
406-443-7871
Fax: 406-862-6357
E-mail: info@namimt.org
www.namimt.org

Gary Popiel, President
Matthew Kuntz, Executive Director

Supports, educates and advocates for Montanans with severe mental illnesses and their families.

Nebraska

1876 Department of Health and Human Services Division of Public Health
Licensure Unit
Lincoln, NE 68508-4986
402-471-2115
Fax: 402-471-3577
E-mail: marie.mcclatchey@nebraska.gov
www.dhhs.ne.gov/crl/crlindex.htm

Dr Joann Schaefer, Chief Medical Officer/Director
Helen Meeks, Administrator of Licensure Unit

The Licensure Unit's mission is to assure the public that health-related practices provided by individuals, facilities and programs are safe, of acceptable quality, and that the cost of expanded services is justified by the need.

1877 Mutual of Omaha's Health and Wellness Programs
Mutual of Omaha Plaza
Omaha, NE 68175-1
402-342-7600
800-238-9354
Fax: 402-351-2775
E-mail: grouphealth@mutualofomaha.com.
www.mutualofomaha.com

Daniel P Neary, CEO

Mutual of Omaha's Health and Wellness Programs provide assistance and professional support in a variety of areas including family concerns; depression/anxiety; gambling and other addictions; parenting issues; drug/alcohol abuse; grief issues and life changes.

1878 National Alliance on Mental Illness: Nebraska

415 South 25th Avenue
Omaha, NE 68131
402-345-8101
877-463-6264
Fax: 402-346-4070
E-mail: nami.nebraska@nami.org
www.ne.nami.org/sites/me

Jonah Deppe, Executive Director

The office of NAMI Nebraska, a non-profit organization dedicated to providing support, education and advocacy to and for anyone whose life has been touched by a mental illness

1879 National Association of Social Workers: Nebraska Chapter

PO Box 83732
Lincoln, NE 68501-3732
402-477-7344
877-816-6279
Fax: 402-476-6547
E-mail: naswne@assocoffice.net
www.naswne.org

June Remington, Executive Director

Nebraska chapter is an affiliate of the National Association of Social Workers with a membership of six hundred plus.

1880 Nebraska Family Support Network

3801 Harney Street
2nd Floor
Omaha, NE 68131-3851
402-505-4608
800-245-6081
Fax: 402-444-7722

1881 Pilot Parents: PP
Ollie Webb Center

1941 S 42nd Street
Suite 122
Omaha, NE 68105-2942
402-346-5220
Fax: 402-346-5253
E-mail: jvarner@olliewebb.org
www.olliewebbinc.org

Laurie Ackermann, Executive Director

Parents, professionals and others concerned with providing emotional and peer support to new parents of children with special needs. Sponsors a parent-matching program which allows parents who have had sufficient experience and training in the care of their own children to share their knowledge and expertise with parents of children recently diagnosed as disabled. Publications: The Gazette, newsletter, published 6 times a year. Also has chapters in Arizona and limited other states.

Nevada

1882 National Alliance on Mental Illness: Carson City, NV

Las Vegas, NV 89701-6122
775-246-7364
E-mail: ruthpax@yahoo.com
www.nami.org

Ruth Paxton, Contact

Part of the nation's leading self-help organization for all those affected by severe brain disorders. Mission is to bring consumers and families with similar experiences together to share information about services, care providers, and ways to cope with the challenges of schizophrenia, manic depression, and other serious mental illnesses.

1883 National Alliance on Mental Illness: Nevada

1170 Curti Drive
Reno, NV 89502-1738
775-329-3260
Fax: 775-329-1618
E-mail: joetyler@sdi.net

Joe Tyler, President

1884 Nevada Principals' Executive Program

2355 Red Rock Street
Suite 106
Las Vegas, NV 89146-3106
702-388-8899
800-216-5188
Fax: 702-388-2966
E-mail: pepinfo@nvpep.org
www.nvpep.org

Karen Taycher

To strengthen and renew the knowledge, skills, and beliefs of public school leaders so that they might help improve the conditions for teaching and learning in schools and school districts.

New Hampshire

1885 Monadnock Family Services

64 Main Street
Suite 301
Keene, NH 03431-3701
603-357-4400
Fax: 603-355-3833
E-mail: rboyd@mfs.org
www.mfs.org

Ken Jue, CEO
Gary Barnes, COO
Peter Skalahan, CFO

A nonprofit community mental health center serving the mental health needs of families, buisness and other public and private organizations with comprehensive continuum of education, prevention and treatment services.

1886 National Alliance on Mental Illness: New Hampshire
15 Green Street
Concord, NH 03301-4020
603-225-5359
800-242-6264
Fax: 603-228-8848
E-mail: info@naminh.org
www.naminh.org

Elizabeth Merry, President
Michael Cohen, Executive Director

A statewide education, support and advocacy organization working for a quality, comprehensive mental health service system.

1887 New Hampshire Alliance for the Mentally Ill
15 Green Street
Concord, NH 03301-4020
603-225-5359
800-242-6264
Fax: 603-228-8848
E-mail: naminh@naminh.org
www.naminh.org

Michael Cohen, Executive Director
Sam Adams, President

Nation's leading self-help organization for all those affected by severe brain disorders. Mission is to bring consumers and families with similar experiences together to share information about services, care providers, and ways to cope with the challenges of schizophrenia, manic depression, and other serious mental illnesses.

New Jersey

1888 Association for Advancement of Mental Health
819 Alexander Road
Princeton, NJ 08540-6303
609-452-2088
Fax: 609-452-0627
E-mail: info@aamh.org

Richard McDonnell, Executive Director
Bruce Moehler, Director of Development

A private, non-profit community-based mental health agency licensed by the NJ State Division of Mental Health and Hospitals, that provides comprehensive services to Mercer County individuals and their families whose lives are adversely affected by emotional distress, psychiatric illness and development disability. Fees are based on ability to pay.

1889 Association for Children of New Jersey
35 Halsey Street
2nd Floor
Newark, NJ 07102-3000
973-643-3876
Fax: 973-643-9153
www.acnj.org

Cecilia Zalkind, Executive Director

Association for Children of New Jersey is a statewide non-profit child advocacy organization. They work on behalf of children and families by conducting research, developing and supporting legislation, and maintaining oversight of the policies and programs of New Jersey administrative agencies. An advocate on a broad range of issues affecting New Jersey's children and families, special areas of interest include: budget advocacy; public policy; early education; child health; community advocacy and outreach. ACNJ operates a Children's Legal Resource Center to meet the demand for information on the status of the law and children's rights. Other ACNJ web sites are: www.kidlaw.org and www.makekidscountnj.org

1890 Disability Rights New Jersey
210 S Broad Street
3rd Floor
Trenton, NJ 08608-2404
609-292-9742
800-922-7233
Fax: 609-777-0187
TTY: 609-633-7106
E-mail: advocate@drnj.org
www.drnj.org

Joseph B Young, Executive Director

Legal and non legal advocacy, information and referral, technical assistance and training, outreach and education in support of the human, civil, and legal rights of people with disabilities in New Jersey.

1891 Eating Disorders Association of New Jersey
10 Station Place
Metuchen, NJ 08840-1919

800-522-2230
Fax: 732-906-9307
E-mail: info@edanj.org
www.edanj.org

A non-profit state organization whose mission is to provide supportive services and resources to individuals affected by eating disorders, including family members and friends.

1892 Jewish Family Service of Atlantic County and Cape
3 S Weymouth Avenue
Ventnor City, NJ 08406-2980
609-822-1108
Fax: 609-882-1106
www.jfsatlantic.org

Multi-service familty counseling agency dedicated to promoting, strengthening and preserving individual, family, and community weel-being in a manner consistent with Jewish philosophy and values.

1893 Mental Health Association of New Jersey
1562 US Highway 130
North Brunswick, NJ 08902-3090
732-940-0991
Fax: 732-940-0355
E-mail: naminj@optonline.net
www.naminj.org

Sylvia Axelrod, Executive Director
Mark Perrin, President

Nation's leading self-help organization for all those affected by severe brain disorders. Mission is to bring consumers and families with similar experiences together to share information about services, care providers, and ways to cope with the challenges of schizophrenia, manic depression, and other serious mental illnesses.

1894 National Alliance on Mental Illness: New Jersey
1562 US Highway 130
North Brunswick, NJ 08902-3090
732-940-0991
Fax: 732-940-0355
E-mail: info@naminj.org
www.naminj.org

Mark Perrin, President
Sylvia Axelrod, Executive Director

A statewide non profit organization dedicated to improving the lives of individuals and families who are affected by mental illness. Also provides education, support and systems advocacy to empower families and persons with mental illness.

1895 New Jersey Association of Mental Health Agencies
The Neuman Building
3575 Quakerbridge Road, Suite 102
Mercerville, NJ 08619-1205
609-838-5488
Fax: 609-838-5489
www.njamha.org

Debra L Wentz, PhD, CEO

To champion opportunities that advance its members' ability to deliver accessible, quality, efficient and effective integrated behavioral health care services to mental health consumers and their families.

1896 New Jersey Psychiatric Association
PO Box 428
Bedminster, NJ 07921
908-719-2222
Fax: 908-719-4747
E-mail: psychnj@optonline.net
www.psychnj.org

Theresa M Miskimen MD, President
Carla A Ross, Executive Director

A professional organization of about 100 physicians qualified by training and experience in the treatment of mental illness.

Year Founded: 1935

1897 New Jersey Support Groups
Anorexia/Bulimia Association of New Jersey
10 Station Place
Metuchen, NJ 08840-1919
609-252-0202

Offers various support groups across the state for anorexics and bulimics.

New Mexico

1898 National Alliance on Mental Illness: New Mexico
6001 Marble NE, Suite 8
PO Box 3086
Alburquerque, NM 87190-3086
505-260-0154
Fax: 505-260-0342
E-mail: naminm@aol.com
www.nm.nami.org

Becky Beckett, President
Kim Ahlbom, Additional Contact

1899 Navajo Nation K'E Project-Shiprock
PO Box 1240
Shiprock, NM 87420
505-368-4479
Fax: 505-368-5582

Evelyn Balwin

Provides community-based behavioral and/or mental health and related services to children and families with serious emotional difficulties.

1900 New Mexico Alliance for the Mentally Ill
6001 Marble NE Suite 8
PO Box 3086
Albuquerque, NM 87190-3086
505-260-0154
Fax: 505-260-0342
E-mail: naminm@aol.com
www.naminm.org

Elaine Jones, Executive Director
Elaine Miller, Administrator Assistant

Nation's leading self-help organization for all those affected by severe brain disorders. Mission is to bring consumers and families with similar experiences together to share information about services, care providers, and ways to cope with the challenges of schizophrenia, manic depression, and other serious mental illnesses.

New York

1901 Babylon Consultation Center
206 Deer Park Avenue
Babylon, NY 11702-2857
631-587-1924

Michael J Beck, Owner
Dr Jacob Kesten PhD, Consulting Psychologist

The Babylon Consultation Center is a community based provider of a full gamut of mental health services for over 20 years, and consists of a multi-disciplinary group of professional independent contractors representing the fields of psychology, social work, marriage and family counseling, mediation also education and business consulting.

1902 Compeer
259 Monroe Avenue
Suite B1
Rochester, NY 14607-3632
585-546-8280
800-836-0475
Fax: 585-325-2558
E-mail: compeerp@rochester.rr.com
www.compeer.org

Dana Frame, Executive Director
Andrea Miller, VP

National nonprofit organization which matches community
volunteers in supportive friendship relationships with children and adults recieving mental health treatment.

1903 Eating Disorder Council of Long Island
50 Charles Lindbergh Boulevard
Suite 400
Uniondale, NY 11553-3600
516-229-2393

The EDCLI is a non-profit organization devoted to prevention, education and support prevention of eating disorders,
and support to sufferers of eating disorders, their families
and their friends.

1904 Families Together in New York State
15 Elk Street
Albany, NY 12207-1002
518-432-0333
888-326-8644
Fax: 518-434-6478
E-mail: info@ftnys.org
www.ftnys.org

Non-profit, parent-run organization that strives to establish
a unified voice for children with emotional, behavioral, and
social challenges.

**1905 Families United Network: Parsons Child
Family Center**
60 Academy Road
Albany, NY 12208-3103
518-426-2600
Fax: 518-447-5234
E-mail: valeryj@parsoncenter.org

Joan Valery

County wide peer support organization providing support
and advocacy for the special needs of families caring for
children suffering from emotional, social and behavioral
disorders. Is a local chapter of the national Federation of
Families for Children's Mental Health.

1906 Finger Lakes Parent Network
25 W Steuben Street
Bath, NY 14810
607-776-2164
800-934-4244
Fax: 607-776-4327
www.flpn.org

Patti DiNardo, Executive Director

A parent-governed organization, focused on the needs of
children and youth with emotional, behavioral, and /or
mental disorders and their families. Supports and empowers families so that they can improve the quality of their
lives and help their child to achieve his/her full potential
within the community

1907 Healthcare Association of New York State
1 Empire Drive
Rensselaer, NY 12144-5729
518-431-7600
Fax: 518-431-7915
E-mail: info@hanys.org
www.hanys.org

Dan Sisto, President

Serves as the primary advocate for more than 550
non-profit and public hospitals, health systems, long-term
care, home care, hospice, and other health care organizations throughout New York State.

1908 Mental Health Association in Albany County
260 S Pearl Street
Albany, NY 12202-1809
518-447-4555
Fax: 518-447-4661

To ensure that persons with mental illness are provided a
full range of services that promote stabilization, rehabilitation and recovery for the purpose of enhancing or improving their lives.

1909 Mental Health Association in Dutchess County
510 Haight Avenue
Poughkeepsie, NY 12603-7204
845-486-3403
E-mail: mhadc@hvc.rr.com

The Mental Health Association in Dutchess County is a
voluntary, not-for-profit dedicated to the promotion of
mental health, the prevention of mental illness and the improved care and treatment of persons with mental illnesses.

**1910 Mental Health Association in Orange County
Inc**
73 County Highway 108
Middletown, NY 10940
845-342-2400
800-832-1200
Fax: 845-343-9665
www.mhaorangeny.com

Jean Pavek, President of the Board
Nadia Allen, Executive Director

Seeks to promote the positive mental health and emotional
well-being of Orange County residents, working towards
reducing the stigma of mental illness, developmental disabilities, and providing support to victims of sexual assault
and other crimes.

1911 Metro Intergroup of Overeaters Anonymous
350 Third Avenue
PO Box 759
New York, NY 10010-2310
212-946-4599
E-mail: NYOAMetroOffice@yahoo.com

Offers various support groups and meetings.

1912 National Alliance on Mental Illness: New York
260 Washington Avenue
Albany, NY 12210-1336
518-462-2000
800-950-3228
Fax: 518-462-3811
E-mail: naminys@naminys.org
www.naminys.org

Sherry Grenz, President

The purpose shall be to serve as an alliance of local mutual support, advocacy, self-help groups and individual members at-large dedicated to improving the quality of life for people with serious mental illness and to the eventual eradication of the severe effects of mental illnesses.

1913 National Association of Social Workers New York State Chapter
188 Washington Avenue
Albany, NY 12210-2394
518-463-4741
Fax: 518-463-6446
E-mail: info@naswnys.com
www.naswnys.org

Reinaldo Cardona, Executive Director

The National Association of Social Workers is the largest membership organization of professional social workers in the world, with more than 155,000 members. NASW works to enhance the professional growth and development of its members, to create and maintain professional standards, and to advance sound social policies.

1914 New York Association of Psychiatric Rehabilitation Services
1 Columbia Place
2nd Floor
Albany, NY 12207-1006
518-436-0008
Fax: 518-436-0044
E-mail: nyaprs@aol.com
www.nyaprs.org

Harvey Rosenthal, Executive Director
Kelly Adams, Administrative Coordinator

New York Association of Psychiatric Services (NYAPRS) is a statewide coalition of New Yorkers, who are in recovery from mental illness and the professionals who work alongside them in rehabilitation and peer support services located throughout New York State. NYAPRS' mission is to promote the partnership of consumers, providers and families seeking to increase opportunities for community integration and independence for persons who have experienced a mental illness.

1915 New York Business Group on Health
386 Park Avenue S
Suite 703
New York, NY 10016-8832
212-252-7440
E-mail: nybgh@nybgh.org

Laurel Pickering, Executive Director
Janaera J Gaston MPA, Programs Director

NYBGH is a not-for-profit coalition of 150 businesses and is the only organization in the New York Metropolitan area exclusively devoted to employer health benefit issues. The mission is to provide leadership and knowledge to employers to promote a value-based, market-driven healthcare system.

1916 New York City Depressive & Manic Depressive Group
100 LaSalle Street
Suite 5A
New York, NY 10027-4726
917-445-2399
Fax: 646-349-1761
E-mail: nycdmdg@aol.com
www.columbia.edu/~jgg17/DMDA/PAGE_1.html

Support groups meets regularly at Mt. Siani Hospital. Web page has helpful information and links to mental health sites.

1917 New York State Alliance for the Mentally Ill
260 Washington Avenue
Albany, NY 12210-1347
518-867-3517
800-950-3228
E-mail: info@naminys.org
www.nysaeyc.org

Kristen Kerr, Executive Director
J David Seay, Executive Director
Jeff Keller, Deputy Director

Organization comprised of families of individuals with mental illness. Members work to improve the quality of life for all people with mental illness and to eradicate the stigma associated with mental illness.

1918 Project LINK
Ibero-American Action League
817 E Main Street
Rochester, NY 14605-2722
585-256-8900
Fax: 585-256-0120
E-mail: eamarlin@iaal.org

Hilda Rosario-Escher, CEO

As well as our other activities in the Hispanic community, we continue to be committed to the betterment and quality of life of the mentally ill. We advocate for the severely and persistently mentally ill individual who is at risk of becoming involved or is involved with the criminal justice system. Project LINK operates in partnership with the University of Rochester, Strong-Memorial Department of Psychiatry, Action for a Better Community, Monroe County Mental Health Clinic for Socio-Legal Services, St.

Mary's Hospital, the Urban League of Rochester and the Ibero-American Action League.

1919 State University of New York at Stony Brook Department of Psychiatry and Behavioral Science

101 Nicolls Road
Stony Brook, NY 11794-1
631-444-1251

Evelyn Petralia, Manager
Gabrielle Carlson, MD, Director of Child Psychiatry
Regina T Cline, JD, Administrator

1920 Westchester Alliance for the Mentally Ill

101 Executive Boulevard
Suite 2
Elmsford, NY 10523-1316
914-592-5458
Fax: 914-592-5458
www.nami.org

Provides support and education for families who are feeling alone and in pain with a member of their family suffering from mental illness; no meeting fee.

1921 Westchester Task Force on Eating Disorders

3 Mount Joy Avenue
Scarsdale, NY 10583-2632
914-472-3701

Karen Cohen

A professionally-led support group for people with eating disorders including anorexia, bulimia and compulsive overeating; families and professionals interested in learning about the disorder are welcome to the meetings.

1922 Yeshiva University: Soundview-Throgs Neck Community Mental Health Center

2527 Glebe Avenue
Bronx, NY 10461-3109
718-597-3434

Nirmala Beharry, Manager

Mental health counseling for adults and children. Accepts Medicaid and private insurance. Sliding scale fee.

North Carolina

1923 Autism Society of North Carolina

505 Oberlin Road
Suite 230
Raleigh, NC 27605-1345
919-743-0204
Fax: 919-743-0208
E-mail: info@autismsociety-nc.org

David Lax, Manager
David Laxton, Director of Communications

Committed to providing support and promoting opportunities which enhance the lives of individuals within the autism spectrum and their families

1924 National Alliance on Mental Illness: North Carolina

309 W Millbrook Road
Suite 121
Raleigh, NC 27609-4394
919-788-0801
800-451-9682
Fax: 919-788-0906
E-mail: mail@naminc.org
www.naminc.org

Carol Matthieu, President
Debra Dihoff, Executive Director

The mission of NAMI North Carolina is to improve the quality of life for individuals and their families living with the debilitating effects of severe and persistent mental illness. We work to protect the dignity of people living with brain disorders through advocacy, education, and support.

1925 National Association of Social Workers: North Carolina Chapter

412 Morson Street
PO Box 27582
Raleigh, NC 27611-7582
919-828-9650
800-280-6207
Fax: 919-828-1341
E-mail: naswnc@naswnc.org
www.naswnc.org

Katherine Boyd, Executive Director

NASW is a membership organization that promotes, develops, and protects the practice of social work and social workers. NASW also seeks to enhance the effective functioning and well-being of individuals, families, and communities through its work and through advocacy.

1926 North Carolina Alliance for the Mentally Ill

309 W Millbrook Road
Suite 121
Raleigh, NC 27609-4394
919-788-0801
800-451-9682
Fax: 919-788-0906
E-mail: mail@naminc.org
www.nami.nc.org

Gloria Harrison, Helpline Director

Nation's leading self-help organization for all those affected by severe brain disorders. Mission is to bring consumers and families with similar experiences together to share information about services, care providers, and ways to cope with the challenges of schizophrenia, manic depression, and other serious mental illnesses.

1927 North Carolina Mental Health Consumers Organization

PO Box 27042
Raleigh, NC 27611-7042
919-832-2286
800-326-3842
Fax: 919-828-6999

NC MHCO is a private non-profit organization not affiliated with NAMI NC. This organization has been providing advocacy and support to adults with mental illness since 1989.

1928 Western North Carolina Families (CAN)
PO Box 665
Arden, NC 28704-665
828-277-7325
E-mail: wncfamilies@bellsouth.net

Ann May

Mutual support and community collaboration, provides resources, referrals, education, and advocacy for families who have children with challenging behaviors and serious emotional disorders.

North Dakota

1929 National Alliance on Mental Illness: North Dakota
PO Box 3215
Minot, ND 58702-3215
701-857-3345
E-mail: weros.diane@jobcorps.com
www.nami.org

Diane Weros, President

1930 National Association of Social Workers: North Dakota Chapter
PO Box 1775
Bismarck, ND 58502-1775
701-223-4161
Fax: 701-224-9824

Tom Tupa, Executive Director

NASW Dakotas, serves the critical and diverse needs of the entire social work profession.

1931 North Dakota Alliance for the Mentally Ill
PO Box 3215
Minot, ND 58702-3215
701-852-8202
Fax: 701-725-4334
E-mail: jsabol@ndak.net
www.nami.org

Janet Sabol

Nation's leading self-help organization for all those affected by severe brain disorders. Mission is to bring consumers and families with similar experiences together to share information about services, care providers, and ways to cope with the challenges of schizophrenia, manic depression, and other serious mental illnesses.

1932 North Dakota Federation of Families for Children's Mental Health: Region V
214 2nd Avenue
W Fargo, ND 58078
701-235-9923
Fax: 701-235-9923

Pat Harles

To provide support and information to families fo children and adolescents with serious emotional, behavioral, or mental disorders.

1933 North Dakota Federation of Families for Children's Mental Health
PO Box 3061
Bismarck, ND 58502-3061
701-222-3310
E-mail: carlottamccleary@bis.midco.net
www.ffcmh.org

Carlotta McCleary, Director

To provide support and informatin to families of children and adolescents with serious emotional, behavioral, or mental disorders.

Ohio

1934 Concerned Advocates Serving Children & Families
9195 2nd Street
Canton, OH 44704
330-454-7917
Fax: 330-455-2026

Connie Truman

Support group for families of children diagnosed with mental illness.

1935 Mental Health Association of Summit
405 Tallmadge Road
PO Box 639
Cuyahoga Falls, OH 44222-639
330-923-0688
Fax: 330-923-7573
E-mail: info@mhasc.net
www.mentalhealthassociationofsummitcounty.org

Rudy Libertini, Executive Director
Sandy Soful, Associate Director

The Mental Health Association of Summit is part of a network of professionals and volunteers committed to improving America's mental health seeking victory over mental illness. To help achieve this national goal we are working to improve mental health services, to initiate services where none exist and to monitor the use of mental health tax dollars in the community.

1936 Mount Carmel Behavioral Healthcare
1808 E Broad Street
Columbus, OH 43203-2003
614-251-8242
800-227-3256
Fax: 614-337-7027
E-mail: mcbhinfo@mchs.com
www.mcbh.com

Mark Ridenour, Executive Director
Marc Clemente MD, MBA, Medical Director

Mount Carmel Behavioral Healthcare is a behavioral healthcare management organization offering a cost-effective, comprehensive continuum of behavioral healthcare services.

1937 National Alliance on Mental Illness: Ohio

747 East Broad Street
Columbus, OH 43205-1001
614-224-2700
800-686-2646
Fax: 614-224-5400
E-mail: amiohio@amiohio.org
www.namiohio.org

James C Mauro, Executive Director
Stacey Smith, Director of Operations

Nation's leading selp-help organization for all those affected by severe brain disorders. Mission is to bring consumers and families with similar experiences together to share information about services, care providers and ways to cope with the challenges of schizophrenia, manic depression, and other serious mental illnesses. Available on FaceBook.

1938 National Association of Social Workers: Ohio Chapter

33 N Third Street
Suite 530
Columbus, OH 43215-3514
614-461-4484
Fax: 614-461-9793
E-mail: ohnasw@ameritech.net
www.naswoh.org

Elaine C Schiwy, Executive Director
Sarah E Hamilton, Membership Coordinator

The mission of NASW is to strengthen, support, and unify the social work profession, to promote the development of social work standards and practice, and to advocate for social policies that advance social justice and diversity.

1939 Ohio Association of Child Caring Agencies

400 E Town Street
Suite G-10
Columbus, OH 43215-4700
614-461-0014
Fax: 614-228-7004
E-mail: PWyman@oacca.org
www.oacca.org

Penny M Wyman, Executive Director
George E Biggs, Assistant Executive Director

The Ohio Association of Child Caring Agencies is to promote and strengthen a fully-integrated, private/public network of high-quality services for Ohio's children and their families through advocacy, education, and support of member agencies.

1940 Ohio Council of Behavioral Healthcare Providers

35 E Gay Street
Suite 401
Columbus, OH 43215-3138
614-228-0747
E-mail: staff@ohiocouncil-bhp.org
www.ohiocouncil-bhp.org

Hugh Wirtz, CEO
Brenda Cornett, Membership Services

A trade association representing provider organizations throughout Ohio which provide behavioral healthcare services to their communities.

1941 Ohio Department of Mental Health

30 E Broad Street
Room 1180
Columbus, OH 43215-3414
614-464-0810
877-275-6364
TDD: 614-752-9696
TTY: 888-636-4889

State agency responsible for oversight and funding of public mental health programs and services.

1942 Planned Lifetime Assistance Network of Northeast Ohio

2490 Lee Boulevard
Suite 204
Cleveland Heights, OH 44118-1269
216-321-3611
Fax: 216-321-0021
E-mail: info@planNEohio.org
www.planneohio.org

Provides individualized home-based social services and advocacy to assist families who have a neurobiologically disabled family member to function at their maximum. LISW staff provides therapy and works with existing service providers to ensure quality of care. Offers a wide range of community-based, social, and recreational activities for its participants.

1943 Positive Education Program

3100 Euclid Avenue
Cleveland, OH 44115-2508
216-361-4400
E-mail: pepgen@pepcleve.org

Frank A Fecser Ph D, Executive Director
Tom Valore Ph D, Program Director

The Positive Education Program (PEP) is to help troubled and troubling children and their families build skills to grow and learn successfully.

1944 Six County

2845 Bell Street
Zanesville, OH 43701-1794
740-454-9766
Fax: 740-588-6452
E-mail: info@sixcounty.org
www.sixcounty.org

Helping community mental health needs in Coshocton, Guernsey, Morgan, Muskingum, Noble and Perry counties. In addition to the traditional treatment services, specialized services have been developed to reach people with ever

changing needs. Employee assistance, sheltered employment, intensive outpatient, and residential services.

Oklahoma

1945 National Alliance on Mental Illness: Oklahoma
1920 N Drexel Blvd
Oklahoma City, OK 73107-3925
405-230-1900
800-583-1264
Fax: 405-230-1903
E-mail: nami-ok@swbell.net
www.ok.nami.org

Wayne Merritt, President
Karina Forrest, Executive Director

1946 OK Parents as Partners
132 N.W. 13th Street
Oklahoma City, OK 73103-4808
405-232-2796
866-492-5437
Fax: 405-232-2799
E-mail: parentsaspartners@coxinet.net
www.ffcmh-ok.org

Janice Garvin, President
Emma Mullendore, Vice President
Etka Ahluwalia, Phd., Oklahoma City Representative
George McCaffrey, Esq., Oklahoma City Representative

Oklahoma Federation of Families for Childrens' Mental
Health dba Parents as Partners seeks to involve families in
the decision making process; assist in meeting the needs of
children with emotional, behavioral, mental health issues or
disabilities; and improving the quality of mental health services the children receive in all settings: inpatient, outpatient, education, and within the juvenile justice system.
Parents as Partners is a family run non-profit organization
dedicated to providing support and advocacy for families of
children and adolescents with emotional, behavioral, or
mental health issues and/or disabilities.

1947 Oklahoma Alliance for the Mentally Ill
500 N Broadway Avenue
Suite 100
Oklamhoma City, OK 73102-6200
405-230-1900
800-583-1264
Fax: 405-230-1903
E-mail: nami-OK@swbell.net
www.ok.nami.org

Jeff Tallent, Executive Director
Hope Ingle, President

Nation's leading self-help organization for all those affected by severe brain disorders. Mission is to bring consumers and families with similar experiences together to
share information about services, care providers, and ways
to cope with the challenges of schizophrenia, manic depression, and other serious mental illnesses.

1948 Oklahoma Mental Health Consumer Council
3200 NW 48th
Suite 102
Oklahoma City, OK 73112-5911
405-604-6975
888-424-1305
www.omhcc.org

Becky Tallent, Executive Director

OMHCC is the statewide advocacy organization of and for
mental health consumers. Offers support groups, speakers'
bureau and advocacy consultations on all issues affecting
consumers.

1949 Oklahoma Psychiatric Physicians Association
PO Box 1328
Norman, OK 73070-1328
405-360-5066
Fax: 405-360-0665
E-mail: oklapsychiatry@yahoo.com

Renee Davenport Mixen, Executive Director

District branch of the American Psychiatric Association, is
a medical specialty society recognized world-wide.
Psysicians specialize in the diagnosis and treatment of
mental and emotional illnesses and substance abuse
disorders.

Oregon

1950 National Alliance for Mental Illness: Oregon
3550sE Woodward Street
Portland, OR 97202-1552
503-230-8009
800-343-6264
Fax: 503-230-2751
E-mail: namioregon@qwestoffice.net
www.nami.org/sites/namioregon

Mike Bowen, President
Christopher Bouneff, Executive Director

Dedicated to improving the quality of life for individuals
with mental illness and their families.

1951 National Alliance on Mental Illness: Oregon
3550 SE Woodward Street
Portland, OR 97202-1552
503-230-8099
800-343-6264
Fax: 503-230-2751
E-mail: namioregon@qwest.net
www.nami.org/sites/namioregon

Christopher Bouneff, President
David Delvallee, Executive Director

A statewide grassroots organization dedicated to improving
the quality of life for individuals with mental illness and
their families through support, education, and advocacy.

1952 Oregon Family Support Network
PO Box 324
Marylhurst, OR 97036
503-675-2294
Fax: 503-697-6932

E-mail: ofsn@ofsn.org
www.ofsn.org

Jammie Farish, Executive Director

Oregon families supporting Oregon families with children and adolescents with emotional, behavioral, mental and/or physical challenges and special needs.

1953 Oregon Psychiatric Association

PO Box 2042
Salem, OR 97308-2042
503-370-7019
800-533-7031
Fax: 503-587-8063
E-mail: info@profadminserv.com

John McCulley, Executive Secretary

To ensure human care and effective treatment for all persons with mental disorder, including mental retardation and substance-related disorders.

Pennsylvania

1954 American Anorexia/Bulimia Association of Philidelphia

PO Box 1287
Langhorne, PA 19047-6287
215-221-1864
Fax: 215-702-8944
E-mail: jbsmje@epix.net
www.aabaphila.org

The American Anorexia/Bulimia Association of Philidelphia is non-profit, providing services and programs for anyone interested in or affected by, Anorexia, Bulimia and/or related disorders. Its purpose is to aid in the education and prevention of these life threatening disorders. Referral programs and support groups assist in the treatment and recovery process.

1955 Health Federation of Philadelphia

1211 Chestnut Street
Suite 801
Philadelphia, PA 19107-4120
215-567-8001
Fax: 215-567-7743
www.healthfederation.org

Natalie Levkovich, Executive Director

A private, non-profit membership organization which provides shared services to a consortium of community and federally qualified health centers in Philadelphia.

1956 Mental Health Association of Southeastern Pennsylvania (MHASP)

1211 Chestnut Street
Philadelphia, PA 19107-4103
215-751-1800
800-688-4226
E-mail: mha@mhasp.org
www.mhasp.org

Joe Rogers, Manager
Jack Boyle, SVP/COO

Maryann E Ludwig, VP Finance/CFO
Stephen P Weinstein, Chairman

The Mental Health Association of Southeastern Pennsylvania (MHASP) is a nonprofit citizen's organization that develops, supports and promotes innovative education and advocacy programs. MHASP serves adults, children and family members through our programs and advocacy efforts. It is the mission of the Mental Health Association of Southeastern Pennsylvania to develop, maintain, and promote innovative education and advocacy programs and mental health services in the five counties we represent in a culturally competent manner, serving as a role model and technical assistance resource for state and national organizations and constituencies.

1957 National Alliance on Mental Illness: Pennsylvania

2149 North 2nd Street
Harrisburg, PA 17110-1005
717-238-1514
800-223-0500
Fax: 717-238-4390
E-mail: nami-pa@nami.org
www.namipa.nami.org

Jyoti Shah, President
James Jordan, Executive Director

A statewide non-profit organization dedicated to helping mental health consumers and their families rebuild their lives and conquer the challenges posed by severe and persistent mental illness.

1958 Parents Involved Network

1211 Chestnut Street
Philadelphia, PA 19107-4103
215-751-1800
800-688-4226
E-mail: pin@pinofpa.org
www.pinofpa.org/

Janet Lonsdale, Director

Parents Involved Network of Pennsylvania is an organization that assists parents or caregivers of children and adolescents with emotional and behavioral disorders. PIN provides information, helps parents find services and will advocate on their behalf with any of the public systems that serve children.

1959 Pennsylvania Alliance for the Mentally Ill

2149 N 2nd Street
Harrisburg, PA 17110-1005
717-238-1514
800-223-0500
Fax: 717-238-4390
E-mail: nami-pa@nami.org
www.namipa.org

James W Jordan Jr, Executive Director
Carol Caruso, President

The largest statewide non-profit organization dedicated to helping mental health consumers and their families rebuild their lives and conquer the challenges posed by severe and persistent mental illness.

1960 Pennsylvania Psychiatric Society

777 East Park Drive
PO Box 8820
Harrisburg, PA 17105-8820
717-558-7750
Fax: 717-558-7841
E-mail: papsych@pamedsoc.org
www.papsych.org

A disctrict branch of the American Psychiatric Association, the PPS has 1,800 member physicians practicing in the field of psychiatry. The mission of the Society is to fully represent Pennsylvania Psychiatrists in advocating for their profession and their patients, and to assure access to psychiatric services of high quality, through activities in education, shaping of legislation and upholding ethical standards.

1961 Pennsylvania Society for Services to Children

415 S 15th Street
Philadelphia, PA 19146-1637
215-875-3400
Fax: 215-875-3411
www.pssckids.org

Michael Vogel, Executive Director
Carla Thompson Neal, Program Director

Philadelphia Society for Services to Children is a recognized leader in child abuse prevention in the Delaware Valley. Provides and advocate for services that will help each child to grow up in a safe, stable and supportive family environment.

1962 Southwestern Pennsylvania Alliance for the Mentally Ill

4721 McKnight Road
Suite 216
Pittsburgh, PA 15237-3415
412-366-3788
888-264-7972
Fax: 412-366-3935
E-mail: www.info@namiswpa.org
www.swpa.nami.org

NAMI Southwestern Pennsylvania is a non-profit organization that serves a ten-county region in Southwestern Pennsylvania. We address the increasing need for families and consumers to have a stronger voice in the mental health system.

1963 University of Pittsburgh Medical Center

200 Lothrop Street
Pittsburgh, PA 15213-2582
412-647-2345
800-533-8762
Fax: 412-647-4801
E-mail: upmcweb@upmc.edu
www.upmc.com

Jeffrey A Romoff, President

The University of Pittsburgh Medical Center is the leading health care system in western Pennsylvania and one of the largest nonprofit integrated health care systems in the United States.

Rhode Island

1964 East Bay Alliance for the Mentally Ill

St. Jean Baptiste
328 Main Street
Warren, RI 02885-4359
401-245-2386
www.namiri.org/

Alice Tupaj, Executive Director

Nation's leading self-help organization for all those affected by severe brain disorders. Mission is to bring consumers and families with similar experiences together to share information about services, care providers, and ways to cope with the challenges of schizophrenia, manic depression, and other serious mental illnesses.

1965 Kent County Alliance for the Mentally Ill

Hillsgrove House
70 Minnesota Avenue
Warwick, RI 02818
401-732-0970

Darlene Rousseau, Manager

Nation's leading self-help organization for all those affected by severe brain disorders. Mission is to bring consumers and families with similar experiences together to share information about services, care providers, and ways to cope with the challenges of schizophrenia, manic depression, and other serious mental illnesses.

1966 National Alliance on Mental Illness: Rhode Island

154 Waterman Street
Suite 5B
Providence, RI 02906-3116
401-331-3060
800-749-3197
Fax: 401-274-3020
E-mail: chaznami@cox.net
www.namirhodeisland.org

Chaz Gross, Executive Director
Charles Gross, Executive Director

The mission of NAMI Rhode Island is to educate the public about mental illness; to offer resources and support to all whose lives are touched by mental illness; to advocate at every level to ensure the rights and dignity of those with mental illness; and to promote research in the science and treatment of mental illness.

1967 National Alliance on Mental Illness: Davis Park

VA Hospital
Room 384
Providence, RI 02908
401-568-7636
www.namiri.org

Gayle Frueh, Executive Director

NAMI Rhode Island (the National Alliance for the Mentally Ill of Rhode Island) was founded in 1983 by family members of people with serious mental illnesses.
NAMI-RI is an independent organization which provides support to people with mental illness and their friends or family members, educates professionals and the public

about mental illness, and advocates for improved services for all people with mental illness.

1968 National Alliance on Mental Illness: Rhode Island

82 Pitman Street
Providence, RI 02906-4312
401-331-3060
Fax: 401-274-3020
E-mail: nicknami@aol.com
www.namiri.org/

Thomas Mack, President
Nicki Sahlin, Executive Director

NAMI Rhode Island (the National Alliance for the Mentally Ill of Rhode Island) was founded in 1983 by family members of people with serious mental illnesses. NAMI-RI is an independent organization which provides support to people with mental illness and their friends or family members, educates professionals and the public about mental illness, and advocates for improved services for all people with mental illness.

1969 New Avenues Alliance for the Mentally Ill

Johnston Mental Health Services
1516 Atwood Avenue
Johnston, RI 02919-3223
401-952-5839
www.namiri.org

Gert Orenberg, Executive Director

Nation's leading self-help organization for all those affected by severe brain disorders. Mission is to bring consumers and families with similar experiences together to share information about services, care providers, and ways to cope with the challenges of schizophrenia, manic depression, and other serious mental illnesses.

1970 Newport County Alliance for the Mentally Ill

Channing Memorial
135 Pelham Street
Newport, RI 02840-3174
401-331-3060
www.namiri.org

Mary Berry, Executive Director

Nation's leading self-help organization for all those affected by severe brain disorders. Mission is to bring consumers and families with similar experiences together to share information about services, care providers, and ways to cope with the challenges of schizophrenia, manic depression, and other serious mental illnesses.

1971 Northern Rhode Island Alliance for the Mentally Ill

Landmark Medical Center
Cass Avenue
Cumberland, RI 02864
401-776-0865
www.namiri.org/

Stella Struzik, Executive Director

Nation's leading self-help organization for all those affected by severe brain disorders. Mission is to bring consumers and families with similar experiences together to share information about services, care providers, and ways to cope with the challenges of schizophrenia, manic depression, and other serious mental illnesses.

1972 Parent Support Network of Rhode Island

400 Warwick Avenue
Suite 12
Warwick, RI 02888-1316
401-467-6855
800-483-8844
Fax: 401-467-6903
E-mail: psnofri@aol.com
www.mentalhealth.samhsa.gov/

Cathy Ciano, Executive Director

Organization of families supporting families with children and youth who are at risk for or have serious behavioral, emotional, and/or mental health challenges, having consideration for their backround and values. The goals of PSN are to: strengthen and preserve families; enable families in advocacy; extend social networks, reduce family isolation and develop social policy systems of care. Parent Support Network accomplishes these goals through providing advocacy, education and training, promoting outreach and public awareness, facilitating social events for families, participating on committees responsible for developing, implementing and evaluating policies and systems of care.

1973 Siblings & Offspring Group Alliance for the Mentally Ill

1255 N Main Street
Providence, RI 02904-1867
401-331-3060
www.namiri.org

Bill Emmet, Executive Director

Nation's leading self-help organization for all those affected by severe brain disorders. Mission is to bring consumers and families with similar experiences together to share information about services, care providers, and ways to cope with the challenges of schizophrenia, manic depression, and other serious mental illnesses.

1974 Spouses & Partners' Group Alliance for the Mentally Ill

Butler Hospital
345 Blackstone Boulevard
Providence, RI 02906-4800
401-331-3060
www.namiri.org

Nicki Sahlin, Executive Director

Nation's leading self-help organization for all those affected by severe brain disorders. Mission is to bring consumers and families with similar experiences together to share information about services, care providers, and ways to cope with the challenges of schizophrenia, manic depression, and other serious mental illnesses.

1975 Washington County Alliance for the Mentally Ill
South Shore Mental Health
33 Cherry Lane
Wakefield, RI 02879
401-295-1956
www.namiri.org

Ginny Eastman, Executive Director

Nation's leading self-help organization for all those affected by severe brain disorders. Mission is to bring consumers and families with similar experiences together to share information about services, care providers, and ways to cope with the challenges of schizophrenia, manic depression, and other serious mental illnesses.

South Carolina

1976 Federation of Families of South Carolina
PO Box 1266
Columbia, SC 29202-1266
803-779-0402
866-779-0402
Fax: 803-779-0017
www.ffcmh.org

Diane Revels-Flashnick, Executive Director

Nonprofit organization established to serve the families of children with any degree of emotional, behavioral or psychiatric disorder. The services and programs by the Federation are designed to meet the individual needs of families around the state. Through support networks, educational materials, publications, conferences, workshops and other activities, the Federation provides many avenues of support for families of children with emotional, behavioral or psychiatric disorders.

1977 National Alliance on Mental Illness: South Carolina
PO Box 1267
Columbia, SC 29202-1267
803-733-9592
800-788-5131
Fax: 803-733-9593
E-mail: namisc@namisc.org
www.namisc.org

John Balling, President
Bill Lindsey, Executive Director

1978 National Mental Health Association: Georgetown County
254 Yadkin Avenue
Georgetown, SC 29440-2237
843-527-1435
Fax: 843-546-8101
www.nmha.org/affiliates/directory/index.cfm?doit=all

Everlena Lance, Executive Director

Advocates for people with mental illness including referrals to counseling and provides education about mental illness.

1979 South Carolina Alliance for the Mentally Ill
PO Box 1267
5000 Thurmond Mall Boulevard, Suite 338
Columbia, SC 29201-2390
803-733-9592
800-788-5131
Fax: 803-733-9593
E-mail: namiofsc@logicsouth.com
www.namisc.org

Ken Howell, President
David Almeida, Executive Director

Non-profit with 17 local groups throughout the state. Provide support, education and advocacy for families and friends of people with serious mental illness.

1980 South Carolina Alliance for the Mentally Ill
PO Box 2538
Columbia, SC 29202-2538
803-779-7849
800-788-5131
Fax: 803-733-9593
www.nami.org

Laurie Flynn, Executive Director

Nation's leading self-help organization for all those affected by severe brain disorders. Mission is to bring consumers and families with similar experiences together to share information about services, care providers, and ways to cope with the challenges of schizophrenia, manic depression, and other serious mental illnesses.

1981 South Carolina Family Support Network
PO Box 2538
Columbia, SC 29202-2538
803-779-7849
800-788-5131
Fax: 803-733-9593
www.ffcmh.org/local.htm

Diane Flashnick

Focused on the needs of children and youth with emotional, behavioral or mental disorders and their families.

South Dakota

1982 Brookings Alliance for the Mentally Ill
211 4th Street
PO Box 221
Brookings, SD 57006-221
605-692-8948
E-mail: zippy@brookings.net
www.nami.org/sites/NAMISouthDakota

Nancy Sonnenburg, Executive Director

Nation's leading self-help organization for all those affected by severe brain disorders. Mission is to bring consumers and families with similar experiences together to share information about services, care providers, and ways to cope with the challenges of schizophrenia, manic depression, and other serious mental illnesses.

1983 Huron Alliance for the Mentally Ill
79 Second Street SW
Huron, SD 57350-1903
605-353-6010
800-551-2531
Fax: 605-352-5573
E-mail: maskipper@ccs-sd.org
www.nami.org/sites/NAMISouthDakota

Marcia Skipper, Executive Director

Dedicated to the eradication of mental illness and the improvement of the quality of life of all whose lives are affected by these diseases.

1984 National Alliance on Mental Illness: South Dakota
PO Box 88808
Sioux Falls, SD 57109-8808
605-271-1871
800-551-2531
Fax: 605-271-1871
E-mail: namisd@midconetwork.com
www.nami.org/sites/namisouthdakota

Shelly Fuller, President
Phyllis Arends, Executive Director

Provides education and support for individuals and families impacted by brain-based disorders (mental illnesses), advocate for the development of a comprehensive system of services and lessen the stigma in the general public.

Tennessee

1985 Bridges: Building Recovery & Individual Dreams & Goals Through Education & Support
480 Craighead Street
#200
Nashville, TN 37204-2343
615-250-1176
800-539-0393
Fax: 615-383-1176
E-mail: bridges@tmhca-tn.org
www.3mhca-tn.org/About_Bridges.html

Irene Russell, Executive Director

Based on the belief that those with mental illness can and do recover a new and valued sense of self and purpose in accepting and overcoming the challenges of a disability that has affected every aspect of life: physical, intellectual, emotional, and spiritual.

1986 Memphis Business Group on Health
5050 Poplar Avenue
Suite 509
Memphis, TN 38157-509
901-767-9585
E-mail: information@memphisbusinessgroup.org
www.memphisbusinessgroup.org

To facilitate the purchase of efficient and effective health care services for the Memphis community.

1987 National Alliance on Mental Illness: Tennessee
1101 Kermit Drive
Suite 608
Nashville, TN 37217-5110
615-361-6608
800-467-3589
Fax: 615-361-6698
E-mail: bstaceyscott@namitn.org
www.namitn.org

Elliot Garret, President
Sita Diehl, Executive Director

NAMI Tennessee is a grassroots, non-profit made up of families, consumers and professionals. We are dedicated to improving quality of life for people with mental illness and their families.

1988 Tennessee Alliance for the Mentally Ill
Cherry Cottage
5908 Lyons View Pike
Knoxville, TN 37919-7520
423-602-7900
800-771-5491
www.namitn.org/

Sita Diehl, Executive Director

Nation's leading self-help organization for all those affected by severe brain disorders. Mission is to bring consumers and families with similar experiences together to share information about services, care providers, and ways to cope with the challenges of schizophrenia, manic depression, and other serious mental illnesses.

1989 Tennessee Association of Mental Health Organization
42 Rutledge Street
Nashville, TN 37210-2043
615-244-2220
800-568-2642
E-mail: tamho@tamho.org
www.tamho.org

Charles Blackburn, Executive Director

State wide trade association representing primarily community mental health centers, community-owned corporations that have historically served the needs of the mentally ill and chemically dependent citizens of Tennessee regardless of their ability to pay.

1990 Tennessee Mental Health Consumers' Association
955 Woodland Street
Nashville, TN 37206
615-250-1176
888-539-0393
Fax: 615-383-1176
E-mail: info@tmhca-tn.org
www.tmhca-tn.org

Anthony Fox, Executive Director

A not for profit organization whose members are mental health consumers and other individuals and groups who support our mission. TMHCA recognizes our members as individuals whose life experiences and dreams for the future are invaluable in the structuring of ourplans and policies.

Year Founded: 1988

1991 Tennessee Voices for Children
701 Bradford Avenue
Nashville, TN 37204
615-269-7751
800-670-9882
Fax: 615-269-8914
E-mail: TVC@tnvoices.org
www.tnvoices.org

Charlotte Bryson, Executive Director

Speaks out as active advocates for the emotional and behavioral well-being of children and their families. A non-profit organization of families, professionals, business and community leaders, and government representatives committed to improving and expanding services related to the emotional and behavioral well-being of children. Available on FaceBook and LinkedIn.

1992 Vanderbilt University: John F Kennedy Center for Research on Human Development
PO Box 40
Peabody College
Nashville, TN 37202
615-322-8240
Fax: 615-322-8236
TDD: 615-343-2958
E-mail: kc@vanderbilt.edu
www.kc.vanderbilt.edu

Pat Leavitt PhD, Center Acting Director
Jan Rosemergy PhD, Director Communications

Research and research training related to disorders of thinking, learning, perception, communication, mood and emotion caused by disruption of typical development. Available services include behavior analysis clinic, referrals, lectures and conferences, and a free quarterly newsletter.

Texas

1993 Children's Mental Health Partnership
1430 Collier Street
Austin, TX 78704-2911
512-445-7780
Fax: 512-445-7701
www.mhatexas.org

A coalition of human services providers, parents, educators and juvenile court professionals who care about the special mental health needs of Austin area youth and families.

1994 Dallas Federation of Families for Children's Mental Health
2629 Sharpview Lane
Dallas, TX 75228-6047
214-320-1825
Fax: 214-320-3750
www.mentalhealth.samhsa.gov/databases/MHDR.asp?D1= TX&T

Susan Rogers

The Dallas Federation is an advocacy service for families in need. They act as a liaison between professionals and families in need of specialized services for children with emotional/behavioral problems. They conduct trainings and workshops on national, state and local levels, regarding children's mental health.

1995 Depression and Bipolar Support Alliance Greater Houston
3800 Buffalo Speedway
Suite 300
Houston, TX 77098
713-600-1131
713-468-5463
Fax: 713-600-1137
E-mail: dbsahouston@dbsahouston.org
www.dbsahouston.org

Glenn Urbach LMSW, Executive Director

Provides free and confidential support groups that assist individuals in the recovery of depression and bipolar disorders.

1996 Fox Counseling Service
1900 Pease Street
Suite 310
Vernon, TX 76384-4625
940-553-3783
800-687-9439

Fred Fox, Owner

Marital counseling using PREP, family counseling, ADHD diagnosis and management. Couseling for mental health issues, depression, anxiety, stress, etc.

1997 Jewish Family Service of Dallas
5402 Arapaho Road
Dallas, TX 75248-6905
972-437-9950
Fax: 972-437-1988
E-mail: info@jfsdallas.org
www.jfsdallas.org

Michael Fleisher, Executive Director

1998 Jewish Family Service of San Antonio
12500 NW Military Hwy
#250
San Antonio, TX 78231-1871
210-302-6920
Fax: 210-349-6952
E-mail: johnsonb@jfs-sa.org

1999 Mental Health Association
505 Orleans
Suite 301
Beaumont, TX 77701
409-833-9657
Fax: 409-833-3522
www.mhatexas.org

Jayne Bordelon, Executive Director

Non-profit agency offering free information, referral services, educational programs, and advocay to all of Jefferson County.

2000 National Alliance on Mental Illness: Texas
Fountain Park Plaza III
2800 South IH35, Suite 140
Austin, TX 78704-5700
512-693-2000
800-633-3760
Fax: 512-693-8000
E-mail: rpeyson@namitexas.org
www.namitexas.org

Patti Haynes, President
Robin Peyson, Executive Director

The mission of NAMI Texas is to improve the lives of all persons affected by serious mental illness by providing support, education and advocacy through a grassroots network.

2001 Texas Counseling Association (TCA)
1204 San Antonio
Suite 201
Austin, TX 78701-1870
512-472-3403
800-580-8144
Fax: 512-472-3756
E-mail: jan@txca.org
www.txca.org

Jan Friese, Executive Director

The Texas Counseling Association is dedicated to providing leadership, advocacy and education to promote the growth and development of the counseling profession and those that are served.

2002 Texas Psychological Association
1005 Congress Avenue
Suite 410
Austin, TX 78701-2491
512-280-4099
888-872-3435
Fax: 512-476-7297
E-mail: itexaspsycholog@austin.rr.com
www.texaspsyc.org/

David White, Executive Director

2003 Texas Society of Psychiatric Physicians
401 W 15th Street
Suite 675
Austin, TX 78701-1665
512-478-0605
E-mail: TxPsychiatry@aol.com
www.tsge.org

John R Bush, Executive Director

2004 University of Texas Southwestern Medical Center
5323 Harry Hines Boulevard
Dallas, TX 75390-7200
214-645-2720

Craig Riggs Malloy, President

Utah

2005 Allies for Youth & Families
2900 S State Street
Suite 301
Salt Lake City, UT 84115-3880
801-467-1500
Fax: 801-467-0328
E-mail: wlolo@sisna.com
www.slsheriff.org

Wilton Lolofie, Program Facilitator

The program is a multi-faceted agency commited to solving community issues. They service families with issues in prevention/intervention of delinquency, drugs, mental health, tracking services, and clinical therapy for youth and adults. An 8-week life skills program features life skills and vocational training for youth weekday evenings. Networking resources allow the agency to work closely with official agencies.

2006 DMDA/DBSA: Uplift
444 W. Stonehedge Drive
Salt Lake City, UT 84107-1270
801-264-8193
www.thewindsofchange.org/by_state.html

John W Kreipl

2007 Healthwise of Utah
2505 Parleys Way
Suite 30270
Salt Lake City, UT 84109-1219
801-333-2000
www.insurance.state.ut.us/Chpt30.html

2008 National Alliance on Mental Illness: Utah
450 2 900 E
Suite 160
Salt Lake City, UT 84117
801-323-9900
Fax: 801-323-9799
E-mail: education@maniut.org
www.namiut.org

Alex Morrison, President
Sherri Wittwer, Executive Director

NAMI Utah's mission is to ensure the dignity and improve the lives of those who live with mental illness and their families through support, education and advocacy.

2009 Utah Parent Center
2290 E 4500 Street S
Suite 110
Salt Lake City, UT 84117-4428
801-272-1051
800-468-1160
Fax: 801-272-8907
E-mail: upcinfo@utahparentcenter.org
www.utahparentcenter.org

Helen Post, Executive Director
Jennie Gibson, Associate Director

The Utah Parent Center is a statewide nonprofit organization founded in 1984 to provide training, information, referral and assistance to parents of children and youth with all disabilities: physical, mental, learning and emotional. Staff at the center are primarily parents of children and youth with disabilities who carry out the philosophy of Parents Helping Parents.

2010 Utah Psychiatric Association

310 E 4500 Sth
Suite 500
Salt Lake City, UT 84107
801-747-3500
Fax: 801-747-3501
E-mail: paige@utahmed.org
www.psych.org/dbs_state_soc/db_list/db_info_dyn.cfm

Paige De Mille, Executive Director

Vermont

2011 Fletcher Allen Health Care

111 Colchester Avenue
Burlington, VT 05401-1416
802-847-3339
800-358-1144

Melinda L Estes, MD, President/CEO
Richarad Magnuson, CFO
Angeline Marano, COO
Theresa Alberghini Dipalma, VP/Government External Affairs

2012 National Alliance on Mental Illness: Vermont

132 South Main Street
Waterbury, VT 05676-1585
802-244-1396
800-639-6480
Fax: 802-244-1405
E-mail: namivt@verizon.net
www.namivt.org

Ann Moore, President
Larry Lewack, Executive Director

NAMI-Vermont is a statewide volunteer organization comprised of family members, friends, and individuals affected by mental illness. We have experienced the struggles and have joined together in membership to help ourselves and others by providing support, information, education and advocacy.

2013 Retreat Healthcare

Anna Marsh Lane
PO Box 803
Brattleboro, VT 05302-803
802-257-7755
800-738-7328
Fax: 802-258-3791
TDD: 802-258-8770
www.retreathealthcare.org/

Richard T Palmisano, President/CEO
Gregory A Miller, VP Medical Affairs
Robert Soucy, COO
John E Blaha, VP/CFO

2014 Vermont Alliance for the Mentally Ill

132 South Main Street
Waterbury, VT 05676-1585
802-244-1396
800-639-6480
Fax: 802-244-1405
E-mail: namivt1@adelphia.net
www.namivt.org

Jerry Goessel, Executive Director

Nation's leading self-help organization for all those affected by severe brain disorders. Mission is to bring consumers and families with similar experiences together to share information about services, care providers, and ways to cope with the challenges of schizophrenia, manic depression, and other serious mental illnesses.

2015 Vermont Employers Health Alliance

104 Church Street
P O Box 987
Burlington, VT 05402-987
802-865-0525
Fax: 805-862-5443

Jeanne Keller, MS/ARM, President

2016 Vermont Federation of Families for Children's Mental Health

95 Main Street
PO Bos 507
Waterbury, VT 05601
802-244-1955
800-639-6071
Fax: 802-828-2135
E-mail: kholsopple@vvfcmh.org
www.vffcmh.org

Kathy Holsopple, Executive Director

Supports families and children where a child or youth,age 0-22, is experiencing or at risk to experience emotional, behavioral, or mental health challenges.

Virginia

2017 Anthem BC/BS of Virginia

2220/2221 Edward Holland Drive
Richmond, VA 23230-2519
804-354-2007
Fax: 804-354-2536

Clark Dumont, Anthem East Coast Media Contact

2018 FHC Health Systems

240 Corporate Boulevard
Norfolk, VA 23502-4900
757-459-5100
866-867-2537
www.fhchealthsystems.com

Ronald I Dozoretz MD, Chief Executive Officer

The umbrella of FHC Health Systems' services covers a wide range of behavioral health services, including behavioral health care management services, administration of and management of drug and alcohol testing programs, creation and provision of web-based programs for the health care industry and the provision of laboratory and pharmaceutical services to health care facilities and physician's practices.

2019 Garnett Day Treatment Center
University of Virginia Health System/UVHS
1 Garnet Center Drive
Charlottesville, VA 22911-8572
434-977-3425
Fax: 434-977-8529
www.healthsystem.virginia.edu/internet/homehealth/

Byrd S Leavell Jr, MD, President UVHS

2020 NAMI
2107 Wilson Boulevard
Suite 300
Arlington, VA 22201-3042
703-524-7600
Fax: 703-524-9094
www.nami.org

Michael Fitzpatrick, Executive Director
Lynn Borton, COO

Dedicated to the eradication of mental illnesses and to the improvement of the quality of life of all whose lives are affected by these diseases.

2021 National Alliance on Mental Illness: Virginia
PO Box 8260
Richmond, VA 23226-260
804-285-8264
888-486-8264
Fax: 804-285-8464
E-mail: namiva@comcast.net
www.namivirginia.org

Bill Farrington, President
Mira Signer, Executive Director

Created in 1985 to provide support, education, and advocacy for consumers and families in Virginia affected by mental illness. It is our mission to improve the lives of all those who are affected by serious brain disorders and to fight the stigma that surrounds mental illness.

2022 Parent Resource Center
Division of Special Education And Student Services
Virginia Department of Education
P O Box 2120
Richmond, VA 23218-2120
804-371-7421
800-422-2083
Fax: 804-559-6835
E-mail: judy.hudgins@doe.virginia.gov
www.doe.virginia.gov/VDOE/sess

Judy Hudgins, Specialist

2023 Richmond Support Group
Warwick Medical & Professional Center
7149 Jahnke Road
Richmond, VA 23225-4017
804-320-7881

Kenneth P Brooks, MD
Richard E Curtis, MD

2024 Virginia Beach Community Service Board
Pembroke 6
Suite 208
Virginia Beach, VA 23462
757-437-5770
Fax: 804-490-5736

Jerry W Brickeen, Media Contact

2025 Virginia Federation of Families for   Children's Mental Health
3212 Cutshaw Avenue
Suite 31
Alexandria, VA 22314-2960
804-257-5455
866-798-2363
Fax: 804-257-5593
E-mail: paulaprice@gmail.com
www.mhav.org

Paula Price, Executive Director
Vicki Hardy-Murrell, Director

Mission is to educate, empower and advocate on behalf of individuals, communities and organizations to take ownership and responsibility for mental wellness.

Washington

2026 A Common Voice
Hope Center, Lakewood Boys/Girls Club
10402 Kline Street SW
Lakewood, WA 98499
253-537-2145
E-mail: acvmarge@comcast.net
www.acommonvoice.org

Marge Critchlow, Director
Sharon Lyons, Assistant Director

A parent driven, nonprofit organization funded by Washington State Mental Health. Their goal is to provide support, technical assistance, and to bring Pierce County parents together who have experience raising children with complex needs, facilitaing partnership between communities, systems, familes, and schools.

2027 Children's Alliance
2017 E Spruce
Seattle, WA 98122-5832
206-324-0340
Fax: 206-325-6291
E-mail: seattle@childrensalliance.org
www.childrensalliance.org

Paola Maranan, Executive Director
Deborah Bowler, Administration
Ruth Schubert, Communications

Washington's statewide child advocacy organization. We champion public policies and practices that deliver the essentials that kids need to thrive — confidence, stability, health and safety.

2028 Good Sam-W/Alliance for the Mentally Ill Family Support Group
325 Pioneer Avenue E
Puyallup, WA 98371
206-848-5571
Fax: 206-845-5355
www.nami.org

Gordon Bopp, Director Washington State Office

Nation's leading self-help organization for all those affected by severe brain disorders. Mission is to bring consumers and families with similar experiences together to share information about services, care providers, and ways to cope with the challenges of schizophrenia, manic depression, and other serious mental illnesses.

2029 Kitsap County Alliance for the Mentally Ill
Health Center
109 Austin Drive NE
Bremerton, WA 98312-1806
360-377-7307
E-mail: blackfish5@comcast.net

Juanita Wiggin, Manager
Myra Clodius

Nation's leading self-help organization for all those affected by severe brain disorders. Mission is to bring consumers and families with similar experiences together to share information about services, care providers, and ways to cope with the challenges of schizophrenia, manic depression, and other serious mental illnesses.

2030 Mental Health & Spirituality Support Group
Nami Eastside-Family Resource Center
16315 NE 87th Street
Suite B-11
Redmond, WA 98052-3537
425-489-4084
E-mail: info@nami-eastside.org
www.nami-eastside.org/

John Radoslovich, Email: Johnrad14@Yahoo.Com
Kendra Perkins, Phone: 253-732-8010

Nation's leading self-help organization for all those affected by severe brain disorders. Mission is to bring consumers and families with similar experiences together to share information about services, care providers, and ways to cope with the challenges of schizophrenia, manic depression, and other serious mental illnesses.

2031 National Alliance on Mental Illnes: Whidbey Island
Oak Harbor, WA 98277-8802
360-675-7358
Fax: 360-675-7358

E-mail: info@namiwi.org
www.namiwi.org

Margaret Houlihan

Nation's leading self-help organization for all those affected by severe brain disorders. Mission is to bring consumers and families with similar experiences together to share information about services, care providers, and ways to cope with the challenges of schizophrenia, manic depression, and other serious mental illnesses.

2032 National Alliance on Mental Illness: Washington
500 108th Avenue NE
Suite 800
Bellevue, WA 98004-5060
425-990-6455
800-782-9264
E-mail: office@namigreaterseattle.org

Gordon Bopp, President

2033 North Sound Regional Support Network
North Sound Mental Health Administration
117 North First Street
Suite 8
Mount Vernon, WA 98273-2858
360-416-7013
800-684-3555
Fax: 360-419-7017
TTY: 360-419-9008
E-mail: nsmha@nsmha.org
www.nsmha.org

Charles Benjamin, Executive Director
Greg Long, Deputy Director
Annette Calder, Executive Assistant

It is the purpose of the North Sound Regional Support Network (NSRSN) to ensure the provision of quality and integrated mental health services for the five counties (San Juan, Skagit, Snohomish, Island, and Whatcom) served by the NSRSN Prepaid Health Plan (PHP). We join together to enhance our community's mental health and support recovery for people with mental illness served in the North Sound region, through high quality culturally competent services.

2034 Nueva Esperanza Counseling Center
720 W Court Street
Suite 8
Pasco, WA 99301-4178
509-545-6506

Maria A Morcuende

2035 Pierce County Alliance for the Mentally Ill
304 7th Avenue NW
Puyallup, WA 98371-4321
253-435-4518
www.nami.org

Eric Renz
Nola Renz

Nation's leading self-help organization for all those affected by severe brain disorders. Mission is to bring consumers and families with similar experiences together to share information about services, care providers, and ways to cope with the challenges of schizophrenia, manic depression, and other serious mental illnesses.

2036 Sharing & Caring for Consumers, Families Alliance for the Mentally Ill
NAMI-Eastside Family Resource Center
16315 NE 87th Street
Suite B-11
Redmond, WA 98052-3537
425-885-6264
E-mail: info@nami-eastside.org
www.nami-eastside.org/

Susan Rynas
Bri Wiechmann

Nation's leading self-help organization for all those affected by severe brain disorders. Mission is to bring consumers and families with similar experiences together to share information about services, care providers, and ways to cope with the challenges of schizophrenia, manic depression, and other serious mental illnesses.

2037 South King County Alliance for the Mentally Ill
515 West Harrison Street
Suite 215
Kent, WA 98032-4403
253-854-6264
E-mail: namisouthking@aol.com
www.nami.org/sites/NAMISouthKingCounty

Jim Adams
Sandy Klungness

Nation's leading self-help organization for all those affected by severe brain disorders. Mission is to bring consumers and families with similar experiences together to share information about services, care providers, and ways to cope with the challenges of schizophrenia, manic depression, and other serious mental illnesses.

2038 Spanish Support Group Alliance for the Mentally Ill
NAMI-Eastside
2601 Elliott Avenue
Suite 4143
Seattle, WA 98121-1399
425-747-7892
E-mail: remmedicalraulmunoz@comcast.net
www.nami-eastside.org/

Gordon Bopp, NAMI-WA Contact Information

Nation's leading self-help organization for all those affected by severe brain disorders. Mission is to bring consumers and families with similar experiences together to share information about services, care providers, and ways to cope with the challenges of schizophrenia, manic depression, and other serious mental illnesses.

2039 Spokane Mental Health
107 South Division Street
Spokane, WA 99202-1510
509-838-4651
Fax: 509-458-7456
www.smhca.org

David Panken, CEO
Jennifer Allen, UC Coordinator

Since 1970, Spokane Mental Health, a not-for-profit organization, has served children, families, adults and elders throughout Spokane County. Our professional staff provides quality treatment and rehabilitation for those with mental illness and co-occurring disorders. These services include crisis response services; individual, family and group therapy; case management and support; vocational rehabilitation; psychiatric and psychological services; medication management and consumer education. We tailor services to the unique needs and strengths of each person seeking care.

2040 Washington Advocates for the Mentally Ill
NAMI Eastside Family Resource Center
16315 NE 87th Street
Suite B-11
Redmond, WA 98052-3537
425-885-6264
800-782-9264
E-mail: info@nami-eastside.org
www.nami-eastside.org/

Gordon Bopp, NAMI-WA Contact Information

Nation's leading self-help organization for all those affected by severe brain disorders. Mission is to bring consumers and families with similar experiences together to share information about services, care providers, and ways to cope with the challenges of schizophrenia, manic depression, and other serious mental illnesses.

2041 Washington Institute for Mental Illness Research and Training
Washington State University, Spokane
PO Box 1495
Spokane, WA 99210-1495
509-358-7514
Fax: 509-358-7619
www.spokane.wsu.edu/research&service/

Michael Hendrix, Director
Sandie Kruse, Training Coordinator

Governmental organization focusing on mental illness research.

2042 Washington State Psychological Association
711 North 35th Street
Suite 206
Seattle, WA 98103-3420
206-547-4220
Fax: 206-547-6366
E-mail: wspa@wapsych.org
www.wapsych.org

Doug Wear, Ph.D, Executive Director
Wren St. Hilaire, Assistant Director

To support, promote and advance the science, education and practice of psychology in the public interest.

West Virginia

2043 CAMC Family Medicine Center of Charleston
1201 Washington Street East
Suite 108
Charleston, WV 25301
304-347-4600
Fax: 304-347-4621
www.hsc.wvu.edu/charleston/familymed/

Robert M D'Alessandri, MD, Vice President Health Sciences

2044 Mountain State Parent Child and Adolescent Contacts
1201 Garfield Street
McMechen, WV 26003-9062
304-233-5399
800-244-5385
Fax: 304-233-3847
www.mspcan.org

Terrie Isaly, Fast Track Program Director

A private non-profit, family-run organization that improves outcomes for children with serious emotional disorders and their families.

2045 National Alliance on Mental Illness: West Virginia
21 Regal Oaks
Barboursville, WV 25504-9639
304-736-2542
800-598-5653
Fax: 304-342-0499
E-mail: namiwv@aol.com
www.namiwv.org

Kathleen Devoge, President

The voice for the families of those individuals with a serious mental illness.

Wisconsin

2046 Child and Adolescent Psychopharmacology Information
Wisconsin Psychiatric Institute and Clinic
6001 Research Park Boulevard
#1568
Madison, WI 53719-1176
608-263-6098
www.psychiatry.wisc.edu

Jeanie Jundt, Manager

2047 Families United of Milwaukee
2733 West Vilet Street
Milwaukee, WI 53205
414-344-7777
Fax: 414-344-0298

E-mail: families@ameritech.net
www.ffcmh.org
Hugh Davis

2048 National Alliance on Mental Illness: Wisconsin
4233 West Beltline Highway
Madison, WI 53711-3814
608-268-6000
800-236-2988
Fax: 608-268-6004
E-mail: nami@namiwisconsin.org
www.namiwisconsin.org

Lannia Syren, Executive Director/CEO

The mission of NAMI Wisconsin is to improve the quality of life of people affected by mental illnesses and to promote recovery.

2049 Stoughton Family Counseling
1520 Vernon Street
Stoughton, WI 53589-2293
608-873-6422
Fax: 608-873-6014

Patricia Renault, Manager

2050 Wisconsin Alliance for the Mentally Ill NAMI-Wisconsin
4233 West Beltline Highway
Madison, WI 53711-3814
608-268-6000
800-236-2988
E-mail: nami@namiwisconsin.org
www.namiwisconsin.org

Lannia Syren, Executive Director
Donna Wren, Executive Director

Self-help organization for all those affected by severe brain disorders. Mission is to bring consumers and families with similar experiences together to share information about services, care providers, and ways to cope with the challanges of schizophrenia, manic depression, and other serious mental illnesses.

2051 Wisconsin Association of Family and Child Agency
131 W Wilson Street
Suite 901
Madison, WI 53703-3259
608-257-5939
www.wafca.org

Linda A Hall, Executive Director

2052 Wisconsin Family Ties
16 N Carroll Street
Suite 640
Madison, WI 53703-2783
608-267-6888
800-422-7145
Fax: 608-267-6801

E-mail: info@wifamilyties.org
www.wifamilyties.org

Hugh Davis, Executive Director
Joan Maynard, Information Referral Coordinator

Wyoming

2053 Central Wyoming Behavioral Health at Lander Valley
1320 Bishop Randall Drive
Lander, WY 82520-3939
307-332-5700
800-788-9446
Fax: 307-335-6465
www.landerhospital.com/patientservices.htm

Rebecca K Smith

2054 National Alliance on Mental Illness: Wyoming
133 W 6th Street
Casper, WY 82601-3124
307-234-0440
888-882-4968
Fax: 307-265-0968
E-mail: nami-wyo@qwest.net
www.nami.org/sites/namiwyoming

Jane Johnson, President
Anna Edwards, Executive Director

To improve the quality of life for those who suffer from depression, bipolar disorder, schizophrenia, obsessive compulsive disorder, panic disorder, autism, borderline personality disorder and other severe and persistent mental illnesses that affect the brain

2055 Uplift
200 West 17th Street
Suite 664
Cheyenne, WY 82001-4434
307-778-8686
888-875-4383
Fax: 307-778-8681
E-mail: uplift@wyoming.com
www.upliftwy.org/

Ron Vigil, President
Peggy Nikkel, Executive Director
Jane Caton, Vice President

Wyoming Chapter of the Federation of Familes for Children's Mental Health. Providing support, education, advocacy, information and referral for parents and professionals focusing on emotional, behavioral and learning needs of children and youth.

2056 Wyoming Alliance for the Mentally Ill
NAMI Wyoming
133 W 6th Street
Casper, WY 82601-3124
307-234-0440
888-882-4968
E-mail: nami-wyo@qwest.net
www.nami.org

Anna Edwards, Executive Director

Nation's leading self-help organization for all those affected by severe brain disorders. Mission is to bring consumers and families with similar experiences together to share information about services, care providers, and ways to cope with the challenges of schizophrenia, manic depression, and other serious mental illnesses.

Government Agencies

Federal

2057 Administration for Children and Families
370 L'Enfant Promenade SW
Washington, DC 20201-1
202-401-4802
Fax: 202-401-5706
www.acf.hhs.gov/index.html

Kenneth Wolfe, Acting Director
Joan E Ohl, Commissioner

Responsible for federal programs that promotes the economic and social well-being of families, children, individuals, and communities.

2058 Administration for Children, Youth and Families
US Department of Health & Human Services
370 L'Enfant Promenade SW
Washington, DC 20201-1
202-401-4802
Fax: 202-401-5706
www.acf.hhs.gov/programs/acyf/acyf.htm

Kenneth Wolfe, Acting Director
Joan E Ohl, Commissioner

Advises Health and Human Services department on plans and programs related to early childhood development; operates the Head Start day care and other related child service programs; provides leadership, advice, and services that affect the general well-being of children and youths.

2059 Administration on Aging
1 Massachusetts Avenue
Suites 4100 & 5100
Washington, DC 20201-1
202-619-0724
E-mail: aoainfo@aoahhs.gov
www.aoa.gov

One of the nation's largest providers of home and community-based care for older persons and their caregivers. The mission is to promote the dignity and independence of older people, and help society prepare for an aging population.

2060 Administration on Developmental Disabilities
US Department of Health & Human Services
370 L'Enfant Promenade SW
Washington, DC 20201-1
202-690-6590
Fax: 202-690-6904
www.acf.hhs.gov/programs/add

Joan Ohl, Commissioner
Kenneth Wolfe, Acting Director

Develops and administers programs protecting rights and promoting independence, productivity and inclusion; funds state grants, protection and advocacy programs, University Affiliated Programs and other national projects.

2061 Agency for Healthcare Research and Quality: Office of Communications and Knowledge Transfer
540 Gaither Road
Suite 2000
Rockville, MD 20850-6649
301-427-1364
www.ahrq.org

Provides policymakers and other health care leaders with information needed to make critical health care decisions.

2062 Association of Maternal and Child Health Programs (AMCHP)
1220 19th Street NW
Suite 801
Washington, DC 20036-2435
202-775-0436
Fax: 202-775-0061
E-mail: lramo@amchp.org
www.amchp.org

Lauren Raskin-Ramos, Director Of Programs
Michael Fraser, CEO

National non-profit organization representing state public health workers. Provides leadership to assure the health and well-being of women of reproductive age, children, youth, including those with special health care needs and their families.

2063 Center for Mental Health Services Homeless Programs Branch
Substance Abuse and Mental Health Services Administration
1 Choke Cherry Road
Rockville, MD 20857-1
240-276-1310
Fax: 240-276-1320
www.samhsa.gov

Federal agency concerned with the prevention and treatment of mental illness and the promotion of mental health. Homeless Programs Branch administers a variety of programs and activities. Provides professional leadership for collaborative intergovernmental initiatives designed to assist persons with mental illnesses who are homeless. Also supports a contract for the National Resource Center on Homelessness and Mental Illness.

2064 Center for Substance Abuse Treatment
Substance Abuse Mental Health Services Administration
1 Choke Cherry Road
Rockville, MD 20857-1
240-276-1660
Fax: 240-276-1670
www.samhsa.gov

2065 Centers for Disease Control & Prevention
1600 Clifton Road
Atlanta, GA 30329-4018

404-639-3311
800-311-3435
www.cdc.gov

Robert Delaney, Plant Manager

Protecting the health and safety of people — at home and abroad, providing credible information to enhance health decisions, and promoting health through strong partnership. Serves as the national focus for developing and applying disease prevention and control, environmental health, and health promotion in education activities designed to improve the health of the people of the United States.

2066 Centers for Medicare & Medicaid Services: Health Policy
7500 Security Blvd
Baltimore, MD 21244-1849
410-786-3000

2067 DC Department of Mental Health
64 New York Avenue, NE
4th Floor
Washington, DC 20002-3329
202-673-7440
888-793-4357
www.dmh.dc.gov

The goal of the Department of Mental Health is to develop, support, and oversee a comprehensive, community-based, consumer-driven, culturally competent, quality mental health system. This system should be responsive and accessible to children, youths, adults, and their families. It should leverage continuous positive change through its ability to learn and to partner. It should also ensure that mental health providers are accountable to consumers and offer services that promote recovery from mental illness.

2068 Equal Employment Opportunity Commission
1801 L Street NW
Washington, DC 20507-1
202-467-8170
800-669-4000
TTY: 800-669-6820
E-mail: info@eeoc.gov

To eradicate employment discrimination at workplace.

2069 Health Care For All(HCFA)
30 Winter Street
10th Floor
Boston, MA 02108-4720
617-832-7300
TTY: 617-350-0974
E-mail: mcdonough@hcfama.org

John E McDonough, Executive Director
Lynn Wickwire, Director Communication/Develop.

2070 Health Systems and Financing Group
Health Resources and Services Administration
5600 Fishers Lane
Rockville, MD 20857-1
301-594-4110

Donald L Weaver, Administrator
Dennis Williams, Deputy Administrator

2071 Health and Human Services Office of Assistant Secretary for Planning & Evaluation
200 Independence Avenue SW
Washington, DC 20201-4
202-619-0257
877-696-6775
www.aspe.hhs.gov

2072 Information Resources and Inquiries Branch
National Institute of Mental Health
6001 Executive Boulevard
Room 8184
Bethesda, MD 20892-1
301-443-4513
866-615-6464
TTY: 301-443-8431
E-mail: nimhinfo@nih.gov

A component of the National Institute of Health, the NIMH conducts and supports research that seeks to understand, treat and prevent mental illness. The Institute's Information Resources and Inquiries Branch (IRIB) responds to information requests from the lay public, clinicians and the scientific community with a variety of publications on subjects such as basic behavioral research, neuroscience of mental health, rural mental, children's mental disorders, schizophrenia, paranoia, depression, bipolar disorder, learning disabilities, Alzheimer's disease, panic, obsessive compulsive and other anxiety disorders. A publication list is available upon request.

2073 National Institutes of Mental Health Division of Intramural Research Programs (DIRP)
10 Center Drive
Room 4N222 MSC 1381
Bethesda, MD 20892-1
301-496-4588

David R Rubinow, Contact

The Division of Intramural Research Programs (DIRP) at the National Institute of Mental Health (NIMH) is the internal research division of the NIMH. NIMH DIRP scientists conduct research ranging from studies into mechanisms of normal brain function, conducted at the behavioral, systems, cellular, and molecular levels, to clinical investigations into the diagnosis, treatment and prevention of mental illness. Major disease entities studied throughout the lifespan include mood disorders and anxiety, schizophrenia, obsessive-compulsive disorder, attention deficit hyperactivity disorder, and pediatric autoimmune neuropsychiatric disorders.

2074 National Center for HIV, STD and TB Prevention
Centers For Disease Control and Prevention
1600 Clifton Road
NE Mailstop E-10
Atlanta, GA 30329-4018
404-639-3311
800-232-4636

TTY: 888-232-6348
E-mail: cdcinfo@cdc.gov
www.cdc.gov
Robert Delaney, Plant Manager

2075 National Clearinghouse for Drug & Alcohol
PO Box 2345
Rockville, MD 20847-2345

800-729-6686
TDD: 800-487-4889
www.ncadi.samhsa.gov

2076 National Institute of Alcohol Abuse and Alcoholism: Treatment Research Branch
5635 Fishers Lane
MSC 9304
Bethesda, MD 20892-1
301-443-3860
E-mail: niaaaweb-r@exchange.nih.gov
www.niaaa.nih.gov/

NIAAA provides leadership in the national effort to reduce alcohol-related problems by conducting and supporting research in a wide range of scientific areas including genetics, neuroscience, epidemiology, health risks and benefits of alcohol consumption, prevention, and treatment.

2077 National Institute of Alcohol Abuse and Alcoholism: Homeless Demonstration and Evaluation Branch
5600 Fishers Lane
Msc 9304
Rockville, MD 20852-1750
301-443-4795
Fax: 301-443-0284
E-mail: niaaaweb-r@exchange.nih.gov

Nelba Chavez, Administrator

NIAAA provides leadership in the national effort to reduce alcohol-related problems by conducting and supporting research in a wide range of scientific areas including genetics, neuroscience, epidemiology, health risks and benefits of alcohol consumption, prevention, and treatment.

2078 National Institute of Alcohol Abuse and Alcoholism: Office of Policy Analysis
The Alcohol Policy Information System (APIS)
5600 Fishers Lane
Room 16-95
Rockville, MD 20857-1
301-443-3864
E-mail: niaaaweb-r@exchange.nih.gov

The Alcohol Policy Information System (APIS) is an online resource that provides detailed information on a wide variety of alcohol-related policies in the United States at both State and Federal levels. It features compilations and analyses of alcohol-related statutes and regulations. Designed primarily as a tool for researchers, APIS simplifies the process of ascertaining the state of the law for studies on the effects and effectiveness of alcohol-related policies.

2079 National Institute of Drug Abuse: NIDA
6001 Executive Boulevard
Room 5213
Bethesda, MD 20892-1
301-443-6245
Fax: 301-443-7397
E-mail: information@nida.nih.gov
www.drugabuse.gov

Beverly Jackson, Manager

Covers the areas of drug abuse treatment and prevention research, epidemiology, neuroscience and behavioral research, health services research and AIDS. Seeks to report on advances in the field, identify resources, promote an exchange of information, and improve communications among clinicians, researchers, administrators, and policymakers. Recurring features include synopses of research advances and projects, NIDA news, news of legislative and regulatory developments, and announcements.

2080 National Institute of Mental Health: Schizophrenia Research Branch
6001 Executive Boulevard
Room 8184, MSC 9663
Bethesda, MD 20892-1
301-443-4513
E-mail: nimhinfo@nih.gov

Information available includes a detailed booklet that provides an overview of schizophrenia and also describes symptoms, causes, and treatments, with information on getting help and coping.

2081 National Institute of Mental Health: Mental Disorders of the Aging
National Institutes of Health
6001 Executive Boulevard
Room 8184, MSC 9663
Bethesda, MD 20892-1
301-443-4513
E-mail: nimhinfo@nih.gov

The Aging Research Consortium was established in January 2002 by NIMH. Its mission is to: Stimulate research on mental health and mental illness to benefit older adults; Maintain an infrastructure to better coordinate aging research throughout the Institute; Provide a linkage to the Institute for researchers, advocates, and the public and advance research training for the study of late life mental disorders.

2082 National Institute of Mental Health: Office of Science Policy, Planning, and Communications
National Institutes of Health
6001 Executive Boulevard
Room 8208 MSC 9667
Bethesda, MD 20892-1
301-443-4513
E-mail: nimhinfo@nih.gov

Plans and directs a comprehensive strategic agenda for national mental health policy, including science program planning and related policy evaluation, research training and coordination, and technology and information transfer.

OSPPC plans and implements portfolio analysis, scientific disease coding, and program evaluations for developing and assessing NIMH strategic plans and portfolio management. OSPPC also creates and implements the Institute's communication efforts, including information dissemination, media relations activities, and internal communications. The Office proposes and guides science education activities concerned with informing the scientific community and public about mental health issues.

2083 National Institute on Drug Abuse: Division of Clinical Neurosciences and Behavioral Research

6001 Executive Boulevard
Room 4123, MSC 9551
Bethesda, MD 20892-1
301-443-6245
Fax: 301-443-7397
E-mail: sgrant@nida.nih.gov
www.drugabuse.gov

Beverly Jackson, Manager

The Clinical Neuroscience Branch (CNB) advances a clinical research and research training program focused on understanding the neurobiological substrates of drug abuse and addiction processes and on characterizing how abused drugs affect the structure, function, development, and maturation of the human central nervous system. Another major emphasis of this program is on etiological studies examining individual differences in neurobiological, genetic, and neurobehavioral factors that underlie increased risk and/or resilience to drug abuse, addiction, and drug-related disorders, as well as on the neurobiological/neurobehavioral factors involved in the transition from drug use to addiction.

2084 National Institute on Drug Abuse: Office of Science Policy and Communications

6001 Executive Boulevard
Room 5153, MSC 9589
Bethesda, MD 20892-1
301-443-6245
Fax: 301-443-7397
www.drugabuse.gov

Beverly Jackson, Manager

The Office of Science Policy and Communications (OSPC) carries out a wide variety of functions in support of the Director, NIDA, and on behalf of the Institute. We're made up of the Office of the Director and the International Program Office, and two branches, the Science Policy Branch and the Public Information and Liaison Branch.

2085 National Institutes of Health: National Center for Research Resources (NCCR)

6701 Democracy Boulevard, MSC 4874
Baltimore, MD
301-435-0888
Fax: 301-480-3558
E-mail: info@ncrr.nih.gov
www.ncrr.nih.gov/

The National Center for Research Resources (NCRR), a component of the National Institutes of Health that supports primary research to create and develop critical resources,

models, and technologies. NCRR funding also provides biomedical researchers with access to diverse instrumentation, technologies, basic and clinical research facilities, animal models, genetic stocks, biomaterials, and more. These resources enable scientific advances in biomedicine that lead to the development of lifesaving drugs, devices, and therapies.

2086 National Institutes of Mental Health: Office on AIDS

National Institutes of Health
6001 Executive Boulevard
Room 6225, MSC 9621
Bethesda, MD 20892-1
301-443-4513

(1) Plans, directs, coordinates, and supports biomedical and behavioral research designed to develop a better understanding of the biological and behavioral causes of HIV (AIDS virus) infection and more effective mechanisms for the diagnosis, treatment, and prevention of AIDS; (2) analyzes and evaluates National needs and research opportunities to identify areas warranting either increased or decreased program emphasis; and (3) consults and cooperates with voluntary and professional health organizations, as well as other NIH components and Federal agencies, to identify and meet AIDS-related needs.

2087 National Library of Medicine

National Instiues of Health
8600 Rockville Pike
Bethesda, MD 20894-1
301-496-2447
Fax: 301-402-0254
E-mail: custserv@nlm.nih.gov/

Pamela G Brooks, Manager

The National Library of Medicine (NLM), on the campus of the National Institutes of Health in Bethesda, Maryland, is the world's largest medical library. The Library collects materials and provides information and research services in all areas of biomedicine and health care.

2088 Office of Applied Studies, SA & Mental Health Services

1 Choke Cherry Road
Rockville, MD 20857-1
240-276-2000
Fax: 240-276-2010
www.oas.samhsa.gov/

The Office of Applied Studies provides the latest national data on alchohol, tobacco, marijuana and other drug abuse in addition to drug related emergency department epidosdes, medical examiner cases and the nation's substance abuse treatment system.

2089 Office of Disease Prevention & Health Promotion

US Department of Health and Human Services
1101 Wootton Parkway, Suite L1100
Rockville, MD 20852-1059
301-435-5646

Bernard Schwetz, Owner

The Office of Disease Prevention and Health Promotion, Office of Public Health and Science, Office of the Secretary, U.S. Department of Health and Human Services, works to strengthen the disease prevention and health promotion priorities of the Department within the collaborative framework of the HHS agencies.

2090 Office of National Drug Control Policy
Drug Policy Information Clearinghouse
P.O. Box 6000
Rockville, MD 20849-6000

800-666-3332
Fax: 301-519-5212
www.whitehousedrugpolicy.gov/

The goal of the Department of Mental Health is to develop, support, and oversee a comprehensive, community-based, consumer-driven, culturally competent, quality mental health system. This system should be responsive and accessible to children, youths, adults, and their families. It should leverage continuous positive change through its ability to learn and to partner. It should also ensure that mental health providers are accountable to consumers and offer services that promote recovery from mental illness.

2091 Office of Program and Policy Development
National Association of Community Health Centers
7200 Wisconcin Ave
Suite 210
Bethesda, MD 20814-4838
301-347-0400
Fax: 301-347-0459
www.nachc.com

Tom Van Coverdan, President

2092 Office of Science Policy OD/NIH
1 Center Drive
Building 1, Room 218
Bethesda, MD 20892-1
301-496-1454
Fax: 301-402-0280
www.ospp.od.nih.gov

Advises the NIH Director on science policy issues affecting the medical research community; Participates in the development of new policy and program initiatives; Monitors and coordinates agency planning and evaluation activities; Plans and implements a comprehensive science education program and Develops and implements NIH policies and procedures for the safe conduct of recombinant DNA and other biotechnology activities.

2093 President's Committee on Mental Retardation
US DHHS, Administration for Children & Families, PCMR
370 L'Enfatne Promenade SW
Washington, DC 20447-1
202-619-0634
www.acf.dhhs.gov/programs/pcmr

Wade F Horn PhD, Author
Curtis L Coy, Deputy Assistant Secretary

The PCMR acts in an advisory capacity to the President and the Secretary of Health and Human Services on matters relating to programs and services for persons with mental retardation. It has adopted several national goals in order to better recognize and uphold the right of all people with mental retardation to enjoy a quality of life that promotes independence, self-determination and participation as productive members of society.

2094 Presidential Commission on Employment of the Disabled
Frances Perkins Building
200 Constitution Avenue, NW
Washington, DC 20210-1

866-633-7365
Fax: 202-693-7888
TTY: 877-889-5627
www.dol.gov/odep

The Office of Disability Employment Policy (ODEP) was authorized by Congress in the Department of Labor's FY 2001 appropriation. Recognizing the need for a national policy to ensure that people with disabilities are fully integrated into the 21 st Century workforce, the Secretary of Labor Elaine L. Chao delegated authority and assigned responsibility to the Assistant Secretary for Disability Employment Policy. ODEP is a sub-cabinet level policy agency in the Department of Labor.

2095 Protection and Advocacy Program for the Mentally Ill
US Department of Health and Human Services
1 Choke Cherry Road
Rockville, MD 20857-1
240-276-1310
Fax: 240-276-1320
www.samhsa.gov/index.aspx

Federal formula grant program to protect and advocate the rights of people with mental illnesses who are in residential facilities and to investigate abuse and neglect in such facilities.

2096 Public Health Foundation
1300 L Street NW
Suite 800
Washington, DC 20005-4208
202-218-4400
Fax: 202-898-5609
E-mail: info@phf.org
www.phf.org

Ricardo Martinez MD, President/CEO/Chairman

A high-performing public health system that protects and promotes health in every community by improving public health infrastructure and performance through innovative solutions and measurable results.

2097 SAMHSA's Fetal Alcohol Spectrum Disorders Center for Excellence (FASD)
2101 Gaither Road
Suite 600
Rockville, MD 20850

866-786-7327
E-mail: fasdcenter@samsa.hhs.gov
www.fascenter.samhsa.gov
Patricia Getty, Contact

Focus on exploring innovative service delivery strategies, developing comprehensive systems of care for FASD prevention and treatment, training staff, families and individuals with an FASD, and preventing alcohol use among women of childbearing age. The mission of the FASD Center for Excellence is to facilitate the development and improvement of prevention and treatment, and care systems in the United States by providing national leadership and facilitating collaboration in the field.

Year Founded: 2001

2098 Substance Abuse & Mental Health Services Administration of the US Dept of Health and Human Services
1 Choke Cherry Road
Rockville, MD 20857
240-276-2000
www.samhsa.gov

Pamela Hyde JD, Administrator
Eric Broderick DDS, MPH, Deputy Adminstrator
Kana Enomoto MA, Advisor to the Administrator
Elaine Parry MS, Director of Program Services

SAMHSA's mission is to reduce the impact of substance abuse and mental illness on America's communities. The Agency was established by Congress to target effectively substance abuse and mental health services to the people most in need and to translate research in these areas more effectively and more rapidly into the general health care system. SAMHSA has demonstrated that prevention works, treatment is effective, and people recover from mental and substance use disorders. Behavioral health services improve health statuse and reduce health care costs to society. The Agency's programs are carried out through: the Center for Mental Health Services (CMHS); The Centers for Substance Abuse Prevention and Treatment (CSAP/T); and the Office of Applied Studies.

Year Founded: 1992

2099 Substance Abuse and Mental Health Services Administration: Center for Mental Health Services
SAMHSA
PO Box 42557
Washington, DC 20015-557
240-221-4022
800-789-2647
Fax: 240-221-4021
TDD: 866-889-2647
www.mentalhealth.samhsa.gov

2100 US Department of Health & Human Services: Indian Health Service
801 Thompson Avenue, Suite 400
Rockville, MD 20852-1627
301-443-3024
E-mail: webmaster@ihs.gov
www.ihs.gov

The mission of Indian Health Service is to raise the physical, mental, social, and spiritual health of American Indians and Alaska Natives to the highest level; to assure that comprehensive, culturally acceptable personal and public health services are available and accessible to American Indian and Alaska Native people; and to uphold the Federal Government's obligation to promote healthy American Indian and Alaska Native people, communities, and cultures and to honor and protect the inherent sovereign rights of Tribes.

2101 US Department of Health and Human Services Planning and Evaluation
200 Independence Ave SW
Washington, DC 20201-4
202-690-7650
877-696-6775

Mike Leavitt, Secretary

Responsible for policy development and for major activities in policy coordination, legislation development, strategic planning, policy research, evaluation, and economic analysis.

2102 US Department of Health and Human Services Bureau of Primary Health
Health Resources and Services Administration
5600 Fishers Lane
Rockville, MD 20857-1
301-594-4110

Donald L Weaver, Administrator

HRSA directs programs that improve the Nation's health by expanding access to comprehensive, quality health care for all Americans. HRSA works to improve and extend life for people living with HIV/AIDS, provide primary health care to medically underserved people, serve women and children through state programs, and train a health workforce that is both diverse and motivated to work in underserved communities.

2103 US Department of Health and Human Services: Office of Women's Health
200 Independence Avenue SW
Washington, DC 20201-4
202-690-7650

Wanda Jones, Deputy Assistant Secretary

The Office on Women's Health (OWH) was established in 1991 within the U.S. Department of Health and Human Services. OWH coordinates the efforts of all the HHS agencies and offices involved in women's health. OWH works to improve the health and well-being of women and girls in the United States through its innovative programs, by educating health professionals, and motivating behavior change in consumers through the dissemination of health information.

2104 US Veterans Administration: Mental Health and Behavioral Sciences Services
810 Vermont Avenue NW
Room 900
Washington, DC 20410-1
202-273-5781

Robert H Roswell, Manager
Michal J Kussman MD, Deputy Secretary for Health

The mission of the Veterans Healthcare System is to serve the needs of America's veterans by providing primary care, specialized care, and related medical and social support services. To accomplish this mission, VHA needs to be a comprehensive, integrated healthcare system that provides excellence in health care value, excellence in service as defined by its customers, and excellence in education and research, and needs to be an organization characterized by exceptional accountability and by being an employer of choice.

By State

Alabama

2105 Alabama Department of Human Resources
Center For Communications
Gordon Persons Building, Suite 2104
50 North Ripley Street
Montgomery, AL 36130-1001
334-242-1850

Nancy Jinright, Manager

Member of the National Leadership Council. The mission of the Alabama Department of Human Resources is to partner with communities to promote family stability and provide for the safety and self-sufficiency of vulnerable Alabamians.

2106 Alabama Department of Mental Health and Mental Retardation
100 North Union Street
PO Box 301410
Montgomery, AL 36130-1410
334-242-3454
800-367-0955
Fax: 334-242-0725
E-mail: dmhmr@mh.alabama.gov
www.mh.alabama.gov

John Houston, Commissioner
Beth Sievers, Administrative Assistant

State agency charged with providing services to citizens with mental illness, mental retardation and substance abuse disorders.

2107 Alabama Department of Public Health
201 Monroe Street
Montgomery, AL 36104-3735
334-206-5300
www.adph.org

Provides public health related information about the State of Alabama.

2108 Alabama Disabilities Advocacy Program
PO Box 870395
Tuscaloosa, AL 35487-395
205-348-4928
800-826-1675
Fax: 205-348-3909
E-mail: adap@adap.ua.edu
www.adap.net/

Ellen Gillespie, Director

Federally mandated, statewide, Protection and Advocacy system serving eligible individuals with disabilities in Alabama. ADAP's five programs are: Protection and Advocacy for Persons with Developmental Disabilities, Protection and Advocacy for Individuals with Mental Illness, Protection and Advocacy of Individual Rights, Protection and Advocacy for Assistive Technology and Protection and Advocacy for Beneficiaries of Social Security.

Alaska

2109 Alaska Council on Emergency Medical Services
20321 Middle Road
Eagle River, AK 99577-7931
907-465-3028
E-mail: shelley.owens@alaska.gov
www.chems.alaska.gov/ems/acems.htm

Shelley K Owens, Public Health Specialist

The mission of the Emergency Medical Services program in Alaska is to reduce both the human suffering and economic loss to society resulting from premature death and disability due to injuries and sudden illness.

2110 Alaska Department of Health & Social Services
350 Main Street, Room 404
Po Box 110601
Juneau, AK 99811-0601
907-465-3030
Fax: 907-465-3068
www.hss.state.ak.us

William H Hogan, Commissioner
Patrick Hefley, Deputy Commissioner
William Streve, Deputy Commissioner

The mission of the Alaska Department of Health and Social Services is to promote and protect the health and well being of Alaskans.

2111 Alaska Division of Mental Health and Developmental Disabilities
PO Box 110620
Juneau, AK 99811-620
907-465-3370
Fax: 907-465-5864
E-mail: stacy.toner@alaska.gov
www.hss.state.ak.us/dbh/resources/contacts/default.htm

Stacy Toner, Deputy Director

The mission of the Division of Behavioral Health is to manage an integrated and comprehensive behavioral health system based on sound policy, effective practices and partnerships.

2112 Alaska Health and Social Services Division of Behavioral Health

3601 C Street,
Suite 934
Anchorage, AK 99503-5932
907-269-3410
Fax: 907-269-3786
E-mail: melissa.stone@alaska.gov
www.hss.state.ak.us/dbh/dir/default.htm

Melissa Witzler Stone, Director

The mission of the Division of Behavioral Health is to manage an integrated and comprehensive behavioral health system based on sound policy, effective practices and partnerships.

2113 Alaska Mental Health Board

431 N Franklin Street
Suite 200
Juneau, AK 99801-1186
907-465-8920
Fax: 907-465-4410
E-mail: kathryn.craft@alaska.gov
www.http://hss.state.ak.us/amhb

Kathryn Craft, Executive Director

Planning and advocacy body for public mental health services. The board works to ensure that Alaska's mental health program is integrated and comprehensive. It recommends operating and capital budgets for the program. The Governor appoints twelve - sixteen members to the board. At least half the members must be consumers of mental health services or family members. Two members are mental health service providers and one an attorney.

2114 Mental Health Association in Alaska

4045 Lake Otis Parkway
Suite 209
Anchorage, AK 99508-5227
907-563-0880
Fax: 907-563-0881
E-mail: mhaa2@pobox.alaska.net
www.alaska.net/~mhaa/

The Mental Health Association in Alaska (MHAA) is a Division of the National Mental Health Association and is dedicated to the promotion of good mental health, the prevention of mental illness and ongoing improvement in the care and treatment of the mentally ill through advocacy, education, referral, research, legislative input and the monitoring of existing programs.

Arizona

2115 Arizona Department of Health Services

150 North 18th Avenue
Phoenix, AZ 85007
602-542-1025
Fax: 602-542-0883
www.azhds.gov

Will Humble, Director

Promotes and protects the health of Arizona's children and adults. Its mission is to set the standard for personal and community health through direct care, science, public policy, and leadership

2116 Arizona Department of Health Services: Behavioral Health Services

150 N. 18th Avenue
#200
Phoenix, AZ 85007-3238
602-364-4558
Fax: 602-364-4570
www.azdhs.gov/bhs/index.htm

Dr. Laura K Nelson, Deputy Director

Administers Arizona's publicly funded behavioral health service system for individuals, families and communities.

Year Founded: 1986

2117 Northern Arizona Regional Behavioral Health Authority

1300 South Yale Street
Flagstaff, AZ 86001-6328
928-774-7128
Fax: 928-774-5665
www.narbha.org

Mick Pattinson, CEO

The Northern Arizona Regional Behavioral Health Authority's (NARBHA) mission is to improve the quality of life for individuals and families across northern Arizona who are eligible for state and federally funded behavioral health services.

Arkansas

2118 Arkansas Department of Human Services

PO Box 1437
Little Rock, AR 72203-1437
501-682-1001
Fax: 501-682-6836
TDD: 501-682-8933
www.arkansas.gov/dhhs/homepage.html

John Selig, Director

The Arkansas Department of Human Services provides Medicaid, mental health and substance abuse resources.

2119 Arkansas Division of Children & Family Service

700 Main Street
P O Box 1437 Slot S 560
Little Rock, AR 72203-1437
501-682-8770
Fax: 501-682-6968
TDD: 501-682-1442
www.arkansas.gov/dhhs/sgChildren.html

The Arkansas Division of Children's Services is a member of the National Leadership Council and provides information and resources on adoption, daycare and child abuse prevention.

2120 Arkansas Division on Youth Services
PO Box 1437
Slot 450
Little Rock, AR 72203-1437
502-682-8654
Fax: 501-682-1339
www.arkansas.gov/dhhs/dys/

The Division of Youth Services (DYS) provides in a manner consistent with public safety, a system of high quality programs to address the needs of the juveniles who come in contact with, or are at risk of coming into contact with the juvenile justice system.

2121 Arkansas State Mental Hospital
4313 West Markham
Little Rock, AR 72205-4023
501-686-9060
E-mail: sheila.duncan@mail.state.ar.us

Glenn Sago, Administrator
Charles Smith, Administrator

The Arkansas State Hospital (ASH) is a 202-bed psychiatric inpatient facility licensed by the Arkansas Department of Health and the Centers for Medicare and Medicaid Services, and accredited by the Joint Commission on Accreditation of Healthcare Organizations (JCAHO). The hospital includes 90 beds for acute psychiatric admission; a 60-bed forensic treatment services program which offers assistance to circuit courts throughout the state; a 16-bed adolescent treatment program for youth 13-18; and a 16-bed program for juvenile sex offenders. The Arkansas State Hospital has been providing quality psychiatric care to the citizens of Arkansas since 1873.

2122 Mental Health Council of Arkansas
501 Woodlane Drive
Suite 104
Little Rock, AR 72201-1058
501-372-7062
Fax: 501-372-8039
E-mail: mhca@mhca.org
www.mhca.org

Kenny Whilock, Executive Director
Tonia Ward, Administrative Assistant

The Mental Health Council of Arkansas is a non-profit organization governed by a board of directors with a representative from each of the 13 participating community mental health centers and their affiliates. The MHCA assists its members to achieve the goal of community based treatment which focuses on the whole person with emphasis on physical, mental and emotional wellness and promotes the comprehensive diagnostic, treatment, and wrap around services provided by the private non-profit community mental health centers of Arkansas. The MHCA is dedicated to improving the overall health and well-being of the citizens and communities of Arkansas.

California

2123 California Department of Alcohol and Drug Programs
1700 K Street
Sacramento, CA 95811-4022
916-445-9338
800-879-2772

Steve Edinger, Administrator

The California Department of Alcohol and Drug Program's mission is to lead California's strategy to reduce alcohol and other drug problems by developing, administering, and supporting prevention and treatment programs.

2124 California Department of Alcohol and Drug Programs: Resource Center
1700 K Street
Sacramento, CA 95811-4022
916-445-9338
800-444-3066

Steve Edinger, Administrator

The Resource Center at the California Department of Alcohol and Drug Programs maintains a comprehensive collection of alcohol, tobacco, and other drug prevention and treatment information. This information is provided to all California residents at no cost through a Clearinghouse, a full-service Library, Internet communication links, and a telephone information and referral system. These services can be accessed by letter, fax, Internet, e-mail, telephone, or in person during the business hours of 8:00 a.m. to 4:30 p.m., Monday through Friday, excluding state holidays.

2125 California Department of Corrections and Rehabilitation
1515 S Street
Suite 502
Sacramento, CA 95811-7243
916-445-7682
Fax: 916-322-2877

Our mission is founded on delivering a balance of quality and cost-effective health care in a safe, secure correctional setting.

2126 California Department of Education: Healthy Kids, Healthy California
PO Box 944272
Sacramento, CA 94244-2720
510-670-4583
888-318-8188
Fax: 510-670-4582
www.californiahealthykids.org

The California Healthy Kids Resource Center was established to assist schools in promoting health literacy. Health literacy is the capacity of an individual to obtain, interpret, and understand basic health information and services and the competence to use such information and services in ways that are health enhancing.

2127 California Department of Health Services: Medicaid
714 P Street
Room 1253
Sacramento, CA 95814-6401
916-445-4171

The mission of the California Department of Health Services is to protect and improve the health of all Californians. Website constains resources and links for detailed information on Medicaid.

2128 California Department of Mental Health
1600 9th Street
Sacramento, CA 95814-6476
916-654-3890
800-896-4042
Fax: 916-654-3198
TTY: 800-896-2512
E-mail: dmh.dmh.ca.gov
www.dmh.ca.gov

2129 California Hispanic Commission on Alcohol Drug Abuse
2101 Capitol Avenue
Sacramento, CA 95816-5720
916-443-5473
Fax: 916-443-1732
www.chcada.org

James Hernandez, Executive Director

Services can consist of developing Latino-based agencies, program management, consultation related to proposal development, Board of Directors training, program planning, and information dissemination. Populations or groups served include Latino alcohol and drug service agencies, groups and/or individuals planning to initiate services to Latinos, other AOD agencies with a commitment to serve the Latino community, and County Alcohol and Drug Program offices.

2130 California Institute for Mental Health
2125 19th Street
2nd Floor
Sacramento, CA 95818-1673
916-556-3477
Fax: 916-556-3483
E-mail: sgoodwin@cimh.org
www.cimh.org

Sandra Naylor-Goodwin, CEO
Bill Carter, Deputy Director

Promoting excellence in mental health services through training, technical asistances, research and policy development.

2131 California Mental Health Directors Association
2125 19th Street
Sacramento, CA 95818-1673
916-556-3477
Fax: 916-446-4519
E-mail: pryan@cmhda.org
www.cmhda.org

Patricia Ryan, Executive Director

The mission of the Association is to provide leadership, advocacy, expertise and support to California's county and city mental health programs (and their system partners) that will assist them in serving persons with serious mental illness and serious emotional disturbance. Our goal is to assist in building a public mental health system that ensures the accessibility of quality, cost-effective mental health care that is consumer-and family-driven, resiliency-based and culturally competent.

Colorado

2132 Colorado Department of Health Care Policy and Financing
1570 Grant Street
Denver, CO 80203-1818
303-866-2993
800-221-3943
E-mail: diane.rodriguez.state.co.us

Joan Henneberry, Manager

The Department of Health Care Policy and Financing manages the Colorado Medicaid Community Mental Health Services program. the program provides mental health care to medicaid clients in Colorado, through Behavioral Health Organization contracts.

2133 Colorado Department of Human Services (CDHS)
1575 Sherman Street
Denver, CO 80203-1702
303-866-5700
Fax: 303-866-4047
www.cdhs.state.co.us/

Karen Beye, Executive Director

CDHS oversees the state's 64 county departments of social/human services, the state's public mental health system, Colorado's system of services for people with developmental disabilities, the state's juvenile corrections system and all state and veterans' nursing homes, through more than 5,000 employees and thousands of community-based service providers. Colorado is a state-supervised, county-administered system for the traditional social services, including programs such as public assistance and child welfare services.

2134 Colorado Department of Human Services: Alcohol and Drug Abuse Division
4055 S. Lowell Blvd.
Denver, CO 80236-3120
303-866-7480
Fax: 303-866-7481
www.cdhs.state.co.us

Roxy Huber, Executive Director

The Alcohol and Drug Abuse Division (ADAD) of the Colorado Department of Human Services was established by state law in 1971 to: promote healthy, drug-free lifestyles; reduce alcohol and other drug abuse and to reduce abuse-associated illnesses and deaths.

2135 Colorado Division of Mental Health
Colorado Department of Human Services
3824 West Princeton Circle
Denver, CO 80236-3111
303-866-7450

The Division of Mental Health administers non-Medicaid community mental health services for people with serious emotional disturbance or serious mental illness of all ages, through contracts with six specialty clinics and seventeen private, nonprofit community mental health centers. The Division of Mental Health strives to ensure high quality, accessible mental health services for Colorado residents, by reviewing community mental health programs; adopting standards, rules and regulations; providing training and technical assistance; and responding to complaints from non-Medicaid consumers.

2136 Colorado Medical Assistance Program
Information Center
Department of Health Care Policy and Financing
1570 Grant Street
Denver, CO 80203-1818
303-866-2993

Joan Henneberry, Manager

Provides numerous resources for policymakers, health care consumers, providers, and all citizens of Colorado.

2137 Colorado Traumatic Brain Injury Trust Fund
Program
1575 Sherman Street
4th Floor
Denver, CO 80203-1702
303-866-4085
Fax: 303-866-4905
www.cdhs.state.co.us

The TBI Trust Fund will strive to support all people in Colorado with traumatic brain injury through services, research and education.

2138 Denver County Department of Social Services
1200 Federal Boulevard
Denver, CO 80204-3221
720-944-3666
Fax: 720-944-3019
E-mail: codhs.fcs-sls@acs-inc.com
www.cdhs.state.co.us/servicebycounty.htm

Roxanne White, Manager

The vision of the Denver Department of Human Services is to help those in need and protect those in harm's way. The mission is to provide and coordinate services with courtesy and respect for each other and for the well being and protection of residents in the Denver community. These services are provided through partnerships that help families and individuals move toward independence, maintain pride and dignity and realize their potential.

2139 El Paso County Human Services
105 North Spruce Street
Colorado Springs, CO 80905-1409
719-636-0000

The mission of the El Paso County Department of Human Services is to strengthen families, assure safety, promote self-sufficiency, eliminate poverty, and improve the quality of life in our community.

Connecticut

2140 Connecticut Department of Mental Health and
Addiction Services
410 Capitol Avenue
P O Box 341431
Hartford, CT 06134-1431
860-418-7000
800-446-7348
TDD: 860-418-6707
www.dmhas.state.ct.us/

The mission of the Department of Mental Health and Addiction Services is to improve the quality of life of the people of Connecticut by providing an integrated network of comprehensive, effective and efficient mental health and addiction services that foster self-sufficiency, dignity and respect.

2141 Connecticut Department of Children and
Families
505 Hudson Street
Hartford, CT 06106-7107
860-550-6301
866-637-4737
www.state.ct.us/dcf/

The mission of the Department of Children and Families is to protect children, improve child and family well-being and support and preserve families. These efforts are accomplished by respecting and working within individual cultures and communities in Connecticut, and in partnership with others. Member of the National Leadership Council

Delaware

2142 Delaware Department of Health & Social
Services
1901 North Dupont Highway
New Castle, DE 19720
302-255-9040
Fax: 302-255-4429
www.dhss.delaware.gov

Rita M Landgraf, Secretary

The mission of the Delaware Department of Health and Social Services is to improve the quality of life for Delaware's citizens by promoting health and well-being, fostering self-sufficiency, and protecting vulnerable populations.

2143 Delaware Division of Child Mental Health
Services
1825 Faulkland Road
Wilmington, DE 19805-1121
302-633-2571
Fax: 302-633-5118
E-mail: cmh.dscyf@state.de.us

Susan Cycyk, Executive Director

The Division of Child Mental Health Services (DCMHS) is part of the Delaware Department of Services for Children, Youth and Their Families. Its primary responsibility is to provide and manage a range of services for children who have experienced abandonment, abuse, adjudication, mental illness, neglect, or substance abuse. Its services include prevention, early intervention, assessment, treatment, permanency, and after care.

2144 Delaware Division of Family Services
1825 Faulkland Road
Wilmington, DE 19805-1121
302-663-2665
E-mail: info.dscyf@state.de.us
www.state.de.us/kids/fs/fs.shtml

The Division of Family Services is mandated by law to investigate complaints about child abuse and neglect. Since 1875, state agencies have been balancing the children's right of safety and the parent's right to choose what is good for the family. The Adoption and Safe Families Act of 1997 clearly puts the focus on the protection, safety and permanency plan of children as the first priority. Services provided are child oriented and family focused.

District of Columbia

2145 California Department of Health and Human Services
200 Independence Avenue SW
Washington, DC 20201-7
202-619-0257
877-696-6775
www.hhs.gov

2146 DC Commission on Mental Health Services
64 New York Avenue, NE
4th Floor
Washington, DC 20002-3329
202-673-7440
888-793-4357
www.dmh.dc.gov/dmh/site/default.asp

Regulates the District's mental health system for adults, children and youth, and their families, and provides mental health services directly through the Community Service Agency (for community-based consumers of mental health services) and St. Elizabeths Hospital.

2147 DC Department of Human Services
801 East Building
2700 Martin Luther King Jr Avenue SE
Washington, DC 20032-2601
202-279-6002
Fax: 202-279-6014

2148 Health & Medicine Counsel of Washington
DDNC Digestive Disease National Coalition
507 Capital Court NE
Suite 200
Washington, DC 20002-7705
202-544-7497
Fax: 202-546-7105
www.ddnc.org
Dale Dirks, Administrator
Linda Aukett, Chair

The Digestive Disease National Coalition (DDNC) is an advocacy organization comprised of the major national voluntary and professional societies concerned with digestive diseases. The DDNC focuses on improving public policy related to digestive diseases and increasing public awareness with respect to the many diseases of the digestive system. The DDNC was founded in 1978 and is based in Washington D.C.

Florida

2149 Florida Department Health and Human Services: Substance Abuse Program
Department of Children and Families
1317 Winewood Boulevard
Building 1 Suite 207
Tallahassee, FL 32399-6570
850-488-5091
Fax: 850-922-6411
Paul Keith, President

The Substance Abuse Program Office is dedicated to the development of a comprehensive system of prevention, emergency/detoxification, and treatment services for individuals and families at risk of or affected by substance abuse; to promote their safety, well-being, and self-sufficiency.

2150 Florida Department of Children and Families
1317 Winewood Boulevard
Building 1, Room 202
Tallahassee, FL 32399-6570
850-488-5091
Fax: 850-922-6411
Paul Keith, President

Provides rules, regulations, monitoring of fifteen district mental health program offices and mental health providers throughout the state.

2151 Florida Department of Health and Human Services
2585 Merchants Row Boulevard
Tallahassee, FL 32399-1
850-245-4444
www.doh.state.fl.us

The mission of the Florida Department of Health and Human Services is to promote and protect the health and safety of all people in Florida through the delivery of quality public health services and the promotion of health care standards.

2152 Florida Department of Mental Health and Rehabilitative Services
Department of Children and Families
1317 Winewood Boulevard
Building 6
Tallahassee, FL 32399-6570
850-488-5091
Fax: 850-922-6411

Paul Keith, President

The Mental Health Program Office is committed to focusing its resources to meet the needs of people who cannot otherwise access mental health care.

2153 Florida Medicaid State Plan
2727 Mahan Drive
Tallahassee, FL 32308-5407

888-419-3456
www.ahca.myflorida.com

Provides information about the Medicare plans, benefits and how to enroll in them. Medicaid is the state and federal partnership that provides health coverage for selected categories of people with low incomes. Its purpose is to improve the health of people who might otherwise go without medical care for themselves and their children. Florida implemented the Medicaid program on January 1, 1970, to provide medical services to indigent people. Over the years, the Florida Legislature has authorized Medicaid reimbursement for additional services. A major expansion occurred in 1989, when the United States Congress mandated that states provide all Medicaid services allowable under the Social Security Act to children under the age of 21.

Georgia

2154 Georgia Department of Human Resources
2 Peachtree Street NW
Suite 3-130
Atlanta, GA 30303-3141
404-656-4374
866-351-0001
Fax: 404-656-9655
www.dca.state.ga.us

Harlold Munter, Manager

Provides programs that control the spread of disease, enable older people to live at home longer, prevent children from developing lifelong disabilities, train single parents to find and hold jobs, and help people with mental or physical disabilities live and work in their communities.

2155 Georgia Department of Human Resources: Division of Public Health
Two Peachtree Street, NW
Atlanta, GA 30303-3141
404-656-4374
Fax: 404-656-9655
E-mail: gdphinfo@dhr.state.ga.us
www.dca.state.ga.us

Harlold Munter, Manager

Our mission is to promote and protect the health of people in Georgia wherever they live, work, and play. We unite

with individuals, families, and communities to improve their health and enhance their quality of life.

2156 Georgia Division of Mental Health Developmental Disabilities and Addictive Diseases (MHDDAD)
2 Peachtree Street NW
Atlanta, GA 30303-3141
404-818-6600
www.mhddad.dhr.georgia.gov

Provides treatment and support services to people with mental illnesses and addictive diseases, and support to people with mental retardation and related developmental disabilities. MHDDAD serves people of all ages with the most severe and likely to be long-term conditions. The division also funds evidenced-based prevention services aimed at reducing substance abuse and related problems.

Hawaii

2157 Hawaii Department of Adult Mental Health
1250 Punchbowl #256
Honolulu, HI 96813-2416
808-586-0343

The mission of the Hawaii Department of Adult Mental Health is to provide a comprehensive, integrated mental health system supporting the recovery of adults with severe mental illness. The Adult Mental Health Division seeks to improve the mental health of Hawai'i's people by reducing the prevalence of emotional disorders, and mental illness. Services include mental health education, treatment and rehabilitation through community-based mental health centers, and an in-patient state hospital facility for the mentally-ill, including those referred through courts and the criminal justice system.

2158 Hawaii Department of Health
1250 Punchbowl Street
Honolulu, HI 96813-2416
808-586-0343

Michelle R Hill, Director Behavioral Health

Idaho

2159 Department of Health and Welfare: Medicaid Division
450 West State Street
Boise, ID 83720-1
208-334-5546
Fax: 208-334-6558
E-mail: APSPortal@idhw.state.id.us

Karl Kurtz, Director

Our mission is to promote and protect the health and safety of all Idahoans. From birth throughout life, we can help enrich and protect the lives of the people of our state.

2160 Department of Health and Welfare: Community Rehab

PO Box 83720
Boise, ID 83720-3
208-332-6910
www.healthandwelfare.idaho.gov/

Our mission is to promote and protect the health and safety of all Idahoans. From birth throughout life, we can help enrich and protect the lives of the people of our state.

2161 Idaho Bureau of Maternal and Child Health

PO Box 83720
Boise, ID 83720-3
208-332-6910
www.healthandwelfare.idaho.gov/

Our mission is to promote and protect the health and safety of all Idahoans. From birth throughout life, we can help enrich and protect the lives of the people of our state.

2162 Idaho Bureau of Mental Health and Substance Abuse, Division of Family & Community Service

PO Box 83720
Boise, ID 83720-3
208-332-6910
www.healthandwelfare.idaho.gov/

Our mission is to promote and protect the health and safety of all Idahoans. From birth throughout life, we can help enrich and protect the lives of the people of our state.

2163 Idaho Department of Health & Welfare

PO Box 83720
Boise, ID 83720-3
208-332-6910
www.healthandwelfare.idaho.gov/DesktopDefault.aspx

Our mission is to promote and protect the health and safety of all Idahoans. From birth throughout life, we can help enrich and protect the lives of the people of our state.

2164 Idaho Department of Health and Welfare: Family and Child Services

PO Box 83720
Boise, ID 83720-3
203-332-6910
www.healthandwelfare.idaho.gov/

Our mission is to promote and protect the health and safety of all Idahoans. From birth throughout life, we can help enrich and protect the lives of the people of our state.

2165 Idaho Mental Health Center

PO Box 83720
Boise, ID 83720-3
208-332-6910
www.healthandwelfare.idaho.gov/

The Idaho Department of Health and Welfare's programs and services are designed to help people live healthy and be productive, strengthening individuals, families and commu-nities. From birth throughout life, we help people improve their lives.

Illinois

2166 Illinois Alcoholism and Drug Dependency Association

937 S 2nd Street
Springfield, IL 62704-2701
217-528-7335
Fax: 217-528-7340
www.iadda.org

Sara Howe, CEO

2167 Illinois Department of Alcoholism and Substance Abuse

100 W Randolph Street
Suite 5-600
Chicago, IL 60601-3224
312-814-3340
Fax: 312-814-1436
E-mail: dhsa48@dhs.state.il.us

Rocco Clapps, Manager

DASA consists of three operational Bureau's designed to reflect our mission and planning goals and objectives. Primary responsibilities are to develop, maintain, monitor and evaluate a statewide treatment delivery system designed to provide screening, assessment, customer-treatment match-ing, referral, intervention, treatment and continuing care services for indigents alcohol and drug abuse and depend-ency problems. These services are provided by numerous community-based substance abuse treatment organizations contracted by DASA according to the needs of various communities and populations.

2168 Illinois Department of Children and Family Services

100 W Randolph Street
Suite 6-200
Chicago, IL 60601-3208
312-814-3340
Fax: 312-814-1436
TDD: 312-814-8783

Rocco Clapps, Manager

The Illinois Department of Children and Family Services provides child welfare services in Illinois. It is also the na-tion's largest state child welfare agency to earn accredita-tion from the Council on Accreditation for Children and Family Services (COA). The Department's organization in-cludes the Divisions of Child Protection, Placement Perma-nency, Field Operations, Guardian & Advocacy, Clinical Practice & Professional Development, Service Interven-tion, Budget & Finance, Planning & Performance Management, and Communications.

2169 Illinois Department of Health and Human Services

401 South Clinton Street
Chicago, IL 60607-3800

800-843-6154
TTY: 312-793-2354
www.dhs.state.il.us/

DHS serves Illinois citizens through seven main programs: Welfare programs, including temporary assistance for needy families, Food Stamps, and child care; Alcoholism and substance abuse treatment and prevention services; Developmental disabilities; Health services for pregnant women and mothers, infants, children, and adolescents; Prevention services for domestic violence and at-risk youth; Mental health and Rehabilitation services.

2170 Illinois Department of Human Services: Office of Mental Health
160 N LaSalle
10th Floor
Chicago, IL 60601-3124
312-793-2800

Bert Rodriguez, Manager

Works to improve the lives of persons with mental illness by integrating state operated services, community based programs, and other support services to create an effective and responsive treatment and care network. Management office which plans, organizes, and controls the activities of the organization, but does not offer services to the public.

2171 Illinois Department of Mental Health and Drug Dependence
Dhs-Division of Alcoholism and Substance Abuse
100 West Randolph Street
Suite 5-600
Chicago, IL 60601-3224
312-814-3840
800-843-6154
Fax: 312-814-2419

Carol L Adams, Director

Primary responsibilities are to develop, maintain, monitor and evaluate a statewide treatment delivery system designed to provide screening, assessment, customer-treatment matching, referral, intervention, treatment and continuing care services for indigents alcohol and drug abuse and dependency problems. These services are provided by numerous community-based substance abuse treatment organizations contracted by DASA according to the needs of various communities and populations.

2172 Illinois Department of Mental Health and Developmental Disabilities
100 South Grand Avenue
2nd Floor
Springfield, IL 62765-1
217-524-7065
www.dhs.state.il.us/mhdd/dd/

Our mission is to provide a full array of quality, outcome-based, person- and community-centered services and supports for individuals with developmental disabilities and their families in Illinois.

2173 Illinois Department of Public Aid
201 S Grand Avenue E
Springfield, IL 62763-1
217-782-1200
Fax: 217-782-5672
www.hfs.illinois.gov/

The Illinois Department of Healthcare and Family Services, formerly the Department of Public Aid, is the state agency dedicated to improving the lives of Illinois' families through health care coverage, child support enforcement and energy assistance.

2174 Illinois Department of Public Health: Division of Food, Drugs and Dairies/FDD
535 W Jefferson Street
Springfield, IL 62761-1
217-785-2033
Fax: 217-785-2038
TTY: 800-547-0466

Damon Arnold, Manager

The mission of the Illinois Department of Public Health is to promote the health of the people of Illinois through the prevention and control of disease and injury.

2175 Mental Health Association in Illinois
70 E Lake Street
Suite 900
Chicago, IL 60601-5995
312-368-9070
www.mhai.org

Carol Wozniewski, Executive Director
Jennifer Okonma, Director Development

Works to promote mental health, prevent mental illnesses, and improve the care and treatment of persons suffering from mental and emotional problems. An affiliate of the National Mental Health Association, MHAI is Illinois' only statewide, non-profit, non-governmental advocacy organization concerned with the entire spectrum of mental and emotional disorders.

Year Founded: 1909

Indiana

2176 Indiana Department of Public Welfare Division of Family Independence: Food Stamps/Medicaid/Training
Family and Social Services Administration
402 W Washington Street
Po Box 7083
Indianapolis, IN 46207-7083
317-232-4946
Fax: 317-233-4693
www.in.gov/fssa

The mission of the Division of Family Independence is to strengthenfamilies and children through temporary assistance to needy families, food stamps, housing, child care, foster care, adoption, energy assistance, homeless services, and job programs.

2177 Indiana Family & Social Services Administration
402 W Washington Street
PO Box 7083
Indianapolis, IN 46207-7083
317-233-4454
Fax: 317-233-4693
www.in.gov/fssa/2474.htm

Ferzelle Jones, Administrative Assistant

The mission of the Indiana Department of Family and Social Services is to strengthen families and children through temporary assistance to needy families, food stamps, housing, child care, foster care, adoption, energy assistance, homeless services, and job programs.

2178 Indiana Family And Social Services Administration
402 W Washington Street
Po Box 7083
Indianapolis, IN 46207-7083
317-233-4454
Fax: 317-233-4693
www.in.gov/fssa//2474.htm

Ferzelle Jones, Administrative Assistant

The mission of the Indiana Bureau of Family Protection is to strengthen families and children through temporary assistance to needy families, food stamps, housing, child care, foster care, adoption, energy assistance, homeless services, and job programs.

2179 Indiana Family and Social Services Administration: Division of Mental Health
402 W Washington Street
Suite W-353
Indianapolis, IN 46204-2779
317-233-4319
Fax: 317-233-3472
www.in.gov/fssa/

The mission of the Indiana Family and Social Services Administration Division of Mental Health is to strengthening families and children through temporary assistance to needy families, food stamps, housing, child care, foster care, adoption, energy assistance, homeless services, and job programs.

2180 The Indiana Consortium for Mental Health Services Research (ICMHSR)
Institute for Social Research Indiana University
1022 East Third Street
Bloomington, IN 47401-3779
812-855-3841
Fax: 812-856-5713
E-mail: acapshew@indiana.edu
www.indiana.edu/~icmhsr/

Bernice A Pescosolido Ph.D, Program Director

The Indiana Consortium for Mental Health Services Research (ICMHSR) focuses on developing high quality scholarly and applied research projects on mental health and related services for people with severe mental disorders. A major commitment of the ICMHSR is to use re-search to foster public awareness and improve public policy and decision-making regarding these devastating illnesses.

Iowa

2181 Iowa Department Human Services
1305 East Walnut
Des Moines, IA 50319-114
515-281-6899
E-mail: fdhs@dhs.state.ia.us
www.dhs.state.ia.us

Kevin W Concannon, Director

The Mission of the Iowa Department of Human Services is to help individuals and families achieve safe, stable, self-sufficient, and healthy lives, thereby contributing to the economic growth of the state. We do this by keeping a customer focus, striving for excellence, sound stewardship of state resources, maximizing the use of federal funding and leveraging opportunities, and by working with our public and private partners to achieve results.

2182 Iowa Department of Public Health
321 E 12th Street
Des Moines, IA 50319-75
515-281-7689
www.idph.state.ia.us

Thomas Newton, Director

Under the direction of the director, the Iowa Department of Public Health exercises general supervision of the state's public health; promotes public hygiene and sanitation; does health promotion activities, prepares for and responds to bioemergency situations; and, unless otherwise provided, enforces laws on public health.

2183 Iowa Department of Public Health: Division of Substance Abuse
321 12th Street
Des Moines, IA 50319-1002
515-242-6514
www.idph.state.ia.us/bh

G. Dean Austin, Bureau Chief

The Office of Substance Abuse Prevention/Staff of the Office of Substance Abuse Prevention provides the following services: technical assistance to individuals, groups, and contracted agencies and organizations; Coordinate and collaborate with multiple state agencies and organizations for assessment, planning, and implementation of statewide prevention initiatives; and Coordinate, train, and monitor funding to local community-based organizations for alcohol, tobacco, and other drug prevention services.

2184 Iowa Division of Mental Health & Developmental Disabilities: Department of Human Services
1305 E Walnut Street
Des Moines, IA 50319
515-281-7277
Fax: 515-242-6036

E-mail: fdhs@dhs.state.ia.us
www.dhs.state.ia.us

Jeanne Nesbit, Director

The Division of Mental Health and Developmental Disabilities (MH/DD) is the agency designated as the state mental health authority by the Governor of Iowa. The Division: provides program support services for persons with mental illness, mental retardation and developmental disabilities; plans for state services; works with counties in the development and implementation of their services plans; develops policy for the state mental health institutes and the state resource centers for persons with developmental disabilities; provides consultation and technical assistance; and, provides accreditation for providers of MH/DD services.

Kansas

2185 Comcare of Sedgwick County
635 North Main
Wichita, KS 67203-3602
316-660-7600
Fax: 316-660-7510
TTY: 316-267-0267
E-mail: mcook@sedgwickcounty.org
www.sedgwickcounty.org

Marilyn Cook LSCSW, Executive Director

Provides a wide array of mental health and substance abuse servicesto residents of Sedgwick County. COMCARE is the safety net for individuals in need of mental health services that cannot afford to obtain them elsewhere in the community

2186 Division of Disability and Behavioral Health Services - Mental Health
Kansas Department of Social and Rehabilitation Services
915 SW Harrison Street
9th Fl
Topeka, KS 66612-1505
785-296-7272
888-582-3759
Fax: 785-296-6142
www.srskansas.org

Rick Shults, Director of Mental Health
Sandy Hashman, Asst Director of Mental Health
Bobbie Graff-Hendrixson, Asst Director of Mental Health

2187 Kansas Council on Developmental Disabilities
Kansas Department of Social and Rehabilitation Services
Docking State Office Building
Room 141
Topeka, KS 66612
785-296-2608

Jane Rhys, Executive Director

2188 Kansas Department of Mental Health and Retardation and Social Services
915 SW Harrison
Dsob 9th Floor
Topeka, KS 66612-1505
785-296-3959
Fax: 785-296-2173
www.srskansas.org

Robbie Berry, Executive Director

The mission of the department of Mental Health in the Division of Health Care Policy is to provide individuals and families who experience mental illness alone or in combination with substance abuse problems, the support they need in order to achieve their personal goals.

Kentucky

2189 Kentucky Cabinet for Health and Human Services
275 East Main Street
1e-B
Frankfort, KY 40621-1
502-564-5497
Fax: 502-564-9523
E-mail: nancy.ovesen@ky.gov
www.chfs.ky.gov/

The goal of the Cabinet for Health and Family Services is to provide the finest health care possible for people in our state facilities; To provide the best preventative services through our public health programs; To provide the most outstanding service for our families and children; To protect and prevent the abuse of children, elders and people with disabilities and To build quality programs across-the-board; and by doing all of these things.

2190 Kentucky Department for Human Support Services
Kentucky Department for Health and Family Services
275 East Main Street
Mail Stop 3W-E
Frankfort, KY 40621-1
502-564-5343
Fax: 502-564-7478
www.chfs.ky.gov/dhss/default.htm

Sam Rodgers, Info Technology Client Manager

Consists of four divisions and one commission, all of which provide vital programs and services to Kentucky families. Divisions include Family Resource and Youth Services Centers, Aging Services, Women's Mental and Physical Health, and Child Abuse and Domestic Violence Services. This department also oversees the Kentucky Commission on Community Volunteerism and Service.

2191 Kentucky Department for Medicaid Services
Cabinet for Health and Family Services
275 East Main Street
1E-B
Frankfort, KY 40621
502-564-5497
Fax: 502-564-9523

E-mail: sherry.carnahan@ky.gov
www.chfs.ky.gov

Steve D Davis, Deputy Inspector General

Purchases quality healthcare and related services that produce positive outcomes for persons eligible for programs administered by the department.

2192 Kentucky Department of Mental Health and Mental Retardation
   C/O The Commissioner's Office
100 Fair Oaks Lane 4E-B
Frankfort, KY 40621-1
502-564-4527
Fax: 502-564-5478
TTY: 502-564-5777
www.chfs.ky.gov/mhmr/

Dr. John M Burt, Commissioner Mental Health Dept

Our mission is to provide leadership, in partnership with others, to prevent disability, build resilience in individuals and their communities, and facilitate recovery for people whose lives have been affected by mental illness, mental retardation or other developmental disability, substance abuse or an acquired brain injury.

2193 Kentucky Justice Cabinet: Department of Juvenile Justice
1025 Capital Center Drive
Frankfort, KY 40601-8205
502-573-2738
www.djj.ky.gov/

J. Ronald Haws, Commissioner

The Kentucky Department of Juvenile Justice's mission is to improve public safety by providing balanced and comprehensive services that hold youth accountable, and to provide the opportunity for youth to develop into productive, responsible citizens.

Louisiana

2194 Louisiana Commission on Law Enforcement and Administration (LCLE)
1885 Wooddale Boulevard
Room 1230
Baton Rouge, LA 70806-1555
225-925-4418
www.cole.state.la.us/

Judy A Dupuy, Executive Director

Lastest news and information on LCLE programs, resources, job openings, and general agency information on a monthly basis and for an in-depth review of our criminal justice programs.

2195 Louisiana Department of Health and Hospitals: Office of Mental Health
Bienville Building
628 N 4th Street
Baton Rouge, LA 70802-5342

225-342-9500
Fax: 225-342-5568
www.dhh.la.gov

Fredrick Cerise, Corporate Secretary

The Mission of the Office of Mental Health (OMH) is to perform the functions of the state which provide or lead to treatment, rehabilitation and follow-up care for individuals in Louisiana with mental and emotional disorders. OMH administers and/or monitors community-based services, public or private, to assure active quality care in the most cost-effective manner in the least restrictive environment for all persons with mental and emotional disorders.

2196 Louisiana Department of Health and Hospitals: Louisiana Office for Addictive Disorders
628 N 4th Street
PO Box 2790, Bin 18
Baton Rouge, LA 70821-2790
225-342-6717
Fax: 225-342-3875
E-mail: lelsie.deville@la.gov
www.dhh.louisiana.gov/offices/?ID=23

Michael Duffy, Assistant Secretary

It is the philosophy of this agency that treatment and prevention services should be of high quality and easily accessible to all citizens of the state. The Office for Addictive Disorders offers comprehensive treatment and prevention services through ten Regional/District Offices throughout the state.

Maine

2197 Maine Department Health and Human Services Children's Behavioral Health Services
11 State House Station
Augusta, ME 04333-11
207-287-3707
888-568-1112
Fax: 207-287-3005
TTY: 207-606-0215
www.maine.gov

Brenda Harvey, Manager

Children's Behavioral Health Services (CBHS), a branch of the Department of Health and Human Services (DHHS) has a long tradition of advocacy for children with special needs. Once known as the Bureau of Children's with Special Needs (BCSN), this part of the Department became known as Children's Services in 1995. In a continuing effort to meet the diverse and growing needs of Maine families, Children's Behavioral Health Services (CBHS) is going through a further transition. Most services formerly provided directly through the Department are now delivered through contracted community agencies.

2198 Maine Department of Behavioral and Developmental Services
Marguardt Building, 3rd Floor
159 State House Station
Augusta, ME 04333-159
207-287-6415
Fax: 207-287-8910

Provides community services to individuals with mental illnesses, mental retardation, substance abuse issues and children with special needs. Provides psychiatric inpatient services at two mental health facilities.

2199 Maine Office of Substance Abuse: Information and Resource Center
11 State House Station
Augusta, ME 04333-11
207-287-8900
800-499-0027
Fax: 207-287-8910
TTY: 800-606-0215
E-mail: osa.ircosa@maine.gov

Jo Mc Caslin, Manager

Provides Maine's citizens with alcohol, tobacco and other drug information, resources and research for prevention, education and treatment.

Maryland

2200 Centers for Medicare & Medicaid Services/CMS: Office of Research, Statisctics, Data and Systems
7500 Security Boulevard
Baltimore, MD 21244-1849
410-786-3000

Information on CMS research, statistics, data & systems.

2201 Centers for Medicare & Medicaid Services
7500 Security Boulevard
Baltimore, MD 21244-1849
410-786-3000

Information about the Centers for Medicare & Medicaid Services (CMS).

2202 Centers for Medicare & Medicaid Services: Office of Policy
7500 Security Boulevard
Baltimore, MD 21244-1849
410-786-3000

The OP assists the CMS Policy Council with immediate/rapid response on timely issues and transforms concepts into institutionalized processes.

2203 Centers for Medicare and Medicaid Services: Office of Financial Management/OFM
7500 Security Boulevard
Baltimore, MD 21244-1849
410-786-3000

OFM has overall reponsibility for the fiscal integrity of CMS' programs.

2204 Maryland Alcohol and Drug Abuse Administration
55 Wade Avenue
Baltimore, MD 21228-4663

410-767-6910
Fax: 410-402-8601
www.maryland-adaa.org

Peter Luongo, Manager

The Alcohol and Drug Abuse Administration (ADAA) is the single state agency responsible for the provision, coordination, and regulation of the statewide network of substance abuse prevention, intervention and treatment services. It serves as the initial point of contact for technical assistance and regulatory interpretation for all Maryland Department of Health and Mental Hygiene (DHMH) prevention and certified treatment programs.

2205 Maryland Department of Health and Mental Hygiene
201 West Preston Street
Baltimore, MD 21201-2301
410-767-6500
877-463-3464
E-mail: webadministrator@dhmh.state.md.us
www.dhmh.state.md.us/health/

Provides information on a variety of services including mental health and substance abuse, health plans and providers, nutrition and maternal care, environmental health and developmental disabilities.

2206 Maryland Department of Human Resources
311 West Saratoga Street
Baltimore, MD 21201-3500

800-332-6347
TTY: 800-925-4434
E-mail: dhrhelp@dhr.state.md.us
www.dhr.state.md.us/help.htm

The mission of the Maryland Department of Human Resources is to assist people in economic need, provide prevention services, and protect vulnerable children and adults.

2207 Maryland Division of Mental Health
2301 Argonne Drive
Baltimore, MD 21218-1628
410-767-6860
Fax: 410-333-7482

Massachusetts

2208 Massachusetts Department of Mental Health
1 Ashburton Place
11th Floor
Boston, MA 02108-1518
617-573-1600
www.mass.gov/dmh/

Judy Ann Bigby, Secretary

The Massachusetts Department of Mental Health provides clinical, rehabilitative and supportive services for adults with serious mental illness, and children and adolescents with serious mental illness or serious emotional disturbance.

2209 Massachusetts Department of Public Health
250 Washington Street
Boston, MA 02108-4603
617-624-6000
Fax: 617-624-5206
TTY: 617-624-6001
www.masspartnership.com

Paul Cote, Manager

Our mission, to serve all the people in the Commonwealth, particularly the under served, and to promote healthy people, healthy families, healthy communities and healthy environments through compassionate care, education and prevention. Your health is our concern.

2210 Massachusetts Department of Public Health: Bureau of Substance Abuse Services
250 Washington Street
Boston, MA 02108-4603
617-624-6000
800-327-5050
Fax: 617-624-5206
TTY: 617-536-5872
www.masspartnership.com

Paul Cote, Manager

The Bureau of Substance Abuse Services oversees the substance abuse prevention and treatment services in the Commonwealth. Responsibilities include: licensing programs and counselors; funding and monitoring prevention and treatment services; providing access to treatment for the indigent and uninsured; developing and implementing policies and programs; and, tracking substance abuse trends in the state.

2211 Massachusetts Department of Social Services
24 Farnsworth Street
Boston, MA 02210-1262
617-748-2000
Fax: 617-261-7435

Mary Ellen Bennard, Executive

The mission of the Massachusetts Department of Social Services is to ensure the safety of children in a manner that holds the best hope of nuturing a sustained, resilent network of relationships to support the child's growth and development into adulthood.

2212 Massachusetts Department of Transitional Assistance
Massachusetts Department of Health and Human Services
600 Washington Street
Boston, MA 02111-1751
617-348-8500
www.mass.gov/dta/

The mission of the Department of Transitional Assistance is to serve the Commonwealth's most vulnerable families and individuals with dignity and respect, ensuring those eligible for our services have access to those services in an accurate, timely and culturally sensitive manner and in a way that promotes client's independence and long term self-sufficiency.

2213 Massachusetts Division of Medical Assistance
MassHealth Program
1 Ashburton Place
11th Floor
Boston, MA 02108-1518
617-573-1600
www.mass/gov/dma/

Judy Ann Bigby, Secretary

The mission of the MassHealth program is to help the financially needy obtain high-quality health care that is affordable, promotes independence, and provides customer satisfacation.

2214 Massachusetts Executive Office of Public Safety
1 Ashburton Place
Suite 2133
Boston, MA 02108-1504
617-727-7775
Fax: 617-727-4764
E-mail: eopsinfo@state.ma.us
www.mass.gov

Plans and manages public safety efforts by supporting, supervising and providing planning and guidance to a variety of state agencies.

Michigan

2215 Michigan Department of Community Health
Department of Mental Health
Capitol View Building
201 Townsend Street
Lansing, MI 48913-1
517-373-3740
E-mail: mccurtisj@michigan.gov
www.michigan.gov/mdch/

Janet Olszewski, Director
James McCurtis, Public Information Officer

Provides information on drug control and substance abuse treatment policies.

2216 Michigan Department of Human Services
235 S Grand Ave
PO Box 30037
Lansing, MI 48909-7537
517-373-2305
Fax: 517-335-6101
TTY: 517-373-8071
www.michigan.gov/dhs/

The Department of Human Services (DHS) is Michigan's public assistance, child and family welfare agency. DHS directs the operations of public assistance and service programs through a network of over 100 county department of human service offices around the state.

2217 Michigan State Representative: Co-Chair
Public Health
S0688 House Office Building
P O Box 30014
Lansing, MI 48909-7514

517-373-1705
Fax: 517-373-5968
E-mail: shanellejackson@house.mi.gov
www.house.michigan.gov/rep.asp?DIST=009
Shanelle Jackson

2218 National Council on Alcoholism and Drug Dependence: Greater Detriot Area

4777 East Outer Drive
Detroit, MI 48234
313-369-5400
Fax: 313-369-5415
E-mail: info@ncadd-detroit.org
www.ncadd-detroit.org/

The National Council on Alcoholism and Drug Dependence-Greater Detroit Area is a voluntary, non-profit agency committed to improving health through providing substance abuse prevention, education, training, treatment and advocacy for the metropolitan Detroit area.

Minnesota

2219 Department of Human Services: Chemical Health Division

PO Box 64977
Saint Paul, MN 55164-977
651-431-2460
Fax: 651-431-7449
www.dhs.state.mn.us

The Chemical Health Division is the state alcohol and drug authority responsible for defining a statewide response to drug and alcohol abuse. This includes providing basic information on chemical health. It also includes planning a broad-based community service system, evaluating the effectiveness of various chemical dependency services, and funding innovative programs to promote reduction of alcohol and other drug problems and their effects on individuals, families and society

2220 Lake Area Youth Services Bureau

244 North Lake Street
Forest Lake, MN 55025-2517
651-464-3685
Fax: 651-464-3687
E-mail: Jeanne.Walz@ysblakesarea.org
www.ysblakesarea.org

Jeanne Walz, Executive Director

Provides enrichment programs and intervention support to youth and families. Available on FaceBook and Twitter

Year Founded: 1976

2221 Minnesota Department of Human Services

444 Lafayette Road
Saint Paul, MN 55155-3899
651-431-3515
Fax: 651-431-7476
www.dhs.state.mn.us/

The Minnesota Department of Human Services helps people meet their basic needs by providing or administering health care coverage, economic assistance, and a variety of services for children, people with disabilities and older Minnesotans.

Mississippi

2222 Mississippi Alcohol Safety Education Program

103 Mississippi Research Park
PO Box 5287
Mississippi State, MS 39762-5287
662-325-3423
Fax: 662-325-9439
www.ssrc.misstate.edu/

MASEP is the statewide program for first-time offenders convicted of driving under the influence of alcohol or another substance which has impaired one's ability to operate a motor vehicle.

2223 Mississippi Department Mental Health Mental Retardation Services

1101 Robert E Lee Building
239 N. Lamar Street
Jackson, MS 39201-1328
601-359-1288
877-210-8513
Fax: 601-359-6295
TDD: 601-359-6230

Margueritte Ransom, Manager

Has the primary responsibility for the development and implementation of services to meet the needs of individuals with mental retardation/developmental disabilities. This public service delivery system is comprised of five state-operated comprehensive regional centers for individuals with mental retardation/developmental disabilities, a state-operated facility for youth who require specialized treatment and have mental retardation/developmental disabilities, 15 regional community mental health/mental retardation centers, and other nonprofit community agencies/organizations that provide community services.

2224 Mississippi Department of Human Services

750 North State Street
Jackson, MS 39202-3033
601-359-4500
800-345-6347
www.mdhs.state.ms.us

Donald Taylor, Executive Director

The mission of the Department of Human Services is to provide services for people in need by optimizing all available resources to sustain the family unit and to encourage traditional family values thereby promoting self-sufficiency and personal responsibility for all Mississippians.

2225 Mississippi Department of Mental Health: Division of Alcohol and Drug Abuse

239 N Lamar Street
1101 Robert F Lee Building
Jackson, MS 39201
601-359-1288
Fax: 601-359-6295

TDD: 601-359-6230
www.dmh.state.ms.us

Edwin Legrand, Executive Director

The Division of Alcohol and Drug Abuse Services is responsible for establishing, maintaining, monitoring and evaluating a statewide system of alcohol and drug abuse services, including prevention, treatment and rehabilitation. The division has designed a system of services for alcohol and drug abuse prevention and treatment reflecting its philosophy that alcohol and drug abuse is a treatable and preventable illness.

2226 Mississippi Department of Mental Health: Division of Medicaid

Sillers Building 550 High Street
Suite 1000
Jackson, MS 39201
601-359-6050
www.dom.state.ms.us/

Robert L Robinson, Executive Director

Medicaid is a national health care program. It helps pay for medical services for low-income people. For those eligible for full Medicaid services, Medicaid is paid to providers of health care. Providers are doctors, hospitals and pharmacists who take Medicaid. We strive to provide financial assistance for the provision of quality health services to our beneficiaries with professionalism, integrity, compassion and commitment. We are advocates for, and accountable to the people we serve.

2227 Mississippi Department of Rehabilitation Services: Office of Vocational Rehabilitation (OVR)

1281 Highway 51
Po Box 1698
Madison, MS 39130-1698
601-853-5100
800-443-1000
www.mdrs.state.ms.us

Dr Norman Miller, Deputy Director

The Office of Vocational Rehabilitation (OVR) provides services designed to improve economic opportunities for individuals with physical and mental disabilities through employment. Work related services are individualized and may include but are not limited to: counseling, job development, job training, job placement, supported employment, transition services and employability skills training program. OVR has a network of 17 community rehabilitation centers (Allied Enterprises) located throughout the state, which provide vocational assessment, job training and actual work experience for individuals with disabilities. Thousands of Mississippians are successfully employed each year through the teamwork at OVR.

Missouri

2228 Missouri Department Health & Senior Services

PO Box 570
Jefferson City, MO 65102-570

573-751-6400
Fax: 573-751-6401
E-mail: info@dhss.mo.gov
www.dhss.mo.gov/

The Missouri Department of Health and Senior Services provides information on a variety of topics including senior services and health, current news and public notices, laws and regulations, and statistical reports.

2229 Missouri Department of Mental Health

1706 E Elm Street
P O Box 687
Jefferson City, MO 65102-687
573-751-4122
800-364-9687
Fax: 573-751-8224
TTY: 573-526-1201
E-mail: dmhmail@dmh.mo.gov
www.dmh.missouri.gov/

State law provides three principal missions for the department: (1) the prevention of mental disorders, developmental disabilities, substance abuse, and compulsive gambling; (2) the treatment, habilitation, and rehabilitation of Missourians who have those conditions; and (3) the improvement of public understanding and attitudes about mental disorders, developmental disabilities, substance abuse, and compulsive gambling.

2230 Missouri Department of Public Safety

301 W. High Street
Hst Building, Rm. 870, PO Box 749
Jefferson City, MO 65101-1517
573-751-8374
E-mail: dpsinfo@dps.mo.gov

Lisa Morrow, Manager

The Office of the Director is the Department of Public Safety's central administrative unit. Our office administers federal and state funds in grants for juvenile justice, victims' assistance, law enforcement, and narcotics control. Other programs in the Director's Office provide support services and resources to assist local law enforcement agencies and to promote crime prevention.

2231 Missouri Department of Social Services

221 West High Street
P O Box 1527
Jefferson City, MO 65102-1527
573-751-4815
Fax: 573-751-3203
TDD: 800-735-2966
www.dss.mo.gov/

Ronald J Levy, Director

A true measure of a society is the extent of its concern for those less fortunate-its intent of keeping families together, preventing abuse and neglect, and encouraging self-sufficiency and independence. In Missouri, programs dealing with these concerns are administered by the state Department of Social Services.

2232 Missouri Department of Social Services: Medical Services Division

615 Howerton Court
P O Box 6500
Jefferson City, MO 65102-6500
573-751-3425
Fax: 573-751-6564
www.dss.mo.gov/mhd/

The purpose of the Division of Medical Services is to purchase and monitor health care services for low income and vulnerable citizens of the State of Missouri. The agency assures quality health care through development of service delivery systems, standards setting and enforcement, and education of providers and recipients. We are fiscally accountable for maximum and appropriate utilization of resources

2233 Missouri Division of Alcohol and Drug Abuse

P O Box 687
1706 E Elm Street
Jefferson City, MO 65101-4130
573-751-4942
E-mail: adamail@dmh.mo.gov
www.dmh.missouri.gov/ada/adaindex.htm

The Division provides funding for prevention, outpatient, residential, and detoxification services to community-based programs that work with communities to develop and implement comprehensive coordinated plans. The Division provides technical assistance to these agencies and operates a certification program that sets standards for treatment programs, qualified professionals, and alcohol and drug related educational programs.

2234 Missouri Division of Comprehensive Psychiatric Service

PO Box 687
1706 E Elm Street
Jefferson City, MO 65101-4130
573-751-8017
E-mail: cpsmail@dmh.mo.gov
www.dmh.missouri.gov/cps/cpsindex.htm

The division is committed to serving four target populations: persons with serious and persistent mental illness (SMI); persons suffering from acute psychiatric conditions; children and youth with serious emotional disturbances (SED) and forensic clients. In addition, CPS has identified four priority groups within the target populations: (1) individuals in crisis, (2) people who are homeless, (3) those recently discharged from inpatient care and (4) substantial users of public funds. These target populations currently constitute the majority of clientele whom the Division serves both in inpatient and ambulatory settings.

2235 Missouri Division of Mental Retardation and Developmental Disabilities

1706 E Elm Street
PO Box 687
Jefferson City, MO 65102-687
573-751-8676
E-mail: mrddmail@dmh.mo.gov
www.dmh.missouri.gov/mrdd/mrddindex.htm

The Division of Mental Retardation and Developmental Disabilities (MRDD), established in 1974, serves a population that has developmental disabilities such as mental retardation, cerebral palsy, head injuries, autism, epilepsy, and certain learning disabilities. Such conditions must have occurred before age 22, with the expectation that they will continue. To be eligible for services from the Division, persons with these disabilities must be substantially limited in their ability to function independently.

Montana

2236 Monatana Department of Human & Community Services

111 N Jackson Street
Helena, MT 59601-4168
406-444-1788
www.dphhs.mt.gov/

The mission of the Montana Department of Human & Community Services is to promote job preparation and work as a means to help needy families become self-sufficient.

2237 Montana Department of Health and Human Services: Child & Family Services Division

Cogswell Building
1400 Broadway
Helena, MT 59601-5231
406-444-5900
www.dphhs.mt.gov/

The Child and Family Services Division (CFSD) is a part of the Montana Department of Public Health and Human Services. Its mission is to keep Montana's children safe and families strong. The division provides state and federally mandated protective services to children who are abused, neglected, or abandoned. This includes receiving and investigating reports of child abuse and neglect, working to prevent domestic violence, helping families to stay together or reunite, and finding placements in foster or adoptive homes.

2238 Montana Department of Public Health & Human Services: Addictive and Mental Disorders

555 Fuller Avenue
Helena, MT 59601-3394
406-444-3964
www.dphhs.mt.gov/

The mission of the Addictive and Mental Disorders Division (AMDD) of the Montana Department of Public Health and Human Services is to implement and improve an appropriate statewide system of prevention, treatment, care, and rehabilitation for Montanans with mental disorders or addictions to drugs or alcohol.

2239 Montana Department of Public Health and Human Services: Montana Vocational Rehabilitation Programs
Disability Services Division
111 Sanders Street
Helena, MT 59601-4520
406-444-5622
www.dphhs.mt.gov/

The mission of the Disability Services Division (DSD) of the Montana Department of Public Health and Human Services is to provide services that help Montanans with disabilities to live, work and fully participate in their communities.

Nebraska

2240 Nebraska Department of Health and Human Services (NHHS)
PO Box 95026
Lincoln, NE 68509-5026
402-471-3121
www.hhs.state.ne.us/

The mission of the NHHS is to help people live better lives through effective health and human services.

2241 Nebraska Health & Human Services: Medicaid and Managed Care Division
Department of Finance & Support
PO Box 95026
Lincoln, NE 68509-5026
402-471-3121
www.hhs.state.ne.us

The Finance and Support agency aligns human resources, financial resources, and information needs for the Nebraska Health and Human Services System and is the designated Title XIX (Medicaid) agency responsible for provider enrollment activities.

2242 Nebraska Health and Human Services Division: Department of Mental Health
P O Box 95026
Lincoln, NE 68509-5026
402-471-3121
www.hhs.state.ne.us

Mental health services are designed for individuals and their families who have a serious and persistent mental illness that can create lifetime disabilities, and in some cases make the individuals dangerous to themselves or others. Services are also designed for people experiencing acute, serious mental illnesses, which in some cases may cause a life threatening event such as suicide attempts. In addition, services are provided for children and to their families.

2243 Nebraska Mental Health Centers
4545 South 86th Street
Lincoln, NE 68526-9227
402-483-6990
888-210-8064
Fax: 402-483-7045
E-mail: drness@nmhc-clinics.com

Reed Campbell, Director

We are a primary mental health care center that is truly committed to being of service to the Lincoln/Lancaster community and Greater Nebraska.

Nevada

2244 Nevada Department of Health & Human Services Health Care Financing and Policy
1100 East William Street, Suite 101
Carson City, NV 89701-3103
775-687-8420
E-mail: techhelp@dhcfp.nv.gov

The Division of Health Care Financing and Policy works in partnership with the Centers for Medicare & Medicaid Services to assist in providing quality medical care for eligible individuals and families with low incomes and limited resources. Services are provided through a combination of traditional fee-for-service provider networks and managed care.

2245 Nevada Department of Health and Human Services
4126 Technology Way
Room 100
Carson City, NV 89706-2013
775-684-4000
E-mail: nvdhs@dhhs.nv.gov
www.dhhs.nv.gov

Michael J Willden, Director

The Department of Health and Human Services (DHHS) promotes the health and well-being of Nevadans through the delivery or facilitation of essential services to ensure families are strengthened, public health is protected, and individuals achieve their highest level of self-sufficiency.

2246 Nevada Division of Mental Health & Developmental Services
4126 Technology Way
2nd Floor
Carson City, NV 89706-2027
775-684-5943
Fax: 775-684-5966
E-mail: mhdswebmaster@mhds.nv.gov
www.mhds.com

Carlos Brandenburg, Administrator

The Nevada Division of Mental Health provides a full array of clinical services to over 24,000 consumers each year. Services include: crisis intervention, hospital care, medication clinic, outpatient counseling, residential support and other mental health services targeted to individuals with serious mental illness.

2247 Nevada Employment Training & Rehabilitation Department
500 East Third Street
Carson City, NV 89713-1
775-684-3849
Fax: 775-684-3850

TTY: 775-687-5353
www.nvdetr.org/

Larry Mosley, Director

The Department of Employment, Training and Rehabilitation (DETR) is comprised of four divisions with numerous bureaus programs, and services housed in offices throughout Nevada to provide citizens the state's premier source of employment, training, and rehabilitative programs.

2248 Nevada State Health Division: Bureau of Alcohol & Drug Abuse
4126 Technology Way
Carson City, NV 89706-2066
775-684-5943
Fax: 775-684-5964
www.state.nv.us

Larry Mosley, Director

The mission of the Bureau of Alcohol and Drug Abuse (BADA) is to reduce the impact of substance abuse in Nevada.

2249 Northern Nevada Adult Mental Health Services
480 Galletti Way
Sparks, NV 89431-5564
775-688-2001
Fax: 775-688-2192
www.mhds.state.nv.us

The mission of Northern Nevada Adult Mental Health Services is to provide psychiatric treatment and rehabilitation services in the least restrictive setting to support personal recovery and enhance quality of life.

2250 Southern Nevada Adult Mental Health Services
6161 W Charleston Boulevard
Las Vegas, NV 89146-1148
702-486-6093

Anuranjan Bist, Director

State operated community mental health center. Provides inpatient and outpatient psychiatric services.

New Hampshire

2251 New Hampshire Department of Health & Human Services: Bureau of Community Health Services
29 Hazen Drive
Concord, NH 03301-6503
603-271-4638
www.dhhs.state.nh.us/DHHS/BCHS/default.htm

The Bureau of Community Health Services oversees grants to community-based agencies for medical and preventive health services, sets policy, provides technical assistance and education, and carries out quality assurance activities in its programmatic areas of expertise.

2252 New Hampshire Department of Health and Human Services: Bureau of Developmental Services
105 Pleasant Street
Concord, NH 03301-3852
603-271-5034
Fax: 603-271-5166
www.dhhs.state.nh.us/DHHS/BDS/default.htm

The NH developmental services system offers its consumers with developmental disabilities and acquired brain disorders a wide range of supports and services within their own communities. BDS is comprised of a main office in Concord and 12 designated non-profit and specialized service agencies that represent specific geographic regions of NH; the community agencies are commonly referred to as Area Agencies. All direct services and supports to individuals and families are provided in accordance with contractual agreements between BDS and the Area Agencies.

2253 New Hampshire Department of Health and Human Services: Bureau of Behavioral Health
105 Pleasant Street
Concord, NH 03301-3852
603-271-5000
Fax: 603-271-5058
www.dhhs.state.nh.us/DHHS/BBH/default.htm

The Bureau of Behavioral Health (BBH) seeks to promote respect, recovery, and full community inclusion for adults, including older adults, who experience a mental illness and children with an emotional disturbance. By law and rule, BBH is mandated to ensure the provision of efficient and effective services to those citizens who are most severely and persistently disabled by mental, emotional, and behavioral dysfunction. To this end, BBH has apportioned the entire state into community mental health regions. Each of the ten regions has a BBH contracted Community Mental Health Center and many regions have Peer Support Agencies.

New Jersey

2254 Juvenile Justice Commission
1001 Spruce Street
Suite 202
Trenton, NJ 08638-3957
609-292-1400
Fax: 609-943-4611
E-mail: commission@njjjc.org
www.state.nj.us/lps/jjc/info.htm

Thomas Flanagan, Acting Executive Director

The Juvenile Justice Commission (JJC) has three primary responsibilities: the care and custody of juvenile offenders committed to the agency by the courts, the support of local efforts to plan for and provide services to at-risk and court-involved youth through County Youth Services Commissions and the state Incentive Program, and the supervision of youth on aftercare/parole.

2255 New Jersey Department of Human Services
P O Box 700
222 S Warren Street
Trenton, NJ 08608-2306

609-292-3717
Fax: 609-292-3824
www.state.nj.us

Jennifer Velez, President

The New Jersey Department of Human Services (DHS) is the state's social services agency, serving more than one million of New Jersey 's most vulnerable citizens, or about one of every eight New Jersey residents. Through the work of DHS and its 13 major divisions, individuals and families in need are able to keep their lives on track, their families together, a roof over their heads, and their health protected. Human Services offers individuals and families the breathing room they need in order to find permanent solutions to otherwise daunting problems.

2256 New Jersey Division of Mental Health Services
50 East State Street
PO Box 727
Trenton, NJ 08625-727

800-382-6717
www.state.nj.us/humanservices/dmhs

Kevin Martone, Assistant Commissioner

The Division of Mental Health Services (DMHS) serves adults with serious and persistent mental illnesses. Central to the Division's mission is the fact that these individuals are entitled to dignified and meaningful lives. With an operating budget of $588,377,000 for FY 2005 and 5,700 employees, services are available to anyone in the state who feels they need help with a mental health problem.

2257 New Jersey Division of Youth & Family Services
P O Box 717
50 East State Street, 5th Floor
Trenton, NJ 08608-1715
609-777-2000
Fax: 609-777-2050
www.state.nj.us/humanservices/dyfs/index.html

Lisa Von Pier, Area Director

The Division of Youth and Family Services (DYFS) is New Jersey's child protection/child welfare agency within the Office of Children's Services (OCS). DYFS is responsible for investigating allegations of child abuse and neglect and if necessary arranging for the child's protection and the family's treatment. 41 local offices handle referrals and investigations statewide. The mission of the Division of Youth and Family Services is to ensure the safety, permanency, and well-being of children and to support families.

2258 New Jersey Office of Managed Care
New Jersey Department of Banking & Insurance
20 West State Street
P O Box 325
Trenton, NJ 08625-325
609-292-7272
800-446-7467
www.state.nj.us/dobi/managed.htm

The Office of Managed Care is responsible for: the day-to-day tasks associated with regulating HMOs; regulating certain aspects of the operations of non-HMO carriers that offer health benefits plans in New Jersey that are managed care plans; regulating the utilization management functions of non-HMO carriers that include utilization management features in the health benefits plans they offer in New Jersey; providing certification of organized delivery systems in New Jersey; and certain review functions for other managed care matters, including review of Workers' Compensation Managed Care Organization applications and renewals, and applications of organized delivery systems that seek to be licensed by the Department of Banking and Insurance.

New Mexico

2259 New Mexico Behavioral Health Collaborative
2025 S Pocheoo Street
Po Box 2348
Santa Fe, NM 87504-2348
505-827-6250
Fax: 505-827-3185
E-mail: deborah.fickling@state.nm.us
www.state.nm.us/hsd/bhdwg/

Deborah Fickling, Director

At the heart of the Collaborative's vision is the expectation that the lives of individuals with mental illness and substance use disorders ("customers") will improve, that customers and family members will have an equal voice in the decisions that affect them and their loved ones, and that those most affected by mental illness and substance abuse can recover to lead full, meaningful lives within their communities. To achieve this will require a paradigm shift not only within the service delivery culture but also within the existing customer/family member networks.

2260 New Mexico Department of Health
1190 S St. Francis Drive
Santa Fe, NM 87505-4173
505-827-2613

Alfredo Vigil, Manager

The mission of the New Mexico Department of Health is to promote health and sound health policy, prevent disease and disability, improve health services systems and assure that essential public health functions and safety net services are available to New Mexicans.

2261 New Mexico Department of Human Services
PO Box 2348
Santa Fe, NM 87504-2348
505-827-7750
Fax: 505-827-6286
E-mail: eckert@state.nm.us
www.state.nm.us/hsd/

The Department strives to provide New Mexicans access to support and services so that they may move toward self-sufficiency.

2262 New Mexico Department of Human Services: Medical Assistance Division
PO Box 2348
Santa Fe, NM 87504-2348
505-827-3100
Fax: 505-827-3185
E-mail: nmmedicaidfraud@state.nm.us
www.state.nm.us/hsd/mad/Index.html

The Medical Assistance Division (MAD) is responsible for direct administration of the New Mexico Medicaid program. Medicaid is a joint federal and state program that pays for health care to New Mexicans who are eligible for Medicaid benefits.

2263 New Mexico Health & Environment Department
1190 St. Francis Drive
Suite N4050
Santa Fe, NM 87505-4173

800-219-6157
www.nmenv.state.nm.us/

Our mission is to provide the highest quality of life throughout the state by promoting a safe, clean and productive environment.

2264 New Mexico Kids, Parents and Families Office of Child Development: Children, Youth and Families Department
760 Motel Blvd
Suite C
Las Cruces, NM 88007-4169
505-827-7946
Fax: 505-476-0490
E-mail: dmhaggard@cyfd.state.nm.us
www.newmexicokids.org/Family/

Dan Haggard, Director

The Children, Youth and Families Department Office of Child Development (OCD) works collaboratively with the State Department of Education, Department of Health, Department of Labor and higher education and community programs to establish a five-year plan for Early Care, Education and Family Support Professional Development. The New Mexico Professional Development Initiative supports OCD's legislative mandate to articulate and implement training and licensure requirements for individuals working in all recognized settings with children from birth to age eight.

New York

2265 New York Office of Alcohol & Substance Abuse Services
1450 Western Avenue
Albany, NY 12203-3526
518-485-1768
E-mail: communications@oasas.state.ny.us
www.oasas.state.ny.us/pio/oasas.htm

Karen M. Carpenter-Paulumbo, Commissioner

State agency responsible for funding, licensing and monitering substance abuse prevention and treatment services in New York State.

2266 New York State Department of Health Individual County Listings of Social Services Departments
Corning Tower
Empire State Plaza
Albany, NY 12237-1
518-447-7300
E-mail: dohweb@health.state.ny.us
www.health.state.ny.us

Provides statewide listing of departments of social services including contact information.

2267 New York State Office of Mental Health
44 Holland Avenue
Albany, NY 12229-1
518-474-5554
800-597-8481

Michael Hogan, Manager

Promoting the mental health of all New Yorkers with a particular focus on providing hope and recovery for adults with serious mental illness and children with serious emotional disturbances.

North Carolina

2268 North Carolina Department of Human Resources
2001 Mail Service Center
Raleigh, NC 27699-2000
919-839-6262
Fax: 919-733-8034
www.ncartmuseum.org

Lawrence J Wheeler, Manager

Whether it is helping applicants find information on available jobs, providing consultation to managers and supervisors, informing current employees of benefits and services, or spearheading efforts to recruit hard-to-fill vacancies, the Division of Human Resources supports the overall mission of the Department of Health and Human Services (DHHS) to serve people.

2269 North Carolina Division of Mental Health
325 North Salisbury Street
Raleigh, NC 27603-1388
919-733-7011
Fax: 919-508-0951
E-mail: contactdmh@ncmail.net

Leza Wainwright, Manager

North Carolina will provide people with, or at risk of, mental illness, developmental disabilities and substance problems and their families the necessary prevention, intervention, treatment, services and supports they need to live successfully in communities of their choice.

2270 North Carolina Division of Social Services
Albemarle Building
325 N Salisbury Street 8th Floor
Raleigh, NC 27601
919-733-3055
Fax: 919-334-1018
www.ncdhhs.gov

Sherry S Bradsher, Director

2271 North Carolina Substance Abuse Professional Certification Board (NCSAPCB)
PO Box 10126
Raleigh, NC 27605-126
919-832-0975
Fax: 919-833-5743
www.ncsapcb.org

Provides guidelines for the certification of professionals in the substance abuse field of human services.

North Dakota

2272 North Dakota Department of Human Services: Medicaid Program
600 E Boulevard Avenue
Dept 325
Bismarck, ND 58505-602
701-328-2455
Fax: 701-328-1717
E-mail: dhsmed@nd.gov

Mark Nelson, Manager

Pays for a wide array of medical services including mental health services for certain low-income residents of North Dakota. Anyone interested in applying for services should contact their local County Social Service Board office.

2273 North Dakota Department of Human Services: Mental Health Services Division
600 E Boulevard Avenue
Dept 325
Bismarck, ND 58505-602
701-328-2455
Fax: 701-328-1717
E-mail: dhsmed@nd.gov

Mark Nelson, Manager

The Department of Human Services' Mental Health and Substance Abuse Services Division provides leadership for the planning, development, and oversight of a system of care for children, adults, and families with severe emotional disorders, mental illness, and/or substance abuse issues.

2274 North Dakota Department of Human Services Division of Mental Health and Substance Abuse Services
1237 West Divide Avenue
Suite 1C
Bismarck, ND 58501-1208
701-328-8920
800-755-2719
Fax: 701-328-8969

E-mail: dhsmhsas@nd.gov
www.nd.gov/dhs/services/mentalhealth

Provides leadership for the planning, development and oversight of a system of care for children, adults and families with severe emotional disorders, mental illness and/or substance abuse issues. Mental health and substance abuse services are delivered through eight Regional Human Services Centers and the North Dakota State Hospital in Jamestown.

Ohio

2275 Ohio Community Drug Board
725 East Market Street
Akron, OH 44305-2421
330-434-4141
Fax: 330-434-7125
TDD: 330-535-4889
www.commhealthcenter.org/

The Community Health Center is committed to enhancing the quality of life by providing a diverse, holistic, patient-centered continuum of care. Our innovative and effective services include addiction treatment, behavioral and primary healthcare, wellness, prevention and housing programs that are responsive to the needs of the community. We have been serving Northeast Ohio since 1974.

2276 Ohio Department of Mental Health
30 East Broad Street
8th Floor
Columbus, OH 43215-3414
614-464-0810
877-275-6364
TTY: 614-752-9696
E-mail: uhricks@mh.state.oh.us

Ensures high quality mental health care is available to all Ohioans, particularly individuals with severe mental illness.

Oklahoma

2277 Oklahoma Department of Human Services
Po Box 25352
Oklahoma City, OK 73125-352
405-521-3646
www.okdhs.org

The mission of the Oklahoma Department of Human Services is to help individuals and families in need help themselves lead safer, healthier, more independent and productive lives.

2278 Oklahoma Department of Mental Health and Substance Abuse Service (ODMHSAS)
1200 NE 13th Street
PO Box 53277
Oklahoma City, OK 73152-3277
405-522-3908
800-522-9054
Fax: 405-522-3650
TDD: 405-522-3851
www.odmhsas.org

State agency responsible for mental health, substance abuse, and domestic violence and sexual assault services.

2279 Oklahoma Healthcare Authority

4545 North Lincoln Boulevard
Suite 124
Oklahoma City, OK 73105-3400
405-522-7300
www.ohca.state.ok.us/

Provides health and medical policy information to Medicaid consumers and providers, administers SoonerCare and other health related programs.

2280 Oklahoma Mental Health Consumer Council

3200 NW 48th
Suite 102
Oklahoma City, OK 73112-5911
405-604-6975
888-424-1305
E-mail: consumercouncil@okmhcc.org
www.omhcc.org

Becky Tallent, Executive Director

Consumer run statewide advocacy organization for education, empowerment, quality of life, encouragement and rights protection of persons with mental illness. Services include empowerment training, systems advocacy, peer support and jail diversion programs.

2281 Oklahoma Office of Juvenile Affairs

3812 North Santa Fe
Suite 400
Oklahoma City, OK 73118-8500
918-530-2800
Fax: 918-530-2890
www.ok.gov/oja/

Robert E Christian, Executive Director

State agency charged with delivery of programs and services to delinquent youth. Services include delinquency prevention, diversion, counseling in both community and secure residential programs. OJA provides counseling services with counselors, social workers and psychologists, as well as contracted service providers.

Year Founded: 1995

Oregon

2282 Marion County Health Department

3180 Center Street NE
Suite 2100
Salem, OR 97310-1
503-588-5057
Fax: 503-361-2268
E-mail: health@co.marion.or.us
www.co.marion.or.us

David Brown, Manager

The Marion County Health Department fosters wellness, monitors health trends, and responds to community health needs.

2283 Office of Mental Health and Addiction Services Training & Resource Center

500 Summer Street Ne E86
Salem, OR 97301-1063
503-945-5763
Fax: 503-378-8467

Robert Nikkel, Administrator

We are a library and clearinghouse, your connection to resources for prevention and treatment of disorders related to the use of alcohol, tobacco, other drugs and problem gambling. Our goal is to provide current, accurate and timely information to professionals and the public. We also seek to promote use of research based practices and promising approaches to prevention and treatment.

2284 Oregon Commission on Children and Families

530 Center Street NE
Suite 405
Salem, OR 97301-3754
503-373-1283

Mickey Lansing, Executive Director

Has various support services for children and families. Includes mental counseling, education training, and community outreach programs.

2285 Oregon Department of Human Resources: Division of Health Services

800 NE Oregon Street
Portland, OR 97232-2162
971-673-1555
Fax: 971-673-1562
TTY: 971-673-0372
www.oregonindependentcontractors.com

Health Services administers low-income medical programs, and mental health and substance abuse services. It provides public health services such as monitoring drinking-water quality and communicable-disease outbreaks, inspecting restaurants and promoting healthy behaviors.

2286 Oregon Department of Human Services: Mental Health Services

500 Summer Street NE
Salem, OR 97301-1063
503-945-5944
Fax: 503-378-2897
TTY: 503-945-6214
E-mail: dhs.info@state.or.us

Bruce Goldberg, Manager

The Office of Mental Health Services oversees a continuum of services and care including crisis services, local acute care, clinic based and outpatient care, state hospital referral, supported housing and employment. Programs include Community Services; Extended Care; Quality Assurance; Medical Director; Planning and Projects Development; Mental Health Planning and Management Advisory Council; Budget, Data and Operations; Contract and Budget Coordination; and Office Operations and Support.

2287 Oregon Department of Human Services: Office of Developmental Disabilities
500 Summer Street NE
Salem, OR 97301-1063
503-945-5944
Fax: 503-378-2897
E-mail: dhs.info@state.or.us
Bruce Goldberg, Manager

The Office of Developmental Disability Services oversees a system of community based programs for individuals with developmental disabilities including residential care, vocational/employment assistance, family support, and crisis/diversion services. Programs include Administration, Protective Services, Contracts, Licensing and Certification, Information and Data, Training, Self-Directed Supports, Medicaid Twenty-Hour Personal Care, Employment/Alternatives to Employment, Development Team, 24-Hour Residential Facilities, Vocational Programs, Diversion/Crisis, Diagnosis and Evaluation, Medical Director, and Housing.

2288 Oregon Health Policy and Research: Policy and Analysis Unit
1225 Ferry Street Se
1st Floor
Salem, OR 97301-4278
503-373-1824
www.oregon.gov/

Facilitates collaborative health services and research and policy analysis on issues affecting the Oregon Health Plan population and works to effectively communicate timely, quality results of health services research and analysis in the interest of informing health policy.

Pennsylvania

2289 Pennsylvania Bureau Drug and Alcohol Programs: Monitoring
2 Kline Plaza
Suite B
Harrisburg, PA 17104-1503
717-783-8200
Fax: 717-787-6285
www.dsf.health.state.pa.us/health/cwp/view.asp?A=173&Q

The Bureau of Drug and Alcohol Programs was established by the Pennsylvania Drug and Alcohol Abuse Control Act and is charged with developing and implementing a comprehensive health, education, and rehabilitation program for the prevention, intervention, treatment and case management of drug and alcohol abuse and dependence. This program is implemented through grant agreements with the 49 Single County Authorities (SCAs) who, in turn, contract with private service providers. BDAP provides for central planning, management, and monitoring; the SCAs provide administrative oversight to the local contracted programs

2290 Pennsylvania Bureau of Community Program Standards: Licensure and Certification
Pennsylvania Department of Health
7th & Forster Streets
Harrisburg, PA 17120-1
717-787-3350
877-724-3258

Perrianne Lurie

The Bureau's mission is to assure that certain healthcare providers are delivering quality services by adhering to established minimum state and federal standards of operation. Bureau staff conduct on-site surveys to assess adherence to the standards, as well as consumer satisfaction with the services provided.

2291 Pennsylvania Bureau of Drug and Alcohol Programs: Information Bulletins
2 Kline Plaza
Suite B
Harrisburg, PA 17104-1503
717-783-8200
Fax: 717-787-6285
www.dsf.health.state.pa.us/health/CWP/view.asp?A=173&Q

The Bureau of Drug and Alcohol Programs was established by the Pennsylvania Drug and Alcohol Abuse Control Act and is charged with developing and implementing a comprehensive health, education, and rehabilitation program for the prevention, intervention, treatment and case management of drug and alcohol abuse and dependence. This program is implemented through grant agreements with the 49 Single County Authorities (SCAs) who, in turn, contract with private service providers. BDAP provides for central planning, management, and monitoring; the SCAs provide administrative oversight to the local contracted programs

2292 Pennsylvania Department of Health: Bureau of Drug and Alcohol Programs
2 Kline Plaza
Suite B
Harrisburg, PA 17104-1503
717-783-8200
Fax: 717-787-6285
www.dsf.health.state.pa.us/health/cwp/view.asp?A=173&Q

The Bureau of Drug and Alcohol Programs was established by the Pennsylvania Drug and Alcohol Abuse Control Act and is charged with developing and implementing a comprehensive health, education, and rehabilitation program for the prevention, intervention, treatment and case management of drug and alcohol abuse and dependence. This program is implemented through grant agreements with the 49 Single County Authorities (SCAs) who, in turn, contract with private service providers. BDAP provides for central planning, management, and monitoring; the SCAs provide administrative oversight to the local contracted programs.

2293 Pennsylvania Department of Public Welfare and Mental Health Services
PO Box 2675
Harrisburg, PA 17105-2675
717-787-6443
www.dpw.state.pa.us/Family/MentalHealthServ/

The Department of Public Welfare is charged with numerous program areas that include all children, youth and family concerns, mental health, mental retardation, income maintenance, medical assistance and social program issues in the Commonwealth. They also license assisted living facilities and day care centers.

2294 Pennsylvania Division of Drug and Alcohol Prevention: Treatment
2 Kline Street
Suite B
Harrisburg, PA 17104-1503
717-783-8200
Fax: 717-787-6285
www.dsf.health.state.pa.us/health/cwp/view.asp?A=173&Q

The Bureau of Drug and Alcohol Programs was established by the Pennsylvania Drug and Alcohol Abuse Control Act and is charged with developing and implementing a comprehensive health, education, and rehabilitation program for the prevention, intervention, treatment and case management of drug and alcohol abuse and dependence. This program is implemented through grant agreements with the 49 Single County Authorities (SCAs) who, in turn, contract with private service providers. BDAP provides for central planning, management, and monitoring; the SCAs provide administrative oversight to the local contracted programs.

2295 Pennsylvania Medical Assistance Programs
Health & Welfare Building
Room 515, PO Box 2675
Harrisburg, PA 17105-2675
717-787-1870
www.dpw.state.pa.us/OMAP/

Mission is to implement mandatory managed care statewide; to expand home and community based services; to improve the quality of services to consumers and providers in all our health care delivery systems; and to improve our technology infrastructure by supporting H-Net Development and re-designing MAMIS.

Rhode Island

2296 Rhode Island Council on Alcoholism and Other Drug Dependence
500 Prospect Street
Pawtucket, RI 02860-6260
401-725-0410
Fax: 401-725-0768
E-mail: info@ricaodd.org

David E Walsh, Executive Director

The Rhode Island Council on Alcoholism and Other Drug Dependence is a private, non-profit corporation whose mission is to help individuals, youth and families who are troubled with alcohol, tobacco and other drug dependence.

2297 Rhode Island Department of Human Services
600 New London Avenue
Cranston, RI 02920-3041
401-462-3019
www.dhs.state.ri.us/

Gary Alexander, Director

We are an organization of opportunity, working hand-in-hand with other resources in Rhode Island to offer a full continuum of services for families, adults, children, the elderly, those with disabilities and veterans.

2298 Rhode Island Division of Substance Abuse
14 Harrington Road
Cranston, RI 02920-3080
401-462-4680
Fax: 401-462-6078
www.mhrh.state.ri.us

Craig Stenning, Executive Director

Substance Abuse Treatment and Prevention Services (SATPS) is responsible for planning, coordinating and administering a comprehensive statewide system of substance abuse, treatment and prevention activities. SATPS develops, supports and advocates for high quality, accessible, comprehensive and clinically appropriate substance abuse prevention and treatment services in order to decrease the negative effects of alcohol, tobacco and other drug use in Rhode Island, and improve the overall behavioral health of Rhode Islanders.

2299 State of Rhode Island Department of Mental Health, Retardation and Hospitals
Division of Behavioral Healthcare Services
14 Harrington Road
Cranston, RI 02920-3080
401-462-2339
Fax: 401-462-1564
www.mhrh.state.ri.us/

Craig S Stenning, Executive Director

Our overall mission will focus on the unique needs and goals of individuals who experience a mental illness, an emotional disturbance, and/or a substance abuse or addiction problem and to prevent, whenever possible, these from ever occurring.

South Carolina

2300 LRADAC The Behavioral Health Center of the Midlands
134 North Hospital Drive
Columbia, SC 29250

800-373-0459
www.lradac.org/

Deborah Francis, President/Coo

The mission of LRADAC is to provide effective, personalized services to prevent or reduce the harm of substance use and addictions. We will provide evidence-based, best practice prevention, intervention and treatment services to the populations of Richland and Lexington Counties and others as appropriate.

2301 Mental Health Association in South Carolina
1823 Gadsden Street
Columbia, SC 29201-2344
803-779-5363
800-375-9894
Fax: 803-929-6147
E-mail: mha@mha-sc.org
www.mha-sc.org

Joy Jay, Executive Director

The Mental Health Association in South Carolina believes in a healthy society in which all people are accorded respect, dignity and the opportunity to achieve their full potential free from stigma and prejudice. The MHASC is dedicated to preventing mental disorders through research and achieving victory over mental illnesses through systems and individual advocacy, education and unmet service development.

2302 South Carolina Department of Alcohol and Other Drug Abuse Services

101 Executive Center Drive
Suite 215
Columbia, SC 29210-8413
803-896-5100
Fax: 803-896-5246
E-mail: leecatoe@daodas.state.sc.us
www.psc.sc.gov

Charles Terreni, Manager

DAODAS is the cabinet-level department responsible for ensuring the availability of comprehensive alcohol and other drug abuse services for the citizens of South Carolina.

2303 South Carolina Department of Mental Health

2414 Bull Street
Columbia, SC 29201-1906
803-898-8319
TTY: 864-297-5130

John H Magill, Executive Director

The administrative offices of the South Carolina Department of Mental Health are located in Columbia and provide support services including long-range planning, performance and clinical standards, evaluation and quality assurance, personnel management, communications, information resource management, legal counsel, financial, and procurement. In addition, the central office administers services for the hearing impaired; children, adolescents and their families; people with developmental disabilities; those needing alcohol and drug treatment; the elderly; and patients who need long-term care.

2304 South Carolina Department of Social Services

1535 Confederate Avenue Extension
P O Box 1520
Columbia, SC 29202-1520
803-898-7601
www.state.sc.us/dss/

Kathleen Hayes, State Director

The mission of the South Carolina Department of Social Services is to ensure the safety and health of children and adults who cannot protect themselves, and to assist those in need of food assistance and temporary financial assistance while transitioning into employment.

South Dakota

2305 South Dakota Department of Human Services: Division of Mental Health

E Highway 34, Hillsview Plaza
Pierre, SD 57501
605-000-1111
800-265-9684

Jeff Pierce, Manager

Serves as the point of contact for state funded services, support and treatment for adults with severe and persistent mental illness (SPMI), and children with serious emotional disturbance (SED).

2306 South Dakota Department of Social Services Office of Medical Services

700 Governors Drive
Pierre, SD 57501-2291
605-773-3131
Fax: 605-773-4950
E-mail: Medical@STATE.SD.US

Dan Siebersma, Manager

The South Dakota Office of Medical Services covers medical care provided to low income people who meet eligibility standards either under Medicaid (Title XIX) or the Children's Health Insurance Program (CHIP). These programs are financed jointly by state and federal government and are managed by the SD Department of Social Services.

2307 South Dakota Human Services Center

3515 Broadway Avenue
PO Box 7600
Yankton, SD 57078-7600
605-668-3100
Fax: 605-668-3460
E-mail: infohsc@state.sd.us
www.dhs.sd.gov/hsc

Cory D. Nelson, Administrator

to provide persons who are mentally ill or chemically dependent   with effective,individualized professional treatment thats enables them to achieve their highest level of personal independence in the most therapeutic environment

Tennessee

2308 Alcohol and Drug Council of Middle Tennessee

Po Box 330189
Nashville, TN 37203-7501
615-269-0029
Fax: 615-269-0299
E-mail: mmckinney@adcmt.org
www.adcmt.org

Mary McKinney, Executive Director
Mr Boyd Smith, President

The Alcohol and Drug Council of Middle Tennessee, Inc. was founded in 1966 by individuals who saw the devastating effects of alcohol and drugs on the individual, the family, and the community. They felt that problems created by chemical dependency must be addressed in a pro-active way with programs of education, prevention and intervention. Since that beginning, the Council continues its commitment to helping people find a better way.

2309 Bureau of TennCare: State of Tennessee

310 Great Circle Road
Nashville, TN 37243-1700

800-342-3145
www.state.tn.us/tenncare/

Darin Gordon, Deputy Commissioner

On January 1, 1994, Tennessee began a new health care reform program called TennCare. This program, which required no new taxes, essentially replaced the Medicaid
program in Tennessee. TennCare was designed as a managed care model. It extended coverage to uninsured and un-
insurable persons who were not eligible for Medicaid.

2310 Council for Alcohol & Drug Abuse Services (CADAS)

207 Spears Avenue
Chattanooga, TN 37405
423-756-7644
877-282-2327
Fax: 423-756-7646
E-mail: info@cadas.org
www.cadas.org

Paul Fuchcar MEd, EdD, Executive Director

Welcome to CADAS, founded in 1964. The CADAS mission is to deliver the highest quality treatment, prevention,
and educational services to the chemically dependent, their
families, and the community at large.

2311 Memphis Alcohol and Drug Council

1430 Poplar Avenue
Memphis, TN 38104-2901
901-274-0056

Provides referrals, alcohol and other drug prevention, intervention and treatment services. Also, regional and county
school prevention coordination, and a clearinghouse for
Shelby County including national data search and materials
distribution.

2312 Middle Tennessee Mental Health Institute

221 Stewarts Ferry Pike
Nashville, TN 37214-3325
615-902-7400
Fax: 615-902-7571
www.state.tn.us

Candance Gilligan, Manager

TDMHDD operates 5 Regional Mental Health Institutes
(RMHIs). Lakeshore Mental Health Institute (Knoxville),
Moccasin Bend Mental Health Institute (Chattanooga) and
Memphis Mental Health Institute provide in-patient psychiatric services for adults; Middle Tennessee Mental Health
Institute (Nashville) and Western Mental Health Institute
(Bolivar) provide in-patient psychiatric services for both
adults and children/youth. Most RMHI admissions are on
an emergency involuntary basis, with a variety of court-or-
dered inpatient evaluation and treatment services also provided. The RMHIs provide psychiatric services based upon
the demonstrated and emerging best practices of each
clinical discipline.

2313 Tennessee Commission on Children and Youth

710 James Robertson Parkway
9th Floor
Nashville, TN 37243-1219
615-741-2633
E-mail: linda.oneal@state.tn.us
www.state.tn.gov/tccy

Linda O'Neal, Executive Director
Pat Wade, Program Director

2314 Tennessee Department of Health

425 5th Avenue N
Cordell Hull Building, 3rd Floor
Nashville, TN 37243-3400
615-741-7213
E-mail: TN.health@state.tn.us

Suzanne Hayes, Manager

Provides information on a wide variety of topics including
community services, health maintenance organizations, immunizations and alcohol and drug services.

2315 Tennessee Department of Health: Alcohol and Drug Abuse

425 5th Avenue N
3rd Fl
Nashville, TN 37243-3400
615-741-7213

Suzanne Hayes, Manager

2316 Tennessee Department of Human Services

400 Deaderick Street
15th Floor
Nashville, TN 37243-1403
615-741-2330
Fax: 615-741-1791
E-mail: Human-Services.Webmaster@state.tn.us

Gina Lodge, Commissioner

Provides information about available programs and services, such as family assistance and child support, community programs, and rehabilitation services.

2317 Tennessee Department of Mental Health and Developmental Disabilities

5th Floor Cordell Hall
425 5th Avenue North
Nashville, TN 37243-3400
615-741-7213
E-mail: opie.tdmhdd@state.tn.us

Suzanne Hayes, Manager
Virginia Trotter Betts, Commissioner

Tennessee's state mental health and developmental disabilities authority. It has responsibility for system planning, setting policy and quality standards, system monitering and
evaluation, disseminating public information and advocating for persons of all ages who have mental illness, serious
emotional disturbance or developmental disabilities.

Texas

2318 Austin Travis County Mental Health: Mental Retardation Center
1430 Collier Street
Austin, TX 78704-2911
512-447-4141
Fax: 512-440-4801
E-mail: webmaster@atcmhmr.com

David Evans, Executive Director

Provides mental health, mental retardation and substance services to the Austin-Travis County community.

2319 Harris County Mental Health: Mental Retardation Authority
7011 Southwest Freeway
Houston, TX 77074-2007
713-970-7000
www.mhmraharris.org

MHMRA of Harris County is one of the largest mental health centers in the United States, serving more than 30,000 persons in the Houston metropolitan area who suffer from mental illness and/or mental retardation. We serve the "priority population" - adults who are diagnosed with severe and persistent mental illness, children with serious

2320 Mental Health Association of Greater Dallas
624 North Good-Latimer
200
Dallas, TX 75204-5818
214-828-4192
Fax: 214-954-0611
www.mhadallas.org

Tim Simmons, President

To lead, coordinate and involve the community in improving mental health by advocating for improved care and treatment of people with mental illness.

2321 Tarrant County Mental Health: Mental Retardation Services
3840 Hulen Street
North Tower
Fort Worth, TX 76107-7277
817-377-6501
Fax: 817-377-6504

Eric Remington, Manager

We serve the citizens in our north Texas community who face the challenges of mental illness, mental retardation, autism, addiction and early childhood developmental delays.

2322 Texas Commission on Alcohol and Drug Abuse
Texas Department of State Health Services
909 West 45th Street
Austin, TX 78751-2803
512-206-5000
E-mail: contact@tcada.state.tx.us
www.tcada.state.tx.us/

The Department of State Health Services promotes optimal health for individuals and communities while providing effective health, mental health and substance abuse services to Texans.

2323 Texas Department of Aging and Disability Services: Mental Retardation Services
701 West 51st St.
Po Box 149030
Austin, TX 78714-9030
512-438-3011
E-mail: mail@dads.state.tx.us
www.dads.state.tx.us

Adelaide Horn, Commissioner
Gordon Taylor, Cfo

State agency which works to improve the quality and efficiency of public and private services and supports for Texans with mental illnesses.

2324 Texas Department of Family and Protective Services
701 W. 51st Street
Po Box 149030
Austin, TX 78714-9030
512-438-4800
www.dfps.state.tx.us/

Ommy Strauch, Chair

The mission of the Texas Department of Family and Protective Services (DFPS) is to protect the unprotected _ children, elderly, and people with disabilities _ from abuse, neglect, and exploitation.

2325 Texas Health & Human Services Commission
4900 N. Lamar Blvd.
Brown-Heatly Building
Austin, TX 78751-2316
512-424-6500
877-787-8999
TTY: 888-425-6889
E-mail: contact@hhsc.state.tx.us
www.hhsc.state.tx.us/

Albert Hawkins, Executive Commissioner

The Health and Human Services Commission provides leadership and direction, and fosters the spirit of innovation needed to achieve an efficient and effective health and human services system for Texans.

Utah

2326 Utah Department of Health
288 N 1460 West
Salt Lake Cty, UT 84116-3231
801-538-6111
www.health.utah.gov/

David Sundwall, MD, Executive Director

Oversees and regulates health care services for children, seniors, the mentally ill, substance abusers, and all residents of Utah.

2327 Utah Department of Health: Health Care Financing
Box 143101
Salt Lake City, UT 84114-3101
801-538-6406
www.health.utah.gov/medicaid

Provides information and assistance on Utah Medicaid programs including eligibility and additional contact info and links for administrators of the program.

2328 Utah Department of Human Services
120 North 200 West, Room 319
Salt Lake City, UT 84103-1550
801-538-4001
800-662-3722
Fax: 801-538-4016
E-mail: dirdhs@utah.gov
www.dhs.utah.gov

Lisa-Michel Church, Executive Director

Provides services for the elderly, substance abusers, people with disabilities,ed children, youthful offenders, mentally ill and others.ple with disabilities,

2329 Utah Department of Human Services: Division of Substance Abuse And Mental Health
120 N 200 W
Room 209
Salt Lake City, UT 84103-1550
801-538-3939
Fax: 801-538-9892
E-mail: dsamhwebmaster@utah.gov
www.dhs.utah.gov

Mark Payne, Executive Director
Paula Bell, Vice Chair

The Utah State Division of Substance Abuse and Mental Health Division is the agency responsible for ensuring that substance abuse and mental health prevention and treatment services are available statewide. The Division also acts as a resource by providing general information, research, and statistics to the public regarding substances of abuse and mental health services.

2330 Utah Department of Mental Health
120 N 200 W
Room 209
Salt Lake City, UT 84103-1550
801-538-3939
Fax: 801-538-9892
www.dhs.utah.gov

Mark Payne, Executive Director

Vermont

2331 State of Vermont Developmental Disabilities Services
103 South Main Street
Weeks Building
Waterbury, VT 05671-9800
802-241-2401
E-mail: AHS-dail-deptweb.master@ahs.state.vt.us

The State of Vermont, Department of Disabilities, Aging and Independent Living, Division of Disability and Aging Services, plans and coordinates state- and federally-funded services for people with developmental disabilities and their families within Vermont. The Division provides funding for services, systems planning, technical assistance, training, quality assurance, program monitoring and standards compliance.

2332 Vermont Department for Children and Families Economic Services Division (ESD)
103 S Main Street
Waterbury, VT 05676-1581
802-241-2131
800-287-0589

Cindy Walcott, Manager

ESD, formerly the Department of Prevention, Assistance, Transition, and Health Access (PATH) and before that the Department of Social Welfare (DSW), administers state and federal programs such as Medicaid, Food Stamps, and Reach Up to assist eligible Vermonters in need. Our mission is to help Vermonters find a path to a better life. To this end, we take on many roles: employment coach, health insurance provider, crisis manager, career planner, champion of families, and promoter of human potential.

2333 Vermont Department of Health: Division of Mental Health Services
108 Cherry Street
Burlington, VT 05401-4295
802-863-7246
800-464-4343

Paul Jarris, Owner

On July 1, 2004 the Department of Developmental and Mental Health Services ceased to exist as an independent department within the Agency of Human Services. Under the Agency's reorganization plan, the division of Mental Health became part of the existing Department of Health. The division of Mental Health includes adult mental health; child, adolescent, and family mental health; emergency services; and the Vermont State Hospital. The division of Developmental Services merged with the Department of Aging and Disabilities to become a new Department of Disability, Aging & Independent Living (DAIL).

Virginia

2334 Virginia Department of Medical Assistance Services
600 E Broad Street
Richmond, VA 23219-1832
804-786-7933
TDD: 800-343-0634
E-mail: info@dmas.virginia.gov
www.dmas.virginia.gov

Patrick Finnerty, Director

2335 Virginia Department of Mental Health, Mental Retardation and Substance Abuse Services (DMHMRSAS)
PO Box 1797
Richmond, VA 23218-1797
804-786-3921
800-451-5544
Fax: 804-371-6638
TDD: 804-371-8977
www.dmhmrsas.virginia.gov/

DMHMRSAS provides leadership and service to improve Virginia's system of quality treatment, habilitation, and prevention services for individuals and their families whose lives are affected by mental illness, mental retardation, or substance use disorders.

2336 Virginia Department of Social Services
Fl 3
801 E Main St
Richmond, VA 23219-2907
804-726-7000
800-552-3431
E-mail: citizen.services@dss.virginia.gov
www.dss.virginia.gov/

Promotes self-reliance, prevention, and protection by serving as a catalyst for healthy families and communities.

2337 Virginia Office of the Secretary of Health and Human Resources
Patrick Henry Building
1111 East Broad Street
Richmond, VA 23219-1934
804-786-7765
Fax: 804-371-6984
www.hhr.virginia.gov/

The DHHR administers programs that benefit the citizens of West Virginia.

Washington

2338 Washington Department of Alcohol and Substance Abuse: Department of Social and Health Service
1115 Washington Street
Olympia, WA 98504-1
360-902-8400
www.dshs.wa.gov

The Division of Alcohol and Substance Abuse promotes strategies that support healthy lifestyles by preventing the misuse of alcohol, tobacco, and other drugs, and support recovery from the disease of chemical dependency.

2339 Washington Department of Social & Health Services
PO Box 45130
Olympia, WA 98504-5130

800-737-0617
www.dshs.wa.gov

The mission of DSHS is to improve the quality of life for individuals and families in need. We help people achieve safe, self-sufficient, healthy and secure lives.

2340 Washington Department of Social and Health Services: Mental Health Division
1115 Washington Street
Po Box 45320
Olympia, WA 98504-5320

800-446-0259
Fax: 360-902-0809
www.dshs.wa.gov/mentalhealth

The mission of the Mental Health Division is to promote recovery and safety.

West Virginia

2341 West Virginia Bureau for Behavioral Health and Health Facilities
West Virginia Department of Health and Human Resources
350 Capitol Street
Room 350
Charleston, WV 25301-1757
304-558-0627
Fax: 304-558-1008
E-mail: obhs@wvdhhr.org
www.wvdhhr.org/bhhf/

John E Bianconi, Commissioner

We ensure that positive meaningful opportunities are available for persons with mental illness, chemical dependency, developmental disabilities and those at risk. We provide support for individuals, families, and communities in assisting persons to achieve their potential and to gain greater control over the direction of their future.

2342 West Virginia Department of Health & Human Resources (DHHR)
350 Capitol Street
Room 730
Charleston, WV 25301-1757
304-558-2974
Fax: 304-558-4194
www.wvdhhr.org/default.asp

The DHHR administers programs that benefit the citizens of West Virginia.

2343 West Virginia Department of Welfare Bureau for Children and Families
West Virginia Department of Health & Human Resources
350 Capitol Street
Room 730
Charleston, WV 25301-1757
304-558-4069
Fax: 304-558-4623
www.wvdhhr.org/bcf/family_assistance/fs.asp

The Bureau for Children and Families provides an accessible, integrated, comprehensive quality service system for

West Virginia's children, families and adults to help them achieve.

Wisconsin

2344 Bureau of Mental Health and Substance Abuse Services
Department of Health and Family Services
1 West Wilson Street
Room 434
Madison, WI 53703-3445
608-266-2900
Fax: 608-261-7824
E-mail: allenjb@dhfs.state.wi.us

Linda Ampe, Manager

The Bureau of Mental Health and Substance Abuse Services' mission is to support and improve the quality and effectiveness of mental health and substance abuse services in order to create a recovery-focused system for the people of Wisconsin.

2345 Dane County Mental Health Center
625 West Washington Avenue
Madison, WI 53703-2637
608-280-2700
Fax: 608-280-2707
E-mail: webmaster@mhcdc.org
www.mhcdc.org

Luanne C Rosa, Manager
William Greer, Executive Director

The mission of the Mental Health Center of Dane County, Inc. is to provide individuals and families with high quality, community based, recovery oriented, mental health, substance abuse, and advocacy services that respect cultural differences and foster hope, strength, and self determination. We will give priority to individuals and families with high needs and low resources.

2346 Department of Health and Family Services: Southern Region
One West Wilson Street
Madison, WI 53703-3445
608-266-2900
Fax: 608-261-7824
E-mail: webmaster@dhfs.state.wi.us

Linda Ampe, Manager

The Wisconsin Department of Health and Family Services administers a wide range.

2347 University of Wisconsin Center for Health Policy and Program Evaluation
610 Walnut Street
Suite 760
Madison, WI 53726-2336
608-263-6294
Fax: 608-262-6404
www.pophealth.wisc.edu/UWPHI/index.htm

The Institute serves as a focal point for applied public health and health policy within the University of Wisconsin-Madison School of Medicine and Public Health as well as a bridge to public health and health policy practitioners in the state. We strive to: address a broad range of real world problems of importance to government, business, providers and the public; and catalyze partnerships of inquiry between researchers and users of research and break down barriers between the academic community and public and private policy makers.

2348 Wisconsin Bureau of Health Care Financing
PO Box 7886
Madison, WI 53707-7886

800-423-1938
Fax: 800-423-1939
www.dhfs.wisconsin.gov/ddb

Disability decisions for Wisconsin residents are made by the Wisconsin Division of Health Care Financing, Disability Determination Bureau (DDB). Applicants who are determined to have a disability, and also meet other specific eligibility requirements, may receive monthly money payments and/or healthcare coverage for many of their medical expenses.

2349 Wisconsin Department of Health and Family Services
1 West Wilson Street
Madison, WI 53703-3445
608-261-0653
TTY: 608-267-7371

Cremear Mims, Manager

The Wisconsin Department of Health and Family Services administers a wide range of services to clients in the community and at state institutions.

Wyoming

2350 Wyoming Department of Family Services
2300 Capitol Avenue
Hathaway Bldg Fl 3
Cheyenne, WY 82002-1
307-777-7564
www.dfsweb.state.wy.us

Jacquie Bensley, Director

The mission of the Wyoming Department of Family Services is to have Families assume more responsibility for raising their own children. Communities will assume more responsibility for their own families. The Department of Family Services will facilitate both.

2351 Wyoming Department of Health: Division of Health Care Finance
401 Hathaway Bldg
Cheyenne, WY 82002-1
307-777-7656
866-571-0944
Fax: 307-777-7439
www.wdh.state.wy.us/main/about.html

Dr Brent Sherard, Director

The Office of Health Care Financing administers the EqualityCare (Medicaid) program, the largest of the State's public health insurance programs. The name EqualityCare reflects Wyoming's history as the Equality State as well as promoting equality of health care benefits and services for all Wyoming citizens regardless of economic status. In addition to providing Medicaid Primary Care services, the Office oversees the administration of Medicaid services provided by the following divisions within the Department: Community and Family Health, Developmental Disabilities, Mental Health, Aging, and Substance Abuse.

2352 Wyoming Mental Health Division
Wyoming State Government
6101 Yellowstone Road
Suite 20
Cheyenne, WY 82002-1
307-777-2432
www.wdh.state.wy.us

State administrative agency of the Department of Health, for mental health in Wyoming.

Professional & Support Services

Accreditation & Quality Assurance

2353 American Board of Examiners in Clinical Social Work
27 Congress Street Suite 501
Shetland Park
Salem, MA 01970-5577
978-825-9311
800-694-5285
Fax: 978-740-5395
E-mail: abe@abecsw.org

Howard Snooks Ph.D BCD, President
Robert Booth, Executive Director
Michael Brooks MSW BCD, Business Development, Policy Dir

Clinical Social Work certifying and standard setting organization. ABE's no cost online and CD ROM directories (both searchable/sortable) are sources used by the healthcare industry nationwide for network development and referrals. They contain verified information about the education, training, experience and practice specialties of over 11,000 Board Certified Diplomates in Clinical Social Work (BCD). Visit our website for the directory, employment resources, continuing education and other services.

2354 American Board of Examiners of Clinical Social Work Regional Offices
414 First Street E
Suite 3
Sonoma, CA 95476-6759
707-938-5833
888-279-9378
Fax: 707-938-3233
E-mail: abe@abecsw.org
www.abecsw.org

Howard Snooks Ph.D BCD, President
Robert Booth, Executive Director
Leonard Hill MSW BCD, Vice President

Sets national practice standards, issues an advance-practice credential, and publishes reference information about its board-certified clinicians.

2355 Brain Imaging Handbook
WW Norton & Company
500 5th Avenue
New York, NY 10110-54
212-354-2907
800-233-4830
Fax: 212-869-0856
E-mail: npb@wwnorton.com

Drake McFeely, CEO

The past 10 years have seen an explosion in the use of brain imaging technologies to aid treatment of medical as well as mental health conditions. MRI, CT ("CAT") scans, and PET scans are now common. This book is the first quick reference to these technologies, rich in illustrations and including discussions of which techniques are best used in particular instances of care.

2356 CARF: Commission on Accreditation of Rehabilitation Facilities
4891 E Grant Road
Tucson, AZ 85712-2704
520-325-1044
Fax: 520-318-1129
TTY: 888-281-6531
www.carf.org

Brian J Boon, CEO
Amanda Birch, Administrator Of Operations

CARF assists organizations to improve the quality of their services, to demonstrate value, and to meet internationally recognized organizational and practice standards.

2357 Cenaps Corporation
6147 Deltona Boulevard
Spring Hill, FL 34606-1000
352-596-8000
E-mail: info@cenaps.com
www.cenaps.com

Tresa Watson, Manager
Tresa Watson, Business Manager

CENAPS is an acronym for the Center for Applied Sciences. They are a private training firm committed to providing advanced clinical skills training for the addiction and behavioral health fields.

2358 CompHealth Credentialing
PO Box 713100
Salt Lake City, UT 84171-3100
801-930-4517
800-453-3030
Fax: 801-930-4517
E-mail: info@comphealth.com
www.comphealth.com

Assists in analyzing the total costs involved in credentialing verifications, including some items frequently overlooked; assesses and/or develops a provider application to meet accreditation standards; can assess current credentialing files; can assist in developing policy and procedures for the verification process.

2359 Consumer Satisfaction Team
1001 Sterigere Street
Building 6
Norristown, PA 19401-5300
610-270-3685
E-mail: watsons@cstmont
www.cstmont.com

Sandra Watson, Executive Director
Sandra F Watson, Executive Director

The central role of CST is to provide the Montgomery County Office of MH/MR/DD with information about satisfaction with the mental health services that adults are receiving and make recommendations for change.

2360 Council on Accreditation (COA) of Services for Families and Children

120 Wall Street
11th Floor
New York, NY 10005-3904
212-785-3705
Fax: 212-797-1428
E-mail: jfulmer@coanet.org

Richard Klarberg, CEO
John Polsky, CFO

The Council of Accreditation of Services for Families and Children, Inc., is an independent, not-for-profit accreditor of behavioral healthcare and social service organizations in the United States and Canada. COA's mission is to promote standards, champion quality services for children, youth and families, and advocate for the value of accreditation. COA accredits programs in more than 1,000 organizations and publishes standards for the full array of community mental health services.

2361 Council on Social Work Education

1725 Duke Street
Suite 500
Alexandria, VA 22314-3457
703-683-8080
Fax: 703-683-8099
E-mail: info@cswe.org
www.cswe.org

Julia M. Watkins, PhD,, Executive Director
Nicole Demarco, Executive Assistant To Exec. Dir

A national association that preserves and enhances the quality of social work education for the purpose of promoting the goals of individual and community well being and social justice. Pursues this mission through setting and maintaining policy and program standards, accrediting bachelors and masters degree programs in social work, promoting research and faculty development, and advocating for social work education.

2362 Healtheast Behavioral Care

559 Capitol Boulevard
Saint Paul, MN 55103-2101
651-232-2228
www.healtheast.org

Robert Beck, President/CEO
Robert D. Gill, VP Finance/CFO
Robert J. Beck, VP Medical Affairs

Assessment and referral for: Psychiatric, Inpatient, Chemical Dependancy.

2363 Joint Commission on Accreditation of Healthcare Organizations

1 Renaissance Boulevard
Oakbrook Terrace, IL 60181-4294
630-792-5000
Fax: 630-792-5617
E-mail: customerservice@jcaho.org
www.jointcommission.org

Mark Chassin, President
Mark Angood, VP/Chief Patient Safety Officer

The Joint Commission evaluates and accredits nearly 20,000 health care organizations and programs in the United States. An independent, not-for-profit organization, the Joint Commission is the nation's predominant standards-setting and accrediting body in health care. The Joint Commission has developed state-of-the-art, professionally-based standards and evaluated the compliance of health care organizations against these benchmarks.

2364 Lanstat Incorporated

517 125th Avenue NE
Lake Stevens, WA 98258
425-334-3124
800-672-3166
Fax: 425-334-3124
E-mail: info@lanstat.com
www.lanstat.com

Landon Kimbrough, President
Sherry Kimbrough, VP/Co-Founder

Provides quality technical assistance to behavioral health treatment agencies nationwide, including tribal and goverment agencies.

2365 Med Advantage

11301 Corporate Boulevard
Suite 300
Orlando, FL 32817-1445
407-282-5131
Fax: 407-282-9240
E-mail: info@med-advantage.com
www.med-advantage.com

John Witty, Owner

Fully accredited by URAC and certified in all 11 elements by NCQA, Med Advantage is one of the oldest credentials verification organizations in the country. Over the past eight years, they have developed sophisticated computer systems and one of the largest data warehouses of medical providers in the nation, containing information on over 900,000 healthcare providers. Their system is continually updated from primary source data required to meet the standards of the URAC, NCQA and JCAHO.

2366 Mertech

PO Box 787
Norwell, MA 02061-787
781-659-0701
Fax: 781-659-2049
E-mail: admin-info@mertech.org
www.mertech.org

John Kopacz, Founder
Leann Johnson, Account Manager

A business development organization that specializes in helping clients capitalize on business opportunities in an efficient and effective manner to meet their goals and objectives. They have three business units: Mertech Health Care Consultants, Mertech Personal Health Improvement Program and Managed Care Information Systems.

2367 National Board for Certified Counselors
3 Terrace Way
Greensboro, NC 27403-3670
336-547-0607
Fax: 336-547-0017
E-mail: nbcc@nbcc.org
www.nbcc.org

Thomas Clawson, President/CEO
Linda Foster, Chairman Of The Board

National voluntary certification board for counselors. Certified counselors have met minimum criteria. Referral lists can be provided to consumers.

2368 National Register of Health Service Providers in Psychology
1120 G Street NW
Suite 330
Washington, DC 20005-3873
202-783-7663
Fax: 202-347-0550
www.nationalregister.org

Judy E Hall, CEO
Greg Hurley, Vice President/Vice-Chair

Nonprofit credentialing organization for psychologists; evaluates education, training, and experience of licensed psychologists. Committed to advancing psychology as a profession and improving the delivery of health services to the public.

Year Founded: 1974

2369 SAFY of America: Specialized Alternatives for Families and Youth
10100 Elida Road
Delphos, OH 45833-9056
419-695-8010
800-532-7239
Fax: 419-695-0004
E-mail: webmaster@safy.org
www.safy.org

Dru Whitaker, CEO
John Hollenkamp, SVP Of Finance

A not-for-profit treatment foster care agency serving more than 1000 children and their families in eight states. Offers programs and services tailored to children's unique needs.

Year Founded: 1984

2370 SUPRA Management
2424 Edenborn Avenue
Suite 660
Metairie, LA 70001-6465
504-837-5557

Associations

2371 Academy of Psychosomatic Medicine
5272 River Road
Suite 630
Bethesda, MD 20816-1453
301-718-6520
Fax: 301-656-0989
E-mail: apm@apm.org
www.apm.org

Kristen Flemming, Academy Coordinator
Norman Wallis Ph.D, Executive Director

Represents psychiatrists dedicated to the advancement of medical science, education, and healthcare for persons with comorbid psychiatric and general medical conditions and provides national and international leadership in the furtherance of those goals.

2372 Advanced Psychotherapy Association
319 Court House Rd
#B
Gulfport, MS 39507-1870
228-897-7730
Fax: 228-897-2121

Karen Seymour, Contact
Philip Schaeffer, Contact

2373 Agency for Healthcare Research & Quality
540 Gaither Road
Suite 2000
Rockville, MD 20850-6649
301-427-1364
Fax: 301-427-1875
www.ahcpr.gov

Carolyn Clancy M.D., Director

2374 Alliance for Children and Families
11700 W Lake Park Drive
Milwaukee, WI 53224-3021
414-359-1040
Fax: 414-359-1074
E-mail: pgoldberg@alliance1.org
www.alliance1.org

Elizabeth Carey, SVP/COO
Peter Goldberg, President/CEO
John Schmidt, CFO

National membership association representing more than three hundred forty private, nonprofit child and family-serving organizations. It's mission is to strengthen members' capacity to serve and advocate for children, families and communities.

2375 American Academy of Addiction Psychiatry (AAAP)
345 Blackstone Boulevard
1st Floor - Weld
Providence, RI 02906-4800
401-524-3076
Fax: 401-272-0922
E-mail: info@aaap.org
www.aaap.org

Kevin A.. Sevarino MD, Head, Treatment Section
Karen P.G. Drexler MD, Head, Education Section
Richard N. Rosenthal MD, Head, Public Policy Section
Laura F. McNicholas MD, PhD, Head, Research Section

Professional membership organization with approximately 1,000 members in the United States and around the world. The membership consists of psychiatrists who work with addiction in their practices, faculty at various academic institutions.

2376 American Academy of Child & Adolescent Psychiatry

3615 Wisconsin Avenue NW
Washington, DC 20016-3007
202-362-1797
E-mail: communications@aacap.org

Robert Hendren, President
David Herzog, Secretary
William Bernet, Treasurer

Provides information on childhood psychiatric disorders.

2377 American Academy of Clinical Psychiatrists

PO Box 458
Glastonbury, CT 06033-458
860-633-6023
Fax: 866-668-9858
E-mail: aacp@cox.net
www.aacp.com

Sanjay Gupta MD, President
John B Reichman MD, Vice President
James Wilcox DO, PhD, Secretary/Treasurer
Donald W Black MD, President-Elect

Practicing board-eligible or board-certified psychiatrists. Promotes the scientific practice of psychiatric medicine. Conducts educational and teaching research. Publications: Annals of Clinical Psychiatry, quarterly journal. Clinical Psychiatry Quarterly, newsletter. Annual conference and exhibits in fall.

2378 American Academy of Medical Administrators

701 Lee Street
Suite 600
Des Plaines, IL 60016-4516
847-759-8601
E-mail: info@aameda.org
www.aameda.org

Renee Schleichar, CEO
Holly Estal, Director Of Education

Their mission is to advance Academy member and the field of healthcare management, and promote excellence and integrity in healthcare delivery and leadership.

Year Founded: 1957

2379 American Academy of Psychiatry and the Law (AAPL)

One Regency Drive
PO Box 30
Bloomfield, CT 06002-30

860-242-5450
800-331-1389
Fax: 860-286-0787
E-mail: execoff@aapl.org
www.aapl.org

Jacquelyn T Coleman, Executive Director
Jeffrey Janofsky MD, President
Kenneth Appelbaum MD, Vice President

Seeks to exchange ideas and experience in areas where psychiatry and the law overlap and develop standards of practice in the relationship of psychiatry to the law and encourage the development of training programs for psychiatrists in this area. Publications: Journal of the American Academy of Psychiatry and the Law, quarterly. Scholarly articles on forensic psychiatry. Newsletter of the American Academy of Psychiatry and Law, 3 year. Membership Directory, annual.

2380 American Academy of Psychoanalysis and Dynamic Psychiatry

One Regency Drive
PO Box 30
Bloomfield, CT 06002-30
888-691-8281
Fax: 860-286-0787
E-mail: info@aapdp.org
www.aapsa.org

Jacquelyn T Coleman CAE, Executive Director
Sherry Katz-Bearnot, President
Carol Filiaci, Secretary

Founded in 1956 to provide an open forum for psychoanalysts to discuss relevant and responsible views of human behavior and to exchange ideas with colleagues and other social behavioral scientists. Aims to develop better communication among psychoanalysts and psychodynamic psychiatrists in other disiplines in science and the humanities. Meetings of the Academy provide a forum for inquiry into the phenomena of individual and interpersonal behavior. Advocates an acceptance of all relevant and responsible psychoanalytic views of human behavior, rather than adherence to one particular doctrine.

2381 American Association for Marriage and Family Therapy

112 S Alfred Street
Alexandria, VA 22314-3061
703-838-9808
Fax: 703-838-9805
E-mail: central@aamft.org
www.wamft.org

Michael Bowers, Executive Director
Linda Schwallie, President-Elect
Douglas Sprenkle, Treasurer

The professional association for the field of marriage and family therapy. They represent the professional interests of more than 23,000 marriage and family therapists throughout the United States, Canada and abroad. They facilitate research, theory development and education. They develop standards for graduate education and training, clinical supervision, professional ethics and the clinical practice of marriage and family therapy. They host an annual national training conference each fall as well as a week-long series of continuing education institutes in the summer.

2382 American Association for Protecting Children
63 Inverness Drive E
Englewood, CO 80112-5117
303-792-9900
Fax: 303-792-5333
www.americanhumane.org

Marie Belew-Wheatley, President/CEO
Bonny Reinmuth, Secretary

Leader in developing programs, policies and services to prevent the abuse and neglect of children, while strengthening families and communities and enhancing social service systems.

2383 American Association of Community Psychiatrists (AACP)
PO Box 570218
Dallas, TX 75357-218
972-613-0985
Fax: 972-613-5532
E-mail: frda1@airmail.net
www.epic.pitt.edu/aacp

Wesley Sowers MD, President
Annelle Primm, Vice President
Francis Bell, Administrative Director

The mission of AACP is to inspire, empower and equip Community Psychiatrists to promote and provide quality care and to integrate practice with policies that improve the well being of individuals and communities.

2384 American Association of Chairs of Departments of Psychiatry (AACDP)
AACDP C/O Lucille Meinsler #319
1594 Cumberland Street
Lebanon, PA 17042-4532
717-270-1673
E-mail: aacdp@verizon.net
www.aacdp.org

Laura Roberts MD, MA, President
Stuart Munro MD, President-Elect
David Baron DO, Secretary/Treasurer
Leighton Huey MD, Advocacy Task Force

Represents the leaders of departments of psychiatry in all the medical schools in the United States and Canada. They are committed to promotion of excellence in psychiatric education, research and clinical care. They are also committed to advocating for health policy to create appropriate and affordable psychiatric care for all.

2385 American Association of Children's Residential Centers
11700 W Lake Park Drive
Milwaukee, WI 53224-3021
877-332-2272
Fax: 877-362-2272
E-mail: kbehling@alliance1.org
www.aacrc-dc.org

Kari Behling, National Coordinator
Steve Elson, President

Funded by the Mental Health Community Support Program. The purpose of the association is to share information about services, providers and ways to cope with mental illnesses. Available services include referrals, professional seminars, support groups and a variety of publications.

2386 American Association of Directors of Psychiatric Residency Training
1594 Cumberland Street
Lebanon, PA 17042-4532
717-270-1673
E-mail: aadprt@verizon.net
www.aadprt.org

Mark Servis, President
Lucille Meinsler, Administrative Manager

To better meet the nation's mental healthcare needs, the mission of the American Association of Directors of Psychiatric Residency Training is to promote excellence in education and training of future psychiatrists.

2387 American Association of Geriatric Psychiatry (AAGP)
7910 Woodmont Avenue
Suite 1050
Bethesda, MD 20814-3069
301-654-7850
Fax: 301-654-4137
E-mail: main@aagponline.org
www.aagponline.org

Christine De Vries, Manager
Annie Williams, Administrative Assistant

Members are psychiatrists interested in promoting better mental health care for the elderly. Maintains placement service and speakers' bureau. Publications: AAGP Membership Directory, annual. Geriatric Psychiatry News, bimonthly newsletter. Growing Older and Wiser, covers consumer and general public information. Annual meeting and exhibits in February or March.

2388 American Association of Health Plans
601 Pennsylvania Avenue NW
South Building, Suite 500
Washington, DC 20004-2601
202-778-3200
Fax: 202-331-7487
E-mail: ahip@ahip.org
www.aahp.org

Michael Abbott, Board Member
Richard Rivers, Board Member

The American Association of Health Plans (AAHP) is the nation's principal association of health plans, representing more than 1,000 plans that provide coverage for approximately 170 million Americans nationwide.

2389 American Association of Healthcare Consultants
5938 N Drake Avenue
Chicago, IL 60659-3203

888-350-2242
Fax: 773-463-3552
E-mail: info@aahcmail.org
www.aahc.net

Billy Adkisson, Chairman

Serve as the preeminent credentialing, professional, and practice development organization for the healthcare consulting profession; to advance the knowledge, quality, and standards of practice for consulting to management in the healthcare industry; and to enhance the understanding and image of the healthcare consulting profession and Member Firms among its various publics.

2390 American Association of Homes and Services for the Aging

2519 Connecticut Avenue NW
Washington, DC 20008-1520
202-783-2242
Fax: 202-783-2255
E-mail: info@aahsa.org
www.aahsa.org

William L Minnix Jr, President
Katrinka Smith Sloan, COO/SVP Member Services

An association committed to advancing the vision of healthy, affordable, ethical long term care for America. The association represents 5,600 million driven, not-for-profit nursing homes, continuing care facilities and community care retirement facilities and community service organizations.

2391 American Association of Mental Health Professionals in Corrections (AAMHPC)

PO Box 160208
Sacramento, CA 95816-208

Fax: 916-649-1080
E-mail: corrmentalhealth@aol.com

Pam Christensen, Contact

Mental health professionals working in correctional settings. Goals include improving the treatment, rehabilitation and care of the mentally ill, retarded and emotionally disturbed. Promotes research and professional education and conducts scientific meetings to advance the therapeutic community in all institutional settings including hospitals, churches, schools, industry and the family. Publications: Corrective and Social Psychiatry, quarterly. Annual conference and symposium and workshops.

2392 American Association of Pastoral Counselors

9504A Lee Highway
Fairfax, VA 22031-2317
703-385-6967
E-mail: info@aapc.org
www.aapc.org

Doug Ronsheim, Executive Director
Dale Kuhn, President
Joretta Marshall, Vice President

Organized in 1963 to promote and support the ministry of pastoral counseling within religious communities and the field of mental health in the United States and Canada.

2393 American Association of Pharmaceutical Scientists

2107 Wilson Boulevard
Suite 700
Arlington, VA 22201-3042
703-243-2800
www.aaps.org

Karen Habucky, President
John Lisack, Executive Director

The American Association of Pharmaceutical Scientists will be the premier organization of all scientists dedicated to the discovery, development and manufacture of pharmaceutical products and therapies through advances in science and technology.

2394 American Association of Retired Persons

601 E Street NW
Washington, DC 20049-2
202-434-2277
888-687-2277
Fax: 202-434-7599
www.aarp.org

A Barry Rand, CEO
Erik Olsen, President

AARP is a non profit membership organization of persons 50 and older dedicated to addressing their needs and interests.

2395 American Association on Intellectual and Developmental Disabilities (AAIDD)

501 3rd Street NW
Suite 200
Washington, DC 20001

800-424-3688
Fax: 202-387-2193
E-mail: anam@aaidd.org
www.aamr.org

M Doreen Croser, Executive Director

AAIDD promotes progressive policies, sound research, effective practices and universal human rights for people with intellectual and developmental disabilities.

2396 American Association on Mental Retardation (AAR)

AAMR
444 N Capitol Street NW
Suite 846
Washington, DC 20001-1569
202-637-0475
800-424-3688
Fax: 202-637-0585
E-mail: dcroser@aaidd.org

Doreen Croser, Executive Director
Paul Aitken, Director Finance/Administration
Bruce Appelgren, Director Of Publications

Books, pamphlets, videos of interest to those who support persons with mental and physical disabilities.

Year Founded: 1962

2397 American Board of Professional Psychology (ABPP)
600 Market Street
Suite 300
Chapel Hill, NC 27516
919-537-8031
Fax: 919-537-8034
E-mail: office@abpp.org
www.abpp.org

Nadine J Kaslow PhD, President

The mission is to increase consumer protection through the examination and certification of psychologists who demonstrate competence in approved specialty areas in professional psychology

2398 American Board of Psychiatry and Neurology (ABPN)
2150 E Lake Cook Road
Suite 900
Buffalo Grove, IL 60089-1875
847-229-6500
Fax: 847-229-6600
www.abpn.com

Burton Reifler, President
Patricia Coyle, Vice President

ABPN is a nonprofit organization that promotes excellence in the practice of psychiatry and neurology through lifelong certification including compentency testing processes.

2399 American College Health Association
891 Elkridge Landing Road
Suite 100
Linthicum, MD 21090
410-859-1500
Fax: 410-859-1510
www.acha.org

Dr. James Turner, Executive Director
Doyle E Randol MS, Executive Director

Principal advocate and leadership organization for college and university health. Provides advocacy, education, communications, products and services as well as promotes research and culturally competent practices to enhance its members' ability to advance the health of all students and the campus community.

2400 American College of Health Care Administrators (ACHCA)
1321 Duke Street
Suite 400
Alexandria, VA 22314
202-536-5120
Fax: 888-874-1585
E-mail: wodonnell@achca.org
www.achca.org

Steve Esdale, Board Chair

A non-profit professional membership association which provides superior educaional programming, professional certification, and career development opportunities for its members. Available on Facebook.

2401 American College of Healthcare Executives
One N Franklin Street
Suite 1700
Chicago, IL 60606-3529
312-424-2800
Fax: 312-424-0023
E-mail: geninfo@ache.org
www.ache.org

Thomas C Dolan, CEO
David Rubenstein, Chairman-Elect

International professional society of nearly 30,000 healthcare executives. ACHE is known for its prestigious credentialing and educational programs. ACHE is also known for its journal, Journal of Healthcare Management, and magazine, Healthcare Executive, as well as groundbreaking research and career development programs. Through its efforts, ACHE works toward its goal of improving the health status of society by advancing healthcare management excellence.

2402 American College of Mental Health Administration (ACMHA)
7804 Loma del Norte Road NE
Albuquerque, NM 87109-5419
505-822-5038
E-mail: executive.director@acmha.org
www.acmha.org

Kris Ericson, Executive Director

Advancing the field of mental health and substance abuse administration and to promote the continuing education of clinical professionals in the areas of administration and policy. Publication: ACMHA Newsletter, quarterly. Annual Santa Fe Summit, conference.

Year Founded: 1979

2403 American College of Osteopathic Neurologists & Psychiatrists
28595 Orchard Lake Road
Suite 200
Farmington Hills, MI 48334-2979
248-553-0010
Fax: 248-553-0818
E-mail: acn-aconp@msn.com
www.osteopathic.org

David Simpson, President
Sue Wesserling, Executive Director

Purpose is to promote the art and science of osteopathic medicine in the fields of neurology and psychiatry; to maintain and further elevate the highest standards of proficiency and training among osteopathic neurologists and psychiatrists; to stimulate original research and investigation in neurology and psychiatry; and to collect and disseminate the results of such work for the benefit of the members of the college, the public, the profession at large, and the ultimate benefit of all humanity.

2404 American College of Psychiatrists
122 S. Michigan Ave
Suite 1360
Chicago, IL 60603-6185
312-662-1020
Fax: 312-662-1025
E-mail: angel@acpsych.org
www.acpsych.org

Maureen Shick, Executive Director
Angel Waszak, Administrative Assistant

Nonprofit honorary association of psychiatrists who, through excellence in their chosen fields, have been recognized for thier significant contributions to the profession. The society's goal is to promote and support the highest standards in psychiatry through education, research and clinical practice.

2405 American College of Psychoanalysts (ACPA)
P.O. Box 570218
Dallas, TX 75357-218
972-613-0985
www.acopsa.org

Elise Snyder, President

Honorary, scientific and professional organization for physician psycholanalysts. Goal is to contribute to the leadership and support high standards in the practice of psychoanalysis, and understanding the relationship between mind and brain.

2406 American Counseling Association
5999 Stevenson Avenue
Alexandria, VA 22304-3304
703-823-9800
800-347-6647
Fax: 703-823-0252
E-mail: webmaster@counseling.org
www.counseling.org

Richard Yep, CAE, Executive Director

ACA serves professional counselors in the US and abroad. Provides a variety of programs and services that support the personal, professional and program development goals of its members. ACA works to provide quality services to the variety of clients who use their services in college, community agencies, in mental health, rehabilitation and related settings. Offers a large catalog of books, manuals and programs for the professional counselor.

2407 American Counseling Association (ACA)
5999 Stevenson Avenue
Alexandria, VA 22304-3304
703-823-9800
Fax: 703-823-0252
E-mail: ryep@counseling.org
www.counseling.org

Richard Yep, Executive Director
Richard Yep, Executive Officer

A not-for-profit, professional and educational organization that is dedicated to the growth and enhancement of the counseling profession.

Year Founded: 1952

2408 American Geriatrics Society
350 5th Avenue, Suite 801
Empire State Building
New York, NY 10118-801
212-308-1414
Fax: 212-832-8646
E-mail: info@americangeriatrics.org
www.americageriatrics.org

Linda H Barondess, Executive VP
Ellen Baumritter, Administrative Assistant

Nationwide, nonprofit association of geriatric health care professionals, research scientists and other concerned individuals dedicated to improving the health, independence and quality of life for all older people. Pivotal force in shaping attitudes, policies and practices regarding health care for older people.

2409 American Group Psychotherapy Association
25 E 21st Street
6th Floor
New York, NY 10010-6207
212-477-2677
877-668-2472
E-mail: info@agpa.org
www.agpa.org

Marsha Block, CEO
Jeffrey Kleinberg, PhD, CGP, President

Interdisciplinary community that has been enhancing practice, theory and research of group therapy for over 50 years. Provides support to enhance your work as a mental health care professional, or your life as a member of a therapeutic group.

Year Founded: 1942

2410 American Health Care Association
1201 L Street NW
Washington, DC 20005-4046
202-842-4444
Fax: 202-842-3860

Bruse Yarwood, President

Nonprofit federation of affiliated state health organizations, together representing nearly 12,000 nonprofit and for profit assisted living, nursing facility, developmentally disabled and subacute care providers that care for more than 1.5 million elderly and disabled individuals nationally. AHCA represents the long term care community at large — to government, business leaders and the general public. It also serves as a force for change within the long term care field, providing information, education, and administrative tools that enhance quality at every level.

2411 American Health Information Management Association
233 N Michigan Avenue
21st Floor
Chicago, IL 60601-5809
312-233-1100
Fax: 312-233-1090

E-mail: info@ahima.org
www.ahima.org

Linda Kloss, Executive Director
Linda L Kloss CAE, CEO

Dynamic professional association that represents more than 46,000 specially educated health information management professionals who work throughout the healthcare industry. Health information management professionals serve the health care industry and the public by managing, analyzing and utilizing data vital for patient care and making it accessible to healthcare providers when it is needed most.

2412 American Hospital Association: Section for Psychiatric and Substance Abuse

1 N Franklin
Chicago, IL 60606-4425
312-893-6800
Fax: 312-422-4500

Mary Grayson, Publisher
Stephen Ahnen, Senior Vice President

AHA represents and serves all types of hospitals, health care networks and their patients and communities. Provides education for health care leaders and is a source of information on health care issues and trends. The AHA Section for Psychiatric and Substance Abuse Services (SPSAS) provides perspective on behavioral health issues.

2413 American Managed Behavioral Healthcare Association

1101 Pennsylvania Avenue NW
6th Floor
Washington, DC 20004-2544
202-756-7726
Fax: 202-756-7308
E-mail: info@abhw.org

Pamela Greenberg, President/CEO

An association of the nation's leading managed behavioral healthcare companies. Member companies are both national and regional and are collectively responsible for managing mental health and substance abuse services in the public and private sector for over 110 million individuals across the country.

2414 American Medical Association

515 N State Street
Chicago, IL 60654-4820
312-464-5000
800-621-8335
Fax: 312-464-4184
www.ama-assn.org

Michael D Maves, CEO
Peter Carmel, Member Board Of Trustees

Speaks out in issues important to patients and the nation's health. AMA policy on such issues is decided through its democratic policy making process, in the AMA House of Delegates, which meets twice a year. The House is comprised of physician delegates representing every state; nearly 100 national medical specialty societies, federal service agents, including the Surgeon General of the US; and 6 sections representing hospital and clinic staffs, resident physicians, medical students, young physicians, medical

schools and international medical graduates. The AMA's envisioned future is to be a part of the professional life of every physician and an essential force for progress in improving the nation's health.

2415 American Medical Directors Association

11000 Broken Land Parkway
Suite 400
Columbia, MD 21044-3532
410-740-9743
800-876-2632
E-mail: info@amda.com

Alva Baker, President
David Brechtelsbauer, Vice President

Professional association of medical directors and physicians practicing in the long-term care continuum, dedicated to excellence in patient care by providing education, advocacy and professional development.

2416 American Medical Group Association

1422 Duke Street
Alexandria, VA 22314-3430
703-838-0033
Fax: 703-548-1890
E-mail: roconnor@amga.org
www.amga.org

Don Fisher, CEO
Francis Marzoni, Secretary

Advocates for the multispecialty group practice model of health care delivery and for the patients served by medical groups, through innovation and information sharing, benchmarking and continuous striving to improve patient care.

2417 American Medical Informatics Association

4915 St. Elmo Avenue
Suite 401
Bethesda, MD 20814-6052
301-657-1291
Fax: 301-657-1296
E-mail: mail@amia.org
www.amia.org

Karen Greenwood, Manager
Don E Detmer MD MA, President/CEO

Nonprofit membership organization of individuals, institutions and corporations dedicated to developing and using information technologies to improve health care. Our members include physicians, nurses, computer and information scientists, biomedical engineers, medical librarians, academic researchers and educators. Holds an annual syposium, 2 congresses, prints a journal and maintains a resource center.

Year Founded: 1990

2418 American Mental Health Counselors Association (AMHCA)

801 N Fairfax Street
Suite 304
Alexandria, VA 22314-1775

703-548-6002
800-326-2642
E-mail: vmoore@amhca.org
www.amhca.org

Mark Hamilton, Executive Director
Virginia Moore, Administration

Professional counselors employed in mental health services and students. Aims to deliver quality mental health services to children, youth, adults, families and organizations and to improve the availability and quality of services through licensure and certification, training standards and consumer advocacy. Publishes an Advocate Newsletter, Journal of Mental Health Counseling, quarterly, Mental Health Brights, brochures. Annual National Conference.

2419 American Neuropsychiatric Association

700 Ackerman Road
Suite 625
Columbus, OH 43202-4505
614-447-2077
E-mail: anpa@osu.edu

Sandy Bornstein, Executive Director
C. Edward Coffey, Treasurer

An association of professionals in neuropsychiatry and clinical neurosciences. Their mission is to promote neuroscience for the benefit of people. They work together in a collegial fashion to provide a forum for learning and provide excellent, scientific and compassionate care. They hold their annual scientific meeting in the early spring.

Year Founded: 1988

2420 American Nurses Association

8515 Georgia Avenue
Suite 400
Silver Spring, MD 20910-3492
301-628-5000
800-274-4262
Fax: 301-628-5001
E-mail: webmaster@ana.org
www.nursingworld.org

Rebecca Patton, President

A full-service professional organization representing the nation's 2.7 million registered nurses through its 54 constituent members associations. The ANA advances the nursing profession by fostering high standards of nursing practice, promoting the economic and general welfare of nurses in the workplace, projecting a positive and realistic view of nursing, and by lobbying the Congress and regulatory agencies on health care issues affecting nurses and the public.

2421 American Pharmacists Association

2215 Constitution Avenue NW
Washington, DC 20037
202-628-4410
800-237-2742
Fax: 202-783-2351
E-mail: feedback@pharmacist.com
www.pharmacist.com

Thomas E Menighan, Executive Vice President/CEO
Harold Godwin, President

National professional society of pharmacists, formerly the American Pharmaceutical Association. Our members include practicing pharmacists, pharmaceutical students, pharmacy scientists, pharmacy technicians, and others interested in advancing the profession. Provides professional information and education for pharmacists and advocates for improved health of the American public through the provision of comprehensive pharmaceutical care.

Year Founded: 1852

2422 American Psychiatric Association (APA)

1000 Wilson Boulevard
Suite 1825
Arlington, VA 22209-3924
703-248-0760
Fax: 703-907-1085
E-mail: apa@psych.org
www.psych.org

Tara L Burkholder, Marketing

The American Psychiatric Association is a medical specialty society comprised of over 35,000 members who work together to ensure appropriate care and effective treatment for all persons with mental disorders, including mental retardation and substance-related disorders.

2423 American Psychiatric Nurses Association

1555 Wilson Boulevard
Suite 602
Arlington, VA 22209-2405
703-243-2443
866-243-2443
Fax: 703-243-3390
E-mail: clement.1@osu.edu
www.apna.org

Nick Croce, Executive Director
Dorothy Hill, Treasurer

Provides leadership to promote the psychiatric-mental health nursing profession, improve mental health care for culturally diverse individuals, families, groups and communities and shape health policy for the delivery of mental health services.

2424 American Psychiatric Publishing

1000 Wilson Boulevard
Suite 1825
Arlington, VA 22209-3924
703-248-0760
800-368-5777
Fax: 703-907-1085
E-mail: appi@psych.org
www.psych.org

Tara L Burkholder, Marketing
Joan Lang, Treasurer

2425 American Psychoanalytic Association (APsaA)

309 E 49th Street
New York, NY 10017-1634
212-752-0450
Fax: 212-593-0571

E-mail: info@apsa.com
www.apsa.org

Dean Stein, Executive Director
Dean Stein, Executive Director

Professional Membership Organization with approximately 3,500 members nationwide, with 43 Affiliate Societies and 29 Training Institutes. Seeks to establish and maintain standards for the training of psychoanalysts and for the practice of psychoanalysis, fosters the integration of psychoanalysis with other disciplines (psychiatry, psychology, social work), and encourages research. Publications include: Journal of the Psychoanalyst (JAPA), American Psychoanalyst, a quarterly newsletter; Ethics Case Book; and Roster. Twice a year the organization sponsors scientific meetings and exhibits.

2426 American Psychologial Association: Division of Family Psychology
750 1st Street NE
Washington, DC 20002-4241
202-336-5500
800-374-2721
Fax: 202-336-5518
E-mail: webmaster@apa.org
www.apa.org

Norman B Anderson, CEO

A division of the American Psychological Association. Psychologists intersted in research, teaching, evaluation, and public interest initiatives in family psychology. Seeks to promote human welfare through the development, dissemination, and application of knowledge about the dynamics, structure, and functioning of the family. Conducts research and specialized education programs.

2427 American Psychological Association
750 1st Street NE
Washington, DC 20002-4242
202-336-5500
800-374-2721
Fax: 202-336-5518
www.apa.org

Norman B Anderson, CEO

Scientific and professional society of psychologists. Students participate as affiliates. Works to advance psychology as a science, as a profession, and as means of promoting human welfare. Annual convention.

2428 American Psychological Association: Applied Experimental and Engineering Psychology
750 First Street NE
Washington, DC 20002-4241
202-336-5500
Fax: 202-336-5518
www.apa.org

Norman B Anderson, CEO

A division of the American Psychological Association. Individuals whose principal fields of study, research, or work are within the area of applied experimental and engineering psychology. Promotes research on psychological factors in the design and use of environments and systems within which human beings work and live.

2429 American Psychology- Law Society (AP-LS)
AP-LS Central Office
PO Box 638
Niwot, CO 80544-638
303-652-9154
E-mail: div41apa@comcast.net
www.ap-ls.org

Margaret Bull Kovera, President
Brad McAuliff, Treasurer

A division of the American Psychological Association. It is an interdisciplinary organization devoted to the scholarship, practice and public service in psychology and law. Their goals include advancing the contributions of psychology to the understanding of law and legal institutions through basic and applied research; promoting the education of psychologists in matters of law and education of legal personnel in matters of psychology.

2430 American Psychosomatic Society
6728 Old McLean Village Drive
McLean, VA 22101-3906
703-556-9222
Fax: 703-556-8729
E-mail: info@psychosomatic.org
www.psychosomatic.org

Laura Degnon, Executive Director
Michael Irwin, Secretary/Treasurer

A worldwide community of scholars and clinicians dedicated to the scientific understanding of the interaction of mind, brain, body and social context in promoting health and contributing to the pathogenesis, course and treatment of disease. Holds an annual meeting in a different location each year.

Year Founded: 1942

2431 American Society for Clinical Pharmacology & Therapeutics
528 N Washington Street
Alexandria, VA 22314-2314
703-836-6981
Fax: 703-836-5223
E-mail: info@ascpt.org
www.ascpt.org

John J Schrogie MD, President
Sharon Swan, Executive Director

Over 1,900 professionals whose primary interest is to promote and advance the science of human pharmacology and theraputics. Most of the members are physicians or other doctoral scientists. Other members are pharmacists, nurses, research coordinators, fellows in training and other professionals.

Year Founded: 1900

2432 American Society of Consultant Pharmacists
1321 Duke Street
Alexandria, VA 22314-3507
703-739-1300
800-355-2727
Fax: 703-739-1321

E-mail: info@ascp.com
www.ascp.com

John Feather, Executive Director
Phylliss M Moret, Associate Executive Director/COO

International professional association that provides leadership, education, advocacy and resources to advance the practice of senior care pharmacy. Consultant pharmacists specializing in senior care pharmacy practice are essential participants in the health care system, ensuring that their patients medications are the most appropriate, effective, the safest possible and are used correctly. They identify, resolve and prevent medication related problems that may interfere with the goals of therapy.

2433 American Society of Group Psychotherapy & Psychodrama

301 N Harrison Street
Suite 508
Princeton, NJ 08540-3512
609-737-8500
E-mail: asgpp@asgpp.org
www.asgpp.org

Jennifer Reis, Executive Director
Eduardo Garcia, Executive Director
Sue Barnum, Secretary

Fosters national and international cooperation among all concerned with the theory and practice of psychodrama, sociometry, and group psychotherapy. Promotes research and fruitful application and publication of the findings. Maintains a code of professional standards.

Year Founded: 1942

2434 American Society of Health System Pharmacists

7272 Wisconsin Avenue
Bethesda, MD 20814-4836
301-657-3000
Fax: 301-664-8877
E-mail: Custserv@ashp.org
www.ashp.org

Mark Woods, President
Janet Silvester, President

Thirty thousand member national professional association that represents pharmacists who practice in hospitals, health maintenance organizations, long-term care facilities, ambulatory care, home care and other components of health care systems. ASHP helps people make the best use of their medications, advances and supports the professional practice of pharmacists in hospitals and health systems and serves as their collective voice on issues related to medication use and public health.

2435 American Society of Psychoanalytic   Physicians (ASPP)

13528 Wisteria Drive
Germantown, MD 20874-1049
301-540-3197
E-mail: cfcotter@aspp.net
www.aspp.net

Christine Cotter, Executive Director

An organization of physicians established for non-profit education, scientific, and professional purposes. Its objective is to futher the study of psyhcoanalytic methods for the treatment and prevention of emotional disorders and mental illnesses. The Society provides scientific meetings to foster its aims and to share information, namely research, evaluation of treatment, dissemination of information, and to publish and recognize achievement and provide professional opportunities among its members.

Year Founded: 1985

2436 American Society of Psychopathology of Expression (ASPE)

74 Lawton Street
Brookline, MA 02446-5801
617-738-9821
Fax: 617-975-0411

Dr. Irene Jakab, President

Psychiatrists, psychologists, art therapists, sociologists, art critics, artists, social workers, linguists, educators, criminologists, writers, and historians. At least two-thirds of the members are physicians. Fosters collaboration among specialists in the United States who are interested in problems of expression and in artistic activities connected with psychiatric, sociological, and pathological research. Disseminates information about research and clinical applications in the field of psychopathology of expression. Sponsors consultations, seminars, and lectures on art therapy.

2437 American Society on Aging

833 Market Street
Suite 511
San Francisco, CA 94105-2938
415-974-9600
800-537-9728
Fax: 415-974-0300
E-mail: info@asaging.org
www.asaging.org

Bob Stein, Executive Director
Robert Lowe, Director Of Operations

Nonprofit organization committed to enhancing the knowledge and skills of those working with older adults and their families. They produce educational programs, publications, conferences and workshops.

Year Founded: 1954

2438 Annie E Casey Foundation

701 St. Paul Street
Baltimore, MD 21202-2311
410-547-6600
Fax: 410-547-6624
E-mail: webmail@aecf.org
www.aecf.org

Douglas W Nelson, President
Ralph Smith, Senior Vice President

Working to build better futures for disadvantaged children and their families in the US. The primary mission of the Foundation is to foster policies, human service reforms and community supports that more effectively meet the needs of today's vulnerable children and families.

Year Founded: 1948

2439 Association for Academic Psychiatry (AAP)
464 Commonwealth Street
#147
Belmont, MA 02478
617-393-3935
Fax: 617-393-1808
E-mail: cberney@mah.harvard.edu
www.academicpsychiatry.org

Carole Berney MA, Administrative Director
Joan Anzia, President

Focuses on education in psychiatry at every level from beginning of medical school through lifelong learning for psychiatrists and other physicians. It seeks to help psychiatrists who are interested in careers in academic psychiatry develop the skills and knowledge in teaching, research and career development that they must have to succeed. The Association provides a forum for members to exchange ideas on teaching techniques, curriculum, and other issues to work together to solve problems. It works with other professional organizations on mutual interests and objectives through committee liaison and collaborative programs.

2440 Association for Ambulatory Behavioral Healthcare
247 Douglas Avenue
Portsmouth, VA 23707-1520
757-673-3741
E-mail: mickey@aabh.org

Mickey Wright, Executive Director

Powerful forum for people engaged in providing mental health services. Promoting the evolution of flexible models of responsive cost-effective ambulatory behavioral healthcare.

2441 Association for Applied Psychophysiology & Biofeedback
10200 W 44th Avenue
Suite 304
Wheat Ridge, CO 80033-2840
303-422-8436
800-477-8892
Fax: 303-422-8894
E-mail: aapb@resourcenter.com

Francine Butler, Executive Director
Steven Baskin, Treasurer

Their purpose is to advance the development, dissemination, and utilization of knowledge about applied psychophysiology and biofeedback to improve health and the quality of life through research, education and practice.

Year Founded: 1969

2442 Association for Behavior Analysis
1219 South Park Street
Kalamazoo, MI 49001
269-492-9310
Fax: 269-492-9316
E-mail: mail@abainternational.org
www.abainternational.org

Janet Twyman, President
Maria E Malott PhD, Executive Director

Their purpose is to develop, enhance and support the growth and vitality of behavior analysis through research, education and practice.

2443 Association for Behavioral and Cognitive Therapies
305 Seventh Avenue
16th Floor
New York, NY 10001-6008
212-647-1890
Fax: 212-647-1865
E-mail: mebrown@abct.org
www.aabt.org

Mary Jane Eimer, Executive Director
Mary Ellen Brown, Administration/Convention

Professional, interdisciplinary organization that is concerned with the application of behavioral and cognitive sciences to understanding human behavior, developing interventions to enhance the human condition and promoting the appropriate utilization of these interventions.

2444 Association for Birth Psychology
P.O. Box 1398
Forestville, CA 95436-1398
707-887-2838
Fax: 707-887-2838
E-mail: apppah@aol.com
www.birthpsychology.com

Maureen Wolfe, Executive Director
David Chamberlain, Treasurer/Website Editor

Obstetricians, pediatricians, midwives, nurses, psychotherapists, psychologists, counselors, social workers, sociologists, and others interested in birth psychology, a developing discipline concerned with the experience of birth and the correlation between the birth process and personality development. Seeks to promote communication among professionals in the field; encourage commentary, research and theory from different points of view; establish birth psychology as an autonomous science of human behavior; develop guidelines and give direction to the field. Annual conference, regional meetings, workshops.

2445 Association for Child Psychoanalysis (ACP)
7820 Enchanted Hills Blvd
#A-233
Rio Rancho, NM 87144
505-771-0372
E-mail: childanalysis@comcast.net
www.childanalysis.org

Kerry Kelly Novick, President
Tricia Hall, Administrator

An international not-for-profit organization in which all members are highly trained child and adolescent psychoanalysts. Provides a forum for the interchange of ideas and clinical experience in order to advance the psychological treatment and understanding of children and adolescents and their families.

2446 Association for Hospital Medical Education
109 Brush Creek Road
Irwin, PA 15642-9504
724-864-7321
866-617-4780
Fax: 724-864-6153
E-mail: info@ahme.org
www.ahme.org

Margie Kleppick, Executive Director
Charles Daschbach, President/Board Chairman

National, nonprofit professional association involved in the continuum of medical education — undergraduate, graduate, and continuing medical education. More than 600 members represent hundreds of teaching hospitals, academic medical centers and consortia nationwide. Promotes improvement in medical education to meet health care needs, serves as a forum and resource for medical education information, advocates the value of medical education in health care.

Year Founded: 1956

2447 Association for Humanistic Psychology
14B Beach Road
PO Box 1190
Tiburon, CA 94920
415-435-1604
Fax: 415-435-1654
E-mail: ahpoffice@aol.com
www.ahpweb.org

Carroy U Ferguson, Co-President
Leland Bagget, Co-President

Enhances the quality of human experience and to advance the evolution of human consciousness.

Year Founded: 1962

2448 Association for Pre- & Perinatal Psychology and Health
PO Box 1398
Forestville, CA 95436-1398
707-887-2838
Fax: 707-887-2838
E-mail: apppah@aol.com
www.birthpsychology.com

Maureen Wolfe, Executive Director
David Chamberlain, Treasurer/Website Editor

Forum for individuals from diverse backgrounds and disciplines interested in psychological dimensions of prenatal and perinatal experiences. Typically, this includes childbirth educators, birth assistants, doulas, midwives, obstetricians, nurses, social workers, perinatologists, pediatricians, psychologists, counselors researchers and teachers at all levels. All who share these interests are welcome to join. Quarterly journal published.

Year Founded: 1983

2449 Association for Psychoanalytic Medicine (APM)
333 Central Park West
New York, NY 10025-7145
718-548-6088
Fax: 212-866-4817

E-mail: gsagi@mac.com
www.theapm.org

Jonah Schein, President
Edith Cooper, Secretary

A non-profit organization that is a component society of both the American Psychoanalytic Association and the International Psychoanalytic Association.

Year Founded: 1942

2450 Association for Psychological Science (APS)
1133 15th Street NW
Suite 1000
Washington, DC 20005
202-293-9300
Fax: 202-293-9350
E-mail: akraut@psychologicalscience.org
www.psychologicalscience.org

Linda Bartoshuk, President
Mahzarin R Banaji, President-Elect
Anne Treisman, Secretary
Alan G Kraut, Executive Director

The APS (previously the American Psychological Society) is a nonprofit organization dedicated to the advancement of scientific psychology and its representation at the national and international levels. The Association's mission is to promote, protect, and advance the interests of scientifically oriented psychology in research, application, teaching and the improvement of human welfare. Available on Facebook and Twitter.

Year Founded: 1988

2451 Association for Research in Nervous and Mental Disease
1300 York Avenue, Box 171
Room F - 1231
New York, NY 10065-4805
570-839-0296
E-mail: amgooder@ptd.net
www.arnmd.org

Dr Annlouise Goodermuth, Executive Director

Keeps practicing physicians in nuerology and psychiatry, and neuroscientists, informed about state of the art research findings of interest to these ever more related disciplines, findings that are beginning to inform the thinking and practice of neurology and psychiatry.

Year Founded: 1920

2452 Association for Women in Psychology
Florida International University
DM 212
University Park
Miami, FL 33199-1
305-348-2408
Fax: 305-348-3143
E-mail: awp@fiu.edu
www.awpsych.org

Suzanna Rose PhD, Director

Nonprofit scientific and educational organization committed to encouraging feminist psychological research, theory and activism. They are an organization with a history of affirming and celebrating differences, deepening challenges, and experiencing growth as feminists.

Year Founded: 1969

2453 Association for the Advancement of Psychology
PO Box 38129
Colorado Springs, CO 80937-8129

800-869-6595
Fax: 719-520-0375
E-mail: Krivard@AAPNet.org
www.AAPNet.org

Stephen M Pfeiffer PhD, Executive Officer
Karen Rivard, Administrator

Promotes the interests of all psychologists before public and governmental bodies. AAP's fundamental mission is the support of candidates for the US Congress who are sympathetic to psychology's concerns, through electioneering activities.

Year Founded: 1974

2454 Association of Black Psychologists
PO Box 55999
Washington, DC 20040-5999
202-722-0808
Fax: 202-722-5941
E-mail: abpsi_office@abpsi.org
www.abpsi.org

Dorothy Holmes, President
Pamela Hall, Secretary
Muriel Kennedy, Treasurer

Members are professional psychologists and others in associated disciplines. Aims to: enhance the psychological well-being of black people in America; define mental health in consonance with newly established psychological concepts and standards, develop policies for local, state, and national decision making that have impact on the mental health of the black community; support established black sister organizations and aid in the development of new, independent black institutions to enhance the psychological educational, cultural, and economic situation. Offers training and information on AIDS. Conducts seminars, workshops and research. Periodic conference, annual convention.

Year Founded: 1968

2455 Association of State and Provincial Psychology Boards
PO Box 241245
Montgomery, AL 36124-1245
334-832-4580
Fax: 334-269-6379
E-mail: aspbb@asppb.org
www.asppb.org

Stephen T DeMers EdD, Executive Officer
Alex Siegel, President
Martha Storie, Secretary/Treasurer

ASPPB is the association of psychology licensing boards in the United States and Canada. They create the Examination for Professional Practice in Psychology which is used in licensing boards to assess candidates for licensure and

certification. They also publish training materials for training programs and for students preparing to enter the profession

Year Founded: 1961

2456 Association of University Centers on Disabilities (UACD)
1010 Wayne Avenuet
Suite 920
Silver Spring, MD 20910-5646
301-588-8252
Fax: 301-588-2842
E-mail: aucdinfo@aucd.org

George Jesien, Executive Director
William Kiernan, President

A network of interdisciplinary centers advancing policy and practice for and with individuals with developmental and other disabilities, their families and communities.

2457 Association of the Advancement of Gestalt Therapy
60 Waller Avenue
White Plains, NY 10605-1408
914-686-3477
E-mail: info@aagt.org
www.aagt.org

Peter Philippson, President
Sylvie Falschlunger, Administrative Assistant

Dynamic, inclusive, energetic nonprofit organization committed to the advancement of theory, philosophy, practice and research in Gestalt Therapy and its various applications. This includes but is not limited to personal growth, mental health, education, organization and systems development, political and social development and change, and the fine and performing arts. Their international member base includes psychiatrists, psychologists, social workers, teachers, academics, artists, writers, organizational consultants, political and social analysts, activists and students.

2458 Bazelon Center for Mental Health Law
1101 15th Street NW
Suite 1212
Washington, DC 20005-5002
202-467-5730
Fax: 202-223-0409
E-mail: webmaster@baxelon.org
www.bazelon.org

Robert Berstein, Executive Director
Albert Archie, Operations Manager

Provides technical support to lawyers and advocates on legal issues affecting children and adults with mental disabilities. Website has extensive legal advocacy resources and an online book store with handbooks, manuals and other publications.

2459 Behavioral Health Systems
2 Metroplex Drive
Suite 500
Birmingham, AL 35209-6827

205-879-1150
800-245-1150
Fax: 205-879-1095
E-mail: generalwebsite@bhs-inc.com
www.behavioralhealthsystems.com

Deborah Stephens, CEO
Kyle Strange, Senior Vice President/COO

Provides behavioral health services to business and industry which are high quality and state of the art, cost effective and accountable, uniformly accessible over a broad geographic area and care continuum, and managed within a least restrictive treatment approach.

2460 Bonny Foundation
PO Box 39355
Baltimore, MD 21212-6355

866-345-5465
E-mail: info@bonnyinstitute.org
www.bonnyfoundation.org

Donald Stoner, President

Nonprofit organization which provides resources and training in the therapeutic use of the arts for professional music therapists, related health professionals, and the general public. The Bonny Foundation Newsletter provides current information on applications of GIM (Guided Imagery and Music), training schedules and publications. Their GIM training program is fully accredited by the Association for Music and Imagery.

2461 CG Jung Foundation for Analytical Psychology
28 E 39th Street
New York, NY 10016-2555
212-697-1945
Fax: 212-953-3989
E-mail: info@cgjungny.org

Janet M Careswell, Executive Director
Maxon McDowell, President
David Rottman, Vice President

Analysts who follow the precepts of Carl G Jung, a Swiss psychologist, and any other persons interested in analytical psychology. Sponsors public lectures, films, continuing education, courses and professional seminars. Operates book service which provides publications on analytical psychology and related topics, and lectures on audio cassettes. Publishes journal, Quadrant.

Year Founded: 1962

2462 California Psychological Association
1231 I Street
Suite 204
Sacramento, CA 95814-2933
916-286-7979
Fax: 916-286-7971
E-mail: membership@cpapsych.org
www.cpapsych.org

Jo Linder-Crow PhD, Executive Director
Patricia VanWoerkom, Administration Director

A non-profit professional association for licensed psychologists and others affiliated with the delivery of psychological services.

Year Founded: 1948

2463 Center for Applications of Psychological Type
2815 NW 13th Street
Suite 401
Gainesville, FL 32609-2865
352-375-0160
800-777-2278
Fax: 352-378-0503
E-mail: customerservice@capt.org
www.capt.org

Nonprofit organization founded to conduct research and develop applications of the Myers-Briggs Type Indicator for the constructive use of differences. The MBTI is based on CG Jung's theory of psychological types. CAPT provides training for users of the MBTI and the Murphy-Meisgeier Type Indicator for Children, publishes and distributes books and resource materials, and maintains the Isabel Briggs Myers memorial library and the MBTI Bibliography. The MBTI is used in counseling individuals and families, to understand differences in learning styles, and for improving leadership and teamwork in organizations.

Year Founded: 1975

2464 Center for Clinical Social Work
27 Congress Street Suite 501
Shetland Park
Salem, MA 01970-5577
978-825-9311
800-694-5285
Fax: 978-740-5395
E-mail: abe@abecsw.org
www.centercsw.org

Hoawrd Snook PhD, BCD President
Robert Booth, Executive Director
Leonard Hill MSW BCD, Vice President

Clinical social work advocacy, certification and standards setting organization.

2465 Child Welfare League of America: Washington
2345 Crystal Drive
Suite 250
Arlington, VA 22202-4815
703-412-2400
E-mail: wtc@cwla.org

Christine James-Brown, CEO

Provides two national conferences each year: Finding Better Ways and Information Technology: Tools That Work; comprehensive training programs for managers, supervisiors, foster parents, adoptive parents and direct care workers. Also provides a range of published materials and training curricula relating to all facets of child welfare service.

2466 Children's Health Council
650 Clark Way
Palo Alto, CA 94304-2340
650-326-5530
Fax: 650-688-3676

E-mail: intake@chconline.org
www.chconline.org

Bruce Fielding, CFO Administration/Finance DIR
Bren Leisure, Secretary
Lawrence Schwab, Treasurer

Working to make a measurable difference in the lives of children who face severe or complex behavioral and developmental challenges by providing interdisciplinary educational, assessment and treatment services and professional training.

2467 Christian Association for Psychological Studies

PO Box 365
Batavia, IL 60510-365
630-639-9478
Fax: 630-454-3799
E-mail: info@caps.net
www.caps.net

Paul Regan EdD, Executive Director

Psychologists, marriage and family therapists, social workers, educators, physicians, nurses, ministers, researchers, pastoral counselors, and rehabilitation workers and others professionally engaged in the fields of psychology, counseling, psychiatry, pastoring and related areas. Association is based upon a genuine commitment to superior clinical, pastoral and scientific enterprise in the theoretical and applied social sciences and theology, assuming persons in helping professions will be guided to professional and personal growth and a greater contribution to others in this way.

Year Founded: 1956

2468 Clinical Social Work Federation

239 N Highland Street
Arlington, VA 22201-1250
703-522-3866
E-mail: nfscswlo@aol.com

Kevin Host, President
Sidney Grossberg, Vice President

A confederation of 31 state societies for clinical social work. The state societies are formed as voluntary associations for the purpose of promoting the highest standards of professional education and clinical practice. Each society is active with legislative advocacy and lobbying efforts for adequate and appropriate mental health services and coverage at their state and national levels of government.

2469 Commission on Accreditation of Rehabilitation Facilities

4891 E Grant Road
Tucson, AZ 85712-2704
520-325-1044
888-281-6531
Fax: 520-318-1129
TTY: 888-281-6531
www.carf.org

Brian J Boon PhD, President/CEO
Amanda Birch, Administrator Of Operations

Promotes the quality, value and optimal outcomes through a consultative accreditation process that centers on enhancing the lives of the people served.

2470 Commonwealth Fund

One E 75th Street
New York, NY 10021-2692
212-606-3800
Fax: 212-606-3500
E-mail: cmwf@cmwf.org

Karen Davis, President
John Craig, COO/Executive Vice President

Private foundation that supports independent research on health and social issues and make grants to improve health care practice and policy.

2471 Community Action Partnership

1140 Connecticut Avenue
Suite 1210
Washington, DC 20036
202-265-7546
Fax: 202-265-5048
E-mail: info@communityactionpartnership.com
www.communityactionpartnership.com

Donald W Mathis, President/CEO

The national organization representing the interests of the 1,000 Community Action Agencies working to fight poverty at the local level.

Year Founded: 1971

2472 Community Anti-Drug Coalitions of America

625 Slaters Lane
Suite 300
Alexandria, VA 22314-1176
703-706-0560
800-542-2322
Fax: 703-706-0565
E-mail: info@cadca.org

Arthur Dean, CEO
Addie Liles, Executive Assistant

With more than five thousand members across the country, CADCA is working to build and strengthen the capacity of community coalitions to create safe, healthy, and drug free communities. CADCA supports its members with technical assistance and training, public policy, media and marketing, conferences and special events.

2473 Corporate Counseling Associates

475 Park Avenue South
Fifth Floor
New York, NY 10016-6901
212-686-6827
800-833-8707
Fax: 212-686-6511
E-mail: info@corporatecounseling.com
www.corporatecounseling.com

Robert Levy, President
Steve Salee, SVP Consultative Services

Customized, integrated workplace solutions designed to enhance business performance by enriching employee productivity.

2474 Council on Social Work Education

1725 Duke Street
Suite 500
Alexandria, VA 22314-3457
703-683-8080
Fax: 703-683-8099
E-mail: info@cswe.org
www.cswe.org

Julia M. Watkins PhD, Executive Director
Nicole Demarco, Executive Assistant To Exec. Dir

A national association that preserves and enhances the quality of social work education for the purpose of promoting the goals of individual and community well being and social justice. Pursues this mission through setting and maintaining policy and program standards, accrediting bachelors and masters degree programs in social work, promoting research and faculty development, and advocating for social work education.

Year Founded: 1952

2475 Developmental Disabilities Nurses Association

P.O. Box 536489
Orlando, FL 32853-6489
407-835-0642
800-888-6733
Fax: 407-426-7440
www.ddna.org

Kathy Brown, Vice President
Richanne Cunningham, Secretary

National nonprofit professional association for nurses working with individuals with developmental disabilities. Publishes a quarterly newsletter.

Year Founded: 1992

2476 Division 42 - the Division of Independent Practice of the American Psychological Association (APADIP)

919 W Marshall Avenue
Phoenix, AZ 85013-1734
602-246-6768
Fax: 602-246-6577
E-mail: div42apa@cox.net
www.division42.org

Lisa Grossman JD, PhD, 2010 President
Pauline Wallin PhD, Internet Editor
Jeannie Beeaff, Administrative Director

Members of the American Psychological Association engaged in independent practice. Works to ensure that the needs and concerns of independent psychology practitioners are considered by the APA. Gathers and disseminates information on legislation affecting the practice of psychology, managed care, and other developments in the health care industries, office management, malpractice risk and insurance, hospital management. Offers continuing professional and educational programs. Semiannual convention, with board meeting.

2477 Employee Assistance Professionals Association

4350 North Fairfax Drive
Suite 410
Arlington, VA 22203-1619

703-387-1000
E-mail: ceo@eap-association.org
www.eapassn.org

Chris Drake, Manager
Mickey McKay, President
Jan Paul, Secretary/Treasurer

International association of approximately 5,000 members who are primarily employee assistance professionals as well as individuals in related fields such as human resources, chemical dependency treatment, mental health treatment, managed behavioral health care, counseling and benefits administration. Hosts annual EAP conference.

Year Founded: 1971

2478 Employee Assistance Society of North America

2001 Jefferson Davis Highway
Suite 1004
Arlington, VA 22202-3617
703-416-0060
Fax: 703-416-0014
E-mail: easnamember@ardel.com

Robert E Mc Lean, Executive Director

International group of professional leaders with competencies in such specialties as workplace and family wellness, employee benefits and organizational development. Maintains accreditation program, membership services and professional training opportunities, promotes high standards of employee assistance programs.

Year Founded: 1985

2479 Gerontoligical Society of America

1030 15th Street NW
Suite 250
Washington, DC 20005-1503
202-842-1150
Fax: 202-842-1150
E-mail: geron@geron.org
www.geron.org

Patricia Walker, Executive Director
Linda Krogh Harootyan, Interim Executive Director

Nonprofit professional organization with more than 5000 members in the field of aging. GSA provides researchers, educators, practitioners and policy makers with opportunities to understand, advance, integrate and use basic and applied research on aging to improve the quality of life as one ages.

2480 Gorski-Cenaps Corporation Training & Consultation

6147 Deltona Boulevard
Spring Hill, FL 34606-1000
352-596-8000
E-mail: info@cenaps.com
www.cenaps.com

Tresa Watson, Manager
Tresa Watson, Business Manager

Cenaps provides advanced clinical skills training for the addiction behavioral health and mental health fields. Their focus is recovery and relapse prevention.

2481 Group for the Advancement of Psychiatry
PO Box 570218
Dallas, TX 75357-218
972-613-3044
Fax: 972-613-5532
E-mail: frad1@airmail.net
www.groupadpsych.org

Frances Roton, Executive Director

An organization of nationally respected psychiatrists dedicated to shaping psychiatric thinking, public programs and clinical practice in mental health. Meets twice a year at the Renaissance Westchester Hotel in White Plains, NY.

Year Founded: 1946

2482 Health Service Providers Verified
1120 G Street NW
Suite 230
Washington, DC 20005-3801
202-783-1270
Fax: 202-783-1269

Judy Hall PhD, President

2483 Institute for the Advancement of Human Behavior (IAHB)
4370 Alpine Road
Suite 209
Portola Valley, CA 94028-7953
650-851-8411
Fax: 650-851-0406
E-mail: staff@iahb.org

Gerald W Piaget, President
Joan Piaget, Executive Director

A non-profit educational organization. They are a fully accredited sponsor of continuing education and continuing medical education for mental health, chemical dependency, and substance abuse treatment providers in the United States and Canada. Their mission is to provide high-quality clinical training to healthcare professionals as well as to companies and individuals with healthcare-related interests. They produce workshops and seminars on timely and important clinical topics conducted by scientist-practitioners who represent the state-of-the art in their chosen fields.

2484 Institute of HeartMath
14700 W Park Avenue
Boulder Creek, CA 95006-9318
831-338-8700
Fax: 831-338-8504
E-mail: ihminquiry@heartmath.org
www.heartmath.org

Katherien Floriana, Executive Director
Rollin McCarty, Executive VP/Dir. Of Research
Brian Kabaker, CFO/Dir. Sales & Marketing

Nonprofit research and education on stress, emotional physiology and heart-brain interactions. Purpose is to reduce stress, school violence, improve mental and emotional attitudes, promote harmony within facilities and communities, improve academic performance and improve workplace health and performance. Research facility provides psychometric assessments for both individual and organizational assessment as well as autonomic assessments for physiological assessment and diagnostic purposes. Education initiative currently developing curriculum for rehabilitation of incarcerated teen felons in drug and alcohol recovery program.

Year Founded: 1991

2485 Institute on Psychiatric Services: American Psychiatric Association
1000 Wilson Boulevard
Suite 1825
Arlington, VA 22209-3924
703-907-7300
E-mail: apa@psych.org
www.psych.org

Carol Robinowitz, President

Open to employees of all psychiatric and related health and educational facilities. Includes lectures by experts in the field and workshops and accredited courses on problems, programs and trends. Offers on-site Job Bank, which lists opportunities for mental health professionals. Organized scientific exhibits. Publications: Psychiatric Services, monthly journal. Annual Institute on Psychiatric Services conference and exhibits in October, Chicago, IL.

2486 International Center for the Study of Psychiatry And Psychology (ISCPP)
1036 Park Avenue
Suite 1B
New York, NY 10028-971
212-861-7400
E-mail: djriccio@aol.com
www.icspp.org

Peter Breggin, Founder/Director Emeritus
Dominick Riccio PhD, Executive Director

Nonprofit research and educational network whose focus is the critical study of the mental health movement. ICSPP is completely independent and their funding consists solely of individual membership dues. Fosters prevention and treatment of mental and emotional disorders. Promotes alternatives to administering psychiatric drugs to children.

2487 International Society for Developmental Psychobiology
8181 Tezel Road
#10269
San Antonio, TX 78250-3092
830-796-9393
866-377-4416
Fax: 830-796-9394
E-mail: isdp@isdpcentraloffice.org
www.isdp.org

Rick Richardson, Secretary
Susan Brunelli, Treasurer

Members are research scientists in the field of developmental psychobiology and biology and psychology students. Promotes research in the field of developmental psychobiology, the study of the brain and brain behavior throughout the life span and in relation to other biological proccesses. Stimulates communication and interaction among scientists in the field. Provides the editorship for the journal, Development Psychobiology. Bestows awards. Compiles statistics. Annual conference.

2488 International Society of Political Psychology
Moynihan Institute of Global Affairs
346 Eggers Hall
Syracuse University
Syracuse, NY 13244-1
315-443-4470
Fax: 315-443-9085
E-mail: ispp@maxwell.syr.edu
www.http://ispp.org

Bruce Dayton, Executive Director

Facilitates communication across disciplinary, geographic and political boundaries among scholars, concerned individuals in government and public posts, the communication media and elsewhere who have a scientific interest in the relationship between politics and psychological processes. ISPP seeks to advance the quality of scholarship in political psychology and to increase the usefulness of work in political psychology.

2489 International Transactional Analysis
Association (ITAA)
2186 Rheem Drive #B-1
Pleasanton, CA 94588-2775
925-600-8110
Fax: 925-600-8112
E-mail: info@itaa-net.org
www.itaa-net.org

Ken Fogleman, Manager
Lee Beer, Webmaster

A non-profit educational organization with members in over 65 countries. Its purpose is to advance the theory, methods and principles of transactional analysis.

2490 Jean Piaget Society: Society for the Study of
Knowledge and Development (JPSSSKD)
Department Of Psychology
Clark University
950 Main St
Worcester, MA 01610-1400
508-793-7250
Fax: 508-793-7265
E-mail: webmaster@piaget.org
www.piaget.org

Nancy Budwig, President
Ashley Maynard, Treasurer

Scholars, teachers, and researchers interested in exploring the nature of the developmental construction of human knowledge. Purpose is to further research on knowledge and development, especially in relation to the work of Jean Piaget, a Swiss developmentalist noted for his work in child psychology, the study of human development, and the origin and growth of human knowledge. Conducts small meetings and programs.

2491 Managed Health Care Association
1299 Pennsylvania Avenue NW
Washington, DC 20004-2400

202-218-4121
Fax: 202-478-1734

2492 Med Advantage
11301 Corporate Boulevard
Suite 300
Orlando, FL 32817-1445
407-282-5131
Fax: 407-282-9240
E-mail: info@med-advantage.com
www.med-advantage.com

John Witty, Owner

Fully accredited by URAC and certified in all 11 elements by NCQA, Med Advantage is one of the oldest credentials verification organizations in the country. Over the past eight years, they have developed sophisticated computer systems and one of the largest data warehouses of medical providers in the nation, containing information on over 900,000 healthcare providers. Their system is continually updated from primary source data required to meet the standards of the URAC, NCQA and JCAHO.

2493 Medical Group Management Association
104 Inverness Terrace E
Englewood, CO 80112-5313
303-799-1111
877-275-6462
Fax: 303-643-9599
E-mail: service@mgma.com
www.mgma.com

William Jessee, CEO
Steve Hellebush, COO

The national membership association providing information networking and professional development for the individuals who manage and lead medical group practices.

Year Founded: 1926

2494 Mental Health Corporations of America
1876-A Eider Court
Tallahassee, FL 32308-4537
850-942-4900
Fax: 850-942-0560
E-mail: heveyd@mhca.com
www.mhca.com

Donald Hevey, President
Tara Boyter, Director Of Communications

Membership in MHCA is by invitation only. It is the organization's intent to include in its network only the highest quality behavioral healthcare organizations in the country. Their alliance is designed to strengthen members' competitive position, enhance their leadership capabilities and facilitate their strategic networking opportunities.

2495 Mental Health Materials Center (MHMC)
PO Box 304
Bronxville, NY 10708-304
914-337-6596
Fax: 914-779-0161

Alex Sareyan, President

Professionals of mental health and health education, seeking to stimulate the development of wider, more effective channels of communication between health educators and the public. Provides consulting services to nonprofit organizations on the implementation of their publishing operations in areas related to mental health and health. Publications: Study on Suicide Training Manual. Survival Manual for Medical Students. Books, booklets and pamphlets. Annual Meeting in New York City.

2496 National Academy of Neuropsychology (NAN)

Ste 525
7555 E Hampden Ave
Denver, CO 80231-4836
303-691-3694
Fax: 303-691-5983
E-mail: office@nanonline.org
www.nanonline.org

Ruben Echemendia, President
John Meyers, Treasurer

Clinical neuropsychologists and others interested in brain-behavior relationships. Works to preserve and advance knowledge regarding the assessment and remediation of neuropsychological disorders. Promotes the development of neuropsychology as a science and profession; develops standard of practice and training guidelines for the field; fosters communication between members, represents the professional interests of members, serves as an information resource, facilitates the exchange of information among related organizations. Offers continuing education programs, conducts research.

2497 National Association For Children's Behavioral Health

1025 Connecticut Avenue NW
Suite 1012
Washington, DC 20036-5417
202-828-1280
Fax: 202-362-5145
E-mail: jmaley@youthconnect.org
www.nacbh.org

Jim Maley, President
Beth Chadwick, President-Elect/Vice President

To promote the availibility and delivery of appropriate and relevant services to children and adolescents with, or at risk of, serious emotional disturbances and their families. Advocate for the full array of mental health and related services necessery, the development and use of assessment and outcome tools based on functional as well as clinical indicators, and the elimination of categorial funding barriers.

2498 National Association for Advancement of Psychoanalysis

80 Eighth Avenue
Suite 1501
New York, NY 10011-5126
212-741-0515
Fax: 212-366-4347
www.naap.org

Margery Quackenbush, Executive Director
Jennifer Harper, President
Kirsty Cardinale, NAAP News Editor

Certified psychoanalysts disseminating psychoanalytic principles to the medical-psychiatric profession and the general community. Conducts scientific meetings. Supports research programs, sponsors public educational lectures. Publications: NAAP News, Quarterly; Registry of Psychoanalysts, Annual.

2499 National Association of Addiction Treatment Providers

313 W Liberty Street
Suite 129
Lancaster, PA 17603-2748
717-392-8480
Fax: 717-392-8481
E-mail: rhunsicker@naatp.org
www.naatp.org

Ronald J Hunsicker, President/CEO

The mission of the National Association of Addiction Treatment Providers (NAATP) is to promote, assist and enhance the delivery of ethical, effective, research-based treatment for alcoholism and other drug addictions. Provides members and the public with accurate, responsible information and other resources related to the treatment of these diseases, advocates for increased access to and availability of quality treatment for those who suffer from alcoholism and other drug addictions; works in partnership with other organizations and individuals that share NAATP's mission and goals.

Year Founded: 1978

2500 National Association of Community Health Centers

7200 Wisconsin Avenue
Suite 210
Bethesda, MD 20814-4838
301-347-0400
Fax: 301-347-0459
www.nachc.com

Tom Van Coverdan, President
Kauila Clark, Treasurer

A non-profit organization whose mission is to enhance and expand access to quality, community-responsive health care for America's medically underserved and uninsured. A major source for information, data, research and advocacy on key issues affecting community-based health centers and the delivery of health care. Provides education, training, technical assistance and leadership development to health center staff, boards and others to promote excellence and cost-effectiveness in health delivery practice and community board governance. Builds partnerships and linkages that stimulate public and private sector investment in the delivery of quality health care services to medically underserved communities.

2501 National Association of Nouthetic Counselors

3600 W 96th Street
Indianapolis, IN 46268-2905
317-337-9100
Fax: 317-337-9199
E-mail: info@nanc.org
www.nanc.org

Randy Patten, Executive Director
Jo Ann Pabody, Office Administrator

NANC is a fellowship of Christian counselors and laymen who have banded together to promote excellence in biblical counseling. NANC was founded in 1975 in service to Christ to address several needs in the counseling community.

Year Founded: 1975

2502 National Association of Psychiatric Health Systems

701 13th Street NW
Suite 950
Washington, DC 20005-3995
202-393-6700
E-mail: naphs@naphs.org
www.naphs.org

Mark Covall, CEO
Debra Osteen, First Vice President

Advocates for behavioral health and represents provider systems that are committed to the delivery of responsive, accountable, and clinically effective treatment and prevention programs for children, adolescents, adults and older adults with mental and substance abuse disorders.

Year Founded: 1933

2503 National Association of School Psychologists (NASP)

4340 East West Highway
Suite 402
Bethesda, MD 20814-4468
301-657-0270
Fax: 301-657-0275
E-mail: sgorin@naspweb.org
www.nasponline.org

Susan Gorin, Executive Director
Ted Feinberg, Assistant Executive Director

School psychologists who serve the mental health and educational needs of all children and youth. Encourages and provides opportunites for professional growth of individual members. Informs the public on the services and practice of school psychology, and advances the standards of the profession. Operates national school psychologist certification system. Sponsers children's services.

2504 National Association of Social Workers

750 First Street NE
Suite 700
Washington, DC 20002-4241
202-408-8600
800-638-8799
Fax: 202-336-8313
www.socialworkers.org

James J Kelly PhD, President

Works to enhance the professional growth and development of its members, to create and maintain professional standards, and to advance sound social policies.

2505 National Association of State Mental Health Program Directors (NASMHPD)

66 Canal Center Plaza
Suite 302
Alexandria, VA 22314-1568
703-739-2120
Fax: 703-548-9517
E-mail: roy.praschil@nasmhpd.org
www.nasmhpd.org

Robert W Glover, Executive Director
Roy Praschil, Director Operations

State commissioners in charge of state mental disability programs for children and youth, aged, legal services, forensic services and adult services. Promotes state government agencies to deliver services to mentally disabled persons and fosters the exchange of scientific and program information in the administration of public mental health programs. Publications: Children and Youth Update, periodic. Federal Agencies, periodic newsletter. State Report, periodic newsletter.

2506 National Business Coalition Forum on Health (NBCH)

1015 18th Street NW
Suite 730
Washington, DC 20036-5207
202-775-9300
Fax: 202-775-1569
E-mail: awebber@nbch.org

Andrew Weber, President
Maria Cornejo, Director Of Operations
Carly McKeon, Office Administrator

A national, non-profit membership organization of employer-based coalitions. Dedicated to value-based purchasing of health care services through the collective action of public and private purchasers. NCBH seeks to accelerate the nations progress towards safe, efficient, high quality health care and the improved health status of the American population.

2507 National Coalition for the Homeless

2201 P Street NW
Washington, DC 20037-1033
202-462-4822
E-mail: info@nationalhomeless.org

M Stoops, Executive Director

A national network of people who are currenlty experiencing or have experienced homelessness, activists and advocates, community-based and faith-based service providers, and others commiited to ending homelessness.

Year Founded: 1984

2508 National Committee for Quality Assurance

1100 13th Street NW
Suite 1000
Washington, DC 20005-4285
202-955-3500
Fax: 202-955-3599
www.ncqa.org

Margaret O'Kane, President
Greg Pawlson, Executive Vice President
Esther Emard, COO

A non-profit organization whose mission is to improve health care quality everywhere and to transform health care quality through measurement, transparency and account-ability.

2509 National Council of Juvenile and Family Court Judges
PO Box 8970
Reno, NV 89507-8970
775-784-6012
Fax: 775-784-6628
E-mail: staff@ncjfcj.org
www.ncjfcj.org

Susan Carbon, President
Mary V Mentaberry, Executive Director

Their mission is to improve courts and systems practice and raise awareness of the core issues that touch the lives of many of our nation's childrens and families.

Year Founded: 1937

2510 National Council on Aging
1901 L Street NW
4th Floor
Washington, DC 20036-3540
202-479-1200
Fax: 202-479-0735
E-mail: info@ncoa.org
www.ncoa.org

James P Firman, CEO
Jay Greenberg, EVP For Business Development

A national network of organizations and individuals dedi-cated to improving the health and independence of older persons and increasing their continuing contributions to communities, society and future generations.

Year Founded: 1950

2511 National Eldercare Services Company
7315 Wisconsin Avenue
Suite 400 East
Bethesda, MD 20814-3202
301-657-3070
Fax: 301-657-3862
E-mail: natleldr@bellatlantic.net
www.macrointernational.com

Chris Bishop, VP

An eldercare benefit management system.

2512 National Mental Health Association
2000 N Beauregard Street
6th Floor
Alexandria, VA 22311-1748
703-684-7722
800-969-6642
Fax: 703-684-5968
TTY: 800-433-5959
www.mentalhealthamerica.net

David Shern, CEO
Kate Gaston, VP Afiliate Services

Dedicated to improving treatments, understanding and ser-vices for adults and children with mental health needs. Working to win political support for funding for school mental health programs. Provides information about a wide range of disorders.

2513 National Nurses Association
1767 Business Center Drive
Suite 150
Reston, VA 20190-5332
703-438-3000
877-662-6253
E-mail: info@nationalnurses.org
www.nationalnurses.org

Laurie Campbell PhD, Executive Director

Purpose is to help enhance the personal development as well as economic well being of its members. They provide services and benefits meaningful to the unique demands of the nursing professional.

Year Founded: 1984

2514 National Pharmaceutical Council
1894 Preston White Drive
Reston, VA 20191-4313
703-620-6390
Fax: 703-476-0904
E-mail: info@npcnow.com

Daniel Leonard, President
Pat Adams, VP Business Operations

NPC sponsors a variety of research and education projects aimed at demonstrating that the appropriate use of pharmaceuticals improves both patient treatment outcomes and the cost effective delivery of overall health care services.

2515 National Psychological Association for Psychoanalysis (NPAP)
150 W 13th Street
New York, NY 10011-7802
212-924-7440
Fax: 212-989-7543
E-mail: info@npap.org
www.npap.org

Paul Kaiser, President
Arlyne Rochlin, Vice President

Professional society for practicing psychoanalysts. Con-ducts training program leading to certification in psycho-analysis. Offers information and private referral service for the public. Operates speakers' bureau. Publications: Na-tional Psychological Association for Psychoanalysis-Bulle-tin, biennial. National Psychological Association for Psychoanalysis-News and Reviews, semiannual. Psychoanalytic Review, bimonthly journal.

Year Founded: 1948

2516 National Register of Health Service Providers in Psychology
1120 G Street NW
Suite 330
Washington, DC 20005-3873
202-783-7663
Fax: 202-347-0550
www.nationalregister.org

Judy E Hall, CEO
Greg Hurley, Vice President/Vice-Chair

Psychologists who are licensed or certified by a state/provincial board of examiners of psychology and who have met council criteria as health service providers in psychology.

Year Founded: 1974

2517 National Treatment Alternative for Safe Communities
1500 N Halsted
Chicago, IL 60642-2517
312-376-0950
Fax: 312-376-5889
E-mail: information@tasc-il.org
www.tasc-il.org

Wil Brown, Manager
Peter Palanca, Vice President

TASC is a not-for-profit organization that provides behavioral health recovery management services for individuals with substance abuse and mental health disorders. They provide direct services, design model programs and build collaborative networks between public systems and community-based human service providers. TASC's purpose is to see that under-served populations gain access to the services they need for health and self-sufficiency, while also ensuring that public and private resources are used most efficiently.

2518 North American Society of Adlerian Psychology (NASAP)
NASAP
614 West Chocolate Avenue
Hershey, PA 17033-1901
717-579-8795
Fax: 717-533-8616
E-mail: info@alfrdadler.org
www.alfredadler.org

Mel Markowski, President
Al Milliren, Vice President

NASAP is a professional organization for couselors, educators, psychologists, parent educators, business professionals, researchers and others who are interested in Adler's Individual Psychology. Membership includes journals, newsletters, conferences and training.

Year Founded: 1952

2519 Pharmaceutical Care Management Association
601 Pennsylvania Avenue NW
7th Floor
Washington, DC 20004-2601
202-756-7210
Fax: 202-207-3623

E-mail: info@pcmanet.org
www.pcmanet.org

Mark Merritt, President/CEO
Missy Jenkins, SVP Federal Affairs

A national association representing Pharmacy Benefit Managers. They are dedicated to enhancing the proven tools and techniques that PBMs have pioneered in the marketplace and working to lower the cost of prescription drugs for more than 200 million Americans.

2520 Physicians for a National Health Program
29 E Madison
Suite 602
Chicago, IL 60602-4406
312-782-6006
E-mail: info@pnhp.org
www.pnhp.org

Ida Hellander, Executive Director
Steffie Woolhandler, Secretary

A single issue organization advocating a universal, comprehensive Single-Payer National Health Program.

Year Founded: 1987

2521 Professional Risk Management Services
The Psychiatrists' Program
1515 Wilson Boulevard
Suite 800
Arlington, VA 22209-2434

800-245-3333
E-mail: aboutus@prms.com
www.prms.com

Martin G Tracy JD ARM, President/CEO
Joseph Detorie, Executive Vice President/CFO

Professional Risk Management Services Inc (PRMS), a managing general agent, specializes in professional liability insurance, risk management, and loss prevention services. Our goal is to protect physicians and improve patient care through the development, design, and delivery of innovative professional liability insurance programs. At PRMS, we excel at providing superior, cost effective products and services that protect and support the demands and needs of our clients, including physicians, physician groups, facilities, and organizations. A key link to the success of PRMS is our staff of dedicated legal, clinical, and insurance professionals who turn their expertise into practice.

2522 Psychiatric Society Of Informatics American Association For Technology In Psychiatry
P.O. Box 11
Bronx, NY 10464-11
718-502-9469
E-mail: aatp@techpsych.org
www.techpsych.org

Robert Kennedy, Executive Director
Carlyle Chan, Secretary
Naakesh Dewan, President

2523 Psychohistory Forum
627 Dakota Trail
Franklin Lakes, NJ 07417-1043
201-891-7486
E-mail: pelovitz@aol.com
www.cliospsyche.org

Paul H Elovitz PhD, Editor

Psychologists, psychiatrists, psychotherapists, social workers, historians, psychohistorians and others having a scholarly interest in the integration of depth psychology and history. Aids individuals in psychohistorical research. Holds lecture series. Publications: Clio's Psyche: Understanding the Why of Current Events and History, quarterly journal. Immigrant Experience: Personal Narrative and Psychological Analysis, monograph. Periodic Meeting.

2524 Psychology of Religion
Doctoral Program in Clinical Psychology
750 First Street NE
Washington, DC 20002-4241
202-336-6013
Fax: 202-218-3599
E-mail: division@apa.org
www.apa.org/divisions/div36

Lisa Miller, President
Michael Donahue, Secretary

A division of the American Psychologial Association. Seeks to encourage and accelerate research, theory, and practice in the psychology of religion and related areas. Facilitates the dissemination of data on religious and allied issues and on the integration of these data with current psychological research, theory and practice.

2525 Psychonomic Society
1710 Fortview Road
Austin, TX 78704-7689
512-462-2442
Fax: 512-462-1101
www.psychonomic.org

Gavin Wilson, Manager
Roger Mellgren, Convention Manager

Persons qualified to conduct and supervise scientific research in psychology or allied sciences; members must hold a PhD degree or its equivalent and must have published significant research other than doctoral dissertation. Promotes the communication of scientific research in psychology and allied sciences.

2526 Rapid Psychler Press
3560 Pine Grove Avenue
Suite 374
Port Huron, MI 48060-1994
519-433-7642
888-779-2453
Fax: 888-779-2457
E-mail: rapid@psychler.com
www.psychler.com

David Robinson, Publisher

Produces books and presentation media for educating mental health professionals. Products cover a wide range of learning needs. Where possible, humor is incorporated as an educational aid to enhance learning and retention.

2527 Risk and Insurance Management Society
1065 Avenue Of The Americas
13th Floor
New York, NY 10018-713
212-286-9292
Fax: 212-986-9716
www.rims.org

Mary Roth, Executive Director
Joseph Restoule, Vice President

2528 Sciacca Comprehensive Services Development
299 Riverside Drive
New York, NY 10025-5278
212-866-5935
Fax: 212-666-1942
E-mail: ksciacca@pobox.com

Kathleen Sciacca MA, Executive Director/Consultant

Provides consulting, education and training for treatment and program development for dual diagnosis of mental illness and substance disorders including severe mental illness. Materials available include manuals, videos, articles, book chapters, journals and books. Trains in Motivational Interviewing. Develops programs across the mental health and substance abuse systems.

2529 Screening for Mental Health
1 Washington Street
Suite 304
Wellesley Hills, MA 02481-1706
781-239-0071
E-mail: smhinfo@mentalhealthscreening.org
www.mentalhealthscreening.org

Yvonne Beyliss, Manager

Nonprofit organization devoted to assisting people with undiagnosed, untreated mental illness connect with local treatment resources via national screening programs for depression, anxiety, eating disorders and alcohol problems.

2530 Sigmund Freud Archives (SFA)
23 The Hemlocks
c/o Harold P Blum, MD
Roslyn, NY 11576-1721
516-621-6850
E-mail: did2005@med.cornell.edu

Harold P Blum, Executive Director

Psychoanalysts interested in the preservation and collection of scientific and personal writings of Sigmund Freud. Assists in research on Freud's life and work and the evolution of psychoanalytic thought. Collects and classifies all documents, papers, publications, personal correspondence and historical data written by, to, and on Freud. Transmits all materials collected to the Library of Congress. Annual meeting in New York City.

2531 Society for Pediatric Psychology (SPP)
Citadel
Department of Phychiatry
Charleston, SC 29409-1
843-953-5320
Fax: 843-953-6797
www.apa.org

Lori Stark, President
Christina Adams, Secretary

Dedicated to research and practice addressing the relationship between children's physical, cognitive, social, and emotional functioning and their physical well-being, including maintenance of health, promotion of positive health behaviors, and treatment of chronic and serious medical conditions. A division of the APA. Bimonthly Journal, Newletter three times a year.

2532 Society for Personality Assessment
6109H Arlington Boulevard
Falls Church, VA 22044-2708
703-534-4772
Fax: 703-564-6905
E-mail: manager@spaonline.org
www.personality.org

Robert E Erard, President
F. Barton Evans, Treasurer
Carol Groves Overton, Secretary

International professional trade association for psychologists, behavioral scientists, anthropologists, and psychiatrists. Promotes the study, research development and application of personality assessment.

2533 Society for Psychophysiological Research
2810 Crossroads Drive
Suite 3800
Madison, WI 53718-7961
608-443-2470
E-mail: spr@reesgroupinc.com
www.scmhr.org

Lisa Nelson, Manager
Karen Quigley, Treasurer

Founded in 1960, the Society for Psychophysiological Research is an international scientific society. The purpose of the society is to foster research on the interrelationship between physiological and phychological aspects of behavior.

2534 Society for Women's Health Research
1025 Connecticut Avenue Nw
Suite 701
Washington, DC 20036-5447
202-466-6069
Fax: 202-833-3472
E-mail: info@womenshealthresearch.org
www.womenshealthresearch.org

Phyllis Greenberger, President
Suzanne Stone, VP Finance And Administration

The nation's only not-for-profit organization whose sole mission is to improve the health of women through research. Founded in 1990, The Society advocates increased funding for research on women's health, encourages the study of sex differences that may affect the prevention, diagnosis and treatment of disease, and promotes the inclusion of women in medical research studies.

2535 Society for the Advancement of Social Psychology (SASP)
630 Convention Tower
Buffalo, NY 14202
301-405-5921
Fax: 301-314-9566
E-mail: sesp@sesp.org
www.sesp.org

Garold Stasser, Secretary
Charles Stangor, Executive Officer

Social psychologists and students in social psychology. Advances social psychology as a profession by facilitating communication among social psychologists and improving dissemination and utilization of social psychological knowledge. Annual meeting every October.

2536 Society for the Psychological Study of Social Issues (SPSSI)
208 I Street NE
Washington, DC 20002-4340
202-543-5347
E-mail: spssi@spssi.org

Susan Dudley, Administrative Director
Anila Balkissoon, Administrative Coordinator

An international group of over 3,500 psychologists, allied scientists, students, and others who share a common interest in research on the psychological aspects of important social issues. The Society seeks to bring theory and practice into focus on human problems of the group, the community, and nations as well as the increasingly important problems that have no national boundaries.

2537 Society of Behavioral Medicine
555 East Wells Street
Suite 1100
Milwaukee, WI 53202-3800
414-918-3156
Fax: 414-276-3349
E-mail: info@sbm.org
www.sbm.org

Michael Long, Executive Director
David Wood, Associate Dir. Member Services

A non-profit organization is a scientific forum for over 3,000 behavioral and biomedical researchers and clinicians to study the interactions of behavior, physiological and biochemical states, and morbidity and mortality. SBM provides an interactive network for education and collaboration on common research, clinical and public policy concerns related to prevention, diagnosis and treatment, rehabilitation, and health promotion.

Year Founded: 1978

2538 Society of Multivariate Experimental Psychology (SMEP)
University of Virginia
102 Gilmer Hall
Department of Psychology
Charlottesville, VA 22903
804-924-0656
E-mail: shrout@psych.nyu.edu
www.smep.org

Steve West, President
Wayne Velicer, President-Elect

An organization of researchers interested in multivariate quantitative methods and their application to substantive problems in psychology. Membership is limited to 65 regular active members. SMEP oversees the publication of a research journal which publishes research articles on multivariate methodology and its use in psychological research. Annual meeting held every October.

Year Founded: 1960

2539 Society of Teachers of Family Medicine
11400 Tomahawk Creek Parkway
Suite 540
Leawood, KS 66211-2681
913-906-6000
800-274-2237
Fax: 913-906-6096
E-mail: stmoffice@stfm.org
www.stfm.org

Stacy Brungardt, Executive Director
Angela Broderick, Deputy Executive Director

Mulitdisciplinary, medical organization that offers numerous faculty development opportunities for individuals involved in family medicine education. STFM publishes a monthly journal, hosts a web site, distributes books, coordinates CME conferences devoted to family medicine teaching and research and other activities designed to improve teaching skills of family medicine educators.

2540 Therapeutic Communities of America
1601 Connecticut Avenue NW
Suite 803
Washington, DC 20009-1055
202-296-3503
E-mail: tca.office@verizon.net
www.therapeuticcommunitiesofamerica.org

Patrcia Beauchemin, Executive Director
Michael Harle, President
Sushma Taylor, First Vice President

National nonprofit membership association representing over 500 substance abuse treatment programs. The member agencies provide services to substance abuse clients of diverse special needs. Members provide a continuum of care including assessment, detoxification, residential care, case management, outpatient treatment, transitional housing, education, vocational and medical care.

2541 United States Psychiatric Rehabilitation Organization (USPRA)
601 Global Way
Suite 106
Linthicum, MD 21090-2265
410-789-7054
Fax: 410-789-7675
E-mail: info@uspra.org
www.uspra.org

Marcia Granahan CAE, CEO
Dave Mank, CFO

The USPRA, formerly IAPSRS, is an organization of psychosocial rehabilitation agencies, practitioners, and interested organizations and individuals dedicated to promoting, supporting and strengthening community-oriented rehabilitation services and resources for persons with psychiatric disabilities.

2542 Wellness Councils of America
9802 Nicholas Stnue
Suite 315
Omaha, NE 68114
402-827-3590
Fax: 402-827-3594
E-mail: wellworkplace@welcoa.org
www.welcoa.org

David Hunnicutt PhD, President
Brittanie Leffelman, Director Of Operations

A national non-profit membership organization dedicated to promoting healthier life styles for all Americans, especially through health promotion initiatives at the worksite. They publish a number of source books, a monthly newsletter, an extensive line of brochures and conducts numerous training seminars.

Year Founded: 1987

2543 WorldatWork
14040 N Northsight Boulevard
Scottsdale, AZ 85260-3627
877-951-9191
480-951-9191
Fax: 866-816-2962
E-mail: customerrelations@worldatwork.org
www.worldatwork.org

Anne Ruddy, President
Marcia Rhodes, Media Relations

A not-for-profit professional association dedicated to knowledge leadership in compensation, benefits and total rewards. Focuses on human resources disciplines associated with attracting, retaining and motivating employees. Provides education programs, a monthly magazine, online information resources, surveys, publications, conferences, research and networking opportunities.

Year Founded: 1955

2544 Yssociation for Psychological Type
9650 Rockville Pike
Bethesda, MD 20814-3999
301-634-7450
800-847-9943
Fax: 301-634-7455

E-mail: web@aptinternational.org
www.aptinternational.org

John Lord, Executive Director
Jane Kise, President

Individuals involved in organizational development, religion, management, education and counseling, and who are interested in psychological type, the Myers-Briggs Type Indicator, and the works of Carl G Jung. Purpose is to share ideas related to the uses of MBTI and the application of personality type theory in any area; promotes research, development, and education in the field. Sponsors seminars, conferences, and training sessions on the use of psychological type.

Alcohol/Substance Abuse & Dependence

2545 American Society of Addiction Medicine
4601 N Park Avenue
Upper Arcade #101
Chevy Chase, MD 20815-4519
301-656-3920
Fax: 301-656-3815
E-mail: email@asam.org
www.asam.org

Eileen McGrath, Executive VP
Eileen McGrath, Executive Vice President

Increase access to and improve the quality of addictions treatment. Educate physicians, medical and osteopathic, and the public.

Psychosomatic (Somatizing) Disorders

2546 American Society for Adolescent Psychiatry (ASAP)
PO Box 570218
Dallas, TX 75357-218
972-613-0985
Fax: 972-613-5532
E-mail: info@adolpsych.org
www.adolpsych.org

Frances Bell, Executive Director
Mohan Nair, President

Psychiatrists concerned with the behavior of adolescents. Provides for the exchange of psychiatric knowledge, encourages the development of adequate standards and training facilities and stimulates research in the psychopathology and treatment of adolescents. Publications: Adolescent Psychiatry, annual journal. American Society for Adolescent Psychiatry Newsletter, quarterly. ASAP Membership Directory, biennial. Journal of Youth and Adolescence, bimonthly. Annual conference. Workshops.

Year Founded: 1967

Books

General

2547 A Family-Centered Approach to People with Mental Retardation
AAMR
444 N Capitol Street NW
Suite 846
Washington, DC 20001-1569
202-637-0475
800-424-3688
Fax: 202-637-0585
E-mail: dcroser@aaidd.org

Doren Croser, Executive Director
Paul Aitken, Director Finance/Administration
Bruce Appelgren, Director Of Publications

Outlines key principles relevant to a family-centered approach to mental retardation and identifies four components to family-centered practice. *$12.95*

53 pages ISBN 0-940898-59-4

2548 A Guide to Consent
AAMR
444 N Capitol Street NW
Suite 846
Washington, DC 20001-1569
202-637-0475
800-424-3688
Fax: 202-637-0585
E-mail: dcroser@aamr.org

Examines current consent issues and explores legal implications of self-determination topics. Focuses on critical life events for people with mental retardation and practical applications of consent law, such as adult guardianship, consent to sexual activity, program placement and home ownership, capacity for and access to legal representation, capacity and other liberty and autonomy issues. *$27.95*

125 pages ISBN 0-940898-58-6

2549 A History of Nursing in the Field of Mental Retardation
AAMR
444 N Capitol Street NW
Suite 846
Washington, DC 20001-1569
202-637-0475
800-424-3688
Fax: 202-637-0585
E-mail: dcroser@aamr.org

For nursing scholars and anyone interested in the history of the treatment of people with mental retardation. *$19.95*

205 pages ISBN 0-940898-68-3

2550 A Primer on Rational Emotive Behavior Therapy
Research Press
Dept 24 W
PO Box 9177
Champaign, IL 61826-9177
217-352-3273
800-519-2707
Fax: 217-352-1221
E-mail: rp@researchpress.com
www.researchpress.com

Dr Windy Dryden, Author
Dennis Wiziecki, Marketing

This concise, systematic guide addresses recent developments in the theory and practice of Rational Emotive Behavior Therapy (REBT). The authors discuss rational versus irrational thinking, the ABC framework, the three basic musts that interfere wtih rational thinking and behavior, two basic biological tendencies, two fundamental human disturbances, and the theory of change in REBT. A detailed case example that includes verbatim dialogue between therapist and client illustrates the 18-step REBT treatment sequence. An appendix by Albert Ellis examines the special features of REBT. *$13.95*

114 pages ISBN 0-878224-78-5

2551 A Research Agenda for DSM-V
American Psychiatric Publishing, Inc.
1000 Wilson Boulevard
Suite 1825
Arlington, VA 22209-3901
703-907-7322
800-368-5777
Fax: 703-907-1091
E-mail: appi@psych.org
www.appi.org

Robert E Hales MD, Editor-in-Chief
Ron McMillen, Chief Executive Officer
John McDuffie, Editorial Director

In the ongoing quest to improve our psychiatric diagnostic system, we are now searching for new approaches to understanding the etiological and pathophysiological mechanisms that can improve the validity of our diagnoses and the consequent power of our preventative and treatment interventions-venturing beyond the current DSM paradigm and DSM-IV framework. This volume represents a far-reaching attempt to stimulate research and discussion in the field in preparation for the start of the DSM-V process, still several years away, and to integrate information from a wide variety of sources and technologies. Copyright 2002. *$38.95*

352 pages ISBN 0-890422-92-3

2552 Adaptive Behavior and Its Measurement Implications for the Field of Mental Retardation
AAMR
444 N Capitol Street NW
Suite 846
Washington, DC 20001-1569
202-637-0475
800-424-3688
Fax: 202-637-0585
E-mail: dcroser@aamr.org

Integrates the concept of adaptive behavior more fully into the AAMR definition of mental retardation.

227 pages ISBN 0-940898-64-0

2553 Addressing the Specific needs of Women with Co-Occuring Disorders in the Criminal Justice System
Policy Research Associates
345 Delaware Avenue
Delmar, NY 12054-1905
518-439-7415
800-444-7415
Fax: 518-439-7612
E-mail: gains@prainc.com
www.prainc.com

Henry Steadman, President

Brochure emphasizes the need for gender specific programs to meet the management needs of female offenders. For law enforcement and justice administrators.

2554 Advances in Projective Drawing Interpetation
Charles C Thomas Publisher
2600 S 1st Street
Springfield, IL 62704-4730
217-789-8980
800-258-8980
Fax: 217-789-9130
E-mail: books@ccthomas.com
www.ccthomas.com

Michael P Thomas, President

Exceptional contributors were chosen for their pertinence, range and inventiveness. This outstanding book assembles the progress in the science and in the clinical art of projective drawings as we enter the twenty-first century. Copyright 1997. *$80.95*

476 pages ISBN 0-398067-43-0

2555 Advancing DSM: Dilemmas in Psychiatric Diagnosis
American Psychiatric Publishing, Inc.
1000 Wilson Boulevard
Suite 1825
Arlington, VA 22209-3901
703-907-7322
800-368-5777
Fax: 703-907-1091
E-mail: appi@psych.org
www.appi.org

Robert E Hales MD, Editor-in-Chief
Ron McMillen, Chief Executive Officer
John McDuffie, Editorial Director

Presents case studies from leading clinicians and researchers that illuminate the need for a revamped system. Each chapter presents a diagnostic dilemma from clinical practice that is intriguing, controversial, unresolved and remarkable in its theoretical and scientific complexity. Chapter by chapter, Advancing DSM raises important questions about the nature of diagnosis under the current DSM system and recommends broad changes. Copyright 2002. *$41.95*

304 pages ISBN 0-890422-93-1

2556 Adverse Effects of Psychotropic Drugs
Gilford Press
72 Spring Street
New York, NY 10012-4019
212-431-9800
Fax: 212-966-6708

Bob Matloff, President

$63.00

2557 Agility in Health Care
Jossey-Bass Publishers
350 Sansome Street
5th Floor
San Francisco, CA 94104-1310
415-394-8677
800-956-7739
Fax: 800-605-2665
www.josseybass.com

$42.95

250 pages ISBN 0-787942-11-1

2558 American Psychiatric Glossary
American Psychiatric Publishing, Inc.
1000 Wilson Boulevard
Suite 1825
Arlington, VA 22209-3901
703-907-7322
800-368-5777
Fax: 703-907-1091
E-mail: appi@psych.org
www.appi.org

Robert E Hales MD, Editor-in-Chief
Ron McMillen, Chief Executive Officer
John McDuffie, Editorial Director

Hardcover. Paperback also available. Copyright 1994.
$28.50

224 pages ISBN 0-880485-26-4

2559 American Psychiatric Publishing Textbook of Clinical Psychiatry
American Psychiatric Publishing, Inc.
1000 Wilson Boulevard
Suite 1825
Arlington, VA 22209-3901
703-907-7322
800-368-5777
Fax: 703-907-1091
E-mail: appi@psych.org
www.appi.org

Robert E Hales MD, Editor-in-Chief
Ron McMillen, Chief Executive Officer
John McDuffie, Editorial Director

This densely informative textbook comprises 40 scholarly, authorative chapters by an astonishing 89 experts and combines junior and senior authors alike to enhance the rich diversity and quality of clinical perspectives. Copyright 2002. *$239.00*

1776 pages ISBN 1-585620-32-7

2560 Americans with Disabilities Act and the Emerging Workforce
AAMR
444 N Capitol Street NW
Suite 846
Washington, DC 20001-1569
202-637-0475
800-424-3688
Fax: 202-637-0585
E-mail: dcroser@aamr.org

Presents an empirical investigation of ADA issues and their effect on the employment of people with disabilities. Filled with legal cases, court opinions, charts, and tables. *$39.95*

303 pages ISBN 0-940898-52-7

2561 Assesing Problem Behaviors
AAMR
444 N Capitol Street NW
Suite 846
Washington, DC 20001-1569
202-637-0475
800-424-3688
Fax: 202-637-0585
E-mail: dcroser@aamr.org

Shows how to conduct a functional assessment, to link assessment results to interventions, and gives an example of completed fuctional analysis. *$21.95*

44 pages ISBN 0-940898-39-X

2562 Basic Personal Counseling: Training Manual for Counslers
Charles C Thomas Publisher
2600 S 1st Street
Springfield, IL 62704-4730
217-789-8980
800-258-8980
Fax: 217-789-9130
E-mail: books@ccthomas.com
www.ccthomas.com

Michael P Thomas, President

Contents: Becoming a Counselor; The Counseling Relationship; An Overview of Skills Training; Attending to the Client and the Use of Minimal Responses; Reflection of Feeling; Reflection of Content and Feeling; The Seeing, Hearing, and Feeling Modes; Asking Questions; Summarizing; Exploring Options; Reframing; Confrontation; Challenging Self-Destructive Beliefs; Termination; Procedure of the Counseling Experience; The Immediacy of the Counseling Experience; The Human Personality as it Emerges in the Counseling Experience; The Angry Client; Loss and Grief Counseling; The Suicidal Client; Arrangement of the Counseling Room; Keeping Records of Counseling Sessions; Confidentiality; Supervision and Ongoing Training; and The Counselor's Own Well-Being. Copyright 1989. *$42.95*

214 pages ISBN 0-398055-40-8

2563 Best of AAMR: Families and Mental Retardation
AAMR
444 N Capitol Street NW
Suite 846
Washington, DC 20001-1569
202-637-0475
800-424-3688
Fax: 202-637-0585
E-mail: dcroser@aamr.org

Provides a comprehensive look at families and mental retardation in the 20th century through the eyes of some of its most respected researchers and service providers. *$59.95*

382 pages ISBN 0-940898-76-4

2564 Boundaries and Boundary Violations in Psychoanalysis
American Psychiatric Publishing, Inc.
1000 Wilson Boulevard
Suite 1825
Arlington, VA 22209-3901
703-907-7322
800-368-5777
Fax: 703-907-1091
E-mail: appi@psych.org
www.appi.org

Robert E Hales MD, Editor-in-Chief
Ron McMillen, Chief Executive Officer
John McDuffie, Editorial Director

Copyright 2002.

240 pages ISBN 1-585620-98-X

2565 Brain Calipers: Descriptive Psychopathology and the Mental Status Examination, Second Edition
Rapid Psychler Press
3560 Pine Grove Avenue
Suite 374
Port Huron, MI 48060-1994
519-433-7642
888-779-2453
Fax: 888-779-2457
E-mail: rapid@psychler.com
www.psychler.com

David Robinson, Publisher

$34.95

ISBN 1-894328-02-7

2566 Breakthroughs in Antipsychotic Medications: A Guide for Consumers, Families, and Clinicians
WW Norton & Company
500 5th Avenue
New York, NY 10110-54
212-354-2907
800-233-4830
Fax: 212-869-0856
E-mail: admalmud@wwnorton.com

Drake McFeely, CEO

Gives patients and their families needed information about the pros and cons of switching medications, possible side effects. Copyright 1999. *$22.95*

240 pages ISBN 0-393703-03-7

2567 Brief Coaching for Lasting Solutions
WW Norton & Company
500 5th Avenue
New York, NY 10110-54
212-354-2907
800-233-4830
Fax: 212-869-0856
E-mail: npb@wwnorton.com

Drake McFeely, CEO

Successful coaching is about finding solutions and optimizing clients' lives. Insoo Kim Berg, one of the founders of solution-focused psychotherapy, collaborates with Peter Szabo in order to show how to help clients achieve their goals by applying their therapeutic approach to coaching.

ISBN 0-393704-72-6

2568 Brief Therapy and Managed Care
Jossey-Bass Publishers
350 Sansome Street
5th Floor
San Francisco, CA 94104-1310
415-394-8677
800-956-7739
Fax: 800-605-2665
www.josseybass.com

Provides focused, time-sensitive treatment to your patients. Pratical guidelines on psychotherapy that are conscientiously managed, appropriate, and sensitive to a client's needs. *$40.95*

443 pages ISBN 0-787900-77-X

2569 Brief Therapy with Intimidating Cases
Jossey-Bass Publishers
350 Sansome Street
5th Floor
San Francisco, CA 94104-1310
415-394-8677
800-956-7739
Fax: 800-605-2665
www.josseybass.com

This hands-on guide shows you how to apply the proven principles of brief therapy to a range of complex psychological problems once thought to be treatable only through long-term therapy or with medication. Learn how to focus on your clients' primary complaint and understand how and in what context the undesired behavior is performed. *$34.95*

224 pages ISBN 0-787943-64-9

2570 CURRENT Diagnosis & Treatment: Psychiatry
McGraw-Hill Medical Publishing Group
2 Penn Plaza
New York, NY 10121

212-904-2000
Fax: 212-904-6030
www.mhprofessional.com/product/php?isbn=0071422927

Michael H Ebert, Co-Author
Peter T Loosen, Co-Author
Barry Nurcombe, Co-Author
James F Leckman, Co-Author

This second edition is a reference for quickly answering day-to-day questions on psychiatric illness in both adults and children. Comprehensive in scope, and streamlined in coverage, this is a time-saving clinical companion. It reviews essential psychopharmacologic and psychotherapeutic approaches to the full range of psychiatric disorders. Copyright 2008. *$72.95*

758 pages ISBN 0-071422-92-7

2571 Cambridge Handbook of Psychology, Health and Medicine
Cambridge University Press
40 W 20th Street
New York, NY 10011-4211
212-924-3900
Fax: 212-691-3239
E-mail: marketing@cup.org
www.cambridge.org

Andrew Baum, Editor

This important text collates international and interdisciplinary expertise to form a unique encyclopedic handbook to this field that will be valuable to medical practitioners as well as psychologists. Copyright 1997. *$85.00*

678 pages ISBN 0-521436-86-9

2572 Challenging Behavior of Persons with Mental Health Disorders and Severe Developmental Disabilities
AAMR
444 N Capitol Street NW
Suite 846
Washington, DC 20001-1569
202-637-0475
800-424-3688
Fax: 202-637-0585
E-mail: dcroser@aamr.org

Provides a valuable compendium of the current knowledge base and empirically tested treatments for individuals with severe developmental disabilities, especially when problematic patterns of behavior are evident. *$39.95*

278 pages ISBN 0-940898-66-7

2573 Changing Health Care Marketplace
Jossey-Bass Publishers
350 Sansome Street
5th Floor
San Francisco, CA 94104-1310
415-394-8677
800-956-7739
Fax: 800-605-2665
www.josseybass.com

$35.95

366 pages ISBN 0-787902-52-7

2574 Clinical Dimensions of Anticipatory Mourning
Research Press
Dept 24 W
PO Box 9177
Champaign, IL 61826-9177
217-352-3273
800-519-2707
Fax: 217-352-1221
E-mail: rp@researchpress.com
www.researchpress.com

Russell Pense, VP Marketing

Dr. Therese Rando is joined by 17 contributing authors to present the most comprehensive resource available on the perspectives, issues, interventions, and changing views associated with anticipatory mourning. *$29.95*

616 pages ISBN 0-878223-80-0

2575 Clinical Integration
Jossey-Bass Publishers
350 Sansome Street
5th Floor
San Francisco, CA 94104-1310
415-394-8677
800-956-7739
Fax: 800-605-2665
www.josseybass.com

Learn how to create information systems that can support care coordination and management across delivery sites, develop a case management model program for multi-provider systems, and more. *$41.95*

272 pages ISBN 0-787940-39-9

2576 Cognitive Therapy in Practice
WW Norton & Company
500 5th Avenue
New York, NY 10110-54
212-354-2907
800-233-4830
Fax: 212-869-0856
E-mail: npd@wwnorton.com

Drake McFeely, CEO

Basic text for graduate studies in psychotherapy, psycholgy nursing social work and counseling. *$29.00*

224 pages Year Founded: 1989 ISBN 0-393700-77-1

2577 Collaborative Therapy with Multi-Stressed Families
Guilford Publications
72 Spring Street
New York, NY 10012-4068
212-431-9800
800-365-7006
Fax: 212-966-6708
E-mail: info@guilford.com

Bob Matloff, President

Written with a clear and fresh style, this is a guide to working in collaboration with clients, therapists and agencies. Experienced and beginning clinicians will appreciate a progressive approach to intricate problems. Copyrigt 1999. *$31.50*

358 pages ISBN 1-572304-90-1

2578 Communicating in Relationships: A Guide for Couples and Professionals
Research Press
Dept 24 W
PO Box 9177
Champaign, IL 61826-9177
217-352-3273
800-519-2707
Fax: 217-352-1221
E-mail: rp@researchpress.com
www.researchpress.com

Russell Pense, VP Marketing

Addresses the behavioral, affective and cognitive aspects of communicating in relationships. The book can be used by couples as a self-help guide, by professionals as an adjunct to therapy, or as a supplementary text for related college courses. Numerous readings are interspersed with 44 exercises that provide a hands-on approach to learning. The authors outline 18 steps for developing communication skills and describe procedures for integrating the skills into relationships. *$29.95*

280 pages ISBN 0-878223-42-8

2579 Community-Based Instructional Support
AAMR
444 N Capitol Street NW
Suite 846
Washington, DC 20001-1569
202-637-0475
800-424-3688
Fax: 202-637-0585
E-mail: dcroser@aamr.org

Offers practical guidelines for applying instructional strategies for adults who are learning community-based tasks. *$12.95*

34 pages ISBN 0-940898-43-8

2580 Comprehensive Textbook of Geriatric Psychiatry
WW Norton & Company
500 5th Avenue
New York, NY 10110-54
212-354-2907
800-233-4830
Fax: 212-869-0856
E-mail: npb@wwnorton.com

Drake McFeely, CEO

Sponsored by the American Association for Geriatric Psychiatry (AAGP), this invaluable reference covers the entire range of geriatric psychiatry, including: the ageing process; psychiatric disorders of the elderly; princpiles of diagnosis and treatment; medical-legal, ethical, and financial issues.

ISBN 0-393704-26-2

2581 Computerization of Behavioral Healthcare
Jossey-Bass Publishers
350 Sansome Street
5th Floor
San Francisco, CA 94104-1310
415-433-1767
800-956-7739
Fax: 800-605-2665
www.josseybass.com

How computers and networked interactive information systems can help to contain costs, improve clinical outcomes, make your organizations more competitive using practical guidelines. Copyright 1996. *$27.95*

304 pages ISBN 0-787902-21-7

2582 Concise Guide to Marriage and Family Therapy
American Psychiatric Publishing, Inc.
1000 Wilson Boulevard
Suite 1825
Arlington, VA 22209-3901
703-907-7322
800-368-5777
Fax: 703-907-1091
E-mail: appi@psych.org
www.appi.org

Robert E Hales MD, Editor-in-Chief
Ron McMillen, Chief Executive Officer
John McDuffie, Editorial Director

Developed for use in the clinical setting, presents the core knowledge in the field in a single quick-reference volume. With brief, to-the-point guidance and step-by-step protocols, it's an invaluable resource for the busy clinician. Copyright 2002. *$29.95*

240 pages ISBN 1-585620-77-7

2583 Concise Guide to Psychiatry and Law for Clinicians
American Psychiatric Publishing, Inc.
1000 Wilson Boulevard
Suite 1825
Arlington, VA 22209-3901
703-907-7322
800-368-5777
Fax: 703-907-1091
E-mail: appi@psych.org
www.appi.org

Robert E Hales MD, Editor-in-Chief
Ron McMillen, Chief Executive Officer
John McDuffie, Editorial Director

Practical information for psychiatrists in understanding legal regulations, legal decisions and present managed care applications. Copyright 1998. *$29.95*

296 pages ISBN 0-880483-29-6

2584 Concise Guide to Psychopharmacology
American Psychiatric Publishing, Inc.
1000 Wilson Boulevard
Suite 1825
Arlington, VA 22209-3901

703-907-7322
800-368-5777
Fax: 703-907-1091
E-mail: appi@psych.org
www.appi.org

Robert E Hales MD, Editor-in-Chief
Ron McMillen, Chief Executive Officer
John McDuffie, Editorial Director

Packed with practical information that is easy to access via detailed tables and charts, this pocket-sized volume (it literally fits into a lab coat or jacket pocket) is designed to be immediately useful for students, residents and clinicians working in a variety of treatment settings, such as inpatient psychiatry units, outpatient clinics, consultation-liaison services and private offices. Copyright 2002. *$29.95*

224 pages ISBN 1-585620-75-0

2585 Consent Handbook for Self-Advocates and Support Staff
AAMR
444 N Capitol Street NW
Suite 846
Washington, DC 20001-1569
202-637-0475
800-424-3688
Fax: 202-637-0585
E-mail: dcroser@aamr.org

Offers options for self-advocates and those for people who cannot consent on their own. *$14.95*

36 pages ISBN 0-904898-69-1

2586 Countertransference Issues in Psychiatric Treatment
American Psychiatric Publishing, Inc.
1000 Wilson Boulevard
Suite 1825
Arlington, VA 22209-3901
703-907-7322
800-368-5777
Fax: 703-907-1091
E-mail: appi@psych.org
www.appi.org

Robert E Hales MD, Editor-in-Chief
Ron McMillen, Chief Executive Officer
John McDuffie, Editorial Director

Overview of countertransference: theory and technique. Copyright 1999. *$37.50*

160 pages ISBN 0-880489-59-6

2587 Crisis: Prevention and Response in the Community
AAMR
444 N Capitol Street NW
Suite 846
Washington, DC 20001-1569
202-637-0475
800-424-3688
Fax: 202-637-0585
E-mail: dcroser@aamr.org

Provides a look at crisis services for people with developmental disabilities and how they impact the surrounding community. *$49.95*

240 pages ISBN 0-940898-74-8

2588 Cross-Cultural Perspectives on Quality of Life
AAMR
444 N Capitol Street NW
Suite 846
Washington, DC 20001-1569
202-637-0475
800-424-3688
Fax: 202-637-0585
E-mail: dcroser@aamr.org

Provides a ground-breaking global outlook on quality-of-life issues for people with mental retardation. *$47.95*

380 pages ISBN 0-940898-70-5

2589 Cruel Compassion: Psychiatric Control of Society's Unwanted
John Wiley & Sons
605 3rd Avenue
New York, NY 10158-180
212-850-6301
E-mail: info@wiley.com

Demonstrates that the main problem that faces mental health policy makers today is adult dependency. A sobering look at some of our most cherished notions about our humane treatment of society's unwanted, and perhaps more importantly, about ourselves as a compassionate and democratic people. Copyright 1994. *$19.95*

264 pages ISBN 0-471010-12-X

2590 Culture & Psychotherapy: A Guide to Clinical Practice
American Psychiatric Publishing, Inc.
1000 Wilson Boulevard
Suite 1825
Arlington, VA 22209-3901
703-907-7322
800-368-5777
Fax: 703-907-1091
E-mail: appi@psych.org
www.appi.org

Robert E Hales MD, Editor-in-Chief
Ron McMillen, Chief Executive Officer
John McDuffie, Editorial Director

Case presentations, analysis, special issues and populations are covered. Copyright 2001. *$51.50*

320 pages ISBN 0-880489-55-3

2591 Cutting-Edge Medicine: What Psychiatrists Need to Know
American Psychiatric Publishing, Inc.
1000 Wilson Boulevard
Suite 1825
Arlington, VA 22209-3901

703-907-7322
800-368-5777
Fax: 703-907-1091
E-mail: appi@psych.org
www.appi.org

Robert E Hales MD, Editor-in-Chief
Ron McMillen, Chief Executive Officer
John McDuffie, Editorial Director

Offers a comprehensive overview of recent developments in cardiovascular illness, gastrointestinal disorders, transplant medicine, and premenstrual mood disorders. Copyright 2003. *$36.95*

164 pages ISBN 1-585620-72-6

2592 Cybermedicine
Jossey-Bass Publishers
350 Sansome Street
5th Floor
San Francisco, CA 94104-1310
415-394-8677
800-956-7739
Fax: 800-605-2665
www.josseybass.com

A passionate plea for the use of computers for initial diagnosis and assessment, treatment decisions, and for self-care, research, prevention, and above all, patient empowerment. *$25.00*

235 pages ISBN 0-787903-43-4

2593 DRG Handbook
Dorland Healthcare Information
1500 Walnut Street
Suite 1000
Philadelphia, PA 19102-3512
215-875-1212
800-784-2332
Fax: 215-735-3966
E-mail: info@dorlandhealth.com
www.dorlandhealth.com

Diagnosis-related groups are the building blocks of hospital reimbursement under the Medicare Prospective Payment System. Also provides the ability to forecast and manage information at DRG-specific levels using comparison groups of like hospitals, a critical tool for both providers and payers. Copyright 1998. *$399.00*

1 per year ISBN 1-573721-39-5

2594 DSM: IV Diagnostic & Statistical Manual of Mental Disorders
American Psychiatric Publishing, Inc.
1000 Wilson Boulevard
Suite 1825
Arlington, VA 22209-3901
703-907-7322
800-368-5777
Fax: 703-907-1091
E-mail: appi@psych.org
www.appi.org

Robert E Hales MD, Editor-in-Chief
Ron McMillen, Chief Executive Officer
John McDuffie, Editorial Director

Focuses on clinical, research and educational findings. Practical and useful for clinicians and researchers of many orientations. Leatherbound. Hardcover and paperback also available. Copyright 1994. *$75.00*

886 pages ISBN 0-890420-64-5

2595 DSM: IV Personality Disorders
Rapid Psychler Press
3560 Pine Grove Avenue
Suite 374
Port Huron, MI 48060-1994
519-433-7642
888-779-2453
Fax: 888-779-2457
E-mail: rapid@psychler.com
www.psychler.com

David Robinson, Publisher

$9.95

ISBN 1-894328-23-x

2596 Designing Positive Behavior Support Plans
AAMR
444 N Capitol Street NW
Suite 846
Washington, DC 20001-1569
202-637-0475
800-424-3688
Fax: 202-637-0585
E-mail: dcroser@aamr.org

Provides a conceptual framework for understanding, designing, and evaluating positive behavior support plans. *$21.95*

43 pages ISBN 0-940898-55-1

2597 Developing Mind: Toward a Neurobiology of Interpersonal Experience
Guilford Publications
72 Spring Street
New York, NY 10012-4068
212-431-9800
800-365-7006
Fax: 212-966-6708
E-mail: info@guilford.com

Bob Matloff, President

Concise research results as to the origins of our behavior based on cognitive neuroscience.

2598 Disability at the Dawn of the 21st Century and the State of the States
AAMR
444 N Capitol Street NW
Suite 846
Washington, DC 20001-1569
202-637-0475
800-424-3688
Fax: 202-637-0585
E-mail: dcroser@aamr.org

Consumate source book on the analysis of financing services and supports for people with developmental disabilities in the United States. A detailed state-by-state analysis of public financial support for persons with MR/DD, mental illness, and physical disabilities.

512 pages ISBN 0-940898-85-3

2599 Diversity in Psychotherapy: The Politics of Race, Ethnicity, and Gender
Praeger
2727 Palisade Avenue
Suite 4H
Bronx, NY 10463-1020
718-796-0971
Fax: 718-796-0971
www.vd6@columbia.edu

Dr. Victor De La Cancela, President/CEO Salud Management

This challenging and insightful work wrestles with difficult treatment problems confronting both culturally and socially oppressed clients and psychotherapists. Case studies offer highly valuable resource material and insights into challenging perpsectives on behavioral health services. Copyright 1993. *$49.95*

224 pages ISBN 0-275941-80-9

2600 Doing What Comes Naturally: Dispelling Myths and Fallacies About Sexuality and People with Developmental Disabilities
High Tide Press
Ste 2n
2081 Calistoga Dr
New Lenox, IL 60451-4833
815-206-2054
888-487-7377
E-mail: managing.editor@hightidepress.com

Diane J Bell, Managing Editor

Uncovers misconceptions about adults whose sexual needs vary greatly, and yet are often treated as children or non-sexual people. Includes heartwarming success stories from adults Mrs. Anderson has supported, as well as suggestions for teaching and a guide to sexual incident reporting. *$19.95*

119 pages ISBN 1-892696-13-4

2601 Dynamic Psychotherapy: An Introductory Approach
American Psychiatric Publishing, Inc.
1000 Wilson Boulevard
Suite 1825
Arlington, VA 22209-3901
703-907-7322
800-368-5777
Fax: 703-907-1091
E-mail: appi@psych.org
www.appi.org

Robert E Hales MD, Editor-in-Chief
Ron McMillen, Chief Executive Officer
John McDuffie, Editorial Director

Principles and techniques. Copyright 1990. *$33.50*

229 pages

2602 Efficacy of Special Education and Related Services
AAMR
444 N Capitol Street NW
Suite 846
Washington, DC 20001-1569
202-637-0475
800-424-3688
Fax: 202-637-0585
E-mail: dcroser@aamr.org

Provides an objective, explicit, and clear evaluation of the existing literature of special education. Also evaluates general education practices adapted and modified for special education. *$31.95*

123 pages ISBN 0-940898-51-9

2603 Electroconvulsive Therapy: A Guide
Madison Institute of Medicine
7617 Mineral Point Road
Suite 300
Madison, WI 53717-1623
608-827-2470
E-mail: mim@miminc.org
www.factsforhealth.org

Margarett Baudhuin, Manager

ECT is an extremely effective method of treatment for severe depression that does not respond to medication. This guidebook explains what ECT is and how it is used today to help patients overcome depression and other serious, treatment resistant psychiatric disorders. *$5.95*

19 pages

2604 Embarking on a New Century: Mental Retardation at the end of the Twentieth Century
AAMR
444 N Capitol Street NW
Suite 846
Washington, DC 20001-1569
202-637-0475
800-424-3688
Fax: 202-637-0585
E-mail: dcroser@aamr.org

This volume of 18 essays summarizes major public policy and service delivery advancements from 1975 to 2000. These changes can be summarized as a siginificant shift in many areas — from services to supports; from passive to active consumer roles; from normalization to quality. *$29.97*

265 pages

2605 Emergencies in Mental Health Practice
Guilford Publications
72 Spring Street
New York, NY 10012-4068
212-431-9800
800-365-7006
Fax: 212-966-6708
E-mail: info@guilford.com

Bob Matloff, President

Focusing on acute clinical situations in which there is an imminent risk of serious harm or death to self or others, this practical resource helps clinicians evaluate and manage a wide range of mental health emergencies. The volume provides guidelines for interviewing with suicidal patients, potentially violent patients, vulnerable victims of violence, as well as patients facing life-and-death medical decisions, with careful attention to risk management and forensic issues. *$24.95*

450 pages ISBN 1-572305-51-7

2606 Essential Guide to Psychiatric Drugs
St. Martin's Press
175 5th Avenue
New York, NY 10010-7848
212-674-5151
Fax: 212-674-3179
E-mail: webmaster@stmartins.com

John Sargent, CEO

Information not found in other drug references. Lists many common drugs and not so common side effects, including drug interaction and the individual's reaction, including sexual side effects. Expert but nontechnical narrative. Copyright 1998. *$6.99*

416 pages ISBN 0-312954-58-1

2607 Essentials of Clinical Psychiatry: Based on the American Psychiatric Press Textbook of Psychiatry
American Psychiatric Publishing, Inc.
1000 Wilson Boulevard
Suite 1825
Arlington, VA 22209-3901
703-907-7322
800-368-5777
Fax: 703-907-1091
E-mail: appi@psych.org
www.appi.org

Robert E Hales MD, Editor-in-Chief
Ron McMillen, Chief Executive Officer
John McDuffie, Editorial Director

51 distinguished experts have created a compelling reference reflecting a biopsychosocial approach to patient treatment that is at once exciting and accessible. Copyright 1999. *$77.00*

1032 pages ISBN 0-880488-48-4

2608 Ethical Way
Jossey-Bass Publishers
350 Sansome Street
5th Floor
San Francisco, CA 94104-1310
415-394-8677
800-956-7739
Fax: 800-605-2665
www.josseybass.com

Leads you through a maze of ethical principles and crucial issues confronting mental health professionals. *$38.95*

254 pages ISBN 0-787907-41-X

2609 Evidence-Based Mental Health Practice: A Textbook
WW Norton & Company
500 5th Avenue
New York, NY 10110-54
212-354-2907
800-233-4830
Fax: 212-869-0856
E-mail: npb@wwnorton.com

Drake McFeely, CEO

The specific term evidence-based medicine was introduced in 1990 to refer to a systematic approach to helping doctors to apply scientific evidence to decision-making at the point of contact with a specific consumer. As support for evidence-based medicine grows in mental health, the need to clarify its fundamental principles also increases. An essential primer for all practitioners and students who are grappling with the new age of evidence-based practice.

ISBN 0-393704-43-2

2610 Executive Guide to Case Management Strategies
Jossey-Bass Publishers
350 Sansome Street
5th Floor
San Francisco, CA 94104-1310
415-394-8677
800-956-7739
Fax: 800-605-2665
www.josseybass.com

A guide to plan, organize, develop, improve and help case management programs reach their full potential in the clinical and financial management of care. *$58.00*

160 pages ISBN 1-556481-28-4

2611 Exemplar Employee: Rewarding & Recognizing Direct Contact Employees
High Tide Press
Ste 2n
2081 Calistoga Dr
New Lenox, IL 60451-4833
815-206-2054
888-487-7377
E-mail: managing.editor@hightidepress.com

Monica Regan, Managing Editor

With staff turnover as high as 90 percent in some agencies, you need to provide direct contact employees with as many incentives to excel as you can. This successful recognition program for non-management, direct contact employees is broken down and explained, with specific advice on how to implement it in your own organization from the people who developed the program. *$10.95*

48 pages ISBN 1-892696-03-7

2612 Family Approach to Psychiatric Disorders
American Psychiatric Publishing, Inc.
1000 Wilson Boulevard
Suite 1825
Arlington, VA 22209-3901

703-907-7322
800-368-5777
Fax: 703-907-1091
E-mail: appi@psych.org
www.appi.org

Robert E Hales MD, Editor-in-Chief
Ron McMillen, Chief Executive Officer
John McDuffie, Editorial Director

Examines how treatment can and should involve the family of the patient. Copyright 1996. *$67.50*

404 pages

2613 Family Stress, Coping, and Social Support
Charles C Thomas Publisher
2600 S 1st Street
Springfield, IL 62704-4730
217-789-8980
800-258-8980
Fax: 217-789-9130
E-mail: books@ccthomas.com
www.ccthomas.com

Michael P Thomas, President

Copyright 1982. *$48.95*

294 pages   ISSN 0-398-06275-7ISBN 0-398046-92-1

2614 Family Therapy Progress Notes Planner
John Wiley & Sons
10475 Crosspoint Boulevard
Indianapolis, IN 46256-3386
317-572-3000
Fax: 317-572-4000
E-mail: consumers@wiley.com
www.wiley.com

Lou Peragallo, Manager

Extends the line into the growing field of family therapy. Included is critical information about HIPAA guidelines, which greatly impact the privacy status of patient progress notes. Helps mental health practitioners reduce the amount of time spent on paperwork by providing a full menu of pre-written progress notes that can be easily and quickly adapted to fit a particular patient need or treatment situation. *$ 49.95*

352 pages   ISBN 0-471484-43-1

2615 Fifty Ways to Avoid Malpractice: A Guidebook
for Mental Health Professionals
Professional Resource Press
PO Box 15560
Sarasota, FL 34277-1560
941-343-9601
800-443-3364
Fax: 941-343-9201
E-mail: orders@prpress.com
www.prpress.com

Debra Fink, Managing Editor

Offers straightforward guidance on providing legally safe and ethically appropriate services to your clients. Copyright 1988. *$ 18.95*

158 pages   ISBN 0-943158-54-0

2616 First Therapy Session
Jossey-Bass Publishers
350 Sansome Street
5th Floor
San Francisco, CA 94104-1310
415-394-8677
800-956-7739
Fax: 800-605-2665
www.josseybass.com

Presents an effective, straightforward approach for conducting first therapy sessions, showing step-by-step, how to identify client problems and help solve them within families. *$27.95*

ISBN 1-555421-94-6

2617 Five-HTP: The Natural Way to Overcome
Depression, Obesity, and Insomnia
Bantam Doubleday Dell Publishing
1745 Broadway
New York, NY 10019-4343
212-782-9000

Jeff Rechtzigel, Publisher

An authorative and comprehensive guide to realizing the health benefits of 5-HTP. Explains how this natural amino acid can safely and effectively regulate low serotonin levels, which have been linked to depression, obesity, insomnia, migraines, and anxiety. 5-HTP is also a powerful antioxidant that can protect the body from free-radical damage, reducing the risk of serious illnesses such as cancer. Copyright 1999. *$11.95*

304 pages   ISBN 0-553379-46-1

2618 Flawless Consulting
Jossey-Bass Publishers
350 Sansome Street
5th Floor
San Francisco, CA 94104-1310
415-394-8677
800-956-7739
Fax: 800-605-2665
www.josseybass.com

This book offers advice on what to say and what to do in specific situations to see your recommendations through. *$39.95*

214 pages   ISBN 0-893840-52-1

2619 Forgiveness: Theory, Research and Practice
Guilford Publications
72 Spring Street
New York, NY 10012-4068
212-431-9800
800-365-7006
Fax: 212-966-6708
E-mail: info@guilford.com

Bob Matloff, President

Scholarly, up-to-date examination of forgiveness ranges many disiplines for mental health professionals. Copyright 2000. *$ 35.00*

334 pages ISBN 1-572305-10-X

2620 Foundations of Mental Health Counseling
Charles C Thomas Publisher
2600 S 1st Street
Springfield, IL 62704-4730
217-789-8980
800-258-8980
Fax: 217-789-9130
E-mail: books@ccthomas.com
www.ccthomas.com

Michael P Thomas, President

The latest writings regarding the explosive growth of mental health counseling over the past twenty years. Leading experts discuss the past, present, and future of the field from their unique positions as practitioners, theoreticians, and educators. Major issues such as professional identity, ethics, assessment, research, and theory are joined with the contemporary problems of managed health care, insurance reimbursement, and private practice. An up-to-date resource in the field of mental health counseling. Copyright 1996. *$89.95*

446 pages ISBN 0-398066-69-8

2621 Fundamentals of Psychiatric Treatment Planning
American Psychiatric Publishing, Inc.
1000 Wilson Boulevard
Suite 1825
Arlington, VA 22209-3901
703-907-7322
800-368-5777
Fax: 703-907-1091
E-mail: appi@psych.org
www.appi.org

Robert E Hales MD, Editor-in-Chief
Ron McMillen, Chief Executive Officer
John McDuffie, Editorial Director

Professional discussion of important basics. Copyright 2002. *$49.00*

368 pages ISBN 1-585620-61-0

2622 Group Involvement Training
New Harbinger Publications
5674 Shattuck Avenue
Oakland, CA 94609-1662
510-652-0215
800-748-6273
Fax: 510-652-5472
E-mail: customerservice@newharbinger.com
www.newharbinger.com

Matthew McKay, Owner

This book shows how training chronically ill mental patients in a series of structured group tasks can be used to treat the symptoms of apathy, withdrawl, poor interpersonal skills, helplessness, and the inability to structure leisure time constructively. Copyright 1988. *$24.95*

160 pages ISBN 0-934986-65-7

2623 Guide to Possibility Land: Fifty One Methods for Doing Brief, Respectful Therapy
WW Norton & Company
500 5th Avenue
New York, NY 10110-54
212-354-2907
Fax: 212-869-0856
E-mail: admalmud@wwnorton.com

Drake McFeely, CEO

The creator of Possibility therapy, William O'Hanlon, outlines acknowledging patient's experience and opinions about their lives while seeing that possibilites for change are explored and underlined. Copyright 1999. *$13.00*

94 pages ISBN 0-393702-97-9

2624 Guide to Treatments That Work
Oxford University Press/Oxford Reference
198 Madison Avenue
New York, NY 10016-4308
212-726-6400
800-451-7556

Michael Cunningham, Manager

A systematic review of various treatments currently in use for virtually all of the recognized mental disorders. Copyright 1997. *$75.00*

624 pages ISBN 0-195102-27-4

2625 Handbook on Quality of Life for Human Service Practitioners
AAMR
444 N Capitol Street NW
Suite 846
Washington, DC 20001-1569
202-637-0475
800-424-3688
Fax: 202-637-0585
E-mail: dcroser@aamr.org

Revolutionary generic model for quality of life that integrates core domains and indicators with a cross-cultural systems prespective that can be used in all human services. *$59.95*

429 pages ISBN 0-940898-77-2

2626 Health Insurance Answer Book
Garner Consulting
630 North Rosemead Blvd
Suite 300
Pasadena, CA 91107
626-351-2300
Fax: 626-371-0447
E-mail: info@garnerconsulting.com
www.garnerconsulting.com

This easy-to-use guide will help you manage a cost effective health insurance plan and ensure that your decisions are in compliance with constantly changing health care legislation. Offers instant access to information on everything from HMOs, PPOs, COBRA, HIPPA, OBRA anad flexible benefits to plan rating, funding, cost containment, and administration. *$290.00*

1100 pages ISBN 0-735582-18-7

42 pages   ISBN 0-965374-46-7

2627 Helper's Journey: Working with People Facing Grief, Loss, and Life-Threatening Illness
Research Press
Dept 24 W
PO Box 9177
Champaign, IL 61826-9177
217-352-3273
800-519-2707
Fax: 217-352-1221
E-mail: rp@researchpress.com
www.researchpress.com

Russell Pense, VP Marketing

Written for both professional and volunteer caregivers, this unique manual provides exercises, activities and specific strategies for more successful caregiving, increased personal growth and effective stress management. The author explores the theory and practice of helping. He includes numerous case examples and verbatim disclosures of fellow caregivers that powerfully convey the joys and sorrows of the helper's journey. Cited as a "Book of the Year" by the American Journal of Nursing. *$21.95*

292 pages   ISBN 0-878223-44-4

2628 High Impact Consulting
Jossey-Bass Publishers
350 Sansome Street
5th Floor
San Francisco, CA 94104-1310
415-394-8677
800-956-7739
Fax: 800-605-2665
www.josseybass.com

Offers a new model for consulting services that shows how to produce short-term successes and use them as a springboard to larger accomplishments and, ultimately, to organization-wide continuous improvement. Also includes specific guidance to assist clients in analyzing their situation, identifying their real needs, and choosing an appropriate consultant. *$26.00*

256 pages   ISBN 0-787903-41-8

2629 Home Maintenance for Residential Service Providers
High Tide Press
Ste 2n
2081 Calistoga Dr
New Lenox, IL 60451-4833
815-206-2054
888-487-7377
E-mail: managing.editor@hightidepress.com

Monica Regan, Managing Editor

What happens when a human service organization becomes a large, commercial landlord, not unlike a real estate firm or condominium management company? Property management for homes supporting persons with disabilities requires a unique blend of human services and physical plant expertise. Provides detailed checklists for all house systems, fixtures and furnishings. Includes a discussion of maintaining an attractive residence that blends with the neighborhood. *$10.95*

2630 How to Partner with Managed Care
John Wiley & Sons
605 3rd Avenue
New York, NY 10158-180
212-850-6301
E-mail: info@wiley.com

A Do It Yourself Kit for Building Working Relationships & Getting Steady Referrals. Copyright 1996.

366 pages

2631 IEP-2005: Writing and Implementing Individualized Education Programs
Charles C Thomas Publishers
PO Box 19265
Springfield, IL 62794-9265
217-789-8980
800-258-8980
Fax: 217-789-9130
www.ccthomas.com

Purpose is to provide guidelines to develop appropriate Individualized Education Programs (IEPs) for children with disabilities based on the Individuals with Disabilities Education Act amendments of 2004 (IDEA-2004) or Pblic LAw 108-446. These guidelines are intended to result in IEPs that are streamlined, focused, and reasonably calculated to provide educational benefit. Available in paperback for $41.95. Copyright 2006. *$61.95*

302 pages   ISBN 0-398076-24-3

2632 Improving Clinical Practice
Jossey-Bass Publishers
350 Sansome Street
5th Floor
San Francisco, CA 94104-1310
415-394-8677
800-956-7739
Fax: 800-605-2665
www.josseybass.com

Enhance your organization's clinical decision making, and ultimately improve the quality of patient care. *$41.95*

342 pages   ISBN 0-787900-93-1

2633 Improving Therapeutic Communication
Jossey-Bass Publishers
350 Sansome Street
5th Floor
San Francisco, CA 94104-1310
415-394-8677
800-956-7739
Fax: 800-605-2665
www.josseybass.com

Improve your communication technique with this definitive guide for counselors, therapists, and caseworkers. Focuses on the four basic skills that facilitate communication in therapy: empathy, respect, authenticity, and confrontation. *$62.95*

394 pages   ISBN 0-875893-08-2

2634 In Search of Solutions: A New Direction in Psychotherapy
WW Norton & Company
500 5th Avenue
New York, NY 10110-54
212-354-2907
800-233-4830
Fax: 212-869-0856
E-mail: npb@wwnorton.com

Drake McFeely, CEO

O'Hanlon and Weiner-Davis provide guidelines for clinicians in implementing solution-oriented language and explain how to aviod dead ends. New material bring the reader up to date on advances in this field since the book's original publication in 1989.

ISBN 0-393704-37-8

2635 Increasing Variety in Adult Life
AAMR
444 N Capitol Street NW
Suite 846
Washington, DC 20001-1569
202-637-0475
800-424-3688
Fax: 202-637-0585
E-mail: dcroser@aamr.org

Step-by-step guidelines for implementing the general-case instructional process and shows how the process can be used across a variety of activities. *$12.95*

38 pages ISBN 0-940898-43-2

2636 Independent Practice for the Mental Health Professional
Brunner/Routledge
325 Chestnut Street
Philadelphia, PA 19106-2614

800-821-8312
Fax: 215-269-0363

Ralph H Earle PhD
Dorothy J Barnes MC

An excellent resource for beginning therapists considering private practice or for experienced therapists moving from agency or institutional settings into private practice. Offers practical, down-to-earth suggestions for practice settings, marketing and working with clients. The authors provide worksheets and examples of successful planning for the growth of a practice. *$24.95*

141 pages ISBN 0-876308-38-8

2637 Infanticide: Psychosocial and Legal Perspectives on Mothers Who Kill
American Psychiatric Publishing, Inc.
1000 Wilson Boulevard
Suite 1825
Arlington, VA 22209-3901
703-907-7322
800-368-5777
Fax: 703-907-1091
E-mail: appi@psych.org
www.appi.org

Robert E Hales MD, Editor-in-Chief
Ron McMillen, Chief Executive Officer
John McDuffie, Editorial Director

Written to help remedy today's dearth of up-to-date, research-based literature, this unique volume brings together a multidisciplinary group of 17 experts who focus on the psychiatric perspective of this tragic cause of infant death. Balanced perspective on a highly emotional issue will find a wide audience among psychiatric and medical professionals, legal professionals, public health professionals and interested laypersons. Copyright 2002. *$53.50*

304 pages ISBN 1-585620-97-1

2638 Innovative Approaches for Difficult to Treat Populations
American Psychiatric Publishing, Inc.
1000 Wilson Boulevard
Suite 1825
Arlington, VA 22209-3901
703-907-7322
800-368-5777
Fax: 703-907-1091
E-mail: appi@psych.org
www.appi.org

Robert E Hales MD, Editor-in-Chief
Ron McMillen, Chief Executive Officer
John McDuffie, Editorial Director

Alternate methods when the usual approaches are not helpful. Copyright 1997. *$86.95*

512 pages

2639 Insider's Guide to Mental Health Resources Online
Guilford Publications
72 Spring Street
New York, NY 10012-4068
212-431-9800
800-365-7006
Fax: 212-966-6708
E-mail: info@guilford.com

Bob Matloff, President

This guide helps readers take full advantage of Internet and world-wide-web resources in psychology, psychiatric, self-help and patient education. The book explains and evaluates the full range of search tools, newsgroups, databases and describes hundreds of specific disorders, find job listings and network with other professionals, obtain needed articles and books, conduct grant searches and much more. *$ 21.95*

338 pages ISBN 1-572305-49-5

2640 Instant Psychopharmacology
WW Norton & Company
500 5th Avenue
New York, NY 10110-54
212-354-2907
Fax: 212-869-0856
E-mail: admalmud@wwnorton.com

Drake McFeely, CEO

Revision of the best selling guide to all the new medications. Straightforward book teaches non medical therapists, clients and their families how the five different classes of drugs work, advice on side effects, drug interaction warnings and much more practical information. Copyright 2002. *$18.95*

168 pages ISBN 0-393703-91-6

2641 Integrated Treatment of Psychiatric Disorders
American Psychiatric Publishing, Inc.
1000 Wilson Boulevard
Suite 1825
Arlington, VA 22209-3901
703-907-7322
800-368-5777
Fax: 703-907-1091
E-mail: appi@psych.org
www.appi.org

Robert E Hales MD, Editor-in-Chief
Ron McMillen, Chief Executive Officer
John McDuffie, Editorial Director

Psychodynamic therapy and medication. Copyright 2001. *$34.95*

208 pages ISBN 1-585620-27-0

2642 Integrating Psychotherapy and Pharmacotherapy: Disolving the Mind-Brain Barrier
WW Norton & Company
500 5th Avenue
New York, NY 10110-54
212-354-2907
800-233-4830
Fax: 212-869-0856
E-mail: npb@wwnorton.com

Drake McFeely, CEO

Will help all mental health clinicians to dissolve their conceptual mind/brain barriers by recognizing the reciprocal influences of psychological and pharmacological interventions. The reader responds to thought-provoking questions and vignettes of problematic cases.

ISBN 0-393704-03-3

2643 Integrative Brief Therapy: Cognitive, Psychodynamic, Humanistic & Neurobehavioral Approaches
Impact Publishers
PO Box 6016
Atascadero, CA 93423-6016
805-466-5917
800-246-7228
Fax: 805-466-5919
E-mail: info@impactpublishers.com
www.impactpublishers.com

Thorough discussion of the factors that contribute to effectiveness in therapy carefully integrates key elements from diverse theoretical viewpoints. Copyright 1998. *$17.95*

272 pages ISBN 1-886230-09-9

2644 International Handbook on Mental Health Policy
Greenwood Publishing Group
88 Post Road W
PO Box 5007
Westport, CT 06881-5007
203-226-3571
Fax: 203-222-1502

Major reference book for academics and practitioners that provides a systematic survey and analysis of mental health policies in twenty representative countries. Copyright 1993. *$125.00*

512 pages ISBN 0-313275-67-X

2645 Interpersonal Psychotherapy
American Psychiatric Publishing, Inc.
1000 Wilson Boulevard
Suite 1825
Arlington, VA 22209-3901
703-907-7322
800-368-5777
Fax: 703-907-1091
E-mail: appi@psych.org
www.appi.org

Robert E Hales MD, Editor-in-Chief
Ron McMillen, Chief Executive Officer
John McDuffie, Editorial Director

An overview of interpersonal psychotherapy for depression, preventative treatment for depression, bulimia nervosa and HIV positive men and women. Copyright 1998. *$37.50*

156 pages ISBN 0-880488-36-0

2646 Introduction to Time: Limited Group Psychotherapy
American Psychiatric Publishing, Inc.
1000 Wilson Boulevard
Suite 1825
Arlington, VA 22209-3901
703-907-7322
800-368-5777
Fax: 703-907-1091
E-mail: appi@psych.org
www.appi.org

Robert E Hales MD, Editor-in-Chief
Ron McMillen, Chief Executive Officer
John McDuffie, Editorial Director

Do more with limited time and sessions. Copyright 1997. *$57.95*

317 pages

2647 Introduction to the Technique of Psychotherapy: Practice Guidelines for Psychotherapists
Charles C Thomas Publisher
2600 S 1st Street
Springfield, IL 62704-4730

217-789-8980
800-258-8980
Fax: 217-789-9130
E-mail: books@ccthomas.com
www.ccthomas.com

Michael P Thomas, President

A basic, simply written book, with a minimum of theory, helpful to the beginning therapist. Discuss how to conduct psychotherapy: by having a format in mind, taking a comprehensive history, and a careful, observing examination of the patient. Copyright 1998. *$34.95*

122 pages   ISSN 0-398-06905-0ISBN 0-398069-04-2

2648 Languages of Psychoanalysis
Analytic Press
101 W Street
Hillsdale, NJ 07642-1421
201-358-9477
800-926-6579
Fax: 201-358-4700
E-mail: TAP@analyticpress.com
www.analyticpress.com

Paul E Stepansky PhD, Managing Director
John Kerr PhD, Sr Editor

A guide to understanding the full range of human discourse, especially behavioral conflicts and communicational deficits as they impinge upon the transactions of the analytic dyad. Available in hardcover. Copyright 1996. *$39.95*

224 pages   ISBN 0-881631-86-8

2649 Leadership and Organizational Excellence
AAMR
444 N Capitol Street NW
Suite 846
Washington, DC 20001-1569
202-637-0475
800-424-3688
Fax: 202-637-0585
E-mail: dcroser@aamr.org

Examines key managerial and organizational strategies that can be used to help ensure high-quality work environments for both staff and service delivery for people with developmental disabilities. *$ 14.95*

65 pages   ISBN 0-940898-78-0

2650 Life Course Perspective on Adulthood and Old Age
AAMR
444 N Capitol Street NW
Suite 846
Washington, DC 20001-1569
202-637-0475
800-424-3688
Fax: 202-637-0585
E-mail: dcroser@aamr.org

Experts in gerontology, sociology, and cognitive disability share the latest research, trends, and thoughtful insights into old age. *$19.95*

229 pages   ISBN 0-940898-31-4

2651 Making Money While Making a Difference: Achieving Outcomes for People with Disabilities
High Tide Press
Ste 2n
2081 Calistoga Dr
New Lenox, IL 60451-4833
815-206-2054
888-487-7377
E-mail: managing.editor@hightidepress.com

Diane J Bell, Managing Editor

Unique handbook for corporations and nonprofits alike. The authors guide readers through a step-by-step process for implementing strategic alliances between nonprofit organizations and corporate partners. Learn the tenets of cause related marketing and much more. *$14.95*

231 pages   ISBN 0-965374-49-1

2652 Managed Mental Health Care in the Public Sector: a Survival Manual
Brunner/Routledge
325 Chestnut Street
Philadelphia, PA 19106-2614

800-821-8312
Fax: 215-269-0363

Manual for administrators, planners, clinicians and consumers with concepts and strategies to maneuver in public sector managed mental healthcare system. Copyright 1996. *$35.00*

410 pages   ISBN 9-057025-37-X

2653 Managing Client Anger: What to Do When a Client is Angry with You
New Harbinger Publications
5674 Shattuck Avenue
Oakland, CA 94609-1662
510-652-0215
800-748-6273
Fax: 510-652-5472
E-mail: customerservice@newharbinger.com
www.newharbinger.com

Matthew McKay, Owner

Guide to help therapists understand their reactions and make interventions when clients express anger toward them. Copyright 1998. *$49.95*

261 pages   ISBN 1-572241-23-3

2654 Manual of Clinical Psychopharmacology
American Psychiatric Publishing, Inc.
1000 Wilson Boulevard
Suite 1825
Arlington, VA 22209-3901
703-907-7322
800-368-5777
Fax: 703-907-1091
E-mail: appi@psych.org
www.appi.org

Robert E Hales MD, Editor-in-Chief
Ron McMillen, Chief Executive Officer
John McDuffie, Editorial Director

Examines the recent changes and standard treatments in psychopharmacology. Copyright 2002. *$63.00*

736 pages ISBN 0-880488-65-4

2655 Mastering the Kennedy Axis V: New Psychiatric Assessment of Patient Functioning
American Psychiatric Publishing, Inc.
1000 Wilson Boulevard
Suite 1825
Arlington, VA 22209-3901
703-907-7322
800-368-5777
Fax: 703-907-1091
E-mail: appi@psych.org
www.appi.org

Robert E Hales MD, Editor-in-Chief
Ron McMillen, Chief Executive Officer
John McDuffie, Editorial Director

Professional evaluation methods. Copyright 2002. *$44.00*

320 pages ISBN 1-585620-62-9

2656 Meditative Therapy Facilitating Inner-Directed Healing
Impact Publishers
PO Box 6016
Atascadero, CA 93423-6016
805-466-5917
800-246-7228
Fax: 805-466-5919
E-mail: info@impactpublishers.com
www.impactpublishers.com

Offers to the professional therapist a full description of the therapeutic procedures that facilitate inner-directed healing and explains the therapist's role in guiding clients' growth psychologically, physiologically and spiritually. Copyright 1999. *$27.95*

230 pages ISBN 1-886230-11-0

2657 Mental Disability Law: Primer, a Comprehensive Introduction
Commission on the Mentally Disabled
1800 M Street NW
Washington, DC 20036-5802
202-331-2240

An updated and expanded version of the 1984 edition provides a comprehensive overview of mental disability law. Part I of the Primer examines the scope of mental disability law, defines the key terms and offers tips on how to provide effective representation for clients. Part II reviews major federal legislative initiatives including the Americans with Disabilities Act. *$15.00*

ISBN 0-897077-98-9

2658 Mental Health Rehabilitation: Disputing Irrational Beliefs
Charles C Thomas Publisher
2600 S 1st Street
Springfield, IL 62704-4730

217-789-8980
800-258-8980
Fax: 217-789-9130
E-mail: books@ccthomas.com
www.ccthomas.com

Michael P Thomas, President

Applicable to a wide variety of disciplines involved with therapeutic counseling of people with mental and/or physical disabilities such as rehabilitation counseling, mental health counseling, pastoral counseling, school counseling, clinical social work, clinical and counseling psychology, and behavioral science oriented medical specialities and related health and therapeutic professionals. Copyright 1995. *$36.95*

106 pages ISBN 0-398065-31-4

2659 Mental Health Resources Catalog
Paul H Brookes Company
PO Box 10624
Baltimore, MD 21285-624
410-337-9580
800-638-3775
Fax: 410-337-8539
E-mail: custserv@brookespublishing.com
www.brookespublishing.com

This catalog offers practical resources for mental health professionals serving young children and their families, including school psychologists, teachers and early intervention professionals. FREE.

2 per year

2660 Mental Retardation: Definition, Classification, and Systems of Supports
AAMR
444 N Capitol Street NW
Suite 846
Washington, DC 20001-1569
202-637-0475
800-424-3688
Fax: 202-637-0585
E-mail: dcroser@aamr.org

Presents a complete system to define and diagnose mental retardation, classify and describe strengths and limitations, and plan a supports needs profile. *$79.95*

250 pages ISBN 0-940898-81-0

2661 Metaphor in Psychotherapy: Clinical Applications of Stories and Allegories
Impact Publishers
PO Box 6016
Atascadero, CA 93423-6016
805-466-5917
800-246-7228
Fax: 805-466-5919
E-mail: info@impactpublishers.com
www.impactpublishers.com

Comprehensive resource aids therapists in helping clients change distorted views of the human experience. Dozens of practical therapeutic activities involving metaphor, drama, fantasy, and meditation. Copyright 1998. *$29.95*

320 pages ISBN 1-886230-10-2

2662 Microcounseling
Charles C Thomas Publisher
2600 S 1st Street
Springfield, IL 62704-4730
217-789-8980
800-258-8980
Fax: 217-789-9130
E-mail: books@ccthomas.com
www.ccthomas.com

Michael P Thomas, President

Innovations in Interviewing, Counseling, Psychotherapy, and Psychoeducation. Copyright 1978. *$91.95*

624 pages ISSN 0-398-06175-0ISBN 0-398037-12-4

2663 Natural Supports: A Foundation for Employment
AAMR
444 N Capitol Street NW
Suite 846
Washington, DC 20001-1569
202-637-0475
800-424-3688
Fax: 202-637-0585
E-mail: dcroser@aamr.org

Step-by-step strategy for developing a network of natural supports aimed at promoting the goals and interests of all individuals in the work setting. *$12.95*

34 pages ISBN 0-940898-65-9

2664 Negotiating Managed Care: Manual for Clinicians
American Psychiatric Publishing, Inc.
1000 Wilson Boulevard
Suite 1825
Arlington, VA 22209-3901
703-907-7322
800-368-5777
Fax: 703-907-1091
E-mail: appi@psych.org
www.appi.org

Robert E Hales MD, Editor-in-Chief
Ron McMillen, Chief Executive Officer
John McDuffie, Editorial Director

Help for professionals to successfully present a case during clinical review. Copyright 2002. *$26.95*

120 pages ISBN 1-585620-42-4

2665 Neurobiology of Violence
American Psychiatric Publishing, Inc.
1000 Wilson Boulevard
Suite 1825
Arlington, VA 22209-3901
703-907-7322
800-368-5777
Fax: 703-907-1091
E-mail: appi@psych.org
www.appi.org

Robert E Hales MD, Editor-in-Chief
Ron McMillen, Chief Executive Officer
John McDuffie, Editorial Director

Important information on the basic science of violence, including genetics, with topics of great practical value to today's clinician, including major mental disorders and violence; alcohol and substance abuse and violence; and psychopharmacological approaches to managing violent behavior. Copyright 2002. *$69.00*

368 pages ISBN 1-585620-81-5

2666 Neurodevelopment & Adult Psychopathology
Cambridge University Press
40 W 20th Street
New York, NY 10011-4211
212-924-3900
Fax: 212-691-3239
E-mail: marketing@cup.org
www.cup.org

2667 Neurology for Clinical Social Work: Theory and Practice
WW Norton & Company
500 5th Avenue
New York, NY 10110-54
212-354-2907
800-233-4830
Fax: 212-869-0856
E-mail: npb@wwnorton.com

Drake McFeely, CEO

Social work educators Jeffrey Applegate and Janet Shapiro demystify the explosion of recent research on neurobiology and present it anew with social workers specifically in mind. Abundant case examples show clinicians how to make use of neurobiological concepts in assessment as well as in designing treatment plans and interventions. Community mental health, family service agencies, and child welfare settings are discussed.

ISBN 0-393704-20-3

2668 Neuropsychiatry and Mental Health Services
American Psychiatric Publishing, Inc.
1000 Wilson Boulevard
Arlington, VA 22209-3901
703-907-7322
800-368-5777
Fax: 703-907-1091
E-mail: appi@psych.org
www.appi.org

Robert E Hales MD, Editor-in-Chief
Ron McMillen, Chief Executive Officer
John McDuffie, Editorial Director

Cognitive therapy practices in conjunction with mental health treatment. Copyright 1999. *$79.95*

448 pages ISBN 0-880487-30-5

2669 Neuropsychology of Mental Disorders: Practical Guide
Charles C Thomas Publisher
2600 S 1st Street
Springfield, IL 62704-4730
217-789-8980
800-258-8980
Fax: 217-789-9130
E-mail: books@ccthomas.com
www.ccthomas.com

Michael P Thomas, President

Discusses the advances in diverse areas such as biology, electrophysiology, genetics, neuroanatomy, pharmacology, psychology, and radiology which are increasingly important for a practical understanding of behavior and its pathology. Copyright 1994. *$70.95*

338 pages ISBN 0-398059-05-5

2670 New Roles for Psychiatrists in Organized Systems of Care
American Psychiatric Publishing, Inc.
1000 Wilson Boulevard
Suite 1825
Arlington, VA 22209-3901
703-907-7322
800-368-5777
Fax: 703-907-1091
E-mail: appi@psych.org
www.appi.org

Robert E Hales MD, Editor-in-Chief
Ron McMillen, Chief Executive Officer
John McDuffie, Editorial Director

Comprehensive view of opportunities, challenges and roles for psychiatrists who are working for or with new organized systems of care. Discusses the ethical dilemmas for psychiatrists in managed care settings and training and identity of the field as well as historical overviews of health care policy. Copyright 1998. *$50.00*

312 pages ISBN 0-880487-58-5

2671 Of One Mind: The Logic of Hypnosis, the Practice of Therapy
WW Norton & Company
500 5th Avenue
New York, NY 10110-54
212-354-2907
800-233-4830
Fax: 212-869-0856
E-mail: admalmud@wwnorton.com

Drake McFeely, CEO

A new approach to an old treatment, the author explains his ideas on connecting with patients in hypno and brief therapies. Copyright 2001. *$30.00*

240 pages ISBN 0-393703-82-7

2672 On Being a Therapist
Jossey-Bass Publishers
350 Sansome Street
5th Floor
San Francisco, CA 94104-1310
415-394-8677
800-956-7739
Fax: 800-605-2665
www.josseybass.com

This thoroughly revised and updated edition shows you how to use the insights gained from your clients' experiences to solve your own problems, realize positive change in yourself, and become a better therapist. *$22.00*

320 pages ISBN 1-555425-55-0

2673 On the Counselor's Path: A Guide to Teaching Brief Solution Focused Therapy
New Harbinger Publications
5674 Shattuck Avenue
Oakland, CA 94609-1662
510-652-0215
800-748-6273
Fax: 510-652-5472
E-mail: customerservice@newharbinger.com
www.newharbinger.com

Matthew McKay, Owner

A teacher's guide for conducting training sessions on solution focused techniques. Copyright 1996. *$24.95*

92 pages ISBN 1-572240-48-2

2674 Opportunities for Daily Choice Making
AAMR
444 N Capitol Street NW
Suite 846
Washington, DC 20001-1569
202-637-0475
800-424-3688
Fax: 202-637-0585
E-mail: dcroser@aamr.org

Provides strategies for increasing choice-making opportunities for people with developmental disabilities. It describes basic principles of choice-making, shows how to teach choice-making skills to the passive learner, describes how to build in multiple choice-making opportunities within daily routines, introduces self-scheduling, and addresses common questions. *$12.95*

48 pages ISBN 0-904898-44-6

2675 Out of Darkness and Into the Light: Nebraska's Experience In Mental Retardation
AAMR
444 N Capitol Street NW
Suite 846
Washington, DC 20001-1569
202-637-0475
800-424-3688
Fax: 202-637-0585
E-mail: dcroser@aamr.org

The Nebraska model for dealing with the condition of mental retardation has been so successful that it has been emulated throughout the United States and other countries. The inspiring story of how this change occured, written by those who made it happen. It is an account of both the changing approach to those once considered less the human, and their successful movement from despondency to hope, and from patient to people. *$29.97*

267 pages

2676 Participatory Evaluation for Special Education and Rehabilitation
AAMR
444 N Capitol Street NW
Suite 846
Washington, DC 20001-1569
202-637-0475
800-424-3688
Fax: 202-637-0585
E-mail: dcroser@aamr.org

Nine-step method for identifying and weighing the importance of disparate goals and outcomes. *$31.95*

90 pages ISBN 0-940898-73-X

2677 Person-Centered Foundation for Counseling and Psychotherapy
Charles C Thomas Publisher
2600 S 1st Street
Springfield, IL 62704-4730
217-789-8980
800-258-8980
Fax: 217-789-9130
E-mail: books@ccthomas.com
www.ccthomas.com

Michael P Thomas, President

Focusing on counseling and psychotherapy, its goals are to renew interest in the person-centered approach in the US, make a signigicant contribution to extending person-centered theory and practice, and promote fruitful dialogue and futher development of person-centered theory. Presents: the rationale for an eclectic application of person-centered counseling; the rationale and process for reflecting clients' feelings; the importance of the theory as the foundation for the counseling process; the importance of values and their influence on the counseling relationship; the modern person-centered counselor's role; and the essential characteristics of a person-centered counseling relationship. Copyright 1999.

260 pages ISSN 0-398-06966-2ISBN 0-398069-64-6

2678 PharmaCoKinetics and Therapeutic Moniltering of Psychiatric Drugs
Charles C Thomas Publisher
2600 S 1st Street
Springfield, IL 62704-4730
217-789-8980
800-258-8980
Fax: 217-789-9130
E-mail: books@ccthomas.com
www.ccthomas.com

Michael P Thomas, President

$52.95

226 pages ISBN 0-398058-41-5

2679 Positive Bahavior Support for People with Developmental Disabilities: A Research Synthesis
AAMR
444 N Capitol Street NW
Suite 846
Washington, DC 20001-1569
202-637-0475
800-424-3688
Fax: 202-637-0585
E-mail: dcroser@aamr.org

Offers a careful analysis documenting that positive behavioral procedures can produce important change in the behavior and lives of people with disabilities. *$31.95*

108 pages ISBN 0-940898-60-8

2680 Positive Behavior Support Training Curriculum
AAMR
444 N Capitol Street NW
Suite 846
Washington, DC 20001-1569
202-637-0475
800-424-3688
Fax: 202-637-0585
E-mail: dcroser@aamr.org

Designed for training supervisors of direct support staff, as well as direct support professionals themselves in the values and practices of positive behavior support.

2681 Practical Guide to Cognitive Therapy
WW Norton & Company
500 5th Avenue
New York, NY 10110-54
212-354-2907
Fax: 212-869-0856
E-mail: admalmud@wwnorton.com

Drake McFeely, CEO

Based on highly successful workshops by the author, this book provides a framework to apply cognitive therapy model to office practices. Copyright 1991. *$22.95*

200 pages ISBN 0-393701-05-0

2682 Practical Psychiatric Practice Forms and Protocols for Clinical Use
American Psychological Publishing
1400 K Street NW
Washington, DC 20005-2403
202-682-6262
800-368-5777
Fax: 202-789-2648
E-mail: appi@psych.org
www.appi.org

Katie Duffy, Marketing Assistant

Designed to aid psychiatrists in organizing their work. Provides rating scales, model letters, medication tracking forms, clinical pathology requests and sample invoices. Handouts on disorders and medication are provided for patients and their families. Spiralbound. Copyright 1998. *$47.50*

312 pages ISBN 0-880489-43-X

296 pages Year Founded: 1997 ISBN 0-881632-74-0

2683 Practice Guidelines for Extended Psychiatric Residential Care: From Chaos to Collaboration
Charles C Thomas Publisher
2600 S 1st Street
Springfield, IL 62704-4730
217-789-8980
800-258-8980
Fax: 217-789-9130
E-mail: books@ccthomas.com
www.ccthomas.com

Michael P Thomas, President
Stanley McCracken, Author/Editor
Joseph Mehr, Author/Editor

Presents a set of practice guidelines that represent state-of-the-art treatments for consumers of extended residential care. Written for line-level staff charged with the day-to-day services: psychiatrists, psychologists, social workers, activity therapists, nurses, and psychiatric technicians who work closely with consumers in residential programs and program administrators who have immediate responsibility for supervising treatment teams. Copyright 1995. *$47.95*

176 pages   ISSN 0-398-06536-5ISBN 0-398065-35-7

2684 Primer of Brief Psychotherapy
WW Norton & Company
500 5th Avenue
New York, NY 10110-54
212-354-2907
Fax: 212-869-0856
E-mail: admalmud@wwnorton.com

Drake McFeely, CEO

Positive guide to brief therapy is a task oriented aid with emphasis on the first session and details of procedures afterward. Copyright 1995. *$19.55*

160 pages ISBN 0-393701-89-1

2685 Primer of Supportive Psychotherapy
Analytic Press
101 W Street
Hillsdale, NJ 07642-1421
201-358-9477
800-926-6579
Fax: 201-358-4700
E-mail: TAP@analyticpress.com
www.analyticpress.com

Paul E Stepansky PhD, Managing Director
John Kerr PhD, Sr Editor

Focuses on the rationale for and techniques of supportive psychotherapy as a form of dyadic intervention distinct from expressive psychotherapies. The realities, ironies, conundrums and opportunities of the therapeutic encounter are vividly portrayed in scores of illustrative dialogues drawn from actual treatments. Among the topics covered are how to provide reassurance in the realistic way, how to handle requests for advice, the role of praise and reinforcement, the appropriate use of reframing techniques and of modeling, negotiating patients' concerns about medication and other collateral forms of treatment. *$45.00*

2686 Psychiatry in the New Millennium
American Psychiatric Publishing, Inc.
1000 Wilson Boulevard
Suite 1825
22209-3901
703-907-7322
800-368-5777
Fax: 703-907-1091
E-mail: appi@psych.org
www.appi.org

Robert E Hales MD, Editor-in-Chieftant
Ron McMillen, Chief Executive Officer
John McDuffie, Editorial Director

Keeping the standards and utilizing advances in diagnosis and treatment. *$66.50*

352 pages Year Founded: 1999 ISBN 0-880489-38-3

2687 Psychoanalysis, Behavior Therapy & the Relational World
American Psychological Association
750 1st St NE
Washington, DC 20002-4242
202-336-5500
Fax: 202-336-5518
www.apa.org

Norman B Anderson, CEO

2688 Psychoanalytic Therapy as Health Care Effectiveness and Economics in the 21st Century
Analytic Press
101 W Street
Hillsdale, NJ 07642-1421
201-358-9477
800-926-6579
Fax: 201-358-4700
E-mail: TAP@analyticpress.com
www.analyticpress.com

Paul E Stepansky PhD, Managing Director
John Kerr PhD, Sr Editor

Drawing on a wide range of clinical and empirical evidence, authors argue that contemporary psychoanalytic approaches are applicable to seriously distressed persons in a variety of treatment contexts. Failure to include such long term therapies within health care delivery systems, they conclude, will deprive many patients of help they need, and help from which they can benefit in enduring ways that far transcend the limited treatment goals of managed care. Available in hardcover. *$ 49.95*

312 pages Year Founded: 1999 ISBN 0-881632-02-3

2689 Psychological Aspects of Women's Health Care
American Psychiatric Publishing, Inc.
1000 Wilson Boulevard
Suite 1825
Arlington, VA 22209-3901

703-907-7322
800-368-5777
Fax: 703-907-1091
E-mail: appi@psych.org
www.appi.org

Robert E Hales MD, Editor-in-Chief
Ron McMillen, Chief Executive Officer
John McDuffie, Editorial Director

The Interface Between Psychiatry and Obstetrics and Gynecology, Second Edition. Discussion from major leaders in the specialties of psychiatry and obstetrics/gynecology covering every major area of contemporary concern. Issues in pregnancy, gynecology, and general issues such as reproductive choices, breast disorders, violence, lesbian health care, and the male perspective are included. *$77.00*

672 pages Year Founded: 2001 ISBN 0-880488-31-X

2690 Psychologists' Desk Reference
Oxford University Press/Oxford Reference Book Society
198 Madison Avenue
New York, NY 10016-4308
212-726-6400
800-451-7556

Michael Cunningham, Manager

For the practicing psychologist; easily accessible, current information on almost any topic by some of the leading thinkers and innovators in the field. *$65.00*

672 pages Year Founded: 1998 ISBN 0-195111-86-9

2691 Psychoneuroendocrinology: The Scientific Basis of Clinical Practice
American Psychiatric Publishing, Inc.
1000 Wilson Boulevard
Suite 1825
Arlington, VA 22209-3901
703-907-7322
800-368-5777
Fax: 703-907-1091
E-mail: appi@psych.org
www.appi.org

Robert E Hales MD, Editor-in-Chief
Ron McMillen, Chief Executive Officer
John McDuffie, Editorial Director

Applications of scientific research.

752 pages Year Founded: 2003 ISBN 0-880488-57-3

2692 Psychopharmacology Desktop Reference
Manisses Communications Group
208 Governor Street
Providence, RI 02906-3246
401-831-6020
800-333-7771
Fax: 401-861-6370
E-mail: manissescs@manisses.com
www.manisses.com

Karienne Stovell, Editor

Covers medications for all types of mental disorders. Provides detailed information on all the latest drugs as well as colored photographs of the different kinds of drugs. Helps you spot side effects and avoid drug interactions. Includes revealing case studies and outcomes data. *$159.00*

ISBN 1-864937-69-1

2693 Psychopharmacology Update
Manisses Communications Group
208 Governor Street
Providence, RI 02906-3246
401-831-6020
800-333-7771
Fax: 401-861-6370
E-mail: manissescs@manisses.com
www.manisses.com

Karienne Stovell, Editor

Offers psychopharmacology advice for general practitioners and nonprescribing professionals in the mental health field. Covers child psychopharmacology and street drugs. Contains case reports. Recurring features include news of research and book reviews. *$147.00*

12 per year ISSN 1068-5308

2694 Psychosocial Aspects of Disability
Charles C Thomas Publishers
PO Box 19265
Springfield, IL 62794-9265
217-789-8980
800-258-8980
Fax: 217-789-9130
www.ccthomas.com

This expanded and updated new edition continues the theme of the first and second editions of emphasizing that attitudinal barriers create environmental barriers for persons with disabilities. The new edition is improved as a primary introductory text or a supplemental text for student helping professionals with the addition of chapters on employment, understanding ethnic groups, concepts, theories, therapies, and issues for the twenty-first century. Available in paperback for $55.95. *$75.95*

424 pages Year Founded: 2004 ISBN 0-398074-86-0

2695 Psychotherapist's Duty to Warn or Protect
Charles C Thomas Publisher
2600 S 1st Street
Springfield, IL 62704-4730
217-789-8980
800-258-8980
Fax: 217-789-9130
E-mail: books@ccthomas.com
www.ccthomas.com

Michael P Thomas, President

$47.95

194 pages Year Founded: 1989 ISBN 0-398055-46-7

2696 Psychotherapist's Guide to Cost Containment: How to Survive and Thrive in an Age of Managed Care
Sage Publications
2455 Teller Road
Thousand Oaks, CA 91320-2234

805-499-0721
800-818-7243
Fax: 805-499-0871
E-mail: info@sagepub.com
www.sagepub.com

Blaise R Simqu, CEO

$23.50

Year Founded: 1998 ISBN 0-803973-81-0

2697 Psychotherapy Indications and Outcomes
American Psychiatric Publishing, Inc.
1000 Wilson Boulevard
Suite 1825
Arlington, VA 22209-3901
703-907-7322
800-368-5777
Fax: 703-907-1091
E-mail: appi@psych.org
www.appi.org

Robert E Hales MD, Editor-in-Chief
Ron McMillen, Chief Executive Officer
John McDuffie, Editorial Director

Clinical approaches to different symptoms. *$66.50*

416 pages Year Founded: 1999 ISBN 0-880487-61-5

2698 Psychotropic Drug Information Handbook
Lexi-Comp
1100 Terex Road
Hudson, OH 44236-4438
330-650-6506
800-837-5394
Fax: 330-656-4307
www.lexi.com

Steven Kerscher, Owner

Concise handbook, designed to fit into your lab coat, is a current and portable psychotropic drug reference with 150 drugs and 35 herbal monographs. Perfect companion to Drug Information Handbook for Psychiatry. *$38.75*

1 per year ISBN 1-591951-15-1

2699 Psychotropic Drugs: Fast Facts
WW Norton & Company
500 5th Avenue
New York, NY 10110-54
212-354-2907
800-233-4830
Fax: 212-869-0856
E-mail: npb@wwnorton.com

Drake McFeely, CEO

Now in its third edition, Psychotropic Drugs: Fast Facts continues to present valuable information in a clear and accessible format. The book organizaes and presents data clinicians need to choose the right treatment for common psychiatric problems and to anticipate and deal with problems that arise in treatment.

ISBN 0-393703-01-0

2700 Quality of Life: Volume II
AAMR
444 N Capitol Street NW
Suite 846
Washington, DC 20001-1569
202-637-0475
800-424-3688
Fax: 202-637-0585
E-mail: dcroser@aamr.org

Focuses on how the concepts and research on quality of life can be applied to people with mental retardation. *$19.95*

267 pages ISBN 0-940898-41-1

2701 Questions of Competence
Cambridge University Press
40 W 20th Street
New York, NY 10011-4211
212-924-3900
Fax: 212-691-3239
E-mail: marketing@cup.org
www.cup.org

2702 Reaching Out in Family Therapy: Home Based, School, and Community Interventions
Guilford Publications
72 Spring Street
New York, NY 10012-4068
212-431-9800
800-365-7006
Fax: 212-966-6708
E-mail: info@guilford.com

Bob Matloff, President

Practical framework for clinicians using multisystems intervention. *$27.00*

244 pages Year Founded: 2000 ISBN 1-572305-19-3

2703 Recognition and Treatment of Psychiatric Disorders: Psychopharmacology Handbook for Primary Care
American Psychiatric Publishing, Inc.
1000 Wilson Boulevard
Suite 1825
Arlington, VA 22209-3901
703-907-7322
800-368-5777
Fax: 703-907-1091
E-mail: appi@psych.org
www.appi.org

Robert E Hales MD, Editor-in-Chief
Ron McMillen, Chief Executive Officer
John McDuffie, Editorial Director

Provides the primary care physician with practical and timely strategies for screening and treating patients who have psychiatric disorders. Includes an overview of the epidemiology, pathophysiology, presentation, diagnostic criteria and screening tests for common psychiatric disorders including anxiety, mood, substance abuse, somatization and eating disorders, as well as insomnia, dementia and schizophrenia. *$35.00*

324 pages

2704 Recognition of Early Psychosis
Cambridge University Press
40 W 20th Street
New York, NY 10011-4211
212-924-3900
Fax: 212-691-3239
E-mail: marketing@cup.org
www.cup.org

2705 Review of Psychiatry
American Psychiatric Publishing, Inc.
1000 Wilson Boulevard
Suite 1825
Arlington, VA 22209-3901
703-907-7322
800-368-5777
Fax: 703-907-1091
E-mail: appi@psych.org
www.appi.org

Robert E Hales MD, Editor-in-Chief
Ron McMillen, Chief Executive Officer
John McDuffie, Editorial Director

Cognitive therapy, repressed memories and obsessive-compulsive disorder across the life cycle. *$59.95*

928 pages Year Founded: 1997 ISBN 0-880484-43-8

2706 Sandplay Therapy: Step By Step Manual for Physchotherapists of Diverse Orientations
WW Norton & Company
500 5th Avenue
New York, NY 10110-54
212-354-2907
Fax: 212-869-0856
E-mail: admalmud@wwnorton.com

Drake McFeely, CEO

Change often occurs on a non-verbal level. This book is for psychotherapists with alternative methods. *$35.00*

256 pages Year Founded: 2000 ISSN 70319-3

2707 Schools for Students with Special Needs
Resources for Children with Special Needs
116 E 16th Street
Fifth Floor
New York City, NY 10003-2112
212-677-4650
Fax: 212-254-4070
E-mail: info@resourcesnyc.org
www.resourcesnyc.org

Rachel Howard, Executive Director

The first complete book listing private day and residential schools for parents, caregivers and professionals seeking schools for students 5 and up with developmental, emotional, physical and learning disabilities in the NYC metro area. More than 400 schools and residential programs that serve children in the elementary through high school grades are listed with contact information, ages and populations served, class sizes and student-teacher ratios, special services and diplomas offered. Includes a 46-page section of Schools for Children with Autism Spectrum Disorders, as well as a guide with a list of websites on autism spectrum disorders. *$25.00*

342 pages

2708 Selecting Effective Treatments: a Comprehensive, Systematic, Guide for Treating Mental Disorders
Jossey-Bass Publishers
350 Sansome Street
5th Floor
San Francisco, CA 94104-1310

800-956-7739
Fax: 800-605-2665
www.josseybass.com

$39.95

416 pages Year Founded: 1998 ISBN 0-787943-07-X

2709 Social Work Dictionary
National Association of Social Workers
750 1st Street NE
Suite 700
Washington, DC 20002-8011
202-408-8600
800-638-8799
Fax: 202-336-8313
E-mail: press@naswdc.org
www.naswpress.org

Elvira Craig De Silva, President

More than 8,000 terms are defined in this essential tool for understanding the language of social work and related disciplines. The resulting reference is a must for every human services professional. *$34.95*

620 pages Year Founded: 1999 ISBN 0-871012-98-7

2710 Strategic Marketing: How to Achieve Independence and Prosperity in Your Mental Health Practice
Professional Resource Press
PO Box 15560
Sarasota, FL 34277-1560
941-343-9601
800-443-3364
Fax: 941-343-9201
E-mail: orders@prpress.com
www.prpress.com

Debra Fink, Managing Editor

Presents ways to reshape your practice to capitalize on new opportunities for success in today's healthcare marketplace. *$21.95*

152 pages Year Founded: 1997 ISBN 1-568870-31-0

2711 Supports Intensity Scale
AAMR
444 N Capitol Street NW
Suite 846
Washington, DC 20001-1569
202-637-0475
800-424-3688

Fax: 202-637-0585

E-mail: dcroser@aamr.org

Designed to help you plan meaningful supports for adults with mental retardation. Consists of a comprehensive scoring system that measures the needs of persons with mental retardation in 57 key life activities based on 7 areas of competence. *$125.00*

128 pages

2712 Surviving & Prospering in the Managed Mental Health Care Marketplace
Professional Resource Press
PO Box 15560
Sarasota, FL 34277-1560
941-343-9601
800-443-3364
Fax: 941-343-9201
E-mail: orders@prpress.com
www.prpress.com

Debra Fink, Managing Editor

Includes examples of different managed care models, extensive references, and checklists. Offers examples of the typical steps in providing outpatient treatment in a managed care milieu, and other extremely useful resources. *$14.95*

106 pages Year Founded: 1994 ISBN 1-568870-04-3

2713 Suzie Brown Intervention Maze
High Tide Press
Ste 2n
2081 Calistoga Dr
New Lenox, IL 60451-4833
815-206-2054
888-487-7377
E-mail: managing.editor@hightidepress.com

Diane J Bell, Managing Editor

Suzie Brown, age 25, has severe developmental disabilities. She lives in a staffed house for six adults, where you work as a team. She has major communication difficulties, is prone to self-injurious behavior, and no longer responds to all the usual calming methods. What can you do? This workbook offers a practical blueprint for group decision making. Each option page presents a new scenario and ideas for moving forward. Decision logs keep track of decisions as they are made. The binder format allows for easy photocopying. *$69.99*

ISBN 1-892696-09-6

2714 Teaching Goal Setting and Decision-Making to Students with Developmental Disabilities
AAMR
444 N Capitol Street NW
Suite 846
Washington, DC 20001-1569
202-637-0475
800-424-3688
Fax: 202-637-0585
E-mail: dcroser@aamr.org

Link four basic steps of goal setting and decision making to twelve instructional principles that engage students in activities. *$12.95*

34 pages ISBN 0-940898-97-7

2715 Teaching Practical Communication Skills
AAMR
444 N Capitol Street NW
Suite 846
Washington, DC 20001-1569
202-637-0475
800-424-3688
Fax: 202-637-0585
E-mail: dcroser@aamr.org

Discusses strategies for teaching students to request their preferences, protest non-preferred activities, and clarify misunderstandings. *$12.95*

30 pages ISBN 0-940898-42-X

2716 Teaching Problem Solving to Students with Mental Retardation
AAMR
444 N Capitol Street NW
Suite 846
Washington, DC 20001-1569
202-637-0475
800-424-3688
Fax: 202-637-0585
E-mail: dcroser@aamr.org

Gives clear teaching strategies for social problem-solving, including role-playing, modeling, and training sequences. *$12.95*

30 pages ISBN 0-940898-62-4

2717 Teaching Students with Severe Disabilities in Inclusive Settings
AAMR
444 N Capitol Street NW
Suite 846
Washington, DC 20001-1569
202-637-0475
800-424-3688
Fax: 202-637-0585
E-mail: dcroser@aamr.org

Presents student-specific strategies for teaching students with severe disabilities in inclusive settings. Strategies include how to write IEPs in inclusive settings; effective scheduling; planning for adaptations of objectives; materials, responses, and settings; and anticipating the need for support. *$12.95*

50 pages ISBN 0-940898-49-7

2718 Textbook of Family and Couples Therapy: Clinical Applications
American Psychiatric Publishing, Inc.
1000 Wilson Boulevard
Suite 1825
Arlington, VA 22209-3901

703-907-7322
800-368-5777
Fax: 703-907-1091
E-mail: appi@psych.org
www.appi.org

Robert E Hales MD, Editor-in-Chief
Ron McMillen, Chief Executive Officer
John McDuffie, Editorial Director

Blending theoretical training and up-to-date clinical strategies. It's a must for clinicians who are currently treating couples and families, a major resource for training future clinicians in these highly effective therapeutic techniques. *$63.00*

448 pages Year Founded: 2002 ISBN 0-880485-18-3

2719 The Annals of Clinical Psychiatry
American Academy of Clinical Psychiatrists
PO Box 458
Glastonbury, CT 06033-458
860-633-6023
Fax: 866-668-9858
E-mail: aacp@cox.net
www.aacp.com

Sanjay Gupta MD, President
John B Reichman MD, Vice President
James Wilcox DO, PhD, Secretary/Treasurer
Donald W Black MD, President-Elect/Author

The journal of the American Academy of Clinical Psychiatrists. The Annals publishes high-quality articles that focus on the advancement of patient care. Contributions furnish professionals and students with a continuing medical perspective on their discipline, addressing problems and concerns that arise in clinical practice as well as their potential solutions. Covers ongoing research and the theories and techniques used by leading authorities in the field.

2720 Theory and Technique of Family Therapy
Charles C Thomas Publisher
2600 S 1st Street
Springfield, IL 62704-4730
217-789-8980
800-258-8980
Fax: 217-789-9130
E-mail: books@ccthomas.com
www.ccthomas.com

Michael P Thomas, President
Ramon Garrido Corrales, Author

Contents: The Family as an Interactional System; The Family as an Intergenerational System; A Model for the Therapeutic Relationship in Family Theory, The Therapeutic Process and Related Concerns; Therapeutic Intervention Techniques and Adjuncts; Marital Group and Multiple Family Therapy; Counseling at Two Critical Stages of Family Development, Formation and Termination of Marriage. Useful information for students and practitioners of family therapy, social workers, the clergy, psychiatrists, psychologists, counselors, and related professionals. *$55.95*

352 pages Year Founded: 1981 ISBN 0-398038-59-7

2721 Thesaurus of Psychological Index Terms
American Psychological Association Database
Department/PsycINFO
750 1st Street NE
Washington, DC 20002-4241
202-336-5500
800-374-2722
Fax: 202-336-5518
TDD: 202-336-6123
E-mail: psycinfo@apa.org
www.apa.org

Norman B Anderson, CEO

Reference to the PsycINFO database vocabulary of over 5,400 descriptors. Provides standardized working to represent each concept for complete, efficient and precise retrieval of psychological information and is updated regularly. 9th edition published 2001. *$60.00*

379 pages ISBN 1-557987-75-0

2722 Three Spheres: Psychiatric Interviewing Primer
Rapid Psychler Press
3560 Pine Grove Avenue
Suite 374
Port Huron, MI 48060-1994
519-433-7642
888-779-2453
Fax: 888-779-2457
E-mail: rapid@psychler.com
www.psychler.com

David Robinson, Publisher

$16.95

ISBN 0-968032-49-4

2723 Through the Patient's Eyes
Jossey-Bass Publishers
350 Sansome Street
5th Floor
San Francisco, CA 94104-1310
415-394-8677
800-956-7739
Fax: 800-605-2665
www.josseybass.com

Jennifer Daley, Editor
Thomas Delbanco, Editor

Learn how providers can improve their ability to meet patient's needs and enhance the quality of care by bringing the patient's perspective to the design and delivery of health services. *$36.95*

347 pages ISBN 7-555425-44-5

2724 Tools of the Trade: A Therapist's Guide to Art
Therapy Assessments
Charles C Thomas Publishers
PO Box 19265
Springfield, IL 62794-9265
217-789-8980
800-258-8980
Fax: 217-789-9130
www.ccthomas.com

Provides critical reviews of art therapy tests along with some new reviews of assessments and updated research in the field. Comprehensive in the approach to consider reliability and validity evidence provided by test authors. Available in paperback for $35.95. *$53.95*

256 pages Year Founded: 2004 ISBN 0-398075-21-2

2725 Total Quality Management in Mental Health and Mental Retardation
AAMR
444 N Capitol Street NW
Suite 846
Washington, DC 20001-1569
202-637-0475
800-424-3688
Fax: 202-637-0585
E-mail: dcroser@aamr.org

Describes how this leadership philosophy helps an organization identify and achive quality outcomes for all its customers. *$14.95*

64 pages ISBN 0-940898-67-5

2726 Training Families to do a Successful Intervention: A Professional's Guide
Hazelden
15251 Pleasant Valley Road
PO Box 176
Center City, MN 55012-176
651-213-2121
800-328-9000
Fax: 651-213-4590
E-mail: customersupport@hazelden.org
www.hazelden.org

Helps professionals explain basic intervention concepts and give clients step-by-step instructions. *$15.95*

152 pages ISBN 1-562461-16-8

2727 Treatment of Complicated Mourning
Research Press
Dept 24 W
PO Box 9177
Champaign, IL 61826-9177
217-352-3273
800-519-2707
Fax: 217-352-1221
E-mail: rp@researchpress.com
www.researchpress.com

Russell Pense, VP Marketing

This is the first book to focus specifically on complicated mourning, often referred to as pathological, unresolved or abnormal grief. It provides caregivers with practical therapeutic strategies and specific interventions that are necessary when traditional grief counseling is unsufficient. The author provides critically important information on the prediction, identification, assessment, classification and treatment of complicated mourning. *$39.95*

768 pages ISBN 0-878223-29-0

2728 Treatments of Psychiatric Disorders
American Psychiatric Publishing, Inc.
1000 Wilson Boulevard
Suite 1825
Arlington, VA 22209-3901
703-907-7322
800-368-5777
Fax: 703-907-1091
E-mail: appi@psych.org
www.appi.org

Robert E Hales MD, Editor-in-Chief
Ron McMillen, Chief Executive Officer
John McDuffie, Editorial Director

Examines customary approaches to the major psychiatric disorders. Diagnostic, etiologic and therapeutic issues are clearly addressed by experts on each topic. *$307.00*

2800 pages Year Founded: 1995 ISBN 0-880487-00-3

2729 Using Computers In Educational and Psychological Research
Charles C Thomas Publishers
PO Box 19265
Springfield, IL 62794-9265
217-789-8980
800-258-8980
Fax: 217-789-9130
www.ccthomas.com

This book has been designed to assist researchers in the social sciences and education fields who are interested in learning how information technologies can help them successfully navigate the research process. Most researchers are familiar with the use of programs like SPSS to analyze data, but many are not aware of other ways informaiton technologies can support the research process. This book is available in paperback for $44.95. *$69.95*

274 pages Year Founded: 2006 ISBN 0-398076-16-2

2730 Values Clarification for Counselors
Charles C Thomas Publisher
2600 S 1st Street
Springfield, IL 62704-4730
217-789-8980
800-258-8980
Fax: 217-789-9130
E-mail: books@ccthomas.com
www.ccthomas.com

Michael P Thomas, President

How Counselors, Social Workers, Psychologists, and Other Human Service Workers Can Use Available Techniques. *$24.95*

104 pages Year Founded: 1978 ISBN 0-398038-47-3

2731 What Psychotherapists Should Know About Disability
Guilford Publications
72 Spring Street
New York, NY 10012-4068
212-431-9800
800-365-7006
Fax: 212-966-6708
E-mail: info@guilford.com

Bob Matloff, President

Available in alternate formats for people with disabilities, this guide confronts biases and relates the human dimesions of disability. Stereotypes and discomfort can get in the way of even a well intentioned therapist, this helps achieve a clearer professional relationship with clients of special need. *$35.00*

368 pages Year Founded: 1999 ISBN 1-572302-27-5

2732 Where to Start and What to Ask: An Assessment Handbook
WW Norton & Company
500 5th Avenue
New York, NY 10110-54
212-354-2907
800-233-4830
Fax: 212-869-0856
E-mail: npb@wwnorton.com

Drake McFeely, CEO

As a life raft for beginners and their supervisors, provides all the necessary tools for garnering information from clients. Offers a framework for thinking about that information and formulating a thorough assessment, helps neophytes organize their approach to the initial phase of treatment. Copyright 1993.

ISBN 0-393701-52-2

2733 Women's Mental Health Services: Public Health Perspecitive
Sage Publications
2455 Teller Road
Thousand Oaks, CA 91320-2234
805-499-0721
800-818-7243
Fax: 805-499-0871
E-mail: info@sagepub.com
www.sagepub.com

Blaise R Simqu, CEO

Paperback, hardcover also available. *$29.95*

Year Founded: 1998 ISBN 0-761905-09-X

2734 Workbook: Mental Retardation
AAMR
444 N Capitol Street NW
Suite 846
Washington, DC 20001-1569
202-637-0475
800-424-3688
Fax: 202-637-0585
E-mail: dcroser@aamr.org

Presents key components from a practical point of view. *$29.95*

64 pages ISBN 0-940898-82-9

2735 Working with the Core Relationship Problem in Psychotherapy
Jossey-Bass Publishers
350 Sansome Street
5th Floor
San Francisco, CA 94104-1310
415-394-8677
800-956-7739
Fax: 800-605-2665
www.josseybass.com

Learn to reveal, understand, and use the core relationship problem, which is formed from earliest childhood and creates an image of the self in relation to others so it can aid in understanding the underlying conflict that repeatedly plays out in a client's behavior. *$39.95*

256 pages ISBN 0-787943-01-0

2736 Writing Behavioral Contracts: A Case Simulation Practice Manual
Research Press
Dept 24 W
PO Box 9177
Champaign, IL 61826-9177
217-352-3273
800-519-2707
Fax: 217-352-1221
E-mail: rp@researchpress.com
www.researchpress.com

Dr William J DeRiski, Author
Dennis Wiziecki, Marketing

The most difficult aspect of using contingency contracting is designing a contract acceptable to and appropriate for all involved parties. This unusually versatile book improves contract-writing skills through practice with typical cases. Valuable for social workers, mental health professionals and educators. *$11.95*

94 pages ISBN 0-878221-23-9

2737 Writing Psychological Reports: A Guide for Clinicians
Professional Resource Press
PO Box 15560
Sarasota, FL 34277-1560
941-343-9601
800-443-3364
Fax: 941-343-9201
E-mail: orders@prpress.com
www.prpress.com

Debra Fink, Managing Editor

Presents widely accepted structured format for writing psychological reports. Numerous useful suggestions for experienced clinicians, and qualifies as essential reading for all clinical psychology students. *$21.95*

158 pages Year Founded: 2002 ISBN 1-568870-76-0

Adjustment Disorders

2738 Ambiguous Loss: Learning to Live with Unresolved Grief
Harvard University Press
79 Garden Street
Cambridge, MA 02138-1400
617-495-1000
Fax: 617-495-5898
E-mail: CONTACT_HUP@harvard.edu
www.hup.harvard.edu

William Sisler, President

$22.00

192 pages Year Founded: 1999 ISBN 0-674017-38-2

2739 Attachment and Interaction
Jessica Kingsley
47 Runway Drive
Suite G
Levittown, PA 19057-4738
215-269-0400
Fax: 215-269-0363
www.taylorandfrancis.com

Available in paperback. *$29.95*

238 pages Year Founded: 1998 ISBN 1-853025-86-0

2740 Body Image: Understanding Body Dissatisfaction in Men, Women and Children
Routledge
2727 Palisade Avenue
Suite 4H
Bronx, NY 10463-1020
718-796-0971
Fax: 718-796-0971
www.vdg@columbia.edu

$75.00

208 pages Year Founded: 1998 ISBN 0-415147-84-0

2741 Cognitive Therapy in Practice
WW Norton & Company
500 5th Avenue
New York, NY 10110-54
212-354-2907
800-233-4830
Fax: 212-869-0856
E-mail: npd@wwnorton.com

Drake McFeely, CEO

Basic text for graduate studies in psychotherapy, psycholgy nursing social work and counseling. *$29.00*

224 pages Year Founded: 1989 ISBN 0-393700-77-1

Alcohol/Substance Abuse & Dependence

2742 Addiction Treatment Homework Planner
John Wiley & Sons
10475 Crosspoint Boulevard
Indianapolis, IN 46256-3386
317-572-3000
Fax: 317-572-4000

E-mail: consumers@wiley.com
www.wiley.com

Lou Peragallo, Manager

Helps clients suffering from chemical and nonchemical addictions develop the skills they need to work through problems. *$ 49.95*

370 pages ISBN 0-471274-59-3

2743 Addiction Treatment Planner
John Wiley & Sons
10475 Crosspoint Boulevard
Indianapolis, IN 46256-3386
317-572-3000
Fax: 317-572-4000
E-mail: consumers@wiley.com
www.wiley.com

Lou Peragallo, Manager

Provides all the elements necessary to quickly and easily develop formal treatment plans that satisfy the demands of HMOs, managed care companies, third-party payers, and state and federal review agencies. *$49.95*

384 pages ISBN 0-471418-14-5

2744 Addictive Behaviors Across the Life Span
Sage Publications
2455 Teller Road
Thousand Oaks, CA 91320-2234
805-499-0721
800-818-7243
Fax: 805-499-0871
E-mail: info@sagepub.com
www.sagepub.com

Blaise R Simqu, CEO

Leading scholars, researchers and clinicians in the field of addictive behavior provide and examination of drug dependency from a life span perspective in this authoritative volume. Four general topic areas include: etiology; early intervention; integrated treatment; and policy issues across the life span. Other topics include biopsychosocial perspectives on the intergenerational transmission of alcoholism to children and reducing the risks of addictive behaviors. *$59.95*

358 pages Year Founded: 1993 ISBN 0-803950-78-0

2745 Addictive Thinking: Understanding Self-Deception
Health Communications
292 Fernwood Avenue
Edison, NJ 08837-3839
732-346-0027
Fax: 732-346-0442
www.hcomm.com

Exposes the irrational and contradictory patterns of addictive thinking, and shows how to overcome them and barriers they create; low self-esteem and relapse.

140 pages ISBN 1-568381-38-7

2746 Adolescents, Alcohol and Drugs: A Practical Guide for Those Who Work With Young People
Charles C Thomas Publisher
2600 S 1st Street
Springfield, IL 62704-4730
217-789-8980
800-258-8980
Fax: 217-789-9130
E-mail: books@ccthomas.com
www.ccthomas.com

Michael P Thomas, President

$41.95

210 pages Year Founded: 1988 ISBN 0-398053-93-6

2747 American Psychiatric Press Textbook of Substance Abuse Treatment
American Psychiatric Publishing, Inc.
1000 Wilson Boulevard
Suite 1825
Arlington, VA 22209-3901
703-907-7322
800-368-5777
Fax: 703-907-1091
E-mail: appi@psych.org
www.appi.org

Robert E Hales MD, Editor-in-Chief
Ron McMillen, Chief Executive Officer
John McDuffie, Editorial Director

Comprehensive view of basic science and psychology underlying addiction and coverage of all treatment modalities. New topics include the neurobiology of alcoholism, stimulants, marijuana, opiates and hallucinogens, club drugs, and addiction in women. *$95.00*

608 pages Year Founded: 1999 ISBN 0-880488-20-4

2748 An Elephant in the Living Room: Leader's Guide for Helping Children of Alcoholics
Hazelden
15251 Pleasant Valley Road
PO Box 176
Center City, MN 55012-176
651-213-2121
800-328-9000
Fax: 651-213-4590
www.hazelden.org

Marion H Typpo PhD, Co-Author
Jill M Hastings PhD, Co-Author

Practical guidance for education and health professionals who help young people cope with a family member's chemical dependency. *$9.95*

129 pages ISBN 1-568380-34-8

2749 Assessing Substance Abusers with the Million Clinical Multiaxial Inventory
Charles C Thomas Publishers
PO Box 19265
Springfield, IL 62794-9265
217-789-8980
800-258-8980

Fax: 217-789-9130
www.ccthomas.com

The construct validity of a psychological test is assessed by a multitrai-multimethod nomothetic matrix, which means that the psychometric properties of an assessment instrument are studied with a variety of populations and in a variety of settings and weighed against a variety of other measures that purportedly assess the same construct. This concept implies that a test might have strong validity with some populations and weak validity with others, and this is the central theme of this book. Also, the book comes in paperback for only $26.95. *$46.95*

164 pages Year Founded: 2005 ISBN 0-398075-91-3

2750 Before It's Too Late: Working with Substance Abuse in the Family
WW Norton & Company
500 5th Avenue
New York, NY 10110-54
212-354-2907
Fax: 212-869-0856
E-mail: admalmud@wwnorton.com

Drake McFeely, CEO

Sometimes, the problem a patient or the family of the patient's root cause to the problem they seek help for, is actually substance abuse. How to present the problem, and step-by-step models for working with families dealing with substance abuse are examined. *$23.95*

224 pages Year Founded: 1989 ISBN 0-393700-68-2

2751 Behind Bars: Substance Abuse and America's Prison Population
Center on Addiction at Columbia University
633 3rd Avenue
19th Floor
New York, NY 10017-8155
212-841-5200
Fax: 212-956-8020
www.casacolumbia.org

William H Foster, CEO

Results of a three year study of American prisons and the reason drugs are responible for the booming prison population and escalating costs. *$25.00*

Year Founded: 1998

2752 Blaming the Brain: The Truth About Drugs and Mental Health
Free Press
866 3rd Avenue
New York, NY 10022-6221
212-744-0379
800-323-7445
www.freepeople.com

Erin Legg, Manager

Exposes weaknesses inherent in the scientific arguments supporting the theory that biochemical imbalances are the main cause of mental illness. It discusses how the accidental discovery of mood-altering drugs stimulated an interest in psychopharmacology. *$25.00*

320 pages Year Founded: 1998 ISBN 0-684849-64-X

2753 Building Bridges: States Respond to Substance Abuse and Welfare Reform
Center on Addiction at Columbia University
633 3rd Avenue
19th Floor
New York, NY 10017-8155
212-841-5200
Fax: 212-956-8020
www.casacolumbia.org

William H Foster, CEO

Prepared in partnership with the American Public Human Services Association, this two year study among the front line workers in the nation's welfare offices, job training programs and substance abuse agencies reveals what they find works and does not work in helping clients. *$15.00*

Year Founded: 1999

2754 CASAWORKS for Families: Promising Approach to Welfare Reform and Substance-Abusing Women
Center on Addiction at Columbia University
633 3rd Avenue
19th Floor
New York, NY 10017-8155
212-841-5200
Fax: 212-956-8020
www.casacolumbia.org

William H Foster, CEO

Designed for TANF recipients, this promising approach to welfare reform is used in 11 cities and nine states. *$5.00*

2755 Clinician's Guide to the Personality Profiles of Alcohol and Drug Abusers: Typological Descriptions Using the MMPI
Charles C Thomas Publisher
2600 S 1st Street
Springfield, IL 62704-4730
217-789-8980
800-258-8980
Fax: 217-789-9130
E-mail: books@ccthomas.com
www.ccthomas.com

Michael P Thomas, President
Dennis M Eshbaugh, Author
Michael A Murphy, Author

$39.95

156 pages Year Founded: 1993 ISSN 0-399-06463-6 ISBN 0-398058-85-7

2756 Critical Incidents: Ethical Issues in Substance Abuse Prevention and Treatment
Hazelden
15251 Pleasant Valley Road
PO Box 176
Center City, MN 55012-176
651-213-2121
800-328-9000

Fax: 651-213-4590
www.hazelden.com

Two hundred critical situations for health care professionals to sharpen their decision-making skills about everyday ethical dilemmas that arise in their field. *$17.95*

276 pages ISBN 0-938475-03-7

2757 Dangerous Liaisons: Substance Abuse and Sex
Center on Addiction at Columbia University
633 3rd Avenue
19th Floor
New York, NY 10017-8155
212-841-5200
Fax: 212-956-8020
www.casacolumbia.org

William H Foster, CEO

An intensive report on the dangerous and sometimes life-threatening connection between alcohol, drug abuse and sexual activity. Parents, guidance professionals and others will find this useful. *$22.00*

170 pages Year Founded: 1999

2758 Determinants of Substance Abuse: Biological, Psychological, and Environmental Factors
Kluwer Academic/Plenum Publishers
233 Spring Street
New York, NY 10013-1522
212-242-1490

Hardcover. *$90.00*

454 pages Year Founded: 1985 ISBN 0-306418-73-8

2759 Drug Information for Teens: Health Tips About the Physical and Mental Effects of Substance Abuse
Omnigraphics
615 Giswold
Detroit, MI 48226-3900
313-961-1340
Fax: 313-961-1383
E-mail: info@omnigraphics.com
www.omnigraphics.com

Provides students with facts about drug use, abuse, and addiction. It describes the physical and mental effects of alcohol, tobacco, marijuana, ecstasy, inhalants and many other drugs and chemicals that are often abused. It includes information about the process that leads from casual use to addiction and offers suggestions for resisting peer pressure and helping friends stay drug free.

452 pages ISBN 0-780804-44-9

2760 Ethics for Addiction Professionals
Hazelden
15251 Pleasant Valley Road
PO Box 176
Center City, MN 55012-176
651-213-2121
800-328-9000
Fax: 651-213-4590
www.hazelden.org

The first on ethics written by and for addiction professionals that addresses complex issues such as patient confidentiality versus mandatory reporting, clinician relapse, personal and social relationships with clients and other important related issues. *$14.95*

60 pages ISBN 0-894864-54-8

2761 Hispanic Substance Abuse
Charles C Thomas Publisher
2600 S 1st Street
Springfield, IL 62704-4730
217-789-8980
800-258-8980
Fax: 217-789-9130
E-mail: books@ccthomas.com
www.ccthomas.com

Michael P Thomas, President

Addresses the concerns of students and professionals who work with Hispanics. Brings together current research on this problem by well-known experts in the fields of alcohol and drug abuse. Useful for scholars and researchers, practitioners in the human services, and the general public. There is shown the extent of substance abuse problems in Hispanic communities, the differences between the Hispanic subgroups and the casual factors that are involved. There are detailed strategies for prevention and the necessary approaches to treatment. *$57.95*

258 pages Year Founded: 1993 ISSN 0-398-06274-9ISBN 0-398058-49-0

2762 Jail Detainees with Co-Occurring Mental Health and Substance Use Disorders
Policy Research Associates
345 Delaware Avenue
Delmar, NY 12054-1905
518-439-7415
800-444-7415
Fax: 518-439-7612
E-mail: gains@prainc.com
www.prainc.com

Henry Steadman, President

Brief report that discusses the issue of keeping federal benefits for jail detainees.

2763 Love First: A New Approach to Intervention for Alcoholism and Drug Addiction
Hazelden
15245 Pleasant Valley Road
PO Box 11-CO 3
Center City, MN 55012-9640
651-257-4010
800-257-7810
Fax: 651-213-4394
www.hazelden.org

Mark Mishek, CEO

A straightforward, simple and practical resource written specifically for families seeking to help a loved one struggling with substance addiction.

280 pages ISBN 1-568385-21-8

2764 Malignant Neglect: Substance Abuse and America's Schools
Center on Addiction at Columbia University
633 3rd Avenue
19th Floor
New York, NY 10017-8155
212-841-5200
Fax: 212-956-8020
www.casacolumbia.org

William H Foster, CEO

Six years of exhaustive research of focus groups, schools, parents and professionals. Findings of the costs of drug abuse in dollars, student behavior, truancy and more. *$22.00*

117 pages Year Founded: 2001

2765 Missed Opportunity: National Survey of Primary Care Physicians and Patients on Substance Abuse
Center on Addiction at Columbia University
633 3rd Avenue
19th Floor
New York, NY 10017-8155
212-841-5200
Fax: 212-956-8020
www.casacolumbia.org

William H Foster, CEO

Findings and recomendations based on a CASA report that revealed 94% of primary care physicians fail to diagnose symptoms of alcohol abuse in adult patients, and 41% of pediatricians missed a diagnosis of drug abuse when presented with a classic description of a teenage patient with these symptoms. The report also sheds light on the fact that many physicians feel unprepared to diagnose substance abuse and have little confidence in the effectiveness of treatments available. *$22.00*

Year Founded: 2000

2766 Motivational Interviewing: Prepare People to Change Addictive Behavior
Hazelden
15251 Pleasant Valley Road
PO Box 176
Center City, MN 55012-176
651-213-2121
800-328-9000
Fax: 651-213-4590
www.hazelden.org

William K Miller, Co-Author
Stephen Rollnick, Co-Author

A key resource for clinical psychologists, social workers and chemical dependency counselors for mastering interviewing skills and working with resistant clients. *$21.95*

348 pages ISBN 0-898624-69-X

2767 Narrative Means to Sober Ends: Treating Addiction and Its Aftermath
Guilford Publications
72 Spring Street
New York, NY 10012-4068

212-431-9800
800-365-7006
Fax: 212-966-6708
E-mail: info@guilford.com

Bob Matloff, President

This eloquently written volume illuminates the devastating power of addiction and describes an array of innovative approaches to facilitating clients' recovery. Demonstrated are creative ways to help clients explore their relationship to drugs and alcohol, take the first steps toward sobriety and develop meaningful ways of living without addiction. *$37.95*

386 pages ISBN 1-572305-66-5

2768 No Place to Hide: Substance Abuse in Mid-Size Cities and Rural America
Center on Addiction at Columbia University
633 3rd Avenue
19th Floor
New York, NY 10017-8155
212-841-5200
Fax: 212-956-8020
www.casacolumbia.org

William H Foster, CEO

Surprisingly to some, young people in smaller cities and rural areas are more likely to use many forms of illegal substances. Tobacco use is also higher away from the major cities. The findings on other statistics of drugs and rural adolescent and teenager use are included. *$10.00*

Year Founded: 2000

2769 No Safe Haven: Children of Substance-Abusing Parents
Center on Addiction at Columbia University
633 3rd Avenue
19th Floor
New York, NY 10017-8155
212-841-5200
Fax: 212-956-8020
www.casacolumbia.org

William H Foster, CEO
Peggy Macchetto, Author
Susan Foster, Author

Comprehensive report with shattering facts and figures reveals the impact of substance abuse on parenting skills and child neglect. The number of children affected by their parent's substance abuse driven behavior has more than doubled in the last ten years, greater than the rise in children's overall population. This report calls for a reworking of the child welfare system, and provides guidelines to when the child should be permanently remove from the home. *$22.00*

Year Founded: 1999

2770 Non Medical Marijuana: Rite of Passage or Russian Roulette?
Center on Addiction at Columbia University
633 3rd Avenue
19th Floor
New York, NY 10017-8155

212-841-5200
Fax: 212-956-8020
www.casacolumbia.org

William H Foster, CEO

The most recent numbers available find that more teens from 19 years old and younger enter treatment for marijuana abuse than for any other drug, including alcohol. Many teens also have a problem with secondary drugs. This report released by CASA at Columbia University, concludes that non medical marijuana is indeed a dangerous substance. *$20.00*

Year Founded: 1999

2771 Perfect Daughters
Health Communications
292 Fernwood Avenue
Edison, NJ 08837-3839
732-346-0027
Fax: 732-346-0442
www.hcomm.com

Identifies what differentiates the adult daughters of alcoholics from other women. Adult daughters of alcoholics operate from a base of harsh and limiting views of themselves and the world. Having learned that they must function perfectly in order to avoid unpleasant situations, these women often assume responsibility for the failures of others. They are drawn to chemically dependent men and are more likely to become addicted themselves. This book collects the thoughts, feelings and experience of twelve hundred perfect daughters, offering readers an opportunity to explore their own life's dynamics and thereby heal and grow.

350 pages ISBN 1-558749-52-7

2772 Principles of Addiction Medicine
American Society of Addiction Medicine
4601 N Park Avenue
Suite 101, Upper Arcade
Chevy Chase, MD 20815-4519
301-656-3920
800-844-8948
Fax: 301-656-3815
E-mail: email@asam.com
www.asam.org

Eileen McGrath, Executive VP

Textbook on the basic and clinical science of prevention and treatment of alcohol, nicotine, and other drug dependencies and addictions. *$155.00*

1338 pages ISBN 1-880425-04-0

2773 Proven Youth Development Model that Prevents Substance Abuse and Builds Communities
Center on Addiction at Columbia University
633 3rd Avenue
19th Floor
New York, NY 10017-8155
212-841-5200
Fax: 212-956-8020
www.casacolumbia.org

William H Foster, CEO

How-to manual developed with nine years of research. The program is a collaboration of local school, law enforcement, social service and health teams to help high risk youth between the ages of 8 - 13 years old and their families prevent substance abuse and violent behavior. Used in 23 urban and rural communities in 11 states and the District of Columbia. *$50.00*

79 pages Year Founded: 2001

2774 Psychological Theories of Drinking and Alcoholism
Guilford Publications
72 Spring Street
New York, NY 10012-4068
212-431-9800
800-365-7006
Fax: 212-966-6708
E-mail: info@guilford.com

Bob Matloff, President

Multidisciplinary approach discusses biological, pharmacological and social factors that influence drinking and alcoholism. Contributors review established and emerging approaches that guide research into the psychological processes influencing drinking and alcoholism. *$47.95*

460 pages Year Founded: 1999 ISBN 1-572304-10-3

2775 Relapse Prevention Maintenance: Strategies in the Treatment of Addictive Behaviors
Guilford Publications
72 Spring Street
New York, NY 10012-4068
212-431-9800
800-365-7006
Fax: 212-966-6708
E-mail: info@guilford.com

Bob Matloff, President

Research on relapse prevention to problem drinking, smoking, substance abuse, eating disorders and compulsive gambling. Analyzes factors that may lead to relapse and offers practical techniques for maintaining treatment gains. *$55.00*

558 pages Year Founded: 1985 ISBN 0-898620-09-0

2776 Relapse Prevention Maintenance: Strategies in the Treatment of Addictive Behaviors
Guilford Publications
72 Spring Street
New York, NY 10012-4068
212-431-9800
800-365-7006
Fax: 212-966-6708
E-mail: info@guilford.com

Bob Matloff, President

Research on relapse prevention to problem drinking, smoking, substance abuse, eating disorders and compulsive gambling. Analyzes factors that may lead to relapse and offers practical techniques for maintaining treatment gains. *$55.00*

558 pages Year Founded: 1985 ISBN 0-898620-09-0

2777 So Help Me God: Substance Abuse, Religion and Spirituality
Center on Addiction at Columbia University
633 3rd Avenue
19th Floor
New York, NY 10017-8155
212-841-5200
Fax: 212-956-8020
www.casacolumbia.org

William H Foster, CEO

Results of a 2 year study, finding that spirituality has enormous power to potentially lower the risks of substance abuse. When this is combined with professional treatment, an individual's religion helps greatly with recovery. *$10.00*

Year Founded: 2001

2778 Solutions Step by Step: Substance Abuse Treatment Manual
WW Norton & Company
500 5th Avenue
New York, NY 10110-54
212-354-2907
Fax: 212-869-0856
E-mail: admalmud@wwnorton.com

Drake McFeely, CEO

Quick tips, questions and examples focusing on successes that can be experienced helping substance abusers help themselves. *$ 25.00*

192 pages Year Founded: 1997 ISSN 70251-0

2779 Substance Abuse and Learning Disabilities: Peas in a Pod or Apples and Oranges?
Center on Addiction at Columbia University
633 3rd Avenue
19th Floor
New York, NY 10017-8155
212-841-5200
Fax: 212-956-8020
www.casacolumbia.org

William H Foster, CEO

Report originating from a conference in 1999 sponsored by CASA, the relationship between learning disabilities that are not addressed, and possible substance abuse by these same children is examined. Attention Deficit/Hyperactivity Disorder and Conduct Disorder and the link to substance abuse is also considered. *$10.00*

00 pages

2780 Substance Abuse: A Comprehensive Textbook
Lippincott Williams & Wilkins
PO Box 1600
Hagerstown, MD 21741-1600
301-714-2300
800-638-3030
Fax: 301-824-7390
www.lww.com

$162.00

956 pages Year Founded: 1997 ISBN 0-683181-79-3

2781 Teens and Alcohol: Gallup Youth Survey Major Issues and Trends
Mason Crest Publishers
370 Reed Road
Suite 302
Broomall, PA 19008-4017
866-627-2665
Fax: 610-543-3878
E-mail: gbrffr@masoncrest.com
www.masoncrest.com

Eighty-seven percent of high school seniors have tried alcohol and, according to a Gallup Youth Survey, 27 percent of teenagers say it is very easy for them to get alcoholic beverages. Alcohol is a contributor to the three leading causes of death for teens and young adults: automobile crashes, homicide and suicides.

112 pages ISBN 1-590847-23-7

2782 Therapeutic Communities for Addictions: Reading in Theory, Research, and Practice
Charles C Thomas Publisher
2600 S 1st Street
Springfield, IL 62704-4730
217-789-8980
800-258-8980
Fax: 217-789-9130
E-mail: books@ccthomas.com
www.ccthomas.com

Michael P Thomas, President
James T Ziegenfuss Jr, Author

Contents: The Therapeutic Community (TC) for Substance Abuse; Democratic TCs or Programmatic TCs or Both?; Motivational Aspects of Heroin Addicts in TCs; A Sociological View of the TC; Psychodynamics of TCs for Treatment of Heroin Addicts; Britain and the Psychoanalytic Tradition in TCs; TC Research; Outcomes of Drug Abuse Treatment; 12-Year Follow-up Outcomes, College Training in a TC; Client Evaluations of TCs and Retention; Side Bets and Secondary Adjustments; Measuring Program Implementation; The TC Looking Ahead; TCs within Prisons; Uses and Abuses of Power and Authority. *$51.95*

282 pages Year Founded: 1986 ISBN 0-398052-06-9

2783 Treating Substance Abuse: Part 1
American Counseling Association
5999 Stevenson Avenue
Alexandria, VA 22304-3304
703-823-9800
800-422-2648
Fax: 703-823-0252
TDD: 703-823-6862
E-mail: webmaster@counseling.org
www.counseling.org

Richard Yep, Executive Director

The first of a two-volume set presents up-to-date findings on the treatment of alcoholism and addiction to cocaine, caffeine, hallucinogens, and marijuana. Techniques and case examples are offered from a variety of approaches, including motivational enhancement therapy, marriage and family therapy as well as cognitive-behavioral. *$26.95*

280 pages ISBN 1-886330-48-4

2784 Treating Substance Abuse: Part 2
American Counseling Association
5999 Stevenson Avenue
Alexandria, VA 22304-3304
703-823-9800
800-422-2648
Fax: 703-823-0252
E-mail: webmaster@counseling.org
www.counseling.org

Richard Yep, Executive Director

For treating select populations of substance-abusing clients, including those with disabilities, psychiatric disorders, schizophrenia and major depression. Also serves adolescents, older adults, pregnant women and clients whose addictions affect their ability to function in the workplace. *$29.95*

311 pages ISBN 1-886330-49-2

2785 Treating the Alcoholic: Developmental Model of Recovery
John Wiley & Sons
605 3rd Avenue
New York, NY 10158-180
212-850-6301
E-mail: info@wiley.com

376 pages Year Founded: 1985

2786 Under the Rug: Substance Abuse and the Mature Woman
Center on Addiction at Columbia University
633 3rd Avenue
19th Floor
New York, NY 10017-8155
212-841-5200
Fax: 212-956-8020
www.casacolumbia.org

William H Foster, CEO

Discusses the fact that millions of mature women are robbed of a healthy and longer lifespan due to a substance abuse problem that they discreetly hide. Their reluctance to get help costs them and the health systems billions. *$25.00*

Year Founded: 1998

2787 Understanding Psychiatric Medications in the Treatment of Chemical Dependency and Dual Diagnoses
Charles C Thomas Publisher
2600 S 1st Street
Springfield, IL 62704-4730
217-789-8980
800-258-8980
Fax: 217-789-9130
E-mail: books@ccthomas.com
www.ccthomas.com

Michael P Thomas, President

Designed to address coexisting chemical dependency and psychiatric disorder (dual diagnoses) and specifically to focus on the appropriate role of psychotropic medications in the treatment of dual diagnonsis patients. The text presents a comprehensive overview of psychiatric medication treatment for dual diagnoses that speaks to a broad professional audience while being sensitive to the values and beliefs of the chemical dependents. *$39.95*

134 pages Year Founded: 1995 ISSN 0-398-05964-0ISBN 0-398059-63-2

2788 Your Drug May Be Your Problem: How and Why to Stop Taking Pyschiatric Medications
Perseus Books Group
550 Central Avenue
Boulder, CO 80301

800-386-5656
Fax: 720-406-7336
E-mail: westview.orders@perseusbooks.com
www.perseusbooksgroup.com

In a very short time, a doctor may prescribe a drug which an individual may take for months, years, even the rest of their lives. This book provides up-to-date, descriptions of the pros and cons of taking psychiatric medication, dangers involved, and explains a safe method of withdrawl if needed. *$17.00*

288 pages Year Founded: 2000 ISBN 0-738203-48-3

Anxiety Disorders

2789 Anxiety Disorders: A Scientific Approach for Selecting the Most Effective Treatment
Professional Resource Press
PO Box 15560
Sarasota, FL 34277-1560
941-343-9601
800-443-3364
Fax: 941-343-9201
E-mail: orders@prpress.com
www.prpress.com

Debra Fink, Managing Editor

Presents descriptive and empirical information on the differential diagnosis of DSM-IV and DSM-III-R categories of anxiety disorders. Explicit decision rules are provided for developing treatment plans based on both scientific research and clinical judgement. *$14.95*

114 pages Year Founded: 1994 ISBN 1-568870-00-0

2790 Applied Relaxation Training in the Treatment of PTSD and Other Anxiety Disorders
New Harbinger Publications
5674 Shattuck Avenue
Oakland, CA 94609-1662
510-652-0215
800-748-6273
Fax: 510-652-5472
E-mail: customerservice@newharbinger.com
www.newharbinger.com

Matthew McKay, Owner

Comes with a one hundred five minute video tape and a 52 page paperback manual. *$100.00*

Year Founded: 1998 ISBN 1-889287-08-3

2791 Assimilation, Rational Thinking, and Suppression in the Treatment of PTSD and Other Anxiety Disorders
New Harbinger Publications
5674 Shattuck Avenue
Oakland, CA 94609-1662
510-652-0215
800-748-6273
Fax: 510-652-5472
E-mail: customerservice@newharbinger.com
www.newharbinger.com

Matthew McKay, Owner

Comes with two videotapes and a ninety four page paperback manual. *$150.00*

Year Founded: 1998 ISBN 1-889287-06-7

2792 Body Remembers: Psychophysiology of Trauma and Trauma Treatment
WW Norton & Company
500 5th Avenue
New York, NY 10110-54
212-354-2907
Fax: 212-869-0856
E-mail: admalmud@wwnorton.com

Drake McFeely, CEO

Unites traditional verbal therapy and body oriented therapies for Post Traumatic Stress Disorder patients, as memories sometimes present in a physical disorder. *$30.00*

224 pages Year Founded: 2000 ISSN 70327-4

2793 Brief Therapy for Post Traumatic Stress Disorder
John Wiley & Sons
605 3rd Avenue
New York, NY 10158-180
212-850-6301
E-mail: info@wiley.com

Discusses a new and exciting treatment technique that has proven to be more effective than the widely used direct theraputic exposure technique. Fills the growing need for a step by step practical treatment manual for PTSD using Traumatic Incident Reduction. It is an ideal companion to training workshops.

192 pages Year Founded: 1998

2794 Client's Manual for the Cognitive Behavioral Treatment of Anxiety Disorders
New Harbinger Publications
5674 Shattuck Avenue
Oakland, CA 94609-1662
510-652-0215
800-748-6273
Fax: 510-652-5472
E-mail: customerservice@newharbinger.com
www.newharbinger.com

Matthew McKay, Owner

$10.00
106 pages Year Founded: 1994 ISBN 1-889287-99-7

2795 Cognitive Processing Therapy for Rape Victims
Sage Publications
2455 Teller Road
Thousand Oaks, CA 91320-2234
805-499-0721
800-818-7243
Fax: 805-499-0871
E-mail: info@sagepub.com
www.sagepub.com

Blaise R Simqu, CEO

Information regarding the assessment and treatment of rape victims. Discusses disorders that result from rape and add to a victim's suffering such as post traumatic stress, depression, poor self-esteem, interpersonal difficulties and sexual dysfunction. *$46.00*

192 pages Year Founded: 1993 ISBN 0-803949-01-4

2796 Cognitive Therapy
American Psychiatric Publishing, Inc.
1000 Wilson Boulevard
Suite 1825
Arlington, VA 22209-3901
703-907-7322
800-368-5777
Fax: 703-907-1091
E-mail: appi@psych.org
www.appi.org

Robert E Hales MD, Editor-in-Chief
Ron McMillen, Chief Executive Officer
John McDuffie, Editorial Director

Cognitive therapy for anxiety, substance abuse, personality, eating and mental disorders. *$37.50*

176 pages Year Founded: 1997 ISBN 0-880484-45-4

2797 Cognitive Therapy in Practice
WW Norton & Company
500 5th Avenue
New York, NY 10110-54
212-354-2907
800-233-4830
Fax: 212-869-0856
E-mail: npd@wwnorton.com

Drake McFeely, CEO

Basic text for graduate studies in psychotherapy, psychology nursing social work and counseling. *$29.00*

224 pages Year Founded: 1989 ISBN 0-393700-77-1

2798 Concise Guide to Brief Dynamic Psychotherapy
American Psychiatric Publishing, Inc.
1000 Wilson Boulevard
Suite 1825
Arlington, VA 22209-3901
703-907-7322
800-368-5777
Fax: 703-907-1091

E-mail: appi@psych.org
www.appi.org

Robert E Hales MD, Editor-in-Chief
Ron McMillen, Chief Executive Officer
John McDuffie, Editorial Director

Seven brief psychodynamic therapy models including supportive, time - limited, interpersonal, time - limited dynamic, short term dynamic for post traumatic stress disorder and brief dynamic for substance abuse. *$21.00*

224 pages Year Founded: 1997 ISBN 0-880483-46-6

2799 Current Treatments of Obsessive-Compulsive Disorder
American Psychiatric Publishing, Inc.
1000 Wilson Boulevard
Suite 1825
Arlington, VA 22209-3901
703-907-7322
800-368-5777
Fax: 703-907-1091
E-mail: appi@psych.org
www.appi.org

Robert E Hales MD, Editor-in-Chief
Ron McMillen, Chief Executive Officer
John McDuffie, Editorial Director

Helps clinicians better match treatment approaches with each patients unique needs.

Year Founded: 01 ISBN 0-880487-79-8

2800 Does Stress Damage the Brain? Understanding Trauma-Related Disorders from a Mind-Body Perspective
WW Norton & Company
500 5th Avenue
New York, NY 10110-54
212-354-2907
800-233-4830
Fax: 212-869-0856
E-mail: npb@wwnorton.com

Drake McFeely, CEO

Shows that extreme stress may result in lasting damage to the brain, especially a part of the brain involved in memory. This new neurobiological understanding of the relation between cognitive problems and trauma has many important implications for both self-understanding of trauma survivors and for the treatment of the effects of trauma.

ISBN 0-393704-74-2

2801 Effective Treatments for PTSD: Practice Guidelines from the International Society for Traumatic Stress Studies
Guilford Publications
72 Spring Street
New York, NY 10012-4068
212-431-9800
800-365-7006
Fax: 212-966-6708
E-mail: info@guilford.com

Bob Matloff, President

Developed under the auspices of the PTSD Treatment Guidelines Task Force of the International Society for Traumatic Stress Studies, this comprehensive volume brings together leading authorities on psychological trauma to offer best practice guidelines for the treatment of PTSD. Approaches covered include acute interventions, cognitive-behavior therapy, pharmacotherapy, EMDR, group therapy, psychodynamic therapy, impatient treatment, psychosocial rehabilitation, hypnosis, creative therapies, marital and family treatment. *$42.00*

388 pages ISBN 1-572305-84-3

2802 Even from a Broken Web: Brief, Respectful Solution Oriented Therapy for Sexual Abuse and Trauma
WW Norton & Company
500 5th Avenue
New York, NY 10110-54
212-354-2907
800-233-4830
Fax: 212-869-0856
E-mail: npb@wwnorton.com

Drake McFeely, CEO

Recent years have shown more people than ever coming to therapy with the after affects of sexual abuse. The authors provide therapists solution oriented treatment that considers a person's inner healing abilities. This method is less traumatic and disruptive to the patient's life than traditional therapies. *$16.95*

208 pages Year Founded: 2002 ISBN 0-393703-94-0

2803 Eye Movement Desensitization and Reprocessing: Basic Principles, Protocols, and Procedures
Guilford Publications
72 Spring Street
New York, NY 10012-4068
212-431-9800
800-365-7006
Fax: 212-966-6708
E-mail: info@guilford.com

Bob Matloff, President

Reviews research and development, discusses theoretical constructs and possible underlying mechanisms, and presents protocols and procedures for treatment of adults and children with a range of presenting complaints. Material is applicable for victims of sexual abuse, crime, combat and phobias. *$45.00*

398 pages Year Founded: 1995 ISBN 0-898629-60-8

2804 Gender Differences in Mood and Anxiety Disorders: From Bench to Bedside
American Psychiatric Publishing, Inc.
1000 Wilson Boulevard
Suite 1825
Arlington, VA 22209-3901
703-907-7322
800-368-5777
Fax: 703-907-1091
E-mail: appi@psych.org
www.appi.org

Robert E Hales MD, Editor-in-Chief
Ron McMillen, Chief Executive Officer
John McDuffie, Editorial Director

Gender differences in neuroimaging. Discusses women, stress and depression, sex differences in hypothalamic-pituitary-adrenal axis regulation, modulation of anxiety by reproductive hormones. Questions if hormone replacement and oral contraceptive therapy induce or treat mood symptoms. *$37.50*

224 pages Year Founded: 1999 ISBN 0-880489-58-8

2805 Generalized Anxiety Disorder: Diagnosis, Treatment and Its Relationship to Other Anxiety Disorders
American Psychiatric Publishing, Inc.
1000 Wilson Boulevard
Suite 1825
Arlington, VA 22209-3901
703-907-7322
800-368-5777
Fax: 703-907-1091
E-mail: appi@psych.org
www.appi.org

Robert E Hales MD, Editor-in-Chief
Ron McMillen, Chief Executive Officer
John McDuffie, Editorial Director

Historical introduction, diagnosis, classification and differential diagnosis. Relationship with depression, panic and OCD. Treatments. *$74.95*

96 pages Year Founded: 1998 ISBN 1-853176-59-1

2806 Group Treatments for Post-Traumatic Stress Disorder
Brunner/Routledge
325 Chestnut Street
Philadelphia, PA 19106-2614

800-821-8312
Fax: 215-269-0363
www.brunner-routledge.com

Contains contributions from renowned PTSD experts who provide group treatment to trauma survivors. It reviews the state-of-the-art applications of group therapy for such survivors of trauma as rape victims, combat veterans, adult survivors of childhood abuse, motor vehicle accident survivors, survivors of disaster, homicide witnesses and disaster relief workers. *$34.95*

216 pages ISBN 0-876309-83-X

2807 Integrative Treatment of Anxiety Disorders
American Psychiatric Publishing, Inc.
1000 Wilson Boulevard
Suite 1825
Arlington, VA 22209-3901
703-907-7322
800-368-5777
Fax: 703-907-1091
E-mail: appi@psych.org
www.appi.org

Robert E Hales MD, Editor-in-Chief
Ron McMillen, Chief Executive Officer
John McDuffie, Editorial Director

Up-to-date look at combined pharmacotherapy and cognitive behavioral therapy in the treatment of anxiety disorders. *$41.50*

320 pages Year Founded: 1995 ISBN 0-880487-15-1

2808 Life After Trauma: Workbook for Healing
Guilford Publications
72 Spring Street
New York, NY 10012-4068
212-431-9800
800-365-7006
Fax: 212-966-6708
E-mail: info@guilford.com

Bob Matloff, President

Useful exercises for clinicians and trauma survivors, very empowering. *$17.95*

352 pages Year Founded: 1999 ISBN 1-572302-39-9

2809 Long-Term Treatments of Anxiety Disorders
American Psychiatric Publishing, Inc.
1000 Wilson Boulevard
Suite 1825
Arlington, VA 22209-3901
703-907-7322
800-368-5777
Fax: 703-907-1091
E-mail: appi@psych.org
www.appi.org

Robert E Hales MD, Editor-in-Chief
Ron McMillen, Chief Executive Officer
John McDuffie, Editorial Director

Treatment of anxiety disorders encapsulating important advances made over the past two decades. *$56.00*

464 pages Year Founded: 1996 ISBN 0-880486-56-2

2810 Memory, Trauma and the Law
WW Norton & Company
500 5th Avenue
New York, NY 10110-54
212-354-2907
Fax: 212-869-0856
E-mail: admalmud@wwnorton.com

Drake McFeely, CEO

Professionals need to be informed of memory in the legal context to avoid malpractice liability suits. Recovered memory research, trauma treatment and the controversy of false memory in some cases are covered. *$100.00*

960 pages Year Founded: 1998 ISSN 70254-5

2811 Obsessive-Compulsive Disorder: Contemporary Issues in Treatment
Lawrence Erlbaum Associates
10 Industrial Avenue
Mahwah, NJ 07430-2253

201-825-3200
800-926-6577
Fax: 201-236-0072
E-mail: orders@erlbaum.com
www.erlbaum.com

Hardcover.

Year Founded: 00 ISBN 0-805828-37-0

2812 Obsessive-Compulsive and Related Disorders in Adults: a Comprehensive Clinical Guide
Cambridge University Press
40 W 20th Street
New York, NY 10011-4211
212-924-3900
Fax: 212-691-3239
E-mail: marketing@cup.org
www.cup.org

The author challenges the current implicit models used in alcohol problem prevention and demonstrates an ecological perspective of the community as a complex adaptive systems composed of interacting subsystems. This volume represents a new and sensible approach to the prevention of alcohol dependence and alcohol-related problems. *$65.00*

380 pages Year Founded: 1999 ISBN 0-521559-75-8

2813 Overcoming Agoraphobia and Panic Disorder
New Harbinger Publications
5674 Shattuck Avenue
Oakland, CA 94609-1662
510-652-0215
800-748-6273
Fax: 510-652-5472
E-mail: customerservice@newharbinger.com
www.newharbinger.com

Matthew McKay, Owner

A twelve to sixteen session treatment. *$11.95*

88 pages Year Founded: 1998 ISBN 1-572241-46-2

2814 Overcoming Obsessive-Compulsive Disorder
New Harbinger Publications
5674 Shattuck Avenue
Oakland, CA 94609-1662
510-652-0215
800-748-6273
Fax: 510-652-5472
E-mail: customerservice@newharbinger.com
www.newharbinger.com

Matthew McKay, Owner

A fourteen session treatment. *$11.95*

72 pages Year Founded: 1998 ISBN 1-572241-29-2

2815 Overcoming Post-Traumatic Stress Disorder
New Harbinger Publications
5674 Shattuck Avenue
Oakland, CA 94609-1662
510-652-0215
800-748-6273
Fax: 510-652-5472

E-mail: customerservice@newharbinger.com
www.newharbinger.com

Matthew McKay, Owner

An eleven to twenty four session treatment. *$11.95*

95 pages Year Founded: 1998 ISBN 1-572241-47-0

2816 Overcoming Specific Phobia
New Harbinger Publications
5674 Shattuck Avenue
Oakland, CA 94609-1662
510-652-0215
800-748-6273
Fax: 510-652-5472
E-mail: customerservice@newharbinger.com
www.newharbinger.com

Matthew McKay, Owner

$9.95

72 pages Year Founded: 1998 ISBN 1-572241-15-2

2817 Panic Disorder: Clinical Diagnosis, Management and Mechanisms
American Psychiatric Publishing, Inc.
1000 Wilson Boulevard
Suite 1825
Arlington, VA 22209-3901
703-907-7322
800-368-5777
Fax: 703-907-1091
E-mail: appi@psych.org
www.appi.org

Robert E Hales MD, Editor-in-Chief
Ron McMillen, Chief Executive Officer
John McDuffie, Editorial Director

Novel and important new discoveries for biological research together with up to date information for the diagnosis and treatment for the practicing clinician. *$75.00*

264 pages Year Founded: 1998 ISBN 1-853175-18-8

2818 Panic Disorder: Theory, Research and Therapy
John Wiley & Sons
605 3rd Avenue
New York, NY 10158-180
212-850-6301
E-mail: info@wiley.com

364 pages Year Founded: 1989

2819 Perturbing the Organism: The Biology of Stressful Experience
University of Chicago Press
5801 S Ellis
Chicago, IL 60637-1546
773-702-1234
Fax: 773-702-0809
E-mail: marketing@press.uchicago.edu

Robert Zimmer, President

Critical analysis of the entire range of research and theory on stress in animals and humans, from the earliest studies in the 30's to present day. Includes empirical and conceptual advances of recent years, but also supplies a new working definition of stressful experience. Hardcover. *$40.50*

358 pages Year Founded: 1992 ISBN 0-226890-41-4

2820 Phobias: Handbook of Theory, Reseach and Treatment
John Wiley & Sons
605 3rd Avenue
New York, NY 10158-180
212-850-6301
E-mail: info@wiley.com

Provides an up-to-date summary of current knowledge of phobias. Psychological treatments available for specific phobias have been refined considerably in recent years. This extensive handbook acknowledges these treatments and includes the description and nature of prevalent phobias, details of symptoms, prevalence rates, individual case histories, and a brief review of of our knowledge of the etiology of phobias.

470 pages Year Founded: 1995

2821 Post Traumatic Stress Disorder
New Harbinger Publications
5674 Shattuck Avenue
Oakland, CA 94609-1662
510-652-0215
800-748-6273
Fax: 510-652-5472
E-mail: customerservice@newharbinger.com
www.newharbinger.com

Matthew McKay, Owner

Includes techniques for managing flashbacks, anxiety attacks, nightmares, insomnia, and dissociation; working through layers of pain; and handling survivor guilt, secondary wounding, low self esteem, victim thinking, anger, and depression. *$49.95*

384 pages Year Founded: 1994 ISBN 1-879237-68-7

2822 Post Traumatic Stress Disorder: Complete Treatment Guide
200 E Joppa Road
Suite 207
Baltimore, MD 21286-3107
410-825-8888
888-825-8249
Fax: 410-337-0747
E-mail: sidran@sidran.org
www.sidran.org

For clinicians who want to work more effectively with trauma survivors, this textbook provides a step by step description of PTSD treatment strategies. Includes chapters on definitions, diagnostic criteria and the biochemistry of PTSD. Reflects a generalized 'ideal' structure of the healing process. Includes cognitive and behavioral techniques for managing flashbacks, anxiety attacks, sleep disturbances and dissociation; a comprehensive program for working through deeper layers of pain; plus PTSD related problems such as survivor guilt, secondary wounding, low self esteem, victim thinking, anger and depression. Presents trauma issues clearly for both general audiences and trauma professionals. *$49.95*

345 pages

2823 Post Traumatic Stress Disorders in Children and Adolescents Handbook
WW Norton & Company
500 5th Avenue
New York, NY 10110-54
212-354-2907
800-233-4830
Fax: 212-869-0856
E-mail: npb@wwnorton.com

Drake McFeely, CEO

The 15 chapters gathered here address different aspects of childhood and adolescent trauma-some consider a distinct therapeutic situation (abuse and neglect), others pertain to standard clinical procedure (assessment), and still others focus on complex research issues (neurobiology and genetics of PSTD).

ISBN 0-393704-12-2

2824 Practice Guideline for the Treatment of Patients with Panic Disorder
American Psychiatric Publishing, Inc.
1000 Wilson Boulevard
Suite 1825
Arlington, VA 22209-3901
703-907-7322
800-368-5777
Fax: 703-907-1091
E-mail: appi@psych.org
www.appi.org

Robert E Hales MD, Editor-in-Chief
Ron McMillen, Chief Executive Officer
John McDuffie, Editorial Director

Summarizes data, evaluation of the patient for coexisting mental disorders and issues specific to the treatment of panic disorders in children and adolescents. *$22.50*

160 pages Year Founded: 1998 ISBN 0-890423-11-3

2825 Rebuilding Shattered Lives: Responsible Treatment of Complex Post-Traumatic and Dissociative Disorders
John Wiley & Sons
605 3rd Avenue
New York, NY 10158-180
212-850-6301
E-mail: info@wiley.com

The most up-to-date, integrative and emperically sound account of trauma theory and practice availible. Based on more than a decade of clinical research and treatment experience at the Harvard Medical School, this comprehensive and nontechnical text offers a stage oriented approach to understanding and treating complex and difficult traumatized patients, integrating modern trauma theory with traditional therapeutic interventions. *$47.50*

256 pages Year Founded: 1998 ISBN 0-471247-32-4

2826 Remembering Trauma: Psychotherapist's Guide to Memory & Illusion
John Wiley & Sons
605 3rd Avenue
New York, NY 10158-180
212-850-6301
E-mail: info@wiley.com

Amy Abzarnik, Conventions Coordinator

2827 Shy Children, Phobic Adults: Nature and Treatment of Social Phobia
American Psychiatric Publishing, Inc.
1000 Wilson Boulevard
Suite 1825
Arlington, VA 22209-3901
703-907-7322
800-368-5777
Fax: 703-907-1091
E-mail: appi@psych.org
www.appi.org

Robert E Hales MD, Editor-in-Chief
Ron McMillen, Chief Executive Officer
John McDuffie, Editorial Director

Describes the similiarities and differences in the syndrome across all ages. Draws from the clinical, social and developmental literatures, as well as from extensive clinical experience. Illustrates the impact of developmental stage on phenomenology, diagnoses and assessment and treatment of social phobia. *$39.95*

321 pages Year Founded: 1998 ISBN 1-557984-61-1

2828 Social Phobia: Clinical and Research Perspectives
American Psychiatric Publishing, Inc.
1000 Wilson Boulevard
Suite 1825
Arlington, VA 22209-3901
703-907-7322
800-368-5777
Fax: 703-907-1091
E-mail: appi@psych.org
www.appi.org

Robert E Hales MD, Editor-in-Chief
Ron McMillen, Chief Executive Officer
John McDuffie, Editorial Director

Comprehensive and practice guide for mental health professionals who encounter individuals with social phobia. *$48.00*

384 pages Year Founded: 1995 ISBN 0-880486-53-8

2829 Standing in the Spaces: Essays on Clinical Process, Trauma, and Dissociation
Analytic Press
101 W Street
Hillsdale, NJ 07642-1421
201-358-9477
800-926-6579
Fax: 201-358-4700
E-mail: TAP@analyticpress.com
www.analyticpress.com

Paul E Stepansky PhD, Managing Director
John Kerr PhD, Sr Editor

Bromberg's essays are delightfully unpredictable, as they strive to keep the reader continually abreast of how words can and cannot capture the subtle shifts in relatedness that characterize the clinical process. Radiating clinical wisdom infused with compassion and wit, Standing in the Spaces, is a classic destined to be read and reread by anlysts and therapists for decades to come. *$55.00*

376 pages Year Founded: 1998 ISBN 0-881632-46-5

2830 The Body Remembers Casebook: Unifying Methods and Models in the Treatment of Trauma and PTSD
WW Norton & Company
500 5th Avenue
New York, NY 10110-54
212-354-2907
800-233-4830
Fax: 212-869-0856
E-mail: npb@wwnorton.com

Drake McFeely, CEO

Emphasizes the importance of tailoring every trauma therapy to the particular needs of each individual client. Each varied and complex case is approached with a combination of methods ranging from traditional psychodynamic approaches and applications of attachment theory to innovative trauma methods including EMDR and Levine's SIBAM model.

ISBN 0-393704-00-9

2831 The Body Remembers: The Psychphysiology of Trauma and Trauma Treatment
WW Norton & Company
500 5th Avenue
New York, NY 10110-54
212-354-2907
800-233-4830
Fax: 212-869-0856
E-mail: npb@wwnorton.com

Drake McFeely, CEO

There is tremendous value in understanding the psychophysiology of trauma and knowing what to do about its manifestations. This book illuminates psychophysiology, casting light on the impact of trauma on the body and the phenomenon of somatic memory. Presents principles and non-touch techniques for giving the body its due.

ISBN 0-393703-27-4

2832 The Pathology of Man: A Study of Human Evil
Charles C Thomas Publishers
PO Box 19265
Springfield, IL 62794-9265
217-789-8980
800-258-8980
Fax: 217-789-9130
www.ccthomas.com

Deals with a topic that is both timely and of enduring importance. Expected to be a unique and important contribution that responds to the concerns of students and professionals in a wide range of diciplines. A comprehensive and solid study of the multi-casual nature of phonomenon that, until now, has been treated almost exclusively in terms of religion, myth, symbolism, moral philosophy, and ethics. Available in paperback for $53.95.
$73.95

376 pages Year Founded: 2005 ISBN 0-398075-57-3

2833 The Trauma Spectrum: Hidden Wounds and Human Resiliency
WW Norton & Company
500 5th Avenue
New York, NY 10110-54
212-354-2907
800-233-4830
Fax: 212-869-0856
E-mail: npb@wwnorton.com

Drake McFeely, CEO

Scaer, a neurologist with over 30 years experience working with car accident victims, extends the conceptual and practical horizons of trauma treatment, redefining trauma as a continuum of variably negative life events occuring over a lifespan-including "little traumas" such as car accidents, risky medical interventions, childhood abuse and neglect, and social discrimination and poverty-that shape every aspect of our existence.

ISBN 0-393704-66-1

2834 Transforming Trauma: EMDR
WW Norton & Company
500 5th Avenue
New York, NY 10110-54
212-354-2907
Fax: 212-869-0856
E-mail: admalmud@wwnorton.com

Drake McFeely, CEO

Has helped thousands of people dealing with abuse histories or recent traumatic events. The author has a unique perspective, as she is both a client of EMDR and a therapist. *$14.95*

288 pages Year Founded: 1996 ISSN 31757-9

2835 Trauma Response
WW Norton & Company
500 5th Avenue
New York, NY 10110-54
212-354-2907
Fax: 212-869-0856
E-mail: admalmud@wwnorton.com

Drake McFeely, CEO

Different causes of psychological trauma and modes of recovery. *$22.36*

240 pages Year Founded: 1993

2836 Traumatic Events & Mental Health
Cambridge University Press
40 W 20th Street
New York, NY 10011-4211

212-924-3900
Fax: 212-691-3239
E-mail: marketing@cup.org
www.cup.org

2837 Treating Anxiety Disorders
Jossey-Bass Publishers
350 Sansome Street
5th Floor
San Francisco, CA 94104-1310
415-394-8677
800-956-7739
Fax: 800-605-2665
www.josseybass.com

$30.95

288 pages ISBN 0-787903-16-7

2838 Treating Anxiety Disorders with a Cognitive
New Harbinger Publications
5674 Shattuck Avenue
Oakland, CA 94609-1662
510-652-0215
800-748-6273
Fax: 510-652-5472
E-mail: customerservice@newharbinger.com
www.newharbinger.com

Matthew McKay, Owner

Behavioral Exposure Based Approach and the Eye Movement Technique comes with a fifty eight minute videotape and a fifty one page paperback manual. *$100.00*

Year Founded: 1998 ISBN 1-889287-02-4

2839 Treating Panic Disorder and Agoraphobia: A Step by Step Clinical Guide
New Harbinger Publications
5674 Shattuck Avenue
Oakland, CA 94609-1662
510-652-0215
800-748-6273
Fax: 510-652-5472
E-mail: customerservice@newharbinger.com
www.newharbinger.com

Matthew McKay, Owner

Treatment program covering breath control training, changing automatic thoughts and underlying beliefs. *$49.95*

296 pages Year Founded: 1997 ISBN 1-572240-84-9

2840 Treatment of Obsessive Compulsive Disorder
Guilford Publications
72 Spring Street
New York, NY 10012-4068
212-431-9800
800-365-7006
Fax: 212-966-6708
E-mail: info@guilford.com

Bob Matloff, President

Provides everything the mental health professional needs for working with clients who suffer from obsessions and compulsions. Supplies background by describing in detail

up-to-date clinically relevant information and a step-by-step guide for conducting behavioral treatment. *$39.95*

224 pages Year Founded: 1993 ISBN 0-898621-84-4

ADHD

2841 ADHD in Adolesents: Diagnosis and Treatment
Guilford Publications
72 Spring Street
New York, NY 10012-4068
212-431-9800
800-365-7006
Fax: 212-966-6708
E-mail: info@guilford.com

Bob Matloff, President

Practical reference with a down to earth approach to diagnosing and treatment of ADHD in adolescents. A structured intervention program with guidelines to using educational, psycholgical and medical components to help patients. Many reproducible handouts, checklists and rating scales. *$24.95*

461 pages Year Founded: 1999 ISBN 1-572305-45-2

2842 ADHD in Adulthood: Guide to Current Theory, Diagnosis and Treatment
Johns Hopkins University Press
2715 North Charles Street
Baltimore, MD 21218-4319
410-516-6900
800-537-5487
Fax: 410-516-6998

William Brody, President

Discusses how ADHD manifests itself in adult life and answers popular questions posed by physicians and by adults with ADHD. Provides health professionals with a practical approach for treatment and diagnosis in adult ADHD patients. *$49.95*

392 pages Year Founded: 1999 ISBN 0-801861-41-1

2843 All About ADHD: Complete Practical Guide for Classroom Teachers
ADD WareHouse
300 NW 70th Avenue
Suite 102
Plantation, FL 33317-2360
954-792-8944
800-233-9273
Fax: 954-792-8545
E-mail: sales@addwarehouse.com
www.addwarehouse.com

Harvey C Parker, Owner

Brings together both the art and science of effective teaching for students with ADHD using the Parallel Teaching Model as the base for blending behavior management and teaching, particularly in regular classroom settings. Real-life examples are used throughout the book and are intended to help you design strategies for you own classrooms to help your students be the best they can be. *$17.00*

175 pages

2844 Attention Deficit Disorder ADHD and ADD Syndromes
Pro-Ed Publications
8700 Shoal Creek Boulevard
Austin, TX 78757-6897
512-451-3246
800-897-3202
Fax: 512-451-8542
E-mail: info@proedinc.com

Donald D Hammill, Owner

This book enters its third edition with even more complete explanations of how ADHD and ADD interfere with: classroom learning, behavior at home, job performance, and social skills development. *$ 19.00*

216 pages Year Founded: 1998 ISBN 0-890797-42-0

2845 Attention Deficit Disorder and Learning Disabilities: Realities, Myths and Controversial Treatments
ADD WareHouse
300 NW 70th Avenue
Suite 102
Plantation, FL 33317-2360
954-792-8944
800-233-9273
Fax: 954-792-8545
E-mail: sales@addwarehouse.com
www.addwarehouse.com

Harvey C Parker, Owner

Designed to help parents and professionals recognize symptoms of learning disabilities and attentional disorders. Covers in detail conventional treatments that have been scientifically validated plus more controversial methods of treatment such as orthomolecular therapies, amino acid supplementation, dietary interventions, EEG biofeedback, cognitive therapy and visual training. *$13.00*

240 pages

2846 Attention Deficit/Hyperactivity Disorder
American Psychiatric Publishing, Inc.
1000 Wilson Boulevard
Suite 1825
Arlington, VA 22209-3901
703-907-7322
800-368-5777
Fax: 703-907-1091
E-mail: appi@psych.org
www.appi.org

Robert E Hales MD, Editor-in-Chief
Ron McMillen, Chief Executive Officer
John McDuffie, Editorial Director

Clinical Guide to Diagnosis and Treatment for Health and Mental Health Professionals making the proper diagnosis, and treatment strategies. *$29.95*

298 pages Year Founded: 1999 ISBN 0-880489-40-5

2847 Attention-Deficit Hyperactivity Disorder: A Handbook for Diagnosis and Treatment
Guilford Publications
72 Spring Street
New York, NY 10012-4068
212-431-9800
800-365-7006
Fax: 212-966-6708
E-mail: info@guilford.com

Bob Matloff, President

This second edition incorporates the latest finding on the nature, diagnosis, assessment and treatment of ADHD. Includes select chapters by seasoned colleagues covering their respective areas of expertise and providing clear guidelines for practice in clinical, school and community settings. *$56.95*

602 pages Year Founded: 1998 ISBN 1-572302-75-5

2848 Attention-Deficit/Hyperactivity Disorder in the Classroom
Pro-Ed Publications
8700 Shoal Creek Boulevard
Austin, TX 78757-6897
512-451-3246
800-897-3202
Fax: 512-451-8542
E-mail: info@proedinc.com

Donald D Hammill, Owner

Provides educators with a complete guide on how to deal effectively with students with attention deficits in their classroom. Emphasizes practical applications for teachers to use that will facilitate the success of students, both academically and socially, in a school setting. *$29.00*

291 pages Year Founded: 1998 ISBN 0-890796-65-3

2849 Family Therapy for ADHD: Treating Children, Adolescents and Adults
Guilford Publications
72 Spring Street
New York, NY 10012-4068
212-431-9800
800-365-7006
Fax: 212-966-6708
E-mail: info@guilford.com

Bob Matloff, President

ADHD affects the entire family. This book helps the clinician evaluate its impact on marital dynamics, parent/sibling/child relationships and the complex treatment of ADHD in a larger context. Includes session by session plans and clinical material. *$32.95*

270 pages Year Founded: 1999 ISBN 1-572304-38-3

2850 How to Operate an ADHD Clinic or Subspecialty Practice
ADD WareHouse
300 NW 70th Avenue
Suite 102
Plantation, FL 33317-2360
954-792-8944
800-233-9273

Fax: 954-792-8545
E-mail: sales@addwarehouse.com
www.addwarehouse.com

Harvey C Parker, Owner

This book goes beyond academic discussions of ADHD and gets down to how to establish and manage an ADHD practice. In addition to practice guidelines and suggestions, this guide presents a compendium of clinic forms and letters, interview formats, sample reports, tricks of the trade and resource listings, all of which will help you develop or refine your clinic/counseling operation. *$65.00*

325 pages

2851 Medications for Attention Disorders and Related Medical Problems: A Comprehensive Handbook
ADD WareHouse
300 NW 70th Avenue
Suite 102
Plantation, FL 33317-2360
954-792-8944
800-233-9273
Fax: 954-792-8545
E-mail: sales@addwarehouse.com
www.addwarehouse.com

Harvey C Parker, Owner

ADHD and ADD are medical conditions and often medical intervention is regarded by most experts as an essential component of the multimodal program for the treatment of these disorders. This text presents a comprehensive look at medications and their use in attention disorders. *$37.00*

420 pages

2852 Parenting a Child With Attention Deficit/Hyperactivity Disorder
Pro-Ed Publications
8700 Shoal Creek Boulevard
Austin, TX 78757-6897
512-451-3246
800-897-3202
Fax: 512-451-8542
E-mail: info@proedinc.com

Donald D Hammill, Owner

Offers proven parenting approaches for helping children between the ages of 5-11 years improve their behavior. *$29.00*

150 pages Year Founded: 1999 ISBN 0-890797-91-9

2853 Pretenders: Gifted People Who Have Difficulty Learning
High Tide Press
Ste 2n
2081 Calistoga Dr
New Lenox, IL 60451-4833
815-206-2054
888-487-7377
E-mail: managing.editor@hightidepress.com

Monica Regan, Managing Editor

Profiles of 8 adults with dyslexia and/or ADD with whom the author has worked. Informative, fascinating, at times heartbreaking, but ultimately inspiring. *$24.50*

177 pages ISBN 1-892696-06-1

Autism Spectrum Disorders

2854 Asperger Syndrome Diagnostic Scale (ASDS)
Pro-Ed
8700 Shoal Creek Boulevard
Austin, TX 78757-6897
512-451-3246
800-897-3202
Fax: 512-451-8542
E-mail: feedback@proedinc.com

Donald D Hammill, Owner
Stacey Bock
Richard Simpson

The ASDS is a quick, easy-to-use rating scale that helps determine whether a child has Asperger Syndrome. Anyone who knows the child or youth well can complete the scale. Parents, teachers, siblings, paraeducators, speech-language pathologists, psychologists, psyciatrists and other professionals can answer the 50 yes/no items in 10 to 15 minutes. *$100.00*

2855 Asperger Syndrome: a Practical Guide for Teachers
ADD WareHouse
300 NW 70th Avenue
Suite 102
Plantation, FL 33317-2360
954-792-8944
800-233-9273
Fax: 954-792-8545
E-mail: sales@addwarehouse.com
www.addwarehouse.com

Harvey C Parker, Owner

A clear and concise guide to effective classroom practice for teachers and support assistants working with children with Asperger Syndrome in school. The authors explain characteristics of children with Asperger Syndrome, discuss methods of assessment and offer practical strategies for effective classroom interventions. *$24.95*

90 pages

2856 Children and Youth with Asperger Syndrome
Program Development Associates
PO Box 2038
Syracuse, NY 13220-2038
315-452-0643
Fax: 315-452-0710
E-mail: info@disabilitytraining.com
www.disabilitytraining.com

Classroom teachers now get special information to accommodate students with Asperger Syndrome, who display symptoms similar to, but milder than, autism. Strategies include research-based instructional, behavioral and environmental modifications. *$35.95*

200 pages

Cognitive Disorders

2857 Cognitive Therapy in Practice
WW Norton & Company
500 5th Avenue
New York, NY 10110-54
212-354-2907
800-233-4830
Fax: 212-869-0856
E-mail: npd@wwnorton.com

Drake McFeely, CEO

Basic text for graduate studies in psychotherapy, psycholgy nursing social work and counseling. *$29.00*

224 pages Year Founded: 1989 ISBN 0-393700-77-1

2858 Geriatric Mental Health Care: A Treatment Guide for Health Professionals
Guilford Publications
72 Spring Street
New York, NY 10012-4068
212-431-9800
800-365-7006
Fax: 212-966-6708
E-mail: info@guilford.com

Bob Matloff, President

Designed for mental health practitioners and primary care providers without advanced training in geriatric psychiatry. Covers depression, anxiety, the dementias, psychosis, mania, sleep disturbances, personality and pain disorders, adapting principles, sexuality, elder issues, alcohol and substance abuse, suicide risk, consultation, legal and ethic issues, exercise and much more. *$39.00*

347 pages ISBN 1-572305-92-4

2859 Guidelines for the Treatment of Patients with Alzheimer's Disease and Other Dementias of Late Life
American Psychiatric Publishing, Inc.
1000 Wilson Boulevard
Suite 1825
Arlington, VA 22209-3901
703-907-7322
800-368-5777
Fax: 703-907-1091
E-mail: appi@psych.org
www.appi.org

Robert E Hales MD, Editor-in-Chief
Ron McMillen, Chief Executive Officer
John McDuffie, Editorial Director

Diagnosis and treatment strategies. *$22.50*

40 pages Year Founded: 1995 ISBN 0-890423-04-0

2860 Loss of Self: Family Resource for the Care of Alzheimer's Disease and Related Disorders
WW Norton & Company
500 5th Avenue
New York, NY 10110-54
212-354-2907
Fax: 212-869-0856
E-mail: admalmud@wwnorton.com

Drake McFeely, CEO

How to help a relative and also meet a family's own needs during the long and tragic period of care involved with Alzheimer's Disease. Challenges are more than medical and can be emotional, involve family conflict, sexuality, abuse, and eventually, dealing with death. As well as the emotional challenges, the latest treatments, drugs and diagnosis information, plus causes and preventative measures are included. *$27.95*

432 pages Year Founded: 2001 ISBN 0-393050-16-5

2861 Neurobiology of Primary Dementia
American Psychiatric Publishing, Inc.
1000 Wilson Boulevard
Suite 1825
Arlington, VA 22209-3901
703-907-7322
800-368-5777
Fax: 703-907-1091
E-mail: appi@psych.org
www.appi.org

Robert E Hales MD, Editor-in-Chief
Ron McMillen, Chief Executive Officer
John McDuffie, Editorial Director

Study of aging and Alzheimer's. Contains investigations of the basic neurobiologic aspects of the etiology of dementia, clear discussions of the diagnostic process with regard to imaging and other laboratory tests, psychopharmacologic treatment and genetic counseling. *$61.50*

440 pages Year Founded: 1998 ISBN 0-880489-15-4

2862 Strange Behavior Tales of Evolutionary Neurology
WW Norton & Company
500 5th Avenue
New York, NY 10110-54
212-354-2907
800-233-4830
Fax: 212-869-0856
E-mail: webmaster@wwnorton.com

Drake McFeely, CEO

Both educational and entertaining, the author presents an array of people with unusual problems who have one thing in common, brain disorder. Carefully constructed, this book outlines the functioning of the brain and evolution of language skills. *$13.95*

256 pages Year Founded: 2001 ISBN 0-393321-84-3

2863 The New Handbook of Cognitive Therapy Techniques
WW Norton & Company
500 5th Avenue
New York, NY 10110-54
212-354-2907
800-233-4830
Fax: 212-869-0856
E-mail: npb@wwnorton.com

Drake McFeely, CEO

Describes, explains, and demonstrates over a hundred cognitive therapy techniques, offering for each the theorretical basis, a thumbnail description of the method, case examples, and resources for further information.

ISBN 0-393703-13-4

2864 Treating Complex Cases: The Cognitive Behavioral Therapy Approach
John Wiley & Sons
605 3rd Avenue
New York, NY 10158-180
212-850-6301
E-mail: info@wiley.com
www.wiley.com

Nicholas Tarrierk, Editor
Adrian Wells, Editor
Gillian Haddock, Editor

This book brings together some of the most experiences and expert cognitive behavioral therapists to share their specialist experience of formulation and treatment of complex problems such as co-morbidity, psychotic conditions, and chronic conditions. The experienced clinician will find: evidence-based approaches to assessment and formulation of complex cases; a wide range of problems not restricted to disorder categories, including anger, low self-esteem, abuse and shame; a concern with the realities of clinical practice which involves complex cases that do not fit into simple case conceptualisations or diagnostic categories. Copyright 2000. *$80.00*

456 pages ISBN 0-471978-39-8

Conduct Disorder

2865 Behavioral Risk Management
Jossey-Bass Publishers
350 Sansome Street
5th Floor
San Francisco, CA 94104-1310
415-394-8677
800-956-7739
Fax: 800-605-2665
www.josseybass.com

Learn to identify potential mental health and behavioral problems on the job and apply effective intervention strategies for behavioral risk. *$41.95*

432 pages ISBN 0-787902-20-9

2866 Beyond Behavior Modification: Cognitive-Behavioral Approach to Behavior Management in the School
Pro-Ed Publications
8700 Shoal Creek Boulevard
Austin, TX 78757-6897
512-451-3246
800-897-3202
Fax: 512-451-8542
E-mail: info@proedinc.com

Donald D Hammill, Owner

Focuses on traditional behavior modification, and presents a social learning theory approach. *$39.00*

643 pages Year Founded: 1995 ISBN 0-890796-63-7

2867 Inclusion Strategies for Students with Learning and Behavior Problems
Pro-Ed Publications
8700 Shoal Creek Boulevard
Austin, TX 78757-6897
512-451-3246
800-897-3202
Fax: 512-451-8542
E-mail: info@proedinc.com

Donald D Hammill, Owner

Provides the components necessary to implement successful inclusion by presenting the experience of those directly impacted by inclusion: an individual with a disability; parents of a student with a disbility; teachers who implement inclusion; and researchers of best practices. Integrates theory and practice in an easy, how-to manner. *$36.00*

416 pages Year Founded: 1997 ISBN 0-890796-98-X

2868 Outrageous Behavior Mood: Handbook of Strategic Interventions for Managing Impossible Students
Pro-Ed Publications
8700 Shoal Creek Boulevard
Austin, TX 78757-6897
512-451-3246
800-897-3202
Fax: 512-451-8542
E-mail: info@proedinc.com

Donald D Hammill, Owner

This handbook is for educators who have had success in managing difficult students. Introduces such methods as planned confusion, disruptive word pictures, unconscious suggestion, double-bind predictions, off the wall interpretations, and even some straight faced paradoxical assignments. *$26.00*

154 pages Year Founded: 1999 ISBN 0-890798-17-6

Dissociative Disorders

2869 Dissociative Identity Disorder: Diagnosis, Clinical Features, and Treatment of Multiple Personality
John Wiley & Sons
605 3rd Avenue
New York, NY 10158-180
212-850-6301
E-mail: info@wiley.com

Comprehensive and interesting, this account of the history of MPD dispells many myths and presents new insight into the treatment of MPD. Perfect for sexual abuse clinics, child abuse agencies, correctional facilities and clinicians of all fields. *$64.50*

Year Founded: 1996 ISBN 0-471132-65-9

2870 Handbook of Dissociation: Theoretical, Empirical, and Clinical Perspectives
Kluwer Academic/Plenum Publishers
233 Spring Street
New York, NY 10013-1522
212-242-1490

Covers both current and emerging theories, research and treatment of dissociative phenomena. Discusses historic, epidemiologic, phenomenologic, etiologic, normative and cross-cultural dimensions of dissociation, providing an empirical foundation for the last chapters. Eight case studies apply dissociation theory and research to specific treatment modalities. *$132.00*

615 pages Year Founded: 1996 ISBN 0-306451-50-6

2871 Rebuilding Shattered Lives: Responsible Treatment of Complex Post-Traumatic and Dissociative Disorders
John Wiley & Sons
605 3rd Avenue
New York, NY 10158-180
212-850-6301
E-mail: info@wiley.com

The most up-to-date, integrative and emperically sound account of trauma theory and practice availible. Based on more than a decade of clinical research and treatment experience at the Harvard Medical School, this comprehensive and nontechnical text offers a stage oriented approach to understanding and treating complex and difficult traumatized patients, integrating modern trauma theory with traditional theraputic interventions. *$47.50*

256 pages Year Founded: 1998 ISBN 0-471247-32-4

Eating Disorders

2872 Biting The Hand That Starves You: Inspiring Resistance to Anorexia/Bulimia
WW Norton & Company
500 5th Avenue
New York, NY 10110-54
212-354-2907
800-233-4830
Fax: 212-869-0856
E-mail: npb@wwnorton.com

Drake McFeely, CEO

Details a unique way of thinking and speaking about anorexia/bulimia (a/b), by having conversations with insiders in which the problem is viewed as an external influence rather than a part of the person. Coercion is sidestepped in favor of practices that are collaborative, accountable, and spirit-nurturing.

ISBN 0-393703-37-1

2873 Drug Therpay and Eating Disorders
Mason Crest Publishers
370 Reed Road
Suite 302
Broomall, PA 19008-4017
610-543-6200
866-627-2665
Fax: 610-543-3878

E-mail: dtaylor@masoncrest.com
www.masoncrest.com

Provides a clear, concise account of the history, symptoms, and current treatment of anorexia nervosa and bulimia nervosa. It is estimated the eating disorders affect five million Americans each year, and many more millions among other nations.

ISBN 1-590845-65-X

2874 Handbook of Treatment for Eating Disorders
Guilford Publications
72 Spring Street
New York, NY 10012-4068
212-431-9800
800-365-7006
Fax: 212-966-6708
E-mail: info@guilford.com

Bob Matloff, President

Includes coverage of binge eating and examines pharmacological as well as therapeutic approaches to eating disorders. Presents cognitive behavioral, psychoeducational, interpersonal, family, feminist, group and psychodynamic approaches, as well as the basics of pharmacological management. Features strategies for handling sexual abuse, substance abuse, concurrent medical conditions, personality disorder, prepubertal eating disorders and patients who refuse therapy. *$56.95*

540 pages Year Founded: 1997 ISBN 1-572301-86-4

2875 Interpersonal Psychotherapy
American Psychiatric Publishing, Inc.
1000 Wilson Boulevard
Suite 1825
Arlington, VA 22209-3901
703-907-7322
800-368-5777
Fax: 703-907-1091
E-mail: appi@psych.org
www.appi.org

Robert E Hales MD, Editor-in-Chief
Ron McMillen, Chief Executive Officer
John McDuffie, Editorial Director

An overview of interpersonal psychotherapy for depression, preventative treatment for depression, bulimia nervosa and HIV positive men and women. *$26.00*

156 pages Year Founded: 1998 ISBN 0-880488-36-0

2876 Sexual Abuse and Eating Disorders
200 E Joppa Road
Suite 207
Baltimore, MD 21286-3107
410-825-8888
888-825-8249
Fax: 410-337-0747
E-mail: sidran@sidran.org
www.sidran.org

This is the first book to explore the complex relationship between sexual abuse and eating disorders. Sexual abuse is both an extreme boundary violation and a disruption of attachment and bonding; victims of such abuse are likely to exhibit symptoms of self injury, including eating disorders.

This volume is a discussion of the many ways that sexual abuse and eating disorders are related, also has accounts by a survivor of both. Investigates the prevalence of sexual abuse amoung individuals with eating disorders. Also examines how a history of sexual violence can serve as a predictor of subsequent problems with food. Looks at related social factors, reviews trauma based theories, more controversial territory and discusses delayed memory versus false memory. *$34.95*

228 pages

Gender Identification Disorder

2877 Gender Loving Care
WW Norton & Company
500 5th Avenue
New York, NY 10110-54
212-354-2907
Fax: 212-869-0856
E-mail: admalmud@wwnorton.com

Drake McFeely, CEO

Understanding and treating gender identity disorder, especially transexuals, who may feel stuck in the wrong-sexed body. *$ 25.00*

196 pages Year Founded: 1999 ISBN 0-393703-40-5

2878 Homosexuality and American Psychiatry: The Politics of Diagnosis
Princeton University Press
Princeton University
Princeton, NJ 08544-1
800-777-4726
Fax: 800-999-1958
www.pup.princeton.edu

$18.00

249 pages Year Founded: 1987 ISBN 0-691028-37-0

2879 Identity Without Selfhood
Cambridge University Press
40 W 20th Street
New York, NY 10011-4211
212-924-3900
Fax: 212-691-3239
E-mail: marketing@cup.org
www.cup.org

Mariam Fraser

Situated at the crossroads of feminism, queer theory and poststructuralist debates around identity, this is a book that shows how key Western concepts such as individuality constrain attempts to deconstruct the self and prevent bisexuality being understood as an identity. *$64.95*

226 pages Year Founded: 1999

2880 Principles and Practice of Sex Therapy
Guilford Publications
72 Spring Street
New York, NY 10012-4068
212-431-9800
800-365-7006

Fax: 212-966-6708
E-mail: info@guilford.com

Bob Matloff, President

Many new developments in theory, diagnosis and treatment of sexual disorders have occured in the past decade. The authors set clear guidlines for assessment and treatment with fresh clinical material. A text for professionals and students in a wide range of mental health fields; sexual disorders, male and female, paraphilias, gender identity disorders, vasoactive drugs and more are covered. *$50.00*

518 pages Year Founded: 2000 ISBN 1-572305-74-6

2881 Psychoanalytic Therapy & the Gay Man
Analytic Press
101 W Street
Hillsdale, NJ 07642-1421
201-358-9477
800-926-6579
Fax: 201-358-4700
E-mail: TAP@analyticpress.com
www.analyticpress.com

Paul E Stepansky PhD, Managing Director
John Kerr PhD, Sr Editor

Explores of the subjectivities of gay men in psychoanalytic psychotherapy. It is a vitally human testament to the richly varied inner experiences of gay men. Offers that sexual identity, which encompass a spectrum of possibilities for any gay man, must be addressed in an atmosphere of honest encounter that allows not only for exploration of conflict and dissasociation but also for restitutive conformation of the patient's right to be himself. Available in hardcover. *$55.00*

384 pages Year Founded: 1998 ISBN 0-881632-08-2

2882 Transvestites and Transsexuals: Toward a Theory of Cross-Gender Behavior
Kluwer Academic/Plenum Publishers
233 Spring Street
New York, NY 10013-1522
212-242-1490

This book proposes a theory of transvestism and transexualism presented with a large amount of important raw data collected from interviews with one hundred ten transvestites and thirty five of their wives. *$54.00*

266 pages Year Founded: 1988 ISBN 0-306428-78-4

Impulse Control Disorders

2883 Abusive Personality: Violence and Control in Intimate Relationships
Guilford Publications
72 Spring Street
New York, NY 10012-4068
212-431-9800
800-365-7006
Fax: 212-966-6708
E-mail: info@guilford.com

Bob Matloff, President

A study of domestic violence, especially male perpetrators. *$26.95*

214 pages Year Founded: 1998 ISBN 1-572303-70-0

2884 Coping With Self-Mutilation: a Helping Book for Teens Who Hurt Themselves
Rosen Publishing Group
29 E 21st Street
New York, NY 10010-6209
212-777-3017
800-237-9932
Fax: 212-777-0277
E-mail: info@rosenpub.com
www.rosenpublishing.com

Roger Rosen, President

Examines the reasons for this phenomenon, and ways one might seek help. *$17.95*

Year Founded: 1999 ISBN 0-823925-59-5

2885 Dealing with Anger Problems:
Rational-Emotive Therapeutic Interventions
Professional Resource Press
PO Box 15560
Sarasota, FL 34277-1560
941-343-9601
800-443-3364
Fax: 941-343-9201
E-mail: orders@prpress.com
www.prpress.com

Debra Fink, Managing Editor

Demonstrates ways to apply rational-emotive therapy techniques to help your clients control their anger. Offers step-by-step anger control treatment program that includes a variety of cognitive, emotive, and behavioral homework assignments, and procedures for modifying behaviors and facilitating change. *$11.95*

68 pages Year Founded: 1990 ISBN 0-943158-59-1

2886 Domestic Violence 2000: Integrated Skills Program for Men
WW Norton & Company
500 5th Avenue
New York, NY 10110-54
212-354-2907
Fax: 212-869-0856
E-mail: admalmud@wwnorton.com

Drake McFeely, CEO

Various theories are examined to deal with this difficult social problem. For group classes. *$23.20*

224 pages Year Founded: 1999 ISSN 70314-2

2887 Sex Murder and Sex Aggression:
Phenomenology Psychopathology,
Psychodynamics and Prognosis
Charles C Thomas Publisher
2600 S 1st Street
Springfield, IL 62704-4730
217-789-8980
800-258-8980
Fax: 217-789-9130

E-mail: books@ccthomas.com
www.ccthomas.com

Michael P Thomas, President

By Eugene Revitch, Robert Wood Johnson School of Medicine, Piscataway, New Jersey, and Louis B Schlesinger, New Jersey Medical School, Newark. With a foreword by Robert R Hazelwood. Contents: The Place of Gynocide and Sexual Aggression in the Classification of Crime; Catathymic Gynocide; Compulsive Gynocide; Psychodynamics, Psychopathology and Differential Diagnosis; Prognostic Considerations. *$43.95*

152 pages Year Founded: 1989 ISSN 0-398-06346-XISBN 0-398055-56-4

2888 Teaching Behavioral Self Control to Students
Pro-Ed Publications
8700 Shoal Creek Boulevard
Austin, TX 78757-6897
512-451-3246
800-897-3202
Fax: 512-451-8542
E-mail: info@proedinc.com

Donald D Hammill, Owner

Demonstrates how teachers, counselors and parents can help children of all ages and ability levels to modify their own behavior. Clear step-by-step methods describe how common childhood problems can be solved by helping children become more responsible and independent. *$ 21.00*

122 pages Year Founded: 1995 ISBN 0-890796-17-3

Mood Disorders

2889 Active Treatment of Depression
WW Norton & Company
500 5th Avenue
New York, NY 10110-54
212-354-2907
Fax: 212-869-0856
E-mail: admalmud@wwnorton.com

Drake McFeely, CEO

A candid discussion on depression and effective, hopeful therapy strategies. *$35.00*

272 pages Year Founded: 2001 ISSN 70322-3

2890 Antidepressant Fact Book: What Your Doctor Won't Tell You About Prozac, Zoloft, Paxil, Celexa and Luvox
Perseus Books Group
550 Central Avenue
Boulder, CO 80301

800-386-5656
Fax: 720-406-7336
E-mail: westview.orders@perseusbooks.com
www.perseusbooksgroup.com

What antidepressants will and won't treat, documented side and withdrawl effects, plus what parents need to know about teenagers and antidepressants. The author has been a medical expert in many court cases invlolving the use and misuse of psychoactive drugs. *$13.00*

240 pages Year Founded: 2001 ISBN 0-738204-51-X

2891 Cognitive Therapy of Depression
Guilford Publications
72 Spring Street
New York, NY 10012-4068
212-431-9800
800-365-7006
Fax: 212-966-6708
E-mail: info@guilford.com

Bob Matloff, President

Shows how psychotherapists can effectively treat depressive disorders. Case examples illustrate a wide range of strategies and techniques. Chapter topics include the role of emotions in cognitive therapy, application of behavioral techniques and cognitive therapy and antidepressant medications. Hardcover. Paperback also available. *$ 46.95*

425 pages Year Founded: 1979 ISBN 0-898620-00-7

2892 Concise Guide to Mood Disorders
American Psychiatric Publishing, Inc.
1000 Wilson Boulevard
Suite 1825
Arlington, VA 22209-3901
703-907-7322
800-368-5777
Fax: 703-907-1091
E-mail: appi@psych.org
www.appi.org

Robert E Hales MD, Editor-in-Chief
Ron McMillen, Chief Executive Officer
John McDuffie, Editorial Director

Designed for daily use in the clinical setting, the Concise Guide to Mood Disorders is a fingertip library of the latest information, easy to understand and quick to access. This practical reference summarizes everything a clinician needs to know to diagnose and treat unipolar and bipolar mood disorders. *$29.95*

320 pages Year Founded: 2002 ISBN 1-585620-56-4

2893 Concise Guide to Women's Mental Health
American Psychiatric Publishing, Inc.
1000 Wilson Boulevard
Suite 1825
Arlington, VA 22209-3901
703-907-7322
800-368-5777
Fax: 703-907-1091
E-mail: appi@psych.org
www.appi.org

Robert E Hales MD, Editor-in-Chief
Ron McMillen, Chief Executive Officer
John McDuffie, Editorial Director

Examines the biological, psychological, and sociocultural factors that influence a woman's mental health and often contribute to psychiatric disorders. Supplies clinicians with important information on gender related differences on differential diagnosis, case formulation and treatment planning. Topics include premenstrual dysphoric disorder,

hormonal contraception and effects on mood, psychiatric disorders in pregnancy, postpartum psychiatric disorders and perimenopause and menopause. *$21.95*

187 pages Year Founded: 1997 ISBN 0-880483-43-1

2894 Depression & Antidepressants
Madison Institute of Medicine
7617 Mineral Point Road
Suite 300
Madison, WI 53717-1623
608-827-2470
E-mail: mim@miminc.org
www.factsforhealth.org

Margarett Baudhuin, Manager

A concise, up-to-date guide to the wide range of medications available today for the treatment of depression. *$5.95*

48 pages ISBN 1-890802-19-0

2895 Depression in Context: Strategies for Guided Action
WW Norton & Company
500 5th Avenue
New York, NY 10110-54
212-354-2907
Fax: 212-869-0856
E-mail: admalmud@wwnorton.com

Drake McFeely, CEO

Description of Behavioral Activation, a new treatment for Depression. *$32.00*

224 pages Year Founded: 2001 ISSN 70350-9

2896 Evaluation and Treatment of Postpartum Emotional Disorders
Professional Resource Press
PO Box 15560
Sarasota, FL 34277-1560
941-343-9601
800-443-3364
Fax: 941-343-9201
E-mail: orders@prpress.com
www.prpress.com

Debra Fink, Managing Editor

Teaches how to recognize and treat postpartum emotional disorders. Procedures for clinical assessment, psychotherapeutic interventions, and medical - psychiatric treatments are described. *$ 13.95*

110 pages Year Founded: 1997 ISBN 1-568870-24-8

2897 Handbook of Depression
Guilford Publications
72 Spring Street
New York, NY 10012-4068
212-431-9800
800-365-7006
Fax: 212-966-6708
E-mail: info@guilford.com

Bob Matloff, President

Brings together well-known authorities who address the need for a comprehensive review of the most current information available on depression. Surveys current theories and treatment models, covering both what the MD and non-MD needs to know. *$65.00*

628 pages Year Founded: 1995 ISBN 0-898628-41-5

2898 Postpartum Mood Disorders
American Psychiatric Publishing, Inc.
1000 Wilson Boulevard
Suite 1825
Arlington, VA 22209-3901
703-907-7322
800-368-5777
Fax: 703-907-1091
E-mail: appi@psych.org
www.appi.org

Robert E Hales MD, Editor-in-Chief
Ron McMillen, Chief Executive Officer
John McDuffie, Editorial Director

$38.50

280 pages Year Founded: 1999 ISBN 0-880489-29-4

2899 Premenstrual Dysphoric Disorder: A Guide
Madison Institute of Medicine
7617 Mineral Point Road
Suite 300
Madison, WI 53717-1623
608-827-2470
E-mail: mim@miminc.org
www.factsforhealth.org

Margarett Baudhuin, Manager

This new 41 page booklet explains what Premenstrual Dysphoric Disorder (PMDD) is, how it is diagnosed, how it differs from PMS, and how it is treated. Anyone seeking information about PMDD and its treatments will find this concise guide of great benefit in their search for accurate, up-to-date information. *$5.95*

41 pages

2900 Scientific Foundations of Cognitive Theory and Therapy of Depression
John Wiley & Sons
605 3rd Avenue
New York, NY 10158-180
212-850-6301
E-mail: info@wiley.com

A synthesis of decades of research and practice, this semminal book presents and critically evaluates this scientific and emprical status of co author Aaron Beck's revised cognitive theory and therapy of depression. The authors explore the evolution of cognitive theory and therapy of depression and discuss the future directions for the treatment of depression.

400 pages Year Founded: 1999

2901 Symptoms of Depression
John Wiley & Sons
605 3rd Avenue
New York, NY 10158-180
212-850-6301
E-mail: info@wiley.com

336 pages Year Founded: 1993

2902 Treating Depressed Children: A Therapeutic Manual of Proven Cognitive Behavioral Techniques
New Harbinger Publications
5674 Shattuck Avenue
Oakland, CA 94609-1662
510-652-0215
800-748-6273
Fax: 510-652-5472
E-mail: customerservice@newharbinger.com
www.newharbinger.com

Matthew McKay, Owner

A full twelve session treatment program incorporates cartoons and role playing games to help children recognize emotions, change negative thoughts, gain confidence and learn crucial interpersonal skills. *$49.95*

160 pages Year Founded: 1996 ISBN 1-572240-61-X

2903 Treating Depression
Jossey-Bass Publishers
350 Sansome Street
5th Floor
San Francisco, CA 94104-1310
415-394-8677
800-956-7739
Fax: 800-605-2665
www.josseybass.com

$27.95

244 pages ISBN 0-787915-85-8

2904 Treatment of Recurrent Depression
American Psychiatric Publishing, Inc.
1000 Wilson Boulevard
Suite 1825
Arlington, VA 22209-3901
703-907-7322
800-368-5777
Fax: 703-907-1091
E-mail: appi@psych.org
www.appi.org

Robert E Hales MD, Editor-in-Chief
Ron McMillen, Chief Executive Officer
John McDuffie, Editorial Director

Five topics covered are, Lifetime Impact of Gender on Recurrent Major Depressive Disorder in Women, Treatment Stategies, Prevention of Recurrences in Bipolar Patients, Potential Applications and Updated Recommondations. *$29.95*

208 pages Year Founded: 2001 ISBN 1-585620-25-4

Personality Disorders

2905 Bad Boys, Bad Men: Confronting Antisocial Personality Disorder
Oxford University Press
198 Madison Avenue
New York, NY 10016-4341
212-726-6400
800-451-7556

Michael Cunningham, Manager

This book examines the mental condition characterized by a serial pattern of bad behavior. Draws on case studies, scientific data, and current events. *$25.00*

256 pages Year Founded: 1999 ISBN 0-195121-13-9

2906 Biological Basis of Personality
Charles C Thomas Publisher
2600 S 1st Street
Springfield, IL 62704-4730
217-789-8980
800-258-8980
Fax: 217-789-9130
E-mail: books@ccthomas.com
www.ccthomas.com

Michael P Thomas, President

$70.95

420 pages Year Founded: 1977 ISBN 0-398005-38-9

2907 Biology of Personality Disorders
American Psychiatric Publishing, Inc.
1000 Wilson Boulevard
Suite 1825
Arlington, VA 22209-3901
703-907-7322
800-368-5777
Fax: 703-907-1091
E-mail: appi@psych.org
www.appi.org

Robert E Hales MD, Editor-in-Chief
Ron McMillen, Chief Executive Officer
John McDuffie, Editorial Director

Content topics include neurotransmitter function in personality disorders, new biological researcher strategies for personality disorders, the genetics psychobiology of the seven - factor model of personality disorders, and significance of biological research for a biopsychosocial model of personality disorders. *$25.00*

166 pages Year Founded: 1998 ISBN 0-880488-35-2

2908 Borderline Personality Disorder: A Therapist Guide to Taking Control
WW Norton & Company
500 5th Avenue
New York, NY 10110-54
212-354-2907
800-233-4830
Fax: 212-869-0856
E-mail: npb@wwnorton.com

Drake McFeely, CEO

From identification to relapse prevention, this guide helps therapists manage a patient's treatment for the rather com-

plex problem of Borderline Personality Disorder, an often difficult and sometimes life threatening condition. *$27.50*

224 pages Year Founded: 2002 ISBN 0-393703-52-5

2909 Borderline Personality Disorder: Tailoring the Psychotherapy to the Patient
American Psychiatric Publishing, Inc.
1000 Wilson Boulevard
Suite 1825
Arlington, VA 22209-3901
703-907-7322
800-368-5777
Fax: 703-907-1091
E-mail: appi@psych.org
www.appi.org

Robert E Hales MD, Editor-in-Chief
Ron McMillen, Chief Executive Officer
John McDuffie, Editorial Director

$34.00

256 pages Year Founded: 1996 ISBN 0-880486-89-9

2910 Cognitive Therapy for Personality Disorders: a Schema-Focused Approach
Professional Resource Press
PO Box 15560
Sarasota, FL 34277-1560
941-343-9601
800-443-3364
Fax: 941-343-9201
E-mail: orders@prpress.com
www.prpress.com

Debra Fink, Managing Editor

A guide to treating the most difficult cases in your practice: personality disorders and other chronic, self - defeating problems. Contains rationale, theory, practical applications, and active cognitive behavioral techniques. *$13.95*

96 pages Year Founded: 1999 ISBN 1-568870-47-7

2911 Cognitive Therapy of Personality Disorders
Guilford Publications
72 Spring Street
New York, NY 10012-4068
212-431-9800
800-365-7006
Fax: 212-966-6708
E-mail: info@guilford.com

Bob Matloff, President

Focuses on the use of cognitive therapy to treat people with personality disorders who do not usually engage in therapy. Emanates the research and practical experience of Beck and his associates and is the first to focus specifically on this diverse and clinically demanding population. Case vignettes are used throughout. *$43.00*

396 pages Year Founded: 1990 ISBN 0-989624-34-7

2912 Dealing With the Problem of Low Self-Esteem: Common Characteristics and Treatment
Charles C Thomas Publisher
2600 S 1st Street
Springfield, IL 62704-4730
217-789-8980
800-258-8980
Fax: 217-789-9130
E-mail: books@ccthomas.com
www.ccthomas.com

Michael P Thomas, President

Considers the practice of psychotherapy from the self-esteem perspective. Describes the common characteristics of low self-esteem that are manifested in clients with diverse problems; focuses on the functions the therapist performs in addressing these characteristics. The third is to consider the modalities of treatment through which the therapist delivers these therapeutic functions. *$ 48.95*

228 pages Year Founded: 1995 ISSN 0-398-05951-9ISBN 0-398059-36-5

2913 Disorders of Personality: DSM-IV and Beyond
John Wiley & Sons
605 3rd Avenue
New York, NY 10158-180
212-850-6301
E-mail: info@wiley.com

Clarifies the distinctions between the vast array of personality disorders and helps clinicians make accurate diagnoses; thoroughly updated to incorporate the recent change in the DSM - IV. Guides the clinicians throught the intricate maze of personality disorders, with special attention on changes in their conceptualization over the last decade. DSM-V due out in 2013 *$85.00*

Year Founded: 1995 ISBN 0-471011-86-X

2914 Group Exercises for Enhancing Social Skills & Self-Esteem
Professional Resource Press
PO Box 15560
Sarasota, FL 34277-1560
941-343-9601
800-443-3364
Fax: 941-343-9201
E-mail: orders@prpress.com
www.prpress.com

Debra Fink, Managing Editor

Includes exercises for enhancing self-esteem utilizing proven social, emotional, and cognitive skill-building techniques. These exercises are useful in therapeutic, psychoeducational, and recreational settings. *$24.95*

150 pages Year Founded: 1996 ISBN 1-568870-20-5

2915 Personality Characteristics of the Personality Disordered
John Wiley & Sons
605 3rd Avenue
New York, NY 10158-180
212-850-6301
E-mail: info@wiley.com

340 pages Year Founded: 1995

2916 Personality Disorders and Culture: Clinical and Conceptual Interactions
John Wiley & Sons
605 3rd Avenue
New York, NY 10158-180
212-850-6301
E-mail: info@wiley.com

Discusses two of the most timely and complex areas in mental health, personality disorders and the impact of cultural variables. Treading on the timeless nature - nurture debate, it suggests that social variables have a dramatic impact on the definition, development, and manifestation of personality disorders.

310 pages Year Founded: 1998

2917 Personality and Stress: Individual Differences in the Stress Process
John Wiley & Sons
605 3rd Avenue
New York, NY 10158-180
212-850-6301
E-mail: info@wiley.com

302 pages Year Founded: 1991

2918 Psychotherapy for Borderline Personality
John Wiley & Sons
605 3rd Avenue
New York, NY 10158-180
212-850-6301
E-mail: info@wiley.com

Based on the work of a research team, this manual offers techniques and strategies for treating patients with Borderline Personality Disorder using Transference Focused Psychology. Provides therapists with an overall strategy for treating BPD patients and helpful tactics for working with individual patients on a session by session basis.

400 pages Year Founded: 1999

2919 Role of Sexual Abuse in the Etiology of Borderline Personality Disorder
200 E Joppa Road
Suite 207
Baltimore, MD 21286-3107
410-825-8888
888-825-8249
Fax: 410-337-0747
E-mail: sidran@sidran.org
www.sidran.org

Presenting the latest generation of research findings about the impact of traumatic abuse on the development of BPD. This book focuses on the theoretical basis of BPD, including topics such as childhood factors associated with the development, the relationship of child sexual abuse to dissociation and self mutilation, severity of childhood abuse, borderline symptoms and family environment. Twenty six contributors cover every aspect of BPD as it relates to childhood sexual abuse. *$42.00*

248 pages

2920 Shorter Term Treatments for Borderline Personality Disorders
New Harbinger Publications
5674 Shattuck Avenue
Oakland, CA 94609-1662
510-652-0215
800-748-6273
Fax: 510-652-5472
E-mail: customerservice@newharbinger.com
www.newharbinger.com

Matthew McKay, Owner

This guide offers approaches designed to help clients stabilize emotions, decrease vulnerability and work toward a more adaptive day to day functioning. *$49.95*

184 pages Year Founded: 1997 ISBN 1-572240-92-X

2921 Treating Difficult Personality Disorders
Jossey-Bass Publishers
350 Sansome Street
5th Floor
San Francisco, CA 94104-1310
415-394-8677
800-956-7739
Fax: 800-605-2665
www.josseybass.com

In this essential resource, experts in the field provide the most current information for the successful assessment and clinical treatment of this challenging client population. This book presents flexible treatment options for clients suffering from borderline, narcissistic, and antisocial personality disorders. *$28.95*

288 pages ISBN 0-787903-15-9

Psychosomatic (Somatizing) Disorders

2922 Anatomy of a Psychiatric Illness: Healing the Mind and the Brain
American Psychiatric Publishing, Inc.
1000 Wilson Boulevard
Suite 1825
Arlington, VA 22209-3901
703-907-7322
800-368-5777
Fax: 703-907-1091
E-mail: appi@psych.org
www.appi.org

Robert E Hales MD, Editor-in-Chief
Ron McMillen, Chief Executive Officer
John McDuffie, Editorial Director

  $22.95

232 pages Year Founded: 1993

2923 Concise Guide to Neuropsychiatry and Behavioral Neurology
American Psychiatric Publishing, Inc.
1000 Wilson Boulevard
Suite 1825
Arlington, VA 22209-3901
703-907-7322
800-368-5777
Fax: 703-907-1091
E-mail: appi@psych.org
www.appi.org

Robert E Hales MD, Editor-in-Chief
Ron McMillen, Chief Executive Officer
John McDuffie, Editorial Director

Provides brief synopsis of the major neuropsychiatric and neurobehavioral syndromes, discusses their clinical assessment, and provides guidelines for management. *$21.00*

368 pages Year Founded: 1995 ISBN 0-880483-43-1

2924 Concise Guide to Psychodynamic Psychotherapy: Principles and Techniques in the Era of Managed Care
American Psychiatric Publishing, Inc.
1000 Wilson Boulevard
Suite 1825
Arlington, VA 22209-3901
703-907-7322
800-368-5777
Fax: 703-907-1091
E-mail: appi@psych.org
www.appi.org

Robert E Hales MD, Editor-in-Chief
Ron McMillen, Chief Executive Officer
John McDuffie, Editorial Director

Thoroughly updated coverage of all the major principles and important issues in psychodynamic psychotherapy and issues not commonly addressed in the standard training curriculum, including the office setting, suicidal and dangerous patients, and what to do when the therapist makes an error. *$21.00*

272 pages Year Founded: 1998 ISBN 0-880483-47-4

2925 Functional Somatic Syndromes
Cambridge University Press
40 W 20th Street
New York, NY 10011-4211
212-924-3900
Fax: 212-691-3239
E-mail: marketing@cup.org
www.cup.org

2926 Manual of Panic: Focused Psychodynamic Psychotherapy
American Psychiatric Publishing, Inc.
1000 Wilson Boulevard
Suite 1825
Arlington, VA 22209-3901
703-907-7322
800-368-5777
Fax: 703-907-1091

E-mail: appi@psych.org
www.appi.org
Robert E Hales MD, Editor-in-Chief
Ron McMillen, Chief Executive Officer
John McDuffie, Editorial Director

A psychodynamic formulation applicable to many or most patients with Axis 1 panic disorders. *$28.00*

112 pages Year Founded: 1997 ISBN 0-880488-71-9

2927 Munchausen Syndrome by Proxy: Issues in Diagnosis and Treatment
Lexington Books
4501 Forbes Boulevard
Suite 200
Lanham, MD 20706-4346
301-459-3365
www.nbooks.com

AV Levin, Editor
MS Sheridan, Editor

Reference/Resource material for professionals.

Year Founded: 1995

2928 Munchausen by Proxy Syndrome: Misunderstood Child Abuse
Sage Publications
2455 Teller Road
Thousand Oaks, CA 91320-2234
805-499-0721
800-818-7243
Fax: 805-499-0871
www.pub.com

Blaise R Simqu, CEO
Deborah O Day

Professional reference/resource book

Year Founded: 1998

2929 Munchausen by Proxy: Identification, Intervention, and Case Management
Haworth Press
10 Alice Street
Binghamton, NY 13904-1503

800-429-6784
Fax: 800-895-0582
E-mail: getinfo@haworthpress.com
www.haworthpress.com

Louisa J Lasher, Author
Mary S Sheridan, Author

A step-by-step guide to help identify and manage cases of this unique form of child maltreatment. *$59.95*

384 pages Year Founded: 2004 ISBN 0-789012-17-0

2930 Somatization, Physical Symptoms and Psychological Illness
American Psychiatric Publishing, Inc.
1000 Wilson Boulevard
Suite 1825
Arlington, VA 22209-3901

703-907-7322
800-368-5777
Fax: 703-907-1091
E-mail: appi@psych.org
www.appi.org

Robert E Hales MD, Editor-in-Chief
Ron McMillen, Chief Executive Officer
John McDuffie, Editorial Director
  $99.95

351 pages Year Founded: 1990 ISBN 0-632028-39-4

2931 Somatoform Dissociation: Phenomena, Measurement, and Theoretical Issues
WW Norton & Company
500 5th Avenue
New York, NY 10110-54
212-354-2907
800-233-4830
Fax: 212-869-0856
E-mail: npb@wwnorton.com

Drake McFeely, CEO

In this first North Americacn edition of his work, Nijenhuis expands upon his theory of somatoform dissociation by providing two new chapters-one on dissociation and the re-call of sexual abuse and a second on the phycometric characteristics of the Traumatic Experiences Checklist (TEC).

ISBN 0-393704-60-2

2932 Somatoform and Factitious Disorders
American Psychiatric Publishing, Inc.
1000 Wilson Boulevard
Suite 1825
Arlington, VA 22209-3901
703-907-7322
800-368-5777
Fax: 703-907-1091
E-mail: appi@psych.org
www.appi.org

Robert E Hales MD, Editor-in-Chief
Ron McMillen, Chief Executive Officer
John McDuffie, Editorial Director

Consise yet thorough, this book covers Factitious disorders, Somatization disorder, Conversion disorder, Hypochondriasis and Body dysmorphic disorder. Explores the latest on these conditions and emphasises the need for further research to improve patient treament and understanding. *$29.95*

208 pages Year Founded: 2001 ISBN 1-585620-29-7

Schizophrenia

2933 Behavioral High-Risk Paradigm in Psychopathology
Springer-Verlag New York
175 5th Avenue
New York, NY 10010-7703
212-477-8200
800-777-4643
Fax: 212-473-6272
E-mail: custserv@springer-ny.com

Examines both traditional clinical research on psychopathology and psychophysiological research on psychopathology, with an emphasis on risk for schizophrenia and for mood disorders. Complementing treatments of risk for psychopathology in other sources which emphasize either genetic factors or large-scale psychosocial factors, chapters focus on research in specific areas of each disorder. Hardcover. *$98.00*

304 pages Year Founded: 1995 ISBN 0-387945-04-0

2934 Cognitive Therapy for Delusions, Voices, and Paranoia
John Wiley & Sons
605 3rd Avenue
New York, NY 10158-180
212-850-6301
E-mail: info@wiley.com

A cognitive view of delusions and voices. The practice of therapy and the problem of engagement.

230 pages Year Founded: 1995

2935 Delusional Beliefs
John Wiley & Sons
605 3rd Avenue
New York, NY 10158-180
212-850-6301
E-mail: info@wiley.com

Unique collection of ideas and empirical data provided by leading experts in a variety of disciplines. Each offers perspectives on questions such as: What criteria should be used to identify, describe and classify delusions? How can delusional individuals be identified? What distinguishes delusions from normal beliefs? *$95.00*

352 pages Year Founded: 1988 ISBN 0-471836-35-4

2936 Families Coping with Schizophrenia: Practitioner's Guide to Family Groups
John Wiley & Sons
605 3rd Avenue
New York, NY 10158-180
212-850-6301
E-mail: info@wiley.com

294 pages Year Founded: 1995

2937 Practice Guideline for the Treatment of Patients with Schizophrenia
American Psychiatric Publishing, Inc.
1000 Wilson Boulevard
Suite 1825
Arlington, VA 22209-3901
703-907-7322
800-368-5777
Fax: 703-907-1091
E-mail: appi@psych.org
www.appi.org

Robert E Hales MD, Editor-in-Chief
Ron McMillen, Chief Executive Officer
John McDuffie, Editorial Director

$22.00

146 pages Year Founded: 1997

2938 Schizophrenia Revealed: From Nuerons to Social Interactions
WW Norton & Company
500 5th Avenue
New York, NY 10110-54
212-354-2907
800-233-4830
Fax: 212-869-0856
E-mail: admalmud@wwnorton.com

Drake McFeely, CEO

Helps explain some of the former mysteries of Schizophrenia that are now possible to study through advances in neuroscience. *$ 10.80*

Year Founded: 1979 ISBN 0-398704-48-1

Sexual Disorders

2939 Assessing Sex Offenders: Problems and Pitfalls
Charles C Thomas Publishers
PO Box 19265
Springfield, IL 62794-9265
217-789-8980
800-258-8980
Fax: 217-789-9130
www.ccthomas.com

This book reviews the scientific evidence relevant to assessing the recidivism risk of sex offenders. Too often, the issues detailed in these chapters have been overlooked and/or misinterpreted. As a result, the likelihood of psychologists misusing and abusing scientific data when assessing sex offenders would not be underestimated. The text identifies numerous instances of such misuse and abuse. Paperback is available for $41.95. *$61.95*

266 pages Year Founded: 2004 ISBN 0-398075-02-6

2940 Cognitive Therapy in Practice
WW Norton & Company
500 5th Avenue
New York, NY 10110-54
212-354-2907
800-233-4830
Fax: 212-869-0856
E-mail: npd@wwnorton.com

Drake McFeely, CEO

Basic text for graduate studies in psychotherapy, psycholgy nursing social work and counseling. *$29.00*

224 pages Year Founded: 1989 ISBN 0-393700-77-1

2941 Erectile Dysfunction: Integrating Couple Therapy, Sex Therapy and Medical Treatment
WW Norton & Company
500 5th Avenue
New York, NY 10110-54
212-354-2907
Fax: 212-869-0856
E-mail: admalmud@wwnorton.com

Drake McFeely, CEO

Helpful to marriage and couple therapists, very up to date and encompassing, with simple and professional writing. *$30.00*

208 pages Year Founded: 2000 ISSN 70330-4

2942 Hypoactive Sexual Desire: Integrating Sex and Couple Therapy
WW Norton & Company
500 5th Avenue
New York, NY 10110-54
212-354-2907
Fax: 212-869-0856
E-mail: admalmud@wwnorton.com

Drake McFeely, CEO

Discussion of treating the couple, not the individual with lack of desire, the authors include distinguishing between organic and psychogenic problems plus how to combine relational and sex therapy. Although lack of desire is one of the most common problems couples face, it is one of the most challenging to treat. *$30.00*

288 pages Year Founded: 2002 ISSN 70344-4

Pediatric & Adolescent Issues

2943 Adolescents in Psychiatric Hospitals: A Psychodynamic Approach to Evaluation and Treatment
Charles C Thomas Publisher
2600 S 1st Street
Springfield, IL 62704-4730
217-789-8980
800-258-8980
Fax: 217-789-9130
E-mail: books@ccthomas.com
www.ccthomas.com

Michael P Thomas, President

A short history of adolescent inpatient psychiatry and its clinical methods, and a month-long, running account of the morning meetings of a typical inpatient ward. For trainees in child and adolescent psychiatry, nurses, social workers, administrators, and psychologists working in the field of adolescent inpatient psychiatry. *$32.95*

208 pages Year Founded: 1998 ISBN 0-398068-60-7

2944 Adolescents, Alcohol and Drugs: A Practical Guide for Those Who Work With Young People
Charles C Thomas Publisher
2600 S 1st Street
Springfield, IL 62704-4730
217-789-8980
800-258-8980
Fax: 217-789-9130
E-mail: books@ccthomas.com
www.ccthomas.com

Michael P Thomas, President
$41.95

210 pages Year Founded: 1988 ISBN 0-398053-93-6

2945 Adolescents, Alcohol and Substance Abuse: Reaching Teens through Brief Interventions
Guilford Press
72 Spring Street
New York, NY 10012-4019
212-431-9800
800-365-7006
Fax: 212-966-6708
E-mail: info@guilford.com

Bob Matloff, President

Reviews a range of empirically supported approachs to dealing with the growing problems of substance use and abuse among young people. While admission to specialized treatment programs is relatively rare in today's health care climate, there are many opportunities for brief interventions. Brief interventions also allow the clinician to work with the teen on his or her home turf, emphasize autonomy and personal responsibility, and can be used across the full range of teens who are engaging in health risk-behavior.

350 pages ISBN 1-572306-58-0

2946 Adolesent in Family Therapy: Breaking the Cycle of Conflict and Control
Guilford Publications
72 Spring Street
New York, NY 10012-4068
212-431-9800
800-365-7006
Fax: 212-966-6708
E-mail: info@guilford.com

Bob Matloff, President

Family relationships that are troubled can be catalysts for change. A guide to treating a wide range of parent/adolescent problems with straightforward advice. *$19.95*

336 pages Year Founded: 1998 ISBN 1-572305-88-6

2947 At-Risk Youth in Crises
Pro-Ed Publications
8700 Shoal Creek Boulevard
Austin, TX 78757-6897
512-451-3246
800-897-3202
Fax: 512-451-8542
E-mail: info@proedinc.com

Donald D Hammill, Owner

This edition has updated material in the chapters covering divorce, loss, abuse, severe depression and suicide. *$31.00*

268 pages Year Founded: 1994 ISBN 0-890795-74-6

2948 Attachment, Trauma and Healing: Understanding and Treating Attachment Disorder in Children and Families
200 E Joppa Road
Suite 207
Baltimore, MD 21286-3107
410-825-8888
888-825-8249
Fax: 410-337-0747

E-mail: sidran@sidran.org
www.sidran.org

An in depth look at the causes of attachment disorder, explains the normal development of attachment, examines the research in this area and present treatment plans. Numerous appendices include a sample intake packet, two brief day in the life accounts of children with attachment disorder, assessment guides, treatment plans and references. *$34.95*

313 pages

2949 Basic Child Psychiatry
American Psychiatric Publishing, Inc.
1000 Wilson Boulevard
Suite 1825
Arlington, VA 22209-3901
703-907-7322
800-368-5777
Fax: 703-907-1091
E-mail: appi@psych.org
www.appi.org

Robert E Hales MD, Editor-in-Chief
Ron McMillen, Chief Executive Officer
John McDuffie, Editorial Director

$46.95

416 pages Year Founded: 1995 ISBN 0-632037-72-5

2950 Behavior Modification for Exceptional Children and Youth
Pro-Ed Publications
8700 Shoal Creek Boulevard
Austin, TX 78757-6897
512-451-3246
800-897-3202
Fax: 512-451-8542
E-mail: info@proedinc.com

Donald D Hammill, Owner

An authoritative textbook for courses in behavior modification. Serves as a practical, comprehensive reference work for clinicians working with people with disabilities and behavior problems. *$37.00*

296 pages Year Founded: 1993 ISBN 1-563720-42-6

2951 Behavior Rating Profile
Pro-Ed Publications
8700 Shoal Creek Boulevard
Austin, TX 78757-6897
512-451-3246
800-897-3202
Fax: 512-451-8542
E-mail: info@proedinc.com

Donald D Hammill, Owner

Provides different evaluations of a student's behavior at home, at school, and in interpersonal relationships from the varied perpsectives of parents, teachers, peers, and the target students themselves. Identifies students whose behavior is perceived to be deviant, the settings in which behavior problems are prominent, and the persons whose perceptions of student's behavior are different from those of other respondents. *$194.00*

Year Founded: 1990

2952 Behavioral Approach to Assessment of Youth with Emotional/Behavioral Disorders
Pro-Ed Publications
8700 Shoal Creek Boulevard
Austin, TX 78757-6897
512-451-3246
800-897-3202
Fax: 512-451-8542
E-mail: info@proedinc.com

Donald D Hammill, Owner

This new book addresses one of the most challenging aspects of special education: evaluating students referred for suspected emotional/behavioral disorders. Geared to the practical needs and concerns of school-based practitioners, including special education teachers, school psychologists and social workers. *$44.00*

729 pages Year Founded: 1996 ISBN 0-890796-25-4

2953 Behavioral Approaches: Problem Child
Cambridge University Press
40 W 20th Street
New York, NY 10011-4211
212-924-3900
Fax: 212-691-3239
E-mail: marketing@cup.org
www.cup.org

2954 Brief Therapy for Adolescent Depression
Professional Resource Press
PO Box 15560
Sarasota, FL 34277-1560
941-343-9601
800-443-3364
Fax: 941-343-9201
E-mail: orders@prpress.com
www.prpress.com

Debra Fink, Managing Editor

Useful book for practicing clinicians and advanced students interested in building new skills for working with depressed young people. Written from the perspective that adaptations of cognitive therapy are necessary when working with adolescents both because of the difference in thinking (relative verses absolute) between adults and adolescents, and because adolescents are deeply embedded in their families of origin and effective treatment rarely can be conducted without intervening with the family. Includes detailed clinical vignettes to illustrate key principles and techniques of this treatment model. *$13.95*

112 pages Year Founded: 1997 ISBN 1-568870-28-0

2955 Candor, Connection and Enterprise in Adolesent Therapy
WW Norton & Company
500 5th Avenue
New York, NY 10110-54
212-354-2907
Fax: 212-869-0856
E-mail: admalmud@wwnorton.com

Drake McFeely, CEO

Suggestions and troubleshooting for therapists dealing with uncooperative adolesent patients. Avoiding the appearence of trying too hard, dialouges that seem to go nowhere, and gaining the faith of a child who may not appreciate efforts on their behalf. *$35.00*

208 pages Year Founded: 2001 ISSN 70356-8

2956 Child Friendly Therapy: Biophysical Innovations for Children and Families
WW Norton & Company
500 5th Avenue
New York, NY 10110-54
212-354-2907
Fax: 212-869-0856
E-mail: admalmud@wwnorton.com

Drake McFeely, CEO

Family centered treatment for children. Suggestions and case studies, therapy room set up and session structure, multi sensory skill building leading to a fresh understanding of often misunderstood children. Family members can be incorporated to work as a team to help with therapy. *$32.00*

256 pages Year Founded: 2002 ISSN 70355-X

2957 Child Psychiatry
American Psychiatric Publishing, Inc.
1000 Wilson Boulevard
Suite 1825
Arlington, VA 22209-3901
703-907-7322
800-368-5777
Fax: 703-907-1091
E-mail: appi@psych.org
www.appi.org

Robert E Hales MD, Editor-in-Chief
Ron McMillen, Chief Executive Officer
John McDuffie, Editorial Director

Provides the essential facts and concepts for everyone involved in child psychiatry, the book includes 200 questions and answers for trainees approaching professional examinations. *$46.95*

336 pages Year Founded: 1987 ISBN 0-632038-85-3

2958 Child Psychopharmacology
American Psychiatric Publishing, Inc.
1000 Wilson Boulevard
Suite 1825
Arlington, VA 22209-3901
703-907-7322
800-368-5777
Fax: 703-907-1091
E-mail: appi@psych.org
www.appi.org

Robert E Hales MD, Editor-in-Chief
Ron McMillen, Chief Executive Officer
John McDuffie, Editorial Director

Includes: Tic disorders and obsessive-compulsive disorder; Attention-deficit/hyperactivity disorder; Children and adolescents with psychotic disorders; Affective disorders in

children and adolescents; Anxiety disorders; Eating disorders. *$26.00*

200 pages ISBN 0-880488-33-6

2959 Child and Adolescent Mental Health Consultation in Hospitals, Schools and Courts
American Psychiatric Publishing, Inc.
1000 Wilson Boulevard
Suite 1825
Arlington, VA 22209-3901
703-907-7322
800-368-5777
Fax: 703-907-1091
E-mail: appi@psych.org
www.appi.org

Robert E Hales MD, Editor-in-Chief
Ron McMillen, Chief Executive Officer
John McDuffie, Editorial Director

Leading experts present a practical guide for mental health professionals. *$38.50*

316 pages Year Founded: 1993 ISBN 0-880484-18-7

2960 Child and Adolescent Psychiatry: Modern Approaches
American Psychiatric Publishing, Inc.
1000 Wilson Boulevard
Suite 1825
Arlington, VA 22209-3901
703-907-7322
800-368-5777
Fax: 703-907-1091
E-mail: appi@psych.org
www.appi.org

Robert E Hales MD, Editor-in-Chief
Ron McMillen, Chief Executive Officer
John McDuffie, Editorial Director

ISBN 0-632028-21-1

2961 Child-Centered Counseling and Psychotherapy
Charles C Thomas Publisher
2600 S 1st Street
Springfield, IL 62704-4730
217-789-8980
800-258-8980
Fax: 217-789-9130
E-mail: books@ccthomas.com
www.ccthomas.com

Michael P Thomas, President

Topics include an introduction to child-centered counseling, counseling as a three-phase process, applying the reflective process, phase three alternatives, counseling through play, consultation, and professional issues. It represents the status of child-centered counseling which also indentifies ideas which can influence its future. *$62.95*

262 pages Year Founded: 1995 ISSN 0-398-06522-5ISBN 0-398065-21-7

2962 Childhood Behavior Disorders: Applied Research and Educational Practice
Pro-Ed Publications
8700 Shoal Creek Boulevard
Austin, TX 78757-6897
512-451-3246
800-897-3202
Fax: 512-451-8542
E-mail: info@proedinc.com

Donald D Hammill, Owner

Provides the balance of theory, research and practical relevance needed by students in graduate and undergraduate introductory courses, as well as practicing teachers and other professionals. *$ 39.00*

550 pages Year Founded: 1998 ISBN 0-890797-19-6

2963 Childhood Disorders
Brunner/Routledge
325 Chestnut Street
Philadelphia, PA 19106-2614

800-821-8312
Fax: 215-269-0363
www.brunner-routledge.com

Provides an up-to-date summary of the current information about the psychological disorders of childhood as well as their causes, nature and course. Together with discussion and evaluation of the major models that guide psychological thinking about the disorders. Gives detailed consideration of the criteria used to make the diagnoses, a presentation of the latest research findings on the nature of the disorder and an overview of the methods used and evaluations conducted for the treatment of the disorders. *$26.95*

240 pages ISBN 0-863776-09-4

2964 Children in Therapy: Using the Family as a Resource
WW Norton & Company
500 5th Avenue
New York, NY 10110-54
212-354-2907
800-233-4830
Fax: 212-869-0856
E-mail: npb@wwnorton.com
www.wwnorton.com

Drake McFeely, CEO

This anthology presents theoretical perspectives of five different competency-based approaches: solution-oriented brief therapy, narrative therapy, collaborative language systems therapy, internal family systems therapy, and emotionally focused family therapy.

ISBN 0-393704-85-8

2965 Childs Work/Childs Play
303 Crossways Park Dr
Woodbury, NY 11797-2099

800-962-1141
Fax: 800-262-1886

E-mail: info@childswork.com
www.childswork.com

Catalog of books, games, toys and workbooks relating to child development issues such as recognizing emotions, handling uncertainty, bullies, ADD, shyness, conflicts and other things that children may need some help navigating.

2966 Clinical & Forensic Interviewing of Children & Families
Jerome M Sattler
PO Box 3557
La Mesa, CA 91944-1060
619-460-3667
Fax: 619-460-2489
www.sattlerpublisher.com

2967 Clinical Application of Projective Drawings
Charles C Thomas Publisher
2600 S 1st Street
Springfield, IL 62704-4730
217-789-8980
800-258-8980
Fax: 217-789-9130
E-mail: books@ccthomas.com
www.ccthomas.com

Michael P Thomas, President

On its way to becoming the classic in the field of projective drawings, this book provides a grounding in fundamentals and goes on to consider differential diagnosis, appraisal of psychological resources as treatment potentials and projective drawing usage in therapy. *$65.95*

688 pages Year Founded: 1980 ISBN 0-398007-68-3

2968 Clinical Child Documentation Sourcebook
John Wiley & Sons
605 3rd Avenue
New York, NY 10158-180
212-850-6301
E-mail: info@wiley.com

This easy to use resource offers child psychologists and therapists a full array of forms, inventories, checklists, client handouts, and clinical records essential to a successful practice in either and organizational or clinical setting. *$49.95*

256 pages Year Founded: 1999 ISBN 0-471291-11-0

2969 Cognitive Behavior Therapy Child
Cambridge University Press
40 W 20th Street
New York, NY 10011-4211
212-924-3900
Fax: 212-691-3239
E-mail: marketing@cup.org
www.cup.org

2970 Concise Guide to Child and Adolescent Psychiatry
American Psychiatric Publishing, Inc.
1000 Wilson Boulevard
Suite 1825
Arlington, VA 22209-3901
703-907-7322
800-368-5777
Fax: 703-907-1091
E-mail: appi@psych.org
www.appi.org

Robert E Hales MD, Editor-in-Chief
Ron McMillen, Chief Executive Officer
John McDuffie, Editorial Director

Topics include evaluation and treatment planning, axis I disorders usually first diagnosed in infancy, childhood or adolescence, attention deficit and disruptive behavior disorders, developmental disorders, special clinical circumstances, psychopharmacology, and psychosocial treatments. *$21.95*

400 pages Year Founded: 1998 ISBN 0-880489-05-7

2971 Counseling Children with Special Needs
American Psychiatric Publishing, Inc.
1000 Wilson Boulevard
Suite 1825
Arlington, VA 22209-3901
703-907-7322
800-368-5777
Fax: 703-907-1091
E-mail: appi@psych.org
www.appi.org

Robert E Hales MD, Editor-in-Chief
Ron McMillen, Chief Executive Officer
John McDuffie, Editorial Director
 $29.95

224 pages Year Founded: 1997 ISBN 0-632041-51-

2972 Creative Therapy with Children and Adolescents
Impact Publishers
PO Box 6016
Atascadero, CA 93423-6016
805-466-5917
800-246-7228
Fax: 805-466-5919
E-mail: info@impactpublishers.com
www.impactpublishers.com

Encourages creativity in therapy, assists therapists in talking with children to facilitate change. From simple ideas to fresh innovations, the activities are to be used as tools to supplement a variety of therapeutic approaches, and can be tailored to each child's needs. *$21.95*

192 pages Year Founded: 1999 ISBN 1-886230-19-6

2973 Defiant Teens
Guilford Publications
72 Spring Street
New York, NY 10012-4068
212-431-9800
800-365-7006

Fax: 212-966-6708
E-mail: info@guilford.com

Bob Matloff, President

Guidelines for best practices in working with families and their teenaged children.

250 pages Year Founded: 1999 ISBN 1-572304-40-5

2974 Developmental Therapy/Developmental Teaching
Pro-Ed Publications
8700 Shoal Creek Boulevard
Austin, TX 78757-6897
512-451-3246
800-897-3202
Fax: 512-451-8542
E-mail: info@proedinc.com

Donald D Hammill, Owner

Provides extensive applications for teachers, counselors, parents and other adults concerned about the behavior and emotional stability of children and teens. The focus is on helping children and youth to cope effectively with the stresses of comtemporary life, with an emphasis on the positive effects adults can have on students when they adjust strategies to the social emotional needs of children. *$41.00*

398 pages Year Founded: 1996 ISBN 0-890796-64-5

2975 Drug Information for Teens: Health Tips About the Physical and Mental Effects of Substance Abuse
Omnigraphics
615 Giswold
Detroit, MI 48226-3900
313-961-1340
Fax: 313-961-1383
E-mail: info@omnigraphics.com
www.omnigraphics.com

Provides students with facts about drug use, abuse, and addiction. It describes the physical and mental effects of alcohol, tobacco, marijuana, ecstasy, inhalants and many other drugs and chemicals that are often abused. It includes information about the process that leads from casual use to addiction and offers suggestions for resisting peer pressure and helping friends stay drug free.

452 pages ISBN 0-780804-44-9

2976 Effective Discipline
Pro-Ed Publications
8700 Shoal Creek Boulevard
Austin, TX 78757-6897
512-451-3246
800-897-3202
Fax: 512-451-8542
E-mail: info@proedinc.com

Donald D Hammill, Owner

Designed to provide principals, counselors, teachers, and college students preparing to become educators with information about research-based techniques that reduce or eliminate school behavior problems. Provides the knowledge to prevent discipline problems, identify specific behaviors that disrupt the environment, match interventions with behavioral infractions, implement a variety of intervention tactics, and evaluate the effectiveness of the intervention program. *$28.00*

220 pages   Year Founded: 1993 ISBN 0-890795-79-7

2977 Empowering Adolesent Girls
WW Norton & Company
500 5th Avenue
New York, NY 10110-54
212-354-2907
Fax: 212-869-0856
E-mail: admalmud@wwnorton.com

Drake McFeely, CEO

Strategies and activities for professionals who work with adolesent girls (teachers, counselors, therapists) to offer support and encouagement through the Go Girls program. *$32.00*

256 pages   Year Founded: 2001 ISSN 70347-9

2978 Enhancing Social Competence in Young Students
Pro-Ed Publications
8700 Shoal Creek Boulevard
Austin, TX 78757-6897
512-451-3246
800-897-3202
Fax: 512-451-8542
E-mail: info@proedinc.com

Donald D Hammill, Owner

Addresses conceptual and practical issues of providing social competence-enhancing interventions for young students in schools, based on research findings. Summarizes recent advances in social skills programming for at-risk students and prevention interventions for all students. Discussions of developmental issues of childhood maladjustment, intervention strategies, implementation issues and assessment/evaluation issues are provided. *$28.00*

281 pages   Year Founded: 1995 ISBN 0-890796-20-3

2979 Group Therapy With Children and Adolescents
American Psychiatric Publishing, Inc.
1000 Wilson Boulevard
Suite 1825
Arlington, VA 22209-3901
703-907-7322
800-368-5777
Fax: 703-907-1091
E-mail: appi@psych.org
www.appi.org

Robert E Hales MD, Editor-in-Chief
Ron McMillen, Chief Executive Officer
John McDuffie, Editorial Director

Explores a major treatment modality often used with adult populations and rarely considered for child and adolescent treatments. With contributions from international experts, this book looks at the effectiveness of treatment and cost of group therapy as it applies to this particular age group. *$52.00*

400 pages   ISBN 0-880484-06-3

2980 Handbook of Child Behavior in Therapy and in the Psychiatric Setting
John Wiley & Sons
605 3rd Avenue
New York, NY 10158-180
212-850-6301
E-mail: info@wiley.com

512 pages   Year Founded: 1994

2981 Handbook of Infant Mental Health
Guilford Publications
72 Spring Street
New York, NY 10012-4068
212-431-9800
800-365-7006
Fax: 212-966-6708
E-mail: info@guilford.com

Bob Matloff, President

Included are chapters on neurobiology, diagnostic issues, parental mental health issues and family dynamics. *$60.00*

588 pages   Year Founded: 2000 ISBN 1-572305-15-0

2982 Handbook of Parent Training: Parents as Co-Therapists for Children's Behavior Problems
John Wiley & Sons
605 3rd Avenue
New York, NY 10158-180
212-850-6301
E-mail: info@wiley.com

This completely revised handbook shows professionals who work with troubled children how to teach parents to become co-therapists. It presents various techniques and behavior modification skills that will help parents to better relate, communicate, and respond to their child. Updates are provided on such problems as noncompliance, ADHD, and conduct disorder, and a new section on special needs parents which includes adolescent mothers, aggressive parents, substance abusing parents, and more.

594 pages   Year Founded: 1994

2983 Handbook of Psychiatric Practice in the Juvenile Court
American Psychiatric Publishing, Inc.
1000 Wilson Boulevard
Suite 1825
Arlington, VA 22209-3901
703-907-7322
800-368-5777
Fax: 703-907-1091
E-mail: appi@psych.org
www.appi.org

Robert E Hales MD, Editor-in-Chief
Ron McMillen, Chief Executive Officer
John McDuffie, Editorial Director

Examines the role that psychiatrists and other mental health professionals are asked to play when children, adolescents, and their families end up in court. *$12.95*

198 pages   ISBN 0-890422-33-8

2984 Helping Parents, Youth, and Teachers Understand Medications for Behavioral and Emotional Problems
American Psychiatric Publishing, Inc.
1000 Wilson Boulevard
Suite 1825
Arlington, VA 22209-3901
703-907-7322
800-368-5777
Fax: 703-907-1091
E-mail: appi@psych.org
www.appi.org

Robert E Hales MD, Editor-in-Chief
Ron McMillen, Chief Executive Officer
John McDuffie, Editorial Director

Valuable resource for anyone involved in evaluating psychiatric disturbances in children and adolescents. Provides a compilation of information sheets to help promote the dialogue between the patient's family, caregivers, and the treating physician. *$39.95*

196 pages Year Founded: 1999 ISBN 0-880487-94-1

2985 How to Teach Social Skills
Pro-Ed Publications
8700 Shoal Creek Boulevard
Austin, TX 78757-6897
512-451-3246
800-897-3202
Fax: 512-451-8542
E-mail: info@proedinc.com

Donald D Hammill, Owner

$8.00

ISBN 0-890797-61-7

2986 In the Long Run... Longitudinal Studies of Psychopathology in Children
American Psychiatric Publishing, Inc.
1000 Wilson Boulevard
Suite 1825
Arlington, VA 22209-3901
703-907-7322
800-368-5777
Fax: 703-907-1091
E-mail: appi@psych.org
www.appi.org

Robert E Hales MD, Editor-in-Chief
Ron McMillen, Chief Executive Officer
John McDuffie, Editorial Director

$29.95

224 pages Year Founded: 1999 ISBN 0-873182-11-1

2987 Infants, Toddlers and Families: Framework for Support and Intervention
Guilford Publications
72 Spring Street
Department 4E
New York, NY 10012-4019
212-431-9800
Fax: 212-966-6708
E-mail: exam@guilford.com

Bob Matloff, President

Examines the complex development in a child's first 3 years of life. Instead of preaching or judging, this book acknowledges the challenges facing all families, especially vulnerable ones, and offers straightforward advice. *$28.95*

204 pages Year Founded: 1999 ISBN 1-572304-87-1

2988 Interventions for Students with Emotional Disorders
Pro-Ed Publications
8700 Shoal Creek Boulevard
Austin, TX 78757-6897
512-451-3246
800-897-3202
Fax: 512-451-8542
E-mail: info@proedinc.com

Donald D Hammill, Owner

This graduate textbook for special education students advocates an eclectic approach toward teaching children with social adjustment problems. Provides how-to information for implementing various techniques to successfully enhance positive sociobehavioral development in children with emotional disorders. *$36.00*

212 pages Year Founded: 1991 ISBN 0-890792-96-8

2989 Interviewing Children and Adolesents: Skills and Strategies for Effective DSM-IV Diagnosis
Guilford Publications
72 Spring Street
New York, NY 10012-4068
212-431-9800
800-365-7006
Fax: 212-966-6708
E-mail: info@guilford.com

Bob Matloff, President

Guide to developmentally appropriate interviewing. *$45.00*

482 pages Year Founded: 99 ISBN 1-572305-01-0

2990 Interviewing the Sexually Abused Child
American Psychiatric Publishing, Inc.
1000 Wilson Boulevard
Suite 1825
Arlington, VA 22209-3901
703-907-7322
800-368-5777
Fax: 703-907-1091
E-mail: appi@psych.org
www.appi.org

Robert E Hales MD, Editor-in-Chief
Ron McMillen, Chief Executive Officer
John McDuffie, Editorial Director

A guide for mental health professionals who need to know if a child has been sexually abused. Presents guidelines on the structure of the interview and covers the use of free play, toys, and play materials by focusing on the investigate interview of the suspected victim. *$15.00*

80 pages Year Founded: 1993 ISBN 0-880486-12-0

2991 Learning Disorders and Disorders of the Self in Children and Adolesents
WW Norton & Company
500 5th Avenue
New York, NY 10110-54
212-354-2907
Fax: 212-869-0856
E-mail: admalmud@wwnorton.com

Drake McFeely, CEO

Clinicians who work with learning disabled children need to understand the complex, integrated framework of learning and self image problems. Specific problems and treatments are discussed. *$32.00*

332 pages Year Founded: 2001 ISSN 70377-0

2992 Living on the Razor's Edge: Solution-Oriented Brief Family Therapy with Self-Harming Adolesents
WW Norton & Company
500 5th Avenue
New York, NY 10110-54
212-354-2907
Fax: 212-869-0856
E-mail: admalmud@wwnorton.com

Drake McFeely, CEO

Research supported stategies and a therapy model for self harming adolesents and their families to devlop a closer and more meaningful relationships. *$25.60*

320 pages Year Founded: 2002 ISSN 70335-5

2993 Making the Grade: Guide to School Drug Prevention Programs
Drug Strategies
1616 P Street NW
Washington, DC 20036-1434
202-289-9070
Fax: 202-414-6199
E-mail: dspoilcy@aol.com

Mathea Falco, President

Updated and expanded from the 1996 original, this guide to drug prevention programs in America helps parents and educators make informed decisions with often limited budgets. *$14.95*

2994 Manual of Clinical Child and Adolescent Psychiatry
American Psychiatric Publishing, Inc.
1000 Wilson Boulevard
Suite 1825
Arlington, VA 22209-3901
703-907-7322
800-368-5777
Fax: 703-907-1091
E-mail: appi@psych.org
www.appi.org

Robert E Hales MD, Editor-in-Chief
Ron McMillen, Chief Executive Officer
John McDuffie, Editorial Director

Addresses current issues such as cost containment, insurance complications, and legal and ethical issues, as well as neuropsychology, alcohol, and substance abuse, and mental retardation and genetics. *$42.50*

528 pages ISBN 0-880485-28-0

2995 Mental Affections Childhood
Cambridge University Press
40 W 20th Street
New York, NY 10011-4211
212-924-3900
Fax: 212-691-3239
E-mail: marketing@cup.org
www.cup.org

$30.00

185 pages Year Founded: 1991

2996 Myth of Maturity: What Teenagers Need from Parents to Become Adults
WW Norton & Company
500 5th Avenue
New York, NY 10110-54
212-354-2907
Fax: 212-869-0856
E-mail: admalmud@wwnorton.com

Drake McFeely, CEO

Debunking outdated and misguided ideas about maturity, the author discusses the amount of support teens need from their parents, what is too much for independence, or not enough. *$24.95*

256 pages Year Founded: 2001 ISBN 0-393049-42-6

2997 Narrative Therapies with Children and Adolescents
Guilford Publications
72 Spring Street
New York, NY 10012-4068
212-431-9800
800-365-7006
Fax: 212-966-6708
E-mail: info@guilford.com

Bob Matloff, President

Many renowned, creative contributors collaborate to bring this professional resource to the shelf. Transcripts of case examples, using many different methods and mediums are shown to engage children of different perspectives and ages. This book can serve as a text for child/adolescent psychotherapy, or is a useful guide for mental health professionals. *$39.95*

469 pages Year Founded: 1997 ISBN 1-572302-53-4

2998 National Survey of American Attitudes on Substance Abuse VI: Teens
Center on Addiction at Columbia University
633 3rd Avenue
19th Floor
New York, NY 10017-8155
212-841-5200
Fax: 212-956-8020
www.casacolumbia.org

William H Foster, CEO

Results of the sixth annual CASA National Survey of teens 12 - 17 years old reveals that parents that are more involved with their children's activities and have house rules and expectations can greatly influence teen behavior choices. Other statistics about availability of illegal substances and who may use them. *$22.00*

2999 No-Talk Therapy for Children and Adolescents
WW Norton & Company
500 5th Avenue
New York, NY 10110-54
212-354-2907
Fax: 212-869-0856
E-mail: admalmud@wwnorton.com

Drake McFeely, CEO

Creative approach to treatment of young people who cannot respond to conversation based therapy. Seemingly sullen patients can be helped to find a voice of their own. *$.27*

288 pages Year Founded: 1999 ISSN 70286-3

3000 Ordinary Families, Special Children: Systems Approach to Childhood Disability
Guilford Publications
72 Spring Street
New York, NY 10012-4068
212-431-9800
800-365-7006
Fax: 212-966-6708
E-mail: info@guilford.com

Bob Matloff, President

Families, including siblings and grandparents are impacted by the special needs of a child's disability. The authors explore personal accounts that shape a family's response to childhood disability and how they come to adapt these unique needs to a satisfactory lifestyle. Available in hardcover and paperback. *$35.00*

324 pages Year Founded: 1999 ISBN 1-572301-55-4

3001 Outcomes for Children and Youth with Emotional and Behavioral Disorders and their Families
Pro-Ed Publications
8700 Shoal Creek Boulevard
Austin, TX 78757-6897
512-451-3246
800-897-3202
Fax: 512-451-8542
E-mail: info@proedinc.com

Donald D Hammill, Owner

This new book addresses one of the most challenging aspects of serving children and youth with emotional and behavioral disorders-evaluating the outcomes of the services you've provided. Also includes information on such topics as: child and family outcomes, system level anaylsis, case study analysis, cost analysis, cultural diversity, managed care, and consumer satisfaction. *$44.00*

730 pages Year Founded: 1998 ISBN 0-890797-50-1

3002 PTSD in Children and Adolesents
American Psychiatric Publishing, Inc.
1000 Wilson Boulevard
Suite 1825
Arlington, VA 22209-3901
703-907-7322
800-368-5777
Fax: 703-907-1091
E-mail: appi@psych.org
www.appi.org

Robert E Hales MD, Editor-in-Chief
Ron McMillen, Chief Executive Officer
John McDuffie, Editorial Director

Mental health and other professionals who work with Post Traumatic Stress Disorder and the young people who suffer from it will find discussions of evaluation, biological treatment strategies, the need for an integrated approach to juvenile offenders who suffer from PTSD and more. *$29.95*

208 pages Year Founded: 2001

3003 Pediatric Psychopharmacology: Fast Facts
WW Norton & Company
500 5th Avenue
New York, NY 10110-54
212-354-2907
800-233-4830
Fax: 212-869-0856
E-mail: npb@wwnorton.com

Drake McFeely, CEO

This new title in the Fast Facts series, full of up-to-date and authoritative infomration, is a critical resource for all health care professionals, including psychiatrists, prescribing psychologists, psychotherapists, pediatricians, family practice physicians, pediatric neurologists, nurse practitioners, and allied mental health professionals. Clear explanations of clinical directions for the prescriber and nonprescriber alike.

ISBN 0-393704-61-0

3004 Play Therapy with Children in Crisis: Individual, Group and Family Treatment
Guilford Publications
72 Spring Street
New York, NY 10012-4068
212-431-9800
800-365-7006
Fax: 212-966-6708
E-mail: info@guilford.com

Bob Matloff, President

$45.00

506 pages Year Founded: 1999 ISBN 1-572304-85-5

3005 Post Traumatic Stress Disorders in Children and Adolescents Handbook
WW Norton & Company
500 5th Avenue
New York, NY 10110-54
212-354-2907
800-233-4830

Fax: 212-869-0856
E-mail: npb@wwnorton.com

Drake McFeely, CEO

The 15 chapters gathered here address different aspects of childhood and adolescent trauma-some consider a distinct therapeutic situation (abuse and neglect), others pertain to standard clinical procedure (assessment), and still others focus on complex research issues (neurobiology and genetics of PSTD).

ISBN 0-393704-12-2

3006 Power and Compassion: Working with Difficult Adolesents and Abused Parents
Guilford Publications
72 Spring Street
New York, NY 10012-4068
212-431-9800
800-365-7006
Fax: 212-966-6708
E-mail: info@guilford.com

Bob Matloff, President

Useful as a supplemental text, or for mental health professionals dealing with aggressive teenagers and their parents. Pragmatic guide to help demoralized parents be more understanding, but more decisive. *$16.95*

196 pages Year Founded: 1999 ISBN 1-572304-70-7

3007 Practical Charts for Managing Behavior
Pro-Ed Publications
8700 Shoal Creek Boulevard
Austin, TX 78757-6897
512-451-3246
800-897-3202
Fax: 512-451-8542
E-mail: info@proedinc.com

Donald D Hammill, Owner

$29.00

160 pages Year Founded: 1998 ISBN 0-890797-36-6

3008 Proven Youth Development Model that Prevents Substance Abuse and Builds Communities
Center on Addiction at Columbia University
633 3rd Avenue
19th Floor
New York, NY 10017-8155
212-841-5200
Fax: 212-956-8020
www.casacolumbia.org

William H Foster, CEO

How-to manual developed with nine years of research. The program is a collaboration of local school, law enforcement, social service and health teams to help high risk youth between the ages of 8 - 13 years old and their families prevent substance abuse and violent behavior. Used in 23 urban and rural communities in 11 states and the District of Columbia. *$50.00*

79 pages Year Founded: 2001

3009 Psychological Examination of the Child
John Wiley & Sons
605 3rd Avenue
New York, NY 10158-180
212-850-6301
E-mail: info@wiley.com

279 pages Year Founded: 1991

3010 Psychotherapies with Children and Adolescents
American Psychiatric Publishing, Inc.
1000 Wilson Boulevard
Suite 1825
Arlington, VA 22209-3901
703-907-7322
800-368-5777
Fax: 703-907-1091
E-mail: appi@psych.org
www.appi.org

Robert E Hales MD, Editor-in-Chief
Ron McMillen, Chief Executive Officer
John McDuffie, Editorial Director

Illustrated with case histories and demonstrates how psychoanalytic techniques can be modified to meet the therapeutic needs of children and adolescents in specific clinical situations. *$47.50*

346 pages ISBN 0-880484-06-3

3011 Safe Schools/Safe Students: Guide to Violence Prevention Stategies
Drug Strategies
1616 P Street NW
Washington, DC 20036-1434
202-289-9070
Fax: 202-414-6199
E-mail: dspoilcy@aol.com

Mathea Falco, President

Practical assistance in rating over 84 violence prevention programs for classroom use, helps examine school policies and possible changes for student protection. *$14.95*

3012 Severe Stress and Mental Disturbance in Children
American Psychiatric Publishing, Inc.
1000 Wilson Boulevard
Suite 1825
Arlington, VA 22209-3901
703-907-7322
800-368-5777
Fax: 703-907-1091
E-mail: appi@psych.org
www.appi.org

Robert E Hales MD, Editor-in-Chief
Ron McMillen, Chief Executive Officer
John McDuffie, Editorial Director

Uniquely blends current research and clinical data on the effects of severe stress on children. Each chapter is written by international experts in their field. *$69.95*

708 pages ISBN 0-880486-57-0

3013 Structured Adolescent Pscyhotherapy Groups
Professional Resource Press
PO Box 15560
Sarasota, FL 34277-1560
941-343-9601
800-443-3364
Fax: 941-343-9201
E-mail: orders@prpress.com
www.prpress.com

Debra Fink, Managing Editor

Provides specific techniques for use in the beginning, middle, and end phase of time-limited structured psychotherapy groups. Offers concrete suggestions for working with hard to reach and difficult adolescents, providing feedback to parents, and dealing with administrative, legal, and ethical issues. Examples of pre/post evaluation forms, therapy contracts, evaluation feedback letters, parent response forms, therapist rating scales, co-therapist rating forms, problem identification forms, supervision and session records, client and patient handouts, and specific group exercises. Solidly anchored to research on the curative factors in group therapy, this book includes empirical data, references, theoretical formulations and examples of group sessions. *$19.95*

164 pages Year Founded: 1994 ISBN 0-943158-74-5

3014 Teaching Buddy Skills to Preschoolers
AAIDD
501 3rd Street NW
Suite 200
Washington, DC 20001

800-424-3688
Fax: 202-387-2193
E-mail: anam@aaidd.org
www.aamr.org

Shows how the rewards of social interactions must outweigh the costs to encouraging friendships between pre-schoolers with and without disabilities. *$12.95*

40 pages ISBN 0-940898-45-4

3015 Teaching Self-Management to Elementary
Students with Developmental Disabilities
AAMR
444 N Capitol Street NW
Suite 846
Washington, DC 20001-1569
202-637-0475
800-424-3688
Fax: 202-637-0585
E-mail: dcroser@aamr.org

This book will help you design and implement self-management systems for elementary students with disabilities including self-monitoring and self-evaluation. *$12.95*

51 pages ISBN 0-940898-48-9

3016 Textbook of Child and Adolescent Psychiatry
American Psychiatric Publishing, Inc.
1000 Wilson Boulevard
Suite 1825
Arlington, VA 22209-3901

703-907-7322
800-368-5777
Fax: 703-907-1091
E-mail: appi@psych.org
www.appi.org

Robert E Hales MD, Editor-in-Chief
Ron McMillen, Chief Executive Officer
John McDuffie, Editorial Director

Includes chapter on changes in DSM-IV classification and discusses the latest research and treatment advances in the areas of epidemiology, fenetics, developmental neurobiology, and combined treatments. A special section covers essential issues such as HIV and AIDS, gender identity disorders, physical and sexual abuse, and substance abuse, for the child and adolescent psychiatrist. *$140.00*

960 pages ISBN 1-882103-03-3

3017 Textbook of Pediatric Neuropsychiatry
American Psychiatric Publishing, Inc.
1000 Wilson Boulevard
Suite 1825
Arlington, VA 22209-3901
703-907-7322
800-368-5777
Fax: 703-907-1091
E-mail: appi@psych.org
www.appi.org

Robert E Hales MD, Editor-in-Chief
Ron McMillen, Chief Executive Officer
John McDuffie, Editorial Director

Comprehensive textbook on pediatric medicine. *$175.00*

1632 pages Year Founded: 1998 ISBN 0-880487-66-6

3018 The Special Education Consultant Teacher
Charles C Thomas Publishers
PO Box 19265
Springfield, IL 62794-9265
217-789-8980
800-258-8980
Fax: 217-789-9130
www.ccthomas.com

This book is intended for special education teachers and other professionals providing special education services with information, guidelines and suggestions relating to the role and responsibilities of the special education consultant teacher. Available in paperback for $ 45.95. *$67.95*

330 pages Year Founded: 2004 ISBN 0-398075-10-7

3019 Through the Eyes of a Child
WW Norton & Company
500 5th Avenue
New York, NY 10110-54
212-354-2907
800-233-4830
Fax: 212-869-0856
E-mail: npb@wwnorton.com

Drake McFeely, CEO

Comprehensive and helpful, this book helps therapists work with children and parents in the application of EMDR with children. *$ 37.00*

288 pages Year Founded: 1999 ISSN 70287-1ISBN 0-393702-87-1

176 pages Year Founded: 1998 ISBN 0-878686-93-2

3020 Transition Matters From School to Independence: a Guide & Directory of Services for Children & Youth with Disabilities & Special Needs in the Metro New York Area
Resources for Children with Special Needs
116 E 16th Street
5th Floor
New York, NY 10003-2164
212-677-4650
Fax: 212-254-4070
E-mail: info@resourcesnyc.org
www.resourcesnyc.org

Rachel Howard, Executive Director

Youth with disabilities need special guidance when moving from school to adult life. Transition Matters covers every aspect of moving from high school to the world of postsecondary education, job training, employment and idependent living. This guide for parents, caregivers and educators presents a wealth of information about the transition process, and lists 1,000 agencies and organizations that provide services for youth 14 and up. It explains entitlements and options and helps families navigate systems and procedures. *$15.00*

500 pages ISBN 0-967836-56-5

3021 Treating Depressed Children: A Therapeutic Manual of Proven Cognitive Behavior Techniques
New Harbinger Publications
5674 Shattuck Avenue
Oakland, CA 94609-1662
510-652-0215
800-748-6273
Fax: 510-652-5472
E-mail: customerservice@newharbinger.com
www.newharbinger.com

Matthew McKay, Owner

Program incorporating cartoons and role playing games to help children recognize emotions, change negative thoughts, gain confidence, and learn interpersonal skills. *$49.94*

160 pages Year Founded: 1996 ISBN 1-572240-61-

3022 Treating the Aftermath of Sexual Abuse: a Handbook for Working with Children in Care
Child Welfare League of America
440 First Street NW
Third Floor
Washington, DC 20001-2028
202-638-2952
Fax: 202-638-4004
www.cwla.org

A handbook for working with children in care who have been sexually abused. The authors review the impact of sexual abuse on a child's physical and emotional development and describe the effect of abuse on basic life experiences. Paperback. *$18.95*

3023 Treating the Tough Adolesent: Family Based Step by Step Guide
Guilford Publications
72 Spring Street
New York, NY 10012-4068
212-431-9800
800-365-7006
Fax: 212-966-6708
E-mail: info@guilford.com

Bob Matloff, President

Model for effective family therapy, with reproducible handouts. *$35.00*

320 pages Year Founded: 1998 ISBN 1-572304-22-7

3024 Troubled Teens: Multidimensional Family Therapy
WW Norton & Company
500 5th Avenue
New York, NY 10110-54
212-354-2907
Fax: 212-869-0856
E-mail: admalmud@wwnorton.com

Drake McFeely, CEO

Based on 17 years of research, this treatment manual is for therapists who work with youth referred for substance abuse and behavior counseling. Treatment involves drug counseling, family and individual sessions and interventions. People or systems of influence outside the family are also considered. *$35.00*

320 pages Year Founded: 2002 ISBN 0-393703-40-1

3025 Understanding and Teaching Emotionally Disturbed Children and Adolescents
Pro-Ed Publications
8700 Shoal Creek Boulevard
Austin, TX 78757-6897
512-451-3246
800-897-3202
Fax: 512-451-8542
E-mail: info@proedinc.com

Donald D Hammill, Owner

Shows how diverse theoretical perspectives translate into practice by exploring forms of therapy and types of interventions currently employed with children and adolescents. *$41.00*

620 pages Year Founded: 1993 ISBN 0-890795-75-4

3026 Ups & Downs: How to Beat the Blues and Teen Depression
Price Stern Sloan Publishing

www.penguingroup.com

Andy Cooke, Illustrator

This book discusses how to recognize depression in teens and what to do about it. Informal, yet informative, using quotes and case studies representing typical young people who are dealing with mood swings, eating disorders and problems at school or at home. The book also demystifies therapy and advises readers on how to seek help, particularly if they, or their friends, have suicidal thoughts. Reading level ages nine to twelve. *$4.99*

90 pages Year Founded: 1999 ISBN 0-843174-50-1

3027 Working with Self-Harming Adolescents: A Collaborative, Strengths-Based Therapy Approach
WW Norton & Company
500 5th Avenue
New York, NY 10110-54
212-354-2907
800-233-4830
Fax: 212-869-0856
E-mail: npb@wwnorton.com

Drake McFeely, CEO

A unique approach to this illness combines flexability, compassion, and candor. His integration of the family in these treatments demonstrates the complex interplay between self-harming teens and their parents, peers, communities, and culture. Originally published in hardcover as Living on the Razor's Edge.

ISBN 0-393704-99-8

3028 Youth Violence: Prevention, Intervention, and Social Policy
American Psychiatric Publishing, Inc.
1000 Wilson Boulevard
Suite 1825
Arlington, VA 22209-3901
703-907-7322
800-368-5777
Fax: 703-907-1091
E-mail: appi@psych.org
www.appi.org

Robert E Hales MD, Editor-in-Chief
Ron McMillen, Chief Executive Officer
John McDuffie, Editorial Director

Based on more than a decade of clinical research and treatment experience, this comprehensive and non-technical book offers a stage-oriented approach to understanding and treating complex and difficult traumatized patients, integrating modern trauma theory with traditional therapeutic interventions. *$48.50*

336 pages Year Founded: 1998 ISBN 0-880488-09-3

Suicide

3029 A Woman Doctor's Guide to Depression
Hyperion
114 Fifth Avenue
New York, NY 10011

www.hyperionbooks.com

Includes information on what depression feels like and how it affects daily life, women's unique risks of developing depression throughout the life cycle from puberty to meno-

pause and current treatment strategies and their risks and benefits, preventive measures and warning signs. *$9.95*

176 pages Year Founded: 1997 ISBN 0-786881-46-1

3030 Antidepressant Fact Book: What Your Doctor Won't Tell You About Prozac, Zoloft, Paxil, Celexa and Luvox
Perseus Books Group
550 Central Avenue
Boulder, CO 80301

800-386-5656
Fax: 720-406-7336
E-mail: westview.orders@perseusbooks.com
www.perseusbooksgroup.com

What antidepressants will and won't treat, documented side and withdrawl effects, plus what parents need to know about teenagers and antidepressants. The author has been a medical expert in many court cases invloving the use and misuse of psychoactive drugs. *$13.00*

240 pages Year Founded: 2001 ISBN 0-738204-51-X

3031 Antipsychotic Medications: A Guide
Madison Institute of Medicine
7617 Mineral Point Road
Suite 300
Madison, WI 53717-1623
608-827-2470
E-mail: mim@miminc.org
www.factsforhealth.org

Margarett Baudhuin, Manager

A number of medications are available today to treat schizophrenia and other illnesses that may lead to psychotic behaviors. This concise guide covers antipsychotic medications available today and provides information about correct dosing and possible side effects. *$5.95*

39 pages

3032 Assessment and Prediction of Suicide
Guilford Publications
72 Spring Street
New York, NY 10012-4068
212-431-9800
800-365-7006
Fax: 212-966-6708
E-mail: info@guilford.com

Bob Matloff, President

Comprehensive reference volume that includes contributions from top suicide experts of the current knowledge in the field of suicide. Covers concepts and theories, methods and quantification, in-depth case histories, specific single predictors applied to the case histories and comorbidity. *$90.00*

697 pages Year Founded: 1992 ISBN 0-898627-91-5

3033 Comprehensive Textbook of Suicidology
Guilford Publications
72 Spring Street
New York, NY 10012-4068

212-431-9800
800-365-7006
Fax: 212-966-6708
E-mail: info@guilford.com

Bob Matloff, President

This volume presents an authoritative overview of current scientific knowledge about suicide and suicide prevention. Multidisciplinary and comprehesive in scope, the book provides a solid foundation in theory, research and clinical applications. Topics covered include the classification and prevalence of suicidal behaviors, psychiatric and medical factors, ethical and legal issues in intervention as well as the social, cultural and gender context of suicide. *$70.00*

650 pages ISBN 1-572305-41-X

3034 Interpersonal Psychotherapy
American Psychiatric Publishing, Inc.
1000 Wilson Boulevard
Suite 1825
Arlington, VA 22209-3901
703-907-7322
800-368-5777
Fax: 703-907-1091
E-mail: appi@psych.org
www.appi.org

Robert E Hales MD, Editor-in-Chief
Ron McMillen, Chief Executive Officer
John McDuffie, Editorial Director

An overview of interpersonal psychotherapy for depression, preventative treatment for depression, bulimia nervosa and HIV positive men and women. *$26.00*

156 pages Year Founded: 1998 ISBN 0-880488-36-0

3035 Practical Art of Suicide Assessment: A Guide for Mental Health Professionals and Substance Abuse Counselors
John Wiley & Sons
10475 Crosspoint Boulevard
Indianapolis, IN 46256-3386
317-572-3000
800-597-3299
Fax: 317-572-4000
E-mail: consumers@wiley.com
www.wiley.com

Lou Peragallo, Manager

Covers the critical elements of suicide assessment, from risk factor analysis to evaluating clients with borderline personality disorders or psychotic process.

316 pages ISBN 0-471237-61-2

3036 Suicide From a Psychological Prespective
Charles C Thomas Publisher
2600 S 1st Street
Springfield, IL 62704-4730
217-789-8980
800-258-8980
Fax: 217-789-9130
E-mail: books@ccthomas.com
www.ccthomas.com

Michael P Thomas, President

$39.95

142 pages Year Founded: 1988 ISBN 0-398057-09-5

3037 Teens and Suicide
Mason Crest Publishers
370 Reed Road
Suite 302
Broomall, PA 19008-4017
866-627-2665
Fax: 610-543-3878
www.masoncrest.com

Suicide is the third-leading cause of death among adolescents in the United States; in a recent study by The Gallup Organization, 47 percent of teenagers between the ages of 13 and 17 said they know someone who has tried to take their own lives. This volume examines the cause of teen-age suicide and explores such issues as teens and guns as well as suicide rates among minorities.

3038 Treatment of Suicidal Patients in Managed Care
American Psychiatric Publishing, Inc.
1000 Wilson Boulevard
Suite 1825
Arlington, VA 22209-3901
703-907-7322
800-368-5777
Fax: 703-907-1091
E-mail: appi@psych.org
www.appi.org

Robert E Hales MD, Editor-in-Chief
Ron McMillen, Chief Executive Officer
John McDuffie, Editorial Director

Suicide is an all too common cause of death and preventable, but the managed care concerns of cost control with rapid diagnosis and treatment of depression puts the clinician in a dilemma. This book guides the professional with advice on knowing who to contact, and getting more of what is needed from the patient's managed care provider. *$39.00*

240 pages Year Founded: 2001 ISBN 0-880488-28-x

Conferences & Meetings

3039 AAIDD Annual Meeting
501 3rd Street NW
Suite 200
Washington, DC 20001

800-424-3688
Fax: 202-387-2193
E-mail: anam@aaidd.org
www.aamr.org

M Doreen Croser, Executive Director

AAIDD promotes progressive policies, sound research, effective practices and universal human rights for people with intellectual and developmental disabilities.

1 per year

3040 AAMA Annual Conference
American Academy of Medical Administrators
701 Lee Street
Suite 600
Des Plaines, IL 60016-4516
847-759-8601
E-mail: info@aameda.org
www.aameda.org

Renee Schleichar, CEO
Merle Hedland, Meeting Planner

Learn the newest trends in healthcare administration; focus on your area of specialty or broaden your knowledge; become energized with new information and contacts in your field; and return to your organization ready to implement new ideas anad face new challenges.

3041 AMA's Annual Medical Communications Conference
American Medical Association
515 N State Street
Chicago, IL 60654-4820
312-464-5000
800-621-8335
Fax: 312-464-4184
www.ama-assn.org

Michael D Maves, CEO

Provides hands-on communications training and hear from top-level medical communicators, government leaders and national journalists

3042 American Academy of Child and Adolescent Psychiatry (AACAP): Annual Meeting
3615 Wisconsin Avenue NW
Washington, DC 20016-3007
202-362-1797
E-mail: communications@aacap.org

Robert Hendren, President
David Herzog, Secretary
William Bernet, Treasurer

Professional society of physicians who have completed an additional five years of stimulate and advance medical contributions to the knowledge and treatment of psychiatric illnesses of children and adolescents. Annual meeting.

3043 American Academy of Addiction Psychiatry (AAAP) Annual Meeting & Symposium
345 Blackstone Boulevard
1st Floor - Weld
Providence, RI 02906-4800
401-524-3076
Fax: 401-272-0922
E-mail: info@aaap.org
www.aaap.org

Joseph G Liberto MD, President of the Board
Frances R Levin MD, President-Elect
Laurence M Westreich MD, Vice President
John A Renner Jr, MD, Secretary

The annual meeting provides researchers and health care practitioners the latest developments in treating mental health and substance abuse disorders. Meeting events include symposia, workshops, poster sessions showcasing new research in the field, Lunch with the Experts, plenary sessions, Breakfast for Trainees, and a case conference with expert discussion.

3044 American Academy of Psychiatry & Law Annual Conference
American Academy of Psychiatry & Law
1 Regency Drive
PO Box 30
Bloomfield, CT 06002-30
860-242-5450
800-331-1389
Fax: 860-286-0787
E-mail: execoff@aapl.org
www.aapl.org

Jacquelyn T. Coleman, Executive Director
Jeffrey Janofsky MD, President
Kenneth Appelbaum MD, Vice President

3045 American Academy of Psychoanalysis Preliminary Meeting
American Academy of Psychoanalysis and Dynamic Psychiatry
One Regency Drive
PO Box 30
Bloomfield, CT 06002-30
888-691-8281
Fax: 860-286-0787
E-mail: info@aapdp.org
www.aapsa.org

Jacquelyn T Coleman CAE, Executive Director
Sherry Katz-Bearnot, President
Carol Filiaci, Secretary

Annual meeting, Toronto, Canada.

3046 American Association of Children's Residential Center Annual Conference
American Association of Children's Residential Centers
11700 W Lake Park Drive
Milwaukee, WI 53224-3021
877-332-2272
Fax: 877-362-2272
E-mail: kbehling@alliance1.org
www.aacrc-dc.org

Kari Behling, National Coordinator
Steve Elson, President

Funded by the Mental Health Community Support Program. The purpose of the association is to share information about services, providers and ways to cope with mental illnesses. Available services include referrals, professional seminars, support groups and a variety of publications.

3047 American Association of Geriatric Psychiatry Annual Meetings
7910 Woodmont Avenue
Suite 1050
Bethesda, MD 20814-3069
301-654-7850
Fax: 301-654-4137
E-mail: main@aagponline.org
www.aagponline.org

Christine De Vries, Manager
Annie Williams, Administrative Assistant

Annual Meeting: March, Puerto Rico

3048 American Association of Health Care Consultants Annual Fall Conference
American Association of Health Care Consultants
5938 Drake Avenue
Chicago, IL 60659-3203
773-866-2770
888-350-2242
E-mail: info@aahcmail.org
www.aahc.net

Linda Campbell, Executive Director

Association hosts an Annual Fall Conference: October.

3049 American Association of Homes & Services for the Aging Annual Convention
American Association of Homes & Services for the Aging
2519 Connecticute Avenue NW
Washington, DC 20008-1520
202-783-2242
Fax: 202-783-2255
E-mail: info@aahsa.org
www.aahsa.org

William L Minnix Jr, President
Katrinka Smith Sloan, COO/SVP Member Services

3050 American Association on Intellectual and Developmental Disabilities Annual Meeting
444 N Capitol Street NW
Suite 846
Washington, DC 20001-1569
202-637-0475
800-424-3688
Fax: 202-637-0585
E-mail: maria@aaidd.org

Doreen M Croser, Executive Director
Maria A Alfaro, Meeting Planner/We Manager

Provides the opportunity of networking with old friends and colleagues, and is a wonderful opportunity to welcome students and new disability professionals to our Association. *$445.00*

3051 American Board of Disability Analysts Annual Conference
Park Plaza Medical Building
345 24th Avenue North
Nashville, TN 37203-1520

615-327-2978
E-mail: americanbd@aol.com
Kenneth N Anchor

3052 American College of Health Care Administrators (ACHCA) Annual Convocation & Exposition
1321 Duke Street
Suite 400
Alexandria, VA 22314
202-536-5120
Fax: 888-874-1585
E-mail: jspence@achca.org
www.achca.org

Steve Esdale, President

A non-profit professional membership association which provides superior educataional programming, professional certification, and career development opportunities for its members.

Year Founded: 1966

3053 American College of Healthcare Executives Educational Events
American College of Healthcare Executives
One N Franklin Street
Suite 1700
Chicago, IL 60606-3529
312-424-2800
Fax: 312-424-0023
E-mail: geninco@ache.org
www.ache.org

Thomas C Dolan, CEO
David Rubenstein, Chairman-Elect

3054 American College of Psychiatrists Annual Meeting
122 S. Michigan Ave
Suite 1360
Chicago, IL 60603-6185
312-662-1020
Fax: 312-662-1025
E-mail: angel@acpsych.org
www.acpsych.org

Maureen Shick, Executive Director
Angel Waszak, Administrative Assistant

Nonprofit honorary association of psychiatrists who, through excellence in their chosen fields, have been recognized for their significant contributions to the profession. The society's goal is to promote and support the highest standards in psychiatry through education, research and clinical practice. Annual Meeting in February.

3055 American Group Psychotherapy Association Annual Conference
American Group Psychotherapy Association
25 E 21st Street
6th Floor
New York, NY 10010-6207

212-477-2677
877-668-2472
E-mail: info@agpa.org
www.agpa.org

Marsha Block, CEO
Jeffrey Kleinberg, PhD, CGP, President

Educational conference with a changing annual focus. February.

Year Founded: 1942

3056 American Health Care Association Annual Convention

1201 L Street NW
Washington, DC 20005-4046
202-842-4444
Fax: 202-842-3860

Bruse Yarwood, President

Exhibits and educational workshops from the nonprofit federation of affiliated state health organizations, together representing nearly 12,000 nonprofit and for profit assisted living, nursing facility, developmentally disabled and subacute care providers that care for more than 1.5 million elderly and disabled individuals nationally. AHCA represents the long term care community at large — to government, business leaders and the general public. It also serves as a force for change within the long term care field, providing information, education, and administrative tools that enhance quality at every level.

3057 American Health Information Management Association Annual Exhibition and Conference

233 N Michigan Avenue
21st Floor
Chicago, IL 60601-5809
312-233-1100
Fax: 312-233-1090
E-mail: info@ahima.org
www.ahima.org

Linda Kloss, Executive Director
Becky Garris-Perry, Executive Vice President/CFO

Exhibits, business and educational conferences of the dynamic professional association that represents more than 46,000 specially educated health information management professionals who work throughout the healthcare industry. Health information management professionals serve the health care industry and the public by manageing, analyzing and utilizing data vital for patient care and making it accessible to healthcare providers when it is needed most.

3058 American Society for Adolescent Psychiatry: Annual Meeting

PO Box 570218
Dallas, TX 75357-218
972-613-0985
Fax: 972-613-5532
E-mail: info@adolpsych.org
www.adolpsych.org

Mohan Nair, President
Frances Bell, Executive Director

Feature presentations by prominent members of the professional community, exhibits, workshops, receptions, award ceremony and installation of officers. Annual meeting held in March.

3059 Annual Meeting & Medical-Scientific Conference

American Society of Addiction Medicine
4601 N Park Avenue
Upper Arcade #101
Chevy Chase, MD 20815-4519
301-656-3920
Fax: 301-656-3815
E-mail: email@asam.org
www.asam.org

Eileen McGrath, Executive VP
Eileen McGrath, Executive Vice President

Goal is to present the most up-to-date information in the addictions field. to attain this goal, program sessions will focus on the latest developments in research and treatment issues and will tanslate them into clinically useful knowledge. Through a mix of symposia, courses, workshops, didactic lectures, and paper and poster presentations based on submitted abstracts, participants will have an opportunity to interact with experts in their field.

3060 Annual Santa Fe Psychiatric Symposium

Psychiatry Department
University of Arizona
Campbell Ave, PO Box 245002
Tucson, AZ 85724-5002
520-626-6254
Fax: 520-626-2004
www.psychiatry.arizona.edu

Designed to meet the educational needs of physicians (psychiatrists, family practitioners, general practitioners), psychologists, nurse practitioners, physician assistants, nurses and other health care professionals. Each half-day will provide practical and clinically relevant information for day-to-day problems. Morning lectures will be followed by panel discussions.

3061 Annual Summit on International Managed Care Trends

Academy for International Health Studies
273 Hebron Avenue
Glastonbury, CT 06033-2116
860-430-1388
Fax: 860-430-1420
www.aihs.com

Bruce A Pollack, President

Global healthcare meeting; 500 people, 47 nations attended previous summits.

3062 Association for Ambulatory Behavioral Healthcare: Training Conference

247 Douglas Avenue
Portsmouth, VA 23707-1520
757-673-3741
E-mail: mickey@aabh.org

Mickey Wright, Executive Director

Powerful forum for people engaged in providing mental health services. Promoting the evolution of flexible models of responsive cost-effective ambulatory behavioral healthcare.

3063 Association for Child Psychoanalysis (ACP) Annual Meeting

7820 Enchanted Hills Blvd
#A-233
Rio Rancho, NM 87144
505-771-0372
E-mail: childanalysis@comcast.net
www.childanalysis.org

Kerry Kelly Novick, President
Tricia Hall, Administrator
Denia Barrett MSW

An international not-for-profit organization in which all members are highly trained child and adolescent psychoanalysts. Provides a forum for the interchange of ideas and clinical experience in order to advance the psychological treatment and understanding of children and adolescents and their families.

3064 Association of Black Psychologists Annual Convention

PO Box 55999
Washington, DC 20040-5999
202-722-0808
Fax: 202-722-5941
E-mail: abpsi_office@abpsi.org
www.abpsi.org

Dorothy Holmes, President
Pamela Hall, Secretary
Muriel Kennedy, Treasurer

Feature presentations, exhibits and workshops held over a four day period focusing on the unique concerns of Black professionals.

3065 California Psychological Association's Annual Convention

1231 I Street
Suite 204
Sacramento, CA 95814-2933
916-286-7979
Fax: 916-286-7971
E-mail: membership@cpapsych.org
www.cpapsych.org

Jo Linder-Crow PhD, Executive Director
Patricia VanWoerkom, Administration Director

Poster sessions, roundtable discussions, CE sessions, ethics discussions and featured speakers. *$680.00*

3066 Georgia Psychological Society First Annual Conference
GPS Proposals

1500 North Patterson Street
Department of Psychology, VSU
Valdosta, GA 31698-100

E-mail: blbrowne@valdosta.edu or crtalor@valdosta.edu
www.georgiapsychologicalsociety.org

Proposals for symposia, papers, posters and workshops on topics in all areas of psychology are invited. Proposals should not exceed 500 words, and each proposal must include a summary that is no longer than 50 words.

3067 Institute for Advancement of Human Behavior

4370 Alpine Road
Suite 209
Portola Valley, CA 94028-7953
650-851-8411
800-258-8411
Fax: 650-851-0406
E-mail: staff@iahb.org

Gerald W Piaget, President
Joan Piaget, Executive Director

Host 10-15 meetings a year. Representing the cutting edge in professional education.

3068 NADD Annual Conference & Exhibit Show
National Association for the Dually Diagnosed

132 Fair Street
Kingston, NY 12401-4802
845-331-4336
800-331-5362
E-mail: info@thenadd.org
www.thenadd.org

Robert Fletcher, Executive Director

3069 NAMI National Convention
National Alliance on Mental Illness

2107 Wilson Boulevard
Suite 300
Arlington, VA 22201-3080
703-524-7600
800-950-6264
Fax: 703-524-9094
TDD: 703-516-7227
E-mail: info@nami.org
www.nami.org

Michael J Fitzpatrick, Executive Director

Join the thousands who will gather to explore strategy and tactics to improve the lives of people who live with mental illnesses.

3070 National Multicultural Conference and Summit

Brakins Consulting & Psychological Svs
13805 60th Avenue North
Phymouth, MN 55446-3583

www.multiculturalsummit.com

The mission is to convene students, practitioners, and scholars in psychology and related fields to inform and inspire multicultural research and practice.

3071 Traumatic Incident Reduction Workshop
E-Productivity-Services.Net
Division of 21st Century Enterprises
13 NW Barry Rd PMB 214
Kansas City, MO 64155-2728
816-468-4945
Fax: 816-468-6656
E-mail: nld@espn.net
www.espn.net

Nancy L Day, Certifien Trauma Specialist

Defines the Conditioned Response Phenomena, establishes a safe environment, analyzes and applies the Unblocking technique to resolve issues relating to emotionally charged persons, places, things and situations, and analyzes and applies Traumatic Incident Reduction (TIR) to resolve known and unknown past traumatic experiences and the unwanted feelings, emotions, sensations, attitutdes and pain associated with them.

3072 YAI/National Institute for People with Disabilities
460 W 34th Street
New York, NY 10001-2382
212-273-6193
Fax: 212-947-7524
www.yai.org

Philip Levy, CEO
Philip H Levy, President/COO

3073 ASHA Annual Convention
American Speech-Language-Hearing Association
2200 Research Blvd
Rockville, MD 20850-3289
301-269-5700
800-638-8255
Fax: 301-296-8580
TTY: 301-296-5650
E-mail: actioncenter@asha.org
www.asha.org

Arlene A Pietranton, Executive Director

ASHA is the professional, scientific and credentialing association for 140,000 members and affiliates who are audiologists, speech-language pathologists and speech, language and hearing scientists.

1 per year

Periodicals & Pamphlets

3074 AACAP News
AACAP
3615 Wisconsin Avenue NW
Washington, DC 20016-3056
202-966-7300
E-mail: communications@aacap.org
www.aacap.org

Eva Brown, Manager
David Herzog, Secretary
William Bernet, Treasurer

The American Academy of Child and Adolescent Psychiatry, (AACAP) publishes a newsletter which focuses events within the Academy, child and adolescent psychiatrists, and AACAP members.

36-64 pages 6 per year

3075 AAMI Newsletter
Arizona Alliance for the Mentally Ill (NAMI Arizona)
2210 N 7th Street
Phoenix, AZ 85006-1604
602-244-8166
800-626-5022
Fax: 602-244-9264
E-mail: namiaz@namiaz.org
www.namiaz.org

Diane McVicker, President
Cheryl Weiner, Educutive Director

Provides support, education, research, and advocacy for individuals and families affected by mental illness. Reports on legislative updates, conventions, psychiatry/psychological practices, and activities of the alliance. Newsletter with membership. *$10.00*

8 pages 4 per year

3076 AAPL Newsletter
American Academy of Psychiatry and the Law
One Regency Drive
PO Box 30
Bloomfield, CT 06002-30
860-242-5450
800-331-1389
Fax: 860-286-0787
E-mail: execoff@aapl.org
www.aapl.org

Jacquelyn T. Coleman, Executive Director
Jeffrey Janofsky MD, President
Kenneth Appelbaum MD, Vice President

Newsletter that discusses psychiatry as it relates to the law. Recurring features include recent legal cases, legislative updates, letters to the editor, notices of publications available, news of educational opportunities, job listings, a calendar of events, and editorial columns. *$25.00*

20 pages 3 per year

3077 AJMR-American Journal on Mental Retardation
AAMR
444 N Capitol Street NW
Suite 846
Washington, DC 20001-1569
202-637-0475
800-424-3688
Fax: 202-637-0585
E-mail: dcroser@aamr.org

Provides updates on the latest program advances, current research, and information on products and services in the developmental disabilities field. *$10.50*

24 per year ISSN 0047-6765

3078 APA Monitor
American Psychological Association
750 1st Street NE
Washington, DC 20002-4242
202-336-5500
800-374-2721
Fax: 202-336-5518
E-mail: letters.monitor@apa.org
www.apa.org

Norman B Anderson, CEO

Magazine of the American Psychological Association.

12 per year   ISSN 1529-4978

3079 ARC News
Association for Retarded Citizens-Pennsylvania
1617 Bald Eagle Avenue
S Williamsport, PA 17702-7066
570-326-6997

Publicizes work of the Association, which is committed to securing for all people with mental retardation the opportunity to choose and realize their goals; promotes reducing the incidence and limiting the consequence of mental retardation through education, research, advocacy, and the support of family, friends, and the community; provides leadership in the field and strives for development of necessary human and financial resources to succeed.

4 pages   12 per year

3080 ASAP Newsletter
American Society for Adolescent Psychiatry
PO Box 570218
Dallas, TX 75357-218
972-613-0985
Fax: 972-613-5532
E-mail: info@adolpsych.org
www.adolpsych.org

Mohan Nair, President
Frances Bell, Executive Director

Contains articles about adolescent psychiatry and society news. Recurring features include news of research, a calendar of events, and book reviews. *$10.00*

16-20 pages   4 per year

3081 Advocate: Autism Society of America
Autism Society of America
7910 Woodmont Avenue
Suite 300
Bethesda, MD 20814-3067
301-657-0881
800-328-8476
Fax: 301-657-0869
www.autism-society.org

Ann Pulley, Manager

Reports news and information of national significance for individuals, families, and professionals dealing with autism. Recurring features include personal features and profiles, research summaries, government updates, book reviews, statistics, news of research, and a calendar of events.

32-36 pages   6 per year   ISSN 0047-9101

3082 Alcohol & Drug Abuse Weekly
John Wiley & Sons
111 River Street
Hoboken, NJ 07030-5790
201-748-6000
Fax: 201-748-6088
www.wiley.com

William J Pesce, CEO

48-issue subsrciption offers significant news and analysis of federal and state policy developments. A resource for directors of addiction treatment centers, managed care executives, federal and state policy makers and healthcare consultants. Topics include the latest findings in treatment and prevention; funding and survival issues for providers; the impact of state and federal policy on treatment and prevention; working under managed care; and co-occurring disorders.

8 pages   48 per year   Year Founded: 1992   ISSN 1042-1394

3083 American Association of Community Psychiatrists (AACP)
PO Box 570218
Dallas, TX 75357-218
972-613-0985
Fax: 972-613-5532
E-mail: frda1@airmail.net
www.wpic.pitt.edu/aacp

Wesley Sowers MD, President
Annelle Primm, Vice President
Francis Bell, Administrative Director

Psychiatrists and psychiatry residents practicing in community mental health centers or similar programs that provide care to the mentally ill regardless of their ability to pay. Addresses issues faced by psychiatrists who practice within CMHCs. Publications: AACP Membership Directory, annual. Community Psychiatrist, quarterly newsletter. Annual meeting, in conjunction with American Psychiatric Association in May. Annual meeting, in conjunction with Institute on Hospital and Community in fall.

4 per year

3084 American Institute for Preventive Medicine
American Institute for Preventive Medicine Press
30445 Northwestern Highway
Suite 350
Farmington Hills, MI 48334-3107
248-539-1800
800-345-2476
Fax: 248-539-1808
E-mail: aipm@healthy.net
www.healthylife.com

Don R Powell, President
Sue Jackson, VP

AIPM is an internationally renowned developer and provider of wellness programs and publications that address both mental and physical health issues. It works with over 11,500 corporations, hospitals, MCOs, universities, and goverment agencies to reduce health care costs, lower absenteeism, and improve productivity. The Institute has a number of publications that address mental health issues, including stress management, depression, self - esteem, and EAP issues.

Year Founded: 1999

3085 Behavioral Health Industry News
Open Minds
163 York Street
Gettysburg, PA 17325-1933
717-334-1329
877-350-6463
Fax: 717-334-0538
E-mail: openminds@openminds.com
www.openminds.com

Monica Oss, Owner

Provides information on marketing, financial, and legal trends in the delivery of mental health and chemical dependency benefits and services. Recurring features include interviews, news of research, a calendar of events, job listings, book reviews, notices of publications available, and industry statistics. *$185.00*

12 pages 12 per year ISSN 1043-3880

3086 Behavioral Health Management
PO Box 20179
Cleveland, OH 44120-179
216-391-9100
Fax: 216-391-9200
www.behavioral.net

Richard Peck, Editorial Director
Douglas J Edwards, Managing Editor

Informs decision makers in managed behavioral healthcare organizations, provider groups, and treatment centers of the ever-changing demands of their field. The magazine publishes analyses, editorials, and organizations case studies to give readers the information they need for best practices in a challenging marketplace.

3087 Brown University: Child & Adolescent
Psychopharmacology Update
John Wiley & Sons
111 River Street
Hoboken, NJ 07030-5790
201-748-6000
Fax: 201-748-6088
E-mail: jbsubs@wiley.com
www.wiley.com

William J Pesce, CEO

Monthly newsletter that gives information on children and adolescent's unique psychotropic medication needs. Delivers updates on new drugs, their uses, typical doses, side effects and interactions, examines generic vs. name brand drugs, reports on new research and new indications for existing medications. Each issue also includes case studies, references for future reading, industry news notes, abstracts of current research and a patient psychotropic medication handout. *$ 190.00*

12 per year ISSN 1527-8395

3088 Brown University: Digest of Addiction Theory
and Application (DATA)
John Wiley & Sons
111 River Street
Hoboken, NJ 07030-5790
201-748-6000
Fax: 201-748-6088
E-mail: jbsubs@wiley.com
www.wiley.com

William J Pesce, CEO

Monthly synopsis of critical research developments in the treatment and prevention of alcoholism and drug abuse, including dozens of research abstracts chosen from over 75 medical journals. *$129.00*

8 pages 12 per year ISSN 1040-6328

3089 Brown University: Geriatric
Psychopharmacology Update
John Wiley & Sons
111 River Street
Hoboken, NJ 07030-5790
201-748-6000
Fax: 201-748-6088
E-mail: jbsubs@wiley.com
www.wiley.com

William J Pesce, CEO

This monthly report is an easy way to keep up to date on the newest breakthroughs in geriatric medicine that have an impact on psychiatric practice. *$190.00*

12 per year ISSN 1529-2584

3090 Brown University: Psychopharmacology
Update
John Wiley & Sons
111 River Street
Hoboken, NJ 07030-5790
201-748-6000
Fax: 201-748-6088
www.wiley.com

William J Pesce, CEO

Each issue examines the pros and cons of specific drugs, drug-drug interactions, side effects, street drugs, warning signs, case reports and more. *$199.00*

12 per year ISSN 1608-5308

3091 Bulletin of Menninger Clinic
Guilford Publications
72 Spring Street
New York, NY 10012-4068
212-431-9800
800-288-3950
Fax: 212-966-6708

Bob Matloff, President

Valuable, practical information for clinicans. Recent topical issues have focused on rekindling the psychodynamic vision, treatment of different clinical populations with panic disorder, and treatment of complicated personality disorders in an era of managed care. All in an integrated, psychodynamic approach. *$75.00*

ISSN 0025-9284

16-28 pages 4 per year

3092 Bulletin of Psychological Type
Association for Psychological Type
9650 Rockville Pike
Bethesda, MD 20814-3999
301-634-7450
800-847-9943
Fax: 301-634-7455
E-mail: web@aptinternational.org
www.aptinternational.org

John Lord, Executive Director
Jane Kise, President

Provides information on regional, national, and international events to keep professionals up-to-date in the study and application of psychological type theory and the Myers-Briggs Type Indicator. Contains announcements of training workshops; international, national, and regional conferences; and awards, along with articles on issues directly related to type theory.

3093 Capitation Report
National Health Information
PO Box 15429
Atlanta, GA 30333-429
404-607-9500
800-597-6300
Fax: 404-607-0095
www.nhionline.net

NHI publishes specialized, targeted information for health care executives on a variety of topics from capitation to disease management.

3094 Child and Adolescent Psychiatry
American Academy of Child and Adolescent Psychiatry
3615 Wisconsin Avenue NW
Washington, DC 20016-3007
202-362-1797
E-mail: communications@aacap.org

Robert Hendren, President
David Herzog, Secretary
William Bernet, Treasurer

Journal focusing on today's psychiatric research and treatment of the child and adolescent. *$175.00*

12 per year ISSN 0890-8567

3095 Chronicle
Association for the Help of Retarded Children (AHRC)
200 Park Avenue South
New York, NY 10003-1503
212-477-9696
E-mail: ahrcnyc@ahrcnyc.org

Covers developmental disabilities, includes legislation and entitlements updates, field news, accessing information and services, advocacy issues, and current research. Recurring features include interviews, news of research, a calendar of events, reports of meetings, book reviews, and notices of publications available.

3096 Clinical Psychiatry News
International Medical News Group
12230 Wilkins Avenue
Rockville, MD 20852-1886
301-816-8700
877-524-9335
Fax: 301-816-8712
E-mail: cpsnews@elsevier.com
www.imng.com

A leading independent newspaper for the Psychiatrist.

3097 Clinical Psychiatry Quarterly
AACP
PO Box 458
Glastonbury, CT 06033-458
860-633-5045
Fax: 860-633-6023
E-mail: info@aacp.com
www.aacp.com

Informs members of of news and events. Recurring features include letters to the editor, news of research, a calendar of events, reports of meetings, and book reviews.

4 per year

3098 Couples Therapy in Managed Care
Haworth Press
10 Alice Street
Binghamton, NY 13904-1503
607-722-5857
800-429-6784
Fax: 607-722-1424
E-mail: getinfo@haworthpressinc.com
www.haworthpress.com

Provides social workers, psychologists and counselors with an overview of the negative effects of the managed care industry on the quality of marital health care.

ISBN 7-890078-86-6

3099 Current Directions in Psychological Science
Association for Psychological Science
1133 15th Street NW
Suite 1000
Washington, DC 20005
202-293-9300
Fax: 202-293-9350
www.psychologicalscience.org

Linda Bartoshuk, President
Mahzarin R Banaji, President-Elect
Randall W Engle, Author
Alan G Kraut, Executive Director

Current Directions publishes reviews by leading experts covering all of scientific psychology and its applications. Each issue features a diverse mix of reports on various topics such as language, memory and cognition, development, the neural basis of behavior and emotions, various aspects of psychopathology, and theory of mind. The articles keep readers apprised of important developments across subfields. The articles are also written to be accessible to non-experts, making them suited for classroom teaching supplements.

6 per year   ISSN 0963-7214

3100 Development & Psychopathology
Cambridge University Press
40 W 20th Street
New York, NY 10011-4211
212-924-3900
Fax: 212-691-3239
E-mail: marketing@cup.org
www.cup.org

This multidisciplinary journal is devoted to the publication of original, empirical, theoretical and review papers which address the interrelationship of normal and pathological development in adults and children. It is intended to serve and intergrate the emerging field of developmental psychopathology which strives to understand patterns of adaptation and maladaptation throughout the lifespan. This journal is of vital interest to psychologists, psychiatrists, social scientists, neuroscientists, pediatricians and researchers. *$66.00*

4 per year   ISSN 0954-5794

3101 Developmental Brain Research
Customer Support Department
PO Box 945
New York, NY 10159-945
212-633-3730
888-437-4636
Fax: 212-633-3680
www.elsevier.com

ISSN 0165-3806

3102 Disability Funding Week
CD Publications
8204 Fenton Street
Silver Spring, MD 20910-4571
301-588-6380
800-666-6380
Fax: 301-588-6385
E-mail: cdpubs@clark.net

Michael Gerecht, President

Up to date news for mental health professionals. *$ 259.00*

14-18 pages   24 per year   Year Founded: 1992   ISSN 1069-1359

3103 EAPA Exchange
Employee Assistance Professionals Association
2101 Wilson Boulevard
Arlington, VA 22201-3086
703-522-6272
Fax: 703-522-4585

3104 ETR Associates
Health Education, Research, Training Curriculum
4 Carbonero Way
Scotts Valley, CA 95066-4200

831-438-4060
800-321-4407
Fax: 831-438-4284
www.etr.org

John Henry Ledwith, National Sales Director

Publishes a complete line of innovative materials covering the full spectrum of health education topics, including maternal/child health, HIV/STD prevention, risk and injury prevention, self esteem, fitness and nutrition, college health, and wellness education, engaging in both extensive training and research endeavors and a comprehensive K-12 health curriculum.

3105 Employee Benefits Journal
International Foundation of Employee Benefit Plans
PO Box 69
Brookfield, WI 53008-69
414-786-6700
Fax: 414-786-8670
E-mail: marybr@ifebp.org
www.ifebp.org

Contains articles on all aspects of employee benefits and related topics. *$70.00*

32-48 pages   4 per year   ISSN 0361-4050

3106 Exceptional Parent
PO Box 5446
Pittsfield, MA 01203
201-634-6550
800-372-7368
Fax: 740-389-6845
www.eparent.com

Magazine for parents and professionals involved in the care and development of children and young adults with special needs, including physical disabilities, developmental disabilities, mental retardation, autism, epilepsy, learning disabilities, hearing/vision impairments, emotional problems, and chronic illnesses. *$36.00*

12 per year

3107 Focal Point: Research, Policy and Practice in Children's Mental Health
Regional Research Institue-Portland State University
PO Box 751
Portland, OR 97207-751
503-725-4040
800-628-1696
Fax: 503-725-4180
E-mail: rtcpubs@pdx.edu
www.rtc.pdx.edu

Janet Walker, Editor

Features information on research, interventions, organizations, strategies, and conferences to aid families that have children with emotional, mental, and/or behavioral disorders.

24 pages

3108 Forty Two Lives in Treatment: a Study of Psychoanalysis and Psychotherapy
Guilford Publications
72 Spring Street
New York, NY 10012-4068
212-431-9800
800-365-7006
Fax: 212-966-6708
E-mail: info@guilford.com

Bob Matloff, President

Comprehensive results of the study of 42 patients undergoing psychoanalysis and analytic psychotherapy. *$79.95*

784 pages Year Founded: 1986 ISBN 0-898623-25-1

3109 From the Couch
Behavioral Health Record Section-AMRA
919 N Michigan Avenue
Suite 1400
Chicago, IL 60611-1692
312-787-2672
Fax: 312-787-5926

From the couch, the newsletter for the Behavioral Health Record section of the American Medical Record Association, covers aspects of the medical records industry that pertain to mental health records.

4 per year

3110 Frontiers of Health Services Management
American College of Healthcare Executives
1 N Franklin Street
Chicago, IL 60606-3529
312-424-2800
Fax: 312-424-0023
E-mail: hap1@ache.org
www.ache.org

Thomas C Dolan, CEO
Janet Davis, Acquisitions Editor

Enhanced by special access to today's healthcare leaders. Frontiers provides you with the cutting edge insight you want. Each quarterly issue engages you in a vigorous debate on a hot healthcare topic. One stimulating article leads the debate, followed by commentaries and perspectives from recognized experts. Unique combination of opinion, practice and research stimulate you to develop new management strategies. *$70.00*

4 per year   ISSN 0748-8157

3111 General Hospital Psychiatry: Psychiatry, Medicine and Primary Care
Elsevier Science
725 Concord Avenue
Suite 4200
Cambridge, MA 02138-1041
617-661-3544
Fax: 617-661-4800
E-mail: don_lipsitt@hms.harvard.edu
www.elsevier.com

Journal that explores the linkages and interfaces between psychiatry, medicine and primary care. As a peer-reviewed journal, it provides a forum for communication among professionals with clinical, academic and research interests in psychiatry's essential function in the mainstream of medicine. *$195.00*

84 pages 6 per year   ISSN 01638343

3112 Geriatrics
Advanstar Communications
7500 Old Oak Boulevard
Cleveland, OH 44130-3343
440-243-8100
Fax: 440-891-2740
E-mail: arossetti@advanstar.com
www.act-europe.org

David Briemer, Sales Manager
Rich Ehrlich, Associate Publisher

Peer-reviewed clinical journal for primary care physicians who care for patients age 50 and older.

100 pages 12 per year

3113 Group Practice Journal
Amerian Medical Group Association
1422 Duke Street
Alexandria, VA 22314-3403
703-838-0033
Fax: 703-548-1890
E-mail: roconnor@amga.org
www.amga.org

Don Fisher, CEO
Donald Fisher, President/CEO

Penned by healthcare professionals, articles in the Group Practice Journal give a view from the trenches of modern medicine on a wide variety of topics, including innovative disease management and clinical best practices. Readers look to the publication to learn strategies and solutions from peers in the profession, healthcare thought leaders, and industry experts.

10 per year

3114 Harvard Mental Health Letter
Harvard Health Publications
10 Shattuck Street
Suite 612
Boston, MA 02115-6030
617-432-4714
E-mail: mental_health@hms.harvard.edu

Anthony Komaroff, Owner

Delivers information on current thinking and debate on mental health issues that concern professionals and layment a like. In the ever-changing and complex field of mental health care, the newsletter has become a trusted source for psychiatrists, psychologists, social workers and therapists of all kinds. *$59.00*

8 pages 12 per year Year Founded: 1983 ISSN 08843783

3115 Harvard Review of Psychiatry
Taylor and Francis
01650 Toebben Drive
Independence, KY 41051

800-634-7064
Fax: 800-248-4724

An authoritative source for scholarly reviews and perspectives on important topics in psychiatry. Founded by the Harvard Medical School's Department of Psychiatry, the Harvard Review of Psychiatry features review papares that summarize and synthesize the key literature in a scholarly and clinically relevant manner. *$185.00*

6 per year

3116 Health & Social Work
National Association of Social Workers
750 1st Street NE
Suite 700
Washington, DC 20002-8011
202-408-8600
Fax: 202-336-8313
www.naswpress.org

Elvira Craig De Silva, President

Articles cover research, policy, specialized servies, quality assurance, inservice training and other topics that affect the delivery of health care services. *$125.00*

3117 Health Data Management
Faulkner & Gray
11 Penn Plaza
New York, NY 10001-2006
212-967-7000
Fax: 212-239-4993

3118 Health Grants & Contracts Weekly
Capitol Publications
1101 K Street
Suite 444
Alexandria, VA 22314
703-583-4100
Fax: 703-739-6517

Provides information on health-related project opportunities in research, training and service

3119 IABMCP Newsletter
IABMCP
3208 N Academy Boulevard, Suite 160
Colorado Springs, CO 80917-5155
719-597-5959
Fax: 719-597-0166
E-mail: iabmcp@att.net

The International Academy of Behavioral Medicine, Counseling, and Psychotherapy, (IABMCP) publishes research articles in the field of behavioral medicine, 'the systematic application of various principles of behavioral science to health care problems.' Contains news of the Academy and its members. Recurring features include book reviews, letters to the editor, and a calendar of events. *$60.00*

4-8 pages 4 per year

3120 Insider
Alliance for Children and Families
1701 K Street NW
Suite 200
Washington, DC 20006-1540
202-296-7116
E-mail: policy@alliance1.org

Neal Gillen, Executive VP
Peter Goldberg, President/CEO
Thomas Harney, VP Membership

Alliance for Children and Families' tool for providing members with accurate and up-to-date information on current legislation, issues the Alliance is advocating on Capitol Hill, summaries of how proposed bills will affect member organizations and the people they serve, and suggestions for local advocacy efforts.

3121 International Drug Therapy Newsletter
Lippincott Williams & Wilkins
351 W Camden Street
Baltimore, MD 21201-2436
410-949-8000
800-882-0483
Fax: 410-528-4414
E-mail: korourke@lww.com
www.lww.com

J Arnold Anthony, Operations

Newsletter that focuses on psychotropic drugs, discussing individual drugs, their effectiveness, and history. Examines illnesses and the drugs used to treat them, studies done on various drugs, their chemical make-up, and new developments and changes in drugs. *$149.00*

8 pages ISSN 0020-6571

3122 International Journal of Neuropsychopharmacology
Cambridge University Press
40 W 20th Street
New York, NY 10011-4211
212-924-3900
Fax: 212-691-3239
E-mail: marketing@cup.org
www.cup.org

3123 International Journal of Aging and Human Developments
Baywood Publishing Company
26 Austin Avenue
Box 337
Amityville, NY 11701-3052
631-691-2048
800-638-7819
Fax: 631-691-1770
E-mail: baywood@baywood.com
www.baywood.com

Stuart Cohen, Owner

$218.00

8 per year Year Founded: 1973 ISSN 0091-4150

3124 International Journal of Health Services
Baywood Publishing Company
26 Austin Avenue
Box 337
Amityville, NY 11701-3052
631-691-2048
800-638-7819
Fax: 631-691-1770
E-mail: baywood@baywood.com
www.baywood.com

Stuart Cohen, Owner

$160.00

4 per year Year Founded: 1970

3125 International Journal of Psychiatry in Medicine
Baywood Publishing Company
26 Austin Avenue
Box 337
Amityville, NY 11701-3052
631-691-2048
800-638-7819
Fax: 631-691-1770
E-mail: baywood@baywood.com
www.baywood.com

Stuart Cohen, Owner

$160.00

4 per year Year Founded: 1970 ISSN 0091274

3126 Journal of AHIMA
**American Health Information Management
Association**
233 N Michigan Avenue
21st Floor
Chicago, IL 60601-5809
312-233-1100
Fax: 312-233-1090
E-mail: info@ahima.org
www.ahima.org

Linda Kloss, Executive Director
Becky Garris-Perry, Executive Vice President/CFO

Monthly magazine with articles, news and event
annoucements from the nonprofit federation of affiliated
state health organizations, together representing nearly
12,000 nonprofit and for profit assisted living, nursing facility, developmentally disabled and subacute care providers that care for more than 1.5 million elderly and disabled
individuals nationally.

**3127 Journal of American Health Information
Management Association**
**American Health Information Management
Association**
233 N Michigan Avenue
21st Floor
Chicago, IL 60601-5809
312-233-1100
Fax: 312-233-1090
E-mail: info@ahima.org
www.ahima.org

Linda Kloss, Executive Director
Becky Garris-Perry, Executive Vice President/CFO

**3128 Journal of American Medical Information
Association**
Hanley & Befus
210 S 13th Street
Philadelphia, PA 19107-5491
215-546-4656

3129 Journal of Drug Education
Baywood Publishing Company
26 Austin Avenue
Box 337
Amityville, NY 11701-3052
631-691-2048
800-638-7819
Fax: 631-691-1770
E-mail: info@baywood.com
www.baywood.com

Stuart Cohen, Owner

$160.00

4 per year Year Founded: 1970

3130 Journal of Education Psychology
American Psychological Association
750 1st Street NE
Washington, DC 20002-4242
202-336-5500
800-374-2721
Fax: 202-336-5518
TDD: 202-336-6123
TTY: 202-336-6123
E-mail: order@apa.org
www.apa.org

Norman B Anderson, CEO

$102.00

4 per year ISSN 0022-0663

3131 Journal of Emotional and Behavioral Disorders
Pro-Ed Publications
8700 Shoal Creek Boulevard
Austin, TX 78757-6897
512-451-3246
800-897-3202
Fax: 512-451-8542
E-mail: info@proedinc.com

Donald D Hammill, Owner

An international, multidisciplinary journal featuring articles on research, practice and theory related to individuals
with emotional and behavioral disorders and to the professionals who serve them. Presents topics of interest to individuals representing a wide range of disciplines including
corrections, psychiatry, mental health, counseling, rehabilitation, education, and psychology. *$39.00*

64 pages 4 per year ISSN 1063-4266

3132 Journal of Intellectual & Development Disability
Taylor & Francis Publishing
875 Massachusetts Avenue
Suite 81
Cambridge, MA 02139-3071
215-625-8900
Fax: 215-269-0363
www.taylorandfrancis.com

3133 Journal of Neuropsychiatry and Clinical Neurosciences
American Neuropsychiatric Association
700 Ackerman Road
Suite 625
Columbus, OH 43202-4505
614-447-2077
E-mail: anpa@osu.edu

Sandy Bornstein, Executive Director
C. Edward Coffey, Treasurer

Official publication of the organization and a benefit of membership. Our mission is to apply neuroscience for the benefit of people. Three core values have been identified for the association: advancing knowledge of brain-behavior relationships, providing a forum for learning, and promoting excellent, scientific and compassionate health care.

3134 Journal of Personality Assessment
Society for Personality Assessment
6109H Arlington Boulevard
Falls Church, VA 22044-2708
703-534-4772
Fax: 703-564-6905
E-mail: manager@spaonline.org
www.personality.org

Gregory J Meyer PhD, Author

Publishes articles dealing with the development, evaluation, refinement and application of personality assessment methods.
102 pages   ISSN 0022-3891

3135 Journal of Positive Behavior Interventions
Pro-Ed Publications
8700 Shoal Creek Boulevard
Austin, TX 78757-6897
512-451-3246
800-897-3202
Fax: 512-451-8542
E-mail: info@proedinc.com

Donald D Hammill, Owner

Deals with principles of positive behavioral support in school, home, and community settings for people with challenges in behavioral adaptation. *$39.00*
64 pages   4 per year   ISSN 1098-3007

3136 Journal of Practical Psychiatry
Williams & Wilkins
351 W Camden Street
Baltimore, MD 21201-2436

410-949-8000
Fax: 410-528-4414
www.lww.com

J Arnold Anthony, Operations

3137 Journal of the American Medical Informatics Association
American Medical Informatics Association
4915 St. Elmo Avenue
Suite 401
Bethesda, MD 20814-6052
301-657-1291
Fax: 301-657-1296
E-mail: mail@amia.org
www.amia.org

Karen Greenwood, Manager
Sarah Ingersoll, Treasurer

JAMIA is a bi-monthly journal that presents peer-reviewed articles on the spectrum of health care informatics in research, teaching, and application. *$212.00*

3138 Journal of the American Psychiatric Nurses Association
Sage Publishing
2455 Teller Road
Thoasand Oaks, CA 91320-2234
805-499-0721
800-818-7243
Fax: 805-499-0871
E-mail: journals@sagepub.com
www.sagepub.com

Blaise R Simqu, CEO

Official Journal of the American Psychiatric Nurses Association *$128.00*
ISSN 1078-3903

3139 Journal of the American Psychoanalytic Association
Analytic Press
101 W Street
Hillsdale, NJ 07642-1421
201-358-9477
800-926-6579
Fax: 201-358-4700
E-mail: TAP@analyticpress.com
www.analyticpress.com

Paul E Stepansky PhD, Managing Director
John Kerr PhD, Sr Editor

JAPA is one of the preeminent psychoanalytic journals. Recognized for the quality of its clinical and theoretical contributions, JAPA is now a major publication source for scientists and humanists whose work elaborates, applies, critiques or impinges on psychoanalysis. Topics include child psychoanalysis and the effectiveness of the intensive treatment of children, boundary violations, problems of memory and false memory syndrome, the concept of working through, the scientific status of psychoanalysis and the relevance or irrevance of infant observation for adult analysis. *$115.00*

300 pages 4 per year Year Founded: 1952 ISSN 0003-0651

3140 Journal of the International Neuropsychological Society
Cambridge University Press
40 W 20th Street
New York, NY 10011-4211
212-924-3900
Fax: 212-691-3239
E-mail: marketing@cup.org
www.cup.org

3141 Key
National Mental Health Consumers Self-Help
1211 Chestnut Street
Lobby 100
Philadelphia, PA 19107-4112
215-751-1810
800-553-4539
Fax: 215-636-6310
TTY: 215-751-9655
E-mail: info@mhselfhelp.org
www.mhselfhelp.org

Violet Phillips, Editor

Provides information for consumers of mental health services/psychiatric survivors on mental health issues, including advocacy and alternative mental health services.
$15.00

12 pages 4 per year

3142 Managed Care Strategies
Managed Care Strategies & Psychotherapy Finances
13901 US Highway 1
Suite 5
Juno Beach, FL 33408-1612
561-624-1155
Fax: 561-624-6006

3143 Mayo Clinic Health Letter
Mayo Clinic
200 1st Street SW
Rochester, MN 55905-2
507-284-9669
E-mail: healthletter@mayo.edu
www.mayoclinic.org

John H Noseworthy, CEO

Helping our subscribers achieve healthier lives by providing useful, easy to understand health information that is timely and of broad interest.

ISSN 0741-6245

3144 Medical Psychotherapist
Americal Board of Medical Psychotherapists & Psychodiagnosticians
345 24th Avenue N
Suite 201
Nashville, TN 37203-1520
615-327-2984
Fax: 615-327-9235

Official newsletter of the American Board of Medical Psychotherapists and Psychodiagnosticians.

3145 Medications
National Institute of Mental Health
6001 Executive Boulevard
Room 8184
Bethesda, MD 20892-1
301-443-4513
866-615-6464
TTY: 301-443-8431
E-mail: nimhinfo@nih.gov

This booklet is designed to help mental health patients and their families understand how and why medications can be used as part of the treatment of mental health problems.
36 pages

3146 Mental & Physical Disability Law Reporter
American Bar Association
740 15th Street NW
9th Floor
Washington, DC 20005-1019
202-662-1000
Fax: 202-662-1032
TTY: 202-662-1012
E-mail: CMPDL@abanet.org
www.abanet.org

Amy Allbright, Managing Editor
Renee Dexter, Production/Marketing Manager

Contains bylined articles and summaries of federal and state court opinions and legislative developments addressing persons with mental and physical disabilities.

6 per year Year Founded: 1976 ISSN 0883-7902

3147 Mental Health Aspects of Developmental Disabilities
Psych-Media
PO Box 57
Bear Creek, NC 27207-57
336-581-3700
Fax: 336-581-3766
E-mail: mhdd@amji.net
www.mhaspectsofdd.com

Margaret Zwilling, Managing Editor
Linda Vollmoeller, Assistant Managing Editor

A practical clinical reference for the hands on clinician. This is a peer-reviewed journal covering the diagnosis, treatment and rehabilitation needs of persons with developmental disabilities. *$ 58.00*

40 pages 4 per year ISSN 1057-3291

3148 Mental Health Law Reporter
Business Publishers
8737 Colesville Road
Suite 1100
Silver Spring, MD 20910-3956
301-587-6300
800-274-6737
Fax: 301-587-1081
E-mail: jbond@bpinews.com
www.bpinews.com

Nancy Biglin, Director Marketing

Summary of court cases pertaining to mental health professionals. *$273.00*

12 per year   ISSN 0741-5141

3149 Mental Health Report
Business Publishers
8737 Colesville Road
Suite 1100
Silver Spring, MD 20910-3956
301-587-6300
800-274-6737
Fax: 301-587-4530
E-mail: jbond@bpinews.com
www.bpinews.com

Nancy Biglin, Director Marketing

Independent, inside Washington coverage of mental health administration, legislation and regulation, state policy plus research and trends. *$396.00*

26 per year   ISSN 0191-6750

3150 Mental Health Views
CD Publications
8204 Fenton Street
Silver Spring, MD 20910-4571
301-588-6380
Fax: 301-588-6385

Michael Gerecht, President

3151 Mental Health Weekly
Manisses Communications Group
PO Box 9758
Providence, RI 02940-9758
401-831-6020
800-333-7771
Fax: 401-861-6370
E-mail: manissescs@manisses.com
www.manisses.com

William Kanapaux, Managing Editor

Economic and policy issues for mental health professionals. *$499.00*

48 per year   ISSN 10581103

3152 Mental Retardation
AAMR
444 N Capitol Street NW
Suite 846
Washington, DC 20001-1569

202-637-0475
800-424-3688
Fax: 202-637-0585
E-mail: dcroser@aamr.org

Newsletter that provides information on the latest program advances, current research, and information on products and services in the developmental disabilities field. Free with membership.

24 per year   ISSN 0895-8033

3153 Mentally Disabled and the Law
William S Hein & Company
1285 Main Street
Buffalo, NY 14209-1987
716-882-2600
800-828-7571
Fax: 716-883-8100
www.wshein.com

Kevin Marmion, President

Offers information on treatment rights, the provider-patient relationship, and the rights of mentally disabled persons in the community. *$80.00*

3154 NAMI Advocate
National Alliance for the Mentally Ill
200 N Glebe Road
Suite 1015
Arlington, VA 22203-3728
703-524-7600
800-950-6264
Fax: 703-524-9094
TDD: 703-516-7227
E-mail: frieda@nami.org
www.nami.org

Newsletter that provides information on latest research, treatment, and medications for brain disorders. Reviews status major policy and legislation at federal, state, and local levels. Recurring features include interviews, news of research, news of educational opportunities, book reviews, politics, legal issues, and columns titled President's Column, Ask the Doctor, and News You Can Use. Included as NAMI membership benefit.

24-28 pages   24 per year

3155 NAMI Beginnings
National Alliance on Mental Illness
2107 Wilson Boulevard
Suite 300
Arlington, VA 22201-3080
703-524-7600
800-950-6264
Fax: 703-524-9094
TDD: 703-516-7227
E-mail: david@nami.org
www.nami.org

David Todd, Director of Publications

A publication dedicated to the Young Minds of America from the Child and Adolescent Action Center, a free newsletter about children and adolescents living with mental illnesses.

4 per year

3156 NASW News
National Association of Social Works
750 1st Street NE
Suite 700
Washington, DC 20002-8011
202-408-8600
Fax: 202-336-8313
www.naswpress.org

Elvira Craig De Silva, President

3157 News & Notes
AAMR
444 N Capitol Street NW
Suite 846
Washington, DC 20001-1569
202-637-0475
800-424-3688
Fax: 202-637-0585
E-mail: dcroser@aamr.org

Doreen Croser, Executive Director

Covers legislative, program, and research developments of interest to the field, as well as international news, Association activities, job ads and other classifieds and upcoming events.

3158 Newsletter of the American Psychoanalytic Association
Analytic Press
101 W Street
Hillsdale, NJ 07642-1421
201-358-9477
800-926-6579
Fax: 201-358-4700
E-mail: TAP@analyticpress.com
www.analyticpress.com

Paul E Stepansky PhD, Managing Director
John Kerr PhD, Sr Editor

A scholarly and clinical resource for all analytic practitioners and students of the field. Articles and essays focused on contemporary social, political and cultural forces as they relate to the practice of psychoanalysis, regular interviews with leading proponents of analysis, essays and reminiscences that chart the evolution of anlaysis in America. The newsletter publishes articles that are rarely if ever found in the journal literature. Sample copies available. *$29.50*

4 per year

3159 North American Society of Adlerian Psychology Newsletter
NASAP
614 W Chocolate Avenue
Hershey, PA 17033-1901
717-579-8795
Fax: 717-533-8616
E-mail: nasap@msn.com
www.alfredadler.org

Becky LaFountain, Administrator

Relates news and events of the North American Society of Alderian Psychology and regional news of affiliated associations. Recurring features include lists of courses and workshops offered by affiliated associations, reviews of new publications in the field, professional employment opportunities, a calendar of events, and a column titled President's Message. *$20.00*

8 pages 24 per year ISSN 0889-9428

3160 ORTHO Update
American Orthopsychiatric Association
2001 Beauregard Street
12th Floor
Alexandria, VA 22311-1739
703-797-2584
Fax: 703-684-5968
E-mail: amerortho@aol.com
www.amerortho.org

Intended for members of the Association, who are concerned with the early signs of mental and behavioral disorder and preventive psychiatry. Provides news notes and feature articles on the trends, issues and events that concern mental health, as well as Association news.

6-16 pages 3 per year

3161 Open Minds
Behavioral Health Industry News
10 York Street
Suite 200
Gettysburg, PA 17325-2301
717-334-1329
Fax: 717-334-0538
E-mail: openminds@openminds.com
www.openminds.com

Provides information on marketing, financial, and legal trends in the delivery of mental health and chemical dependency benefits and services. Recurring features include interviews, news of research, a calendar of events, job listings, book reviews, notices of publications available, and industry statistics. *$185.00*

12 pages 12 per year ISSN 1043-3880

3162 Perspective on Psychological Science
Association for Psychological Science
1133 15th Street NW
Suite 1000
Washington, DC 20005
202-293-9300
Fax: 202-293-9350
www.psychologicalscience.org

Linda Bartoshuk, President
Mahzarin R Banaji, President-Elect
Ed Deiner, Author
Alan G Kraut, Executive Director

Perspectives publishes an eclectic mix of provocative reports and articles, including board integrative reviews, overviews of research programs, meta-analysis, theoretical statements, book reviews, and articles on topics such as the philosophy of science, opnion pieces about major issues in the field, autobiographical reflections of senior members in the field, and the occasional humorous essay and sketch.

6 per year ISSN 1745-6916

3163 Professional Counselor
3201 SW 15th Street
Deerfield Beach, FL 33442-8157
954-360-0909
800-851-9100
Fax: 954-360-0034
www.professionalcounselor.com

The number one publication serving the addictions and mental health fields.

3164 Provider Magazine
American Health Care Association
1201 L Street NW
Washington, DC 20005-4046
202-842-4444
Fax: 202-842-3860

Bruse Yarwood, President

Of interest to the professionals who work for the nearly 12,000 nonprofit and for profit assisted living, nursing facility, developmentally disabled and subacute care providers that care for more than 1.5 million elderly and disabled individuals nationally. Provides information, education, and administrative tools that enhance quality at every level.

3165 PsycINFO News
American Psychological Association Database Department/PsycINFO
750 1st Street NE
Washington, DC 20002-4241
202-336-5500
800-374-2722
Fax: 202-336-5518
TDD: 202-336-6123
TTY: 202-336-6123
E-mail: psycinfo@apa.org
www.apa.org

Norman B Anderson, CEO

Free newsletter that keeps you up to date on enhancements to PsycINFO products.

4 per year

3166 PsycSCAN Series
PsycINFO/American Psychological Association
750 1st Street NE
Washington, DC 20002-4241
202-336-5500
800-374-2722
Fax: 202-336-5518
TDD: 202-336-6123
E-mail: psycinfo@apa.org
www.apa.org

Norman B Anderson, CEO

Quarterly current awareness print publications in the fields of clinical, developmental, and applied psychology, as well as learning disorders/mental retardation and behavior analysis and therapy. Contains relevant citations and abstracts from the PsycINFO database. PyscScan: Psychopharmacology is an electronic only publication.

4 per year

3167 Psych Discourse
Association of Black Psychologists
PO Box 55999
Washington, DC 20040-5999
202-722-0808
Fax: 202-722-5941
E-mail: admin@abpsi.org
www.abpsi.org

Halford Fairchild, Editor

Publishes news of the Association. Recurring features include editorials, news of research, letters to the editor, a calendar of events, and columns titled Social Actions, Chapter News, Publications, and Members in the News. *$110.00*

32-64 pages 12 per year Year Founded: 1969 ISSN 1091-4781

3168 Psychiatric News
American Psychiatric Publishing, Inc.
1000 Wilson Boulevard
Suite 1825
Arlington, VA 22209-3901
703-907-7322
800-368-5777
Fax: 703-907-1091
E-mail: appi@psych.org
www.appi.org

Robert E Hales MD, Editor-in-Chief
Ron McMillen, Chief Executive Officer
John McDuffie, Editorial Director

Psychiatric News is the official newspaper for the American Psychiatric Association. It is published twice a month and mailed to all APA members as a member benefit as well as to about 2,000 subscribers.

3169 Psychiatric Rehabilitation Journal
International Association of Psychosocialogy
10025 Gover
Columbia, MD 21044
410-730-5965

3170 Psychiatric Times
Continuing Medical Education
806 Plaza Three
Jersey City, NJ 07311-1112
949-250-1008
800-993-2632
Fax: 949-250-0445
E-mail: pt@mhsource.com
www.psychiatrictimes.com

John Schwartz MD, Editor-in-Chief

Allows you to earn CME credit every month with a clinical article, as well as keeping you up to date on the current news in the field. *$54.95*

12 per year

3171 Psychiatry Drug Alerts
MJ Powers & Company
65 Madison Avenue
Ssite 220
Morristown, NJ 07960-7354
973-889-5398
800-875-0058
E-mail: psych@alertpubs.com

Evelyn Powers, Owner

Discusses drugs used in the psychiatric field, including side effects and risks. *$63.00*

8 pages 12 per year ISSN 0894-4873

3172 Psychiatry Research
Customer Support Department
PO Box 945
New York, NY 10159-945
212-633-3730
888-437-4636
Fax: 212-633-3680
www.elsevier.nl/locate/psychres

ISSN 0165-1781

3173 Psychohistory News
International Psychohistorical Assocation (IPA)
34 Plaza Street E
Suite 1109
Brooklyn, NY 11238-5061
718-638-1414

Includes news of Association events, conference announcements, events in the psychohistorical field, and interviews and reviews. *$15.00*

8-10 pages 4 per year

3174 Psychological Abstracts
PsycINFO/American Psychological Association
750 1st Street NE
Washington, DC 20002-4241
202-336-5500
800-374-2722
Fax: 202-336-5518
TDD: 202-336-6123
E-mail: psycinfo@apa.org
www.apa.org

Norman B Anderson, CEO

Print index containing citations and abstracts for journal articles, books, and book chapters in psychology and related disciplines. Annual indexes.

12 per year

3175 Psychological Assessment Resources
PO Box 998
Odessa, FL 33556
813-968-3003
Fax: 813-968-2598

3176 Psychological Science
Association for Psychological Science
1133 15th Street NW
Suite 1000
Washington, DC 20005
202-293-9300
Fax: 202-293-9350
E-mail: akraut@psychologicalscience.org
www.psychologicalscience.org

Linda Bartoshuk, President
Mahzarin R Banaji, President-Elect
Robert V Kail, Author
Alan G Kraut, Executive Director

The flagship journal of the APS, it publishes cutting edge research articles, short reports, and research reports spanning the entire spectrum of the science of psychology. The Journal is the source for the latest findings in cognitive, social, developmental and health psychology, as well as behavioral neuroscience and biopsychology.

12 per year Year Founded: 1988 ISSN 0956-7976

3177 Psychological Science Agenda
Science Directorate-American Psychological Association
750 1st Street NE
Washington, DC 20002-4241
202-336-6000
800-374-2721
Fax: 202-336-5953
E-mail: science@apa.org
www.apa.org/science/psa/psacover.html

This newsletter disseminates information on scientific psychology, including news on activities of the Association and congressional and federal advocacy efforts of the Directorate. Recurring features include reports of meetings, news of research, notices of publications available, interviews, and the columns titled Science Directorate News, On Behalf of Science, Science Briefs, Announcements, and Funding Opportunities.

16-20 pages 6 per year ISSN 1040-404X

3178 Psychological Science in the Public Interest
Association for Psychological Science
1133 15th Street NW
Suite 1000
Washington, DC 20005
202-293-9300
Fax: 202-293-9350
www.psychologicalscience.org

Linda Bartoshuk, President
Mahzarin R Banaji, President-Elect
Elaine Walker, Author
Alan G Kraut, Executive Director

PSPI is a unique journal featuring comprehensive and compelling views of issues that are of direct relevance to the general public. Reviews are written by teams of award-winning specialists representing a range of viewpoints, and are intended to assess the current state-of-the-science with regard to the topic.

3 per year ISSN 1529-1006

3179 Psychology Teacher Network Education Directorate
750 1st Street NE
Washington, DC 20002-4241
202-336-5500
Fax: 202-336-5518
E-mail: jrg.apa@email.apa.org
www.apa.org

Norman B Anderson, CEO

Provides descriptions of experiments and demonstrations aimed at introducing topics as a basis for classroom lectures or discussion. Recurring features include news and announcements of courses, workshops, funding sources, and meetings; reviews of teaching aids; and reports of innovative programs or curricula occurring in schools, interviews and brief reports from prominent psychologists. *$15.00*

16 pages 5 per year

3180 Psychophysiology
Cambridge University Press
40 W 20th Street
New York, NY 10011-4211
212-924-3900
Fax: 212-691-3239
E-mail: marketing@cup.org
www.cup.org

3181 Psychosomatic Medicine
American Psychosomatic Society
6728 Old McLean Village Drive
McLean, VA 22101-3906
703-556-9222
Fax: 703-556-8729
E-mail: info@psychosomatic.org
www.psychosomatic.org

Laura Degnon, Executive Director
William Lovallo, President

News and event annoucements, examines the scientific understanding of the interrelationships among biological, psychological, social and behavioral factors in human health and disease, and the integration of the fields of science that separately examine each.

3182 Psychotherapy Bulletin
American Psychological Association
750 First Street NE
Washington, DC 20002-4242
202-336-5500
800-374-2721
Fax: 202-336-5518
www.apa.org

Norman B Anderson, CEO

Recurring features include letters to the editor, news of research, reports of meetings, news of educational opportunities, committee reports, legislative issues, and columns titled Washington Scene, Finance, Marketing, Professional Liability, Medical Psychology Update, and Substance Abuse. *$8.00*

50 pages 4 per year

3183 Psychotherapy Finances
Managed Care Strategies & Psychotherapy Finances
13901 US Highway 1
Suite 58979
Juno Beach, FL 33408-1612
561-624-1155
800-869-8450
Fax: 561-624-6006

3184 Research and Training for Children's Mental Health-Update
University of South Florida
13301 Bruce B Downs Boulevard
Florida Mental Health Institute
Tampa, FL 33612-3807
813-974-4565

Services and research on children with emotional disorders.

2 per year

3185 Rural Mental Health Journal
NARMH
300 33rd Avenue South
Suite 101
Waite Park, MN 56387
320-202-1820
Fax: 320-202-1833
E-mail: info@narmh.org
www.narmh.org

Provides a information for rural mental health professionals and advocates.

4 per year

3186 Smooth Sailing
Depression and Related Affective Disorders Association
600 N Wolfe Street
John Hopkins Hospital Meyer 3-181
Baltimore, MD 21287-5

Fax: 410-614-3241
www.med.jhu.edu/drada/

Outreach to students and parents through schools.

4 per year

3187 Social Work
National Association of Social Works
750 1st Street NE
Suite 700
Washington, DC 20002-8011
202-408-8600
Fax: 202-336-8313
www.naswpress.org

Elvira Craig De Silva, President

3188 Social Work Abstracts
National Association of Social Works
750 1st Street NE
Suite 700
Washington, DC 20002-8011
202-408-8600
Fax: 202-336-8313
www.naswpress.org

Elvira Craig De Silva, President

3189 Social Work Research
National Association of Social Works
750 1st Street NE
Suite 700
Washington, DC 20002-8011
202-408-8600
Fax: 202-336-8313
www.naswpress.org

Elvira Craig De Silva, President

3190 Social Work in Education
National Association of Social Works
750 1st Street NE
Suite 700
Washington, DC 20002-8011
202-408-8600
Fax: 202-336-8313
www.naswpress.org

Elvira Craig De Silva, President

3191 Society for Adolescent Psychiatry Newsletter
PO Box 570218
Dallas, TX 75357-218
972-613-0985
Fax: 972-613-5532
E-mail: info@adolpsych.org
www.adolpsych.org

Frances Bell, Executive Director
Mohan Nair, President

Puts psychiatrists in touch with an informed cross-section of the profession from all over North America. Dedicated to education development and advocacy of adolescents and the adolescent psychiatric field.

3192 The Bulletin
American Society of Psychoanalytic Physicians
13528 Wisteria Drive
Germantown, MD 20874-1049
301-540-3197
E-mail: cfcotter@aspp.net
www.aspp.net

Christine Cotter, Executive Director

The Bulletin of the American Society of Psychoanalustic Physicians is a professional publication containing articles by members, meeting speakers and other professionals in addition to newes about the society. Papers are accepted based on a peer review process.

15 pages 1 per year

3193 World Federation for Mental Health Newsletter
World Federation for Mental Health
PO Box 16810
Alexandria, VA 22302-810
703-838-7525
Fax: 703-519-7648
E-mail: info@wfmh.com
www.wfmh.com

Gwen Dixon, Office Administrator

World-wide mental health reports. Education and advocacy on mental health issues. Working to protect the human rights of those defined as mentally ill.

8 pages 1 per year Year Founded: 1984

3194 Journal of Professional Counseling: Practice, Theory & Research
Texas Counseling Association (TCA)
1204 San Antonio
Suite 201
Austin, TX 78701-1870
512-472-3403
800-580-8144
Fax: 512-472-3756
E-mail: jan@txca.org
www.txca.org

Jan Friese, Executive Director

The Texas Counseling Association is dedicated to providing leadership, advocacy and education to promote the growth and development of the counseling profession and those that are served. *$150.00*

50 pages 2 per year

Pediatric & Adolescent Issues

3195 Children and Youth Funding Report
CD Publications
8204 Fenton Street
Silver Spring, MD 20910-4571
301-588-6380
800-666-6380
Fax: 301-588-6385
E-mail: fsr@cdpublications.com

Michael Gerecht, President

Helps social service professionals stay up-to-date on changing federal priorities and legislative developments in Washington, with insight from agency officials, Congressional staff, and advocates on what's likely to happen in the months ahead. Also provides updates on national and local news, with in-depth reports on welfare reform, the federal budget, and entitlement programs. Features program ideas from around the country, to help children and youth service providers learn about innovative new strategies they can implement in their communities. *$399.00*

18 pages 24 per year ISSN 1524-9484

Testing & Evaluation

3196 Assessment and Treatment of Anxiety Disorders in Persons with Mental Retardation
NADD
132 Fair Street
Kingston, NY 12401-4802
845-331-4336
800-331-5362
E-mail: info@thenadd.org
www.thenadd.org

Robert Fletcher, Executive Director

Anxiety disorders as a group are the commonest mental health disorders seen in the general population, as they probably also are in people with developmental disorders. This upgraded version of a book first published in 1996 describes issues of diagnosis and treatment of various anxiety disorders, and includes modalities for staff training in those conditions. *$19.95*

ISBN 1-572560-01-0

3197 Assessment of Neuropsychiatry and Mental Health Services
American Psychiatric Publishing, Inc.
1000 Wilson Boulevard
Suite 1825
Arlington, VA 22209-3901
703-907-7322
800-368-5777
Fax: 703-907-1091
E-mail: appi@psych.org
www.appi.org

Robert E Hales MD, Editor-in-Chief
Ron McMillen, Chief Executive Officer
John McDuffie, Editorial Director

Examines the importance of an integrated approach to neuropsychiatric conditions and looks at ways to overcome the difficulties in assessing medical disorders in psychiatric populations. Addresses neuropsychiatric disorders and their costs and implications on policy. *$94.00*

448 pages Year Founded: 1999 ISBN 0-880487-30-5

3198 Attention-Deficit/Hyperactivity Disorder Test: a Method for Identifying Individuals with ADHD
Pro-Ed Publications
8700 Shoal Creek Boulevard
Austin, TX 78757-6897
512-451-3246
800-897-3202
Fax: 512-451-8542
E-mail: info@proedinc.com

Donald D Hammill, Owner

An effective instrument for identifying and evaluating attention - deficit disorders in persons ages three to twenty-three. Designed for use in schools and clinics, the test is easily completed by teachers, parents and others who are knowledgeable about the referred individual. *$110.00*

Year Founded: 1995

3199 Behavioral and Emotional Rating Scale
Pro-Ed Publications
8700 Shoal Creek Boulevard
Austin, TX 78757-6897
512-451-3246
800-897-3202
Fax: 512-451-8542
E-mail: info@proedinc.com

Donald D Hammill, Owner

Helps to measure the personal strengths of children ages five through eighteen. Contains 52 items that measure five aspects of a child's strength: interpersonal strength, involvement with family, intrapersonal strength, school functioning, and affective strength. Provides overall strength score and five subtest scores. Identifies individual behavioral and emotional strengths of children, the areas in which individual strengths need to be developed, and the goals for individual treatment plans. *$165.00*

Year Founded: 1998

3200 CPP Incorporated
1055 Joaquin Rd
2nd Floor
Mountain View, CA 94043-1243
650-969-8901
800-624-1765
Fax: 650-969-8608
E-mail: custserv@cpp.com

David Krantz, President

3201 Childhood History Form for Attention Disorders
ADD WareHouse
300 NW 70th Avenue
Suite 102
Plantation, FL 33317-2360
954-792-8944
800-233-9273
Fax: 954-792-8545
E-mail: websales@addwarehouse.com
www.addwarehouse.com

Harvey C Parker, Owner

This form is completed by parents prior to a history taking session. It is designed to be used in conjunction with standardized assessment questionaires utilized in the evaluation of attention disorders. 25 per package. *$45.00*

10 pages

3202 Children's Depression Inventory
ADD WareHouse
300 NW 70th Avenue
Suite 102
Plantation, FL 33317-2360
954-792-8944
800-233-9273
Fax: 954-792-8545
E-mail: websales@addwarehouse.com
www.addwarehouse.com

Harvey C Parker, Owner

A self-report, symptom-oriented scale which requires at least a first grade reading level and was designed for school-aged children and adolescents. The CDI has 27 items, each of which consists of three choices. Quickscore form scoring make the inventories easy and economical to administer. The profile contains the following five factors plus a total score normed according to age and sex: negative mood, interpersonal problems, ineffectiveness, anhedonia and negative self-esteem. Contains ten items and provides a general indication of depressive symptoms. *$148.00*

3203 Clinical Evaluations of School Aged Children
Professional Resource Press
PO Box 15560
Sarasota, FL 34277-1560

800-443-3364
Fax: 941-343-9201
www.prpress.com

This book delineates the specific symptoms and behaviors associated with each DSM - IV diagnostic syndrome and provides an exceptionally well designed system for communicating diagnostic findings with great clarity when working with parents and professionals from different disciplines. *$34.95*

376 pages Year Founded: 1998 ISBN 1-568870-27-2

3204 Clinical Interview of the Adolescent: From Assessment and Formulation to Treatment Planning
Charles C Thomas Publisher
2600 S 1st Street
Springfield, IL 62704-4730
217-789-8980
800-258-8980
Fax: 217-789-9130
E-mail: books@ccthomas.com
www.ccthomas.com

Michael P Thomas, President

This book addresses the process of interviewing troubled and psychologically disturbed adolescents who are seen in hospital settings, schools, courts, clinics, and residential facilities. Interviews with adolescents, younger children or adults should follow a logical, sequential and integrated procedure, accomplishing diagnostic closure and the development of a treatment formulation. The nine chapters cover the theoretical and developmental concerns of adolescence; the initial referral; meeting with parents; the therapist; getting acquainted; getting to the heart of the matter; making order out of disorder; the reasons and rationale for the behavior problems. *$59.95*

234 pages Year Founded: 1997 ISBN 0-398067-79-1

3205 Concise Guide to Assessment and Management of Violent Patients
American Psychiatric Publishing, Inc.
1000 Wilson Boulevard
Suite 1825
Arlington, VA 22209-3901

703-907-7322
800-368-5777
Fax: 703-907-1091
E-mail: appi@psych.org
www.appi.org

Robert E Hales MD, Editor-in-Chief
Ron McMillen, Chief Executive Officer
John McDuffie, Editorial Director

Written by an expert on violence, this edition provides current information on psychopharmacology, safety of clinicians and how to deal with threats of violence to the clinician. *$32.95*

180 pages Year Founded: 1996 ISBN 0-880483-44-X

3206 Conducting Insanity Evaluations
Guilford Publications
72 Spring Street
New York, NY 10012-4068
212-431-9800
800-365-7006
Fax: 212-966-6708
E-mail: info@guilford.com

Bob Matloff, President

Great resource for both psychologists and lawyers. Covers legal standards and their applications to clinical work. Mental health professionals who evaluate defendants or consult to courts on criminal matters will find this a useful resource. *$50.00*

342 pages Year Founded: 2000 ISBN 1-572305-21-5

3207 Conners' Rating Scales
Pro-Ed Publications
8700 Shoal Creek Boulevard
Austin, TX 78757-6897
512-451-3246
800-897-3202
Fax: 512-451-8542
E-mail: info@proedinc.com

Donald D Hammill, Owner

Conner's Rating Scales are a result of 30 years of research on childhood and adolescent psychopathology and problem behavior. This revision adds a number of enhancements to a set of measures that has long been the standard instruments for the measurement of attention-deficit/hyperactivity disorder in children and adolescents. *$153.00*

Year Founded: 1997

3208 Depression and Anxiety in Youth Scale
Pro-Ed Publications
8700 Shoal Creek Boulevard
Austin, TX 78757-6897
512-451-3246
800-897-3202
Fax: 512-451-8542
E-mail: info@proedinc.com

Donald D Hammill, Owner

A unique battery of three norm-referenced scales useful in identifying major depressive disorder and overanxious disorders in children and adolescents. *$150.00*

Year Founded: 1994

3209 Diagnosis and Treatment of Multiple Personality Disorder
Guilford Publications
72 Spring Street
New York, NY 10012-4068
212-431-9800
800-365-7006
Fax: 212-966-6708
E-mail: info@guilford.com

Bob Matloff, President

Comprehensive and integrated approach to a complex psychotherapeutic process. From first interview to crisis management to final post-integrative treatment each step is systematically reviewed, with detailed instructions on specific diagnostic and therapeutic techniques and examples of clinical applications. Specially geared to the needs of therapists, novice or expert alike, struggling with their first MPD case. *$48.00*

351 pages Year Founded: 1989 ISBN 0-898621-77-1

3210 Diagnosis and Treatment of Sociopaths and Clients with Sociopathic Traits
New Harbinger Publications
5674 Shattuck Avenue
Oakland, CA 94609-1662
510-652-0215
800-748-6273
Fax: 510-652-5472
E-mail: customerservice@newharbinger.com
www.newharbinger.com

Matthew McKay, Owner

This text presents a full course of treatment, with special attention to safety issues and other concerns for different client populations in a range of treatment settings. *$49.95*

208 pages Year Founded: 1996 ISBN 1-572240-47-4

3211 Diagnostic Interview Schedule for Children: CDISC
Columbia DISC Development Group
Columbia University
1051 Riverside Drive, Unit 78
New York, NY 10032-1007
212-543-5298
Fax: 212-543-1000
E-mail: jjwebsite@childpsycho.columbia.edu

David Shaffer MD, Executive Director

Automated diagnostic interview assessing 34 common child and adolescent mental health disorders, using DSM-IV criteria. A valuable aid to research, as well as clinical and school assessments.

3212 Draw a Person: Screening Procedure for Emotional Disturbance
Pro-Ed Publications
8700 Shoal Creek Boulevard
Austin, TX 78757-6897
512-451-3246
800-897-3202

Fax: 512-451-8542
E-mail: info@proedinc.com

Donald D Hammill, Owner

Helps identify children and adolescents ages six through seventeen who have emotional problems and require further evaluation. *$140.00*

Year Founded: 1991

3213 Functional Assessment and Intervention: Guide to Understanding Problem Behavior
High Tide Press
Ste 2n
2081 Calistoga Dr
New Lenox, IL 60451-4833
815-206-2054
800-469-9461

These experienced practitioners in behavior analyses provide a hands-on, practical approach to recognizing, analyzing, understanding and modifying problem behaviors. Learn the fundamentals of functional assessment and behavior management. *$12.95*

62 pages ISBN 1-892696-31-2

3214 Handbook of Psychological Assessment
John Wiley & Sons
605 3rd Avenue
4th Floor
New York, NY 10158-180
212-850-6301
800-225-5945
E-mail: info@wiley.com

Gary Groth-Marnat, Author

Classic, revised and new psychological tests are all considered for validity and overall reliability in the light of current clinical thought and scientific development. The new edition has expanded coverage of neuropsychological assessment and reports on assessment and treatment planning in the age of managed care. *$95.00*

862 pages Year Founded: 1997 ISBN 0-471419-79-6

3215 Harvard Medical School Guide to Suicide Assessment and Intervention
Jossey-Bass Publishers
989 Market Street
San Francisco, CA 94103-1708
415-433-1740
Fax: 415-433-0499
www.leadertoleader.org

Debra Hunter, President

The definitive guide for helping mental health professionals determine the risk for suicide and appropriate treatment strategies for suicidal or at-risk patients. *$85.00*

736 pages ISBN 0-787943-03-7

3216 Health Watch
28 Maple Avenue
Medford, MA 02155-7118

781-395-5515
800-643-2757
Fax: 781-395-6547
www.healthwatch.cc

Bill Govostes, Owner

On site performer of preventative health screening services and disease risk management programming. Specializing in point of care testing, we perform fast and accurate health screening tests and services to assist in indentifying participant's risk for developing future disease.

Year Founded: 1987

3217 Scale for Assessing Emotional Disturbance
Pro-Ed Publications
8700 Shoal Creek Boulevard
Austin, TX 78757-6897
512-451-3246
800-897-3202
Fax: 512-451-8542
E-mail: info@proedinc.com

Donald D Hammill, Owner

Helps you identify children and adolescents who qualify for the federal special education category Emotional Disturbance. *$100.00*

Year Founded: 1998

3218 Screening for Brain Dysfunction in Psychiatric Patients
Charles C Thomas Publisher
2600 S 1st Street
Springfield, IL 62704-4730
217-789-8980
800-258-8980
Fax: 217-789-9130
E-mail: books@ccthomas.com
www.ccthomas.com

Michael P Thomas, President

This book presents how medical diseases can be misdiagnosed as psychiatric disorders and how clinicians without extensive training in the neurosciences can do a competent job of screening psychiatric clients for possible brain disorders. The research cited in this book, dating back to the 1890's, establishes beyond a doubt that such misdiagnoses are more common than most clinicians would guess. This book focuses on one type of medical condition that is likely to be misdiagnosed: brain injuries and illnesses. *$36.95*

148 pages Year Founded: 1998 ISBN 0-398069-21-2

3219 Sexual Dysfunction: Guide for Assessment and Treatment
Guilford Publications
72 Spring Street
New York, NY 10012-4068
212-431-9800
800-365-7006
Fax: 212-966-6708
E-mail: info@guilford.com

Bob Matloff, President

Designed as a succinct guide to contemporary sex therapy, this book provides an empirically based overview of the most common sexual dysfunctions and a step-by-step manual for their assessment and treatment. Provides a biopsychosocial model of sexual function and dysfunction and describes the authors' general approach to management of sexual difficulties. *$25.00*

212 pages Year Founded: 1991 ISBN 0-898622-07-7

3220 Social-Emotional Dimension Scale
Pro-Ed Publications
8700 Shoal Creek Boulevard
Austin, TX 78757-6897
512-451-3246
800-897-3202
Fax: 512-451-8542
E-mail: info@proedinc.com

Donald D Hammill, Owner

A rating scale for teachers, counselors, and psychologists to screen age 5 1/2 through 18 1/2 who are at risk for conduct disorders, behavior problems, or emotional disturbance. It assesses physical/fear reaction, depressive reaction, avoidance of peer interaction, avoidance of teacher interaction, aggressive interaction, and inappropriate behaviors. *$149.00*

Year Founded: 1986

3221 Test Collection at ETS
Educational Testing Service
Brigham Library
Rosedale Road
Princeton, NJ 08541-1
609-921-9000
Fax: 609-734-5410

Kurt M Landgraf, CEO

Provides 1,200 plus tests available in microfiche or downloadable for reaserch.

Training & Recruitment

3222 Ackerman Institute for the Family
149 E 78th Street
New York, NY 10075-486
212-879-4900
E-mail: ackerman@ackerman.org
www.ackerman.org

Peter J Steinglass
Marcia Steinberg CSW, Director Training

A not-for-profit agency devoted to the treatment and study of families and to the training of family therapists. One of the first training institutions in the United States committed to promoting family functioning and family mental health, Acker is dedicated to helping all families at all stages of family life.

3223 Active Intervention
735 Whitney Avenue
Gretna, LA 70056-3832
504-367-5766

3224 Alfred Adler Institute (AAI)
594 Broadway
Suite 1213
New York, NY 10012-3257
212-254-1048
E-mail: director@alfredadler-ny.org
www.alfredadler-ny.org

Offers training in psychotherapy and analysis to psychiatrists, psychologists, social workers, teachers, clergymen and other related professional persons. Conducts three-year program to provide an understanding of the dynamics of personality and interpersonal relationships and to teach therapeutic methods and techniques. Presents the theory of Individual Psychology as formulated by Alfred Adler. Publications: Journal of Individual Psychology, quarterly. Annual meeting. Semi-annual seminar.

3225 Alliance Behavioral Care: University of Cincinnati Psychiatric Services
222 Piedmont Avenue
Suite 8800
Cincinnati, OH 45219-4231
513-475-8622
800-926-8862
www.alliance-behavioral.com

A regional managed behavioral healthcare organization committed to continuously improving the resources and programs that serve their members and providers. Their goal is to provide resources that improve the well-being of those they serve and to integrate the behavioral healthcare within the overall healthcare systems.

3226 Alton Ochsner Medical Foundation, Psychiatry Residency
1514 Jefferson Highway
New Orleans, LA 70121-2429
504-842-3000
Fax: 504-736-4978
E-mail: gme@ochsner.org
Doris Ratcliff, Manager

3227 American Academy of Child and Adolescent Psychiatry
3615 Wisconsin Avenue NW
Washington, DC 20016-3007
202-966-7300
Fax: 202-966-2891
www.aacap.org
Laurence Lee Greenhill, President

A non-profit membership based organization composed of over 7,500 child and adolescent psychiatrists and other interested physicians. Promotes mentally healthy children, adolescents and families through research, training, advocacy, prevention, comprehensive diagnosis and treatment, peer support and collaboration.

Year Founded: 1953

3228 American College of Healthcare Executives
One N Franklin Street
Suite 1700
Chicago, IL 60606-3529
312-424-2800
Fax: 312-424-0023
E-mail: geninfo@ache.org
www.ache.org
Thomas C Dolan, CEO
David Rubenstein, Chairman-Elect

International professional society of nearly 30,000 healthcare executives. ACHE is known for its prestigious credentialing and educational programs. ACHE is also known for its journal, Journal of Healthcare Management, and magazine, Healthcare Executive, as well as ground-breaking research and career development programs. Through its efforts, ACHE works toward its goal of improving the health status of society by advancing healthcare management excellence.

3229 American College of Women's Health Physicians
1100 E Woodfield Road
Suite 520
Schaumburg, IL 60173-5125
847-969-0283
Fax: 847-517-7229
E-mail: info@acwhp.org
www.aclm.org
Sue O'Sullivan, Manager

The mission of ACWHP is to advance women-centered healthcare.

3230 Andrus Children's Center
Julia Dyckman Andrus Memorial
1156 N Broadway
Yonkers, NY 10701-1108
914-965-3700
Tecla Critelli, President/CEO

Vision is to "give opportunity to youth." A private, non-profit community agency that provides assessment, treatment, education and preventive services for children and their families in residential, day and other restorative programs. Mission is to serve families, without regard to background or financial status, who have or are at risk for developing behavioral health problems. A highly qualified and caring staff uses established techniques and innovative programs to accomplish these purposes.

3231 Asian Pacific Development Center for Human Development
1825 York Street
Denver, CO 80206-1213
303-393-0304
Fax: 303-388-1172
www.apdc.org
Christine Wanifuchi, CEO

A community-based non-profit organization that serves the needs of a growing population of Asian American and Pacific Islander residents throughout Colorado. APDC operates a licensed Community Mental Health Clinic and a multicultural Interpreters Bank.

Year Founded: 1980

3232 Behavioral Healthcare Center
464 Commonwealth Street
#147
Belmont, MA 02478
617-393-3935
Fax: 617-393-1808
E-mail: cberney@mah.harvard.edu
www.academicpsychiatry.org

Carole Berney, Administrative Director
Joan Anzia, President

A behavorial health facility providing consultation in psychiatry, psychopharmacology and psychotherapy to primary care physicians and their patients.

3233 Behavioral Medicine and Biofeedback Consultants
150 SW 12th Avenue
Suite 330
Pompano Beach, FL 33069-3238
954-783-5100
E-mail: behmed@aol.com
www.behavioralmedicine.com

Gary S Traub, Owner

3234 Brandeis University/Heller School
415 South Street
Waltham, MA 02453-2700
781-736-2000
Fax: 781-736-4416
www.brandeis.edu

Jehuda Reinharz, Administrator

3235 Breining Institute College for the Advanced Study of Addictive Disorders
8894 Greenback Lane
Orangevale, CA 95662-4019
916-987-0662
E-mail: college@breining.edu
www.breininginstitute.net

Kathy Breining, Administrator

The mission of Breining Institute faculty and staff is to ensure a consistent standard of higher education, training, testing and certification of professionals working in the field of addictions.

Year Founded: 1986

3236 Brown Schools Behavioral Health System
PO Box 150459
Austin, TX 78715-459

800-848-9090

3237 California Institute of Behavioral Sciences
701 Welch Road
Suite 203
Palo Alto, CA 94304-1705
650-325-1501

Sanjay Jasuja, Medical Director

Provides the following services for children, adolescents, adults and families on national and international level: Objective testing and comprehensive treatment for ADHD/ADD, depression, manic depressive disorder or Bipolar disorder, anxiety disorders, including obsessive compulsive disorder, panic attacks, phobias, post-traumatic stress disorder, Tourette's syndrome, stuttering, psychopharmacology, stress and anger control, violence and workplace issues, learning and behavior problems, and parenting support groups.

3238 Cambridge Hospital: Department of Psychiatry
1493 Cambridge Street
Cambridge, MA 02139-1047
617-665-1000

3239 Center for Health Policy Studies
10440 Little Patuxent Parkway
10th Floor
Columbia, MD 21044-3561
410-715-9400

3240 College of Health and Human Services: SE Missouri State
901 S National Ave
Springfield, MO 65897-27
417-836-4176
www.missouristate.edu

3241 College of Southern Idaho
315 Falls Avenue
P.O. Box 1238
Twin Falls, ID 83303-1238
208-732-6221
800-680-0274
Fax: 208-736-4705
E-mail: info@csi.edu
www.csi.edu

Jerry Beck, President
Jerry Gee, Executive VP/CAO

Addiction Studies

3242 Colonial Services Board
1657 Merrimac Trail
Williamsburg, VA 23185-5624
757-220-3200
Fax: 757-229-7173
www.colonialcsb.org

David Coe, Executive Director

MR and substance abuse

3243 Columbia Counseling Center

900 St. Andrews Road
Columbia, SC 29210-5816
803-731-4708
Fax: 803-798-7607
www.columbiacounselingcenter.com

Darrel G Shaver, President

3244 Copper Hills Youth Center

5899 Rivendell Drive
West Jordan, UT 84081-6500
801-561-3377
800-776-7116
Fax: 801-569-2959

Residential treatment center for boys and girls ages 12-17. Mental health and substance abuse treatment. Also specialized programs for Autism and sexual misconduct

3245 Corphealth

1300 Summit Avenue
6th Floor
Fort Worth, TX 76102-4414
817-333-6400
800-240-8388
E-mail: businessdevelopment@corphealth.com

Patrick D Gotchen II, President/CEO
Brae Jacobson, COO
Michael Baker, CFO

Privately owned and managed behavioral health care company which serves its customers by facilitating the resolution of behavioral health problems in a manner which balances the needs of purchasers, patients and providers. Provides services that bring added value to insurers and health plans while delivering quality care for their members and customers.

3246 Daniel and Yeager Healthcare Staffing Solutions

6767 Old Madison Pike
Suite 690
Huntsville, AL 35806-2198
256-551-1070
800-955-1919
Fax: 256-551-5075
www.dystaffing.com

Susie Brown, COO

Setting the standard for excellence in health care staffing.

3247 Department of Psychiatry: Dartmouth University

Dartmouth Medical School
Lebanon, NH 03756
603-650-5834
Fax: 603-650-5842

3248 Distance Learning Network

111 Boal Ave
Boalsburg, PA 16827-1444
814-466-7808

Eric Porterfield, Director

Broadcast and multimedia company dedicated solely to meeting the medical education and communications needs of physicians through the use of both traditional and innovative media formats. More than 150,000 physicians, nurses and pharmacists turn to DLN each year for their medical education.

Year Founded: 1996

3249 Downstate Mental Hygiene Association

370 Lenox Road
Brooklyn, NY 11226-2206
718-287-4806
Fax: 718-287-0337

3250 East Carolina University Department of Psychiatric Medicine

600 Moye Boulevard
Room 4E-98
Greenville, NC 27834-4300
252-744-4440

Joseph B Webster

3251 Eastern County Mental Health Center

100 West Laurel
Sheridan County Courthouse
Plentywood, MT 59254-1647
406-765-2550
Fax: 406-228-4553

Mental health and chemical dependency help for over 17 counties in Montana.

3252 Emory University School of Medicine, Psychology and Behavior

1440 Clifton Road NE
Atlanta, GA 30322-1053
404-727-5630
Fax: 404-727-0473

3253 Emory University: Psychological Center

532 Kilgo Circle
Atlanta, GA 30322-1122
404-727-7438
Fax: 404-727-0372
E-mail: psych@emory.edu
www.psychology.emory.edu

Nonprofit community clinic providing low cost counseling and psychological testing services for children and adults.

3254 Fletcher Allen Health Care

111 Colchester Avenue
Burlington, VT 05401-1416
802-847-3339

Fletcher Allen Health Care is both a community hospital and, in partnership with the University of Vermont, the state's academic health center. Their mission is to improve the health of the people in the communities they serve by integrating patient care, education and research in a caring environment.

3255 Genesis Learning Center (Devereux)
430 Allied Drive
Nashville, TN 37211-3304
615-832-4222
Fax: 615-832-4577
www.genesislearn.org

Terance Adams, Executive Director

3256 George Washington University
2121 1 Street
Washington, DC 20052-1
202-994-2083

Steven Knapp, President

3257 Harper House: Change Alternative Living
2940 E Eight Mile Road
Detroit, MI 48234-1017
313-891-4976

3258 Haymarket Center, Professional Development
932 W Washington
Chicago, IL 60607-2217
312-226-7984
Fax: 312-226-8048
E-mail: info@hcenter.org
www.hcenter.org

Raymond Soucek, President
Donald Musil, Executive Vp

drug and alcohol treatment programs.

3259 Heartshare Human Services
12 Metro Tech Center
29th Floor
Brooklyn, NY 11201-3858
718-422-4200
E-mail: info@heartshare.org
www.heartshare.org

Ralph A. Subbiondo, Chairman
William R. Guarinello, President/ Ceo
Mia Higgins, Executive Vp
Lynette Fernandez, Assistant Comptroller

a nonprofit human services agency dedicated to improving the lives of people in need of special services and support.

3260 Hillcrest Utica Psychiatric Services
1120 S Utica Street
South Physician Bldg Suite 1000
Tulsa, OK 74104-4012
918-579-1000
www.helmerichwomenscenter.com

Steve Dobbs, CEO

3261 Institute for Behavioral Healthcare
4370 Alpine Road
Suite 209
Portola Valley, CA 94028-7953
650-851-8411
800-258-8411
Fax: 650-851-0406
E-mail: staff@iahb.org
www.iahb.org

Gerry Piaget, President
Joan Piaget, Executive Director

Non-profit educational organization that is a fully accredited sponsor of continuing education and continuing medical education for mental health, chemical dependency, and substance abuse treatment providers in the United States and Canada. Mission is to provide high-quality training to healthcare professionals as well as to companies and individuals with healthcare-related interests.

3262 Jacobs Institute of Women's Health
2021 K Street
Nw Suite 800
Washington, DC 20006-1003
202-530-2376
Fax: 202-296-0025
E-mail: whieditor@gwu.edu
www.jiwh.org

Richard Mauery, Managing Staff Director

Working to improve health care for women through research, dialogue and information dissemination. Mission is to identify and study women's health care issues involving the interaction of medical and social systems; facilitate informed dialogue and foster awareness among consumers and providers alike; and promote problem resolution, interdisciplinary coordination and information dissemination at the regional, national and international levels.

3263 Jefferson Drug/Alcohol
833 Chestnut East
Suite 210
Philadelphia, PA 19107-4405
215-503-2818

Michael Vergare MD, Chair Dpt Psychiatry/Human Bhvr

Provides clinical and consultation services to Thomas Jefferson University Hospital and its medical community. In addition, its staff focuses special attention on the consultation and treatment of the most common psychiatric problems of anxiety, depression, insomnia, substance abuse, eating disorders and sleep disorders.

3264 John A Burns School of Medicine Department of Psychiatry
1356 Lusitana Street
Floor 4
Honolulu, HI 96813-2409
808-586-2900
Fax: 808-586-2940
www.jabsom.hawaii.edu

Naleen Andrade, Chair

Medical School Programs and Residency Programs, general, geriatric, addictive and, child and adolescent.

3265 Langley Porter Psych Institute at UCSF Parnassus Campus

401 Parnassus Avenue
San Francisco, CA 94143-2211
415-476-7500

Alissa M Peterson

3266 Laurelwood Hospital and Counseling Centers

35900 Euclid Avenue
Willoughby, OH 44094-4648
440-953-3000
800-438-4673
Fax: 440-602-3938

Farshid Afsarifard, Administrator

Full-service behavioral healthcare system-(comprehensive outpatient and inpatient services).

3267 Life Science Associates

1 Fenimore Road
Bayport, NY 11705-2115
631-472-2111
Fax: 631-472-8146
E-mail: lifesciassoc@pipeline.com
www.lifesciassoc.home.pipeline.com

Publishes over fifty computer programs for individuals impaired by head trauma and stroke. Also produces EDS, a software/hardware system for assessing driving.

3268 Locumtenens.com

3650 Mansell Road
Suite 310
Alpharetta, GA 30022-3068

800-930-0748
www.locumtenens.com

Richard M Jackson, CEO
David Roush, President/COO
Harrison L Rogers Jr, MD, Medical Director

Specializing in temporary and permanant placement of psychiatrists. Physicians tell us where and when they want to work and locumtenens.com will find a jop that fits those needs.

3269 MCG Telemedicine Center

1120 15th Street
Augusta, GA 30912-6
706-721-0211
E-mail: decisionsupport@mcg.edu
www.mcg.edu

Daniel W. Rahn, President

Involved in the delivery of mental health services via telemedicine. In addition, the Telemedicine Center maintains the Georgia Mental Health Network website, a comprehensive listing of mental health resources in the State.

3270 MCW Department of Psychiatry and Behavioral Medicine

8701 Watertown Plank Road
Milwaukee, WI 53226-3548
414-456-4362
E-mail: webmaster@mcw.edu

3271 Management Recruiters of Washington, DC

Ste 704
1109 Spring St
Silver Spring, MD 20910-4032
301-625-5100
Fax: 301-625-3001
E-mail: info@mr-twg.com
www.mr-twg.com

Frank Black Jr., Partner,President
John Marty, Managing Director

3272 Marsh Foundation

1229 Lincoln Highway
PO Box 150
Van Wert, OH 45891-150
419-238-1695
Fax: 419-238-1747
E-mail: marshfound@embarqmail.com
www.marshfoundation.org

Jeff Grothouse, Executive Secretary/Treasurer
Terry Geiger, Coordinator

Nonprofit center serving children and families with special emphasis in juvenile sex offender population. Services include individual therapy, group therapy, case management and diagnostic assessment.

3273 Masters of Behavioral Healthcare Management California School of Professional Psychology

Los Angeles Campus
1000 South Fremont Avenue, Unit 5
Alhambra, CA 91803-8835
626-284-2777
866-825-5426
TDD: 800-585-5087
www.alliant.edu

Geoffrey Cox PhD, President

Offers industry-specific training to mid-management and supervisory personnel employed in behavioral healthcare organizations.

3274 Medical College of Georgia

1120 15th Street
Augusta, GA 30912-6
706-721-2361
Fax: 706-721-6126
www.mcghealthinc.com

Dennis Roemer, VP

The mission of the Medical College of Georgia is to improve health and resuce the burden of illness in society by discovering, disseminating, and applying knowledge of human health and disease.

3275 Medical College of Ohio, Psychiatry
3000 Arlington Avenue
Toledo, OH 43614-2595
419-383-4117
Fax: 419-383-6140

Mission is to improve the human condition through the creation, dissemination and application of knowledge using wisdom and compassion as our guides.

3276 Medical College of Pennsylvania
3300 Henry Avenue
Philadelphia, PA 19129-1191
215-842-6000

A tertiary care educational facility that reaches out to a regional referral base for select specialty services while continuing to offer primary and secondary service to the residents of its immediate community.

3277 Medical College of Wisconsin
8701 Watertown Plank Road
Milwaukee, WI 53226-4801
414-456-8296
www.mcw.edu

Dougals R Campell, Finance Executive

3278 Medical Doctor Associates
145 Technology Parkway NW
Norcross, GA 30092-2913
770-246-9191
800-780-3500
Fax: 770-246-0882
www.mdainc.com

Ken Shumard, President
Mike Pretiger, Cfo

Committed to providing the most complete staffing services available to the healthcare industry. The family of services offered by Medical Doctor Associates includes Locum Tenens, Contract, and Permanent Placement staffing for physicians, allied health and rehabilitation staffing, and credentials verification and licensing services.

3279 Medical University of South Carolina Institute of Psychiatry, Psychiatry Access Center
171 Ashley Avenue
Charleston, SC 29425-100
843-792-8100
Fax: 843-792-4854

Robert J Black

3280 Meharry Medical College
1005-David B Todd Boulevard
Nashville, TN 37208
615-327-6862
Fax: 615-321-2932
www.mmc.edu

Fatima Barnes, Manager

3281 Menninger Division of Continuing Education
Menninger Clinic Department of Research
2801 Gessner Drive
Houston, TX 77080-2503
713-275-5000
800-351-9058
Fax: 713-275-5117

Ian Aitken, CEO
Lynn Bodenhamer, Executive Assistant

The international psychiatric center of excellence, restoring hope to each person through innovative programs in treatment, research and education.

3282 NEOUCOM-Northeastern Ohio Universities College of Medicine
4209 State Route 44
PO Box 95
Rootstown, OH 44272-95

800-686-2511
www.neoucom.edu

Mission is to graduate qualified physicians who are passionate about serving their communities. All of our graduates, regardless of specialty, have a solid background in community and public health. NEOUCOM strives to improve the quality of health care throughout northeast Ohio by instilling in each graduate the desire to serve the public and the highest ideals of the medical profession.

3283 Nathan S Kline Institute for Psychiatric Research
140 Old Orangeburg Road
Orangeburg, NY 10962-1157
845-398-5500
Fax: 845-398-5510
E-mail: webmaster@nki.rfmh.org
www.rfmh.org/nki

Bennet L Leventhal, MD, Deputy Director

Research programs in Alzheimers disease, analytical psychopharmacology, basic and clinical neuroimaging, cellular and molecular neurobiology, clinical trial data management, co-occuring disorders and many other mental health studies.

3284 National Association of Alcholism and Drug Abuse Counselors
901 N Washington Street
Suite 600
Alexandria, VA 22314-1535
703-741-7686
800-548-0497
E-mail: ncac@naadac.org
www.naadac.org

NAADAC is the only professional membership organization that serves counselors who specialize in addiction treatment. With 14,000 members and 47 state affiliates representing more than 80,000 addiction counselors, it is the nation's largest network of alcoholism and drug abuse treatment professionals. Among the organization's national certifacation programs are the National Certified Addiction Counselor and the Masters Addiction Counselor designations.

3285 National Association of School Psychologists

4340 E West Highway
Suite 402
Bethesda, MD 20814-4468
301-657-0270
866-331-6277
Fax: 301-657-0275
www.nasponline.org

Susan Gorin, Executive Director

3286 New York University Behavioral Health Programs

530 1st Avenue
Suite 7D
New York, NY 10016-6402
212-263-7419

David Ginsberg, Director

Outpatient psychiatry group for Tisch Hospital at NYU Medical Center. Our multidisciplinary team of licensed psychiatrists and social workers offers you the most up-to-date and scientifically validated treatments.

3287 Nickerson Center

7025 N Lombard Street
Portland, OR 97203-3203
503-289-9071

3288 Northwestern University Medical School Feinberg School of Medicine

710 North Lakeshore Drive
Chicago, IL 60611-3128
312-503-8722
Fax: 312-503-8700
E-mail: clinpsych@northwestern.edu

Eva Erskine, Manager

The Mental Health Services and Policy Program is a multidisciplinary research/educational program on the development and implementation of outcomes management technology.

3289 Ochester Psychological Service

1924 Copper Oaks Circle
Blue Springs, MO 64015-8300
816-224-6500

Jeffery L Miller PhD, Psychologist/Owner

Offers a full range of outpatient mental health services including individuals, couples and family therapy. Offers psychological testing and evaluation. Adults, adolescents and children served.

3290 Onslow County Behavioral Health

165 Center Street
Jacksonville, NC 28546-5708

910-219-8000
Fax: 910-219-8072
www.ocbhs.org

Daniel Jones, Executive Director

3291 PRIMA A D D Corp.

13140 Coit RoadRoad
Suite 500
Dallas, TX 75240
972-386-8599
Fax: 972-386-8597

Robin Binnig, Owner

Prima ADD Corp specializes in the diagnosis and treatment of Attention-Deficit/Hyperactivity Disorder (ADHD). We treat children and adults. Services include: psychological assessment (including intellectual, achievement and pesonality testing), counseling, coaching and consultation. We also carry books and CD's concerning ADHD.

3292 Parent Child Center

2001 W Blue Heron Blvd
W Palm Beach, FL 33404-5003
561-841-3500
Fax: 561-844-3577
E-mail: information@parent-childcenter.org

Patrick Mc Namara, CEO

3293 Penn State Hershey Medical Center

500 University Drive
Hershey, PA 17033-2390
717-531-6955
Fax: 717-531-4077
www.hmc.psu.edu

Harold L Paz, CEO

3294 Pepperdine University, Graduate School of Education and Psychology

6100 Center Drive
Los Angeles, CA 90045-9200
310-506-4000
800-347-4849

Andrew Benton, President

Offers graduate degree programs designed to prepare psychologists, marriage and family therapists, and mental health practitioners. Many programs accommodate a full-time work schedule with evening and weekend classes available in a trimester schedule. The average class size is 15. There are five educational centers in southern California and three community counseling clinics available to the surrounding community.

3295 Postgraduate Center for Mental Health

71 W 23rd St
New York, NY 10010-4102
212-576-4168
E-mail: crichards@pgcmh.org
www.pgcmh.org

Information on mental health.

3296 Pressley Ridge Schools
530 Marshall Avenue
Pittsburgh, PA 15214-3098
412-321-6995
Fax: 412-321-5313
www.pressleyridge.org

Lynn Boley, Principal
Scott Erickson, Executive VP/CfO

Provides an array of social services, special education programs, and mental health services for troubled children and their families in Delaware, Maryland, Ohio, Pennsylvania, Virginia, Washngton, DC and West Virginia as well as worldwide.

3297 Psych-Med Association, St. Francis Medical
2616 Wilmington Road
New Castle, PA 16105-1504
724-652-2323

Lynda Circelli, Manager

3298 PsychTemps
2404 Auburn Avenue
Cincinnati, OH 45219-2735
513-651-9500
888-651-8367
Fax: 513-651-9558
E-mail: info@psychtemps.com
www.psychtemps.com

Holly D Dorna MA LPCC, President/CEO

Specialized recruiting and staffing company that fills temporary, permanent, and temp-to-hire job placement for the behavioral healthcare field.

3299 Psychiatric Associates
2216 W Alto Road
Kokomo, IN 46902
765-453-9338

3300 Psychological Center
135 Oakland Street
Pasadena, CA 91101
626-584-5500

Winston Gooden, Manager

3301 Psychology Department
Bowling Green University
Bowling Green, OH 43403-1
419-372-2835
Fax: 419-372-6013

3302 QuadraMed Corporation
12110 Sunset Hills Road
Reston, VA 20190-5852
703-709-2300
800-393-0278
Fax: 703-709-2490
E-mail: boardofdirectors@quadramed.com
www.quadramed.com

Duncan W James, CEO

3303 Regional Research Institute for Human Services of Portland University
1600 Sw 4th Ave
Suite 900
Portland, OR 97201-5521
503-725-4040
Fax: 503-725-4180
www.rri.pdx.edu

3304 Research Center for Children's Mental Health, Department of Children and Family
University of South Florida
13301 Bruce B Downs Boulevard
Tampa, FL 33612-3807
813-974-4565

The center conducts research, synthesized and shared existingknowledge, provided training and consultation, and served as a resource for other researchers, policy makers, administrators in the public system, and organizations representing parents, consumers, advocates, professional societies and practitioners.

3305 River City Mental Health Clinic
2265 Como Avenue
Suite 201
Saint Paul, MN 55108-5298
651-646-8985
Fax: 651-646-3959
www.rivercityclinic.com

Doug Jensen, Owner

Psychotherapy and assessment for all ages.

3306 Riveredge Hospital
8311 W Roosevelt
Forest Park, IL 60130-2500
708-771-7000
Fax: 708-209-2280
www.riveredgehospital.com

Carey Carlock, CEO

Striving to foster an environment that demonstrates compassion and caring with timely and effective communication through comprehensive behavioral health care services of clinical excellence.

3307 Riverside Center
PO Box 2259
671 Sw Main
Winston, OR 97496-2259
541-679-6129
www.riversidecenter.org

3308 Rockland Children's Psychiatric Center
599 Convent Road
Orangeburg, NY 10962
845-359-7400
E-mail: rocklandcpc@omh.state.ny.us

Josefina M Moneda

RCPC is a JCAHO accredited children's psychiatric center. We provide inpatient care to youngsters 10 - 18 years of age from the lower Hudson Valley. An array of local, school-based outpatient services are available in each of the seven counties in the area.

3309 Rosemont Center
2440 Dawnlight Avenue
Columbus, OH 43211-1934
614-471-2626
800-753-0424
Fax: 614-478-3234
www.rosemont.org

Yolanda Lewis, Finance Executive
Kate Tesoriero, Director Of Development

Provides for the physical, emotional, mental and spiritual well being of our community's most troubled young people and their families. the caring people of rosemont offer a more comprehensive program to address a wider range of cases and ages than other central Ohio mental health providers.

3310 SAFY of America
10100 Elida Road
Delphos, OH 45833-9056
419-695-8010
800-532-7239
Fax: 419-695-0004
E-mail: webmaster@safy.org
www.safy.org

Dru Whitaker, CEO
John Hollenkamp, SVP of Finance

3311 Schneider Institute for Health Policy
The Heller School for Social Policy & Management
Brandeis University
415 South Street, Mailstop 035
Waltham, MA 02453-2728
781-736-3900
Fax: 781-736-3905
E-mail: colnon@brandeis.edu
www.sihp.brandeis.edu

Stanley S Wallack, Executive Director

Committed to developing an objective, university-based entity capable of providing research assistance to the Federal government on the major problems it faced in financing and delivering care to the elderly, disabled and poor. Our role has always been to solve complex health care problems, and to link research studies to policy change.

3312 School of Nursing, UCLA
PO Box 951702
Los Angeles, CA 90095-1702
310-825-7181
Fax: 310-267-0330
E-mail: sonsaff@sonnet.ucla.edu
www.nursing.ucla.edu

Rene Dennis, Director Development

3313 Southern Illinois University School of Medicine: Department of Psychiatry
PO Box 19621
Springfield, IL 62794-9621
217-545-2155
www.siumed.edu

3314 Southern Illinois University School of Medicine
SIU School of Medicine
PO Box 19621
Springfield, IL 62794-9621
217-545-8000
www.siumed.edu

Stephen M Soltys MD, Pfr/Chair Dpt. of Psychiatry
Philip Pan MD, Division Chief

Provides high quality clinical treatment,outstanding teaching and solid efforts in research and community service.

3315 St. Francis Medical Center
400 45th Street
Pittsburgh, PA 15201-1115
412-622-4343

3316 St. Joseph Behavioral Medicine Network
861 Corporate Drive
Suite 103
Lexington, KY 40503-5433
859-224-2022
Fax: 859-224-2024

Carla Zelzenlik, Manager

3317 St. Louis Behavioral Medicine Institute
1129 Macklind Avenue
Saint Louis, MO 63110-1440
314-534-0200
877-245-2688
www.slbmi.com

Debbie Milfelt, Manager

Offers exceptional quality, result-focused treatment. Have remained true to our commitment of providing excellence in clinical care and customer service. We offer comprehensive treatment plans to meet the individual needs of children, adolescents, adults, older adults, and their families suffering from emotional and behavioral problems.

3318 Stonington Institute
75 Swantown Hill Road
N Stonington, CT 06359-1022
860-535-1010
800-832-1022
Fax: 860-535-4820

E-mail: andrea.keeney@uhsinc.com
www.stoningtoninstitute.com

William Aniskovich, CEO

3319 Success Pros
Skills Unlimited
2060 Ocean Ave
Suite 3
Ronkonkoma, NY 11779-6533
631-580-5319
Fax: 631-580-5394
E-mail: success@skillsunlimited.org
www.skillsunlimited.org

Jeffrey Koppelson, Program Director

SUCCESS provides rehabilitative services to indivduals who are recovering from mental illness. In addition to offering clinical treatment, SUCCESS has a schedule of classes and other services that help to identify and achieve personally meaningful goals in the areas of employment, housing, education, health and socialization. Transportation is generally available free of charge. The program is open Monday through Saturday and has ectended hours two evenings per week.

3320 Topeka Institute for Psychoanalysis
PO Box 829
Topeka, KS 66601-829

800-288-3950

A training facility for health care professionals, the Topeka Institute for Psychoanalysis has the tripartite mission of promoting research to expand the knowledge base in its field of expertise; providing didactic education and clinical supervision to trainees; and caring for patients in need of its services through a low-fee clinic.

3321 Training Behavioral Healthcare Professionals
Jossey-Bass Publishers
350 Sansome Street
5th Floor
San Francisco, CA 94104-1310

800-956-7739

Provides text on strategies for training mental health professionals in the skills necessary for providing services in a framework of limited resources. *$46.00*

180 pages Year Founded: 1997 ISBN 0-787907-95-2

3322 UCLA Neuropsychiatric Institute and Hospital
700 Westwood Plaza
Los Angeles, CA 90024
310-825-0291

Gary W Small

Multidisciplinary institute of human neurosciences, and is unifying focus of scholarly activity at UCLA in this area. Scientific advances recent decades have shown the value in approaches that cut across traditional academic departments, and which emphasize interdisciplinary collaborations.

3323 UCSF-Department of Psychiatry, Cultural Competence
1001 Potrero Avenue
San Francisco, CA 94110-3518
415-206-8313
www.reprogenetics.com

Philip C Hopewell

3324 USC Psychiatry and Psychology Associates
1640 Marengo Street
Suite 510
Los Angeles, CA 90033-1075
323-221-0854

3325 USC School of Medicine
Health Sciences Campuses
Name/Department USC
Los Angeles, CA 90089-1
323-442-1100
www.usc.edu/schools/medicine/

3326 Ulster County Mental Health Department
239 Golden Hill Lane
Kingston, NY 12401-6441
845-340-4000
Fax: 845-340-4094
www.co.ulster.ny.us

Marshall Beckman, Executive Director

Responsible for planning, funding and monitoring of community mental health, mental retardation/developmental disability and alcohol and substance abuse services in Ulster County.

3327 Union County Psychiatric Clinic
117 Roosevelt Avenue
Plainfield, NJ 07060-1331
908-412-9792

3328 University Behavioral Healthcare
671 Hoes Lane
Piscataway, NJ 08854-8021
732-235-5500
800-969-5300

Christopher Kosseff, President

3329 University of California at Davis Psychiatry and Behavioral Sciences Department
2315 Stockton Boulevard
Sacramento, CA 95817-2201
916-734-2011

Offers opportunities for students and faculty for clinical and research applications in all aspects of psychiatry and behavioral sciences.

3330 University of Cincinnati College of Medical Department of Psychiatry
231 Albert Sabin Way
Medical Sciences Building/Ml 0559
Cincinnati, OH 45267-2827
513-558-5190

Todd Palumbo, Contact

Researches eating disorders, bipolar disorder, and chemical dependency.

3331 University of Colorado Health Sciences Center
4200 E 9th Avenue
Box A-080
Denver, CO 80262-1000
720-848-1840
877-472-2586
E-mail: alumni@uchsc.edu

John C Slocumb

3332 University of Connecticut Health Center
263 Farmington Avenue
Farmington, CT 06030-1
860-679-2719
TDD: 860-679-2242

3333 University of Iowa Hospital
200 Hawkins Drive
Iowa City, IA 52242-1007
319-356-3574
800-777-8442
TDD: 319-356-4999
E-mail: uihc-webcomments@uiowa.edu

3334 University of Kansas Medical Center
3901 Rainbow Boulevard
Kansas City, KS 66160-1
913-588-3606
TDD: 913-588-7963

E K Reddy
Barbara Atkinson, Executive Vice Chancellor

An integral and unique component of the University of Kansas and the Kansas Board of Regents system, is composed of the School of Medicine, the School of Nursing, the School of Allied Health, the University of Kansas Hospital, and a Graduate School. KU Medical Center is a complex institution whose basic functions include research, education, patient care, and community service involving multiple constituencies at state and national levels.

3335 University of Kansas School of Medicine
1010 N. Kansas
Wichita, KS 67214-3124
316-293-2607
E-mail: kusmw@kumc.edu
www.kumc.edu

Debbie Bennett, Manager

3336 University of Louisville School of Medicine
Abell Administration Center
323 E. Chestnut Street
Louisville, KY 40292-1
502-562-3000
E-mail: meddean@louisville.edu

Wes Allison

Mission is to be a vital component in the University of Louisville's quest to become a premier, nationally recognized metropolitan research university, to excel in the education of physicians and scientists for careers in teching, research, patient care and community service, and to bring the fundamental discoveries of our basic and clinical scientists to the bedside.

3337 University of Maryland Medical Systems
701 W Pratt Street
Suite 388
Baltimore, MD 21201-1023
410-328-2132

John Talbott

3338 University of Maryland School of Medicine
655 West Baltimore Street
Baltimore, MD 21201-1509
410-706-3681

Nancy Ryan Lowitt, Dean/Vp Medical Affairs

Dedicated to providing excellence in biomedical education, basic and clinical research, quality patient care and service to improve the health of the citizens of Maryland and beyond.

3339 University of Massachusetts Medical Center
55 Lake Avenue N
Worcester, MA 01655-1
508-856-8989

Aaron Lazare, Administrator

Mission is to serve the people of the commonwealth through national distinction in health sciences, education, research, public service and clinical care.

3340 University of Miami - Department of Psychology
PO Bo 248185
Coral Gables, FL 33124-8185
305-284-2814
Fax: 305-284-3402
E-mail: webmaster@psy.miami.edu
www.psy.miami.edu

A facility that publishes approximately 100 journal articles, chapters, and books, and make numerous convention presentations, invited addresses, and colliquia.

3341 University of Michigan
400 E Eisenhower Parkway
Ann Arbor, MI 48108-3302
734-936-2938
E-mail: info@umich.edu

3342 University of Minnesota Fairview Health Systems
2450 Riverside Ave
Minneapolis, MN 55454-1450
612-273-2229
Fax: 612-273-2211
TTY: 612-672-7300
www.fairview.org

Gordon Alexander, President

Mission is to improve the health of the communities we serve. We commit our skills and resources to the benefit of the whole person by providing the finest in healthcare, while addressing the physical, emotional and spiritual needs of individuals and their families. Pledge to support the research and education efforts of our partner, the University of Minnesota, and its tradition of excellence.

3343 University of Minnesota, Family Social Science
290 McNeal Hall
1985 Buford Avenue
Saint Paul, MN 55108-6140
612-625-1900
Fax: 612-625-4227
E-mail: fsosinfo@umn.edu

Jan Mc Culloch, Manager

Mission is to enhance the well-being of diverse families in a changing world through teaching, research, and outreach.

3344 University of New Mexico, School of Medicine Health Sciences Center
Ofc of the Executive VP for Health Svs
MSC09 5300 1 University Of New Mexi
Albuquerque, NM 87131-1
505-277-8267
Fax: 505-277-8626

Theresa Anderson, Manager

Established in 1994, the University of New Mexico Health Sciences Center is the largest academic health complex in the state. Located on the University of New Mexico campus in Albuquerque, New Mexico, the HSC combines its four mission area-education, research, patient care and partnership-the provide New Mexicans with the highest level of health care.

3345 University of North Carolina School of Social Work
Behavioral Healthcare Resource Institute
301 Pittsboro Street
Cb # 3550
Chapel Hill, NC 27599-1
919-843-3018
E-mail: bhrinstitute@listserv.unc.edu
www.behavioralhealthcareinstitute.org

3346 University of North Carolina, School of Medicine
4030 Bondurant Hall
Cb# 7000
Chaple Hill, NC 27599-1
919-962-8331
E-mail: admissions@med.unc.edu
www.med.unc.edu

Mission is to improve the health of North carolinians and others whom we serve. We will accomplish this by achieving excellence and providing leadership in the interrelated areas of patient care, education, and research.

3347 University of Pennsylvania Health System
399 S 34th Street
Suite 2002 Penn Tower
Philadelphia, PA 19104-4316
215-662-6995

3348 University of Pennsylvania, Department of Psychiatry
PENN Behavioral Health
1019 Blockley Hall
423 Guardian Drive
Philadelphia, PA 19104-4865
215-662-2560
Fax: 215-573-6410
E-mail: vdongen@mail.med.upenn.edu
www.uphs.upenn.edu

3349 University of Tennessee Medical Group: Department of Medicine and Psychiatry
135 N Pauline Street
Suite 122
Memphis, TN 38105-3816
901-448-4572
Fax: 901-448-1684
E-mail: jgreen41@uthsc.edu
www.uthsc.edu/psych

James A. Greene, Professor/Chair

3350 University of Texas Medical Branch Managed Care
301 University Boulevard
Galveston, TX 77555-5302
409-772-1506
800-228-1841
Fax: 409-772-6216
E-mail: public.affairs@utmb.edu
www.utmb.edu

3351 University of Texas, Southwestern Medical Center
5323 Harry Hines Boulevard
Dallas, TX 75390-7200
214-645-2720

Craig Riggs Malloy

3352 University of Texas-Houston Health Science Center
7000 Fannin
Suite 1200
Houston, TX 77030-5400
713-500-4472

Larry R Kaiser, President

A comprehensive health sciences health science university composed of six schools, an institute of molecular medicine and a psychiatric center. UTHSC-H's mission is to treat, cure and prevent disease now and in the future of educating health science professionals; discovering and translating advances in socials and biomedical sciences; and modeling the best practices in clincal care.

3353 University of Utah Neuropsychiatric
501 Chipeta Way
Salt Lake City, UT 84108-1222
801-583-2500
E-mail: sarah.latta@hsc.utah.edu

Kristin Fontaine, Manager

Located in the University's Research Park, is a full service 90-bed psychiatric hospital providing mental health and substance abuse treatment. Services include inpatient, day treatment, intensive outpatient, and ooutpatient services for children, adolescents and adults. Confidential assessments, referrals, and intervention education are available.

3354 Wake Forest University
1834 Wake Forest Road
Winston Salem, NC 27109-6000
336-758-5000
Fax: 336-759-6074
www.wfu.edu

William C Gordon, CEO

3355 Wayne University-University of Psychiatric Center-Jefferson: Outpatient Mental Health for Children, Adolescents and Adults
2751 E Jefferson Avenue
Suite 436 Upc Jefferson
Detroit, MI 48207-4180
313-993-3434
E-mail: rmarcian@med.wayne.edu

Humera Athar, Director Of Clinical Programs

The University Psychiatric Centers' Early Childhood Intervention (ECI) provides services to preschool children with emotional and behavioral problems and their families. The program works to increase parental understanding of the child's developmental and emotional issues. this is achieved through education, support, and the observation of child management techniques. The program places a strong emphasis on family involvement and preventing more serious difficulties later in the child's life.

3356 West Jefferson Medical Center
1101 Medical Center Boulevard
Marrero, LA 70072-3191
504-347-5511
www.wjmc.org

A Gary Muller, CEO

Not-for-profit community hospital on the West Bank of Jefferson Parish. Continues to strengthen its community base while maintaining its mission and values. Dedicated to considerate and respectful quality healthcare, the institution welcomes patient, family, and visitor feedback regarding programs, services, and community needs.

3357 Western Psychiatric Institute and Clinic
3811 Ohara Street
Pittsburgh, PA 15213-2597
412-624-2000
877-624-4100

Rizwan Parvez

A national leader in the diagnosis, management, and treatment of mental health and addictive disorders. Providing the most comprehensive range of behavioral health services available today, but also shaping tomorrow's behavioral health care through clinical innovation, research, and education.

3358 Wordsworth
3905 Ford Road
Philadelphia, PA 19131-2824
215-452-5176
E-mail: info@wordsworth.org

Debra Lacks, CEO

The mission of Wordsworth, a not-for-profit institution, is to provide quality education, treatment and care to children and families with special needs.

Year Founded: 1952

3359 Yale University School of Medicine: Child Study Center
230 S Frontage Road
New Haven, CT 06519-1124
203-785-3413

Yann Poncin, Director

Provides a comprehensive range of in-depth diagnostic and treatment services for children with psychiatric and developmental disorders. These services include specialized developmental evaluations for children ages zero-four, and psychological and psychiatric evaluations for children 5-18. Individualized treatment plans following evaluation make use for a range of theraputic interventions, including psychotherapy, group therapy, family therapy, psycho-pharmacological treatment, parent counseling, consultation and service planning. Immediate access for children needing to be seen within 24 hours and walk-in service is also available.

Video & Audio

3360 Asperger's Diagnostic Assessment with Dr. Tony Attwood
Program Development Associates
PO Box 2038
Syracuse, NY 13220-2038
315-452-0643
Fax: 315-452-0710
E-mail: info@disabilitytraining.com
www.disabilitytraining.com

New from acclaimed autism expert Dr. Tony Attwood, this 4-hour DVD set with program guide offers diagnostic characteristics of Asperger's Syndrome in children and adults, patient interviews and impacts on girls. An essential guide for Child Psychologists, Special Ed teachers and Parents. *$129.95*

3361 Cognitive Behavioral Assessment
New Harbinger Publications
5674 Shattuck Avenue
Oakland, CA 94609-1662
510-652-0215
800-748-6273
Fax: 510-652-5472
E-mail: customerservice@newharbinger.com
www.newharbinger.com

Matthew McKay, Owner

A videotape that guides three clients through PAC (Problem, Antecedents, Consequences) method of cognitive behavioral assessment. *$49.95*

ISBN 1-572243-15-5

3362 Couples and Infertility - Moving Beyond Loss
Guilford Publications
72 Spring Street
New York, NY 10012-4068
212-431-9800
800-365-7006
Fax: 212-966-6708
E-mail: info@guilford.com

Bob Matloff, President

A VHS video explores the biological and resulting psychological and social issues of infertility. *$95.00*

Year Founded: 1995 ISBN 1-572302-86-0

3363 Educating Clients about the Cognitive Model
New Harbinger Publications
5674 Shattuck Avenue
Oakland, CA 94609-1662
510-652-0215
800-748-6273
Fax: 510-652-5472
E-mail: customerservice@newharbinger.com
www.newharbinger.com

Matthew McKay, Owner

Videotape that helps three clients understand their symptoms as they work toward developing a working contract to begin cognitive restructing. *$49.95*

ISBN 1-572243-19-8

3364 Gender Differences in Depression: Marital Therapy Approach
Guilford Publications
72 Spring Street
New York, NY 10012-4068
212-431-9800
800-365-7006
Fax: 212-966-6708
E-mail: info@guilford.com

Bob Matloff, President

Male-female treatment team is shown working with a markedly depressed couple to improve communication and sense of well being in their marriage. *$85.50*

Year Founded: 1996 ISBN 1-572302-87-9

3365 Group Work for Eating Disorders and Food Issues
American Counseling Association
5999 Stevenson Avenue
Alexandria, VA 22304-3304
703-823-9800
800-422-2648
Fax: 703-823-0252
www.counseling.org

Richard Yep, Executive Director

A plan for working with high school and college age females who are at risk for eating disorders. This video provides a method for identifying at-risk clients, a session-by-session desciption of the group, exercises and information on additional resources. *$89.95*

Year Founded: 1995 ISSN 79801

3366 Help This Kid's Driving Me Crazy - the Young Child with Attention Deficit Disorder
Pro-Ed Publications
8700 Shoal Creek Boulevard
Austin, TX 78757-6897
512-451-3246
800-897-3202
Fax: 512-451-8542
E-mail: info@proedinc.com

Donald D Hammill, Owner

This videotape provides information about the behavior and special needs of young children with ADD and offers suggestions on fostering appropriate behaviors. *$89.00*

3367 I Love You Like Crazy: Being a Parent with Mental Illness
Mental Illness Education Project
PO Box 470813
Brookline Village, MA 02447-813
617-562-1111
800-343-5540
Fax: 617-779-0061
E-mail: miep@tiac.net
www.miepvideos.org

Christine Ledoux, Executive Director

In this videotape, eight mothers and fathers who have mental illness discuss the challenges they face as parents. Most of these parents have faced enormous obstacles from homelessness, addictions, legal difficulties and hospitalizations, yet have maintained a positive and loving relationship with their children. The tape introduces issues of work, fear, stigma, relationships with children and the rest of the family, with professionals, and with the community at large. Discounted price for families/consumers. *$79.95*

Year Founded: 1999

3368 Inner Health Incorporated
Christopher Alsten, PhD
1260 Lincoln Avenue
San Diego, CA 92103-2322
619-299-7273
800-283-4679
Fax: 619-291-7753
E-mail: sleepenhancement@aol.com

Provides a series of prerecorded therapeutic audio programs for anxiety, insomnia and chemical dependency, both for adults and children. Developed over a 15 year period by a practicing psychiatrist and recording engineer they employ state-of-the-art 3-D sound technologies and the latest relaxation and psychological techniques (but no stimulants). Clients include: US Air Force, US Navy, National Institute of Health, National Institute of Aging and various psychiatric and chemical dependency facilities and companies with shiftworkers.

3369 Know Your Rights: Mental Health Private Practice & the Law
American Counseling Association
5999 Stevenson Avenue
Alexandria, VA 22304-3304
703-823-9800
800-347-6647
Fax: 703-823-0252
E-mail: webmaster@counseling.org
www.counseling.org

Richard Yep, Executive Director

Whether you are in private practice or are thinking about opening your own practice, this forum lead by national experts, offers answers to important questions and provides invaluable information for every practitioner. Helps to orientate practitioners on the legally permissible boundaries, legal liabilities that are seldom known and how to respond in the face of legal action. *$145.00*

ISSN 79062

3370 Life Is Hard: Audio Guide to Healing Emotional Pain
Impact Publishers
PO Box 6016
Atascadero, CA 93423-6016
805-466-5917
800-246-7228
Fax: 805-466-5919
E-mail: info@impactpublishers.com
www.impactpublishers.com

In a very warm and highly personal style, psychologist Preston offers listeners powerful advice — realistic, practical, effective, on dealing with the emotional pain life often inflicts upon us. *$11.95*

Year Founded: 1996 ISBN 0-915166-99-2

3371 Life Passage in the Face of Death, Vol II: Psychological Engagement of the Physically Ill Patient
American Psychiatric Publishing, Inc.
1000 Wilson Boulevard
Suite 1825
Arlington, VA 22209-3901
703-907-7322
800-368-5777
Fax: 703-907-1091
E-mail: appi@psych.org
www.appi.org

Robert E Hales MD, Editor-in-Chief
Ron McMillen, Chief Executive Officer
John McDuffie, Editorial Director

Ongoing explanation of therapy from a recognized expert. Valuable to clinicians and students alike.

3372 Life Passage in the Face of Death, Volume I: A Brief Psychotherapy
American Psychiatric Publishing, Inc.
1000 Wilson Boulevard
Suite 1825
Arlington, VA 22209-3901
703-907-7322
800-368-5777
Fax: 703-907-1091
E-mail: appi@psych.org
www.appi.org

Robert E Hales MD, Editor-in-Chief
Ron McMillen, Chief Executive Officer
John McDuffie, Editorial Director

A senior psychoanalyst demonstrates the extraordinary impact of a very brief dynamic psychotherapy on a patient in a time of crisis — the terminal illness and death of a spouse. We not only meet the patient and observe the therapy, but our understanding is guided by the therapist's ongoing explanation of the process. He vividly illustrates concepts such as transference, clarification, interpretation, insight, denial, isolation and above all the relevance of understanding the past for changing the present. This unique opportunity to see a psychotherapy as it is conducted will be of immense value for all mental health clinicians and trainees.

3373 Medical Aspects of Chemical Dependency The Neurobiology of Addiction
Hazelden
15251 Pleasant Valley Road
PO Box 176
Center City, MN 55012-176
651-213-2121
800-328-9000
Fax: 651-213-4590
www.hazelden.org

This interactive curriculum helps professionals educate clients in treatment and other settings about medical effects of chemical use and abuse. The program includes a video that explains body and brain changes that can occur when using alcohol or other drugs, a workbook that helps clients apply the information from the video to their own situations, a handbook that provides in-depth information on addiction, brain chemistry and the physiological effects of chemical dependency and a pamphlet that answers critical questions clients have about the medical effects of chemical dependency. Total price of $244.70, available to purchase separately. Program value packages available for $395.00, with 25 workbooks, two handbooks, two video and 25 pamphlets. *$225.00*

Year Founded: 2003 ISBN 1-568389-87-6

3374 Mental Illness Education Project

PO Box 470813
Brookline Village, MA 02447-813
617-562-1111
800-343-5540
Fax: 617-779-0061
E-mail: info@miepvideos.org
www.miepvideos.org

Christine Ledoux, Executive Director

Engaged in the production of video-based educational and support materials for the following specific populations: people with psychiatric disabilities; families, mental health professionals, special audiences, and the general public. The Project's videos are designed to be used in hospital, clinical and educational settings, and at home by individuals and families.

3375 Personality and Stress Center for Applications of Psychological Type

2815 NW 13th Street
Suite 401
Gainesville, FL 32609-2865
352-375-0160
800-777-2278
Fax: 352-378-0503
E-mail: customerservice@capt.org
www.catp.org

Alecia Perkins, Director Customer Service

Humorous and energetic presentation of the use of type and rational-emotive therapy concepts in stress management. The authors share years of experience using this model in a hospital setting. Useful to the counselor, educator, or anyone working with stress management. *$11.00*

audio pages Year Founded: 1989

3376 Physicians Living with Depression
American Psychiatric Publishing, Inc.

1000 Wilson Boulevard
Suite 1825
Arlington, VA 22209-3901
703-907-7322
800-368-5777
Fax: 703-907-1091
E-mail: appi@psych.org
www.appi.org

Robert E Hales MD, Editor-in-Chief
Ron McMillen, Chief Executive Officer
John McDuffie, Editorial Director

Designed to help doctors see the signs of depression in their fellow physicians and to alert psychiatrists to the severity of the illness in their physician patients, the tape contains two fifteen-minute interviews, one with an emergency physician and one with a pediatrician. *$25.00*

ISBN 0-890422-78-8

3377 Rational Emotive Therapy
Research Press

Dept 26 W
PO Box 9177
Champaign, IL 61826-9177
217-352-3273
800-519-2707
Fax: 217-352-1221
E-mail: rp@researchpress.com
www.researchpress.com

Dennis Wiziecki, Marketing
Dr Albert Ellis, Author

This video illustrates the basic concepts of Rational Emotive Therapy (RET). It includes demonstrations of RET procedures, informative discussions and unstaged counseling sessions. Viewers will see Albert Ellis and his colleagues help clients overcome such problems as guilt, social anxiety, and jealousy. Also, Dr. Ellis shares his perspectives on the evolution of RET. *$195.00*

3378 Solutions Step by Step - Substance Abuse Treatment Videotape
WW Norton & Company

500 5th Avenue
New York, NY 10110-54
212-354-2907
Fax: 212-869-0856
E-mail: admalmud@wwnorton.com

Drake McFeely, CEO

Quick tips, questions and examples focusing on successes that can be experienced helping substance abusers help themselves. *$ 100.00*

Year Founded: 1997 ISSN 70260-X

3379 Testing Automatic Thoughts with Thought Records
New Harbinger Publications

5674 Shattuck Avenue
Oakland, CA 94609-1662
510-652-0215
800-748-6273
Fax: 510-652-5472
E-mail: customerservice@newharbinger.com
www.newharbinger.com

Matthew McKay, Owner

Videotape that helps a client explore the hot thoughts that contribute to depression. *$49.95*

ISBN 1-572243-17-1

Web Sites

3380 www.42online.org
Psychologists In Independent Practice - American Psych Assn (APADIP)

E-mail: div42apa@cox.net
www.42online.org

Members of the American Psychological Association engaged in independent practice. Works to ensure that the needs and concerns of independent psychology practitioners are considered by the APA. Gathers and disseminates information on legislation affecting the practice of psychology, managed care, and other developments in the health care industries, office management, malpractice risk and insurance, hospital management. Offers continuing professional and educational programs. Semiannual convention, with board meeting.

3381 www.aacap.org
American Academy of Child and Adolescent Psychiatry

Represents over 6,000 child and adolescent psychiatrists, brochures availible online which provide concise and up-to-date material on issues ranging from children who suffer from depression and teen suicide to stepfamily problems and child sexual abuse.

3382 www.aan.com
American Academy of Neurology

Provides information for both professionals and the public on neurology subjects, covering Alzheimer's and Parkinson's diseases to stroke and migraine, includes comprehensive fact sheets.

3383 www.aapb.org
Association for Applied Psychophysiology and Biofeedback

Represents clinicians interested in psychopsysiology or biofeedback, offers links to their mission statement, membership information, research, FAQ about biofeedback, conference listings, and links.

3384 www.abecsw.org
American Board of Examiners in Clinical Social Work

Fax: 978-740-5395

Information about the American Board of Examiners, credentialing, and ethics.

3385 www.about.com
About.Com

Network of comprehensive Web sites for over 600 mental health topics.

3386 www.abpsi.org
American Association of Black Psychologists

Includes information about the Association's history and objectives, contact and member information, upcoming events, and publications of interest.

3387 www.ama-assn.org
American Medical Association

Offers a wide range of medical information and links, full-text abstracts of each journal's current and past articles.

3388 www.americasdoctor.com
AmericasDoctor.com

Center researching for new medicine.

3389 www.apa.org
American Psychological Association

Information about journals, press releases, professional and consumer information related to the psychological profession; resources include ethical principles and guidelines, science advocacy, awards and funding programs, testing and assessment information, other on-line and real world resources.

3390 www.apna.org
American Psychiatric Nurses Association

Includes membership information, contact information, organizational information, announcements and related links.

3391 www.appi.org
American Psychiatric Publishing Inc

Informational site about mental disorders, 'Lets Talk Facts' brochure series.

3392 www.apsa.org
American Psychoanalytic Asssociation

Includes searchable bibliographic database containing books, reviews and articles of a psychoanalytical orientation, links and member information.

3393 www.askdrlloyd.wordpress.com
Ask Dr Lloyd

Helps individuals understand mental illnesses and addictions, what treatments and services have been proven scientifically effective, how to manage yourself or help your loved one, and how to beat a mental health system.

3394 www.assc.caltech.edu
Association for the Scientific Study of Consciousness

Electronic journal dedicated to interdisciplinary exploration on the nature of consciousness and its relationship to the brain, congitive science, philosophy, psychology, physics, neuroscience, and artificial intelligence.

3395 www.blarg.net/~charlatn/voices
Compilation of Writings by People Suffering from Depression

3396 www.bpso.org
BPSO-Bipolar Significant Others

3397 www.bpso.org/nomania.htm
How to Avoid a Manic Episode

3398 www.cape.org
Cape Cod Institute

Offers symposia every summer for keeping mental health professionals up-to-date on the latest developments in psychology, treatment, psychiatry, and mental health, outlines available workshops, links and other relevant information.

3399 www.chadd.org
CHADD

Peg Nichols, Director Communications
National non-profit organization representing children and adults with attention deficit/hyperactivity disorder (AD/HD).

3400 www.cnn.com/Health
CNN Health Section

Updated with health and mental health-related stories three to four times weekly.

3401 www.compuserve.com
IQuest/Knowledge Index

On-line research and database information provider.

3402 www.counseling.com
American Counseling Association

Hosts information about the American Counseling Association, membership, legislative and news updates, a conference and workshop calendar, and links to related resources and publications.

3403 www.counselingforloss.com
Counseling for Loss and Life Changes

Look under articles for reprints of writings and links.

3404 www.cyberpsych.org
CyberPsych

Hosts the American Psychoanalyists Foundation, American Association of Suicideology, Society for the Exploration of Psychotherapy Intergration, and Anxiety Disorders Association of America. Also subcategories of the anxiety disorders, as well as general information, including panic disorder, phobias, obsessive compulsive disorder (OCD), social phobia, generalized anxiety disorder, post traumatic stress disorder, and phobias of childhood. Book reviews and links to web pages sharing the topics.

3405 www.factsforhealth.org
Madison Institute of Medicine

Resource to help identify, understand and treat a number of medical conditions, including social anxiety disorder and posttraumatic stress disorder.

3406 www.geocities.com
Have a Heart's Depression Home

Several fine essays and seven triggers for suicide.

3407 www.geocities.com/enchantedforest/1068
Bipolar Kids Homepage

Set of links.

3408 www.goaskalice.columbia.edu
GoAskAlice/Healthwise Columbia University

Oriented toward students, information on sexuality, sexual health, general health, alcohol and other drugs, fitness and nutrition, emotional wellbeing and relationships.

3409 www.grieftalk.com/help1.html
Grief Journey

Short readings for clients.

3410 www.habitsmart.com/cogtitle.html
Cognitive Therapy Pages

Offers accessible explanations.

3411 www.healthgate.com/
HealthGate

On-line reference and database information service, $.75/record.

3412 www.healthtouch.com
Healthtouch Online

Healthtouch Online is a resource that brings together valuable information from trusted health organizations.

3413 www.healthy.net
HealthWorld Online

Consumer-oriented articles on a wide range of health and mental health topics, including: Welcome Center, QuickN'Dex, Site Search, Free Medline, Health Conditions, Alternative Medicine, Referral Network, Health Columns, Global Calendar, Discussion, Cybrarian,

Professional Center, Free Newsletter, Opportunities, Healthy Travel, Homepage, Library, University, Marketplace, Health Clinic, Wellness Center, Fitness Center, News Room, Association Network, Public Health, Self Care Central, and Nutrition Center.

3414 www.helix.com
Helix MEDLINE: GlaxoSmithKline

Helix is an Education, Learning and Information exchange. Developed especially for healthcare practitioners by GlaxoSmithKline, HELIX is a premire source of on-line education and professional resources on a range of therapeutic and practice-management issues.

3415 www.human-nature.com/odmh
On-line Dictonary of Mental Health

Global information resource and research tool. It is compiled by Internet mental health resource users for Internet mental health resource users, and covers all the disciplines contributing to our understanding of mental health.

3416 www.infotrieve.com
Infotrieve Medline Services Provider

Infotrieve is a library services company offering full-service document delivery, databases on the web and a variety of tools to simplify the process of identifying, retrieving and paying for published literature.

3417 www.intelihealth.com
InteliHealth

3418 www.krinfo.com
DataStar/Dialog

Information provider: reference and databases.

3419 www.lollie.com/blue/suicide.html
Comprehensive Approach to Suicide Prevention

Readings for anyone contemplating suicide.

3420 www.mayohealth.org/mayo
Mayo Clinic Health Oasis Library

Healthcare library and resources.

3421 www.med.jhu.edu/drada/creativity.html
Creativity and Depression and Manic-Depression

3422 www.med.nyu.edu/Psych/index.html
NYU Department of Psychiatry

General mental health information, screening tests, reference desk, continuing educations in psychiatry program, interactive testing in psychiatry, augmentation of antidepressants, NYU Psychoanalytic Institute, Psychology Internship Program, Internet Mental Health Resources links.

3423 www.medinfosource.com
CME, Medical Information Source

Medical information and education, fully accredited for all medical specialties.

3424 www.medscape.com
Medscape

Oriented toward physicians and medical topics, but also carries information relevant to the field of psychology and mental health.

3425 www.medweb.emory.edu/MedWeb/
MedWeb Emory University Health Sciences Center Library

Hundreds of links for mental health, psychology, and pscyhiatry. Recognized nationally for clinical, educational and research programs, and its hospitals and professional schools are ranked among the top in the nation. Webpage includes General Information Links, Emory Healthcare, Schools and Research Centers, Libraries and Research Tools, Health Sciences Communications Office, Employment Opportunities, Frequently Requested Contact Information, and much more.

3426 www.members.aol.com/dswgriff
Now Is Not Forever: A Survival Guide

Print out a no-suicide contract, do problem solving, and other exercises.

3427 www.mentalhealth.com/book
Schizophrenia: A Handbook for Families

Mostly unique information.

3428 www.mentalhealth.com/p20-grp.html
Manic-Depressive Illness

Click on Bipolar and then arrow down to Booklets.

3429 www.mentalhealth.com/story
How to Help a Person with Depression

Valuable family education.

3430 www.mentalhealthamerica.net
Mental Health America

Mental Health America is the nation's largest and oldest community-based network dedicated to helping all Americans live mentally healthier lives. With more than 300 affiliates across the country, Mental Health America touches the lives of millions - advocating for changes in policy; educating the public and providing critical information; & delivering urgently needed programs and services.

3431 www.metanoia.org/suicide/
If You Are Thinking about Suicide...Read This First

Excellent suggestions, information and links for the suicidal.

3432 www.mhsource.com
CME Mental Health InfoSource

Mental health information and education, fully accredited for all medical specialties.

3433 www.mhsource.com/
CME Psychiatric Time

Select articles published online from the Psychiatric Times, topics relevant to all mental health professionals.

3434 www.mindfreedom.org
Support Coalition Human Rights & Psychiatry Home Page

Support Coalition is an independent alliance of several dozen grassroots groups in the USA, Canada, Europe, New Zealand; has used protests, publications, letter-writing, e-mail, workshops, Dendron News, the arts and performances. Led by psychiatric survivors, and open to the public, membership is open to anyone who supports its mission and goals.

3435 www.mirror-mirror.org/eatdis.htm
Mirror, Mirror

Relapse prevention for eating disorders.

3436 www.moodswing.org/bdfaq.html
Bipolar Disorder Frequently Asked Questions

Excellent for those newly diagnosed.

3437 www.naphs.org
National Association of Psychiatric Health Systems

The NAPHS advocates for behavioral health and represents provider systems that are committed to the delivery of responsive, accountable and clinically effective prevention, treatment and care for children, adolescents and adults with mental and substance use disorders.

3438 www.naswdc.org/
National Associaton of Social Workers

Central resource for clinical social workers, includes information about the federation, a conference and workshop calender, information on how to subscribe to social worker mailing lists, legislative and news updates, links to state agencies and social work societies, and publications.

3439 www.ndmda.org/justmood.htm
Just a Mood...or Something Else

A brochure for teens.

3440 www.nimh.nih.gov
National Institute of Mental Health (NIMH)

The mission of NIMH is to diminish the burden of mental illness through research of the biological, behavioral, clinical, epidemiological, economic, and social science aspects of mental illnesses.

3441 www.nmha.org
National Mental Health Association

Dedicated to promoting mental health, preventing mental disorders and achieving victory over mental illness through advocacy, education, research and service. NMHA's collaboration with the National GAINS Center for People with Co-Occuring Disorders in the Justice System has produced the Justice for Juveniles Initiative. This program battles to reform the juvenile justice system so that the inmates mental needs are addressed. Envisions a just, humane and healthy society in which all people are accorded respect, dignity and the opportunity to achieve their full potential free from stigma and prejudice.

3442 www.oclc.org
EPIC

On-line reference and database information provider, $40/hour (plus connection fees) and $.75/record.

3443 www.oznet.ksu.edu/library/famlf2/
Family Life Library

3444 www.pace-custody.org
Professional Academy of Custody Evaluators

Nonprofit corporation and membership organization to acknowledge and strengthen the professionally prepared comprehensive custody evaluation; psychologicals legal knowledge base, assessment procedures, courtroom testimony, provides continuing education courses, conferences, conventions and seminars.

3445 www.paperchase.com
PaperChase

Searches may be conducted through a browsable list of topics, search engine recognizes queries made in natural language.

3446 www.parenthoodweb.com
Blended Families

Resolving conflicts.

3447 www.planetpsych.com
Planetpsych.com

Learn about disorders, their treatments and other topics in psychology. Articles are listed under the related topic areas. Ask a therapist a question for free, or view the directory of professionals in your area. If you are a therapist sign up for the directory. Current features, self-help, interactive, and newsletter archives.

3448 www.positive-way.com/step.htm
Stepfamily Information

Introduction and tips for stepfathers, stepmothers and re-married parents.

3449 www.psych.org
American Psychiatric Association

A medical specialty society recognized world-wide. Its 40,500 US and international physicians specializing in the diagnosis and treatment of mental and emotional illness and substance use disorders.

3450 www.psychcentral.com
Psych Central

Personalized one-stop index for psychology, support, and mental health issues, resources, and people on the Internet.

3451 www.psychcrawler.com
American Psychological Association

Indexing the web for the links in psychology.

3452 www.psychology.com/therapy.htm
Therapist Directory

Therapists listed geographically plus answers to frequently asked questions.

3453 www.psycom.net/depression.central.html
Dr. Ivan's Depression Central

Medication-oriented site.

3454 www.recovery-inc.com
Recovery

Describes the organizations approach.

3455 www.reutershealth.com
Reuters Health

Relevant and useful clinical information on mental disorders, news briefs updated daily.

3456 www.save.org
SA/VE - Suicide Awareness/Voices of Education

3457 www.schizophrenia.com
Schizophrenia.com

Offers basic and in-depth information, discussion and chat.

3458 www.schizophrenia.com/ami
Alliance for the Mentally Ill

Information on mental disorders, reducing the stigmatization of them in our society today, and how you can be more active in your local community. Includes articles, press information, media kits, mental disorder diagnostic and treatment information, coping issues, advocacy guides and announcements.

3459 www.schizophrenia.com/newsletter
Schizophrenia.com

Comprehensive psychoeducational site on schizophrenia.

3460 www.shpm.com
Self-Help and Psychology Magazine

General psychology and self-help magazine online, offers informative articles on general well being and psychology topics. Features Author of the Month, Breaking News Stories of the Month, Most Popular Pages, What's Hot, Departments, and Soundoff (articles and opinion page). This online compendium of hundreds of readers and professionals.

3461 www.shpm.com/articles/depress
Placebo Effect Accounts for Fifty Percent of
Improvement

3462 www.siop.org
Society for Industrial and Organizational
Psychology

Home to the Industrial-Organizational Pyschologist newsletter, links and resources, member information, contact information for doctoral and master's level program in I/O
psychology, and announcements of various events and
conferences.

3463 www.stepfamily.org/tensteps.htm
Ten Steps for Steps

Guidelines for stepfamilies.

3464 www.stepfamilyinfo.org/sitemap.htm
Stepfamily in Formation

3465 www.usatoday.com
USA Today

'Mental Health' category includes news and in-depth reports.

3466 www.webmd.com
WebMD

3467 www.wingofmadness.com
Wing of Madness: A Depression Guide

Accurate information, advice, support, and personal experiences.

Workbooks & Manuals

3468 **Activities for Adolescents in Therapy**
Charles C Thomas Publisher
2600 S 1st Street
Springfield, IL 62704-4730

217-789-8980
800-258-8980
Fax: 217-789-9130
E-mail: books@ccthomas.com
www.ccthomas.com
Michael P Thomas, President

In this practical resource manual, professionals will find
more than 100 therapeutic group activities for use in counseling troubled adolescents. This new edition provides spe-
cifics on establishing an effective group program while, at
the same time, outlining therapeutic activities that can be
used in each phase of a therapy group. Step-by-step instructions have been provided for setting up, planning and
facilitating adolescent groups with social and emotional
problems. The interventions provided have been designed
specifically for initial, middle and termination phases of
group. $39.95 *$46.95*

264 pages Year Founded: 1998 ISBN 0-398068-07-0

3469 **Activities for Children in Therapy: Guide for
Planning and Facilitating Therapy with
Troubled Children**
Charles C Thomas Publisher
2600 S 1st Street
Springfield, IL 62704-4730
217-789-8980
800-258-8980
Fax: 217-789-9130
E-mail: books@ccthomas.com
www.ccthomas.com
Michael P Thomas, President

Provides the mental health professional with a wide variety
of age-appropriate activities which are simultaneously fun
and therapeutic for the five-to-twelve-year-old troubled
child. Activities have been designed as enjoyable games in
the context of therapy. Provides a comprehensive listing of
books with other therapeutic intervention ideas,
bibliotherapy materials, assessment scales for evaluating
youngsters, and a sample child assessment for individual
therapy. For professionals who provide counseling to children, such as social workers, psychologists, guidance counselors, speech/language pathologists, and art therapists.
$52.95

302 pages Year Founded: 1999 ISBN 0-398069-71-9

3470 **Chemical Dependency Treatment Planning
Handbook**
Charles C Thomas Publisher
2600 S 1st Street
Springfield, IL 62704-4730
217-789-8980
800-258-8980
Fax: 217-789-9130
E-mail: books@ccthomas.com
www.ccthomas.com
Michael P Thomas, President

Provides the entry-level clinician with a broad data base of
treatment planning illustrations from which unpretentious
treatment plans for the chemically dependent client can be
generated. They are simple, largely measurable, and pur-
posefully, with language that is cognizant of comprehen-

sion and learning needs of clients. It will be of interest to drug and alcohol counselors. *$29.95*

174 pages Year Founded: 1997 ISBN 0-398067-76-7

3471 Clinical Manual of Supportive Psychotherapy
American Psychiatric Publishing, Inc.
1000 Wilson Boulevard
Suite 1825
Arlington, VA 22209-3901
703-907-7322
800-368-5777
Fax: 703-907-1091
E-mail: appi@psych.org
www.appi.org

Robert E Hales MD, Editor-in-Chief
Ron McMillen, Chief Executive Officer
John McDuffie, Editorial Director

New approaches and ideas for your practice. *$64.00*

362 pages Year Founded: 1993

3472 Concise Guide to Laboratory and Diagnostic Testing in Psychiatry
American Psychiatric Publishing, Inc.
1000 Wilson Boulevard
Suite 1825
Arlington, VA 22209-3901
703-907-7322
800-368-5777
Fax: 703-907-1091
E-mail: appi@psych.org
www.appi.org

Robert E Hales MD, Editor-in-Chief
Ron McMillen, Chief Executive Officer
John McDuffie, Editorial Director

Basic strategies for applying laboratory testing and evaluation. *$19.50*

176 pages Year Founded: 1989 ISBN 0-880483-33-4

3473 Creating and Implementing Your Strategic Plan: Workbook for Public and Nonprofit Organizations
Jossey-Bass Publishers
1110 Mar Street
Suite E
Tiburon, CA 94920
415-435-9821
Fax: 415-435-9092
www.josseybass.com

Step-by-step workbook to conducting strategic planning in public and nonprofit organizations. *$30.00*

192 pages Year Founded: 2004 ISBN 0-787967-54-8

3474 Handbook for the Study of Mental Health
Cambridge University Press
40 W 20th Street
New York, NY 10011-4211
212-924-3900
Fax: 212-691-3239

E-mail: marketing@cup.org
www.cup.org

Offers the first comprehensive presentation of the sociology of mental health illness, including original, contemporary contributions by experts in the relevant aspects of the field. Divided into three sections, the chapters cover the general perspectives in the field, the social determinants of mental health and current policy areas affecting mental health services. Designed for classroom use in sociology, social work, human relations, human services and psychology. With its useful definitions, overview of the historical, social and institutional frameworks for understanding mental health and illness, and nontechnical style, the text is suitable for advanced undergraduate or lower level graduate students. *$90.00*

694 pages Year Founded: 1999 ISBN 0-521561-33-7

3475 Handbook of Clinical Psychopharmacology for Therapists
New Harbinger Publications
5674 Shattuck Avenue
Oakland, CA 94609-1662
510-652-0215
800-748-6273
Fax: 510-652-5472
E-mail: customerservice@newharbinger.com
www.newharbinger.com

Matthew McKay, Owner

This newly revised classic includes updates on new medications, and expanded quick reference section, and new material on bipolar illness, the treatment of psychosis, and the effect of severe trauma. *$55.95*

264 pages Year Founded: 2005 ISBN 1-572240-94-6

3476 Handbook of Constructive Therapies
Jossey-Bass Publishers
350 Sansome Street
5th Floor
San Francisco, CA 94104-1310
415-394-8677
800-956-7739
Fax: 800-605-2665
www.josseybass.com

Learn techniques that focus on the strengths and resources of your clients and look to where they want to go rather than where they have been. *$64.00*

500 pages Year Founded: 1998 ISBN 0-787940-44-5

3477 Handbook of Counseling Psychology
John Wiley & Sons
605 3rd Avenue
New York, NY 10158-180
212-850-6301
E-mail: info@wiley.com

Provides a cross-disciplinary survey of the entire field and offers analysis of important areas of counseling psychology activity. the book elaborates on future directions for research, highlighting suggestions that may advance knowledge and stimulate further inquiry. Specific advice is presented from the literature in counseling psychology and related disciplines to help improve one's counseling practice. *$ 120.00*

880 pages Year Founded: 2000 ISBN 0-471254-58-4

3478 Handbook of Managed Behavioral Healthcare
Jossey-Bass Publishers
350 Sansome Street
5th Floor
San Francisco, CA 94104-1310
415-394-8677
800-956-7739
Fax: 800-605-2665
www.josseybass.com

A comprehensive curriculum to understanding managed care. *$43.00*

240 pages Year Founded: 1998 ISBN 0-787941-53-0

3479 Handbook of Medical Psychiatry
Mosby
11830 Westline Industrial Drive
Saint Louis, MO 63146-3318
314-872-8370
800-325-4177
Fax: 314-432-1380

This large-format handbook covers almost every psychiatric, neurologic and general medical condition capable of causing disturbances in thought, feeling, or behavior and includes almost every psychopharmacologic agent available in America today. *$61.95*

544 pages Year Founded: 1996 ISBN 0-323029-11-6

3480 Handbook of Mental Retardation and Development
Cambridge University Press
40 W 20th Street
New York, NY 10011-4211
212-924-3900
Fax: 212-691-3239
E-mail: marketing@cup.org
www.cup.org

This book reviews theoretical and empirical work in the developmental approach to mental retardation. Armed with methods derived from the study of typically developing children, developmentalists have recently learned about the mentally retarded child's own development in a variety of areas. These now encompass many aspects of cognition, language, social and adaptive functioning, as well as of maladaptive behavior and psychopathology. In addition to a focus on individuals with mental retardation themselves, other ecological factors have influenced developmental approaches to mental retardation. Comprised of twenty seven chapters on various aspects of development, this handbook provides a comprehensive guide to understanding mental retardation. *$80.00*

764 pages Year Founded: 1998

3481 Handbook of Psychiatric Education and Faculty Development
American Psychiatric Publishing, Inc.
1000 Wilson Boulevard
Suite 1825
Arlington, VA 22209-3901
703-907-7322
800-368-5777
Fax: 703-907-1091
E-mail: appi@psych.org
www.appi.org

Robert E Hales MD, Editor-in-Chief
Ron McMillen, Chief Executive Officer
John McDuffie, Editorial Director

Putting education to work in the real world. *$68.50*

496 pages Year Founded: 1999 ISBN 0-880487-80-1

3482 Handbook of Psychiatric Practice in the Juvenile Court
American Psychiatric Publishing, Inc.
1000 Wilson Boulevard
Suite 1825
Arlington, VA 22209-3901
703-907-7322
800-368-5777
Fax: 703-907-1091
E-mail: appi@psych.org
www.appi.org

Robert E Hales MD, Editor-in-Chief
Ron McMillen, Chief Executive Officer
John McDuffie, Editorial Director

How your practice can work with the court system, so your patients can get the help they need. *$27.95*

198 pages Year Founded: 1992 ISBN 0-890422-33-8

3483 Living Skills Recovery Workbook
Elsevier Science
Po Box 28430
Saint Louis, MO 63146-930
314-453-7010
800-545-2522
Fax: 314-453-7095
E-mail: orders@bhusa.com or custserv@bhusa.com
www.bh.com

Katie Hennessy, Medical Promotions Coordinator

Provides clinicians with the tools necessary to help patients with dual diagnoses acquire basic living skills. Focusing on stress management, time management, activities of daily living, and social skills training, each living skill is taught in relation to how it aids in recovery and relapse prevention for each patient's individual lifestyle and pattern of addiction.

224 pages ISBN 0-750671-18-1

3484 On the Client's Path: A Manual for the Practice of Brief Solution - Focused Therapy
New Harbinger Publications
5674 Shattuck Avenue
Oakland, CA 94609-1662

510-652-0215
800-748-6273
Fax: 510-652-5472
E-mail: customerservice@newharbinger.com
www.newharbinger.com

Matthew McKay, Owner

Provides everything you need to master the solution - focused model. *$49.95*

157 pages Year Founded: 1995 ISBN 1-572240-21-0

3485 Relaxation & Stress Reduction Workbook
New Harbinger Publications
5674 Shattuck Avenue
Oakland, CA 94609-1662
510-652-0215
800-748-6273
Fax: 510-652-5472
E-mail: customerservice@newharbinger.com
www.newharbinger.com

Matthew McKay, Owner

Details effective stress reduction methods such as breathing exercises, meditation, visualization, and time management. Widely reccomended by therapists, nurses, and physicians throughout the US, this fourth edition has been substantially revised and updated to reflect current research. Line drawings and charts. *$19.95*

276 pages Year Founded: 2005 ISBN 1-879237-82-2

3486 Skills Training Manual for Treating Borderline Personality Disorder, Companion Workbook
Guilford Publications
72 Spring Street
New York, NY 10012-4068
212-431-9800
800-365-7006
Fax: 212-966-6708
E-mail: info@guilford.com

Bob Matloff, President

A vital component in Dr. Linehan's comprehensive treatment program, this step-by-step manual details precisely how to implement the skills training procedures and includes practical pointers on when to use the other treatment strategies described. It includes useful, clear-cut handouts that may be readily photocopied. *$27.95*

180 pages Year Founded: 1993 ISBN 0-898620-34-1

3487 Step Workbook for Adolescent Chemical Dependency Recovery
American Psychiatric Publishing, Inc.
1000 Wilson Boulevard
Suite 1825
Arlington, VA 22209-3901
703-907-7322
800-368-5777
Fax: 703-907-1091
E-mail: appi@psych.org
www.appi.org

Robert E Hales MD, Editor-in-Chief
Ron McMillen, Chief Executive Officer
John McDuffie, Editorial Director

Strategies for younger patients in your practice. *$ 62.00*

72 pages Year Founded: 1990 ISBN 0-882103-00-9

3488 Stress Management Training: Group Leader's Guide
Professional Resource Press
PO Box 15560
Sarasota, FL 34277-1560
941-343-9601
800-443-3364
Fax: 941-343-9201
E-mail: orders@prpress.com
www.prpress.com

This practical guide will help you define the concept of stress for group members and teach them various intervention techniques ranging from relaxation training to communication skills. Includes specific exercises, visual aids, stress response index, stress analysis form and surveys for evaluating program effectiveness. *$13.95*

96 pages Year Founded: 1990 ISBN 0-943158-33-8

3489 Stress Owner's Manual: Meaning, Balance and Health in Your Life
Impact Publishers
PO Box 6016
Atascadero, CA 93423-6016
805-466-5917
800-246-7228
Fax: 805-466-5919
E-mail: info@impactpublishers.com
www.impactpublishers.com

Offers specific solutions: maps, checklists and rating scales to help you assess your life; dozens of stress buffer activities to help you deal with stress on the spot; life-changing strategies to prepare you for a lifetime of effective stress management. *$15.95*

224 pages Year Founded: 2003 ISBN 1-886230-54-4

3490 The Comprehensive Directory
Resources For Children with Special Needs
116 E 16th Street
5th Floor
New York, NY 10003-2164
212-677-4650
Fax: 212-254-4070
E-mail: info@resourcesnyc.org
www.resourcesnyc.org

Rachel Howard, Executive Director

The directory for everyone who needs to find services for children with disabilities and special needs. Designed for parents, caregivers and professionals, it includes more than 2,500 agencies providing more than 4,000 services and programs. *$30.00*

1200 pages ISBN 0-967836-51-4

3491 Therapist's Workbook
Jossey-Bass Publishers
350 Sansome Street
5th Floor
San Francisco, CA 94104-1310
415-394-8677
800-956-7739
Fax: 800-605-2665
www.josseybass.com

This workbook nourishes and challenges counselors, guiding them on a journey of self-reflection and renewal.
$35.00

192 pages Year Founded: 1999 ISBN 0-787945-23-4

3492 Treating Alcohol Dependence: a Coping Skills Training Guide
Guilford Publications
72 Spring Street
New York, NY 10012-4068
212-431-9800
800-365-7006
Fax: 212-966-6708
E-mail: info@guilford.com

Bob Matloff, President

Treatment program based on a cognitive-social learning theory of alcohol abuse. Presents a straight-forward treatment strategy that copes with how to stop drinking and provides the training skills to make it possible. *$21.95*

240 pages Year Founded: 1989 ISBN 0-898622-15-8

3493 Uniquity
PO Box 10
Galt, CA 95632-10
209-745-2111
800-521-7771
Fax: 209-745-4430
E-mail: uniquity@uniquitypsych.com
www.uniquitypsych.com

Reuven E Epstein, Owner

Mail order and internet supplier of mental health materials, anger tools, play therapy, foster care, adoption, attachment, group therapy, child abuse and more.

Directories & Databases

3494 AAHP/Dorland Directory of Health Plans
Dorland Healthcare Information
1500 Walnut Street
Suite 1000
Philadelphia, PA 19102-3512
215-875-1212
800-784-2332
Fax: 215-735-3966
E-mail: info@dorlandhealth.com
www.dorlandhealth.com

Paperback, published yearly. *$215.00*

3495 American Academy of Child and Adolescent Psychiatry - Membership Directory
3615 Wisconsin Avenue NW
Washington, DC 20016-3007
202-362-1797
800-333-7636
E-mail: communications@aacap.org

Robert Hendren, President
David Herzog, Secretary
William Bernet, Treasurer

$30.00

179 pages 2 per year

3496 American Academy of Psychoanalysis and Dynam ic Psychiatry
American Academy of Psychoanalysis and Dynamic Psychiatry
One Regency Drive
PO Box 30
Bloomfield, CT 06002-30
888-691-8281
Fax: 860-286-0787
E-mail: info@aapdp.org
www.aapsa.org

Jacquelyn T Coleman CAE, Executive Director
Sherry Katz-Bearnot, President
Carol Filiaci, Secretary

The journal of the American Academy of Psychoanalysis and Dynamic Psychiatry. Publishes articles by members and other authors who have a significant contribution to make to the community of scholars or practitioners interested in a psychodynamic understanding of human behavior. *$50.00*

70 pages

3497 American Network of Community Options and Resources-Directory of Members
ANCOR
1101 King Street
Suite 380
Alexandria, VA 22314-2962
703-535-7850
Fax: 703-535-7860
E-mail: ancor@ancor.org
www.ancor.org

Renee L Pietrangelo, CEO

Covers 650 agencies serving people with mental retardation and other developmental disabilities. *$25.00*

179 pages 1 per year

3498 American Psychiatric Association-Membership Directory
Harris Publishing
2500 Westchester Avenue
Suite 400
Purchase, NY 10577-2515

800-326-6600
Fax: 914-641-3501
www.bcharrispub.com

$59.95
816 pages

3499 American Psychoanalytic Association - Roster
American Psychological Association
750 1st Street NE
Washington, DC 20002-4242
202-336-5500
800-374-2721
Fax: 202-336-5518
E-mail: webmaster@apa.org
www.apa.org

Norman B Anderson, CEO

$40.00
194 pages

3500 Association for Advancement of Behavior Therapy: Membership Directory
305 Seventh Avenue
16th Floor
New York, NY 10001-6008
212-647-1890
Fax: 212-647-1865
E-mail: mebrown@aabt.org

Mary Jane Eimer, Executive Director
Mary Ellen Brown, Administration/Convention
Rosemary Park, Membership Services

Covers over 4,500 psychologists, psychiatrists, social workers and other interested in behavior therapy. *$50.00*

240 pages 2 per year

3501 At Health
14241 NE Woodinville-Duvall Road
Suite 104
Woodinville, WA 98072-8564
360-668-3808
888-284-3258
Fax: 360-668-2216
E-mail: support@athealth.com
www.athealth.com

Providing trustworthy online information, tools, and training that enhance the ability of practitioners to furnish high quality, personalized care to those they serve. For the meantl health consumer, find practitioners, treatment center, learn about disorders and conditions, and about medications being used, news and resources.

3502 Behavioral Measurement Database Services
PO Box 110287
Pittsburgh, PA 15232-787
412-687-6850
Fax: 412-687-5213
E-mail: bmds@aol.com

Service health and psychosocial instruments, a database of over 75,000 records on measurement instruments enriching the health and psychosocial sciences. Records include questionnaires, interview schedules, vignettes/scenarios, coding schemes, and other scales, checklists, indexes, and tests in medicine, nursing, public health, psychology, social work, sociology, and communicaiton. Also provides copies of selected instruments cited in the HAPI database through its instrument delivery service. Contact Ovid Technologies 1-800-950-2035

3503 CARF Directory of Organizations with Accredited Programs
Rehabilitation Accreditation Commission
4891 E Grant Road
Tucson, AZ 85712-2704
520-325-1044
Fax: 520-318-1129
TTY: 888-281-6531
www.carf.org

Brian J. Boom, President/CEO
Amanda Birch, Administrator Of Operations

Covers about three thousand organizations in seven thousand locations offering more than eighteen hundred medical rehabilitation, behavioral health, and employment and community support services that have been accredited by CARF. *$100.00*

200 pages 1 per year Year Founded: 1999

3504 Case Management Resource Guide
Dorland Healthcare Information
1500 Walnut Street
Suite 1000
Philadelphia, PA 19102-3512
215-875-1212
800-784-2332
Fax: 215-735-3966
E-mail: info@dorlandhealth.com
www.dorlandhealth.com

Extensive directory of healthcare services used by case managers, discharge planners, managed care contracting staff, sales and marketing professionsal, search firms and information and referral agencies. $175 for four-volume set or $49 for each regional edition.

1 per year

3505 Case Management Resource Guide (Health Care)
Dorland Healthcare Information
1500 Walnut Street
Suite 1000
Philadelphia, PA 19102-3512
215-875-1212
800-784-2332
Fax: 215-735-3966
E-mail: info@dorlandhealth.com
www.dorlandhealth.com

In four volumes, over 110,000 health care facilities and support services are listed, including homecare, rehabilitation, psychiatric and addiction treatment programs, hospices, adult day care and burn and cancer centers.

5,200 pages 1 per year ISBN 1-880874-84-9

3506 Case Manager Database
Dorland Healthcare Information
1500 Walnut Street
Suite 1000
Philadelphia, PA 19102-3512
215-875-1212
800-784-2332
Fax: 215-735-3966
E-mail: info@dorlandhealth.com
www.dorlandhealth.com

Largest database of information on case managers in US, especially of case managers who work for health plans and health insurers. Covers over 15,000 case managers and includes detailed data such as work setting and clinical specialty, which can be used to carefully target marketing communications. $2500 for full database, other prices available.

3507 Community Mental Health Directory
Department of Community Health
320 S Walnut
Suite 6
Lansing, MI 48913-1
517-373-3500

Covers about 51 public community mental health services and programs in Michigan.

20 pages 2 per year

3508 Complete Directory for People with Disabilities
Grey House Publishing
4919 Route 22
PO Box 56
Amenia, NY 12501
518-789-8700
800-562-2139
Fax: 845-373-6390
E-mail: books@greyhouse.com
www.greyhouse.com

Leslie Mackenzie, Publisher
Laura Mars-Proietti, Editor

This one-stop annual resource provides immediate access to the latest products and services available for people with disabilities, such as Periodicals & Books, Assistive Devices, Employment & Education Programs, Camps and Travel Groups. *$165.00*

1200 pages ISBN 1-592370-07-1

3509 Complete Learning Disabilities Directory
Grey House Publishing
4919 Route 22
PO Box 56
Amenia, NY 12501
518-789-8700
800-562-2139
Fax: 845-373-6390
E-mail: books@greyhouse.com
www.greyhouse.com

Leslie Mackenzie, Publisher
Laura Mars-Proietti, Editor

This annual resource includes information about Associations & Organizations, Schools, Colleges & Testing Materi-

als, Government Agencies, Legal Resources and much more. *$195.00*

745 pages ISBN 1-930956-79-7

3510 Complete Mental Health Directory
Grey House Publishing
4919 Route 22
PO Box 56
Amenia, NY 12501
518-789-8700
800-562-2139
Fax: 845-373-6390
E-mail: books@greyhouse.com
www.greyhouse.com

Leslie Mackenzie, Publisher
Laura Mars-Proietti, Editor

This bi-annual directory offers understandable descriptions of 25 Mental Health Disorders as well as detailed information on Associations, Media, Support Groups and Mental Health Facilities. *$ 165.00*

800 pages ISBN 1-592370-46-2

3511 DSM-IV Psychotic Disorders: New Diagnostic Issue
American Psychiatric Publishing, Inc.
1000 Wilson Boulevard
Suite 1825
Arlington, VA 22209-3901
703-907-7322
800-368-5777
Fax: 703-907-1091
E-mail: appi@psych.org
www.appi.org

Robert E Hales MD, Editor-in-Chief
Ron McMillen, Chief Executive Officer
John McDuffie, Editorial Director

Updates on clinical findings. *$39.95*

Year Founded: 1995

3512 Detwiler's Directory of Health and Medical Resources
Dorland Healthcare Information
1500 Walnut Street
Suite 1000
Philadelphia, PA 19102-3512
215-875-1212
800-784-2332
Fax: 215-735-3966
E-mail: info@dorlandhealth.com
www.dorlandhealth.com

An invaluable guide to healthcare information sources. This directory lists information on over 2,000 sources of information on the medical and healthcare industry. *$195.00*

1 per year Year Founded: 1999 ISBN 1-880874-57-1

3513 Directory for People with Chronic Illness
Grey House Publishing
4919 Route 22
PO Box 56
Amenia, NY 12501
518-789-8700
800-562-2139
Fax: 845-373-6390
E-mail: books@greyhouse.com
www.greyhouse.com

Leslie MacKenzie, Publisher
Laura Mars-Proietti, Editor

This bi-annual resource provides a comprehensive overview of the support services and information resources available for people diagnosed with a chronic illness. Includes 12,000 entries. *$165.00*

1200 pages ISBN 1-592370-81-0

3514 Directory of Developmental Disabilities Services
Nebraska Health and Human Services System
PO Box 94728
Department of Services
Lincoln, NE 68509-4728
402-471-2851
800-833-7352
Fax: 402-479-5094

Covers agencies and organizations that provide developmental disability services and programs in Nebraska.

28 pages

3515 Directory of Health Care Professionals
Dorland Healthcare Information
1500 Walnut Street
Suite 1000
Philadelphia, PA 19102-3512
215-875-1212
800-784-2332
Fax: 215-735-3966
E-mail: info@dorlandhealth.com
www.dorlandhealth.com

Helps you easily locate the key personnel and facilities you want by hospital name, system head-quarters, or job title. Valuable for locating industry professionals, recruiting, networking, and prospecting for industry business. *$299.00*

1 per year Year Founded: 1998 ISBN 1-573721-40-9

3516 Directory of Hospital Personnel
Grey House Publishing
185 Millerton Road
PO Box 860
Millerton, NY 12546-860
518-789-8700
800-562-2139
Fax: 518-789-0545
E-mail: books@greyhouse.com
www.greyhouse.com

Leslie MacKenzie, Publisher
Laura Mars-Proietti, Editor

Best annual resource for researching or marketing a product or service to the hospital industry. Includes 6,000 hospitals and over 80,000 key contacts. *$275.00*

2400 pages ISBN 1-592370-26-8

3517 Directory of Physician Groups & Networks
Dorland Healthcare Information
1500 Walnut Street
Suite 1000
Philadelphia, PA 19102-3512
215-875-1212
800-784-2332
Fax: 215-735-3966
E-mail: info@dorlandhealth.com
www.dorlandhealth.com

This directory offers the most comprehensive and current data on these fast-changing organizations. Includes valuable lists and rankings such as the top 200 group practices, plus, five industry experts provide exclusive reviews of current dynamics and trends in the physician marketplace. *$349.00*

3518 Directory of Physician Groups and Networks
Dorland Healthcare Information
1500 Walnut Street
Suite 1000
Philadelphia, PA 19102-3512
215-875-1212
800-784-2332
Fax: 215-735-3966
E-mail: info@dorlandhealth.com
www.dorlandhealth.com

Reference tool with over 4,000 entries covering IPAs, PHOs, large medical group practices with 20 or more physicians, MSOs and PPMCs. Paperback, published yearly. *$345.00*

Year Founded: 1998 ISBN 1-880874-50-4

3519 Dorland's Medical Directory
Dorland Healthcare Information
1500 Walnut Street
Suite 1000
Philadelphia, PA 19102-3512
215-875-1212
800-784-2332
Fax: 215-735-3966
E-mail: info@dorlandhealth.com
www.dorlandhealth.com

Contains expanded coverage of healthcare facilities with profiles of 616 group practices, 661 hospitals and 750 rehabilitation, subacute, hospice and long term care facilities. *$699.00*

1 per year ISBN 1-880874-82-2

3520 Drug Information Handbook for Psychiatry
Lexi-Comp
1100 Terex Road
Hudson, OH 44236-4438
330-650-6506
800-837-5394
Fax: 330-656-4307
www.lexi.com

Steven Kerscher, Owner

Written specifically for mental health professionals. Addresses the fact that mental health patients may be taking additional medication for the treatment of another medical condition in combination with their psychtropic agents. With that in mind, this book contains information on all drugs, not just the psychotropic agents. Specific fields of information contained within the drug monograph include Effects on Mental Status and Effects on Psychiatric Treatment. *$38.75*

1 per year ISBN 1-591951-14-3

3521 HMO & PPO Database & Directory
Dorland Healthcare Information
1500 Walnut Street
Suite 1000
Philadelphia, PA 19102-3512
215-875-1212
800-784-2332
Fax: 215-735-3966
E-mail: info@dorlandhealth.com
www.dorlandhealth.com

Delivers comprehensive and current information on senior-level individuals at virtually all US HMOs and PPOs at an affordable price. *$400.00*

3522 HMO/PPO Directory
Grey House Publishing
185 Millerton Road
PO Box 860
Millerton, NY 12546-860
518-789-8700
800-562-2139
Fax: 518-789-0545
E-mail: books@greyhouse.com
www.greyhouse.com

Leslie MacKenzie, Publisher
Laura Mars-Proetti, Editor

This annual resource provides detailed information about health maintenance organizations and preferred provider organizations nationwide. *$275.00*

500 pages ISBN 1-592370-22-5

3523 Innovations in Clinical Practice: Source Book - Volumes 4-20
Professional Resource Press
PO Box 15560
Sarasota, FL 34277-1560
941-343-9601
800-443-3364
Fax: 941-343-9201
E-mail: orders@prpress.com
www.prpress.com

Debra Fink, Managing Editor

Provides a comprehensive source of practical information and applied techniques that can be put to immediate use in your practice. *$64.95*

524 pages Year Founded: 1999

3524 Medi-Pages On-Line Directory
Medi-Pages
719 Main Street
Niagara Falls, NY 14301-1703
716-284-4277
800-554-6661
Fax: 716-284-4401
E-mail: marilyn@medipages.com
www.medipages.com

Marilyn Gould, Executive Assistant

On-line service covers more than 1.5 million listings of hospitals, nursing homes, clinics, home healthcare providers, HMOs, PPOs, CPOs, health associations, professional associations, federal government agencies, international health organizations, medical libraries, hospital management companies, case managers, HFCA offices, AT&T numbers as well as an online medical product locater.

3525 Medical & Healthcare Marketplace Guide Directory
Dorland Healthcare Information
1500 Walnut Street
Suite 1000
Philadelphia, PA 19102-3512
215-875-1212
800-784-2332
Fax: 215-735-3966
E-mail: info@dorlandhealth.com
www.dorlandhealth.com

Contains valuable data on pharmaceutical, medical advice, and clinical and non-clinical healthcare service companies worldwide. *$499.00*

3526 Mental Health Directory
Office of Consumer, Family & Public Information
5600 Fishers Lane, Room 15-99
Center For Mental Health Services
Rockville, MD 20857-1
301-443-2792
Fax: 301-443-5163

Covers hospitals, treatment centers, outpatient clinics, day/night facilities, residential treatment centers for emotionally disturbed children, residential supportive programs such as halfway houses, and mental health centers offering mental health assistance. *$23.00*

468 pages

3527 National Association of Psychiatric Health Systems: Membership Directory
325 Seventh Street NW
Suite 625
Washington, DC 20004-2805
202-393-6700
Fax: 202-783-6041
E-mail: naphs@naphs.org
www.naphs.org

Mark Covall, Executive Director
Carole Szpak, Director Communications

Contact information of professional groups working to coordinate a full spectrum of treatment services, including inpatient, residential, partial hospitalization and outpatient programs as well as prevention and management services. *$32.10*

48 pages 1 per year Year Founded: 1933

3528 National Directory of Medical Psychotherapists and Psychodiagnosticians

345 24th Avenue N
Park Plaza Medical Building Suite 2
Nashville, TN 37203-1520
615-327-2984
Fax: 615-327-9235
E-mail: americanbd@aol.com

Includes the following: Disability Analysis in Practice: Fundamental Framework for an Interdisciplinary Science, and The Disability Handbook: Tools for Independent Practice. *$45.00*

240 pages 1 per year

3529 National Register of Health Service Providers in Psychology

1120 G Street NW
Suite 330
Washington, DC 20005-3873
202-783-7663
Fax: 202-347-0550
www.nationalregister.org

Judy E Hall, CEO
Greg Hurley, Vice President/Vice-Chair

Psychologists who are licensed or certified by a state/provincial board of examiners of psychology and who have met council criteria as health service providers in psychology.

Year Founded: 1974

3530 National Registry of Psychoanalysts
National Association for the Advancement of Psychoanalysis

80 8th Avenue
Suite 1501
New York, NY 10011-5126
212-741-0515
Fax: 212-366-4347
E-mail: dfmaxwell@mac.com
www.naap.org

Mary Quackenburh, Executive Director
Douglas Maxwell, President

NAAP provides information to the public on psychoanalysis. Publishes quarterly NAAP News, annual Registry of Psychoanalysts. *$ 15.00*

175 pages

3531 Patient Guide to Mental Health Issues: Desk Chart
Lexi-Comp

1100 Terex Road
Hudson, OH 44236-4438
330-650-6506
800-837-5394

Fax: 330-656-4307
www.lexi.com

Steven Kerscher, Owner

Designed specifically for healthcare professionals dealing with mental health patients. Combines eight of our popular Patient Chart titles into one, convienient desktop presentation. This will assist in explaining the most common mental health issue to your patients on a level that they will understand. *$38.75*

1 per year ISBN 1-591950-54-6

3532 PsycINFO Database
PsycINFO, American Psychological Association

750 1st Street NE
Washington, DC 20002-4241
202-336-5500
800-374-2722
Fax: 202-336-5518
TDD: 202-336-6123
E-mail: psycinfo@apa.org
www.apa.org

Norman B Anderson, CEO

PsycINFO is a database that contains citations and summaries of journal articles, book chapters, books, dissertations and technical reports in the field of psychology and the psychological aspects of related disciplines, such as medicine, psychiatry, nursing, sociology, education, pharmacology, physiology, linguistics, anthropology, business and law. Journal coverage, spanning 1887 to present, includes international material from 1,800 periodicals written in over 30 languages. Current chapter and book coverage includes worldwide English language material published from 1987 to present. Over 75,000 references are added annually through weekly updates.

52 per year

3533 Rating Scales in Mental Health
Lexi-Comp

1100 Terex Road
Hudson, OH 44236-4438
330-650-6506
800-837-5394
Fax: 330-656-4307
www.lexi.com

Steven Kerscher, Owner

Ideal for clinicians as well as administrators, this title provides an overview of over 100 recommended rating scales for mental health assessment. This book is also a great tool to assist mental healthcare professionals determine the appropriate psychiatric rating scale when assessing their clients. *$38.75*

1 per year ISBN 1-591950-52-X

3534 Roster: Centers for the Developmentally Disabled
Nebraska Health and Human Services

301 Centennial Mall S
Lincoln, NE 68508-2529
402-471-4363
Fax: 402-471-0555

TDD: 070-119-99
www.2.hhs.state.ne.us/

Joann Erickson RN, Program Manager

Covers approximately 160 licensed facilities in Nebraska
for the developmentally disabled.

40 pages   1 per year

3535 Roster: Health Clinics
Nebraska Health and Human Services
301 Centennial Mall S
Lincoln, NE 68508-2529
402-471-4363
Fax: 402-471-0555
www.2.hhs.state.ne.us/

Joann Erickson RN, Section Administrator

Covers approximately 90 licensed health clinic facilities in
Nebraska.

11 pages   1 per year

3536 Roster: Substance Abuse Treatment Centers
Nebraska Health and Human Services
301 Centennial Mall S
Lincoln, NE 68508-2529
402-471-4363
Fax: 402-471-0555
www.2.hhs.state.ne.us/

Joann Erickson RN, Program Manager

Covers approximately 56 licensed substance abuse treatment centers in Nebraska.

12 pages   1 per year

Publishers

Books

3537 Active Parenting Publishers
1955 Vaughn Road NW
Suite 108
Kennesaw, GA 30144-7808
770-429-0565
800-825-0060
Fax: 770-429-0334
E-mail: cservice@activeparenting.com

Delivers quality education programs for parents, children and teachers to schools, hospitals, social service organizations, churches and corporate market. Innovator in the educational market.

3538 American Psychiatric Publishing (APPI)
1000 Wilson Boulevard
Suite 1825
Arlington, VA 22209-3924
703-907-7322
800-368-5777
Fax: 703-907-1091
E-mail: appi@psych.org
www.appi.org

Ron McMillen, CEO
Joan Lang, Treasurer

Publisher of books, journals, and multi-media on psychiatry, mental healths and behavioral science. Offers authoratative, up-to-date and affordable information geared toward psychiatrists, other mental health professionals, psychiatric residents, medical students and the general public.

3539 Analytic Press
10 Industrial Avenue
Mahwah, NJ 07430-2253
201-258-2200
Fax: 201-760-3735
www.analyticpress.com

Publishes works of substance and originality that constitute genuine contributions to their respective disciplines and professions.

3540 Baker and Taylor
2550 West Tyvola Road
Suite 300
Charlotte, NC 28217-4579
704-357-3500
800-775-1800
Fax: 704-998-3316
www.libraryplace.com

Thomas Morgan, CEO
Robert Agres, Executive VP/CFO

Provides quality information and entertainment services. Worldwide distributor of books, videos, music and games in all disciplines.

3541 Brookes Publishing
PO Box 10624
Baltimore, MD 21285-624
410-337-9580
800-638-3775
Fax: 410-337-8539
E-mail: custserv@brookespublishing.com
www.brookespublishing.com

Paul H Brookes, President
Melissa A Behm, Vice President

Publishes highly respected resources in early childhood, early interventions, inclusive and special education, developmental disabilities, learning disabilities, communication and language, behavior, and mental health

3542 Brookline Books/Lumen Editions
34 University Road
Brookline, MA 02445-4533
617-734-6772
Fax: 617-734-3952
www.brooklinebooks.com

Publishes books on learning disabilities, study skills, self-advocacy for the disabled, early childhood intervention, and more, in readable language that reaches beyond the academic community.

3543 Brunner-Routledge Mental Health
270 Madison Avenue
New York, NY 10016-601
212-695-6599
800-634-7064

Maura May, Publisher

he Routledge imprint publishes books and journals on clinical psychology, psychiatry, psychoanalysis, analytical psychology, psychotherapy, counseling, mental health and other professional subjects.

3544 Bull Publishing Company
Bull Publishing Company
PO Box 1377
Boulder, CO 80306-1377

800-676-2855
Fax: 303-545-6354
E-mail: jim.bullpubco@comcast.net
www.bullpub.com

Jim Bull, Publisher

Publisher of books focused on addressing the growing need for sound health information and good advice.

3545 Cambridge University Press
40 West 20th Street
New York, NY 10011-4211
212-924-3900
Fax: 212-691-3239
www.cambridge.org/americas

Printing and publishing house that is an integral part of the University and has similar charitable objectives in advancing knowledge, education, learning and research.

3546 Charles C Thomas Publishers
2600 South First Street
Po Box 19265
Springfield, IL 62794-9265
217-789-8980
800-258-8980
Fax: 217-789-9130
E-mail: books@ccthomas.com
www.ccthomas.com

Producing a strong list of specialty titles and textbooks in the biomedical sciences. Also very active in producing books for the behavioral sciences, education and special education, speech language and hearing, as well as rehabilitation and long-term care. One of the largest producers of books in all areas of criminal justice and law enforcement.

3547 Crossroad Publishing
831 Chestnut Ridge Rd
Spring Valley, NY 10977-6356
212-868-1801
Fax: 212-868-2171
E-mail: ask@crossroadspublishing.com
www.cpcbooks.com

Publishes words of thoughtfulness and hope. A leading independent publishing house.

3548 EBSCO Publishing
10 Estes Street
Ipswich, MA 01938-2106
978-356-1372
800-653-2726
Fax: 978-356-6565

Timothy S Collins, President
Daniel Boutchie, Inside Sales Representative
Jeffery Greaves, Inside Sales Representative

EBSCO Publishing offers electronic access to a variety of health data: full text databases containing aggregate journals, access to publishers' electronic journals, and the citational databases produced by the American Psychiatric Association to name just a few. Offers a free, nonobligation, on-line trial.

3549 Family Experiences Productions
PO Box 5879
Austin, TX 78763-5879
512-494-0338
Fax: 512-494-0340
E-mail: info@fepi.com
www.fepi.com

R Geyer, Executive Producer

Consumers Health videos; available individually, or in large volume (private branded) for health providers to give to patients, professionals, staff. Postpartum Emotions, Parenting Preschoolers, Facing Death (5-tape series) and teen grief English and Spanish.

ISSN 1-930772-00-9

3550 Fanlight Productions
4196 Washington Street
Boston, MA 02131-1731
617-469-4999
800-937-4113
Fax: 617-469-3379
E-mail: info@fanlight.com
www.fanlight.com

Distributor of innovative film and video works on the social issues of our time, with a special focus on healthcare, mental health, profesional ethics, aging and gerontology, disabilites, the workplace, and gender and family issues.

3551 Franklin Electronic Publishers
Frankling Electronic Publishers
1 Franklin Plaza
Burlington, NJ 08016-4907
609-386-2500
800-266-5626
Fax: 609-387-2666
www.franklin.com

Barry J Lipsky, CEO

Publishes materials for healthcare.

3552 Free Spirit Publishing
217 Fifth Avenue North
Suite 200
Minneapolis, MN 55401-1299
612-338-2068
866-703-7322
Fax: 612-337-5050
www.freespirit.com

Judy Galbraith, Owner

Publisher of learning tools that support young people's social and emotional health. Known for unique understanding of what young adults want and need to know to navigate life successfully.

3553 Greenwood Publishing Group
88 Post Road West
Westport, CT 06880-4208
203-226-3571
Fax: 203-222-1502
E-mail: webmaster@greenwood.com
www.greenwood.com

Wayne Smith, President

Publisher of reference titles, academic and general interest books, texts, books for librarians and other profesionals, and electronic resources.

3554 Grey House Publishing
4919 Route 22
PO Box 56
Amenia, NY 12501
518-789-8700
800-562-2139
Fax: 845-373-6360

E-mail: books@greyhouse.com
www.greyhouse.com

Leslie Mackenzie, Publisher
Richard Gottlieb, Editor

Publishes over 100 titles including reference directories in the areas of business, education, health, statistics and demographics, as well as educational encyclopedias and business handbooks. All titles offer detailed information in well-organized formats. Many titles available online.

3555 Guilford Publications

72 Spring Street
New York, NY 10012-4068
212-431-9800
800-365-7006
Fax: 212-966-6708
E-mail: info@guilford.com

Bob Matloff, President

Publisher of books, periodicals, software and audiovisual programs in mental health, education, and the social sciences.

Year Founded: 1973

3556 Gurze Books

PO Box 2238
Carisbad, CA 92018-2238
760-434-7533
800-756-7533
Fax: 760-434-5476
E-mail: mylo@gurze.net
www.gurze.com

Publishing company that specializes in resources and education on eating disorders. Offers high quality materials on understanding and overcoming eating disorders of all kinds.

3557 Harper Collins Publishers

10 East 53rd Street
New York, NY 10022-5299
212-207-7000
Fax: 212-207-6964
www.harpercollins.com

Brian Murray, CEO

A subsidiary of News Corporation, Harper Collins produces literary and commercial fiction, business books, children's books, cookbooks, mystery, romance, reference, religious, healthcare and spiritual books.

3558 Harvard University Press

79 Garden Street
Cambridge, MA 02138-1400
617-495-1000
800-405-1619
Fax: 617-495-5898
E-mail: contact_hup@harvard.edu
www.hup.harvard.edu

William Sisler, President

Publishes material on varied topics including healthcare.

3559 Haworth Press

10 Alice Street
Binghamton, NY 13904-1503
607-722-5857
800-429-6784
Fax: 800-895-0582
E-mail: getinfo@haworthpress.com
www.haworthpress.com

Publishers of library science, social work and human services, gerontology and aging, marketing, gay/lesbian/bisexual studies, and additional subject fields.

3560 Hazelden

CO3 PO Box 11
Center City, MN 55012-11
651-213-4200
800-257-7810
Fax: 651-213-4590
E-mail: info@hazelden.org
www.hazelden.org

A nonprofit organization that helps people transform their lives by providing the highest quality treatment and continuing care services, education, research, and publishing products available today.

3561 Health Communications

3201 SW 15th Street
Deerfield Beach, FL 33442-8157
954-360-0909
800-441-5569
Fax: 954-360-0034
www.hcibooks.com

Peter Vegso, CEO

Original publisher of informational pamphlets for the recovery community; publishes inspriation, soul/spirituality, relationships, recovery/healing, women's issues and self-help material.

3562 High Tide Press

Ste 2N
2081 Calistoga Dr
New Lenox, IL 60451-4833
815-206-2054
800-469-9461

Art Dykstra, Executive Director
Steve Baker, Director

Provides high quality books, training materials and seminars to people working in the field of human services. Seek to provide the best resources in developmental, mental and learning disabilities, as well as psychology, leadership and management.

3563 Hogrefe & Huber Publishers

218 Main Street
Suite 485
Kirkland, WA 98033-6108
866-823-4726
Fax: 617-354-6875
E-mail: info@hhpub.com
www.hhpub.com

Publisher of journals and books of all different variety titles including healthcare.

3564 Hope Press
110 Mill Run
Monrovia, CA 91016-1658
626-303-0644
800-321-4039
Fax: 626-358-3520
E-mail: dcomings@mail.earthlink.net
www.hopepress.com

Specializes in the publication of books on Tourette Syndrome, Attention Deficit Hyperactivity Disorder (ADHD, ADD), Conduct Disorder, Oppositional Defiant Disorder and other psychological, psychiatric and behavioral problems.

3565 Hyperion Books
77 West 66th Street
11th Floor
New York, NY 10023-6201

Fax: 212-456-1980
www.hyperionbooks.com

Publishes general-interest fiction and nonfiction books for adults including healthcare titles. Includes the Miramax, ESPN Books, ABC Daytime Press, Hyperion East and Hyperion Audiobooks.

3566 Impact Publishers
PO Box 6016
Atascadero, CA 93423-6016

E-mail: info@impactpublishers.com
www.impactpublishers.com

Produces a select list of psychology and self improvement books and audio-tapes for adults, children, families, organizations, and communities. Written by highly respected psychologists and other human service professionals.

3567 Jason Aronson Publishers
4501 Forbes Blvd
Suite 200
Lanham, MD 20706-4346
301-459-3366
800-462-6420
Fax: 301-429-5748
www.aronson.com

Publisher of highly regarded books in psychotherapy. Dedicated to publishing professional, scholarly works by respected and gifted authors.

3568 Jerome M Sattler Publisher
PO Box 3557
La Mesa, CA 91944-1060
619-460-3667
Fax: 619-460-2489
E-mail: sattlerpublisher@sbcglobal.net
www.sattlerpublisher.com

Publishes books that represent the cutting edge of clinical assessment of children and families. Designed for students in training as well as for practitioners ans clinicians.

3569 Jessica Kingsley Publishers
116 Pentonville Road
London United Kingdom
N1 9JB,

E-mail: post@jkp.com
www.jkp.com

Wholly independent company, committed to publishing books for professional and general readers in a range of subjects including the autism spectrum, social work, and the arts therapies. Recent titles include mental health, counseling, palliative care, and practical theology.

3570 John Wiley & Sons
111 River Street
Hoboken, NJ 07030-5790
201-748-6000
Fax: 201-748-6088
E-mail: custserv@wiley.com
www.wiley.com

William J Pesce, CEO

A global publisher of print and electronic products, specializing in scientific, technical, and medical books and journals professional and consumer books and subscription services; also textbooks and other educational materials for undergraduate and graduate students as well as lifelong learners.

3571 Johns Hopkins University Press
2715 North Charles Street
Baltimore, MD 21218-4319
410-516-6900
Fax: 410-516-6998
E-mail: webmaster@jhupress.jhu.edu

William Brody, President

Publishes 58 scholarly periodicals and more than 200 new books each year. A leading online provider of scholarly journals, bringing more than 250 periodicals to the desktops of 9 million students, scholars, and others worldwide.

3572 Jossey-Bass
111 River Street
Hoboken, NJ 07030-5773
201-748-6000
Fax: 201-748-6088
E-mail: custserv@wiley.com
www.wiley.com

Jossey-Bass publishes books, periodicals, and other media to inform and inspire those interested in developing themselves, their organizations and their communities. The publications feature the work of some of the world's best-known authors in leadership, business, education, religion and spirituality, parenting, nonprofit, public health and health administration, conflict resolution and relationships.

3573 Lawrence Erlbaum Associates
10 Industrial Avenue
Mahwah, NJ 07430-2253
201-258-2200
800-926-6579
Fax: 201-236-0072
www.erlbaum.com

An international academic publisher and distributor of a full range of books, journals, and software, as well as electronic media. Dedicated to providing quality scholarship and knowledge that will contribute to each representative field, including healthcare, and offer promising new direction for teachers, researchers, and practitioners.

3574 Lexington Books
4501 Forbes Blvd
Suite 200
Lanham, MD 20706-4346
301-459-3366
800-462-6420
Fax: 301-429-5748
www.lexingtonbooks.com

John Sisk, Publisher

Publisher of specialized new work by established and emerging scholars, including material for the healthcare community.

3575 Lippincott Williams & Wilkins
530 Walnut Street
Philadelphia, PA 19106-3691
215-521-8300
Fax: 215-521-8902
www.lww.com

Gordon Macomber, CEO

Publishes specialized publications and software for physicians, nurses, students and specialized clinicians. Products include drug guides, medical journals, nursing journals, medical textbooks and medical pda software.

3576 Love Publishing
9101 East Kenyon Avenue
Suite 2200
Denver, CO 80237-1854
303-221-7333
Fax: 303-221-7444
E-mail: lpc@lovepublishing.com
www.lovepublishing.com

Stan Love, Owner

Publishes books that offer therapy options to children of all ages, adults, and adolescents.

3577 Mason Crest Publishers
370 Reed Road
Suite 302
Broomall, PA 19008-4017

866-627-2665
Fax: 610-543-3878
www.masoncrest.com

Publishes core-related materials for grades K-12. Current catalog includes many titles for health care and mental health curriculums.

3578 Nelson Thornes
Delta Place
27 Berth Road
Cheltenham Glos GL53 7TH, UK
124-226-7100
www.nelsonthornes.com

Leading educational publisher of books, CD-Rom and electronic teaching and learning resources, formed through the merger of two UK publishing businesses — Thomas Nelson and Stanley Thornes.

3579 New Harbinger Publications
5674 Shattuck Avenue
Oakland, CA 94609-1662
510-652-0215
800-748-6273
Fax: 510-652-5472
www.newharbinger.com

Matthew McKay, Owner
Patrick Fanning, Co-Founder

Publisher of self-help books that teach the reader skills they could use to significantly improve the quality of their lives.

Year Founded: 1973

3580 New World Library
14 Pamaron Way
Nopvato, CA 94949-6215
415-884-2199
800-972-6657
Fax: 415-884-2199
www.newworldlibrary.com

Marc Allen, CEO

Publishes books and audios that inspire and challenge us to improve the quality of our lives and our world.

3581 New York University Press
838 Broadway
3rd Floor
New York, NY 10003-4812
212-998-2575
800-996-6987
Fax: 212-995-3833
E-mail: information@nyupress.org
www.nyupress.nyu.edu

Steve Maikowski, Director
Eric Zinner, Editor-In-Chief

Publishes approximately 100 new books each year, and enjoys a backlist of over 1500 titles that includes health care and academic materials.

3582 Omnigraphics
615 Griswold
PO Box 624
Detroit, MI 48231-624

800-234-1340
Fax: 800-875-1340
E-mail: info@omnigraphics.com
www.omnigraphics.com

Fred Ruffner, Co-Founder
Peter Ruffner, Co-Founder

Quality reference resources for libraries and schools.

Year Founded: 1985

3583 Oxford University Press

2001 Evans Road
Cary, NC 27513-2010
919-677-0977
800-445-9714
Fax: 919-677-2673
E-mail: custserv.us@oup.com

Publishes works that further Oxford University's objective of excellence in research, scholarship, and education, including titles in the health care and mental health field.

3584 Penguin Group

345 Hudson Street
New York, NY 10014-4592
212-366-2000
Fax: 212-366-2933

David Shanks, CEO

Publishes under a wide range of prominent imprints and trademarks, among them Berkeley Books, Dutton, Grosset & Dunlap, New American Library, Penguin, Philomel, G.P. Putnam's Sons, Riverhead Books, Viking and Frederick Warne. Includes a variety of titles in health care and mental health subjects.

3585 Perseus Books Group

1094 Flex Drive
Jackson, TN 38301-5070
731-423-1973
800-371-1669
Fax: 731-422-4044
E-mail: perseus.orders@perseusbooks.com

Chris Wagner, VP

Titles include science, public issues, military history, modern maternity, health care and mental health.

3586 Princeton University Press

41 William Street
Princeton, NJ 08540-5223
609-258-4900
Fax: 609-258-6305

Peter Dougherty, Manager

Independent publisher with close connection to Princeton Unviersity. Fundamental mission is to disseminate through books, journals, and electronic media, with both academia and society at large on a variety of social issues, including health care and mental health.

3587 Pro-Ed Publications

8700 Shoal Creek Blvd
Austin, TX 78757-6897
512-451-3246
800-897-3202
Fax: 512-451-8542
E-mail: feedback@proedinc.com

Donald D Hammill, Owner

Leading publisher of nationally standardized tests, resource and reference texts, curricular and therapy materials, and professional journals covering: speech, language and hearing; psychology and counseling; special education including developmental disabilities, rehabilitation, and gifted education; early childhood intervention; and occupational and physical therapy.

3588 Professional Resource Press

Professional Resource Press
PO Box 15560
Sarasota, FL 34277-1560
941-343-9601
800-443-3364
Fax: 941-343-9201
E-mail: orders@prpress.com
www.prpress.com

Debra Fink, Managing Editor

Publisher of books, continuing education programs and other applied resources for mental health professionals, including psychologists, psychiatrists, clinical social workers, counselors, OTs, and recreational therapists.

3589 Rapid Psychler Press

3560 Pine Grove Avenue
Suite 374
Port Huron, MI 48060-1994

888-779-2453
Fax: 888-779-2457
E-mail: rapid@psychler.com
www.psychler.com

Produces textbooks and presentation graphics for use in mental health education (mainly psychiatry). Products are thoroughly researched and clinically oriented. Designed by students, instructors and clinicians.

3590 Research Press Publishers

Department 26W
Po Box 9177
Champaign, IL 61826-9177
217-352-3273
800-519-2707
Fax: 217-352-1221
E-mail: rp@researchpress.com
www.researchpress.com

Publishes books and videos in school counseling, special education, psychology, counseling and therapy, parenting, death and dying, and developmental disabilities.

3591 Riverside Publishing
425 Spring Lake Drive
Itasca, IL 60143-2076
630-467-7000
800-323-9540
Fax: 630-467-7192
www.riverpub.com

Dedicated to providing society with the finest professional testing products and services available. Division of Houghton Mifflin Company.

3592 Sage Publications
2455 Teller Road
Thousand Oaks, CA 91320-2234
805-499-0721
800-818-7243
Fax: 805-499-0871
E-mail: info@sagepub.com
www.sagepub.com

Blaise R Simqu, CEO

An independent international publisher of journals, books, and electronic media, known for commitment to quality and innovation in scholarly, educational and professional markets.

3593 Sidran Institute
200 East Joppa Road
Suite 207
Towson, MD 21286-3107
410-825-8888
Fax: 410-337-0747
E-mail: sidran@sidran.org
www.sidran.org

Esther Giller, President

Leader in traumatic stress education and advocacy. Devoted to helping people who have experienced traumatic life events by publishing books and educational materials on traumatic stress and dissociative conditions.

3594 Simon & Schuster
100 Front Street
Riverside, NJ 08075-1181
856-461-6500
Fax: 856-824-2402
www.simonandschuster.com

David Schaeffer, VP

Leader in the field of general interest publishing, providing consumers worldwide with a diverse range of quality books and multimedia products across a wide variety of genres and formats, including health care and mental health.

3595 Springer Science and Business Media
233 Spring Street
New York, NY 10013-1578
212-460-1500
Fax: 212-460-1575
E-mail: service-ny@springer.com

William Curtis, President
Martin Mos, COO

Develops, manages and disseminates knowledge through books, journals and the internet in a variety of subjects, including health care and mental health.

3596 St. Martin's Press
175 5th Avenue
New York, NY 10010
212-674-5151
Fax: 212-674-3179

John Sargent, CEO

Publishes 700 titles a year, including those titles in a variety of health care and mental health subjects.

3597 Taylor & Francis Group
325 Chestnut Street
Suite 800
Philadelphia, PA 19106-2608
215-625-8900
800-354-1420
Fax: 215-625-2940
E-mail: beverley.acreman@tandf.co.uk
www.taylorandfrancis.com

Kevin Bradley, CEO

Publishes more than 1000 journals and 1800 new books each year with a books backlist in excess of 20,000 specialty titles. Providers of quality information and knowledge that enable our customers to perform their jobs efficiently, continue their education, and help contribute to the advancement of their chosen markets.

3598 Therapeutic Resources
PO Box 16814
Cleveland, OH 44116-814

888-331-7114
Fax: 440-331-7118
E-mail: contact@therapeuticresources.com
www.therapeuticresources.com

Publishers of a variety of titles including ADD/ADHD, Alzheimer/Dimentia, Anger Management, Autism/PDD, Bereavement/Adjustment Disorders, Substance Abuse and more.

3599 Time Warner Bookmark
1271 Avenue of the Americas
New York, NY 10020-1300

800-759-0190
Fax: 800-331-1664

Formerly known as Time Warner Trade Publishing, consists of Warner Books and its various imprints: the Mysterious Press, Warner Vision, Warner Business Books, Aspect, Warner Faith, and Little, Brown and Company. Includes a variety of titles in health care and mental health.

3600 Underwood Books
PO Box 1919
Nevada City, CA 95959-1919

800-788-3123
E-mail: contact@underwoodbooks.com
www.underwoodbooks.com

A publisher specializing in fantasy art, science fiction, and self-help/health related titles.

3601 University of California Press
2120 Berkeley Way
Berkeley, CA 94704-5804
510-642-4247
Fax: 510-643-7127
E-mail: askucp@ucpress.edu
www.ucpress.edu

Pamela Wimberly, Plant Manager

Distinguished university press that enriches lives around the world by advancing scholarships in the humanities, social sciences, and natural sciences.

3602 University of Chicago Press
1427 East 60th Street
Chicago, IL 60637-2902
773-834-0555
E-mail: marketing@press.uchicago.edu

Holds an obligation to disseminate scholarship of the highest standard and to publish serious works that promote education, foster public understanding, and enrich cultural life.

3603 University of Minnesota Press
111 Third Avenue South
Suite 290
Minneapolis, MN 55401-2520
612-627-1970
Fax: 612-627-1980
E-mail: ump@umn.edu
www.upress.umn.edu

Doug Armato, Manager

Publisher of groundbreaking work in social and cultural thought, critical theory, race and ethnic studies, urbanism, feminist criticism, and media studies.

3604 WW Norton
500 Fifth Avenue
New York, NY 10110-54
212-354-2907
Fax: 212-869-0856

Drake McFeely, CEO

Publishing house owned by its employees, and publishes books in fiction, nonfiction, poetry, college, cookbooks, art, and professional subjects, including health care and mental health.

3605 Woodbine House
6510 Bells Mill Road
Bethesda, MD 20817-1636
301-897-3570
800-843-7323

Fax: 301-897-5838
www.woodbinehouse.com

Irv Shapell, Owner

Publishes special needs books for parents, children, teachers and professionals.

Facilities

By State

Alabama

3606 Bryce Hospital
200 University Boulevard
Tuscaloosa, AL 35401-1294
205-759-0799
Fax: 205-759-0890

Charles Cutts, CEO

3607 Greil Memorial Psychiatric Hospital
2140 Upper Wetumpka Road
Montgomery, AL 36107-1342
334-262-0363
Fax: 334-834-4562

Allen Stewart, Executive Director

Greil Hospitalis a 50-bed acute care psychiatric hospital located in Montgomery, the capital city. Fully accredited by the Joint Commission on Accreditation of Healthcare Organizations and certified by Medicare, Greil services as a regional facility for 11 counties in central Alabama. The hospital's facilities are among the newest and most recently renovated in the Alabama Mental Health system.

3608 Mary Starke Harper Geriatric Psychiatry Center
201 University Boulevard
Tuscaloosa, AL 35401
205-759-0900
Fax: 205-759-0931

Bob White, Manager

3609 North Alabama Regional Hospital
Highway 31 S
Decatur, AL 35609
256-560-2200
Fax: 256-560-2203

Randy Phillips, Manager

3610 Searcy Hospital
Coy Smith Highway
PO Box 1001
Mount Vernon, AL 36560-1001
251-662-6700

John T Bartlett, Contact

3611 Taylor Hardin Secure Medical Facility
1301 Jack Warner Parkway NE
Tuscaloosa, AL 35404-1098
205-556-7060
Fax: 205-556-1198
www.mh.alabama.gov

James Redick, Executive Director

Alaska

3612 Alaska Psychiatric Institute
2800 Providence Drive
Anchorage, AK 99508-4677
907-269-7100
Fax: 907-269-7128

Ronald Adler, CEO
R Duane Hopson MD, Medical Director

In partnership with individuals, their families and the community, natural network and providers, API's Alaska Recovery Center provides therapeutic services which assist individuals to achieve a personal level of satisfaction and success in their recovery.

Arizona

3613 Arizona State Hospital
2500 East Van Buren
Phoenix, AZ 85008-6079
602-244-1331
Fax: 602-220-6355
www.azdhs.gov/azsh/index.htm

John C Cooper, CEO
M Megan Mitscher LMSW, Admissions & Tribal Liaison

The Arizona State Hospital provides specialized psychiatric services to support people in achieving mental health recovery in a safe and respectful environment.

Year Founded: 1887

3614 Southwest Behavorial Health Services
3450 North 3rd Street
Phoenix, AZ 85012-2331
602-257-9339
Fax: 602-265-8377
E-mail: ifno@sbhservices.org
www.sbhservices.org

Bob Bohanske, Executive Director

Inspire people to feel better and reach their potential.

Arkansas

3615 Arkansas State Hospital
305 South Palm Street
Little Rock, AR 72205
501-686-9400
Fax: 501-686-9464
E-mail: barbra.brooks@arkansas.gov
www.arkansas.gov/dhs/dmhs/ar_state_hospital.htm

Charles Smith, Administrator
Albert Kittrell, MD, Medical Director

The Arkansas State Hospital is a psychiatric inpatient treatment facility for those with mental or emotional disorders which includes 90 beds for acute psychiatric admission; a 60-bed forensic treatment services program which offers assistance to circuit courts throughout the state; a 16-bed adolescent treatment program for youth 13-18; and a program for juvenile sex offenders.

3616 Center for Outcomes and Evidence
Agency for Healthcare Research and Quality
John M Eisenberg Building
540 Gaither Road
Rockville, MD 20850
301-427-1600
Fax: 301-427-1520
www.ahrq.gov

Formerly the Center for Outcomes and Effectiveness Research. Conducts and supports research and assessment of health care practices, technologies, processes, and systems.

3617 UAMS Psychiatric Research Institute
5800 W 10th Street
Suite 605
Little Rock, AR 72204-1773
501-660-7559
Fax: 501-660-7542
E-mail: kramerteresal@uams.edu
www.uams.edu

Combining research, education and clinical services into one facility, PRI offers inpatiend and outpatient services, with 40 psychiatric beds, therapy options, and specialized treatment for specific disorders, including: addictive eating, anxiety, deppressive and post-traumatic stress disorders. Research focuses on evidence-based care takes into consideration the education of future medical personnel while relying on research scientists to provide innovative forms of treatment. PRI includes the Center for Addiction Research as well as a methadone clinic.

California

3618 ANKA Behavioral Health
1875 Willow Pass Road
Suite 300
Concord, CA 94520-2527
925-825-4700
Fax: 925-825-2610
www.ankabhs.org

Michael Jacquemet-Barrington, President/CEO
Chris Withrow, Deputy CEO/Exec VP
Maryann Silva, Corporate Compliance Officer

Offers comprehensive services and programs designed to promote a client's overall wellness and to attain an enhanced quality of life.

3619 Atascadero State Hospital
10333 El Camino Real
Atascadero, CA 93422-5808
805-468-2000
www.dmh.cahwnet.gov/Services_and_Programs

Jon DeMorales, Executive Director

A maximum security forensic hosptial, providing inpatient forensic services for adult males who are court committed throughout the State of California. The staff members of Atascadero State Hospital (ASH) proudly serve the people of the State of California by providing protection for the community, expert evaluations for the courts, and state-of-the-science psychiatric recovery services for individuals referred to us from across the state.

3620 Augustus F Hawkins Community Mental Health Center
Los Angeles County Department of Mental Health
1720 E 120th Street
Los Angeles, CA 90059-3052
310-668-4790

James C Allen, Deputy Director

Provides community and client crisis intervention, case management, community promotion and outpatient services. Clinical facilities for professional field training.

3621 Campobello Chemical Dependency Treatment Services
3250 Guerneville Road
Santa Rosa, CA 95401-4030
707-579-4066
800-806-1833
Fax: 707-579-1603
www.campobello.org

Jim Cody, Executive Director
Kathy Leigh Willis, Executive Director

Innovative chemical dependency treatment center with the belief in the 12 step self-help programs of Alcoholics Anonymous, Narcotics Anonymous and Al-Anon for friends and family.

3622 Changing Echoes
7632 Pool Station Road
Angels Camp, CA 95222-9620
209-785-3666
800-633-7066
Fax: 209-785-5238
www.changingechoes.com

J R Maughan, Executive Director

Established as a social model chemical dependency facility with the intent to render high-quality treatment for affordable prices to men and women who suffer from the disease of addiction.

Year Founded: 1989

3623 Combined Addicts and Professionals Services CAPS/Residential Unit
398 South 12th Street
San Jose, CA 95112-2228
408-294-5425

Timmie Kase, Information Services

Providing individualized substance abuse treatment and recovery services. Provides a continuum of care to help clients' transition from one level of intensity to another.

3624 Department of Mental Health Vacaville Psychiatric Program
PO Box 2297
Vacaville, CA 95696-8297
707-449-6597
Fax: 707-453-7047
www.dmh.ca.gov/services_and_programs/State_Hospitals

Victor Brewer, Executive Director

The mission of Vacaville Psychiatric Program is to provide quality mental health evaluation and treatment to inmate-patients. This is accomplished in a safe and therapeutic environment, and as part of a continuum of care.

3625 Exodus Recovery Center

3828 Delmas Terrace
Tower 6
Culver City, CA 90232-2713
310-253-9494
800-829-3923
E-mail: lezlie@exodusrecovery.com
www.exodusrecoveryinc.com

Connie Dinh, Manager

Mission is that we believe that chemically dependent men and women can achieve freedom from the bondage of drugs and alcohol. Teaching patients and their families that the devastation of addiction can be overcome. Produce personal action plans that can produce a lifetime of recovery.

3626 Family Service Agency

123 W Gutierrez Street
Santa Barbara, CA 93101-3424
805-965-1001
E-mail: hr@fsacares.org
www.fsacares.org

William EG Batty III, Executive Director
Jeff Hurley, Program Director

A non-profit human service agency whose programs help people help themselves. FSA services prevent family breakdown, intervene effectively where problems are known to exist and help individuals and families build on existing strengt

3627 Fremont Hospital
Psychiatric Solutions

39001 Sundale Drive
Fremont, CA 94538-2005
510-796-1100
www.fremonthospital.com

Joey A Jacobs, President/CEO/Chairman

A private, modern 96-bed behavioral healthcare facility that provides services to adolescents (ages 12-17) and adults.

3628 Life Steps Pasos de Vida

1431 Pomeroy Road
Arroyo Grande, CA 93420-5943
805-481-2505
800-530-5433
www.lifestepsfoundation.org

Virginia Franco, Founder/CEO
Allen C Haile, President

Develops innovative programs that target underserved populations. Goal is to help participants develop healthy lifestyles free of alcohol and drugs.

3629 Lincoln Child Center

4368 Lincoln Avenue
Oakland, CA 94602-2529
510-531-3111
Fax: 510-530-8083
E-mail: info@lincolncc.org
www.lincolncc.org

Christina Stoner-Mertz, CEO
Toni Taylor, Chief Program Officer

Enables vulnerable and emotionally troubled children and their families to lead independent and fulfilling live

3630 Mental Health Association of Orange County

822 Town & Country Road
Orange, CA 92868
714-547-7559
Fax: 717-543-4431
E-mail: mhainfo@mhaoc.org
www.mhaoc.org

Dedicated to improving the quality of life of Orange County residents impacted by mental illness through direct service, advocacy, education and information dissemination.

3631 Merit Behavioral Care of California
California Department of Managed Health Care

300 Continental Blvd.
Suite 240
El Segundo, CA 90245-5043
310-726-7090
800-424-1565
Fax: 650-742-0988
E-mail: FAVivaldo@magellanhealth.com
www.dmhc.ca.gov/mcp/details.asp?id=137

Lucinda Ehnes, Director
G Lewis Chartrand Jr, Chief Deputy Director

The people of the Department of Managed Health Care work toward an affordable, accountable and robust managed care delivery system that promotes healthier Californians. Through leadership and partnership, the Department shares responsibility with everyone in managed care to ensure aggressive prevention and high quality health care, as well as cost-effective regulatory oversight.

3632 Metropolitan State Hospital

11401 Bloomfield Avenue
Norwalk, CA 90650-2015
562-863-7011
Fax: 562-929-3131
TDD: 562-863-1743
www.dmh.cahwnet.gov/services_and_programs

Sharon Smith Nevins, Executive Director

The mission of Metropolitan State Hospital is to work in partnership with individuals to assist in their recovery by using rehabilitation services as their tool, thus preparing clients for community living.

3633 Mills-Peninsula Hospital: Behavioral Health

1783 El Camino Real
Burlingame, CA 94010-3205

650-696-5900

Community hospital mental health and chemical dependency care. Our team is uniquely qualified to evaluate, diagnose and treat a wide range of behavioral conditions.

3634 Napa State Hospital

2100 Napa-Vallejo Highway
Napa, CA 94558-6293
707-253-5000
Fax: 707-253-5379
TDD: 707-253-5768
E-mail: nshcontact@dmhnsh.state.ca.us
www.dmh.cahwnet.gov/services_and_programs

Jennifer Marshall CTRS, RTC, Chief, Rehabilitation Therapy

Napa State Hospital provides treatment and support to adults with serious mental illness, and assists each individual in achieving his/her highest potential for independence and quality of life, leading to recovery and integrating safely and successfully into society.

3635 New Life Recovery Centers

782 Park Avenue
Suite 1
San Jose, CA 95126-4800
408-297-1182
866-894-6572
Fax: 408-297-7450
www.newliferecoverycenters.com

Kevin Richardson, President
Gary Ruble, Founder

Strives to provide our clients with the very best services available. We value our employees as our greatest asset, while collectively and continuously working to adopt and implement the latest and most effective medical, clinical, and social model treatment modalities.

3636 Northridge Hospital Medical Center

18300 Roscoe Boulevard
Northridge, CA 91325-4167
818-885-8500
Fax: 818-885-5439
www.northridgehospital.org

Mike Wall, CEO

Northridge Hospital Medical Center offers a comprehensive Behavioral Health program for both adults and adolescents.

3637 PacifiCare Behavioral Health

PO Box 31053
Laguna Hills, CA 92654-1053

800-999-9585
www.pbhi.com

Richard J Kelliher PsyD, Clinical Director

Provides behavioral health services to children, adolescents, adults, and seniors.

3638 Patton State Hospital
California Department of Mental Health

3102 E Highland Avenue
Patton, CA 92369
909-425-7000
Fax: 909-425-7520
TDD: 909-862-5730
E-mail: cbarrett@dmhpsh.state.ca.us
www.dmh.ca.gov/Statehospitals/Patton/default.asp

Octavio C Luna, Executive Director

Patton State Hospital's mission is to empower forensic and civilly committed individuals to recover from mental illness utilizing Recovery principles and evidenced based practices within a safe, structured, and secure environment.

3639 Phoenix Programs Inc

1401 West 4th Street
Antioch, CA 94509-1024
925-778-3750
Fax: 925-778-7412
www.ankabhi.org

Kassie L Perkins, Manager
Chris Withrow, Executive VP/DCEO

Offers an array of services and programs designed to promote overall wellness while making it possible for all to obtain a higher quality of life.

3640 Presbyterian Intercommunity Hospital Mental Health Center

12401 Washington Boulevard
Whittier, CA 90602-1006
562-698-0811
www.whittierpres.com

James West, CEO

Offers an inpatient program for those with a variety of mental disorders.

3641 South Coast Medical Center

Ste A
12 Mason
Irvine, CA 92618-2733
714-380-1552
E-mail: info@southcoastmedcenter.com

3642 Twin Town Treatment Centers

4388 E Katella Avenue
Los Alamitos, CA 90720-3565
562-594-8844
Fax: 562-596-0058
www.twintowntreatmentcenters.com

David Lisonbee, CEO

Mission is to introduce new solutions for people who find that chemically induced coping no longer works.

3643 Walden House Transitional Treatment Center

520 Townsend Street
San Francisco, CA 94103-6241

415-554-1100
Fax: 415-554-1122
TDD: 415-431-1067
www.waldenhouse.org

Rod Lippey, CEO
Vitka Eisen, COO

A national leader in developing strategies to help addicts recover and maintain their lives.

Colorado

3644 Centennial Mental Health Center

211 W Main Street
Sterling, CO 80751-3168
970-522-4392
E-mail: webmaster@centennialmhc.org
www.centennialmhc.org

Daniel D Hammond, Manager

A non-profit organization dedicated to providing the highest quality comprehensive mental health services to the rural communities of northeastern Colorado.

3645 Colorado Mental Health Institute at Fort Logan

3520 West Oxford Avenue
Denver, CO 80236-3108
303-866-7066
Fax: 303-866-7048
www.colorado.gov

Keith Lagrenade, CEO

The mission of the Colorado Mental Health Institute at Fort Logan is to provide the highest quality mental health services to persons of all ages with complex, serious and persistent mental illness within the resources available.

3646 Colorado Mental Health Institute at Pueblo

1600 West 24th Street
Pueblo, CO 81003-1411
719-546-4000
Fax: 719-546-4484
www.cdhs.state.co.us

John De Quardo, Administrator

Provides quality mental health services focused on sustaining hope and promoting recovery.

3647 Emily Griffith Center

PO Box 95
Larkspur, CO 80118-95
303-681-2400
Fax: 303-681-2401
www.emilygriffith.com

Howard Shiffman, CEO
Beth Miller, Deputy Director/COO
John Smrcka, Program Director

Provides troubled children the environment and opportunities to become healthy, participating and productive members of society.

Connecticut

3648 Cedarcrest Hospital

525 Russell Road
Newington, CT 06111-1595
860-666-4613
Fax: 860-666-7642
E-mail: thomas.kirk@po.state.ct.us
www.stateofct.com

Brenda Thorington, CEO
Richard Stillson Ph.D, Director of Psychology
Thomas A Kirk Jr, Commissioner

The mission of Cedarcrest Hospital is to improve the quality of life of the people of Connecticut by providing an integrated network of comprehensive, effective and efficient mental health and addiction services that foster self-sufficiency, dignity and respect.

3649 Connecticut Valley Hospital General Psychiatric Division

PO Box 351
Middletown, CT 06457-7023
860-262-5529

Thomas A Kirk, Commissioner
Pat Rehem, Deputy Commissioner
Garrell S Mullaney, CEO

The mission of Connecticut Valley Hospital is to improve the quality of life of the people of Connecticut by providing an integrated network of comprehensive, effective and efficient mental health services that foster self-sufficiency, dignity and respect.

3650 Daytop Residential Services Division

425 Grant Street
Bridgeport, CT 06610-3222
203-337-9943
Fax: 203-337-9986
www.aptfoundation.org/daytop.htm

Nancy Moak, Intake Services

Long-term substance abuse treatment facility based on the Therapeutic Community model. Combines current research and treatment methods with traditional therapeutic community concepts.

3651 Greater Bridgeport Community Mental Health Center

1635 Central Avenue
PO Box 5117
Bridgeport, CT 06610-902
203-551-7400
Fax: 203-551-7446

James M LeHene MPH, Contact

3652 High Watch Farm

62 Carter Road
Kent, CT 06757
860-927-3772
Fax: 860-927-1840

E-mail: admissions@highwatchfarm.com
www.highwatchfarm.com

Janina J Kean, President/CEO

A spiritually nurturing environment dedicated to providing treatment to alcohol and substance dependent individuals based on the 12-step principles of Alcoholics Anonymous.

3653 Jewish Family Service
733 Summer Street
Suite 602
Stamford, CT 06901-1035
203-921-4161

Michelle T Presser, Executive Director
Isrella Knopf, LMSW, Director Senior Services
Eve Moskowitz LCSW, Clinical Services Director

Offers a wide range of innovative programs designed to address contemporary problems and issues through counseling and therapy, crisis intervention, Jewish Family Life Education, Depression, Aging and senior mental health, Obsessions and compulsions.

Year Founded: 1978

3654 Klingberg Family Centers
370 Linwood Street
New Britain, CT 06052-1998
860-826-1739
Fax: 860-826-1739
E-mail: markj@klingberg.org
www.klingberg.org

Rosemarie Burton, President

To uphold, preserve and restore families in a therapeutic environment, valuing the absolute worth of every child, while adhering to the highest ethical principles in accordance with our Judaeo-Christian heritage.

3655 McCall Foundation
58 High Street
PO Box 806
Torrington, CT 06790-806
860-496-2107
E-mail: mccallfoundation@snet.net
www.northwestunitedway.org/mccall.htm

Provides outpatient, partial hospital, intensive outpatient, residential, parenting and prevention programs for substance abusers and/or their family members; and helps to reduce area substance abuse in the local community. Funding is provided by the United Way.

3656 Mountainside Treatment Center
PO Box 717
Canaan, CT 06018-717
860-824-1397
800-762-5433
Fax: 860-824-5691
E-mail: admissions@mountainside.org
www.mountainside.org

Program is based on strategies and principles that promote healing and enhance the quality of life. Through the utilization of Motivational Interviewing, Directional Therapy,

Gender-Specific Groups, the 12-Step Principles and Adventure Based Initiatives, individuals qwill encounter, confront and experience the challenges of recovery.

3657 Silver Hill Hospital
208 Valley Road
New Canaan, CT 06840-3899
203-966-1380
800-899-4455
E-mail: info@silverhillhospital.org
www.silverhillhospital.org

Siguard Ackerman, President
Elizabeth Moore, Chief Operating Officer

A nationally recognized, independent, not-for-profit psychiatric hospital that is focused exclusively on providing patients the best possible treatment of psychiatric illnesses and substance use disorders, in the best possible environment.

Year Founded: 1931

Delaware

3658 Delaware Psychiatric Center
1901 N Dupont Highway
New Castle, DE 19720-1199
302-577-4000

Karen Kovacic RN, MSN, CAP, Director, DSAMH

Providing integrated services to adults suffering from severe and persistent mental illness.

District of Columbia

3659 St. Elizabeth's Hospital
2700 Martin Luther King Jr Avenue SE
Washington, DC 20032-2698
202-562-4000

Dr Patrick J Canavan Psy.D., Contact

Florida

3660 Archways-A Bridge To A Brighter Future
919 NE 13th Street
Fort Lauderdale, FL 33304-2009
954-763-2030
Fax: 954-763-9847
E-mail: intake@archways.org
www.archways.org

Andrea Katz, CEO

A not-for-profit, privately-governed organization whose mission is to provide quality comprehensive behavioral health care to individuals and families who are in need of improving their quality of life.

3661 Fairwinds Treatment Center
1569 South Fort Harrison
Clearwater, FL 33756-2004
727-449-0300
800-226-0300

Fax: 727-446-1022
E-mail: fairwinds@fairwindstreatment.com
www.fairwindstreatment.com

Mazhar Al-Abed, Administrator
Thomas H Lewis, Clinical Director

As a dually licensed psychiatric and substance abuse center, reaches far beyond standard treatment to offer medical services for substance abuse, eating disorders, and emotional/mental health issues.

3662 First Step of Sarasota
1726 18th Street
Sarasota, FL 34234-8638
941-366-5333
800-266-6866
Fax: 941-351-5161

Marlene Minzey, VP
Brenda Asher, CFO

Provides high quality, affordable substance abuse treatment and recovery programs on Florida's Gulf Coast. Offers a variety of programs including a medical detox, residential and outpatient services for adolescents, adults and families.

3663 Florida State Hospital
100 N Main Street
Chattahoochee, FL 32324-1107
850-663-7536
www.dcf.state.fl.us/facilities/fsh/index.shtml

Diane James, Administrator

FSH provides person-centered treatment and rehabilitations in order to propel the client toward their personal recovery and to prepare for roles and environments that have personal and social value.

Year Founded: 1876

3664 G Pierce Wood Memorial Hospital
5847 SE Highway 31
Arcadia, FL 33821
863-494-3323

Myers R Kurtz, Contact

3665 Gateway Community Services
555 Stockton Street
Jacksonville, FL 32204-2597
904-387-4661
Fax: 904-384-5753
www.gatewaycommunity.com

Gary Powers, CEO
Laura Dale, CFO
Randy Jennings, Sr VP Operations

Provides a full continuum of care that delivers effective treatment and rehabilitation services to individuals suffering from alcoholism, substance abuse and related mental health problems.

3666 Genesis House Recovery Residence
4865 40th Way South
Lake Worth, FL 33461-5301
561-439-4070
800-737-0933
E-mail: genesishouse@yahoo.com
www.genesishouse.net

James Dodge, Program Director
Kathryn Shafer, Clinical Director

Works closely with both local and out of state courts. Provides the suffering person with a safe, secure, professional environment to glean the care, answers and support they so desperately need in their lives.

3667 Manatee Glens
391 6th Avenue W
Bradenton, FL 34205-8820
941-782-4800

Mary Ruiz, CEO/President
Deborah Kostroun, COO
John Denaro, CFO
Dr Jose Zaglul, CMO

Helps families in crisis with mental health and addictions services and supports the community through prevention and recovery.

3668 Manatee Palms Youth Services
4480 51st Street W
Bradenton, FL 34210-2857
941-795-4083
Fax: 941-795-4359

Jeff Turiczek, CEO
Timothy Macsuga, Business Development Director

Committed to providing the highest quality comprehensive mental health care and education services for at-risk children, adolescents, families and our community.

3669 New Horizons of the Treasure Coast
4500 W Midway Road
Ft Pierce, FL 34981-4823
772-468-5600
Fax: 772-468-5606
www.nhtcinc.org

John Romano, CEO
Dr Charles Buscema, Medical Director

To improve the quality of life in the community through the provision of accessible, person-centered behavioral health resources.

3670 North Florida Evaluation and Treatment Center
1200 NE 55th Boulevard
Gainesville, FL 32641-2759
352-375-8484
Fax: 352-264-8283

William Baxter, Administrator

Dedicated to serving you while fulfilling our responsibilities for safety, security and a positive, caring environment.

3671 North Star Centre
9033 Glades Road
Boca Raton, FL 33434-3939
561-479-0501
Fax: 561-479-0384
E-mail: info@northstar-centre.com
www.northstar-centre.com

Jody Kaufman, Manager
Randi Katz, Administrative Assistant

A uniquely comprehensive facility dedicated to restoring
your sense of emotional and physical well being.

3672 Northeast Florida State Hospital
7487 South State Road 121
MacClenny, FL 32063-5480
904-259-6211
Fax: 904-259-7101

Joe Infantino, Administrator
Rufus Johnson, Evening Administrator

To provide comprehensive mental health treatment services
to ensure a timely transition to the community.

Year Founded: 1959

3673 Renaissance Manor
1401 16th Street
Sarasota, FL 34236-2519
941-365-8645
Fax: 941-955-0520

Heather Eller, Administrator

Community based assisted living facility with a limited
mental health license, specializes in serving adults with
neuro-biological disorders and mood disorders along with
other special mental health needs. Our not-for-profit organization is a program designed to encourage positive mental health while meeting the various interest of our
residents.

3674 Seminole Community Mental Health Center
237 Fernwood Blvd
Fern Park, FL 32730-2116
407-831-2411
Fax: 407-831-0195
E-mail: scmhc@scmhc.com

Jim Berko, Manager

A private, nonprofit organization whose goal is to provide
comprehensive, biopsychosocial rehabilitation programming in the areas of mental health and substance abuse.

**3675 South Florida Evaluation and Treatment
Center**
2200 NW 7th Avenue
Miami, FL 33127-4202
305-637-2500

Cheryl Brantley, Contact

3676 Starting Place
351 North State Road 7
Suite 200
Plantation, FL 33317
954-327-4060
www.startingplace.org

Sheldon Shaffer, CEO

Improves the lives through education, treatment and support services related to substance abuse, mental illness and
co-occurring disorders

3677 The Transition House
1224 12 Street
St Cloud, FL 34769
407-891-1551
E-mail: counselor@thetransitionhouse.org
www.thetransitionhouse.org

The adress above is the men's house. The address for the
women's house is: 505 N Clyde Street Kissimmee, FL
34741. All other information is the same. Mission is to provide a milieu of comprehensive educational, health, prevention and human services to Central Florida's most
disenfranchised populations.

3678 Turning Point of Tampa
6227 Sheldon Road
Tampa, FL 33615-3100
813-882-3003
800-397-3006
www.tpoftampa.com

Robin Piper, CEO
Robin Piper, Clinical Director/CEO
Michelle Ratcliff, Owner

Provides high-quality, 12 step based addiction treatment
programs specifically designed to be cost effective; to continually monitor and evaluate industry research and our
own outcome data in an effort to develop our own
programming.

3679 University Pavilion Psychiatric Services
7425 N University Drive
Tamarac, FL 33321-2955
954-722-9933
Fax: 954-722-7756
www.uhmchealth.com

David Hughes, Manager

Offers psychiatric services on an inpatient and outpatient
basis for all individuals.

3680 Willough Healthcare System
9001 Tamiami Trail East
Naples, FL 34113-3304
239-775-4500
800-722-0100
E-mail: info@thewilloughatnaples.com
www.thewilloughatnaples.com/

James O'Shea, Administrator

Specializes in the treatment of eating disorders and chemical dependency.

Georgia

3681 Candler General Hospital: Rehabilitation Unit
5353 Reynolds Street
Savannah, GA 31405-6015
912-819-6000

Paul P Hinchey, President/CEO

Our vision is to set the standards of excellence in the delivery of health care throughout the regions we serve. Candler Hospital is an affiliate of St. Joseph's/Candler, the largest health care system in Southeast Georgia and the only faith based health system in Savannah. Candler Hospital is the second oldest continuously operating hospitals in the United States and the oldest hospital in Georgia.

3682 Central State Hospital
620 Broad Street
Milledgeville, GA 31062-7525
478-445-4128
Fax: 478-445-6034
E-mail: info@centralstatehospital.org
www.centralstatehospital.org

Marvin Bailey, Chief Executive Officer
Scot Van Sant MD, Chief Medical Officer
Lee Ann Molini, Director of Nursing

Central State Hospital (CSH) is Georgia's largest facility for persons with mental illness and developmental disabilities. The scope of our services is extensive and includes: short-stay acute treatment for consumers with mental illness; residential units and habilitation programs for individuals with developmental disabilities; recovery programs for consumers requiring longer stays; and specialized skilled and ICF nursing centers. Some of our programs serve primarily our central Georgia region while other programs serve many counties throughout the state.

3683 Georgia Regional Hospital at Atlanta
3073 Panthersville Road
Decatur, GA 30034-3800
404-243-2100
Fax: 404-212-4621
E-mail: grha@dhr.state.ga.us
www.atlantareg.dhr.state.ga.us

Susan Trueblood, CEO
Gwen Skinner, Director

Located on 174 Acres in DeKalb County, Georgia Regional Hospital/Atlanta operates 366 licensed, accredited inpatient beds in five major program areas: Adult Mental Health, Adolescent Mental Health, Child Mental Health, Forensic Services, and Developmental Disabilities. In addition, GRH/Atlanta also offers inpatient and outpatient Dental Services and an Outpatient Forensic Evaluation Program for juveniles and adults. Finally, GRH/Atlanta operates the Fulton County Collaborative Crisis Service System which provides mobile crisis and residential services to adults experiencing mental health problems in Fulton County.

3684 Georgia Regional Hospital at Augusta
3405 Old Savannah Road
Augusta, GA 30906-3897

706-792-7019
Fax: 706-792-7041
Ben Waker EdD, Contact

3685 Georgia Regional Hospital at Savannah
1915 Eisenhower Drive
PO Box 13607
Savannah, GA 31416-607
912-356-2045
Douglas Osborne, Contact

3686 Northwest Georgia Regional Hospital
1305 Redmond Circle
Rome, GA 30165-9655
706-295-6600

Karl Schwarzkopf, President
Karl H Schwarzkopf, Administrator

3687 Southwestern State Hospital
400 Pinetree Boulevard
PO Box 1378
Thomasville, GA 31792-1378
229-227-2850
www.swsh.org

Hillary Hooyou, Manager

Provides extensive behavioral healthcare services in community and hospital settings, including: residential MRDD services; inpatient, residential and case management psychiatric services; and residential care for dual-diagnosed persons.

3688 West Central Georgia Regional Hospital
PO Box 12435
Columbus, GA 31917-2435
706-568-5204
E-mail: wcgrh@dhr.state.ga.us
www.wcgrh.org

Mission is to treat customers with respect and dignity while providing comprehensive, person-centered behavioral healthcare.

Idaho

3689 Children of Hope Family Hospital
Po Box 1829
Boise, ID 83701-1829
208-658-8013
E-mail: drharper@afo.net
www.chfhosp.dmi.net

Rev Anthony R Harper PhD, Founder

3690 State Hospital North
300 Hospital Drive
Orofino, ID 83544-9034
208-476-4511
Fax: 208-476-7898
www.hospitalnorth.com

Gary Moore, Administrator

3691 State Hospital South
700 E Alice Street
PO Box 400
Blackfoot, ID 83221-400
208-785-8401
Fax: 208-785-8448
Raymond Laible, Contact

Illinois

3692 Advocate Ravenswood Hospital Medical Center
2025 Windsor Avenue
Oakbrook, IL 60523-1586
630-572-9393
Fax: 630-990-4752
www.advocatehealth.com
James H Skogsbergh, CEO

Provides a comprehensive array of services for inpatient (Adult, Adolescent, Substance Abuse), Partial Hospital, Intensive Outpatient, Psychological Rehabilitation, Emergency-Crisis, Assertive Community Outreach, Case Management, Program for Deaf and Hard of Hearing at multiple sites on the Northside of Chicago.

3693 Alexian Brothers Bonaventure House
825 W Wellington Avenue
Chicago, IL 60657-9249
773-327-9921
Fax: 773-327-9113
E-mail: info@abam.org
Bart Winters, CEO
Marty Hansen, Director Programs/Services

Offers adult men and women with HIV/AIDS-who are homeless or at-risk for homelessness- a chance to rebuild and reclaim their lives. Bonaventure House has a wide array of on-site supportive services-case management, occupational therapy, recovery, and spiritual care-most residents are able to return to independent life in the community within a 24-month period.

3694 Alton Mental Health Center
4500 College Avenue
Alton, IL 62002-5099
618-474-3200
Fax: 618-474-3967
www.illinois.gov
Susan Shobe, Administrator

3695 Andrew McFarland Mental Health Center
901 Southwind Road
Springfield, IL 62703-5125
217-786-6900
Fax: 217-786-7167
Karen Schweighart, Administrator

3696 Chester Mental Health Center
Chester Road
Chester, IL 62233
618-826-4571
Stephen Hardy PhD, Contact

3697 Choate Mental Health and Development Center
1000 N Main Street
Anna, IL 62906-1652
618-833-5161
Fax: 618-833-4191
Cindy Flamm, CEO

3698 Cornell Interventions Lifeworks
1611 Jefferson Street
Joliet, IL 60435-6724
815-730-7521
www.cornellcompanies.com
Karen Monroe, Manager

Provides outpatient addiction counseling, education and life skills services to adolescents and adults.

3699 Delta Center
1400 Commercial Avenue
Cairo, IL 62914-1978
618-734-3626
Fax: 618-734-1999
TTY: 618-734-1350
E-mail: delta1@midwest.net
www.deltacenter.org
Lisa Tolbert, Executive Director

A non-profit mental health center, substance abuse counseling facility, and also provides various community services to Alexander and Pulaski County, Illinois

3700 Elgin Mental Health Center
750 S State Street
Elgin, IL 60123-7692
847-742-1040
Fax: 847-429-4910
Raul Almazar, Administrator

3701 FHN Family Counseling Center
421 W Exchange Street
Freeport, IL 61032-4008
815-599-6900
Fax: 815-599-6106
Lisa Mahoney, VP

3702 Franklin-Williamson Human Services
1307 W Main Street
Marion, IL 62959-1139
618-997-5336
David Melby, Plant Manager

A place where people with mental, emotional, behavioral, family, developmental or substance abuse problems can get help. Our programs help people learn to prevent problems, acquire new skills, develop abilities and adjust to community life.

3703 H Douglas Singer Mental Health Center
4402 N Main Street
Rockford, IL 61103-1278
815-987-7096
Fax: 815-987-7559

Mohammad Yunus, Administrator

3704 Habilitative Systems
415 S Kilpatrick Avenue
Chicago, IL 60644-4958
773-854-1680
Fax: 773-854-8300
TDD: 773-854-8364
E-mail: hsi@habilitative.org
www.habilitative.org

Donald Dew, President
Joyce Wade, VP Finance
Karen Barbee-Dixon, EdD, COO

To provide integrated human services to children, adults, families, and persons with disabling conditions that help them to achieve their highest level of self-sufficiency

Year Founded: 1978

3705 Harriet Tubman Women and Children Treatment Facility Residential Program
11352 South State Street
Chicago, IL 60628-4836
773-785-4955

Primary focus is the mix of mental health and substance abuse services. Providing residential long-term treatment which is longer than 30 days.

3706 John J Madden Mental Health Center
1200 S 1st Avenue
Hines, IL 60141-800
708-338-7400
Fax: 708-338-7057

Fred Nirde, Administrator

3707 John R Day and Associates
3716 W Brighton Avenue
Peoria, IL 61615-2938
309-692-7755
Fax: 309-692-2262
www.christianpsychological.org

John R Day, Partner

3708 Keys To Recovery
100 North River Road
Des Plaines, IL 60016-1209
847-298-9355
www.keystorecovery.org

Philip Kolski, Director
Debra Ayanian, Nurse Manager

A leading Alcoholism and Drug Treatment Center in the Midwest, providing innovative and effective Alcoholism and Drug Treatment.

3709 MacNeal Hospital
3231 South Euclid Avenue
Berwyn, IL 60402-3471
708-783-3705
888-622-6325
TTY: 708-783-3058
E-mail: inf@macnealfp.com

Randall K Mc Givney, Program Director
Davis Yang, Center Director
John Gong, Clinical Faculty
Edward C Foley MD, Director Of Research

The MacNeal Family Practice Residency Program was one of the first family practice programs in the country and the first in Illinois. We have continue a progressive tradition in all aspects of our curriculum. Our program is at the forefront of contemporary family medicine offering diverse academic and clinical opportunites and building on the innovative ideas of our residents.

3710 McHenry County Mental Health Board
620 Dakota Street
Crystal Lake, IL 60012-3732
815-455-2828
Fax: 815-455-2925
www.mc708.org

Sandy Lewis, Executive Director
Robert Lesser, Deputy Director

To provide leadership and ensure the prevention and treatment of mental illness, developmental disabilities and chemical abuse by coordinating, developing, and contracting for quality services for all citizens of McHenry County, Illinois. This is not a provider organization.

3711 Metro Child and Adolescent Network
Chicago Read MHC Annex
4200 North Oak Park Avenue
Chicago, IL 60634-1417
773-794-4010

James Brunner MD, Hospital Administrator
Randy Thompson, Medical Director
Thomas Simpatico MD, Facility Director

An important psychiatric hospital which is part of the Department of Human Services of the State of Illinois. Provides comprehensive psychiatric inpatient services for adults in cooperation with a broad spectrum of community mental health service providers.

3712 Pfeiffer Treatment Center and Health Research Institute
4575 Weaver Parkway
Warrenville, IL 60555-4039
630-505-0300
866-504-6076
Fax: 630-836-0667

E-mail: info@hriptc.org
www.hriptc.org

Scott Filer, MPH, Executive Director
Allen Lewis MD, Medical Director
William Walsh, PhD, Research/Found Dir/Co-Founder

A not-for-profit, outpatient medical facility for children, teens and adults seeking a biochemical assessment and treatment for their symptons caused by a biochemical imbalance, or to support health and promote wellness. PTC physician precribes individualized program of vitamins, minerals, and amino acids to address the patient's unique biochemical needs. Common conditions: anxiety, ADHA, autism spectrum disorder, post traumatic stress syndrome, depression, bipolar disorder, schozophrenia and Alzheimer's disease.

3713 Salem Children's Home

15161 N 400 E Road
Flanagan, IL 61740-9143
815-796-4561
Fax: 815-796-4565
E-mail: info@salemranch.com
www.salemranch.com

Brent Ketring, Executive Director

Salem Children's Home is a Christian organization which provides a variety of individualized services of superior quality to meet the spiritual, social, educational, emotional and psysical needs of boys and their families. We gladly accept the responsibility to provide this care in a personal, nurtuing manner to reconcile familes, develop positive self-images and build healthy relationships among those we serve.

3714 Sonia Shankman Orthogenic School

1365 E 60th Street
Chicago, IL 60637-2890
773-834-2728
Fax: 773-702-1304
www.orthogenicschool.uchicago.edu

Henry J Roth PhD, Executive Director

A coeducational residential treatment program for children and adolescents in need of support for emotional issues which cause the student to act in disruptive ways and experience unfulfilling social and educational experiences

3715 Stepping Stones Recovery Center

1621 Theodore Street
Joliet, IL 60435-1958
815-744-4555
Fax: 815-744-4670
E-mail: info@steppingstonestreatment.com
www.steppingstonestreatment.com

Dedicated to providing effective treatment for persons suffering from the illness of addiction to alcohol and/or other drugs, even if these persons are unable to pay for the cost of such services.

3716 Tinley Park Mental Health Center

7400 W 183rd Street
Tinely Park, IL 60477-3688

708-614-4000
Fax: 708-614-4495

Thomas Monahan, Manager

3717 Transitions Mental Health Rehabilitation

805 19th Street
PO Box 4238
Rock Island, IL 61204-4238
309-793-4993
Fax: 309-793-9053
E-mail: transitions@revealed.net
www.transrehab.org

Transitions is dedicated to promoting, enhancing, and improving the health, recovery, and well-being of individuals, families, and the community impacted by mental health issues.

3718 Way Back Inn-Grateful House

1915 W Roosevelt Road
Braodview, IL 60155-2925
708-344-3301
E-mail: frankl@waybackinn.org
www.waybackinn.org

Frank Lieggi, Executive Director
Anita Pindiur, Clinical Director

Provides a high level clinical treatment program specializing in addressing the needs of men and women suffering from both chemical dependence (Alcohol and Drugs) and also Gambling Dependence.

3719 Wells Center

1300 Lincoln Avenue
Jacksonville, IL 62650-4007
217-243-1871
Fax: 217-243-2278
TDD: 217-243-0470
E-mail: bcarter@wellscenter.org
www.wellscenter.org

Bruce Carter, Executive Director

Mission has been to improve the health and welfare of individuals and families affected by the ause of alcohol and other substances and by mental health issues. Dedicates its efforts to providing levels of care and support services in settings approval to the individual needs of the patient.

3720 White Oaks Companies of Illinois

130 Richard Pryor Place
Peoria, IL 61605-2484
309-671-8960
800-475-0257
E-mail: whiteoaks@fayettecompanies.org
www.whiteoaks.com

Non profit agency offering comprehensive, state-of-the-art chemical dependency services, individually designed for each client.

Indiana

3721 Community Hospital Anderson

1515 N Madison Avenue
Anderson, IN 46011-3457
765-298-4242
www.communityhospitalanderson.com

William Vanness, CEO

The mission of Community Hospital is to serve the medical, health and human service needs to the people in Anderson-Madison County and contiguous counties with compassion dignity, repect and excellence. Service, although focused on injury, illness and disease will also embrace prevention, education and alternative systems of health care delivery.

3722 Crossroad: Fort Wayne's Children's Home

2525 Lake Avenue
Fort Wayne, IN 46805-5457
260-484-4153
800-976-2306
Fax: 260-484-2337
www.crossroad-fwch.org

Randy Rider, President/CEO
Mick Thiel, Chief Program Officer
A Wayne Burton, CFO

A not-for-profit treatment center for emotionally troubled youth.

3723 Hamilton Center

620 Eighth Avenue
Terre Haute, IN 47804-2771
812-231-8200

Gaylan Good, CEO
Richard Pittelkow, Vice President
Cary Sparks, Treasurer
Virginia Gilman, Secretary

Provides the full continuum of psychological health and addiction services to children, adolescents, adults and families.

3724 Mental Health America of Indiana

1431 North Delaware Street
Indianapolis, IN 46202
317-638-3501
800-555-6424
Fax: 317-638-3540
E-mail: mha@mentalhealthassociation.com
www.mentalhealthamerica.net

Stephen C McCaffrey JD, President/CEO

A statewide organization, with over sicty local chapters, making it the largest Mental Health Association in the country.

3725 Parkview Hospital Rehabilitation Center

2200 Randilla Drive
Ft. Wayne, IN 46805-4638
260-373-6450
888-480-5151
E-mail: paulette.fisher@parkview.com
www.parkview.com

Sue Ehinger, CEO

31 bed inpatient rehabilitation unit serving a wide variety of diagnoses. CARF accredited for both comprehensive and B1 programs. Outpatient services are offered at several sites throughout the community.

3726 Richmond State Hospital

498 NW 18th Street
Richmond, IN 47374-2851
765-966-0511
Fax: 765-935-9504
www.richmondstatehospital.org

Jeff Butler, Manager

A public behavioral health facility operated by the State of Indiana that provides psychiatric and chemical dependency treatment to citizens on a state wide basis.

3727 Universal Behavioral Service

820 Fort Wayne Avenue
Indianapolis, IN 46204-1309
317-684-0442
Fax: 317-684-0679

Iowa

3728 Cherokee Mental Health Institute

1251 W Cedar Loop
Cherokee, IA 51012-1599
712-225-2594
Fax: 712-225-6925

Tony Morris, Manager

3729 Clarinda Mental Health Treatment Complex

1800 N 16th Street
PO Box 338
Clarinda, IA 51632-610
712-542-2161

Mark Lund, Contact

3730 Four Seasons Counseling Clinic

2015 West Bay Drive
Muscatine, IA 52761-2228
563-263-3869
Fax: 563-263-3869

Ruth Evans, Owner

3731 Independence Mental Health Institute

2277 Iowa Avenue
Independence, IA 50644-9215
319-334-2583

Bhasker Dave, Manager

3732 Mount Pleasant Mental Health Institute

1200 E Washington Street
Mount Pleasant, IA 52641-1898

319-385-7231
Fax: 319-385-8465

John Mathes, Contact

Kansas

3733 Larned State Hospital
Route 3
Box 89
Larned, KS 67550-5353
620-285-4703

Mark Schutter, Superintendent

3734 Osawatomie State Hospital
PO Box 500
Osawatomie, KS 66064-500
913-755-7000
Fax: 913-755-2637

Gregory Valentine, Superintendent

JCAHO accredited state psychiatric hospital.

3735 Prairie View
1901 E First Street
Newton, KS 67114-5010
316-284-6400
800-362-0180

Stan Wright, CEO

A behavioral and mental health facility which consists of the main campus in Newton that consists of outpatient services, a 38-bed inpatient hospital and various other divisions of our organization. Also maintain outpatient offices in Hutchinson, KS; Marion, KS; McPherson, KS; along with two outpatient offices in Wichita, KS.

Year Founded: 1954

3736 Rainbow Mental Health Facility
2205 W 36th Avenue
Kansas City, KS 66103-2198
913-785-5800
www.kumc.edu/rainbow

Roz Underdahl, Contact

3737 Via Christi Research
1100 N St. Francis Street
Suite 300
Wichita, KS 67214-2871
316-291-4774
800-362-0070
Fax: 316-291-7704
www.privia.org

Joe Carrithers, Manager
Joe Carrithers, PhD, Research Operations Director

Provide people with mental health conditions such as depression, suicidal thoughts, schizophrenia or dementia have a unique set of needs. They receive highly skilled, compassionate treatment.

Kentucky

3738 ARH Psychiatric Center
102 Medical Center Drive
Hazard, KY 41701-9421
606-439-1331
Fax: 606-439-6701

Wendy Morris, Contact

3739 Central State Hospital
10510 LaGrange Road
Louisville, KY 40223-1228
502-253-7000
Fax: 502-253-7435

Patricia Brodie, Manager

3740 Cumberland River Regional Board
PO Box 568
Corbin, KY 40702-568
606-528-7010
www.cumberlandriver.com/crccc.html

For children with emotional, behavioral and/or mental challenges.

3741 Eastern State Hospital
627 W Fourth Street
Lexington, KY 40508-1294
859-246-7000
E-mail: mjdaniluk@bluegrass.org
www.bluegrass.org

Janet Warren, Plant Manager

3742 Kentucky Correctional Psychiatric Center
1612 Dawkins Road
PO Box 67
La Grange, KY 40031-67
502-222-7161
Fax: 502-222-7798

Gregory Taylor, Contact

3743 Our Lady of Bellefonte Hospital
St. Christopher Drive
Ashland, KY 41101
606-833-3333
Fax: 606-833-3946
www.careyoucantrust.com

Tim O'Toole, Manager

3744 Western State Hospital
2400 Russeville Road
PO Box 2200
Hopkinsville, KY 42241-2200
270-889-6025
Fax: 502-886-4487

Steven Wiggins, Contact

Louisiana

3745 Central Louisiana State Hospital
242 West Shamrock Avenue
PO Box 5031
Pineville, LA 71361-5031
318-484-6200
Fax: 318-484-6501
E-mail: clshmail@dhh.state.la.us
www.dhh.state.la.us

Thomas L Davis, Facility Director

The free-standing inpatient facility of Area C - Mental Health Services. The mission of Area C is to provide a comprehensive, integrated continuum of care (system of services) for adults with serious mental illness and children/youth with serious emotional/behavioral disturbance in need, in accordance with state and national accrediting organizations' standards for service access, quality, outcome, and cost.

3746 East Division Greenwell Springs Campus
PO Box 549
Greenwell Springs, LA 70739-549
225-261-2730
Fax: 225-261-9080

Mark Anders, Contact

3747 Eastern Louisiana Mental Health System
PO Box 498
Jackson, LA 70748-498
225-634-0100
Fax: 225-634-5827

Mark Anders, Contact

3748 Forensic Division
PO Box 888
Jackson, LA 70748-888
225-634-0100
Fax: 225-634-5827

Mark Anders, Contact

3749 Medical Center of LA: Mental Health Services
1532 Tulane Avenue
New Orleans, LA 70112-2860
504-903-3000

Genaro F Arriola Jr, Contact

3750 New Orleans Adolescent Hospital
Po Box 3850
Mandeville, LA 70470-3850
504-897-3400
Fax: 504-896-4959
www.dhh.louisiana.gov

Provides a fully integrated hospital and community based continuum of mental health services for children and adolescents, with serious emotional and behavioral problems, residing in Louisiana.

3751 River Oaks Hospital
1525 River Oaks Road W
New Orleans, LA 70123-2199
504-734-1740
800-366-1740
Fax: 504-733-7020
E-mail: kim.epperson@uhsinc.com

Evelyn Nolting, CEO

A private psychiatric facility for adults, adolescents and children.

3752 Southeast Louisiana Hospital
23515 Highway 190
PO Box 3850
Mandeville, LA 70470-3850
985-626-6300
Fax: 985-626-6658
www.dhh.louisiana.gov

Patricia Gonzalez, Facility Director

Maine

3753 Dorthea Dix Psychiatric Center
656 State Street
PO Box 926
Bangor, ME 04402-926
207-941-4000
E-mail: larry.larson@maine.gov
www.maine.gov/dhhs/ddpc/home.html

N Lawrence Ventura, Contact

DDPC is a 100 bed psychiatric hospital serving two-thirds of the State's geographic area that provides services for people with severe mental illness.

3754 Good Will-Hinckley Homes for Boys and Girls
PO Box 159
Hinckley, ME 04944
207-238-4000
E-mail: info@gwh.org
www.gwh.org

Donald H Marden, Chairman
Kathryn Hunt, Vice Chair
David Kimball, President

Provides a home for the reception and support of needy boys and girls who are in needs maintaining and operates a school for them; attends to the physical, industrial, moral and spiritual development of those who shall be placed in its care.

3755 Riverview Psychiatric Center
250 Arsenal Street
11 SHS
Augusta, ME 04333-0011
207-624-4600
Fax: 207-287-6123
www.maine.gov/dhhs/riverview/index.shtml

Mary Louise McEwen, Superintendent
William Nelson MD, Medical Director
Lauret Grommett RN, Director of Nursing

Acute care psychiatric hospital owned and operated by the state of Maine.

3756 Spring Harbor Hospital
123 Andover Road
Westbrook, ME 04092-3850
207-761-2200
888-524-0080

Dennis P King, President
Rick Hamley, COO
Girard Robinson, Chief Medical Officer

Southern Maine's premier provider of inpatient services for individuals who experience acute mental illness or dual disorders issues.

Maryland

3757 Clifton T Perkins Hospital Center
ATTN: (Dept or General Information)
8450 Dorsey Run Road
Jessup, MD 20794
410-724-3000
Fax: 410-724-3249
www.dhmh.state.maryland.gov/perkins

Sheilah Davenport, JD,MS,RN, CEO
Muhammed M Ajanah MD, Clinical Director
Steve Mason, COO

CTPHC is a maximum security facility. The mission of the facilty is to perform timely pretrial evaluations of defendants referred by the judicial circuit of Maryland, provide quality assessment of and treatment for all patients, and provide maximum security custody of patients to ensure public safety.

3758 Eastern Shore Hospital Center
Po Box 800
Cambridge, MD 21613-800
410-221-2300
Fax: 410-221-2534

Mary K Noren, Contact

3759 John L. Gildner Regional Institute for Children and Adolescents
15000 Broschart Road
Rockville, MD 20850-3303
301-251-6800
Fax: 301-309-9004
www.dhmh.state.md.us/jlgrica/

Thomas E. Pukalski, CEO
Claudette Bernstein, Medical Director
Debra K. VanHorn, Director of Comm. Res. & Dev.

John L. Gildner Regional Institute for Children and Adolescents (JLG-RICA) is a community-based, public residential, clinical, and educational facility serving children and adolescents with severe emotional disabilities. The program is designed to provide residential and day treatment for students in grades 5-12. JLG-RICA's goal is to successfully return its students to an appropriate family, community, and academic or vocational setting that will lead to happy and successful lives.

3760 Kennedy Krieger Institute
707 North Broadway
Baltimore, MD 21205-1888
443-923-9200
E-mail: info@kennedykrieger.org

Gary W Goldstein, CEO

Dedicated to improving the lives of children and adolescents with pediatric developmental disabilities through patient care, special education, research, and professional training.

3761 Laurel Regional Hospital
7300 Van Dusen Road
Laurel, MD 20707-9463
410-792-2270
www.dimensionhealth.org

Marilyn Davis, Data Processing

Laurel Regional Hospital is a full-service community hospital serving northern Prince George's County and Montgomery, Howard, and Anne Arundel Counties with 146 beds and 670 employees.

3762 RICA: Baltimore
605 S Chapel Gate Lane
Baltimore, MD 21229-3906
410-368-7800
877-203-5179
E-mail: pmakris@dhmh.state.md.us

Penny Makris, Contact

3763 RICA: Southern Maryland
55 Wade Ave
Catonsville, MD 21228-4663
301-372-1840
Fax: 301-372-1906
www.pgcps.org/~rica/

Mary Sheperd, Contact

3764 Sheppard Pratt at Ellicott City
4100 College Avenue
PO Box 0836
Ellicott City, MD 21041-836
410-465-3322
800-883-3322
Fax: 410-465-1988
www.taylorhealth.com

To provide personal, high quality mental health services for your family, by our family of health care professionals.

3765 Spring Grove Hospital Center
Wade Avenue
Catonsville, MD 21228

410-402-6000

Patrick Sokas, Contact

3766 Springfield Hospital Center
6655 Sykesville Road
Sykesville, MD 21784-7966
410-795-2100
800-333-7564
E-mail: shc_admin@dhmh.state.md.us
www.dhmh.state.md.us

Paula Langmead, CEO
Janice Bowen, COO
Jonathan Book, Clinical Director

A regional psychiatric hospital operated by the State of Maryland, Department of Health and Mental Hygiene, Mental Hygiene Administration.

3767 Thomas B Finan Center
10102 Country Club Road
PO Box 1722
Cumberland, MD 21501-1722
301-777-2240
Fax: 301-777-2364

Judy Hott, Contact

3768 Walter P Carter Center
630 W Fayette Street
Baltimore, MD 21201-1585
410-209-6200
Fax: 410-209-6355

Archie T Wallace, CEO

Massachusetts

3769 Arbour-Fuller Hospital
200 May Street
S Attleboro, MA 02703-5520
508-761-8500
800-828-3934
Fax: 508-761-4240
TTY: 800-974-6006
E-mail: arbourhealth@mindspring.com
www.uhsinc.com

Robert Mansfield, CEO
Frank Kahr MD, Medical Director
Judith Merel, Director Marketing

Psychiatric hospital providing services to adults, adolesents and adults with developmental disabilities.

3770 Baldpate Hospital
83 Baldpate Road
Georgetown, MA 01833-2303
978-352-2131
Fax: 978-352-6755

Lucille M Batal, President

3771 Berkshire Center
18 Park Street
Lee, MA 01238-1702
413-243-2576
www.berkshirecenter.org

Michael McManmon, Executive Director

3772 Choate Health Management
23 Warren Avenue
Woburn, MA 01801-7906
781-933-6700

3773 Concord Family and Adolescent Services
A Division of Justice Resource Institute, Inc
380 Massachusetts Avenue
Acton, MA 01720-3743
978-263-3006
Fax: 978-263-3088
www.jri.org

Gregory Canfield, Executive Director

Provides professional residential schools, group home, residence for homeless teens, alternative, therapeutic high school, education and parenting programs for children, adults and families throughouth Massachusetts.

3774 First Connections and Healthy Families
A Division of Justice Resource Institute, Inc
111 Old Road to NAC
Concord, MA 01742-4141
978-287-0221
www.jri.org

Ellen Weistein, Director

First Conneections provides resources, education and support to families with children birth through age three. First Connections is dedicated to providing quality, comprehensive parenting support services to a diverse communities seeking resources to compliment and enrich their parenting experience.

3775 Grip Project
A Division of Justice Resource Institute, Inc
174 Central Square
Suite 433
Lowell, MA 01852-1926
978-458-3622
www.jri.org

Rachel McNamara, Program Director

A by teens, for teens young people's program with residential services as a foundation. Grip serves young people, ages 16-20, who are homeless or aging out of foster-care/group homes and are committed to being independent. There is a separate residence for young women and men, both located in Lowell, MA.

3776 Littleton Group Home
A Division of Justice Resource Institute, Inc
22 King Street
Littleton, MA 01460-1519

978-952-6809
www.jri.org

Donna Grisi, Program Director

Prepares young men, ages 13-18 for independent living by helping them to live respectful, dignified and increasingly responsible lives. The young men participate in after school activities and have daily access to the community.

3777 Meadowridge Pelham Academy
A Division of Justice Resource Institute, Inc
13 Pelham Road
Lexington, MA 02421-5707
781-274-6800
www.jri.org

Andre Solomita, Program Director

A residential treatment program that focuses on the special challenges of adolescent girls with emotional and behavioral difficulties. The students, between the ages of 12-22, have typically experienced trauma and poor functioning in their personal, educational and/or family life.

3778 Meadowridge Walden Street School
A Division of Justice Resource Institute, Inc
148 Walden Street
Concord, MA 01742-3614
978-369-7611
www.jri.org

Kari Beserra, Program Director

A residential school program that focuses on the challenges and special needs of adolescent females age 12-22 whom are coping with educational, emotional and behavioral difficulties.

3779 New England Home for Little Wanderers
271 Huntington Avenue
Boston, MA 02115-4554
617-267-3700
888-466-3321
Fax: 617-267-8142
www.thehome.org

Joan Wallace-Benjamin, President/CEO
Susan P Curnan, VP Opeations/Outcomes
Kenneth E Hamberg, Executive VP/CFO

To ensure the healthy, emotional, mental and social development of children at risk, their families and communities.

3780 Sleep Disorders Unit of Beth Israel Hospital
330 Brookline Avenue
Boston, MA 02215-5400
617-667-7000
Fax: 617-667-1134
www.bidmc.harvard.edu/home.asp

Jean K Matheson MD, Contact

Provides testing and treatment for those with sleep disorders and offers educational workshops, plus support for their families.

3781 Taunton State Hospital
PO Box 4007
Taunton, MA 02780-997
508-977-3000

Katherine Chmiel, Contact

3782 Victor School
A Division of Justice Resource Institute, Inc
380 Massachusetts
Acton, MA 01720-3743
978-266-1991
www.jri.org

Wendy Rosenblum, Program Director

A private, co-ed, therapeutic day school for students in grades 8-12 with a school philosophy that children learn when they can. Provides innovative and specialized educational and emotional support and treatment.

3783 Westboro State Hospital
Lyman Street
PO Box 288
Westboro, MA 01581-288
508-616-2100
Fax: 508-616-2875

Joel Skolnick, COO

3784 Windhorse Integrative Mental Health
211 North Street
Suite 1
Northampton, MA 01060-2386
413-586-0207
Fax: 413-585-1521
www.windhorseimh.org

Jack Rockefeller JD, MPH, Executive Director
Jeff Bliss MSW, Director, Admissions/Marketing
Sara Watters MA, LMHC, Director, Clinical Operations

Windhorse is a nonprofit treatment and education organization with a whole person approach to recovery from serious psychiatric distress. Services are tailored in close communication with each client and their family.

Michigan

3785 Caro Center
2000 Chambers Road
Caro, MI 48723-9296
989-673-3191
Fax: 989-673-6749

Rose Laskowski, Administrator

3786 E Lansing Center for Family
425 W Grand River Avenue
E Lansing, MI 48823-4201
517-332-8900

Provides mental health treatment.

3787 Hawthorn Center
18471 Haggerty Road
Northville, MI 48168-9575
248-349-3000
Fax: 248-349-6893
www.michigan.gov

Shobhana Joshi, Executive Director

To provide high quality inpatient mental health services to emotionally disturbed children and adolescents.

3788 Kalamazoo Psychiatric Hospital
1312 Oakland Drive
PO Box A
Kalamazoo, MI 49008-1205
269-337-3000

James J Coleman, Executive Director

3789 Mount Pleasant Center
30901 Palmer Rd
Westland, MI 48186-9529
989-773-7921

George Garland, Contact

3790 Northpointe Behavioral Healthcare Systems
715 Pyle Drive
Kingsford, MI 49802-4456
906-774-0522
Fax: 906-779-1306
E-mail: info@nbhs.org
www.nbhs.org

Karen Thekan, CEO

Northpointe strives to improve the well being of individuals and families through the delivery of excellent person-centered mental health services.

3791 Samaritan Counseling Center
29887 W Eleventh Mile Road
Farmington Hills, MI 48336
248-474-4701
Fax: 248-474-1518
E-mail: info@samaritancounselingmichigan.com
www.samaritancounselingmichigan.com

Paul Melrose, Executive Director

Provides professional therapeutic counseling and educational services to all God's people seeking wholeness through emotional and spiritual growth.

3792 Walter P Ruther Psychiatric Hospital
30901 Palmer Road
Westland, MI 48186-5389
734-367-8400

Ronald Denstedt, CEO

3793 Westlund Child Guidance Clinic
3253 Congress Avenue
Saginaw, MI 48602-3199

989-793-4790
Fax: 989-793-1641

Matt Muempfer, Manager

Provides mental health services.

Minnesota

3794 Metro Regional Treatment Center: Anoka
3300 4th Avenue N
Anoka, MN 55303-1161
763-576-5500
Fax: 763-712-4013

Judith Krohn, Contact

3795 St. Peter Regional Treatment Center
100 Freeman Drive
Saint Peter, MN 56082-3504
507-985-2000
TDD: 507-931-7825

Larry Te Brake, Forensic Site Director
Jim Behrends, Regional Administrator

3796 Willmar Regional Treatment Center
1550 Highway 71 NE
Willmar, MN 56201-9504
320-231-5100

James E Becker, Site Director

Mississippi

3797 East Mississippi State Hospital
PO Box 4128, W Station
Meridian, MS 39304-4128
601-482-6186
Fax: 601-483-5543
www.emsh.state.ms.us

Charles Carlisle, Director

To provide a continuum of behavioral health and long term care services for adults and adolescents in a caring, compassionate environment in which ethical principles guide decision making and resources are used responsibly and creatively.

3798 Mississippi State Hospital
PO Box 157-A
Whitfield, MS 39193-157
601-351-8018
E-mail: info@msh.state.ms.us
www.msh.state.ms.us

Facilitates improvement in the quality of life for Mississippians who are in need of psychiatric, chemical dependency or nursing home survices by rehabilitating to the least restrictive environment utilizing a reange of psychiatric and medical services that reflect the accepted standard of care and are in compliance with statutory and regulatory guidlelines.

3799 North Mississippi State Hospital
1937 Briar Ridge Road
Tupelo, MS 38804-5963
662-690-4200
Fax: 662-690-4261
www.nmsh.state.ms.us

Paul Callens, Executive Director

3800 South Mississippi State Hospital
823 Highway 589
Purvis, MS 39475-4194
601-794-0100
Fax: 601-794-0210
www.smsh.state.ms.us

Wynona Winfield, Executive Director

Provides the highest quality acute psychiatric care for
adults who live in southern Mississippi

Missouri

3801 Edgewood Children's Center
330 N Gore Avenue
Saint Louis, MO 63119-1699
314-968-2060
Fax: 314-968-8308
E-mail: info@eccstl.org

Wayne Crull, CEO
Latriece N Kimbrough, CFO

Provides compassionate care and treatmetn to restore children and strengthen families through intensive therapy, special education, case management and support services.

3802 Hyland Behavioral Health System
10020 Kennerly Road
Sappington, MO 63128-2106
314-525-7200
800-525-2032

Adult and pediatric psychiatric inpatient/partial services located at St. Anthony's Medical Center.

**3803 Northwest Missouri Psychiatric Rehabilitation
Center**
3505 Frederick Avenue
Saint Joseph, MO 64506-2914
816-387-2300
Fax: 816-387-2329
www.mo.gov

Mary Attebury, Manager

Inpatient care for long-term psychiatric/adult.

3804 Southeast Missouri Mental Health Center
1010 W Columbia Street
Farmington, MO 63640-2902
573-218-6792
Fax: 573-218-6703
E-mail: cynthia.forsyth@dmh.mo.gov

Karen Adams, CEO

People shall receive services focusing on strenghts and promoting opportunities beyond the limitations of mental
illness.

3805 Western Missouri Mental Health Center
1000 E 24th Street
Kansas City, MO 64108-2776
816-512-7000
Fax: 816-512-7509

Scott Carter, Manager

Offers services in alcoholism, drug, family, group and individual counseling, crisis intervention, group psychiatric
therapy, and suicide prevention as well as hospital inpatient
care, mental health aftercare and psychiatric care.

Nebraska

3806 Norfolk Regional Center
1700 N Victory Road
PO Box 1209
Norfolk, NE 68702-1209
402-370-3400
Fax: 402-370-3194

William Gibson, CEO
TyLynne Bauer, Facility Operating Officer

A progressive 120-bed state psychiatric hospital providing
specialized psychiatric care to adults.

Nevada

**3807 Behavioral Health Options: Sierra Health
Services**
2724 N Tenaya Way
Las Vegas, NV 89128-424

877-393-6094
www.sierrahealth.com

Anthony M Marlon, Chairman/CEO

to manage behavioral health services in the private and
public sectors on a national basis, creating value for our
customers, including brokers, employers, members, providers and shareholders

3808 Northern Nevada Adult Mental Health Services
480 Galletti Way
Sparks, NV 89431-5564
775-688-2001
Fax: 775-688-2052

David Rosin MD, Contact

3809 Southern Nevada Adult Mental Health Services
6161 W Charleston Boulevard
Las Vegas, NV 89146-1148
702-486-6093

Anuranjan Bist, Contact

New Hampshire

3810 Hampstead Hospital

218 E Road
Hamptead, NH 03841-5303
603-329-5311
Fax: 603-329-4746
www.hamsteadhospital.com

Phillip Kubiak, President

Provides a full range of psychiatric and chemical dependency services for children, adolescents, adults and the
elderly.

3811 New Hampshire State Hospital

36 Clinton Street
Concord, NH 03301-2359
603-271-5300
Fax: 603-271-5395
www.dhhs.state.nh.us

Chester G Batchelder, CEO

a state operated, publicly funded hospital providing a range
of specialized psychiatric services. NHH advocates for and
provides services that support an individual's recovery.

New Jersey

3812 Ancora Psychiatric Hospital

202 Spring Garden Road
Ancora, NJ 08037
609-561-1700
Fax: 609-567-7294
E-mail: donna.ingram@dhs.state.nj.us

Allan Boyer, CEO

Provides quality comprehensive psychiatric, medical and
rehabilitative services that encourage maximun patient independence and movement towards community reintegration with an enviroment that is safe and caring.

3813 Ann Klein Forensic Center

Stuyvesant Avenue
PO Box 7717
W Trenton, NJ 08628-717
609-633-0900
Fax: 609-633-0971
E-mail: mhs.affc-infoline@dhs.state.nj.us
www.state.nj.us/humanservices/pfnurse/ak-forensic.htm

A 200-bed psychiatric hospital serving a unique population
that requires a secured environment. The facility provides
care and treatment to individuals suffering from mental illness who are also within the legal system.

3814 Arthur Brisbane Child Treatment Center

Route 524
Farmingdale, NJ 07727
732-938-7803
Fax: 732-938-3102
E-mail: judy.gnad@dhs.state.nj.us
www.stae.nj.us/humanservices/pfnurses/brisbane.htm

Judy Gnad, Contact

A state-run facility for the treatment of youth between the
ages of eleven and seventeen who require post acute psychiatric care.

3815 Greystone Park Psychiatric Hospital

Greystone Park, NJ 07950
973-292-4096
Fax: 973-993-8782
E-mail: william.lanni@dhs.state.nj.us
www.state.nj.us/humanservices/pfnurses/greystone.htm

William Lanni, Contact

A 550 bed psychiattric hospital.

3816 Jersey City Medical Center Behavioral Health Center

50 Baldwin Avenue
Jersey City, NJ 07304-3154
201-915-2542

Surasak Puvabanditsin

3817 Senator Garrett Hagedorn Psychiatric Hospital

200 Sanitarium Road
Glen Gardner, NJ 08826-3288
908-537-2141
E-mail: jdecker@state.nj.us

Debra Smith, CEO

A 288 bed psychiatric hospital that provides quality interdisciplinary psychiatric services that maximize potential
and community reintegration within a safe and caring
environment.

New Mexico

3818 Life Transition Therapy

110 Delgado Street
Santa Fe, NM 87501-2781
505-982-4183
800-547-2574
E-mail: info@lifetransition.com

Sabina Schulze, Manager
Ralph Steele, Founder

To eliminate the fear, ignorance and conditioning that fuel
racism and social injustice within the individual as well as
in relationships, families, communities, and the world at
large.

3819 New Mexico State Hospital

3695 Hot Springs Boulevard
Las Vegas, NM 87701-9550
505-454-2100
Fax: 505-454-2346

Felix Alderete, Contact

3820 Northern New Mexico Rehabilitation Center
Las Vegas Medical Center
PO Box 1388
Las Vegas, NM 87701-1388
505-454-5100

Felix Alderete, Contact

3821 Sequoyah Adolescent Treatment Center
3405 W Pan American Freeway NE
Albuquerque, NM 87107-4786
505-222-0300
www.health.state.nm.us

Henry Gardner, Manager

A 36 bed residential treatment center whose purpose is to provide care, treatment, and reintegration into society for adolescents who are violent or who have a history of violence and have a mental disorder and who are amenable to treatment.

New York

3822 Arms Acres
75 Seminary Hill Road
Carmel, NY 10512-1921
845-225-3400
888-227-4641

Frederick R Hesse, CEO
Sultan Niazi, CFO
Michele Saari, Health Information Management

A private health care system providing high quality, cost-effective care to those suffering from alcoholism and chemical dependency and to the many whose lives are affected by the diseases of addiction.

3823 Berkshire Farm Center and Services for Youth
13640 State Route 22
Canaan, NY 12029-3506
518-781-4567
Fax: 518-781-4577
E-mail: info@berkshirefarm.org
www.berkshirefarm.org

Timothy Giacchetta, CEO

Mission is to strengthen children and their families so they can lives safely, independently and productively within their home communities.

3824 Bronx Children's Psychiatric Center
1000 Waters Place
Bronx, NY 10461
718-239-3639
Fax: 718-239-3669
www.omh.state.ny.us

3825 Bronx Psychiatric Center
1500 Waters Place
Bronx, NY 10461-2796
718-829-3440
E-mail: bronxpc@omh.state.ny.us

Lalitakala Sundar

A 360 bed facility that has three impatient services and a comprehensive outpatient program.

3826 Brooklyn Children's Center
1819 Bergen Street
Brooklyn, NY 11233-4513
718-221-4500
Fax: 718-221-4581
E-mail: bcc@omh.state.ny.us
www.omh.state.ny.us/omhweb/facilities/bkpc/facility.ht

Provides high quality comprehensive individualized mental health treatment services to serious emotionally disturbed children and adolescents in Brooklyn, and to continuously strive to improve the quality of those services.

3827 BryLin Hospitals
1263 Delaware Avenue
Buffalo, NY 14209-2497
716-886-8200
800-727-9546
Fax: 716-886-1986
E-mail: info@brylin.com
www.brylin.com

Eric Pleskow, CEO

Provides inpatient psychiatric services for children, adolescents, adults and geriatric patients. Outpatient services are offered to persons experiencing substance abuse problems.

3828 Buffalo Psychiatric Center
400 Forest Avenue
Buffalo, NY 14213-1298
716-885-2261
Fax: 716-885-4852
E-mail: bufflopc@omh.state.ny.us

Tom Dodson, Manager

Provides psychiatric quality inpatient, outpatient, residential, vocational, and wellness services to adults with serious mental illnesses

3829 Cabrini Medical Center
227 East 19th Street
New York, NY 10003-2693
212-995-6658
E-mail: info@cabrininy.org

Voluntary hospital, sponsored by the Missionary Sisters of the Sacred Heart of Jesus that seeks to promote the teachings of the Gospel and of its foundress, St. Frances Xavier Cabrini.

3830 Capital District Psychiatric Center
75 New Scotland Avenue
Albany, NY 12208-3474
518-447-9611
Fax: 518-436-3620

Lewis Campbell, CEO

Provides inpatient psychiatric treatment and rehabilitation to patients who have been diagnosed with serious and persistenet mental illnesses and for whom brief or short-term treatment in a community hospital mental health unit has been unable to provide sympton stability.

3831 Central New York Psychiatric Center

PO Box 300
Marcy, NY 13403-300
315-765-3600
Fax: 315-765-3629
E-mail: cnypc@omh.state.ny.us
www.omh.state.ny.us/omhweb/facilities/cnpc/facility.ht

A comprehensive mental health service delivery system providing a full range of care and treatment to persons incarcerated in the New York State and county correctional system.

3832 Cornerstone of Rhinebeck

500 Milan Hollow Road
Rhinebeck, NY 12572-2970
845-266-3481
800-266-4410
Fax: 845-266-8335
E-mail: admin@cornerstoneny.com
www.cornerstoneny.com

Eileen Mc Curdy, Senior VP

Provides inpatient chemical dependency treatment and offers a comprehensive range of inpatient and outpatient treatment services for alcohol and substance abuse.

3833 Creedmoor Psychiatric Center

79-25 Winchester Boulevard
Queens Village, NY 11427-2128
718-264-5029
E-mail: crpc_info@omh.state.ny.us

Prema Rayappa, Executive Director

Provides a continuum of inpatient, outpatient and related psychiatric services with inpatient hospitalization at the main campus and five outpatient sites in the boroughs of Queens.

3834 Elmira Psychiatric Center

100 Washington Street
Elmira, NY 14901-2898
607-737-4700
Fax: 607-737-4722
E-mail: elmirapc@omh.state.ny.us

Mark Stephany, Manager

Provides a wide array of comprehensive psychiatric services.

3835 Freedom Ranch

PO Box 24
Lakemont, NY 14857-24
607-243-8126
800-842-8679
E-mail: 14jd@freedomvillageusa.com
www.freedomvillageusa.com

Dr Fletcher Brothers, Founder

An extension of Freedom Village, Freedom Ranch offers a residential program for men 21 and older with substance abuse and emotional problems. Freedom Ranch is a faith-based program seeking to help men become productive members of society.

3836 Freedom Village USA

PO Box 24
Lakemont, NY 14857-24
607-243-8126
800-842-8679
E-mail: 14jd@freedomvillageusa.com
www.freedomvillageusa.com

Dr Fletcher Brothers, Founder

A not-for-profit residential campus for troubled teens. Offers a faith-based approach to teenagers in crisis or at risk. Students are required to make a voluntary one-year commitment to the program. Freedom Village has an 80% success rate with troubled teenagers.

3837 Gift of Life Home

PO Box 24
Lakemont, NY 14857-24
607-243-8126
800-842-8679
E-mail: 14jd@freedomvillageusa.com
www.freedomvillageusa.com

Dr Fletcher Brothers, Founder

An affiliate program of Freedom Village, USA, a residential program for troubled teenagers, the Gift of Life Home offers pregnant girls a safe haven, a place of refuge, where they can come and have their baby while transforming their life as well. Freedom Village is a faith-based alternative to other residential placements.

3838 Graham-Windham Services for Children and Families: Manhattan Mental Health Center

151 W 136th Street
Lenox & 7th Avenue
New York, NY 10030-2606
212-368-4100
E-mail: info@graham-windham.org

Offers mental health services to children from birth through 18 years and their families: individual, family and group therapy, psychiatric evaluation and medication management, psychological assessment. Family support services program offering advocacy, support and referrals to families with seriously emotionally disturbed children.

3839 Greater Binghamton Health Center

425 Robinson Street
Binghamton, NY 13904-1775
607-773-4520
E-mail: binghamton@omh.state.ny.us

Pamela Vredenburgh, Manager

Provides comprehensive outpatient and inpatient services for adults and children who are seriously mentally ill.

3840 Hope House
517 Western Avenue
Albany, NY 12203-1653
518-482-4673
Fax: 518-482-0873
E-mail: information@hopehouseinc.org
www.hopehouseinc.org

Don Smith, Executive Director
Mathhew Kawola, Dir Human Resources/Quality Ass.

Started helping the community in need of education, intervention and treatment for the persons affected by substance abuse.

3841 Hudson River Psychiatric Center
10 Ross Circle
Poughkeepsie, NY 12601-1078
845-452-8000

Pushpa Patil

Serves the seriously and persistently mentally ill through inpatient care for 150 patients, including psychotherapy, psychoeducation groups, medication and a range of rehabilitation activities.

3842 Hutchings Psychiatric Center
620 Madison Street
Syracuse, NY 13210-2338
315-426-3600
Fax: 315-426-3603

Colleen Sawyer, Executive Director

A comprehensive, community-based mental health facility providing an integrated network of inpatient and outpatient services for children and adults residing in the Central New York Region.

3843 Kingsboro Psychiatric Center
681 Clarkson Avenue
Brooklyn, NY 11203-2199
718-363-2159
Fax: 718-221-7297
E-mail: kingsboro@omh.state.ny.us

Mark Lerman, Manager

Provides competent compassionate psychiatric care to people with serious mental illness with a purpose of reintegrating them to the community.

3844 Kirby Forensic Psychiatric Center
600 E 125th Street
New York, NY 10035-6000
646-672-6767
E-mail: kirbypc@omh.state.ny.us
www.omh.state.ny.us

Steve Rabinowitz, Manager

A maximum security hospital of the New York State Office of Mental Health that provides secure treatment and evaluation for the forensic patients and courts of New York City and Long Island.

3845 Liberty Resources
1065 James Street
Suite 200
Syracuse, NY 13203
315-425-1004
E-mail: info@liberty-resource.org
www.liberty-resource.org

Carl Coyle, CEO
Michael Sayles, President

Provides residential and non-residential services to individuals and families, our present array of services include Mental Health; Mental Retardation and Developmental Disabilities; services for individuals living with HIV/AIDS, families and youth involved in the child welfare system, domestic violence services; services to persons in recovery; and diversified case management services.

3846 Manhattan Psychiatric Center
600 E 125th Street
New York, NY 10035-6000
646-672-6767
Fax: 646-369-0980
E-mail: mpcinfo@omh.state.ny.us
www.omh.state.ny.us

Steve Rabinowitz, Manager

Offers inpatient and outpatient treatment for adults with mental illness.

3847 Mid-Hudson Forensic Psychiatric Center
Box 158, Route 17-M
New Hampton, NY 10958
845-374-8700
E-mail: midhudsonfpc@omh.state.ny.us

Barbara Daria, Manager

A secure adult psychiatric center that provides a comprehensive program of evaluation, treatment, and rehabilitation for patients admitted by court order.

3848 Middletown Psychiatric Center
122 Dorothea Dix Drive
Middletown, NY 10940-1907
845-342-5511
Fax: 845-342-4975
E-mail: midokmw@lmh.state.ny.us
www.omh.state.ny.us/omhweb/facilities/mipc/facility.ht

Offers contemporary treatment for adults with complex mental illnesses.

3849 Mohawk Valley Psychiatric Center
1400 Noyes at York
Utica, NY 13502
315-738-3800
E-mail: mvpc@omh.state.ny.us
www.omh.state.ny.us

Sarah Rudes, CEO

Provides quality, individualized psychiatric treatment and rehabilitation services that promote recovery.

3850 Nathan S Kline Institute for Psychiatric Research
140 Old Orangeburg Road
Orangeburg, NY 10962-1157
845-398-5500
Fax: 845-398-5510
E-mail: webmaster@nki.rfmh.org
www.rfmh.org/nki

Bennett L Leventhal, MD, Deputy Director

Research programs in Alzheimers disease, analytical psychopharmacology, basic and clinical neuroimaging, cellular and molecular neurobiology, clinical trial data management, co-occuring disorders and many other mental health studies.

3851 New York Psychiatric Institute
1051 Riverside Drive
New York, NY 10032-1098
212-543-6283

John Caleb Markowitz, Chairman

3852 Odyssey House
95 Pine Street
New York, NY 10005-3904
212-361-1600
Fax: 212-361-1666
E-mail: info@odysseyhouseinc.org
www.odysseyhouseinc.org

Peter Provet, President

Develops innovative treatment models to ensure that our systems take into account current research, utilizing what works most effectively to help these individuals overcome their difficulties and build a stable, producitve, drug-free life.

3853 Pahl Transitional Apartments
559-565 Sixth Avenue
Troy, NY 12182-2620
518-237-9891
Fax: 518-237-9409
E-mail: michael_kennedy@pahlinc.org
www.pahlinc.org

Michael Kennedy, Clinical Director

A 9-12 month residential, chemical dependency treatment facility for males ages 16-25. The goal for the residents is to learn the skills necessary for long-term recovery and independent living.

3854 Phoenix House
164 West 74th Street
New York, NY 10023-2301
646-505-2000
Fax: 646-721-2164
www.phoenixhouse.org

Howard Meitiner, CEO

Reclaims disordered lives, encourages individual responsibility, positive behavior, and personal growth, also strengthens families and communities, and safeguards public health. Also, promotes a drug-free society through prevention, treatment, education and training, research, and advocacy.

3855 Pilgrim Psychiatric Center
998 Crooked Hill Road
West Brentwood, NY 11717-1019
631-761-3500
Fax: 631-761-2600
E-mail: pilgriminfo@omh.state.ny.us

Dean Wienstock, Manager

Provides excellent, integrated care in evaluation, treatment, crisis intervention, rehabilitation, support, and self help/empowerment service to individuals with serious psychiatric illness.

3856 Queens Children's Psychiatric Center
74-03 Commonwealth Boulevard
Bellerose, NY 11426-1839
718-264-4500
E-mail: queenscpc@omh.state.ny.us

Keith Little, Executive Director

Serves seriously emotionally disturbed children and adolescents from the ages of 5 through 18 in a range of programs including Inpatient hospitalization, outpatient clinic treatment, intensive case management, homemaker services and community education and consultation services.

3857 Rochester Psychiatric Center
1111 Elmwood Avenue
Rochester, NY 14620-3090
585-241-1200
Fax: 585-241-1424
TTY: 585-241-1982
E-mail: rochesterpc@omh.state.ny.us

Michael Vuber, Executive Director

Provides quality comprehensive treatment and rehabilitation services to people with psychiatric disabilities working toward recovery.

3858 Rockland Children's Psychiatric Center
599 Convent Road
Orangeburg, NY 10962
845-359-7400
800-597-8481
E-mail: rocklandcpc@omh.state.ny.us

Josefina M Moneda

A psychiatric hospital exclusively for children and adolescents

3859 Rockland Psychiatric Center
140 Old Orangeburg Road
Orangeburg, NY 10962
845-359-1000
Fax: 845-359-3478
E-mail: rpamz01@omh.state.ny.us
www.omh.state.ny.us

Provides treatment, rehabilitation, and support to adults 18 and older with severe and complex mental illness.

3860 Sagamore Children's Psychiatric Center
197 Half Hollow Road
Dix Hills, NY 11746-5859
631-370-1700
E-mail: scisdcc@omh.state.ny.us

Dennis Dubey, Executive Director

Programs for youngsters and their families include inpatient hospitalization, day hospitalization, day treatment, outpatient clinic treatment, mobile mental health team crisis services, information and referral, and community consultation and training.

3861 Samaritan Village
138-02 Queens Blvd
Briarwood, NY 11435
718-206-2000
800-532-4357
www.samaritanvillage.org

Tino Hernandez, President/CEO

Mission is to eliminate the devastating impact of substance abuse on individuals, families and communities by helping addicted men and women take responsibility for their own recovery.

3862 South Beach Psychiatric Center
777 Seaview Avenue
Staten Island, NY 10305-3409
718-667-2300
E-mail: sbcsmss@omh.state.ny.us

William Henri, Administrator

Provides intermediate level inpatient services to persons living in western Brooklyn, southern Staten Island, and Manhattan south of 42nd street.

3863 St. Lawrence Psychiatric Center
1 Chimney Point Drive
Ogdensburg, NY 13669-2291
315-541-2001
E-mail: slpcinfo@omh.state.ny.us

Sam Bastien, Executive Director

3864 Veritas Villa
5 Ridgeview Road
Kerhonkson, NY 12446-1555
845-626-3555
Fax: 845-626-3840
E-mail: info@veritasvilla.com
www.veritasvilla.com

Joseph Stoeckeler, CEO

Inpatient rehabilitation and wellness center

3865 Western New York Children's Psychiatric Center
1010 E & W Road
W Seneca, NY 14224-3698

716-674-6300
E-mail: westernnewyorkcpc@omh.state.ny.us
www.cs.state.ny.us

Deborah Shiffner, Manager

Provides high quality, comprehensive behavioral health care services to seriously emotionally disturbed children and adolescents, and to partner with their families throughout the continuum of care.

North Carolina

3866 Broughton Hospital
1000 S Sterling Street
Morganton, NC 28655-3999
828-433-2111
E-mail: BH.Information@NCMail.net
www.broughtonhospital.org

Dr Art Robarge, Interim Hospital Director/CEO

3867 Central Regional Hospital
1003 12th Street
Butner, NC 27509-1626
919-575-7100
www.dhhs.state.nc.us/mhddsas/centralhospital/index.htm

Formed by the merger of Dorothea Dix Hospital and John Umstead Hospital. Services include adult psychiatric services, clinical research services, child and adolescent services, medical services, and geropsychiatric services.

3868 Cherry Hospital
201 Stevens Mill Road
Goldsboro, NC 27530-1057
919-731-3206

Phillip Cook, Manager

North Dakota

3869 North Dakota State Hospital
2605 Circle Drive
Jamestown, ND 58401-6905
701-253-3650
Fax: 701-253-3999
TTY: 701-253-3880
www.nd.gov

Alex Schweitzer, CEO

Ohio

3870 Appalachian Behavioral Healthcare System
Athens Campus
100 Hospital Drive
Athens, OH 45701-2301
740-594-5000
800-372-8862

Michael Anikeev, CEO
Mark McGee MD, CCO
Kelly Douglas-Markins, Hospital Manager

40 Bed inpatient psychiatric facility.

3871 Central Behavioral Healthcare
5965 Renaissance Place
Toledo, OH 43623-4728
419-841-5934
Fax: 419-882-7446
www.centralbehavioralhealthcare.com

Dennis W Kogut, Owner

Provides patients with a broad range of high-quality behavioral healthcare in a professional and personal matter.

3872 Clermont Counseling Center
4 Cecelia Drive
Amelia, OH 45102-1906
513-947-7025
800-732-9805
Fax: 513-947-7055
TTY: 513-947-0333

Patricia Burke, Executive Director

Provides comprehensive mental health services to adults and families who are confronted with emotional difficulties, family and relationship problems or abuse and mental illness.

Year Founded: 1973

3873 Hannah Neil Center for Children
301 Obetz Road
Columbus, OH 43207-4092
614-491-5784
E-mail: suzan@worldofchildren.org

Randy Copas, Director

The Hannah Neil Center for Children serves children who suffer from severe behavioral and emotional difficulties.

3874 Heartland Behavioral Healthcare
3000 Erie Street S
Massillon, OH 44646-7976
330-833-3135

G Eric Carpenter, MPA, CEO

3875 Medina CFIT
Heartland Behavioral Healthcare
3076-A Remsen Road
Medina, OH 44256-9225
330-722-0750
Fax: 330-723-0068

Charles Johnston, Contact

3876 Millcreek Children's Services
6600 Paddock Road
PO Box 16006
Cincinnati, OH 45216-6
513-948-3983

Peter Steele, Contact

3877 Northcoast Behavioral Healthcare System
Cleveland Campus
1708 Southpoint Drive
Cleveland, OH 44109-1911
216-787-0500
Fax: 216-787-0656

Dave Coletti, Manager

3878 Northcoast Behavioral Healthcare System
Northfield Campus
PO Box 305
Northfield, OH 44067
330-467-7131
Fax: 330-467-2420

George P Gintoli, Contact

3879 Northwest Psychiatric Hospital
930 S Detroit Avenue
Toledo, OH 43614-2701
419-381-0228
Fax: 419-389-1967

Terry Smith, Administrator

3880 Twin Valley Behavioral Healthcare
Dayton Campus, 2611 Wayne Avenue
Dayton, OH 45420-1833
937-258-0440
Fax: 937-258-6218
TDD: 937-258-6257

Robert Short, CEO

State operated BHD serving severley mentally ill adults in partnership with the community.

3881 Twin Valley Psychiatric System
Columbus Campus, 2200 W Broad Street
Columbus, OH 43223-1297
614-752-0333

James Ignelzi, Chief Executive Officer

Oklahoma

3882 Griffin Memorial Hospital
900 E Main Street
PO Box 151
Norman, OK 73070-151
405-321-4880
Fax: 405-522-8320

Don Bowen, Contact

3883 Northwest Center for Behavioral Health
1222 10th Street
Woodward, OK 73801-3156
580-256-8615
Fax: 580-256-8643
www.odmhsas.org

Trudy Hoffman, Executive Director

Comprehensive regional behavioral health center.

3884 Oklahoma Forensic Center
PO Box 69
Vinita, OK 74301-0069
918-256-7841
Fax: 918-256-4491

William Burkett, Contact

3885 Oklahoma Youth Center
320 12th Avenue
PO Box 1008
Norman, OK 73070-1008
405-364-9004
Fax: 405-573-3804

Paul Bouffard, Contact

3886 Willow Crest Hospital
130 A Street Southwest
Miami, OK 74354-6800
918-542-1836
Fax: 918-542-8730
www.willowcresthospital.com

Anne Anthony, CEO

Oregon

3887 Blue Mountain Recovery Center
2600 Westgate
Pendleton, OR 97801-9604
541-276-0810
Fax: 541-278-2209

Kerry Kelly, Contact

3888 Oregon State Hospital: Portland
1121 NE 2nd Avenue
Portland, OR 97232-2043
503-731-8620

Nena Strickland, Executive Director

3889 Oregon State Hospital: Salem
2600 Center Street NE
Salem, OR 97301-2682
503-945-2800

Pam Dickinson, Manager

3890 St. Mary's Home for Boys
16535 SW Tualatin Valley Highway
Beaverton, OR 97006-5199
503-649-5651
Fax: 503-649-7405
E-mail: reception@stmaryshomeforboys.org
www.stmaryshomeforboys.com

Francis Maher, Executive Director

Founded in 1889 as an orphanage for abandoned and wayward children, today St. Mary's is a private, non-profit organization that offers comprehensive residential, day treatment and mental health services to at-risk boys between the ages of 10 and 17 who are emotionally disturbed and/or disruptive behavior disordered.

Pennsylvania

3891 Allentown State Hospital
1600 Hanover Avenue
Allentown, PA 18109-2498
610-740-3200

Gregory Smith, CEO

3892 Clarks Summit State Hospital
1451 Hillside Drive
Clarks Summit, PA 18411-9505
570-586-2011

Thomas P Comerford Jr, CEO

3893 Craig Academy
751 N Negley Avenue
Pittsburg, PA 15206-2059
412-361-2801
Fax: 412-361-6775
www.craigacademy.org

Denise Sedlacek, Manager

Operates a psychiatric partial day program and private elementary, middle, and high school programs.

3894 MHNet
1060 First Avenue
Suite 201
King of Prussia, PA 19406-1336

888-638-7491
E-mail: edwynl@integra-ease.com
www.integra-ease.com

Wesley J Brockhoeft, PhD, President/CEO
Peter Harris, MD, Corporate Medical Director
Robert Wilson, CFO
Richard T Wright, SVP Business Development

MHNet is an outgrowth of the Center for Individual and Family Counseling, a multi-disciplinary outpatient treatment clinic with a full spectrum behavioral health organization with national service delivery capability.

Year Founded: 1981

3895 Mayview State Hospital
1601 Mayview Road
Bridgeville, PA 15017-1599
412-257-6826

Laszlo Petras, Contact

3896 Montgomery County Project SHARE
538 Dekalb Street
Norristown, PA 19401-4931
610-278-3555
800-688-4226
E-mail: mcps@mhasp.org

Ronald Ahlbrandt, Executive Director

Serving people with mental health disabilities in Montgomery County.

Year Founded: 1988

3897 National Mental Health Self-Help Clearinghouse
1211 Chestnut Street
Suite 1207
Philadephia, PA 19107-4103
215-751-1810
800-553-4539
Fax: 215-636-6312
www.mhselfhelp.org

Joseph Rogers, Executive Director

A national consumer technical assistance center, has played a major role in the development of the mental health consumer movement.

Year Founded: 1986

3898 Norristown State Hospital
1001 Sterigere Street
Norristown, PA 19401-5397
610-270-1000
Fax: 610-313-1013

Gerry Kent, CEO

3899 Renfrew Center Foundation
475 Spring Lane
Philadelphia, PA 19128-3918
215-482-5353
Fax: 215-482-7390
E-mail: foundation@renfrew.org
www.renfrewcenter.com

Sam Menaged, President

A tax-exempt, nonprofit organization advancing the education, prevention, research, and treatment of eating disorders.

3900 State Correctional Institution at Waymart
Forensic Treatment Center
PO Box 256
Waymart, PA 18472-256
570-488-5811
Fax: 570-488-2558

Stephen A Zoburt PhD, Contact

3901 Torrance State Hospital
PO Box 111
Torrance, PA 15779-111
724-459-4511

Richard Stillwagon, Contact

3902 Warren State Hospital
33 Main Drive
N Warren, PA 16365-5099
814-723-5500
Fax: 814-726-4447

Dave Kucherawy, Executive Director

3903 Wernersville State Hospital
PO Box 300
Wernersville, PA 19565-300
610-678-3411
Fax: 610-670-4101

Kenneth Ehrhart, Contact

Rhode Island

3904 Butler Hospital
345 Blackstone Boulevard
Providence, RI 02906-4829
401-455-6200
E-mail: info@butler.org
www.butler.org

Patricia Recupero, President

Rhode Island's only private, nonprofit psychiatric and substance abuse hospital for adults, adolescents, children and seniors.

3905 Gateway Healthcare
249 Roosevelt Avenue
Suite 205
Pawtucket, RI 02860-2134
401-724-8400
E-mail: developmentoffice@gatewayhealth.org
www.gatewayhealth.org

Kim Walker, Manager
Scott W DiChristofero, VP Finance
Stephen Chabot MD, Medical Director

To promote resiliency and to assist people in their recovery from mental health, substance abuse, and behavioral and emotional disorder

3906 Groden Center
86 Mount Hope Avenue
Providence, RI 02906-1648
401-274-6310
Fax: 401-421-3280
E-mail: grodencenter@grodencenter.org
www.grodencenter.org

June Groden, President

Groden Center has been providing day and residential treatment and educational services to children and youth who have developmental and behavioral difficulties and their families. By providing a broad range of individualized services in the most normal and least restrictive settings possible, children and youth learn skills that will help them engage in typical experiences and interact more successfully with others. Education and treatment take place in Groden Center classrooms, in the student's homes, and in the community with every effort made to maintain typical family and peer relationships. Call or visit our web site for more information about the Center and the publications and materials we have available.

Year Founded: 1976

South Carolina

3907 CM Tucker Jr Nursing Care Center

2200 Harden Street
Columbia, SC 29203-7107
803-737-5300

Jaclynn Upfield, Manager

Provides excellence in resident care in an environment of concern and compassion that is respectful to others, adaptive to change and accountable for outcome.

3908 Earle E Morris Jr Alcohol & Drug Treatment Center

610 Faison Drive
Columbia, SC 29203-3218
803-935-7100
Fax: 803-935-7329
www.scdmh.org

George Mc Connell, Manager

Provides effective treatment of chemical dependence through comprehensive evaluation, safe detoxification, and state-of-the-art treatment servies.

3909 G Werber Bryan Psychiatric Hospital

220 Faison Drive
Columbia, SC 29203-3210
803-935-7140
Fax: 803-935-5397

A 277 bed short term intensive care facility that serves adult and geriatric patients ages 16 years and older. Provides therapeutic services in a warm and nurturing environment for individuals in crisis.

3910 James F Byrnes Medical Center

2100 Bull Street
Box 119
Columbia, SC 29201-2104
803-254-9325

Jaime E Condom MD, Contact

3911 Patrick B Harris Psychiatric Hospital

130 Highway 252
PO Box 2907
Anderson, SC 29622-2907
864-231-2600
Fax: 864-225-3297
www.patrickbharrispsychiatrichospital.com

John Fletcher, CEO

Provides intensive, short-term, psychiatric diagnostic and treatment services on a 24 hour, emergency voluntary and involuntary basis.

3912 South Carolina State Hospital

2100 Bull Street
Columbia, SC 29201-2147
803-434-4260

Miroslav Cuturic, Contact

Psychiatric hospital

3913 William S Hall Psychiatric Institute

1800 Colonial Drive
PO Box 202
Columbia, SC 29202-202
803-898-1693

Dalmer Sercy, Contact

South Dakota

3914 South Dakota Human Services Center

3515 Broadway Avenue
PO Box 7600
Yankton, SD 57078-7600
605-668-3100
Fax: 605-668-3460
www.dhs.sd.gov/hsc

Cory Nelson, Administrator

Tennessee

3915 Cherokee Health Systems

2018 Weestern Avenue
Knoxville, TN 37921-5718
865-544-0406
www.cherokeehealth.com

Tracey Trench, Manager

Uses an integrated model to provide behavioral health and primary care services in a community-based setting.

Year Founded: 1960

3916 Lakeshore Mental Health Institute

5908 Lyons View Drive
Knoxville, TN 37919-7598
865-584-1561
Fax: 865-450-5203

Richard L Thomas, CEO

3917 Memphis Mental Health Institute

951 Court Avenue
Memphis, TN 38103-2813
901-577-1800
Fax: 901-577-1434
www.tennessee.gov

Jeanne West Freeman, CEO

3918 Middle Tennessee Mental Health Institute
221 Stewarts Ferry Pike
Nashville, TN 37214-3325
615-902-7400
Fax: 615-902-7571
www.state.tn.us

Candance Gilligan, Manager

3919 Moccasin Bend Mental Health Institute
Moccasin Bend Road
Chattanooga, TN 37405
423-265-2271
Fax: 423-785-3347
www.tennessee.gov

William Ventress, CEO

3920 Western Mental Health Institute
Highway 64 W
Bolivar, TN 38008
731-228-2000

Roger Pursley, Chief Officer

3921 Woodridge Hospital
403 State of Franklin Road
Johnson City, TN 37604-6034
423-928-7111
800-346-8899
www.msha.com

Kim Moore, Manager
Kim Cudebec, Clinical Director

Texas

3922 Austin State Hospital
4110 Guadalupe Street
Austin, TX 78751-4223
512-452-0381
Fax: 512-419-2812

Carl Schock, CEO

Provides adult psychiatric services, specialty adult services and child and adolescent psychiatric services.

3923 Big Spring State Hospital
1901 N Highway 87
Big Spring, TX 79720-283
432-267-8216
E-mail: edward.moughon@dshs.state.tx.us

Ed Mougon, CEO

A 195-bed psychiatric hospital that provides hospitalization for people 18 years of age and older with psychiatric illnesses in a 57-county area in West Texas and the Texas Panhandle.

3924 Choices Adolescent Treatment Center
4521 Karnack Hwy
Marshall, TX 75672-8734

903-938-4455
800-638-0880
Fax: 903-938-8906
E-mail: choices@sydcom.net
www.choicestreatment.com

C G Bowman, CEO

Choices residential treatment program focuses on adolescents which abuse substances and addresses related psychiatric disorders.

3925 Dallas Metrocare Services
1380 Riverbend Drive
Dallas, TX 75247
214-743-1200
877-283-2121
Fax: 214-630-3469
www.metrocareservices.org

North Texas' leading nonprofit dedicated to helping people with mental illness, developmental disabilities, and severe emotional problems live healthier lives. Provides a comprehensive array of individually-tailored services to help the people we serve toward meaningful and satisfying lives.

Year Founded: 1967

3926 El Paso Psychiatric Center
4615 Alameda Avenue
El Paso, TX 79905-2702
915-532-2202
E-mail: zulema.carrillo@dshs.state.tx.us
www.dshs.state.tx.us

Zulema Carrillo, Administrator

A 74-bed psychiatric hospital that provides hospitalization to the citizens of far West Texas.

3927 Green Oaks Behavioral Healthcare Service
7808 Clodus Fields Drive
Dallas, TX 75251-2206
972-991-9504
Fax: 972-789-1865
www.greenoakspsych.com

Committed to developing and emulating the latest, most effective clinical practices always, and, in all things, to promote dignity, holding compassion and respect for patients and their families as the absolute standard.

3928 Homeward Bound
233 West 10th Street
Dallas, TX 75208-4524
214-941-3500
Fax: 214-941-3517
E-mail: ddenton@homewardboundinc.org
www.homewardboundinc.org

Douglas Denton, Executive Director

Offers chemical dependence treatment for the indigent population anad those referred by the criminal justice system, local hospitals and private practitioners.

3929 Jewish Family and Children's Services
12500 NW Military Highway
Suite 250
San Antonio, TX 78231-1871
210-302-6920
Fax: 210-302-6952
www.jfs-sa.org

M H Levine, Executive Director
Frank J Villani, Executive Director
LaDina Epstein, Associate Director

To strengthen community values, promote human dignity and enhance self-sufficiency of individuals and families through social, psychological, health educaitonal and financial support programs.

Year Founded: 1974

3930 Kerrville State Hospital
721 Thompson Drive
Kerrville, TX 78028-5199
830-896-2211
Fax: 830-792-4926

Linda Highsmith, President

provides care for persons with major mental illnesses who need the safety, structure, and resources of an in-patient setting

3931 La Hacienda Treatment Center
Hunt, TX 78024

800-749-6160
E-mail: info@lahacienda.com
www.lahacienda.com

Provides treatment for alcoholism and other chemical dependencies

3932 Laurel Ridge Treatment Center
17720 Corporate Woods Drive
San Antonio, TX 78259-3500
210-491-9400
Fax: 210-491-3550
www.psysolutions.com

Dan Thomas, CEO

A psychiatric hospital offering a comprehensive continuum of behavioral healthcare services including acute programs for children, adolescents and adults and residential treatment for children and adolescents.

3933 Macon W Freeman Center
1401 Columbus Avenue
Waco, TX 76701-1120
254-753-8251
Fax: 254-753-5881
E-mail: dworley@thefreemancenter.org
www.thefreemancenter.org

Tim Martindale, Medical Director
Gerald Elliot, Program Manager

Provides a chemical free environment in which professional guidance and peer support allow each client to work toward achievement of individualized treatment goals.

3934 New Horizons Ranch and Center
PO Box 549
Goldthwaite, TX 76844-549
915-938-5518
www.newhorizonsinc.com

To provide an environment where children, families and staff are able to heal and grow through caring relationships and unconditional love and acceptance.

3935 North Texas State Hospital: Vernon Campus
4730 College Drive
Vernon, TX 76384-4009
940-552-9901
Fax: 940-553-2500
E-mail: jamese.smith@dshs.state.tx.us
www.dshs.state.tx.us

James E Smith, CEO

3936 North Texas State Hospital: Wichita Falls Campus
6515 Lake Road
Wichita Falls, TX 76308-5419
940-692-1220
Fax: 940-689-5538
E-mail: jamese.smith@dshs.state.tx.us

Jim Smith, Administrator

3937 Rio Grande State Center
1401 South Rangerville
Harlingen, TX 78552-7638
956-364-8000

Maria G Dill, Superintendent

The only public provider south of San Antonio, Texas that offers healthcare, inpatient mental health services and long term mental retardation services.

3938 Rusk State Hospital
805 North Dickinson Drive
Rusk, TX 75785
903-683-3421
E-mail: ted.debbs@dshs.state.tx.us

Lakshmi Srinivasan, Manager

An inpatient hospital providing psychiatric treatment and care for citizens primarily from the East Texas region.

3939 San Antonio State Hospital
6711 South New Braunfels
Suite 100
San Antonio, TX 78223-3006
210-532-8811
Fax: 210-531-7780
E-mail: robert.arizpe@dshs.state.tx.us
www.dshs.state.tx.us

Robert Arizpe, Superintendent

Provides intensive inpatient diagnostic, treatment, rehabilitative, and referral servious for seriously mentally ill persons from South Texas regardless of their financial status.

3940 Shades of Hope Treatment Center
PO Box 639
Buffalo Gap, TX 79508-639

800-588-4673
www.shadesofhope.com
Tennie McCarty, Founder/CEO

A residential and outpatient all-addictions treatment center specializing in the intensive treatment of eating disorders.

3941 Starlite Recovery Center
230 Mesa Verde Drive East
PO Box 317
Center Point, TX 78010-317

866-220-1626
Fax: 830-634-2532
E-mail: info@starliterecovery.com
www.starliterecovery.com

Kirk Kureska, Executive Director

Provides the highest quality of care in a cost-effective manner, insuring that our valued clients receive treatment that will allow them to return to a productive way of life.

3942 Terrell State Hospital
1200 East Brin
Terrell, TX 75160-2938
972-563-6452

Fred Hale, CEO

A 316 bed, Joint Commission accredited and Medicare certified, psychiatric inpatient hospital, that is responsible for providing services for individuals with mental illnesses residing within a 19 county, 12,052 square mile service region, with a population of over 3 million.

3943 University of Texas Harris County Psychiatric Center
2800 S MacGregor Way
Houston, TX 77021-1032
713-741-5000

Robert Guynn MD, Executive Director

Delivers a comprehensive program of psychiatric services to children, adolescents and adults suffering from mental illness.

3944 Waco Center for Youth
3501 N 19th Street
Waco, TX 76708-2097
254-756-2171
Fax: 254-745-5398
E-mail: eddie.greenfield@dshs.state.tx.us
www.dshs.state.tx.us

Eddie Greenfield, Executive Director

A psychiatric residential treatment facility that serves teen-agers, ages 13 through 17, with emotional difficulties and/or behavioral problems.

Utah

3945 Utah State Hospital
1300 E Center Street
Provo, UT 84606-3554
801-344-4400
E-mail: jgierisch@utah.gov

Mark I Payne, Manager

provides excellent care in a safe and respectful environment to promote hope and quality of life for individuals with mental illness

Vermont

3946 Brattleboro Retreat
Anna Marsh Lane
PO Box 803
Brattleboro, VT 05302-803
802-257-7785
Fax: 802-258-3791
www.bratretreat.org

Robert E Simpson Jr, President/CEO

A not-for-profit health services organization which, above all else, is committed to assisting individuals to improve their health and functioning.

3947 Spring Lake Ranch
1169 Spring Lake Road
Cuttingville, VT 05738-4418
802-492-3322
Fax: 802-492-3331
E-mail: admissions@springlakeranch.org
www.springlakeranch.org

Pam Grace, Admissions
Jim Taggart, Executive Director

Offers an alternative therapeutic treatment program for adults with mental illness and/or substance abuse. Our work program and community life help residents grow and recover in the beautiful Green Mountains of Vermont. Our goal is to help people move from hospitalization or period of crisis to an independent life.

Year Founded: 1932

3948 Vermont State Hospital
103 South Main Street
Waterbury, VT 05671-9800
802-241-3246
Fax: 802-241-3001
www.vtbass.com

Bertold Francke MD, Contact

Virginia

3949 Catawba Hospital
5525 Catawba Hospital Drive
Catawba, VA 24070-2115
540-375-4200
800-451-5544
Fax: 540-375-4394

Jack Wood, CEO

To support the continuous process of recovery by providing quality psychiatric services to those individuals entrusted to our care

3950 Central State Hospital
26317 West Washington Street
PO Box 4030
Petersburg, VA 23803-30
804-524-7000
www.csh.dmhmrsas.virginia.gov/default.htm

to provide state of the art mental health care and treatment to forensic and civilly committed patients in need of a structured, secure environment. The major components of the hospital's mission include Evaluation, Treatment, Protection, and Disposition

3951 Commonwealth Center for Children & Adolescents
PO Box 4000
Staunton, VA 24402-4000
540-332-2100
Fax: 540-332-2201
www.ccca.dmhmrsas.virginia.gov

William J Tuell, Contact

CCCA is an acute care mental health facility for minors under the age of 18 years, operated by the State of Virginia, Department of Behavioral Health and Developmental Services.

Year Founded: 1996

3952 Dominion Hospital
2960 Sleepy Hollow Road
Falls Church, VA 22044-2082
703-536-2000
Fax: 703-538-2810
www.dominionhospital.com

Trula Minton, CEO

Offers individuals and families hope and help. Treats children, adolescents and adults who suffer from debilitating disorders such as anxiety, panic, depression, delusions, eating disorders, schizophrenia, school refusal, and self-injurious behavior.

3953 Eastern State Hospital
4601 Ironbound Road
Williamsburg, VA 23188-2652
757-253-5161
Fax: 757-253-5065
www.esh.dmhmrsas.virginia.gov

John M Favret, Manager

3954 Hiram W Davis Medical Center
PO Box 4030
Petersburg, VA 23803-30
804-524-7344

David A Rosenquist, Contact

3955 Northern Virginia Mental Health Institute
3302 Gallows Road
Falls Church, VA 22042-3398
703-207-7100
Fax: 703-207-7146
www.nvmhi.dmhmrsas.virginia.gov

Lynn De Lacy, Executive Director

Actively promoting recovery of individuals with serious mental illness through the use of safe, efficient, and effective treatment

3956 Piedmont Geriatric Hospital
5001 East Patrick Henry Highway
PO Box 427
Burkeville, VA 23922-427
434-767-4401
Fax: 434-767-4500
E-mail: steve.herrick@pgh.dmhmrsas.virginia.gov
www.pgh.dmhmrsas.virginia.gov

Stephen Herrick, Director

A 135-bed psychiatric hospital that provides recovery based MH services to enable the elderly to thrive in the community.

3957 Southern Virginia Mental Health Institute
382 Taylor Drive
Danville, VA 24541-4096
434-799-6220
Fax: 434-773-4241
E-mail: naomi.gibson@svmhi.dmhmrsas.virginia.gov
www.svmhi.dmhmrsas.virginia.gov

David Lyon, Manager

To be an inpatient mental health service provider within our Regional Service Area that responds to the patient's and area needs.

3958 Southwestern Virginia Mental Health Institute
340 Bagley Circle
Marion, VA 24354-3126
276-783-1200
Fax: 276-783-9712
www.swvmhi.dmhmrsas.virginia.gov

Cynthia Mc Clure, CEO

3959 Western State Hospital
1301 Richmond Avenue
Staunton, VA 24401-9146
540-332-8000
Fax: 540-332-8385
www.wsh.dmhmrsas.virginia.gov

Jack W Barber, Executive Director

Western State Hospital is a state psychiatric hospital which is licensed and operated by the Virginia Department of Mental Health, Mental Retardation, and Substance Abuse Services. Provides safe and effective individualized treatment in a recovery focused environment.

Washington

3960 Child Study & Treatment Center
8805 Steilacoom Boulevard SW
Lakewood, WA 98498-4771
253-756-2504
800-283-8639
Fax: 253-756-3911
www.clipadministration.org

Rick Mehlman, CEO

Treats children from age 5 to 17 who can not be served in less restrictive setting within the community.

3961 Eastern State Hospital
Maple Street
PO Box 800 Mail Stop B 32-23
Medical Lake, WA 99022-0800
509-565-4000
Fax: 509-565-4705
E-mail: eshinfo@dshs.wa.gov
www.dshs.wa.gov/mentalhealth/eshcontacts.shtml

Shirley Maike, Information Coordinator

Eastern State Hospital is a key partner in assisting adults with psychiatric illness in their recovery through expert in-patient treatment whenever needs exceed community resources.

3962 Ryther Child Center
2400 NE 95th Street
Seattle, WA 98115-2499
206-525-5050
Fax: 206-525-9795
TDD: 800-883-6388
www.ryther.org

Lee Grogg, Executive Director

Offers and develops safe places and opportunities for children, youth and families to heal and grow so that they can reach their highest potential.

3963 Western State Hospital
9601 Steilacoom Boulevard SW
Tacoma, WA 98498-4798
253-582-8900

Sukhinderpa Aulakh, Public Information Officer

West Virginia

3964 Highland Hospital
300 56th Street SE
Charleston, WV 25304-2361
304-926-1600
800-250-3806

Fax: 304-925-1524
www.highlandhosp.com

Phylis Spangler, Manager

Our mission is to identify and respond to mental health needs, and promote physical, social emotional and intellectual well-being.

3965 Mildred Mitchell-Bateman Hospital
1530 Norway Avenue
PO Box 448
Huntington, WV 25709-448
304-525-7801
800-644-9318
www.wvs.state.wv.us/newhh

Mary Beth Carlisle, CEO

Provides inpatient psychiatric treatment for the adult citizens of southern West Virginia.

3966 Weirton Medical Center
601 Colliers Way
Weirton, WV 26062-5091
304-797-6000
www.weirtonmedical.com

Joseph Endrich, CEO

Weirton Medical Center is a 238 bed, non-profit, acute-care, general community hospital located in the city of Weirton in Brooke County, West Virginia. Weirton Medical Center offers health care services to the residents of West Virginia, Ohio and Pennsylvania.

3967 William R Sharpe, Jr Hospital
936 Sharpe Hospital Road
Weston, WV 26452-8550
304-269-1210
Fax: 304-269-6235

Kevin Stalnaker, CEO

Wisconsin

3968 Bellin Psychiatric Center
301 E St. Joseph Street
PO Box 23725
Green Bay, WI 54305-3725
920-433-3630
E-mail: Isroet@bellin.org
www.bellin.org/psych

3969 Mendota Mental Health Institute
301 Troy Drive
Madison, WI 53704-1599
608-244-3262

A psychiatric hospital operated by the Wisconsin Department of Health and Family Services, Division of Disability and Elder Services, specializes in serving patients with complex psychiatric conditions, often combined with certain problem behaviors.

3970 Wheaton Franciscan Healthcare: Elmbrook Memorial
19333 W North Avenue
Brookfield, WI 53045-4132
262-785-4766

3971 Winnebago Mental Health Institute
1300 South Drive
PO Box 9
Winnebago, WI 54985-9
920-235-4910
Fax: 920-237-2043
TDD: 888-241-9438
www.dhfs.wisconsin.gov/mh_winnebago

Winnebago Mental Health Institute (WMHI) serves as a specialized component in a community-based mental health delivery system.

Wyoming

3972 Wyoming State Hospital
831 Highway 150 South
Evanston, WY 82930-5340
307-789-3464
Fax: 307-789-7373

William L Matchinski, Manager

A center for treatment, rehabilitation and recovery.

Clinical Management

Management Companies

3973 ABE American Board of Examiners in Clinical Social Work
27 Congress Street Suite 501
Shetland Park
Salem, MA 01970-5577
978-825-9311
800-694-5285
Fax: 978-740-5395
E-mail: abe@abecsw.org

Robert Booth, CEO
Robert Booth, Executive Director
Leonard Hill MSW BCD, Vice President

The American Board of Examiners in Clinical Social Work (ABE) sets national practice standards, issues an advanced-practice credential, and publishes reference information about its board-certified clinicians

3974 APOGEE
489 Devon Park Drive
Suite 301
Wayne, PA 19087-1809
610-688-1227
877-337-3200
Fax: 610-337-2337
E-mail: info@apogeeinsgroup.com

Tom Katona, Partner
Chris Hoxie, Account Executive

3975 Academy of Managed Care Providers
1945 Palo Verde Avenue
Suite 202
Long Beach, CA 90815-3445
562-682-3559
800-297-2627
Fax: 562-799-3355
E-mail: membership@academymcp.org
www.academymcp.org

Dr. John Russell, President
William Adams, Advisory Board Member

National organization of clinicans and MCO professionals. Provides many services to members including continuing education, diplomate certification, notification of panel openings and practice opportunities, newsletter, group health insurance and many other benefits.

3976 Access Behavioral Care
117 S 17th Street
Suite 900
Philadelphia, PA 19103-5025
215-567-3638
Fax: 215-567-5572

3977 Action Healthcare Management
6245 N. 24th Parkway
Suite 112
Phoenix, AZ 85016-2029
602-265-0681
800-433-6915
Fax: 602-265-0202
E-mail: jeanr@actionhealthcare.com
www.actionhealthcare.com

Jean Rice, President

Action Healthcare Management has been an independent healthcare management company offering a full range of services that can be tailored to meet your organization's needs-from pre-certification and utilization review, management of high risk pregnancy and workers' compensation cases, to cases involving serious illness, catastrophic injury and cases requiring transplants. AHM works within your budget to assure provision of quality, affordable healthcare, negotiation of provider agreements and cost containment in the structuring of quality utilization management plans. In today's complicated healthcare system, Action Healthcare Management is a partner to both your organization and your insured. We're by your side, every step of the way.

3978 Adanta Group-Behavioral Health Services
259 Parkers Mill Road
Somerset, KY 42501-3152
606-679-4782
Fax: 606-376-3467
E-mail: klworley@adanta.org
www.adanta.org

Jamie Burton, CEO

Adanta is composed of three major divisions which include Human Development Services, Clinical Services and the Regional Prevention Center. While each division is responsible for providing separate and distinct services, each relies on the expertise and resources available within the overall corporation. The three major divisions are made up of many smaller specialized areas, each of which include many professionals, staff and support personnel who take great pride in the quality of their work. Their professional skills, combined with time, energy and caring, have yielded and continue to yield positive results and many success stories across the region.

3979 Adult Learning Systems
1954 S Industrial Highway
Suite A
Ann Arbor, MI 48104-8601
734-668-7447

Sherri Turner, Contact

3980 Aetna-US HealthCare
151 Farmington Avenue
Hartford, CT 06156-1
860-273-0123
800-323-9930
Fax: 860-273-3971
www.aetna.com

Ronald A Williams, CEO

3981 Aldrich and Cox
3075 Southwestern Boulevard
Suite 202
Orchard Park, NY 14127-1287
716-675-6300
Fax: 716-675-2098
E-mail: cox@aldrichandcox.com
www.aldrichandcox.com

Charles Cox, President
Herbert Cox, Chairman
James Hood Jr, Exec. VP/ Secretary

Aldrich and Cox provides independent, fee-based Risk Management, Insurance and Employee Benefit Consulting services to a wide range of clientele.

3982 Alliance Behavioral Care
Po Box 19947
Cincinnati, OH 45219-947
513-475-8622
800-926-8862
E-mail: allen.daniels@uc.edu
www.alliance-behavioral.com

Allen Daniels, CEO

Alliance Behavioral Care is a regional managed behavioral healthcare organization located in Cincinnati, Ohio. They are committed to continuously improving the resources and programs that serve their members and providers. Their goal is to provide resources that improve the well-being of those they serve and to integrate the behavioral healthcare within the overall healthcare systems.

3983 Alliance For Community Care
2001 The Alameda
San Jose, CA 95126-1136
408-261-7777
Fax: 408-248-6520

3984 Allina Hospitals & Clinics Behavioral Health Services
2925 Chicago Avenue
Minneapolis, MN 55407-1321
612-775-5000
800-877-7878

Kenneth Paulus, CEO
Michael McAnder, CFO

Provides clinically and geographically integrated care delivery. Innovative programs and services across comprehensive continuum of care. Practicing guideline development, outcomes data and quality managment programs to enhance care delivery.

3985 AmeriChoice
8045 Leesburg Pike, Ste.650
Wanamaker Building
Vienna, VA 22182-2787
703-506-3500
Fax: 703-506-3556
E-mail: webmaster@americhoice.com

Rick Jelinek, CEO

3986 American Managed Behavioral Healthcare Association
1101 Pennsylvania Avenue NW
6th Floor
Washington, DC 20004-2544
202-756-7726
Fax: 202-756-7308
E-mail: info@abhw.org

Pamela Greenberg, President/CEO

A non-profit trade association representing the nation's leading managed behavioral healthcare organizations. These organizations collectively manage mental health and substance abuse services for its over 100 million individuals.

Year Founded: 1994

3987 Analysis Group
111 Huntington Avenue
Tenth Floor
Boston, MA 02199
617-547-0029
Fax: 617-425-8001
www.analysisgroup.com

Martha Samuelson, President/CEO
Bruce F Deal, Managing Principal

Provides economic, financial, and business strategy consulting to law firms, corporations and government agencies

Year Founded: 1981

3988 Aon Consulting Group
200 East Randolph Street
Chicago, IL 60601-6408
312-381-1000
Fax: 312-701-3100
www.aon.com

Gregory C Case, CEO

Aon Corporation is a leading provider of risk management services, insurance and reinsurance brokerage, human capital and management consulting, and specialty insurance underwriting.

3989 Arizona Center For Mental Health PHD
5070 N 40th Street
Suite 200
Phoenix, AZ 85018-2135
602-954-6700
Fax: 602-954-0190

Allan H Gelber, Owner

3990 Arthur S Shorr and Associates
4710 Deseret Drive
Woodland Hills, CA 91364-3720
818-225-7055
800-530-5728
E-mail: arthur@arthurshorr.com
www.arthurshorr.com

Arthur S Shorr, Owner
Nancy Daniels, Senior Consultant-Principal

Consultants to Health Care Providers

3991 Associated Counseling Services
8 Roberta Drive
Dartmouth, MA 02748-2020
508-992-9376

Douglas Riley, Owner

3992 Barbanell Associates
3629 Sacramento Street
San Francisco, CA 94118-1731
415-929-1155
Fax: 415-929-8485

Harriet Barbanell, Owner

3993 Barry Associates
6807 Knotty Pine Drive
Chapel Hill, NC 27517-8660
919-490-8474
Fax: 765-381-1100
E-mail: info@barryonline.com
www.barry-online.com

John S Barry MSW MBA, President

Provides technical assistance services to behavioral health
and social service organizations in the areas of performance
measurement, survey research, program evaluation, compensation system design and other selected human resource
management areas.

3994 Behavioral Health Care
6801 S Yosemite Street #201
Centennial, CO 80112-1411
303-889-4806
E-mail: bhi@bhicares.org

Julie Holtz, Chief Executive Officer
Joe Pastor M.D., Medical Director

BHI is committed to excellence in mental health service delivery. They strive to promote recovery by focusing on the
unique needs, strengths and hopes of consumers and
families.

3995 Behavioral Health Care Consultants
12 Windham Lane
Beverly, MA 01915-1568
978-921-5968
E-mail: mkatzenstein@bhcconsult.com
www.bhcconsult.com

Michael L Katzenstein, President

3996 Behavioral Health Management Group
1025 Main Street
Suite 708
Wheeling, WV 26003-2726

304-232-7232
Fax: 304-232-7245
E-mail: user655349@aol.com

William R Coburn, Practice Manager

They offer a wide range of services for men, women, adolescents, and children. The professional staff specializes in
mental and emotional disorders, marital and family counseling, group therapy, vocational counseling, alcohol and
substance abuse, academic adjustment counseling, psychological testing, biofeedback, and hypnotherapy.

3997 Behavioral Health Services
2925 Chicago Avenue
Minneapolis, MN 55407-1321
612-262-5000
www.allina.com

Richard Pettingill, President/CEO
Mary Foarde, General Counsel/Corp Secretary

Provides clinically and geographically integrated delivery
system, innovative programs and services across comprehensive continuum of care, practice guidelines development, outcomes data and quality management programs to
enhance care delivery systems.

3998 Behavioral Health Systems
2 Metroplex Drive
Suite 500
Birmingham, AL 35209-6827
205-879-1150
800-245-1150
Fax: 205-879-1095
E-mail: generalwebsite@bhs-inc.com
www.behavioralhealthsystems.com

Deborah Stephens, CEO
Kyle Strange, Senior Vice President/COO

Provides managed psychiatric and substance abuse and
drug testing services to more than 20,000 employees nationally through a network of 7,600 providers.

3999 Berkowitz Chassion and Sklar
9911 W Pico Blvd
Suite 685W
Los Angeles, CA 90035-2703
310-659-3823

Elaine D Chaisson, Contact

4000 Broward County Health Care Services
115 S Andrews Avenue
Soom A330
Fort Lauderdale, FL 33301
954-327-5390
Fax: 954-357-5897
TTY: 800-995-8711
www.broward.org/healthcare

The Health Care Section of the Community Partnership Division provide mental health, primary health care, and special health care services, as well as funding, Mahogany
Project, and the Ryan White Part A Program offices.

4001 Brown Consulting

121 N Erie Street
Toledo, OH 43604-5915
419-241-8547
800-495-6786
E-mail: info@danbrownconsulting.com
www.danbrownconsulting.com

Daniel C Brown, Owner
David Galbraith, CFO

Provides a full range of consulting services to behavioral healthcare providers. Has relationships with national, regional and state behavioral healthcare organizations.

Year Founded: 1987

4002 CBCA

10900 Hampshire Avenue S
Bloomington, MN 55438-2384
952-829-3500
800-824-3882
Fax: 952-946-7694
E-mail: info@cbca.com
www.cbca.com

Mary Dixon, Senior VP

Provides total health plan management including 24 hours a day, seven days a week patient access and demand management, care management, behavioral health care management, disease management and disability workers' compensation management, all supported by QualityFIRST clinical decision guidelines. These services are electronically integrated with HRM's national provider networks and electronic claims management. HRM's clients include HMOs, hospital systems, insurance and self-insured plans, workers' compensation and disability plans and Medicare/Medicaid plans throughout the US, Canada and New Zealand.

4003 CBI Group

310 Busse Highway
#369
Park Ridge, IL 60068-3251
847-292-6676
Fax: 847-823-0740
E-mail: jlemmer@cbipartners.com
www.cbipartners.com

4004 CIGNA Behavioral Care

11095 Viking Drive
Suite 350
Eden Prairie, MN 55344-7234
952-996-2000
800-334-8925
Fax: 952-996-2579
www.cignabehavioral.com

Keith Dixon, CEO

Provides behavioral care benefit management, EAPs, and work/life programs to consumers through health plans offered by large U.S. employers, national and regional HMOs, Taft-Hartley trusts and disability insurers.

Year Founded: 1974

4005 Cameron and Associates

6100 Lake Forrest Drive
Suite 550
Atlanta, GA 30328-3889
404-843-3399
800-334-6014
Fax: 404-843-3572
www.caiquality.com

William Cameron, Owner

Assists troubled employees and their dependents in resolving personal problems in order to provide their employer a level of acceptable job performance and efficiency, and to provide a safe working environment for all employees.

4006 Carewise

1501 4th Avenue
Suite 700
Seattle, WA 98101-3624
206-749-1100
800-755-2136
Fax: 206-749-1125
www.shps.net

Rishabh Mehrotra, President/CEO
John McCarty, Executive Vice President/CFO

4007 Casey Family Services

127 Church Street
New Haven, CT 06510-2001
203-401-6900
Fax: 203-401-6901
E-mail: info@caseyfamilyservices.org
www.caseyfamilyservices.org

Raymond L Torres, Executive Director
Michael Brennan, Co-Chairman

Year Founded: 1976

4008 Center for Health Policy Studies

40 Beaver Street
Albany, NY 12207-1530
518-426-4315

Jack Knowlton, Executive Vice President

4009 Center for the Advancement of Health

2000 Florida Avenue NW
Suite 210
Washington, DC 20009-1231
202-387-2829
Fax: 202-387-2857
E-mail: cfah@cfah.org
www.cfah.org

Jessie Gruman, Executive Director
Jessie Gruman, President

4010 Century Financial Services

185 NW Spanish River Boulevard
Boca Raton, FL 33431-4227
407-362-0111

4011 Children's Home of the Wyoming Conference, Quality Improvement
1182 Chenango Street
Binghamton, NY 13901-1653
607-772-6904
800-772-6904
Fax: 607-723-2617
E-mail: info@chowc.org

Chip Houser, President
Patricia Giglio, CFO/Chief Admin. Officer

Child care agency referred to various departments of social services, court systems, school systems for children who are at risk, have trouble in the home, or have been abused or abandoned.

4012 ChoiceCare
655 Eden Park Drive, Suite 400
Grand Baldwin Building
Cincinnati, OH 45202-6039
513-241-1400
800-543-7158
Fax: 513-684-7461
www.choicecare.com

4013 College Health IPA
7711 Center Avenue
Suite 300
Huntington Beach, CA 92647-9100
562-467-5555
800-779-3825
Fax: 562-402-2666
E-mail: info@chipa.com
www.chipa.com

Randy Davis, President/CEO
Kevin Gardiner, VP Of Financial Operations

Culturally sensitive mental health referral service.

4014 College of Dupage
425 Fawell Boulevard
Glen Ellyn, IL 60137-6599
630-790-1085
Fax: 630-942-2947
www.cod.edu

Sunil Chand, President

4015 College of Southern Idaho
315 Falls Avenue
PO Box 1238
Twin Falls, ID 83303-1238
208-733-9554
800-680-0274
Fax: 208-736-4743
E-mail: info@csi.edu
www.csi.edu

Jerry Beck, President
Jerry Gee, Executive VP/CAO

4016 Columbia Hospital M/H Services
2201 45th Street
W Palm Beach, FL 33407-2095
561-842-6141
Fax: 561-844-8955
www.columbiahospital.com

Valerie Jackson, CEO
Oon Soo Ung, CFO
Brenda Logan, CNO

250-bed acute-care facility with dedicated psychiatry, emergency psychiatry, geriatric psychiatry, inpatient and outpatient psychiatry, and partial day psychiatry units and programs.

4017 ComPsych
455 N City Front Plaza Drive
NBC Tower
Chicago, IL 60611-5377
312-595-4000
800-755-3050
Fax: 312-660-1057
E-mail: mpaskell@compsych.com
www.compsych.com

Richard A Chaifetz, CEO

Worlwide leader in guidance resources, including employee assistance programs, managed behavioral health, work-life, legal, financial, and personal convenience services. ComPsych provides services worldwide covering millions of individuals. Clients range from Fortune 100 to smaller public and private concerns, government entities, health plans and Taft-Hartley groups. Guidance Resources transforms traditionally separate services into a seamless integration of information, resources and creative solutions that address personal life challenges and improve workplace productivity and performance.

4018 Comprehensive Care Corporation
3405 W. Martin Luther King Jr. Blvd
Suite 101
Tampa, FL 33607
813-288-4808
Fax: 813-288-4844
E-mail: info@comprehensivecare.com
www.compcare.com

John M Hill, CEO
Robert Landis, Chairman/CFO/Treasurer

Offers a flexible system of services to provide comprehensive, compassionate and cost-effective mental health and substance abuse services to managed care organizations both public and private. CompCare is committed to providing state-of-the-art comprehensive care management services for all levels and phases of behavioral health care.

4019 Comprehensive Center For Pain Management
7053 W Central Avenue
Toledo, OH 43617-1114
419-843-1370
877-446-6724
E-mail: ccpminfo@cc4pm.com
www.cc4pm.com

Ron Loeffler, Manager

4020 Corphealth
1300 Summit Avenue
6th Floor
Fort Worth, TX 76102-4414
817-333-6400
800-240-8388
E-mail: businessdevelopment@corphealth.com

Patrick Gotcher II, President/CEO
Brae Jacobson, COO
Michael Baker, CFO

4021 Corporate Health Systems
15153 Technology Drive
Suite B
Eden Prairie, MN 55344-2221
952-939-0911
Fax: 952-939-0990
www.corphealthsys.com

Bob Hanalon, President

Benefits consulting firm to partner with clients to find the most flexible and comprehensive benefits packages for their investments.

4022 Counseling Associates
109 High Street
Salisbury, MD 21801-4276
410-546-1692
888-546-1692
Fax: 410-548-9056
E-mail: tim@catherapy.com
www.catherapy.com

Anne M Bass, Manager

Provides therapeutic counseling to help individuals lead productive and fulfilled lives.

4023 Covenant Home Healthcare
3615 19th Street
Lubbock, TX 79410-1209
806-725-2328
www.covenanthealth.org

Melinda Clark, CEO

Provides quality home care to patients when hospitalization may be unneccessary, or when the length of stay may be shorter than expected.

4024 Coventry Health Care of Iowa
211 Lake Drive
Newark, DE 19702-3320
302-283-6500
800-752-7242

Al Redmen, CEO

4025 Creative Health Concepts
305 Madison Avenue
Suite 2022
New York, NY 10165-2017
212-697-7207
Fax: 212-697-3509
E-mail: info@creativegroupny.com
www.creativegroupny.com

Ira Gottlieb, President/CEO
Harry Blair, Vice Chairman

4026 Cypruss Communications
430 Myrtle Ave
Suite A
Fort Lee, NJ 07024-3913
201-735-7730
800-750-5231
E-mail: peterm@cypruss.com
www.cypruss.com

Peter Miller, VP/CFO

4027 DD Fischer Consulting
8105 White Oak Road
Quincy, IL 62305-8148
217-656-3000

D D Fisher, Owner

4028 DML Training and Consulting
4228 Boxelder Place
Davis, CA 95618-6062
530-753-4300
Fax: 530-753-7500
E-mail: info@dmlmd.com
www.dmlmd.com

David Mee-Lee, Founder

4029 Deloitte and Touche LLP Management Consulting
1700 Market Street
Philadelphia, PA 19103-3913
215-405-5555

Barry Salzberg, CEO
Sharon Allen, Chairman Of The Board

4030 DeltaMetrics
600 Public Ledger Building
150 S Independence Mall West
Philadelphia, PA 19106-3413
215-399-0988
800-238-2433
Fax: 215-399-0989
www.deltametrics.com

Jack Durell, President/CEO
John Cacciola, Senior Vice President

National research, evaluation, and consulting organization dedicated to the improvement of substance abuse and other behavioral health care treatment.

4031 Diversified Group Administrators
6345 Flank Drive
PO Box 6250
Harrisburg, PA 17112-250
717-652-8040
800-877-6490
Fax: 717-652-8328
E-mail: jhoellman@dgatpa.com
www.dgatpa.com

James Hoellman, Contact

4032 Dorenfest Group
455 N Cityfront Plaza Drive
NBC Tower Suite 2725
Chicago, IL 60611-5503
312-464-3000
E-mail: info@dorenfest.com

Sheldon Dorenfest, CEO

4033 Dougherty Management Associates Health Strategies
9 Meriam Street
Suite 4
Lexington, MA 02420-5312
781-863-8003
800-817-7802
E-mail: mail@dmahealth.com
www.dmahealth.com

Richard Dougherty, Owner

Providing the public and private sectors with superior management conusulting services to improve healthcare delivery systems and manage complex organizational change.

4034 Dupage County Health Department
111 North County Farm Road
Wheaton, IL 60187-3988
630-682-7400
Fax: 630-462-9261
TDD: 630-932-1447
www.dupagehealth.org

Maureen Mc Hugh, Executive Director

4035 Echo Management Group
15 Washington Street
PO Box 2150
Conway, NH 03818-2150
603-447-8600
800-635-8209
Fax: 603-447-8680
E-mail: info@echoman.com
www.echoman.com

John Raden, CEO

Provides financial, clinical, and administrative software applications for behavioral health and social service agencies; comprehensive, fully-intergrated Human Service Information System is a powerful management tool that enables agencies to successfully operate their organizations within the stringent guidelines of managed care mandates. Provides implementation planning, training, support and systems consulting services.

4036 Elon Homes for Children
1717 Sharon Road West
Charlotte, NC 28210
704-369-2500
Fax: 704-688-2961
E-mail: info@elonhomes.org
www.elonhomes.org

Dr Frederick Grosse, President/CEO

Provides over 1,000 children and families a year in North Carolina an excellent opportunity for safe haven, life skills and education

Year Founded: 1907

4037 Employee Assistance Professionals
1234 Summer Street
Stamford, CT 06905-5558
203-977-2446

4038 Employee Benefit Specialists
Ste 400
789 Sherman St
Denver, CO 80203-3532
303-757-1234
Fax: 303-861-8147
E-mail: cfankhouser@clickebs.com

Alan Curtis, Chairman/CEO
Curtis Fankhouser, President

4039 Employee Network
1040 Vestal Parkway E
Vestal, NY 13850-2354
607-754-1043
800-364-4748
Fax: 607-754-1629
www.eniweb.com

Gene Raymondi, Owner

4040 Entropy Limited
345 South Great Road
Lincoln, MA 01773-4303
781-259-8901
Fax: 781-259-1255
E-mail: clientservices@entropylimited.com
www.entropylimited.com

Ron Christensen, Owner

Uses pattern recognition, statistics, and computer simulation to track past behavior, see current behavior and predict future behavior. Used by insuranch companies and the healthcare industry.

4041 Essi Systems
70 Otis Street
San Francisco, CA 94103-1236
415-252-8224
800-252-3774
Fax: 415-252-5732

E-mail: essi@essisystems.com
www.sesystems.com

Esther Orioli, CEO
Karen Trocki, Research Director

4042 Ethos Consulting
3219 E Camelback Road
Suite 515
Phoenix, AZ 85018-2307
480-296-3801
E-mail: conrad@ethosconsulting.com
www.ethosconsulting.com

Conrad E Prusak, President
Julie Prusak, CEO

4043 Evaluation Center at HSRI
2336 Massachusetts Avenue
Cambridge, MA 02140-1813
617-876-0426
Fax: 617-492-7401
E-mail: sjohniken@hsri.org
www.hsri.org

Sebrina Johniken, Office Manager

4044 FCS
1711 Ashley Circle
Suite 6
Bowling Green, KY 42104-5801
502-782-9152
800-783-9152
Fax: 270-782-1055
E-mail: admin@fcspsy.com
www.fcspsy.com

Bob Toth, President
Brian Browning, VP Of Client Services

4045 FPM Behavioral Health: Corporate Marketing
1276 Minnesota Avenue
Winter Park, FL 32789-4833
407-647-1781

4046 Family Managed Care
5745 Essen Lane
Suite 100
Baton Rouge, LA 70810-1104
225-215-2100
E-mail: webmaster@calaishealth.com
www.calaishealth.com

Leslie Yander, Director Human Resources
Tuan Nguyen, Information Services

Provider of managed behavioral healthcare and employee assistance programs.

4047 Findley, Davies and Company
300 Madison Avenue
Suite 1000
Toledo, OH 43604-1525

419-255-1360
Fax: 419-259-5685
www.findleydavies.com

Marc Stockwell, VP

4048 First Consulting Group
1160 West Swedesford Road
Building One, Suite 200
Berwyn, PA 19312

800-345-7672
www.csc.com

Larry Ferguson, CEO
Thomas Watford, COO/CFO

Around the world and across the healthcare spectrum, First Consulting Group is transforming healthcare with better information for better decisions.

4049 First Corp-Health Consulting
38 W Fulton Street
Suite 300
Grand Rapids, MI 49503-2644
616-676-3258
Fax: 616-676-0846
www.corphealth.com

Patrick Gotcher, President and CEO
Brae Jacobson, Chief Operating Officer

Year Founded: 1989

4050 Fowler Healthcare Affiliates
2000 Riveredge Parkway
Suite 920
Atlanta, GA 30328-4600
770-261-6363
800-784-9829
Fax: 770-261-6361
www.fowler-consulting.com

Frances J Fowler, Owner

Developed innovative solutions for managing cost of high cost patients.

4051 Freedom To Fly
27871 Medical Center Road
Ste. 285
Mission Viejo, CA 92691-6404
949-364-1833
Fax: 949-364-1365

Ralph J Tassinari, Owner

4052 Full Circle Programs
70 Skyview Terrace
San Rafael, CA 94903-1845
415-499-3320
E-mail: dmeshel@fc-fi.org
www.fullcircleprograms.org

David Meshel, Contact

Actively disseminates knowledge through training and technical assistace, advocating for policies that support best practices, services and outcomes for children and families.

Year Founded: 1971

4053 GMR Group
755 Business Center Drive
Suite 250
Horsham, PA 19044-3491
215-653-7401
Fax: 215-653-7982
E-mail: webmaster@gmrgroup.com
www.gmrgroup.com

Barron J Ginnetti, CEO
Thomas Bishop, Vice President/COO

Provides strategic and tactical solutions to the marketing and sales challenges their clients face in the managed healthcare environment.

4054 Garner Consulting
630 North Rosemead Blvd
Suite 300
Pasadena, CA 91107-2138
626-351-2300
Fax: 626-371-0447
E-mail: info@garnerconsulting.com
www.garnerconsulting.com

John Garner, CEO
Gerti Reagan Garner, President

Provides innovative consultation, which produces immediate, bottom line results and long term value.

4055 Gaynor and Associates
100 Whitney Avenue
New Haven, CT 06510-1265
203-865-0865
Fax: 203-865-0093
E-mail: mlg110@columbia.edu

Mark Gaynor LCSW, Principle

Clinical social work provider, EAP services, and clinical practice. Specialty weight management

4056 Geauga Board of Mental Health, Alcohol and Drug Addiction Services
13244 Ravenna Road
Chardon, OH 44024-9012
440-285-2282
E-mail: info@geauga.org
www.geauga.org

Jim Adams, Executive Director

4057 Glazer Medical Solutions
P.O. Box 121
Beach Plum Lane
Menemsha, MA 02552
508-645-9635
Fax: 508-645-3212

E-mail: glazermedicalsol@aol.com
www.glazmedsol.com

William Glazer, President/Founder

Glazer Medical Solutions is a national medical education consortium that has facilitated a comprehensive matrix of medical education services since 1994.

4058 HCA Healthcare
1 Park Plaza
Nashville, TN 37203-6527
615-344-9551
www.hcahealthcare.com

Richard Bracken, President/CEO

4059 HPN Worldwide
119 W Vallette Street
Elmhurst, IL 60126-4419
630-941-9030
Fax: 630-941-9064
E-mail: info@hpn.com
www.hpn.com

Bob Gorsky, Owner
Year Founded: 1983

4060 HSP Verified
1120 G Street NW
Suite 330
Washington, DC 20005-3893
202-783-7663
Fax: 202-347-0550
www.nationalregister.org

Judy E Hall, CEO

Offers comprehensive, innovative credential verification services designed to help you find that precious time. It relieves health care providers and management of tedious administrative activities-leaving time and resources to focus on quality health care. Provides valuable information and cultivates alliances between cutting edge health care organizations/plans and qualified health care providers.

4061 Hays Group
1133 20th Street NW
Suite 450
Washington, DC 20036-3452
202-263-4000
E-mail: info@hayscompanies.com

4062 Health Alliance Plan
2850 W Grand Boulevard
Detroit, MI 48202-2692
313-872-8100
800-422-4641
Fax: 313-664-8479
TDD: 313-664-8000

Fran Parker, CEO
Ronald Berry, Senior Vice President/CFO

4063 Health Capital Consultants

1143 Olivette Executive Pkwy
Saint Louis, MO 63132-3205
314-994-7641
800-394-8258
Fax: 314-991-3435
E-mail: solutions@healthcapital.com
www.healthcapital.com

Robert Cimasi, President

4064 Health Decisions

409 Plymouth Road
Suite 220
Plymouth, MI 48170-1834
734-451-2230
www.healthdecisions.com

Si Nahra, Owner

4065 Health Management Associates

5811 Pelican Bay Boulevard
Suite 500
Naples, FL 34108-2711
239-598-3131
Fax: 239-597-5794
www.hma.com

Gary D Newsome, CEO
Robert Farnham, Senior Vice President/CFO

4066 Health Systems Research

1200 18th Street NW
Suite 700
Washington, DC 20036-2531
202-828-5100
Fax: 202-728-9469
www.hsrnet.com

Lincoln Smith, President/CEO
Mark Kielb, Senior Vice President/CFO

4067 HealthPartners

2701 University Avenue SE
Minneapolis, MN 55414-3233
952-967-7992
TTY: 612-627-3584

Mary Brainerd, President/CEO

4068 Healthcare Value Management Group

3200 Highland Avenue
Downers Grove, IL 60515-1282
630-434-1678

Ronald Blaine Faulkner, COO

Consulting practice providing information technology, operations and provider contracting consultitative services.

4069 Healthcare in Partnership

3230 73rd Avenue SE
Mercer Island, WA 98040-3415

206-232-6300
E-mail: mhrnllc@comcast.net

Lawrence Jacobson, Manager

Health care consulting including managed care contract negotiation, IPA development, provider support. Specializes in behavioral health.

4070 Healthwise

2601 N Bogus Basin Road
Boise, ID 83702-909
208-345-1161
800-706-9646
Fax: 208-345-1897
www.healthwise.org

Donald W Kemper, CEO
Jim Giuffre, President/COO

4071 Healthy Companies

2101 Wilson Boulevard
Suite 1002
Arlington, VA 22201-3048
703-351-9902
www.healthycompanies.com

Robert Rosen, Owner
Eric Sass, COO
Robert Rosen, Chairman/CEO

4072 HeartMath

14700 W Park Avenue
Boulder Creek, CA 95006-9318
831-338-8700
Fax: 831-338-9861
E-mail: ihminquiry@heartmath.org

Bruce Cryer, President

HeartMath's Freze-Framer Interactive Learning System is an innovative approach to stress relief based on learning to change the heart rhythm pattern and create physiological coherence in the body. The Freeze-Framer has been widely used with clients to help them develop internal awareness, self-recognition and emotional management skills. Clients can learn to prevent stress by becoming aware of when the stress response starts and stopping it in the moment and taking a more active role in preventing stress, managing the emotions associated with stress, creating better health and improving performance.

4073 Helms & Company

1 Pillsbury Street
Suite 200
Concord, NH 03301-3556
603-225-6633
Fax: 603-225-4739
E-mail: info@helmsco.com
www.helmsco.com

J Michael Degnan, President

They are a New Hampshire based behavioral health management company offering managed behavioral healthcare services, community service programs, and employee assistance programs for health care insurers, members, employers and their employees.

4074 Horizon Behavioral Services
2941 South Lake Vista Drive
Lewisville, TX 75067-3801
972-420-8300
800-931-4646
Fax: 972-420-8252

Mike Saul, President

Provider of national managed care, utilization management and employee assistance programs. Horizon will work in collaboration with HMOs, insurance companies, employers and hospitals to develop seamless, cost-effective managed care services including practitioner panel formation, information system development, utilization management services, EAPs, outcomes measurement systems and sales and marketing functions.

4075 Horizon Mental Health Management
2941 South Lake Vista Drive
Lewisville, TX 75067-3801
972-420-8200
800-931-4646
Fax: 972-420-8383
E-mail: cindy.novak@horizonhealth.com

Johan Smith, VP

Inpatient, outpatient, partial hospitalization and home health psychiatric programs.

4076 Human Affairs International
10150 Centennial Parkway
Sandy, UT 84070-4103
801-256-7000
Fax: 801-256-7669

4077 Human Behavior Associates
1350 Hayes Street
Suite B-100
Benicia, CA 94510-2970
707-747-0117
800-937-7770
Fax: 707-747-6646
E-mail: jameswallace@callhba.com
www.callhba.com

James B Wallace PhD, President
Yolanda Calderon, Operations Manager

National provider of emploee assistance programs, managed behavioral healthcare services, critical incident stress management services, conflict management, organizational consultation, and substance abuse professional services. Maintains a network of 6500 licensed mental health care providers and 650 hospitals and treatment centers nationwide.

4078 Human Services Research Institute
2336 Massachusetts Avenue
Cambridge, MA 02140-1886
617-876-0426
Fax: 617-491-7902

E-mail: sjohniken@hsri.org
www.hsri.org
Val Bradley, President

4079 Hyde Park Associates
1515 E 52nd Place
3rd Floor
Chicago, IL 60615-4390
773-493-8212

Darlene Clark, Manager

4080 IHC Behavioral Health Network
36 S State Street
Floor 22
Salt Lake City, UT 84111-1624
801-442-3462
E-mail: contactus@intermountainmail.org

Kem Gardner, Chairman
Kent Murdock, Vice Chairman

4081 Insurance Management Institute
6 Stafford Court
Mount Holly, NJ 08060-3281
609-267-8998
Fax: 609-267-2472
E-mail: TIMInstitute@aol.com
www.timinstitute.com

Michael C Hill, Management Consultant/Author

4082 Interface EAP
10370 Richmond Avenue
Suite 1100
Houston, TX 77042-4174
713-781-3364
Fax: 713-784-3241
E-mail: info@ieap.com

Fred Newman, Owner
Tina Pace, CFO

4083 Interim Physicians
1040 Crown Pointe Pkwy
Ste. 120
Atlanta, GA 30338-4777
770-379-1245
800-226-6347
E-mail: info@interimphysicians.com

Jane Hinton, Vice President Of Operations
Michael Slupecki, CFO/Treasurer

4084 Interlink Health Services
4660 Belknap Court
Suite 209
Hillsboro, OR 97124-8401
503-640-2000
800-599-9119
Fax: 503-640-2028

E-mail: administration@interlinkhealth.com
www.interlinkhealth.com

Sherrie Simmons, Manager
Scott Ray, SVP/General Counsel

4085 JM Oher and Associates
10 Tanglewild Plaza
Suite 100
Chappaqua, NY 10514
914-238-0607
www.oherandassociates.com

Jim Oher, Founder

4086 Jeri Davis Marketing Consultants
P.O. Box 770534
Memphis, TN 38177-534
901-763-0696
E-mail: inquiries@jeridavisinternational.com
www.jeridavisinternational.com

Jeri Davis, Founder/President

4087 John Maynard and Associates
258 Spruce Street
Suite 1000
Boulder, CO 80302-4906
303-444-6300
E-mail: ceo@eap-association.org

4088 Johnson, Bassin and Shaw
8630 Fenton Street
12th Floor
Silver Spring, MD 20910-3806
301-495-1080
Fax: 301-587-4352
E-mail: info@jbsinternational.com
www.jbs.biz

Jerri Shaw, President
Gail Bassin, Chair Of The Board/Treasurer

4089 KAI Associates
6001 Montrose Road
Suite 920
Rockville, MD 20852-4874
301-770-2730
Fax: 301-770-4183
E-mail: kai@kai-research.com
www.kai-research.com

Selma Kunitz, President
Rene Kozloff, Executive Vice President

4090 Kushner and Company
1050 17th Street NW
Suite 810
Washington, DC 20036-5514
202-857-8009
E-mail: info@kushnerco.com

Hallock Northcott, President

4091 Lake Mental Health Consultants
54 Hospital Drive
Osage Beach, MO 65065-3050
573-348-8000
www.lakeregional.com

Michael Henze, CEO
Vicki Franklin, SVP Of Operations/COO

4092 Legacy Consulting Insurance Services
811 W. Fremont Street
Suite B
Stockton, CA 95203-2703
209-546-0402
E-mail: charless@legacyconsult.com

Charlynn Harless, President/CEO

4093 Lewin Group
3130 Fairview Park Drive
Suite 800
Falls Church, VA 22042-4517
703-269-5500
Fax: 703-269-5501
E-mail: lisa.chimento@lewin.com
www.lewin.com

Tracy Tsutaki, Senior VP

4094 Lifelink Corporation
331 S York Road
Suite 206
Bensenville, IL 60106-2673
630-521-8281
Fax: 630-860-5130
www.lifelink.org

Timothy Rhodes, President/CEO

Provides therapy services in Spanish for children, families and couples. Offers substance abuse treatment and educational groups for men who batter in English and Spanish. Provides comprehensive services to Latina victims of domestic violence and their children in Spanish.

4095 Lifespan Care Management Agency
600 Frederick Street
Santa Cruz, CA 95062-2203
831-469-4900
Fax: 831-469-4950
E-mail: info@lifespancare.com
www.lifespancare.com

Pamela Goodman, Owner
Pamela Goodman, President

Comprehensive care management for adults who need care.

4096 MCF Consulting
25 Bragg Drive
Lake Meade, PA 17316-9342

717-259-6631
Fax: 717-259-6537
E-mail: mcfconsulting@pa.aldelphia.net

Mark C Fox, President

MCF Consulting has demonstrated accomplishments in: developing managed care and management service organization (MSO) capabilities; managed Medicaid strategic planning efforts; Information System analysis and design contracts; product development projects; pricing and product positioning; business plan and marketing plan development; proposal development; organizational change; and creating joint ventures and partnerships. Clients have included managed care firms, provider groups, hospital systems, state and county governments and diverse contract agencies.

4097 MCG Telemedicine Center
1120 15th Street
EA - 100
Augusta, GA 30912-6
706-721-6616
Fax: 706-721-7270
E-mail: ekhasanshina@mail.mcg.edu
www.mcg.edu/telehealth

Max Stachura, Director
Brenda Starnes, Center Manager

Involved with the delivery of mental health services via telemedicine. In addition, the Telemedicine Center maintains the Georgia Mental Health Network website, a comprehensive listing of mental health resources in the State.

4098 MCW Department of Psychiatry and Behavioral Medicine
8701 Watertown Plank
Milwaukee, WI 53226-3548
414-456-4362
E-mail: aodya@mcw.edu

Laura Roberts, Chair

4099 MMHR
2550 University Avenue W
Suite 4358
Saint Paul, MN 55114-1052
651-647-1900
Fax: 651-647-1861
E-mail: tquesnell@hmr.net
www.mentalhealthinc.com

Tim Quesnell, Administrator

4100 MSI International
245 Peachtree Center Avenue
Suite 2500
Atlanta, GA 30303-1248
404-659-5236
800-511-0383
Fax: 404-659-7139
E-mail: wayne-whatley@msi-intl.com
www.msi-intl.com

Eric Lindberg, President/CEO
Mike Didomenico, Vice President

4101 Magellan Health Service
6950 Columbia Gateway Drive
Columbia, MD 21046-3308
410-953-1000
800-458-2740
www.magellanhealth.com

Maryann Owens, Manager
Mark Demilio, CFO

Provides members with high quality, clinically appropriate, affordable health care which is tailored to each individual's needs.

4102 Magellan Public Solutions
222 Berkeley Street
Suite 1350
Boston, MA 02116-3777
617-661-2851
800-947-0071
Fax: 617-790-4848

4103 Managed Care Concepts
PO Box 812032
Boca Raton, FL 33481-2032
561-750-2240
800-899-3926
Fax: 561-750-4621
E-mail: info@theemployeeassistanceprogram.com
www.theemployeeassistanceprogram.com

Beth Harrell, Corporate Contacts Director
Ginger Minnelonica, Administrative Assistant

Provides comprehensive EAP services to large and small companies in the United States and parts of Canada. Also provides child/elder care referrals, drug free workplace program services, consultation and training services.

4104 Managed Care Consultants
11461 N 109 Way
Scottsdale, AZ 85259-3029
480-391-2992

4105 Managed Health Network
503 Canal Boulevard
Port Richmond, CA 94804-3517
415-491-7200
800-327-2133
TDD: 800-735-2929
E-mail: mhnfeedback@mhn.com
www.mhn.com

Steven Sell, President/CEO
Juanell Hefner, COO

Provides high-quality, cost-effective behavioral health care services to the public sector.

4106 Managed Healthcare Consultants
1907 London Lane
Wilmington, NC 28405-4210
910-256-6196

Daniel Patterson, Contact

4107 Managed Networks of America
905 E Horseshoe Court
Virginia Beach, VA 23451-5924
757-425-2173
E-mail: mnamerica@aol.com

Matthew Weinstein, Owner

Management services that include strategic and business plan development, new corporate formations and contractual affiliations, product and infrastructure development, implementation, and management. Organizes cost effective provider networks which include a full continuum of care and services while supplying the necessary clinical, administrative, and financial systems to enable effective management of populations across varied geographic areas.

4108 Maniaci Insurance Services
500 Silver Spur Road
Suite 121
Palos Verdes, CA 90275-3674
310-541-4824
866-541-4824
Fax: 310-377-2016
E-mail: mail@maniaciinsurance.com
www.maniaciinsurance.com

Dan Maniaci, Owner
Dan Maniaci, President
Kristy Maniaci, Director Of Operations

4109 Marin Institute
24 Belvedere Street
San Rafael, CA 94901-4817
415-456-5692
Fax: 415-456-0491
E-mail: info@marininstitute.org
www.marininstitute.org

Bruce Livingston, Executive Director
Julio Rodriguez, Vice President
Larry Meredith, Treasurer

4110 Mayes Group
PO Box 399
Saint Peters, PA 19470-399
610-469-6900
Fax: 610-469-6088

Abby Mayes, President/Founder

Retained executive search firm that specializes exclusively in managed care/behavioral healthcare since 1982. Offices in Pennsylvania and Florida.

Year Founded: 1982

4111 McGladery and Pullen CPAs
3600 American Blvd W.
Third Floor
Bloomington, MN 55431-1082
952-835-9930
888-214-1416

Fax: 952-921-7702
www.mcgladrey.com

Tony Ceci, Partner

4112 McGraw Hill Healthcare Management
1221 Avenue of the Americas
New York, NY 10020-1001
212-512-2000
Fax: 212-512-3840
E-mail: customer.service@mcgraw-hill.com

Glenn S Goldberg, President
Robert Bahash, Executive Vice President/CFO

4113 McKesson HBO and Company
5995 Windwrad Parkway
Alphretta, GA 30005-4184
404-338-6000
Fax: 404-338-5112

Craig Niemiec, Senior VP

4114 Menninger Care Systems
4006 Belt Line Road
Suite 205
Addison, TX 75001-5831

800-866-7242
Fax: 972-931-1938
E-mail: servicenow@mhnet.com
www.mhneteap.com

Wesley Brockhoeft, President/CEO
Robert Wilson, CFO

4115 Mental Health Network
Stonebridge Plaza I
9606 N MoPac Expressway, Suite 600
Austin, TX 78759-5952
512-347-7900
Fax: 512-347-1810
www.mhnet.com

Wesley Brockhoeft, President/CEO
Robert Wilson, CFO

Health care management and solutions company providing employee assistance programs (EAP), work life programs, managed behavioral health care and consulting services.

4116 Mercer Consulting
200 Clarendon Street
Boston, MA 02116-5026
617-424-3930
Fax: 617-424-3300

M. Michele Burns, Chairman/CEO
Tom Elliott, Chief Operating Officer

4117 Meridian Resource Corporation
1401 Enclave Parkway
Suite 300
Houston, TX 77077-2054

281-597-7000
Fax: 281-597-8880

Paul Ching, CEO
Lloyd Delano, SVP/Chief Accounting Officer
Michael Mayell, President/COO

4118 Mesa Mental Health
PO Box 90607
Albuquerque, NM 87199-607
505-816-6791
800-333-8829
Fax: 505-816-6702
E-mail: chr@mesamentalhealth.com
www.mesamentalhealth.com

4119 Mihalik Group
1300 W Belmont
Suite 500
Chicago, IL 60657-3242
773-929-4276
E-mail: zorinag@themihalikgroup.com
www.themihalikgroup.com

Zorina Granjean, Contact

4120 Milliman, Inc
1099 18th Street
Suite 3100
Denver, CO 80202-1931
303-299-9400
Fax: 303-299-9018
www.milliman.com

Megan Maguire, Manager

Assist plans and payors in measuring and analyzing their healthcare costs arising from behavioral health conditions, identifying specific value opportunities, and designing innovative ways to obtain increased quality and value from behavioral health care delivery.

4121 Murphy-Harpst-Vashti
740 Fletcher Street
Cedartown, GA 30125-3297
770-748-1500
Fax: 770-749-1094
E-mail: contact@murphyharpst.org
www.murphyharpst.org

Joanne Simmons, President
Emily Saltino, VP Of Development

4122 NASW JobLink
750 First Street NE
Suite 700
Washington, DC 20002-8011
202-408-8600
Fax: 202-336-8313
E-mail: membership@naswdc.org
www.naswnc.org

Robert Arnold, Manager
Willie Walker, Vice President

4123 National Empowerment Center
599 Canal Street
Lawrence, MA 01840-1244
978-685-1494
800-769-3728
Fax: 978-681-6426
E-mail: info4@power2u.org

Dan Fisher, Executive Director

Consumer/survivor/ex-patient run organization that carries a message of recovery, empowerment, hope and healing to people who have been diagnosed with mental illness.

4124 New Day
49 Music Square W
Suite 502
Nashville, TN 37203-3272
615-321-5577
Fax: 615-321-5566
E-mail: info@seniorhealthinc.com
www.seniorhealthinc.com

William Kaupas, VP Of Business Development
Kerri Kelley Frye, Vice President/CFO

Develops and manages successful mental health units by utilizing clinical operations and information systems to set quality, low cost standards in diagnosing and treating psychiatric conditions.

4125 New England Psych Group
10 Langley Road
Suite 305
Newton Center, MA 02459-1972
617-527-4055
Fax: 617-527-2571

4126 Newbride Consultation
280 Madison Avenue
Suite 1004
New York, NY 10016-808
516-665-7889
E-mail: info@couplesandfamilies.com
www.couplesandfamilies.com

Cari Sans, Founder And Director

4127 Northpointe Behavioral Healthcare Systems
715 Pyle Drive
Kingsford, MI 49802-4456
906-774-0522
Fax: 906-779-1306
E-mail: info@nbhs.org
www.nbhs.org

Karen Thekan, CEO
Anastasia Babladelis, Secretary

Michigan Community Mental Health agency serving Dickinson, Menominee and Iron counties. Provides a full spectrum of managed behavioral healthcare services to the chronically mentally ill and developmentally disabled. A corporate services division provides employee assistance programs both in Michigan and outside the state.

4128 Oklahoma Mental Health Consumer Council
3200 NW 48th Street
Suite 102
Oklahoma City, OK 73112-5911
405-604-6975
888-424-1305
E-mail: consumercouncil@okmhcc.org
www.omhcc.org

Becky Tallent, Executive Director
Jerry Risenhoover, Vice President

4129 One Hundred Top Series
Dorland Healthcare Information
1500 Walnut Street
Suite 1000
Philadelphia, PA 19102-3512
215-875-1212
800-784-2332
Fax: 215-735-3966
E-mail: info@dorlandhealth.com
www.dorlandhealth.com

A leader in health and managed care business information.
$495.00

Year Founded: 1999

4130 Optimum Care Corporation
30011 Ivy Glenn Drive
Suite 219
Laguna Niguel, CA 92677-5018
949-495-1100
Fax: 949-495-4316
www.optimumcare.net

Edward A Johnson, CEO

4131 Options Health Care
240 Corporate Boulevard
Norfolk, VA 23502-4900
757-393-0859
www.valueoptions.com

Barbara B Hill, CEO
Michele Alfano, Chief Operating Officer

Specializes in creating innovative services for a full range of at-risk and administrative services only benefits, including behavioral health programs, customized provider and facility networks, utilization and case management, EAPs and youth services.

4132 PMHCC
123 S Broad Street
23rd Floor
Philadelphia, PA 19109-1029
215-546-0300
Fax: 215-732-1606
E-mail: PMHCCExecOffice@pmhcc.org
www.pmhcc.org

Bernard Borislow, Executive Director
Jay Centifanti, Treasurer

4133 PRO Behavioral Health
7600 E Eastman Avenue
Ste. 500
Denver, CO 80231-4375
303-695-8007
888-687-6755
Fax: 303-695-0100
E-mail: webmaster@probh.com
www.probh.com

Martin Dubin, Senior Vice President
Theodore Wirecki, Chair

A managed behavioral health care company dedicated to containing psychiatric and substance abuse costs while providing high-quality health care. Owned and operated by mental health care professionals, PRO has exclusive, multi-year contracts with HMOs and insurers on both coasts and in the Rocky Mountain region.

4134 PSIMED Corporation
725 Town & Country
Suite 200
Orange, CA 92868-4723
714-689-1544
E-mail: response@arbormed.com
www.psimed-ambs.com

Suzanne Beals, Contact

4135 Paris International Corporation
185 Great Neck Rd
Ste. 305
Great Neck, NY 11021-3352
516-487-2630
Fax: 516-466-6255
E-mail: info@parisintl.com
www.parisint.com

Stuart Paris, Owner

4136 Pearson
5601 Green Valley Drive
Bloomington, MN 55437-1187
952-681-3000
800-627-7271
Fax: 952-681-3549
E-mail: pearsonassessments@pearson.com

Jerry Wesbecher, VP

pearson is a publisher of assessment tools and instructional materials in the special needs behavior management, speech, language, and mental health markets. Among their numerous products are the MMPI-2, million inventories, BASC-2, BASC monitor for ADHD, vineland adaptive behavior scales(vineland II) and the Peabody picture vocabulary test (PPVT-4).

4137 Persoma Management
2540 Monroeville Blvd
Monroeville, PA 15146-2329

412-823-5155
Fax: 412-823-8262
www.persoma.com

James Long, President
Richard Heil Jr., Staff Member

4138 Perspectives
20 N Clark Street
Suite 2650
Chicago, IL 60602-5104
312-558-5318
800-866-7556
Fax: 312-558-1570
E-mail: info@perspectivesltd.com
www.perspectivesltd.com

Bernard Dyme, Owner

4139 Philadelphia Health Management
260 S Broad Street
18th Floor
Philadelphia, PA 19102-5000
215-985-2500
Fax: 215-985-2550
E-mail: info@phmc.org

Richard J Cohen, CEO
John Loeb, Senior Vice President

4140 Pinal Gila Behavioral Health Association
2066 W Apache Trail
Suite 116
Apache Junction, AZ 85120-3733
480-982-1317
800-982-1317
Fax: 480-982-7320
E-mail: info@pgbha.org
www.pgbha.org

Sandie Smith, President
Bryan Chambers, Vice President

4141 Porter Novelli
75 Varick Street
6th Floor
New York, NY 10013-1946
212-601-8400
Fax: 212-601-8101
E-mail: chris.lynch@porternovelli.com
www.porternovelli.com

Gary Stockman, CEO
Gloria Ketenbaum, VP Of Marketing/Public Relations

4142 Practice Management Resource Group
4100 Redwood Road #283
Oakland, CA 94619-2363
708-623-8200
Fax: 708-507-2932
E-mail: info@medicalpmrg.com
www.medicalpmrg.com

Ron Rosenberg, President/Founder

4143 Preferred Mental Health Management
401 E. Douglas
Suite 300
Wichita, KS 67202-3411
316-262-0444
800-264-7496
Fax: 316-262-0003
E-mail: info@pmhm.com
www.pmhm.com

Courtney Ruthven, Owner

Offers managed care services and EAP services.

4144 ProMetrics CAREeval
480 American Avenue
King of Prussia, PA 19406-4060
610-265-6353
Fax: 610-265-8377
E-mail: admin@prometrics.com
www.prometrics.com

Marc Duey, Owner

A joint venture formed by Father Flanagan's Home (Boys Town), Susquehanna Pathfinders and ProMetrics Consulting. These organizations combine years of experience as service providers and technical resource developers. Provides innovative ways to collect, store and analyze service outcome data to improve the effectiveness of your services.

4145 ProMetrics Consulting & Susquehanna PathFinders
480 American Avenue
King of Prussia, PA 19406-4060
610-265-6353
Fax: 610-265-8377
E-mail: admin@prometrics.com
www.prometrics.com

Marc Duey, Owner

4146 Process Strategies Institute
1418 D MacCorkle Ave SW
Charleston, WV 25303-1331
304-348-1436
Fax: 304-348-1262
www.highlandhospital.com

Lois Nelson, Manager

4147 Professional Risk Management Services
1515 Wilson Boulevard
Suite 800
Arlington, VA 22209-2434
703-907-3800
800-245-3333
Fax: 703-276-9530
E-mail: tracy@prms.com
www.prmsva.com

Martin Tracy, CEO
Joseph Detorie, Executive Vice President/CFO

4148 Providence Behavioral Health Connections
10300 SW Eastridge Street
Portland, OR 97225-5004
503-216-4984

4149 Psy Care
4550 Kearny Villa Road
Suite 116
San Diego, CA 92123-1583
858-279-1223

James Adams, Board Certified Psychiatrist
Lauren Beauchamp, Psychologist

4150 PsycHealth
922 Davis Street
Evanston, IL 60201-3605
847-864-4961
800-753-5456
Fax: 847-864-9930
E-mail: administration@psychealthltd.com
www.psychealthltd.com

Janet O'Brien, Manager

Specialists providing mental health services, managed care
and referrals.

4151 Psychiatric Associates
6720 Las Colinas Dr
Temple, TX 76502-5569
765-453-9338
Fax: 765-455-2710

Alok Sarda M.D., Contact

4152 Psycho Medical Chirologists
11612 Lockwood Drive
Suite 103
Silver Spring, MD 20904-2314
301-681-6614

Robert F Spiegel, Director

4153 Public Consulting Group
148 State Street
10th Floor
Boston, MA 02109-2589
617-426-2026
800-210-6113
Fax: 617-426-4632

William S Mosakowski, CEO

4154 Pyrce Healthcare Group
7325 Greenfield Street
River Forest, IL 60305-1256
708-383-7700
E-mail: phg-inc@ix.netcom.com

Janice M Pyrce, President/Founder

A national consulting firm, founded in 1990, with a focus
on behavioral health. The firm specializes in strategic planning, market research, integrated delivery systems, business
development, retreat facilitation and
management/organizational development. PHG offers significant depth of resources, with direct involvement of experienced senior staff. Clients include hospitals, healthcare
systems, academic medical centers, human service agencies, physician/allied practices, professional/trade associations and investor groups. The firm has over 200
organizations with locations in over 40 states.

4155 Quinco Behavioral Health Systems
720 N Marr Road
Columbus, IN 47201-6660
812-379-2341
800-266-2341
E-mail: quincobhs@quincoinc.com
www.centerstone.org

Robert Williams, CEO

Nonprofit mental health care provider serving south central
Indiana. 24 hour crisis line and full continuum of mental
health services.

4156 Sandra Fields-Neal and Associates
535 S Burdick Street
Suite 165
Kalamazoo, MI 49007-5261
269-381-5213
Fax: 269-381-4375

Sandra Fields Neal, Owner

4157 Sarmul Consultants
1 Strawberry Hill Court
Stamford, CT 06902-2548
203-327-1596
Fax: 203-325-1639

4158 Schafer Consulting
602 Hemlock Road
Coraopolis, PA 15108-9140
724-695-0652
E-mail: ask@schaferconsulting.com
www.schaferconsulting.com

Steve Schafer, Owner

4159 Scheur and Associates
1 Gateway Center
Suite 810
Newton, MA 02458-2804
617-969-7500
Fax: 617-969-7508
E-mail: webmaster@scheur.com
www.scheur.com

Barry Scheur, President

**4160 Sciacca Comprehensive Service Development
for MIDAA**
299 Riverside Drive
New York, NY 10025-5278

212-866-5935
Fax: 212-666-1942
E-mail: ksciacca@pobox.com

Kathleen Sciacca MA, Executive Director/Consultant

Provides consulting, education, and training for treatment and program development for dual diagnosis of mental illness and substance disorders including severe mental illness. Materials available include manuals, videos, articles, book chapters, journals, and books. Trains in Motivational Interviewing.

4161 Seelig and Company: Child Welfare and Behavioral Healthcare
140 E 45th Street
19th Floor
New York, NY 10017-7143
212-655-3500
www.meisterseelig.com

Mark J Seelig, President

4162 Sheppard Pratt Health Plan
6501 N Charles Street
Baltimore, MD 21204-6893
410-938-3800
E-mail: info@sheppardpratt.org
www.sheppardpratt.org

Steven S Sharfstein, CEO
Diana Ramsay, Executive Vice President/COO

4163 Shueman and Associates
PO Box 90024
Pasadena, CA 91109
626-585-8248

4164 Specialized Alternatives for Families & Youth of America (SAFY)
10100 Elida Road
Delphos, OH 45833-9056
419-695-8010
800-532-7239
Fax: 419-695-0004
E-mail: webmaster@safy.org
www.safy.org

Dru Whitaker, CEO
John Hollenkamp, SVP Of Finance

Not-for-profit managerial service organization providing a full continuum of quality care to families and youth across the nation.

4165 Specialized Therapy Associates
83 Summit Avenue
Hackensack, NJ 07601-1262
201-488-6678
Fax: 201-488-6224
E-mail: stadocs@hotmail.com
www.specializedtherapy.com

Vanessa Gourdine, Executive Director
Linda Mack, Assistant Director

4166 St. Anthony Behavioral Medicine Center, Behavioral Medicine
1000 N Lee Avenue
Oklahoma City, OK 73102-1036
405-272-7000
800-227-6964
Fax: 405-272-7075
E-mail: st_anthony@ssmhc.com

Joe Hodges, President

4167 Suburban Research Associates
107 Chesley Drive
Unit 4
Media, PA 19063-1760
610-891-9024
Fax: 610-891-9699
E-mail: mmcnichol@suburbanresearch.com
www.suburbanresearch.com

Mary Beth Mc Nichol, Manager

4168 Sue Krause and Associates
15 Jutland Road
Binghamton, NY 13903-1336
607-771-8009

Sue Krause, Contact

4169 Supportive Systems
25 Beachway Drive
Suite C
Indianapolis, IN 46224-8506
317-788-4111
800-660-6645
Fax: 317-788-7783
E-mail: staff@supportivesystems.com
www.supportivesystems.com

Pam Ruster, Owner

4170 TASC
1500 N Halsted Street
Chicago, IL 60642-2588
312-376-0950
Fax: 312-376-5889
E-mail: information@tasc-il.org
www.tasc-il.org

Wil Brown, Manager
Pamela Rodriguez, Executive Vice President
Roy Fesmire, Vice President/CFO

4171 The Kennion Group Inc
1200 Corporate Drive
Suite G-50
Birmingham, AL 35242-2942
205-972-0110
800-645-8058
Fax: 205-969-1199
www.kennion.com

W. Hal Shepherd, President/CEO

4172 Towers Perrin Integrated Heatlh Systems Consulting
335 Madison Avenue
New York, NY 10017-4611
212-309-3400
www.towersperrin.com

Mark Mactas, Chairman/CEO
Maureen Breakiron-Evans, CFO

Managed behavorial health care consultants specializing in strategy and operations, clinical effectiveness, actuarial and reimbursement and human resources for both the provider and the payer sides.

4173 Traumatic Incident Reduction Newsletter
Traumatic Incident Reduction Association
5145 Pontiac Trail
Ann Arbor, MI 48105-9279
734-761-6268
800-499-2751
Fax: 734-663-6861
E-mail: info@tir.org
www.tirbook.org

Victor Volkam, Author

Traumatic Incident Reduction is a brief, person-sentered treatment for the affects of trauma and loss. This newsletter offers part of the larger subject of Applied Metapsychology, which addresses relationship, self-esteem and well-being issues of all sorts, including traumatic stress. Additional web site for TIR: www.tir.org.

16 pages 2 per year

4174 United Behavioral Health
425 Market Street
27th Floor
San Francisco, CA 94105-2406
415-547-5000
800-888-2998
www.unitedbehavioralhealth.com

Gregory A Bayer, CEO
Rhonda Robinson-Beale, Chief Medical Officer

4175 University of North Carolina School of Social Work, Behavioral Healthcare
Tate-Turner-Kuralt Building
325 Pittsboro Street Cb#3550
Chapel Hill, NC 27599-1
919-962-1225
Fax: 919-962-0890
E-mail: ssw@unc.edu
www.http://ssw.unc.edu

4176 Value Health
525 Knotter Dr
Cheshire, CT 06410-1100
203-272-3856

4177 ValueOptions
240 Corporate Blvd
Norfolk, VA 23502-4900
757-393-0859
www.valueoptions.com

Barbara B Hill, CEO
Michele Alfano, COO

Designs and operates innovative administrative and full-risk services for a wide range of behavioral health and chemical dependency programs, Medicaid, child welfare and other human services, and Employee Assistance Programs. Develops collaborative relationships with government agencies, community providers, consumer groups, health plans, insurers, and others to foster a deeper understanding of the needs of the various populations they serve. Develops child welfare programs based upon the principles of managed care.

4178 ValueOptions Jacksonville Service Center
10199 Southside Blvd
Building 100 Suite 300
Jacksonville, FL 32256-757

800-700-8646
www.valueoptions.com

Barbara Hill, Chief Executive Officer
E. Paul Dunn Jr., Chief Financial Officer
Michele D Alfano, Chief Operating Officer

4179 Vedder Price
222 N LaSalle Street
Chicago, IL 60601-1003
312-609-7500
Fax: 312-609-5005
E-mail: kwendrickx@vedderprice.com
www.vedderprice.com

Michael Nemeroff, President
Richard Thomas, Director Of Finance

4180 VeriCare
47415 Viewridge Avenue
Suite 230
San Diego, CA 92123
858-454-3610
800-257-8715
Fax: 858-874-8212
E-mail: contactus@vericare.com
www.vericare.com

Joe Casciani, President
Thomas Cooper, Chairman Of The Board

4181 VeriTrak
179 Niblick Road
Suite 149
Paso Robles, CA 93446-4845

800-370-2440
E-mail: support@veritrak.com
www.veritrak.com

4182 Verispan

114 Melrich Road
Suite A
Cranbury, NJ 08512-3510
609-235-3300
Fax: 609-235-3400
www.kwsp.com

Wayne Yetter, CEO
Peter Bird, Senior Vice President

4183 Webman Associates

4 Brattle Street
Cambridge, MA 02138-3714
617-864-6769
www.webmanassociates.com

Dorothy Webman, Owner

4184 WellPoint Behavioral Health

9655 Graniteridge Drive
Sixth Floor
San Diego, CA 92123-2674
858-571-8100
800-728-9498

Lori Wright, Manager

Software Companies

4185 ACS Healthcare Solutions

5225 Auto Club Drive
Dearborn, MI 48126-2620
248-386-8300
Fax: 248-386-8301
www.superiorconsultant.com

Lynn Blodgett, CEO

We focus on the unique needs of your healthcare business through out diversified service offerings.

4186 AHMAC

140 Allens Creek Road
Rochester, NY 14618-3307
800-638-0890
E-mail: sales@ahmac.com
www.hewitsoftware.com

CareManager is a microcomputer based system targeted at small to medium sized HMOs, PPOs and PHOs as well as vertical markets such as Medicaid and managed mental health. Easily customized to meet the needs and require- ments of the client.

4187 AIMS

485 Underhill Boulevard
Syosset, NY 11791-3434
516-496-7700
Fax: 516-496-7069

Ann Elbirt, Marketing Administration Mgr

Provider of systems for payers and providers. AIMS client centered, integrated care systems respond to payer cost containment strategies. The system features clinical integ- rity, outcome-oriented service plans with integrated notes and documentation.

4188 AMCO Computers

750 W Golden Grove Way
Covina, CA 91722-3255
626-859-6292

Yohanes Nugroho, President

Medical consultants, business computing consulting, com- puter software.

4189 Accumedic Computer Systems

11 Grace Avenue
Suite 401
Great Neck, NY 11021-2427
516-466-6800
800-765-9300
Fax: 516-466-6880
www.accumedic.com

Mark Kollenscher, President

Medical practice management software and healthcare in- formation systems (HCIS) solutions.

4190 Adam Software

1600 RiverEdge Parkway
Suite 100
Atlanta, GA 30328-4696
770-980-0888
www.adam.com

Provides products to connect consumers and their families to trustworthy and relevant health information.

4191 Advanced Data Systems

700 Mount Hope Avenue
Suite 101
Bangor, ME 04401-5667
207-947-4494
800-779-4494
Fax: 207-947-0650
E-mail: info@adspro.com
www.adspro.com

Advanced Data Systems (ADS) is a New England-based software developer and reseller of accounting information systems with over 23 years of experience. We specialize in developing, implementing and supporting administrative software. As a complement to our software we also pro- vide technical services. Advanced Data Systems is your "total accounting solution".

4192 Agilent Technologies

5301 Stevens Creek Blvd
Santa Clara, CA 95051-7201
408-553-7777
408-345-8886
Fax: 408-345-8474
www.agilent.com

William P Sullivan, CEO

Clinical measurement and diagnostic solutions for healthcare organizations.

4193 American Medical Software
PO Box 236
Edwardsville, IL 62025-236
618-692-1300
800-423-8836
Fax: 618-692-1809
E-mail: sales@americanmedical.com
www.americanmedical.com

Practice management software for billing, electronic claims, appointments and electronic medical records.

4194 American Psychiatric Press Reference Library CD-ROM
American Psychiatric Publishing, Inc.
1000 Wilson Boulevard
Suite 1825
Arlington, VA 22209-3901
703-907-7322
800-368-5777
Fax: 703-907-1091
E-mail: appi@psych.org
www.appi.org

Robert E Hales MD, Editor-in-Chief
Ron McMillen, Chief Executive Officer
John McDuffie, Editorial Director

$395.00
Year Founded: 1998

4195 Anasazi Software
9831 S 51st Street
Suite C117
Phoenix, AZ 85044-5673
480-503-8321
800-651-4411
Fax: 480-496-8089
E-mail: sales@anasazisoftware.com
www.anasazisoftware.com

Melani Jolly, VP

Developed by and for behavioral healthcare and social service professionals, helps you provide the best care possible to your clients.

4196 Andrew and Associates
PO Box 9226
Winter Haven, FL 33883-9226
813-299-4767

William F Andrew, PE, President

IT consulting and clinical IS for computer based patient records.

4197 Aries Systems Corporation
200 Sutton Street
N Andover, MA 01845-1656

978-975-7570
Fax: 978-975-3811
E-mail: kfinder@kfinder.com
www.kfinder.com

Lyndon Holmes, President

Provides technical innovations that empower all of the participants in the knowledge retrieval chain: publishers, database developers, librarians.

4198 Ascent
Ruby Creek Road
PO Box 230
Naples, ID 83847-230
208-267-3626
800-974-1999
Fax: 208-267-2295
E-mail: claudia.peterson@uhsinc.com

4199 Askesis Development Group
One Chatham Center
112 Washington Place Ste 300
Pittsburgh, PA 15219-3458
412-803-2400
Fax: 412-803-2099
E-mail: info@askesis.com
www.askesis.com

Askesis Development Group's PsychConsult is a complete informatics solution for behavioral health organizations: inpatient or outpatient behavioral health facilities, managed care organizations, and provider networks. PsychConsult is Windows NT based, and Y2K compliant. ADG development is guided by the PsychConsult Consortium, a collaborative effort of leading institutions in behavioral health.

4200 Assist Technologies
2501 N Hayden Road
Suite 104
Scottsdale, AZ 85257-2326
480-874-9400
Fax: 480-874-9414
E-mail: info@assistek.com

Joy Hebert, Owner

The Touch Outcomes Collector system greatly increase the quality of questionnaire data collected in clinical trials, which results in more usable data to support FDA claims.

4201 Austin Travis County Mental Health Mental Retardation Center
1430 Collier Street
Austin, TX 78704-2911
512-447-4141
Fax: 512-440-4801

David Evans, Executive Director

Provides mental health, mental retardation and substance services to the Austin-Travis County community.

4202 Aware Resources
PO Box 247
Munroe Falls, OH 44262-247
330-475-0060
800-254-1532
Fax: 330-475-0066
E-mail: info@awareresources.com
www.awareresources.com

Susan Searl, RN, President

Provides behavior management consultation, staff training and client counseling.

4203 BOSS Inc
2639 N Downer Avenue
Suite 9
Milwaukee, WI 53211

800-964-4789
E-mail: bmiller@healthcareboss.com
www.healthcareboss.com

Bob Miller, President

Practice management software that is easy to use and is in more than 29,000 practices nationally. Outcome management software products for social workers and hospitals. *$1499.00*

Year Founded: 1986

4204 Beaver Creek Software
525 SW 6th Street
Corvallis, OR 97333-4323
541-752-5039
800-895-3344
E-mail: sales@beaverlog.com

Peter Gysegem, Owner

"The THERAPIST" practice management and billing software for Windows operating systems comes in Pro and EZ versions. The EZ version is powerful yet simple to use and is tailored to needs of smaller offices. The Pro version is designed to handle the complex needs of busy practices. Use Pro to create HIPAA compliant electronic insurance claims. Both versions let you have an unlimited number of providers at no additional cost. *$249.00*

Year Founded: 1989

4205 Behavioral Health Advisor
McKesson Clinical Reference Systems
335 Interlocken Parkway
Broomfield, CO 80021-3484

800-782-1334
www.mckesson.com

The Behavioral Health Advisor software program provides consumer health information for more than 600 topics covering pediatric and adult mental illness, disorders and behavioral problems. Includes behavioral health topics from the American Academy of Child and Adolescent Psychiatry. Many Spanish translations available. *$4.75*

Year Founded: 1998

4206 Behaviordata
20833 Stevens Creek Boulevard
Suite 100
Cupertino, CA 95014-2154
408-342-0600
800-627-2673
Fax: 408-342-0617
www.behaviordat.com

Diana Everstine, President
Dr David Nichols, Contact

4207 BetaData Systems
2365 E Edison St
Tucson, AZ 85719-3807
520-917-1028
Fax: 520-733-5659
E-mail: sales@betadata.net
www.betadata.net

Providing computer software, hardware, consulting, service, and support to the industry.

Year Founded: 1978

4208 Body Logic
PO Box 162101
Austin, TX 78716-2101
512-327-0050
Fax: 512-307-6770

designs and consults information technology solutions for clinical delivery.

4209 Bull HN Information Systems
296 Concord Road
Billerica, MA 01821-6618
978-294-6000
Fax: 978-244-0085

David W Bradbury, President

Provides solutions and services to key markets, including the public sector, finance, manufacturing, and telecommunications.

4210 Business Objects
3410 Hillview Ave
Palo Alto, CA 94304-1395
408-953-6000
800-527-0580
Fax: 408-953-6001
www.businessobjects.com

Our software helps organizations gain better insight into their business, improving decision making and enterprise performance.

Year Founded: 1990

4211 CLARC Services
3500 Tamiami Trail
Port Charlotte, FL 33952-8100

800-246-5488

E-mail: dclaise@clarc.com
www.clarc.com

Dave Claise, Sales Manager

Computer consultancy which provides software, software training and support, custom programming, modifications to packaged products and education. We help your business with hardware and software installation and setup as well as data migration, integration and data conversion. Creators of Mental Health Organizational System Interface (MHOSI).

Year Founded: 1989

4212 CSI Software

3333 Richmond
2nd Floor
Houston, TX 77098-3007
713-942-7779
800-247-3431
Fax: 713-942-7731
E-mail: sales@csisoftwareusa.com
www.csisoftwareusa.com

Frank Mc Duff, VP

CSI Software designs software for the membership industry utilizing the most sophisticated software technologies, coupled with unsurpassed and experience and support.

4213 Cardiff Software: Vista

3220 Executive Ridge
Vista, CA 92081-8571
760-936-4500
Fax: 760-936-4800
E-mail: info@verity.com
www.cardiff.com

Provider of adaptive business process management (BPM) and content capture solutions. Cardiff enables organizations to capture data from electronic and paper sources and adapt to existing processes by managing structured, exception and people driven actions.

4214 Center for Clinical Computing

350 Longwood Avenue
Boston, MA 02115-5726
617-732-5925

Warner V Slack

4215 Center for Health Policy Studies

10400 Little Patuxent Parkway
Suite 10
Columbia, MD 21044-3518
410-715-9400
www.heritage.org

Robert E Moffit, PhD, Director

Provides thorough analyses and develops major policy prescriptions to address matters of affordability, insurance, and quality of care.

4216 Ceridian Corporation

3311 E Old Shackopee Road
Minneapolis, MN 55425-1640
952-548-5000
Fax: 952-548-5100
www.ceridian.com

Lee A Kennedy, CEO

A computer services and manufacturing company.

Year Founded: 1957

4217 Chartman Software

PO Box 551
Santa Barbara, CA 93102-551
805-563-5363

A complete electronic patient chart management solution.

4218 Cincom Systems

55 Merchant Street
Cincinnati, OH 45246-3761
513-612-2300
800-224-6266
Fax: 513-612-2000
E-mail: info@cincom.com
www.cinapps.com

Thomas M Nies, CEO

Cincom provides software and service solutions that help our clients create, manage and grow relationships with their customers through adaptive e-business information systems.

4219 Client Management Information System
WilData Systems Group

255 Bradenton Avenue
Dublin, OH 43017-2546
614-734-4719
800-860-4222
Fax: 614-734-1063
E-mail: cmis@wildatainc.com
www.wildatainc.com

A total Electronic Health Records (EHR) solution for behavioral health care organization like mental health centers, substance abuse providers, human service organizations, and family service agencies. Become 100% paperless by using CMIS in-house or by accessing our web based version called e-CMIS to minimize the up front capital expenditure and ongoing maintenance costs.

4220 CliniSphere version 2.0
Facts and Comparisons

77 Westport Plaza
Suite 450
Saint Louis, MO 63146-3125
314-216-2100
800-223-0554
www.factsandcomparisons.com

Access to all information in a clinical drug reference library, by drug, disease, side-effects; thousands of drugs (prescription, OTC, investigational) all included; contains information from Drug Facts and Comparisons, most definitive and comprehensive source for comparative drug information.

4221 Clinical Nutrition Center

7555 E Hampden Avenue
Suite 301
Denver, CO 80231-4834
303-750-9454
www.clinicalnutritioncenter.com

Ethan Lazarus, President

Our programs are based on the latest development in the field of nutrition, weight loss and weight control, behavior modification.

4222 Compu-Care Management and Systems

3737 Executive Center Drive
Austin, TX 78731-1647
512-219-8025

Application service provider for the behavioral health industry dedicated to helping providers meet their goals for efficiency and productivity.

4223 CompuLab Healthcare Systems Corporation

PO Box 11739
Fort Lauderdale, FL 33339-1739

800-266-7852
E-mail: webmaster@compulab.com
www.compulab.com

For the development of innovative computer technology and data processing systems in a variety of industries.

4224 Computer Transition Services

3223 S Loop
Suite 556
Lubbock, TX 79423
806-793-8961
Fax: 806-793-8968

David Baucum, Owner

Improve the life and business success of clients by providing integrated solutions and professional services to meet their technological and organizational needs.

4225 Control-0-Fax Corporation

3070 W Airline Highway
Waterloo, IA 50703-9591
319-234-4651
800-344-7777
Fax: 319-236-7332
E-mail: info@controlofax.com
www.controlofax.com

Ken Weber, Manager

Our product offering includes printed forms, clinical records, color-coded filing, chart management and four-color promotional printing. Additional services include file conversion, print and mail services and a complete array of EDI applications.

4226 Cornucopia Software

PO Box 6111
Albany, CA 94706-111
510-528-7000
E-mail: supportstaff@practicemagic.com
www.practicemagic.com

Providers of Practice MAGIC, the billing and practice management software that counts for your psychotherapy practice.

4227 Creative Socio-Medics Corporation

3500 Sunrise Highway
Suite D122
Great River, NY 11739-1001
631-581-7643

Creative has pioneered delivery of information systems to the health and human services industry.

4228 DB Consultants

198 Tabor Road
PO Box 580
Ottsville, PA 18942-580
610-847-5065
Fax: 610-847-2298
E-mail: sales@dbconsultants.com
www.dbconsultants.com

AS/PC includes electronic claims submission. Healtcare professionals rely on AS/PC every day to help them provide quality care.

4229 DST Output

2600 Sw Blvd
Kansas City, MO 64108-2349
816-221-1234
800-441-7587
E-mail: sales_marketing@dstoutput.com
www.dstoutput.com

Steven J Towle, CEO
Frank Delfer, CTO
Jim Reinert, EVP Business Development

Providing a customer communications solution offering myriad benefits to healthcare payor organizations, including the ability to manage both inbound and outbound communications; ensure document control and content compliance; integrate data from portal entry; distribute data, information, and material to the right place and audience with integrity.

4230 DataMark

2305 Presidents Drive
Salt Lake City, UT 84120-7230
801-886-2002
800-279-9335
Fax: 801-886-0102
E-mail: info@datamark.com
www.datamark-inc.com

Tom Dearden, CEO

Dedicated to providing innovative solutions that work to ease administrative burdens through automation, improved data capture, reduced duplication of effort and improved reporting capabilities: Custom Software Development, Data Analysis, Data Capture, Reporting, Statistic Anslysis.

4231 DeltaMetrics

600 Public Ledger Building
150 South Independence Mall West
Philadelphia, PA 19106-3413
215-399-0988
Fax: 215-399-0989
www.deltametrics.com

Jack Durell, MD, President/CEO

DeltaMetrics is now assisting treatment agencies to design and implement programs of Continuous Quality Improvement (CQI) within their systems of care.

4232 Distance Learning Network

111 Boal Ave
Boalsburg, PA 16827-1444
814-466-7808

Eric Porterfield, Director

Broadcast and multimedia company dedicated solely to meeting the medical education and communications needs of physicians through the use of both traditional and innovative media formats. More than 150,000 physicians, nurses and pharmacists turn to DLN each year for their medical education.

Year Founded: 1996

4233 Docu Trac

20140 Scholar Drive
Suite 218
Hagerstown, MD 21742-6575
301-766-4130
800-850-8510
E-mail: sales@quicdoc.com

Arnie Schuster, Owner

Offering Quic Doc clinical documentation software, a comprehensive software system designed specifically for behavioral healthcare providers.

Year Founded: 1993

4234 DocuMed

3518 West Liberty Road
Ann Arbor, MI 48103-9013
734-930-9053
800-321-5595
E-mail: info@documed.com

DocuMed 2002 is a comprehensive system for automated documentation of physician/patient encounters in ambulatory settings for solo practitioners or multiple physician groups.

4235 E Services Group

7340 Executive Way
Suite M
Frederick, MD 21704-9405

301-698-1900
Fax: 301-698-1909
E-mail: sales@esrv.com

Dave Walsh, Owner

Our primary focus is on finding that perfect marriage of savvy business logic and technologies so that our healthcare IT applications solve the real world business problems of our clients.

4236 EAP Technology Systems

PO Box 1650
Yreka, CA 96097-1650

800-755-6965
E-mail: information@eaptechnology.com
www.eaptechnology.com

Provider of technologies that automate work flow and enhance the business value of Employee Assistance Programs.

4237 Echo Group

519 17th Street
Suite 400
Oakland, CA 94612-3461
510-238-2727
800-635-8209
Fax: 510-238-2730
E-mail: info@echoman.com
www.echoman.com

David Allen, Manager

Echo Group has been helping behavioral healthcare organizations to succeed in their missions of healing.

4238 Eclipsys Corporation

1750 Clint Moore Road
Boca Raton, FL 33487-2707
561-322-4321
www.eclipsys.com

R Andrew Eckert, President/CEO

Eclipsys empowers healthcare organizations to improve patient safety, financial strength, operational efficiency and customer satisfaction through innovative information software and service solutions.

Year Founded: 1995

4239 Electronic Healthcare Systems

Ehs One Metroplex Drive
Suite 500
Birmingham, AL 35209
205-871-1031
888-879-7302
Fax: 205-871-1185
E-mail: marketing@ehsmed.com
www.ehsmed.com

EHS develops and markets system solutions to a select group of physicians who are leading the way to clinical excellence and practice efficiency trhough automation.

Year Founded: 1995

ware County area, the Young Resources Database is a condensed version of the above.

4240 Emedeon Practice Services
2202 N West Shore Boulevard
Suite 300
Tampa, FL 33607-5776

877-932-6301
E-mail: lynne.durham@sage.com
www.sagehealth.com

Lynne Durham, Contact

Provides comprehensive systems that include all aspects of billing, scheduling, electronic data interchange(EDI), electronic health records(EHR), and enterprise data management with advanced reporting solutions.

4241 Entre Technology Services
2727 Central Ave
Billings, MT 59102-3151
406-256-5700
Fax: 406-256-0201
www.entremt.com

Mike Keene, Owner

Computer Networking.

4242 Experior Corporation
5710 Coventry Lane
Fort Wayne, IN 46804-7141
260-432-2020
800-595-2020
Fax: 260-432-4753
E-mail: sales@experior.com
www.experior.com

Experior provides Innovative Information systems to practice management and ASC marketplace. Out products, SurgeOn and EMS provide scheduling, case costing and billing.

4243 Facts Services
1575 San Ignacio Avenue
Suite 406
Coral Gables, FL 33146-3000
305-284-7400
Fax: 305-661-6710
E-mail: sales@factsservices.com
www.factsservices.com

Provides fully automated and integrated software and hardware solutions for employee benefit administration, specializing in claims and encounter processing, risk management and managed care systems.

4244 Family Services of Delaware County
600 N Olive Street
Media, PA 19063-2418
610-566-7540
Fax: 610-566-7677
www.fcsdc.org

Tracy Segal, Director Development

The Where to Turn Database is the most comprehensive listing of Non-Profit Human Service programs in the Dela-

4245 First Data Bank
1111 Bayhill Drive
San Bruno, CA 94066-3027
650-827-4564
800-633-3453
Fax: 650-588-4003
www.firstdatabank.com

Donald M Nielsen, CEO

Provides thousands of drug knowledge base implementations ranging from pharmacy dispensing and claims processing to emerging applications including computerized physician order entry (CPOE), electronic health records (EHR), e-Prescribing and electronic medication administration records (EMAR).

4246 Gelbart and Associates
423 S Pacific Coast Highway
Suite 102
Redondo Beach, CA 90277-3731
310-792-1823
www.refuse2lose.com

Robert Cutrow, Contact

Comprehensive Psychological and Psychiatric services for individuals, families, couples and groups, treating: anxiety, depression, relationship conflicts and medication management.

4247 GenSource Corporation
25572 Stanford Avenue
Valencia, CA 91355

800-949-9192
Fax: 661-294-1310
E-mail: sales@gensourcecorp.com
www.gensourcecorp.com

Greg Fisher, President/Coo
Chris Sullivan, Vp Operations

Offers a comprehensive set of fully integrated software systems for administering insurance related claims and managing risk, including workers compensation, non-ocupational disability, property and casualty claims.

Year Founded: 1977

4248 Genelco Software Solutions
325 McDonnell Blvd
Hazelwood, MO 63042-2513

800-548-2040
Fax: 314-593-3517
E-mail: info@genelco.com
www.genelco.com

Offers its flagship software systems in an ASP financial model. An ASP arrangement allows an organization to maintain control over operations without maintaining the software onsite.

4249 HMS Healthcare Management Systems
3102 W End Avenue
Suite 400
Nashville, TN 37203-1623
615-383-7300
800-383-3317
Fax: 615-383-6093
www.hmstn.com

Thomas M Stephenson, CEO

Automates processes including billing, scheduling and auditing within healthcare organizations.

4250 HSA-Mental Health
1080 Emeline Avenue
Santa Cruz, CA 95060-1966
831-454-4000
Fax: 831-454-4770
TDD: 831-454-2123
E-mail: info@santacruzhealth.org
www.santacruzhealth.org

Exists to protect and improve the health of the people in Santa Cruz County. Provides programs in environmental health, public health, medical care, substance abuse prevention and treatment, and mental health. Clients are entitled to information on the costs of care and their options for getting health insurance coverage through a variety of programs.

4251 HZI Research Center
150 White Plains Road
Tarrytown, NY 10591-5535
914-631-3315

Tele-Map EEG Service provides the most advanced neuroimaging technologies.

4252 Habilitation Software
204 N Sterling Street
Morganton, NC 28655-3345
828-438-9455
Fax: 828-438-9488
E-mail: info@habsoft.com
www.habsoft.com

Randy Herson, President

Personal Planning System, Windows-based computer program which assists agencies serving people with developmental disabilities with the tasks of person-centered planning; tracks outcomes, services and supports, assists with assesments and quarterly reviews, and maintains a customizable library of training programs. Also includes a census system for agencies which must maintain an exact midnight census, as well as an Accident/Incident system.

4253 Hanover Insurance
440 Lincoln Street
Worcester, MA 01653-2
508-855-1000
800-853-0456
Fax: 508-853-6332
www.allmerica.com

Frederick H Eppinger Jr, CEO

Offers hospice programs, rehabilitation groups and mental health services.

4254 Health Probe
5693 Bear Wallow Road
Suite 100
Morgantown, IN 46160-9315
765-342-9947
E-mail: support@healthprobe.com
www.healthprobe.com

EMR created to eliminate the need for paper with electronic medical records.

4255 HealthLine Systems
17085 Camino San Bernardo
San Diego, CA 92127-5709
858-673-1700
800-733-8737
Fax: 858-673-9866
E-mail: sales@healthlinesystems.com
www.healthlinesystems.com

Dan Littrell, CEO

Provide peerless information management solutions and services that maximize the quality and delivery of healthcare.

4256 HealthSoft
PO Box 536489
Orlando, FL 32853-6489
407-648-4857
800-235-0882
Fax: 407-426-7440
E-mail: admin@healthsoftonline.com
www.healthsoftonline.com

CD - ROM and web based software for professionals on mental health nursing and developmental disabilities nursing.

4257 Healthcare Vision
2601 Scott Avenue
Suite 600
Fort Worth, TX 76103-2307
817-531-8992
888-836-7428
Fax: 817-531-2360
E-mail: sales1@healthcaare-vision.com
www.healthcare-vision.com

HCV's innovative telemedicine software solutions and research and development capability enables HCV to deliver high-tech software solutions with features and benefits for quality healthcare, today and in the future.

Year Founded: 1992

4258 Healthline Systems
17085 Camino San Bernardo
San Diego, CA 92127-5709
858-673-1700
800-254-7347
Fax: 858-673-9866

E-mail: sales@healthlinesystems.com
www.healthlinesystems.com

Dan Littrell, CEO

Provider of Document Management and Physician Credentialing software solutions.

4259 Healthport

120 Bluegrass Valley Parkway
Alpharetta, GA 30005-2204

800-367-1500
www.healthport.com

Develops and sells Companion EMR, an electronic medical record system that eliminates paperwork, improves accuracy of information, provides instant access to patient and clinical information, and helps cuts costs while increasing revenue.

4260 Hogan Assessment Systems

2622 East 21st Street
Tulsa, OK 74114-1768
918-293-2300
800-756-0632
Fax: 918-749-0635

Joyce Hogan, Owner

Focuses on five dimensions of personality including emotional stability, extroversion, likeability, conscientiousness and the degree to which a person needs stimulation.

4261 IBM Global Healthcare Industry

404 Wyman Street
Waltham, MA 02451-1212
781-895-2911
Fax: 617-361-2485
E-mail: tgaffin@us.ibm.com
www.ibm.com/industries/healthcare

IBM has been strategically involved in assisting the healthcare industry in addressing numerous IT challenges. IBM provides clients and partners with the industry's broadest portfolio of technology, services, skills, and insight.

4262 IDX Systems Corporation

40 IDX Drive
South Burlington, VT 05403-7771
802-862-1022
Fax: 802-862-6848
www.idx.com

Provides information technology solutions to maximize value in the delivery of healthcare, improve the quality of patient service, enhance medical outcomes, and reduce the costs of care.

Year Founded: 1969

4263 IMNET Systems

3015 Windward Plaza
Alpharetta, GA 30005-8715

770-521-5600
800-329-2777

Develops, markets, installs and services electronic information and document management systems for the healthcare industry and other document intensive businesses.

4264 InfoMC

101 W Elm Street
Suite G10
Conshohocken, PA 19428-2075
484-530-0100
Fax: 484-530-0111
E-mail: sales@infomc.com
www.infomc.com

Develops software solutions for Managed Care organizations, EAP/Work-Life organizations, and Health and Human Services agencies.

Year Founded: 1994

4265 Information Management Solutions

2422 Freedom Street
San Antonio, TX 78217-4423
210-826-4994
800-255-3190
Fax: 210-826-2676
E-mail: john@totalims.com
www.business-document-management.com

Henry Minten, Owner
John Reed, Sales Contact

Provides complete electronic Document Imaging Services to covert paper, microfilm, microfiche and engineering drawings to electronic images.

4266 Informix Software
IBM Corporation

1133 Westchester Avenue
White Plains, NY 10604-3599
877-426-6006
www.ibm.com/software

IBM Informix® software includes a comprehensive array of high-performance, stand-alone and integration tools that enable efficient application and Web development, information integration , and database administration.

4267 Inforum

777 E Eisenhower Parkway
Ann Arbor, MI 48108-3273
734-913-3000
www.medstat.com

Medstat has designed information solutions to strengthen healthcare policy and management decision-making.

Year Founded: 1981

4268 Inhealth Record Systems

5076 Winters Chapel Road
Atlanta, GA 30360-1832
770-396-4994
800-477-7374

Fax: 770-396-0475
E-mail: sales@inhealth.us
www.inhealthrecords.com

Sue Kay, President

Provides variety of record keeping system products for health care practices and organizations.

Year Founded: 1979

4269 Innovative Data Solutions
386 Newberry Drive
Suite 100
Elk Grove Village, IL 60007-2778
847-923-1926
E-mail: info@idsincp.com
www.idsincp.com

Mark Parianos, President/CEO

Provide effective web based and software solutions for business, small offices and fortune 500 clients.

Year Founded: 1991

4270 Innovative Health Systems/SoftMed
160 Blue Ravine Road
Suite A
Folsom, CA 95630-4718
916-605-2050
800-695-4447
Fax: 916-605-2065
www.softmed.com

Don Ratcliff, Founder/President/EVP

4271 Integrated Business Services
736 N Western Ave
125
Lake Forest, IL 60045-1820
847-735-1690
800-451-5478
E-mail: info@medbase200.com

Sam Tartamella, Manager

A medical research and information marketing firm providing access to highly selectable medical databases.

Year Founded: 1982

4272 Keane Care
8383 158th Avenue NE
Suite 100
Redmond, WA 98052-3846
425-869-9000
800-426-2675
Fax: 425-307-2220
E-mail: kim_A_Allen@keane.com
www.keanecare.com

Thomas Weitzel, Executive
Jim Ingalls, Director Sales

Develops, markets, and supports a range of clinical and financial software.

Year Founded: 1969

4273 Lexical Technologies
151 W Atlantic Avenue
Alameda, CA 94501-7546
501-865-8500

Provide the delivery of healthcare across enterprises through the application of integrated component solutions.

Year Founded: 1984

4274 M/MGMT Systems
2335 American River Drive
Suite 402
Sacramento, CA 95825-7065
916-648-9010
800-664-8797
Fax: 916-648-9040
E-mail: mlab@mmgmt.com
www.mmgmt.com

Provides a comprehensive support and maintenance program to service the public health laboratories and license M/LAB.

Year Founded: 1982

4275 MEDCOM Information Systems
2117 Stonington Avenue
Hoffman Estates, IL 60169-2016
847-885-1553
800-213-2161
Fax: 847-885-1591
E-mail: medcom@emirj.com
www.emirj.com

John Holub, President

Provides a wide variety of products and services to the independent physician clinic as well as the hospital and private clinical laboratories.

Year Founded: 1991

4276 MEDecision
601 Lee Road
Chesterbrook Corporate Center
Wayne, PA 19087-5607
610-540-0202
Fax: 610-540-0270
E-mail: salesinfo@medecision.com
www.medecision.com

Scott A Storrer, CEO

Providing managed care organizations with powerful and flexible care management solutions. MEDecision's tools help managed care organizations improve care management processes and align more closely with their members and providers to improve the quality and cost outcomes of healthcare.

Year Founded: 1988

4277 McHenry County M/H Board
620 Dakota Street
Crystal Lake, IL 60012-3732
815-455-2828
Fax: 815-455-2925

E-mail: webadmin@mc708.org
www.mc708.org
Sandy Lewis, Executive Director
Robert Lesser, Deputy Director

Our misson is to provide leadership and be accountable for the provision of prevention and treatment of mental illness, developmental disabilities, and chemical abuse by coordinative, developing and contracting services for all citizens of McHenry County.

4278 McKesson HBOC

2700 Snelling Ave N
Roseville, MN 55113-1719
651-697-5900
Fax: 651-697-5910

Chris Bauleke, VP

Our products and services are designed to meet the information needs of all participants in the integrated health system.

4279 Med Data Systems

1950 Old Cuthbert Road
Suite L
Cherry Hill, NJ 08034-1439
856-428-1550
800-842-0011
Fax: 856-428-8172
E-mail: information@md-systems.com
www.md-systems.com

Jerold Zebrick, President/CEO

Provides an extensive suite of software programs to the healthcare and industrial markets which encompass Outcome Measurements, Baseline-Progress-Discharge Reports as well as Ergonomic and Work Hardening Analysis.

4280 MedPLus

4690 Parkway Drive
Mason, OH 45040-8172
513-229-5500
800-444-6235
E-mail: info@medplus.com
www.medplus.com

Richard A Mahoney, President
Thomas R Wagner, CTO
Philip S Present, II, COO

Developer and integrator of clinical connectivity and data management solutions for health care organizations and clinicians.

Year Founded: 1991

4281 Medai

Millenia Park One
4901 Vineland Rd Suite 450
Orlando, FL 32811-7192
321-281-4480
800-446-3324

Steve Epstein, Owner
Diane Lee, EVP/Co Founder
Swati Abbott, President

Provides solutions for the improvement of healthcare delivery. Utilizing cutting-edge technology, payers are able to predict patients at risk, identify cost drivers for their high-risk population, predict future health plan costs, evaluate patient patterns over time, and improve outcomes.

4282 Medcomp Software

PO Box 16687
Golden, CO 80402-6010
303-277-0772
Fax: 303-277-9801
E-mail: customerservice@medcompsoftware.com
www.medcompsoftware.com

Developing and designing case management systems for a wide variety of applications.

Year Founded: 1995

4283 Medi-Span

8425 Woodfield Crossing Boulevard
Suite 490
Indianapolis, IN 46240-7300
317-735-5300
800-388-8884
Fax: 317-735-5350
E-mail: medispan-support@wolterskluwer.com
www.medi-span.com

Travis Rothrock, Manager

Medi-Span offers a complete line of drug databases, including clinical decision support and disease suite modules, application programming interfaces, and stand-alone PC products.

4284 Medical Records Institute

425 Boylston Street
Boston, MA 02116-3315
617-964-3923
Fax: 617-964-3926
E-mail: peter@medrecinst.com
www.medrecinst.com

Peter Waegemann, CEO

Promote and enhance the journey towards electronic health records, e-health, mobile health, mental health assessment, and related applications of information technologies (IT).

4285 Medical Records Solution
Creative Solutions Unlimited

203 Gilman Street
PO Box 550
Sheffield, IA 50475-550

800-253-7697
E-mail: mkoch@csumail.com
www.creativesolutionsunlimited.com

Martha Koch, Vp

Reliable, comprehensive, intuitive, fully-integrated clinical software able to manage MDS 2.0 electronic submission, RUGs/PPS, triggers, Quick RAP's, survey reports, QI's, assessments, care plans, Quick Plans, physician orders, CQI, census, and hundreds of reports. Creative Solutions Unlimited provides outstanding toll-free support, training, updates, user groups, newsletters, and continuing education.

Year Founded: 1988

4286 Medipay
620 SW 5th Avenue
Suite 610
Portland, OR 97204-1421
503-227-6491
Fax: 503-299-6490

Medipay's information technology products and services monitor and control quality, manage clinical and financial risk, collaborate and integrate with external stakeholders, and empower front line staff.

4287 Medix Systems Consultants
17050 S Park Avenue
Suites C-D
S Holland, IL 60473-3374
708-331-1271
Fax: 708-331-1272
E-mail: info@imsci.com
www.imsci.com

Systems integration and development company committed to client/server multi vendor(open systems) solutions for a diverse vertical market ranging from education and healthcare.

Year Founded: 1987

4288 Medware
2650 North Dixie Freeway
New Smyrna Beach, FL 32168-5774

877-932-6301
E-mail: medwaresales@sage.com
www.medware.com

Integrated medical management software.

4289 Mental Health Connections
21 Blossom Street
Lexington, MA 02421-8103
617-510-1318
www.mhc.com

Robert Patterson, MD, Founder/Principal

Developer of medical management software for physicians and research scientists. Their primary product is desigend to identify drug interactions based on the mainstream of drug metabolism research.

4290 Mental Health Outcomes
2941 S Lake Vista Drive
Lewisville, TX 75067-3801

800-266-4440
Fax: 972-420-8215
E-mail: johan.smith@horizonhealth.com
www.mho-inc.net

Johan Smith, VP Operations/Development

Designs and implements custom outcome measurement systems specifically for behavioral helath programs through its CQI Outcomes Measurement System. This system provides information for a wide range of patient and treatment focused variables for child, adolesent, adult, geriatric and substance abuse programs in the inpatient, partial hospital, residential treatment and outpatient settings.

Year Founded: 1994

4291 Meritcare Health System
PO Box M.C
Fargo, ND 58122-1
701-234-6000
800-437-4010
www.meritcare.com

Roger Gilbertson, CEO
Craig Hewitt, CIO

MeritCare is able to track your employees' health trends due to a new software program called Occusource.

4292 Micro Design International
45 Skyline Drive
Suite 1017
Lake Mary, FL 32746-6224
407-804-0727
800-228-0891
E-mail: sales@mdi.com
www.mdi.com

Martin Legat, President

Provides optical (CD/DVD/MO) storage solutions through innovative achivements, easy-to-use data access, and exceptional service and support.

Year Founded: 1978

4293 Micro Office Systems
3825 Severn Road
Cleveland, OH 44118-1910
216-297-1240
E-mail: normane@micro-officesystems.com

Norman Efroymson, Contact

4294 Micromedex
6200 S Syracuse Way
Suite 300
Englewood, CO 80111-4705

800-525-9083
Fax: 303-486-6450
www.micromedex.com

A comprehensive suite of alerts, answers, protocols, and interventions directly addresses clinicians need for evidence-based information. This vital information is used to support patient care and improve outcomes.

Year Founded: 1974

4295 Misys Health Care Systems
8529 Six Forks Road
Raleigh, NC 27615-2963

866-647-9787
www.misyshealthcare.com

Develops and supports software and services for physicians and caregivers.

4296 MphasiS(BPO)
5353 N 16th Street
Suite 400
Phoenix, AZ 85016-3205
602-604-3100
Fax: 602-604-3115
E-mail: fred.thierbach@mphasis.com
www.eldocomp.com

W Thomas Castleberry, CEO

Focused on financial services, logistics and technology verticals and spans across architecture, application development and integration, application management and business process outsourcing, including the operation of large scale customer contact centers.

4297 National Families in Action
2957 Clairmont Road Ne
Suite 150
Atlanta, GA 30329-1647
404-248-9676
Fax: 404-248-1312
E-mail: nfia@nationalfamilies.org
www.nationalfamilies.org

Sue Rusche, President

An interactive database of ever-changing names of drugs that people use and abuse for illnesses.

Year Founded: 1977

4298 National Medical Health Card Systems
Ste 610
2441 Warrenville Rd
Lisle, IL 60532-3642

800-251-3883
Fax: 516-605-6981
www.nmhc.com

Software to electronically manage combined medical and Rx deductibles for the healthcare industry.

4299 NetMeeting
Microsoft Corporation
Customer Advocate Center
One Microsoft Way
Redmond, WA 98052-8300
425-882-8080
800-642-7676
Fax: 425-936-7329
www.microsoft.com

Steve Ballmer, CEO

NetMeeting delivers a complete Internet conferencing solution for all Window users with multi-point data conferencing, text chat, whiteboard, and file transfer, as well as point-to-point audio and video.

4300 Netsmart Technologies
570 Metro Place N
Dublin, OH 43017-5317
614-764-0143
800-434-2642
Fax: 614-764-0362
www.ntst.com

John Paton, Chairman

Offers information systems for mental health, behavioral and public health organizations.

4301 Nightingale Vantagemed Corporation
10670 White Rock Road
Suite 300
Rancho Cordova, CA 95670-6162
916-638-4744
Fax: 916-638-0504
E-mail: info@nightingale.md

Liesel Loesch, VP

Therapist Helper, the leading practice management software program, processes patient and insurance billing transactins, accounts receivable, statements, and tracks payments. Therapist Helper will also assist in scheduling managed care tracking, and electronic claims submission. Will network at no additional charge. All you'll need is IMB or compatible Pentium with 16 MB RAM and at least 25 MB available hard drive space. Download a free, full working demo at our website.

4302 Northwest Analytical
111 SW 5th Avenue
Suite 800
Portland, OR 97204-3606
503-224-7727
888-692-7638
Fax: 503-224-5236
E-mail: info@nwasoft.com
www.nwasoft.com

Jeff Cawley, VP

Provides comprehensive SPC software tools meeting technically stringent mental health industry requirements.

4303 OPTAIO-Optimizing Practice Through Assessment, Intervention and Outcome
Harcourt Assessment/PsychCorp
19500 Bulverde Road
San Antonio, TX 78259-3701
210-339-5000
800-622-3231
Fax: 210-339-5046

Mike Cook, Executive

Provides the clinical information necessary for proactive decision making.

4304 Occupational Health Software
6609 NE Tara Lane
Bainbridge Island, WA 98110-4030
206-842-5838

Provides a wide range of consulting and training services, addressing occupational health and safety, workers compensation management, medical surveillance and industrial hygiene.

4305 Optio Software
3015 Windward Plaza
Windward Fairways II
Alpharetta, GA 30005-8715
770-576-3500
Fax: 770-576-3699
E-mail: info@optio.com
www.optiosoftware.com

C Wayne Cape, Chairman/President/CEO
Caroline Bembry, CFO
Daryl G Hatton, CTO
Donald French, SVP Research/Development

Provides software solutions that enable organizations to achieve unprecedented speed, accuracy, functionality and quality in their document processes such as procure-to-pay, order-to-case, manufacturing and healthcare.

Year Founded: 1981

4306 Oracle Corporation
500 Oracle Parkway
Redwood Shores, CA 94065-1675
650-506-7000
Fax: 650-506-7200
www.oracle.com

Lawrence J Ellison, CEO
Larry Ellison, CEO

PeopleSoft provides a range of applications from traditional human resources, payroll and benefits to financials.

Year Founded: 1977

4307 Orion Healthcare Technology
1016 Leavenworth Street
Omaha, NE 68102-2944
402-341-8880
800-324-7966
Fax: 402-341-8911
E-mail: info@orionhealthcare.com
www.myaccucare.com

Bill Allan, Owner

Orion provides technology solutions to meet the ever changing needs of the healthcare industry. To accomodate the behavioral health field, Orion developed the AccuCare software system, a highly integrated and adaptive approach to the clinical practice environment. AccuCare enables clinicians to quickly realize value, effiency and standardization without disrupting their primary focus to provide excellence in health care.

4308 P and W Software
5655 Lindero Canyon Road
Suite 403
Westlake Village, CA 91362-4046
818-707-7690
Fax: 818-707-9097
E-mail: pwsoft@pwsoftware.com
www.pwsoftware.com

Tom Philipps, Owner
Bud Bockoven, Director Marketing/Sales

POWERPLUS was developed as a flexible toolkit, one which would allow each user to administer benefits according to his or her specific model. With user-defined codes and values and company level processing defaults.

Year Founded: 1984

4309 Parrot Software
PO Box 250755
W Bloomfield, MI 48325-755
248-788-3223
800-727-7681
Fax: 248-788-3224
E-mail: support@parrotsoftware.com
www.parrotsoftware.com

Provide 60 different software programs for the remediation of speech, cognitive, language, attention, and memory deficits seen in individuals who have suffered aphasia from stroke or head injury.

Year Founded: 1981

4310 Perot Systems
2300 West Plano Parkway
Plano, TX 75075-8427
972-535-1900
888-317-3768
Fax: 972-535-1997
E-mail: americas@ps.net

Steven Blasnik, President

Deliveres technology based business solutions to help organizations worldwide control costs and cultivate growth.

Year Founded: 1988

4311 Primary Care Medicine on CD
Facts and Comparisons
77 West Port Plaza
Suite 450
Saint Louis, MO 63146-3125

800-223-0554
Fax: 314-216-2100
www.factsandcomparisons.

Current, comprehensive coverage of what's happening in the discipline; quarterly updates include summary, analysis and critique of relevant studies on ambulatory care, family medicine, internal medicine, pharmacology, cardiology, therapeutic advances, plus twelve critical reviews of major new studies in the field of medical practice.

4312 Psychological Assessment Resources
16204 N Florida Avenue
Lutz, FL 33549-8119
813-968-3003
800-331-8378
Fax: 813-968-2598

Robert Smith Iii, President

This program produces normative-based interpretive hypotheses based on your client's scores. It produces a profile of T scores, a listing of the associated raw and percentile scores, and interpretive hypotheses for each scale. Although this program is not designed to produce a finished clinical report, it allows you to integrate BRS and SRI data with other sources of information about your client. The report can be generated as a text file for editing.

Year Founded: 1978

4313 Psychological Software Services
6555 Carrollton Avenue
Indianapolis, IN 46220-1664
317-257-9672
Fax: 317-257-9674
E-mail: nsc@netdirect.net
www.neuroscience.cnter.com

Comprehensive and easy-to-use multimedia cognitive rehabilitation software. Packages include 64 computerized therapy tasks with modifiable parameters that will accommodate most requirements. Exercises extend from simple attention and executive skills, through multiple modalities of visuospatial and memory skills. For clinical and educational use with head injury, stroke, LD/ADD and other brain compromises. Price range: $260-$2,500.

Year Founded: 1984

4314 Psychometric Software
2210 Front Street
Suite 208
Melbourne, FL 32901-7506
407-729-6390
800-882-9811
Fax: 321-951-9508
E-mail: psi@digital.net
www.psipsych.com

Specializes in behavioral medicine, neuropsychological assessment, cognitive rehabilitation and biofeedback software.

Year Founded: 1978

4315 QuadraMed Corporation
12110 Sunset Hills Road
Reston, VA 20190-5852
703-709-2300
800-393-0278
Fax: 703-709-2490
E-mail: boardofdirectors@quadramed.com
www.quadramed.com

Duncan W James, CEO
James Milligan, Svp Sales/Government Programs

4316 RCF Information Systems
4200 Colonel Glenn Highway
Suite 100
Beavercreek, OH 45431-1670
937-427-5680
Fax: 937-427-5689
www.rcfinfo.com

Roger Harris, President
Healthcare software.

4317 Raintree Systems
28765 Single Oak Drive
Suite 200
Temecula, CA 92590
951-252-9400
800-333-1033
www.raintreeinc.com

Richard Welty, President/CTO

Provides practice management software for commerical, not-for-profit, government healthcare providers, rehabilitation facilities, and social service agencies.

Year Founded: 1983

4318 Right On Programs/PRN Medical Software
778 New York Avenue
Huntington, NY 11743-4413
631-424-7777
Fax: 631-424-7207
E-mail: riteonsoft@aol.com

Barbara Feinstein, Owner

Computer software for mental health, medical and other organizations requiring cataloging and searching a wide range of materials. Software is especially easy to learn and use. Programs include The Circulation Desk for cataloging and circulation of books, CDs, videos, photos, booklets, etc., Computer Access Catalog for cataloging without the circulation module, and Periodical Manager for periodicals including supplements.

Year Founded: 1980

4319 SHS Computer Service
759 Main Street
Stroudsburg, PA 18360-2062
570-424-5676
E-mail: sales@shscomputer.com

Sheryl Hope Shay, President

Client and Fund Tracking System with HIPAA Billing, Pennsylvania CCRS/POMS State Reporting, and adhoc reports for behavioral health organizations.

Year Founded: 1986

4320 SPSS
233 S Wacker Drive
11th Floor
Chicago, IL 60606-6306
312-651-3000
Fax: 312-651-3668
www.spss.com

Jack Noonan, CEO

Worldwide provider of predictive analytics software and solutions.

Year Founded: 1968

4321 Saner Software
761 N 17th Street
Unit 11
Saint Charles, IL 60174-1664
630-762-9440
Fax: 630-562-9443
E-mail: sales@sanersoftware.com
www.tssphotography.com

John Parkinson, Owner

Develops health practice management software.

Year Founded: 1988

4322 Scinet
11117 Mockingbird Drive
Omaha, NE 68137-2332
402-331-6660
E-mail: info@scinetinc.com
www.scinetinc.com

Provides all payer electronic claims transactions, electronic remittance advice, and electronic patient statements.

Year Founded: 1986

4323 Sls Residential
2505 Carmel Ave
Suite 210
Brewster, NY 10509-1122

888-822-7348
www.slshealth.com

Fully intergrated informatics software solutions; clinical, billing/AR, administration, outcomes.

4324 Star Systems Corporation
4083 North Shiloh Drive
Suite 8
Fayetteville, AR 72703-5201
501-587-0882
Fax: 501-587-9449
E-mail: frank@starsyscorp.com
www.starsyscorp.com

Frank W Woods, Founder

Provides healthcare software.

Year Founded: 1980

4325 Stephens Systems Services
267 5th Avenue
Suite 812
New York, NY 10016-7506
212-545-7788
www.stephenssystems.com

Mike Stephens, Owner

Provides healthcare software.

4326 Strategic Advantage
3353 Peachtree Road NE
Suite 400
Atlanta, GA 30326-1413
404-231-8676
800-330-8889
Fax: 404-237-1291
www.gscpa.org

4327 SumTime Software®
4713 Goodrich Avenue NE
Albuquerque, NM 87110-1164

888-821-0771
Fax: 505-888-2653
E-mail: sumtime@sumtime.com
www.sumtime.com

Is the practice management solution for health care professionals. We offer the most comprehensive means for preparing billing statements and tracking payments and maintaining records.

4328 Sun Microsystems
4150 Network Circle
Santa Clara, CA 95054-1778
650-960-1300
800-555-9786
Fax: 650-786-4557
www.sun.com

Gregory M Papadopoulos, Executive VP

Provider of healthcare software.

Year Founded: 1982

4329 SunGard Pentamation
3 West Broad Street
Bethlehem, PA 18018-6799
610-691-3616
866-905-8989
www.pentamation.com

Provides secure and reliable K-12 student information systems, special education management, financial and human resource management software to school districts.

Year Founded: 1992

4330 Synergistic Office Solutions (SOS Software)
17445 E Apshawa Road
Clermont, FL 34715-9049
352-242-9100
Fax: 352-242-9104
E-mail: sales@sosoft.com
www.sosoft.com

Seth R Krieger, PhD, President

Produce patient management software for behavioral health service providers, including billing, scheduling and clinical records.

Year Founded: 1985

4331 Tempus Software
225 Water Street
Suite 250
Jacksonville, FL 32202-5185

Fax: 904-355-3322

Keith B Hagen, President/CEO

Provide the most comprehensive range of innovative, installable and practical healthcare information technology solutions that increase efficiencies, and empower clinicians to improve patient care through smarter healthcare technology solutions.

Year Founded: 1993

4332 Thomson ResearchSoft
2141 Palomar Airport Road
Suite 350
Carlsbad, CA 92011-1451
760-438-5526
800-722-1227
Fax: 760-438-5573
www.scientific.thomsonrueters.com

Software for wherever research is performed worldwide including all leading academic, corporate and government institutions, healthcare.

4333 TriZetto Group
567 San Nicolas Drive
Suite 360
Newport Beach, CA 92660-6500
949-718-4940
800-569-1222
Fax: 949-219-2197
E-mail: salesinfo@trizetto.com
www.trizetto.com

Jeffrey H Margolis, CEO
Kathleen Earley, President/COO

Focuses on the business of healthcare and offers a broad portfolio of technology products and services.

Year Founded: 1997

4334 Turbo-Doc EMR
771 Buschmann Road
Suite G
Paradise, CA 95969-5848
530-877-8650
800-977-4868
Fax: 530-877-8621
E-mail: turbodoc@turbodoc.com
www.turbodoc.net

Lyle B Hunt, CEO

An electronic medical record system designed to assist physicians and other health care workers in completing medical record tasks.

4335 UNI/CARE Systems
540 North Tamiami Trail
Sarasota, FL 34236-4823

941-954-3403
Fax: 941-954-2033
E-mail: sales@unicaresys.com
www.unicaresys.com

May Ahdab, President

UNI/CARE's mission is to offer enterprise-based solutions designed to improve clinical recovery outcomes, standardize workflows and maximize revenue cycles within a technical environment, fostering collaboration and informed decision-making. Pro-Filer is a .NETcentric Human Service Enterprise (HSE) platform designed to support the requirements of data processing and use by healthcare organizations providing an array of clinical services. It's viable in a single organization or across a consortium, offering users customized workflows, best practice guides, revenue management tools, and the ability to concurrently meet clinical and financial compliance standards.

Year Founded: 1981

4336 Universal Behavioral Service
3590 N Meridian Street
Indianapolis, IN 46208-4425
317-684-0442

4337 Vann Data Services
1801 Dunn Avenue
Daytona Beach, FL 32114-1250
386-238-1200
Fax: 386-238-1454
E-mail: sales@vanndata.com
www.vanndata.com

Janice Huffstickler, President

Healthcare practice software.

4338 Velocity Healthcare Informatics
8441 Wayzata Boulevard
Suite 105
Minneapolis, MN 55426-1349

800-844-5648
E-mail: info@velocity.com

Ellen B White, President/CEO

Provides outcomes management system.

4339 VersaForm Systems Corporation
591 W Hamilton Avenue
Suite 230
Campbell, CA 95008-521

800-678-1111
www.versaform.com

Electronic medical records and practice management.

4340 Virtual Software Systems
PO Box 815
Bethel Park, PA 15102-815
412-835-9417
Fax: 412-835-9419

E-mail: sales@vss3.com
www.vss3.com

Thomas Palmquist, Contact

Easy to use practice management, billing, and scheduling software. *$3500.00*

4341 Woodlands
195 Union Street
Suite B1
Newark, OH 43055-3998
740-349-7066
800-686-2756
Fax: 740-345-6028
www.thewoodland.org

Tricia Hufford, Executive Director

4342 Zy-Doc Technologies
1455 Veterans Highway
Hauppauge, NY 11749

800-546-5633
Fax: 516-908-3718
E-mail: sales@zydoc.com
www.zydoc.com

Information Services

4343 3m Health Information Systems
575 Murray Boulevard
Murray, UT 84123-4611
801-265-4400
Fax: 801-263-3657

George W Buckley, CEO

4344 ADL Data Systems
9 Skyline Drive
Hawthorne, NY 10532-2100
914-591-1800
Fax: 914-591-1818
E-mail: sales@mail.adldata.com
www.adldata.com

David Pollack, President

The most comprehensive software solution for MH/MRDD and the continuum of care. 38 modules to choose from. Designed to meet all financial, clinical, and administrative needs. For organizations requiring greater flexiblity and processing power. Ask about new Windows-based products utilizing the latest in technology, including bar coding, scanning, etc.

Year Founded: 1977

4345 Accumedic Computer Systems
11 Grace Avenue
Suite 401
Great Neck, NY 11021-2427

516-466-6800
800-765-9300
Fax: 516-466-6880
E-mail: sales@accumedic.com
www.accumedic.com

Mark Kollenscher, President

Practice management solutions for mental health facilities: scheduling, billing, EMR, HIPAA.

4346 American Institute for Preventive Medicine
30445 Northwestern Highway
Suite 350
Farmington Hills, MI 48334-3107
248-539-1800
800-345-2476
Fax: 248-539-1808
E-mail: aipm@healthylife.com
www.healthylife.com

4347 American Nurses Foundation: National Communications
8515 Georgia Ave
Suite 400 W
Silver Spring, MD 20910-3403
301-628-5000
Fax: 301-628-5001
E-mail: anf@ana.org
www.nursingworld.org

4348 Apache Medical Systems
1650 Tysons Boulevard
Suite 300
McLean, VA 22102-4840
703-847-1400
Fax: 703-847-1401

4349 Applied Computing Services
2764 Allen Road W
Elk, WA 99009

800-553-4055

4350 Applied Informatics (ILIAD)
295 Chipeta Way
Salt Lake City, UT 84108-1287
801-584-6485

4351 Arbour Health System-Human Resource Institute Hospital
227 Babcock Street
Brookline, MA 02446-6773
617-731-3200
www.arbourhealth.com

Patrick Moallemian, CEO

4352 Arservices, Limited
7767 Armistead Rd
Suite 160
Lorton, VA 22079
703-824-6298
Fax: 703-824-6438
www.arserviceslimited.com

Jay A McCargo, President

4353 Association for Ambulatory Behavioral Healthcare
247 Douglas Ave
Portsmouth, VA 23707-1520
757-673-3741
E-mail: mickey@aabh.org

Mickey Wright, Executive Director

Powerful forum for people engaged in providing mental health services. Promoting the evolution of flexible models of responsive cost-effective ambulatory behavioral healthcare.

4354 Behavioral Intervention Planning: Completing a Functional Behavioral Assessment and Developing a Behavioral Intervention Plan
Pro-Ed Publications
8700 Shoal Creek Boulevard
Austin, TX 78757-6897
512-451-3246
800-897-3202
Fax: 512-451-8542

Donald D Hammill, Owner

Provides school personnel with all tools necessary to complete a functional behavioral assessment, determine whether a behavior is related to the disability of the student, and develop a behavioral intervention plan. *$22.00*

4355 Breining Institute College for the Advanced Study of Addictive Disorders
8894 Greenback Lane
Orangevale, CA 95662-4019
916-987-0662
E-mail: college@breining.edu
www.breininginstitute.net

Kathy Breining, Administrator

4356 Brief Therapy Institute of Denver
1333 W 120th Ave
Suite 220
Westminster, CO 80234-2749
303-426-8757
www.btid.com

Marne Wine, Therapist

Our form of psychotherapy emphasizes goals, active participation between therapist and client, client strengths, resources, resiliencies and accountability of the therapy process.

4357 Buckley Productions
238 E Blithedale Avenue
Mill Valley, CA 94941-2083
415-383-2009
877-508-3979
Fax: 415-383-5031
E-mail: buckleypro@aol.com
www.buckleyproductions.com

Richard Buckley, Owner

Alcohol and drug education handbooks, videos, and web-based products for safety sensitive employers, supervisiors and employees who are covered by the Department of Transportaion rules. We provide training materials for Substance Abuse Professional (SAPs) and urine collectors.

4358 CBI Group
100 S Prospect Avenue
Park Ridge, IL 60068-4057
847-698-1090

4359 CMHC Systems
570 Metro Place N
Dublin, OH 43017-1300
614-764-0143

4360 CareCounsel
68 Mitchell Boulevard
Suite 200
San Rafael, CA 94903-2018
415-472-2366
www.carecounsel.com

Larry Gelb, Owner

4361 Catholic Community Services of Western Washington
100 23rd Avenue S
Seattle, WA 98144-2302
206-328-5097
Fax: 206-324-4835
E-mail: info@ccsww.org
www.ccsww.org

Michael Reichert, President

4362 Center for Creative Living
2011 Crooks Road
Royal Oak, MI 48073-4049
248-414-4051
Fax: 248-414-4053
E-mail: cclro@aol.com
www.centerforcreativeliving.com

Diane Braun, Owner

4363 Central Washington Comprehensive M/H
PO Box 959
402 S 4th Ave
Yakima, WA 98902-3546

509-575-4084
800-572-8122
Fax: 509-575-4811
Rick Weaver, CEO

4364 Child Welfare Information Gateway
1250 Maryland Avenue, SW
8th Floor
Washington, DC 20024-2141
703-385-7565
800-394-3366
Fax: 703-385-3206
www.childwelfare.gov

The clearinghouse serves as a facilitator of information and knowledge exchange; the Children's Bureau and its training and technical assistant network; the child abuse and neglect, child welfare, and adoption communities; and allied agencies and professions.

4365 Cirrus Technology
403 Chris Drive
Building 4 Suite H
Huntsville, AL 35802
256-539-2241
Fax: 256-539-3885
E-mail: info@cirrusti.com
www.cirrusti.com

Jerry Harris, Owner

4366 Community Psychiatric Clinic
4319 Stone Way North
Seattle, WA 98103-7444
206-461-3614
www.cpcwa.org

4367 Community Solutions
PO Box 546
Morgan Hill, CA 95038-546
408-842-7138
Fax: 408-778-9672
E-mail: cs@communitysolutions.org
www.communitysolutions.org

4368 Consumer Health Information Corporation
8300 Greensboro Drive
Suite 1220
McLean Va, VA 22102-3661
703-734-0650
Fax: 703-734-1459

Dorothy L Smith, President

4369 Control-O-Fax Corporation
3070 W Airline Highway
Waterloo, IA 50703-9591
319-234-4651
800-553-0070
Fax: 319-236-7332

E-mail: info@controlofax.com
www.controlofax.com
Ken Weber, Manager

4370 DCC/The Dependent Care Connection
500 Nyla Farms
Westport, CT 06880-6270
203-226-2680

4371 Dean Foundation for Health, Research and Education
2711 Allen Boulevard
Suite 300
Middleton, WI 53562-2287
608-824-4800
800-844-6015

Ann C Federman

The Dean Foundation is the non-profit research and education entity of DHS. The Foundation currently encompasses Dean's Educational Services Department, supports community service and health education projects, funds research grants, and conducts its own ancillary research including several outcomes management studies and computer-assisted, voice-activated programs for behavioral medicine.

4372 Distance Learning Network
111 Boal Ave
Boalsburg, PA 16827-1444
814-466-7808

Eric Porterfield, Director

Broadcast and multimedia company dedicated solely to meeting the medical education and communications needs of physicians through the use of both traditional and innovative media formats. More than 150,000 physicians, nurses and pharmacists turn to DLN each year for their medical education.

Year Founded: 1996

4373 Dorland Healthcare Information
PO Box 25128
Salt Lake City, UT 84125-128

800-784-2332
Fax: 801-365-2300
E-mail: info@dorlandhealth.com
www.dorlandhealth.com

4374 FOCUS: Family Oriented Counseling Services
PO Box 921
1435 Hauck Drive
Rolla, MO 65401-2586
573-364-7551
800-356-5395
Fax: 573-364-4898
www.rollanet.org

4375 Federation of Families for Children's Mental Health
9605 Medical Center Drive
Suite 280
Rockville, MD 20850-6390
240-403-1901
Fax: 240-403-1909
E-mail: ffcmh@ffcmh.org
www.ffcmh.org

National family-run organization dedicated exclusively to children and adolesents with mental health needs and their families. Our voice speaks through our work in policy, training and technical assistance programs. Publishes a quarterly newsletter and sponsors an annual conference and exhibits.

4376 HSA-Mental Health
1080 Emeline Avenue
Santa Cruz, CA 95060-1966
831-454-4000
Fax: 831-454-4770
TDD: 831-454-2123
E-mail: info@santacruzhealth.org
www.santacruzhealth.org

Exists to protect and improve the health of the people in Santa Cruz County. Provides programs in environmental health, public health, medical care, substance abuse prevention and treatment, and mental health. Clients are entitled to information on the costs of care and their options for getting health insurance coverage through a variety of programs.

4377 Hagar and Associates
164 W Hospitality Lane
San Bernardino, CA 92408-3316
909-890-4050

Deborah Hagar, Owner

Provides clients with data, from national databases, of outcomes, patient demographics, and benchmark data. Can provide technology and/or automated data connection. Provides support in objective outcomes measurement.

4378 Healthcare Management Systems
3102 W End Avenue
Suite 400
Nashville, TN 37203-1623
615-383-7300
Fax: 615-383-6093
www.hmstn.com

Thomas M Stephenson, CEO

4379 Healthcheck
3954 Youngfield Street
Wheat Ridge, CO 80033-3865
916-556-1880

4380 Human Resources Consulting Group
1202 Dover Drive
Provo, UT 84604-5240

801-765-4417
Fax: 801-765-4418
www.hrconsultinggroup.com

Consultants in Human Resoures and benefits plan design. Software systems and evolutions nation wide.

4381 INMED/MotherNet America
45449 Severn Way
Suite 161
Sterling, VA 20166-8918
703-444-4477
Fax: 703-444-4471
www.inmed.org

4382 Information Access Technology
1100 E 6600 S
Suite 300
Salt Lake City, UT 84121-7411
801-265-8800
800-574-8801
Fax: 801-265-8880
www.iat-cti.com

David H Rudd, CEO

4383 Informedics
4000 Kruse Way Place
Lake Oswego, OR 97035-5545
503-697-3000
www.informedics.com

4384 Lad Lake
PO Box 158
W350 S1401 Waterville Rd
Dousman, WI 53118-9020
262-965-2131
Fax: 262-965-4107
www.ladlake.org

Donna Thompson, Owner

4385 Lanstat Incorporated
517 125th Ave NE
Lake Stevens, WA 98258
425-377-2540
800-672-3166
Fax: 425-334-3124
E-mail: info@lanstat.com
www.lanstat.com

Landon Kimbrough, President
Sherry Kimbrough, VP/Co-Founder

Provides quality technical assistance to behavioral health treatment agencies nationwide, including tribal and government agencies.

4386 Liberty Healthcare Management Group
75 Seminary Hill Road
Carmel, NY 10512-1921
845-225-3400

Liberty provides individualized programs and a continuum of services for psychiatric and substance abuse treatment at our centers located throughout the Northeast, Oklahoma and Florida. Liberty's commitment to medical excellence within an environment of results-oriented care is evident in our outstanding record of clinical success.

4387 Lifelink Corporation/Bensenville Home Society
331 S York Road
Bensenville, IL 60106-2673
630-766-3570
www.lifelink.org

4388 Managed Care Local Market Overviews
Dorland Healthcare Information
PO Box 25128
Salt Lake City, UT 84125-128

800-784-2332
Fax: 801-365-2300
E-mail: info@dorlandhealth.com
www.dorlandhealth.com

Delivers valuable intelligence on local health and managed care marekts. Each of these 71 reports describes key market participants and competitive environment in one US market, including information on: local trends in events, key players, alliances among MCOs and providers, legislative developments, regulatory development, statistics on Managed Penetration. *$475.00*

4389 Manisses Communication Group
Manisses Communications Group
208 Governor Street
Providence, RI 02906-3246
401-831-6020
Fax: 401-861-6370
www.manisses.com

Fraser Lang, President/Publisher
Paul Newman, Director Of Sales

4390 Mayo HealthQuest/Mayo Clinic Health Information
200 1st Street SW
Rochester, MN 55905-1
507-284-2511
Fax: 507-284-5824

Dennis Cortese, CEO

4391 Medical Data Research
5225 Wiley Post Way
Suite 500
Salt Lake City, UT 84116-2825
801-536-1110

Karen Beckstead, Contact

4392 Medipay
521 SW 11th Avenue
Suite 200
Portland, OR 97205-2620
503-227-6491

Complete information technology solutions for integrated continuum of managed behavioral health care.

4393 Meridian Resource Corporation
1401 Enclave Parkway
Suite 300
Houston, TX 77077-2054
281-597-7000
Fax: 281-597-8880

Paul Ching, CEO

4394 Microsoft Corporation
1 Microsoft Way
Redmond, WA 98052-8300
425-882-8080
800-642-7676
Fax: 425-936-7329
www.microsoft.com

Steve Ballmer, CEO

4395 NASW West Virginia Chapter
1608 Virginia Street E
Charleston, WV 25311-2114
304-345-6279
E-mail: naswwv@aol.com
www.naswpress.org

Sam Hickman, Executive Director

4396 National Child Support Network
PO Box 1018
Fayetteville, AR 72702-1018
479-582-2300
www.childsupport.org

4397 National Council on Alcoholism and Drug Dependence
244 East 58th Street
4th Floor
New York, NY 10022-2001
212-269-7797
Fax: 212-269-7510
E-mail: national@ncadd.org
www.ncadd.org

4398 National Families in Action
2957 Clairmont Road NE
Suite 150
Atlanta, GA 30329-1647
404-248-9676
Fax: 404-248-1312
E-mail: nfia@nationalfamilies.org
www.nationalfamilies.org

Sue Rusche, President

4399 National Mental Health Self-Help Clearinghouse
1211 Chestnut Street
Suite 1207
Philadelphia, PA 19107-4103
215-751-1810
800-553-4539
Fax: 215-636-6312
E-mail: info@mhselfhelp.org
www.mhselfhelp.org

4400 North Bay Center for Behavioral Medicine
1100 Trancas Street
Suite 244
Napa, CA 94558-2960
707-255-7786
www.behavioralmed.org

Frank Lucchetti, Psychologist

Represents comprehensive assessment and a balanced schedule of medical and/or psychological treatments for individuals with disabilities needing relief from chronic pain, disabling conditions and stress related to depression, anxiety, and unhealthy work, community or family conditions.

4401 On-Line Information Services
Po Box 1489
Winterville, NC 28590-1489
252-758-4141
800-765-8268
www.onlineinfoservices.com

4402 Open Minds
Behavioral Health Industry News
163 York Street
Gettysburg, PA 17325-1933
717-334-1329
877-350-6463
Fax: 717-334-0538
E-mail: openminds@openminds.com
www.openminds.com

Provides information on marketing, financial, and legal trends in the delivery of mental health and chemical dependency benefits and services. Recurring features include interviews, news of research, a calendar of events, job listings, book reviews, notices of publications available, and industry statistics. *$185.00*

12 pages 12 per year ISSN 1043-3880

4403 Optum
Mail Route MN010-S203
6300 Olson Memorial Highway
Golden Valley, MN 55427-4946
763-595-3200
888-262-4614
Fax: 763-595-3333

David Elton, Senior VP

A market leader in providing comprehensive information, education and support services that enhance quality of life through improved health and well-being. Through multiple access points-the telephone, audio tapes, print materials, in-person consultations and the Internet-Optum helps participants address daily living concerns, make appropriate health care decisions, and become more effective managers of their own health and well-being.

4404 Our Town Family Center
3830 E Bellevue
Street 85716
Tucson, AZ 85716-4012
520-323-1708
Fax: 520-323-9077

Sue Eggleston, Executive Director

A general social services agency which focuses on serving children, youth, and their families. We offer low or no cost assistance with counseling, prevention, services for homeless youth and runaways (their families too) mediation, services for at risk youth, residential programs, parent mentoring, and much more. Our Town has made a conscious decision to keep its services focused in Pima County, in order to better serve our community. We are nonprofit, and funded by United Way, private donations, and grants with the state, county and city.

4405 Ovid Online
Ovid Technologies
333 7th Avenue
New York, NY 10001-5004
212-563-3006
800-950-2035
Fax: 212-674-6301
E-mail: sales@ovid.com
www.ovid.com

Karen Abramson, CEO

Online reference and database information provider.
$.50/record

4406 Patient Medical Records
901 Tahoka Road
Brownfield, TX 79316-3817
806-637-2556
800-285-7627

4407 Penelope Price
4281 MacDuff Pl
Dublin, OH 43016-9510
614-793-0165

4408 Physicians' ONLINE
560 White Plains Road
Tarrytown, NY 10591-5113
914-333-5800

4409 Piedmont Community Services
24 Clay Street
Martinsville, VA 24112-2810
276-632-7128
Fax: 276-638-5450
www.piedmontcsb.org

Mary Kay Berger, Manager

4410 Point of Care Technologies
6 Taft Court
Rockville, MD 20850-5331
301-610-2400

4411 Quadramed
12110 Sunset Hills Road
Reston, VA 20190-5852
703-709-2300
800-393-0278
Fax: 703-709-2490
www.quadramed.com

Duncan W James, CEO

4412 Servisource
40520 Hayes Road
Clinton Township, MI 48038-2543
586-286-1101

Bob Byrne, Owner

4413 SilverPlatter Information
100 River Ridge Drive
Suite 200
Norwood, MA 02062-5041
781-769-2599
Fax: 781-769-8763

4414 Stress Management Research Associates
10609-B Grant Road
Houston, TX 77070-4462
281-890-8575
E-mail: relax@stresscontrol.com
www.stresscontrol.com

Edward Charlesworth, Contact

4415 Supervised Lifestyles
2505 Carmel Ave
Suite 210
Brewster, NY 10509-1122
845-279-5639
888-822-7348
Fax: 845-279-7678
E-mail: sls@slshealth.com

4416 Technical Support Systems
775 E 3300 S
1
Salt Lake City, UT 84106-4078

801-484-1283
www.tssutah.com

Harry Heightman, Manager

4417 Telepad Corporation
380 Herndon Parkway
Suite 1900
Herndon, VA 20170-4881
703-834-9000

4418 Traumatic Incident Reduction Association
5145 Pontiac Trail
Ann Arbor, MI 48105-9279
734-761-6268
800-499-2751
Fax: 734-663-6861
E-mail: info@tir.org
www.tir.org

Traumatic Incident Reduction is a brief, person-sentered treatmetn for the affects of all sorts of trauma and loss. It is part of the larger subject of Applied Metapsychology, which addresses relationship, self-esteem and well-being issues of all sorts, including traumatic stress. Additional web site for TIR: www.tirbook.com

4419 UNISYS Corporation
8008 Westpark Drive
McLean, VA 22102-3109
703-847-2412

4420 Universal Behavioral Service
3590 N Meridian Street
Indianapolis, IN 46208-4425
317-684-0442

4421 Virginia Beach Community Service Board
289 Independence Blvd
#138
Virginia Beach, VA 23462-5492
757-437-6150

4422 Well Mind Association
1201 Western Ave
Seattle, WA 98101-2936
206-728-9770
800-556-5829
Fax: 206-728-1500
www.speakeasy.net

Well Mind Association distributes information on current research and promotes alternative therapies for mental illness and related disorders. WMA believes that physical conditions and treatable biochemical imbalances are the causes of many mental, emotional and behavioral problems.

Pharmaceutical Companies

Manufacturers A-Z

4423 Abbott Laboratories
100 Abbott Park Road
Abbott Park, IL 60064-3500
847-937-6100
www.abbott.com

Miles D White, CEO

Manufactures the following psychological drugs: Cylert, Desoxyn, Depakote, Nembutal, Placidyl, Prosom, Tranxene.

4424 Akzo Nobel
525 W Van Buren Street
Chicago, IL 60607-3845
312-544-7000
800-906-9977
Fax: 312-544-7188
E-mail: csrusa@sc.akzonobel.com
www.akzonobel.com

Phil Radtke, President
Rob Frohn, CFO

Manufactures the following psychological drugs: Tolvon.

4425 Astra Zeneca Pharmaceuticals
1800 Concord Pike
PO Box 15437
Wilmington, DE 19850-5437
302-886-3000
Fax: 302-886-3119
www.astrazeneca-us.com

Tony Zook, President/CEO
David Elkins, Vice President/CFO

Full range of products in six therapeutic areas; gastrointestinal, oncology, anesthesia, cardiovascular, central nervous system and respiratory.

4426 Bristol-Myers Squibb
345 Park Avenue
New York, NY 10154-28
212-546-4000
Fax: 212-546-4020
www.bms.com

James M Cornelius, CEO

Manufactures the following psychological drugs: Avapro, Enfamil, Abilify, Provachol, and Serzone.

4427 Cephalon
41 Moores Road
Frazer, PA 19355-1113
610-344-0200
Fax: 610-738-6590
E-mail: humanresources@cephalon.com
www.cephalon.com

Frank Baldino Jr, CEO
Frank Baldino, Chairman/CEO

Manufactures the following pharmaceuticals: Provigil, Amrix, Fentora, Vivitrol, Trisenox, Nuvigil.

4428 Eisai
100 Tice Blvd
Woodcliff Lake, NJ 07677-8404
201-692-1100

Judee Shuler, Dir. Corp. Plans/Communications
Robert Feeney, Dir. Investor & Gov. Relations

Manufactures the following psychological drug: Aricept, Aciphex, Fragmin, Zonegran.

4429 Eli Lilly and Company
Lilly Corporate Center
Indianapolis, IN 46285
317-276-2000
www.lilly.com

John C Lechleiter, Chairman, President & CEO
Robert Armitage, Senior VP, General Counsel
E Paul Ahern PhD, SVP, Global API Manufacturing

Manufactures the following psychological drugs: Prozac, Ceclor, Zyprexa, Cialis, Strattera, and Symbyax.

4430 First Horizon Pharmaceutical
6195 Shiloh Road
Alpharetta, GA 30005-8413
770-442-9707
Fax: 770-442-9594
www.horizonpharm.com

Manufactures the following products:Triglide, Fortamet, and Altopren.

4431 Forest Laboratories
909 Third Avenue
New York, NY 10022-4748
212-421-7850
800-947-5227
Fax: 212-750-9152
www.frx.com

Howard Solomon, CEO

Manufactures the following psychological drugs: Lexapro, Benicar, Campral, Celexa, Namenda, and Tiazac.

4432 GlaxoSmithKline
5 Moore Drive
PO Box 13398
Research Triangle Park, NC 27709-3398

888-825-5249
Fax: 919-483-5249
www.gsk.com

JP Garnier, CEO

Manufactures the following psychological drugs: Lamictal, Paxil, Parnate.

4433 Hoffman-La Roche
340 Kingsland Street
Nutley, NJ 07110-1199
973-235-3091
Fax: 973-235-5477

George Abercrombie, President/CEO

Manufactures the following psychological drugs: Boniva
Valium, Klonopin, Valcyte, Zenapax.

4434 Janssen
1125 Trenton-Harbourton Road
PO Box 200
Titusville, NJ 08560-1002
609-730-2000
800-526-7736
www.janssen.com

Timothy Cost, Senior VP Corporate Affairs

Janssen markets prescription medications for the treatment
of schizophrenia and bipolar disorder. Medications include:
Invega and Risperdal.

4435 Jazz Pharmaceuticals
3180 Porter Drive
Palo Alto, CA 94304
650-496-3777
Fax: 650-496-3781
www.jazzpharma.com

Bruce C Cozadd, Chairman & CEO
Robert M Myers, President
Kathryn E Falberg, SVP & Chief Financial Officer

Manufactures the following medications: Luvox, Xyrem.

4436 Johnson & Johnson
One Johnson & Johnson Plaza
New Brunswick, NJ 08933-1
732-524-0400
www.jnj.com

William C Weldon, CEO

Manufactures the following: Concerta, Haldol, Reminyl,
Daktarin, Ertaczo, Levaquin.

4437 King Pharmaceuticals
501 Fifth Street
Bristol, TN 37620-2304
423-989-8000
800-776-7637
Fax: 423-274-8677
www.kingpharm.com

Brian A Markison, CEO
David Robinson, Senior Dir. Corporate Affairs

Manufactures some of the following medications: Sonata,
Corgard, Cytomel, Humatin, Levoxyl, Procanbid, and
Septra.

4438 Mallinckrodt
Corporate Headquarters
675 McDonnell Boulevard
Hazelwood, MO 63042-2379
314-654-2000

Douglas McKinney, VP Of Finance/CFO
Lisa Britt, VP Of Human Resources

Manufactures the following psychological drugs: Dexedrine, Methylin, Anafranil.

4439 Merck
One Merck Drive
PO Box 100
Whitehouse Station, NJ 08889-100
908-423-1000
www.merck.com

Peter Kellogg, Executive VP/CFO
Mirian Graddick-Weir, Executive VP Human Resources

Manufactures: Vioxx, Zocor, Fosamax, Cozaar, Januvia,
Triavil and others.

4440 Mylan
1500 Corporate Drive
Canonsburg, PA 15317
724-514-1800
www.mylan.com

Robert J Coury, Chairman & CEO
Heather Bresch, President
Rajiv Malik, Chief Operating Officer

Manufactures the following psychological drugs: Ativan,
BuSpar, Klonopin, Tranxene, Valium, Xanax, Xanax XR

4441 Novartis
400 Technology Square
Cambridge, MA 02139-3545
617-871-8000
Fax: 617-871-8911
www.novartis.com

Daniel Vasella, Chairman/CEO
Raymund Breu, CFO

Manufactures the following products: Diovan, Glivec,
Lamisil, Zometa, Focalin and more.

4442 Organon Schering Plough
56 Livingston Avenue
Roseland, NJ 07068-1733
973-325-4500
Fax: 973-325-4589
www.schering-plough.com

Fred Hassan, CEO

Manufactures the following: Remeron, Nuvaring, Follistia,
Ganirelix, and Zemuron.

4443 Ortho-McNeil Pharmaceutical
1125 Trenton Harbourton Road
P.O. Box 200
Titusville, NJ 08560-1002

800-526-7736
www.ortho-mcneil.com

Manufactures the following: Elmiron, Modicon, Ortho-Novum, and Terazol 3.

4444 Otsuka Pharmaceutical Group

One Embarcadero Center
Suite 2020
San Francisco, CA 94111
415-986-5300
Fax: 415-986-5361
www.otsuka-global.com

Taro Iwamoto, President

Manufactures the following psychological drugs: Abilify

4445 Pfizer

235 E 42nd Street
New York, NY 10017-5703
212-573-2323
www.pfizer.com

Jeffrey B Kindler, CEO

Manufactures the following psychological drugs: Geodon, Halcion, Navane, Navane IM, Neurontin, Reboxetine, Relpax, Sinequan, Vistaril, Xanax, Zoloft.

4446 Roxane Laboratories

1809 Wilson Road
PO Box 16532
Columbus, OH 43216-6532
614-276-4000
Fax: 614-274-0974

Manufactures detoxification medication: Dolophine.

4447 Sanofi-Aventis

55 Corporate Drive
Bridgewater, NJ 08807-1265
908-981-5000
Fax: 908-231-4744

Paul Chew, President

Manufacturer of medication for cardiovascular disease, thrombosis, oncology, diabetes, central nervous system, internal medicine, and vaccines. Medication includes Wellbutrin, Wellbutrin SR, and Wellbutrin XL.

4448 Sepracor Pharmaceuticals

84 Waterford Drive
Marlborough, MA 01752-7010
508-481-6700
800-586-3782
Fax: 508-357-7478
E-mail: info@sepracor.com
www.sepracor.com

Adrian Adams, CEO
Mark Iwicki, Exeecutive Vice President/COO

Manufactures sleep disorder drug Lunesta,as well as other medications Xopenex, and Brovana.

4449 Shire Richwood

725 Chesterbrook Blvd
Wayne, PA 19087-5649
484-595-8800
Fax: 484-595-8200

Angus Russell, CEO
Barbara Deptula, Exec. VP Bussiness Development

Manufactures the following psychological drugs: Adderall, DextroStat.

4450 Solvay Pharmaceuticals

901 Sawyer Road
Marietta, GA 30062-2250
770-578-9000
Fax: 770-578-5597
www.solvaypharmaceuticals.com

Stephen Hill, CEO
Jessica Mumaw, Contact

Manufactures the following psychological drugs: Klonopin, Lithobid, Lithonate.

4451 Somerset Pharmaceuticals

5415 W Laurel Street
Tampa, FL 33607-1729
813-288-0040
www.somersetpharm.com

Manufactures the following psychological drug: Eldepryl.

4452 Synthon Pharmaceuticals

9000 Development Drive
PO Box 110487
Research Triangle, NC 27709-5487
919-493-6006
Fax: 919-493-6104
E-mail: info@synthon.com
www.synthon-usa.com

Develops, produces and sells high quality alternatives to innovative medicines. Our products are marketed at the earliest possible opportunity and we sell them at competitive prices.

4453 Takeda Pharmaceuticals North America

One Takeda Parkway
Deerfield, IL 60015-5713
847-383-3000
877-582-5332
Fax: 847-383-3080

Shinji Honda, CEO

Manufacturer of Rozerem, Duetact, Amitiza, and Actos.

4454 Valeant Pharmaceuticals International

One Enterprise
Aliso Viejo, CA 92656-2606
949-461-6000
800-548-5100

Fax: 949-461-6609
www.valeant.com

J Michael Pearson, CEO

Develops, manufactures and markets pharmaceutical products primarily in the areas of neurology, dermatology and infectious disease.

4455 Validus Pharmaceuticals

119 Cherry Hill Road
Suite 310
Parsippany, NJ 07054
973-265-2777
Fax: 973-265-2770
E-mail: jhunter@validuspharma.com
www.validuspharma.com

James R Hunter, President
Lee Rios, Chief Operating Officer

Manufactures the following psychological drugs: Marplan, Equetro.

4456 Watson Pharmaceuticals

311 Bonnie Circle
Corona, CA 92880-2882
951-493-5300

Paul M Bisaro, CEO

Manufactures the following medications: Ferrlecit, Quasense, Androderm, Nicotine Polacrilex Gum USP, Trelstar, Oxycodone and Acetaminophen Tablets USP, Oxytrol.

4457 Wyeth

5 Giralda Farms
Madison, NJ 07940-1021
973-660-5000
Fax: 973-660-5103

Bernard J Poussot, CEO

Manufactures the following products: Advil brands, Alavert, Anbesol, Ativan, Caltrate, Centrum brands, Dimetapp, FiberCon, Preparation H, and Loxitane.

Drugs A-Z

4458 Abilify
Generic: aripiprazole

Used in the treatment of psychotic disorders and bipolar disorder. This product is manufactured by Bristol-Myers Squibb and Otsuka. See manufacturers section for company information.

4459 Adderall/Adderall XR
Generic: amphetamine/dextroamphetamine

Used to manage anxiety disorders and some cases of attention deficit hyperactivity disorder. This product is manufactured by Shire Richwood. See Manufacturers section for company information.

4460 Ambien/Ambien CR
Generic: zolpidem

Used in the treatment of insomnia, also sold as Tovalt. This product is manufactured by Sanofi-Aventis. See Manufacturers section for company information.

4461 Anafranil
Generic: clomipramine

Used in the treatment of obsessive-compulsive disorder. This product is manufactured by Mallinckrodt Pharmaceuticals. See Manufacturers section for company information.

4462 Antabuse
Generic: disulfiram

Used in the treatment of alcohol and substance abuse. This product is manufactured by Wyeth-Ayers. See Manufacturers section for company information.

4463 Aricept
Generic: donepezil

Used in the treatment of Alzheimer's disease. This product is manufactured by and Eisai. See Manufacturers section for company information.

4464 Asenapine
Generic: saphris

Sublingual tablets used in the treatment for schizophreina. Manufactured by Schering-Plough. See Manufacturers section for company information.

4465 Ativan
Generic: lorazepam

Used in the treatment of anxiety and as a preanesthetic medication in adults. This product is manufactured by Wyeth. See Manufacturers section for company information.

4466 BuSpar
Generic: buspirone

Used in the treatment of anxiety. This product is manufactured by Mylan. See Manufacturers section for company information.

4467 Campral
Generic: acamprosate

Used for alcohol abstinence. This product is manufactured by Forest Laboratories. See Manufacturers section for company information.

4468 Celexa
Generic: citalopram

Used in the treatment of depression. This product is manufactured by Forest Laboratories. See Manufacturers section for company information.

4469 Clozaril
Generic: clozapine

Used in the treatment of severe schizophrenia, and also sold as Clozaril and Fazaclo. This product is manufactured by Novartis. See Manufacturers section for company information.

4470 Cognex
Generic: tacrine

Used in the treatment of dementia. This product is manufactured by First Horizon Pharmaceutical. See Manufacturers section for company information.

4471 Concerta
Generic: methylphenidate

Used in the treatment of attention deficit disorder, and also sold as Daytrana and Desoxyn. This product is manufactured by Johnson & Johnson. See Manufacturers section for company information.

4472 Cymbalta
Generic: dulozetine

Used in the treatment of depression. Manufactured by Eli Lilly and Company. See Manufacturers section for company information.

4473 Depakote
Generic: valproic acid

Used in the treatment of manic episodes associated with bipolar disorder and mania, and also sold as Depakene. This product is manufactured by Abbott Laboratories. See Manufacturers section for company information.

4474 Desoxyn
Generic: methamphetamine

Used in the treatment of attention deficit hyperactivity disorder. This product is manufactured by Abbott Laboratories. See Manufacturers section for company information.

4475 Desvenlafaxine
Generic: pristiq

Used in the treatment of fibromyalgia. Manufacturered by Wyeth. See Manufacturers section for company information.

4476 Dexedrine
Generic: dextroamphetamine

Used in the treatment of attention deficit hyperactivity disorder, and also sold as DextroState, Focalin (by Novartis), Metadate, and Methylin. This product is manufactured by Mallinckrodt. See Manufacturers section for company information.

4477 Dolophine
Generic: methadone

Used in the treatment of detoxifcation and opioid addiction. This product is manufactured by Roxane Laboratories. See manufacturers section for company information.

4478 Effexor
Generic: venlafazine

Used in the treatment of depression and generalized anxiety disorder. This product is manufactured by Wyeth-Ayerst Laboratories. See Manufacturers section for company information.

4479 Elavil
Generic: amitryptiline

Used in the treatment of depression, also sold as Limbitrol (by Valeant). This product is manufactured by Astra Zeneca Pharmaceuticals. See Manufacturers section for company information.

4480 Emsam
Generic: selegiline

Used in the treatment of major depressive disorder. This product is manufactured by Bristol-Myers Squibb. See manufacturers section for company information.

4481 Equetro
Generic: carbarnazepine

Used in the treatment of bipolar disorder. Manufactured by Validus. See Manufacturers section for company information.

4482 Eskalith
Generic: lithium

Used in the treatment of bipolar disorder. This product is manufactured by GlaxoSmithKline. See Manufacturers section for company information.

4483 Exelon
Generic: rivastigmine

Used in the treatment of Alzheimer's disease. This product is manufactured by Novartis. See Manufacturers section for company information.

4484 Focalin/Focalin XR
Generic: dexmethylphenidate

Used in the treatment of attention deficit hyperactivity disorder. This product is manufactured by Novartis. See Manufacturers section for company information.

4485 Geodon
Generic: ziprasidone

Used in the treatment of psychoses and bipolar disorder. This product is manufactured by Pfizer. See Manufacturers section for company information.

4486 Halcion
Generic: triazolam

Used in the treatment of insomnia. This product is manufactured by Pfizer. See Manufacturers section for company information.

4487 Haldol
Generic: haloperidol

Used in the treatment of Schizophrenia. This product is manufactured by Johnson & Johnson. See manufacturers section for company information.

4488 Invega
Generic: paliperidone

Used in the treatment of Schizophrenia. This product is manufactured by Janssen. See manufacturers section for company information.

4489 Klonopin
Generic: clonazepam

Used in the treatment of panic attacks/anxiety. This product is manufactured by Hoffman-La Roche. See Manufacturers section for company information.

4490 Lamictal
Generic: lamotrigine

Used in the treatment of bipolar disorder. This product is manufactured by GlaxoSmithKline. See Manufacturers section for company information.

4491 Leponex
Generic: clozapine

Used in the treatment of Schizophrenia. This product is manufactured by Novartis. See Manufacturers section for company information.

4492 Lexapro
Generic: escitalopram

Used in the treatment of depression. This product is manufactured by Forest Laboratories. See Manufacturers section for company information.

4493 Lithobid
Generic: lithium; eskalith

Used in the treatment of bipolar disorder and depression. This product is manufactured by Solvay Pharmaceuticals. See Manufacturers section for company information.

4494 Loxitane
Generic: loxapine

Used in the treatment of Schizophrenia. This product is manufactured by Lederle Pharmaceuticals. See manufacturers section for company information.

4495 Lunesta
Generic: eszopiclone

Used in the treatment of insomnia. This product is manufactured by Sepracor. See Manufacturers section for company information.

4496 Luvox
Generic: fluvoxamine

Used in the treatment of obsessive compulsive disorder and depression. This product is manufactured by Jazz Pharmaceuticals. See Manufacturers section for company information.

4497 Marplan
Generic: isocarboxazid

Used in the treatment of depression, anxiety and panic disorders. Manufactured by Validus. See Manufacturers section for company information.

4498 Methylin
Generic: methylphenidate

Used in the treatment of attention deficit hyperactivity disorder. This product is manufactured by Mallinckrodt. See Manufacturers section for company information.

4499 Milnacipran HCl
Generic: savella

Used in the treatment for major depressive disorder. Manufactured by Forest Laboratories. See Manufacturers section for company information.

4500 Namenda
Generic: memantine

Used in the treatment of dementia. This product is manufactured by Forest Pharmaceuticals. See Manufacturers section for company information.

4501 Nardil
Generic: phenelzine

Used in the treatment of depression. This product is manufactured by Pfizer. See Manufacturers section for company information.

4502 Navane, Navane IM
Generic: thiothiyene

Used in the treatment of psychotic disorders such as Schizophrenia. This product is manufactured by Pfizer. See Manufacturers section for company information.

4503 Neurontin
Generic: gabapentin

Used in the treatment of seizures and neuropathic pais. This product is manufactured by Pfizer. See Manufacturers section for company information.

4504 Norpramin
Generic: desipramine

Used in the treatment of depression. This product is manufactured by Aventis Pharmaceuticals. See Manufacturers section for company information.

4505 Nuvigil
Generic: amodafinil

Used in the treatment of narcolepsy. This product is manufactured by Cephalon. See Manufacturers section for company information.

4506 Pamelor
Generic: nortriptyline

Used in the treatment of depression. This product is manufactured by Sandoz Pharmaceuticals. See Manufacturers section for company information.

4507 Parnate
Generic: tranylcypromine

Used to help manage depression. This product is manufactured by GlaxoSmithKline. See Manufacturers section for company information.

4508 Paxil
Generic: parozetine

Used in the treatment of depression, and anxiety disorders. This product is manufactured by GlaxoSmithKline. Sold also as Pexeva by Synthon. See Manufacturers section for company information.

4509 Prolixin
Generic: fluphenazine

Used in the treatment of psychotic disorders. This product is manufactured by Bristol-Myers Squibb. See Manufacturers section for company information.

4510 Provigil
Generic: modafinil

Used in the treatment of narcolepsy. This product is manufactured by Cephalon. See Manufacturers section for company information.

4511 Prozac
Generic: fluozetine

Used in the treatment of depression and anxiety disorders. This product is manufactured by Eli Lilly and Company. See Manufacturers section for company information.

4512 Razadyne ER
Generic: galantamine

Used in the treatment of dementia. This product is manufactured by Ortho-McNeil. See Manufacturers section for company information.

4513 Reboxetine
Generic: vestra

Used in the treatment of depression. This product is manufactured by Pfizer. See Manufacturers section for company information.

4514 Relpax
Generic: eletriptan

Used in the treatment of migraines. This product is manufactured by Pfizer. See Manufacturers section for company information.

4515 Remeron
Generic: mirtazapine

Used in the treatment of manage depression. This product is manufactured by Organon. See Manufacturers section for company information.

4516 Reminyl
Generic: razadyne

Used in the treatment of Alzheimer's disease. This product is manufactured by Johnson & Johnson. See Manufacturers section for company information.

4517 Risperdal
Generic: risperidone

Used in the treatment of schizophrenia and other mental illnesses such as psychosis. This product is manufactured by Janssen. See Manufacturers section for company information.

4518 Ritalin
Generic: methylphenidate

Used in the treatment of attention deficit hyperactivity disorders and in some forms of narcolepsy. This product is manufactured by Novartis. See Manufacturers section for company information.

4519 Rozerem
Generic: ramelteon

Used in the treatment of insomnia. This product is manufactured by Takeda Pharmaceuticals. See Manufacturers section for company information.

4520 Seroquel
Generic: quetiapine

Used in the treatment of Schizophrenia. This product is manufactured by AstraZeneca Pharmaceuticals. See Manufacturers section for company information.

4521 Serzone
Generic: nefazodone

Used in the treatment of depression. This product is manufactured by Bristol-Meyers Squibb. See Manufacturers section for company information.

4522 Sinequan
Generic: doxepin hcl

Used in the treatment of psychosis. This product is manufactured by Pfizer. See Manufacturers section for company information.

4523 Sonata
Generic: zalplon

Used in the treatment of insomnia. This product is manufactured by King Pharmaceuticals. See Manufacturers section for company information.

4524 Strattera
Generic: atomoxetine

Used in the treatment of attention deficit disorder. This product is manufactured by Eli Lilly & Company. See Manufacturers section for company information.

4525 Surmontil
Generic: trimipramine

Used in the treatment of depression. This product is manufactured by Wyeth-Ayerst Laboratories. See Manufacturers section for company information.

4526 Symbyax
Generic: fluoxetine

Used in the treatment of depression and anxiety disorders. This product is manufactured by Eli-Lilly & Company. See Manufacturers section for company information.

4527 Tofranil
Generic: imipramine

Used in the treatment of depression. This product is manufactured by Novartis Pharmaceuticals. See Manufacturers section for company information.

4528 Tolvon
Generic: mianserin hydrochloride

Used in the treatment of depression. This product is manufactured by Akzo Nobel. See Manufacturers section for company information.

4529 Topamax
Generic: topiramate

Used in the treatment of seizures and migraines. This product is manufactured by Ortho-McNeil Pharmaceutical. See Manufacturers section for company information.

4530 Tranxene
Generic: clorazepate

Used in the treatment of anxiety. This product is manufactured by Abbott Laboratories. See Manufacturers section for company information.

4531 Triavil
Generic: perphenazine+amitriptyline

Used in the treatment of depression with psychosis, agitation and anxiety. This product is manufactured by Merck. See Manufacturers section for company information.

4532 Valium
Generic: diazepam

Used in the treatment of anxiety. This product is manufactured by Hoffman-La Roche. See Manufacturers section for company information.

4533 Vistaril
Generic: hydroxyzine pamoate

Used in the treatment of anxiety and tension associated with psychoneuroses. This product is manufactured by Pfizer. See Manufacturers section for company information.

4534 Vyvanse
Generic: lixdexamfetamine

Used in the treatment of attention deficit hyperactivity disorder. This product is manufactured by Shire Richwood. See Manufacturers section for company information.

4535 Wellbutrin, Wellbutrin SR, Wellbutrin XL
Generic: bupropion

Used in the treatment of depression. This product is manufactured by Sanofi-Aventis. See Manufacturers section for company information.

4536 Xanax
Generic: alprazolam

Used in the treatment of anxiety. This product is manufactured by Pfizer. See Manufacturers section for company information.

4537 Xyrem
Generic: sodium oxybate

Used in the treatment of narcolepsy. This product is manufactured by Jazz Pharmaceuticals. See Manufacturers section for company information.

4538 Zoloft
Generic: sertraline

Used in the treatment of depression and anxiety disorders. This product is manufactured by Pfizer. See Manufacturers section for company information.

4539 Zyprexa
Generic: olanzapine

Used in the treatment of Schizophrenia. This product is manufactured by Eli Lilly and Company. See Manufacturers section for company information.

Alcohol/Substance Abuse & Dependence

Anxiety Disorders

Cognitive Disorders

Conduct Disorder

Dissociative Disorders

Eating Disorders

Gender Identity Disorder

Impulse Control Disorders

Mood Disorders

Paraphilias (Perversions)

Pediatric & Adolescent Issues

Personality Disorders

Professional & Support Services

Psychosomatic (Somatizing) Disorders

Publishers

Schizophrenia

Sexual Disorders

Sleep Disorders

Suicide

Tic Disorders

Behaviordata, 4206
Behind Bars: Substance Abuse and America's Prison Population, 2751
Bellefaire Jewish Children's Bureau, 1588
Bellin Psychiatric Center, 3968
Bereaved Parents of the USA, 32, 29
Bereaved Parents' Network, 44
Berkowitz Chassion and Sklar, 3999
Berkshire Center, 3771
Berkshire Farm Center and Services for Youth, 3823
Best Buddies International (BBI), 1609
Best of AAMR: Families and Mental Retardation, 2563
BetaData Systems, 4207
Bethesda Lutheran Homes and Services, 1610
Beyond Anorexia, 889
Beyond Anxiety and Phobia, 289
Beyond Behavior Modification: Cognitive-Behavioral Approach to Behavior Management in the School, 2866
Beyond Gentle Teaching, 636
Beyond Ritalin, 502
Bibliotherapy Starter Set, 1457

Big Spring State Hospital, 3923
Bill Ferguson's How to Divorce as Friends, 51
Binge Drinking, 211
Binge Drinking: Am I At Risk?, 163
Binge Eating: Nature, Assessment and Treatment, 890
Biological Basis of Personality, 2906
Biology of Anxiety Disorders, 290
Biology of Personality Disorders, 2907
Biology of Personality Disorders, Review of Psychiatry, 1219
Biology of Schizophrenia and Affective Disease, 1294
Biology of the Autistic Syndromes, 637
Bipolar Affective Disorder in Children and Adolescents, 1530
Bipolar Children and Teens Homepage, 1526
Bipolar Clinic and Research Program, 1141
Bipolar Disorder, 1117
Bipolar Disorder Frequently Asked Questions, 1184, 3436
Bipolar Disorder Survival Guide: What You and Your Family Need to Know, 1058
Bipolar Disorder for Dummies, 1059
Bipolar Disorders Clinic, 1142
Bipolar Disorders Treatment Information Center, 1033, 1183
Bipolar Disorders: A Guide to Helping Children and Adolescents, 1060
Bipolar Disorders: Clinical Course and Outcome, 1061
Bipolar Kids Homepage, 1176, 1524, 3407
Bipolar Puzzle Solution, 1062
Bipolar Research at University of Pennsylvania, 1143
Birds-Eye View of Life with ADD and ADHD: Advice from Young Survivors, Second Edition, 503
Biting The Hand That Starves You: Inspiring Resistance to Anorexia/Bulimia, 2872
Black Mental Health Alliance (BMHA), 1611
Blackwell Publishing, 133
Blaming the Brain: The Truth About Drugs and Mental Health, 2752
Blended Families, 1544, 3446
Blue Mountain Recovery Center, 3887
Body Image, 935
Body Image Workbook: An 8 Step Program for Learning to Like Your Looks, 891

Body Image, Eating Disorders, and Obesity in Youth, 892
Body Image: Understanding Body Dissatisfaction in Men, Women and Children, 2740
Body Logic, 4208
The Body Remembers Casebook: Unifying Methods and Models in the Treatment of Trauma and PTSD, 2830
Body Remembers: Psychophysiology of Trauma and Trauma Treatment, 2792
The Body Remembers: The Psychphysiology of Trauma and Trauma Treatment, 2831
Bolton Press Atlanta, 1571
Bonnie Tapes, 1339
The Bonnie Tapes Mental Illness in the Family; Recovering from Mental Illness; My Sister is Mentally Ill, 1163
Bonny Foundation, 2460
Book of Psychotherapeutic Homework, 1458
A Book: A Collection of Writings from the Advocate, 609
Borderline Personality Disorder, 1220
Borderline Personality Disorder Sanctuary, 1246
The Borderline Personality Disorder Survival Guide, 1242
Borderline Personality Disorder: A Patient's Guide to Taking Control, 1222
Borderline Personality Disorder: A Therapist Guide to Taking Control, 2908
Borderline Personality Disorder: Etilogy and Treatment, 1223
Borderline Personality Disorder: Multidimensional Approach, 1221
Borderline Personality Disorder: Tailoring the Psychotherapy to the Patient, 1224, 2909
Borgess Behavioral Medicine Services, 1845
Boundaries and Boundary Violations in Psychoanalysis, 2564
Boy Who Couldn't Stop Washing, 291
Boysville of Michigan, 1846
Brain Calipers: Descriptive Psychopathology and the Mental Status Examination, Second Edition, 2565
Brain Imaging Handbook, 2355
Brain Lock: Free Yourself from Obsessive Compulsive Behavior, 292
Brandeis University/Heller School, 3234
Branden Publishing Company, 630
Brattleboro Retreat, 3946
Breaking the News, 1523
Breaking the Patterns of Depression, 1063
Breaking the Silence: Teaching the Next Generation About Mental Illness, 1459
Breakthroughs in Antipsychotic Medications: A Guide for Consumers, Families, and Clinicians, 1295, 2566
Breakthroughs: How to Reach Students with Autism, 715
Breining Institute College for the Advanced Study of Addictive Disorders, 3235, 4355
Bridges: Building Recovery & Individual Dreams & Goals Through Education & Support, 1985
Bridgewell, 1835
Brief Coaching for Lasting Solutions, 2567
Brief Therapy Institute of Denver, 4356
Brief Therapy and Eating Disorders, 893
Brief Therapy and Managed Care, 2568
Brief Therapy for Adolescent Depression, 2954
Brief Therapy for Post Traumatic Stress Disorder, 2793
Brief Therapy with Intimidating Cases, 2569
Brilliant Madness: Living with Manic-Depressive Illness, 1064
Bristol-Myers Squibb, 4426
Broadway Books, 316

Broadway Books a Division of Random House, 1573
Broken, 106
Broken Connection: On Death and the Continuity of Life, 1065
Bronx Children's Psychiatric Center, 3824
Bronx Psychiatric Center, 3825
Brookes Publishing, 3541
Brookings Alliance for the Mentally Ill, 1982
Brookline Books/Lumen Editions, 3542, 672
Brooklyn Children's Center, 3826
Broughton Hospital, 3866
Broward County Health Care Services, 4000
Brown Consulting, 4001
Brown Schools Behavioral Health System, 3236
Brown University: Child & Adolescent Psychopharmacology Update, 3087
Brown University: Digest of Addiction Theory and Application (DATA), 3088
Brown University: Geriatric Psychopharmacology Update, 3089
Brown University: Psychopharmacology Update, 3090
Brunner-Routledge Mental Health, 3543
Brunner/Routledge, 2636, 2652, 2806, 2963
BryLin Hospitals, 3827
Bryce Hospital, 3606
BuSpar, 4466
Buckley Productions, 4357
Buffalo Psychiatric Center, 3828
Building Bridges: States Respond to Substance Abuse and Welfare Reform, 2753
Bulimia, 894, 936
Bulimia Nervosa, 895
Bulimia Nervosa & Binge Eating: A Guide To Recovery, 896
Bulimia: News & Discussion Forum, 960
Bulimia: a Guide to Recovery, 897
Bull HN Information Systems, 4209
Bull Publishing Company, 3544
The Bulletin, 3192
Bulletin of Menninger Clinic, 3091
Bulletin of Psychological Type, 3092
Bundle of Blues, 1155
Bureau of Mental Health and Substance Abuse Services, 2344
Bureau of TennCare: State of Tennessee, 2309
Business Objects, 4210
Business Publishers, 3148, 3149
Butler Hospital, 3904

C

CAFCA, 1743
CAMC Family Medicine Center of Charleston, 2043
CARE Child and Adolescent Risk Evaluation: A Measure of the Risk for Violent Behavior, 1460
CARF Directory of Organizations with Accredited Programs, 3503
CARF: Commission on Accreditation of Rehabilitation Facilities, 2356
CASAWORKS for Families: Promising Approach to Welfare Reform and Substance-Abusing Women, 2754
CASCAP, 1836
CBCA, 4002
CBI Group, 4003, 4358
CD Publications, 3102, 3150, 3195
CG Jung Foundation for Analytical Psychology, 2461
CHADD, 3399
CHADD: Children/Adults with Attention Deficit/Hyperactivity Disorder, 1505
CHINS UP Youth and Family Services, 1744

G

H

I

J

N

O

U

X

Y

Z

Nightingale Vantagemed Corporation, 4301
Northern California Psychiatric Society, 1738
Optimum Care Corporation, 4130
Oracle Corporation, 4306
Orange County Psychiatric Society, 1739
Otsuka Pharmaceutical Group, 4444
P and W Software, 4308
PSIMED Corporation, 4134
Parents Helping Parents, 1446, 1677
Pepperdine University, Graduate School of
    Education and Psychology, 3294
Phobics Anonymous, 421
Postpartum Support International, 1052
Practice Management Resource Group, 4142
Psy Care, 4149
Psychological Center, 3300
Raintree Systems, 4317
Rational Recovery, 206
Research Center for Severe Mental Illnesses, 1686
School of Nursing, UCLA, 3312
Shueman and Associates, 4163
Sun Microsystems, 4328
Thomson ResearchSoft, 4332
Training Behavioral Healthcare Professionals,
    3321
TriZetto Group, 4333
Trichotillomania Learning Center, 1003, 1017
Turbo-Doc EMR, 4334
UCLA Department of Psychiatry & Biobehavioral
    Sciences, 1740
UCLA Neuropsychiatric Institute and Hospital,
    3322
UCSF-Department of Psychiatry, Cultural
    Competence, 3323
USC Psychiatry and Psychology Associates, 3324
USC School of Medicine, 3325
United Advocates for Children of California, 1741
United Behavioral Health, 4174
University of California at Davis Psychiatry and
    Behavioral Sciences Department, 3329
Valeant Pharmaceuticals International, 4454
VeriCare, 4180
VeriTrak, 4181
VersaForm Systems Corporation, 4339
Watson Pharmaceuticals, 4456
We Insist on Natural Shapes, 886
WellPoint Behavioral Health, 4184

Colorado

Adolescent and Family Institute of Colorado, 1742
American Association for Protecting Children,
    2382
American Psychology- Law Society (AP-LS), 2429
Asian Pacific Development Center for Human
    Development, 3231
Association for Applied Psychophysiology &
    Biofeedback, 2441
Association for the Advancement of Psychology,
    2453
Behavioral Health Advisor, 4205
Behavioral Health Care, 3994
CAFCA, 1743
CHINS UP Youth and Family Services, 1744
Clinical Nutrition Center, 4221
Colorado Department of Health Care Policy and
    Financing, 2132
Colorado Department of Human Services (CDHS),
    2133
Colorado Department of Human Services: Alcohol
    and Drug Abuse Division, 2134
Colorado Division of Mental Health, 2135
Colorado Health Networks-Value Options, 1745
Colorado Medical Assistance Program Information
    Center, 2136

Colorado Traumatic Brain Injury Trust Fund
    Program, 2137
Craig Counseling & Biofeedback Services, 1746
Denver County Department of Social Services,
    2138
El Paso County Human Services, 2139
Employee Benefit Specialists, 4038
Federation of Families for Children's Mental
    Health: Colorado Chapter, 1747
John Maynard and Associates, 4087
Medcomp Software, 4282
Medical Group Management Association, 2493
Mental Health Association of Colorado, 1748
Micromedex, 4294
Milliman, Inc, 4120
National Academy of Neuropsychology (NAN),
    2496
PRO Behavioral Health, 1676, 4133
University of Colorado Health Sciences Center,
    3331

Connecticut

Aetna-US HealthCare, 3980
American Academy of Clinical Psychiatrists, 2377
American Academy of Psychiatry & Law Annual
    Conference, 3044
American Academy of Psychiatry and the Law
    (AAPL), 2379
American Academy of Psychoanalysis Preliminary
    Meeting, 3045
American Academy of Psychoanalysis and
    Dynamic Psychiatry, 2380
Annual Summit on International Managed Care
    Trends, 3061
Casey Family Services, 4007
Connecticut Department of Mental Health and
    Addiction Services, 2140
Connecticut Department of Children and Families,
    2141
Connecticut Families United for Children's Mental
    Health, 1750
Connecticut National Alliance on Mental Illness,
    1751
Family & Community Alliance Project, 1752
Gaynor and Associates, 4055
Infoline, 199
Institute of Living Anxiety Disorders Center, 1642
Largesse, The Network for Size Esteem, 876
Mental Health Association: Connecticut, 1753
Sarmul Consultants, 4157
Stonington Institute, 3318
Thames Valley Programs, 1755
University of Connecticut Health Center, 3332
Value Health, 4176
Women's Support Services, 1756
Yale Mood Disorders Research Program, 1150
Yale University School of Medicine: Child Study
    Center, 3359
Yale University: Depression Research Program,
    1151

Delaware

Astra Zeneca Pharmaceuticals, 4425
Coventry Health Care of Iowa, 4024
Delaware Alliance for the Mentally Ill, 1757
Delaware Department of Health & Social Services,
    2142
Delaware Division of Child Mental Health
    Services, 2143
Delaware Division of Family Services, 2144
Delaware Guidance Services for Children and
    Youth, 1758

Mental Health Association of Delaware, 1759

District of Columbia

AAIDD Annual Meeting, 3039
AAMR: American Association on Mental
    Retardation, 1589
Administration for Children and Families, 2057
Administration for Children, Youth and Families,
    2058
Administration on Aging, 2059
Administration on Developmental Disabilities US
    Department of Health & Human Services, 2060
Alliance of Genetic Support Groups, 1593
American Academy of Child and Adolescent
    Psychiatry (AACAP): Annual Meeting, 3042
American Academy of Child & Adolescent
    Psychiatry, 2376
American Academy of Child and Adolescent
    Psychiatry, 1433, 1594, 3227, 3227
American Association of Health Plans, 2388
American Association of Homes & Services for the
    Aging Annual Convention, 3049
American Association of Homes and Services for
    the Aging, 2390
American Association of Retired Persons, 2394
American Association on Intellectual and
    Developmental Disabilities Annual Meeting,
    1598, 2395, 3050, 3050
American Association on Mental Retardation
    (AAR), 2396
American Foundation for Suicide Prevention
    (SPAN USA), 1581
American Health Care Association, 2410
American Health Care Association Annual
    Convention, 3056
American Managed Behavioral Healthcare
    Association, 1600, 3986, 2413, 2413
American Pharmacists Association, 2421
American Psychologial Association: Division of
    Family Psychology, 2426
American Psychological Association, 1604, 2427
American Psychological Association: Applied
    Experimental and Engineering Psychology, 2428
American Public Human Services Association, 80
Association for Psychological Science (APS), 2450
Association of Black Psychologists, 2454
Association of Black Psychologists Annual
    Convention, 3064
Association of Maternal and Child Health
    Programs (AMCHP), 2062
Bazelon Center for Mental Health Law, 1608, 2458
California Department of Health and Human
    Services, 2145
Center For Mental Health Services, 4, 469
Center for the Advancement of Health, 4009
Change for Good Coaching and Counseling, 873
Community Action Partnership, 2471
DC Alliance for the Mentally Ill, 1762
DC Commission on Mental Health Services, 2146
DC Department of Human Services, 2147
DC Department of Mental Health, 2067
Department of Health and Human Services/OAS,
    1763
Equal Employment Opportunity Commission, 2068
Family Advocacy & Support Association, 1631,
    1764
George Washington University, 3256
Gerontoligical Society of America, 2479
HSP Verified, 4060
Hays Group, 4061
Health & Medicine Counsel of Washington DDNC
    Digestive Disease National Coalition, 2148
Health Service Providers Verified, 2482
Health Systems Research, 4066

Health and Human Services Office of Assistant Secretary for Planning & Evaluation, 2071
Jacobs Institute of Women's Health, 3262
Kushner and Company, 4090
Managed Health Care Association, 2491
NASW JobLink, 4122
National Association Councils on Developmental Disabilities, 768
National Association For Children's Behavioral Health, 2497
National Association of Protection and Advocacy Systems, 1656
National Association of Psychiatric Health Systems, 2502
National Association of Social Workers, 1775, 1913, 2504, 2504
National Association of State Alcohol and Drug Abuse Directors, 88
National Business Coalition Forum on Health (NBCH), 2506
National Coalition for the Homeless, 2507
National Committee for Quality Assurance, 2508
National Council on Aging, 2510
National Dissemination Center for Children with Disabilities, 476, 1444
National Gay and Lesbian Task Force, 976
National Organization on Disability, 1670
National Organization on Fetal Alcohol Syndrome, 94
National Register of Health Service Providers in Psychology, 2368, 2516
National Technical Assistance Center for Children's Mental Health, 1445, 1674
Parents and Friends of Lesbians and Gays, 979
Parents, Families and Friends of Lesbians and Gays, 980
Pharmaceutical Care Management Association, 2519
President's Committee on Mental Retardation, 2093
Presidential Commission on Employment of the Disabled, 2094
Psychology of Religion, 2524
Public Health Foundation, 2096
SAMHSA'S National Mental Health Information Center, 1260, 1293, 1355, 1355, 1381, 1399, 1562
SAMHSA's National Mental Health Information Center, 97, 275, 478, 478, 608, 774, 848, 884, 981, 1002, 1053, 1203, 1216
Society for Women's Health Research, 2534
Society for the Psychological Study of Social Issues (SPSSI), 2536
Substance Abuse and Mental Health Services Administration: Center for Mental Health Services, 2099
Therapeutic Communities of America, 2540
US Department of Health and Human Services Planning and Evaluation, 2101
US Department of Health and Human Services: Office of Women's Health, 2103
US Veterans Administration: Mental Health and Behavioral Sciences Services, 2104
ZERO TO THREE: National Center for Infants, Toddlers, and Families, 1454, 1699

Florida

Andrew and Associates, 4196
Association for Women in Psychology, 2452
Association of Mental Health Librarians (AMHL), 1607
Behavioral Medicine and Biofeedback Consultants, 3233
Best Buddies International (BBI), 1609

Broward County Health Care Services, 4000
CLARC Services, 4211
Career Assessment & Planning Services, 81, 261, 818, 818, 996, 1034, 1210, 1252, 1285
Cenaps Corporation, 2357
Center for Applications of Psychological Type, 2463
Century Financial Services, 4010
Columbia Hospital M/H Services, 4016
Comprehensive Care Corporation, 4018
CompuLab Healthcare Systems Corporation, 4223
Department of Human Services For Youth & Families, 1766
Developmental Disabilities Nurses Association, 2475
Eclipsys Corporation, 4238
Emedeon Practice Services, 4240
FPM Behavioral Health: Corporate Marketing, 4045
Facts Services, 4243
Family Network on Disabilities, 1767
Florida Alcohol and Drug Abuse Association, 1768
Florida Department Health and Human Services: Substance Abuse Program, 2149
Florida Department of Children and Families, 2150
Florida Department of Health and Human Services, 2151
Florida Department of Mental Health and Rehabilitative Services, 2152
Florida Federation of Families for Children's Mental Health, 1769
Florida Health Care Association, 1770
Florida Health Information Management Association, 1771
Florida Medicaid State Plan, 2153
Florida National Alliance for the Mentally Ill, 1772
Food Addicts Anonymous, 953
Gorski-Cenaps Corporation Training & Consultation, 2480
Health Management Associates, 4065
HealthSoft, 4256
Managed Care Concepts, 4103
Med Advantage, 2365, 2492
Medai, 4281
Medware, 4288
Mental Health Association of West Florida, 1773
Mental Health Corporations of America, 2494
Micro Design International, 4292
National Alliance on Mental Illness: Florida, 1774
Parent Child Center, 3292
Psychological Assessment Resources, 4312
Psychometric Software, 4314
Research Center for Children's Mental Health, Department of Children and Family, 3304
Research and Training Center for Children's Mental Health, 1448
Somerset Pharmaceuticals, 4451
Synergistic Office Solutions (SOS Software), 4330
Tempus Software, 4331
UNI/CARE Systems, 4335
United Families for Children's Mental Health, 1451, 1692
University of Miami - Department of Psychology, 3340
ValueOptions Jacksonville Service Center, 4178
Vann Data Services, 4337
Youth Services International, 1453, 1698

Georgia

Adam Software, 4190
Cameron and Associates, 4005
Center for the Study of Adolescence, 947
Centers for Disease Control & Prevention, 2065

Eating Disorders Research and Treatment Program, 949
Emory University School of Medicine, Psychology and Behavior, 3252
Emory University: Psychological Center, 3253
First Horizon Pharmaceutical, 4430
Fowler Healthcare Affiliates, 4050
Georgia Association of Homes and Services for Children, 1776
Georgia Department of Human Resources, 2154
Georgia Department of Human Resources: Division of Public Health, 2155
Georgia Division of Mental Health Developmental Disabilities and Addictive Diseases (MHDDAD), 2156
Georgia National Alliance for the Mentally Ill, 1777
Georgia Parent Support Network, 1778
Georgia Psychological Society First Annual Conference, 3066
Grady Health Systems: Central Fulton CMHC, 1779
Healthport, 4259
IMNET Systems, 4263
Inhealth Record Systems, 4268
Interim Physicians, 4083
Locumtenens.com, 3268
MCG Telemedicine Center, 4097, 3269
MSI International, 4100
McKesson HBO and Company, 4113
Medical College of Georgia, 3274
Medical Doctor Associates, 3278
Murphy-Harpst-Vashti, 4121
National Alliance on Mental Illness: Georgia, 1780
National Center for HIV, STD and TB Prevention, 2074
National Families in Action, 4297
Optio Software, 4305
Solvay Pharmaceuticals, 4450
Strategic Advantage, 4326

Hawaii

Hawaii Department of Adult Mental Health, 2157
Hawaii Department of Health, 2158
Hawaii Families As Allies, 1781
John A Burns School of Medicine Department of Psychiatry, 3264
National Alliance on Mental Illness: Hawaii, 1782

Idaho

Ascent, 4198
College of Southern Idaho, 4015, 3241
Department of Health and Welfare: Medicaid Division, 2159
Department of Health and Welfare: Community Rehab, 2160
Healthwise, 4070
Idaho Alliance for the Mentally Ill, 1783
Idaho Bureau of Maternal and Child Health, 2161
Idaho Bureau of Mental Health and Substance Abuse, Division of Family & Community Service, 2162
Idaho Department of Health & Welfare, 2163
Idaho Department of Health and Welfare: Family and Child Services, 2164
Idaho Mental Health Center, 2165
National Alliance on Mental Illness: Idaho, 1784

Illinois

AAMA Annual Conference, 3040

AMA's Annual Medical Communications Conference, 3041
Abbott Laboratories, 4423
Akzo Nobel, 4424
Allendale Association, 1785
Alzheimer's Association National Office, 763
American Academy of Medical Administrators, 2378
American Academy of Pediatrics, 1434, 1595
American Academy of Sleep Medicine, 1376
American Association of Health Care Consultants Annual Fall Conference, 3048
American Association of Healthcare Consultants, 2389
American Board of Psychiatry and Neurology (ABPN), 2398
American College of Healthcare Executives, 2401, 3053, 3228, 3228
American College of Psychiatrists, 2404
American College of Psychiatrists Annual Meeting, 3054
American College of Women's Health Physicians, 3229
American Health Information Management Association Annual Exhibition and Conference, 2411, 3057
American Hospital Association: Section for Psychiatric and Substance Abuse, 2412
American Medical Association, 2414
American Medical Software, 4193
Aon Consulting Group, 3988
Baby Fold, 1786
Bereaved Parents of the USA, 32
CBI Group, 4003
Chaddock, 1787
Chicago Child Care Society, 1788
Child and Adolescent Bipolar Foundation, 1037
Children's Home Association of Illinois, 1789
Christian Association for Psychological Studies, 2467
Coalition of Illinois Counselors Organization, 1790
College of Dupage, 4014
ComPsych, 4017
Community Service Options, 1625
Compassionte Friends, Inc, 33
DD Fischer Consulting, 4027
Depression & Bi-Polar Support Alliance, 1038
Depression & BiPolar Support Alliance, 1039
Depression and Bi-Polar Alliance, 1042
Depressive and Bipolar Support Alliance (DBSA), 1866
Dorenfest Group, 4032
Dupage County Health Department, 4034
Family Service Association of Greater Elgin Area, 1791
HPN Worldwide, 4059
Haymarket Center, Professional Development, 3258
Healthcare Value Management Group, 4068
Human Resources Development Institute, 1792
Hyde Park Associates, 4079
Illinois Alcoholism and Drug Dependency Association, 1793, 2166
Illinois Alliance for the Mentally Ill, 1794
Illinois Department of Alcoholism and Substance Abuse, 2167
Illinois Department of Children and Family Services, 2168
Illinois Department of Health and Human Services, 2169
Illinois Department of Human Services: Office of Mental Health, 2170
Illinois Department of Mental Health and Drug Dependence, 2171
Illinois Department of Mental Health and Developmental Disabilities, 2172

Illinois Department of Public Aid, 2173
Illinois Department of Public Health: Division of Food, Drugs and Dairies/FDD, 2174
Illinois Federation of Families for Children's Mental Health, 1795
Innovative Data Solutions, 4269
Integrated Business Services, 4271
International Association of Eating Disorders Professionals, 875
International Society for Traumatic Stress Studies, 268
International Society for the Study of Dissociation, 845
Joint Commission on Accreditation of Healthcare Organizations, 2363
Larkin Center, 1796
Lifelink Corporation, 4094
Little City Foundation (LCF), 1797
MEDCOM Information Systems, 4275
McHenry County M/H Board, 4277
Medix Systems Consultants, 4287
Mental Health Association in Illinois, 2175
Metropolitan Family Services, 1798
Mihalik Group, 4119
National Association of Anorexia Nervosa and Associated Disorders (ANAD), 879
National Medical Health Card Systems, 4298
National Treatment Alternative for Safe Communities, 2517
Northwestern University Medical School Feinberg School of Medicine, 3288
Perspectives, 4138
Physicians for a National Health Program, 2520
Professional Assistance Center for Education (PACE), 1681
PsycHealth, 4150
Psychiatric Clinical Research Center, 1682
Pyrce Healthcare Group, 4154
Rainbows, 37, 1495
Recovery, 422, 1154, 1684, 1684
Riveredge Hospital, 3306
SAFE Alternatives, 1243
SPSS, 4320
Saner Software, 4321
Section for Psychiatric and Substance Abuse Services (SPSPAS), 98
Southern Illinois University School of Medicine: Department of Psychiatry, 3313
Southern Illinois University School of Medicine, 3314
TASC, 4170
Takeda Pharmaceuticals North America, 4453
Thresholds, 1691
Vedder Price, 4179
Voice of the Retarded, 1693

Indiana

Eli Lilly and Company, 4429
Experior Corporation, 4242
Health Probe, 4254
Indiana Department of Public Welfare Division of Family Independence: Food Stamps/Medicaid/Training, 2176
Indiana Family & Social Services Administration, 2177
Indiana Family And Social Services Administration, 2178
Indiana Family and Social Services Administration: Division of Mental Health, 2179
Indiana Resource Center for Autism (IRCA), 599, 705, 1800, 1800
Indiana University Psychiatric Management, 1801
Medi-Span, 4283

Mental Health Association in Marion County Consumer Services, 1802
More Advanced Autistic People Services (MAAPS), 600
National Alliance on Mental Illness: Indiana, 1803
National Association of Nouthetic Counselors, 2501
Psychiatric Associates, 4151, 3299
Psychological Software Services, 4313
Quinco Behavioral Health Systems, 4155
Supportive Systems, 4169
The Indiana Consortium for Mental Health Services Research (ICMHSR), 2180
Universal Behavioral Service, 4336

Iowa

Control-0-Fax Corporation, 4225
Iowa Alliance for the Mentally Ill, 1804
Iowa Department Human Services, 2181
Iowa Department of Public Health, 2182
Iowa Department of Public Health: Division of Substance Abuse, 2183
Iowa Division of Mental Health & Developmental Disabilities: Department of Human Services, 2184
Iowa Federation of Families for Children's Mental Health, 1805
Medical Records Solution, 4285
National Alliance on Mental Illness: Iowa, 1806
University of Iowa Hospital, 3333
University of Iowa, Mental Health: Clinical Research Center, 1807

Kansas

Comcare of Sedgwick County, 2185
Council for Learning Disabilities, 1626
Division of Disability and Behavioral Health Services - Mental Health, 2186
Kansas Council on Developmental Disabilities Kansas Department of Social and Rehabilitation Services, 2187
Kansas Department of Mental Health and Retardation and Social Services, 2188
Keys for Networking: Kansas Parent Information & Resource Center, 1808
National Alliance on Mental Illness: Kansas, 1809
Preferred Mental Health Management, 4143
Society of Teachers of Family Medicine, 2539
Topeka Institute for Psychoanalysis, 3320
University of Kansas Medical Center, 3334
University of Kansas School of Medicine, 3335

Kentucky

Adanta Group-Behavioral Health Services, 3978
Depressed Anonymous, 1152
FCS, 4044
KY-SPIN, 1811
Kentucky Alliance for the Mentally Ill, 1812
Kentucky Cabinet for Health and Human Services, 2189
Kentucky Department for Human Support Services, 2190
Kentucky Department for Medicaid Services, 2191
Kentucky Department of Mental Health and Mental Retardation, 2192
Kentucky IMPACT, 1813
Kentucky Justice Cabinet: Department of Juvenile Justice, 2193

Kentucky Partnership for Families and Children, 1814
Kentucky Psychiatric Association, 1815
National Anxiety Foundation, 270
St. Joseph Behavioral Medicine Network, 3316
University of Louisville School of Medicine, 3336

Louisiana

Active Intervention, 3223
Alton Ochsner Medical Foundation, Psychiatry Residency, 3226
Family Managed Care, 4046
Louisiana Alliance for the Mentally Ill, 1819
Louisiana Commission on Law Enforcement and Administration (LCLE), 2194
Louisiana Department of Health and Hospitals: Office of Mental Health, 2195
Louisiana Department of Health and Hospitals: Louisiana Office for Addictive Disorders, 2196
Louisiana Federation of Families for Children's Mental Health, 1820
SUPRA Management, 2370
West Jefferson Medical Center, 3356

Maine

Advanced Data Systems, 4191
Maine Department Health and Human Services Children's Behavioral Health Services, 2197
Maine Department of Behavioral and Developmental Services, 2198
Maine Office of Substance Abuse: Information and Resource Center, 2199
Maine Psychiatric Association, 1822
National Alliance on Mental Illness: Maine, 1823
United Families for Children's Mental Health, 1824

Maryland

ASHA Annual Convention, 3073
Academy of Psychosomatic Medicine, 2371
Agency for Healthcare Research & Quality, 2373
Agency for Healthcare Research and Quality: Office of Communications and Knowledge Transfer, 2061
Alzheimer's Disease Education and Referral Center, 764
American Association for Geriatric Psychiatry, 1596
American Association of Geriatric Psychiatry (AAGP), 2387
American Association of Geriatric Psychiatry Annual Meetings, 3047
American College Health Association, 2399
American Health Assistance Foundation, 765
American Medical Directors Association, 2415
American Medical Informatics Association, 2417
American Nurses Association, 2420
American Society of Addiction Medicine, 2545
American Society of Health System Pharmacists, 2434
American Society of Psychoanalytic Physicians (ASPP), 2435
American Speech-Language-Hearing Association, 1605
Annie E Casey Foundation, 2438
Annual Meeting & Medical-Scientific Conference, 3059
Anxiety Disorders Association of America, 258
Asher Meadow, 1277

Association of University Centers on Disabilities (UACD), 2456
Autism Society, 592
Autism Society of America (ASA), 593

Black Mental Health Alliance (BMHA), 1611
Bonny Foundation, 2460
Center for Health Policy Studies, 4008, 4215, 3239, 3239
Center for Mental Health Services (CMHS), 7, 83, 263, 263, 471, 596, 767, 844, 872, 974, 998, 1036, 1200, 1212, 1254, 1287, 1617
Center for Mental Health Services Homeless Programs Branch, 2063
Center for Substance Abuse Treatment, 2064
Centers for Medicare & Medicaid Services/CMS: Office of Research, Statisctics, Data and Systems, 2200
Centers for Medicare & Medicaid Services, 2201
Centers for Medicare & Medicaid Services: Office of Policy, 2066, 2202
Centers for Medicare and Medicaid Services: Office of Financial Management/OFM, 2203
Chemically Dependent Anonymous, 197
Children and Adults with AD/HD (CHADD), 472, 554
Community Behavioral Health Association of Maryland: CBH, 1825
Community Services for Autistic Adults and Children, 597
Council on Quality and Leadership, 1627
Counseling Associates, 4022
Depression & Related Affective Disorders Association (DRADA), 1040
Docu Trac, 4233
E Services Group, 4235
Epidemiology-Genetics Program in Psychiatry, 1144
Families Involved Together, 1826
Federation of Families for Children's Mental Health, 1439, 1634
First Candle/SIDS Alliance, 8
Health Resources and Services Administration, 1827
Health Systems and Financing Group, 2070
Information Resources and Inquiries Branch, 2072
International Critical Incident Stress Foundation, 266
Johnson, Bassin and Shaw, 4088
KAI Associates, 4089
Magellan Health Service, 4101
Management Recruiters of Washington, DC, 3271
Maryland Alcohol and Drug Abuse Administration, 2204
Maryland Department of Health and Mental Hygiene, 2205
Maryland Department of Human Resources, 2206
Maryland Division of Mental Health, 2207
Maryland Psychiatric Research Center, 1828
Mental Health Association of Maryland, 1829
National Institutes of Mental Health Division of Intramural Research Programs (DIRP), 2073
National Association of Community Health Centers, 2500
National Association of School Psychologists, 2503, 3285
National Clearinghouse for Alcohol and Drug Information, 89
National Clearinghouse for Drug & Alcohol, 2075
National Council for Community Behavioral Healthcare, 90, 1662
National Eldercare Services Company, 2511
National Family Caregivers Association, 770

National Federation of Families for Children's Mental Health, 1832
National Institute of Alcohol Abuse and Alcoholism: Treatment Research Branch, 2076
National Institute of Alcohol Abuse and Alcoholism: Homeless Demonstration and Evaluation Branch, 2077
National Institute of Alcohol Abuse and Alcoholism: Office of Policy Analysis, 2078
National Institute of Drug Abuse (NIDA), 1665
National Institute of Drug Abuse: NIDA, 2079
National Institute of Mental Health Information Resources and Inquiries Branch, 603, 882, 977, 977, 1050, 1666
National Institute of Mental Health: Schizophrenia Research Branch, 2080
National Institute of Mental Health: Mental Disorders of the Aging, 2081
National Institute of Mental Health: Office of Science Policy, Planning, and Communications, 2082
National Institute of Neurological Disorders and Stroke, 771
National Institute of Neurological Disorders and Stroke Brain Information Network (BRAIN), 604
National Institute on Alcohol Abuse and Alcoholism, 92
National Institute on Deafness and Other Communication Disorders Information Clearinghouse, 605
National Institute on Drug Abuse: Division of Clinical Neurosciences and Behavioral Research, 2083
National Institute on Drug Abuse: Office of Science Policy and Communications, 2084
National Institutes of Health: National Center for Research Resources (NCCR), 2085
National Institutes of Mental Health: Office on AIDS, 2086
National Library of Medicine, 2087
New Hope Foundation, 1675
Office of Applied Studies, SA & Mental Health Services, 2088
Office of Disease Prevention & Health Promotion, 2089
Office of National Drug Control Policy, 2090
Office of Program and Policy Development, 2091
Office of Science Policy OD/NIH, 2092
Protection and Advocacy Program for the Mentally Ill, 2095
Psycho Medical Chirologists, 4152
SAMHSA's Fetal Alcohol Spectrum Disorders Center for Excellence (FASD), 95, 2097
SAMHSA's National Clearinghouse For Alcohol And Drug Information, 96
Schizophrenia Research Branch: Division of Clinical and Treatment Research, 1335
Sheppard Pratt Health Plan, 4162
Sheppard Pratt Health System, 1833
Sidran Traumatic Stress Institute, 1689
Substance Abuse & Mental Health Services Administration of the US Dept of Health and Human Services, 99, 2098
Survey & Analysis Branch, 1834
US Department of Health & Human Services: Indian Health Service, 2100
US Department of Health and Human Services Bureau of Primary Health, 2102
United States Psychiatric Rehabilitation Organization (USPRA), 2541
University of Maryland Medical Systems, 3337
University of Maryland School of Medicine, 3338
Warren Grant Magnuson Clinical Center, 1694
Yssociation for Psychological Type, 2544

Massachusetts

ABE American Board of Examiners in Clinical Social Work, 3973
Advocates for Human Potential, 1591
American Board of Examiners in Clinical Social Work, 2353
American Society of Psychopathology of Expression (ASPE), 2436
Analysis Group, 3987
Aries Systems Corporation, 4197
Asperger's Association of New England (AANE), 587
Associated Counseling Services, 3991
Association for Academic Psychiatry (AAP), 2439
Autism Research Foundation, 590
Behavioral Health Care Consultants, 3995
Behavioral Healthcare Center, 3232
Bipolar Clinic and Research Program, 1141
Brandeis University/Heller School, 3234
Bridgewell, 1835
Bull HN Information Systems, 4209
CASCAP, 1836
Cambridge Hospital: Department of Psychiatry, 3238
Center for Clinical Computing, 4214
Center for Clinical Social Work, 2464
Concord Family and Youth Services A Division of Justice Resource Institute, 1837
Depression and Bipolar Support Alliance of Boston, 1838
Dougherty Management Associates Health Strategies, 4033
Entropy Limited, 4040
Evaluation Center at HSRI, 4043
Federation for Children with Special Needs (FCSN), 1438, 1633
Glazer Medical Solutions, 4057
Hanover Insurance, 4253
Health Care For All(HCFA), 2069
Human Services Research Institute, 1639, 4078
IBM Global Healthcare Industry, 4261
International OCD Foundation, 418
International Obsessive Compulsive Disorder Foundation, 267
Jean Piaget Society: Society for the Study of Knowledge and Development (JPSSSKD), 2490
Jewish Family and Children's Services, 1839
Join Together Online, 200
Judge Baker Children's Center, 1645
MEDA, 954
Magellan Public Solutions, 4102
Massachusetts Alliance for the Mentally Ill, 1840
Massachusetts Behavioral Health Partnership, 1841
Massachusetts Department of Mental Health, 2208
Massachusetts Department of Public Health, 2209
Massachusetts Department of Public Health: Bureau of Substance Abuse Services, 2210
Massachusetts Department of Social Services, 2211
Massachusetts Department of Transitional Assistance, 2212
Massachusetts Division of Medical Assistance MassHealth Program, 2213
Massachusetts Executive Office of Public Safety, 2214
Medical Records Institute, 4284
Mental Health Connections, 4289
Mental Health and Substance Abuse Corporations of Massachusetts, 1842
Mental Illness Education Project, 1651
Mercer Consulting, 4116
Mertech, 2366
National Empowerment Center, 1663, 4123
New England Center for Children, 607
New England Psych Group, 4125
Novartis, 4441

Parent Professional Advocacy League, 1844
Public Consulting Group, 4153
Refuah, 1685
SADD: Students Against Destructive Decisions, 207, 1496
Scheur and Associates, 4159
Schneider Institute for Health Policy, 3311
Screening for Mental Health, 2529
Sepracor Pharmaceuticals, 4448
University of Massachusetts Medical Center, 3339
Webman Associates, 4183

Michigan

ACS Healthcare Solutions, 4185
Adult Learning Systems, 3979
Agoraphobics in Motion, 257
American College of Osteopathic Neurologists & Psychiatrists, 2403
Association for Behavior Analysis, 2442
Borgess Behavioral Medicine Services, 1845
Boysville of Michigan, 1846
Christian Horizons, 1622
DocuMed, 4234
First Corp-Health Consulting, 4049
Harper House: Change Alternative Living, 3257
Health Alliance Plan, 4062
Health Decisions, 4064
Inforum, 4267
Justice in Mental Health Organizations, 1847
Lapeer County Community Mental Health Center, 1848
Macomb County Community Mental Health, 1849
Manic Depressive and Depressive Association of Metropolitan Detroit, 1850
Metropolitan Area Chapter of Federation of Families for Children's Mental Health, 1851
Michigan Alliance for the Mentally Ill, 1852
Michigan Association for Children with Emotional Disorders: MACED, 1853
Michigan Association for Children's Mental Health, 1442, 1854
Michigan Department of Community Health, 2215
Michigan Department of Human Services, 2216
Michigan State Representative: Co-Chair Public Health, 2217
Mississippi Alliance for the Mentally Ill, 1863
National Council on Alcoholism and Drug Dependence: Greater Detriot Area, 91, 2218
Northpointe Behavioral Healthcare Systems, 1856, 4127
Parrot Software, 4309
Rapid Psychler Press, 2526
Sandra Fields-Neal and Associates, 4156
Save Our Sons And Daughters (SOSAD), 14
Schizophrenics Anonymous Forum, 1338
Southwest Counseling & Development Services, 1857
TransYouth Family Allies, 985
Traumatic Incident Reduction Newsletter, 4173
University of Michigan, 3341
Wayne University-University of Psychiatric Center-Jefferson: Outpatient Mental Health for Children, Adolescents and Adults, 3355
Woodlands Behavioral Healthcare Network, 1858

Minnesota

Allina Hospitals & Clinics Behavioral Health Services, 3984
Behavioral Health Services, 3997
CBCA, 4002
CIGNA Behavioral Care, 4004
Ceridian Corporation, 4216

Corporate Health Systems, 4021
Department of Human Services: Chemical Health Division, 2219
Emotions Anonymous International Service Center, 417, 1153, 1628, 1628
HealthPartners, 4067
Healtheast Behavioral Care, 2362
Lake Area Youth Services Bureau, 2220
MMHR, 4099
McGladery and Pullen CPAs, 4111
McKesson HBOC, 4278
Minnesota Department of Human Services, 2221
NASW Minnesota Chapter, 1859
National Association for Rural Mental Health, 1654
National Multicultural Conference and Summit, 3070
North American Training Institute: Division of the Minnesota Council on Compulsive Gambling, 1861
Pacer Center, 1862
Pearson, 4136
River City Mental Health Clinic, 3305
University of Minnesota Fairview Health Systems, 3342
University of Minnesota, Family Social Science, 3343
Velocity Healthcare Informatics, 4338

Mississippi

Advanced Psychotherapy Association, 2372
Mississippi Alcohol Safety Education Program, 2222
Mississippi Department Mental Health Mental Retardation Services, 2223
Mississippi Department of Human Services, 2224
Mississippi Department of Mental Health: Division of Alcohol and Drug Abuse, 2225
Mississippi Department of Mental Health: Division of Medicaid, 2226
Mississippi Department of Rehabilitation Services: Office of Vocational Rehabilitation (OVR), 2227
Mississippi Families as Allies, 1864

Missouri

CliniSphere version 2.0, 4220
College of Health and Human Services: SE Missouri State, 3240
DST Output, 4229
E-Productivity-Services.Net, 264
Genelco Software Solutions, 4248
Health Capital Consultants, 4063
Lake Mental Health Consultants, 4091
Mallinckrodt, 4438
Mental Health Association of Greater St. Louis, 1867
Missouri Alliance for the Mentally Ill, 1868
Missouri Department Health & Senior Services, 2228
Missouri Department of Mental Health, 2229
Missouri Department of Public Safety, 2230
Missouri Department of Social Services, 2231
Missouri Department of Social Services: Medical Services Division, 2232
Missouri Division of Alcohol and Drug Abuse, 2233
Missouri Division of Comprehensive Psychiatric Service, 2234
Missouri Division of Mental Retardation and Developmental Disabilities, 2235
Missouri Institute of Mental Health, 1869

North Carolina

North Dakota

Ohio

Parents of Murdered Children, 36
Planned Lifetime Assistance Network of Northeast
Ohio, 1942
Positive Education Program, 1943
PsychTemps, 3298
Psychology Department, 3301
RCF Information Systems, 4316
Rosemont Center, 3309
Roxane Laboratories, 4446
SAFY of America, 3310
SAFY of America: Specialized Alternatives for
Families and Youth, 2369
SMART-Self Management and Recovery Training,
208
Six County, 1944
Specialized Alternatives for Families & Youth of
America (SAFY), 4164
University of Cincinnati College of Medical
Department of Psychiatry, 3330
Woodlands, 4341

Oklahoma

Hillcrest Utica Psychiatric Services, 3260
Hogan Assessment Systems, 4260
OK Parents as Partners, 1946
Oklahoma Alliance for the Mentally Ill, 1947
Oklahoma Department of Human Services, 2277
Oklahoma Department of Mental Health and
Substance Abuse Service (ODMHSAS), 2278
Oklahoma Healthcare Authority, 2279
Oklahoma Mental Health Consumer Council, 1948,
2280, 4128, 4128
Oklahoma Office of Juvenile Affairs, 2281
Oklahoma Psychiatric Physicians Association,
1949
St. Anthony Behavioral Medicine Center,
Behavioral Medicine, 4166

Oregon

Anorexia Nervosa and Related Eating Disorders,
870
Beaver Creek Software, 4204
Deborah MacWilliams, 1255
Interlink Health Services, 4084
Marion County Health Department, 2282
Medipay, 4286
National Alliance for Mental Illness: Oregon, 1950
National Alliance on Mental Illness: Oregon, 1951
Nickerson Center, 3287
Northwest Analytical, 4302
Office of Mental Health and Addiction Services
Training & Resource Center, 2283
Oregon Commission on Children and Families,
2284
Oregon Department of Human Resources: Division
of Health Services, 2285
Oregon Department of Human Services: Mental
Health Services, 2286
Oregon Department of Human Services: Office of
Developmental Disabilities, 2287
Oregon Family Support Network, 1952
Oregon Health Policy and Research: Policy and
Analysis Unit, 2288
Oregon Psychiatric Association, 1953
Providence Behavioral Health Connections, 4148
Regional Research Institute for Human Services of
Portland University, 3303
Research and Training Center on Family Support
and Children's Mental Health, 1449, 1687
Riverside Center, 3307

Pennsylvania

APOGEE, 3974
Access Behavioral Care, 3976
American Anorexia/Bulimia Association of
Philidelphia, 1954
American Association of Chairs of Departments of
Psychiatry (AACDP), 2384
American Association of Directors of Psychiatric
Residency Training, 2386
Askesis Development Group, 4199
Association for Hospital Medical Education, 2446
Bipolar Research at University of Pennsylvania,
1143
Cephalon, 4427
Consumer Satisfaction Team, 2359
DB Consultants, 4228
Deloitte and Touche LLP Management Consulting,
4029
DeltaMetrics, 4030, 4231
Distance Learning Network, 4232, 3248
Diversified Group Administrators, 4031
Family Services of Delaware County, 4244
First Consulting Group, 4048
GMR Group, 4053
Health Federation of Philadelphia, 1955
InfoMC, 4264
International Society of Psychiatric-Mental Health
Nurses, 1644
Jefferson Drug/Alcohol, 3263
Kidspeace National Centers, 1493
Learning Disabilities Association of America, 473,
1646
MCF Consulting, 4096
MEDecision, 4276
Mayes Group, 4110
Medical College of Pennsylvania, 3276
Mental Health Association of Southeastern
Pennsylvania (MHASP), 1956
Mylan, 4440
National Association of Addiction Treatment
Providers, 2499
National Association of Therapeutic Wilderness
Camps, 1658
National Mental Health Consumers' Self-Help
Clearinghouse, 12, 93, 272, 272, 477, 606, 772,
821, 847, 883, 978, 1001, 1051, 1202, 1215,
1259, 1292
North American Society of Adlerian Psychology
(NASAP), 2518
One Hundred Top Series, 4129
PMHCC, 4132
Parents Involved Network, 1958
Penn State Hershey Medical Center, 3293
Pennsylvania Alliance for the Mentally Ill, 1959
Pennsylvania Bureau Drug and Alcohol Programs:
Monitoring, 2289
Pennsylvania Bureau of Community Program
Standards: Licensure and Certification, 2290
Pennsylvania Bureau of Drug and Alcohol
Programs: Information Bulletins, 2291
Pennsylvania Department of Health: Bureau of
Drug and Alcohol Programs, 2292
Pennsylvania Department of Public Welfare and
Mental Health Services, 2293
Pennsylvania Division of Drug and Alcohol
Prevention: Treatment, 2294
Pennsylvania Medical Assistance Programs, 2295
Pennsylvania Psychiatric Society, 1960
Pennsylvania Society for Services to Children,
1961
Persoma Management, 4137
Philadelphia Health Management, 4139
Pressley Ridge Schools, 3296
ProMetrics CAREeval, 4144

ProMetrics Consulting & Susquehanna
PathFinders, 4145
Psych-Med Association, St. Francis Medical, 3297
SHS Computer Service, 4319
Schafer Consulting, 4158
Shire Richwood, 4449
Southwestern Pennsylvania Alliance for the
Mentally Ill, 1962
St. Francis Medical Center, 3315
Suburban Research Associates, 4167
SunGard Pentamation, 4329
Systems Advocacy, 1690
UNITE Inc Grief Support, 18
University of Pennsylvania Health System, 3347
University of Pennsylvania Weight and Eating
Disorders Program, 952
University of Pennsylvania, Department of
Psychiatry, 3348
University of Pittsburgh Medical Center, 1963
Virtual Software Systems, 4340
Western Psychiatric Institute and Clinic, 3357
Wordsworth, 3358

Rhode Island

American Academy of Addiction Psychiatry
(AAAP) Annual Meeting & Symposium, 78,
2375, 3043, 3043
East Bay Alliance for the Mentally Ill, 1964
Kent County Alliance for the Mentally Ill, 1965
National Alliance on Mental Illness: Davis Park,
1967
National Alliance on Mental Illness: Rhode Island,
1968
New Avenues Alliance for the Mentally Ill, 1969
Newport County Alliance for the Mentally Ill,
1970
Northern Rhode Island Alliance for the Mentally
Ill, 1971
Parent Support Network of Rhode Island, 1972
Rhode Island Council on Alcoholism and Other
Drug Dependence, 2296
Rhode Island Department of Human Services, 2297
Rhode Island Division of Substance Abuse, 2298
Siblings & Offspring Group Alliance for the
Mentally Ill, 1973
Spouses & Partners' Group Alliance for the
Mentally Ill, 1974
State of Rhode Island Department of Mental
Health, Retardation and Hospitals, 2299
Washington County Alliance for the Mentally Ill,
1975

South Carolina

Columbia Counseling Center, 3243
Federation of Families of South Carolina, 1976
LRADAC The Behavioral Health Center of the
Midlands, 2300
Medical University of South Carolina Institute of
Psychiatry, Psychiatry Access Center, 3279
Mental Health Association in South Carolina, 2301
National Mental Health Association: Georgetown
County, 1978
Society for Pediatric Psychology (SPP), 2531
South Carolina Alliance for the Mentally Ill, 1979
South Carolina Alliance for the Mentally Ill, 1980
South Carolina Department of Alcohol and Other
Drug Abuse Services, 2302
South Carolina Department of Mental Health, 2303
South Carolina Department of Social Services,
2304
South Carolina Family Support Network, 1981

Washington

West Virginia

Wisconsin

Wyoming

General Reference

American Environmental Leaders: From Colonial Times to the Present
An African Biographical Dictionary
Encyclopedia of African-American Writing
Encyclopedia of American Industries
Encyclopedia of Emerging Industries
Encyclopedia of Global Industries
Encyclopedia of Gun Control & Gun Rights
Encyclopedia of Invasions & Conquests
Encyclopedia of Prisoners of War & Internment
Encyclopedia of Religion & Law in America
Encyclopedia of Rural America
Encyclopedia of the United States Cabinet, 1789-2010
Encyclopedia of Warrior Peoples & Fighting Groups
Environmental Resource Handbook
From Suffrage to the Senate: America's Political Women
Global Terror & Political Risk Assessment
Historical Dictionary of War Journalism
Human Rights in the United States
Nations of the World
Political Corruption in America
Speakers of the House of Representatives, 1789-2009
The Environmental Debate: A Documentary History
The Evolution Wars: A Guide to the Debates
The Religious Right: A Reference Handbook
The Value of a Dollar: 1860-2009
The Value of a Dollar: Colonial Era
University & College Museums, Galleries & Related Facilities
Weather America
World Cultural Leaders of the 20th & 21st Centuries
Working Americans 1880-1999 Vol. I: The Working Class
Working Americans 1880-1999 Vol. II: The Middle Class
Working Americans 1880-1999 Vol. III: The Upper Class
Working Americans 1880-1999 Vol. IV: Their Children
Working Americans 1880-2003 Vol. V: At War
Working Americans 1880-2005 Vol. VI: Women at Work
Working Americans 1880-2006 Vol. VII: Social Movements
Working Americans 1880-2007 Vol. VIII: Immigrants
Working Americans 1770-1869 Vol. IX: Revol. War to the Civil War
Working Americans 1880-2009 Vol. X: Sports & Recreation
Working Americans 1880-2010 Vol. XI: Entrepreneurs & Inventors

Bowker's Books In Print®Titles

Books In Print®
Books In Print® Supplement
American Book Publishing Record® Annual
American Book Publishing Record® Monthly
Books Out Loud™
Bowker's Complete Video Directory™
Children's Books In Print®
El-Hi Textbooks & Serials In Print®
Forthcoming Books®
Large Print Books & Serials™
Law Books & Serials In Print™
Medical & Health Care Books In Print™
Publishers, Distributors & Wholesalers of the US™
Subject Guide to Books In Print®
Subject Guide to Children's Books In Print®

Business Information

Directory of Business Information Resources
Directory of Mail Order Catalogs
Directory of Venture Capital & Private Equity Firms
Food & Beverage Market Place
Grey House Homeland Security Directory
Grey House Performing Arts Directory
Hudson's Washington News Media Contacts Directory
New York State Directory
Sports Market Place Directory
The Rauch Guides – Industry Market Research Reports

Statistics & Demographics

America's Top-Rated Cities
America's Top-Rated Small Towns & Cities
America's Top-Rated Smaller Cities
Comparative Guide to American Suburbs
Comparative Guide to Health in America
Profiles of... Series – State Handbooks

Health Information

Comparative Guide to American Hospitals
Comparative Guide to Health in America
Complete Directory for Pediatric Disorders
Complete Directory for People with Chronic Illness
Complete Directory for People with Disabilities
Complete Mental Health Directory
Directory of Health Care Group Purchasing Organizations
Directory of Hospital Personnel
HMO/PPO Directory
Medical Device Register
Older Americans Information Directory

Education Information

Charter School Movement
Comparative Guide to American Elementary & Secondary Schools
Complete Learning Disabilities Directory
Educators Resource Directory
Special Education

TheStreet.com Ratings Guides

TheStreet.com Ratings Consumer Box Set
TheStreet.com Ratings Guide to Bank Fees & Service Charges
TheStreet.com Ratings Guide to Banks & Thrifts
TheStreet.com Ratings Guide to Bond & Money Market Mutual Funds
TheStreet.com Ratings Guide to Common Stocks
TheStreet.com Ratings Guide to Credit Unions
TheStreet.com Ratings Guide to Exchange-Traded Funds
TheStreet.com Ratings Guide to Health Insurers
TheStreet.com Ratings Guide to Life & Annuity Insurers
TheStreet.com Ratings Guide to Property & Casualty Insurers
TheStreet.com Ratings Guide to Stock Mutual Funds
TheStreet.com Ratings Ultimate Guided Tour of Stock Investing

Canadian General Reference

Associations Canada
Canadian Almanac & Directory
Canadian Environmental Resource Guide
Canadian Parliamentary Guide
Financial Services Canada
History of Canada
Libraries Canada

Grey House Publishing

4919 Route 22, PO Box 56, Amenia NY 12501-0056 | (800) 562-2139 | www.greyhouse.com | books@greyhouse.com